2026 EDITION

Greenberg's GUIDES®

LIONEL® TRAINS

POCKET PRICE GUIDE 1901-2026

Edited by Roger Carp

This book belongs to:

Firecrown
405 Cherry Street
Chattanooga, TN 37402

Shop.Trains.com

Published in 2025

Forty-fifth Edition

Manufactured in China

ISBN: 979-8-89491-055-0
EISBN: 979-8-89491-056-7

Front cover photo: Lionel No. 8774 Southern GP7 diesel engine, courtesy Jack and Joey Sommerfeld, Sommerfeld's Trains & Hobbies, Butler, Wis., with input from Max Kirksey

Back cover photo: Lionel No. 395 Floodlight Tower, courtesy Joe Algozzini

Lionel does not set prices and valuations; these are developed independently as third party estimates.

We constantly strive to improve Greenberg's Pocket Price Guides. If you find missing items or detect misinformation, please contact us. Send your comments, new information, or corrections via e-mail to books@firecrown.com or by mail to Lionel Pocket Price Guide Editor, 18650 W. Corporate Dr., Ste. 103, Brookfield, WI 53045.

CONTENTS

INTRODUCTION

Whether you are a longtime Lionel enthusiast or a newcomer to the toy train hobby, this guide contains the information you need to identify and evaluate thousands of items made by Lionel since 1901. Most of all, you'll have at your fingertips the most up-to-date prices for locomotives, freight cars, passenger cars, stations, tunnels, signals, track sections, transformers, and other items.

What is listed

Almost every Lionel Standard, O, O-27, and OO gauge toy train and accessory produced over the years is listed in the pages that follow.

This edition of the *Lionel Pocket Price Guide* contains information about new additions to the product line as described in Lionel catalogs, press releases, and other sources. Any additions that Lionel makes to its line after this book is printed will be reported in the next edition.

In addition, the *Lionel Pocket Price Guide* provides information about items associated with Lionel yet not mentioned in its catalogs. These uncataloged or promotional items include unique models and specially decorated locomotives and cars that Lionel produces for national and regional toy train collecting and operating groups, museums, local railroad clubs, and other customers.

When to consult this guide

Many readers of the *Lionel Pocket Price Guide* use it after the fact. They already have some trains and accessories and now want to identify and evaluate those items. Maybe someone lucked upon a bridge at a garage sale and wants to know whether it's a No. 300 Hellgate Bridge or a No. 314 Deck Girder Bridge. Somebody else needs to provide his or her insurance agent with a complete list of O gauge locomotives that includes their conditions and current values. This guide contains the information needed to identify that bridge as well as determining present values for that engine roster.

In addition, the *Lionel Pocket Price Guide* can help you think about what to acquire in the future. That's really when the fun begins! You just have to spend some time considering how you want to approach the hobby. Collect, operate, or both? Prewar, postwar, or modern? Particular types of locomotives or cars? Favorite railroads? Promotional items?

Once you have a general idea of how to enjoy this hobby, you can make informed decisions about which trains you want.

UNDERSTANDING VALUES

The values presented here are an averaged reflection of prices for items bought and sold across the country during the year prior to the publication of this edition. These values are offered as guidelines and should be viewed as starting points that buyers and sellers can use to begin informed and reasonable negotiations.

In a listing for a steam locomotive, the value includes a tender, even if the tender is not listed in the description. The value of steam locomotives, particularly prewar items, may be affected significantly by the type of tender included.

Values for individual items may differ from what is listed in this price guide due to a few key factors. Where collectible trains are scarce and demand outruns supply, actual values may exceed what is shown. Values may also rise where certain items are especially popular, often because of their road names. And as with all collectibles, national and local economic conditions will impact values, which tend to drop when times are tough and demand falls.

Original packaging

Items in Like New or better condition require their original packaging to maintain their high level of value. The values given for items in Good and Excellent condition are not based on the expectation that a box and other associated items are present.

Items that do have their original packaging, especially if it is complete and undamaged, command a premium among collectors of prewar and postwar trains. No hard-and-fast rules can be stated as to how much higher their value is over the same items in Excellent condition. Generally speaking, though, boxed items in Like New condition are valued about 50 percent above the same item without a box.

Using the values

The values listed are what a consumer would pay — more or less — to get a particular item in a specific condition. One collector selling that item to another would probably ask the stated value and expect to get something close to it.

However, someone selling that same item to a person or business that intends to resell it (a train dealer) is unlikely to receive the stated value. Experience shows that sellers get about half the amount. Dealers offer less so they can earn a profit when reselling an item.

When buying or selling a toy train, you should learn more about it. Start by consulting this price guide and then look for more about it in a reference guide or website on toy trains. You can also ask more experienced hobbyists for their opinion about the item's condition and value.

FINDING A PRODUCT

The *Lionel Pocket Price Guide* has been divided into eight major sections.

Section 1: Prewar 1901–1942

Section 1 of the *Lionel Pocket Price Guide* is devoted to the pre-World War II period. The entries cover just about every train, accessory, and transformer associated with Lionel's line during its first 42 years.

The only outfits (sets) listed are those of articulated streamlined trains that consist of a powered unit and attached unpowered cars.

In an item's listing, the basic description specifies its gauge (the distance between the inside of the outermost rails). During this time, Lionel catalogued models in four sizes. It is noted in parentheses whether an item is 2⅞-inch, Standard (2⅛ inches), O (1¼ inches), or OO (¾ inches). O gauge models intended to run on tighter 27-inch-diameter track belong to Lionel's O-27 gauge line and are identified as such.

Transformers, rheostats, and many accessories were not limited to a single gauge, so their descriptions do not specify a gauge.

Section 2: Postwar 1945–1969

Section 2 concentrates on the post-World War II period of production. Nearly every train and accessory (except outfits) that Lionel cataloged between 1945 and 1969 has its own listing. By this time, Lionel no longer made trains in 2⅞-inch, Standard, or OO gauge. Instead, it offered trains that ran on track that had a diameter of either 31 inches (O gauge) or 27 inches (O-27 gauge). However, the entries in this section do not distinguish between O and O-27 since only a handful of locomotives and cars could operate solely on the wider curves.

Section 3: Modern Era 1970–2025

Section 3 shows the trains, accessories, transformers, and other items that Lionel has cataloged since 1970. The modern era encompasses the products of three companies: General Mills (Model Products Corp. and Fundimensions divisions), 1970–85; Lionel Trains Inc. (LTI), 1986–95; and Lionel LLC (LLC), 1996–2025.

These incarnations of Lionel are responsible for an enormous inventory of trains, rolling stock, transformers, and accessories. Cataloged and uncataloged O gauge items (ranging from the near-scale Standard O to the toy-like O-27) can be found within the pages of this section. All items in Section 3 are arranged according to their Lionel catalog number (omitting the numeral 6 used as a prefix). The descriptions of products made during the modern era may include information that relates to where in the product line a particular item belongs. Models derived from older designs have been described as traditional. Rolling stock whose dimensions and features approach scale realism may be designated as Standard O (abbreviated as std O). Locomotives equipped with TrainMaster Command Control or its successor, Legacy, are identified with the abbreviation CC.

Section 4: Lionel Corporation Tinplate

Section 4 features 800 products developed jointly by Lionel and MTH Electric Trains since 2009. These Lionel Corporation trains and accessories are reproductions of Lionel (and some American Flyer) tinplate items from the prewar era. You'll find trains here that operate as tinplate trains did prior to 1942 as well as others that have been updated with modern features and technology, such as Proto-Sound. The retail prices are listed for these products.

Section 5: Modern tinplate

Section 4 covers a category of modern-era trains that is referred to as modern tinplate. Here you'll find reissues of Standard and O gauge trains and accessories dating from the prewar period that LTI and LLC brought out for the purpose of satisfying a growing market. Also included in this section are a few Standard gauge trains that Lionel LLC has created, based on new designs.

Section 6: Club Cars and Special Production

Section 5 gathers the various items, principally locomotives and rolling stock, Lionel has made or sponsored for different hobby organizations, museums, and businesses since the 1970s. These uncataloged club cars and special production items are arranged according to the groups that offered them for sale. These groups are listed alphabetically; regional divisions of national organizations follow the parent organization's listing. Within each subordinate section, items are listed in numerical (not chronological) order, with a description similar to that used for cataloged entries.

Section 7: Boxes

Over the past 25 years, original boxes and other forms of packaging have assumed significance for some collectors. These hobbyists insist that the trains they buy come in the boxes and have the paperwork and ancillary pieces (inserts, instruction sheets, and envelopes) that the manufacturer packed with them before offering them for sale.

Cardboard boxes, inserts, and assorted sheets of paper are more fragile than die-cast metal or plastic trains. They were also deemed to be less important to the children playing with toy trains long ago and so were not treated with the same care. Instruction sheets were lost, and boxes were discarded. As a result, fewer boxes and instruction sheets have survived than have the trains and accessories that went with them. In some cases, the box that a particular locomotive, car, or even set came in is now valued more than the item itself. Boxes are evaluated according to standards and conditions established by the Train Collectors Association, similar to those developed for toy trains and accessories:

P-10 **Mint:** Brand new, complete, all original as made, and unused. Flaps appear to never have been opened, and edges are crisp. No tears, fading, or wear marks. Contains original contents and all applicable sealing tape, wrap, and staples.

P-9 **Store New:** Complete, all original, and unused. May have merchant additions such as store stamps and price tags. Must have appropriate inner liners.

P-8 **Like New:** Complete and all original. There is evidence of light use and aging. Box may have notations (discrete) added since leaving the manufacturer.

P-7 **Excellent:** Complete and all original. Box shows moderate signs of being opened and closed including edge and corner wear. All flaps must be intact.

P-6 **Very Good:** Complete and all original. Box shows signs of usage such as minor abrasions, small tears, color changes, and minor soiling. Inner liners may be missing, and inner flaps may require strengthening. The box can still safely store its original contents.

P-5 **Good:** Box shows substantial wear, and edges may be damaged. Box may have extensive color fading but no evident water damage or cardboard deterioration. Exterior flaps are present, but their connection to the box may require repair. Inner liners may be missing. With care, the box can still store contents. (Any box that has been repaired cannot be graded above P-5.)

P-4 **Fair:** Box shows heavy damage and may have been repaired. Inner flaps may be missing. Box cannot store its original contents. Water damage may be present.

Values for postwar boxes in this section are shown for Good (P-5) and Excellent (P-7) conditions.

Lionel used these box types during the postwar years:

Art Deco: Original postwar box with bold orange and blue design and lettering. It was used in 1946 and 1947.

Classic: More understated design than Art Deco. It was the main component box from 1948 through 1958. Boxes can be divided into Early (1948–49), Middle (1949–55), and Late (1956–58) Classic designs, which are marked by minor lettering changes.

Orange Perforated: This was a significant change from the Classic design. The solid orange box features white lettering and a tear-out perforated front panel. It was used in 1959 and 1960.

Orange Picture: Instead of a perforated panel, this version of the Orange Perforated box features an illustration of a steam locomotive and an F3 diesel on the front. It was used from 1961 to 1964.

Hillside Orange Picture: Similar to an Orange Picture box, it is labeled with Hillside, N.J., where Lionel's plant was located. It was used in 1965.

Cellophane: Used in 1966, this box features a clear cellophane window on the front.

Hagerstown Checkerboard: It has a Lionel checkerboard pattern and Hagerstown, Maryland, printed on end flap bottoms. The box was used in 1968.

Hillside Checkerboard: This 1969 box is the same as the Hagerstown Checkerboard box, but with Hillside, New Jersey, printed on it.

Lionel also used brown corrugated and plain white boxes.

Section 8: Sets

This section lists boxed train sets cataloged by Lionel during the postwar years, 1945–69. When collecting sets, it is important that the sets, or outfits, contain all the items, including ancillary ones, that Lionel packed with them. These items include the locomotive (and tender if a steam engine) rolling stock, any accessories, track, transformer, instructions and other paper pieces, component boxes, and the set box.

The listings include the set's catalog number, a short description, and product numbers for the locomotives, rolling stock, and any major accessories. Sets came with O-27 gauge, O gauge, or Super O track. O-27 and Super O track are listed in the set's description. If no track is listed, the set came with O gauge.

Set values are listed for Excellent (C-7) condition. The presence and condition of original component boxes, set boxes, inserts and other packaging materials can have a significant effect on a set's value. The values reflect the inclusion of these materials. Values of individual set and component boxes can be found in Section 7.

Due to space constraints, not every item found in a set is listed in the description. You can find more complete information on a set's contents on various websites and in the third volume of *Greenberg's Guide to Lionel Trains 1945–1969: Cataloged Sets* by Paul Ambrose and Harold J. Lovelock. Even though the book is out of print, copies can be found from booksellers on the internet.

USING THE GUIDE

Number	Description	Good	Exc	
2561	Vista Valley Observation Car, *59–61* *	75	230	___
X6454	NYC Boxcar, *48*			
	(A) Brown body	15	35	___
	(B) Orange body	50	140	___
	(C) Tan body	20	60	___
6475	Libby's Crushed Pineapple Vat Car, *63u*	35	90	___

Condition → Good Exc

Identifying a catalog number

A Lionel catalog number is usually stamped, printed, or painted on an item. However, some products do not contain a catalog number. In these cases, you can match the product with its catalog number using a comprehensive reference book or website, including Lionel.com, which contains current and some past catalogs.

Two-, three-, and four-digit numbers predominated during the prewar (1901–42) and postwar (1945–69) periods. Four- and five-digit numbers, and now seven digit numbers, have been most common during the modern era (1970–2024).

On the models, catalog numbers often double as road numbers, although sometimes separate road numbers were added.

Locating an item

Sections are arranged in numerical order of catalog numbers. Items having one or more zeroes as placeholders are listed before those without placeholders. For example, a 004 4-6-4 Locomotive is listed before a 4 Electric Locomotive.

In the prewar and postwar sections, some items, such as transformers and track pieces, are identified by a letter. These products follow the numbered items.

Reading an entry

Every entry begins with the product's catalog number assigned by Lionel. (Club and special production cars may have numbers that were assigned by the group.)

A basic description of the model follows. It gives the type of product, lists the name of any railroad identified with it, and includes identifying characteristics, such as color or lettering. If the item has a road number that differs from its catalog number, that number is shown in quotation marks. (Most of these are seen in Section 3). Abbreviations used in the descriptions, including those of railroad names, are listed at the back of the price guide.

Next, you'll find the year or years during which that item was part of Lionel's cataloged product line. The years are shown in italics. If a year is followed by a u, this item is considered to be uncataloged. It was not part of the cataloged line but a promotional item that Lionel made or sponsored for an outside business or group.

Entries that show an asterisk (*) after the year have had one or more reissues of the item made.

Many entries feature variations, each indicated by a separate letter (A, B, and so forth). Variations amount to slight yet noteworthy differences in appearance that distinguish models that otherwise seem identical. These differences can relate to color, lettering, and details that were added or deleted. For items having many variations, an entry may not include every variation.

An entry concludes with an indication of the value of the item for several common conditions.

Condition

Lionel enthusiasts should be familiar with the condition and grading standards established by the Train Collectors Association, which are used as the basis for evaluating the condition of toy trains and accessories:

C-10 **Mint:** Brand new—all original, unused, and unblemished.

C-9 **Factory New:** Same condition as Mint but with evidence of factory rubs or slight signs of handling, shipping, and being test run at the factory.

C-8 **Like New:** Complete and all original with no rust or no missing parts; may show effects of being displayed or signs of age and may have been run.

C-7 **Excellent:** All original and may have minute scratches and paint nicks; no rust, no missing parts, and no distortion of component parts.

C-6 **Very Good:** Has minor scratches, paint nicks, or minor spots of surface rust; is free of dents and may have minor parts replaced.

C-5 **Good:** Shows evidence of heavy use and signs of play wear—small dents, scratches, minor paint loss, and minor surface rust.

C-4 **Fair:** Shows evidence of heavy use—scratches and dents, moderate paint loss, missing parts, and surface rust.

C-3 **Poor:** Requires major body repair and is a candidate for restoration; major rust, missing parts, and heavily scratched.

C-2 **Restoration:** Needs to be restored.

C-1 **Junk:** Parts value only.

Values are listed for prewar and postwar trains in Good (C-5) and Excellent (C-7) conditions. For modern-era trains, including special production and club cars, the values for Excellent (C-7) and Mint (C-10) are shown.

You may also see NRS listed as a value. NRS (No Reported Sales) refers to an item with limited pricing data since only a handful of these scarce items may have been reported.

Determining a model's condition

Look over a model carefully to see whether it has suffered serious damage, including warping and breaking. Then note whether any parts are missing. Feel for dents in metal and cracks in plastic. Check for areas marred by rust, mildew, or chipped paint.

The TCA condition standards will assist you in evaluating your model, such as deciding whether a prewar or postwar model falls below Good or above Excellent.

The assessment of a toy train's value is based on the expectations that it has not been modified and that all parts are present and original to it. Repainting or relettering a model seriously undermines a train's value, regardless of how beat-up and scratched it may have been before undergoing modification. Any model that has been altered should be labeled as a restoration; potential buyers deserve to be informed about how it has been modified, so they do not mistake it for an original.

A model that is missing some parts should be sold as is or have those parts replaced by identical originals. A tank car cataloged in 1935 that needs a brake wheel must have a part from 1935 put on it to be considered a true original. Adding a brake wheel from 1936 undermines the car's legitimacy as much as adding one from 2023 does.

The same rule applies to the ancillary items that came with various models. The value of a flatcar may depend largely on the miniature airplane or rocket packed with it; therefore, having a load that is a genuine original is essential to maintaining the value of that flatcar. Similarly, freight loaders must have whatever cargo came with them (coal, logs, trailers, and so forth). Reproductions should be identified as such.

NOTES

Section 1
PREWAR 1901–1942

			Good	Exc
___	**001**	4-6-4 Locomotive (00), 38-42	195	360
___	**1**	Bild-A-Motor (0), 28-31	60	140
___	**1**	Trolley (std), 06-14		
___		(A) Cream body, orange band and roof	1900	4750
___		(B) White body, blue band and roof	1750	4750
___		(C) Cream body, blue band and roof	1300	3150
___		(D) Cream body, blue band and roof, Curtis Bay	2150	5550
___		(E) Blue, cream band, blue roof	1450	3150
___	**1/111**	Trolley Trailer (std), 06-14	1000	2700
___	**002**	4-6-4 Locomotive (00), 39-42	160	285
___	**2**	Bild-A-Motor (std), 28-31	100	180
___	**2**	Trolley (std), 06-16*		
___		(A) Yellow, red band	1575	3575
___		(B) Red, yellow band	1200	5175
___	**2/200**	Trolley Trailer (std), 06-16	1000	1800
___	**003**	4-6-4 Locomotive (00), 39-42		
___		(A) 003W whistling Tender	190	395
___		(B) 003T nonwhistling Tender	175	355
___	**3**	Trolley (std), 06-13		
___		(A) Cream, orange band	1400	3100
___		(B) Cream, dark olive green band	1400	3100
___		(C) Orange, dark olive green band	1400	3100
___		(D) Dark green, cream windows	1400	3100
___		(E) Green, cream windows, Bay Shore	1650	3700
___	**3/300**	Trolley Trailer (std), 06-13	1500	3500
___	**004**	4-6-4 Locomotive (00), 39-42		
___		(A) 004W whistling Tender	210	350
___		(B) 004T nonwhistling Tender	190	310
___	**4**	Electric Locomotive 0-4-0 (0), 28-32*		
___		(A) Orange, black frame	550	875
___		(B) Gray, apple green stripe	580	1050
___	**4**	Trolley (std), 06-12		
___		(A) Cream, dark olive green band	3000	4950
___		(B) Green or olive green, cream roof	3000	4950
___	**4U**	No. 4 Kit Form (0), 28-29	1150	2050
___	**5**	0-4-0 Locomotive, no tender, early (std), 06-07		
___		(A) NYC & HRR	1000	1450
___		(B) Pennsylvania	1400	2300
___		(C) NYC & HRRR (3 Rs)	992	2050
___		(D) B&O RR	2850	6200
___	**5**	0-4-0 Locomotive, tender, early Special (std), 06-09	980	1300
___	**5**	0-4-0 Locomotive, no tender, later (std), 10-11	750	1150
___	**5**	0-4-0 Locomotive, tender, later Special (std), 10-11	920	1200

PREWAR 1901-1942		Good	Exc	
5/51	0-4-0 Locomotive, tender, latest (std), 12-23	800	1100	___
6	4-4-0 Locomotive (std), 06-23	860	2075	___
6	0-4-0 Locomotive Special (std), 08-09	1700	2950	___
7	Steam 4-4-0 Locomotive (std), 10-23*	1850	2550	___
8	Electric Locomotive 0-4-0 (std), 25-32			___
	(A) Maroon or mojave, brass windows and trim	130	250	___
	(B) Olive green, brass windows	155	205	___
	(C) Red, brass or cream windows	166	265	___
	(D) Peacock, orange windows	520	750	___
8	Trolley (std), 08-14*			___
	(A) Cream, orange band and roof	3000	5400	___
	(B) Dark green, cream windows	2825	6100	___
8E	Electric Locomotive 0-4-0 (std), 26-32			___
	(A) Mojave, brass windows and trim	175	250	___
	(B) Red, brass or cream windows	150	238	___
	(C) Peacock, orange windows	370	590	___
	(D) Pea green, cream stripe	465	670	___
9	Electric Locomotive 0-4-0 (std), 29*	1200	2150	___
9	Motor Car (std), 09-12		NRS	___
9	Trolley (std), 09	3000	18200	___
9E	Electric Locomotive (std), 28-35*			___
	(A) 0-4-0, orange	833	1083	___
	(B) 2-4-2, two-tone green	880	2550	___
	(C) 2-4-2, gunmetal gray	514	1100	___
9U	Electric Locomotive 0-4-0 Kit (std), 28-29	817	1975	___
10	Electric Locomotive 0-4-0 (std), 25-29*			___
	(A) Mojave, brass trim	145	215	___
	(B) Gray, brass trim	105	228	___
	(C) Peacock, brass inserts	145	165	___
	(D) Red, cream stripe	580	880	___
10	Interurban (std), 10-16			___
	(A) Maroon	3000	5750	___
	(B) Dark olive green	1200	2150	___
10E	Electric Locomotive 0-4-0 (std), 26-30			___
	(A) Olive green, black frame		NRS	___
	(B) Peacock, dark green or black frame	260	400	___
	(C) State brown, dark green frame	435	630	___
	(D) Gray, black frame	165	220	___
	(E) Red, cream stripe	620	890	___
011	Non derailing switches, 33-37	18	38	___
11	Flatcar, early (std), 06-08	150	360	___
11	Flatcar, later (std), 09-15	45	90	___
11	Flatcar, latest (std), 16-18	50	90	___
11	Flatcar, Lionel Corp. (std), 18-26	50	80	___
012	Switches, pair (O), 27-33	20	40	___
12	Gondola, early (std), 06-08	150	755	___

	PREWAR 1901-1942		Good	Exc
___	12	Gondola, later (std), 09-15	50	100
___	12	Gondola, latest (std), 16-18	33	70
___	12	Gondola, Lionel Corp. (std), 18-26	50	70
___	013	012 Switches and 439 panel board, 27-33	120	190
___	13	Cattle Car, early (std), 06-08	300	950
___	13	Cattle Car, later (std), 09-15	150	225
___	13	Cattle Car, latest (std), 16-18	65	115
___	13	Cattle Car, Lionel Corp. (std), 18-26	65	115
___	0014	Boxcar (OO), 38-42		
___		(A) Yellow, Lionel Lines	80	155
___		(B) Tuscan, Pennsylvania	40	75
___	14	Boxcar, early (std), 06-08	195	909
___	14	Boxcar, later (std), 09-15	80	105
___	14	Boxcar, latest (std), 16-18	75	105
___	14	Boxcar, Lionel Corp. (std), 18-26	2090	2153
___	0015	Tank Car (OO), 38-42		
___		(A) Silver, Sunoco	40	90
___		(B) Black, Shell	50	83
___	15	Oil Car, early (std), 06-08	200	580
___	15	Oil Car, later (std), 09-15	75	115
___	15	Oil Car, latest (std), 16-18	75	115
___	15	Oil Car, Lionel Corp. (std), 18-26	75	115
___	0016	Hopper Car (OO), 38-42		
___		(A) Gray	75	160
___		(B) Black	58	115
___	16	Ballast Dump Car, early (std), 06-11	400	1350
___	16	Ballast Dump Car, later (std), 09-15	95	175
___	16	Ballast Dump Car, latest (std), 16-18	95	175
___	16	Ballast Dump Car, Lionel Corp. (std), 18-26	95	175
___	0017	Caboose (OO), 38-42	40	90
___	17	Caboose, early (std), 06-08	220	1115
___	17	Caboose, later (std), 09-15	70	135
___	17	Caboose, latest (std), 16-18	75	135
___	17	Caboose, Lionel Corp. (std), 18-26	50	90
___	18	Pullman Car (std), 08		
___		(A) Dark olive green, nonremovable roof	700	2150
___		(B) Dark olive green, removable roof	88	215
___		(C) Yellow-orange, removable roof	315	870
___		(D) Orange, removable roof	90	205
___		(E) Mojave, removable roof	305	890
___	18	Pullman Car (std), 11-13	600	900
___	18	Pullman Car (std), 13-15	150	270
___	18	Pullman Car (std), 15-18	150	270
___	18	Pullman Car (std), 18-22	90	155
___	18	Pullman Car (std), 23-26	270	530

PREWAR 1901-1942		Good	Exc	
19	Combine Car (std), 08			___
	(A) Dark olive green, nonremovable roof	1100	2600	___
	(B) Dark olive green, removable roof	80	148	___
	(C) Yellow-orange, removable roof	260	430	___
	(D) Orange, removable roof	115	205	___
	(E) Mojave, removable roof	305	890	___
19	Combine Car (std), 11-13	600	900	___
19	Combine Car (std), 13-15	200	270	___
19	Combine Car (std), 15-18	200	270	___
19	Combine Car (std), 18-22	90	155	___
19	Combine Car (std), 23-26	265	520	___
020	90-degree Crossover (O), 15-42	4	13	___
020X	45-degree Crossover (O), 17-42	3	10	___
20	90-degree Crossover (std), 09-32	4	10	___
20	Direct Current Reducer, 06	95	195	___
20X	45-degree Crossover (std), 28-32	5	10	___
021	Switches, pair (O), 15-37	20	50	___
21	90-degree Crossover (std), 06	10	20	___
21	Switches, pair (std), 15-25	35	70	___
022	Remote Control Switches, pair (O), 38-42	40	70	___
22	Manual Switches, pair (std), 06-25	45	75	___
023	Bumper (O), 15-33	15	35	___
23	Bumper (std), 06-23	15	40	___
0024	Pennsylvania Boxcar (OO), 39-42	45	75	___
24	Open Railway Station (std), 06	300	1500	___
025	Bumper (O), 28-42	15	54	___
0025	Tank Car (OO), 39-42			___
	(A) Black, Shell	40	90	___
	(B) Silver, Sunoco	40	80	___
25	Open Station (std), 06		NRS	___
25	Bumper (std), 27-42	25	45	___
26	Passenger Bridge (std), 06	15	40	___
0027	Caboose (OO), 39-42	40	70	___
27	Lighting Set, 11-23	15	40	___
27	Station (std), 09-12		NRS	___
28	Double Station with dome, 09-12		NRS	___
29	Day Coach (std), 07-22			___
	(A) Dark olive green, 9 windows	2100	3000	___
	(B) Maroon, 10 windows	1200	1500	___
	(C) Dark green, 10 windows	3000	4500	___
	(D) Dark olive green, 10 windows	485	1000	___
	(E) Dark green, 10 windows	450	900	___
0031	2-rail 13" Curve Track (OO), 39-42	5	10	___
31	Combine Car (std), 21-25			___
	(A) Maroon	70	90	___
	(B) Orange	125	195	___

		PREWAR 1901-1942	Good	Exc
___		(C) Dark olive green	65	90
___		(D) Brown	75	95
___	**0032**	2-rail 12" Straight Track (OO), 39-42	10	15
___	**32**	Mail Car (std), 21-25		
___		(A) Maroon	85	125
___		(B) Orange	120	185
___		(C) Dark olive green	65	85
___		(D) Brown	70	90
___	**32**	Miniature Figures, 09-18	95	250
___	**33**	Electric Locomotive 0-6-0, early (std), 13		
___		(A) Dark olive green, NYC in oval	105	188
___		(B) Black, NYC	320	950
___		(C) Dark olive green, NYC	440	950
___		(D) Pennsylvania RR	580	1250
___	**33**	Electric Locomotive 0-4-0, later (std), 13-24		
___		(A) Dark olive green or black, NYC	105	170
___		(B) Black, lettered C&O	395	720
___		(C) Maroon, red, or peacock	340	620
___	**0034**	2-rail 13" Curve Track, electrical connectors (OO), 39-42	10	15
___	**34**	Electric Locomotive 0-6-0, early (std), 12	520	860
___	**34**	Electric Locomotive 0-4-0 (std), 13	200	385
___	**35**	Pullman Car (std), 12-13		
___		(A) Dark blue	470	900
___		(B) Dark olive green	170	235
___	**35**	Pullman Car (std), 14-16		
___		(A) Dark olive green, maroon windows	35	70
___		(B) Maroon, green windows	75	105
___		(C) Orange, maroon windows	125	195
___	**35**	Pullman Car (std), 15-18	40	70
___	**35**	Pullman Car (std), 18-23		
___		(A) Dark olive green, maroon windows	30	50
___		(B) Maroon, green windows	25	45
___		(C) Orange, maroon windows	120	210
___		(D) Brown, green windows	30	50
___	**35**	Boulevard Street Lamp, 6 1/8" high, 40-42	27	50
___	**35**	Pullman Car (std), 24	40	55
___	**35**	Pullman Car (std), 25-26	40	55
___	**36**	Observation Car (std), 12-13		
___		(A) Dark blue	315	810
___		(B) Dark olive green	145	205
___	**36**	Observation Car (std), 14-16		
___		(A) Dark olive green, maroon windows	60	95
___		(B) Maroon, green windows	50	70
___		(C) Orange, maroon windows	180	290
___		(D) Brown, green windows	50	75
___	**36**	Observation Car (std), 15-18	60	80

PREWAR 1901-1942		Good	Exc	
36	Observation Car (std), 18-23			___
	(A) Dark olive green, maroon windows	40	55	___
	(B) Maroon, green windows	40	55	___
	(C) Orange, maroon windows	130	215	___
	(D) Brown, green windows	40	55	___
36	Observation Car (std), 24	40	55	___
36	Observation Car (std), 25-26	40	55	___
38	Electric Locomotive 0-4-0 (std), 13-24			___
	(A) Black	100	163	___
	(B) Red	475	680	___
	(C) Mojave or pea green	405	820	___
	(D) Dark green	270	360	___
	(E) Brown	270	315	___
	(F) Red, cream trim	405	540	___
	(G) Maroon	170	270	___
	(H) Gray	70	125	___
41	Accessory Contactor, 37-42	3	12	___
042	Switches, pair (O), 38-42	15	40	___
42	Electric Locomotive 0-4-4-0, square hood, early (std), 12*	760	1650	___
42	Electric Locomotive 0-4-4-0 , round hood, later (std), 3-23			___
	(A) Black or gray	300	510	___
	(B) Maroon	1250	3325	___
	(C) Dark gray	388	600	___
	(D) Dark green or mojave	600	800	___
	(E) Peacock	1100	3200	___
	(F) Olive or dark olive green	750	1200	___
043/43	Bild-A-Motor Gear Set, 29	40	85	___
0044	Boxcar (OO), 39-42	40	80	___
0044K	Boxcar Kit (OO), 39-42	75	120	___
0045	Tank Car (OO), 39-42			___
	(A) Black, Shell	40	95	___
	(B) Silver, Sunoco	40	80	___
0045K	Tank Car Kit (OO), 39-42	75	120	___
045	Automatic Gateman (O), 35-36	15	149	___
45	Automatic Gateman (std), 35-36	20	45	___
45N	Automatic Gateman (std, O), 37-42	58	159	___
0046	Hopper Car (OO), 39-42	50	90	___
0046K	Hopper Car Kit (OO), 39-42			___
	(A) Southern Pacific	75	135	___
	(B) Reading		NRS	___
46	Single Crossing Gate, 39-42	75	120	___
0047	Caboose (OO), 39-42	30	60	___
0047K	Caboose Kit (OO), 39-42	75	135	___
47	Double Crossing Gate, 39-42	63	140	___
48W	Whistle Station, 37-42	20	65	___

	PREWAR 1901-1942		Good	Exc
___	**50**	Electric Locomotive 0-4-0 (std), 24		
___		(A) Dark green or dark gray	133	250
___		(B) Maroon	315	600
___		(C) Mojave	175	345
___	**50**	Cardboard Train, Cars, Accessory (0), 43*	275	360
___	**0051**	7" Curve Track (00), 39-42	5	15
___	**51**	0-4-0 Locomotive, late, 8-wheel (std), 12-23	638	2375
___	**0052**	7" Straight Track (00), 39-42	10	15
___	**52**	Lamp Post, 33-41	45	112
___	**53**	Electric Locomotive 0-4-4-0, early (std), 12-14	1200	2450
___	**53**	Electric Locomotive 0-4-0, later (std), 15-19		
___		(A) Maroon	550	950
___		(B) Mojave	670	1350
___		(C) Dark olive green	560	1150
___	**53**	Electric Locomotive 0-4-0, latest (std), 20-21	200	450
___	**53**	Electric Locomotive 0-6-6-0, early (std), 11		NRS
___	**53**	Lamp Post, 31-42	30	65
___	**0054**	7" Curve Track, electrical connectors (00), 39-42	10	15
___	**54**	Electric Locomotive 0-4-4-0, early (std), 12*	2500	4050
___	**54**	Electric Locomotive 0-4-4-0, late (std), 13-23	1775	2700
___	**54**	Lamp Post, 29-35	60	244
___	**56**	Lamp Post, removable lens and cap, 24-42		
___		(A) Mojave	110	185
___		(B) Dark gray	55	110
___		(C) 45N green	25	45
___		(D) Pea green	30	225
___		(E) Aluminum	30	45
___		(F) Copper	60	160
___		(G) Dark green	30	45
___	**57**	Lamp Post with street names, 22-42		
___		(A) Orange post, Main St. & Broadway	35	55
___		(B) Orange post, Fifth Ave. & 42nd St.	40	95
___		(C) Orange post, Broadway & 21st St.	45	90
___		(D) Orange post, Broadway, 42nd St., Fifth Ave. & 21st St.	70	165
___		(E) Yellow post, Main St. & Broadway	35	89
___	**58**	Lamp Post, 7 3/8" high, 22-42		
___		(A) Cream	32	60
___		(B) Peacock	30	118
___		(C) Pea green	30	60
___		(D) Maroon	33	155
___		(E) Dark green	28	50
___		(F) Orange	30	60
___	**59**	Lamp Post, 8 3/4" high, 20-36	40	108
___	**060**	Telegraph Post (0), 29-42	10	25
___	**60**	Telegraph Post (std), 20-28	10	73
___	**60**	Electric Locomotive 0-4-0, FAO Schwartz (std), 15 u		NRS

PREWAR 1901-1942		Good	Exc	
0061	7" Curve Track, tubular (00), 38	3	10	___
61	Lamp Post, one globe, 14-36	35	65	___
61	Electric Locomotive 0-4-4-0, FAO Schwartz (std), 15 u		NRS	___
0062	7" Straight Track, tubular (00), 38	5	10	___
62	Semaphore, 20-32	30	50	___
62	Electric Locomotive 0-4-0, FAO Schwartz (std), 24-32 u		NRS	___
0063	Half Curve Track, tubular (00), 38-42	8	15	___
63	Semaphore, single arm, 15-21	25	50	___
63	Lamp Post, two globes, 33-42	135	265	___
0064	7" Curve Track, tubular, electrical connectors (00), 38	8	15	___
64	Lamp Post, 40-42	35	70	___
64	Semaphore, double arm, 15-21	30	60	___
0065	Half Straight Track, tubular (00), 38-42	10	15	___
65	Semaphore, one-arm, 15-26	30	60	___
65	Whistle Controller, 35	8	15	___
0066	5 5/8" Straight Track (00), 38-42	10	15	___
66	Semaphore, two-arm, 15-26	35	70	___
66	Whistle Controller, 36-39	5	10	___
67	Lamp Post, 15-32	85	145	___
67	Whistle Controller, 36-39	12	30	___
068	Warning Signal (0), 25-42	7	202	___
68	Warning Signal (std), 20-39	12	30	___
069	Electric Warning Bell Signal (0), 21-35	37	75	___
69	Electric Warning Bell Signal (std), 21-35	40	76	___
69N	Electric Warning Bell Signal (std, 0), 36-42	35	85	___
0070	90-degree Crossing, 38-42	5	10	___
70	Outfit: 62 (2), 59 (1), 68 (1), 21-32	60	815	___
071	060 Telegraph Post Set, 6 pieces (0), 29-42	70	160	___
71	60 Telegraph Post Set, 6 pieces (std), 21-31	35	173	___
0072	Remote Control Switches, pair (00), 38-42	155	290	___
0072L	Remote Control Switch, left hand (00), 38-42	50	95	___
0072R	Remote Control Switch, right hand (00)	50	95	___
0074	Boxcar (00), 39-42	35	85	___
0075	Tank Car (00), 39-42	50	145	___
076	Block Signal (0), 23-28	35	105	___
76	Warning Bell and Shack, 39-42	47	180	___
0077	Caboose (00), 39-42	30	60	___
77/077	Automatic Crossing Gate, 23-35	13	63	___
78/078	Train Signal, 24-32	45	100	___
79	Flashing Signal, 28-42	97	175	___
80/080	Semaphore, 26-35	75	120	___
81	Controlling Rheostat, 27-33	5	17	___
82/082	Semaphore, 27-35	40	120	___
83	Flashing Traffic Signal, 27-42	88	213	___
084	Semaphore (0), 27-32	60	100	___
84	Semaphore (std), 27-32	43	85	___

PREWAR 1901-1942			Good	Exc
___	**85**	Telegraph Pole (std), 29-42	18	30
___	**86**	Telegraph Poles, 6 pieces, 29-42	60	278
___	**87**	Flashing Crossing Signal, 27-42	168	308
___	**88**	Rheostat, 15-27	3	10
___	**88**	Direction Controller, 33-42	4	12
___	**89**	Flagpole, 23-34	40	132
___	**90**	Flagpole, 27-42	40	98
___	**91**	Circuit Breaker, 30-42	30	50
___	**092**	Signal Tower, 23-27	85	190
___	**92**	Floodlight Tower, 31-42*	149	243
___	**93**	Water Tower, 31-42	55	152
___	**94**	High Tension Tower, 32-42*	150	470
___	**95**	Controlling Rheostat, 34-42	5	15
___	**096**	Telegraph Post (O), 34-35	15	25
___	**96**	Coal Elevator, manual, 38-40	165	390
___	**097**	Telegraph Post and Signal Set (O), 34-35	45	75
___	**97**	Coal Elevator, 38-42	118	558
___	**98**	Coal Bunker, 38-40	107	320
___	**99N**	Train Control Block Signal, 36-42	45	153
___	**100**	Wooden Gondola (2 7/8"), 01		NRS
___	**100**	Bridge Approaches, 2 ramps (std), 20-31	20	40
___	**100**	Electric Locomotive (2 7/8"), 03-05*	2900	5200
___	**100**	Trolley (std), 10-16		
___		(A) Blue, white windows	1300	2700
___		(B) Blue, cream windows	1425	6733
___		(C) Red, cream windows	1300	2700
___	**101**	Bridge, span (104) and 2 approaches (100), 20-31	53	120
___	**101**	Summer Trolley (std), 10-13	1533	4200
___	**102**	Bridge, 2 spans (104) and 2 approaches (100), 20-31	70	175
___	**103**	Bridge (std), 13-16	40	75
___	**103**	Bridge, 3 spans (104) and 2 approaches (100), 20-31	60	145
___	**104**	Bridge Center Span (std), 20-31	20	45
___	**104**	Tunnel, papier mache (std), 09-14	50	135
___	**105**	Bridge (std), 11-14	40	70
___	**105**	Bridge Approaches, 2 ramps (O), 20-31	50	70
___	**106**	Bridge, span (110) and 2 approaches (105), 20-31	30	72
___	**106**	Rheostat, 11-14	3	10
___	**107**	DC Reducer, 110V, 23-32		NRS
___	**108**	Bridge, 2 spans (110) and 2 approaches (105), 20-31	50	90
___	**109**	Bridge, 3 spans, (110) and 2 approaches (105), 20-32	50	115
___	**109**	Tunnel, papier mache (std), 13-14	30	70
___	**110**	Bridge Center Span (O), 20-31	10	25
___	**111**	Box of 50 Bulbs, 20-31	55	105
___	**112**	Gondola, early (std), 10-12	225	400
___	**112**	Gondola, later (std), 12-16	40	65
___	**112**	Gondola, latest (std), 16-18	40	65

PREWAR 1901-1942		Good	Exc	
112	Gondola, Lionel Corp. (std), 18-26	40	65	___
112	Station, 31-35	133	270	___
113	Cattle Car, later (std), 12-16	50	70	___
113	Cattle Car, latest (std), 16-18	50	70	___
113	Cattle Car, Lionel Corp. (std), 18-26	30	55	___
113	Station with light fixtures, 31-34	150	310	___
114	Boxcar, later (std), 12-16	50	90	___
114	Boxcar, latest (std), 16-18	40	70	___
114	Boxcar, Lionel Corp. (std), 18-26	40	70	___
114	Station with light fixtures, 31-34	502	1200	___
115	Station with train control, 35-42*	128	370	___
116	Ballast Car, early and later (std), 10-16	85	115	___
116	Ballast Car, latest (std), 16-18	65	105	___
116	Ballast Car, Lionel Corp. (std), 18-26	55	95	___
116	Station with train control, 35-42*	419	997	___
117	Caboose, early (std), 12	40	75	___
117	Caboose, later (std), 12-16	40	75	___
117	Caboose, latest (std), 16-18	40	75	___
117	Caboose, Lionel Corp. (std), 18-26	30	60	___
117	Station, 36-42	87	235	___
118	Tunnel, metal, 8" long (O), 20-32	23	65	___
118L	Tunnel, metal, lighted, 8" long, 27	20	55	___
119	Tunnel, metal, 12" long, 20-42	25	115	___
119L	Tunnel, metal, lighted, 12" long, 27-33	20	55	___
120	Tunnel, metal, 17" long, 22-27	30	75	___
120L	Tunnel, metal, lighted, 17" long, 27-42	75	165	___
121	Station, lighted (std), 09-16			___
	(A) 14" x 10" x 9"		NRS	___
	(B) 13" x 9" x 13"	150	300	___
121	Station (std), 20-26	75	165	___
121X	Station (std), 17-19	110	255	___
122	Station (std), 20-30	55	190	___
123	Station (std), 20-23	75	210	___
123	Tunnel, paperboard base, 18 1/2" long (O), 33-42	105	255	___
124	Lionel City Station, 20-36*			___
	(A) Tan or gray base, pea green roof	77	240	___
	(B) Pea green base, red roof	234	360	___
125	Lionelville Station, 23-25	80	185	___
125	Track Template, 38	1	5	___
126	Lionelville Station, 23-36	95	205	___
127	Lionel Town Station, 23-36	95	160	___
128	115 Station and 129 Terrace, 35-42*	900	1900	___
128	124 Station and 129 Terrace, 31-34*	900	1900	___
129	Terrace, 28-42*	425	1100	___
130	Tunnel, 26" long (O), 20-36	100	415	___
130L	Tunnel, lighted, 26" long, 27-33	150	450	___

			Good	Exc
___	**131**	Corner Display, 24-28	125	295
___	**132**	Corner Grass Plot, 24-28	125	295
___	**133**	Heart-shaped Plot, 24-28	125	295
___	**134**	Lionel City Station with stop, 37-42	173	445
___	**134**	Oval-shaped Plot, 24-28	125	300
___	**135**	Circular Plot, 24-28	125	295
___	**136**	Large Elevation, 24-28		NRS
___	**136**	Lionelville Station with stop, 37-42	123	415
___	**137**	Station with stop, 37-42	97	160
___	**140L**	Tunnel, lighted, 37" long, 27-32	460	1875
___	**150**	Electric Locomotive 0-4-0, early (O), 17	93	590
___	**150**	Electric Locomotive 0-4-0, late (O), 18-25		
___		(A) Brown, brown or olive windows	95	225
___		(B) Maroon, dark olive windows	90	135
___	**152**	Electric Locomotive 0-4-0 (O), 17-27		
___		(A) Dark green	90	135
___		(B) Gray	100	160
___		(C) Mojave	340	680
___		(D) Peacock	340	1240
___	**152**	Crossing Gate, 40-42	20	40
___	**153**	Block Signal, 40-42	25	45
___	**153**	Electric Locomotive 0-4-0 (O), 24-25		
___		(A) Dark green	100	268
___		(B) Gray	100	160
___		(C) Mojave	100	160
___	**154**	Electric Locomotive 0-4-0 (O), 17-23	100	428
___	**154**	Highway Signal, 40-42		
___		(A) Black base	25	50
___		(B) Orange base	123	245
___	**155**	Freight Shed, 30-42*		
___		(A) Cream base, terra cotta floor	197	320
___		(B) Ivory base, red floor	133	400
___	**156L**	Electric Locomotive 0-4-0 (O), 17-23	400	720
___	**156**	Station Platform, 39-42	78	115
___	**156**	Electric Locomotive 4-4-4 (O), 17-23		
___		(A) Dark green	475	810
___		(B) Maroon	540	890
___		(C) Olive green	600	1050
___		(D) Gray	670	1200
___	**156X**	Electric Locomotive 0-4-0 (O), 23-24		
___		(A) Maroon	330	495
___		(B) Olive green	200	400
___		(C) Gray	530	1755
___		(D) Brown	420	600
___	**157**	Hand Truck, 30-32	20	40

PREWAR 1901-1942		Good	Exc	
158	Electric Locomotive 0-4-0 (0), 19-23			___
	(A) Gray or red windows	75	205	___
	(B) Black	95	250	___
158	Station Set: 136 Station and 2 platforms (156), 40-42	120	280	___
159	Block Actuator, 40	10	30	___
161	Baggage Truck, 30-32*	40	80	___
162	Dump Truck, 30-32*	40	80	___
163	Freight Accessory Set: 2 hand trucks (157), baggage truck (161), and dump truck (162), 30-42*	215	360	___
164	Log Loader, 40-42	120	743	___
165	Magnetic Crane, 40-42	182	245	___
165-22	Scrap Steel with bag, 40-42	50	125	___
165-83	Steel Blanks with bag, 40-42	50	177	___
166	Whistle Controller, 40-42	3	10	___
167	Whistle Controller, 40-42	8	25	___
167X	Whistle Controller (00), 40-42	5	15	___
168	Magic Electrol Controller, 40-42	25	75	___
169	Controller, 40-42	4	18	___
170	DC Reducer, 220V, 14-38	5	10	___
171	DC to AC Inverter, 110V, 36-42	5	15	___
172	DC to AC Inverter, 229V, 39-42	3	7	___
180	Pullman Car (std), 11-13			___
	(A) Maroon body and roof	145	205	___
	(B) Brown body and roof	145	255	___
180	Pullman Car (std), 13-15	80	160	___
180	Pullman Car (std), 15-18	80	160	___
180	Pullman Car (std), 18-22	80	135	___
181	Combine Car (std), 11-13			___
	(A) Maroon, dark olive doors	145	205	___
	(B) Brown, dark olive doors	145	205	___
	(C) Yellow-orange, orange doors	350	495	___
181	Combine Car (std), 13-15	80	160	___
181	Combine Car (std), 15-18	80	160	___
181	Combine Car (std), 18-22	80	135	___
182	Observation Car (std), 11-13			___
	(A) Maroon, dark olive doors	145	205	___
	(B) Brown, dark olive doors	145	205	___
	(C) Yellow-orange, orange doors	300	495	___
182	Observation Car (std), 13-15	80	160	___
182	Observation Car (std), 15-18	80	160	___
182	Observation Car (std), 18-22	80	135	___
184	Bungalow, illuminated, 23-32*	65	123	___
185	Bungalow, 23-24	50	115	___
186	184 Bungalows, set of 5, 23-32	195	630	___
186	Log Loader Outfit, 40-41	130	340	___
187	185 Bungalows, set of 5, 23-24	170	590	___
188	Elevator and Car Set, 38-41	115	370	___

	PREWAR 1901-1942		Good	Exc
___	**189**	Villa, illuminated, 23-32*	125	400
___	**190**	Observation Car (std), 08		
___		(A) Dark olive green, nonremovable roof	1150	2600
___		(B) Dark olive green, removable roof	115	205
___		(C) Yellow-orange, removable roof	320	620
___		(D) Orange, removable roof	115	205
___		(E) Mojave, removable roof	345	870
___	**190**	Observation Car (std), 11-13	600	900
___	**190**	Observation Car (std), 13-15	200	295
___	**190**	Observation Car (std), 15-18	200	295
___	**190**	Observation Car (std), 18-22	80	135
___	**190**	Observation Car (std), 23-26	230	475
___	**191**	Villa, illuminated, 23-32*	142	413
___	**192**	Illuminated Villa Set: 189, 191, 184 (2), 27-32	388	800
___	**193**	Automatic Accessory Set (O), 27-29	150	325
___	**194**	Automatic Accessory Set (std), 27-29	100	325
___	**195**	Terrace, 27-30	350	2130
___	**196**	Accessory Set, 27	200	335
___	**200**	Electric Express (2 7/8"), 03-05*	4000	11400
___	**200**	Trailer, matches No. 2 Trolley (std), 11-16	1200	2400
___	**200**	Turntable (std), 28-33*	85	190
___	**201**	0-6-0 Locomotive (O), 40-42		
___		(A) 2201B Tender, bell	296	760
___		(B) 2201T Tender, no bell	345	690
___	**202**	Summer Trolley (std), 10-13		
___		(A) Electric Rapid Transit	1300	2700
___		(B) Preston St.	3250	4500
___	**203**	Armored 0-4-0 (O), 17-21	1187	2067
___	**203**	0-6-0 Locomotive (O), 40-42		
___		(A) 2203B Tender, bell	400	495
___		(B) 2203T Tender, no bell	325	550
___	**204**	2-4-2 Locomotive (O), 40-42 u		
___		(A) Black	55	105
___		(B) Gunmetal gray	80	165
___	**205**	Merchandise Containers, 3 pieces, 30-38*	110	373
___	**206**	Sack of Coal, 38-42	5	20
___	**208**	Tool Set: 6 assorted tools, 34-42*	65	300
___	**0209**	Barrels, wooden, 6 pieces (O), 34-42		
___		(A) Solid barrels	10	25
___		(B) 2-piece barrels	53	153
___	**209**	Barrels, wooden, 4 pieces (std), 34-42	10	146
___	**210**	Switches, pair (std), 26, 34-42	40	75
___	**211**	Flatcar (std), 26-40*	135	248
___	**212**	Gondola (std), 26-40*		
___		(A) Gray or light green	100	389
___		(B) Maroon	69	488

PREWAR 1901-1942		Good	Exc	
213	Cattle Car (std), 26-40*			___
	(A) Mojave, maroon roof	160	658	___
	(B) Terra-cotta, pea green roof	130	470	___
	(C) Cream, maroon roof	300	775	___
214	Boxcar (std), 26-40*			___
	(A) Terra-cotta, dark green roof	195	704	___
	(B) Cream body, orange roof	138	315	___
	(C) Yellow, brown roof	300	573	___
214R	Refrigerator Car (std), 29-40*			___
	(A) Ivory or white, peacock roof	263	548	___
	(B) White, light blue roof	435	790	___
215	Tank Car (std), 26-40*			___
	(A) Pea green	153	295	___
	(B) Ivory	220	1028	___
	(C) Aluminum	315	798	___
216	Hopper Car (std), 26-38*			___
	(A) Dark green, brass plates	125	348	___
	(B) Dark green, nickel plates	445	1450	___
217	Caboose (std), 26-40*			___
	(A) Orange, maroon roof	257	673	___
	(B) Red, peacock roof	99	388	___
	(C) Red body and roof, ivory doors	200	390	___
217	Lighting Set, 14-23		NRS	___
218	Dump Car (std), 26-38*	220	533	___
219	Crane Car (std), 26-40*			___
	(A) Peacock, red boom	124	456	___
	(B) Yellow, light green or red boom	198	452	___
	(C) Ivory, light green boom	243	748	___
220	Floodlight Car (std), 31-40*			___
	(A) Terra-cotta base	217	580	___
	(B) Green base	340	728	___
220	Switches, pair (std), 26*	25	90	___
222	Switches, pair (std), 26-32	40	100	___
223	Switches, pair (std), 32-42	35	120	___
224/224E	2-6-2 Locomotive (O), 38-42			___
	(A) Black, die-cast 2224 Tender	110	294	___
	(B) Black, plastic 2224 Tender	110	195	___
	(C) Gunmetal, die-cast 2224 Tender	380	900	___
	(D) Gunmetal, sheet-metal 2689 Tender	120	306	___
225	222 Switches and 439 Panel, 29-32	115	260	___
225/225E	2-6-2 Locomotive (O), 38-42			___
	(A) Black, 2235 or 2245 Tender	190	372	___
	(B) Black, 2235 plastic Tender	185	320	___
	(C) Gunmetal, 2225 or 2265 Tender	203	360	___
	(D) Gunmetal, 2235 die-cast Tender	355	1040	___
226/226E	2-6-4 Locomotive (O), 38-41	291	946	___

PREWAR 1901-1942			Good	Exc
___	**227**	0-6-0 Locomotive (O), 39-42		
___		(A) 2227B Tender, bell	513	1413
___		(B) 2227T Tender, no bell	577	1200
___	**228**	0-6-0 Locomotive (O), 39-42		
___		(A) 2228B Tender, bell	600	1250
___		(B) 2228T Tender, no bell	600	1150
___	**229**	2-4-2 Locomotive (O), 39-42		
___		(A) Black or gunmetal, 2689W Tender	155	240
___		(B) Black or gunmetal, 2689T Tender	120	200
___		(C) Black, 2666W whistle Tender	155	280
___		(D) Black, 2666T nonwhistling Tender	120	200
___	**230**	0-6-0 Locomotive (O), 39-42	1050	2050
___	**231**	0-6-0 Locomotive (O), 39	1000	3150
___	**232**	0-6-0 Locomotive (O), 40-42	1000	1800
___	**233**	0-6-0 Locomotive (O), 40-42	900	1800
___	**238**	4-4-2 Locomotive (O), 39-40 u	430	710
___	**238E**	4-4-2 Locomotive (O), 36-38		
___		(A) 265W or 2225W whistle Tender	280	345
___		(B) 265 or 2225T nonwhistling Tender	275	360
___	**248**	Electric Locomotive 0-4-0 (O), 27-32	150	240
___	**249/249E**	2-4-2 Locomotive (O), 36-39		
___		(A) Gunmetal, 265T or 265W Tender	100	270
___		(B) Black, 265W Tender	110	210
___	**250**	Electric Locomotive 0-4-0, early (O), 26	125	220
___	**250**	Electric Locomotive 0-4-0, late (O), 34		
___		(A) Yellow-orange body, terra-cotta frame	145	245
___		(B) Terra-cotta body, maroon frame	160	270
___	**250E**	4-4-2 Hiawatha Locomotive (O), 35-42*	400	995
___	**250W**	Hiawatha Tender (O), 35-42*	125	250
___	**251**	Electric Locomotive 0-4-0 (O), 25-32		
___		(A) Gray body, red windows	190	340
___		(B) Red body, ivory stripe	215	455
___		(C) Red body, no ivory stripe	200	380
___	**251E**	Electric Locomotive 0-4-0 (O), 27-32		
___		(A) Red body, ivory stripe	225	425
___		(B) Red body, no ivory stripe	215	395
___		(C) Gray, red trim	153	513
___	**252**	Electric Locomotive 0-4-0 (O), 26-32		
___		(A) Peacock or olive green	87	187
___		(B) Terra-cotta or yellow-orange	113	560
___	**252E**	Electric Locomotive 0-4-0 (O), 33-35		
___		(A) Terra-cotta	145	250
___		(B) Yellow-orange	125	205
___	**253**	Electric Locomotive 0-4-0 (O), 24-32		
___		(A) Maroon	225	537
___		(B) Dark green	93	250

		Good	Exc	
	(C) Mojave	105	235	___
	(D) Terra-cotta	180	430	___
	(E) Peacock	95	195	___
	(F) Red	210	475	___
253E	Electric Locomotive 0-4-0 (O), 31-36			___
	(A) Green	158	205	___
	(B) Terra-cotta	190	305	___
254	Electric Locomotive 0-4-0 (O), 24-32	210	308	___
254E	Electric Locomotive 0-4-0 (O), 27-34	180	292	___
255E	2-4-2 Locomotive (O), 35-36	485	1000	___
256	Electric Locomotive 0-4-4-0 (O), 24-30*			___
	(A) Rubber-stamped lettering	397	2083	___
	(B) no outline around Lionel	419	770	___
	(C) Lionel Lines and No. 256 on brass	388	1050	___
257	2-4-0 Locomotive (O), 30-35 u			___
	(A) Black tender	145	250	___
	(B) Black crackle-finish tender	240	435	___
258	2-4-0 Locomotive, early (O), 30-35 u			___
	(A) 4-wheel 257 Tender	85	185	___
	(B) 8-wheel 258 Tender	100	195	___
258	2-4-2 Locomotive, late (O), 41 u			___
	(A) Black	60	100	___
	(B) Gunmetal	85	135	___
259	2-4-2 Locomotive (O), 32	70	144	___
259E	2-4-2 Locomotive (O), 33-42	88	193	___
259T	Tender	15	30	___
260E	2-4-2 Locomotive (O), 30-35*			___
	(A) Black body, green or black frame	362	507	___
	(B) Dark gunmetal body and frame	435	693	___
261	2-4-2 Locomotive (O), 31	125	210	___
261E	2-4-2 Locomotive (O), 35	175	285	___
262	2-4-2 Locomotive (O), 31-32	153	320	___
262E	2-4-2 Locomotive (O), 33-36			___
	(A) Gloss black, copper and brass trim	110	270	___
	(B) Satin black, nickel trim	150	237	___
263E	2-4-2 Locomotive (O), 36-39*			___
	(A) Gunmetal gray	272	610	___
	(B) 2-tone blue, from Blue Comet	415	950	___
263W	Tender, gunmetal	99	200	___
264E	2-4-2 Locomotive (O), 35-36			___
	(A) Red, Red Comet	135	310	___
	(B) Black	200	380	___
265E	2-4-2 Locomotive (O), 35-40			___
	(A) Black or gunmetal	160	345	___
	(B) Light blue, Blue Streak	460	800	___
265T	Tender	15	28	___

			Good	Exc
___	**267E/W**	Set: 616, 617 (2), 618, 35-41	275	655
___	**270**	Bridge, 10" long (O), 31-42	30	133
___	**270**	Lighting Set, 15-23		NRS
___	**271**	270 Bridges, set of 2, 31-33, 35-40	65	150
___	**271**	Lighting Set, 15-23		NRS
___	**272**	270 Bridges, set of 3, 31-33, 35-40	60	165
___	**280**	Bridge, 14" long (std), 31-42	60	176
___	**281**	280 Bridges, set of 2, 31-33, 35-40	90	205
___	**282**	280 Bridges, set of 3, 31-33, 35-40	105	265
___	**289E**	2-4-2 Locomotive (O), 37 u	120	305
___	**300**	Electric Trolley Car (2 7/8"), 01-05	2000	3600
___	**300**	Hellgate Bridge (std), 28-42*		
___		(A) Cream towers, green truss	613	1375
___		(B) Ivory towers, aluminum truss	704	1600
___	**303**	Summer Trolley, 10-13	1500	3150
___	**308**	Signs, set of 5 (O), 40-42	30	70
___	**309**	Electric Trolley Trailer (2 7/8"), 01-05	2500	4050
___	**309**	Pullman Car (std), 26-39		
___		(A) Maroon body and roof, mojave windows	100	160
___		(B) Mojave body and roof, maroon windows	100	160
___		(C) Light brown body, dark brown roof	120	190
___		(D) Medium blue body, dark blue roof	170	280
___		(E) Apple green body, dark green roof	170	280
___		(F) Pale blue body, silver roof	100	185
___		(G) Maroon body, terra-cotta roof	130	195
___	**310**	Rails and Ties, complete section (2 7/8"), 01-02	5	15
___	**310**	Baggage Car (std), 26-39		
___		(A) Maroon body and roof, mojave windows	100	160
___		(B) Mojave body and roof, maroon windows	85	160
___		(C) Light brown body, dark brown roof	115	185
___		(D) Medium blue body, dark blue roof	170	280
___		(E) Apple green body, dark green roof	170	280
___		(F) Pale blue body, silver roof	100	175
___	**312**	Observation Car (std), 24-39		
___		(A) Maroon body and roof, mojave windows	100	160
___		(B) Mojave body and roof, maroon windows	85	160
___		(C) Light brown body, dark brown roof	120	185
___		(D) Medium blue body, dark blue roof	170	280
___		(E) Apple green body, dark green roof	170	280
___		(F) Pale blue body, silver roof	100	175
___		(G) Maroon body, terra-cotta roof	130	195
___	**313**	Bascule Bridge (O), 40-42		
___		(A) Silver bridge	330	500
___		(B) Gray bridge	180	590
___	**314**	Girder Bridge (O), 40-42	25	40
___	**315**	Illuminated Trestle Bridge (O), 40-42	30	80

PREWAR 1901-1942		Good	Exc	
316	Trestle Bridge (O), 40-42	25	50	___
318	Electric Locomotive 0-4-0 (std), 24-32			___
	(A) Gray, dark gray, or mojave	150	300	___
	(B) Pea green	150	250	___
	(C) State brown	250	395	___
318E	Electric Locomotive 0-4-0, 26-35			___
	(A) Gray, mojave, or pea green	190	250	___
	(B) State brown	275	440	___
	(C) Black	550	1275	___
319	Pullman Car (std), 24-27	105	175	___
320	Baggage Car (std), 25-27	100	175	___
320	Switch and Signal (2 7/8"), 02-05		NRS	___
322	Observation Car (std), 24-27, 29-30 u	100	175	___
330	90-degree Crossing (2 7/8"), 02-05		NRS	___
332	Baggage Car (std), 26-33			___
	(A) Red body and roof, cream doors	80	120	___
	(B) Peacock body and roof, orange doors	75	115	___
	(C) Gray body and roof, maroon doors	75	115	___
	(D) Olive green body and roof, red doors	90	145	___
	(E) State brown body, dark brown roof	190	430	___
337	Pullman Car (std), 25-32			___
	(A) Red body and roof, cream doors	95	190	___
	(B) Mojave body and roof, maroon doors	68	190	___
	(C) Olive green body and roof, red doors	105	225	___
	(D) Olive green body and roof, maroon doors	95	190	___
	(E) Pea green body and roof, cream doors	210	500	___
338	Observation Car (std), 25-32			___
	(A) Red body and roof, cream doors	95	190	___
	(B) Mojave body and roof, maroon doors	68	190	___
	(C) Olive green body and roof, red doors	105	225	___
	(D) Olive green body and roof, maroon doors	95	190	___
339	Pullman Car (std), 25-33			___
	(A) Peacock body and roof, orange doors	55	90	___
	(B) Gray body and roof, maroon doors	55	100	___
	(C) State brown body, dark brown roof	135	380	___
	(D) Peacock body, dark green roof	75	130	___
	(E) Mojave body, maroon roof and doors	145	230	___
340	Suspension Bridge (2 7/8"), 02-05*		NRS	___
341	Observation Car (std), 25-33			___
	(A) Peacock body and roof, orange doors	50	70	___
	(B) Gray body and roof, maroon doors	50	70	___
	(C) State brown body, dark brown roof	75	160	___
	(D) Peacock body, dark green roof	65	95	___
	(E) Mojave body, maroon roof and doors	135	165	___
350	Track Bumper (2 7/8"), 02-05	225	550	___
380	Elevated Pillars (2 7/8"), 04-05*	30	70	___

	PREWAR 1901-1942		Good	Exc
___	**380**	Electric Locomotive 0-4-0 (std), 23-27	310	440
___	**380E**	Electric Locomotive 0-4-0 (std), 26-29		
___		(A) Mojave	445	630
___		(B) Maroon	295	400
___		(C) Dark green	370	460
___	**381**	Electric Locomotive 4-4-4 (std), 28-29*	1600	2100
___	**381E**	Electric Locomotive 4-4-4 (std), 28-36*		
___		(A) State green, apple green subframe	1112	2385
___		(B) State green, red subframe	1900	3250
___	**381U**	Electric Locomotive 4-4-4 Kit (std), 28-29	1600	4100
___	**384**	2-4-0 Locomotive (std), 30-32*	490	730
___	**384E**	2-4-0 Locomotive (std), 30-32*	425	650
___	**385E**	2-4-2 Locomotive (std), 33-39*	370	670
___	**390**	2-4-2 Locomotive (std), 29*	460	798
___	**390E**	2-4-2 Locomotive (std), 29-31*		
___		(A) Black, with or without orange stripe	430	690
___		(B) 2-tone blue, cream-orange stripe	650	1050
___		(C) 2-tone green, orange or green stripe	990	3175
___	**392E**	4-4-2 Locomotive (std), 32-39*		
___		(A) Black, 384 Tender	788	1250
___		(B) Black, large 12-wheel tender	838	1850
___		(C) Gunmetal gray	988	1800
___	**400**	Express Trail Car (2 7/8"), 03-05*	3500	5850
___	**400E**	4-4-4 Locomotive (std), 31-39*		
___		(A) Black	1400	2425
___		(B) Blue	1500	2350
___		(C) Gunmetal or light blue	1350	3650
___		(D) Black crackle finish	1600	3500
___	**402**	Electric Locomotive 0-4-4-0 (std), 23-27	342	570
___	**402E**	Electric Locomotive 0-4-4-0 (std), 26-29	337	550
___	**404**	Summer Trolley (std), 10		NRS
___	**408E**	Electric Locomotive 0-4-4-0 (std), 27-36*		
___		(A) Apple green or mojave, red pilots	818	1600
___		(B) State brown, brown pilots	2000	3950
___		(C) State green, red pilots	2000	3800
___	**412**	California Pullman Car (std), 29-35*		
___		(A) Light green body, dark green roof	590	1750
___		(B) Light brown body, dark brown roof	735	2100
___	**413**	Colorado Pullman Car (std), 29-35*		
___		(A) Light green body, dark green roof	590	1750
___		(B) Light brown body, dark brown roof	620	2100
___	**414**	Illinois Pullman Car (std), 29-35*		
___		(A) Light green body, dark green roof	590	2825
___		(B) Light brown body, dark brown roof	620	2050

PREWAR 1901-1942		Good	Exc	
416	New York Observation Car (std), 29-35*			___
	(A) Light green body, dark green roof	590	1750	___
	(B) Light brown body, dark brown roof	620	2100	___
418	Pullman Car (std), 23-32*	225	320	___
419	Combination (std), 23-32*	190	280	___
420	Faye Pullman Car (std), 30-40*			___
	(A) Brass trim	555	900	___
	(B) Nickel trim	450	1200	___
421	Westphal Pullman Car (std), 30-40*			___
	(A) Brass trim	500	900	___
	(B) Nickel trim	500	1200	___
422	Tempel Observation Car (std), 30-40*			___
	(A) Brass trim	555	900	___
	(B) Nickel trim	500	1200	___
424	Liberty Bell Pullman Car (std), 31-40*			___
	(A) Brass trim	350	530	___
	(B) Nickel trim	385	650	___
425	Stephen Girard Pullman Car (std), 31-40*			___
	(A) Brass trim	350	530	___
	(B) Nickel trim	385	650	___
426	Coral Isle Observation Car (std), 31-40*			___
	(A) Brass trim	350	530	___
	(B) Nickel trim	385	650	___
428	Pullman Car (std), 26-30*			___
	(A) Dark green body and roof	250	385	___
	(B) Orange body and roof, apple green windows	390	890	___
429	Combine Car (std), 26-30*			___
	(A) Dark green body and roof	250	385	___
	(B) Orange body and roof, apple green windows	390	890	___
430	Observation Car (std), 26-30*			___
	(A) Dark green body and roof	250	385	___
	(B) Orange body and roof, apple green windows	390	890	___
431	Diner (std), 27-32*			___
	(A) Mojave body, screw-mounted roof	350	540	___
	(B) Mojave body, hinged roof	465	720	___
	(C) Dark green body, orange windows	410	720	___
	(D) Orange body, apple green windows	410	720	___
	(E) Apple green body, red windows	410	720	___
435	Power Station, 26-38*	218	783	___
436	Power Station, 26-37*			___
	(A) Power Station plate	88	295	___
	(B) Edison Service plate	270	610	___
437	Switch Signal Tower, 26-37*	183	1263	___
438	Signal Tower, 27-39*			___
	(A) Mojave base, orange house	158	363	___
	(B) Black base, white house	174	640	___

PREWAR 1901-1942			Good	Exc
____	**439**	Panel Board, 28-42*	85	148
____	**440/0440**	Signal Bridge, 32-35*	170	472
____	**440C**	Panel Board, 32-42	90	145
____	**441**	Weighing Station (std), 32-36	359	1325
____	**442**	Landscaped Diner, 38-42	117	420
____	**444**	Roundhouse (std), 32-35*	1350	3475
____	**444-18**	Roundhouse Clip, 33		NRS
____	**450**	Electric Locomotive 0-4-0, Macy's (0), 30 u		
____		(A) Red, black frame	295	700
____		(B) Apple green, dark green frame	415	880
____	**450**	Set: 450, matching 605, 606 (2), 30 u	750	1800
____	**490**	Observation Car (std), 23-32*	190	255
____	**500**	Electric Derrick Car (2 7/8"), 03-04*	5000	6750
____	**511**	Flatcar (std), 27-40		
____		(A) Dark green	65	95
____		(B) Medium green	75	165
____	**512**	Gondola (std), 27-39		
____		(A) Peacock	30	143
____		(B) Light green	50	95
____	**513**	Cattle Car (std), 27-38		
____		(A) Olive green, orange roof	70	360
____		(B) Orange, pea green roof	120	255
____		(C) Cream, maroon roof	80	250
____	**514**	Boxcar (std), 29-40		
____		(A) Cream, orange roof	90	327
____		(B) Yellow, brown roof	115	285
____	**514**	Refrigerator Car, ivory or white, peacock roof, (std), 27-28	240	400
____	**514R**	Refrigerator Car (std), 29-40		
____		(A) Ivory, peacock roof	113	190
____		(B) White, light blue roof	350	545
____	**515**	Tank Car (std), 27-40		
____		(A) Terra-cotta	90	145
____		(B) Ivory	105	378
____		(C) Aluminum	90	325
____		(D) Orange, red Shell decal	230	750
____	**516**	Hopper Car (std), 28-40		
____		(A) Red	170	280
____		(B) Red, rubber-stamped data	200	300
____		(C) Light red, nickel trim	200	325
____	**517**	Caboose (std), 27-40		
____		(A) Pea green body, red roof	50	133
____		(B) Red body and roof	90	155
____		(C) Red body, black roof, orange windows	355	640
____	**520**	Floodlight Car (std), 31-40		
____		(A) Terra-cotta base	110	210
____		(B) Green base	118	240

		Good	Exc	
529	Pullman Car (O), 26-32			___
	(A) Olive green body and roof	25	45	___
	(B) Terra-cotta body and roof	25	60	___
530	Observation Car (O), 26-32			___
	(A) Olive green body and roof	25	45	___
	(B) Terra-cotta body and roof	25	60	___
550	Miniature Figures, boxed (std), 32-36*	175	503	___
551	Engineer (std), 32	25	45	___
552	Conductor (std), 32	20	40	___
553	Porter with stool (std), 32	25	50	___
554	Male Passenger (std), 32	25	45	___
555	Female Passenger (std), 32	25	45	___
556	Red Cap with suitcase (std), 32	25	65	___
600	Derrick Trailer (2 7/8"), 03-04*	5000	8550	___
600	Pullman Car, early (O), 15-23			___
	(A) Dark green	65	170	___
	(B) Maroon or brown	45	85	___
600	Pullman Car, late (O), 33-42			___
	(A) Light red or gray, red roof	50	90	___
	(B) Light blue, aluminum roof	70	120	___
601	Observation Car, late (O), 33-42			___
	(A) Light red body and roof	50	85	___
	(B) Light gray, red roof	50	90	___
	(C) Light blue body, aluminum roof	70	120	___
601	Pullman Car, early (O), 15-23	50	70	___
602	Lionel Lines Baggage Car, late (O), 33-42			___
	(A) Light red or gray, red roof	60	110	___
	(B) Light blue, aluminum roof	90	150	___
602	NYC Baggage Car (O), 15-23	33	45	___
602	Observation Car (O), 22 u	30	45	___
603	Pullman Car, early (O), 22 u	40	70	___
603	Pullman Car, later (O), 20-25	20	45	___
603	Pullman Car, latest (O), 31-36			___
	(A) Light red body and roof	45	85	___
	(B) Red body, black roof	35	60	___
	(C) Stephen Girard green body, dark green roof	35	60	___
	(D) Maroon body and roof, Macy Special	60	125	___
604	Observation Car, later (O), 20-25	35	60	___
604	Observation Car, latest (O), 31-36			___
	(A) Light red body and roof	45	85	___
	(B) Red body, black roof	35	60	___
	(C) Yellow-orange body, terra-cotta roof	35	60	___
	(D) Stephen Girard green body, dark green roof	35	60	___
	(E) Maroon body and roof	70	150	___

			Good	Exc
___	**605**	Pullman Car (O), 25-32		
___		(A) Gray, Lionel Lines	85	170
___		(B) Gray, Illinois Central	85	170
___		(C) Red, Lionel Lines	170	255
___		(D) Red, Illinois Central	255	340
___		(E) Orange, Lionel Lines	170	255
___		(F) Orange, Illinois Central	300	430
___		(G) Olive green, Lionel Lines	255	340
___	**606**	Observation Car (O), 25-32		
___		(A) Gray, Lionel Lines	130	215
___		(B) Gray, Illinois Central	90	170
___		(C) Red, Lionel Lines	170	255
___		(D) Red, Illinois Central	255	340
___		(E) Orange, Lionel Lines	170	255
___		(F) Orange, Illinois Central	170	255
___		(G) Olive green, Lionel Lines	255	340
___	**607**	Pullman Car (O), 26-27		
___		(A) Peacock, Lionel Lines	50	70
___		(B) Peacock, Illinois Central	75	115
___		(C) 2-tone green, Lionel Lines	50	75
___		(D) Red, Lionel Lines	75	110
___	**608**	Observation Car (O), 26-37		
___		(A) Peacock, Lionel Lines	50	70
___		(B) Peacock, Illinois Central	75	115
___		(C) 2-tone green, Lionel Lines	50	75
___		(D) Red, Lionel Lines	75	110
___	**609**	Pullman Car (O), 37	60	85
___	**610**	Pullman Car, early (O), 15-25		
___		(A) Dark green body and roof	50	65
___		(B) Maroon body and roof	60	95
___		(C) Mojave body and roof	60	95
___	**610**	Pullman Car, late (O), 26-30		
___		(A) Olive green body and roof	65	80
___		(B) Mojave body and roof	55	80
___		(C) Terra-cotta body, maroon roof	100	155
___		(D) Pea green body and roof	70	115
___		(E) Light blue body, aluminum roof	130	260
___		(F) Light red body, aluminum-painted roof	100	155
___	**611**	Observation Car (O), 37	55	80
___	**612**	Observation Car, early (O), 15-25		
___		(A) Dark green body and roof	40	60
___		(B) Maroon body and roof	70	90
___		(C) Mojave body and roof	70	90
___	**612**	Observation Car, late (O), 26-30		
___		(A) Olive green body and roof	55	80
___		(B) Mojave body and roof	55	80

		Good	Exc	
	(C) Terra-cotta body, maroon roof	100	155	___
	(D) Pea green body and roof	70	115	___
	(E) Light blue body, aluminum roof	130	260	___
	(F) Light red body, aluminum-painted roof	100	155	___
613	Pullman Car (O), 31-40*			___
	(A) Terra-cotta body, maroon/terra-cotta roof	85	195	___
	(B) Light red body, light red/aluminum roof	175	350	___
	(C) Blue, two-tone blue roof	115	354	___
614	Observation Car (O), 31-40*			___
	(A) Terra-cotta body, maroon/terra-cotta roof	100	190	___
	(B) Light red body, light red/aluminum roof	175	350	___
	(C) Blue, two-tone blue roof	100	228	___
615	Baggage Car (O), 33-40*	150	260	___
616E/W	Diesel only (O), 35-41	90	215	___
616E/W	Set: 616, 617 (2), 618	225	570	___
617	Coach (O), 35-41			___
	(A) Blue and white	55	85	___
	(B) Chrome, gunmetal skirts	55	180	___
	(C) Chrome, chrome skirts	55	85	___
	(D) Silver-painted	55	85	___
618	Observation Car (O), 35-41			___
	(A) Blue and white	55	85	___
	(B) Chrome, gunmetal skirts	55	85	___
	(C) Chrome, chrome skirts	55	85	___
	(D) Silver-painted	55	85	___
619	Combine Car (O), 36-38			___
	(A) Blue, white windows band	100	205	___
	(B) Chrome, chrome skirts	100	205	___
620	Floodlight Car (O), 37-42	39	85	___
629	Pullman Car (O), 24-32			___
	(A) Dark green body and roof	25	40	___
	(B) Orange body and roof	25	40	___
	(C) Red body and roof	20	35	___
	(D) Light red body and roof	30	55	___
630	Observation Car, 24-32			___
	(A) Dark green body and roof	25	40	___
	(B) Orange body and roof	25	40	___
	(C) Red body and roof	20	35	___
	(D) Light red body and roof	30	55	___
636W	Diesel only (O), 36-39	90	175	___
636W	Set: 636W, 637 (2), 638, 36-39	322	640	___
637	Coach (O), 36-39	70	105	___
638	Observation Car (O), 36-39	70	105	___
651	Flatcar (O), 35-40	30	65	___
652	Gondola (O), 35-40	28	55	___
653	Hopper Car (O), 34-40	35	65	___

PREWAR 1901-1942		Good	Exc
___ **654**	Tank Car (0), 34-42		
___	(A) Orange or aluminum	35	60
___	(B) Gray	40	75
___ **655**	Boxcar (0), 34-42		
___	(A) Cream, maroon roof	35	60
___	(B) Cream, tuscan roof	45	75
___ **656**	Cattle Car (0), 35-40		
___	(A) Light gray, vermilion roof	40	100
___	(B) Burnt orange, tuscan roof	70	125
___ **657**	Caboose (0), 34-42		
___	(A) Red body and roof	20	35
___	(B) Red body, tuscan roof	25	40
___ **659**	Dump Car (0), 35-42	40	82
___ **700**	Electric Locomotive 0-4-0 (0), 15-16	360	690
___ **700E**	4-6-4 NYC Hudson "5344," scale (0), 37-42*	1433	4517
___ **700K**	4-6-4 Locomotive, unbuilt gray primer (0), 38-42	4400	5950
___ **701**	0-6-0 PRR Locomotive "8976," 41	900	2100
___ **701**	Electric Locomotive 0-4-0 (0), 15-16	376	780
___ **702**	Baggage Car (0), 17-21	115	803
___ **703**	Electric Locomotive 4-4-4 (0), 15-16	711	2547
___ **706**	Electric Locomotive 0-4-0 (0), 15-16	375	1465
___ **708**	0-6-0 PRR Locomotive "8976" (0), 39-42*	1450	2850
___ **710**	Pullman Car (0), 24-34		
___	(A) Red, Lionel Lines	200	300
___	(B) Orange, Lionel Lines	150	225
___	(C) Orange, New York Central	175	225
___	(D) Orange, Illinois Central	300	450
___	(E) 2-tone blue, Lionel Lines	300	415
___	(F) Orange, New York Central	200	260
___ **711**	Remote Control Switches, pair (072), 35-42	83	236
___ **712**	Observation Car (0), 24-34		
___	(A) Red, Lionel Lines	185	355
___	(B) Orange, Lionel Lines	140	265
___	(C) Orange, New York Central	160	310
___	(D) Orange, Illinois Central	315	530
___	(E) 2-tone blue, Lionel Lines	280	485
___ **714**	Boxcar (0), 40-42*	333	610
___ **714K**	Boxcar, unbuilt (0), 40-42	220	480
___ **715**	Tank Car (0), 40-42*		
___	(A) SEPS 8124 decal	340	610
___	(B) SUNX 715 decal	313	880
___ **715K**	Tank Car, unbuilt (0), 40-42	250	530
___ **716**	Hopper Car (0), 40-42*	290	400
___ **716K**	Hopper Car, unbuilt (0), 40-42	350	730
___ **717**	Caboose (0), 40-42*	340	510
___ **717K**	Caboose, unbuilt (0), 40-42	275	590

PREWAR 1901-1942		Good	Exc	
720	90-degree Crossing (072), 35-42	20	40	___
721	Manual Switches, pair (072), 35-42	50	105	___
730	90-degree Crossing (072), 35-42	20	40	___
731	Remote Control Switches, pair, T-rail (072), 35-42	80	237	___
751E/W	Set: 752, 753 (2), 754 (0), 34-41*	587	943	___
752E	Diesel only (0), 34-41*			___
	(A) Yellow and brown	170	348	___
	(B) Aluminum	145	340	___
753	Coach (0), 36-41			___
	(A) Yellow and brown	68	143	___
	(B) Aluminum	75	180	___
754	Observation Car (0), 36-41			___
	(A) Yellow and brown	68	145	___
	(B) Aluminum	75	180	___
760	Curved Track, 16 pieces, (072), 35-42	40	80	___
761	Curved Track (072), 34-42	1	2	___
762	Straight Track (072), 34-42	1	2	___
762S	Insulated Straight Track (072), 34-42	2	5	___
763E	4-6-4 Locomotive (0), 37-42			___
	(A) Gunmetal, 263 or 2263W Tender	1125	2385	___
	(B) Gunmetal, 2226X or 2226WX Tender	1150	2950	___
	(C) Black, 2226WX Tender	965	2725	___
771	Curved Track, T-rail (072), 35-42	3	10	___
772	Straight Track, T-rail (072), 35-42	5	25	___
772S	Insulated Straight Track, T-rail (072), 35-42	15	30	___
773	Fishplate Set, 50 plates (072), 36-42	15	67	___
782	Hiawatha Combine Car (0), 35-41*	230	380	___
783	Hiawatha Coach (0), 35-41*	140	290	___
784	Hiawatha Observation Car (0), 35-41*	205	445	___
792	Rail Chief Combine Car (0), 37-41*	215	580	___
793	Rail Chief Coach (0), 37-41*	290	800	___
794	Rail Chief Observation Car (0), 37-41*	250	800	___
800	Boxcar (2 7/8"), 04-05*	2500	7775	___
800	Boxcar (0), 15-26			___
	(A) Light orange body, brown-maroon roof	45	70	___
	(B) Orange body and roof, PRR	25	45	___
801	Caboose (0), 15-26	30	50	___
802	Stock Car (0), 15-26	40	60	___
803	Hopper Car, early (0), 23-28	25	55	___
803	Hopper Car, late (0), 29-34	30	55	___
804	Tank Car (0), 23-28	11	45	___
805	Boxcar (0), 27-34			___
	(A) Pea green, terra-cotta roof	33	55	___
	(B) Pea green, maroon roof	45	115	___
	(C) Orange, maroon roof	45	95	___

	PREWAR 1901-1942		Good	Exc
___	**806**	Stock Car (O), 27-34		
___		(A) Pea green, terra-cotta roof	40	75
___		(B) Orange, various color roofs	35	50
___	**807**	Caboose (O), 27-40		
___		(A) Peacock body, dark green roof	20	35
___		(B) Red body, peacock roof	20	93
___		(C) Light red body and roof	20	40
___	**809**	Dump Car (O), 31-41		
___		(A) Orange bin	40	136
___		(B) Green bin	40	85
___	**810**	Crane Car (O), 30-42		
___		(A) Terra-cotta cab, maroon roof	170	260
___		(B) Cream cab, vermilion roof	110	205
___	**811**	Flatcar (O), 26-40		
___		(A) Maroon	40	83
___		(B) Aluminum	50	100
___	**812**	Gondola (O), 26-42	40	70
___	**812T**	Tool Set: pick, shovel, hammer, 30-41	40	105
___	**813**	Stock Car (O), 26-42		
___		(A) Orange body, pea green roof	76	145
___		(B) Orange body, maroon roof	55	135
___		(C) Cream body, maroon roof	100	225
___		(D) Tuscan body and roof	650	1900
___	**814**	Boxcar (O), 26-42		
___		(A) Cream, orange roof	50	145
___		(B) Cream, maroon roof	118	140
___		(C) Yellow, brown roof	95	120
___	**814R**	Refrigerator Car (O), 29-42		
___		(A) Ivory, peacock roof	100	213
___		(B) White, light blue roof	103	315
___		(C) Flat white, brown roof	600	1325
___	**815**	Tank Car (O), 26-42		
___		(A) Pea green, maroon frame	250	510
___		(B) Pea green, black frame	70	155
___		(C) Aluminum, black frame	50	100
___		(D) Orange-yellow, black frame	150	255
___	**816**	Hopper Car (O), 27-42		
___		(A) Olive green	85	155
___		(B) Red body	65	140
___		(C) Black body	370	680
___	**817**	Caboose (O), 26-42		
___		(A) Peacock body, dark green roof	45	323
___		(B) Red body, peacock roof	45	80
___		(C) Light red body and roof	45	80
___	**820**	Boxcar (O), 15-26		
___		(A) Orange, Illinois Central	40	80

	PREWAR 1901-1942	Good	Exc	
	(B) Orange, Union Pacific	50	105	___
820	Floodlight Car (0), 31-42			___
	(A) Terra-cotta	100	180	___
	(B) Green	100	175	___
	(C) Light green	105	180	___
821	Stock Car (0), 15-16, 25-26	45	85	___
822	Caboose (0), 15-26	35	65	___
831	Flatcar (0), 27-34	20	130	___
840	Industrial Power Station, 28-40*	1292	3050	___
900	Ammunition Car (0), 17-21	120	340	___
900	Box Trail Car (2 7/8"), 04-05*	2000	4350	___
901	Gondola (0), 19-27	25	50	___
902	Gondola (0), 27-34	25	45	___
910	Grove of Trees, 32-42	70	502	___
911	Country Estate, 32-42	241	547	___
912	Suburban Home	463	620	___
913	Landscaped Bungalow, 40-42	168	562	___
914	Park Landscape, 32-35	160	270	___
915	Tunnel, 65" or 60" long, 32-33, 35	170	1290	___
916	Tunnel, 29¼" long, 35	95	665	___
917	Scenic Hillside, 34" x 15", 32-36	90	205	___
918	Scenic Hillside, 30" x 10", 32-36	90	205	___
919	Park Grass, cloth bag, 32-42	10	20	___
920	Village, 32-33	600	3350	___
921	Scenic Park, 3 pieces, 32-33	980	2600	___
921C	Park Center, 32-33	400	1050	___
922	Terrace, 32-36	90	298	___
923	Tunnel, 40¼" long, 33-42	125	225	___
924	Tunnel, 30" long (072), 35-42	50	135	___
925	Lubricant, 35-42	25	120	___
927	Flag Plot, 37-42	70	408	___
1000	Passenger Car (2 7/8"), 05*	4500	6750	___
1000	Trolley Trailer (std), 10-16	1400	2250	___
1010	Electric Locomotive 0-4-0, Winner Lines (0), 31-32	90	160	___
1010	Interurban Trailer (std), 10-16	1000	1800	___
1011	Pullman Car, Winner Lines (0), 31-32	45	75	___
1012	Station, 32	40	70	___
1015	0-4-0 Locomotive (0), 31-32	100	205	___
1017	Winner Station, 33	25	70	___
1019	Observation Car (0), 31-32	50	70	___
1020	Baggage Car (0), 31-32	65	110	___
1021	90-degree Crossover (027), 32-42	1	5	___
1022	Tunnel, 18¾" long (0), 35-42	15	165	___
1023	Tunnel, 19" long, 34-42	20	40	___
1024	Switches, pair (027), 37-42	5	33	___
1025	Bumper (027), 40-42	15	25	___

PREWAR 1901-1942			Good	Exc
___	**1027**	Transformer Station, 34	50	115
___	**1028**	Transformer, 40 watts, 39	3	10
___	**1029**	Transformer, 25 watts, 36	5	20
___	**1030**	Electric Locomotive 0-4-0 (O), 32	75	135
___	**1030**	Transformer, 40 watts, 35-38	6	25
___	**1035**	0-4-0 Locomotive (O), 32	75	115
___	**1037**	Transformer, 40 watts, 40-42	7	25
___	**1038**	Transformer, 30 watts, 40	2	5
___	**1039**	Transformer, 35 watts, 37-40	7	20
___	**1040**	Transformer, 60 watts, 37-39	10	30
___	**1041**	Transformer, 60 watts, 39-42	15	30
___	**1045**	Watchman, 38-42	30	68
___	**1050**	Passenger Car Trailer (2 7/8"), 05*	3900	7200
___	**1100**	Summer Trolley Trailer (std), 10-13		NRS
___	**1100**	Mickey Mouse Handcar, 35-37*		
___		(A) Red base	325	677
___		(B) Apple green base, orange shoes	500	880
___		(C) Orange base	538	1225
___	**1103**	Peter Rabbit Handcar (O), 35-37*	490	820
___	**1105**	Santa Claus Handcar (O), 35-36*		
___		(A) Red base	755	1050
___		(B) Green base	720	1200
___	**1107**	Transformer Station, 33	25	70
___	**1107**	Donald Duck Handcar (O), 36-37*		
___		(A) White dog house, red roof	475	1200
___		(B) White dog house, green roof	380	1100
___		(C) Orange dog house, green roof	640	1850
___	**1121**	Switches, pair (027), 37-42	15	35
___	**1506L**	0-4-0 Locomotive (O), 33-34	95	125
___	**1506M**	0-4-0 Locomotive (O), 35	250	430
___	**1508**	0-4-0 Commodore Vanderbilt with 1509 Mickey Mouse stoker Tender, 35	420	690
___	**1511**	0-4-0 Locomotive (O), 36-37	110	280
___	**1512**	Gondola (O), 31-33, 36-37	25	33
___	**1514**	Boxcar (O), 31-37	25	40
___	**1515**	Tank Car (O), 33-37	25	40
___	**1517**	Caboose (O), 31-37	25	40
___	**1518**	Mickey Mouse Circus Dining Car (O), 35	120	260
___	**1519**	Mickey Mouse Band Car (O), 35	120	260
___	**1520**	Mickey Mouse Circus Car (O), 35	120	260
___	**1536**	Mickey Mouse Circus Set: 1508, 1509, 1518, 1519, 1520, 35	770	1350
___	**1550**	Switches, for windup trains, pair, 33-37	2	5
___	**1555**	90-degree Crossover, for windup trains, 33-37	1	2
___	**1560**	Station, 33-37	15	35
___	**1569**	Accessory Set, 8 pieces, 33-37	35	70

		Good	Exc	
1588	0-4-0 Locomotive (O), 36-37	150	250	___
1630	Pullman Car (O), 38-42			___
	(A) Aluminum windows	35	70	___
	(B) Light gray windows	45	80	___
1631	Observation Car (O), 38-42			___
	(A) Aluminum windows	35	70	___
	(B) Light gray windows	45	80	___
1651E	Electric Locomotive 0-4-0 (O), 33	130	240	___
1661E	2-4-0 Locomotive (O), 33	75	160	___
1662	0-4-0 Locomotive (027), 40-42	154	365	___
1663	0-4-0 Locomotive (027), 40-42	200	385	___
1664/E	2-4-2 Locomotive (027), 38-42			___
	(A) Gunmetal	60	188	___
	(B) Black	60	95	___
1666/E	2-6-2 Locomotive (027), 38-42			___
	(A) Gunmetal	115	170	___
	(B) Black	78	150	___
1668/E	2-6-2 Locomotive (027), 37-41			___
	(A) Gunmetal	75	115	___
	(B) Black	75	130	___
1673	Coach (O), 36-37			___
	(A) Aluminum windows	35	75	___
	(B) Light gray windows	45	90	___
1674	Pullman Car (O), 36-37	35	75	___
1675	Observation Car (O), 36-37	30	70	___
1677	Gondola (O), 33-35, 39-42			___
	(A) Light blue, Ives	40	60	___
	(B) Blue or red, Lionel	20	40	___
1679	Boxcar (O), 33-42			___
	(A) Cream, Ives	25	40	___
	(B) Cream, Lionel	25	40	___
	(C) Cream or yellow, Baby Ruth	20	40	___
1680	Tank Car (O), 33-42			___
	(A) Aluminum, Ives Tank Lines	60	95	___
	(B) Aluminum, no Ives lettering	11	35	___
	(C) Orange, Shell Oil	15	32	___
1681	2-4-0 Locomotive (O), 34-35			___
	(A) Black, red frame	55	120	___
	(B) Red, red frame	110	145	___
1681E	2-4-0 Locomotive (O), 34-35			___
	(A) Black, red frame	65	130	___
	(B) Red, red frame	130	165	___
1682	Caboose (O), 33-42			___
	(A) Vermilion, Ives	35	70	___
	(B) Red or tuscan, Lionel	6	40	___

			Good	Exc
____	**1684**	2-4-2 Locomotive (027), 41-42		
____		(A) Black	45	70
____		(B) Gunmetal	45	70
____	**1685**	Coach (0), 33-37 u		
____		(A) Gray, maroon roof	240	495
____		(B) Red, maroon roof	170	335
____		(C) Blue, silver roof	170	315
____	**1686**	Baggage Car (0), 33-37 u		
____		(A) Gray, maroon roof	240	495
____		(B) Red, maroon roof	170	335
____		(C) Blue, silver roof	170	315
____	**1687**	Observation Car (0), 33-37 u		
____		(A) Gray, maroon roof	170	315
____		(B) Red, maroon roof	180	315
____		(C) Blue, silver roof	170	315
____	**1688/E**	2-4-2 Locomotive (027), 36-40	50	125
____	**1689E**	2-4-2 Locomotive (027), 36-37		
____		(A) Gunmetal	75	118
____		(B) Black	60	100
____	**1689T**	Tender, black	15	38
____	**1690**	Pullman Car (0), 33-40	35	60
____	**1691**	Observation Car (0), 33-40	35	60
____	**1692**	Pullman Car (027), 39 u	45	70
____	**1693**	Observation Car (027), 39 u	45	70
____	**1700E**	Diesel, power unit only (027), 35-37	45	75
____	**1700E**	Set: 1700, 1701 (2), 1702, 35-37 u		
____		(A) Aluminum and light red	140	250
____		(B) Chrome and light red	140	250
____		(C) Orange and gray	155	285
____	**1701**	Coach (027), 35-37		
____		(A) Chrome sides and roof	20	45
____		(B) Silver sides and roof	30	55
____		(C) Orange and gray	75	150
____	**1702**	Observation Car (027), 35-37		
____		(A) Chrome sides and roof	20	45
____		(B) Silver sides and roof	30	55
____		(C) Orange and gray	75	150
____	**1703**	Observation Car, hooked coupler, 35-37 u	50	110
____	**1717**	Gondola (0), 33-40 u	30	50
____	**1717X**	Gondola (0), 40 u	25	50
____	**1719**	Boxcar (0), 33-40 u	30	50
____	**1719X**	Boxcar (0), 41-42 u	30	50
____	**1722**	Caboose (0), 33-42 u	25	50
____	**1722X**	Caboose (0), 39-40 u	25	40
____	**1766**	Pullman Car (std), 34-40*		
____		(A) Terra-cotta, maroon roof, brass trim	300	650

		Good	Exc	
	(B) Red, maroon roof, nickel trim	300	540	___
1767	Baggage Car (std), 34-40*			___
	(A) Terra-cotta, maroon roof, brass trim	295	850	___
	(B) Red, maroon roof, nickel trim	295	700	___
1768	Observation Car (std), 34-40*			___
	(A) Terra-cotta, maroon roof, brass trim	300	650	___
	(B) Red, maroon roof, nickel trim	300	540	___
1811	Pullman Car (0), 33-37	35	70	___
1812	Observation Car (0), 33-37	30	65	___
1813	Baggage Car (0), 33-37	60	135	___
1816/W	Diesel (0), 35-37	100	240	___
1817	Coach (0), 35-37	25	50	___
1818	Observation Car (0), 35-37	25	50	___
1835E	2-4-2 Locomotive (std), 34-39	448	730	___
1910	Electric Locomotive 0-6-0, early (std), 10-11	920	1550	___
1910	Electric Locomotive 0-6-0, late (std), 12	550	1350	___
1910	Pullman Car (std), 09-10 u	860	3525	___
1911	Electric Locomotive 0-4-0, early (std), 10-12	860	1700	___
1911	Electric Locomotive 0-4-0, late (std), 13	700	1100	___
1911	Electric Locomotive 0-4-4-0 Special (std), 11-12	860	2500	___
1912	Electric Locomotive 0-4-4-0 (std), 10-12*			___
	(A) New York, New Haven & Hartford	1550	3200	___
	(B) New York Central Lines	1300	2700	___
1912	Electric Locomotive 0-4-4-0 Special (std), 11*	2500	4500	___
2200	Summer Trolley Trailer (std), 10-13	1100	2250	___
2203B	Tender	40	99	___
2224W	Tender	55	137	___
2225W	Tender	30	60	___
2226WX	Tender, 38	75	100	___
2228B	Tender	140	280	___
2235W	Tender	25	65	___
2600	Pullman Car (0), 38-42	80	155	___
2601	Observation Car (0), 38-42	60	115	___
2602	Baggage Car (0), 38-42	90	185	___
2613	Pullman Car (0), 38-42*			___
	(A) Blue, 2-tone blue roof	145	300	___
	(B) State green, 2-tone green roof	200	440	___
2614	Observation Car (0), 38-42*			___
	(A) Blue, 2-tone blue roof	100	300	___
	(B) State green, 2-tone green roof	200	440	___
2615	Baggage Car (0), 38-42*			___
	(A) Blue, 2-tone blue roof	115	300	___
	(B) State green, 2-tone green roof	200	420	___
2620	Floodlight Car (0), 38-42	65	100	___
2623	Pullman Car (0), 41-42			___
	(A) Irvington	175	843	___

			Good	Exc
___		(B) Manhattan	220	310
___	**2624**	Pullman Car (O), 41-42	750	1700
___	**2630**	Pullman Car (O), 38-42	30	70
___	**2631**	Observation Car (O), 38-42	30	70
___	**2640**	Pullman Car, illuminated (O), 38-42		
___		(A) Light blue, aluminum roof	30	120
___		(B) State green, dark green roof	30	70
___	**2641**	Observation Car, illuminated (O), 38-42		
___		(A) Light blue, aluminum roof	30	100
___		(B) State green, dark green roof	30	70
___	**2642**	Pullman Car (O), 41-42	30	70
___	**2643**	Observation Car (O), 41-42	30	65
___	**2651**	Flatcar (O), 38-42	30	80
___	**2652**	Gondola (O), 38-41	25	65
___	**2653**	Hopper Car (O), 38-42		
___		(A) Stephen Girard green	35	70
___		(B) Black	60	130
___	**2654**	Tank Car (O), 38-42		
___		(A) Aluminum, Sunoco	35	60
___		(B) Orange, Shell	35	60
___		(C) Light gray, Sunoco	40	70
___	**2655**	Boxcar (O), 38-42		
___		(A) Cream, maroon roof	35	65
___		(B) Cream, tuscan roof	40	70
___	**2656**	Stock Car (O), 38-41		
___		(A) Light gray, red roof	45	75
___		(B) Burnt orange, tuscan roof	39	67
___	**2657**	Caboose (O), 40-41	30	45
___	**2657X**	Caboose (O), 40-41	25	40
___	**2659**	Dump Car (O), 38-41	40	70
___	**2660**	Crane Car (O), 38-42	80	266
___	**2672**	Caboose (O27), 41-42	20	50
___	**2677**	Gondola (O27), 39-41	25	40
___	**2679**	Boxcar (O27), 38-42	13	30
___	**2680**	Tank Car (O27), 38-42		
___		(A) Aluminum, Sunoco	15	40
___		(B) Orange, Shell	15	40
___	**2682**	Caboose (O27), 38-42	6	30
___	**2682X**	Caboose (O27), 38-42	20	35
___	**2689T**	Tender	15	35
___	**2689W**	Tender	35	50
___	**2717**	Gondola (O), 38-42 u	20	40
___	**2719**	Boxcar (O), 38-42 u	30	50
___	**2722**	Caboose (O), 38-42 u	25	50
___	**2755**	Tank Car (O), 41-42	71	195
___	**2757**	Caboose (O), 41-42	25	61

PREWAR 1901-1942		Good	Exc	
2757X	Caboose (O), 41-42	25	40	___
2758	Automobile Boxcar (O), 41-42	35	60	___
2810	Crane Car (O), 38-42	130	160	___
2811	Flatcar (O), 38-42	50	95	___
2812	Gondola (O), 38-42			___
	(A) Green	40	143	___
	(B) Dark orange	53	95	___
2813	Stock Car (O), 38-42	120	363	___
2814	Boxcar (O), 38-42			___
	(A) Cream, maroon roof	85	150	___
	(B) Orange, brown roof, rubber-stamped lettering	288	825	___
2814R	Refrigerator Car (O), 38-42			___
	(A) White, light blue roof, nickel plates	129	260	___
	(B) White, brown roof, no plates	375	660	___
2815	Tank Car (O), 38-42			___
	(A) Aluminum	85	165	___
	(B) Orange	113	215	___
2816	Hopper Car (O), 35-42			___
	(A) Red	100	320	___
	(B) Black	110	220	___
2817	Caboose (O), 36-42			___
	(A) Light red body and roof	78	140	___
	(B) Flat red body, tuscan roof	115	371	___
2820	Floodlight Car (O), 38-42			___
	(A) Stamped nickel searchlights	118	205	___
	(B) Gray die-cast searchlights	120	260	___
2954	Boxcar (O), 40-42*	132	375	___
2955	Sunoco Tank Car (O), 40-42*			___
	(A) Shell decal	198	500	___
	(B) Sunoco decal	279	690	___
2956	Hopper Car (O), 40-42*	130	400	___
2957	Caboose (O), 40-42*	110	501	___
3300	Summer Trolley Trailer (std), 10-13	1400	2250	___
3651	Operating Lumber Car (O), 39-42	25	55	___
3652	Operating Gondola (O), 39-42	27	75	___
3659	Operating Dump Car (O), 39-42	20	40	___
3811	Operating Lumber Car (O), 39-42	35	88	___
3814	Operating Merchandise Car (O), 39-42	72	195	___
3859	Operating Dump Car (O), 38-42	45	90	___
Other Transformers and Motors				
A	Miniature Motor, 04	50	95	___
A	Transformer, 40, 60 watts, 21-37	10	41	___
B	New Departure Motor, 06-16	75	135	___
B	Transformer, 50, 75 watts, 16-38	7	25	___
C	New Departure Motor, 06-16	100	180	___
D	New Departure Motor, 06-14	100	180	___

	PREWAR 1901-1942		Good	Exc
___	E	New Departure Motor, 06-14	100	180
___	F	New Departure Motor, 06-14	100	180
___	G	Fan Motor, battery-operated, 06-14	100	180
___	K	Transformer, 150, 200 watts, 13-38	18	73
___	L	Transformer, 50, 75 watts, 13-16, 33-38	10	25
___	M	Peerless Motor, battery-operated, 15-20	30	80
___	N	Transformer, 50 watts, 41-42	7	20
___	Q	Transformer, 50 watts, 14-15	10	21
___	Q	Transformer, 75 watts, 38-42	12	28
___	R	Peerless Motor, battery-operated, reversing, 15-20	30	75
___	R	Transformer, 100 watts, 38-42	20	45
___	S	Transformer, 50 watts, 14-17	13	28
___	T	Transformer, 75, 100, 150 watts, 14-28	8	30
___	U	Transformer, Aladdin, 32-33	5	15
___	V	Transformer, 150 watts, 39-42	40	200
___	W	Transformer, 75 watts, 32-33	10	35

Track, Lockons, and Contactors				
___		0 Straight		1
___		0 Curve		1
___		072 Straight	1	3
___		072 Curve	1	3
___		027 Straight		1
___		027 Curve		1
___		Standard Straight	1	3
___		Standard Curve	1	2
___		Standard Insulated Straight, 33-42	2	4
___		Standard Insulated Curve, 33-42	1	2
___		0 Gauge Lockon	0	4
___		Standard Gauge Lockon		1
___		UTC Lockon		1
___		145C Contactor	3	9
___		153C Contactor	3	7
___		Track Clips, dozen (0), 37	5	10

Section 2
POSTWAR 1945–1969

		Good	Exc
011-11	Fiber Pins, dozen (0), 46-50	1	3 ___
011-43	Insulating Pins, dozen (0), 61	1	3 ___
020	90-degree Crossover (0), 45-61	3	6 ___
020X	45-degree Crossover (0), 46-59	4	8 ___
022	Remote Control Switches, pair (0), 45-69	23	65 ___
022-500	Adapter Set (0), 57-61	2	7 ___
022A	Remote Control Switches, pair (0), 47	21	57 ___
022C-1	Switch Controller	5	11 ___
25	Bumper (0), 46-47		___
26	Bumper, 48-50		___
	(A) Red, 49-50	5	14 ___
	(B) Gray, 48	16	48 ___
027C-1	Track Clips, box of 12 (027), 47, 49	3	13 ___
027C-1	Track Clips, box of 50 (027)	8	30 ___
30	Water Tower, 47-50		___
	(A) Single-walled	16	64 ___
	(B) Double-walled	29	86 ___
31	Curved Track (Super 0), 57-66	2	5 ___
31-5	Track Ground Pins, Dozen (Super 0), 57-60	2	5 ___
31-7	Power Blade Connection, dozen (Super 0), 57-60	7	11 ___
31-15	Ground Rail Pin, dozen (Super 0), 57-66	3	11 ___
31-45	Power Blade Connection, dozen (Super 0), 61-66	4	10 ___
32	Straight Track (Super 0), 57-66	2	5 ___
32-10	Insulating Pin, dozen (Super 0), 57-60	5	11 ___
32-20	Power Blade Insulator, dozen (Super 0), 57-60	2	8 ___
32-25	Insulating Pin (Super 0), 57-61		1 ___
32-30	Ground Pin (Super 0), 57-61		1 ___
32-31	Power Pin, Dozen (Super 0), 57-61	3	10 ___
32-32	Insulating Pin, Dozen (Super 0), 57-61	3	8 ___
32-33	Ground Pin, Dozen (Super 0), 57-61	3	9 ___
32-34	Power Pin (Super 0), 57-61	3	9 ___
32-35	Insulating Pin, dozen (Super 0 to 027), 57-61	4	8 ___
32-45	Power Blade Insulators, dozen (Super 0), 61-66	3	11 ___
32-55	Insulating Pins, dozen (Super 0), 61-66	3	10 ___
33	Half Curved Track (Super 0), 57-66	2	5 ___
34	Half Straight Track (Super 0), 57-66	3	6 ___
35	Boulevard Lamp, 45-49	11	28 ___
36	Operating Car Remote Control Set (Super 0), 57-66	10	31 ___
37	Uncoupling Track Set (Super 0), 57-66	10	18 ___
38-85	Accessory Adapter Tracks, pair (Super 0), 57-61	9	27 ___
38	Operating Water Tower, 46-47	77	176 ___
39	Operating Set (Super 0), 57	7	14 ___
39-5	Operating Set (Super 0), 57-58	4	89 ___

	POSTWAR 1945-1969		Good	Exc
___	**39-6**	Operating Set (Super O), 57-58	4	9
___	**39-10**	Operating Set (Super O), 58	4	8
___	**39-15**	Operating Set with blade (Super O), 57-58	4	8
___	**39-20**	Operating Set (Super O), 57-58	4	8
___	**39-25**	Operating Set (Super O), 61-66	8	46
___	**39-35**	Operating Set (Super O), 59	8	24
___	**40**	Hookup Wire, 50-51, 53-63		
___		(A) Single reel, orange or gray, with tape	7	50
___		(B) 8 sealed reels in dealer box	97	397
___	**40-25**	Conductor Wire with envelope, 56-59	10	47
___	**40-50**	Cable Reel with envelope, 60-61	12	42
___	**41**	U.S. Army Switcher, 55-57		
___		(A) Unpainted black body	48	106
___		(B) Black-painted body	286	884
___	**042/42**	Manual Switches, pair (O), 46-59	11	25
___	**42**	Picatinny Arsenal Switcher, 57	130	275
___	**43**	Power Track (Super O), 59-66	6	15
___	**44**	U.S. Army Mobile Launcher, 59-62	68	255
___	**44-80**	Missiles, 59-60	12	30
___	**45**	U.S. Marines Mobile Launcher, 60-62	113	264
___	**45**	Automatic Gateman, 46-49	11	39
___	**45N**	Automatic Gateman, 45	14	40
___	**48**	Insulated Straight Track (Super O), 57-66	5	13
___	**49**	Insulated Curved Track (Super O), 57-66	5	10
___	**50**	Section Gang Car, 54-64		
___		(A) Gray bumpers, rotating blue man and fixed olive men, center horn, 54	286	719
___		(B) Blue bumpers, rotating olive man and fixed blue men, center horn	25	61
___		(C) Blue bumpers, rotating olive man and fixed blue men, off-center horn	25	60
___	**51**	Navy Yard Switcher, 56-57	61	228
___	**52**	Fire Car, 58-61	59	146
___	**53**	Rio Grande Snowplow, 57-60		
___		(A) Backwards “a” in Rio Grande	63	244
___		(B) Correctly printed “a”	145	438
___	**54**	Ballast Tamper, 58-61, 66, 68-69	53	139
___	**55**	PRR Tie-Jector Car, 57-61		
___		(A) Ventilation slot behind motorman	49	161
___		(B) No slot behind motorman	36	92
___	**55-150**	Ties, 24 pieces, 57-60	15	29
___	**56**	Lamp Post, 46-49	13	39
___	**56**	M&StL Mine Transport, 58	195	334
___	**57**	AEC Switcher, 59-60	199	707
___	**58**	GN Snowplow, 59-61	137	396
___	**58**	Lamp Post, 46-50	15	71
___	**59**	Minuteman Switcher, 62-63	283	544

POSTWAR 1945-1969		Good	Exc	
60	Lionelville Rapid Transit Trolley, 55-58			___
	(A) Metal motorman silhouettes	75	220	___
	(B) No motorman silhouettes	36	100	___
61	Ground Lockon (Super O), 57-66	3	6	___
61-25	Super O Ground clips, dozen, with dealer envelope	9	17	___
62	Power Lockon (Super O), 57-66	3	6	___
64	Highway Lamp Post, 45-49	13	52	___
65	Handcar, 62-66			___
	(A) Light yellow	71	244	___
	(B) Dark yellow	65	214	___
68	Executive Inspection Car, 58-61	70	151	___
69	Maintenance Car, 60-62	74	164	___
70	Yard Light, 49-50	10	33	___
71	Lamp Post, 49-59	6	14	___
75	Goose Neck Lamps, set of 2, 61-63	13	33	___
76	Boulevard Street Lamps, set of 3, 59-66, 68-69	19	67	___
80	Controller, 60	7	18	___
88	Controller, 46-60	6	20	___
89	Flagpole, 56-58	16	80	___
90	Controller, 55-66			___
	(A) Metal clip	5	12	___
	(B) No metal clip	6	10	___
91	Circuit Breaker, 57-60	10	27	___
92	Circuit Breaker, 59-66, 68-69	7	20	___
93	Water Tower, 46-49	17	148	___
96C	Controller, 45-54	4	8	___
97	Coal Elevator, 46-50	73	172	___
108	Trestle Set, 12 black piers,	9	21	___
109	Partial Trestle Set, 61	5	14	___
110	Graduated Trestle Set, 22 or 24 piers, 55-69	10	26	___
110-75	Graduated Trestle Set with 110-78 envelope	18	128	___
111	Elevated Trestle Set, 10 A piers, 56-69	11	25	___
111-100	Elevated Trestle Piers, set of 2, 60-63	13	73	___
112	Remote Control Switches, pair (Super O), 57-66	40	116	___
114	Newsstand with horn, 57-59	29	80	___
115	Passenger Station, 46-49	109	252	___
118	Newsstand with whistle, 57-58	33	85	___
119	Landscaped Tunnel, 57-58	175	400	___
120	90-degree Crossing (Super O), 57-66	5	13	___
121	Landscaped Tunnel, 59-66	5	30	___
122	Lamp Assortment, 48-52	33	257	___
123	Lamp Assortment, 55-59	63	281	___
123-60	Lamp Assortment, 60-63	31	204	___
125	Whistle Shack, 50-55			___
	(A) Gray base	14	45	___
	(B) Green base	21	56	___

	POSTWAR 1945-1969		Good	Exc
___	**128**	Animated Newsstand, 57-60	45	84
___	**130**	60-degree Crossing (Super O), 57-66	6	16
___	**131**	Curved Tunnel, 59-66	9	39
___	**132**	Passenger Station, 49-55	25	92
___	**133**	Passenger Station, 57, 61-62, 66	19	43
___	**138**	Water Tower, 53-57	25	85
___	**140**	Automatic Banjo Signal, 54-66	13	56
___	**142**	Manual Switches, pair (Super O), 57-66	22	50
___	**145**	Automatic Gateman, 50-66		
___		(A) Red roof	17	57
___		(B) Maroon roof	10	55
___	**145C**	Contactor, 50-60	4	15
___	**147**	Whistle Controller, 61-66	2	6
___	**148**	Dwarf Trackside Signal, 57-60	22	92
___	**148-100**	Controller (SPDT switch), 57-60	5	21
___	**150**	Telegraph Pole Set, 47-50	17	42
___	**151**	Automatic Semaphore, 47-69		
___		(A) Green base, yellow blade, 47	40	82
___		(B) Black base, yellow blade	13	57
___		(C) Black base, red blade, 47	186	437
___	**152**	Automatic Crossing Gate, 45-49	10	34
___	**153**	Automatic Block Control Signal, 45-59	16	89
___	**153C**	Contactor	3	10
___	**154**	Automatic Highway Signal, 45-69	14	56
___	**154C**	Contactor	4	15
___	**155**	Blinking Light Signal with bell, 55-57	21	74
___	**156**	Station Platform, 46-49	28	85
___	**156-5**	Station Platform Fence with envelope	23	50
___	**157**	Station Platform, 52-59		
___		(A) Maroon base	14	54
___		(B) Red base	26	85
___	**157-23**	Station Platform Fence with envelope	14	43
___	**160**	Unloading Bin, 52-57		
___		(A) Black plastic, long	2	5
___		(B) Black metal, short	43	70
___		(C) Multicolor Bakelite, short	7	31
___		(D) Black Bakelite, short	3	8
___	**161**	Mail Pickup Set, 61-63	33	93
___	**163**	Single Target Block Signal, 61-69	13	44
___	**164**	Log Loader, 46-50	44	134
___	**164-64**	Log Set, 5 pieces, separate sale w/box, 52-58	26	69
___	**167**	Whistle Controller, 45-50, 52-57	3	7
___	**175**	Rocket Launcher, 58-60	48	283
___	**175-50**	Extra Rocket, 59-60	10	23
___	**182**	Magnetic Crane, 46-49	83	222
___	**182-22**	Steel Scrap with bag, 46-49	48	108

POSTWAR 1945-1969		Good	Exc	
192	Operating Control Tower, 59-60	87	254	___
193	Industrial Water Tower, 53-55			___
	(A) Red	43	83	___
	(B) Black, 53	62	171	___
195	Floodlight Tower, 57-69			___
	(A) Medium tan base, rubber-stamped lettering	23	74	___
	(B) All other variations	19	57	___
195-75	Floodlight Extension, 8-bulb (with box), 58-60	29	99	___
196	Smoke Pellets, 46-47	38	93	___
197	Rotating Radar Antenna, 57-59			___
	(A) Orange platform	43	155	___
	(B) Gray platform	30	82	___
197-75	Separate Sale Radar Head with box	58	155	___
199	Microwave Relay Tower, 58-59	23	68	___
202	UP Alco Diesel A Unit, 57	24	67	___
204	Santa Fe Alco Diesel AA Units, 57	62	344	___
205	Missouri Pacific Alco Diesel AA Units, 57-58			___
	(A) Pilot without support	53	120	___
	(B) Pilot with painted metal support	71	172	___
206	Artificial Coal, large bag, 46-68	14	20	___
207	Artificial Coal, small bag, 46-48	9	14	___
208	Santa Fe Alco Diesel AA Units, 58-59	80	437	___
209	New Haven Alco Diesel AA Units, 58	178	565	___
209	Wooden Barrels, set of 6, 46-50	9	15	___
210	Texas Special Alco Diesel AA Units, 58	57	121	___
211	Texas Special Alco Diesel AA Units, 62-66	60	209	___
212	Santa Fe Alco Diesel AA Units, 64-66			___
	(A) With Built Date "8-57," 64-65	43	112	___
	(B) Without Built Date, 66	61	145	___
212T	Santa Fe Alco Diesel Dummy A Unit, 64-66			___
	(A) With Built Date 8-57, 64-65	21	46	___
	(B) Without Built Date, 66	30	64	___
212	USMC Alco Diesel A Unit, 58-59	56	137	___
212T	USMC Diesel Dummy A Unit, 58 u	408	1332	___
213	M&StL Alco Diesel AA Units, 64	72	187	___
214	Plate Girder Bridge, 53-69	9	25	___
215	Santa Fe Alco Diesel Units, 65 u			___
	(A) AB Units	63	130	___
	(B) AA Units	77	161	___
215	Santa Fe Alco Diesel Powered A Unit, 65 u	25	54	___
216	Burlington Alco Diesel A Unit, 58	119	408	___
216	M&StL Alco Diesel AA Units (213T dummy A unit), 64 u	67	179	___
217	B&M Alco Diesel AB Units, 59	75	187	___
217C	B&M Alco Diesel B Unit, 59	30	70	___
218	Santa Fe Alco Diesel Units, 59-63			___
	(A) AA Units	77	295	___

			Good	Exc
___		(B) AB Units	62	184
___		(C) AA Units, solid nose decal	71	200
___	**218C**	Santa Fe Alco B Unit, 61-63	33	78
___	**219**	Missouri Pacific Alco Diesel AA Units, 59 u	65	147
___	**220**	Santa Fe Alco Diesel Units, 60-61		
___		(A) A Unit	39	90
___		(B) AA Units	69	159
___	**221**	2-6-4 Locomotive, 221W Tender, 46-47		
___		(A) Gray body, black drivers	65	138
___		(B) Black body, nickel-rimmed black drivers, 47	60	136
___		(C) Gray body, cast-aluminum drivers, 46	112	292
___	**221**	Rio Grande Alco Diesel A Unit, 63-64	29	58
___	**221**	Santa Fe Alco Diesel A Unit, 63-64 u	335	664
___	**221**	U.S. Marine Corps Alco Diesel A Unit, 63-64 u	340	630
___	**221T**	Tender		
___		(A) Gray	17	38
___		(B) Black	16	39
___	**221W**	Whistle Tender	24	59
___	**222**	Rio Grande Alco Diesel A Unit, 62	27	62
___	**223**	Santa Fe Alco Diesel AB Units, 63	62	173
___	**224**	2-6-2 Locomotive, 2466W or 2466WX Tender, 45-46		
___		(A) Blackened handrails, 45	119	240
___		(B) Silver handrails	61	126
___	**224**	US Navy B Unit	37	79
___	**224**	U.S. Navy Alco Diesel AB Units, 60	107	372
___	**225**	C&O Alco Diesel A Unit, 60	30	63
___	**226**	B&M Alco Diesel AB Units, 60 u	78	255
___	**226C**	B&M Alco Diesel B Unit, 60 u	31	73
___	**227**	CN Alco Diesel A Unit, 60 u	57	157
___	**228**	CN Alco Diesel A Unit, 61 u	64	234
___	**229**	M&StL Alco Diesel Units, 61-62		
___		(A) A Unit, 61	42	97
___		(B) AB Units, 62	79	314
___	**229C**	M&StL Alco Diesel B Unit, 61-62	30	80
___	**230**	C&O Alco Diesel A Unit, 61	32	185
___	**231**	Rock Island Alco Diesel A Unit, 61-63		
___		(A) With red stripe	40	92
___		(B) Without red stripe	131	367
___	**232**	New Haven Alco Diesel A Unit, 62	50	133
___	**233**	2-4-2 Scout Locomotive, 233W Tender, 61-62	32	73
___	**233W**	Whistle Tender	16	34
___	**234T**	Lionel Lines Tender	9	24
___	**234T**	Pennsylvania Tender	17	42
___	**234W**	Lionel Whistle Tender	21	51
___	**234W**	Pennsylvania Whistle Tender	33	84

POSTWAR 1945-1969		Good	Exc	
235	2-4-2 Scout Locomotive, 1130T or 1060T Tender, 60 u	82	262	___
236	2-4-2 Scout Locomotive, 61-62			___
	(A) 1050T slope-back Tender	15	37	___
	(B) 1130T Tender	15	36	___
237	2-4-2 Scout Locomotive, 63-66			___
	(A) 1060T Tender	24	51	___
	(B) 234W Tender	31	69	___
238	2-4-2 Scout Locomotive, stripe on running board, 234W Tender, 63-64	41	102	___
239	2-4-2 Scout Locomotive, 234W Tender, 65-66	37	78	___
240	2-4-2 Scout Locomotive, 242T Tender, 64 u	74	238	___
241	2-4-2 Scout Locomotive, 65 u			___
	(A) Narrow stripe, 234W Tender	31	74	___
	(B) Wide stripe, 1130T Tender	25	62	___
242	2-4-2 Scout Locomotive, 1060T or 1062T Tender, 62-66	23	49	___
243	2-4-2 Scout Locomotive, 243W Tender, 60	32	72	___
243W	Whistle Tender	19	45	___
244	2-4-2 Scout Locomotive, 244T or 1130T Tender, 60-61	21	47	___
244T	Tender	9	24	___
245	2-4-2 Scout Locomotive, 1130T Tender, 59 u	25	105	___
246	2-4-2 Scout Locomotive, 244T or 1130T Tender, 59-61	19	59	___
247	2-4-2 Scout Locomotive, 247T Tender, 59			___
	(A) Closed pilot	22	59	___
	(B) Open pilot	35	96	___
247T	B&O Tender	15	43	___
248	2-4-2 Scout Locomotive, 1130T Tender, 58	25	60	___
249	2-4-2 Scout Locomotive, 250T Tender, 58	21	124	___
250	2-4-2 Scout Locomotive, 250T Tender, 57	27	98	___
250T	Tender	12	25	___
251	2-4-2 Scout Locomotive, 66 u			___
	(A) 1062T slope-back Tender	62	139	___
	(B) 250T-type Tender	62	139	___
252	Crossing Gate, 50-62	10	45	___
253	Block Control Signal, 56-59	12	39	___
256	Illuminated Freight Station, 50-53			___
	(A) Standard	25	79	___
	(B) Light green roof	40	95	___
257	Freight Station with diesel horn, 56-57			___
	(A) Maroon base	28	63	___
	(B) Brown base	38	81	___
	(C) Maroon or brown base, light green roof	58	125	___
260	Bumper, 51-69			___
	(A) Die-cast	10	27	___
	(B) Black plastic	13	45	___
262	Highway Crossing Gate, 62-69	13	61	___

	POSTWAR 1945-1969		Good	Exc
____	**264**	Operating Forklift Platform, 57-60	92	251
____	**282**	Portal Gantry Crane, 54-57	69	165
____	**282R**	Portal Gantry Crane, 56-57	65	163
____	**299**	Code Transmitter Beacon Set, 61-63	33	137
____	**308**	Railroad Sign Set, die-cast, 45-49	13	31
____	**309**	Yard Sign Set, plastic, 50-59	8	21
____	**309-100**	Yard Sign Set in Plastic Packaging, 66-69 u	10	51
____	**310**	Billboard Set, 50-68	3	8
____	**313**	Bascule Bridge, 46-49	71	243
____	**313-82**	Fiber Pins, dozen, 46-60	1	3
____	**313-121**	Fiber Pins, dozen, 61	2	4
____	**314**	Scale Model Girder Bridge, 45-50	10	37
____	**315**	Illuminated Trestle Bridge, 46-48	31	85
____	**316**	Trestle Bridge, 49	16	35
____	**317**	Trestle Bridge, 50-56	15	37
____	**321**	Trestle Bridge, 58-64	15	36
____	**321-100**	Trestle Bridge	21	81
____	**332**	Arch-Under Trestle Bridge, 59-66	16	35
____	**334**	Operating Dispatching Board, 57-60	63	144
____	**342**	Culvert Loader, 56-58	55	161
____	**345**	Culvert Unloader, 57-59	51	213
____	**346**	Culvert Unloader, manual, 65 u	41	136
____	**347**	Cannon Firing Range Set, 64 u	273	749
____	**348**	Culvert Unloader, manual, 66-69	51	127
____	**350**	Engine Transfer Table, 57-60	97	233
____	**350-50**	Transfer Table Extension, 57-60	50	134
____	**352**	Ice Depot with 6352 Ice Car, 55-57	73	122
____	**353**	Trackside Control Signal, 60-61	11	27
____	**356**	Operating Freight Station, 52-57		
____		(A) Dark green roof, 52-57	33	76
____		(B) Light green roof, 57	58	146
____	**362**	Barrel Loader, 52-57		
____		(A) Gold lettering	23	80
____		(B) Red lettering	115	312
____	**362-78**	Wooden Barrels, 6 pieces, 52-57		
____		(A) Brown	8	35
____		(B) Red	96	225
____	**364**	Conveyor Lumber Loader, 48-57	28	82
____	**364C**	On/Off Switch, 48-64	7	22
____	**365**	Dispatching Station, 58-59	34	86
____	**365-35**	Set of Delivery Carts, 52	10	32
____	**375**	Turntable, 62-64	52	144
____	**390C**	Switch, double-pole, double-throw, 60-64	6	24
____	**394**	Rotary Beacon, 49-53		
____		(A) Steel tower, red platform	15	48
____		(B) Steel tower, green platform	50	267

POSTWAR 1945-1969		Good	Exc
	(C) Aluminum tower, platform, and base	12	65
	(D) Aluminum tower, red steel base	32	99
	(E) Steel tower, red platform, stick-on nameplate	36	81
395	Floodlight Tower, 49-56		
	(A) Light green, silver, or unpainted aluminum	13	112
	(B) Red	32	313
	(C) Dark green	77	262
	(D) Yellow	44	262
397	Operating Coal Loader, 48-57		
	(A) Yellow generator, 48	118	449
	(B) Blue generator, 49-57	28	79
400	B&O Passenger Rail Diesel Car, 56-58	64	235
404	B&O Baggage-Mail Rail Diesel Car, 57-58	101	319
410	Billboard Blinker, 56-58	20	51
413	Countdown Control Panel, 62	17	119
415	Diesel Fueling Station, 55-57	46	120
419	Heliport Control Tower, 62	144	305
443	Missile Launching Platform with ammo dump, 60-62	27	62
445	Switch Tower, lighted, 52-57	18	65
448	Missile Firing Range Set, 61-63	44	152
450	Operating Signal Bridge, 52-58	21	84
450L	Signal Light Head, 52-58	11	35
452	Overhead Gantry Signal, 61-63	34	97
455	Operating Oil Derrick, 50-54		
	(A) Dark green tower, green top	49	233
	(B) Dark green tower, red top	108	237
	(C) Apple green tower, red top	99	325
456	Coal Ramp with 3456 Hopper, 50-55		
	(A) Light gray ramp	36	97
	(B) Dark gray ramp	52	116
456C	Coal Ramp Controller	13	26
460	Piggyback Transportation Set, 55-57		
	(A) Metal stick-on signs on lift truck	43	79
	(B) Rubber-stamped lettering on lift truck	52	112
460P	Piggyback Platform, 55-57	19	44
460-150	Separate Sale 2 Trailers in Box	56	280
461	Platform with truck and trailer, 66	54	142
462	Derrick Platform Set, 61-62	129	268
464	Lumber Mill, 56-60	39	91
465	Sound Dispatching Station, 56-57	62	87
470	Missile Launching Platform w/6470 exploding boxcar, 59-62	55	93
479-1	Truck for 6362 Truck Car with envelope, 55-56	23	56
480-25	Conversion Magnetic Coupler, 50-60	1	5
480-32	Conversion Magnetic Coupler, 61-69	1	7

	POSTWAR 1945-1969		Good	Exc
___	**494**	Rotary Beacon, 54-66		
___		(A) Painted steel	23	44
___		(B) Unpainted aluminum	17	44
___	**497**	Coaling Station, 53-58	42	122
___	**497C**	Controller, 53-58	11	25
___	**520**	LL Boxcab Electric Locomotive, 56-57		
___		(A) Black pantograph	31	69
___		(B) Copper-colored pantograph	39	81
___	**600**	MKT NW2 Switcher, 55		
___		(A) Black frame, black end rails	44	94
___		(B) Gray frame, yellow or black end rails	73	256
___	**601**	Seaboard NW2 Switcher, 56		
___		(A) Red stripes with square ends	72	199
___		(B) Red stripes with round ends	64	130
___	**602**	Seaboard NW2 Switcher, 57-58	65	161
___	**610**	Erie NW2 Switcher, 55		
___		(A) Black frame, one-axle Magna-Traction	45	72
___		(B) Black frame, two-axle Magne-Traction	91	229
___		(C) Yellow frame, two-axle Magne-Traction	176	493
___		(D) Replacement body with nameplates	87	261
___	**611**	Jersey Central NW2 Switcher, 57-58	62	128
___	**613**	UP NW2 Switcher, 58	92	304
___	**614**	Alaska NW2 Switcher, 59-60		
___		(A) Plastic bell, no brake	71	145
___		(B) No bell, yellow brake	108	369
___		(C) "Built by Lionel" outlined in yellow near nose	139	277
___	**616**	Santa Fe NW2 Switcher, 61-62		
___		(A) Open E-unit slot and bell/horn slots	67	141
___		(B) Plugged E-unit slot and open bell/horn slots	90	197
___		(C) Plugged E-unit slot and bell/horn slots	96	220
___	**617**	Santa Fe NW2 Switcher, 63	102	235
___	**621**	Jersey Central NW2 Switcher, 56-57	56	104
___	**622**	Santa Fe NW2 Switcher, 49-50		
___		(A) Large GM decal on cab	101	256
___		(B) Small GM decal on side	80	174
___	**623**	Santa Fe NW2 Switcher, 52-54	66	187
___	**624**	C&O NW2 Switcher, 52-54	65	161
___	**625**	LV GE 44-ton Switcher, 57-58	38	95
___	**626**	B&O GE 44-ton Switcher, 56-57, 59	100	242
___	**627**	LV GE 44-ton Switcher, 56-57	28	79
___	**628**	NP GE 44-ton Switcher, 56-57	36	254
___	**629**	Burlington GE 44-ton Switcher, 56	125	318
___	**633**	Santa Fe NW2 Switcher, 62	56	127
___	**634**	Santa Fe NW2 Switcher, 63, 65-66		
___		(A) Safety stripes	63	130
___		(B) No safety stripes	44	87

		Good	Exc	
635	UP NW2 Switcher, 65 u	55	104	___
637	2-6-4 Locomotive, 2046 736W Tender, 59-63			___
	(A) 2046W Lionel Lines Tender	50	116	___
	(B) 736W Pennsylvania Tender	72	272	___
638-2361	Van Camp's Pork & Beans Boxcar, 62 u	15	33	___
645	Union Pacific NW2 Switcher, 69	66	142	___
646	4-6-4 Locomotive, 2046W Tender, 54-58	67	341	___
665	4-6-4 Locomotive, 2046W, 6026W, or 736W Tender, 54-59, 66	72	374	___
671	6-8-6 Steam Turbine Locomotive, 46-49			___
	(A) Bulb smoke unit, 671W Tender, 46	40	147	___
	(B) E-unit slot, heater smoke unit, 671W Tender, 47	59	163	___
	(C) Thin nickel rims, 2671WX Tender with functioning backup lights, 48	63	208	___
	(D) Thin nickel rims, 2671W Tender, nonfunctioning backup lights, 48	56	135	___
	(E) Thin nickel rims, 2671W Tender, no backup light lenses, 48	52	113	___
	(F) No rims on drivers, 49	50	110	___
671-75	Smoke Lamp, 12 volt, 46	11	22	___
671R	6-8-6 Steam Turbine Locomotive, 4424W or 4671 Tender, 46-49	170	354	___
671RR	6-8-6 Steam Turbine Locomotive, 2046W-50 Tender, 52	76	193	___
671S	Smoke Conversion Kit	20	72	___
671W	Whistle Tender, 46-48	26	69	___
675	2-6-2 Locomotive, 2466WX or 6466WX Tender, 47-49			___
	(A) Aluminum smokestack, 47	74	207	___
	(B) Black smokestack, 48-49	56	151	___
	(C) 2-6-4 Locomotive, 2046W Tender, 52	69	216	___
681	6-8-6 Steam Turbine Locomotive, 50-51, 53			___
	(A) 2671W Tender, 50-51	68	157	___
	(B) 2046W-50 Tender, 53	48	144	___
682	6-8-6 Steam Turbine Locomotive, 2046W-50 Tender, 54-55	142	424	___
685	4-6-4 Hudson Locomotive, 6026W Tender, 53	83	236	___
703-10	Smoke Lamp, 18 volt, 46	11	26	___
726	2-8-4 Berkshire, 46-49			___
	(A) Turned stanchions, no front coupler, bulb smoke unit, 2426W Tender, 46	271	708	___
	(B) Cotter pin stanchions, E-unit slot, no front coupler, heater smoke unit, 2426W Tender, 47	212	560	___
	(C) Simulated front coupler, 2426W Tender, 48-49	105	342	___
726RR	2-8-4 Berkshire Locomotive, 2046W Tender, 52	117	260	___
726S	Smoke Conversion Kit	33	84	___
736	2-8-4 Berkshire Locomotive, 50-66			___
	(A) No headlight wedge brace, hexagonal flagstaff base, 2671WX Tender , 50-51	120	311	___

			Good	Exc
___		(B) Headlight wedge brace, round flagstaff brace, 2046W Tender, 53-54	134	216
___		(C) Sheet metal and plastic trailing truck, 55-56	113	198
___		(D) Smaller typeface on cab number, 57-60	110	169
___		(E) 736W Tender, 61-66	73	184
___	**736W**	PRR Whistle Tender	29	103
___	**746**	N&W 4-8-4 Class J Northern, 57-60		
___		(A) Tender with long stripe	406	1011
___		(B) Tender with short stripe	339	764
___	**746W**	N&W Tender		
___		(A) Short stripe	66	196
___		(B) Long stripe	100	190
___	**760**	Curved Track, 16 sections (072), 54-57	35	75
___	**773**	4-6-4 Hudson Locomotive, 50, 64-66		
___		(A) Valve guides cast in steam chest, 2426W Tender, 50	788	1314
___		(B) No valve guides in steam chest, 736W Pennsylvania Tender, 64	548	955
___		(C) No valve guides in steam chest, 773W New York Central Tender, 64-66	555	1040
___	**773W**	NYC Whistle Tender, 64-66		
___		(A) Closed spaced lettering	250	500
___		(B) Widely spaced lettering	175	350
___	**902**	Elevated Trestle Set, 60, u	29	91
___	**908**	Union Station, 59, u	335	791
___	**909**	Smoke Fluid, large or small bottle, 57-66, 68-69		
___		(A) 1/2-ounce bottle	8	40
___		(B) 2-ounce bottle	15	36
___	**B909**	Smoke Fluid, 2-ounce bottle in blister pack, 66	88	285
___	**919**	Artificial Grass, 46-64	8	18
___	**920**	Scenic Display Set, 57-58	30	93
___	**920-2**	Tunnel Portals, pair, 58-59	141	283
___	**920-3**	Green Grass, 57	5	13
___	**920-4**	Yellow Grass, 57	9	18
___	**920-5**	Artificial Rock, 57-58	7	21
___	**920-6**	Dry Glue, 57-58	4	13
___	**920-8**	Dyed Lichen, 57-58	5	15
___	**925**	Lubricant, 2 ounce tube, 46-69	3	15
___	**925-1**	Lubricant, 1 ounce tube, 50-69	2	6
___	**926**	Lubricant, 1/2 ounce tube, 55	2	3
___	**926-5**	Instruction Booklet, 46-48	1	4
___	**927**	Lubricating Kit, 50-59	10	37
___	**927-3**	Track Cleaner	4	12
___	**927-3**	Track Cleaner	4	14
___	**928**	Maintenance and Lubricating Kit, 60-63	19	42
___	**943**	Ammo Dump, 59-61	17	37
___	**950**	U.S. Railroad Map, 58-66	12	60

POSTWAR 1945-1969		Good	Exc
951	Farm Set, 13 pieces, 58	35	85 ___
952	Figure Set, 30 pieces, 58	31	86 ___
953	Figure Set, 32 pieces, 59-62	36	78 ___
954	Swimming Pool and Playground Set, 30 pieces, 59	45	145 ___
955	Highway Set, 22 pieces, 58	28	59 ___
956	Stockyard Set, 18 pieces, 59	34	73 ___
957	Farm Building and Animal Set, 35 pieces, 58	50	104 ___
958	Vehicle Set, 24 pieces, 58	47	165 ___
959	Barn Set, 23 pieces, 58	76	157 ___
960	Barnyard Set, 29 pieces, 59-61	50	117 ___
961	School Set, 36 pieces, 59	47	211 ___
962	Turnpike Set, 24 pieces, 58	49	112 ___
963	Frontier Set, 18 pieces, 59-60	52	112 ___
963-100	Boxed Frontier Set, 60	125	400 ___
964	Factory Site Set, 18 pieces, 59	70	191 ___
965	Farm Set, 36 pieces, 59	61	168 ___
966	Firehouse Set, 45 pieces, 58	64	139 ___
967	Post Office Set, 25 pieces, 58	52	180 ___
968	TV Transmitter Set, 28 pieces, 58	55	113 ___
969	Construction Set, 23 pieces, 60	60	122 ___
970	Ticket Booth, 58-60	29	85 ___
971	Lichen with box, 60-64	26	90 ___
972	Landscape Tree Assortment, 61-64	30	108 ___
973	Complete Landscaping Set, 60-64	41	127 ___
974	Scenery Set, 58	63	181 ___
980	Ranch Set, 14 pieces, 60	45	108 ___
981	Freight Yard Set, 10 pieces, 60	46	133 ___
982	Suburban Split Level Set, 18 pieces, 60	60	168 ___
983	Farm Set, 7 pieces, 60-61	26	110 ___
984	Railroad Set, 22 pieces, 61-62	50	117 ___
985	Freight Area Set, 32 pieces, 61	51	313 ___
986	Farm Set, 20 pieces, 62	103	251 ___
987	Town Set, 24 pieces, 62	43	289 ___
988	Railroad Structure Set, 16 pieces, 62	58	322 ___
1001	2-4-2 Scout Locomotive, plastic body, 1001T Tender, 48		___
	(A) Silver rubber-stamped cab number	28	69 ___
	(B) White heat-stamped cab number	13	35 ___
1001T	Tender	6	15 ___
1002	Gondola, 48-52		___
	(A) Black, white lettering	4	120 ___
	(B) Blue, white lettering	4	9 ___
	(C) Silver, black lettering	185	484 ___
	(D) Yellow, black lettering	154	599 ___
	(E) Red, white lettering	178	465 ___
X1004	PRR Baby Ruth Boxcar, 48-52	4	10 ___
1005	Sunoco 1-D Tank Car, 48-50	3	9 ___

			Good	Exc
___	**1007**	LL SP-type Caboose, 48-52		
___		(A) Red body	2	6
___		(B) Red body, raised board on roofwalk	7	19
___		(C) Tuscan body	154	381
___	**1008**	Uncoupling Unit (027), 57-62	2	3
___	**1008-50**	Uncoupling Track Section (027), 57-62	1	5
___	**1009**	Manumatic Track Section (027), 48-52	2	3
___	**1010**	Transformer, 35 watts, 61-66	3	10
___	**1011**	Transformer, 25 watts, 48-49	2	9
___	**1012**	Transformer, 35 watts, 50-54	3	9
___	**1013**	Curved Track (027), 45-69		1
___	**1013-17**	Steel Pins, dozen (027), 46-60		1
___	**1013-42**	Steel Pins, dozen (027), 61-68		2
___	**1014**	Transformer, 40 watts, 55	4	10
___	**1015**	Transformer, 45 watts, 56-60	4	9
___	**1016**	Transformer, 35 watts, 59-60	3	7
___	**1018**	Half Straight Track (027), 55-69		1
___	**1018**	Straight Track (027), 45-69		1
___	**1019**	Remote Control Track Set (027), 46-48	2	7
___	**1020**	90-degree Crossing (027), 55-69	2	4
___	**1021**	90-degree Crossing (027), 45-54	2	4
___	**1022**	Manual Switches, pair (027), 53-69	6	11
___	**1023**	45-degree Crossing (027), 56-69	2	5
___	**1024**	Manual Switches, pair (027), 46-52	5	11
___	**1025**	Illuminated Bumper (027), 46-47	5	11
___	**1025**	Transformer, 45 watts, 61-69	3	9
___	**1026**	Transformer, 25 watts, 61-64	2	15
___	**1032**	Transformer, 75 watts, 48	7	19
___	**1033**	Transformer, 90 watts, 48-56	18	30
___	**1034**	Transformer, 75 watts, 48-54	10	34
___	**1035**	Transformer, 60 watts, 47	6	36
___	**1037**	Transformer, 40 watts, 46-47	4	8
___	**1041**	Transformer, 60 watts, 45-46	7	15
___	**1042**	Transformer, 75 watts, 47-48	8	18
___	**1043**	Transformer, 50 watts, 53-57	4	14
___	**1043-500**	Transformer, 60 watts, ivory, 57-58	68	241
___	**1044**	Transformer, 90 watts, 57-69	13	29
___	**1045**	Operating Watchman, 46-50	13	62
___	**1045C**	Contactor	4	9
___	**1047**	Operating Switchman, 59-61	33	119
___	**1050**	0-4-0 Scout Locomotive, 1050T Tender, 59 u	33	77
___	**1050T**	Tender	6	15
___	**1053**	Transformer, 60 watts, 56-60	6	14
___	**1055**	Texas Special Alco Diesel A Unit, 59-60	22	54
___	**1060**	2-4-2 Locomotive, 1050T or 1060T Tender, 60-62	15	30
___	**1060T**	Lionel Lines Tender	6	13

POSTWAR 1945-1969		Good	Exc	
1060T-50	Southern Pacific Tender, 63-64 u	11	25	___
1061	0-4-0 or 2-4-2 Scout Locomotive, 1061T Tender, 64, 69			___
	(A) Slope-back Lionel Lines tender	9	24	___
	(B) Paper number labels	28	87	___
	(C) No number stamped on cab	19	50	___
1061T	Tender	4	16	___
1062	0-4-0 or 2-4-2 Scout Locomotive, 63-64			___
	(A) Streamlined Southern Pacific Tender	25	53	___
	(B) Other tenders	15	39	___
1063	Transformer, 75 watts, 60-64	11	26	___
1063	Transformer 75 watts, with green whistle control	58	87	___
1065	Union Pacific Alco Diesel A Unit, 61	23	60	___
1066	Union Pacific Alco Diesel A Unit, 64 u	25	60	___
1073	Transformer, 60 watts, 61-66	6	15	___
1101	Transformer, 25 watts, 48	2	5	___
1101	2-4-2 Scout Locomotive, 1001T Tender, 48 u			___
	(A) Cab correctly marked "1101"	13	29	___
	(B) Cab marked "1001"	58	133	___
1110	2-4-2 Locomotive, 1001T Tender, 49, 51-52	15	31	___
1120	2-4-2 Scout Locomotive, 1001T Tender, 50	19	32	___
1121	Remote Control Switches, pair (027), 46-51	11	27	___
1122	Remote Control Switches, pair (027), 52-53	12	24	___
1122E	Remote Control Switches, pair (027), 53-69	11	26	___
1122-34	Remote Control Switches, pair, 52-53	11	26	___
1122-500	Gauge Adapter (027), 57-66	3	7	___
1130	2-4-2 Locomotive, 6066T or 1130T Tender, 53-54			___
	(A) Plastic body	14	34	___
	(B) Die-cast body	28	63	___
1130T	Tender			___
	(A) Black-painted shell	22	51	___
	(B) Black plastic shell	6	14	___
1130T-500	Tender, pink, from Girls Set	113	276	___
1144	Transformer, 75 watts, 61-66	10	25	___
1232	Transformer, 75 watts, made for export, 48	17	38	___
1615	0-4-0 Locomotive, 1615T Tender, 55-57			___
	(A) No grab irons	55	109	___
	(B) Grab irons on locomotive and tender	91	208	___
1615T	Tender	15	30	___
1625	0-4-0 Locomotive, 1625T Tender, 58	135	328	___
1625T	Tender	22	48	___
1640-100	Presidential Kit, 60	53	145	___
1654	2-4-2 Locomotive, 1654W Tender, 46-47	32	70	___
1654T	Tender	10	24	___
1654W	Whistling Tender	13	33	___
1655	2-4-2 Locomotive, 6654W Tender, 48-49	30	70	___

POSTWAR 1945-1969		Good	Exc
____ **1656**	0-4-0 Locomotive, 6403B Tender, 48-49		
____	(A) Large silver cab number	105	291
____	(B) Small silver cab number	106	277
____ **1665**	0-4-0 Locomotive, 2403B Tender, 46	141	316
____ **1666**	2-6-2 Locomotive, 2466W or 2466WX Tender, 46-47		
____	(A) Number plate and two-piece bell	57	122
____	(B) Rubber-stamped number and one-piece bell	59	122
____ **1666T**	Tender	10	23
____ **1862**	4-4-0 Civil War General, 1862T Tender, 59-62		
____	(A) Gray smokestack	67	141
____	(B) Black smokestack	72	150
____ **1862T**	Tender	21	43
____ **1865**	Western & Atlantic Coach, 59-62	21	48
____ **1866**	Western & Atlantic Mail-Baggage Car, 59-62	21	49
____ **1872**	4-4-0 Civil War General, 1872T Tender, 59-62	102	301
____ **1872T**	Tender	29	57
____ **1875**	Western & Atlantic Coach, 59-62	77	247
____ **1875W**	Western & Atlantic Coach, whistle, 59-62	51	122
____ **1876**	Western & Atlantic Baggage Car, 59-62	38	111
____ **1877**	Flatcar with fence and horses, 59-62	46	118
____ **1882**	4-4-0 Civil War General, 1882T Tender, 60 u	186	368
____ **1882T**	Tender, 60 u	41	91
____ **1885**	Western & Atlantic Coach, 60 u	90	223
____ **1887**	Flatcar with fences and horses, 60 u	85	174
____ **2001**	Track Make-up Kit (027), 63	288	760
____ **2002**	Track Make-up Kit (027), 63	495	1181
____ **2003**	Track Make-up Kit (027), 63	600	3267
____ **2016**	2-6-4 Locomotive, 6026W Tender, 55-56	39	87
____ **2018**	2-6-4 Locomotive, 56-59, 61		
____	(A) 6026T Tender	32	58
____	(B) 6026W Tender	41	87
____	(C) 1130T Tender	32	107
____ **2020**	6-8-6 Steam Turbine Locomotive, 2020W or 2466WX Tender, smoke lamp, 46	82	213
____ **2020**	6-8-6 Steam Turbine Locomotive, 2020W or 6020W Tender, 47-49	74	176
____ **2020W**	Whistling Tender	28	61
____ **2023**	Union Pacific Alco Diesel AA Units, 50-51		
____	(A) Yellow body	64	276
____	(B) Gray nose and side frames	1393	4048
____	(C) Silver body	71	172
____ **2024**	C&O Alco Diesel A Unit, 69	30	68
____ **2025**	2-6-2 Locomotive, 2466WX or 6466WX Tender, 47-49		
____	(A) Black smokestack, 48-49	73	160
____	(B) Aluminum smokestack, 47	78	183
____ **2025**	2-6-4 Locomotive, 6466W Tender, 52	82	202
____ **2026**	2-6-2 Locomotive, 6466WX Tender, 48-49	51	279

		Good	Exc	
2026	2-6-4 Locomotive, 6466W, 6466T, or 6066T Tender, 51-53	39	70	___
2028	Pennsylvania GP7 Diesel, 55			___
	(A) Gold lettering	117	245	___
	(B) Yellow lettering	87	184	___
	(C) Tan frame	179	502	___
2029	2-6-4 Locomotive, 64-69			___
	(A) 234W Lionel Lines Tender	47	138	___
	(B) LL Tender with "Hagerstown" on bottom	61	126	___
	(C) 234W Pennsylvania Tender	71	152	___
2031	Rock Island Alco Diesel AA Units, 52-54	75	200	___
2032	Erie Alco Diesel AA Units, 52-54	90	246	___
2033	Union Pacific Alco Diesel AA Units, 52-54	71	155	___
2034	2-4-2 Scout Locomotive, 6066T Tender, 52	30	63	___
2035	2-6-4 Locomotive, 6466W Tender, 50-51	58	113	___
2036	2-6-4 Locomotive, 6466W Tender, 50	41	195	___
2037	2-6-4 Locomotive, 54-55, 57-63			___
	(A) 6026T or 1130T Tender	35	132	___
	(B) 6026W, 233W, or 234W whistle Tender	49	177	___
2037-500	2-6-4 Locomotive, pink, 1130T-500 Tender, 57-58	404	1045	___
2041	Rock Island Alco Diesel AA Units, 69	61	170	___
2046	4-6-4 Locomotive, 2046W Tender, 50-51, 53	104	266	___
2046T	Tender, for export	54	146	___
2046W	Whistle Tender	29	121	___
2046W-50	PRR Whistle Tender	34	118	___
2055	4-6-4 Locomotive, 2046W or 6026W Tender, 53-55	90	190	___
2056	4-6-4 Locomotive, 2046W Tender, 52	71	199	___
2065	4-6-4 Locomotive, 2046W or 6026W Tender, 54-56	83	238	___
2203B	Tender with bell	47	108	___
2203T	Tender, 45-46	36	54	___
2224W	Whistle Tender	28	66	___
2240	Wabash F3 AB Units, 56	189	419	___
2242	New Haven F3 AB Units, 58-59	385	939	___
2242C	New Haven F3 B Unit, 58-59	99	312	___
2243	Santa Fe F3 AB Units, 55-57			___
	(A) Gray body mold, raised molded cab door ladder	100	250	___
	(B) Typical molded cab door ladder	180	388	___
2243C	Santa Fe F3 B Unit, 55-57	46	129	___
2245	Texas Special F3 A Unit, 54-55	133	255	___
2245C	Texas Special F3 B Unit, 54-55			___
	(A) With Portholes, 54	171	387	___
	(B) Without Portholes, 55	191	570	___
2257	SP-type caboose, 47			___
	(A) Red body, no smokestack	5	18	___
	(B) Tuscan body and smokestack	107	287	___
	(C) Red body and smokestack	153	512	___

			Good	Exc
____	**2321**	Lackawanna FM Train Master Diesel, 54-56		
____		(A) Gray roof	141	356
____		(B) Maroon roof	208	499
____	**2322**	Virginian FM Train Master Diesel, 65-66		
____		(A) Unpainted blue body, yellow stripes	210	458
____		(B) Blue or black body, painted blue and yellow stripes	216	529
____	**2328**	Burlington GP7 Diesel, 55-56	84	247
____	**2329**	Virginian GE E-33 or EL-C Electric Locomotive, 58-59	164	404
____	**2330**	Pennsylvania GG1 Electric Locomotive, green, 50	301	890
____	**2331**	Virginian FM Train Master Diesel, 55-58		
____		(A) Black and yellow stripes, gray mold, 55	282	703
____		(B) Yellow stripes, blue mold, 56-58	209	558
____		(C) Blue and yellow stripes, gray mold	318	801
____	**2332**	Pennsylvania GG1 Electric Locomotive, 47-49		
____		(A) Black	498	1786
____		(B) Dark green	205	779
____	**2333**	NYC F3 Diesel AA Units, 48-49		
____		(A) Rubber-stamped lettering	209	599
____		(B) Heat-stamped lettering	159	473
____	**2333**	Santa Fe F3 Diesel AA Units, 48-49	161	422
____	**2337**	Wabash GP7 Diesel, 58	98	204
____	**2338**	Milwaukee Road GP7 Diesel, 55-56		
____		(A) Orange band around shell	440	1328
____		(B) Interrupted orange band	104	210
____	**2339**	Wabash GP7 Diesel, 57	116	230
____	**2340**	Pennsylvania GG1 Electric Locomotive, 55		
____		(A) Tuscan	436	1135
____		(B) Dark green	284	1073
____	**2341**	Jersey Central FM Train Master Diesel, 56		
____		(A) High-gloss orange	869	2673
____		(B) Dull orange	831	2041
____	**2343**	Santa Fe F3 Diesel AA Units, 50-52	178	423
____	**2343C**	Santa Fe F3 B Unit, 50-55		
____		(A) Screen roof vents	88	225
____		(B) Louver roof vents	64	160
____	**2344**	NYC F3 Diesel AA Units, 50-52	172	417
____	**2344C**	NYC F3 B Unit, 50-55	88	268
____	**2345**	Western Pacific F3 Diesel AA Units, 52	435	965
____	**2346**	B&M GP9 Diesel, 65-66	112	273
____	**2347**	C&O GP7 Diesel, 65 u	1568	4190
____	**2348**	M&StL GP9 Diesel, 58-59	175	315
____	**2349**	Northern Pacific GP9 Diesel, 59-60	131	435
____	**2350**	New Haven EP-5 Electric Locomotive, 56-58		
____		(A) Painted nose trim, white N and orange H	171	397
____		(B) Decaled nose trim, white N and orange H	92	251

		Good	Exc	
	(C) Painted nose trim, orange N and black H	757	2796	___
	(D) Decaled nose trim, orange N and black H	386	858	___
	(E) Orange and white stripes go through doorjambs	276	851	___
2351	Milwaukee Road EP-5 Electric Locomotive, 57-58	135	409	___
2352	Pennsylvania EP-5 Electric Locomotive, 58-59			___
	(A) Tuscan body	167	384	___
	(B) Chocolate brown body	214	404	___
2353	Santa Fe F3 Diesel AA Units, 53-55	146	411	___
2354	NYC F3 Diesel AA Units, 53-55	186	422	___
2355	Western Pacific F3 Diesel AA Units, 53	409	1499	___
2356	Southern F3 Diesel AA Units, 54-56	297	730	___
2356C	Southern F3 B Unit, 54-56	124	308	___
2357	SP-type Caboose, 47-48			___
	(A) Red body and smokestack	212	530	___
	(B) Tuscan body and smokestack	14	40	___
	(C) Tile red, no smokestack, "6357" stamped on bottom	51	137	___
2358	Great Northern EP-5 Electric Locomotive, 59-60	202	548	___
2359	Boston & Maine GP9 Diesel, 61-62	116	315	___
2360	Pennsylvania GG1 Electric Locomotive, 56-58, 61-63			___
	(A) Tuscan, 5 gold stripes	469	1624	___
	(B) Dark green, 5 gold stripes	354	786	___
	(C) Tuscan, gold stripe, heat-stamped letters	378	727	___
	(D) Tuscan, gold stripe, decaled lettering	341	668	___
2363	Illinois Central F3 Diesel AB Units, 55-56			___
	(A) Black lettering	340	917	___
	(B) Brown lettering	366	917	___
2363C	Illinois Central "B" Unit	61	230	___
2365	C&O GP7 Diesel, 62-63	127	331	___
2367	Wabash F3 Diesel AB Units, 55	309	1065	___
2367C	Wabash F3 Diesel B Unit, 55	88	219	___
2368	B&O F3 Diesel AB Units, 56	708	1663	___
2368C	B&O F3 Diesel B Unit, 56	150	510	___
2373	CP F3 Diesel AA Units, 57	582	1555	___
2378	Milwaukee Road F3 Diesel AB Units, 56			___
	(A) Yellow roof line stripes	441	779	___
	(B) No roof line stripes	399	904	___
2378C	Milwaukee Road F3 Diesel B Unit, yellow roof line stripe, 56	201	480	___
2379	Rio Grande F3 Diesel AB Units, 57-58	351	940	___
2379C	Rio Grande B Unit	84	275	___
2383	Santa Fe F3 Diesel AA Units, 58-66	166	603	___
2400	Maplewood Pullman Car, green, 48-49	39	79	___
2401	Hillside Observation Car, green, 48-49	29	70	___
2402	Chatham Pullman Car, green, 48-49	34	81	___
2403B	Tender, 46	20	47	___
2404	Santa Fe Vista Dome Car, 64-65	26	58	___

POSTWAR 1945-1969		Good	Exc
___ 2405	Santa Fe Pullman Car, 64-65	26	58
___ 2406	Santa Fe Observation Car, 64-65	21	51
___ 2408	Santa Fe Vista Dome Car, 66	29	61
___ 2409	Santa Fe Pullman Car, 66	30	62
___ 2410	Santa Fe Observation Car, 66	24	54
___ 2411	Lionel Lines Flatcar, 46-48		
___	(A) With pipes, 46	32	62
___	(B) With logs, 47-48	17	33
___ 2412	Santa Fe Vista Dome Car, 59-63	33	98
___ 2414	Santa Fe Pullman Car, 59-63	37	98
___ 2416	Santa Fe Observation Car, 59-63	29	82
___ 2419	DL&W Work Caboose, 46-47	17	42
___ 2420	DL&W Work Caboose with searchlight, 46-48	23	167
___	(A) Light or dark gray, heat-stamped lettering	37	78
___	(B) Light or dark gray, rubber-stamped lettering	60	131
___ 2421	Maplewood Pullman Car, 50-53		
___	(A) Gray roof	26	60
___	(B) Silver roof	21	61
___ 2422	Chatham Pullman Car, 50-53		
___	(A) Gray roof	24	61
___	(B) Silver roof	21	79
___ 2423	Hillside Observation Car, 50-53		
___	(A) Gray roof	25	60
___	(B) Silver roof	21	52
___ 2426W	Whistle Tender, 50	184	373
___ 2429	Livingston Pullman Car, 52-53	47	121
___ 2430	Pullman Car, blue, 46-47	21	76
___ 2431	Observation Car, blue, 46-47	20	70
___ 2432	Clifton Vista Dome Car, 54-58	26	95
___ 2434	Newark Pullman Car, 54-58	25	94
___ 2435	Elizabeth Pullman Car, 54-58	42	114
___ 2436	Mooseheart Observation Car, 57-58	23	60
___ 2436	Summit Observation Car, 54-56	23	58
___ 2440	Pullman Car, green, 46-47		
___	(A) Silver lettering	28	62
___	(B) White lettering	25	53
___ 2441	Observation Car, green, 46-47		
___	(A) Silver lettering	25	59
___	(B) White lettering	21	51
___ 2442	Clifton Vista Dome Car, 56	33	81
___ 2442	Pullman Car, brown, 46-48		
___	(A) Silver lettering	32	68
___	(B) White lettering	29	71
___ 2443	Observation Car, brown, 46-48		
___	(A) Silver lettering	32	65
___	(B) White lettering	26	75

POSTWAR 1945-1969		Good	Exc	
2444	Newark Pullman Car, 56	38	85	___
2445	Elizabeth Pullman Car, 56	124	172	___
2446	Summit Observation Car, 56	38	80	___
2452	Pennsylvania Gondola, 45-47			___
	(A) Whirly wheels, 45	29	78	___
	(B) Regular wheels	9	19	___
	(C) Early flying shoe trucks, two holes in floor, 45	38	92	___
2452X	Pennsylvania Gondola, 46-47	11	24	___
X2454	Baby Ruth Boxcar, PRR logo, 46-47	15	56	___
X2454	Pennsylvania Boxcar, 46			___
	(A) Brown door	59	180	___
	(B) Orange door	111	395	___
2456	Lehigh Valley Hopper, 48			___
	(A) Flat black, 2 lines of data, 48	11	27	___
	(B) Flat black, 3 lines of data, 48	59	161	___
2457	PRR N5-type Caboose 477618, tintype, 45-47			___
	(A) Brown body, white lettering centered, red window frames, 45	15	45	___
	(B) Brown body, white lettering not centered, 45	88	332	___
	(C) Red body, red window frames, 46-47	10	28	___
	(D) Red body, black window frames, 46-47	13	46	___
	(E) Red body, no "Eastern Division" markings, 46-47	10	20	___
	(F) Same as E, but black smokejack, 46-47	10	21	___
X2458	PRR Automobile Boxcar, 46-48	22	134	___
2460	Bucyrus Erie Crane Car, 12-wheel, 46-50			___
	(A) Gray cab	69	222	___
	(B) Black cab	36	103	___
2461	Transformer Car, die-cast, 47-48			___
	(A) Red transformer	27	74	___
	(B) Black transformer	23	60	___
	(C) Red transformer, number rubber-stamped on bottom	52	125	___
2465	Sunoco 2-D Tank Car, 46-48			___
	(A) "Gas, Sunoco, and Oils" in diamond, centered	266	553	___
	(B) "Sunoco" in diamond	6	20	___
	(C) "Sunoco" extends beyond diamond	6	16	___
	(D) "Sunoco" in diamond, centered	63	120	___
2466T	Tender	16	33	___
2466W	Whistle Tender, 46-48			___
	(A) Number heat-stamped on front, 46	64	151	___
	(B) Number missing from front, 47-48	12	30	___
2466WX	Whistle Tender, 45-48	23	66	___
2472	PRR N5-type Caboose, tintype, 46-47	12	36	___
2481	Plainfield Pullman Car, yellow, 50	82	215	___
2482	Westfield Pullman Car, yellow, 50	82	224	___
2483	Livingston Observation Car, yellow, 50	69	211	___
2521	President McKinley Observation Car, 62-66	57	137	___

POSTWAR 1945-1969			Good	Exc
___	**2522**	President Harrison Vista Dome Car, 62-66	65	150
___	**2523**	President Garfield Pullman Car, 62-66	74	155
___	**2530**	REA Baggage Car, 54-60		
___		(A) Large doors	137	451
___		(B) Small doors	63	201
___	**2531**	Silver Dawn Observation Car, 52-60		
___		(A) Ribbed channels, round rivets	30	85
___		(B) Ribbed channels, hex rivets	36	85
___		(C) Ribbed channels, hex rivets, red center taillight	62	136
___		(D) Flat channels, glued nameplates	39	110
___	**2532**	Silver Range Vista Dome Car, 52-60		
___		(A) Ribbed channels, or hex rivets	33	86
___		(B) Flat channels, glued nameplates	37	119
___	**2533**	Silver Cloud Pullman Car, 52-59		
___		(A) Ribbed channels, or hex rivets	33	84
___		(B) Flat channels, glued nameplates	39	97
___	**2534**	Silver Bluff Pullman Car, 52-59		
___		(A) Ribbed channels, or hex rivets	43	88
___		(B) Flat channels, glued nameplates	38	92
___	**2541**	Alexander Hamilton Observation Car, 55-56*	59	124
___	**2542**	Betsy Ross Vista Dome Car, 55-56*	62	131
___	**2543**	William Penn Pullman Car, 55-56*	62	133
___	**2544**	Molly Pitcher Pullman Car, 55-56*	62	132
___	**2550**	B&O Baggage-Mail Rail Diesel Car, 57-58	146	480
___	**2551**	Banff Park Observation Car, 57*	84	205
___	**2552**	Skyline 500 Vista Dome Car, 57*	105	240
___	**2553**	Blair Manor Pullman Car, 57*	152	335
___	**2554**	Craig Manor Pullman Car, 57*	152	311
___	**2555**	Sunoco 1-D Tank Car, 46-48	18	49
___	**2559**	B&O Passenger Rail Diesel Car, 57-58	120	280
___	**2560**	Lionel Lines Crane Car, 8-wheel, 46-47		
___		(A) Black boom	24	78
___		(B) Brown boom	25	67
___		(C) Green boom	31	82
___	**2561**	Vista Valley Observation Car, 59-61*	77	173
___	**2562**	Regal Pass Vista Dome Car, 59-61*	82	203
___	**2563**	Indian Falls Pullman Car, 59-61*	80	198
___	**2625**	Irvington Pullman Car, 46-50*		
___		(A) No silhouettes	62	141
___		(B) Silhouettes	73	194
___	**2625**	Madison Pullman Car, 46-47*	54	144
___	**2625**	Manhattan Pullman Car, 46-47*	54	145
___	**2627**	Madison Pullman Car, 48-50*		
___		(A) No silhouettes	52	150
___		(B) Silhouettes	71	191

POSTWAR 1945-1969		Good	Exc	
2628	Manhattan Pullman Car, 48-50*			___
	(A) No silhouettes	57	176	___
	(B) Silhouettes	77	220	___
2666T	Tender	9	18	___
2671T	PRR Tender, for export	47	120	___
2671W	Whistle Tender	35	96	___
2671W	PRR Tender with silver letters and back-up light	180	346	___
2671WX	Whistle Tender	44	202	___
2755	Sunoco 1-D Tank Car, 45	24	67	___
X2758	PRR Automobile Boxcar, 45-46	27	61	___
2855	Sunoco 1-D Tank Car, 46-47			___
	(A) Black	62	190	___
	(B) Black, decal without "Gas" and "Oils"	54	175	___
	(C) Gray	47	135	___
3309	Turbo Missile Launch Car, red body, 63-64	16	46	___
3309-50	Turbo Missile Launch Car, olive body, 63-64	195	425	___
3330	Flatcar with submarine kit, 60-62	51	247	___
3330-100	Operating Submarine Kit with box, 60-61	151	382	___
3349	Turbo Missile Launch Car, red body, 62-65	19	72	___
3356	Operating Horse Car and Corral Set, 56-60, 64-66	62	290	___
3356	Operating Horse Car only, 56-60, 64-66			___
	(A) Built date, bar-end trucks, 56-60	40	88	___
	(B) No built date, AAR trucks, 64-66	48	104	___
3356-100	Black Horses, 9 pieces, 56-59	18	33	___
3356-150	Horse Car Corral, 57-60	37	165	___
3357	Hydraulic Maintenance Car, 62-64			___
	(A) Blue, 62-64	10	33	___
	(B) Teal, 62-64	40	91	___
3357-27	Trestle Components for Cop and Hobo Car, 62	26	53	___
3359	Lionel Lines Twin-bin Coal Dump Car, 55-58	18	100	___
3360	Operating Burro Crane, self-propelled, 56-57	72	152	___
3361	Operating Log Dump Car, 55-58	16	52	___
3362	Helium Tank Unloading Car, 61-63, 69	23	87	___
3364	Operating Dump Car with 3 logs, 65-66, 68	18	59	___
3366	Circus Car Corral Set, 59-62	98	221	___
3366	Circus Car Corral only, 59-62	18	95	___
3366	Circus Car only, 59-62	42	90	___
3366-100	White Horses, 9 pieces, 59-62	32	62	___
3370	W&A Sheriff and Outlaw Car, 61-64			___
	(A) AAR trucks	19	62	___
	(B) Archbar trucks	25	60	___
3376	Bronx Zoo Car, 60-66, 69			___
	(A) Blue, white lettering	17	75	___
	(B) Green, yellow lettering	23	57	___
	(C) Blue, yellow lettering	73	203	___

		POSTWAR 1945-1969	Good	Exc
___	**3386**	Bronx Zoo Car, 60	22	56
___	**3409**	Helicopter Car, 61	32	80
___	**3410**	Helicopter Car, 61-63		
___		(A) 2 operating couplers, gray Navy helicopter	27	69
___		(B) 1 operating coupler, yellow helicopter, 63	51	113
___	**3413**	Mercury Capsule Car, 62-64	42	132
___	**3419**	Helicopter Car, 59-65	31	107
___	**3424**	Wabash Operating Boxcar, 56-58	17	80
___	**3424-75**	Low Bridge Signal, 56-57	54	185
___	**3424-100**	Low Bridge Signal Set, 56-58	23	104
___	**3428**	U.S. Mail Operating Boxcar, 59-60	34	102
___	**3429**	USMC Helicopter Car, 60	226	575
___	**3434**	Poultry Dispatch Car, 59-60, 64-66		
___		(A) Gray man	52	137
___		(B) Blue man	44	100
___	**3435**	Traveling Aquarium Car, 59-62		
___		(A) Gold lettering, tank designations, and circle around L	375	719
___		(B) Gold lettering, tank designations, no circle around L	237	624
___		(C) Gold lettering, no tank designations, no circle around L	88	416
___		(D) Yellow lettering, no tank designations, no circle around L	50	160
___	**3444**	Erie Operating Gondola, 57-59	32	75
___	**3451**	Operating Log Dump Car, 46-48		
___		(A) Heat-stamped lettering	14	34
___		(B) Rubber-stamped lettering	24	62
___	**3454**	PRR Operating Merchandise Car, 46-47		
___		(A) Red lettering	1803	3646
___		(B) Blue lettering	37	138
___	**3456**	N&W Operating Hopper, 50-55	23	59
___	**3459**	LL Operating Coal Dump Car, 46-48		
___		(A) Aluminum bin	115	301
___		(B) Black bin	17	41
___		(C) Green bin	23	64
___	**3460**	Flatcar with trailers, 55-57	33	70
___	**3461**	LL Operating Log Car, 49-55		
___		(A) Black car, heat-stamped lettering	19	76
___		(B) Black car, rubber-stamped lettering	135	390
___	**3461-25**	LL Operating Log Car, green	23	75
___	**3462**	Automatic Milk Car, 47-48		
___		(A) Flat white or cream, steel base mechanism	12	43
___		(B) Flat white or cream, brass base mechanism	22	58
___		(C) Glossy cream	64	199
___	**3462-70**	Magnetic Milk Cans, 52-59	11	16
___	**3462P**	Milk Car Platform, 47-48	6	20

POSTWAR 1945-1969		Good	Exc	
X3464	ATSF Operating Boxcar, 49-52			___
	(A) Orange body, corner steps, 49	8	14	___
	(B) Orange body, no steps, 50-52	9	35	___
	(C) Tan body	444	1088	___
X3464	NYC Operating Boxcar, 49-52			___
	(A) Corner steps, 49	8	15	___
	(B) No steps, 50-52	6	13	___
3469	LL Operating Coal Dump Car, 49-55	18	61	___
3470	Target Launching Car, dark blue, 62-64	26	111	___
3470-100	Target Launching Car, light blue, 63	53	149	___
3472	Automatic Milk Car, 49-53	19	50	___
3474	Western Pacific Operating Boxcar, 52-53	23	167	___
3482	Automatic Milk Car, 54-55			___
	(A) "RT3472" on right	38	89	___
	(B) "RT3482" on right	17	48	___
3484	Pennsylvania Operating Boxcar, 53	21	52	___
3484-25	ATSF Operating Boxcar, 54			___
	(A) White lettering	30	67	___
	(B) Black lettering	564	1631	___
3494-1	NYC Operating Boxcar, 55	32	90	___
3494-150	MP Operating Boxcar, 56	42	107	___
3494-275	State of Maine Operating Boxcar, 56-58			___
	(A) "3494275" on side	38	107	___
	(B) No number on side	60	177	___
3494-550	Monon Operating Boxcar, 57-58	222	441	___
3494-625	Soo Operating Boxcar, 57-58	222	404	___
3509	Satellite Launching Car, 61			___
	(A) Chrome satellite cover	28	69	___
	(B) Gray satellite cover	80	192	___
3510	Satellite Launching Car, 62	33	78	___
3512	Fireman and Ladder Car, 59-61			___
	(A) Black extension ladder	33	80	___
	(B) Silver extension ladder	62	169	___
3519	Satellite Launching Car, 61-64	22	61	___
3520	Searchlight Car, 52-53			___
	(A) Serif lettering	17	40	___
	(B) Sans serif lettering	15	85	___
3530	GM Generator Car, 56-58			___
	(A) Blue fuel tank	43	136	___
	(B) Black fuel tank	37	105	___
	(C) "3530" underscored	664	1880	___
3530-50	Searchlight with pole and base, 56-56	23	73	___
3535	Security Car with searchlight, 60-61	48	110	___
3540	Operating Radar Car, 59-60	40	114	___
3545	Operating TV Monitor Car, 61-62	50	137	___

			Good	Exc
___	**3559**	Operating Coal Dump Car, 46-48		
___		(A) Black coil housing	18	52
___		(B) Brown coil housing	37	79
___	**3562-1**	ATSF Operating Barrel Car, 54		
___		(A) Black, black unloading trough	70	200
___		(B) Black, yellow unloading trough	65	174
___		(C) Gray, red lettering	1150	2643
___	**3562-25**	ATSF Operating Barrel Car, gray, 54		
___		(A) Red lettering, no bracket tab	189	452
___		(B) Blue lettering, no bracket tab	20	67
___		(C) Blue lettering, bracket tab	25	69
___	**3562-50**	ATSF Operating Barrel Car, yellow, 55-56		
___		(A) Painted	35	83
___		(B) Unpainted	23	62
___	**3562-75**	ATSF Operating Barrel Car, orange, 57-58	35	112
___	**3619**	Helicopter Reconnaissance Car, 62-64		
___		(A) Light yellow	46	132
___		(B) Dark yellow	64	154
___	**3620**	Searchlight Car, orange generator, 54-56		
___		(A) Unpainted gray plastic searchlight	20	38
___		(B) Gray-painted gray plastic searchlight	26	56
___		(C) Unpainted orange plastic searchlight	53	117
___		(D) Gray-painted orange plastic searchlight	75	277
___	**3650**	Extension Searchlight Car, 56-59		
___		(A) Light gray	29	91
___		(B) Dark gray	60	159
___		(C) Olive gray	111	260
___	**3656**	Armour Operating Cattle Car, some with an open coil, 49-55		
___		(A) Black letters, Armour sticker	126	310
___		(B) White letters, Armour sticker	19	43
___		(C) Black letters, no Armour sticker	94	204
___		(D) White letters, no Armour sticker	16	40
___	**3656**	Stockyard with cattle, 49-55	18	42
___	**3656-34**	Cattle, black, 9 pieces, 49-58		
___		(A) Rounded ridge on base, 49	60	92
___		(B) Plain base	15	27
___	**3656-150**	Corral Platform, yellow tray	225	539
___	**3662**	Automatic Milk Car, 55-60, 64-66	30	118
___	**3662-79**	Nonmagnetic Milk Cans, 7 pieces, white envelope	18	34
___	**3662-80**	Nonmagnetic Milk Cans, 7 pieces, manila envelope	16	32
___	**3665**	Minuteman Operating Car, 61-64		
___		(A) Medium blue roof	85	210
___		(B) Dark blue roof	34	103
___	**3666**	Minuteman Boxcar with cannon, 64 u	254	485

POSTWAR 1945-1969		Good	Exc	
3672	Bosco Operating Milk Car, 59-60			___
	(A) Unpainted yellow body	78	168	___
	(B) Painted yellow body	122	347	
3672-79	Bosco Can Set, 7 pieces in envelope, 59-60	39	66	___
3820	USMC Operating Submarine Car, 60-62	117	255	___
3830	Operating Submarine Car, 60-63	39	102	___
3854	Automatic Merchandise Car, 46-47	181	601	___
3927	Lionel Lines Track Cleaning Car, 56-60	29	112	___
3927-38	Track Cleaning Fluid Bottle	8	15	___
3927-50	Track Wiping Cylinders, 25 pieces, 57-60	16	33	___
3927-75	Track-Clean Detergent, can, 56-69	5	12	___
4357	SP-type Caboose, electronic, die-cast stack, 48-49			___
	(A) Die-cast metal smokestack	75	180	___
	(B) Matching plastic smokestack	104	237	___
	(C) Matching plastic smokestack, raised board on roofwalk	110	255	___
4452	PRR Gondola, electronic, 46-49	61	134	___
4454	Baby Ruth PRR Boxcar, electronic, 46-49	62	148	___
4457	PRR N5-type Caboose, tintype, electronic, 46-47	52	149	___
4671W	Whistle Tender	86	204	___
5102	Railroad and Roadway Crossing	10	45	___
5159-50	Maintenance and Lube Kit, 66-69	23	54	___
5160	Viewing Stand, 63	40	209	___
5459	LL Coal Dump Car, electronic, 46-49	60	157	___
6001T	Tender	7	15	___
6002	NYC Gondola, 50	3	6	___
X6004	Baby Ruth PRR Boxcar, 50	4	8	___
6007	Lionel Lines SP-type Caboose, 50	3	6	___
6009	Remote Control Uncoupling Track, 53-54	2	5	___
6012	Gondola, 51-56	2	15	___
6014	Bosco PRR Boxcar, 58			___
	(A) White body	14	36	___
	(B) Red body	4	13	___
	(C) Orange body	5	14	___
6014	Chun King Boxcar, 57 u	44	125	___
6014	Frisco Boxcar, 57, 63-69			___
	(A) White body	9	31	___
	(B) Red body	5	9	___
	(C) White body, coin slot	16	40	___
	(D) Orange body, 57	12	31	___
	(E) Orange body, 69	9	20	___
X6014	Baby Ruth PRR Boxcar, 51-56			___
	(A) White body	5	9	___
	(B) Red body	4	10	___
6014-100	Airex Boxcar, 60 u	14	49	___
6014-150	Wix Boxcar, 59 u	124	211	___

	POSTWAR 1945-1969		Good	Exc
___	6015	Sunoco 1-D Tank Car, 54-55		
___		(A) Painted tank	73	420
___		(B) Unpainted tank	7	16
___	6017	Lionel Lines SP-type Caboose, 51-62		
___		(A) Common unpainted red or Tuscan-red body	4	14
___		(B) Glossy Tuscan-painted, orange mold	22	58
___		(C) Semi-glossy Tuscan-painted, orange mold	12	30
___		(D) Light or dark tile red-painted, blue mold	14	36
___		(E) Common-brown painted body	2	7
___	6017	Lionel SP-type Caboose, unpainted maroon, 56	7	20
___	6017-50	U.S. Marine Corps SP-type Caboose, 58	28	74
___	6017-85	Lionel Lines SP-type Caboose, gray-painted, 58	22	75
___	6017-100	B&M SP-type Caboose, 59, 62, 65-66		
___		(A) Dark purple-blue	95	387
___		(B) Medium or light blue	14	40
___	6017-185	ATSF SP-type Caboose, gray-painted, 59-60	17	35
___	6017-200	U.S. Navy SP-type Caboose, 60	53	157
___	6017-235	ATSF SP-type Caboose, red-painted, 62	17	43
___	6019	Remote Control Track (027), 48-66	2	8
___	6020W	Whistle Tender	24	59
___	6024	Nabisco Shredded Wheat Boxcar, 57	10	28
___	6024	RCA Whirlpool Boxcar, 57 u	27	167
___	6025	Gulf 1-D Tank Car, 56-58		
___		(A) Gray body, blue lettering	5	15
___		(B) Orange body, blue lettering	11	23
___		(C) Black body, red-orange Gulf emblem	5	14
___	6026T	Tender	12	30
___	6026W	Whistle Tender	24	103
___	6027	Alaska SP-type Caboose, 59	31	74
___	6029	Remote Control Uncoupling Track, 55-63	2	8
___	6032	Short Gondola, black (027), 52-54	3	7
___	X6034	Baby Ruth PRR Boxcar, 53-54		
___		(A) Orange, blue lettering	5	13
___		(B) Orange, black lettering	5	11
___	6035	Sunoco 1-D Tank Car, 52-53	4	10
___	6037	Lionel Lines SP-type Caboose, 52-54		
___		(A) Tuscan	3	6
___		(B) Red	4	8
___	6042	Short Gondola, 59-61, 62-64	4	8
___	6044	Airex Boxcar, orange lettering, 59-60 u		
___		(A) Medium blue	8	21
___		(B) Teal blue	23	59
___		(C) Purple-blue	103	236
___	6044-1X	Nestles/McCall's Boxcar, 62-63 u	322	1137
___	6045	Lionel Lines 2-D Tank Car, 59-64		
___		(A) Gray	9	21

POSTWAR 1945-1969		Good	Exc
	(B) Orange	12	27
	(C) Beige	9	21
6045	Cities Service 2-D Tank, 60 u	14	31
6047	Lionel Lines SP-type Caboose, 62		
	(A) Unpainted, medium red	2	7
	(B) Painted, brown	164	466
	(C) Unpainted, coral pink	16	42
6050	Lionel Savings Bank Boxcar, 61		
	(A) Type I body, "Blt by Lionel"	17	41
	(B) Type I body, "Built by Lionel"	39	150
	(C) Type IIa body, "Blt by Lionel"	125	260
6050-110	Swift Boxcar, 62-63		
	(A) Red body	9	26
	(B) Dark red body, 2 open holes in roof walk	33	84
6050-175	Libby's Tomato Juice Boxcar, 63 u		
	(A) Green stems on tomatoes	15	45
	(B) Green stems missing	23	57
	(C) No white lines between glass and tomatoes	20	53
6057	Lionel Lines SP-type Caboose, 59-62		
	(A) Unpainted, red	4	16
	(B) Painted, red	22	89
	(C) Unpainted, coral pink	20	50
6057-50	LL SP-type Caboose, orange, 62	18	57
6058	C&O SP-type Caboose, 61		
	(A) Blue lettering	17	43
	(B) Black lettering	25	59
6059	M&StL SP-type Caboose, 61-69		
	(A) Painted, red	14	33
	(B) Unpainted, red	6	15
	(C) Unpainted, maroon	5	11
6062	NYC Gondola with 3 cable reels, 59-62		
	(A) No metal undercarriage	12	28
	(B) Metal undercarriage	20	49
	(C) No metal undercarriage, no paint on bottom	30	65
6062-50	NYC Gondola with 2 canisters, 69	10	20
6066T	Tender	8	20
6067	SP-type Caboose, unmarked, 61-62		
	(A) Red	3	7
	(B) Yellow	5	12
	(C) Brown	5	14
6076	ATSF Hopper, 63 u	7	17
6076	Lehigh Valley Hopper, short, 61-63		
	(A) Gray body	6	16
	(B) Black body	6	12
	(C) Red body	6	13
	(D) Yellow body, painted	391	1103

POSTWAR 1945-1969		Good	Exc
___ **6076-100**	Hopper, gray, unmarked, 63	6	20
___ **6110**	2-4-2 Locomotive, 6001T Tender, 50-51	16	37
___ **6111**	Flatcar with logs, 55-57		
___	(A) Yellow with black lettering	11	35
___	(B) Yellow with white lettering	133	374
___ **6112**	Short Gondola with 4 canisters, 56-58		
___	(A) Black body	8	18
___	(B) Blue body	8	18
___	(C) White body	18	44
___ **6112-5**	Canister, 56-58		
___	(A) Red or white	2	4
___	(B) Red with black letters	23	46
___ **6112-25**	Canister Set, 4 pieces, red or white, with box, 56-58	50	190
___ **6119**	DL&W Work Caboose, red, 55-56	11	24
___ **6119-25**	DL&W Work Caboose, orange, 56-59	19	57
___ **6119-50**	DL&W Work Caboose, brown, 56	24	73
___ **6119-75**	DL&W Work Caboose, 57		
___	(A) Heat-stamped letters on frame	15	45
___	(B) Closely spaced rubber-stamped letters on frame	63	198
___	(C) Widely spaced rubber-stamped letters on frame	63	203
___ **6119-100**	DL&W Work Caboose, red cab, gray tool tray, 57-66, 69		
___	(A) Black frame, white letters	10	22
___	(B) "Built By Lionel" builders plate, 66	21	62
___	(C) Black frame, red-painted cab	49	131
___	(D) Santa Fe cab, gray tool box	10	30
___ **6119-125**	Rescue Caboose, unpainted olive tray, black frame, white lettering, 64	72	241
___ **6120**	Work Caboose, yellow, unmarked, 61-62	6	12
___ **6121**	Flatcar with pipes, 56-57		
___	(A) Yellow, red, or gray	12	43
___	(B) Maroon	17	55
___ **6130**	ATSF Work Caboose, 61, 65-69		
___	(A) Red painted, no builders plate	13	38
___	(B) Red unpainted, builders plate	10	26
___	(C) Red painted, builders plate	63	248
___ **6139**	Remote Control Uncoupling Track (027), 63	1	4
___ **6142**	Short Gondola, green, blue, or black, with 2 canisters, 63-66, 69	8	44
___ **6142-175**	Short Gondola, olive drab, with 2 canisters	75	220
___ **6149**	Remote Control Uncoupling Track (027), 64-69	1	4
___ **6151**	Flatcar with patrol truck, 58		
___	(A) Yellow frame	35	153
___	(B) Orange frame	26	84
___	(C) Cream frame	35	84
___ **6162**	NYC Gondola with 3 white canisters, 59-68		
___	(A) Blue body	15	77

		Good	Exc
	(B) Red body	66	245
	(C) Teal body/or green body	25	54
6162-60	Alaska Gondola with 3 red canisters, 59	42	84
6162-100	NYC Gondola		
	(A) Red body with 3 red canisters	80	160
	(B) Teal or green body with 3 white canisters	15	33
6167	LL SP-type Caboose, red, 63-64		
	(A) Unpainted	5	11
	(B) Painted	31	85
6167	SP-type Caboose, unmarked, no end rails, 63-64		
	(A) Red body	4	8
	(B) Brown body	6	15
6167-50	SP-type Caboose, unmarked, yellow	5	14
6167-85	Union Pacific SP-type Caboose, 69	9	26
6167-175	SP-type Caboose, unmarked, olive	108	272
6175	Flatcar with rocket, 58-61		
	(A) Black frame	26	92
	(B) Red frame	26	69
6176	Hopper, unmarked, 63-69		
	(A) Dark yellow	11	28
	(B) Gray	8	15
	(C) Red	7	16
	(D) Bright yellow	19	49
6176-75	Lehigh Valley Hopper, 64-66, 69		
	(A) Dark yellow	5	15
	(B) Gray	6	11
	(C) Black	4	10
	(D) Red	11	24
	(E) Bright yellow	19	41
6176-100	Olive Drab Hopper, unmarked	80	140
6219	C&O Work Caboose, 60	17	41
6220	Santa Fe NW2 Switcher, 49-50		
	(A) Large GM decal on cab	101	250
	(B) Small GM decal on side	69	170
6250	Seaboard NW2 Switcher, 54-55		
	(A) Seaboard decal	71	225
	(B) Widely spaced rubber-stamped letters	92	256
	(C) Closely spaced rubber-stamped letters	134	364
6257	SP-type Caboose, 48-52		
	(A) Dark red, matching plastic smokestack	163	461
	(B) All other variations	8	15
6257-25	SP-type Caboose, circled-L logo, 53-55		
	(A) Painted, red	7	16
	(B) Unpainted, red	5	11
6257-50	SP-type Caboose, 56	8	20
6257-100	Lionel Lines SP-type Caboose, smokestack, 63-64	12	25

		POSTWAR 1945-1969	Good	Exc
___	**6257X**	SP-type Caboose, red, 2 couplers, with box, 48	30	105
___	**6262**	Flatcar with wheel load, 56-57		
___		(A) Black frame, 56-57	27	72
___		(B) Red frame, 56	376	858
___	**6264**	Flatcar with lumber for 264 Fork Lift Platform, 57-60		
___		(A) Bar-end trucks	28	62
___		(B) Plastic trucks	32	67
___		(C) Separate-sale box and envelope	129	363
___	**6311**	Flatcar with 3 pipes, 55	20	44
___	**6315**	Gulf 1-D Chemical Tank Car, 56-59, 68-69		
___		(A) Early, painted	32	78
___		(B) Late, unpainted	23	50
___		(C) Late, unpainted, built date	49	136
___	**6315**	Lionel Lines 1-D Tank Car, 63-66		
___		(A) Unpainted orange body	15	32
___		(B) Painted orange body	88	561
___	**6342**	NYC Gondola with culvert channel and 7 pipes, 56-58, 64-66	19	55
___	**6343**	Barrel Ramp Car with 6 barrels, 61-62	19	52
___	**6346**	Alcoa Quad Hopper, 56	31	99
___	**6352-1**	PFE Ice Car from 352 Ice Depot, 55-57		
___		(A) 3 lines of data	53	115
___		(B) 4 lines of data	29	82
___		(C) Separate-sale box	524	2521
___	**6356**	NYC Stock Car, 2-level, 54-55		
___		(A) Heat-stamped lettering	22	44
___		(B) Rubber-stamped lettering	29	76
___	**6357**	SP-type Caboose, SP logo, 48-53		
___		(A) Tile red, Tuscan, or maroon	12	26
___		(B) Tile red, extra board on roofwalk	100	306
___	**6357**	SP-type Caboose, no logo, 57-61		
___		(A) Number to left	12	25
___		(B) Number to right	19	96
___	**6357-25**	SP-type Caboose, circle L logo, 53-56		
___		(A) Maroon or tuscan body, black metal smokestack	12	25
___		(B) Maroon body, matching metal smokestack	89	317
___	**6357-50**	ATSF SP-type Caboose, lighted, 60	474	974
___	**6361**	Timber Transport Car, 60-61, 64-69		
___		(A) White lettering	35	87
___		(B) No lettering	51	140
___	**6362**	Truck Car with 3 trucks, 55-56		
___		(A) Shiny orange	19	43
___		(B) Dull orange	34	144
___	**6376**	LL Circus Stock Car, 56-57	34	65
___	**6401**	Flatcar, gray, no load, 60	5	12

POSTWAR 1945-1969		Good	Exc	
6401-25	Flatcar, gray with load, 64-67			___
	(A) Jeep and cannon	119	235	___
	(B) Tank	100	212	___
	(C) Payton automobile	27	54	___
	(D) Logs	14	28	___
6402	Flatcar with 2 Cable Reels, 62, 64-66, 69			___
	(A) Gray car with orange reels	5	13	___
	(B) Maroon car with orange reels	6	13	___
	(C) Brown car with gray or orange reels	8	15	___
	(D) Gray car with gray reels	8	15	___
	(E) Gray car with green reels	10	25	___
6402	Flatcar with blue boat, 69	27	61	___
6402-25	Flatcar with 2 cable reels (gray or orange), 62, 64-66	14	30	___
6402-150	Maroon Flatcar with white trailer	18	35	___
6403B	Tender	40	87	___
6404	Black Flatcar with auto, 60 u			___
	(A) Red auto	33	64	___
	(B) Yellow auto	62	111	___
	(C) Brown auto	108	186	___
	(D) Green auto	118	251	___
6405	Flatcar with piggyback van, 61	22	48	___
6406	Flatcar with auto, 61			___
	(A) Maroon frame, red auto	34	58	___
	(B) Maroon frame, yellow auto	71	121	___
	(C) Gray frame, dark brown auto	106	220	___
	(D) Gray frame, green auto	130	244	___
	(E) Gray frame, yellow auto	60	109	___
	(F) Gray frame, red auto	26	50	___
6407	Flatcar with rocket, 63	233	539	___
6408	Flatcar with pipes, 63 u	18	36	___
6408-50	Flatcar with 2 orange cable reels, 67 u	16	33	___
6409-25	Flatcar with pipes, 63 u	17	39	___
6410-25	Flatcar with 2 automobiles, 63 u			___
	(A) Yellow autos	146	327	___
	(B) Brown autos	143	334	___
6411	Flatcar with logs, 48-50	17	49	___
6413	Mercury Capsule Carrying Car, 62-63			___
	(A) Medium blue frame	66	189	___
	(B) Aquamarine frame	81	185	___
	(C) Teal frame	92	409	___
6414	Evans Auto Loader with 4 cars, 55-66			___
	(A) Premium cars (chrome bumpers, windows, rubber wheels): red, yellow, blue-green, and white	40	184	___
	(B) Cheapie cars (no wheels): 2 red and 2 yellow	167	284	___
	(C) Red cars with gray bumpers	110	253	___

			Good	Exc
___		(D) Yellow cars with gray bumpers	261	484
___		(E) Brown cars with gray bumpers	378	847
___		(F) Green cars with gray bumpers	467	895
___		(H) Metal trucks, number right of Lionel without nubs on axle	51	116
___		(G) Metal trucks, number right of Lionel, premium cars with nubs on axle first run	79	145
___	**6414-25**	Set of 4 Automobiles, separate sale box, 55-58	146	338
___	**6415**	Sunoco 3-D Tank Car, 53-55, 64-66, 69	18	37
___	**6416**	Boat Transport Car, 4 boats, 61-63	119	327
___	**6417**	PRR N5c Porthole Caboose, 53-57		
___		(A) New York Zone	16	36
___		(B) Without New York Zone	106	220
___	**6417-25**	Lionel Lines N5c Porthole Caboose, 54	17	45
___	**6417-50**	Lehigh Valley N5c Porthole Caboose, 54		
___		(A) Gray	53	266
___		(B) Tuscan	477	1853
___	**6418**	Machinery Car with 2 steel girders, 55-57		
___		(A) Black girders, "Lionel" in raised letters	51	105
___		(B) Orange girders, "Lionel" in raised letters	44	91
___		(C) Pinkish orange girders, U.S. Steel	65	217
___		(D) Black girders, U.S. Steel	59	116
___	**6419**	DL&W Work Caboose, 48-50, 52-55	15	39
___	**6419-25**	DL&W Work Caboose, one coupler, 54-55	19	39
___	**6419-50**	DL&W Work Caboose, short smokestack, 56-57	16	38
___	**6419-75**	DL&W Work Caboose, one coupler, 56-57	15	40
___	**6419-100**	N&W Work Caboose, 57-58	55	168
___	**6420**	DL&W Work Caboose with searchlight, 48-50		
___		(A) Heat-stamped serif lettering	38	78
___		(B) Rubber-stamped sans serif lettering	60	126
___	**6424**	Twin Auto Flatcar, 56-59		
___		(A) Black frame, premium cars	29	121
___		(B) 6805 slots, no rail stops	46	104
___		(C) AAR trucks, number on right	33	67
___	**6424-110**	Twin Auto Flatcar, 6805 slots and rail stops, 58-59	65	145
___	**6425**	Gulf 3-D Tank Car, 56-58	16	70
___	**6427**	Lionel Lines N5c Porthole Caboose, 54-60	19	47
___	**6427-60**	Virginian N5c Porthole Caboose, 58	223	464
___	**6427-500**	PRR N5c Porthole Caboose, sky blue, from Girls Set, 57-58*	155	320
___	**6428**	U.S. Mail Boxcar, 60-61, 65-66	20	64
___	**6429**	DL&W Work Caboose, AAR trucks, 63	101	597
___	**6430**	Flatcar with 2 trailers, 56-58		
___		(A) Gray Cooper-Jarrett trailers	33	78
___		(B) White Cooper-Jarrett trailers	37	95
___		(C) Green Fruehauf trailers	26	53
___		(D) Gray Cooper-Jarrett trailers with Fruehauf stickers	35	76

POSTWAR 1945-1969		Good	Exc
6431	Flatcar with 2 vans and Midgetoy tractor, 66		___
	(A) White vans, 66	59	125 ___
	(B) Yellow vans, 66	141	310 ___
6434	Poultry Dispatch Stock Car, 58-59	35	113 ___
6436-1	LV Open Quad Hopper, black, 55-56, 66		___
	(A) No spreader brace holes	44	96 ___
	(B) Spreader brace with holes	11	36 ___
6436-25	LV Open Quad Hopper, maroon, 55-57		___
	(A) No spreader brace holes	74	170 ___
	(B) Spreader brace with holes	22	63 ___
6436-110	LV Quad Hopper, red, 63-68		___
	(A) No built date	17	86 ___
	(B) Built date "New 3-55"	35	77 ___
6436-500	LV Open Quad Hopper, lilac, from Girls Set, 57-58*		___
	(A) No spreader brace holes	152	354 ___
	(B) Spreader brace with holes	119	292 ___
6436-1969	TCA (Train Collectors Association) Open Quad Hopper, 69 u	44	110 ___
6437	PRR N5c Porthole Caboose, 61-68	18	53 ___
6440	Flatcar with gray vans, 61-63	32	75 ___
6440	Green Pullman Car, 48-49	29	68 ___
6441	Green Observation Car, 48-49	24	61 ___
6442	Brown Pullman Car, 49	29	68 ___
6443	Brown Observation Car, 49	23	58 ___
6445	Fort Knox Gold Reserve Boxcar with coin slot, 61-63	42	144 ___
6446	N&W Covered Quad Hopper, black or gray, 54-55	28	78 ___
6446-25	N&W Covered Quad Hopper, 55-57		___
	(A) Black, white lettering	26	67 ___
	(B) Gray, black lettering	31	66 ___
	(C) Gray, AAR truck, spreader brace holes	57	136 ___
6446-60	LV Covered Quad Hopper, 63	72	276 ___
6447	PRR N5c Porthole Caboose, 63	123	453 ___
6448	Exploding Target Range Boxcar, 61-64		___
	(A) Red sides, white roof and ends	14	60 ___
	(B) White sides, red roof and ends	13	42 ___
6452	Pennsylvania Gondola, black, 48-49		___
	(A) Numbered "6462," 48	18	43 ___
	(B) Numbered "6452," 49	8	17 ___
X6454	Baby Ruth PRR Boxcar, 48	75	234 ___
X6454	Santa Fe Boxcar, 48	13	41 ___
X6454	NYC Boxcar, 48		___
	(A) Brown body	14	38 ___
	(B) Orange body	45	118 ___
	(C) Tan body	17	46 ___
X6454	Erie Boxcar, 49-52		___
	(A) Corner steps, 49	14	34 ___

		POSTWAR 1945-1969	Good	Exc
___		(B) No steps, 50-52	10	26
___	**X6454**	PRR Boxcar, 49-52		
___		(A) Corner steps, 49	15	32
___		(B) No steps, 50-52	10	26
___	**X6454**	SP Boxcar, 49-52		
___		(A) Corner steps, break in herald circle between "R" and "N," 49	27	76
___		(B) No steps, full circle in herald, 50	16	48
___		(C) No steps, red-brown body, 51-52	16	37
___	**6456**	Lehigh Valley Short Hopper, 48-55		
___		(A) Black	11	22
___		(B) Maroon	9	26
___	**6456-25**	Lehigh Valley Short Hopper, gray, 54-55	18	59
___	**6456-50**	Lehigh Valley Short Hopper, enamel red, white lettering, 54	243	740
___	**6456-75**	Lehigh Valley Short Hopper, enamel red, yellow lettering, 54	86	189
___	**6457**	SP-type Caboose, 49-52		
___		(A) Tuscan body and plastic smokejack	14	25
___		(B) Tuscan body and brown metal smokejack	9	15
___		(C) Tuscan body and black metal smokejack	12	22
___		(D) Maroon body and black metal smokejack	12	20
___	**6460**	Bucyrus Erie Crane Car, black cab, 8-wheel, 52-54	19	38
___	**6460-25**	Bucyrus Erie Crane Car, red cab, 8-wheel, 54	32	85
___	**6461**	Transformer Car, 49-50	28	63
___	**6462**	NYC Gondola, black or red, with 6 barrels, 49-54	9	26
___	**6462-25**	NYC Gondola, green, with 6 barrels, 54-57		
___		(A) "N" in second panel, 2 lines of data	14	34
___		(B) "N" in third panel, 3 lines of data	16	42
___	**6462-75**	NYC Gondola, red-painted, with 6 barrels, 52-55	14	33
___	**6462-125**	NYC Gondola, red plastic, with 6 barrels, 55-57	9	21
___	**6462-500**	NYC Gondola, pink, from Girls Set, with 4 canisters, 57-58*	101	248
___	**6463**	Rocket Fuel 2-D Tank Car, 62-63	20	53
___	**6464-1**	WP Boxcar, 53-54		
___		(A) Blue lettering	25	102
___		(B) Red lettering	517	2012
___	**6464-25**	GN Boxcar, 53-54	51	97
___	**6464-50**	M&StL Boxcar, 53-56	35	110
___	**6464-75**	RI Boxcar, green, 53-54, 69		
___		(A) Built date, 53-54	29	91
___		(B) No built date, 69	37	121
___	**6464-100**	Western Pacific Boxcar, 54-55		
___		(A) Silver body, yellow feather	41	199
___		(B) Orange body, blue feather	349	856
___	**6464-125**	NYC Pacemaker Boxcar, 54-56	34	109

POSTWAR 1945-1969		Good	Exc	
6464-150	MP Boxcar, 54-55, 57			___
	(A) Unpainted royal blue or navy blue body	42	94	___
	(B) Painted royal blue or navy blue body	40	92	___
	(C) Herald in fifth panel (first panel to left of door)	500	1200	___
	(D) New 3 54 on left and XME on lower right	45	98	___
6464-175	Rock Island Boxcar, 54-55			___
	(A) Blue lettering	36	148	___
	(B) Black lettering	348	956	___
6464-200	Pennsylvania Boxcar, 54-55, 69			___
	(A Built date NEW 5-53) , 54-55	60	130	___
	(B) No built date , 69	56	127	___
6464-225	SP Boxcar, 54-56	42	121	___
6464-250	WP Boxcar, 66	72	209	___
6464-275	State of Maine Boxcar, 55, 57-59			___
	(A) Striped doors	34	85	___
	(B) Solid doors	57	209	___
	(C) Striped doors, AAR trucks, 59	22	46	___
6464-300	Rutland Boxcar, 55-56			___
	(A) Rubber-stamped lettering	40	173	___
	(B) Split door with bottom painted green	347	1042	___
	(C) Rubber-stamped lettering with solid shield	1753	3770	___
	(D) Heat-stamped lettering	63	743	___
	(E) Painted yellow body, rubber-stamped lettering	500	1500	___
				___
	(F) Painted yellow body, heat-stamped lettering	1350	3938	___
6464-325	B&O Sentinel Boxcar, 56	159	416	___
6464-350	MKT Boxcar, 56	136	317	___
6464-375	Central of Georgia Boxcar, 56-57, 66			___
	(A) Unpainted maroon body	40	105	___
	(B) Painted red body	700	2393	___
6464-400	B&O Time-Saver Boxcar, 56-57, 69			___
	(A) BLT 5-54	38	86	___
	(B) BLT 2-56	93	255	___
	(C) No built date	53	124	___
	(D) "BLT 5-54" on one side/"BLT 2-56" on other side	500	975	___
6464-425	New Haven Boxcar, 56-58, 69	27	72	___
6464-450	Great Northern Boxcar, 56-57, 66	53	141	___
6464-475	B&M Boxcar, 57-60, 65-66, 68			___
	(A) Medium blue-painted or unpainted plastic	28	92	___
	(B) Dark purple-painted, gray or blue mold	71	207	___
	(C) Dark blue-painted, yellow mold	128	356	___
6464-500	Timken Boxcar, white side band and charcoal lettering, 57-59, 69			___
	(A) Unpainted yellow body	45	128	___
	(B) Painted yellow body, Type II	137	409	___
	(C) Painted yellow body, Type IV	63	201	___

			Good	Exc
___	**6464-510**	NYC Pacemaker Boxcar (pastel blue), 57-58	300	571
___	**6464-515**	MKT Boxcar (pastel yellow), 57-58	305	577
___	**6464-525**	M&StL Boxcar, 57-58, 64-66		
___		(A) Red, white lettering	33	113
___		(B) Maroon, white lettering	94	269
___	**6464-650**	D&RGW Boxcar, 57-58, 66		
___		(A) Yellow body, silver roof, black stripe	65	138
___		(B) Yellow body, type II, silver roof, no black stripe	512	1277
___		(C) Painted yellow body and yellow roof	694	1939
___		(D) Yellow body, silver roof, no black stripe on one side only	400	1100
___		(E) Yellow body, type IV, silver roof, black stripe on one side only	400	1100
___	**6464-700**	Santa Fe Boxcar, 61, 66	45	145
___	**6464-725**	New Haven Boxcar, 62-66, 68		
___		(A) Orange body	27	65
___		(B) Black body	94	296
___	**6464-825**	Alaska Boxcar, 59-60	139	313
___	**6464-900**	NYC Boxcar, 60-63, 65-66		
___		(A) Green Doors	33	65
___		(B) Black Doors	30	62
___	**6465**	Gulf 2-D Tank Car, 58		
___		(A) Black tank	14	41
___		(B) Gray tank	11	23
___	**6465**	Sunoco 2-D Tank Car, 48-56		
___		(A) Silver tank, rubber-stamped "6465"	9	15
___		(B) Silver tank, rubber-stamped "6455"	14	42
___		(C) Silver tank, no number on frame	8	16
___		(D) Glossy gray tank	10	28
___	**6465-85**	LL 2-D Tank Car, black, 59	14	116
___	**6465-110**	Cities Service 2-D Tank, 60-62	19	55
___	**6465-160**	LL 2-D Tank Car, orange with black ends, 63-64	13	33
___	**6466T**	Tender, 49-53	15	30
___	**6466W**	Whistle Tender, 49-53	22	48
___	**6466WX**	Whistle Tender, 49-53	25	54
___	**6467**	Miscellaneous Car, 56	21	49
___	**6468**	B&O Auto Boxcar, blue, 53-55	17	43
___	**6468X**	B&O Auto Boxcar, Tuscan, 53-55	125	295
___	**6468-25**	NH Auto Boxcar, 56-58		
___		(A) Black N over white H, black doors	24	82
___		(B) White N over black H, black doors	88	274
___		(C) Black N over white H, painted Tuscan doors	53	231
___	**6469**	Liquified Gas Tank Car, 63	35	102
___	**6470**	Explosives Boxcar, 59-60	14	32
___	**6472**	Refrigerator Car, 50-53	12	26
___	**6473**	Horse Transport Car, 62-69	15	58
___	**6475**	Libby's Crushed Pineapple Vat Car, 63 u	46	129

	POSTWAR 1945-1969	Good	Exc
6475	Pickles Vat Car, 60-62	22	58
6476	LV Short Hopper, 57-63		
	(A) Red body	6	16
	(B) Gray body	8	20
	(C) Black body	6	16
6476-75	LV Short Hopper, black, Type VI body, 63	7	16
6476-135	LV Short Hopper, yellow, 64-66, 68	7	50
6476-160	LV Short Hopper, black, 69	6	16
6476-185	LV Short Hopper, yellow, 69	6	16
6477	Miscellaneous Car with pipes, 57-58	25	57
6480	Explosives Boxcar, red, 61	16	33
6482	Refrigerator Car, 57	16	30
6500	Flatcar with Bonanza airplane, 62, 65		
	(A) Plane, red top and wings	343	579
	(B) Plane, white top and wings	437	796
6501	Flatcar with jet boat, 62-63	62	140
6502	Flatcar with Girder, 62		
	(A) Black flatcar	21	58
	(B) Red flatcar	29	70
6502-50	Flatcar, blue or teal, no lettering, with bridge girder, 62	17	53
6511	Flatcar with pipes, 53-56		
	(A) Die-cast metal truck plates, 53	17	48
	(B) Red car, stamped metal truck plates	15	76
	(C) Brown car, stamped metal truck plates	7	25
6511-24	Set of 6 pipes with box, 55-58	62	145
6512	Cherry Picker Car, 62-63	30	81
6517	LL Bay Window Caboose, 55-59		
	(A) Built date underscored	23	57
	(B) Built date not underscored	23	76
	(C) Built date not underscored, lettering higher	21	52
6517-75	Erie Bay Window Caboose, 66	166	547
6518	Transformer Car, 56-58	25	59
6519	Allis-Chalmers Flatcar, 58-61		
	(A) Dark or medium orange base	26	94
	(B) Dull light orange base	42	140
6520	Searchlight Car, 49-51		
	(A) Tan generator	722	1534
	(B) Green generator	145	268
	(C) Maroon generator	20	55
	(D) Orange generator	15	36
	(E) Green generator, black searchlight housing	154	638
6530	Firefighting Instruction Car, 60-61		
	(A) Red body, white lettering	24	75
	(B) Black body, white lettering	119	259
6536	M&StL Open Quad Hopper, 58-59, 63		
	(A) AAR trucks, 59, 63	26	58

	Item	Description	Good	Exc
___		(B) Bar-end trucks, 58	42	92
___	**6544**	Missile Firing Car, 4 missiles, 60-64		
___		(A) White-lettered console	43	136
___		(B) Black-lettered console	111	473
___	**6555**	Sunoco 1-D Tank Car, 49-50	13	54
___	**6556**	MKT Stock Car, 58	139	272
___	**6557**	SP-type Smoking Caboose, 58-59		
___		(A) Tuscan, with non-reverse lettering	106	290
___		(B) Brown, with reverse lettering	517	1267
___	**6560**	Bucyrus Erie Crane Car, smokestack, 55-58, 68-69		
___		(A) Black frame, unpainted red-orange cab	27	70
___		(B) Black frame, painted red cab, no "6560"	45	168
___		(C) Black frame, unpainted gray cab	22	55
___		(D) Black frame, unpainted red cab, closed crank spokes	11	21
___		(E) Black frame, unpainted red cab, no "6560" on frame	13	24
___		(F) Black frame, unpainted red cab, open crank spokes	10	20
___		(G) Black frame, black cab	46	102
___		(H) Dark blue frame, bronze hook	19	56
___	**6560-25**	Bucyrus Erie Crane Car, 8-wheel, marked "656025", 56	35	108
___	**6561**	Cable Car, 2 reels, 53-56		
___		(A) Orange reels	15	60
___		(B) Gray reels	27	102
___	**6562**	NYC Gondola with 4 red canisters, 56-58		
___		(A) Gray body, 56	21	85
___		(B) Red body, 56, 58	16	52
___		(C) Black body, 57	14	29
___	**6572**	REA Refrigerator Car, 58-59, 63		
___		(A) Passenger trucks	68	156
___		(B) Bar-end trucks	37	83
___		(C) AAR trucks, 63	29	66
___	**6630**	Missile Launching Car, 61	25	58
___	**6636**	Alaska Open Quad Hopper, 59-60	36	94
___	**6640**	USMC Missile Launching Car, 60	120	220
___	**6646**	Lionel Lines Stock Car, 57	15	34
___	**6650**	IRBM Rocket Launcher, 59-63		
___		(A) "6650" stamped on left	24	57
___		(B) "6650" stamped on right	79	235
___	**6650-80**	Missile, 60	5	72
___	**6651**	USMC Cannon Car, 64 u	95	206
___	**6654W**	Whistle Tender	17	39
___	**6656**	Lionel Lines Stock Car, 49-55		
___		(A) Brown Armour decal	21	44
___		(B) No decal	11	30
___	**6657**	Rio Grande SP-type Caboose, 57-58		
___		(A) With ladder slots	49	132
___		(B) Without ladder slots	135	311

		Good	Exc	
6660	Boom Car, 58	29	90	___
6670	Derrick Car, 59-60			___
	(A) "6670" stamped on left	27	68	___
	(B) "6670" stamped on right	59	171	___
6672	Santa Fe Refrigerator Car, 54-56			___
	(A) Blue lettering, 2 lines of data	20	46	___
	(B) Black lettering, 2 lines of data	24	68	___
	(C) Blue lettering, 3 lines of data	78	189	___
6736	Detroit & Mackinac Open Quad Hopper, 60-62	22	85	___
6800	Flatcar with airplane, 57-60			___
	(A) Plane, black top and wings	40	84	___
	(B) Plane, yellow top and wings	61	110	___
6800-60	Airplane, separate sale w/box, 57-58	88	209	___
6801	Flatcar with boat, white hull, brown deck, 57	29	62	___
6801-50	Flatcar with boat, yellow hull, white deck, 58-60	39	107	___
6801-60	Boat, separate sale w/box, 57-58	56	129	___
6801-75	Flatcar with boat, blue hull, white deck, 58-60	32	78	___
6802	Flatcar with 2 U.S. Steel girders, 58-59	25	60	___
6803	Flatcar with USMC tank and sound truck, 58-59	104	230	___
6804	Flatcar with USMC antiaircraft and sound trucks, 58-59	132	228	___
6805	Atomic Energy Disposal Flatcar, 58-59	66	239	___
6806	Flatcar with USMC radar and medical trucks, 58-59	98	221	___
6807	Flatcar with amphibious vehicle, 58-59	90	184	___
6808	Flatcar with USMC tank and searchlight truck, 58-59	105	243	___
6809	Flatcar with USMC antiaircraft and medical trucks, 58-59	98	229	___
6810	Flatcar with trailer, 58	21	44	___
6812	Track Maintenance Car, 59			___
	(A) Dark yellow superstructure	26	163	___
	(B) Black base, gray platform and crank handle	23	58	___
	(C) Gray base, black platform and crank handle	23	62	___
	(D) Cream superstructure	60	223	___
	(E) Light yellow superstructure	23	65	___
6814	Rescue Caboose, 59-61	44	114	___
6816	Flatcar with Allis-Chalmers bulldozer, 59-60			___
	(A) Red car	163	581	___
	(B) Black car	770	1318	___
6816-100	Allis-Chalmers Bulldozer, 59-60			___
	(A) No box	69	183	___
	(B) Separate-sale box	250	608	___
6817	Flatcar with Allis-Chalmers motor scraper, 59-60			___
	(A) Red car	165	404	___
	(B) Black car	650	1094	___
6817-100	Allis-Chalmers motor scraper, 59-60			___
	(A) No box	115	277	___
	(B) Separate-sale box	225	926	___
6818	Flatcar with transformer, 58	19	51	___

			Good	Exc
___	**6819**	Flatcar with helicopter, 59-60	25	62
___	**6820**	Aerial Missile Transport Car with helicopter, 60-61		
___		(A) Light blue frame	89	439
___		(B) Medium blue frame	86	200
___	**6821**	Flatcar with crates, 59-60	19	49
___	**6822**	Searchlight Car, 61-69		
___		(A) Black base, gray light	17	39
___		(B) Gray base, black light	20	39
___	**6823**	Flatcar with 2 IRBM missiles, 59-60	39	102
___	**6824**	USMC Work Caboose, 60	90	261
___	**6824-50**	Rescue Caboose, white, 64	34	79
___	**6825**	Flatcar with arch trestle bridge, 59-62	17	40
___	**6826**	Flatcar with Christmas trees, 59-60	48	93
___	**6827**	Flatcar with Harnischfeger power shovel, 60-63	83	250
___	**6827-100**	Harnischfeger power shovel, 60		
___		(A) No box	52	143
___		(B) Separate-sale box	120	268
___	**6828**	Flatcar with Harnischfeger crane, 60-63, 66		
___		(A) Black flatcar, light yellow crane cab	73	235
___		(B) Black flatcar, dark yellow crane cab	82	258
___		(C) Red flatcar, dark yellow crane cab	485	1150
___	**6828-100**	Harnischfeger Construction Crane, 60		
___		(A) No box	43	118
___		(B) Separate-sale box	86	249
___	**6830**	Flatcar with submarine, 60-61	49	111
___	**6844**	Missile Carrying Car, 6 missiles, 59-60		
___		(A) Black frame	30	69
___		(B) Red frame	468	1141

Other Track, Transformers, and Assorted Items

			Good	Exc
___	**A**	Transformer, 90 watts, 47-48	10	32
___	**CO-1**	Track Clips, dozen, with envelope (0), 49	5	44
___	**CO-1**	Track Clips, box of 100 (0), 49	32	77
___	**CTC**	Lockon (0 and 027), 47-69	1	4
___	**CTC-14**	Lockons, dozen, with envelope	14	53
___	**ECU-1**	Electronic Control Unit, 46	33	89
___	**KW**	Transformer, 190 watts, 50-65	46	77
___	**LTC**	Lockon (0 and 027), 50-69	5	13
___	**LW**	Transformer, 125 watts, 55-56	34	60
___	**OC**	Curved Track (0), 45-61	1	3
___	**OC1/2**	Half Section Curved Track (0), 45-66	1	3
___	**OCS**	Curved Insulated Track (0), 46-50	5	12
___	**OS**	Straight Track (0), 45-61	1	3
___	**OSS**	Straight Insulated Track, 46-50	5	15
___	**OTC**	Lockon Track (0 and 027)	2	4
___	**Q**	Transformer, 75 watts, 46	11	24
___	**R**	Transformer, 110 watts, 46-47	16	33

POSTWAR 1945-1969		Good	Exc
RCS	Remote Control Track (0), 45-48	3	8 ___
RW	Transformer, 110 watts, 48-54	22	33 ___
RX	Transformer, 100 watts, 47-48	13	79 ___
S	Transformer, 80 watts, 47	8	21 ___
SP	Smoke Pellets, bottle, 48-69		18 ___
	(A) Tall, light amber bottle	11	33 ___
	(B) Tall, dark amber bottle	11	33 ___
	(C) Short, light amber bottle	14	35 ___
	(D) All other bottles	10	20 ___
	(E) Bottle on blister pack, 65	23	58 ___
SP-12	Dealer Display Box with 12 full smoke bottles	133	300 ___
ST-295	Nut Driver, 5/32-inch		29 ___
ST-296	Nut Driver, 3/16-inch		43 ___
ST-297	Nut Driver, 7/32-inch		58 ___
ST-300	Nut Driver Set with holder, service station item	604	911 ___
ST-301	Wheel Puller, service station item	81	146 ___
ST-302	Spring Adjusting Tool	108	169 ___
ST-303	E Unit Spreader, service station item	50	84 ___
ST-311	Wheel Puller, service station item	109	183 ___
ST-320	Phillips Screwdriver, service station item	111	175 ___
ST-321	Flathead Screwdriver, short, service station item	131	203 ___
ST-322	Flathead Screwdriver, long, service station item	77	128 ___
ST-325	Screwdriver Set, service station item	575	938 ___
ST-342	Track Pliers, service station item	79	157 ___
ST-343	0 Gauge Track Pliers, service station item	223	369 ___
ST-350	Rivet Press, service station item	391	689 ___
ST-350-6	Rivet Press Tool Block with tools, service station item	391	503 ___
ST-350-17	Sliding Shoe Anvil, service station item	28	45 ___
ST-375	Wheel Cup Tool Set, service station item	538	805 ___
ST-378	E Unit Vice, service station item	187	348 ___
ST-384	Track Pliers, service station item	91	185 ___
SW	Transformer, 130 watts, 61-66	22	55 ___
TW	Transformer, 175 watts, 53-60	35	69 ___
TOC	Curved Track (0), 62-66, 68-69	1	2 ___
TOC1/2	Half Section Straight Track (0), 62-66	1	3 ___
TOS	Straight Track (0), 62-69	1	3 ___
UCS	Remote Control Track (0), 45-69	7	16 ___
UTC	Lockon (0, 027, Standard), 45	2	4 ___
V	Transformer, 150 watts, 46-47	35	66 ___
VW	Transformer, 150 watts, 48-49	39	77 ___
Z	Transformer, 250 watts, 45-47	59	105 ___
ZW	Transformer, 250 watts, 48-49	60	146 ___
ZW	Transformer, 275 watts, 50-56	81	146 ___
ZW	Transformer, 275 watts, R type, 57-66	86	172 ___

Section 3
MODERN 1970–2025

			Exc	Like New
____	2438120	2024 Personalized Happy Birthday Boxcar, 24		100
____	79C95204C	Sears Santa Fe Diesel Freight Set, 71 u	150	165
____	79C9715C	Sears 4-unit Diesel Freight Set, 75 u	50	65
____	79C9717C	Sears 7-unit Steam Freight Set, 75 u	150	165
____	79N95223C	Sears 6-unit Diesel Freight Set, 74 u	150	165
____	79N9552C	Sears 6-unit Steam Freight Set, 72 u	150	165
____	79N9553C	Sears 6-unit Diesel Freight Set, 72 u	150	165
____	79N96178C	Sears 4-unit Steam Freight Set, 74 u	50	65
____	79N97082C	Sears Steam Freight Set, 70 u		NRS
____	79N97101C	Sears 5-unit Steam Freight Set, 72 u	150	165
____	79N98765C	Sears Logging Empire Set, 78 u	100	115
____	**366**	Menards C&NW 4-4-2 Locomotive with tender, 09	45	75
____	**400**	Menards C&NW Chicago Combine Car, 09	25	40
____	**403**	Menards C&NW Lake Superior Observation Car, 09	25	40
____	**410**	Menards C&NW Lake Michigan Coach, 09	40	65
____	**0512**	Toy Fair Reefer, 81 u	60	70
____	**550C**	31" Diameter Curved Track (O), 70	1	2
____	**550S**	Straight Track (O), 70	1	2
____	**665E**	Johnny Cash Blue Train 4-6-4 Locomotive, 71 u		NRS
____	**1050**	New Englander Set, 80-81	155	205
____	**1051**	Texas & Pacific Diesel Set, 80	150	175
____	**1052**	Chesapeake Flyer Set, 80	140	150
____	**1053**	James Gang Set, 80-82	145	195
____	**1070**	Royal Limited Set, 80	238	350
____	**1071**	Mid Atlantic Limited Set, 80	225	230
____	**1072**	Cross Country Express Set, 80-81	197	385
____	**1081**	Wabash Cannonball Set, 70-72	105	120
____	**1082**	Yard Boss Set, 70	110	165
____	**1083**	Pacemaker Set, 70	105	120
____	**1084**	Grand Trunk Western Freight Set, 70	120	140
____	**1085**	Santa Fe Express Diesel Freight Set, 70	175	190
____	**1086**	Mountaineer Train Set, 70	120	145
____	**1087**	Midnight Express Train Set, 70	125	150
____	**1091**	Sears Special Steam Freight Set, 70 u	150	165
____	**1092**	Sears GTW Steam Freight Set, 70 u	150	165
____	**1100**	Happy Huff n' Puff, 74-75 u	55	70
____	**1150**	L.A.S.E.R. Train Set, 81-82	152	203
____	**1151**	Union Pacific Thunder Freight Set, 81-82	150	175
____	**1153**	JCPenney Thunderball Freight Set, 81 u	165	180
____	**1154**	Reading Yard King Set, 81-82	170	190
____	**1155**	Cannonball Freight Set, 82	75	85
____	**1157**	Lionel Leisure Wabash Cannonball Set, 81 u		250
____	**1158**	Maple Leaf Limited Set, 81	298	435
____	**1159**	Toys "R" Us Midnight Flyer Set, 81 u	135	145
____	**1160**	Great Lakes Limited Set, 81	178	330
____	**T-1171**	CN Locomotive Set, 71 u	240	275
____	**T-1172**	Yardmaster Set, 71 u		200
____	**T-1173**	Grand Trunk Western Freight Set, 71-73 u	175	195
____	**T-1174**	Canadian National Set, 71-73 u	265	300
____	**1182**	Yardmaster Set, 71-72	85	105

MODERN 1970-2025		Exc	Like New	
1183	Silver Star Set, 71-72	65	80	___
1184	Allegheny Set, 71	120	150	___
1186	Cross Country Express Set, 71-72	210	260	___
1187	Illinois Central Set (SSS), 71	363	485	___
1190	Sears Special #1 Set, 71 u	88	103	___
1195	JCPenney Special Set, 71 u	150	165	___
1198	Unnamed Set, 71 u		175	___
1199	Ford-Autolite Allegheny Set, 71 u	187	207	___
1200	Gravel Gus, 75 u	75	100	___
1223	Seattle & North Coast Hi-Cube Boxcar, 86	25	225	___
1250	New York Central Set (SSS), 72	345	380	___
1252	Heavy Iron Set, 82-83	90	130	___
1253	Quicksilver Express Set, 82-83	265	340	___
1254	Black Cave Flyer Set, 82	75	105	___
1260	Continental Limited Set, 82	183	388	___
1261	Sears Black Cave Flyer Set, 82 u	165	195	___
1262	Toys 'R' Us Heavy Iron Set, 82 u	150	165	___
1263	JCPenney Overland Freight Set, 82 u	150	165	___
1264	NIBCO Express Set, 82 u	190	215	___
1265	Tappan Special Set, 82 u	130	155	___
T-1272	Yardmaster Set, 72-73 u	150	165	___
T-1273	Silver Star Set, 72-73 u	90	115	___
1280	Kickapoo Valley & Northern Set, 72	55	75	___
1284	Allegheny Set, 72	140	165	___
1285	Santa Fe Twin Diesel Set, 72	95	140	___
1287	Pioneer Dockside Switcher Set, 72	95	100	___
1290	Sears Steam Freight Set, 72 u	150	165	___
1291	Sears Steam Freight Set, 72 u	150	165	___
1300	Gravel Gus Junior, 75 u	70	90	___
1350	Canadian Pacific Set (SSS), 73	405	620	___
1351	Baltimore & Ohio Set, 83-84	205	280	___
1352	Rocky Mountain Freight Set, 83-84	75	95	___
1353	Southern Streak Set, 83-85	75	95	___
1354	Northern Freight Flyer Set, 83-85	230	280	___
1355	Commando Assault Train, 83-84	158	270	___
1359	Display Case for Set 1355, 83 u	75	95	___
1361	Gold Coast Limited Set, 83	167	400	___
1362	Lionel Leisure BN Express Set, 83 u	200	300	___
1380	U.S. Steel Industrial Switcher Set, 73-75	55	83	___
1381	Cannonball Set, 73-75	70	75	___
1382	Yardmaster Set, 73-74	110	135	___
1383	Santa Fe Freight Set, 73-75	100	125	___
1384	Southern Express Set, 73-76	75	120	___
1385	Blue Streak Freight Set, 73-74	100	120	___
1386	Rock Island Express Set, 73-74	120	140	___
1387	Milwaukee Road Special Set, 73	146	285	___
1388	Golden State Arrow Set, 73-75	215	240	___
1390	Sears 7-unit Steam Freight Set, 73 u	170	190	___
1392	Sears 8-unit Steam Freight Set, 73 u	150	165	___
1393	Sears 6-unit Diesel Freight Set, 73 u	150	165	___
1395	JCPenney Set, 73 u	150	165	___
1400	Happy Huff n' Puff Junior, 75 u	130	140	___
1402	Chessie System Set, 84-85	125	150	___
1403	Redwood Valley Express Set, 84-85	170	205	___

			Exc	Like New
___	**1450**	D&RGW Set (SSS), 74	217	394
___	**1451**	Erie-Lackawanna Limited Set, 84	293	443
___	**1460**	Grand National Set, 74	180	330
___	**1461**	Black Diamond Set, 74 u, 75	100	120
___	**1463**	Coca-Cola Special Set, 74 u, 75	170	284
___	**1487**	Broadway Limited Set, 74-75	160	255
___	**1489**	Santa Fe Double Diesel Set, 74-76	140	165
___	**1492**	Sears 7-unit Steam Freight Set, 74 u	150	165
___	**1493**	Sears 7-unit Steam Freight Set, 74 u	150	165
___	**1499**	JCPenney Great Express Set, 74 u	150	165
___	**1501**	Midland Freight Set, 85-86	75	95
___	**1502**	Yard Chief Set, 85-86	153	230
___	**1506**	Sears Centennial Chessie System Set, 85 u	165	195
___	**1512**	JCPenney Midland Freight Set, 85 u	90	115
___	**1549**	Toys “R” Us Heavy Iron Set, 85-89 u	160	218
___	**1552**	Burlington Northern Limited Set, 85	264	570
___	**1560**	North American Express Set, 75	275	365
___	**1562**	Fast Freight Flyer Set, 85 u	120	140
___	**1577**	Liberty Special Set, 75 u	212	275
___	**1579**	Milwaukee Road Set (SSS), 75	253	410
___	**1581**	Thunderball Freight Set, 75-76	90	100
___	**1582**	Yard Chief Set, 75-76	115	155
___	**1584**	N&W “Spirit of America” Set, 75	140	180
___	**1585**	75th Anniversary Special Set, 75-77	192	239
___	**1586**	Chesapeake Flyer Set, 75-77	160	190
___	**1587**	Capitol Limited Set, 75	248	300
___	**1593**	Sears Set, 75 u		100
___	**1595**	Sears 6-unit Diesel Freight Set, 75 u	150	165
___	**1602**	Nickel Plate Special Set, 86-91	120	125
___	**1606**	Sears Centennial Nickel Plate Set, 86 u	165	195
___	**1608**	American Express General Set, 86 u	205	320
___	**1615**	Cannonball Express Set, 86-90	65	75
___	**1632**	Santa Fe Work Train (SSS), 86	152	210
___	**1652**	B&O Freight Set, 86	135	185
___	**1658**	Town House TV and Appliances Set, 86 u	80	95
___	**1660**	Yard Boss Set, 76	100	115
___	**1661**	Rock Island Line Set, 76-77	80	100
___	**1662**	Black River Freight Set, 76-78	75	95
___	**1663**	Amtrak Lake Shore Limited Set, 76-77	193	265
___	**1664**	Illinois Central Freight Set, 76-77	265	355
___	**1665**	NYC Empire State Express Set, 76	229	417
___	**1672**	Northern Pacific Set (SSS), 76	215	280
___	**1685**	True Value Freight Flyer Set, 86-87 u	60	75
___	**1686**	Kay Bee Toys Freight Flyer Set, 86 u	150	165
___	**1687**	Freight Flyer Set, 87-90	39	47
___	**1693**	Toys ‘R’ Us Rock Island Line Set, 76 u	110	130
___	**1694**	Toys ‘R’ Us Black River Freight Set, 76 u	115	135
___	**1696**	Sears Steam Freight Set, 76 u	110	130
___	**1698**	True Value Rock Island Line Set, 76 u	125	145
___	**1760**	Trains n’ Truckin’ Steel Hauler Set, 77-78	105	110
___	**1761**	Trains n’ Truckin’ Cargo King Set, 77-78	95	165
___	**1762**	Wabash Cannonball Set, 77	135	190
___	**1764**	Heartland Express Set, 77	185	240

MODERN 1970-2025		Exc	Like New	
1765	Rocky Mountain Special Set, 77	210	315	___
1766	B&O Budd Car Set (SSS), 77	335	390	___
1776	Seaboard U36B Diesel w/wo printing on chassis, 74-76	74	123	___
1790	Lionel Leisure Steel Hauler Set, 77 u	150	200	___
1791	Toys 'R' Us Steel Hauler Set, 77 u	130	175	___
1792	True Value Rock Island Line Set, 77 u	100	135	___
1793	Toys 'R' Us Black River Freight Set, 77 u	120	155	___
1796	JCPenney Cargo Master Set, 77 u		200	___
1860	"Workin' on the Railroad" Timberline Set, 78	65	85	___
1862	"Workin' on the Railroad" Logging Empire Set, 78	85	110	___
1864	Santa Fe Double Diesel Set, 78-79	155	190	___
1865	Chesapeake Flyer Set, 78-79	155	180	___
1866	Great Plains Express Set, 78-79	172	285	___
1867	Milwaukee Road Limited Set, 78	153	275	___
1868	M&StL Set (SSS), 78	215	255	___
1892	JCPenney Logging Empire Set, 78 u	95	125	___
1893	Toys 'R' Us Logging Empire Set, 78 u	175	225	___
1960	Midnight Flyer Set, 79-81	55	75	___
1962	Wabash Cannonball Set, 79	90	105	___
1963	Black River Freight Set, 79-81	75	85	___
1965	Smokey Mountain Line Set, 79	65	85	___
1970	Southern Pacific Limited Set, 79 u	172	365	___
1971	Quaker City Limited Set, 79	153	335	___
1990	Mystery Glow Midnight Flyer Set, 79 u	75	90	___
1991	JCPenney Wabash Cannonball Deluxe Express Set, 79 u	150	165	___
1993	Toys 'R' Us Midnight Flyer Set, 79 u	115	135	___
2110	Graduated Trestle Set, 22 pieces, 70-88	9	13	___
2111	Elevated Trestle Set, 10 pieces, 70-88	8	11	___
2113	Tunnel Portals, pair, 84-87	11	16	___
2115	Dwarf Signal, 84-87	9	13	___
2117	Block Target Signal, 84-87	23	29	___
2122	Extension Bridge, rock piers, 76-87	24	34	___
2125	Whistling Freight Shed, 71	36	43	___
2126	Whistling Freight Shed, 76-87	18	26	___
2127	Diesel Horn Shed, 76-87	25	30	___
2128	Operating Switchman, 83-86	26	29	___
2129	Illuminated Freight Station, 83-86	30	33	___
2133	Lighted Freight Station, 72-78, 80-84	34	44	___
2140	Automatic Banjo Signal, 70-84	17	21	___
2145	Automatic Gateman, 72-84	31	48	___
2151	Operating Semaphore, 78-82	15	19	___
2152	Automatic Crossing Gate, 70-84	21	25	___
2154	Automatic Highway Flasher, 70-87	19	24	___
2156	Illuminated Station Platform, 70-71	26	34	___
2162	Automatic Crossing Gate and Signal "262," 70-87, 94, 96-98, 05	16	28	___
2163	Block Target Signal, 70-78	14	19	___
2170	Street Lamps, set of 3, 70-87	13	19	___
2171	Gooseneck Street Lamps, set of 2, 80-81, 83-84	15	18	___
2175	"Sandy Andy" Gravel Loader Kit, 76-79	34	55	___
2180	Road Signs, 16 pieces, 77-98		6	___
2181	Telephone Pole Set "150," 77-98		5	___
2195	Floodlight Tower, 70-71	38	50	___

		MODERN 1970-2025	Exc	Like New
____	2199	Microwave Tower, 72-75	30	39
____	2214	Girder Bridge, 70-71, 72 u, 73-87	5	9
____	2256	Station Platform, 73-81	12	18
____	2260	Illuminated Bumper, 70-71, 72 u, 73	23	35
____	2280	Nonilluminated Bumpers, set of 3, 73-84	2	4
____	2282	Die-cast Bumpers, pair, 83 u	12	18
____	2283	Die-cast Illuminated Bumpers "260," 84-99	10	16
____	2290	Illuminated Bumpers, pair, 75 u, 76-86	7	11
____	2292	Station Platform, 85-87	5	9
____	2300	Operating Oil Drum Loader, 83-87	80	90
____	2301	Operating Sawmill, 80-84	60	65
____	2302	Union Pacific Manual Gantry Crane, 80-82	24	31
____	2303	Santa Fe Manual Gantry Crane, 80-81, 83 u	17	21
____	2305	Getty Operating Oil Derrick, 81-84	105	115
____	2306	Operating Ice Station with 6700 Ice Car, 82-83	90	125
____	2307	Lighted Billboard, 82-86	12	13
____	2308	Animated Newsstand, 82-83	82	120
____	2309	Mechanical Crossing Gate, 82-92	4	7
____	2310	Mechanical Crossing Gate, 73-77	2	4
____	2311	Mechanical Semaphore, 82-92	4	7
____	2312	Mechanical Semaphore, 73-77	2	4
____	2313	Floodlight Tower, 75-86	22	27
____	2314	Searchlight Tower, 75-84	22	27
____	2315	Operating Coaling Station, 83-84	80	89
____	2316	N&W Operating Gantry Crane, 83-84	90	125
____	2317	Operating Drawbridge, 75 u, 76-81	100	130
____	2318	Operating Control Tower, 83-86	40	52
____	2319	Illuminated Watchtower, 75-78, 80	29	56
____	2320	Flagpole Kit, 83-87	10	14
____	2321	Operating Sawmill, 84, 86-87	115	133
____	2323	Operating Freight Station, 84-87	43	47
____	2324	Operating Switch Tower, 84-87	60	65
____	2390	Lionel Mirror, 82 u	97	130
____	2494	Rotary Beacon, 72-74	37	44
____	2709	Rico Station Kit, 81-98		42
____	2710	Billboards, set of 5, 70-84	4	10
____	2714	Tunnel, 75 u, 76-77	36	43
____	2716	Short Extension Bridge, 88-98	3	8
____	2717	Short Extension Bridge, 77-87	2	4
____	2718	Barrel Platform Kit, 77-84	3	5
____	2719	Watchman's Shanty Kit, 77-87	3	5
____	2720	Lumber Shed Kit, 77-84, 87	3	5
____	2721	Operating Log Mill Kit, 78	2	4
____	2722	Barrel Loader Kit, 78	2	4
____	2783	Freight Station Kit, 84	8	15
____	2784	Freight Platform Kit, 81-90	5	8
____	2785	Engine House Kit, 73-77	31	39
____	2786	Freight Platform Kit, 73-77	4	6
____	2787	Freight Station Kit, 73-77, 83	7	10
____	2788	Coal Station Kit, 75 u, 76-77	18	30
____	2789	Water Tower Kit, 75-77, 80	19	24
____	2791	Cross Country Set, 70-71	22	30
____	2792	Whistle Stop Set, 70-71	24	34
____	2792	Layout Starter Pack, 80-84	9	21

MODERN 1970-2025		Exc	Like New	
2793	Alamo Junction Set, 70-71	22	30	___
2796	Grain Elevator Kit, 76 u, 77	43	47	___
2797	Rico Station Kit, 76-77	23	37	___
2900	Lockon, 70-98	3	8	___
2901	Track Clips, dozen (027), 71-98		8	___
2905	Lockon and Wire, 74-00		3	___
2909	Smoke Fluid, 70-98		8	___
2910	OTC Contactor, 84-86, 88	4	7	___
2911	Smoke Pellets, 70-73	18	35	___
2925	Lubricant, 70-71, 72 u, 73-75		2	___
2927	Maintenance Kit, 70, 78-98		11	___
2928	Oil, 71		2	___
2951	Track Layout Book, 70-86	1	2	___
2952	Train and Accessory Manual, 70-74	1	2	___
2953	Train and Accessory Manual, 75-86	1	2	___
2960	Lionel 75th Anniversary Book, 75 u, 76	15	30	___
2980	Magnetic Conversion Coupler, 70-71	1	2	___
2985	The Lionel Train Book, 86-98		18	___
3100	Great Northern 4-8-4 (FARR 3), 81	238	388	___
4044	Transformer, 45-watt, 70-71	2	7	___
4045	Safety Transformer, 70-71	2	3	___
4050	Safety Transformer, 72-79	2	3	___
4060	Power Master Transformer, 80-93	4	13	___
4090	Power Master Transformer, 70-84	50	65	___
4125	Transformer, 25-watt, 72	2	3	___
4150	Trainmaster Transformer, 72-73, 75-77	6	15	___
4250	Trainmaster Transformer, 74	5	10	___
4651	Trainmaster Transformer, 78-79	1	2	___
4690	MW Transformer, 86-89	60	80	___
4851	AC Transformer, red or black, 85-91, 94-96	5	10	___
5012	27" Diameter Curved Track, card of 4 (027), 70-96		17	___
5013	27" Diameter Curved Track (027), 70-78		1	___
5014	Half Curved Track (027), 70-98		1	___
5016	36" Straight Track (027), 87-88	1	2	___
5017	Straight Track, card of 4 (027), 70-96		4	___
5018	Straight Track (027), 70-78		1	___
5019	Half Straight Track (027), 70-98		1	___
5020	90-degree Crossover (027), 70-98		7	___
5021	27" Manual Switch, left hand (027), 70-98		15	___
5022	27" Manual Switch, right hand (027), 70-98		15	___
5023	45-degree Crossover (027), 70-98		6	___
5024	35" Straight Track (027), 88-98, 05		3	___
5025	Manumatic Uncoupler, 71-72	1	2	___
5027	27" Manual Switches, pair (027), 74-84	13	21	___
5030	Track Expander Set (027), 71-84	18	26	___
5031	Ford-Autolite Layout Expander Set, 71 u	50	65	___
5033	27" Diameter Curved Track (027), 79-98		1	___
5038	Straight Track (027), 79-98		1	___
5041	Insulator Pins, dozen (027), 70-98		1	___
5042	Steel Pins, dozen (027), 70-98		1	___
5045	54" Diameter Curved Track Ballast (027), 87-88	1	2	___
5046	27" Diameter Curved Track Ballast (027), 87-88	1	2	___
5047	Straight Track Ballast (027), 87-88	1	2	___

	MODERN 1970-2025		Exc	Like New
___	**5049**	42" Diameter Curved Track (027), 88-98	1	2
___	**5090**	27" Manual Switches, 3 pair (027), 78-84	55	70
___	**5113**	54" Diameter Curved Track (027), 79-98	1	2
___	**5121**	27" Remote Switch, left hand (027), 70-98	18	22
___	**5122**	27" Remote Switch, right hand (027), 70-98	20	22
___	**5125**	27" Remote Switches, pair (027), 71-83	20	30
___	**5132**	31" Remote Switch, right hand (0), 80-94	29	30
___	**5133**	31" Remote Switch, left hand (0), 80-94	22	30
___	**5149**	Remote Uncoupling Section (027), 70-98		15
___	**5165**	72" Remote Switch, right hand (0), 87-98	23	65
___	**5166**	72" Remote Switch, left hand (0), 87-98	23	75
___	**5167**	42" Remote Switch, right hand (027), 88-98	25	37
___	**5168**	42" Remote Switch, left hand (027), 88-98	25	37
___	**5193**	27" Remote Switches, 3 pair (027), 78-83	80	95
___	**5500**	10" Straight Track (0), 71-98		1
___	**5501**	31" Diameter Curved Track (0), 71-98		1
___	**5502**	Remote Uncoupling Section (0), 71-72	7	9
___	**5504**	Half Curved Track (0), 83-98		1
___	**5505**	Half Straight Track (0), 83-98		1
___	**5520**	90-degree Crossover (0), 71-72	6	9
___	**5522**	36" Straight, 87-88		3
___	**5523**	40" Straight Track (0), 88-98		4
___	**5530**	Remote Uncoupling Section (0), 81-98	10	19
___	**5540**	90-degree Crossover (0), 81-98		10
___	**5543**	Insulator Pins, dozen (0), 70-98		1
___	**5545**	45-degree Crossover (0), 83-98		11
___	**5551**	Steel Pins, dozen (0), 70-98		1
___	**5554**	54" Diameter Curved Track (0), 90-98		2
___	**5560**	72" Diameter Curved Track Ballast (0), 87-88	1	2
___	**5561**	31" Diameter Curved Track Ballast (0), 87-88	1	2
___	**5562**	Straight Track Ballast (0), 87-88	1	2
___	**5572**	72" Diameter Curved Track (0), 79-98	2	3
___	**5600**	Curved Track (Trutrack), 73-74	1	2
___	**5601**	Curved Track, card of 4 (Trutrack), 73-74	6	10
___	**5602**	Curved Track Ballast, card of 4 (Trutrack), 73-74	5	9
___	**5605**	Straight Track (Trutrack), 73-74	1	2
___	**5606**	Straight Track, card of 4 (Trutrack), 73-74	5	9
___	**5607**	Straight Track Ballast, card of 4 (Trutrack), 73-74	5	9
___	**5620**	Manual Switch, left hand (Trutrack), 73-74	4	13
___	**5625**	Remote Switch, left hand (Trutrack), 73-74	9	17
___	**5630**	Manual Switch, right hand (Trutrack), 73-74	4	13
___	**5635**	Remote Switch, right hand (Trutrack), 73-74	9	17
___	**5640**	Left Switch Ballast, card of 2 (Trutrack), 73-74	5	9
___	**5650**	Right Switch Ballast, card of 2 (Trutrack), 73-74	5	9
___	**5655**	Lockon (Trutrack), 73-74	1	2
___	**5660**	Terminal Track with lockon (Trutrack), 74	1	3
___	**5700**	Oppenheimer Reefer, 81	32	39
___	**5701**	Dairymen's League Reefer, 81	21	23
___	**5702**	National Dairy Despatch Reefer, 81	16	21
___	**5703**	North American Despatch Reefer, 81	22	26
___	**5704**	Budweiser Reefer, 81-82	69	78
___	**5705**	Ball Glass Jars Reefer, 81-82	30	35
___	**5706**	Lindsay Brothers Reefer, 81-82	26	29

MODERN 1970-2025		Exc	Like New	
5707	American Refrigerator Transit Reefer, 81-82	17	20	___
5708	Armour Reefer, 82-83	16	21	___
5709	REA Reefer, 82-83	22	26	___
5710	Canadian Pacific Reefer, 82-83	22	25	___
5711	Commercial Express Reefer, 82-83	13	15	___
5712	Lionel Lines Reefer, 82 u	47	75	___
5713	Cotton Belt Reefer, 83-84	19	22	___
5714	Michigan Central Reefer, 83-84	17	24	___
5715	Santa Fe Reefer, 83-84	19	26	___
5716	Vermont Central Reefer, 83-84	20	23	___
5717	Santa Fe Bunk Car, 83	22	30	___
5719	Canadian National Reefer, 84	11	17	___
5720	Great Northern Reefer, 84	75	90	___
5721	Soo Line Reefer, 84	21	23	___
5722	NKP Reefer, 84	16	18	___
5724	PRR Bunk Car, 84	15	23	___
5726	Southern Bunk Car, 84 u	22	27	___
5727	USMC Bunk Car, 84-85	25	30	___
5728	Canadian Pacific Bunk Car, 86	17	24	___
5730	Strasburg Reefer, 85-86	20	27	___
5731	L&N Reefer, 85-86	19	24	___
5732	Jersey Central Reefer, 85-86		24	___
5733	Lionel Lines Bunk Car, 86 u	18	24	___
5735	NYC Bunk Car, 85-86	33	35	___
5739	B&O Tool Car, 86	32	37	___
5745	Santa Fe Bunk Car (SSS), 86	39	45	___
5760	Santa Fe Tool Car (SSS), 86	30	35	___
5900	AC/DC Converter, 79-83	3	10	___
6076	LV Hopper (027), 70 u	17	21	___
6100	Ontario Northland Covered Quad Hopper, 81-82	30	34	___
6101	BN Covered Quad Hopper, 81-82	17	31	___
6102	GN Covered Quad Hopper (FARR 3), 81	26	28	___
6103	Canadian National Covered Quad Hopper, 81	35	39	___
6104	Southern Quad Hopper with coal (FARR 4), 83	39	60	___
6105	Reading Operating Hopper, 82	34	40	___
6106	N&W Covered Quad Hopper, 82	30	40	___
6107	Shell Covered Quad Hopper, 82	13	26	___
6109	C&O Operating Hopper, 83	29	41	___
6110	MP Covered Quad Hopper, 83-84	17	27	___
6111	L&N Covered Quad Hopper, 83-84	13	20	___
6113	Illinois Central Hopper (027), 83-85	15	25	___
6114	C&NW Covered Quad Hopper, 83	54	80	___
6115	Southern Hopper (027), 83-86	15	19	___
6116	Soo Line Ore Car, 84	21	27	___
6117	Erie Operating Hopper, 84	29	39	___
6118	Erie Covered Quad Hopper, 84	31	45	___
6122	Penn Central Ore Car, 84	20	25	___
6123	PRR Covered Quad Hopper (FARR 5), 84-85	55	105	___
6124	D&H Covered Quad Hopper, 84	19	32	___
6126	Canadian National Ore Car, 86	18	24	___
6127	Northern Pacific Ore Car, 86	20	24	___
6131	Illinois Terminal Covered Quad Hopper, 85-86	15	21	___
6134	BN 2-bay ACF Hopper (std O), 86 u	95	115	___

			Exc	Like New
____	**6135**	C&NW 2-bay ACF Hopper (std O), 86 u	65	80
____	**6137**	NKP Hopper (027), 86-91	13	17
____	**6138**	B&O Quad Hopper with coal, 86	21	28
____	**6142**	Gondola, black, 70	20	33
____	**6150**	Santa Fe Hopper (027), 85-86, 92 u	10	15
____	**6177**	Reading Hopper (027), 86-90	14	19
____	**6200**	FEC Gondola with canisters, 81-82	13	24
____	**6201**	Union Pacific Animated Gondola, 82-83	19	25
____	**6202**	WM Gondola with coal, 82	34	36
____	**6203**	Black Cave Gondola (027), 82	2	4
____	**6205**	CP Gondola with canisters, 83	18	26
____	**6206**	C&IM Gondola with canisters, 83-85	18	26
____	**6207**	Southern Gondola with canisters (027), 83-85	6	8
____	**6208**	Chessie System Gondola with canisters, 83 u	21	24
____	**6209**	NYC Gondola with coal (std O), 84-85	42	46
____	**6210**	Erie-Lackawanna Gondola with canisters, 84	21	30
____	**6211**	C&O Gondola with canisters, 84-85		10
____	**6214**	Lionel Lines Gondola with canisters, 84 u	38	45
____	**6230**	Erie-Lackawanna Reefer (std O), 86 u	95	120
____	**6231**	Railgon Gondola with coal (std O), 86 u	46	76
____	**6232**	Illinois Central Boxcar (std O), 86 u	65	80
____	**6233**	CP Flatcar with stakes (std O), 86 u	36	43
____	**6234**	Burlington Northern Boxcar (std O), 85	55	75
____	**6235**	Burlington Northern Boxcar (std O), 85	33	43
____	**6236**	Burlington Northern Boxcar (std O), 85	33	43
____	**6237**	Burlington Northern Boxcar (std O), 85	33	49
____	**6238**	Burlington Northern Boxcar (std O), 85	33	43
____	**6239**	Burlington Northern Boxcar (std O), 86 u	38	55
____	**6251**	NYC Coal Dump Car, 85	25	42
____	**6254**	NKP Gondola with canisters, 86-91	6	11
____	**6258**	Santa Fe Gondola with canisters (027), 85-86, 92 u	3	5
____	**X6260**	NYC Gondola with canisters, 85-86	13	15
____	**6272**	Santa Fe Gondola with cable reels (SSS), 86	20	25
____	**6300**	Corn Products 3-D Tank Car, 81-82	19	25
____	**6301**	Gulf 1-D Tank Car, 81	20	26
____	**6302**	Quaker State 3-D Tank Car, 81	42	46
____	**6304**	GN 1-D Tank Car (FARR 3), 81	32	53
____	**6305**	British Columbia 1-D Tank Car, 81	46	64
____	**6306**	Southern 1-D Tank Car (FARR 4), 83	45	50
____	**6307**	PRR 1-D Tank Car (FARR 5), 84-85	70	75
____	**6308**	Alaska 1-D Tank Car (027), 82-83	27	35
____	**6310**	Shell 2-D Tank Car (027), 83-84	19	24
____	**6312**	C&O 2-D Tank Car (027), 84-85	18	26
____	**6313**	Lionel Lines 1-D Tank Car, 84 u	40	50
____	**6314**	B&O 3-D Tank Car, 86	31	38
____	**6317**	Gulf 2-D Tank Car (027), 84-85	18	22
____	**6357**	Frisco 1-D Tank Car, 83	42	50
____	**6401**	Virginian Bay Window Caboose, 81	37	47
____	**6403**	Amtrak Vista Dome Car (027), 76-77	24	31
____	**6404**	Amtrak Passenger Coach (027), 76-77	24	31
____	**6405**	Amtrak Passenger Coach (027), 76-77	24	31
____	**6406**	Amtrak Observation Car (027), 76-77	22	29
____	**6410**	Amtrak Passenger Coach (027), 77	28	48

MODERN 1970-2025		Exc	Like New	
6411	Amtrak Passenger Coach (027), 77	24	35	___
6412	Amtrak Vista Dome Car (027), 77	22	32	___
6420	Reading Transfer Caboose, 81-82	20	28	___
6421	Joshua L. Cowen Bay Window Caboose, 82	34	40	___
6422	DM&IR Bay Window Caboose, 81	32	38	___
6425	Erie-Lackawanna Bay Window Caboose, 83-84	35	43	___
6426	Reading Transfer Caboose, 82-83	14	24	___
6427	BN Transfer Caboose, 83-84	12	21	___
6428	C&NW Transfer Caboose, 83-85	22	25	___
6430	Santa Fe SP-type Caboose, 83-89	4	14	___
6431	Southern Bay Window Caboose (FARR 4), 83	42	55	___
6432	Union Pacific SP-type Caboose, 81-82	6	10	___
6433	Canadian Pacific Bay Window Caboose, 81	50	70	___
6435	U.S. Marines Transfer Caboose, 83-84	9	17	___
6438	GN Bay Window Caboose (FARR 3), 81	48	65	___
6439	Reading Bay Window Caboose, 84-85	22	30	___
6441	Alaska Bay Window Caboose, 82-83	45	50	___
6446-25	N&W Covered Quad Hopper, 70 u	212	389	___
6449	Wendy's N5c Caboose, 81-82	64	74	___
6464-500	Timken Boxcar, orange, 70 u	225	319	___
6464-500	Timken Boxcar, yellow, 70 u	210	358	___
6476-135	LV Hopper "25000" (027), 70-71 u	6	11	___
6478	Black Cave SP-type Caboose, 82	5	9	___
6482	Nibco Express SP-type Caboose, 82 u	26	34	___
6485	Chessie System SP-type Caboose, 84-85	6	10	___
6486	Southern SP-type Caboose, 83-85	5	7	___
6490	NKP N5c Caboose, 84 u		0	___
6491	Erie-Lackawanna Transfer Caboose, 85-86	9	17	___
6493	L&C Bay Window Caboose, 86-87	21	36	___
6494	Santa Fe Bobber Caboose, 85-86	7	9	___
6496	Santa Fe Work Caboose (SSS), 86	21	29	___
6504	L.A.S.E.R. Flatcar with helicopter (027), 81-82	18	26	___
6505	L.A.S.E.R. Radar Car, 81-82	17	25	___
6506	L.A.S.E.R. Security Car, 81-82	18	26	___
6507	L.A.S.E.R. Flatcar with cruise missile, 81-82	21	30	___
6508	Canadian Pacific Crane Car, 81	50	70	___
6509	Depressed Center Flatcar with girders, 81	60	85	___
6510	Union Pacific Crane Car, 82	55	60	___
6515	Union Pacific Flatcar (027), 83-84, 86	5	13	___
6521	NYC Flatcar with stakes (std 0), 84-85	29	35	___
6522	C&NW Searchlight Car, 83-85	27	30	___
6524	Erie Crane Car, 84	55	60	___
6526	Searchlight Car, 84-85	23	25	___
6529	NYC Searchlight Car, 85-86	21	27	___
6531	Express Mail Flatcar with trailers, 85-86	23	32	___
6560	Bucyrus Erie Crane Car, 71	100	130	___
6561	Flatcar with cruise missile (027), 83-84	13	26	___
6562	Flatcar with fences (027), 83-84	13	21	___
6564	U.S. Marines Flatcar with 2 tanks (027), 83-84	13	21	___
6573	Redwood Valley Express Log Dump Car (027), 84-85	8	13	___
6574	Redwood Valley Express Crane Car (027), 84-85	7	13	___

	MODERN 1970-2025		Exc	Like New
	6575	Redwood Valley Express Flatcar with fences (027), 84-85	7	13
	6576	Santa Fe Crane Car (027), 85-86, 92 u	7	10
	6579	NYC Crane Car, 85-86	36	44
	6585	PRR Flatcar with fences (027), 86-90	5	9
	6587	W&ARR Flatcar with horses, 86 u	18	26
	6593	Santa Fe Crane Car (SSS), 86	41	48
	6700	PFE Ice Car, 82-83		70
	6900	N&W Extended Vision Caboose, 82	60	65
	6901	Ontario Northland Extended Vision Caboose, 82 u	44	55
	6903	Santa Fe Extended Vision Caboose, 83	80	95
	6904	Union Pacific Extended Vision Caboose, 83	115	135
	6905	NKP Extended Vision Caboose, 83 u	50	65
	6906	Erie-Lack. Extended Vision Caboose, 84	75	90
	6907	NYC Wood-sided Caboose (std 0), 86 u	90	92
	6908	PRR N5c Caboose (FARR 5), 84-85	43	47
	6910	NYC Extended Vision Caboose, 84 u	55	60
	6912	Redwood Valley Express SP-type Caboose, 84-85	9	16
	6913	Burlington Northern Extended Vision Caboose, 85	60	90
	6916	NYC Work Caboose, 85-86	16	22
	6917	Jersey Central Extended Vision Caboose, 86	36	50
	6918	B&O SP-type Caboose, 86	10	15
	6919	Nickel Plate Road SP-type Caboose, 86-91	5	9
	6920	B&A Wood-sided Caboose (std 0), 86 u	65	80
	6921	PRR SP-type Caboose, 86-90	5	9
	7200	Quicksilver Passenger Coach (027), 82-83	26	34
	7201	Quicksilver Passenger Coach (027), 82-83	26	34
	7202	Quicksilver Observation Car (027), 82-83	26	34
	7203	N&W Diner "491," 82 u	130	180
	7204	Southern Pacific Diner, 82 u	190	235
	7207	NYC Diner, 83 u	70	140
	7208	PRR Diner, 83 u	80	90
	7210	Union Pacific Diner, 84	85	110
	7211	Southern Pacific Vista Dome Car, 83 u	145	185
	7215	B&O Passenger Coach, 83-84	43	50
	7216	B&O Passenger Coach, 83-84	43	50
	7217	B&O Baggage Car, 83-84	43	50
	7220	Illinois Central Baggage Car, 85, 87	105	135
	7221	Illinois Central Combination Car, 85, 87	85	105
	7222	Illinois Central Passenger Coach, 85, 87	85	105
	7223	Illinois Central Passenger Coach, 85, 87	85	105
	7224	Illinois Central Diner, 85, 87	75	90
	7225	Illinois Central Observation Car, 85, 87	95	115
	7227	Wabash Diner (FF 1), 86-87	115	130
	7228	Wabash Baggage Car (FF 1), 86-87	90	100
	7229	Wabash Combination Car (FF 1), 86-87	90	100
	7230	Wabash Passenger Coach (FF 1), 86-87	90	100
	7231	Wabash Passenger Coach (FF 1), 86-87	90	100
	7232	Wabash Observation Car (FF 1), 86-87	88	98
	7241	W&ARR Passenger Coach, 86 u	43	50
	7242	W&ARR Baggage Car, 86 u	43	50
	7301	Norfolk & Western Stock Car, 82	34	45
	7302	Texas & Pacific Stock Car (027), 83-84	9	14
	7303	Erie Stock Car, 84	41	50

MODERN 1970-2025		Exc	Like New	
7304	Southern Stock Car (FARR 4), 83 u	41	45	___
7309	Southern Stock Car (027), 85-86	12	16	___
7312	W&ARR Stock Car (027), 86 u	25	30	___
7401	Chessie System Stock Car (027), 84-85	13	17	___
7404	Jersey Central Boxcar, 86	26	40	___
7500	Lionel 75th Anniversary U36B Diesel, 75-77	153	181	___
7501	Lionel 75th Anniversary Boxcar, 75-77	28	39	___
7502	Lionel 75th Anniversary Reefer, 75-77	30	41	___
7503	Lionel 75th Anniversary Reefer, 75-77	41	47	___
7504	Lionel 75th Anniversary Covered Quad Hopper, 75-77	28	40	___
7505	Lionel 75th Anniversary Boxcar, 75-77	41	50	___
7506	Lionel 75th Anniversary Boxcar, 75-77	20	25	___
7507	Lionel 75th Anniversary Reefer, 75-77	27	39	___
7508	Lionel 75th Anniversary N5c Caboose, 75-77	24	29	___
7509	Kentucky Fried Chicken Reefer, 81-82	88	98	___
7510	Red Lobster Reefer, 81-82	79	88	___
7511	Pizza Hut Reefer, 81-82	70	81	___
7512	Arthur Treacher's Reefer, 82	69	76	___
7513	Bonanza Reefer, 82	70	78	___
7514	Taco Bell Reefer, 82	80	438	___
7515	Denver Mint Car, 81	64	81	___
7517	Philadelphia Mint Car, 82	38	39	___
7518	Carson City Mint Car, 83	34	43	___
7519	Toy Fair Reefer, 82 u	35	42	___
7520	Nibco Express Boxcar, 82 u	280	458	___
7521	Toy Fair Reefer, 83 u	50	65	___
7522	New Orleans Mint Car, 84	33	38	___
7523	Toy Fair Reefer, 84 u	44	49	___
7524	Toy Fair Reefer, 85 u	55	60	___
7525	Toy Fair Boxcar, 86 u	65	80	___
7530	Dahlonega Mint Car, 86	37	48	___
7600	Frisco Spirit of '76 N5c Caboose, 74-76	33	39	___
7601	Delaware Boxcar, 74-76	11	22	___
7602	Pennsylvania Boxcar, 74-76	11	27	___
7603	New Jersey Boxcar, 74-76	13	24	___
7604	Georgia Boxcar, 74 u, 75-76	22	26	___
7605	Connecticut Boxcar, 74 u, 75-76	11	32	___
7606	Massachusetts Boxcar, 74 u, 75-76	25	29	___
7607	Maryland Boxcar, 74 u, 75-76	13	34	___
7608	South Carolina Boxcar, 75 u, 76	38	50	___
7609	New Hampshire Boxcar, 75 u, 76	38	46	___
7610	Virginia Boxcar, 75 u, 76	141	200	___
7611	New York Boxcar, 75 u, 76	50	65	___
7612	North Carolina Boxcar, 75 u, 76	35	60	___
7613	Rhode Island Boxcar, 75 u, 76	36	50	___
7700	Uncle Sam Boxcar, 75 u	44	51	___
7701	Camel Boxcar, 76-77	73	83	___
7702	Prince Albert Boxcar, 76-77	65	84	___
7703	Beechnut Boxcar, 76-77	39	58	___
7704	Toy Fair Boxcar, 76 u	110	120	___
7705	Canadian Toy Fair Boxcar, 76 u	130	145	___
7706	Sir Walter Raleigh Boxcar, 77-78	56	88	___
7707	White Owl Boxcar, 77-78	71	80	___

MODERN 1970-2025			Exc	Like New
___	7708	Winston Boxcar, 77-78	70	85
___	7709	Salem Boxcar, 78	70	78
___	7710	Mail Pouch Boxcar, 78	69	79
___	7711	El Producto Boxcar, 78	44	75
___	7712	Santa Fe Boxcar (FARR 1), 79	30	50
___	7800	Pepsi Boxcar, 76 u, 77	83	93
___	7801	A&W Boxcar, 76 u, 77	54	67
___	7802	Canada Dry Boxcar, 76 u, 77	44	57
___	7803	Trains n' Truckin' Boxcar, 77 u	20	26
___	7806	Season's Greetings Boxcar, 76 u	70	95
___	7807	Toy Fair Boxcar, 77 u	70	95
___	7808	Northern Pacific Stock Car, 77	37	43
___	7809	Vernors Boxcar, 77 u, 78	50	65
___	7810	Orange Crush Boxcar, 77 u, 78	45	60
___	7811	Dr Pepper Boxcar, 77 u, 78	51	65
___	7813	Season's Greetings Boxcar, 77 u	65	90
___	7814	Season's Greetings Boxcar, 78 u	70	95
___	7815	Toy Fair Boxcar, 78 u	65	85
___	7816	Toy Fair Boxcar, 79 u	65	85
___	7817	Toy Fair Boxcar, 80 u	95	105
___	7900	D&RGW Operating Cowboy Car (027), 82-83	22	26
___	7901	LL Cop and Hobo Car (027), 82-83	24	27
___	7902	Santa Fe Boxcar (027), 82-85	5	9
___	7903	Rock Island Boxcar (027), 83	8	13
___	7904	San Diego Zoo Giraffe Car (027), 83-84	44	55
___	7905	Black Cave Boxcar (027), 82	6	9
___	7908	Tappan Boxcar (027), 82 u	39	55
___	7909	L&N Boxcar (027), 83-84	40	49
___	7910	Chessie System Boxcar (027), 84-85	18	23
___	7912	Toys 'R' Us Giraffe Car (027), 82-84 u	70	80
___	7913	Turtleback Zoo Giraffe Car (027), 85-86	50	60
___	7914	Toys 'R' Us Giraffe Car (027), 85-89 u	70	90
___	7920	Sears Centennial Boxcar (027), 85-86 u	39	44
___	7925	Erie-Lackawanna Boxcar (027), 86-90	10	18
___	7926	NKP Boxcar (027), 86-91	8	10
___	7930	True Value Boxcar (027), 86-87 u	34	50
___	7931	Town House TV and Appliances Boxcar (027), 86 u	31	39
___	7932	Kay Bee Toys Boxcar (027), 86-87 u	40	49
___	8001	NKP 2-6-4 Locomotive, 80 u	55	65
___	8002	Union Pacific 2-8-4 Locomotive (FARR 2), 80	210	345
___	8003	Chessie System 2-8-4 Locomotive, 80	333	542
___	8004	Rock Island 4-4-0 Locomotive, 80-82	190	220
___	8005	Santa Fe 4-4-0 Locomotive, 80-82	65	75
___	8006	ACL 4-6-4 Locomotive, 80 u	202	340
___	8007	NYNH&H 2-6-4 Locomotive, 80-81	65	75
___	8008	Chessie System 4-4-2 Locomotive, 80	65	75
___	8010	Santa Fe NW2 Switcher, 70, 71 u	48	79
___	8020	Santa Fe Alco Diesel A Unit, dummy, 70	45	60
___	8020	Santa Fe Alco Diesel A Unit, 70-72, 74-76	65	85
___	8021	Santa Fe Alco Diesel B Unit, 71-72, 74-76	49	67
___	8022	Santa Fe Alco Diesel A Unit, 71 u	80	105
___	8025	CN Alco Diesel A Unit, 71-73 u	85	105
___	8025	CN Alco Diesel A Unit, dummy, 71-73 u	45	65

MODERN 1970-2025		Exc	Like New	
8030	Illinois Central GP9 Diesel, 70-72	75	140	___
8031	Canadian National GP7 Diesel, 71-73 u	80	150	___
8031	Illinois Central GP9 Diesel, unpowered, 70	40	127	___
8040	Canadian National 2-4-2 Locomotive, 71 u	43	85	___
8040	NKP 2-4-2 Locomotive, 70-72	26	34	___
8041	NYC 2-4-2 Locomotive, 70	55	65	___
8041	PRR 2-4-2 Locomotive, 71 u	55	65	___
8042	GTW 2-4-2 Locomotive, 70, 71-73 u	26	34	___
8043	NKP 2-4-2 Locomotive, 70 u	45	65	___
8050	D&H U36C Diesel, 80	105	220	___
8051	D&H U36C Diesel Dummy Unit, 80	95	115	___
8054/55	Burlington F3 Diesel AA Set, 80	335	385	___
8056	C&NW FM Train Master Diesel, 80	137	202	___
8057	Burlington NW2 Switcher, 80	100	115	___
8059	Pennsylvania F3 Diesel B Unit, 80 u	190	290	___
8060	Pennsylvania F3 Diesel B Unit, 80 u	335	420	___
8061	Chessie System U36C Diesel, 80	93	140	___
8062	Burlington F3 Diesel B Unit, 80 u	205	255	___
8063	Seaboard SD9 Diesel, 80	80	100	___
8064	Florida East Coast GP9 Diesel, 80	150	200	___
8065	Florida East Coast GP9 Diesel Dummy Unit, 80	95	120	___
8066	TP&W GP20 Diesel, 80-81, 83 u	65	80	___
8071	Virginian SD18 Diesel, 80 u	135	155	___
8072	Virginian SD18 Diesel Dummy Unit, 80 u	75	110	___
8100	Norfolk & Western 4-8-4 “611”, 81	290	402	___
8101	Chicago & Alton 4-6-4 Locomotive “659”, 81	275	445	___
8102	Union Pacific 4-4-2 Locomotive, 81-82	49	65	___
8104	Union Pacific 4-4-0 Locomotive “3”, 81 u	180	235	___
8111	DT&I NW2 Switcher, 71-74	55	65	___
8140	Southern 2-4-0 Locomotive, 71 u	22	30	___
8141	PRR 2-4-2 Locomotive, 71-72	41	43	___
8142	C&O 4-4-2 Locomotive, 71-72		55	___
8150	PRR GG1 Electric Locomotive “4935”, 81	220	395	___
8151	Burlington SD28 Diesel, 81	120	145	___
8152	Canadian Pacific SD24 Diesel, 81	155	185	___
8153	Reading NW2 Switcher, 81-82	100	155	___
8154	Alaska NW2 Switcher, 81-82	120	160	___
8155	Monon U36B Diesel, 81-82	110	135	___
8156	Monon U36B Diesel Dummy Unit, 81-82		65	___
8157	Santa Fe FM Train Master, 81	230	325	___
8158	DM&IR GP35 Diesel, 81-82	90	150	___
8159	DM&IR GP35 Diesel Dummy Unit, 81-82	55	75	___
8160	Burger King GP20 Diesel, 81-82	106	128	___
8161	L.A.S.E.R. Switcher, 81-82	23	55	___
8162	Ontario Northland SD18 Diesel, 81 u	150	210	___
8163	Ontario Northland SD18 Diesel Dummy Unit, 81 u	95	140	___
8164	Pennsylvania F3 Diesel B Unit, 81 u	340	370	___
8182	Nibco Express NW2 Switcher, 82 u	90	130	___
8190	Diesel Horn Kit, 81 u		30	___
8200	Kickapoo Dockside 0-4-0T, 72	28	39	___
8203	PRR 2-4-2 Locomotive, 72, 74 u, 75	26	34	___
8204	C&O 4-4-2 Locomotive, 72	55	60	___
8206	NYC 4-6-4 Locomotive, 72-75	140	155	___

			Exc	Like New
___	**8209**	Pioneer Dockside 0-4-0T with tender, 72	45	65
___	**8209**	Pioneer Dockside 0-4-0T, no tender, 73-76	42	55
___	**8210**	Joshua L. Cowen 4-6-4 Locomotive, 82	245	350
___	**8212**	Black Cave 0-4-0 Locomotive, 82	30	49
___	**8213**	D&RGW 2-4-2 Locomotive, 82-83, 84-91 u	65	70
___	**8214**	Pennsylvania 2-4-2 Locomotive, 82-83	55	65
___	**8215**	Nickel Plate Road 2-8-4 Locomotive "779," 82 u	245	285
___	**8250**	Santa Fe GP9 Diesel, 72, 74-75	120	145
___	**8251-50**	Horn/Whistle Controller, 72-74	1	2
___	**8252**	D&H Alco Diesel A Unit, 72	85	125
___	**8253**	D&H Alco Diesel B Unit, 72	50	70
___	**8254**	Illinois Central GP9 Diesel Dummy Unit, 72	60	65
___	**8255**	Santa Fe GP9 Diesel Dummy Unit, 72	60	65
___	**8258**	Canadian National GP7 Diesel Dummy Unit, 72-73 u	65	85
___	**8260/62**	Southern Pacific F3 Diesel AA Set, 82	358	520
___	**8261**	Southern Pacific F3 Diesel B Unit, 82 u	330	395
___	**8263**	Santa Fe GP7 Diesel, 82	65	80
___	**8264**	CP Vulcan Switcher Snowplow, 82	80	100
___	**8265**	Santa Fe SD40 Diesel, 82	165	225
___	**8266**	Norfolk & Western SD24 Diesel, 82	113	225
___	**8268**	Quicksilver Alco Diesel A Unit, 82-83	85	105
___	**8269**	Quicksilver Alco Diesel A Unit, dummy, 82-83	55	65
___	**8272**	Pennsylvania EP-5 Electric Locomotive, 82 u	205	265
___	**8300**	Santa Fe 2-4-0 Locomotive, 73-74	22	25
___	**8302**	Southern 2-4-0 Locomotive, 73-76	29	30
___	**8303**	Jersey Central 2-4-2 Locomotive, 73-74	55	59
___	**8304**	B&O 4-4-2 Locomotive, 75	75	105
___	**8304**	Rock Island 4-4-2 Locomotive, 73-75	85	105
___	**8304**	Pennsylvania 4-4-2 Locomotive, 74-75	75	105
___	**8304**	C&O 4-4-2 Locomotive, 75-77	75	105
___	**8305**	Milwaukee Road 4-4-2 Locomotive, 73	95	120
___	**8307**	Southern Pacific 4-8-4 Locomotive "4449," 83	305	560
___	**8308**	Jersey Central 2-4-2 Locomotive, 73-74 u	36	43
___	**8309**	Southern 2-8-2 Locomotive "4501" (FARR 4), 83	385	495
___	**8310**	Nickel Plate Road 2-4-0 Locomotive, 73 u	26	50
___	**8310**	Santa Fe 2-4-0 Locomotive, 74-75 u	26	34
___	**8310**	Jersey Central 2-4-0 Locomotive, 74-75 u	26	50
___	**8311**	Southern 0-4-0 Locomotive, 73 u	26	34
___	**8313**	Santa Fe 0-4-0 Locomotive, 83-84	13	17
___	**8314**	Southern 2-4-0 Locomotive, 83-85	17	21
___	**8315**	B&O 4-4-0 Locomotive, 83-84	85	120
___	**8341**	ACL SP-type Caboose, 86 u, 87-90	6	8
___	**8350**	U.S. Steel Switcher, 73-75	18	26
___	**8351**	Santa Fe Alco Diesel A Unit, 73-75	60	65
___	**8352**	Santa Fe GP20 Diesel, 73-75	65	105
___	**8353**	Grand Trunk Western GP7 Diesel, 73-75	90	120
___	**8354**	Erie NW2 Switcher, 73, 75	80	105
___	**8355**	Santa Fe GP20 Diesel Dummy Unit, 73-74	65	90
___	**8356**	Grand Trunk Western GP7 Diesel Dummy Unit, 73-75	65	75
___	**8357**	PRR GP9 Diesel, 73-75	108	120
___	**8358**	PRR GP9 Diesel Dummy Unit, 73-75	55	100
___	**8359**	Chessie System GP7 Diesel, 73	123	158
___	**8360**	Long Island GP20 Diesel, 73-74	70	105

MODERN 1970-2025		Exc	Like New	
8361	Western Pacific Alco Diesel A Unit, 73-75	50	70	___
8362	Western Pacific Alco Diesel B Unit, 73-75	45	65	___
8363	B&O F3 Diesel A Unit, 73-75	280	310	___
8364	B&O F3 Diesel A Unit, dummy, 73-75	120	160	___
8365/66	CP F3 Diesel AA Set (SSS), 73	355	405	___
8367	Long Island GP20 Diesel Dummy Unit, 73-75	80	100	___
8368	Alaska Vulcan Switcher, 83	120	129	___
8369	Erie-Lackawanna GP20 Diesel, 83-85	125	140	___
8370/72	NYC F3 Diesel AA Set, 83	330	435	___
8371	NYC F3 Diesel B Unit, 83	105	150	___
8374	Burlington Northern NW2 Switcher, 83-85	105	120	___
8375	C&NW GP7 Diesel, 83-85	135	165	___
8376	Union Pacific SD40 Diesel, 83	175	200	___
8377	U.S. Marines Switcher, 83-84	55	65	___
8378	Wabash FM Train Master Diesel "550," 83 u	500	690	___
8379	PRR Fire Car, 83 u	80	100	___
8380	Lionel Lines SD28 Diesel, 83 u	235	315	___
8402	Reading 4-4-2 Locomotive, 84-85	47	55	___
8403	Chessie System 4-4-2 Locomotive, 84-85	55	65	___
8404	PRR 6-8-6 Turbine "6200" (FARR 5), 84-85	250	460	___
8406	NYC 4-6-4 Locomotive "783," 84	309	571	___
8410	Redwood Valley Express 4-4-0 Locomotive, 84-85	34	50	___
8452	Erie Alco Diesel A Unit, 74-75	75	95	___
8453	Erie Alco Diesel B Unit, 74-75	55	75	___
8454	D&RGW GP7 Diesel, 74-75	80	110	___
8455	D&RGW GP7 Diesel Dummy Unit, 74-75	50	85	___
8458	Erie-Lackawanna SD40 Diesel, 84	145	190	___
8459	D&RGW Vulcan Rotary Snowplow, 84	125	146	___
8460	MKT NW2 Switcher, 74-75	45	65	___
8463	Chessie System GP20 Diesel, 74 u	130	200	___
8464/65	D&RGW F3 Diesel AA Set (SSS), 74	220	325	___
8466	Amtrak F3 Diesel A Unit, 74-76	225	250	___
8467	Amtrak F3 Diesel A Unit, dummy, 74-76	80	90	___
8468	B&O F3 Diesel B Unit, 74-75	82	100	___
8469	CP F3 Diesel B Unit (SSS), 74	85	110	___
8470	Chessie System U36B Diesel, 74	80	110	___
8471	Pennsylvania NW2 Switcher, 74-76	170	195	___
8473	Coca-Cola NW2 Switcher, 74 u, 75	120	130	___
8474	D&RGW F3 Diesel B Unit (SSS), 74	110	125	___
8475	Amtrak F3 Diesel B Unit, 74	85	105	___
8477	NYC GP9 Diesel, 84 u	150	205	___
8480/82	Union Pacific F3 Diesel AA Set, 84	280	365	___
8481	Union Pacific F3 Diesel B Unit, 84	104	155	___
8485	USMC NW2 Switcher, 84-85	87	135	___
8500	Pennsylvania 2-4-0 Locomotive, 75-76	17	21	___
8502	Santa Fe 2-4-0 Locomotive, 75	17	21	___
8506	PRR 0-4-0 Locomotive, 75-77	75	90	___
8507	Santa Fe 2-4-0 Locomotive, 75 u	25	30	___
8512	Santa Fe 0-4-0T Locomotive, 85-86	22	30	___
8516	NYC 0-4-0 Locomotive, 85-86	115	140	___
8550	Jersey Central GP9 Diesel, 75-76	120	163	___
8551	Pennsylvania EP-5 Electric Locomotive, 75-76	108	120	___
8552/3/4	SP Alco Diesel ABA Set, 75-76	170	245	___

			Exc	Like New
___	**8555/57**	Milwaukee Road F3 Diesel AA Set (SSS), 75	240	315
___	**8556**	Chessie System NW2 Switcher, 75-76	115	160
___	**8558**	Milwaukee Road EP-5 Electric Locomotive, 76-77	128	185
___	**8559**	N&W GP9 Diesel "1776," 75	115	145
___	**8560**	Chessie System U36B Diesel Dummy Unit, 75	105	143
___	**8561**	Jersey Central GP9 Diesel Dummy Unit, 75-76	70	95
___	**8562**	Missouri Pacific GP20 Diesel, 75-76	95	138
___	**8563**	Rock Island Alco Diesel A Unit, 75-76 u	65	90
___	**8564**	Union Pacific U36B Diesel, 75	110	155
___	**8565**	Missouri Pacific GP20 Diesel Dummy Unit, 75-76	48	70
___	**8566**	Southern F3 Diesel A Unit, 75-77	220	370
___	**8567**	Southern F3 Diesel A Unit, dummy, 75-77	105	135
___	**8568**	Preamble Express F3 Diesel A Unit, 75 u	90	115
___	**8569**	Soo Line NW2 Switcher, 75-77	60	65
___	**8570**	Liberty Special Alco Diesel A Unit, 75 u	75	90
___	**8571**	Frisco U36B Diesel, 75-76	58	95
___	**8572**	Frisco U36B Diesel Dummy Unit, 75-76	23	55
___	**8573**	Union Pacific U36B Diesel Dummy Unit, 75 u	103	138
___	**8575**	Milwaukee Road F3 Diesel B Unit (SSS), 75	105	160
___	**8576**	Penn Central GP7 Diesel, 75 u, 76-77	90	120
___	**8578**	NYC Ballast Tamper, 85, 87	85	90
___	**8580/82**	Illinois Central F3 Diesel AA Set, 85, 87	420	485
___	**8581**	Illinois Central F3 Diesel B Unit, 85, 87	130	155
___	**8585**	Burlington Northern SD40 Diesel, 85	355	385
___	**8587**	Wabash GP9 Diesel "484," 85 u	250	280
___	**8600**	NYC 4-6-4 Locomotive, 76	175	195
___	**8601**	Rock Island 0-4-0 Locomotive, 76-77	13	33
___	**8602**	D&RGW 2-4-0 Locomotive, 76-78	16	26
___	**8603**	C&O 4-6-4 Locomotive, 76-77	135	190
___	**8604**	Jersey Central 2-4-2 Locomotive, 76 u	39	44
___	**8606**	B&A 4-6-4 Locomotive "784," 86 u	353	760
___	**8610**	Wabash 4-6-2 "672" (FF 1), 86-87	324	610
___	**8615**	L&N 2-8-4 Locomotive "1970," 86 u	540	630
___	**8616**	Santa Fe 4-4-2 Locomotive, 86	60	65
___	**8617**	Nickel Plate Road 4-4-2 Locomotive, 86-91	60	65
___	**8625**	Pennsylvania 2-4-0 Locomotive, 86-90	21	34
___	**8630**	W&ARR 4-4-0 Locomotive "3," 86 u	125	150
___	**8635**	Santa Fe 0-4-0 (SSS), 86	80	100
___	**8650**	Burlington Northern U36B Diesel, 76-77	100	145
___	**8651**	Burlington Northern U36B Diesel Dummy Unit, 76-77	60	93
___	**8652**	Santa Fe F3 Diesel A Unit, 76-77	260	510
___	**8653**	Santa Fe F3 Diesel A Unit, dummy, 76-77	135	160
___	**8654**	Boston & Maine GP9 Diesel, 76-77	143	178
___	**8655**	Boston & Maine GP9 Diesel Dummy Unit, 76-77	90	115
___	**8656**	Canadian National Alco Diesel A Unit, 76	150	193
___	**8657**	Canadian National Alco Diesel B Unit, 76	60	75
___	**8658**	CN Alco Diesel A Unit, dummy, 76	85	170
___	**8659**	Virginian Electric Locomotive, 76-77	113	134
___	**8660**	CP Rail NW2 Switcher, 76-77	112	138
___	**8661**	Southern F3 Diesel B Unit, 76	145	165
___	**8662**	B&O GP7 Diesel, 86	120	130
___	**8664**	Amtrak Alco Diesel A Unit, 76-77	85	120
___	**8665**	BAR Jeremiah O'Brien GP9 Diesel "1776," 76 u	100	170

MODERN 1970-2025		Exc	Like New	
8666	Northern Pacific GP9 Diesel (SSS), 76	128	183	___
8667	Amtrak Alco Diesel B Unit, 76-77	60	80	___
8668	Northern Pacific GP9 Diesel Dummy Unit (SSS), 76	100	130	___
8669	Illinois Central Gulf U36B Diesel, 76-77	118	153	___
8670	Chessie System Switcher, 76	30	55	___
8679	Northern Pacific GP20 Diesel, 86	90	105	___
8687	Jersey Central FM Train Master Diesel, 86	189	258	___
8690	Lionel Lines Trolley, 86	105	115	___
8701	W&ARR 4-4-0 Locomotive "3," 77-79	157	210	___
8702	Southern 4-6-4 Locomotive, 77-78	280	398	___
8703	Wabash 2-4-2 Locomotive, 77	22	30	___
8750	Rock Island GP7 Diesel, 77-78	110	125	___
8751	Rock Island GP7 Diesel Dummy Unit, 77-78	50	70	___
8753	Pennsylvania GG1 Electric Locomotive, 77 u	290	315	___
8754	New Haven Electric Locomotive, 77-78	100	115	___
8755	Santa Fe U36B Diesel, 77-78	130	150	___
8756	Santa Fe U36B Diesel Dummy Unit, 77-78	75	95	___
8757	Conrail GP9 Diesel, 76 u, 77-78	111	138	___
8758	Southern GP7 Diesel Dummy Unit, 77 u, 78	75	95	___
8759	Erie-Lackawanna GP9 Diesel, 77-79	117	175	___
8760	Erie-Lackawanna GP9 Diesel Dummy Unit, 77-79	95	115	___
8761	GTW NW2 Switcher, 77-78	95	130	___
8762	Great Northern EP5 Electric Locomotive, 77-78	130	140	___
8763	Norfolk & Western GP9 Diesel, 76 u, 77-78	110	120	___
8764	B&O Budd RDC Passenger (SSS), 77	110	135	___
8765	B&O Budd RDC Baggage Dummy Unit (SSS), 77	80	100	___
8766	B&O Budd RDC Baggage (SSS), 77		310	___
8767	B&O Budd RDC Passenger Dummy Unit (SSS), 77	85	105	___
8768	B&O Budd RDC Passenger Dummy Unit (SSS), 77	85	105	___
8769	Republic Steel Switcher, 77-78	22	39	___
8770	NW2 Switcher, 77-78		65	___
8771	Great Northern U36B Diesel, 77	110	130	___
8772	GM&O GP20 Diesel, 77	85	95	___
8773	Mickey Mouse U36B Diesel, 77-78	497	655	___
8774	Southern GP7 Diesel, 77 u, 78	115	135	___
8775	Lehigh Valley GP9 Diesel, 77 u, 78	85	105	___
8776	C&NW GP20 Diesel, 77 u, 78	87	129	___
8777	Santa Fe F3 Diesel B Unit (SSS), 77	160	175	___
8778	Lehigh Valley GP9 Diesel Dummy Unit, 77 u, 78	90	110	___
8779	C&NW GP20 Diesel Dummy Unit, 77 u, 78	73	109	___
8800	Lionel Lines 4-4-2 Locomotive, 78-81	58	105	___
8801	Blue Comet 4-6-4 Locomotive, 78-80	385	505	___
8803	Santa Fe 0-4-0 Locomotive, 78	14	24	___
8850	Penn Central GG1 Electric Locomotive, 78 u, 79	178	305	___
8851/52	New Haven F3 Diesel AA Set, 78 u, 79	320	430	___
8854	CP Rail GP9 Diesel, 78-79	100	120	___
8855	Milwaukee Road SD18 Diesel, 78		115	___
8857	Northern Pacific U36B Diesel, 78-80	140	180	___
8858	Northern Pacific U36B Diesel Dummy Unit, 78-80	55	85	___
8859	Conrail Electric Locomotive, 78-82	105	150	___
8860	Rock Island NW2 Switcher, 78-79	85	100	___
8861	Santa Fe Alco Diesel A Unit, 78-79	65	85	___
8862	Santa Fe Alco Diesel B Unit, 78-79	36	43	___

		MODERN 1970-2025	Exc	Like New
___	**8864**	New Haven F3 Diesel B Unit, 78	85	105
___	**8866**	M&StL GP9 Diesel (SSS), 78	85	120
___	**8867**	M&StL GP9 Diesel Dummy Unit (SSS), 78	65	95
___	**8868**	Amtrak Budd RDC Baggage, 78, 80	195	235
___	**8869**	Amtrak Budd RDC Passenger Dummy Unit, 78, 80	75	95
___	**8870**	Amtrak Budd RDC Passenger Dummy Unit, 78, 80	85	115
___	**8871**	Amtrak Budd RDC Baggage Dummy Unit, 78, 80	85	105
___	**8872**	Santa Fe SD18 Diesel, 78 u	125	155
___	**8873**	Santa Fe SD18 Diesel Dummy Unit, 78 u	60	85
___	**8900**	Santa Fe 4-6-4 Locomotive (FARR 1), 79	270	310
___	**8902**	ACL 2-4-0 Locomotive, 79-82, 86 u, 87-90	13	17
___	**8903**	D&RGW 2-4-2 Locomotive, 79-81	17	21
___	**8904**	Wabash 2-4-2 Locomotive, 79, 81 u	30	34
___	**8905**	Smokey Mountain Dockside 0-4-0T Locomotive, 79	9	17
___	**8950**	Virginian FM Train Master Diesel, 79	185	285
___	**8951**	Southern Pacific FM Train Master Diesel, 79	185	335
___	**8952/53**	PRR F3 Diesel AA Set, 79	350	500
___	**8955**	Southern U36B Diesel, 79	120	195
___	**8956**	Southern U36B Diesel Dummy Unit, 79	80	125
___	**8957**	Burlington Northern GP20 Diesel, 79	120	150
___	**8958**	Burlington Northern GP20 Diesel Dummy Unit, 79	85	90
___	**8960**	Southern Pacific U36C Diesel, 79 u	130	180
___	**8961**	Southern Pacific U36C Diesel Dummy Unit, 79 u	70	80
___	**8962**	Reading U36B Diesel, 79	115	130
___	**8970/71**	PRR F3 Diesel AA Set, 79 u, 80	330	425
___	**9001**	Conrail Boxcar (027), 86-87 u, 88-90	5	10
___	**9010**	GN Hopper (027), 70-71	6	8
___	**9011**	GN Hopper (027), 70 u, 75-76, 78-83	8	10
___	**9012**	TA&G Hopper (027), 71-72	7	8
___	**9013**	Canadian National Hopper (027), 72-76	5	8
___	**9015**	Reading Hopper (027), 73-75	17	21
___	**9016**	Chessie System Hopper (027), 75-79, 87-88, 89 u	4	6
___	**9017**	Wabash Gondola with canisters (027), 78-82	3	5
___	**9018**	DT&I Hopper (027), 78-79, 81-82	6	7
___	**9019**	Flatcar (027), 78	2	3
___	**9020**	Union Pacific Flatcar (027), 70-78	3	5
___	**9021**	Santa Fe Work Caboose, 70-71, 73-75	27	75
___	**9022**	Santa Fe Bulkhead Flatcar (027), 70-72, 75-79	7	13
___	**9023**	MKT Bulkhead Flatcar (027), 73-74	7	10
___	**9024**	C&O Flatcar (027), 73-75	3	6
___	**9025**	DT&I Work Caboose, 71-74, 77-78	8	10
___	**9026**	Republic Steel Flatcar (027), 75-82	5	7
___	**9027**	Soo Line Work Caboose, 75-76	7	9
___	**9030**	Kickapoo Gondola (027), 72, 79	5	9
___	**9031**	NKP Gondola with canisters (027), 73-75, 82-83, 84-91 u	5	8
___	**9032**	SP Gondola with canisters (027), 75-78	3	5
___	**9033**	PC Gondola w/canisters (027), 76-78, 82, 86 u, 87-90, 92 u	3	5
___	**9034**	Lionel Leisure Hopper (027), 77 u	30	34
___	**9035**	Conrail Boxcar (027), 78-82	5	12
___	**9036**	Mobilgas 1-D Tank Car (027), 78-82	7	19
___	**9037**	Conrail Boxcar (027), 78 u, 80	7	10
___	**9038**	Chessie System Hopper (027), 78 u, 80	15	19
___	**9039**	Mobilgas 1-D Tank Car (027), 78 u, 80	10	15

MODERN 1970-2025		Exc	Like New	
9040	General Mills Wheaties Boxcar (027), 70-72	9	13	___
9041	Hershey's Boxcar (027), 70-71, 73-76	18	28	___
9042	Ford-Autolite Boxcar (027), 71 u, 72 74-76	13	21	___
9043	Erie-Lackawanna Boxcar (027), 73-75	13	20	___
9044	D&RGW Boxcar (027), 75-76	5	8	___
9045	Toys 'R' Us Boxcar (027), 75 u	35	42	___
9046	True Value Boxcar (027), 76 u	26	34	___
9047	Toys 'R' Us Boxcar (027), 76 u	40	43	___
9048	Toys 'R' Us Boxcar (027), 76 u	33	41	___
9049	Toys 'R' Us Boxcar (027), 78 u		87	___
9050	Sunoco 1-D Tank Car (027), 70-71	17	23	___
9051	Firestone 1-D Tank Car (027), 74-75, 78	15	19	___
9052	Toys 'R' Us Boxcar (027), 77 u	26	34	___
9053	True Value Boxcar (027), 77 u	28	40	___
9054	JCPenney Boxcar (027), 77 u	14	19	___
9055	Republic Steel Gondola with canisters, 78 u	9	10	___
9057	CP Rail SP-type Caboose, 78-79	10	15	___
9058	Lionel Lines SP-type Caboose, 78-79, 83	5	7	___
9059	Lionel Lines SP-type Caboose, 79 u, 81 u	7	9	___
9060	Nickel Plate Road SP-type Caboose, 70-72	5	7	___
9061	Santa Fe SP-type Caboose, 70-76	5	8	___
9062	Penn Central SP-type Caboose, 70-72, 74-76	7	9	___
9063	GTW SP-type Caboose, 70, 71-73 u	15	19	___
9064	C&O SP-type Caboose, 71-72, 75-77	7	10	___
9065	Canadian National SP-type Caboose, 71-73 u	19	24	___
9066	Southern SP-type Caboose, 73-76	7	9	___
9067	Kickapoo Valley Bobber Caboose, 72	6	9	___
9068	Reading Bobber Caboose, 73-76	5	7	___
9069	Jersey Central SP-type Caboose, 73-74, 75-76 u	5	8	___
9070	Rock Island SP-type Caboose, 73-74	13	17	___
9071	Santa Fe Bobber Caboose, 74 u, 77-78	7	9	___
9073	Coca-Cola SP-type Caboose, 74 u, 75	33	38	___
9075	Rock Island SP-type Caboose, 75-76 u	13	17	___
9076	"We The People" SP-type Caboose, 75 u	19	28	___
9077	D&RGW SP-type Caboose, 76-83, 84-91 u	7	8	___
9078	Rock Island Bobber Caboose, 76-77	5	7	___
9079	GTW Hopper (027), 77	28	32	___
9080	Wabash SP-type Caboose, 77	9	10	___
9085	Santa Fe Work Caboose, 79-82	4	5	___
9090	General Mills Mini-Max Car, 71	27	32	___
9106	Miller Vat Car, 84-85	33	52	___
9107	Dr Pepper Vat Car, 86-87	30	36	___
9110	B&O Quad Hopper, 71			___
	(A) White Lettering	25	30	___
	(B) Gray Lettering	25	35	___
	(C) Yellow Lettering	50	70	___
9111	N&W Quad Hopper, 72-75	15	20	___
9112	D&RGW Covered Quad Hopper, 73-75	20	23	___
9113	Norfolk & Western Quad Hopper (SSS), 73	27	32	___
9114	Morton Salt Covered Quad Hopper, 74-76	18	27	___
9115	Planter's Covered Quad Hopper, 74-76	21	33	___
9116	Domino Sugar Covered Quad Hopper, 74-76	22	29	___
9117	Alaska Covered Quad Hopper (SSS), 74-76	29	33	

MODERN 1970-2025			Exc	Like New
___	**9118**	Corning 4-Bay Covered Hopper, 74 u		45
___	**9119**	Detroit & Mackinac Covered Hopper, 75 u		20
___	**9120**	Northern Pacific Flatcar with trailers, 70-71	33	38
___	**9121**	L&N Flatcar with bulldozer and scraper, 71-79	47	54
___	**9122**	Northern Pacific Flatcar with trailers, 72-75	19	32
___	**9123**	C&O Auto Carrier, 3-tier, 72 u, 73-74	34	79
___	**9124**	P&LE Flatcar with logs, 73-74	18	25
___	**9125**	Norfolk & Western Auto Carrier, 2-tier, 73-77	23	28
___	**9126**	C&O Auto Carrier, 3-tier, 73-75	23	34
___	**9128**	Heinz Vat Car, 74-76	19	36
___	**9129**	N&W Auto Carrier, 3-tier, 75-76	17	19
___	**9130**	B&O Quad Hopper, 70	23	24
___	**9131**	D&RGW Gondola with canisters, 73-77	5	8
___	**9132**	Libby's Vat Car (SSS), 75-77	16	23
___	**9133**	BN Flatcar with trailers, 76-77, 80	20	28
___	**9134**	Virginian Covered Quad Hopper, 76-77		32
___	**9135**	N&W Covered Quad Hopper, 70 u, 71, 75	12	26
___	**9136**	Republic Steel Gondola with canisters, 72-76, 79	9	11
___	**9138**	Sunoco 3-D Tank Car (SSS), 78	33	37
___	**9139**	PC Auto Carrier, 3-tier, 76-77	21	29
___	**9140**	Burlington Gondola with canisters, 70, 73-82, 87-89	7	9
___	**9141**	BN Gondola with canisters, 70-72	8	10
___	**9142**	Republic Steel Gondola w/2 canisters, 77 u	15	23
___	**9143**	CN Gondola with canisters, 71-73 u	30	34
___	**9144**	D&RGW Gondola with canisters (SSS), 74-76	9	13
___	**9145**	ICG Auto Carrier, 3-tier, 77-80	21	29
___	**9146**	Mogen David Vat Car, 77-81	21	26
___	**9147**	Texaco 1-D Tank Car, 77-78	46	63
___	**9148**	Du Pont 3-D Tank Car, 77-81	25	28
___	**9149**	CP Rail Flatcar with trailers, 77-78	22	35
___	**9150**	Gulf 1-D Tank Car, 70 u, 71	22	28
___	**9151**	Shell 1-D Tank Car, 72	27	31
___	**9152**	Shell 1-D Tank Car, 73-76	25	34
___	**9153**	Chevron 1-D Tank Car, 74-76	33	39
___	**9154**	Borden 1-D Tank Car, 75-76	33	47
___	**9155**	Monsanto 1-D Tank Car, 75 u	38	47
___	**9156**	Mobilgas 1-D Tank Car, 76-77	30	40
___	**9157**	C&O Crane Car, 76-78, 81-82	35	44
___	**9158**	PC Flatcar with shovel, 76-77, 80	40	55
___	**9159**	Sunoco 1-D Tank Car, 76	35	50
___	**9160**	Illinois Central N5c Caboose, 70-72	17	23
___	**9161**	CN N5c Caboose, 72-74	14	25
___	**9162**	PRR N5c Caboose, 72-76	25	30
___	**9163**	Santa Fe N5c Caboose, 73-76	17	24
___	**9165**	Canadian Pacific N5c Caboose (SSS), 73	21	30
___	**9166**	D&RGW SP-type Caboose (SSS), 74-75	20	25
___	**9167**	Chessie System N5c Caboose, 74-76	24	31
___	**9168**	Union Pacific N5c Caboose, 75-77	17	19
___	**9169**	Milwaukee Road SP-type Caboose (SSS), 75	18	35
___	**9170**	N&W N5c Caboose "1776," 75	27	30
___	**9171**	MP SP-type Caboose, 75 u, 76-77	19	20
___	**9172**	Penn Central SP-type Caboose, 75 u, 76-77	23	31
___	**9173**	Jersey Central SP-type Caboose, 75 u, 76-77	22	33

MODERN 1970-2025		Exc	Like New	
9174	NYC (P&E) Bay Window Caboose, 76	65	70	___
9175	Virginian N5c Caboose, 76-77	24	26	___
9176	BAR N5c Caboose, 76 u	16	30	___
9177	Northern Pacific Bay Window Caboose (SSS), 76	20	35	___
9178	ICG SP-type Caboose, 76-77	19	24	___
9179	Chessie System Bobber Caboose, 76	7	11	___
9180	Rock Island N5c Caboose, 77-78	12	23	___
9181	B&M N5c Caboose, 76 u, 77	28	49	___
9182	N&W N5c Caboose, 76 u, 77-80	20	26	___
9183	Mickey Mouse N5c Caboose, 77-78	32	54	___
9184	Erie Bay Window Caboose, 77-78	24	30	___
9185	GTW N5c Caboose, 77	21	28	___
9186	Conrail N5c Caboose, 76 u, 77-78	27	29	___
9187	Gulf, Mobile & Ohio SP-type Caboose, 77	10	16	___
9188	GN Bay Window Caboose, 77	22	27	___
9189	Gulf 1-D Tank Car, 77	40	60	___
9193	Budweiser Vat Car, 83-84	92	121	___
9200	Illinois Central Boxcar, 70-71	19	25	___
9201	Penn Central Boxcar, 70	17	25	___
9202	Santa Fe Boxcar, 70	20	24	___
9203	Union Pacific Boxcar, 70		21	___
9204	Northern Pacific Boxcar, 70		21	___
9205	Norfolk & Western Boxcar, 70	22	25	___
9206	Great Northern Boxcar, 70-71		20	___
9207	Soo Line Boxcar, 71	11	18	___
9208	CP Rail Boxcar, 71	21	23	___
9209	Burlington Northern Boxcar, 71-72	16	25	___
9210	B&O DD Boxcar, 71	16	20	___
9211	Penn Central Boxcar, 71	17	28	___
9212	Seaboard Coast Line Flatcar with trailers, 76 u	22	31	___
9213	M&StL Covered Quad Hopper (SSS), 78	20	29	___
9214	Northern Pacific Boxcar, 71-72	16	21	___
9215	Norfolk & Western Boxcar, 71	19	24	___
9216	Great Northern Auto Carrier, 3-tier, 78	25	39	___
9217	Soo Line Operating Boxcar, 82-84	29	36	___
9218	Monon Operating Boxcar, 81	23	33	___
9219	Missouri Pacific Operating Boxcar, 83	29	37	___
9220	Borden Operating Milk Car, 83-86	95	113	___
9221	Poultry Dispatch Operating Chicken Car, 83-85	45	50	___
9222	L&N Flatcar with trailers, 83-84	38	60	___
9223	Reading Operating Boxcar, 84	33	40	___
9224	Churchill Downs Operating Horse Car, 84-86	85	110	___
9225	Conrail Operating Barrel Car, 84	42	55	___
9226	Delaware & Hudson Flatcar with trailers, 84-85	31	34	___
9228	Canadian Pacific Operating Boxcar, 86	23	42	___
9229	Express Mail Operating Boxcar, 85-86	21	27	___
9230	Monon Boxcar (SSS), 71, 72 u	17	24	___
9231	Reading Bay Window Caboose, 79	24	32	___
9232	Allis-Chalmers Condenser Car, 80-81, 83 u	42	53	___
9233	Depressed Center Flatcar with transformer, 80	55	65	___
9234	Radioactive Waste Car, 80	53	78	___
9235	Union Pacific Derrick Car, 83-84	16	22	___
9236	C&NW Derrick Car, 83-85	22	30	

			Exc	Like New
___	**9237**	UPS Express Operating Boxcar, 84	32	99
___	**9238**	Northern Pacific Log Dump Car, 84	16	24
___	**9239**	Lionel Lines N5c Caboose, 83 u	50	60
___	**9240**	NYC Operating Hopper, 86	32	39
___	**9240**	NYC Hopper (027), 87 u	20	29
___	**9241**	PRR Log Dump Car, 85-86	21	27
___	**9250**	WaterPoxy 3-D Tank Car, 70-71	23	34
___	**9260**	Reynolds Aluminum Covered Quad Hopper, 75-77	19	22
___	**9261**	Sun-Maid Raisins Covered Quad Hopper, 75 u, 76	25	31
___	**9262**	Ralston Purina Covered Quad Hopper, 75 u, 76	36	58
___	**9263**	PRR Covered Quad Hopper, 75 u, 76-77	23	30
___	**9264**	Illinois Central Covered Quad Hopper, 75 u, 76-77	28	39
___	**9265**	Chessie System Covered Quad Hopper, 75 u, 76-77	21	27
___	**9266**	Southern "Big John" Covered Quad Hopper, 76	46	65
___	**9267**	Alcoa Covered Quad Hopper (SSS), 76	20	25
___	**9268**	Northern Pacific Bay Window Caboose, 77 u	30	40
___	**9269**	Milwaukee Road Bay Window Caboose, 78	37	59
___	**9270**	Northern Pacific N5c Caboose, 78	14	27
___	**9271**	M&StL Bay Window Caboose (SSS), 78-79	18	30
___	**9272**	New Haven Bay Window Caboose, 78-80	20	34
___	**9273**	Southern Bay Window Caboose, 78 u	36	45
___	**9274**	Santa Fe Bay Window Caboose, 78 u	40	47
___	**9276**	Peabody Quad Hopper, 78	19	28
___	**9277**	Cities Service 1-D Tank Car, 78	41	45
___	**9278**	Life Savers 1-D Tank Car, 78-79	80	156
___	**9279**	Magnolia 3-D Tank Car, 78, 79 u	13	19
___	**9280**	Santa Fe Operating Stock Car (027), 77-81	16	24
___	**9281**	Santa Fe Auto Carrier, 3-tier, 78-80	21	27
___	**9282**	GN Flatcar with trailers, 78-79, 81-82	22	28
___	**9283**	Union Pacific Gondola with canisters, 77	15	21
___	**9284**	Santa Fe Gondola with canisters, 77	16	27
___	**9285**	ICG Flatcar with trailers, 77	47	48
___		(A) Unpainted yellow	20	39
___	**9286**	B&LE Covered Quad Hopper, 77	14	26
___	**9287**	Southern N5c Caboose, 77 u, 78	18	30
___	**9288**	Lehigh Valley N5c Caboose, 77 u, 78, 80	25	31
___	**9289**	C&NW N5c Caboose, 77 u, 78, 80	25	36
___	**9290**	Union Pacific Operating Barrel Car, 83	65	75
___	**9300**	PC Log Dump Car, 70-75, 77	18	24
___	**9301**	U.S. Mail Operating Boxcar, 73-84	32	42
___	**9302**	L&N Searchlight Car, 72 u, 73-78	21	24
___	**9303**	Union Pacific Log Dump Car, 74-78, 80	17	22
___	**9304**	C&O Coal Dump Car, 74-78	11	25
___	**9305**	Santa Fe Operating Cowboy Car (027), 80-82	16	23
___	**9306**	Santa Fe Flatcar with horses, 80-82	18	26
___	**9307**	Erie Animated Gondola, 80-84	55	70
___	**9308**	Aquarium Car, 81-84	125	129
___	**9309**	TP&W Bay Window Caboose, 80-81, 83 u	19	25
___	**9310**	Santa Fe Log Dump Car, 78 u, 79-83	13	24
___	**9311**	Union Pacific Coal Dump Car, 78 u, 79-82	13	24
___	**9312**	Conrail Searchlight Car, 78 u, 79-83	18	27
___	**9313**	Gulf 3-D Tank Car, 79 u	43	50
___	**9315**	Southern Pacific Gondola with canisters, 79 u	16	23

MODERN 1970-2025		Exc	Like New	
9316	Southern Pacific Bay Window Caboose, 79 u	47	50	___
9317	Santa Fe Bay Window Caboose, 79	21	36	___
9320	Fort Knox Mint Car, 79 u	110	135	___
9321	Santa Fe 1-D Tank Car (FARR 1), 79	25	31	___
9322	Santa Fe Covered Quad Hopper (FARR 1), 79	30	38	___
9323	Santa Fe Bay Window Caboose (FARR 1), 79	39	49	___
9324	Tootsie Roll 1-D Tank Car, 79-81	69	98	___
9325	Norfolk & Western Flatcar with fences, 79-81 u	6	10	___
9326	Burlington Northern Bay Window Caboose, 79-80	34	44	___
9327	Bakelite 3-D Tank Car, 80	19	29	___
9328	Chessie System Bay Window Caboose, 80	33	42	___
9329	Chessie System Crane Car, 80	40	47	___
9330	Kickapoo Dump Car, 72, 79	3	7	___
9331	Union 76 1-D Tank Car, 79	39	44	___
9332	Reading Crane Car, 79	37	50	___
9333	Southern Pacific Flatcar with trailers, 79-80	33	47	___
9334	Humble 1-D Tank Car, 79	21	26	___
9335	B&O Log Dump Car, 86	16	22	___
9336	CP Rail Gondola with canisters, 79	16	29	___
9338	Pennsylvania Power & Light Quad Hopper, 79	60	75	___
9339	GN Boxcar (027), 79-83, 85 u, 86	8	10	___
9340	Illinois Central Gondola with canisters (027), 79-81, 82 u, 83	5	9	___
9341	ACL SP-type Caboose, 79-82, 86 u 87-90	6	8	___
9344	Citgo 3-D Tank Car, 80	23	38	___
9345	Reading Searchlight Car, 84-85	20	25	___
9346	Wabash SP-type Caboose, 79	6	10	___
9347	NIagara Falls 3-D Tank Car, 79 u	38	46	___
9348	Santa Fe Crane Car (FARR 1), 79 u	60	70	___
9349	San Francisco Mint Car, 80	55	70	___
9351	PRR Auto Carrier, 3-tier, 80	23	40	___
9352	Trailer Train Flatcar with C&NW trailers, 80	29	55	___
9353	Crystal Line 3-D Tank Car, 80	18	26	___
9354	Pennzoil 1-D Tank Car, 80, 81 u	60	85	___
9355	Delaware & Hudson Bay Window Caboose, 80	37	45	___
9357	Smokey Mountain Bobber Caboose, 79	8	10	___
9359	National Basketball Association Boxcar (027), 79-80 u	19	24	___
9360	National Hockey League Boxcar (027), 79-80 u	21	26	___
9361	C&NW Bay Window Caboose, 80	47	50	___
9362	Major League Baseball Boxcar (027), 79-80 u	17	21	___
9363	N&W Log Dump Car "9325" (027), 79	4	7	___
9364	N&W Crane Car "9325" (027), 79	7	9	___
9365	Toys 'R' Us Boxcar (027), 79 u	30	37	___
9366	UP Covered Quad Hopper (FARR 2), 80	19	23	___
9367	Union Pacific 1-D Tank Car (FARR 2), 80	21	30	___
9368	Union Pacific Bay Window Caboose (FARR 2), 80	30	36	___
9369	Sinclair 1-D Tank Car, 80	60	85	___
9370	Seaboard Gondola with canisters, 80	19	21	___
9371	Atlantic Sugar Covered Quad Hopper, 80	19	22	___
9372	Seaboard Bay Window Caboose, 80	35	40	___
9373	Getty 1-D Tank Car, 80-81, 83 u	31	42	___
9374	Reading Covered Quad Hopper, 80-81, 83 u	39	40	___
9376	Soo Line Boxcar (027), 81 u	40	50	___
9378	Derrick Car, 80-82	18	22	___

			Exc	Like New
___	**9379**	Santa Fe Gondola with canisters, 80-81, 83 u	22	30
___	**9380**	NYNH&H SP-type Caboose, 80-81	7	10
___	**9381**	Chessie System SP-type Caboose, 80	7	9
___	**9382**	Florida East Coast Bay Window Caboose, 80	34	48
___	**9383**	UP Flatcar with trailers (FARR 2), 80 u	27	34
___	**9384**	Great Northern Operating Hopper, 81	50	55
___	**9385**	Alaska Gondola with canisters, 81	27	34
___	**9386**	Pure Oil 1-D Tank Car, 81	38	50
___	**9387**	Burlington Bay Window Caboose, 81	46	52
___	**9388**	Toys 'R' Us Boxcar (027), 81 u	38	45
___	**9389**	Radioactive Waste Car, 81-82	65	78
___	**9398**	PRR Coal Dump Car, 83-84	28	38
___	**9399**	C&NW Coal Dump Car, 83-85	17	22
___	**9400**	Conrail Boxcar, 78	14	20
___	**9401**	Great Northern Boxcar, 78	18	23
___	**9402**	Susquehanna Boxcar, 78	30	36
___	**9403**	Seaboard Coast Line Boxcar, 78	12	17
___	**9404**	NKP Boxcar, 78	19	21
___	**9405**	Chattahoochee Boxcar, 78	14	19
___	**9406**	D&RGW Boxcar, 78-79	17	21
___	**9407**	Union Pacific Stock Car, 78	18	25
___	**9408**	Lionel Lines Circus Stock Car (SSS), 78	31	40
___	**9411**	Lackawanna Phoebe Snow Boxcar, 78	35	43
___	**9412**	RF&P Boxcar, 79	21	27
___	**9413**	Napierville Junction Boxcar, 79	18	24
___	**9414**	Cotton Belt Boxcar, 79	19	23
___	**9415**	Providence & Worcester Boxcar, 79	17	25
___	**9416**	MD&W Boxcar, 79, 81	13	19
___	**9417**	CP Rail Boxcar, 79	45	50
___	**9418**	FARR Boxcar, 79 u	50	60
___	**9419**	Union Pacific Boxcar (FARR 2), 80	22	31
___	**9420**	B&O Sentinel Boxcar, 80	21	26
___	**9421**	Maine Central Boxcar, 80	10	17
___	**9422**	EJ&E Boxcar, 80	12	20
___	**9423**	NYNH&H Boxcar, 80	14	22
___	**9424**	TP&W Boxcar, 80	17	21
___	**9425**	British Columbia DD Boxcar, 80	26	35
___	**9426**	Chesapeake & Ohio Boxcar, 80	19	30
___	**9427**	Bay Line Boxcar, 80-81	12	17
___	**9428**	TP&W Boxcar, 80-81, 83 u		23
___	**9429**	"The Early Years" Boxcar, 80	13	27
___	**9430**	"The Standard Gauge Years" Boxcar, 80	12	25
___	**9431**	"The Prewar Years" Boxcar, 80	12	25
___	**9432**	"The Postwar Years" Boxcar, 80	22	55
___	**9433**	"The Golden Years" Boxcar, 80	33	43
___	**9434**	Joshua Lionel Cowen "The Man" Boxcar, 80 u	29	37
___	**9436**	Burlington Boxcar, 81	25	30
___	**9437**	Northern Pacific Stock Car, 81	22	36
___	**9438**	Ontario Northland Boxcar, 81	25	31
___	**9439**	Ashley Drew & Northern Boxcar, 81	11	19
___	**9440**	Reading Boxcar, 81	50	65
___	**9441**	Pennsylvania Boxcar, 81	32	42
___	**9442**	Canadian Pacific Boxcar, 81	12	31

MODERN 1970-2025		Exc	Like New	
9443	Florida East Coast Boxcar, 81	19	24	___
9444	Louisiana Midland Boxcar, 81	14	18	___
9445	Vermont Northern Boxcar, 81	14	17	___
9446	Sabine River & Northern Boxcar, 81	15	21	___
9447	Pullman Standard Boxcar, 81	16	21	___
9448	Santa Fe Stock Car, 81-82	34	40	___
9449	Great Northern Boxcar (FARR 3), 81	22	35	___
9450	Great Northern Stock Car (FARR 3), 81 u	50	60	___
9451	Southern Boxcar (FARR 4), 83	26	32	___
9452	Western Pacific Boxcar, 82-83	12	16	___
9453	MPA Boxcar, 82-83	14	19	___
9454	New Hope & Ivyland Boxcar, 82-83	21	27	___
9455	Milwaukee Road Boxcar, 82-83	15	29	___
9456	PRR DD Boxcar (FARR 5), 84-85	24	30	___
9461	Norfolk & Southern Boxcar, 82	25	43	___
9462	Southern Pacific Boxcar, 83-84	18	23	___
9463	Texas & Pacific Boxcar, 83-84	15	19	___
9464	NC&StL Boxcar, 83-84	16	22	___
9465	Santa Fe Boxcar, 83-84	12	19	___
9466	Wanamaker Boxcar, 82 u	60	70	___
9467	Tennessee World's Fair Boxcar, 82 u	26	31	___
9468	Union Pacific DD Boxcar, 83	31	34	___
9469	NYC Pacemaker Boxcar (std O), 84-85	37	53	___
9470	Chicago Beltline Boxcar, 84	15	20	___
9471	Atlantic Coast Line Boxcar, 84	13	20	___
9472	Detroit & Mackinac Boxcar, 84	22	26	___
9473	Lehigh Valley Boxcar, 84	13	28	___
9474	Erie-Lackawanna Boxcar, 84	31	35	___
9475	D&H "I Love NY" Boxcar, 84 u	28	37	___
9476	PRR Boxcar (FARR 5), 84-85	27	36	___
9480	MN&S Boxcar, 85-86	15	18	___
9481	Seaboard System Boxcar, 85-86	15	18	___
9482	Norfolk & Southern Boxcar, 85-86	13	17	___
9483	Manufacturers Railway Boxcar, 85-86	14	19	___
9484	Lionel 85th Anniversary Boxcar, 85	22	26	___
9486	GTW "I Love Michigan" Boxcar, 86	23	34	___
9490	Christmas Boxcar for Lionel Employees, 85 u	140	300	___
9491	Christmas Boxcar, 86 u	26	37	___
9492	Lionel Lines Boxcar, 86	23	29	___
9500	Milwaukee Road Passenger Coach, 73	28	75	___
9501	Milwaukee Road Passenger Coach, 73 u, 74-76	33	37	___
9502	Milwaukee Road Observation Car, 73	30	48	___
9503	Milwaukee Road Passenger Coach, 73	33	48	___
9504	Milwaukee Road Passenger Coach, 73 u, 74-76	33	37	___
9505	Milwaukee Road Passenger Coach, 73 u, 74-76	35	38	___
9506	Milwaukee Road Combination Car, 74 u, 75-76	32	37	___
9507	PRR Passenger Coach, 74-75	34	55	___
9508	PRR Passenger Coach, 74-75	32	50	___
9509	PRR Observation Car, 74-75	41	60	___
9510	PRR Combination Car, 74 u, 75-76	30	47	___
9511	Milwaukee Road Passenger Coach, 74 u	33	48	___
9513	PRR Passenger Coach, 75-76	25	44	___
9514	PRR Passenger Coach, 75-76	23	36	___

			Exc	Like New
___	**9515**	PRR Passenger Coach, 75-76	22	34
___	**9516**	B&O Passenger Coach, 76	27	42
___	**9517**	B&O Passenger Coach, 75	45	65
___	**9518**	B&O Observation Car, 75	45	65
___	**9519**	B&O Combination Car, 75	55	85
___	**9521**	PRR Baggage Car, 75 u, 76	65	95
___	**9522**	Milwaukee Road Baggage Car, 75 u, 76	65	80
___	**9523**	B&O Baggage Car, 75 u, 76	60	70
___	**9524**	B&O Passenger Coach, 76	27	37
___	**9525**	B&O Passenger Coach, 76	30	43
___	**9527**	Milwaukee Road Campaign Observation Car, 76 u	39	61
___	**9528**	PRR Campaign Observation Car, 76 u	49	76
___	**9529**	B&O Campaign Observation Car, 76 u	38	62
___	**9530**	Southern Baggage Car, 77-78	45	65
___	**9531**	Southern Combination Car, 77-78	29	37
___	**9532**	Southern Passenger Coach, 77-78	33	47
___	**9533**	Southern Passenger Coach, 77-78	27	38
___	**9534**	Southern Observation Car, 77-78	31	47
___	**9536**	Blue Comet Baggage Car, 78-80	39	55
___	**9537**	Blue Comet Combination Car, 78-80	35	50
___	**9538**	Blue Comet Passenger Coach, 78-80	35	47
___	**9539**	Blue Comet Passenger Coach, 78-80	35	48
___	**9540**	Blue Comet Observation Car, 78-80	16	40
___	**9541**	Santa Fe Baggage Car, 80-82	21	30
___	**9545**	Union Pacific Baggage Car, 84	135	200
___	**9546**	Union Pacific Combination Car, 84	85	105
___	**9547**	Union Pacific Observation Car, 84	85	105
___	**9548**	UP Placid Bay Passenger Coach, 84	90	110
___	**9549**	UP Ocean Sunset Passenger Coach, 84	85	105
___	**9551**	W&ARR Baggage Car, 77 u, 78-80	36	48
___	**9552**	W&ARR Passenger Coach, 77 u, 78-80	46	60
___	**9553**	W&ARR Flatcar with horses, 77 u, 78-80	32	50
___	**9554**	Chicago & Alton Baggage Car, 81	55	85
___	**9555**	Chicago & Alton Combination Car, 81	50	75
___	**9556**	Chicago & Alton Wilson Passenger Coach, 81	50	75
___	**9557**	Chicago & Alton Webster Groves Passenger Coach, 81	45	65
___	**9558**	Chicago & Alton Observation Car, 81	50	75
___	**9559**	Rock Island Baggage Car, 81-82	42	65
___	**9560**	Rock Island Passenger Coach, 81-82	43	65
___	**9561**	Rock Island Passenger Coach, 81-82	42	65
___	**9562**	N&W Baggage Car "577," 81	80	110
___	**9563**	N&W Combination Car "578," 81	80	105
___	**9564**	N&W Passenger Coach "579," 81	90	100
___	**9565**	N&W Passenger Coach "580," 81	85	100
___	**9566**	N&W Observation Car "581," 81	90	95
___	**9567**	N&W Vista Dome Car "582," 81 u	160	255
___	**9569**	PRR Combination Car, 81 u	115	160
___	**9570**	PRR Baggage Car, 79	85	115
___	**9571**	PRR Passenger Coach, 79	125	145
___	**9572**	PRR Passenger Coach, 79	110	125
___	**9573**	PRR Vista Dome Car, 79	95	120
___	**9574**	PRR Observation Car, 79	75	100
___	**9575**	PRR Passenger Coach, 79-80 u	100	135

MODERN 1970-2025		Exc	Like New	
9576	Burlington Baggage Car, 80	145	175	___
9577	Burlington Passenger Coach, 80	95	105	___
9578	Burlington Passenger Coach, 80	105	110	___
9579	Burlington Vista Dome Car, 80	95	110	___
9580	Burlington Observation Car, 80	95	110	___
9581	Chessie System Baggage Car, 80	55	64	___
9582	Chessie System Combination Car, 80	47	53	___
9583	Chessie System Passenger Coach, 80	40	50	___
9584	Chessie System Passenger Coach, 80	34	43	___
9585	Chessie System Observation Car, 80	57	68	___
9586	Chessie System Diner, 86 u	85	93	___
9588	Burlington Vista Dome Car, 80 u	110	120	___
9589	Southern Pacific Baggage Car, 82-83	110	135	___
9590	Southern Pacific Combination Car, 82-83	90	105	___
9591	Southern Pacific Pullman Passenger Coach, 82-83	85	105	___
9592	Southern Pacific Pullman Passenger Coach, 82-83	85	105	___
9593	Southern Pacific Observation Car, 82-83	100	130	___
9594	NYC Baggage Car, 83-84	76	130	___
9595	NYC Combination Car, 83-84	75	85	___
9596	NYC Wayne County Passenger Coach, 83-84	80	95	___
9597	NYC Hudson River Passenger Coach, 83-84	70	85	___
9598	NYC Observation Car, 83-84	75	85	___
9599	Chicago & Alton Diner, 86 u	80	90	___
9600	Chessie System Hi-Cube Boxcar, 75 u, 76-77	19	25	___
9601	ICG Hi-Cube Boxcar, 75 u, 76-77	20	21	___
9602	Santa Fe Hi-Cube Boxcar, 75 u, 76-77	17	20	___
9603	Penn Central Hi-Cube Boxcar, 76-77	12	18	___
9604	Norfolk & Western Hi-Cube Boxcar, 76-77	23	26	___
9605	NH Hi-Cube Boxcar, 76-77	17	21	___
9606	Union Pacific Hi-Cube Boxcar, 76 u, 77	10	17	___
9607	Southern Pacific Hi-Cube Boxcar, 76 u, 77	12	15	___
9608	Burlington Northern Hi-Cube Boxcar, 76 u, 77	21	23	___
9610	Frisco Hi-Cube Boxcar, 77	25	34	___
9620	NHL Wales Boxcar, 80	27	35	___
9621	NHL Campbell Boxcar, 80	27	34	___
9622	NBA Western Boxcar, 80	24	30	___
9623	NBA Eastern Boxcar, 80	26	34	___
9624	National League Baseball Boxcar, 80	27	34	___
9625	American League Baseball Boxcar, 80	27	35	___
9626	Santa Fe Hi-Cube Boxcar, 82-84	10	14	___
9627	Union Pacific Hi-Cube Boxcar, 82-83	15	21	___
9628	Burlington Northern Hi-Cube Boxcar, 82-84	14	19	___
9629	Chessie System Hi-Cube Boxcar, 83-84	24	36	___
9660	Mickey Mouse Hi-Cube Boxcar, 77-78	34	46	___
9661	Goofy Hi-Cube Boxcar, 77-78	57	66	___
9662	Donald Duck Hi-Cube Boxcar, 77-78	38	49	___
9663	Dumbo Hi-Cube Boxcar, 77 u, 78	43	52	___
9664	Cinderella Hi-Cube Boxcar, 77 u, 78	56	63	___
9665	Peter Pan Hi-Cube Boxcar, 77 u, 78	49	77	___
9666	Pinocchio Hi-Cube Boxcar, 78	120	175	___
9667	Snow White Hi-Cube Boxcar, 78	365	473	___
9668	Pluto Hi-Cube Boxcar, 78	149	193	___
9669	Bambi Hi-Cube Boxcar, 78 u	67	105	___

MODERN 1970-2025			Exc	Like New
___	**9670**	Alice In Wonderland Hi-Cube Boxcar, 78 u	61	91
___	**9671**	Fantasia Hi-Cube Boxcar, 78 u	56	91
___	**9672**	Mickey Mouse 50th Anniversary Hi-Cube Boxcar, 78 u	384	484
___	**9700**	Southern Boxcar, 72-73	22	30
___	**9700**	Hoboken Shore RR Boxcar "1029," 98 u		20
___	**9701**	B&O DD Boxcar, 72	14	19
___	**9702**	Soo Line Boxcar, 72-73	15	21
___	**9703**	CP Rail Boxcar, 72	30	40
___	**9704**	Norfolk & Western Boxcar, 72	10	17
___	**9705**	D&RGW Boxcar, 72	13	20
___	**9706**	C&O Boxcar, 72	11	19
___	**9707**	MKT Stock Car, 72-75	14	22
___	**9708**	U.S. Mail Toy Fair Boxcar, 73 u	85	95
___	**9708**	U.S. Mail Boxcar, 72-75	18	23
___	**9709**	BAR State of Maine Boxcar (SSS), 72-74	29	32
___	**9710**	Rutland Boxcar (SSS), 72-74	24	28
___	**9711**	Southern Boxcar, 74-75	19	25
___	**9712**	B&O DD Boxcar, 73-74	31	34
___	**9713**	CP Rail "Season's Greetings" Boxcar, 74 u	95	120
___	**9713**	CP Rail Boxcar, 73-74	24	30
___	**9714**	D&RGW Boxcar, 73-74	16	20
___	**9715**	C&O Boxcar, 73-74	17	22
___	**9716**	Penn Central Boxcar, 73-74	15	20
___	**9717**	Union Pacific Boxcar, 73-74	18	28
___	**9718**	Canadian National Boxcar, 73-74	23	31
___	**9719**	New Haven DD Boxcar, 73 u	23	32
___	**9723**	Western Pacific Toy Fair Boxcar, 74 u	20	60
___	**9723**	Western Pacific Boxcar (SSS), 73-74	27	29
___	**9724**	Missouri Pacific Boxcar (SSS), 73-74	21	24
___	**9725**	MKT Stock Car (SSS), 73-75	15	18
___	**9726**	Erie-Lackawanna Boxcar (SSS), 78	25	30
___	**9729**	CP Rail Boxcar, black, 78		34
___	**9730**	CP Rail Boxcar, silver, 74-75	23	27
___	**9731**	Milwaukee Road Boxcar, 74-75	18	28
___	**9732**	Southern Pacific Boxcar, 79 u	24	31
___	**9734**	Bangor & Aroostook Boxcar, 79	30	38
___	**9735**	Grand Trunk Western Boxcar, 74-75	15	21
___	**9737**	Vermont Central Boxcar, 74-76	27	34
___	**9738**	Illinois Terminal Boxcar, 82	33	45
___	**9739**	D&RGW Boxcar (SSS), 74-76	17	25
___	**9740**	Chessie System Boxcar, 74-75	15	19
___	**9742**	M&StL Boxcar, 73 u	12	19
___	**9742**	M&StL "Season's Greetings" Boxcar, 73 u	85	105
___	**9743**	Sprite Boxcar, 74 u, 75	19	27
___	**9744**	Tab Boxcar, 74 u, 75	17	24
___	**9745**	Fanta Boxcar, 74 u, 75	19	29
___	**9747**	Chessie System DD Boxcar, 75-76	24	28
___	**9748**	CP Rail Boxcar, 75-76	16	20
___	**9749**	Penn Central Boxcar, 75-76	16	21
___	**9750**	DT&I Boxcar, 75-76	13	20
___	**9751**	Frisco Boxcar, 75-76	15	23
___	**9752**	L&N Boxcar, 75-76	20	23
___	**9753**	Maine Central Boxcar, 75-76	16	22

MODERN 1970-2025		Exc	Like New	
9754	NYC Pacemaker Boxcar (SSS), 75-77	20	30	___
9755	Union Pacific Boxcar, 75-76	20	24	___
9757	Central of Georgia Boxcar, 74 u	16	17	___
9758	Alaska Boxcar (SSS), 75-77	24	31	___
9759	Paul Revere Boxcar, 75 u	36	43	___
9760	Liberty Bell Boxcar, 75 u	30	40	___
9761	George Washington Boxcar, 75 u	36	43	___
9762	Toy Fair Boxcar, 75 u	125	170	___
9763	D&RGW Stock Car, 76-77	15	20	___
9764	GTW DD Boxcar, 76-77	40	63	___
9767	Railbox Boxcar, 76-77	15	20	___
9768	B&M Boxcar, 76-77	18	27	___
9769	B&LE Boxcar, 76-77	13	21	___
9770	Northern Pacific Boxcar, 76-77	14	18	___
9771	Norfolk & Western Boxcar, 76-77	16	24	___
9772	Great Northern Boxcar, 76	49	81	___
9773	NYC Stock Car, 76	32	39	___
9775	M&StL Boxcar (SSS), 76	19	23	___
9776	SP Overnight Boxcar (SSS), 76	32	34	___
9777	Virginian Boxcar, 76-77	19	25	___
9778	"Season's Greetings" Boxcar, 75 u	165	185	___
9780	Johnny Cash Boxcar, 76 u	50	61	___
9781	Delaware & Hudson Boxcar, 77-78	19	23	___
9782	Rock Island Boxcar, 77-78	14	17	___
9783	B&O Time-Saver Boxcar, 77-78	18	27	___
9784	Santa Fe Boxcar, 77-78	13	17	___
9785	Conrail Boxcar, 77-78	20	23	___
9786	C&NW Boxcar, 77-79	18	27	___
9787	Jersey Central Boxcar, 77-79	12	19	___
9788	Lehigh Valley Boxcar, 77-79	17	21	___
9789	Pickens Boxcar, 77	25	33	___
9801	B&O Sentinel Boxcar (std O), 73-75	18	26	___
9802	Miller High Life Reefer (std O), 73-75	30	38	___
9803	Johnson Wax Boxcar (std O), 73-75	27	33	___
9805	Grand Trunk Western Reefer (std O), 73-75	20	31	___
9806	Rock Island Boxcar (std O), 74-75	38	46	___
9807	Stroh's Beer Reefer (std O), 74-76	72	90	___
9808	Union Pacific Boxcar (std O), 75-76	36	50	___
9809	Clark Reefer (std O), 75-76	33	41	___
9811	Pacific Fruit Express Reefer (FARR 2), 80	26	33	___
9812	Arm & Hammer Reefer, 80	24	30	___
9813	Ruffles Reefer, 80	20	28	___
9814	Perrier Reefer, 80	21	30	___
9815	NYC "Early Bird" Reefer (std O), 84-85	34	40	___
9816	Brach's Candy Reefer, 80	21	26	___
9817	Bazooka Bubble Gum Reefer, 80	24	31	___
9818	Western Maryland Reefer, 80	18	23	___
9819	Western Fruit Express Reefer (FARR 3), 81	22	29	___
9820	Wabash Gondola with coal (std O), 73-74	24	38	___
9821	SP Gondola with coal (std O), 73-75	28	32	___
9822	GTW Gondola with coal (std O), 74-75	24	29	___
9823	Santa Fe Flatcar with crates (std O), 75-76	34	44	___
9824	NYC Gondola with coal (std O), 75-76	41	56	___

			Exc	Like New
___	**9825**	Schaefer Reefer (std O), 76-77	45	60
___	**9826**	P&LE Boxcar (std O), 76-77	34	39
___	**9827**	Cutty Sark Reefer, 84	45	55
___	**9828**	J&B Reefer, 84	37	49
___	**9829**	Dewar's White Label Reefer, 84	45	51
___	**9830**	Johnnie Walker Red Label Reefer, 84	36	44
___	**9831**	Pepsi Cola Reefer, 82	93	103
___	**9832**	Cheerios Reefer, 82	171	197
___	**9833**	Vlasic Pickles Reefer, 82	23	29
___	**9834**	Southern Comfort Reefer, 83-84	34	47
___	**9835**	Jim Beam Reefer, 83-84	48	62
___	**9836**	Old Grand-Dad Reefer, 83-84	44	54
___	**9837**	Wild Turkey Reefer, 83-84	76	110
___	**9840**	Fleischmann's Gin Reefer, 85	39	44
___	**9841**	Calvert Gin Reefer, 85	44	49
___	**9842**	Seagram's Gin Reefer, 85	44	49
___	**9843**	Tanqueray Gin Reefer, 85	45	50
___	**9844**	Sambuca Reefer, 86	37	49
___	**9845**	Baileys Irish Cream Reefer, 86	62	86
___	**9846**	Seagram's Vodka Reefer, 86	41	49
___	**9847**	Wolfschmidt Vodka Reefer, 86	38	43
___	**9849**	Lionel Lines Reefer, 83 u	20	32
___	**9850**	Budweiser Reefer, 72 u, 73-75	58	70
___	**9851**	Schlitz Reefer, 72 u, 73-75	30	36
___	**9852**	Miller Reefer, 72 u, 73-77	32	38
___	**9853**	Cracker Jack Reefer, 72 u, 73-75		
___		(A) White body, black border on logo	24	34
___		(B) Caramel body, clear background logo	23	28
___		(C) Caramel body, white background logo	23	28
___	**9854**	Baby Ruth Reefer, 72 u, 73-76	22	26
___	**9855**	Swift Reefer, 72 u, 73-77	16	28
___	**9856**	Old Milwaukee Reefer, 75-76	33	40
___	**9858**	Butterfinger Reefer, 73 u, 74-76	22	28
___	**9859**	Pabst Reefer, 73 u, 74-75	43	50
___	**9860**	Gold Medal Reefer, 73 u, 74-76	12	21
___	**9861**	Tropicana Reefer, 75-77	23	35
___	**9862**	Hamm's Reefer, 75-76	35	42
___	**9863**	REA Reefer (SSS), 74-76	24	28
___	**9866**	Coors Reefer, 76-77	42	58
___	**9867**	Hershey's Reefer, 76-77	80	93
___	**9869**	Santa Fe Reefer (SSS), 76	32	37
___	**9870**	Old Dutch Cleanser Reefer, 77-78, 80	15	21
___	**9871**	Carling Black Label Reefer, 77-78, 80	33	45
___	**9872**	Pacific Fruit Express Reefer, 77-79	24	28
___	**9873**	Ralston Purina Reefer, 78	25	38
___	**9874**	Miller Lite Beer Reefer, 78-79	58	63
___	**9875**	A&P Reefer, 78-79	23	31
___	**9876**	Vermont Central Reefer, 78	26	31
___	**9877**	Gerber Reefer, 79-80	68	78
___	**9878**	Good and Plenty Reefer, 79	24	31
___	**9879**	Hills Bros. Reefer, 79-80	24	29
___	**9880**	Santa Fe Reefer (FARR 1), 79	27	31
___	**9881**	Rath Packing Reefer, 79 u	22	31

MODERN 1970-2025		Exc	Like New	
9882	NYC "Early Bird" Reefer, 79	25	29	___
9883	Nabisco Oreo Reefer, 79	95	104	___
9884	Fritos Reefer, 81-82	26	34	___
9885	Lipton Tea Reefer, 81-82	30	38	___
9886	Mounds Reefer, 81-82	24	30	___
9887	Fruit Growers Express Reefer (FARR 4), 83	29	38	___
9888	Green Bay & Western Reefer, 83	42	49	___
11000	Holiday Express Freight Set, 08		280	___
11004	NASCAR Diesel Freight Set, 06-07	150	325	___
11005	Dale Earnhardt Jr. Diesel Freight Set, 06-07	65	240	___
11006	Lionel Lion Set, 03 u		230	___
11006	Kasey Kahne Expansion Pack, 06-07		130	___
11007	Dale Earnhardt Sr. Expansion Pack, 06-07		130	___
11008	Dale Earnhardt Jr. Expansion Pack, 06-07		130	___
11009	Tony Stewart Expansion Pack, 06-07		130	___
11010	Jimmie Johnson Expansion Pack, 06-07		130	___
11011	Jeff Gordon Expansion Pack, 06-07		130	___
11020	Harry Potter Hogwarts Express Steam Passenger Set, 08-13	80	330	___
11025	Jimmie Johnson 2006 Champion Boxcar, 07		45	___
11038	Snow-covered Straight Track 4-pack, 08		14	___
11041	Holiday Calliope Car, 08		45	___
11067	Lionel Bear, 08		25	___
11077	Harry Potter Figures, 08		27	___
11096	Engineer Hat, 08		20	___
11098	Holiday Toy Soldier Car, 08		50	___
11099	Pennsylvania Flyer Steam Freight Set, 08	136	210	___
11100	PRR 2-8-2 Mikado Locomotive "9631," CC, 07		370	___
11101	LL 2-8-4 Berkshire Locomotive "737," CC, 06		350	___
11103	Southern PS4 4-6-2 Pacific Locomotive "1403," CC, 06		1000	___
11104	UP Big Boy Locomotive "4014," CC, 06		1800	___
11105	NYC L-2A 4-8-2 Mohawk Locomotive "2770," CC, 06		1100	___
11106	N&W 4-8-4 Northern Locomotive "746," CC, 06-07	610	750	___
11107	LionMaster SP Cab Forward "4276," RailSounds, 06-07		850	___
11108	C&O F19 4-6-2 Pacific Locomotive "494," CC, 06-07		1160	___
11109	C&O 0-8-0 Locomotive "79," TrainSounds, 06		420	___
11110	NYC 0-8-0 Locomotive "7805," TrainSounds, 06		420	___
11114	NYC 4-8-2 Mohawk Locomotive "2795," CC, 06		1000	___
11116	UP 4-8-4 FEF-3 Locomotive "844," gray, CC, 08-09		1160	___
11117	Santa Fe E6 4-4-2 Atlantic Locomotive "1484," CC, 07-09		600	___
11119	Southern 0-8-0 Locomotive "6535," TrainSounds, 07	113	420	___
11122	UP Big Boy Locomotive "4024," CC, 06		1700	___
11123	UP Big Boy Locomotive "4023," CC, 06	433	1700	___
11126	UP Big Boy Locomotive "4012," CC, 06		1700	___
11127	SP GS-4 4-8-4 Northern Locomotive "4436," CC, 07-09		1200	___
11128	C&O F19 4-6-2 Pacific Locomotive "490," CC, 07		1160	___
11129	C&O 2-8-4 Berkshire Locomotive "2696," CC, 07		1160	___
11129	C&O 2-8-4 Berkshire Locomotive "2699," CC, 07-09		1200	___
11130	Postwar "736" 2-8-4 Berkshire Locomotive, 07		300	___
11131	UP 4-8-4 FEF-3 Locomotive "844," black, CC, 08-09	520	1160	___
11132	Reading 2-8-0 Consolidation Locomotive "1914," RailSounds, 08		450	___
11133	NYC 2-8-0 Consolidation Locomotive "1149," RailSounds, 08		450	___
11134	WM 2-8-0 Consolidation Locomotive "729," RailSounds, 08		450	___

	MODERN 1970-2025		Exc	Like New
___	**11135**	B&O 2-8-0 Consolidation Locomotive "2784," RailSounds, 08		450
___	**11136**	WP 2-8-2 Mikado Locomotive "322," CC, 08		800
___	**11137**	UP 2-8-2 Mikado Locomotive "1925," CC, 08		800
___	**11138**	ATSF 2-8-2 Mikado Locomotive "3156," CC, 08		800
___	**11139**	MILW 2-8-2 Mikado Locomotive "462," CC, 08		800
___	**11140**	Cass Scenic Shay Locomotive "7," CC, 07	238	800
___	**11141**	Birch Valley Lumber Shay Locomotive "5," CC, 07		800
___	**11142**	Hogwarts Express Add-on 2-pack, 09-10		120
___	**11143**	SP AC-4 Cab Forward Locomotive "4100," CC, 08		1670
___	**11145**	CNJ G3s 4-6-2 Pacific Locomotive "835," CC, 08		1290
___	**11145**	CNJ G3s 4-6-2 Pacific Locomotive "835," CC, 08		1290
___	**11146**	Pere Marquette 2-8-4 Berkshire Locomotive "1225," CC, 08		1290
___	**11147**	PRR 4-8-2 Mib Locomotive "6750," CC, 08		1290
___	**11148**	NYC Dreyfuss J-3a 4-6-4 Hudson Locomotive "5448," CC, 08		1130
___	**11149**	LionMaster UP Big Boy 4-8-8-4 Locomotive "4006," CC, 08		860
___	**11150**	NYC F-12e 4-6-0 10-wheel Locomotive "827," CC, 08	200	700
___	**11151**	Polar Express Tender, RailSounds, 08-10		440
___	**11152**	D&RGW LionMaster 4-6-6-4 Challenger Locomotive "3805," CC, 09		900
___	**11153**	Stourbridge Lion Steam Locomotive, 09-10		430
___	**11154**	PRR CC2s 0-8-8-0 Mallet Locomotive "8183," CC, 09-10		2000
___	**11155**	ATSF 2-10-10-2 Mallet Locomotive "3000," CC, 09-10		2500
___	**11156**	C&O 4-6-0 Ten-Wheeler Locomotive, CC, 10	213	740
___	**11157**	WM Shay Locomotive "6," CC, 10		800
___	**11162**	Lone Ranger Add-on 3-pack, 10		165
___	**11164**	Dewitt Clinton Passenger Set, 10		630
___	**11165**	Dewitt Clinton Add-on Coach, 10		70
___	**11166**	CSX Merger Freight 2-pack #1, 10-11		130
___	**11167**	CSX Merger Freight 2-pack #2, 10-11		105
___	**11168**	CSX Merger Freight 2-pack #3, 10-11		130
___	**11169**	Strasburg Freight Add-on 2-pack, 10		100
___	**11170**	Three Rivers Fast Freight Set, 10-12		400
___	**11172**	Santa Fe 4-4-2 Steam Freight Set, 13		200
___	**11173**	Texan Freight Add-on 2-pack, 10-11		130
___	**11174**	Maple Leaf Freight Add-on 2-pack, 10-11		110
___	**11175**	Operation Eagle Justice Add-on 2-pack, 10-11		125
___	**11180**	Motor City Express Diesel Freight Train Set, CC, 12-13		1175
___	**11181**	CN GP9 Diesel Piggyback Train Set, CC, 12		850
___	**11182**	Dixie Special FT Diesel Freight Set, 11		700
___	**11183**	Lincoln Funeral Train, 13		1140
___	**11194**	Texas Special Diesel Passenger Set, CC, 13-14		1110
___	**11195**	PRR Diesel Passenger Set, CC, 13-14		1110
___	**11196**	BNSF Gondola "670591," 13		35
___	**11197**	ATSF Caboose "999471," 13		48
___	**11199**	UP NW2 Diesel Switcher Work Train Set, CC, 12		600
___	**11200**	UP LionMaster Challenger Locomotive "3985," CC, 10		900
___	**11201**	WM LionMaster Challenger Locomotive "1204," CC, 10		900
___	**11202**	CP 4-6-0 Ten-Wheeler Locomotive "914," CC, 10	200	740
___	**11203**	Pere Marquette Berkshire Locomotive "1225," CC, 09		980
___	**11204**	Pere Marquette Tender, RailSounds, 09-10		440
___	**11206**	DeWitt Clinton Locomotive and Tender, 11		800
___	**11207**	PRR LionMaster T1 Duplex Locomotive "5511," CC, 10		800

MODERN 1970-2025		Exc	Like New	
11208	UP LionMaster Big Boy Locomotive "4011," CC, 10		900	___
11209	Vision NYC Hudson Locomotive "5344," CC, 10	550	1600	___
11210	UP Challenger Locomotive "3967," CC, 10		1825	___
11211	UP 4-6-6-4 Challenger Locomotive "3976," CC, 10		1825	___
11212	NKP Berkshire Locomotive "765," CC, 10		1350	___
11215	LV 4-6-0 Camelback Locomotive "1598," CC, 10		550	___
11216	Jersey Central 4-6-0 Camelback Locomotive, CC, 10		550	___
11217	PRR 4-6-0 Camelback Locomotive "822," CC, 10		550	___
11218	Vision NYC Hudson Locomotive "5331," CC, 10		1600	___
11219	Clinchfield Challenger Locomotive "672," CC, 10		1825	___
11220	UP Challenger Locomotive "3989," CC, 10		1825	___
11221	UP Challenger Locomotive "3983," CC, 10		1825	___
11224	PRR Atlantic Locomotive "460," CC, 10-11		700	___
11225	B&O Atlantic Locomotive "1440," CC		700	___
11226	UP Water Tender, black, CC, 11		300	___
11227	UP Water Tender, gray, CC, 11		300	___
11228	Clinchfield Water Tender, CC, 11		300	___
11229	MILW 4-8-4 Northern Locomotive "261," CC, 11		995	___
11230	MILW 4-8-4 Northern Locomotive "267," CC, 11		995	___
11232	Reading Atlantic Locomotive "351," CC, 11		700	___
11233	Pennsylvania Power & Light 2-Truck Shay Locomotive, CC, 11	263	900	___
11234	Pennsylvania Power & Light 2-Truck Shay Locomotive, 11		750	___
11235	West Side Lumber 2-Truck Shay Steam Locomotive, CC, 11		900	___
11236	West Side Lumber 2-Truck Shay Steam Locomotive, 11		750	___
11237	Sugar Pine Lumber Shay Locomotive "4," CC, 11		900	___
11238	Sugar Pine Lumber Shay Locomotive "5", 11		750	___
11239	Merrill & Ring Lumber 2-Truck Shay Steam Locomotive, CC, 11		900	___
11240	Merrill & Ring Lumber 2-Truck Shay Steam Locomotive, 11		750	___
11247	Erie USRA 0-8-0 Steam Switcher "121," CC, 11-12		700	___
11248	Erie USRA 0-8-0 Steam Switcher "127," 11-12		550	___
11249	L&N USRA 0-8-0 Steam Switcher "2119," CC, 11-12		700	___
11250	L&N USRA 0-8-0 Steam Switcher "2121," 11-12	55	550	___
11251	Pere Marquette USRA 0-8-0 Steam Switcher "1300," CC, 11-12		700	___
11252	Pere Marquette USRA 0-8-0 Steam Switcher "1307," 11-12		550	___
11253	NH 0-8-0 Steam Switcher "3603," CC, 11-13		700	___
11254	NH 0-8-0 Steam Switcher "3606," 11-13		550	___
11255	C&O 2-8-2 Mikado Steam Locomotive "1062," CC, 12		900	___
11256	NH 2-8-2 Mikado Steam Locomotive "3021," CC, 12		900	___
11257	PRR 2-8-2 Mikado Steam Locomotive "8631," CC, 12	138	900	___
11258	Southern 2-8-2 Mikado Steam Locomotive "4501," CC, 12		900	___
11259	UP 2-8-2 Mikado Steam Locomotive "2840," CC, 12		900	___
11260	Rio Grande 2-8-2 Mikado Steam Locomotive "1207," CC, 12		900	___
11261	DM&I 2-8-2 Mikado Steam Locomotive "1305," CC, 12		900	___
11262	Erie 2-8-2 Mikado Steam Locomotive "3007," CC, 12	263	900	___
11264	PRR K4 4-6-2 Pacific Steam Locomotive "1361," CC, 11		900	___
11265	PRR K4 4-6-2 Pacific Steam Locomotive "1330," CC, 11		900	___
11266	PRR K4 4-6-2 Pacific Locomotive "1361," 11		750	___
11267	Undecorated S-3 4-8-4 Northern Locomotive, CC, 11		995	___
11268	Strasburg 2-6-0 Mogul Steam Locomotive "89," 11		550	___
11269	RI 2-6-0 Mogul Steam Locomotive "750," 11-13		550	___
11270	GN 2-6-0 Mogul Steam Locomotive "453," 11		550	___
11271	C&O 2-6-0 Mogul Steam Locomotive "49," 11-12		550	___

			Exc	Like New
___	**11272**	ATSF 2-6-0 Mogul Steam Locomotive "573," 11		550
___	**11273**	Central Pacific 2-6-0 Mogul Locomotive "1470,"11-13		550
___	**11274**	MKT USRA 0-8-0 Steam Switcher "46," CC, 11-12		700
___	**11275**	MKT 0-8-0 Steam Switcher "51," CC, 11		550
___	**11276**	Lionelville & Western 0-8-0 Steam Switcher "1," CC, 11-13		700
___	**11277**	Lionelville & Western 0-8-0 Steam Switcher "2," 11-13		550
___	**11278**	WP 2-8-2 Mikado Steam Locomotive "322," CC, 11		900
___	**11279**	WP 2-8-2 Mikado Steam Locomotive "327," 11		750
___	**11280**	B&O 2-8-2 Mikado Steam Locomotive "4507," CC, 11	195	900
___	**11281**	B&O 2-8-2 Mikado Steam Locomotive "451," 11		750
___	**11282**	GN 2-8-2 Mikado Locomotive "3125," CC, 11		900
___	**11283**	GN 2i-8-2 Mikado Locomotive "3130," traditional, 11		750
___	**11284**	MP 2-8-2 Mikado Locomotive "1310," CC, 11		900
___	**11285**	MP 2-8-2 Mikado Locomotive "1312," traditional, 11		750
___	**11286**	RI 2-8-2 Mikado Steam Locomotive "2302," CC, 11		900
___	**11287**	RI 2-8-2 Mikado Steam Locomotive "2305," 11		750
___	**11288**	T&P 2-8-2 Mikado Steam Locomotive "552," CC, 11		900
___	**11289**	T&P 2-8-2 Mikado Steam Locomotive "557," 11		750
___	**11290**	Bethlehem Steel 2-6-0 Mogul Steam Locomotive "28," 11		550
___	**11291**	Weyerhaeuser 2-6-0 Mogul Locomotive "288," 11-13		550
___	**11292**	Nashville 4-4-0 General Locomotive, 13		500
___	**11295**	Elk River Lumber 2-Truck Shay Locomotive "1," CC, 11		900
___	**11296**	Elk River Lumber 2-Truck Shay Locomotive "2", 11		750
___	**11297**	P. Bunyan Lumber 2-Truck Shay Locomotive "18," CC, 11		900
___	**11298**	P. Bunyan Lumber 2-Truck Shay Locomotive "23," 11		750
___	**11299**	C&O 2-6-6-2 Mallet Steam Locomotive "875," CC, 12		1300
___	**11300**	PRR 2-10-4 Texas Steam Locomotive "6479," CC, 11		1300
___	**11301**	PRR 2-10-4 Texas Steam Locomotive "6498," CC, 11		1300
___	**11303**	C&O 2-10-4 Texas Steam Locomotive "3011," CC, 11		1300
___	**11304**	C&O 2-10-4 Texas Steam Locomotive "3025," CC, 11		1300
___	**11306**	NKP 2-10-4 Texas Steam Locomotive "801," CC, 11		1300
___	**11308**	Erie 2-10-4 Texas Steam Locomotive "3405," CC, 11		1300
___	**11310**	Pere Marquette 2-10-4 Texas Locomotive "1241," CC, 11		1300
___	**11312**	MILW S3 4-8-4 Northern Steam Locomotive "265," CC, 11		995
___	**11315**	Pennsylvania-Reading Seashore Atlantic Locomotive, 11		550
___	**11316**	PRR 4-4-2 Atlantic Steam Locomotive "272," 11		550
___	**11317**	Southern 4-4-2 Atlantic Steam Locomotive "1910," 11		550
___	**11318**	CN 4-4-2 Atlantic Steam Locomotive "1630," 11		550
___	**11319**	PRR K4 4-6-2 Pacific Locomotive "5409," 13		900
___	**11320**	PRR K4 4-6-2 Pacific Locomotive, "5436," 13		750
___	**11321**	C&O 2-6-6-2 Mallet Steam Locomotive "1525," CC, 12		1300
___	**11322**	NKP 2-6-6-2 Mallet Steam Locomotive "943," CC, 12		1300
___	**11323**	W&LE 2-6-6-2 Mallet Steam Locomotive "8002," CC, 12		1300
___	**11327**	PRR Prewar K4 4-6-2 Pacific Locomotive "3667," CC, 11		900
___	**11328**	PRR Prewar K4 4-6-2 Pacific Locomotive "3672," CC, 11		900
___	**11329**	PRR Prewar K4 4-6-2 Pacific Locomotive "3678," 11	113	750
___	**11330**	Polar K4 4-6-2 Pacific Locomotive, CC, 11-14		900
___	**11331**	Polar K4 4-6-2 Pacific Locomotive, 11		750
___	**11332**	ATSF 4-8-4 Northern Steam Locomotive "3751," CC, 12	432	1300
___	**11333**	ATSF 4-8-4 Northern Steam Locomotive "3759," CC, 12		1300
___	**11334**	Southern Crescent Limited 4-6-2 Pacific Locomotive, CC, 12		1100
___	**11335**	Blue Comet 4-6-2 Pacific Locomotive "832," CC, 12		1100
___	**11336**	Undecorated EM-1 2-8-8-4 Pilot Locomotive, CC, 12		1300

MODERN 1970-2025		Exc	Like New	
11337	B&O 2-8-8-4 Steam Locomotive "7621," CC, 12		1300	____
11338	Alton Limited 4-6-2 Pacific Steam Locomotive "657," CC, 12		1100	____
11339	N&W 2-6-6-2 Mallet Steam Locomotive "1409," CC, 12		1300	____
11340	B&O 2-8-8-4 Steam Locomotive "659," CC, 12		1300	____
11341	Pilot 4-12-2 Locomotive, CC, 13		1300	____
11342	UP 4-12-2 Steam Locomotive "9004," CC, 12-13		1300	____
11343	UP 4-12-2 Steam Locomotive, black, "9000," CC, 12-13		1300	____
11344	UP 4-12-2 Steam Locomotive, greyhound, "9000," CC, 12		1300	____
11363	Cass Scenic RR 2-Truck Shay Steam Locomotive "3," CC, 12		900	____
11364	Meadow River 2-Truck Shay Locomotive "1," CC, 12-13		900	____
11365	Weyerhaeuser 2-Truck Shay Locomotive "3," CC, 12-13		900	____
11366	Pickering Lumber 2-Truck Shay Locomotive "3," CC, 12-13		900	____
11367	CP 2-Truck Shay Steam Locomotive "111," CC, 12-13		900	____
11368	WM 2-Truck Shay Steam Locomotive "2," CC, 12		900	____
11369	Bethlehem Steel 2-Truck Shay Locomotive "5," CC, 12-13		900	____
11374	DM&I 2-8-8-4 Steam Locomotive "223," CC, 12		1300	____
11375	WP 2-8-8-4 Steam Locomotive "258," CC, 12		1300	____
11376	NP 2-8-8-4 Steam Locomotive "5000," CC, 12		1300	____
11377	GN 2-8-8-4 Steam Locomotive "2060," CC, 12		1300	____
11379	PRR 0-4-0 Shifter Steam Locomotive "112," 12		450	____
11380	PRR 0-4-0 Shifter Steam Locomotive "94" , 12		450	____
11381	North Pole Central 0-4-0 Switcher (std O), 12		450	____
11382	Transylvania 0-4-0 Shifter Steam Locomotive "13," 12		450	____
11383	Bethlehem Steel 0-4-0 Shifter Steam Locomotive "134," 12		450	____
11384	ATSF 0-4-0 Shifter Steam Locomotive "2301," 13		450	____
11385	UP 0-4-0 Shifter Steam Locomotive "206," 13		450	____
11386	B&M 2-8-4 Berkshire Steam Locomotive "4018," CC, 12-13	225	1250	____
11387	ATSF 2-8-4 Berkshire Steam Locomotive "4199," CC, 12-13		1250	____
11388	SP 2-8-4 Berkshire Steam Locomotive "3505," CC, 12-13		1250	____
11389	B&A 2-8-4 Berkshire Steam Locomotive "1404," CC, 12-13		1250	____
11390	Lima Demonstrator 2-8-4 Berkshire "1," CC, 12-13		1250	____
11391	IC 2-8-4 Berkshire Steam Locomotive "7020," CC, 12-13		1250	____
11392	Michigan Central 2-8-4 Berkshire "1420," CC, 12-13		1250	____
11399	UP H7 Class 2-8-8-2 Steam Locomotive "3595," CC, 13-14		1350	____
11400	C&O H7 Class 2-8-8-2 Steam Locomotive "1578," CC, 13-14		1350	____
11401	Pilot H7 Class 2-8-8-2 Locomotive, CC, 14-15		1350	____
11402	Virginian USRA Y3 2-8-8-2 Locomotive, CC, 13-14		1350	____
11403	Pilot USRA 2-8-8-2 Locomotive, CC, 13-15		1350	____
11404	ATSF USRA Y3 2-8-8-2 Locomotive, CC, 13-14		1350	____
11405	N&W USRA Y3 2-8-8-2 Locomotive, CC, 13-14		1350	____
11410	Pilot 4-8-2 Mohawk Locomotive, CC, 13-15		1300	____
11411	NYC 4-8-2 Mohawk Locomotive "2854," CC, 12-13		1300	____
11412	NYC 4-8-2 Mohawk Locomotive "2867," CC, 12-13		1300	____
11413	Pilot 4-8-4 J-Class Locomotive, CC, 13-15		1300	____
11414	N&W 4-8-4 Steam Locomotive "612," CC, 12-13		1300	____
11415	Pilot S2 6-8-6 Turbine Locomotive, CC, 14-15		1300	____
11416	PRR S2 6-8-6 Steam Turbine Locomotive "6200," CC, 12-14		1300	____
11417	PRR S2 6-8-6 Steam Turbine Locomotive "6200," CC, 12-13		1300	____
11418	Pilot GS-6 Locomotive, CC, 13-14		1300	____
11419	SP 4-8-4 GS-2 Locomotive, black, CC, 12-13		1300	____
11420	SP 4-8-4 GS-2 Locomotive, Daylight, CC, 12		1300	____
11421	SP 4-8-4 GS-6 Locomotive, black, CC, 12		1300	____
11422	WP 4-8-4 GS-64 Locomotive "482," CC, 12		1300	____

MODERN 1970-2025		Exc	Like New
11423	CNJ Blue Comet Locomotive "833," CC, 12-13		1100
11425	Alaska 0-4-0 Locomotive, RailSounds, 12-13		1100
11426	Rio Grande 0-4-0 Locomotive, RailSounds, 12-13		450
11427	SP 0-4-0 Locomotive "14," RailSounds, 12-13		450
11428	MILW 0-4-0 Locomotive, RailSounds, 12-13		450
11429	Southern 0-4-0 Locomotive, RailSounds, 12-13		450
11430	GN 0-4-0 Locomotive "1066," RailSounds, 12-13		450
11431	N&W 4-8-4 Locomotive "611," CC, 12		1300
11432	LL S2 6-8-6 Steam Turbine Locomotive, CC, 13-14		1300
11433	PRR S2 6-8-6 Steam Turbine Locomotive CC, 13-14		1300
11434	UP Big Boy Locomotive "4006," CC, 14	1167	2700
11435	UP Big Boy Locomotive "4018," CC, 14		2700
11436	UP Big Boy Locomotive "4005," CC, 14		2700
11437	UP Big Boy Locomotive "4014," CC, 14		2992
11438	UP Big Boy Locomotive "4017," CC, 14		2700
11446	UP USRA Y3 2-8-8-2 Locomotive "3671," CC, 13-14		1350
11447	PRR USRA Y3 2-8-8-2 Locomotive "376," CC, 13-14		1350
11448	UP Big Boy Locomotive "4012," CC, 14		2700
11449	UP Big Boy Locomotive "4004," CC, 14		2700
11450	Polar Express Berkshire Scale Locomotive, gold, CC, 14		1500
11451	Polar Express Berkshire Scale Locomotive, black, CC, 14	1000	1835
11452	C&O 2-8-4 Berkshire Locomotive "2687," CC, 14		1500
11453	Erie 2-8-4 Berkshire Locomotive "3321," CC, 14		1500
11454	NKP 2-8-4 Berkshire Locomotive "765," CC, 14		1500
11455	Pere Marquette 2-8-4 Berkshire Locomotive "1225," CC, 14		1500
11456	Pere Marquette 2-8-4 Berkshire Locomotive "1227," CC, 14		1500
11462	SP AC-12 Cab-Forward Locomotive "4291," CC, 14		1700
11463	SP AC-12 Cab-Forward Locomotive "4286," CC, 14		1700
11464	SP AC-12 Cab-Forward Locomotive "4294," CC, 14		1700
11465	SP AC-12 Cab-Forward Locomotive "4275," CC, 14		1700
11469	Pilot AC-12 Cab-Forward Locomotive, CC, 14-15		1700
11528	Frosty the Snowman Figure Pack, 14, 16		30
11650	Alderney Dairy General American Milk Car 2-pack (std O), 07		130
11651	Freeport General American Milk Car 2-pack (std O), 07		130
11652	BNSF Mechanical Reefer 2-pack (std O), 07-09		140
11653	SPFE Mechanical Reefer 2-pack (std O), 07		140
11654	UPFE Mechanical Reefer 2-pack (std O), 07		140
11655	GN WFE Mechanical Reefer 2-pack (std O), 07		140
11657	PFE Wood-sided Reefer 3-pack (std O), 06		190
11658	John Bull Add-on Coach, 08		80
11700	Conrail Limited Set, 87	203	370
11701	Rail Blazer Set, 87-88	30	114
11702	Black Diamond Set, 87	168	265
11703	Iron Horse Freight Set, 88-91	100	105
11704	Southern Freight Runner Set (SSS), 87	150	285
11705	Chessie System Unit Train, 88	218	450
11706	Dry Gulch Line Set (SSS), 88	195	260
11707	Silver Spike Set, 88-89	175	245
11708	Midnight Shift Set, 88 u, 89	60	83
11710	CP Rail Freight Set, 89	321	415
11711	Santa Fe F3 Diesel ABA Set, 91	330	745
11712	Great Lakes Express Set (SSS), 90	205	340
11713	Santa Fe Dash 8-40B Set, 90	235	480

MODERN 1970-2025		Exc	Like New	
11714	Badlands Express Set, 90-91	49	60	___
11715	Lionel 90th Anniversary Set, 90	163	378	___
11716	Lionelville Circus Special Set, 90-91	155	190	___
11717	CSX Freight Set, 90	230	240	___
11718	Norfolk Southern Dash 8-40C Unit Train, 92	294	481	___
11719	Coastal Freight Set (SSS), 91	165	215	___
11720	Santa Fe Special Set, 91	49	60	___
11721	Mickey's World Tour Train Set, 91, 92 u	105	154	___
11722	Girls Train Set, 91	659	903	___
11723	Amtrak Maintenance Train, 91, 92 u	210	245	___
11724	GN F3 Diesel ABA Set, 92	383	840	___
11726	Erie-Lackawanna Freight Set, 91 u	225	275	___
11727	Coastal Limited Set, 92	90	110	___
11728	High Plains Runner Set, 92	120	130	___
11733	Feather River Set (SSS), 92	210	330	___
11734	Erie Alco Diesel ABA Set (FF 7), 93	225	305	___
11735	NYC Flyer Freight Set "1735WS," 93-99	99	160	___
11736	Union Pacific Express Set, 93-95	110	130	___
11738	Soo Line Set (SSS), 93	205	280	___
11739	Super Chief Set, 93-94	138	165	___
11740	Conrail Consolidated Set, 93	200	240	___
11741	Northwest Express Set, 93	130	155	___
11742	Coastal Limited Set, 93 u	90	115	___
11743	Chesapeake & Ohio Freight Set, 94	240	280	___
11744	NYC Passenger/Freight Set (SSS), 94	196	335	___
11745	U.S. Navy Set, 94-95	164	248	___
11746	Seaboard Freight Set, 94, 95 u	90	183	___
11747	Lionel Lines Steam Set, 95	310	340	___
11748	Amtrak Alco Diesel Passenger Set, 95-96	145	235	___
11749	Western Maryland Set (SSS), 95	167	300	___
11750	McDonald's Nickel Plate Special Set, 87 u	143	153	___
11751	Sears PRR Passenger Set, 87 u	120	155	___
11752	JCPenney Timber Master Set, 87 u	75	115	___
11753	Kay Bee Toys Rail Blazer Set, 87 u	80	100	___
11754	Key America Set, 87 u	150	165	___
11755	Timber Master Set, 87 u	150	165	___
11756	Hawthorne Freight Flyer Set, 87-88 u	65	85	___
11757	Chrysler Mopar Express Set, 88 u	327	387	___
11758	Desert King Set (SSS), 89	158	250	___
11759	JCPenney Silver Spike Set, 88 u	175	250	___
11761	JCPenney Iron Horse Freight Set, 88 u	120	125	___
11762	True Value Cannonball Express Set, 89 u	95	145	___
11763	United Model Freight Hauler Set, 88 u	135	145	___
11764	Sears Iron Horse Freight Set, 88 u	155	190	___
11765	Spiegel Silver Spike Set, 88 u	175	250	___
11767	Shoprite Freight Flyer Set, 88 u	80	125	___
11769	JCPenney Midnight Shift Set, 89 u	100	175	___
11770	Sears Circus Set, 89 u	185	220	___
11771	K-Mart Microracers Set, 89 u	80	110	___
11772	Macy's Freight Flyer Set, 89 u	170	220	___
11773	Sears NYC Passenger Set, 89 u	175	200	___
11774	Ace Hardware Cannonball Express Set, 89 u	145	175	___
11775	Anheuser-Busch Set, 89-92 u	261	355	___

			Exc	Like New
___	**11776**	Pace Iron Horse Freight Set, 89 u	115	135
___	**11777**	Sears Lionelville Circus Set, 90 u	175	190
___	**11778**	Sears Badlands Express Set, 90 u	49	60
___	**11779**	Sears CSX Freight Set, 90 u	190	230
___	**11780**	Sears NP Passenger Set, 90 u	155	190
___	**11781**	True Value Cannonball Express Set, 90 u	75	115
___	**11783**	Toys 'R' Us Heavy Iron Set, 90-91 u	138	165
___	**11784**	Pace Iron Horse Freight Set, 90 u	115	135
___	**11785**	Costco Union Pacific Express Set, 90 u	200	230
___	**11789**	Sears Illinois Central Passenger Set, 91 u	170	200
___	**11793**	Santa Fe Set, 91 u	49	60
___	**11794**	Mickey's World Tour Set, 91 u	80	100
___	**11796**	Union Pacific Express Set, 91 u	150	160
___	**11797**	Sears Coastal Limited Set, 92 u	80	100
___	**11800**	Toys 'R' Us Heavy Iron Thunder Limited Set, 92-93 u	238	298
___	**11803**	Nickel Plate Special Set, 92 u	135	145
___	**11804**	K-Mart Coastal Limited Set, 92 u	80	100
___	**11809**	Village Trolley Set, 95-97	55	85
___	**11810**	Budweiser Modern Era Set, 93-94 u	220	231
___	**11811**	United Auto Workers Set, 93 u	189	447
___	**11812**	Coastal Limited Special Set, 93 u	95	115
___	**11813**	Crayola Activity Train Set, 94 u, 95	117	153
___	**11814**	Ford Limited Edition Set, 94 u	196	266
___	**11818**	Chrysler Mopar Set, 94 u	173	268
___	**11819**	Georgia Power Set, 95 u	540	563
___	**11820**	Red Wing Shoes NYC Flyer Set, 95 u	264	324
___	**11821**	Sears Zenith Set, 95 u	368	807
___	**11822**	Chevrolet Set, 96 u	287	337
___	**11825**	Bloomingdale's Set, 96 u	150	333
___	**11826**	Sears NYC Zenith Express Freight Set, 95-96 u	380	776
___	**11827**	Zenith Employees Set, 96 u	340	823
___	**11828**	NJ Transit Passenger Set, 96 u	70	180
___	**11833**	NJ Transit GP38 Diesel Passenger Set, 97	275	300
___	**11837**	Union Pacific GP9 Diesel Set, 97	113	520
___	**11838**	ATSF Warhorse Hudson Freight Set, 97	449	810
___	**11839**	SP&S 4-6-2 Steam Freight Set, 97	95	280
___	**11841**	Bloomingdale's Set, 97 u	157	332
___	**11843**	Boston & Maine GP9 Diesel ABA Set, 98		510
___	**11844**	Union Pacific Die-cast Ore Cars 4-pack, 98		225
___	**11846**	Kal Kan Pet Care Train Set, 97 u	271	879
___	**11849**	Lionel Centennial Series Reefer 4-pack, 98	80	123
___	**11850**	Rice A Roni Trolley Set, 02 u		271
___	**11851**	PFE Reefer 6-pack (std 0), 02	225	255
___	**11852**	Clinchfield PS-2 2-bay Hopper, 04		70
___	**11853**	B&M PS-2 2-bay Hopper 2-pack, 05		128
___	**11854**	N&W PS-2 Covered Hopper 2-pack, 04		70
___	**11855**	GN Offset Hopper with coal, 2-pack, 05		120
___	**11856**	Green Bay & Western Offset Hopper 2-pack, 05		120
___	**11857**	Baltimore & Ohio Offset Hopper 2-pack, 05		120
___	**11858**	PRR PS-4 Flatcar with trailers, 2-pack (std 0), 05		160
___	**11859**	GN PS-4 Flatcar with trailers (std 0), 05		160
___	**11860**	SP PS-4 Flatcar with trailers (std 0), 05		160
___	**11861**	C&O PS-4 Flatcar with trailers (std 0), 05		160

MODERN 1970-2025		Exc	Like New	
11863	Southern Pacific GP9 Diesel "2383," 98	59	225	___
11864	New York Central GP9 Diesel "2383," 98		275	___
11865	Alaska GP7 Diesel "1802," 98-99		90	___
11866	Govt. of Canada Cylindrical Hopper 2-pack (std O), 05		120	___
11867	CN Cylindrical Hopper 2-pack (std O), 05		120	___
11868	BN Husky Stack Car 2-pack (std O), 05		160	___
11869	SP Husky Stack Car 2-pack (std O), 05		160	___
11870	CSX Husky Stack Car 2-pack (std O), 05		220	___
11871	TTX Trailer Train Stack Car 2-pack (std O), 05		160	___
11872	PFE Orange Steel-sided Reefer 3-pack (std O), 05		130	___
11873	C&O Offset Hopper 3-pack (std O), 05		130	___
11874	PFE Orange Steel-sided Reefer 3-pack (std O), 05		130	___
11875	NP Steel-sided Reefer 3-pack (std O), 05	68	131	___
11876	PFE Silver Steel-sided Reefer 3-pack (std O), 05		165	___
11877	C&NW Steel-sided Reefer 3-pack (std O), 05		130	___
11878	Santa Fe PS-2 2-bay Covered Hopper 3-pack (std O), 06		125	___
11879	MKT PS-2 2-bay Covered Hopper 3-pack (std O), 06		125	___
11880	Boraxo PS-2 2-bay Covered Hopper 3-pack (std O), 06		125	___
11881	PRR PS-2 2-bay Covered Hopper 3-pack (std O), 06		125	___
11882	RI Offset Hopper with gravel, 3-pack (std O), 06		125	___
11883	CNJ Offset Hopper 3-pack (std O), 06		145	___
11884	Maine Central Offset Hopper 3-pack (std O), 06		145	___
11891	Pennsylvania 3-bay Hopper 3-pack (std O), 06		155	___
11892	Conrail ACF 3-bay Hopper 3-pack (std O), 06		155	___
11893	N&W 3-bay Hopper 3-pack (std O), 06		155	___
11894	UP 3-bay Hopper 3-pack (std O), 06		155	___
11895	GN Steel-sided Reefer 3-pack (std O), 06		145	___
11896	Santa Fe Steel-sided Reefer 3-pack (std O), 06		145	___
11897	Pepper Packing Steel-sided Reefer 3-pack (std O), 06		145	___
11900	SF Steam Freight Set, 96-01		130	___
11903	ACL F3 Diesel ABA Set, 96	225	716	___
11905	U.S. Coast Guard Set, 96	149	205	___
11906	Factory Selection Special Set, 95 u	43	93	___
11909	N&W J 4-8-4 Warhorse Set, 96	358	720	___
11910	Lionel Lines Set (027), 96	100	160	___
11912	"57" Switcher Service Exclusive, 96	129	310	___
11913	SP GP9 Diesel Freight Set, 97	100	440	___
11914	NYC GP9 Diesel Freight Set, 97		370	___
11918	Conrail SD20 Service Exclusive "X1144" (SSS), 97	142	255	___
11919	Docksider Set, 97		70	___
11920	Port of Lionel City Dive Team Set, 97		185	___
11921	Lionel Lines Freight Set, 97		130	___
11929	ATSF Warbonnet Passenger Set, 97-99		132	___
11930	ATSF Warbonnet Passenger Car 2-pack, 97-99		80	___
11931	Chessie Flyer Freight Set "1931S," 97-99	105	185	___
11933	Dodge Motorsports Freight Set, 96 u	189	323	___
11934	Virginian Electric Locomotive Freight Set, 97-99		260	___
11935	NYC Flyer Freight Set, 97		155	___
11936	Little League Baseball Steam Set, 97	250	321	___
11939	SP&S 4-6-2 Steam Freight Set, 97		220	___
11940	Southern Pacific SD40 Warhorse Coal Set, 98		600	___
11944	Lionel Lines 4-4-2 Steam Freight Set, 98		175	___
11956	UP GP9 Diesel Set, 97	330	380	___

		MODERN 1970-2025	Exc	Like New
___	**11957**	Mobil Oil Steam Special Set, 97	100	458
___	**11971**	D&H 4-4-2 Steam Freight Set, 98	125	155
___	**11972**	Alaska GP7 Diesel Set, 98-99	165	215
___	**11974**	Station Accessory Set, 98		22
___	**11975**	Freight Accessory Pack, 98		23
___	**11977**	NP Freight Cars 4-pack, 98	60	185
___	**11979**	N&W 4-4-2 Steam Freight Set, 98	38	120
___	**11981**	1998 Holiday Trolley Set, 98		75
___	**11982**	New Jersey Transit Ore Car Set, 98		250
___	**11983**	Farmrail GP7 Agricultural Freight Set, 99	195	493
___	**11984**	Corvette GP7 Diesel Set, 99	254	424
___	**11988**	NYC Firecar "18444" and Instruction Car "19853," 99		210
___	**12000**	NY Yankees Berkshire Passenger Set, 13		380
___	**12004**	Philadelphia Phillies Berkshire Passenger Set, 13	188	388
___	**12008**	Boston Red Sox Berkshire Passenger Set , 13		380
___	**12012**	Chicago Cubs Berkshire Passenger Set, 13	175	380
___	**12013**	NY Mets and Yankees Subway Series Set, 13		400
___	**12014**	FasTrack 10" Straight Track, 03-25		6
___	**12015**	FasTrack 036 Curved Track, 03-25		6
___	**12016**	FasTrack 10" Terminal Track, 03-25		10
___	**12017**	FasTrack 036 Manual Switch, left hand, 03-25		55
___	**12018**	FasTrack 036 Manual Switch, right-hand, 03-25		55
___	**12019**	FasTrack 90-degree Crossover, 03-25		29
___	**12020**	FasTrack 5" Uncoupling Track, 03-25		46
___	**12022**	FasTrack 036 Half Curved Track, 03-25		5
___	**12023**	FasTrack 036 Quarter Curved Track, 03-25		5
___	**12024**	FasTrack 5" Straight Track, 03-24		5
___	**12025**	FasTrack 4½" Straight Track, 03-25		5
___	**12026**	FasTrack 1¾" Straight Track, 03-25		5
___	**12027**	FasTrack 10" Insulated Track Accessory Activation Extender, 03-25		5
___	**12028**	FasTrack Inner Passing Loop Track Pack, 03-25		127
___	**12029**	FasTrack Accessory Activator Pack, 03-25		23
___	**12030**	FasTrack Figure 8 Track Pack, 03-25		83
___	**12031**	FasTrack Outer Passing Loop Track Pack, 03-25	63	160
___	**12032**	FasTrack 10" Straight Track,4-pack, 03-25		25
___	**12033**	FasTrack 036 Curved Track, 4-pack, 03-25		25
___	**12035**	FasTrack Lighted Bumper, 2-pack, 05-25		37
___	**12036**	FasTrack 10" Grade Crossing, 2-pack, 05-25		22
___	**12037**	FasTrack Graduated Trestle Set, 05-25		94
___	**12038**	FasTrack Elevated Trestle Set, 05-25		50
___	**12039**	FasTrack Railer, 04-25		11
___	**12040**	FasTrack 5" O Gauge Transition Piece, 04-25		11
___	**12041**	FasTrack 072 Curved Track, 04-25		8
___	**12042**	FasTrack 30" Straight Track, 04-25		19
___	**12043**	FasTrack 048 Curved Track, 04-25		7
___	**12044**	FasTrack Siding Track Add-on Track Pack, 04-25		132
___	**12045**	036 Remote Switch, left hand (FasTrack), 04-17		95
___	**12046**	036 Remote Switch, right hand (FasTrack), 04-17		95
___	**12047**	072 Wye Remote Switch (FasTrack), 04-14		97
___	**12048**	072 Remote Switch, left hand (FasTrack), 04-14		104
___	**12049**	072 Remote Switch, right hand (FasTrack), 04-14		104
___	**12050**	FasTrack 22.5-degree Crossover, 04-25		55

MODERN 1970-2025		Exc	Like New	
12051	FasTrack 45-degree Crossover, 04-25		33	____
12052	FasTrack Grade Crossing w/Flashers, 05-25	45	110	____
12053	FasTrack Accessory Power Wire, 04-25		4	____
12054	FasTrack 10" Straight Uncoupling Track, 05-25		50	____
12055	FasTrack 072 Half Curved Track , 04-25		7	____
12056	FasTrack 060 Curved Track, 05-25		8	____
12057	060 Remote Switch, left hand, 05-14		110	____
12058	060 Remote Switch, right hand (FasTrack), 05-14		110	____
12059	FasTrack Earthen Bumper, 04-25		15	____
12060	FasTrack 5" Insulated Block Section, 05-25		13	____
12061	FasTrack 084 Curved Track, 05-25		8	____
12062	FasTrack Grade Crossing w/Gates and Flashers, 06-24		187	____
12065	048 Remote Switch, left hand (FasTrack), 07-14		104	____
12066	048 Remote Switch, right hand (FasTrack), 07-14		104	____
12073	FasTrack 1 3/8" Track Section, 07-25		5	____
12074	FasTrack 1 3/8" Track Section, no roadbed, 07-25		5	____
12080	42" Path Remote Switch, right hand, 07-12		80	____
12081	42" Path Remote Switch, left hand, 07-12		80	____
12700	Erie Magnetic Gantry Crane, 87	125	150	____
12701	Operating Fueling Station, 87	60	74	____
12702	Control Tower, 87	60	75	____
12703	Icing Station, 88-89	60	65	____
12704	Dwarf Signal, 88-93	9	11	____
12705	Lumber Shed Kit, 88-99		9	____
12706	Barrel Loader Building Kit, 87-99		10	____
12707	Billboards, set of 3, 87-99		5	____
12708	Street Lamps, set of 3, 88-93	6	9	____
12709	Banjo Signal, 87-91, 95-00		29	____
12710	Engine House Kit, 87-91	21	25	____
12711	Water Tower Kit, 87-99		13	____
12712	Automatic Ore Loader, 87-88	17	21	____
12713	Automatic Gateman, 87-88, 94-00	30	40	____
12714	No. 252 Automatic Crossing Gate, 87-25		55	____
12715	Illuminated Bumpers, set of 2, 87-15		18	____
12716	Searchlight Tower, 87-89, 91-92	15	22	____
12717	Nonilluminated Bumpers, set of 3, 87-17		7	____
12718	Barrel Shed Kit, 87-99		10	____
12719	Animated Refreshment Stand, 88-89	65	70	____
12720	Rotary Beacon, 88-89	40	45	____
12721	Illuminated Extension Bridge, rock piers, 89	26	38	____
12722	Roadside Diner, smoke, 88-89	27	38	____
12723	Microwave Tower, 88-91, 94-95	14	19	____
12724	Double Signal Bridge, 88-90	39	50	____
12725	Lionel Tractor and Trailer, 88-89	10	18	____
12726	Grain Elevator Kit, 88-91, 94-99		31	____
12727	Operating Semaphore, 89-99		26	____
12728	Illuminated Freight Station, 89	29	38	____
12729	Mail Pickup Set, 88-91, 95	12	16	____
12730	Lionel Girder Bridge, 88-03, 08-25		21	____
12731	Station Platform, 88-00		8	____
12732	Coal Bag, 88-25		8	____
12733	Watchman Shanty Kit, 88-99		5	____
12734	Passenger/Freight Station Kit, 89-99	18	41	____

MODERN 1970-2025			Exc	Like New
____	**12735**	Diesel Horn Shed, 88-91	22	30
____	**12736**	Coaling Station Kit, 88-91	21	31
____	**12737**	Whistling Freight Shed, 88-99	12	32
____	**12739**	Lionel Gas Company Tractor and Tanker, 89	20	25
____	**12740**	Genuine Wood Logs, set of 3, 88-92, 94-95, 97-99		5
____	**12741**	Union Pacific Intermodal Crane, 89	138	185
____	**12742**	Gooseneck Lamps, set of 2, 89-00		21
____	**12743**	Track Clips, dozen (0), 89-16		12
____	**12744**	Rock Piers, set of 2, 89-25		19
____	**12745**	Barrel Pack, set of 6, 89-25		10
____	**12746**	Operating/Uncoupling Track (027), 89-16		10
____	**12748**	Illuminated Passenger Platform, 89-99		18
____	**12749**	Rotary Radar Antenna, 89-92, 95	28	38
____	**12750**	Crane Kit, 89-91	8	10
____	**12751**	Shovel Kit, 89-91	8	10
____	**12752**	History of Lionel Trains Video, 89-92, 94	19	21
____	**12753**	Ore Load, set of 2, 89-91, 95	1	2
____	**12754**	Graduated Trestle Set, 22 pieces, 89-15		27
____	**12755**	Elevated Trestle Set, 10 pieces, 89-15		34
____	**12756**	The Making of the Scale Hudson Video, 91-94	20	22
____	**12759**	Floodlight Tower, 90-00		25
____	**12760**	Automatic Highway Flasher, 90-91	23	27
____	**12761**	Animated Billboard, 90-91, 93, 95	12	23
____	**12763**	Single Signal Bridge, 90-91, 93	31	35
____	**12767**	Steam Clean and Wheel Grind Shop, 92-93, 95	240	290
____	**12768**	Burning Switch Tower, 90, 93	85	94
____	**12770**	Arch-Under Bridge, 90-03, 08-25		30
____	**12771**	Mom's Roadside Diner, smoke, 90-91	40	68
____	**12772**	Truss Bridge, flasher and piers, 90-16, 18, 20		70
____	**12773**	Freight Platform Kit, 90-98		32
____	**12774**	Lumber Loader Kit, 90-99		19
____	**12777**	Chevron Tractor and Tanker, 90-91	9	15
____	**12778**	Conrail Tractor and Trailer, 90	9	16
____	**12779**	Lionelville Grain Company Tractor and Trailer, 90	11	19
____	**12780**	RS-1 50-watt Transformer, 90-93	95	130
____	**12781**	N&W Intermodal Crane, 90-91	133	160
____	**12782**	Lift Bridge, 91-92	263	518
____	**12783**	Monon Tractor and Trailer, 91	11	19
____	**12784**	Intermodal Containers, set of 3, 91	12	17
____	**12785**	Lionel Gravel Company Tractor and Trailer, 91	9	15
____	**12786**	Lionel Steel Company Tractor and Trailer, 91	10	16
____	**12791**	Animated Passenger Station, 91	45	60
____	**12794**	Lionel Tractor, 91	7	13
____	**12795**	Cable Reels, pair, 91-98	3	5
____	**12798**	Forklift Loader Station, 92-95	34	53
____	**12800**	Scale Hudson Replacement Pilot Truck, 91 u	13	17
____	**12802**	Chat & Chew Roadside Diner, smoke and lights, 92-95	41	50
____	**12804**	Highway Lights, 4-pack, 92-04, 13-25	9	35
____	**12805**	Intermodal Containers, set of 3, 92	10	14
____	**12806**	Lionel Lumber Company Tractor and Trailer, 92	10	15
____	**12807**	Little Caesars Tractor and Trailer, 92	9	14
____	**12808**	Mobil Tractor and Tanker, 92	8	13
____	**12809**	Animated Billboard, 92-93	12	22

MODERN 1970-2025		Exc	Like New	
12810	American Flyer Tractor and Trailer, 94	12	18	___
12811	Alka Seltzer Tractor and Trailer, 92	11	19	___
12812	Illuminated Freight Station, 93-00		27	___
12818	Animated Freight Station, 92, 94-95	50	60	___
12819	Inland Steel Tractor and Trailer, 92	9	16	___
12821	Lionel Catalog Video, 92	13	17	___
12826	Intermodal Containers, set of 3, 93	10	16	___
12831	Rotary Beacon, 93-95	20	41	___
12832	Block Target Signal, 93-98		25	___
12833	RoadRailer Tractor and Trailer, 93	9	15	___
12834	Pennsylvania Magnetic Gantry Crane, 93	130	170	___
12835	Operating Fueling Station, 93	55	60	___
12836	Santa Fe Quantum Tractor and Trailer, 93	8	14	___
12837	Humble Oil Tractor and Tanker, 93	9	16	___
12838	Crate Load, set of 2, 93-97		3	___
12839	Grade Crossings, set of 2, 93-16		7	___
12840	Insulated Straight Track (0), 93-16		8	___
12841	Insulated Straight Track (027), 93-16		5	___
12842	Dunkin' Donuts Tractor and Trailer, 92 u	13	25	___
12843	Die-cast Sprung Trucks, pair, 93-99		10	___
12844	Coil Covers, pair (0), 93-98		3	___
12847	Animated Ice Depot, 94-99		65	___
12848	Lionel Oil Company Derrick, 94	55	75	___
12849	Lionel Controller with wall pack, 94, 95 u	22	40	___
12852	Die-cast Intermodal Trailer Frame, 94-01		6	___
12853	Coil Covers, pair (std 0), 94-98		7	___
12854	U.S. Navy Tractor and Tanker, 94-95		33	___
12855	Intermodal Containers, set of 3, 94-95	9	13	___
12860	Lionel Visitor's Center Tractor and Trailer, 94 u	10	14	___
12861	Lionel Leasing Company Tractor, 94	8	13	___
12862	Oil Drum Loader, 94-95	75	85	___
12864	Little Caesars Tractor and Trailer, 94	8	14	___
12865	Wisk Tractor and Trailer, 94	12	55	___
12866	TMCC 135-watt PowerHouse Power Supply, 94 u, 95-03	15	46	___
12867	TMCC 135 PowerMaster Power Distribution Center, 94 u, 95-04		49	___
12868	TMCC CAB-1 Remote Controller, 94 u, 95-09		115	___
12869	Marathon Oil Tractor and Tanker, 94	15	22	___
12873	Operating Sawmill, 95-97	40	95	___
12874	Classic Street Lamps, set of 3, 94-00		13	___
12877	Operating Fueling Station, 95	75	85	___
12878	Control Tower, 95	49	60	___
12881	Chrysler Mopar Tractor and Trailer, 94 u	51	62	___
12882	Lighted Billboard, 95	9	14	___
12883	No. 148 Dwarf Signal, 95-24		30	___
12884	Truck Loading Dock Kit, 95-98		16	___
12885	40-watt Control System, 94 u, 95-05		35	___
12886	Floodlight Tower, 95-98		31	___
12888	No. 154 Railroad Crossing Flasher, 95-25		60	___
12889	Operating Windmill, 95-98	15	47	___
12890	Big Red Control Button, 94 u, 95-00		43	___
12891	Lionel Refrigerator Lines Tractor and Trailer, 95	12	16	___
12892	Automatic Flagman, 95-96		25	___

MODERN 1970-2025			Exc	Like New
____	12893	TMCC PowerMaster Adapter Cable, 94 u, 95-25		25
____	12894	Signal Bridge, 95-01		22
____	12895	Double-track Signal Bridge, 95-00	13	49
____	12896	Tunnel Portals, set of 2, 95-25		22
____	12897	Engine House Kit, 96-98		29
____	12898	Flagpole, 95-97		9
____	12899	Searchlight Tower, 95-98	10	25
____	12900	Crane Kit, 95-98		9
____	12901	Shovel Kit, 95-98		7
____	12902	Marathon Oil Derrick, 94 u, 95	109	161
____	12903	Diesel Horn Shed, 95-98		29
____	12904	Coaling Station Kit, 95-98		19
____	12905	Factory Kit, 95-98		20
____	12906	Maintenance Shed Kit, 95-98		20
____	12907	Intermodal Containers, set of 3, 95	9	14
____	12911	TMCC Command Base, 95-09		80
____	12912	Oil Pumping Station, 95-98	38	65
____	12914	SC-1 Switch and Accessory Controller, 95-98		35
____	12915	Log Loader, 96	40	120
____	12916	Water Tower, 96-97		56
____	12917	Animated Switch Tower, 96-98		29
____	12922	NYC Operating Gantry Crane, coil covers, 96	78	90
____	12923	Red Wing Shoes Tractor and Trailer, 95 u	34	38
____	12925	42" Diameter Curved Track Section (O), 96-16		4
____	12926	Black Globe Street Lamps, 3-pack, 96-03, 08-09, 16-24		30
____	12927	No. 65 Yard Light, 3-pack, 96-25		35
____	12929	Rail-truck Loading Dock, 96		44
____	12930	Lionelville Oil Company Derrick, 95 u, 96	55	75
____	12931	Electrical Substation, 96		22
____	12932	Laimbeer Packaging Tractor and Trailer Set, 96		14
____	12933	GM Parts Tractor and Trailer, 95	17	29
____	12935	Zenith Tractor and Trailer, 96		25
____	12936	SP Intermodal Crane, 97		195
____	12937	NS Intermodal Crane, 97		200
____	12938	PowerStation Controller/PowerHouse 135-watt Supply, 97-00		150
____	12943	Illuminated Station Platform, 97-00		24
____	12944	Sunoco Oil Derrick, 97		85
____	12945	Sunoco Pumping Oil Station, 97		80
____	12948	Bascule Bridge, 97	137	315
____	12949	Billboards, set of 3, 97-00		7
____	12951	Airplane Hangar Kit, 97-98		29
____	12952	Big L Diner Kit, 97		24
____	12953	Linex Gas Tall Oil Tank, 97		9
____	12954	Linex Gas Wide Oil Tank, 97		10
____	12955	Road Runner and Wile E. Coyote Ambush Shack, 97		100
____	12958	Industrial Water Tower, 97-98		53
____	12960	Rotary Radar Antenna, 97		26
____	12961	Newsstand with diesel horn, 97		30
____	12962	LL Passenger Service Train Whistle, 97-99		30
____	12964	Donald Duck Radar Antenna, 97		77
____	12965	Goofy Rotary Beacon, 97		58
____	12966	Rotary Aircraft Beacon, 97-00		35

MODERN 1970-2025		Exc	Like New	
12968	Girder Bridge Building Kit, 97		22	___
12969	TMCC Command Set, 97-09		199	___
12974	Blinking Light Billboard, 97-00		15	___
12975	Steiner Victorian Building Kit, 97-98		33	___
12976	Dobson Victorian Building Kit, 97-98		24	___
12977	Kindler Victorian Building Kit, 97-98		35	___
12982	Culvert Loader, conventional, 98-00	38	170	___
12983	Culvert Unloader, conventional, 99		185	___
12987	Intermodal Containers, set of 3, 98		15	___
12989	Lionel Tractor and Trailer, 98		16	___
12991	Linex Gas Tractor-Tanker, 98		16	___
14000	Operating Forklift Platform, 00		160	___
14001	Operating Belt Lumber Loader, 00		95	___
14002	ZW Amp/Volt Meter, 00-04		80	___
14003	80-watt Transformer/Controller, 00-03		70	___
14004	Operating Coal Loader, 00		135	___
14005	Operating Coal Ramp, 00	50	165	___
14018	ElectroCoupler Kit for Command Upgradeable GP9s, 00		20	___
14062	31" Path Remote Switch, left hand, 01-14		55	___
14063	31" Path Remote Switch, right hand, 01-14		75	___
14065	Nuclear Reactor, 00	110	233	___
14071	Yard Light 3-pack, 00-18		35	___
14072	Haunted House, 01		181	___
14073	History of Lionel, The First 90 Years Video, 00		15	___
14075	A Century of Lionel, 1900-1969 Video, 00		15	___
14076	A Century of Lionel, 1970-2000 Video, 00		15	___
14077	ZW Amp/Volt Meter, 00-03		70	___
14078	Die-cast Sprung Trucks, 2-pack, 00-25		35	___
14079	Operating North Pole Pylon, 01		70	___
14080	Hobo Hotel, 01	30	65	___
14081	Shell Oil Derrick, 01		100	___
14082	Pedestrian Walkover, speed sensor, 01-03		50	___
14083	Pedestrian Walkover, 01-03, 08, 12-16		55	___
14084	Lionel Heliport, 01		85	___
14085	Newsstand, 01		75	___
14086	Water Tower, 00		109	___
14087	Lighthouse, 01		115	___
14090	No. 140 Banjo Signal, 01-24		60	___
14091	Automatic Gateman, 01-03, 07-09		38	___
14092	Floodlight Tower, 01-05, 08-16		48	___
14093	Single Signal Bridge, 01-04, 08		22	___
14094	Double Signal Bridge, 01-04, 08		30	___
14095	Illuminated Station Platform, 01-04		20	___
14096	Station Platform, 01-04		10	___
14097	Rotary Aircraft Beacon, 01-04, 07-10	15	50	___
14098	Auto Crossing Gate 2-pack, 01-25		120	___
14099	Block Target Signal, 01-04, 07-08		29	___
14100	Blinking Light Billboard, 01-03		23	___
14101	Red Baron Pylon, 01		85	___
14102	Rocket Launcher, 01	130	280	___
14104	Burning Switch Tower, 00		70	___
14105	Aquarium, 01		175	___
14106	Operating Freight Station, 00	25	85	___

MODERN 1970-2025			Exc	Like New
____	14107	Coaling Station, 01-03		95
____	14109	Carousel, 01		265
____	14110	Operating Ferris Wheel, 01-02, 04	128	279
____	14111	1531R Controller, 00-25	20	53
____	14112	Lighted Lockon, 01-10, 13-16		6
____	14113	Engine Transfer Table, 01	90	210
____	14114	Engine Transfer Table Extension, 01		75
____	14116	PRR Die-cast Girder Bridge, 01		20
____	14117	NYC Die-cast Girder Bridge, 01		20
____	14119	Gooseneck Lamps, set of 2, 01-04, 07		24
____	14121	Classic Billboards, set of 3, 01-03		10
____	14124	ZW Controller with 2 transformers, 01		300
____	14125	Christmas Tree with 400E Train, 00		65
____	14126	Exploding Ammo Dump		55
____	14133	Madison Hobby Shop, 01	197	368
____	14134	Triple Action Magnetic Crane, 01		230
____	14135	NS Black Die-cast Girder Bridge, 02		15
____	14137	Die-cast Girder Bridge, 01-07		25
____	14138	Snap-On Tool Animated Billboard, 01 u	27	40
____	14142	Industrial Smokestack, 02-04		50
____	14143	Industrial Tank, 02-04		40
____	14145	Operating Lumberjacks, 02-03		65
____	14147	Die-cast Old Style Clock Tower, 02-04, 08-25		30
____	14148	Operating Billboard Signmen, 02-03		60
____	14149	Scale-sized Banjo Signal, 02-05		40
____	14151	Mainline Dwarf Signal, 02-08		43
____	14152	Passenger Station, 02-04		37
____	14153	Lion Oil Derrick, 02-03		50
____	14154	Water Tower, 01-02		65
____	14155	Floodlight Tower, 02-03		55
____	14156	Lion Oil Diesel Fueling Station, 02-03		70
____	14157	Coal Loader, 01-03		120
____	14158	Icing Station, 01-02		75
____	14159	Animated Billboard, 02-04		20
____	14160	Frank's Hotdog Stand, 03-04		55
____	14161	Smoking Hobo Shack, 02		60
____	14162	Missile Launching Platform, 02-03		48
____	14163	Industrial Power Station, 02-03		550
____	14164	Lionelville Bandstand, 02		140
____	14166	Train Orders Building, 04-05		49
____	14167	Operating Lift Bridge, 02	222	410
____	14168	Operating Harry's Barber Shop, 02-04		100
____	14170	Amusement Park Swing Ride, 03-04	73	150
____	14171	Pirate Ship Ride, 02-04		177
____	14172	NYC Railroad Tugboat, 02		215
____	14173	Drawbridge, 02-04		70
____	14175	Santa Fe Die-cast Girder Bridge, 01-03		17
____	14176	Norfolk Southern Die-cast Girder Bridge, 02-03		18
____	14178	TMCC Direct Lockon, 02-03		25
____	14179	TMCC Track Power Controller, 02-13		230
____	14180	B&O Railroad Tugboat, 02-03		155
____	14181	TMCC Action Recorder Controller, 02-13	60	115
____	14182	TMCC Accessory Switch Controller, 02-13		115

		Exc	Like New	
14183	TMCC Accessory Motor Controller, 02-13		115	___
14184	TMCC Block Power Controller, 02-12		90	___
14185	TMCC Operating Track Controller, 02-13		100	___
14186	TMCC Accessory Voltage Controller, 02-13		160	___
14187	TMCC How-to Video, 02-04		11	___
14189	TMCC Track Power Controller, 02-13		175	___
14190	The Lionel Train Book, 04-14		30	___
14191	TMCC Command Base Cable, 6 feet, 02-13		14	___
14192	TMCC 3-wire Command Base Cable, 02-13		15	___
14193	TMCC Controller to Controller Cable, 1 foot, 02-13		6	___
14194	TMCC TPC Cable Set, 02-13		16	___
14195	TMCC Command Base Cable, 20 feet, 02-07		12	___
14196	TMCC Controller to Controller Cable, 6 feet, 02-13		9	___
14197	TMCC Controller to Controller Cable, 20 feet, 02-07		9	___
14198	CW-80 80-watt Transformer, 03-18	65	150	___
14199	Playground Swings, 03-04, 08-09		50	___
14201	Burning Switch Tower, 05-06		70	___
14202	Water Tower, 05		140	___
14203	Amusement Park Swing Ride, 06-07		230	___
14209	U.S. Steel Gantry Crane, 05		180	___
14210	Pony Ride, 06-07		70	___
14211	Road Crew, 06-08		90	___
14214	Lionelville Mini Golf, 06		80	___
14215	Tug-of-War, 06-08		60	___
14217	Helicopter Pylon, 06-09		140	___
14218	Downtown People Pack, 05-19		27	___
14219	Ice Rink, 06-08		80	___
14220	Lionelville Water Tower, 06-08		21	___
14221	Witches Cauldron, 06-08		70	___
14222	Die-cast Girder Bridge, 06-09		30	___
14225	Sunoco Industrial Tank, 06-09		70	___
14227	Yard Tower, 06-08		45	___
14229	Crossing Shanty, 06-09		20	___
14230	Milk Bottle Toss Midway Game, 06		20	___
14231	Cotton Candy Midway Booth, 06		20	___
14236	Operating Freight Station, 06-07		105	___
14237	Rocket Launcher, 06-07		320	___
14240	Ice Block 10-Pack, 06-25		7	___
14241	Work Crew People Pack, 05-19		27	___
14242	Hard Rock Cafe, 06		50	___
14243	U.S. Army Water Tower, 06-08		95	___
14244	Ammo Loader, 06-07		105	___
14251	Die-cast Sprung Trucks, rotating bearing caps, set of 2, 07-24		40	___
14255	Sand Tower, 06-18		35	___
14257	Passenger Station, 06-13		60	___
14258	North Pole Passenger Station, 06-10		53	___
14259	Christmas People Pack, 06-12		23	___
14260	Christmas Tractor and Trailer, 06-08		25	___
14261	Christmas Tree Lot, 06		70	___
14262	Elevated Tank, 07		70	___
14265	Sawmill with sound, 08		130	___
14267	Sir Topham Hatt Gateman, 07-12		80	___

		MODERN 1970-2025	Exc	Like New
___	**14273**	Polar Express Add-on Figures, 06-07, 12-25		30
___	**14289**	Operating Santa Gateman, 08		80
___	**14290**	UPS Store, 06		30
___	**14291**	Operating Milk Loading Depot, K-Line, 08		100
___	**14294**	993 Legacy Expansion Set, 07-16, 18-20		335
___	**14295**	990 Legacy Command Set, 07-16, 18-20	267	678
___	**14297**	Halloween Witch Pylon, 07-08	80	150
___	**14500**	KCS F3 Diesel AA Set, Railsounds, CC, 01	328	660
___	**14512**	F3 Diesel ABA Demonstrator "291," CC, 01	360	425
___	**14517**	Santa Fe F3 Diesel B Unit "2343C," powered, 01		280
___	**14518**	CP F3 Diesel B Unit "2373C," RailSounds, CC, 01		345
___	**14520**	Texas Special F3 Diesel B Unit, RailSounds, 01		360
___	**14521**	Rock Island E6 Diesel AA Set, 01	343	612
___	**14524**	Atlantic Coast Line E6 Diesel AA Set, 01	213	630
___	**14536**	Santa Fe F3 Diesel AA Set, RailSounds, CC, 03-04	217	800
___	**14539**	Santa Fe F3 Diesel B Unit, 03		300
___	**14540**	D&RGW F3 Diesel B Unit, RailSounds, CC, 01		315
___	**14541**	C&O F3 Diesel B Unit, RailSounds, CC, 01		300
___	**14542**	KCS F3 Diesel B Unit "2388C," RailSounds, CC, 01		375
___	**14543**	SP F3 Diesel B Unit, RailSounds, CC, 01		282
___	**14544**	Southern E6 AA Diesel Set, CC, 02	275	560
___	**14547**	Burlington E5 AA Diesel Set, CC, 02	200	570
___	**14552**	NYC F3 Diesel AA Set, RailSounds, CC, 03-04		740
___	**14555**	NYC F3 Diesel B Unit, 03		200
___	**14557**	WP F3 Diesel B Unit, nonpowered, 03-04		190
___	**14558**	B&O F3 Diesel B Unit, nonpowered, 03-04		155
___	**14559**	D&RGW F3 Diesel AA Set, 01		620
___	**14560**	NP F3 Diesel A Unit "2390B," freight, 02	NRS	200
___	**14561**	NP F3 Diesel A Unit "2390B," passenger, 02		190
___	**14562**	Milwaukee Road F3 Diesel A Unit "75C," 02	80	190
___	**14563**	Erie-Lackawanna F3 Diesel A Unit "7094," 02		175
___	**14564**	CP F3 Diesel B Unit "237C," CC, 02	80	350
___	**14565**	B&O F3 Diesel AA Set, 03-04		650
___	**14568**	WP F3 Diesel AA Set, 03-04		780
___	**14571**	Santa Fe PA Diesel AA Set, CC, 03		660
___	**14574**	D&H PA Diesel AA Set, CC, 03		580
___	**14579**	UP Alco PA-1 Diesel A Unit "600," powered, 03		450
___	**14580**	UP Alco PA-1 Diesel B Unit "600B," unpowered, 03		150
___	**14581**	UP Alco PA-1 Diesel A Unit "601," unpowered, 03		150
___	**14584**	Wabash F3 Diesel A Unit, nonpowered, 03		180
___	**14586**	D&H PB Unit, 03		125
___	**14587**	Santa Fe PB Unit, 03		125
___	**14588**	Santa Fe F3 Diesel ABA Set, CC, 04-05		980
___	**14592**	PRR F3 Diesel ABA Set, CC, 04-05		750
___	**14596**	NH Alco PA Diesel AA Set, 04-05		700
___	**14599**	NH Alco PB Diesel B Unit "0767-B," 04-05		150
___	**15000**	D&RGW Waffle-sided Boxcar, 95	12	18
___	**15001**	Seaboard Waffle-sided Boxcar, 95	14	19
___	**15002**	Chesapeake & Ohio Waffle-sided Boxcar, 96	16	20
___	**15003**	Green Bay & Western Waffle-sided Boxcar, 96	16	20
___	**15004**	Bloomingdale's Boxcar, 97 u		40
___	**15005**	"I Love NY" Boxcar, 97 u		65
___	**15008**	CP Rail Boxcar		30

MODERN 1970-2025		Exc	Like New	
15013	L&N Waffle-sided Boxcar "102402," 00		29	___
15014	Seaboard Waffle-sided Boxcar "125925," 00		25	___
15015	C&NW Waffle-sided Boxcar "161013," 03		18	___
15016	IC Waffle-sided Boxcar "12981," 04		20	___
15017	CSX Waffle-sided Boxcar, 05		27	___
15018	D&H Waffle-sided Boxcar "24052," 06		30	___
15020	NH Waffle-sided Boxcar, 07		30	___
15021	MKT Waffle-sided Boxcar, 08		35	___
15024	UP Waffle Boxcar "960860," 09-11		40	___
15028	Southern Waffle-sided Boxcar "539889," 10		40	___
15029	Western & Atlantic Wood-sided Reefer, 10		53	___
15033	MTK Stock Car, 10		65	___
15036	NPC Bass Pro Shops Boxcar, 11		22	___
15038	CSX Hi-Cube Boxcar, 11-12		40	___
15039	NS Waffle-sided Boxcar, 11-12		40	___
15041	BNSF Hi-Cube Boxcar, 10		50	___
15042	CSX Waffle-sided Boxcar, 11		40	___
15051	Lionel Lines Boxcar, 11-12		40	___
15052	Amtrak Hi-Cube Boxcar, 11-12		40	___
15053	REA Waffle-sided Boxcar, 11-12		40	___
15054	C&NW Wood-sided Reefer, 11-12		40	___
15060	K-Line Boxcar, 06		40	___
15063	U.S.A.F. Minuteman Boxcar, 11		55	___
15069	Coke Wood-sided Reefer #1, 09-16		65	___
15071	Coca-Cola Christmas Boxcar, 12		70	___
15072	Halloween Boxcar, 09-11		55	___
15074	Mr. Goodbar Wood-sided Reefer, 09-11		55	___
15075	Boy Scouts of America Eagle Scout Boxcar, 11-14		60	___
15077	ATSF Stock Car , 11		55	___
15078	Pabst Wood-sided Reefer, 11		65	___
15079	Schlitz Wood-sided Reefer, 11		58	___
15080	C&O 40' Boxcar , 11		55	___
15083	CP Rail Waffle-sided Boxcar, 13		43	___
15084	GN Hi-Cube Boxcar, 13-14		43	___
15086	Alaska Wood-Sided Reefer, 12		40	___
15091	Angela Trotta Thomas "High Hopes" Hi-Cube Boxcar, 12		55	___
15094	Sleepy Hollow Halloween Reefer, 14-15		60	___
15095	1953 Lionel Catalog Art Reefer, 13		55	___
15096	Hershey's Kisses Christmas Boxcar, 12		70	___
15097	Peanuts Christmas Boxcar, 12-13		70	___
15098	Lone Ranger Boxcar, 12-14		60	___
15100	Amtrak Passenger Coach, 95-97		35	___
15101	Reading Baggage Car (027), 96		34	___
15102	Reading Combination Car (027), 96		23	___
15103	Reading Passenger Coach (027), 96		23	___
15104	Reading Vista Dome Car (027), 96		26	___
15105	Reading Full Vista Dome Car (027), 96		26	___
15106	Reading Observation Car (027), 96		23	___
15107	Amtrak Vista Dome Car, 96		38	___
15108	Northern Pacific Vista Dome Car, 96		34	___
15109	ATSF Combine Car "2407," 97		35	___
15110	ATSF Vista Dome Car 2404," 97		35	___
15111	ATSF Observation Car "2406," 97		35	___

			Exc	Like New
___	**15112**	ATSF Albuquerque Coach "2405," 97		34
___	**15113**	ATSF Culebra Vista Dome Car "2404," 97		34
___	**15114**	NJ Transit Coach "5610," 96 u		45
___	**15115**	NJ Transit Coach "5611," 96 u		45
___	**15116**	NJ Transit Coach "5612," 96 u		45
___	**15117**	Annie Passenger Coach, 97		26
___	**15118**	Clarabel Passenger Coach, 97		26
___	**15122**	NJ Transit Passenger Coach "5613," 97 u		45
___	**15123**	NJ Transit Passenger Coach "5614," 97 u		45
___	**15124**	NJ Transit Passenger Coach "5615," 97 u		45
___	**15125**	Amtrak Observation Car, 97 u		50
___	**15126**	Stars & Stripes Abraham Lincoln General Coach, 99		60
___	**15127**	Stars & Stripes Ulysses S. Grant General Coach, 99		60
___	**15128**	Pride of Richmond Robert E. Lee General Coach, 99		60
___	**15129**	Pride of Richmond Jefferson Davis General Coach, 99		60
___	**15136**	Custom Series Short Observation Car, blue, 99		40
___	**15137**	Custom Series Short Observation Car, red, 99		34
___	**15138**	Pratt's Hollow Baggage Car, 98		100
___	**15139**	Pratt's Hollow Vista Dome Car, 98		100
___	**15140**	Pratt's Hollow Coach, 98		100
___	**15141**	Pratt's Hollow Observation, 98		100
___	**15142**	U.S. Army Baby Heavyweight Coach, 00		50
___	**15143**	U.S. Army Baby Heavyweight Coach, 00		50
___	**15153**	Pullman Baby Madison Set 4-pack, 01		190
___	**15163**	T&P Baby Heavyweight Coach, 01		30
___	**15166**	Union Pacific Whistling Baggage Car, 04		41
___	**15169**	C&O Streamliner Car 4-pack, 03	55	140
___	**15170**	L&N Streamliner Car 4-pack, 03		140
___	**15180**	NYC Streamliner Car 4-pack, 04		340
___	**15185**	UP Streamliner Car 4-pack, 04		340
___	**15300**	NYC Superliner Aluminum Passenger Car 4-pack, 02		360
___	**15301**	NYC Manhattan Superliner Passenger Coach, 02		90
___	**15302**	NYC Queens Superliner Passenger Coach, 02		90
___	**15304**	NYC Staten Island Superliner Passenger Coach, 02		90
___	**15305**	NYC Brooklyn Superliner Passenger Coach, 02		90
___	**15311**	CB&Q California Zephyr Aluminum Passenger Car 4-pack, 03		350
___	**15312**	Santa Fe Super Chief Aluminum Passenger Car 4-pack, 03		275
___	**15313**	D&H Aluminum Passenger Car 4-pack, 03		415
___	**15314**	Amtrak Superliner 2-pack, 03		220
___	**15315**	Santa Fe Superliner 2-pack, 03		200
___	**15316**	NYC Superliner 2-pack, 03		195
___	**15317**	Southern Aluminum Passenger Car 4-pack, 03		350
___	**15318**	Lionel Lines Aluminum Passenger Car 2-pack, 03		125
___	**15319**	Santa Fe Superliner Aluminum Passenger Car 2-pack, 03	50	145
___	**15326**	NYC 20th Century Limited Aluminum Passenger Car 6-pack, 02	243	564
___	**15333**	N&W Powhatan Arrow Aluminum Passenger Car 6-pack, 02-03		435
___	**15334**	N&W Powhatan Arrow Aluminum Baggage Car "117," 02-03		70
___	**15335**	N&W Powhatan Arrow Aluminum Combine, 02-03		70
___	**15336**	N&W Powhatan Arrow Aluminum Coach "537," 02-03		70
___	**15337**	N&W Powhatan Arrow Aluminum Coach "553," 02-03		70
___	**15338**	N&W Powhatan Arrow Aluminum Coach "641," 02-03		70

MODERN 1970-2025		Exc	Like New	
15339	N&W Powhatan Arrow Aluminum Observation, 02-03		70	___
15340	PRR South Wind Aluminum Passenger Car 6-pack, 02-03	218	525	___
15341	PRR South Wind Aluminum Baggage Car "6529," 02-03		100	___
15342	PRR South Wind Aluminum Combine "6700," 02-03		100	___
15343	PRR South Wind Aluminum Coach "4021," 02-03		100	___
15344	PRR South Wind Aluminum Coach "4022," 02-03		100	___
15345	PRR South Wind Aluminum Coach "4022," 02-03		100	___
15346	PRR South Wind Aluminum Observation "1126," 02-03		100	___
15350	Amtrak Superliner Aluminum Sleeper, 02-03		100	___
15351	Amtrak Superliner Aluminum Lounge Car, 02-03		100	___
15352	ATSF Superliner Hi-Level Sleeper "712," 03		100	___
15353	ATSF Superliner Hi-Level Lounge Car "575,", 03		100	___
15364	ATSF Super Chief Aluminum Baggage Car "3425," 03		100	___
15365	ATSF Super Chief Aluminum Sleeper "Palm Leaf,", 03		100	___
15366	ATSF Super Chief Aluminum Vista Dome, 03		100	___
15368	UP Streamlined Aluminum Baggage Car "5608," 03		100	___
15369	UP Streamlined Aluminum Combination Car "Clifton," 03		100	___
15370	UP Streamlined Aluminum Diner w/StationSounds, 03		230	___
15371	UP Streamlined Aluminum Coach "Chatham", 03		100	___
15372	UP Streamlined Aluminum Offset Dome Car "Plainfield," 03		100	___
15373	UP Streamlined Aluminum Offset Dome Car "Westfield"		100	___
15374	UP Streamlined Aluminum Observation "Elizabeth," 03		100	___
15375	Southern Aluminum Combination Car "Mississippi," 03		100	___
15376	Southern Aluminum Coach "North Carolina," 03		100	___
15377	Southern Aluminum Coach "Maryland," 03		100	___
15378	Southern Aluminum Observation "Louisiana," 03		100	___
15379	Lionel Lines Silver Valley Aluminum Combination Car, 03		100	___
15380	Lionel Lines Silver Spoon Aluminum Diner, 03		100	___
15381	Santa Fe Aluminum Baggage Car "2571," 03		100	___
15382	Santa Fe Regal Dome Aluminum Vista Dome Car, 03		100	___
15383	NYC 20th Century Limited Diner, StationSounds, 03		195	___
15384	N&W Powhatan Arrow Diner, StationSounds, 03		190	___
15385	Pennsylvania South Wind Diner, StationSounds, 03		190	___
15394	Amtrak Streamliner Car 4-pack, 03-04		450	___
15395	Alaska Streamliner Car 4-pack, 03-04		365	___
15396	Amtrak Superliner Diner, StationSounds, 03		220	___
15397	Santa Fe Superliner Diner, StationSounds, 03	80	200	___
15398	NYC Superliner Diner, StationSounds, 03		225	___
15405	50th Anniversary Hillside Heavyweight Diner, StationSounds, 02		195	___
15406	Blue Comet Giacobini Heavyweight Diner, StationSounds, 02		300	___
15504	Alton Limited Diner, StationSounds, 03		230	___
15506	Alton Limited Heavyweight Baggage Car "R.S. Brauer," 03		115	___
15506	Alton Limited Heavyweight Coach "Oak Park," 03		115	___
15507	Phantom III Passenger Car 4-pack, 02		245	___
15508	Phantom III Baggage Car, 02		65	___
15509	Phantom II Vista Dome, 02		65	___
15510	Phantom III Coach, 02		65	___
15512	Phantom III Observation, 02		65	___
15512	Phantom II Passenger Car 4-pack, 02		250	___
15517	Southern Crescent Limited Heavyweight Car 2-pack, 03-04		205	___
15520	Southern Crescent Limited Diner, StationSounds, 03-04		220	___

			Exc	Like New
___	**15521**	NYC 20th Century Limited Heavyweight Passenger Car 4-pack, 04		345
___	**15526**	Santa Fe Chief Heavyweight Passenger Car 4-pack, 04		370
___	**15538**	NYC 20th Century Limited Heavyweight Passenger Car 2-pack, 04		200
___	**15541**	NYC 20th Century Limited Diner, StationSounds, 04		200
___	**15542**	Santa Fe Chief Heavyweight Passenger Car 2-pack, 04		195
___	**15545**	Santa Fe Chief Heavyweight Diner, StationSounds, 04		200
___	**15546**	Napa Valley Wine Train Heavyweight 2-pack, 05		250
___	**15547**	Napa Valley Wine Train Heavyweight Coach "1015," 05		125
___	**15548**	Napa Valley Wine Train Heavyweight Coach "1100," 05		125
___	**15549**	Napa Valley Wine Train Diner, StationSounds, 05		280
___	**15550**	Napa Valley Wine Train Heavyweight Combination Car "1052," 05		100
___	**15551**	Napa Valley Wine Train Heavyweight Coach "1017," 05		100
___	**15552**	Napa Valley Wine Train Heavyweight Coach "1014," 05		100
___	**15553**	Napa Valley Wine Train Heavyweight Observation "1011," 05		100
___	**15554**	Pennsylvania Heavyweight Car 3-pack (std O), 05		375
___	**15558**	Pennsylvania Heavyweight Add-on Coach (std O), 05		140
___	**15559**	PRR Reading Seashore Heavyweight Car 3-pack (std O), 05	95	370
___	**15563**	PRR Reading Seashore Heavyweight Add-on Coach, 05		130
___	**15564**	LIRR Heavyweight Car 3-pack (std O), 05		370
___	**15568**	LIRR Heavyweight Add-on Coach (std O), 05		130
___	**15570**	LIRR Heavyweight Car 3-pack (std O), 06		230
___	**15574**	LIRR Heavyweight Car Add-on (std O), 06		140
___	**15575**	C&O Heavyweight Diner, StationSounds (std O), 06-07		295
___	**15576**	C&O Heavyweight Passenger Car 2-pack (std O), 06-07		265
___	**15577**	NYC Heavyweight 3-pack (std O), 05-06		370
___	**15581**	NYC Heavyweight Add-on Coach (std O), 05-06		130
___	**15584**	Amtrak Acela Passenger Car 3-pack (std O), 06	175	670
___	**15588**	Southern Heavyweight Passenger Car 4-pack, 06	125	495
___	**15593**	Southern Heavyweight Passenger Car 2-pack, 06		265
___	**15596**	Southern Heavyweight Diner, StationSounds, 06		295
___	**15597**	C&O Heavyweight Passenger Car 4-pack (std O), 06-07		495
___	**15906**	RailSounds Trigger Button, 90-95		12
___	**16000**	PRR Vista Dome Car (027), 87-88	37	55
___	**16001**	PRR Passenger Coach (027), 87-88	33	41
___	**16002**	PRR Passenger Coach (027), 87-88	24	29
___	**16003**	PRR Observation Car (027), 87-88	24	29
___	**16009**	PRR Combination Car (027), 88	36	38
___	**16010**	Virginia & Truckee Passenger Coach (SSS), 88	36	47
___	**16010**	Railbox Modern Boxcar 6-pack, LionScale, 16		360
___	**16011**	Virginia & Truckee Passenger Coach (SSS), 88	36	47
___	**16012**	Virginia & Truckee Baggage Car (SSS), 88	36	47
___	**16013**	Amtrak Combination Car (027), 88-89	21	34
___	**16014**	Amtrak Vista Dome Car (027), 88-89	21	34
___	**16015**	Amtrak Observation Car (027), 88-89	21	34
___	**16016**	NYC Baggage Car (027), 89	36	55
___	**16017**	NYC Combination Car (027), 89	21	29
___	**16018**	NYC Passenger Coach (027), 89	21	29
___	**16019**	NYC Vista Dome Car (027), 89	21	29
___	**16020**	NYC Passenger Coach (027), 89	23	33
___	**16020**	BNSF Modern Boxcar 6-pack, LionScale, 16		360

		Exc	Like New	
16021	NYC Observation Car (027), 89	20	28	___
16022	Pennsylvania Baggage Car (027), 89	27	38	___
16023	Amtrak Passenger Coach (027), 89	21	30	___
16024	Northern Pacific Diner (027), 92	39	44	___
16027	LL Combination Car (027, SSS), 90	39	48	___
16028	LL Passenger Coach (SSS, 027), 90	32	42	___
16029	LL Passenger Coach (SSS, 027), 90	35	42	___
16030	LL Observation Car (SSS, 027), 90	35	42	___
16030	CSX Modern Boxcar 6-pack, LionScale, 16		360	___
16031	Pennsylvania Diner (027), 90	35	39	___
16033	Amtrak Baggage Car (027), 90	28	38	___
16034	NP Baggage Car (027), 90-91	30	45	___
16035	NP Combination Car (027), 90-91	18	26	___
16036	NP Passenger Coach (027), 90-91	21	30	___
16037	NP Vista Dome Car (027), 90-91	18	26	___
16038	NP Passenger Coach (027), 90-91	17	25	___
16039	NP Observation Car (027), 90-91	21	30	___
16040	Southern Pacific Baggage Car, 90-91	22	30	___
16040	NS Modern Boxcar 6-pack, LionScale, 16		360	___
16041	NYC Diner (027), 91	37	47	___
16042	Illinois Central Baggage Car (027), 91	24	34	___
16043	Illinois Central Combination Car (027), 91	22	30	___
16044	Illinois Central Passenger Coach (027), 91	24	34	___
16045	Illinois Central Vista Dome Car (027), 91	22	30	___
16046	Illinois Central Passenger Coach (027), 91	24	34	___
16047	Illinois Central Observation Car (027), 91	24	34	___
16048	Amtrak Diner (027), 91-92	33	40	___
16049	Illinois Central Diner (027), 92	27	38	___
16050	C&NW Baggage Car "6620," 93	44	55	___
16050	AT&SF 3-bay Offset Hopper 6-pack, LionScale, 16		330	___
16051	C&NW Combination Car "6630," 93	40	50	___
16052	C&NW Passenger Coach "6616," 93	34	42	___
16053	C&NW Passenger Coach "6602," 93	37	46	___
16054	C&NW Observation Car "6603," 93	38	47	___
16055	Santa Fe Passenger Coach (027), 93-94	29	38	___
16056	Santa Fe Vista Dome Car (027), 93-94	25	32	___
16057	Santa Fe Passenger Coach (027), 93-94	30	40	___
16058	Santa Fe Combination Car (027), 93-94	27	35	___
16059	Santa Fe Vista Dome Car (027), 93-94	26	34	___
16060	Santa Fe Observation Car (027), 93-94	25	31	___
16060	B&O 3-bay Offset Hopper 6-pack, LionScale, 16		330	___
16061	N&W Baggage Car "6061," 94	60	85	___
16062	N&W Combination Car "6062," 94	38	50	___
16063	N&W Passenger Coach "6063," 94	43	55	___
16064	N&W Passenger Coach "6064," 94	43	55	___
16065	N&W Observation Car "6065," 94	36	48	___
16066	NYC Combination Car "6066" (SSS), 94	55	70	___
16067	NYC Passenger Coach "6067" (SSS), 94	38	47	___
16068	UP Baggage Car "6068" (027), 94	50	65	___
16069	UP Combination Car "6069" (027), 94	36	43	___
16070	UP Passenger Coach "6070" (027), 94	36	43	___
16070	B&M 3-bay Offset Hopper 6-pack, LionScale, 16		330	___
16071	UP Diner "6071" (027), 94	36	46	___

	MODERN 1970-2025		Exc	Like New
___	16072	UP Vista Dome Car "6072" (027), 94	36	43
___	16073	UP Passenger Coach "6073" (027), 94	36	42
___	16074	UP Observation Car "6074" (027), 94	36	43
___	16075	Missouri Pacific Baggage Car "6620," 95	44	55
___	16076	Missouri Pacific Combination Car "6630," 95	34	41
___	16077	Missouri Pacific Passenger Coach "6616," 95	34	41
___	16078	Missouri Pacific Passenger Coach "7805," 95	34	39
___	16079	Missouri Pacific Observation Car "6609," 95	34	41
___	16080	New Haven Baggage Car "6080" (027), 95	35	44
___	16080	C&O 3-bay Offset Hopper 6-pack #1, LionScale, 16		330
___	16081	New Haven Combination Car "6081" (027), 95	28	37
___	16082	New Haven Passenger Coach "6082" (027), 95	28	37
___	16083	New Haven Vista Dome Car "6083" (027), 95	30	39
___	16084	New Haven Full Vista Dome Car "6084" (027), 95	33	39
___	16086	New Haven Observation Car "6086" (027), 95	31	40
___	16087	NYC Baggage Car "6087" (SSS), 95	48	65
___	16088	NYC Passenger Coach "6088" (SSS), 95	36	43
___	16089	NYC Diner "6089" (SSS), 95	36	43
___	16090	NYC Observation Car "6090" (SSS), 95	38	46
___	16090	C&O 3-bay Offset Hopper 6-pack #2, LionScale, 16		330
___	16091	NYC Passenger Cars, set of 4 (SSS), 95	140	165
___	16092	Santa Fe Full Vista Dome Car (027), 95	30	38
___	16093	Illinois Central Full Vista Dome Car (027), 95	29	38
___	16094	Pennsylvania Full Vista Dome Car (027), 95	30	39
___	16095	Amtrak Combination Car (027), 95	19	23
___	16096	Amtrak Vista Dome Car (027), 95	19	23
___	16097	Amtrak Observation Car (027), 95	19	23
___	16098	Amtrak Passenger Coach, 95-97	20	33
___	16099	Amtrak Vista Dome Car, 95-97	20	33
___	16100	Alaska RR 3-bay 9-panel Hopper 6-pack, LionScale, 16		330
___	16102	Southern 3-D Tank Car (SSS), 87	23	30
___	16103	Lehigh Valley 2-D Tank Car (027), 88	19	25
___	16104	Santa Fe 2-D Tank Car (027), 89	19	23
___	16105	D&RGW 3-D Tank Car (SSS), 89	48	65
___	16106	Mopar Express 3-D Tank Car, 88 u	105	156
___	16107	Sunoco 2-D Tank Car (027), 90	16	20
___	16108	Racing Fuel 1-D Tank Car "6108" (027), 89 u, 92 u	9	13
___	16109	B&O 1-D Tank Car (SSS), 91	29	34
___	16110	Circus Animals Operating Stock Car "1989" (027), 89 u	24	34
___	16110	Chessie 3-bay 9-panel Hopper 6-pack, LionScale, 16		330
___	16111	Alaska 1-D Tank Car (027), 90-91	22	27
___	16112	Dow Chemical 3-D Tank Car, 90	20	26
___	16113	Diamond Shamrock 2-D Tank Car (027), 91	20	25
___	16114	Hooker Chemicals 1-D Tank Car (027), 91	13	17
___	16115	MKT 3-D Tank Car, 92	13	16
___	16116	U.S. Army 1-D Tank Car, 91 u	36	42
___	16119	MKT 2-D Tank Car (027), 92, 93 u	14	19
___	16120	Southern 3-bay 9-panel Hopper 6-pack, LionScale, 16		330
___	16121	C&NW Stock Car (SSS), 92	33	43
___	16123	Union Pacific 3-D Tank Car, 93-95	16	22
___	16124	Penn Salt 3-D Tank Car, 93	21	26
___	16125	Virginian Stock Car, 93	19	24
___	16126	Jefferson Lake 3-D Tank Car, 93	22	26

MODERN 1970-2025		Exc	Like New	
16127	Mobil 1-D Tank Car, 93	28	33	___
16128	Alaska 1-D Tank Car, 94	24	29	___
16129	Alaska 1-D Tank Car (027), 93 u, 94	21	28	___
16130	SP Stock Car (027), 93 u, 94	10	13	___
16130	WM 3-bay 9-panel Hopper 6-pack, LionScale, 16		330	___
16131	T&P Reefer, 94	19	24	___
16132	Deep Rock 3-D Tank Car, 94	25	30	___
16133	Santa Fe Reefer, 94	22	28	___
16134	Reading Reefer, 94	17	21	___
16135	C&O Stock Car, 94	23	27	___
16136	B&O 1-D Tank Car, 94	28	32	___
16137	Ford 1-D Tank Car "12," 94 u	34	39	___
16138	Goodyear 1-D Tank Car, 95	28	34	___
16140	Domino Sugar 1-D Tank Car, 95	17	29	___
16140	Klemme Coop PS-2CD Covered Hopper 6-pack, LionScale, 16		360	___
16141	Erie Stock Car, 95	22	30	___
16142	Santa Fe 1-D Tank Car, 95	26	30	___
16143	Reading Reefer, 95	18	23	___
16144	San Angelo 3-D Tank Car, 95	22	25	___
16146	Dairy Despatch Reefer, 95	15	20	___
16147	Clearly Canadian 1-D Tank Car (027), 94 u	25	40	___
16149	Zep Chemical 1-D Tank Car (027), 95 u	68	81	___
16150	Sunoco 1-D Tank Car "6315," 97	35	39	___
16150	D&RGW PS-2CD Covered Hopper 6-pack, LionScale, 16		360	___
16152	Sunoco 3-D Tank Car "6415", 97		26	___
16153	AEC Reactor Fluid 1-D Tank Car "6515-1," 97		94	___
16154	AEC Reactor Fluid 1-D Tank Car "6515-2," 97	39	107	___
16155	AEC Reactor Fluid 1-D Tank Car "6515-3," 97	60	109	___
16157	Gatorade Little League Baseball 1-D Tank Car "6315," 97 u	30	64	___
16160	AEC Tank Car "6515" with reactor fluid, 98		85	___
16160	MILW PS-2CD Covered Hopper 6-pack, LionScale, 16		360	___
16162	Hooker 1-D Tank Car "6315-1," 97		50	___
16163	Hooker 1-D Tank Car "6315-2," 97		50	___
16164	Hooker 1-D Tank Car "6315-3," 97		50	___
16165	Mobilfuel 3-D Tank Car "6415," 97 u		50	___
16170	RFMX PS-2CD Covered Hopper 6-pack, LionScale, 16		360	___
16171	Alaska 1-D Tank Car "6171," 98-99		33	___
16173	Harold the Helicopter Flatcar, 98	45	60	___
16175	NJ Transit Port Morris Ore Car "9125," 98		45	___
16176	NJ Transit Raritan Yard Ore Car "9126," 98 u		45	___
16177	NJ Transit Gladstone Yard Ore Car "9127," 98 u		45	___
16178	NJ Transit Bay Head Yard Ore Car "9128," 98 u	7	45	___
16179	NJ Transit Dover Yard Ore Car "9129," 98 u		45	___
16180	Tabasco 1-D Tank Car, 98	67	84	___
16181	Biohazard Tank Car with Lights, 98	50	90	___
16182	Gatorade 1-D Tank Car "6315," 98 u		64	___
16187	Linex 3-D Tank Car "6425," 99		30	___
16188	Kodak 1-D Tank Car "6515," 99	74	93	___
16199	UP 1-D Tank Car "6035," 99-00		25	___
16200	Rock Island Boxcar (027), 87-88	5	10	___
16201	Wabash Boxcar (027), 88-91	7	10	___
16203	Key America Boxcar (027), 87 u	45	65	___
16204	Hawthorne Boxcar (027), 87 u	50	85	___

	MODERN 1970-2025		Exc	Like New
____	**16205**	Mopar Express Boxcar "1987" (027), 87-88 u	55	65
____	**16206**	D&RGW Boxcar (SSS), 89	37	42
____	**16207**	True Value Boxcar (027), 88 u	32	115
____	**16208**	PRR Auto Carrier, 3-tier, 89	24	41
____	**16209**	Disney Magic Boxcar (027), 88 u	90	110
____	**16211**	Hawthorne Boxcar (027), 88 u	45	65
____	**16213**	Shoprite Boxcar (027), 88 u	55	80
____	**16214**	D&RGW Auto Carrier, 90	22	37
____	**16215**	Conrail Auto Carrier, 90	27	38
____	**16217**	Burlington Northern Auto Carrier, 92	24	36
____	**16219**	True Value Boxcar (027), 89 u	55	75
____	**16220**	Ace Hardware Boxcar (027), 89 u	58	81
____	**16221**	Macy's Boxcar (027), 89 u	55	80
____	**16222**	Great Northern Boxcar (027), 90-91	8	15
____	**16223**	Budweiser Reefer, 89-92 u	73	93
____	**16224**	True Value "Lawn Chief" Boxcar (027), 90 u	45	60
____	**16225**	Budweiser Vat Car, 90-91 u	61	105
____	**16226**	Union Pacific Boxcar "6226" (027), 90-91 u	15	19
____	**16227**	Santa Fe Boxcar (027), 91	13	17
____	**16228**	Union Pacific Auto Carrier, 92	26	33
____	**16229**	Erie-Lackawanna Auto Carrier, 91 u	45	55
____	**16232**	Chessie System Boxcar, 92, 93 u, 94, 95 u	25	30
____	**16233**	MKT DD Boxcar, 92	20	29
____	**16234**	ACY Boxcar (SSS), 92	34	41
____	**16235**	Railway Express Agency Reefer, 92	19	23
____	**16236**	NYC Pacemaker Boxcar, 92 u	18	24
____	**16237**	Railway Express Agency Boxcar, 92 u	21	23
____	**16238**	NYNH&H Boxcar, 93-95	10	14
____	**16239**	Union Pacific Boxcar, 93-95	15	20
____	**16241**	Toys 'R' Us Boxcar, 92-93 u	35	45
____	**16242**	Grand Trunk Western Auto Carrier, 93	35	40
____	**16243**	Conrail Boxcar, 93	26	34
____	**16244**	Duluth, South Shore & Atlantic Boxcar, 93	20	24
____	**16245**	Contadina Boxcar, 93	16	20
____	**16247**	ACL Boxcar, 94	15	19
____	**16248**	Budweiser Boxcar, 93-94 u	52	70
____	**16249**	United Auto Workers Boxcar, 93 u		55
____	**16250**	Santa Fe Boxcar (027), 93 u, 94	8	10
____	**16251**	Columbus & Greenville Boxcar, 94	8	15
____	**16252**	U.S. Navy Boxcar "6106888", 94-95		30
____	**16253**	Santa Fe Auto Carrier, 94	32	38
____	**16255**	Wabash DD Boxcar, 95	20	26
____	**16256**	Ford DD Boxcar, 94 u	30	34
____	**16257**	Crayola Boxcar, 94 u, 95	17	23
____	**16258**	Lehigh Valley Boxcar, 95	17	22
____	**16259**	Chrysler Mopar Boxcar, 97 u	33	43
____	**16260**	Chrysler Mopar Auto Carrier, 96 u	59	69
____	**16261**	Union Pacific DD Boxcar, 95	26	29
____	**16263**	ATSF Boxcar, 96-99		25
____	**16264**	Red Wing Shoes Boxcar, 95	26	32
____	**16265**	Georgia Power "Atlanta '96" Boxcar, 95 u	213	241
____	**16266**	Crayola Boxcar, 95	17	23
____	**16267**	Sears Zenith Boxcar, 95-96 u	18	55

MODERN 1970-2025		Exc	Like New	
16268	GM/AC Delco Boxcar, 95 u		51	___
16269	Lionel Lines Boxcar, 96	5	18	___
16272	Christmas Boxcar, 97	16	51	___
16273	Lionel Employee Christmas Boxcar, 97		55	___
16274	Marvin the Martian Boxcar, 97		60	___
16279	Dodge Motorsports Boxcar, 96 u	153	197	___
16280	Rawlings Little League Boxcar, 97	25	30	___
16281	MacGregor Little League Boxcar, 97	25	30	___
16282	Wisk Detergent Boxcar, 97	25	30	___
16284	Galveston Wharves Boxcar, 98		28	___
16285	Savannah State Docks Boxcar, 98		26	___
16291	Christmas Boxcar, 98		34	___
16292	Lionel Employee Christmas Boxcar, 98	309	369	___
16293	JCPenney Boxcar, 97		100	___
16294	Pedigree Boxcar, 97	148	168	___
16295	Kal Kan Boxcar, 97	159	180	___
16296	Whiskas Boxcar, 97	142	168	___
16297	Sheba Boxcar, 97	136	160	___
16298	Mobil Boxcar, 97		50	___
16300	Rock Island Flatcar with fences (027), 87-88	8	10	___
16301	Lionel Barrel Ramp Car, 87	14	19	___
16303	PRR Flatcar with trailers, 87	26	33	___
16304	RI Gondola with cable reels (027), 87-88	5	9	___
16305	Lehigh Valley Ore Car, 87	80	130	___
16306	Santa Fe Barrel Ramp Car, 88	13	18	___
16307	NKP Flatcar with trailers, 88	30	40	___
16308	Burlington Northern Flatcar with trailer, 88-89	20	25	___
16309	Wabash Gondola with canisters, 88-91	9	13	___
16310	Mopar Express Gondola with canisters, 87-88 u	35	39	___
16311	Mopar Express Flatcar with trailers, 87-88 u	117	162	___
16313	PRR Gondola with cable reels (027), 88 u, 89	5	10	___
16314	Wabash Flatcar with trailers, 89	26	30	___
16315	PRR Flatcar with fences (027), 88 u, 89	7	9	___
16317	PRR Barrel Ramp Car, 89	18	22	___
16318	LL Depressed Center Flatcar with cable reels, 89	22	26	___
16320	Great Northern Barrel Ramp Car, 90	13	19	___
16321/22	Sealand TTUX Flatcar Set with trailers, 90	65	73	___
16323	Lionel Lines Flatcar with trailers, 90	21	25	___
16324	PRR Depressed Center Flatcar with cable reels, 90	16	20	___
16325	Microracers Exhibition Ramp Car, 89 u	21	28	___
16326	Santa Fe Depressed Center Flatcar with cable reels, 91	16	21	___
16327	The Big Top Circus Gondola with canisters, 89 u	19	24	___
16328	NKP Gondola with cable reels, 90-91	17	23	___
16329	SP Flatcar with horses (027), 90-91	19	24	___
16330	MKT Flatcar with trailers, 91	25	30	___
16332	LL Depressed Center Flatcar with transformer, 91	28	33	___
16333	Frisco Bulkhead Flatcar with lumber, 91	17	22	___
16334	C&NW Flatcar Set (16337, 16338) with trailers, 91	55	60	___
16335	NYC Pacemaker Flatcar with trailer (SSS), 91	46	65	___
16336	UP Gondola "6336" with canisters, 90-91 u	17	21	___
16337	C&NW Flatcar w/trailer, 91	28	30	___
16338	C&NW Flatcar w/trailer, 91	28	30	___
16339	Mickey's World Tour Gondola with canisters (027), 91, 92 u	17	21	___

			Exc	Like New
____	**16341**	NYC Depressed Center Flatcar with transformer, 92	29	32
____	**16342**	CSX Gondola with coil covers, 92	18	23
____	**16343**	Burlington Gondola with coil covers, 92	20	23
____	**16345/46**	SP TTUX Flatcar Set with trailers, 92	55	65
____	**16347**	Ontario Northland Bulkhead Flatcar with pulp load, 92	22	26
____	**16348**	Erie Liquefied Petroleum Car, 92	23	25
____	**16349**	Allis Chalmers Condenser Car, 92	28	35
____	**16350**	CP Rail Bulkhead Flatcar with lumber, 91 u	20	29
____	**16351**	Flatcar with U.S. Navy submarine, 92	27	39
____	**16352**	U.S. Military Flatcar with cruise missile, 92	33	43
____	**16353**	B&M Gondola with coil covers, 91 u	33	39
____	**16355**	Burlington Gondola, 92, 93 u, 94-95	11	17
____	**16356**	MKT Depressed Center Flatcar with cable reels, 92	17	21
____	**16357**	L&N Flatcar with trailer, 92	24	31
____	**16358**	L&N Gondola with coil covers, 92	17	21
____	**16359**	Pacific Coast Gondola with coil covers (SSS), 92	33	38
____	**16360**	N&W Maxi-Stack Flatcar Set w/containers, 93	44	55
____	**16361**	N&W Maxi-Stack Flatcar w/containers, 93	22	28
____	**16362**	N&W Maxi-Stack Flatcar w/containers, 93	22	28
____	**16363**	Southern TTUX Flatcar Set w/trailers, 93	38	49
____	**16364**	Southern TTUX Flatcar w/trailer, 93	19	25
____	**16365**	Southern TTUX Flatcar w/trailer, 93	19	25
____	**16367**	Clinchfield Gondola with coil covers, 93	18	21
____	**16368**	MKT Liquid Oxygen Car, 93	21	22
____	**16369**	Amtrak Flatcar with wheel load, 92 u	19	28
____	**16370**	Amtrak Flatcar with rail load, 92 u	19	28
____	**16371**	BN I-Beam Flatcar with load, 92 u	23	30
____	**16372**	Southern I-Beam Flatcar with load, 92 u	24	34
____	**16373**	Erie-Lackawanna Flatcar with stakes, 93	19	23
____	**16374**	D&RGW Flatcar with trailer, 93	25	28
____	**16375**	NYC Bulkhead Flatcar, 93-95	21	25
____	**16376**	UP Flatcar with trailer, 93-95	31	37
____	**16378**	Toys 'R' Us Flatcar with trailer, 92-93 u	60	95
____	**16379**	NP Bulkhead Flatcar with pulp load, 93	16	23
____	**16380**	UP I-Beam Flatcar with load, 93	20	26
____	**16381**	CSX I-Beam Flatcar with load, 93	20	30
____	**16382**	Kansas City Southern Bulkhead Flatcar, 93	14	18
____	**16383**	Conrail Flatcar with trailer, 93	50	58
____	**16384**	Soo Line Gondola with cable reels, 93	14	19
____	**16385**	Soo Line Ore Car, 93	65	75
____	**16386**	SP Flatcar with lumber, 94	15	19
____	**16387**	KCS Gondola with coil covers, 94	13	16
____	**16388**	LV Gondola with canisters, 94	16	20
____	**16389**	PRR Flatcar with wheel load, 94	27	32
____	**16390**	Flatcar with water tank, 94	24	27
____	**16391**	Lionel Lines Gondola, 93 u	11	15
____	**16392**	Wabash Gondola with canisters (027), 93 u, 94	7	9
____	**16393**	Wisconsin Central Bulkhead Flatcar, 94	13	19
____	**16394**	Vermont Central Bulkhead Flatcar, 94	20	30
____	**16395**	CP Flatcar with rail load, 94	19	29
____	**16396**	Alaska Bulkhead Flatcar, 94	17	22
____	**16397**	Milwaukee Road I-Beam Flatcar with load, 94	30	34
____	**16398**	C&O Flatcar with trailer, 94	80	85

		Exc	Like New	
16399	Western Pacific I-Beam Flatcar with load, 94	31	35	___
16400	PRR Hopper (027), 88 u, 89	15	18	___
16402	Southern Quad Hopper with coal (SSS), 87	30	42	___
16406	CSX Quad Hopper with coal, 90	29	34	___
16407	B&M Covered Quad Hopper (SSS), 91	28	37	___
16408	UP Hopper "6408" (027), 90-91 u	17	21	___
16410	MKT Hopper (027), 92, 93 u	19	24	___
16411	L&N Quad Hopper with coal, 92	28	32	___
16412	C&NW Covered Quad Hopper, 94	16	21	___
16413	Clinchfield Quad Hopper with coal, 94	16	22	___
16414	CCC&StL Hopper (027), 94	16	23	___
16416	D&RGW Covered Quad Hopper, 95	16	20	___
16417	Wabash Quad Hopper with coal, 95	19	21	___
16418	C&NW Hopper with coal (027), 95	15	21	___
16419	Tennessee Central Hopper, 96		17	___
16420	WM Quad Hopper with coal (SSS), 95	30	34	___
16421	WM Quad Hopper with coal (SSS), 95	30	33	___
16422	WM Quad Hopper with coal (SSS), 95		33	___
16423	WM Quad Hopper with coal (SSS), 95		30	___
16424	WM Covered Quad Hopper (SSS), 95	34	39	___
16425	WM Covered Quad Hopper (SSS), 95	25	29	___
16426	WM Covered Quad Hopper (SSS), 95	24	27	___
16427	WM Covered Quad Hopper (SSS), 95	27	30	___
16429	WM Quad Hopper with coal, set of 2		70	___
16430	Georgia Power Quad Hopper "82947" with coal, 95 u		109	___
16431	Lionel Corporation 2-bay Hopper "6456-1," 96		30	___
16432	Lionel Corporation 2-bay Hopper "6456-2," 96		64	___
16433	Lionel Corporation 2-bay Hopper "6456-3," 96		18	___
16434	LV 2-bay Hopper "6456," "TLDX," 97		25	___
16435	Virginian 2-bay Hopper "6456-1," 97		30	___
16436	N&W 2-bay Hopper "6456-2," 97		33	___
16437	C&O 2-bay Hopper "6456-3," 97		33	___
16438	Frisco 4-bay Covered Hopper "87538," 98		34	___
16439	Southern 4-bay Covered Hopper "77836," 98		34	___
16440	Alaska 2-bay Hopper "7100," 98-99		35	___
16441	New York Central 4-bay Hopper, 99		26	___
16442	Bethlehem Gondola "6462" (SSS), 99		40	___
16443	GN 2-bay Hopper "172364," 99-00		20	___
16444	CNJ 2-bay Hopper "643," 00		20	___
16445	Frisco 2-bay Hopper "93108," 00		20	___
16446	Burlington 2-bay Hopper, 00		20	___
16447	PRR Tuscan 2-bay Hopper, 00 u		30	___
16448	PRR Gray 2-bay Hopper, 00 u		30	___
16449	PRR Black 2-bay Hopper, 00 u		30	___
16450	PRR Green 2-bay Hopper, 00 u		30	___
16451	Lionel Mines 2-bay Hopper, 00 u		50	___
16453	SP 2-bay Hopper "460604," 01		15	___
16454	Bethlehem Steel Hopper "41025," 01		37	___
16455	Pioneer Seed 2-bay Hopper, 00 u		50	___
16456	B&O 2-bay Hopper, 01		20	___
16459	LV 2-bay Hopper "51102," 01		23	___
16460	Reading 2-bay Hopper "79636," 02		25	___
16463	Rio Grande Icebreaker Tunnel Car "18936," 02		32	___

	MODERN 1970-2025		Exc	Like New
___	**16464**	NYC Icebreaker Tunnel Car "X3200," 02		32
___	**16465**	WP 2-bay Hopper "100340," 03		19
___	**16466**	Pennsylvania Icebreaker Tunnel Car, 03		33
___	**16467**	Naughty and Nice Hopper 2-pack, 02		60
___	**16468**	ACL Wood-chip Hopper, 02		20
___	**16469**	B&O Hopper "435351," 02		22
___	**16470**	Naughty and Nice Ore Car 2-pack, 03		43
___	**16473**	Rock Island Ore Car "99122," 03		18
___	**16474**	Alaska Ore Car "16474," 04		21
___	**16475**	Santa Fe Hopper "16475," 04		18
___	**16480**	Lionelville Snow Transport Quad Hopper, 04		45
___	**16482**	Norfolk Southern Hopper, traditional, 05		27
___	**16487**	Alaska 2-bay Hopper, 05		35
___	**16489**	BNSF Ore Car, traditional, 05		15
___	**16490**	Sodor Mining Hopper, 05, 13		35
___	**16491**	CNJ Hopper "60714," 06		30
___	**16492**	C&NW Ore Car "114023," 06		30
___	**16493**	Christmas Ice Breaker Car, 06		55
___	**16500**	Rock Island Bobber Caboose, 87-88	9	13
___	**16501**	Lehigh Valley SP-type Caboose, 87	19	24
___	**16503**	NYC Transfer Caboose, 87	16	22
___	**16504**	Southern N5c Caboose (SSS), 87	17	30
___	**16505**	Wabash SP-type Caboose, 88-91	10	15
___	**16506**	Santa Fe Bay Window Caboose, 88	18	28
___	**16507**	Mopar Express SP-type Caboose, 87-88 u	42	54
___	**16508**	Lionel Lines SP-type Caboose "6508," 89 u	13	17
___	**16509**	D&RGW SP-type Caboose (SSS), 89	19	24
___	**16510**	New Haven Bay Window Caboose, 89	25	30
___	**16511**	PRR Bobber Caboose, 88 u, 89	9	13
___	**16513**	Union Pacific SP-type Caboose, 89	14	21
___	**16515**	Lionel Lines SP-type Caboose, RailScope, 89	20	23
___	**16516**	Lehigh Valley SP-type Caboose, 90	15	26
___	**16517**	Atlantic Coast Line Bay Window Caboose, 90	21	26
___	**16518**	Chessie System Bay Window Caboose, 90	41	50
___	**16519**	Rock Island Transfer Caboose, 90	13	17
___	**16520**	Welcome to the Show Circus SP-type Caboose, 89 u	13	21
___	**16521**	PRR SP-type Caboose, 90-91	8	11
___	**16522**	Chills & Thrills Circus N5c Caboose, 90-91	10	15
___	**16523**	Alaska SP-type Caboose, 91	24	31
___	**16524**	Anheuser-Busch SP-type Caboose, 89-92 u	36	47
___	**16525**	D&H Bay Window Caboose (SSS), 91	30	39
___	**16526**	Kansas City Southern SP-type Caboose, 91	17	21
___	**16528**	UP SP-type Caboose "6528", 90-91 u	17	21
___	**16529**	Santa Fe SP-type Caboose "16829," 91	9	13
___	**16530**	Mickey's World Tour SP-type Caboose "16830," 91, 92 u	13	17
___	**16531**	Texas & Pacific SP-type Caboose, 92	18	23
___	**16533**	C&NW Bay Window Caboose, 92	22	30
___	**16534**	Delaware & Hudson SP-type Caboose, 92	14	19
___	**16535**	Erie-Lackawanna Bay Window Caboose, 91 u	42	50
___	**16536**	Chessie System SP-type Caboose, 92, 93 u, 94, 95 u		23
___	**16537**	MKT SP-type Caboose, 92, 93 u	17	21
___	**16538**	L&N Bay Window Caboose "1041," 92 u	29	33
___	**16539**	WP Steelside Caboose "539," smoke, SSS (std O), 92	50	55

		Exc	Like New	
16541	Montana Rail Link Extended Vision Caboose "10131" with smoke, 93	50	73	___
16543	NYC SP-type Caboose, 93-95		20	___
16544	Union Pacific SP-type Caboose, 93-95	22	26	___
16546	Clinchfield SP-type Caboose, 93	22	26	___
16547	Happy Holidays SP-type Caboose, 93-95	46	55	___
16548	Conrail SP-type Caboose, 93	15	20	___
16549	Soo Line Work Caboose, 93	18	26	___
16550	U.S. Navy Searchlight Caboose, 94-95	16	21	___
16551	Budweiser SP-type Caboose, 93-94 u	30	33	___
16552	Frisco Searchlight Caboose, 94	23	26	___
16553	United Auto Workers SP-type Caboose, 93 u		40	___
16554	GT Extended Vision Caboose "79052," smoke, 94	40	47	___
16555	C&O SP-type Caboose, 94	22	26	___
16557	Ford SP-type Caboose, 94 u	19	24	___
16558	Crayola SP-type Caboose, 94 u, 95	17	21	___
16559	Seaboard Center Cupola Caboose "5658," 95	23	24	___
16560	Chrysler Mopar Caboose, 94 u	24	26	___
16561	UP Center Cupola Caboose "25766," 95	27	31	___
16562	Reading Center Cupola Caboose, 95	25	29	___
16563	Lionel Lines SP-type Caboose, 95	22	26	___
16564	Western Maryland Center Cupola Caboose (SSS), 95	30	34	___
16565	Milwaukee Road Bay Window Caboose, 95	45	70	___
16566	U.S. Army SP-type Caboose "907," 95		28	___
16568	ATSF SP-type Caboose, 96-99		23	___
16571	Georgia Power SP-type Caboose "52789," 95 u		68	___
16575	Sears Zenith SP-type Caboose, 95		38	___
16577	U.S. Coast Guard Work Caboose, 96		26	___
16578	Lionel Lines SP-type Caboose, 95 u		20	___
16579	GM/AC Delco, SP-type Caboose, 95		35	___
16580	SP-type Caboose, 96-99		11	___
16581	UP Illuminated Caboose, 96		30	___
16586	SP Illuminated Caboose "6357", 97		42	___
16589	Zenith SP-type Caboose, 97	20	45	___
16590	Dodge Motorsports SP-type Caboose "6950," 96		58	___
16591	Little League Baseball SP-type Caboose "6397," 97		45	___
16593	Lionel Belt Line Caboose "6257," 98		32	___
16594	Caboose "6357", 98		29	___
16600	Illinois Central Coal Dump Car, 88	14	23	___
16601	Canadian National Searchlight Car, 88	19	24	___
16602	Erie-Lackawanna Coal Dump Car, 87	16	26	___
16603	Detroit Zoo Giraffe Car (027), 87	40	49	___
16604	NYC Log Dump Car, 87	15	27	___
16605	Bronx Zoo Giraffe Car (027), 88	39	44	___
16606	Southern Searchlight Car, 87	13	21	___
16607	Southern Coal Dump Car "16707" (SSS), 87	18	26	___
16608	Lehigh Valley Searchlight Car, 87	11	30	___
16609	Lehigh Valley Derrick Car, 87	22	30	___
16610	Track Maintenance Car, 87-88	15	25	___
16611	Santa Fe Log Dump Car, 88	15	23	___
16612	Soo Line Log Dump Car, 89	14	24	___
16613	MKT Coal Dump Car, 89	17	26	___
16614	Reading Cop and Hobo Car (027), 89	24	25	___

			Exc	Like New
___	**16615**	Lionel Lines Extension Searchlight Car, 89	20	28
___	**16616**	D&RGW Searchlight Car (SSS), 89	22	30
___	**16617**	C&NW Boxcar with ETD, 89	23	34
___	**16618**	Santa Fe Track Maintenance Car, 89	11	19
___	**16619**	Wabash Coal Dump Car, 90	14	25
___	**16620**	C&O Track Maintenance Car, 90-91	16	19
___	**16621**	Alaska Log Dump Car, 90	24	31
___	**16622**	CSX Boxcar with ETD, 90-91	20	28
___	**16623**	MKT DD Boxcar with ETD, 91	16	23
___	**16624**	NH Cop and Hobo Car (027), 90-91	23	31
___	**16625**	NYC Extension Searchlight Car, 90	22	30
___	**16626**	CSX Searchlight Car, 90	18	26
___	**16627**	CSX Log Dump Car, 90	19	23
___	**16628**	Cop and Hobo Circus Gondola, 90-91	36	43
___	**16629**	Operating Circus Elephant Car (027), 90-91	38	50
___	**16630**	SP Operating Cowboy Car (027), 90-91	22	26
___	**16631**	RI Boxcar, steam RailSounds, 90	110	130
___	**16632**	BN Boxcar, diesel RailSounds, 90	82	98
___	**16634**	WM Coal Dump Car, 91	26	31
___	**16636**	D&RGW Log Dump Car, 91	19	25
___	**16637**	WP Extension Searchlight Car, 91	27	30
___	**16638**	Operating Circus Animal Car (027), 91	50	55
___	**16639**	B&O Boxcar, steam RailSounds, 91	100	120
___	**16640**	Rutland Boxcar, diesel RailSounds, 91	100	120
___	**16641**	Toys 'R' Us Giraffe Car (027), 90-91 u	48	68
___	**16642**	Mickey's World Tour Goofy Car (027), 91, 92 u	33	41
___	**16644**	Amtrak Crane Car, 91, 92 u	36	42
___	**16645**	Amtrak Searchlight Caboose, 91	27	30
___	**16649**	Railway Express Agency Boxcar, steam RailSounds, 92	110	140
___	**16650**	NYC Pacemaker Boxcar, diesel RailSounds, 92	100	135
___	**16651**	Operating Circus Clown Car (027), 92	24	30
___	**16652**	Radar Car, 92	25	29
___	**16653**	Western Pacific Crane Car (SSS), 92	44	60
___	**16655**	Steam Tender "1993," RailSounds, 93	115	140
___	**16656**	Burlington Log Dump Car, 92 u	18	25
___	**16657**	Lehigh Valley Coal Dump Car, 92 u	22	29
___	**16658**	Erie-Lackawanna Crane Car, 93	47	65
___	**16659**	Union Pacific Searchlight Car, 93-95	15	18
___	**16660**	Fire Car with ladders, 93-94	28	33
___	**16661**	Flatcar with boat, 93	20	22
___	**16662**	Bugs Bunny and Yosemite Sam Outlaw Car (027), 93-94	25	34
___	**16663**	Missouri Pacific Searchlight Car, 93	16	19
___	**16664**	L&N Coal Dump Car, 93	22	25
___	**16665**	Maine Central Log Dump Car, 93	23	27
___	**16666**	Toxic Waste Car, 93-94	25	32
___	**16667**	Conrail Searchlight Car, 93	27	30
___	**16668**	Ontario Northland Log Dump Car, 93	20	24
___	**16669**	Soo Line Searchlight Car, 93	17	21
___	**16670**	TV Car, 93-94	12	22
___	**16673**	Lionel Lines Tender, whistle, 94-97	33	44
___	**16674**	Pinkerton Animated Gondola, 94	28	32
___	**16675**	Great Northern Log Dump Car, 94	21	25
___	**16676**	Burlington Coal Dump Car, 94	23	28

MODERN 1970-2025		Exc	Like New	
16677	NATO Flatcar with Royal Navy submarine, 94	34	44	___
16678	Rock Island Searchlight Car, 94	12	23	___
16679	U.S. Mail Operating Boxcar, 94	45	50	___
16680	Cherry Picker Car, 94	25	28	___
16681	Aquarium Car, 95	35	44	___
16682	Lionelville Farms Operating Stock Car (027), 94	23	27	___
16683	Los Angeles Zoo Elephant Car (027), 94	22	26	___
16684	U.S. Navy Crane Car, 94-95	35	40	___
16685	Erie Extension Searchlight Car, 95	30	34	___
16686	Mickey Mouse Animated Boxcar, 95	32	38	___
16687	U.S. Mail Operating Boxcar, 94	29	37	___
16688	Fire Car with ladders, 94	35	43	___
16689	Toxic Waste Car, 94	29	32	___
16690	Bugs Bunny and Yosemite Sam Outlaw Car (027), 94	30	34	___
16701	Southern Tool Car (SSS), 87	43	55	___
16702	Amtrak Bunk Car, 91, 92 u	25	27	___
16703	NYC Tool Car, 92	24	31	___
16704	TV Car, 94	27	29	___
16705	Chesapeake & Ohio Cop and Hobo Car, 95	28	34	___
16706	Animal Transport Service Giraffe Car, 95	27	30	___
16708	C&NW Track Maintenance Car, 95	24	31	___
16709	New York Central Derrick Car, 95	22	28	___
16710	U.S. Army Operating Missile Car, 95	40	46	___
16711	Pennsylvania Searchlight Car, 95	27	31	___
16712	Pinkerton Animated Gondola, 95	34	39	___
16715	ATSF Log Dump Car, 96-99		24	___
16717	Jersey Central Crane Car, 96		41	___
16718	USMC Missile Launching Flatcar, 96	26	31	___
16719	Exploding Boxcar, 96		38	___
16720	Lionel Lines Searchlight Car "3650," 96-97		50	___
16724	Mickey and Friends Submarine Car, 96		39	___
16725	Rhino Transport Car, 97		31	___
16726	U.S. Army Fire Ladder Car, 96		43	___
16734	U.S. Coast Guard Searchlight Car, 96		30	___
16735	U.S. Coast Guard Flatcar with radar, 96	28	35	___
16736	U.S. Coast Guard Derrick Car, 96		34	___
16737	Road Runner and Wile E. Coyote Gondola "3444," 96		66	___
16738	Pepe LePew Boxcar "3370," 96		40	___
16739	Foghorn Leghorn Animated Poultry Car "3434," 96		44	___
16740	Lionel Corporation Mail Car "3428," 96		37	___
16741	Union Pacific Illuminated Bunk Car, 97		25	___
16742	Trout Ranch Aquarium Car "3435," 96		32	___
16744	Port of Lionel City Searchlight Car, 97		30	___
16745	Port of Lionel City Flatcar with radar, 97		30	___
16746	Port of Lionel City Derrick Car, 97		30	___
16747	Breyer Animated Horse Car "6473," 97		34	___
16748	U.S. Forest Service Log-Dump Car "3361," 97		30	___
16749	Midget Mines Ore-Dump Car "3479," 97		36	___
16750	Lionel City Aquarium Car "3436," 97		32	___
16751	AIREX Sports Channel TV Car "3545", 97		25	___
16752	Marvin the Martian Missile Launching Flatcar "6655," 97	149	167	___
16754	Porky Pig and Instant Martians Flatcar "6805," 97	100	147	___
16755	Daffy Duck Animated Balloon Car "3470," 97	149	187	___

	MODERN 1970-2025		Exc	Like New
___	**16760**	Pluto and Cats Animated Gondola "3444," 97		55
___	**16765**	Bureau of Land Management Log Car "3351," 98		30
___	**16766**	Bureau of Land Management Ore Car "3479," 98		31
___	**16767**	New York Central Ice Docks Ice Car "6352," 98		47
___	**16776**	Holiday Boxcar, RailSounds, 98		68
___	**16777**	Animated Cola Car and Platform, 98		100
___	**16782**	Bethlehem Ore Dump Car "3479," 99	24	95
___	**16783**	Westside Lumber Log Dump Car "3351," 99		32
___	**16784**	Pratt's Hollow Seed Dump Car "3479," 99		36
___	**16785**	Happy Holidays Music Reefer "5700," 99	23	100
___	**16789**	Easter Operating Boxcar, 99		39
___	**16790**	UP Stock Car "3356," Crowsounds, 99		90
___	**16791**	New York City Lights Boxcar, 99		44
___	**16792**	Constellation Boxcar "9600," 99		37
___	**16793**	Animated Glow-in-the-Dark Alien Boxcar, 99		44
___	**16794**	Wicked Witch Halloween Boxcar, 99		46
___	**16795**	Elf Chasing Rudolph Gondola "6462," 99		55
___	**16796**	Snowman Loading Ice Car "6352," 99		55
___	**16805**	Budweiser Malt Nutrine Reefer "3285," 91-92 u	82	109
___	**16806**	Toys 'R' Us Boxcar, 92 u	21	26
___	**16807**	H.J. Heinz Reefer "301," 93	23	27
___	**16808**	Toys 'R' Us Boxcar, 93 u	28	30
___	**16817**	Ambassador 1-D Tank Car, 00 u		184
___	**16818**	Engineer Award Tank Car, 00 u		715
___	**16819**	JLC Award Tank Car, 00 u		760
___	**16820**	Ambassador Boxcar, 00 u	322	523
___	**16822**	CSX Water Tower, 08		23
___	**16824**	036 Command Control Switch, left hand (FasTrack), 09-14		110
___	**16825**	036 Command Control Switch, right hand (FasTrack), 09-14		110
___	**16826**	072 Command Control Switch, left hand (FasTrack), 09-14		120
___	**16827**	072 Command Control Switch, right hand (FasTrack), 09-14		120
___	**16828**	060 Command Control Switch, left hand (FasTrack), 09-14		120
___	**16829**	060 Command Control Switch, right hand (FasTrack), 09-14		120
___	**16830**	048 Command Control Switch, left hand (FasTrack), 09-14		120
___	**16831**	048 Command Control Switch, right hand (FasTrack), 09-14		120
___	**16832**	072 Command Control Wye Switch (FasTrack), 09-14		115
___	**16834**	FasTrack 048 Half-Curved Track, 09-25		7
___	**16835**	FasTrack 048 Quarter-Curved Track, 09-25		5
___	**16836**	Christmas Girder Bridge, 09		21
___	**16837**	Christmas Operating Billboard, 09		45
___	**16841**	Halloween Gateman, 09		80
___	**16842**	Big Moe Crane, 10		70
___	**16843**	City and Western Diorama, 10-11		15
___	**16845**	Bookstore, 09-10		60
___	**16846**	Burning Hobo Depot, 09		90
___	**16847**	Legacy Hotel, 10-11		70
___	**16848**	Creature Comforts Pet Store, sound, 09-10		80
___	**16849**	Rotary Dumper with coal conveyor, CC, 10		600
___	**16850**	Operating Wind Turbine, 3-pack, 09-11		225
___	**16851**	Sunoco Cylindrical Oil Tank, gray, 10-11		100
___	**16852**	Sunoco Cylindrical Oil Tank, yellow, 10-11		90
___	**16853**	Polar Express Diorama, 09-11, 13		18
___	**16854**	MTA LIRR Blinking Billboard, 09		30

MODERN 1970-2025		Exc	Like New	
16855	MTA LIRR Illuminated Station Platform, 09		37	___
16856	MTA LIRR Passenger Station, 09		60	___
16857	Thomas & Friends Diorama, 10-16, 20		18	___
16859	Grand Central Terminal, 09		1500	___
16861	50,000-gallon Water Tank, 09-11		150	___
16863	Santa's Christmas Wish Station, 09-11		125	___
16868	Straight O Gauge Tunnel, 09-17		55	___
16871	Winter Wonderland Diorama, 09-11		15	___
16872	Illuminated Christmas Station Platform, 09		35	___
16873	Bathtub Gondola Coal Load 3-pack, 10-19		20	___
16874	Coaling Station, 10-11		80	___
16880	Freight Platform, 10-12		30	___
16881	Barrel Shed, 10-11		30	___
16882	12" Covered Bridge, 10-18		60	___
16883	Neil's Guitar Shop, 10-11		60	___
16889	Coal Tipple Pack, 11-20		15	___
16891	Tank Car Accident, 10-11		130	___
16896	Flagpole with lights, 10-16		28	___
16897	75th Anniversary Gateman, 10		80	___
16903	CP Bulkhead Flatcar with pulp load (SSS), 94	22	25	___
16904	NYC Pacemaker Flatcar Set with trailers, 94	55	60	___
16907	Flatcar with farm tractors, 94	27	33	___
16908	U.S. Navy Flatcar "04039" with submarine, 94-95	39	46	___
16909	U.S. Navy Gondola "16556" with canisters, 94-95	16	22	___
16910	Missouri Pacific Flatcar with trailer, 94	22	27	___
16911	B&M Flatcar with trailer, 94	28	34	___
16912	CN Maxi-Stack Flatcar Set with containers, 94	70	75	___
16915	Lionel Lines Gondola (027), 93-94 u	7	10	___
16916	Ford Flatcar with trailer, 94 u	38	45	___
16917	Crayola Gondola with crayons, 94 u, 95	8	9	___
16919	Chrysler Mopar Gondola with coil covers, 94-96	33	36	___
16922	Chesapeake & Ohio Flatcar with trailer, 95	25	31	___
16923	Intermodal Service Flatcar with wheel chocks, 95	15	22	___
16924	Lionel Corporation Flatcar "6424" with trailer, 96		24	___
16925	New York Central Flatcar with trailer, 95	65	85	___
16926	Frisco Flatcar with trailers, 95	24	31	___
16927	New York Central Flatcar with gondola, 95	17	22	___
16928	Soo Line Flatcar with dump bin (027), 95	12	15	___
16929	BC Rail Gondola with cable reels, 95	21	25	___
16930	Santa Fe Flatcar with wheel load, 95	20	25	___
16932	Erie Flatcar with rail load, 95	17	22	___
16933	Lionel Lines Flatcar with autos, 95	23	25	___
16934	Pennsylvania Flatcar with Ertl road grader, 95	28	39	___
16935	UP Depressed Center Flatcar with Ertl bulldozer, 95	22	35	___
16936	Sealand Maxi-Stack Flatcar Set with containers, 95	61	85	___
16939	U.S. Navy Flatcar "04040" with boat, 95	25	30	___
16940	ATSF Flatcar with trailer, 96-99		40	___
16941	ATSF Flatcar with autos, 96-99		25	___
16943	Jersey Central Gondola, 96		18	___
16944	Georgia Power Flatcar "31438" with transformer, 95 u		50	___
16945	Georgia Power Flatcar "31950" with cable reels, 95 u		53	___
16946	C&O F9 Well Car "3840," 96		31	___
16951	Southern I-Beam Flatcar "9823" with load, 97		25	___

		MODERN 1970-2025	Exc	Like New
___	**16952**	U.S. Navy Flatcar with Ertl helicopter, 96		25
___	**16953**	NYC Flatcar with Red Wing Shoes trailer, 95 u	39	45
___	**16954**	NYC Flatcar "6424" with Ertl scraper, 96		30
___	**16955**	ATSF Flatcar with Ertl Challenger, 96		30
___	**16956**	Zenith Flatcar with trailer, 95 u	50	141
___	**16957**	Depressed Center Flatcar "6461" with Ertl Case tractor, 96		29
___	**16958**	Flatcar with Ertl New Holland loader, 96		26
___	**16960**	U.S. Coast Guard Flatcar with boat, 96		40
___	**16961**	GM/AC Delco Flatcar with trailer, 95		73
___	**16963**	Lionel Corporation Flatcar "6411," 96-97		34
___	**16964**	Lionel Corporation Gondola "6462," 97		22
___	**16965**	Scout Flatcar "6424" with stakes, 96-97		20
___	**16967**	Depressed Center Flatcar "6461" with transformer, 96		21
___	**16968**	Depressed Center Flatcar "6461" with Ertl Helicopter, 96	10	40
___	**16969**	Flatcar "6411" with Beechcraft Bonanza, 96		33
___	**16970**	LA County Flatcar "6424" with motorized powerboat, 96	11	20
___	**16971**	Port of Lionel City Flatcar with boat, 97		35
___	**16972**	P&LE Gondola "6462," 97		22
___	**16975**	Well Car Doublestack Set, 97		75
___	**16978**	MILW Flatcar "6424" with P&H shovel, 97		43
___	**16980**	Speedy Gonzales Missile Flatcar "6823," 97	30	56
___	**16982**	BC Rail Bulkhead Flatcar "9823" with lumber, 97		28
___	**16983**	PRR F9 Well Car "6983" with cable reels, 97		39
___	**16986**	Sears Zenith Bulkhead Flatcar, 96 u		45
___	**16987**	Musco Lighting Bulkhead Flatcar, 97 u		35
___	**16997**	Lionel Lines Recovery Crane Car, 99		50
___	**17002**	Conrail 2-bay ACF Hopper (std 0), 87	42	47
___	**17003**	Du Pont 2-bay ACF Hopper (std 0), 90	39	45
___	**17004**	MKT 2-bay ACF Hopper (std 0), 91	23	27
___	**17005**	Cargill 2-bay ACF Hopper (std 0), 92	26	37
___	**17006**	Soo Line 2-bay ACF Hopper (std 0, SSS), 93	31	36
___	**17007**	GN 2-bay ACF Hopper "173872" (std 0), 94	26	31
___	**17008**	D&RGW 2-bay ACF Hopper "10009" (std 0), 95		31
___	**17009**	New York Central 2-bay ACF Hopper, 96		35
___	**17010**	Govt. of Canada ACF 2-bay Covered Hopper "7000," 98	23	35
___	**17010**	NP PS-1 Boxcar 6-pack, LionScale, 17		360
___	**17011**	NP ACF 2-bay Covered Hopper "75052," 98		44
___	**17012**	Govt. of Canada ACF 2-bay Covered Hopper "7001," 98	15	36
___	**17013**	NYC Graffiti 2-bay Covered Hopper "7000," 99		55
___	**17014**	Graffiti 2-bay Covered Hopper "7000" (std 0), 99		45
___	**17015**	Corning 2-bay Hopper "90409" (std 0), 01		40
___	**17016**	C&NW 2-bay Hopper "96644" (std 0), 01		46
___	**17017**	Chessie System 2-bay Hopper "605527" (std 0), 02		32
___	**17018**	Nickel Plate Road Offset Hopper "33074," 02		43
___	**17019**	Santa Fe Offset Hopper "78299", 02		43
___	**17020**	Frisco Offset Hopper "92092," 02		43
___	**17020**	UP PS-1 Boxcar 6-pack, LionScale, 17		360
___	**17021**	NYC Offset Hopper "867999," 02		43
___	**17022**	Burlington 2-bay ACF Hopper "183925" (std 0), 03		30
___	**17023**	BNSF 2-bay Hopper "409038" (std 0), 04		30
___	**17024**	Reading Offset Hopper "81089" (std 0), 03-04		43
___	**17025**	C&O Offset Hopper "300027" (std 0), 03-04		43
___	**17026**	D&H Offset Hopper "7215" (std 0), 03-04		41

MODERN 1970-2025		Exc	Like New	
17027	IC Offset Hopper "92142" (std O), 03-04		49	___
17028	GE PS-2 2-bay Covered Hopper "326" (std O), 03-04		35	___
17029	CNJ PS-2 2-bay Covered Hopper "803" (std O), 03-04		35	___
17030	MILW PS-2 2-bay Covered Hopper "99708" (std O), 03-04	18	43	___
17030	Reading PS-1 Boxcar 6-pack, LionScale, 17		360	___
17031	SP PS-2 2-bay Covered Hopper "401306" (std O), 03-04		38	___
17038	Clinchfield PS-2 Covered Hopper, 05		70	___
17039	Boston & Maine PS-2 2-bay Covered Hopper, 05		55	___
17040	Norfolk & Western PS-2 2-bay Covered Hopper, 05		55	___
17040	NYC PS-1 Boxcar 6-pack, LionScale, 17		360	___
17041	Great Northern Offset Hopper, 05		60	___
17042	Green Bay & Western Offset Hopper, 05		60	___
17043	Baltimore & Ohio Offset Hopper, 05		60	___
17044	DT&I PS-2 Covered Hopper (std O), 05-06	15	38	___
17050	NYC 14-panel Hopper 6-pack, LionScale, 17		330	___
17060	D&RGW 14-panel Hopper 6-pack, LionScale, 17		330	___
17063	Santa Fe PS-2 2-bay Covered Hopper "82297" (std O), 06		55	___
17064	MKT PS-2 2-bay Covered Hopper "1311" (std O), 06		55	___
17065	Boraxo PS-2 2-bay Covered Hopper "31062" (std O), 06		55	___
17066	PRR PS-2 2-bay Covered Hopper "256177" (std O), 06		55	___
17067	Rock Island Offset Hopper "89500" with gravel (std O), 06		65	___
17068	CNJ Offset Hopper "61261" (std O), 06		65	___
17069	Maine Central Offset Hopper "3785" (std O), 06		65	___
17070	P&LE Offset Hopper "4990" (std O), 06		65	___
17070	Conrail 14-panel Hopper 6-pack, LionScale, 17		330	___
17075	MKT PS-2 2-bay Covered Hopper "1314" (std O), 06		55	___
17080	EL 14-panel Hopper 6-pack, LionScale, 17		330	___
17083	C&O Offset Hopper "47386" (std O), 05		40	___
17090	Trailer Train 50' Flatcar 6-pack, 17		330	___
17100	Chessie System 3-bay ACF Hopper	49	85	___
17100	BN 50' Flatcar 6-pack, 17		330	___
17101	Chessie System 3-bay ACF Hopper (std O), 88	37	45	___
17102	Chessie System 3-bay ACF Hopper (std O), 88	35	41	___
17103	Chessie System 3-bay ACF Hopper (std O), 88	31	34	___
17104	Chessie System 3-bay ACF Hopper (std O), 88	38	46	___
17105	Chessie System 3-bay ACF Hopper (std O), 88	39	46	___
17107	Sinclair 3-bay ACF Hopper (std O), 89	40	48	___
17108	Santa Fe 3-bay ACF Hopper (std O), 90	42	48	___
17109	N&W 3-bay ACF Hopper (std O), 91	24	31	___
17110	UP Hopper with coal (std O), 91	24	30	___
17110	AT&SF 50' Flatcar 6-pack, 17		330	___
17111	Reading Hopper with coal (std O), 91	23	28	___
17112	Erie-Lack. 3-bay ACF Hopper (std O), 92	24	34	___
17113	LV Hopper with coal (std O), 92-93	25	32	___
17114	Peabody Hopper with coal (std O), 92-93	26	30	___
17118	Archer Daniels Midland 3-bay ACF Hopper "60029" (std O), 93	28	35	___
17120	CSX Hopper "295110" with coal (std O), 94	28	30	___
17120	PRR 50' Flatcar 6-pack, 17		330	___
17121	ICG Hopper "72867" with coal (std O), 94	26	33	___
17122	RI 3-bay ACF Hopper "800200" (std O), 94	32	39	___
17123	Cargill Covered Grain Hopper "844304" (std O), 95	26	37	___
17124	Archer Daniels Midland 3-bay ACF Hopper "50224" (std O), 95	24	30	___
17127	Delaware & Hudson 3-bay Hopper, 96	11	34	___

		MODERN 1970-2025	Exc	Like New
____	**17128**	Chesapeake & Ohio 3-bay Hopper, 96		30
____	**17129**	WM 3-bay Hopper "9300" with coal (std 0), 97		34
____	**17130**	ACFX ACF 4-bay Covered Hopper 6-pack, LionScale, 17		360
____	**17132**	PRR 3-bay ACF Hopper "260815," 98		40
____	**17133**	BNSF ACF 3-bay Covered Hopper "403698," 98	16	39
____	**17134**	BNSF 3-bay Covered Hopper "403698" (std 0), 01		38
____	**17135**	BNSF ACF 3-bay Covered Hopper with ETD, 98	16	39
____	**17137**	Cargill 3-bay Covered Hopper "1219" (std 0), 99		45
____	**17138**	Farmers Elevator 3-bay Covered Hopper (std 0), 99		45
____	**17139**	Grain Train 3-bay Hopper "BLMR 1025," 99-00	29	52
____	**17140**	Virginian 3-bay Hopper 6-pack, "5260-5265", 99		230
____	**17140**	GN ACF 4-bay Covered Hopper 6-pack, LionScale, 17		360
____	**17147**	C&O 3-bay Hopper 6-pack, "156330-156335," 99		230
____	**17150**	AT&SF ACF 4-bay Covered Hopper 6-pack, LionScale, 17		360
____	**17154**	Alberta Cylindrical Hopper "628373" (std 0), 01		40
____	**17155**	Shell Cylindrical Hopper "3527" (std 0), 01		40
____	**17156**	ACF Pressureaide 3-bay Hopper "59267" (std 0), 01		27
____	**17157**	Wonder Bread "56670" 3-bay Hopper (std 0), 01		45
____	**17158**	Conrail Coal Hopper "487739" (std 0), 01		42
____	**17159**	N&W Coal Hopper "1776" (std 0), 01		45
____	**17160**	C&NW (UP) B145ACF 4-bay Covered Hopper 6-pack, LionScale, 17		360
____	**17163**	C&O 3-bay Hopper (std 0), 01		30
____	**17170**	General Mills 3-bay Covered Hopper (std 0), 00 u		60
____	**17170**	PFE 57' Mechanical Reefer, 6-pack, LionScale, 17		390
____	**17171**	Lionel Lion Cylindrical Hopper (std 0), 01		45
____	**17172**	CP Rail Cylindrical Hopper "385206" (std 0), 02		37
____	**17173**	Govt. of Canada Cylindrical Hopper "111031" (std 0), 02		33
____	**17174**	GN 3-bay Hopper "171250" (std 0), 02		29
____	**17175**	IC PS-2CD 4427 Covered Hopper "57031" (std 0), 02		40
____	**17176**	Cargill PS-2CD 4427 Covered Hopper "2514" (std 0), 02		46
____	**17177**	PS-2CD 4427 Covered Hopper "2500" (std 0), 02		40
____	**17178**	Santa Fe PS-2CD 4427 Covered Hopper "304774" (std 0), 02		40
____	**17179**	Indianapolis Power & Light Coal Hopper "10074" (std 0), 02		40
____	**17180**	Rock Island Coal Hopper "700665" (std 0), 02		40
____	**17180**	SPFE 57' Mechanical Reefer 6-pack, LionScale, 17		390
____	**17181**	NYC 4-bay ACF Centerflow Hopper "892138" (std 0), 03		45
____	**17182**	Sigco Hybrids 4-bay ACF Centerflow Hopper "1100" (std 0), 03		46
____	**17183**	C&O Hopper "156341" (std 0), 01		30
____	**17184**	Virginian Hopper "5271" (std 0), 01		30
____	**17185**	LLCX Bathtub Gondola "877900" (std 0), 01		36
____	**17186**	Cannonaide 4-bay ACF Centerflow Hopper "96169" (std 0), 03		40
____	**17187**	Rio Grande 4-bay ACF Centerflow Hopper "15521" (std 0), 03		40
____	**17188**	Govt. of Canada 3-bay Cylindrical Hopper (std 0), 03		48
____	**17189**	Saskatchewan Grain 3-bay Cylindrical Hopper (std 0), 03		48
____	**17190**	Soo/CP 3-bay ACF Hopper "119303" (std 0), 03		37
____	**17190**	UPFE 57' Mechanical Reefer 6-pack, LionScale, 17		390
____	**17191**	BN PS-2CD 4427 Hopper "450669" (std 0), 03-04		45
____	**17192**	Lehigh Valley PS-2CD 4427 Hopper "51118" (std 0), 03-04		40
____	**17193**	Chessie System/WM PS-2CD 4427 Hopper "4673" (std 0), 03-04		30
____	**17194**	MKT PS-2CD 4427 Hopper "1122" (std 0), 03-04		40

MODERN 1970-2025		Exc	Like New	
17195	L&N 3-bay Hopper "240850" (std O), 04		40	___
17196	Firestone 4-bay Hopper "53240" (std O), 04		40	___
17197	Diamond Chemicals 4-bay Hopper "53286" (std O), 04		40	___
17198	Hercules 4-bay Hopper "50503" (std O), 04		40	___
17199	Conrail 4-bay Hopper "888367" (std O), 04		46	___
17200	Canadian Pacific Boxcar (std O), 89	26	32	___
17200	BNFE 57' Mechanical Reefer 6-pack, LionScale, 17		390	___
17201	Conrail Boxcar (std O), 87	33	38	___
17202	Santa Fe Boxcar (std O), diesel RailSounds, 90	80	85	___
17203	Cotton Belt DD Boxcar (std O), 91	34	38	___
17204	Missouri Pacific DD Boxcar (std O), 91	27	30	___
17207	C&IM DD Boxcar (std O), 92	36	42	___
17208	Union Pacific DD Boxcar (std O), 92	32	40	___
17209	B&O DD Boxcar "296000" (std O), 93	37	43	___
17210	Chicago & Illinois Midland Boxcar "16021" (std O), 92 u	30	39	___
17210	BN 100-Ton, 4-Bay Hopper 6-pack, 17		330	___
17211	Chicago & Illinois Midland Boxcar "16022" (std O), 92 u	30	39	___
17212	Chicago & Illinois Midland Boxcar "16023" (std O), 92 u	24	31	___
17213	Susquehanna Boxcar "501" (std O), 93	28	31	___
17214	Railbox Boxcar (std O), diesel RailSounds, 93	75	85	___
17216	PRR DD Boxcar "60155" (std O), 94	34	38	___
17217	New Haven State of Maine Boxcar "45003" (std O), 95	28	35	___
17218	BAR State of Maine Boxcar "2184" (std O), 95	23	36	___
17219	Tazmanian Devil 40th Birthday Boxcar (std O), 95	40	50	___
17220	Pennsylvania Boxcar (std O), 96		23	___
17220	CSX 100-Ton, 4-Bay Hopper 6-pack, 17		330	___
17221	NYC Boxcar (std O), 96	19	33	___
17222	Western Pacific Boxcar (std O), 96	28	34	___
17223	Milwaukee Road DD Boxcar (std 0), 96		34	___
17224	Central of Georgia Boxcar "9464-197" (std O), 97	15	29	___
17225	Penn Central Boxcar "9464-297" (std O), 97	13	26	___
17226	Milwaukee Road Boxcar "9464-397" (std O), 97	13	27	___
17227	UP DD Boxcar "9200" (std O), 97		35	___
17230	NS 100-Ton, 4-Bay Hopper 6-pack, 17		330	___
17231	Wisconsin Central DD Boxcar "9200" with auto frames, 98		40	___
17232	SP/UP Merger DD Boxcar "9200," 98		33	___
17233	Western Pacific Boxcar "9464-198," 98		27	___
17234	Port Huron & Detroit Boxcar "9464-298," 98		33	___
17235	Boston & Maine Boxcar "9464-398," 98		41	___
17239	ATSF Texas Chief Boxcar "9464-1," 97		50	___
17240	ATSF Super Chief Boxcar "9464-2," 97		50	___
17240	UP 100-Ton, 4-Bay Hopper 6-pack, 17		330	___
17241	ATSF El Capitan Boxcar "9464-3," 97		50	___
17242	ATSF Grand Canyon Boxcar "9464-4," 97		60	___
17243	NP Boxcar "8722," 98		48	___
17244	Santa Fe Chief Boxcar, 98		37	___
17245	C&O Boxcar with Chessie kitten, 98		44	___
17246	NYC Pacemaker Rolling Stock 4-pack, 98		200	___
17247	NYC 9464 Boxcar "174940," 98		135	___
17248	NYC 9464 Boxcar "174945," 98	50	115	___
17249	NYC 9464 Boxcar "174949," 98		60	___
17250	UP Boxcar "507406" (std O), 99		45	___
17250	AT&SF Stockcar 6-pack, 17		360	___

	MODERN 1970-2025		Exc	Like New
___	**17251**	BNSF Boxcar "103277," 99		41
___	**17252**	NS Boxcar "564824" (std 0), 99		41
___	**17253**	CSX Boxcar "141756" (std 0), 99		35
___	**17254**	UP Boxcar "551967" (std 0), 99		42
___	**17255**	Chevy DD Boxcar "9200" (std 0), 99		38
___	**17257**	Atlantic Coast Line Boxcar "28809" (std 0), 99		36
___	**17258**	D&H 9464 Boxcar "29055" std 0, 99		41
___	**17259**	MKT 9464 Boxcar "1422" (std 0), 99		34
___	**17260**	CP Rail 9464 Boxcar "286138" (std 0), silver, 00		45
___	**17260**	PRR Stockcar 6-pack, 17		360
___	**17261**	CP Rail 9464 Boxcar "85154," green, 00	20	45
___	**17262**	CP Rail 9464 Boxcar "56776," red (std 0), 00		48
___	**17263**	NYC Boxcar "45725" (std 0), 00		46
___	**17264**	C&O Boxcar "6054" (std 0), 00		44
___	**17265**	U.S. Army Boxcar (std 0), 00		35
___	**17266**	Monon Boxcar "911" (std 0), 00		45
___	**17268**	C&O 9464 Boxcar "12700" (std 0), 01		44
___	**17269**	Western Maryland 9464 Boxcar "29140" (std 0), 01		44
___	**17270**	B&O Time-Saver 9464 Boxcar "467439" (std 0), 01		42
___	**17270**	Nickel Plate Road Stockcar 6-pack, 17		360
___	**17271**	The Rock Boxcar "300324" (std 0), 01		37
___	**17272**	Railbox Boxcar "15150" (std 0), 01		27
___	**17273**	DT&I DD Boxcar "26852" (std 0), 01		44
___	**17274**	Soo Line DD Boxcar "177587" (std 0), 01		42
___	**17275**	NYC PS-1 Boxcar "175008" (std 0), 02		43
___	**17276**	Cotton Belt PS-1 Boxcar "75000" (std 0), 02		44
___	**17277**	Rio Grande PS-1 Boxcar "69676" (std 0), 02		40
___	**17278**	WP PS-1 Boxcar "1953" (std 0), 02		44
___	**17279**	Ontario Northland Boxcar "7428" (std 0), 02		40
___	**17280**	Santa Fe Boxcar "600194" with auto frames (std 0), 02		45
___	**17280**	UP Stockcar 6-pack, 17		360
___	**17281**	PRR DD Boxcar "83158" (std 0), 04		42
___	**17282**	UP DD Boxcar "160300" (std 0), 04		42
___	**17283**	GM&O DD Boxcar "9077" (std 0), 04		41
___	**17284**	Erie DD Boxcar "66000" (std 0), 04		41
___	**17285**	CSX Big Blue Boxcar "151296" (std 0), 03		36
___	**17287**	BAR Boxcar "5976" (std 0), 03		35
___	**17288**	NYC PS-1 Boxcar "175012" (std 0), 03-04		38
___	**17289**	GN PS-1 Boxcar "18485" (std 0), 03	29	43
___	**17290**	Seaboard PS-1 Boxcar "24452" (std 0), 03-04		42
___	**17290**	Portland Terminal Wood-chip Hopper 6-pack, 17		360
___	**17291**	RI PS-1 Boxcar "21110" (std 0), 03-04		42
___	**17292**	B&M PS-1 Boxcar "76182" (std 0), 04		34
___	**17293**	IC PS-1 Boxcar "400666" (std 0), 04		40
___	**17294**	TP&W PS-1 Boxcar "5036" (std 0), 04	18	47
___	**17295**	Santa Fe PS-1 Boxcar "276749" (std 0), 04		40
___	**17296**	C&O PS-1 Boxcar (std 0), 04		40
___	**17297**	UP PS-1 Boxcar, 03		100
___	**17298**	Southern PS-1 Boxcar w/box load (std 0), 05-06	18	42
___	**17300**	Canadian Pacific Reefer (std 0), 89	28	33
___	**17300**	Chessie System Wood-chip Hopper 6-pack, 17		360
___	**17301**	Conrail Reefer (std 0), 87	35	42
___	**17302**	Santa Fe Reefer with ETD (std 0), 90	27	41

MODERN 1970-2025		Exc	Like New	
17303	C&O Reefer "7890" (std 0), 93	23	30	___
17304	Wabash Reefer "26269" (std 0), 94	29	37	___
17305	Pacific Fruit Express Reefer "459400" (std 0), 94	27	40	___
17306	Pacific Fruit Express Reefer "459401" (std 0), 94	19	27	___
17307	Tropicana Reefer "300" (std 0), 95	44	65	___
17308	Tropicana Reefer "301" (std 0), 95	22	35	___
17309	Tropicana Reefer "302" (std 0), 95	21	29	___
17310	Tropicana Reefer "303" (std 0), 95	20	27	___
17310	GM&O Wood-chip Hopper 6-pack, 17		360	___
17311	REA Reefer (std 0), 96	28	30	___
17314	PFE Reefer "9800-198," 98		42	___
17315	PFE Reefer "9800-298," 98		39	___
17316	NP Reefer "98583," 98		50	___
17317	PRR Reefer FGE "91904," 98		36	___
17318	UP Reefer "170650" (std 0), 99		47	___
17319	PFE Reefer 6-pack (std 0), 01	240	300	___
17320	WM Wood-chip Hopper 6-pack, 17		360	___
17331	Hood's General American Milk Car "802" (std 0), 02	33	88	___
17332	Pfaudler General American Milk Car "501" (std 0), 02	33	70	___
17334	REA General American Milk Car "1741" (std 0), 02	21	77	___
17335	New Haven General American Milk Car "102" (std 0), 02	25	69	___
17336	PFE Steel-sided Reefer "17760" (std 0), 03		45	___
17337	CN Steel-sided Reefer "209712" (std 0), 03		38	___
17338	Merchants Dispatch Transit Steel-sided Reefer "12322" (std 0), 03		39	___
17339	Burlington Steel-sided Reefer "74825" (std 0), 03		45	___
17340	White Bros. General American Milk Car "891" (std 0), 03		44	___
17341	Dairymen's League General American Milk Car "779" (std 0), 03		43	___
17342	Miller Beer Steel-sided Reefer American Eagle (std 0), 03 u	40	63	___
17343	Miller Beer Steel-sided Reefer Lady and Moon (std 0), 03 u	40	64	___
17349	NYC General American Milk Car "6581" (std 0), 03 u		42	___
17350	Hood's General American Milk Car "503" (std 0), 03 u		45	___
17351	Santa Fe Steel-sided Reefer "3526" (std 0), 04		43	___
17352	PFE Steel-sided Reefer "20043" (std 0), 04		41	___
17353	Needham Packing Steel-sided Reefer "60507" (std 0), 04		44	___
17354	Swift Steel-sided Reefer "15392" (std 0), 04		42	___
17355	Hood's Steel-sided Reefer "550" (std 0), 04	15	40	___
17356	Nestle Nesquik Steel-sided Reefer (std 0), 04		44	___
17357	Borden's Steel-sided Reefer "522" (std 0), 04		47	___
17358	Fairfield Farms Steel-sided Reefer (std 0), 04		44	___
17360	Hood's General American Milk Car "810" (std 0), 03	25	53	___
17361	Hood's General American Milk Car "811" (std 0), 03		43	___
17362	Pfaudler General American Milk Car "502" (std 0), 03		47	___
17363	Pfaudler General American Milk Car "503" (std 0), 03		40	___
17364	REA General American Milk Car "1742" (std 0), 03		38	___
17365	REA General American Milk Car "1743" (std 0), 03		44	___
17366	NH General American Milk Car "103" (std 0), 03	25	50	___
17367	NH General American Milk Car "104" (std 0), 03		47	___
17368	White Brothers General American Milk Car "892" (std 0), 03		43	___
17369	White Brothers General American Milk Car "893" (std 0), 03		47	___
17370	Dairymen's League General American Milk Car "780" (std 0), 03		47	___
17371	Dairymen's League Milk Car "781" (std 0), 03		47	___

		Exc	Like New
____ **17372**	NYC General American Milk Car "6582" (std 0), 03		47
____ **17373**	NYC General American Milk Car "6583" (std 0), 03		40
____ **17374**	Hood's General American Milk Car "504" (std 0), 03	28	54
____ **17375**	Hood's General American Milk Car "505" (std 0), 03	25	54
____ **17377**	Railway Express General American Milk Car "302" (std 0), 05	69	163
____ **17378**	Supplee General American Milk Car (std 0), 05		63
____ **17379**	NP Steel-sided Reefer "91353" (std 0), 05	33	60
____ **17380**	PFE Silver Steel-sided Reefer "45698" (std 0), 05		60
____ **17381**	North Western Steel-sided Reefer "751" (std 0), 05		40
____ **17397**	PFE Steel-sided Reefer "47767" (std 0), 05		45
____ **17398**	A&P General American Milk Car "737" (std 0), 06		65
____ **17399**	Bowman Dairy General American Milk Car "117" (std 0), 06		65
____ **17400**	CP Rail Gondola with coal (std 0), 89	30	34
____ **17401**	Conrail Gondola with coal (std 0), 87	24	26
____ **17402**	Santa Fe Gondola with coal (std 0), 90	19	25
____ **17403**	Chessie System Gondola "371629" w/coil covers (std 0), 93	18	25
____ **17404**	ICG Gondola "245998" with coil covers (std 0), 93	26	32
____ **17405**	Reading Gondola "24876" with coil covers (std 0), 94	27	31
____ **17406**	PRR Gondola "385405" with coil covers (std 0), 95	37	42
____ **17407**	NKP Gondola with scrap load, 96		24
____ **17408**	Cotton Belt Gondola "9820" with scrap load (std 0), 97		32
____ **17410**	UP Gondola "903004" with scrap load (std 0), 99		30
____ **17412**	Gondola, blue, online store, 98		20
____ **17413**	Service Center Gondola with parts load (SSS), 00		24
____ **17414**	Nickel Plate PS-5 Gondola "44801" (std 0), 01-02		40
____ **17415**	Frisco PS-5 Gondola "61878" (std 0), 01-02		35
____ **17416**	D&H Gondola "14011" with scrap load (std 0), 01		33
____ **17417**	BN Rotary Bathtub Gondola 3-pack, 01		140
____ **17421**	CSX Rotary Bathtub Gondola 3-pack, 01		135
____ **17425**	Western Maryland PS-5 Gondola "354903" (std 0), 01-02		36
____ **17426**	Maine Central PS-5 Gondola "1116" (std 0), 01-02		40
____ **17427**	CSX Rotary Bathtub Gondola Add-on Unit (std 0), 02		47
____ **17428**	BN Rotary Bathtub Gondola Add-on Unit (std 0), 02		42
____ **17429**	Conrail Rotary Bathtub Gondola 3-pack (std 0), 02-03		115
____ **17433**	BNSF Rotary Bathtub Gondola 3-pack (std 0), 02-03		145
____ **17439**	UP PS-5 Gondola "229606" (std 0), 03		35
____ **17440**	Algoma Central PS-5 Gondola "801" (std 0), 03		32
____ **17441**	Conrail Rotary Bathtub Gondola "507673" (std 0), 03		39
____ **17442**	BNSF Rotary Bathtub Gondola "668330" (std 0), 03		46
____ **17443**	NS Rotary Bathtub Gondola 3-pack (std 0), 03		90
____ **17447**	UP Rotary Bathtub Gondola 3-pack (std 0), 03		100
____ **17457**	GN PS-5 Gondola "72839" (std 0), 03		35
____ **17458**	Reading PS-5 Gondola "33267" (std 0), 03		35
____ **17459**	CP Rail PS-5 Gondola "338966" (std 0), 04		35
____ **17460**	NYC PS-5 Gondola "749592" (std 0), 04		40
____ **17461**	Pennsylvania PS-5 Gondola "374256" (std 0), 04		36
____ **17462**	Santa Fe PS-5 Gondola "167340" (std 0), 04		35
____ **17463**	NS Bathtub Gondola "10303" (std 0), 04		40
____ **17464**	UP Bathtub Gondola "28100" (std 0), 04		35
____ **17465**	CP Rail Bathtub Gondola 3-pack (std 0), 04		105
____ **17469**	B&O/Chessie System PS-5 Drop-end Gondola (std 0), 05-06	15	38
____ **17470**	CP Rail Bathtub Gondola, 05		50

MODERN 1970-2025		Exc	Like New	
17471	Burlington PS-5 Gondola with covers (std 0), 05		44	____
17472	New Haven PS-5 Gondola with covers (std 0), 05		53	____
17473	NYC PS-5 Gondola "502351" (std 0), 06-07		65	____
17474	D&H PS-5 Gondola "13816" (std 0), 06-07		65	____
17475	Koppers PS-5 Gondola "213" (std 0), 06-07		65	____
17477	L&N PS-5 Gondola "170012" (std 0), 06-07		46	____
17478	N&W PS-5 Gondola "275005" with containers (std 0), 08		70	____
17479	LV PS-5 Gondola "33455" with containers (std 0), 08		70	____
17480	RI PS-5 Gondola with coke containers (std 0), 08-09		70	____
17488	UP Bathtub Gondola 3-pack (std 0), 09		190	____
17500	CP Flatcar with logs (std 0), 89	22	37	____
17501	Conrail Flatcar with stakes (std 0), 87	37	45	____
17502	Santa Fe Flatcar with trailer (std 0), 90	70	75	____
17503	NS Flatcar with trailer (std 0), 92	55	65	____
17504	NS Flatcar with trailer (std 0), 92	55	65	____
17505	NS Flatcar with trailer (std 0), 92	50	55	____
17506	NS Flatcar with trailer (std 0), 92	46	55	____
17507	NS Flatcar with trailer (std 0), 92	50	55	____
17510	NP Flatcar "61200" with logs (std 0), 94	28	35	____
17511	WM Flatcar with logs, set of 3 (std 0), 95	60	145	____
17512	WM Flatcar with logs (std 0), 95	35	41	____
17513	WM Flatcar with logs (std 0), 95	43	50	____
17514	WM Flatcar with logs (std 0), 95	39	45	____
17515	Norfolk Southern Flatcar with tractors (std 0), 95	24	42	____
17516	T&P Flatcar "9823" with 2 Beechcraft Bonanzas (std 0), 97		50	____
17517	WP Flatcar "9823" with Ertl Caterpillar frontloader (std 0), 97		39	____
17518	PRR Flatcar "9823" with 2 Corgi Mack trucks (std 0), 97	32	53	____
17522	Flatcar with Plymouth Prowler, 98		41	____
17522	Lake Superior & Ishpeming PS-1 Boxcar, 98u		45	____
17524	Lake Superior & Ishpeming PS-1 Boxcar, 98u		45	____
17527	Flatcar with 2 Dodge Vipers, 98		38	____
17529	ATSF Flatcar "90010" with Ford milk truck, 99		55	____
17533	MTTX Ford Flatcar with auto frames, 99		38	____
17534	Diamond T Flatcar with Mack trucks "9823", 99		55	____
17536	Route 66 Flatcar "9823-3" with 2 luxury coupes, 99		37	____
17537	Route 66 Flatcar "9823-4" with 2 touring coupes, 99		32	____
17538	NYC Flatcar with Ford tow truck, 99		43	____
17539	Flatcar "9823" with 2 Corvettes (std 0), 99		70	____
17540	Flatcar "9823" with 2 Corvettes (std 0), 99		70	____
17546	LL Recovery Flatcar "6424" with rail load, 99		50	____
17547	Lionel Lines Recovery Flatcar "6429" with machinery, 99		50	____
17548	Route 66 Flatcar "9823-6" with 2 luxury coupes, 99		42	____
17549	Route 66 Flatcar "9823-5" with station wagon and trailer, 99		42	____
17550	BN Center Beam Flatcar "6216" with lumber (std 0), 99		39	____
17551	NYC Flatcar with NYC pickups "499," 99		49	____
17553	Trailer Train Flatcar "98102" with combine (std 0), 99		125	____
17554	GN Flatcar "61042" with logs, 00		32	____
17555	Ford Mustang Flatcar with 2 cars (std 0), 01		0	____
17556	Ford Mustang Flatcar with 2 cars (std 0), 01		0	____
17557	Route 66 Flatcar "9823-7" with black sedans, 99-00		39	____
17558	Route 66 Flatcar "9823-8" with brown sedans, 99		39	____
17559	Route 66 Flatcar "9823-9" with 2 wagons (std 0), 01		40	____
17560	Route 66 Flatcar "9823-10" with 2 sedans (std 0), 01		40	____

		MODERN 1970-2025	Exc	Like New
___	**17563**	Santa Fe Flatcar "90011" with pickup trucks (std 0), 01		49
___	**17564**	West Side Lumber Shay Log Car 3-pack #2 (std 0), 01		95
___	**17568**	PRR Flatcar "470333" with pickup trucks (std 0), 02		50
___	**17571**	UP Flatcar "909231" with pickup trucks (std 0), 03		50
___	**17572**	Pioneer Seed Flatcar with pedal cars, 02 u		220
___	**17573**	WM PS-4 Flatcar "2631" (std 0), 03		35
___	**17574**	Santa Fe PS-4 Flatcar "90081" (std 0), 03		35
___	**17575**	NYC PS-4 Flatcar "506098" (std 0), 03		40
___	**17576**	Ontario Northland PS-4 Flatcar "2020" (std 0), 03		35
___	**17577**	B&O PS-4 Flatcar "8651" (std 0), 04		35
___	**17578**	B&M PS-4 Flatcar "34007" (std 0), 04		35
___	**17579**	Milwaukee Road PS-4 Flatcar "64073" (std 0), 04		35
___	**17580**	UP PS-4 Flatcar "54603" (std 0), 04		35
___	**17581**	GN Flatcar "X4168" with pickup trucks (std 0), 04		42
___	**17582**	PRR PS-4 Flatcar "469617" with trailers (std 0), 05		110
___	**17583**	GN PS-4 Flatcar with trailers, 05	43	90
___	**17584**	SP PS-4 Flatcar with trailers, 05		80
___	**17585**	C&O PS-4 Flatcar "81000" with trailers (std 0), 05		80
___	**17586**	BN Husky Stack Car "63322" (std 0), 05		80
___	**17587**	SP Husky Stack Car "513915" (std 0), 05		80
___	**17588**	CSX Husky Stack Car "620350" (std 0), 05		80
___	**17589**	TTX Trailer Train Husky Stack Car "456249" (std 0), 05		65
___	**17590**	Penn Central PS-4 Flatcar w/stakes (std 0), 05-06	15	38
___	**17600**	NYC Wood-sided Caboose (std 0), 87 u	35	45
___	**17601**	Southern Wood-sided Caboose (std 0), 88	35	44
___	**17602**	Conrail Wood-sided Caboose (std 0), 87	65	75
___	**17603**	RI Wood-sided Caboose (std 0), 88	19	34
___	**17604**	Lackawanna Wood-sided Caboose (std 0), 88	42	53
___	**17605**	Reading Wood-sided Caboose (std 0), 89	34	37
___	**17606**	NYC Steel-sided Caboose, smoke (std 0), 90	49	65
___	**17607**	Reading Steel-sided Caboose, smoke (std 0), 90	55	65
___	**17608**	C&O Steel-sided Caboose, smoke (std 0), 91	46	55
___	**17610**	Wabash Steel-sided Caboose, smoke (std 0), 91	39	55
___	**17611**	NYC Wood-sided Caboose "6003" (std 0), 90 u	40	55
___	**17612**	NKP Steel-sided Caboose, smoke (FF 6), 92	60	65
___	**17613**	Southern Steel-sided Caboose "7613," smoke (std 0), 92	60	65
___	**17615**	NP Wood-sided Caboose, smoke (std 0), 92	65	70
___	**17617**	D&RGW Steel-sided Caboose (std 0), 95	43	63
___	**17618**	Frisco Wood-sided Caboose (std 0), 95	65	75
___	**17620**	NP Wood-sided Caboose "1746", 98		70
___	**17623**	Farmrail Extended Vision Caboose, 99		74
___	**17624**	Conrail Extended Vision Caboose "6900", 99		43
___	**17625**	Burlington Northern Steel-sided Caboose "7606," 99		65
___	**17626**	Service Center Extended Vision Caboose (SSS), 00		29
___	**17627**	C&O Extended Vision Caboose, 01		65
___	**17628**	BNSF Extended Vision Caboose, 01		65
___	**17629**	Santa Fe Extended Vision Caboose, 01		80
___	**17630**	UP Extended Vision Caboose, 01	25	85
___	**17631**	Virginian Bay Window Caboose, 01		90
___	**17632**	CSX Bay Window Caboose, 01		75
___	**17633**	NYC Bay Window Caboose, 01	25	90
___	**17634**	Delaware & Hudson Bay Window Caboose, 01		75
___	**17635**	100th Anniversary Die-cast Gold Caboose, 00	195	597

MODERN 1970-2025		Exc	Like New	
17636	NYC Die-cast Caboose "18096," 00-01		100	___
17637	NYC "Quicker via Peoria" Die-cast Caboose, 00		135	___
17638	RI Extended Vision Caboose "17011" (std O), 02		83	___
17639	Chessie Extended Vision Caboose "3322" (std O), 02		63	___
17640	CP Extended Vision Caboose "434604" (std O), 02		57	___
17641	Soo Line Extended Vision Caboose "2" (std O), 02		55	___
17642	Conrail Bay Window Caboose "21023" (std O), 02		65	___
17643	NKP Bay Window Caboose "480" (std O), 02		65	___
17644	Erie Bay Window Caboose "C307," (std O), 02		55	___
17645	N&W Bay Window Caboose "C-6," (std O), 02		55	___
17646	UP Bay Window Caboose "24555," (std O), 02		65	___
17647	B&O Caboose "C-2820" (std O), 03-04		65	___
17648	Chessie System Caboose "C-2800" (std O), 03-04		75	___
17649	Lionel Lines Caboose "7649" (std O), 03-04		65	___
17650	Rio Grande Extended Vision Caboose "01500" (std O), 03		65	___
17651	BN Extended Vision Caboose "10531" (std O), 03-05		80	___
17652	NYC Bay Window Caboose "20200" (std O), 03		75	___
17653	SP Bay Window Caboose "1337" (std O), 03		65	___
17654	Alaska Extended Vision Caboose "989" (std O), 03		75	___
17655	WP Bay Window Caboose "448" (std O), 03-04		75	___
17657	Norman Rockwell Holiday Caboose, 03		30	___
17658	Burlington Extended Vision Caboose "13611" (std O), 04		70	___
17659	CN Extended Vision Caboose "79646" (std O), 04	33	85	___
17660	Seaboard Extended Vision Caboose "5700" (std O), 04		65	___
17661	C&NW Bay Window Caboose "10871" (std O), 04		65	___
17662	PC Bay Window Caboose "21001" (std O), 04		65	___
17663	Southern Bay Window Caboose "X546" (std O), 04		65	___
17664	B&O Caboose "C-2824" (std O), 03-04		65	___
17665	Chessie System Caboose "C-2802" (std O), 03-04		75	___
17669	NYC Bay Window Caboose, smoke, 05		85	___
17670	CP Rail Bay Window Caboose, smoke, 05		85	___
17671	BN Extended Vision Caboose, 05		85	___
17672	GN Extended Vision Caboose "X-106" (std O), 05		85	___
17673	Santa Fe Extended Vision Caboose, 05		85	___
17674	Reading Extended Vision Caboose "94119" (std O), 05		75	___
17675	Rio Grande Extended Vision Caboose "01507" (std O), 06		90	___
17676	NYC Bay Window Caboose "20300," 07		60	___
17677	Erie-Lack. Bay Window Caboose "C359" (std O), 06		90	___
17678	B&O I-12 Caboose "C2421" (std O), 06		90	___
17679	Long Island Bay Window Caboose "C-62" (std O), 06		90	___
17682	Reading Northeastern Caboose "92841" (std O), 06-07		85	___
17683	Chessie System Northeastern Caboose "1893" (std O), 07		85	___
17684	Conrail Northeastern Caboose "18873" (std O), 07		85	___
17685	Jersey Central Northeastern Caboose "91533" (std O), 07		85	___
17687	B&O/Chessie System Smoking Caboose (std O), 05-06	45	92	___
17690	UP CA-4 Caboose "3826" (std O), 06	21	90	___
17691	UP CA-4 Caboose "25103" (std O), 06		90	___
17692	LL CA-4 Caboose "7629" (std O), 06		90	___
17693	Chessie Extended Vision Caboose "3285" (std O), 06		90	___
17694	NS Extended Vision Caboose "555582" (std O), 06		90	___
17695	Alaska I-12 Caboose "1001" (std O), 06		90	___
17696	CP Bay Window Caboose "437266" (std O), 06		90	___
17697	CN Extended Vision Caboose "78128" (std O), 06		90	___

			Exc	Like New
___	**17699**	UP Ca-4 Caboose "25193" (std O), 07		90
___	**17700**	UP ACF 40-ton Stock Car "47456" (std O), 01-02		85
___	**17701**	Rio Grande ACF 40-ton Stock Car "39269" (std O), 01-02		60
___	**17702**	CP ACF 40-ton Stock Car "277083" (std O), 01-02		75
___	**17703**	NYC ACF 40-ton Stock Car "23334" (std O), 01-02		85
___	**17703**	Crayola 2-bay Hopper, LionScale, 17-18		70
___	**17704**	B&O ACF 40-ton Stock Car "110234" (std O), 02		40
___	**17705**	CB&Q ACF 40-ton Stock Car "52886" (std O), 02		40
___	**17707**	PRR ARF 40-ton Stock Car "128994" (std O), 03		35
___	**17708**	CP Rail ACF 40-ton Stock Car "277313" (std O), 03	12	47
___	**17709**	UP Stock Car "48154" (std O), 04		45
___	**17710**	Great Northern Stock Car "56385" (std O), 04		40
___	**17711**	C&O ACF 40-ton Stock Car "95237" (std O), 06		60
___	**17712**	N&W ACF 40-ton Stock Car "33000" (std O), 06		60
___	**17713**	MKT ACF 40-ton Stock Car "47150" (std O), 06		60
___	**17714**	CN 40-ton Stock Car "172755" (std O), 06		60
___	**17715**	MP 40-ton Stock Car "52428" (std O), 06		60
___	**17716**	CGW 40-ton Stock Car "838," 08		60
___	**17717**	UP 40-ton Stock Car "48217," 08		60
___	**17718**	NS Heritage 3-bay Hopper 2-pack (std O), 12		160
___	**17719**	C&BQ ACF Stock Car "52925" (std O), 09	30	70
___	**17720**	UP ACF Stock Car (std O), 10		70
___	**17721**	Postwar Scale Stock Car 2-pack, 10-11		140
___	**17724**	CN Scale Steel-sided Reefer "210552," (std O), 11		80
___	**17725**	NP Scale Steel-sided Reefer "98528," (std O), 11		80
___	**17726**	IC Scale Steel-sided Reefer "16644," (std O), 11		80
___	**17727**	Mopac/Wabash Scale Steel-sided Reefer "30790," (std O), 11		80
___	**17729**	C&O Scale PS-1 Boxcar "2992" (std O), 12		70
___	**17730**	Seaboard Scale Round-roof Boxcar "19293" (std O), 11		70
___	**17731**	Pere Marquette Scale Boxcar "81805" (std O), 12		70
___	**17732**	L&N Scale PS-1 Boxcar "4798" (std O) , 12		70
___	**17733**	PRR Scale Round-roof Boxcar "78948" (std O), 11		70
___	**17734**	PRR Scale Round-roof Boxcar "76644" (std O), 11		70
___	**17735**	PRR Round-roof DD Boxcar "77851" (std O), 12		70
___	**17736**	PRR Round-roof DD Boxcar "60156" (std O), 12		70
___	**17737**	N&W Scale Round-roof Boxcar "46494" (std O), 11		70
___	**17738**	NP Round-roof DD Boxcar "39300" (std O), 12		70
___	**17739**	DT&I Round-roof DD Boxcar "12250" (std O), 12		70
___	**17740**	Alaska Scale Round-roof Boxcar "27781" (std O), 11		70
___	**17741**	Santa Fe Scale Slogan Reefer 5-car Set (std O), 12		320
___	**17747**	Santa Fe Scale Boxcar "39009" (std O), 12		70
___	**17748**	Grave's Mortuary Supply Scale PS-1 Boxcar (std O), 12-13		70
___	**17749**	Erie Scale PS-1 Boxcar "90300" (std O), 12		70
___	**17750**	NYC Round-roof DD Boxcar "77147" (std O), 12		70
___	**17751**	NKP Scale PS-1 Boxcar "6605" (std O), 12		70
___	**17752**	Polar Round-roof Boxcar "1202" (std O), 12-13, 16-17		70
___	**17753**	LV Scale PS-1 Boxcar "65124" (std O), 12		70
___	**17754**	EL DD Boxcar "65000" (std O), 12		75
___	**17755**	D&H DD Boxcar "25025" (std O), 12		75
___	**17756**	CP Rail DD Boxcar "42630" (std O), 12		75
___	**17757**	Milwaukee Road DD Boxcar "13441" (std O), 12		75
___	**17758**	ATSF Map and Slogan Reefer 3-pack, 12		190
___	**17762**	BN 57' Mechanical Reefer "9618" (std O), 12		85

MODERN 1970-2025		Exc	Like New	
17763	NYC 57' Mechanical Reefer "6762" (std 0), 12		85	___
17764	ATSF 57' Mechanical Reefer "56244" (std 0), 12		85	___
17765	Virginian Round-roof DD Boxcar "3131" (std 0), 13-14		80	___
17766	NH Round-roof Boxcar "39303" (std 0), 13		70	___
17767	SP Round-roof DD Boxcar "166052" (std 0), 13-14		80	___
17768	Grave's Mortuary Supply Round-roof Boxcar (std 0), 13		70	___
17769	D&RGW PS-1 Boxcar "60046" (std 0), 13		70	___
17770	MILW PS-1 Boxcar "8777" (std 0), 13		70	___
17771	CNJ PS-1 Boxcar "23522" (std 0), 13-14		80	___
17772	Central of Georgia PS-1 Boxcar (std 0), 13		70	___
17773	D&M Round-roof Boxcar "3148" (std 0), 13-14		80	___
17774	D&M PS-1 Boxcar "2833" (std 0), 13		70	___
17775	NS Heritage 3-bay Hopper 3-pack (std 0), 13-15		240	___
17779	NS Heritage 3-bay Hopper 3-pack (std 0), 13-15		240	___
17783	NS Heritage 3-bay Hopper 3-pack (std 0), 13-15		240	___
17787	NS Heritage 3-bay Hopper 3-pack (std 0), 13		240	___
17791	NS Heritage 3-bay Hopper 3-pack (std 0), 13		240	___
17795	NS Heritage 3-bay Hopper 3-pack (std 0), 13		240	___
17800	Ontario Northland Ore Car "6126", 00		30	___
17801	CN Ore Car "345165," 00		37	___
17802	CP Ore Car "377249," 00		28	___
17803	DMIR Ore Car "31456," 00		30	___
17804	UP Ore Car "8023," 01		29	___
17805	CP Rail Ore Car "377238," 01		29	___
17806	UP Ore Car "27250," 03		30	___
17807	BN Ore Car "95887," 02		28	___
17900	Santa Fe Unibody Tank Car (std 0), 90	37	46	___
17901	Chevron Unibody Tank Car (std 0), 90	26	32	___
17902	NJ Zinc Unibody Tank Car (std 0), 91	26	34	___
17903	Conoco Unibody Tank Car (std 0), 91	24	30	___
17904	Texaco Unibody Tank Car (std 0), 92	39	48	___
17905	Archer Daniels Midland Unibody Tank Car (std 0), 92	24	33	___
17906	SCM Unibody Tank Car "78286" (std 0), 93	47	55	___
17908	Marathon Oil Unibody Tank Car (std 0), 95	55	60	___
17909	Hooker Chemicals Unibody Tank Car (std 0), 96	25	55	___
17910	Sunoco Unibody Tank Car "7900," 97		37	___
17913	J.M. Huber Tank Car, 98		29	___
17914	Englehard Tank Car, 98		36	___
17915	Gulf Unibody Tank Car "8438," 00		43	___
17916	Burlington Unibody Tank Car "130000," 00	24	38	___
17918	Southern Unibody Tank Car, 01		32	___
17919	Koppers Unibody Tank Car, 01		39	___
17924	Safety Kleen Unibody Tank Car "77603" (std 0), 02	20	55	___
17925	Beefmaster Unibody Tank Car "120021" (std 0), 02		38	___
17926	Cargill Unibody 1-D Tank Car "5836" (std 0), 03		40	___
17927	Union Starch Unibody 1-D Tank Car "59137" (std 0), 03		35	___
17928	Merck 1-D Tank Car "25421" (std 0), 03		35	___
17929	Wyandotte Chemicals 1-D Tank Car "1325" (std 0), 03		34	___
17930	CSX Unibody Tank Car "993369" (std 0), 04		35	___
17931	UP Unibody Tank Car "6" (std 0), 04		35	___
17932	CIBRO TankTrain Intermediate Car "26263" (std 0), 04		35	___
17933	GATX TankTrain Intermediate Car 3-pack (std 0), 04		100	___
17946	Candy Cane Unibody Tank Car (std 0), 04		60	___

		MODERN 1970-2025	Exc	Like New
___	**17947**	Domino Sugar Unibody Tank Car (std O), 04		50
___	**17948**	Philadelphia Quartz 1-D Tank Car "806" (std O), 06		55
___	**17949**	Skelly Oil 1-D Tank Car "2293" (std O), 06		55
___	**17950**	ADM Unibody Tank Car "19020" (std O), 06		60
___	**17951**	Cerestar Unibody Tank Car "190177" (std O), 06		60
___	**17959**	Dow 1-D Tank Car "310101" (std O), 07		55
___	**17960**	Amaizo 1-D Tank Car "15440" (std O), 07		55
___	**17962**	Domino Sugar 1-D Tank Car "3008" (std O), 07		60
___	**17966**	Procor 1-D Tank Car "82607" (std O), 07		60
___	**17971**	Simonin's 1-D Tank Car "9569" (std O), 07		60
___	**17972**	Union Starch 1-D Tank Car "724" (std O), 08		60
___	**17973**	UP 1-D Tank Car "907838" (std O), 08		60
___	**17975**	Cargill Foods Unibody Tank Car 3-pack (std O), 08-09		195
___	**17976**	Huber Unibody Tank Car 3-pack (std O), 08-09		195
___	**17983**	GATX TankTrain Intermediate Car 3-pack, 08		195
___	**18000**	PRR 0-6-0 Locomotive "8977," 89, 91	145	405
___	**18001**	Rock Island 4-8-4 Locomotive "5100," 87	208	315
___	**18002**	NYC 4-6-4 Locomotive "785," 87 u	287	421
___	**18003**	DL&W 4-8-4 Locomotive "1501," 88	162	278
___	**18004**	Reading 4-6-2 Locomotive "8004," 89	159	205
___	**18005**	NYC 4-6-4 Locomotive "5340," display case, 90	393	729
___	**18006**	Reading 4-8-4 Locomotive "2100," 89 u	329	528
___	**18007**	Southern Pacific 4-8-4 Locomotive "4410," 91	221	379
___	**18008**	Disneyland 35th Anniversary 4-4-0 Locomotive, display case, 90	266	315
___	**18009**	NYC 4-8-2 Locomotive "3000," 90 u, 91	243	561
___	**18010**	PRR 6-8-6 Steam Turbine Locomotive "6200," 91-92	650	1041
___	**18010**	L&NE AC-2 Covered Hopper 6-pack, 18		360
___	**18011**	Chessie System 4-8-4 Locomotive "2101," 91	402	533
___	**18012**	NYC 4-6-4 Locomotive "5340," 90	615	750
___	**18013**	Disneyland 35th Anniversary 4-4-0 Locomotive, 90	255	296
___	**18014**	Lionel Lines 2-6-4 Locomotive "8014," 91	145	190
___	**18016**	Northern Pacific 4-8-4 Locomotive "2626," 92	293	440
___	**18018**	Southern 2-8-2 Locomotive "4501," 92	399	650
___	**18020**	N&W AC-2 Covered Hopper 6-pack, 18		360
___	**18021**	Frisco 2-8-2 Mikado Locomotive, 93	530	640
___	**18022**	Pere Marquette 2-8-4 Locomotive "1201," 93	550	650
___	**18023**	Western Maryland Shay Locomotive "6," 92	519	1350
___	**18024**	Sears T&P 4-8-2 Locomotive "907," display case, 92 u	750	790
___	**18025**	T&P 4-8-2 Locomotive "907,", 92 u	138	640
___	**18026**	NYC 4-6-4 Dreyfuss Hudson Locomotive, 2-rail, 92 u		2350
___	**18027**	NYC 4-6-4 Dreyfuss Hudson Locomotive, 3-rail, 93 u	250	1450
___	**18028**	Smithsonian PRR 4-6-2 Locomotive "3768," 2-rail, 93 u		2150
___	**18029**	NYC 4-6-4 Dreyfuss Hudson Locomotive, 3-rail, 93 u	1900	2150
___	**18030**	Frisco 2-8-2 Locomotive "4100", 93 u	378	625
___	**18030**	Pere Marquette AC-2 Covered Hopper 6-pack, 18		360
___	**18031**	2-10-0 Bundesbahn BR-50 Locomotive, 2-rail, 93 u		1500
___	**18034**	Santa Fe 2-8-2 Locomotive "3158," 94	340	620
___	**18035**	2-10-0 Reichsbahn BR-50 Locomotive, 2-rail, 93 u		1500
___	**18036**	2-10-0 French BR-50 Locomotive, 2-rail, 93 u		1500
___	**18040**	N&W 4-8-4 Locomotive "612," 95	294	710
___	**18040**	WM AC-2 Covered Hopper 6-pack, 18		360
___	**18041**	WM AC-2 Covered Hopper "5125," 18		60
___	**18042**	Boston & Albany 4-6-4 Locomotive "618," 95		250

		Exc	Like New	
18043	Chesapeake & Ohio 4-6-4 Locomotive "490," 95	435	750	___
18044	Southern 4-6-2 Locomotive "1390," 96		242	___
18045	Commodore Vanderbilt Locomotive "777," 96	260	678	___
18046	Wabash 4-6-4 Locomotive "700," 96	175	375	___
18049	N&W Warhorse 4-8-4 Locomotive "600," 96	145	490	___
18050	JCPenney 4-6-2 Pacific Locomotive "2055," 96	235	245	___
18050	Continental Grain ACF 3-Bay Covered Hopper 6-pack, 18		360	___
18051	Continental Grain ACF 3-Bay Covered Hopper "46611," 18		60	___
18052	Pennsylvania Torpedo Locomotive "238E," 97	90	455	___
18053	LL 2-8-4 Berkshire Locomotive "726," 96-97	310	400	___
18054	NYC 0-4-0 Switcher "1665," black, 97		145	___
18055	Continental Grain ACF 3-Bay Covered Hopper "46615," 18		60	___
18056	NYC J1-e Hudson Locomotive "763E," Vanderbilt tender, 97	384	603	___
18057	PRR 6-8-6 Turbine Locomotive "671," 96-98	280	450	___
18058	NYC 4-6-4 Hudson Locomotive "773," 96-97	300	550	___
18060	PRR ACF 3-Bay Covered Hopper 6-pack, 18		360	___
18062	ATSF 4-6-4 Hudson Locomotive "3447," 97		680	___
18063	NYC 4-6-4 Commodore Vanderbilt Locomotive, 99	579	952	___
18064	NYC 4-8-2 Mohawk L-3A Locomotive "3005," tender, 98	318	450	___
18067	NYC Weathered Commodore Vanderbilt Scale Hudson, 97	313	840	___
18068	PRR S2 Steam Tender, 99	145	250	___
18070	Tenneco ACF 3-Bay Covered Hopper 6-pack, 18		360	___
18071	SP Daylight Locomotive "4449," 98	60	680	___
18072	Lionel Lines Torpedo Locomotive, tender, 98		360	___
18079	NYC 2-8-2 Mikado Locomotive "1967," 99		710	___
18080	D&RGW 2-8-2 Mikado Locomotive "1210," 99		720	___
18080	BN ACF 3-Bay Covered Hopper 6-pack, 18		360	___
18082	NYC 4-6-4 Hudson Locomotive "5404," 99		230	___
18083	C&O 4-6-4 Hudson Locomotive "305," 99		205	___
18084	Santa Fe 4-6-4 Hudson Locomotive "305," 99		225	___
18085	NH 4-6-2 Pacific Locomotive "1334," 99		275	___
18086	NYC 4-6-2 Pacific Locomotive "4929," 99		235	___
18087	Santa Fe 4-6-2 Pacific Locomotive "3448," 99		265	___
18088	SP 4-6-2 Pacific Locomotive "1407," 99		350	___
18089	CNJ 4-6-0 Camelback Locomotive "771," 99		405	___
18090	Vesuvius Crucible PS-1 Boxcar 6-pack, 18	55	360	___
18091	PRR 4-6-0 Camelback Locomotive "821," 99		405	___
18092	SP 4-6-0 Camelback Locomotive "2283," 99	113	395	___
18093	C&NW 4-6-0 Camelback Locomotive "3006," 99		285	___
18094	B&O 4-4-2 E6 Atlantic Locomotive, CC, 99-00		345	___
18095	PRR 4-4-2 E6 Atlantic Locomotive, CC, 99-00	275	455	___
18096	ATSF 4-4-2 E6 Atlantic Locomotive, CC, 99-00		370	___
18097	CNJ 4-6-0 Camelback Locomotive "770," 99		330	___
18098	PRR 4-6-0 Camelback Locomotive "820," 99		355	___
18099	SP 4-6-0 Camelback Locomotive "2282," 99		360	___
18100	Santa Fe F3 Diesel A Unit "8100," powered, 91		300	___
18100	EJ&E PS-1 Boxcar 6-pack, 18		360	___
18101	Santa Fe F3 Diesel B Unit "8101," powered, 91		250	___
18102	Santa Fe F3 Diesel A Unit "8102," unpowered, 91		200	___
18103	Santa Fe F3 Diesel B Unit "8103," unpowered, 91 u	180	190	___
18104	GN F3 Diesel A Unit "366A," powered, 92		500	___
18105	GN F3 Diesel B Unit "370B," unpowered, 92		220	___
18106	GN F3 Diesel A Unit "351C," unpowered, 92		260	___

	MODERN 1970-2025		Exc	Like New
___	**18107**	D&RGW Alco PA1 Diesel ABA Set, 92	323	740
___	**18108**	Great Northern F3 Diesel B Unit “371B,” 93	85	105
___	**18109**	Erie Alco Diesel A Unit “725A,” powered, 93		250
___	**18110**	Erie Alco Diesel B Unit “725B,” unpowered, 93		160
___	**18110**	Monon PS-1 Boxcar 6-pack, 18		360
___	**18111**	Erie Alco Diesel A Unit “736A,” unpowered, 93		170
___	**18115**	Santa Fe F3 Diesel B Unit, 93	90	115
___	**18116**	Erie-Lackawanna Alco PA1 Diesel AA Set, 93	310	490
___	**18117**	ATSF F3 Diesel AA Set, 93		375
___	**18117/18**	Santa Fe F3 Diesel AA Set “200,” 93	290	410
___	**18118**	ATSF F3 Diesel A Unit, unpowered, 93		200
___	**18119/20**	UP Alco Diesel AA Set, 94	250	350
___	**18119**	UP Alco FA-2 Diesel AA Set, 94	150	300
___	**18120**	UP Alco FA-2 Diesel A Unit, 94		120
___	**18120**	Rutland PS-1 Boxcar 6-pack, 18		360
___	**18121**	Santa Fe F3 Diesel B Unit “200A,” 94	75	95
___	**18122**	Santa Fe F3 Diesel B Unit “200B,” 95	140	150
___	**18123**	ACL F3 Diesel A Unit “342,” powered, 96		250
___	**18124**	ACL F3 Diesel B Unit “342B,” unpowered, 96		185
___	**18125**	ACL F3 Diesel A Unit “343,” unpowered, 96		190
___	**18128**	Santa Fe F3 Diesel A Unit “2343,” 96		435
___	**18129**	Santa Fe F3 Diesel B Unit “2343C,” 96		245
___	**18130**	Santa Fe F3 Diesel AB Set, 96	237	600
___	**18130**	NYC AAR 3-Bay Hopper 6-pack, 18		360
___	**18131**	NP F3 Diesel AB Set, “2390A, 2390C,” 97	323	480
___	**18132**	NP F3 Diesel A Unit, powered		300
___	**18133**	NP F3 Diesel B Unit, dummy		150
___	**18134**	Santa Fe F3 Diesel A Unit “2343,” dummy, 97	75	195
___	**18135**	NYC F3 AA Diesel Set “2333,” 99		650
___	**18135**	NYC F3 Diesel AA Set “2333,” 96-99	300	520
___	**18136**	Santa Fe F3 Diesel B Unit “2343C,” 97	120	240
___	**18138**	Milwaukee Road F3 Diesel A Unit “75A,” 98		400
___	**18139**	Milwaukee Road F3 Diesel B Unit “2378B,” 98		250
___	**18140**	Milwaukee Road F3 Diesel AB Set, 98	380	600
___	**18140**	Nickel Plate Road AAR 3-Bay Hopper 6-pack, 18		360
___	**18145**	NP F3 Diesel A Unit “2390A,” powered, 97	300	360
___	**18146**	NP F3 Diesel B Unit “2390C,” 97		170
___	**18147**	NP F3 Diesel AB Set, 97	438	580
___	**18149**	UP Veranda Gas Turbine Locomotive “61,” 98	705	900
___	**18150**	LG Everist AAR 3-Bay Hopper 6-pack, 18		360
___	**18154**	Deluxe Santa Fe FT Diesel AA Set, 98-00		375
___	**18155**	Deluxe Santa Fe FT Diesel A Unit, powered, 98-00		200
___	**18156**	Deluxe Santa Fe FT Diesel A Unit, unpowered, 98-00		160
___	**18157**	Santa Fe FT Diesel AA Set, 98-00		240
___	**18158**	Santa Fe FT Diesel A Unit, powered, 98-00		220
___	**18159**	Santa Fe FT Diesel A Unit, unpowered, 98-00		120
___	**18160**	NYC Deluxe FT Diesel AA Set, “1602”/”1603”, 98-00		500
___	**18160**	UP AAR 3-Bay Hopper 6-pack, 18		360
___	**18161**	NYC Deluxe FT Diesel A Unit “1603,” powered, 98-00		350
___	**18162**	NYC Deluxe FT Diesel A Unit “1602,” unpowered, 98-00		120
___	**18163**	NYC FT Diesel AA Set, “1600, 2400,” 98-00		300
___	**18164**	NYC FT Diesel A Unit “1600,” powered, 98-00		200
___	**18165**	NYC FT Diesel A Unit “2400,” unpowered, 98-00		110

MODERN 1970-2025		Exc	Like New	
18166	B&O FT Diesel AA Set, CC, 99-00		340	___
18167	B&O FT Diesel A Unit "8167," CC, 99-00		230	___
18168	B&O FT Diesel A Unit "8168," unpowered, 99-00		110	___
18169	B&O FT Diesel AA Set, traditional, 99-00		240	___
18170	B&O FT Diesel A Unit, traditional, 99-00		140	___
18171	B&O FT Diesel A Unit, unpowered, 99-00		90	___
18178	NYC F3 Diesel B Unit, unpowered, 99		275	___
18189	Army of Potomac Operating Stock Car, 99		45	___
18190	McNeil's Rangers Operating Stock Car "2", 99		45	___
18191	WP F3 Diesel AA Set, 98	227	570	___
18192	WP F3 Diesel A Unit, powered, 98		485	___
18193	WP F3 Diesel A Unit, unpowered, 98		495	___
18194	EL F3 Diesel AB Set, 99		450	___
18195	EL F3 Diesel A Unit "7091, powered", 99		300	___
18196	EL F3 B Unit, nonpowered, 99		150	___
18197	WP F3 Diesel B Unit "2355C," 99	88	255	___
18198	WP F3 Diesel B Unit "2345C" CC, 99		360	___
18200	Conrail SD40 Diesel "8200," 87	180	200	___
18201	Chessie System SD40 Diesel "8201," 88	245	340	___
18202	Erie-Lack. SD40 Diesel Unit "8459," dummy, 89 u	90	140	___
18203	CP Rail SD40 Diesel "8203," 89	168	250	___
18204	Chessie SD40 Diesel Unit "8204," dummy, 90 u	135	190	___
18205	Union Pacific Dash 8-40C Diesel "9100," 89	198	335	___
18206	Santa Fe Dash 8-40B Diesel "8206," 90	195	293	___
18207	Norfolk Southern Dash 8-40C Diesel "8689," 92	230	270	___
18208	BN SD40 Diesel Dummy Unit "8586," 91 u	115	165	___
18209	CP Rail SD40 Diesel Dummy Unit "8209," 92 u	118	165	___
18210	Illinois Central SD40 "6006," 93	210	250	___
18210	Northwestern Refrigerated Wood-sided Reefer 6-pack, 18		360	___
18211	Susquehanna Dash 8-40B Diesel "4002," 93	145	165	___
18212	Santa Fe Dash 8-40B Diesel Dummy Unit "8212," 93	155	180	___
18213	Norfolk Southern Dash 8-40C Diesel "8688," 94	168	240	___
18214	CSX Dash 8-40C Diesel "7500," 94	235	255	___
18215	CSX Dash 8-40C Diesel "7643," 94	240	260	___
18216	Conrail SD-60M Diesel "5500," 94	162	380	___
18217	Illinois Central SD40 Diesel "6007," 94	170	175	___
18218	Susquehanna Dash 8-40B Diesel "4004," 94	205	225	___
18219	C&NW Dash 8-40C Diesel "8501," 95	325	330	___
18220	C&NW Dash 8-40C Diesel "8502," 95	215	315	___
18220	PFE Wood-sided Refrigerator Car 6-pack, 18		360	___
18221	D&RGW SD50 Diesel "5512," 95	455	520	___
18222	D&RGW SD50 Diesel "5517," 95	280	325	___
18223	Milwaukee Road SD40 Diesel "154," 95	268	380	___
18224	Milwaukee Road SD40 Diesel "155," 95	190	265	___
18226	GE Dash 9 Diesel, 97	85	295	___
18228	SP Dash 9 Diesel "8228," gray with red nose, 97		340	___
18229	SP SD40 Diesel "7333," 98	300	425	___
18230	Swift Wood-sided Refrigerator Car 6-pac, 18		360	___
18231	BNSF Dash 9 Diesel "739," 98		435	___
18232	Soo Line SD60 Diesel "5500," 97		350	___
18233	BNSF Dash 9 Diesel "745,", 98		330	___
18234	BNSF Dash 9 Diesel "740," CC, 98-99		405	___
18235	BNSF Dash 9 Diesel 2-pack, "739, 740," 98		710	___

			Exc	Like New
___	**18238**	Conrail SD70 Diesel "4145", 99-00		300
___	**18239**	SP SD40 Diesel "7340", 98		300
___	**18240**	Conrail Dash 8-40B Diesel "5065" CC, 98		260
___	**18240**	Rath Wood-sided Refrigerator Car 6-pac, 18		360
___	**18241**	BN SD70 Diesel "9413," 99-00		345
___	**18245**	PRR Alco PA1 Diesel AA Set, 99		495
___	**18246**	PRR Alco PA1 Diesel A Unit "5750A," powered, 99		350
___	**18247**	PRR Alco PA-1 A Unit, unpowered, 99		240
___	**18248**	PRR Alco PB-1 Diesel "5750B," 99	93	215
___	**18249**	Erie Alco PB-1 Diesel "850B," 00		250
___	**18250**	BNSF SD70 Diesel "9870," 99-00		365
___	**18251**	CSX SD60 Diesel "8701," 99-00	113	300
___	**18252**	Amtrak Dash 9 Diesel, CC, 99	118	285
___	**18253**	BNSF Dash 9 Diesel, CC, 99		305
___	**18254**	ATSF Dash 9 Diesel, CC, 99		340
___	**18255**	NS Dash 9 Diesel, CC, 99	95	315
___	**18256**	Amtrak Dash 9 Diesel, traditional, 99		200
___	**18257**	BNSF Dash 9 Diesel, traditional, 99		190
___	**18258**	ATSF Dash 9 Diesel, traditional, 99	75	205
___	**18259**	NS Dash 9 Diesel, traditional, 99		215
___	**18260**	Conrail SD70 Diesel "4144," 99-00		280
___	**18261**	BN SD60 Diesel "9412," 99-00		255
___	**18262**	BNSF SD70 Diesel "9869," 99-00		250
___	**18263**	CSX SD60 Diesel "8700," 99-00	100	255
___	**18264**	Southern Pacific SD70M Diesel "8238," 99-00		245
___	**18265**	Southern Pacific SD70M Diesel "9803," 99-00		340
___	**18266**	Norfolk Southern SD60 Diesel "6552," CC, 01-02	90	400
___	**18268**	Lionel Centennial SD90MAC Diesel, CC, 00	113	428
___	**18269**	UP SD90MAC Diesel "8006," CC, 00		405
___	**18270**	UP SD90MAC Diesel "8004," traditional, 00		330
___	**18271**	CP SD90MAC Diesel "9129," CC, 00	160	440
___	**18272**	CP SD90MAC Diesel "9127," traditional, 00		330
___	**18273**	UP SD40 Diesel "8071," 99-00		330
___	**18274**	Burlington U30C Diesel "891," CC, 01		370
___	**18276**	Seaboard U30C Diesel "7274," CC, 01		325
___	**18278**	UP U30C Diesel "2938," CC, 01		330
___	**18280**	Maersk SD70 Diesel, CC, 00		345
___	**18281**	BNSF Dash 9-44CW Diesel "788," CC, 00		340
___	**18282**	BNSF Dash 9-44CW Diesel "789," traditional, 00		225
___	**18283**	CSX Dash 9-44CW Diesel "9019," CC, 00	125	340
___	**18284**	CSX Dash 9-44CW Diesel "9020," traditional, 00		300
___	**18285**	UP Dash 9-44C Diesel "9659," CC, 01		325
___	**18286**	UP Dash 9-44CW Diesel "9717," CC, 01		355
___	**18287**	CN Dash 9-44C Diesel "2529," CC, 01		460
___	**18288**	Odyssey System SD70 Diesel, CC, 00 u	85	400
___	**18289**	CN Dash 9-44C Diesel "2528," traditional, 01		220
___	**18290**	Amtrak Dash 8-32BWH Diesel "509," CC, 01		325
___	**18291**	BNSF Dash 8-32BWH Diesel "580," CC, 02		340
___	**18292**	Chessie GE U30C Diesel "3312," CC, 02	100	340
___	**18293**	Santa Fe U30C Diesel, CC, 03	95	395
___	**18294**	Alaska SD70MAC Diesel "4005," CC, 01-02		435
___	**18295**	Conrail SD80MAC Diesel "7200," CC, 02-03		365
___	**18296**	CSX SD80MAC Diesel "801,", CC, 02-03	125	405

MODERN 1970-2025		Exc	Like New	
18297	NYC SD80MAC Diesel "9914," CC, 02-03	138	405	___
18298	UP "Desert Victory" SD40-2 Diesel "3593," CC, 02-03		380	___
18299	CP Rail SD40-2 Diesel "5420," CC, 02-03		375	___
18300	PRR GG1 Electric Locomotive "8300," 87	285	335	___
18301	Southern FM Train Master Diesel "8301," 88	140	204	___
18302	GN EP-5 Electric Locomotive "8302" (FF 3), 88	140	260	___
18303	Amtrak GG1 Electric Locomotive "8303," 89	189	338	___
18304	Lackawanna MU Commuter Car Set, 91	278	435	___
18305	Lackawanna MU Commuter Car Dummy Set, 92	165	255	___
18306	PRR MU Commuter Car Set, 92	218	330	___
18307	PRR FM Train Master Diesel "8699," 94	150	202	___
18308	PRR GG1 Electric Locomotive "4866," 92	148	264	___
18309	Reading FM Train Master Diesel "863," 93	173	212	___
18310	PRR MU Commuter Car Dummy Set, 93	265	345	___
18311	Disney EP-5 Electric Locomotive "8311," 94	202	412	___
18313	Pennsylvania GG1 Electric Locomotive "4907," 96	139	271	___
18314	PRR GG1 Electric Locomotive "2332," 5 gold stripes, 97	185	507	___
18315	Virginian E33 Electric Locomotive "2329," 97		240	___
18319	New Haven EP-5 Electric Locomotive, 99	200	365	___
18321	CNJ Train Master Diesel "2341," 99	85	405	___
18322	Lackawanna Train Master Diesel "2321," 99	163	435	___
18323	Amtrak HHP-8 Diesel "656F," CC, 09		500	___
18326	PRR Congressional GG1 Electric Locomotive, 00		600	___
18327	Virginian FM Train Master Diesel "2331," 99-00	195	410	___
18328	NH MU Commuter Car Set, CC, 00		385	___
18329	NH MU Commuter Car "4082," powered, 00		240	___
18330	NH MU Commuter Car "4083," unpowered, 00		140	___
18331	Reading MU Commuter Car Set, CC, 00		460	___
18332	Reading MU Commuter Car "9109," powered, 00		340	___
18333	Reading MU Commuter Car "9110," unpowered		140	___
18334	NH MU Commuter Car Set, unpowered, 01		180	___
18335	NH MU Commuter Car "4084," unpowered, 01		90	___
18336	NH MU Commuter Car "4085," unpowered, 01		90	___
18337	Reading MU Commuter Car Set, unpowered, 01		200	___
18338	Reading MU Commuter Car "9111," unpowered, 01		100	___
18339	Reading MU Commuter Car "9112," unpowered, 01		100	___
18340	Train Master Demonstrator AA Set, CC, 00		650	___
18341	Train Master Demonstrator A Unit "TM-1," CC, 00		350	___
18342	Train Master Demonstrator A Unit "TM-2," CC, 00		350	___
18343	PRR GG1 Electric Locomotive "2332," CC, 01		610	___
18344	LIRR MU Commuter Car Set, CC, 01		470	___
18345	LIRR MU Commuter Car "1163," CC, 01		360	___
18346	LIRR MU Commuter Car "1163," unpowered, 01		120	___
18347	IC MU Commuter Car Set, CC, 01		470	___
18348	IC MU Commuter Car "1204," CC, 01		360	___
18349	IC MU Commuter Car "1204," unpowered, 01		120	___
18350	Archive No. 2350 NH EP-5 electric, 01		375	___
18351	NYC S1 Electric Locomotive, 03		400	___
18352	JCPenney SP MU Commuter Car, display case, 02		140	___
18353	Pennsylvania E33 Electric Locomotive "4403," CC, 02		280	___
18354	PRR GG1 Electric Locomotive "4918," tuscan, CC, 04	307	790	___
18355	PRR GG1 Electric Locomotive "4876," green, CC, 04	393	900	___
18356	Penn Central GG1 Electric Locomotive "4901," CC, 04	288	1050	___

	MODERN 1970-2025		Exc	Like New
___	**18357**	Amtrak Acela Power Unit "2026," CC, 04-05		530
___	**18358**	Amtrak Acela Power Unit "2029," unpowered, 04-05		270
___	**18359**	PRR GG1 Electric Locomotive "2360," CC, 04		430
___	**18360**	New York City R27 Subway Power Unit "8026," CC, 06-07		220
___	**18361**	New York City R27 Subway Power Unit "8027," unpowered, 04		120
___	**18362**	New York City R27 Subway Power Unit "8028," unpowered, 06-07		120
___	**18363**	New York City R27 Subway End Car "8029," unpowered, 06-07		120
___	**18364**	PRR BB1 Electric Locomotive Set "3900, 3901," CC, 05-07	150	530
___	**18365**	PRR BB1 Electric Locomotive "3900," CC, 05-07		370
___	**18366**	PRR BB1 Electric Locomotive "3901," unpowered, 05-07		160
___	**18367**	LIRR BB3 Electric Locomotive Set "328A, 329B," CC, 05		530
___	**18368**	LIRR BB3 Electric Locomotive "328 A," CC, 05		360
___	**18369**	LIRR BB3 Electric Locomotive "329B," unpowered, 05		160
___	**18370**	Postwar Virginian Train Master Diesel "2331," CC, 05-07		340
___	**18371**	PRR GG1 Electric "4912," Tuscan, 5 stripes, CC, 05-07	225	780
___	**18372**	PRR GG1 Electric Locomotive "4925," green, 1 stripe, CC, 05-07		780
___	**18373**	NYC S2 Electric Locomotive "125," CC, 05-07	93	410
___	**18374**	PRR GG1 Electric Locomotive "4866," silver, CC, 06-08		900
___	**18375**	Lackawanna FM Train Master Diesel "850," CC, 06		400
___	**18376**	Lackawanna FM Train Master Diesel "851," nonpowered (std O), 06		130
___	**18378**	New York City R27 Subway Car 2-pack, 07		360
___	**18379**	New York City R27 Subway Car "8030," unpowered, 06-07		100
___	**18380**	New York City R27 Subway Car "8031," unpowered, 06-07		100
___	**18381**	PRR BB1 Electric Locomotive "4751," CC, 06		500
___	**18383**	Postwar GN EP-5 Electric "2358," CC, 06-08		740
___	**18384**	MILW EP-2 Electric Locomotive, CC, 07-08		950
___	**18385**	NYC H-16-44 Diesel "7001," 07-09		202
___	**18386**	NYC H-16-44 Diesel "7002," nonpowered (std O), 07-09		123
___	**18388**	CNJ Train Master Diesel "2341," CC, 08-09		500
___	**18389**	MILW EP-2 Electric Locomotive "E-1," CC, 07-08		950
___	**18399**	NH EF-4 Rectifier Locomotive "306," CC, 09		360
___	**18400**	Santa Fe Vulcan Rotary Snowplow "8400," 87	135	170
___	**18401**	Workmen Handcar, 87-88	30	37
___	**18402**	Lionel Lines Burro Crane, 88	65	87
___	**18403**	Santa Claus Handcar, 88	26	33
___	**18404**	San Francisco Trolley "8404," 88	55	85
___	**18405**	Santa Fe Burro Crane, 89	70	83
___	**18406**	Track Maintenance Car, 89, 91	34	49
___	**18407**	Snoopy and Woodstock Handcar, 90-91	96	115
___	**18408**	Santa Claus Handcar, 89	26	35
___	**18410**	PRR Burro Crane, 90	100	115
___	**18411**	Canadian Pacific Fire Car, 90	70	98
___	**18412**	UP Fire Car, 91	70	100
___	**18413**	Charlie Brown and Lucy Handcar, 91	40	61
___	**18416**	Bugs Bunny and Daffy Duck Handcar, 92-93	129	179
___	**18417**	Section Gang Car, 93	65	80
___	**18419**	Lionelville Electric Trolley "8419," 94	75	90
___	**18421**	Sylvester and Tweety Handcar, 94	44	50
___	**18422**	Santa and Snowman Handcar, 94	32	37
___	**18423**	On-track Step Van, 95	23	28

MODERN 1970-2025		Exc	Like New	
18424	On-track Pickup Truck, 95	20	32	___
18425	Goofy and Pluto Handcar, 95	45	58	___
18426	Santa and Snowman Handcar, 95	25	30	___
18427	Tie-Jector Car "55," 97	35	75	___
18429	Workmen Handcar, 96	28	34	___
18430	Crew Car, 96		28	___
18431	Trolley Car, 96-97		46	___
18433	Mickey and Minnie Handcar, 96-97	48	87	___
18434	Porky and Petunia Handcar, 96		35	___
18436	Dodge Ram Track Inspection Vehicle, 97		40	___
18438	PRR High-rail Inspection Vehicle, 98		50	___
18439	Union Pacific High-rail Inspection Vehicle, 98		42	___
18440	NJ Transit High-rail Inspection Vehicle, 98		50	___
18444	Lionelville Fire Car (SSS), 98		150	___
18445	NYC Fire Car, 98		90	___
18446	Postwar "58" GN Rotary Snowplow, 99		181	___
18447	Executive Inspection Vehicle, 99		125	___
18452	Boston Trolley "3321," 99-00		65	___
18454	Executive Inspection Vehicle, blue, 00	48	118	___
18455	NYC Tie-Jector Car "X-2," 00-01		74	___
18456	Postwar "59" Minuteman Motorized Unit, 01-02		290	___
18457	Postwar "65" Handcar, 00-01		45	___
18458	Postwar "53" D&RGW Snowplow, 00		160	___
18459	Christmas Handcar, 01		35	___
18461	Track Cleaning Car, 02-03		90	___
18463	Hot Rod Inspection Vehicle, 01-02		100	___
18464	Postwar "54" Track Ballast Tamper, 02-03		170	___
18465	Postwar "50" Gang Car, 03		78	___
18466	UP Rotary Snow Plow, 01-02		150	___
18467	Train Robbery Handcar, 02		45	___
18468	CN Railroad Speeder, 03-04		49	___
18469	Chessie System Railroad Speeder, 03-04		49	___
18470	Postwar "52" Fire Car, 02		105	___
18471	UP GP20 Diesel "1977," 03		105	___
18473	Lehigh Valley GP38 Diesel "310," 03		160	___
18474	Postwar "41" U.S. Army Switcher, 03-04		145	___
18475	Toy Story Handcar, 03		55	___
18476	Mickey and Minnie Mouse Handcar, 03-04	30	60	___
18477	UP Burro Crane "MOW 10166", 03		95	___
18479	Postwar "45" USMC Mobile Missile Launcher, 03-04		125	___
18480	Hobo Motorized Handcar, 03-04		35	___
18481	Christmas Yuletide Trolley, 03		50	___
18482	New Haven Rail Bonder "16," 04		35	___
18483	C&O Ballast Tamper "48," 04		55	___
18484	NS Dodge Inspection Vehicle, 04-05		55	___
18485	NYC Gang Car, 04-05		100	___
18486	Donald and Daisy Duck Handcar, 04-05		63	___
18487	Postwar "56" M&StL Mine Transport Car, 04-05		230	___
18488	CP Rotary Snow Plow, 03-05		160	___
18489	Great Northern Rail Bonder "HR-73", 04		35	___
18490	UP Ballast Tamper, 04-05		150	___
18491	MOW Ballast Tamper "325," 04		44	___
18492	MOW Rail Bonder "58," 04		35	___

			Exc	Like New
___	**18493**	Santa's Speeder, 05		60
___	**18497**	N&W Speeder "541005," traditional, 05		65
___	**18498**	New York Central Rotary Snowplow, 05		210
___	**18500**	Milwaukee Road GP9 Diesel "8500" (FF 2), 87	148	198
___	**18501**	WM NW2 Switcher "8501" (FF 4), 89	185	215
___	**18502**	LL 90th Anniversary GP9 Diesel "1900," 90	148	173
___	**18503**	Southern Pacific NW2 Switcher "8503," 90	143	280
___	**18504**	Frisco GP7 Diesel "504" (FF 5), 91	155	240
___	**18505**	NKP GP7 Diesel Set "400, 401" (FF 6), 92	295	365
___	**18506**	CN Budd RDC Set, "D202, D203," 92	180	261
___	**18507**	CN Budd RDC Baggage Car "D202," powered, 92	50	75
___	**18508**	CN Budd RDC Passenger Dummy Unit "D203," 92	125	150
___	**18510**	CN Budd RDC Passenger Dummy Unit "D200," 93	50	75
___	**18511**	CN Budd RDC Passenger Dummy Unit "D250," 93	50	75
___	**18512**	CN Budd RDC Dummy Set, "D200, D250," 93	125	195
___	**18513**	NYC GP7 Diesel "7420," 94	90	165
___	**18514**	Missouri Pacific GP7 Diesel "4124," 95	213	310
___	**18515**	Lionel Steel Vulcan Diesel "57" (SSS), 96		190
___	**18516**	Phantom III Locomotive, CC, 02		345
___	**18517**	Phantom IV Locomotive, CC, 08		390
___	**18550**	JCPenney MILW GP9 Diesel "8500," display case, 87 u	180	245
___	**18551**	JCPenney Susquehanna RS3 Diesel "8809," display case, 89 u	180	195
___	**18552**	JCPenney DM&IR SD18 Diesel "8813," display case, 90 u	170	195
___	**18553**	Sears UP GP9 Diesel "150," display case, 91 u	100	150
___	**18554**	JCPenney GM&O RS3 "721," display case, 92-93 u	160	180
___	**18555**	Sears C&IM SD9 Diesel "52," 92 u	165	190
___	**18556**	Sears Chicago & Illinois Midland Freight Car Set, 92 u	110	120
___	**18557**	Chessie System 4-8-4 Locomotive "2101," display case, export, 92 u		NRS
___	**18558**	JCPenney MKT GP9 Diesel "91," display case, 94 u	160	180
___	**18562**	SP GP9 Diesel "2380," 96	85	195
___	**18563**	NYC GP9 Diesel "2380," 96	83	215
___	**18564**	CP GP9 Diesel "2380," 97		265
___	**18565**	Milwaukee Road GP9 Diesel "2338", 97	93	220
___	**18566**	CR SD20 Diesel "8495" (SSS), 97		150
___	**18567**	PRR GP9 Diesel "2028", 97	60	225
___	**18569**	CB&Q GP9 Diesel "2380", 98		190
___	**18570**	B&M GP7 Diesel "2380," CC, 98		190
___	**18571**	B&M GP7 Diesel I "2381," unpowered, 98		135
___	**18572**	B&M GP7 Diesel "2389," CC, 98		190
___	**18573**	Santa Fe GP9 Diesel "2380," 98	80	155
___	**18574**	Milwaukee Road GP20 Diesel "975," 98	110	270
___	**18575**	Custom Series I GP9 Diesel "2398," 98		350
___	**18576**	SP GP9 Diesel B Unit "2385," nonpowered, 98		135
___	**18577**	NYC GP9 Diesel B Unit "2385," nonpowered, 98		145
___	**18578**	NYC Ballast Tamper "8578," 98		150
___	**18579**	MILW GP9 Diesel "2384," nonpowered, 99		135
___	**18580**	Pennsylvania GP9 Diesel B Unit "2027," 98	75	165
___	**18582**	Seaboard NW2 Switcher, 98	250	455
___	**18583**	AEC Switcher "57," 98	75	214
___	**18585**	Centennial SD40 Diesel, 99	NRS	463
___	**18587**	NKP Alco C420 Switcher "577," CC, 99-01	178	255
___	**18588**	D&H Alco C420 Switcher "412," CC, 99-01	250	275
___	**18589**	LV Alco C420 Switcher "409," CC, 99-01	255	300

MODERN 1970-2025		Exc	Like New	
18590	NKP Alco C420 Switcher "578," traditional, 99-01		170	___
18591	D&H Alco C420 Switcher "411," traditional, 99-01		215	___
18592	LV Alco C420 Switcher "410," traditional, 99-01		175	___
18594	Farmrail GP7 Diesel "8252," traditional, 99		155	___
18595	D&H RS11 Diesel "5002," traditional, 99-00		160	___
18596	D&H Alco RS11 Diesel "5001," CC, 99-01		370	___
18597	NYC RS11 Diesel "8011," traditional, 99-00		160	___
18598	NYC Alco RS11 Switcher "8010," CC, 99-01		380	___
18599	C&O GP38 Diesel "3855," 99-00		145	___
18600	ACL 4-4-2 Locomotive "8600," 87 u	65	75	___
18601	Great Northern 4-4-2 Locomotive "8601," 88	80	95	___
18602	PRR 4-4-2 Locomotive "8602," 87	75	85	___
18604	Wabash 4-4-2 Locomotive "8604," 88-91	65	75	___
18605	Mopar Express 4-4-2 Locomotive "1987,", 87-88 u	75	120	___
18606	NYC 2-6-4 Locomotive "8606," 89	170	190	___
18607	Union Pacific 2-6-4 Locomotive "8607," 89	130	155	___
18608	D&RGW 2-6-4 Locomotive "8608" (SSS), 89	90	105	___
18609	Northern Pacific 2-6-4 Locomotive "8609," 90	170	195	___
18610	Rock Island 0-4-0 Locomotive "8610," 90	105	115	___
18611	Lionel Lines 2-6-4 Locomotive (SSS), 90	125	140	___
18612	C&NW 4-4-2 Locomotive "8612," 89	75	100	___
18613	NYC 4-4-2 Locomotive "8613," 89 u	75	95	___
18614	Circus Train 4-4-2 Locomotive "1989," 89 u	95	125	___
18615	GTW 4-4-2 Locomotive "8615," 90	70	85	___
18616	Northern Pacific 4-4-2 Locomotive "8616," 90 u	85	110	___
18617	Adolphus III 4-4-2 Locomotive, 89-92 u	100	125	___
18618	B&O 4-4-2 Atlantic Locomotive, 91	105	125	___
18620	Illinois Central 2-6-2 Locomotive "8620," 91	165	190	___
18622	Union Pacific 4-4-2 Locomotive "8622," 90-91 u	65	80	___
18623	Texas & Pacific 4-4-2 Locomotive "8623," 92	80	110	___
18625	Illinois Central 4-4-2 Locomotive "8625," 91 u	70	95	___
18626	Delaware & Hudson 2-6-2 Locomotive "8626," 92	105	115	___
18627	C&O 4-4-2 Locomotive "8627" or "8633," 92, 93 u, 94, 95 u	75	95	___
18628	MKT 4-4-2 Locomotive "8628," 92, 93 u	70	85	___
18630	C&NW 4-6-2 Locomotive "2903," 93	325	370	___
18632	NYC 4-4-2 Locomotive "8632," 93-95	75	95	___
18632	C&O Columbia 4-4-2 Locomotive "8632," 97-99	75	95	___
18633	C&O 4-4-2 Locomotive "8633," 94-95	65	85	___
18633	UP 4-4-2 Locomotive "8633," 93-95	65	85	___
18635	Santa Fe 2-6-4 Locomotive "8625," 93	135	155	___
18636	B&O 4-6-2 Locomotive "5300," 94	215	315	___
18637	United Auto Workers 4-4-2 Locomotive "8633," 93 u		90	___
18638	Norfolk & Western 2-6-4 Locomotive "638," 94	150	220	___
18639	Reading 4-6-2 Locomotive "639," 95	145	170	___
18640	Union Pacific 4-6-2 Locomotive "8640," 95	110	130	___
18641	Ford 4-4-2 Locomotive "8641," 94 u	65	85	___
18642	Lionel Lines 4-6-2 Locomotive, 95	110	130	___
18644	ATSF 4-4-2 Columbia Locomotive "8644," 96-99	75	90	___
18648	Sears Zenith 4-4-2 Locomotive "8632," 96 u		140	___
18649	Chevrolet 4-4-2 Locomotive "USA-1," 96 u		150	___
18650	LL 4-4-2 Columbia Locomotive "X-1110," 96-99	95	120	___
18653	B&A 4-6-2 Pacific Locomotive "2044," 97		140	___
18654	SP 4-6-2 Pacific Locomotive "2044," 97		140	___

MODERN 1970-2025			Exc	Like New
___	**18656**	Bloomingdale's 4-4-2 Columbia Locomotive "8632," 96		112
___	**18657**	Sears Zenith 4-4-2 Columbia Locomotive "8632," 96		120
___	**18658**	LL Little League 4-4-2 Columbia Locomotive "X-1110," 97		90
___	**18660**	CN 4-6-2 Locomotive "2044," tender, 98		175
___	**18661**	N&W 4-6-2 Locomotive "2044," tender, 98		160
___	**18662**	Pennsylvania 0-4-0 Switcher, 98	165	230
___	**18666**	SP&S 4-6-2 Pacific Locomotive "2044," 97		200
___	**18668**	Bloomingdale's 4-4-2 Columbia Locomotive "8632," 97		130
___	**18669**	JCPenney IC 4-6-2 Pacific Locomotive "2099," 98		205
___	**18670**	D&H Columbia 4-4-2 Locomotive "1400," 98		80
___	**18671**	N&W Columbia 4-4-2 Locomotive "1201," 98		70
___	**18673**	N&W 0-4-0 Locomotive "203," 99		110
___	**18676**	Safari RR 0-4-0 Locomotive, 99		110
___	**18678**	Quaker Oats Columbia 4-4-2 Locomotive "8632," 98		162
___	**18679**	JCPenney T&P 4-6-2 Locomotive "2000," traditional, 99, 00 u	45	250
___	**18680**	LRRC Century Club 4-6-4 Hudson "2000," 00		200
___	**18681**	PRR 4-4-2 Locomotive "460," 99		75
___	**18682**	Santa Fe 4-4-2 Columbia Locomotive "524," traditional, 00-01		70
___	**18683**	Mickey's Holiday Express 4-4-2 Atlantic, 99		90
___	**18684**	LRRC Inside Track Special Edition 4-6-2 Pacific, 99		185
___	**18685**	NYC 4-4-2 Atlantic "8632," 99		100
___	**18686**	Tinsel Town Express 4-4-2 Atlantic "3766," 00-01		95
___	**18689**	NS Dash 8-40C Diesel "8689," 92		200
___	**18690**	Centennial Express 4-4-2 Atlantic "100," 00		90
___	**18691**	PRR -4-4-2 Atlantic "201," 00		70
___	**18692**	PRR 4-6-4 Hudson, 00		80
___	**18693**	Lionel Mines 4-6-4 Hudson "49," 00		80
___	**18694**	Whirlpool Limited 4-4-2 Atlantic "201," 00		75
___	**18695**	Mickey's Millennium Express 2000, 00		250
___	**18696**	ACL 4-6-4 Locomotive "1800," 01		120
___	**18697**	Santa Fe 4-6-4 Locomotive "3465," 01		100
___	**18698**	Wabash 4-4-2 Atlantic , 07		85
___	**18699**	Alaska 4-4-2 Locomotive "64", 01		105
___	**18700**	Rock Island 0-4-0T Locomotive "8700," 87-88	36	43
___	**18701**	Polar Express LionScale 3-Bay Covered Hopper, 18		65
___	**18702**	V&TRR 4-4-0 Locomotive "8702" (SSS), 88	160	195
___	**18703**	Merry Christmas LionScale 3-Bay Covered Hopper, 18		60
___	**18704**	Lionel Lines 2-4-0 Locomotive, 89 u	36	43
___	**18704**	Halloween ELX 3-Bay Hopper, LionScale, 18		65
___	**18705**	Neptune 0-4-0T Locomotive "8705," 90-91	35	42
___	**18706**	Santa Fe 2-4-0 Locomotive "8706", 91	36	43
___	**18707**	Mickey's World Tour 2-4-0 Locomotive "8707," 91, 92 u	58	68
___	**18709**	Lionel Employee Learning Center 0-4-0T Locomotive, 92 u		140
___	**18710**	SP 2-4-0 Locomotive "2000," 93	30	38
___	**18711**	Southern 2-4-0 Locomotive "2000," 93	30	38
___	**18712**	Jersey Central 2-4-0 Locomotive "2000," 93	30	38
___	**18713**	Chessie System 2-4-0 Locomotive "1993," 94-95	30	38
___	**18716**	Lionelville Circus 4-4-0 Locomotive, 90-91	90	110
___	**18718**	LL 0-4-0 Dockside Switcher "8200," 97-98		40
___	**18719**	Thomas the Tank Engine "1," 97		158
___	**18720**	Union 4-4-0 General Locomotive "1865," 99		175
___	**18721**	Confederate 4-4-0 General Locomotive "1861," 99		175
___	**18722**	Percy the Tank Engine "6," 99		170

MODERN 1970-2025		Exc	Like New	
18723	Union Pacific 4-4-0 General Locomotive, 05		100	___
18725	World of Disney General Locomotive, 03		100	___
18728	Thomas the Tank Engine "1," 04-07		120	___
18730	Transylvania RR 4-4-0 Locomotive "13," traditional, 05		105	___
18731	PH-1 PowerHouse Transformer, 97	75	120	___
18732	North Pole Central 4-4-0 Locomotive "25," 06		110	___
18733	Percy the Tank Engine "6," 05-12		120	___
18734	James the Tank Engine "5," 06-12		120	___
18736	PRR 4-4-2 Atlantic "1645," 06-07		60	___
18738	North Pole Central 4-4-2 Atlantic "25," 08-09		90	___
18739	Great Western 4-4-0 General Locomotive, traditional, 07-09		80	___
18740	Walter E. Disney 4-4-0 General Locomotive, traditional, 06		90	___
18741	Thomas the Tank Engine, 08-13		120	___
18742	Nutcracker 4-4-0 General Locomotive, 08		140	___
18744	PRR 0-8-0 Locomotive "565," 08		125	___
18745	Hallow's Eve 4-6-0 Steam Locomotive, 11-12		190	___
18749	Rio Grande General Locomotive "346," 11-12		145	___
17850	SP 0-8-0 Locomotive w/Vanderbilt tender "4508," 12		140	___
18751	Santa Flyer 0-8-0 Locomotive, 11-13		120	___
18753	Route of the Reindeer RS3 Diesel, 11		190	___
18754	Polar Express 2-8-4 Berkshire Steam Locomotive, 11, 13		300	___
18755	C&O Berkshire Steam Locomotive "2751," TrainSounds, 11		290	___
18756	Coca-Cola 4-4-0 General Locomotive "125," 11-12		175	___
18765	PRR 2-8-4 Berkshire Locomotive "2331," 12-13		190	___
18769	Thomas, remote system, 12		140	___
18770	Christmas Thomas the Tank Engine "1," 13-15		90	___
18771	Percy, remote system, 13-16		140	___
18773	UP 0-8-0 Locomotive "4500," 12-13		105	___
18774	James, remote system, 13-16		140	___
18775	Diesel, remote system, 13-16		140	___
18776	Hershey's 0-8-0 Locomotive, 12-13		140	___
18778	GN 0-8-0 Locomotive w/Vanderbilt Tender '819," 12-13		130	___
18780	NYC 0-8-0 Locomotive "7794," 11-13		150	___
18783	Menard's C&NW 0-8-0 Locomotive "1009," 12 u		135	___
18784	Silver Bells 2-4-2 Columbia Locomotive, 13-15		110	___
18787	PRR 4-4-0 General Locomotive "1510," 94-95		125	___
18788	U.S. Military 4-4-0 General Locomotive, 13-14		300	___
18789	Peanuts LC 2-4-2 Columbia Locomotive "1031," 13-16		155	___
18790	Gingerbread Junction 0-6-0 Docksider "1226," 13-15		130	___
18791	PRR 0-8-0 LC Locomotive, 13-17		140	___
18799	Bethlehem Steel Switcher "44," 99		100	___
18800	Lehigh Valley GP9 Diesel "8800,"87	88	100	___
18801	Santa Fe U36B Diesel "8801," 87	100	120	___
18802	Southern GP9 Diesel "8802" (SSS), 87	100	115	___
18803	Santa Fe RS3 Diesel "8803," 88	90	105	___
18804	Soo Line RS3 Diesel "8804," 88	95	115	___
18805	Union Pacific RS3 Diesel "8805," 89	113	132	___
18806	New Haven SD18 Diesel "8806," 89	108	123	___
18807	Lehigh Valley RS3 Diesel "8807," 90	98	120	___
18808	ACL SD18 Diesel "8808," 90	83	105	___
18809	Susquehanna RS3 Diesel "8809," 89 u		130	___
18810	CSX SD18 Diesel "8810," 90	95	130	___
18811	Alaska SD9 Diesel "8811," 91	95	135	___

	MODERN 1970-2025		Exc	Like New
____	**18812**	Kansas City Southern GP38 Diesel "4000," 91	120	140
____	**18813**	DM&IR SD18 Diesel "8813," 90 u	90	145
____	**18814**	D&H RS3 Diesel "8814" (SSS), 91	90	120
____	**18815**	Amtrak RS3 Diesel "1815," 91, 92 u	100	130
____	**18816**	C&NW GP38-2 Diesel "4600," 92	105	135
____	**18817**	UP GP9 Diesel "150" (see 18553), 91 u		135
____	**18818**	LRRC GP38-2 Diesel, 92 u	100	117
____	**18819**	L&N GP38-2 Diesel "4136," 92	115	145
____	**18820**	WP GP9 Diesel "8820" (SSS), 92	120	140
____	**18821**	Clinchfield GP38-2 Diesel "6005," 93	125	150
____	**18822**	Gulf, Mobile & Ohio RS3 Diesel "721," 92-93 u		NRS
____	**18823**	Chicago & Illinois Midland SD9 Diesel "52," 92 u		235
____	**18824**	Montana Rail Link SD9 Diesel "600," 93	133	230
____	**18825**	Soo Line GP38-2 Diesel "4000" (SSS), 93	120	145
____	**18826**	Conrail GP7 Diesel "5808," 93	100	120
____	**18827**	Happy Holidays RS3 Diesel "8827," 93	165	220
____	**18830**	Budweiser GP9 Diesel "1947," 93-94 u	125	165
____	**18831**	SP GP20 Diesel "4060," 94	105	120
____	**18832**	PRR RSD4 Diesel "8446," 95	110	135
____	**18833**	Milwaukee Road RS3 Diesel "2487," 94	100	110
____	**18834**	C&O SD28 Diesel "8834," 94	110	140
____	**18835**	NYC RS3 Diesel "8223" (SSS), 94	135	195
____	**18836**	CN (Grand Trunk) GP38-2 Diesel "5800," 94	135	160
____	**18837**	Happy Holidays RS3 Diesel "8837," 94-95	150	190
____	**18838**	Seaboard RSC3 Diesel "1538," 95	110	140
____	**18840**	U.S. Army GP7 Diesel "1821," 95	85	124
____	**18841**	Western Maryland GP20 Diesel "27" (SSS), 95	120	150
____	**18842**	JCPenney B&LE SD38 Diesel "868," 95 u	80	265
____	**18843**	Great Northern RS3 Diesel "197," 96		145
____	**18844**	Nacionales de Mexico GP38 Diesel, 96		150
____	**18845**	D&RGW RS3 Diesel "5204," 97		100
____	**18846**	Lionel Centennial Series GP9 Diesel, 98	265	426
____	**18847**	Santa Fe H-12-44 Switcher "602," 99	149	385
____	**18848**	PRR H-12-44 Switcher "9087," 99	113	420
____	**18853**	JCPenney Santa Fe GP9 Diesel "2370," 97 u	60	150
____	**18854**	UP GP9 Diesel Dummy Set, "2380, 2387," 97		450
____	**18855**	UP GP9 Diesel "2381," unpowered, 97		210
____	**18856**	NJ Transit GP38-2 Diesel "4303," 99	143	320
____	**18857**	Union Pacific GP9 Diesel "2397," 97		240
____	**18858**	Lionel Centennial GP20 Diesel, 98	183	450
____	**18859**	Phantom II Locomotive, 99		360
____	**18860**	Pratt's Hollow Collection I: Phantom, 98	150	400
____	**18864**	Southern Pacific GP9 Diesel B Unit, 98		140
____	**18865**	New York Central GP9 Diesel B Unit, 98		170
____	**18866**	Milwaukee Road GP7 Diesel "2383," 98		205
____	**18868**	NJ Transit GP38-2 Diesel "4300," 98 u		140
____	**18870**	Pennsylvania GP9 Diesel "2029," 98		180
____	**18872**	Wabash GP7 Diesel Set, "453, 454, 455," 99	213	560
____	**18873**	Wabash GP7 Diesel "454," unpowered, 99		125
____	**18874**	Wabash GP7 Diesel "455," CC, 99		260
____	**18876**	C&NW H-12-44 Switcher "1053," 99	128	319
____	**18877**	Union Pacific GP9 Diesel "2399," nonpowered, 99		175
____	**18878**	Alaska GP7 Diesel "1803", 99	55	115

		Exc	Like New	
18879	B&O GP9 Diesel "5616," 99	90	260	___
18881	Custom GP9 Diesel "5616," 99		350	___
18890	UP RS3 Diesel "8805," 89		85	___
18892	Burlington GP9 Diesel "2328," 99	75	205	___
18893	Corvette GP7 Diesel, traditional, 99		230	___
18897	Christmas GP7 Diesel "1999," 99	66	200	___
18900	PRR Switcher "8900," 88 u, 89	26	34	___
18901	PRR Alco Diesel AA Set "8901, 8902," 88		320	___
18901/02	PRR Alco Diesel AA Set, 88	110	130	___
18902	PRR Alco Diesel FA-2 Unit, unpowered, 88		80	___
18903	Amtrak "Mopar Express," 99		500	___
18904	Amtrak Alco Diesel FA-2, unpowered, 88-89		80	___
18903/04	Amtrak Alco Diesel AA Set, 88-89	90	130	___
18905	PRR 44-ton Switcher "9312," 92	80	116	___
18906	Erie-Lackawanna RS3 Diesel "8906," 91 u	70	90	___
18907	Rock Island 44-ton Switcher "371," 93	95	110	___
18908	NYC Alco Diesel AA Units "8908, 8909," 93	60	150	___
18908/09	NYC Alco Diesel AA Set, 93	113	123	___
18909	NYC Alco FA-2 Diesel "8909," unpowered, 93	50	80	___
18910	CSX Switcher "8910," 93	40	46	___
18911	UP Switcher "8911," 93	33	37	___
18912	Amtrak Switcher "8912," 93	37	43	___
18913	Santa Fe Alco Diesel A Unit "8913," 93-94	55	65	___
18915	WM Alco Diesel A Unit "8915," 93	65	80	___
18916	WM Alco Diesel A Unit "8916," dummy, 93	38	42	___
18917	Soo Line NW2 Switcher, 93	65	75	___
18918	B&M NW2 Switcher "8918," 93	75	90	___
18919	Santa Fe Alco Diesel A Unit "8919," dummy, 93-94	36	55	___
18920	Frisco NW2 Switcher "254," 94	70	75	___
18921	C&NW NW2 Switcher "1017," 94	60	80	___
18922	New Haven Alco Diesel A Unit "8922," 94	75	120	___
18923	New Haven Alco Diesel A Unit "8923," dummy, 94	50	55	___
18924	IC Switcher "8924," 94-95	37	44	___
18925	D&RGW Switcher "8925," 94-95	32	37	___
18926	Reading Switcher "8926," 94-95	31	39	___
18927	U.S. Navy NW2 Switcher "65-00637,"94-95	65	85	___
18928	C&NW NW2 Switcher Calf Unit, 95	50	55	___
18929	B&M NW2 Switcher Calf Unit, 95	44	48	___
18930	Crayola Switcher, 94 u, 95	27	30	___
18931	Chrysler Mopar NW2 Switcher "1818," 94 u	76	88	___
18932	Jersey Central NW2 Switcher "8932," 96		65	___
18933	Jersey Central NW2 Switcher Calf Unit "8933," 96		55	___
18934/35	Reading Alco Diesel AA Set, 95	75	95	___
18934	Reading Alco Diesel A-A Set, 95		220	___
18935	Reading Alco FA-2 Diesel "8935," unpowered, 95		80	___
18936	Amtrak Alco Diesel A Unit "8936," 95	40	80	___
18937	Amtrak FA2 Alco Diesel, nonpowered, 95-97		50	___
18938	U.S. Navy NW2 Switcher Calf Unit, 95	55	65	___
18939	Union Pacific NW2 Switcher Set, 96		145	___
18940	UP NW2 Switcher, unpowered, 96		75	___
18943	Georgia Power NW2 Switcher "1960," 95 u		170	___
18945	MP NW2 Switcher, 96		168	___
18946	U.S. Coast Guard NW2 Switcher "8946," 96		80	___

		MODERN 1970-2025	Exc	Like New
____	**18947**	Port of Lionel City Alco FA2 Diesel "2030," 97		70
____	**18948**	Port of Lionel City Alco FB-2 Diesel "2030B," 97		45
____	**18949**	NYC NW2 Switcher, 97		170
____	**18951**	Erie NW2 Switcher "6220," 97		165
____	**18952**	ATSF Alco PA1 Diesel "2000," 97	138	345
____	**18953**	NYC Alco PA1 Diesel "2000," 97	65	260
____	**18954**	ATSF Alco FA2 Diesel "212," powered, 97-99		80
____	**18955**	NJ Transit NW2 Switcher "500," 96 u		110
____	**18956**	Dodge Motorsports NW2 Switcher "8956," 96 u		172
____	**18959**	New York Central NW2 Switcher "622," 97	70	475
____	**18961**	Erie Alco PA1 Diesel "850," 98		315
____	**18965**	Santa Fe Alco PB1 Diesel, 98	150	235
____	**18966**	New York Central Alco BP1 Diesel "2008", 98	45	250
____	**18971**	Alco Diesel A Unit, nonpowered, 98		60
____	**18972**	RI Alco FA Diesel AA Set, 98		180
____	**18973**	RI Alco FA2 Diesel "2031," powered, 98-99		165
____	**18974**	RI Alco FA2 Diesel Dummy Unit, 98-99		80
____	**18975**	Southern 44-ton Switcher "1955," 99		190
____	**18978**	C&O NW2 Switcher "624," 99-00		410
____	**18979**	Area 51 Groom Lake RR Alco FA-2 Diesel, 02		170
____	**18981**	Pennsylvania Railroad Speeder "16", 04		45
____	**18982**	Santa Fe Railroad Speeder "122", 04-05		65
____	**18988**	MP15 Diesel, K-Line, 06		140
____	**18989**	Bethlehem Steel Plymouth Switcher, traditional, K-Line, 06		100
____	**18992**	SP S2 Diesel Switcher "1440," CC, 08		410
____	**18993**	C&NW S2 Diesel Switcher "1031," CC, 08		410
____	**18994**	Lionel Lines FA Diesel, traditional, 08-09		90
____	**19000**	Blue Comet Diner, 87 u	60	75
____	**19001**	Southern Diner, 87 u	55	65
____	**19002**	Pennsylvania Diner, 88 u	29	41
____	**19003**	Milwaukee Road Diner, 88 u	29	44
____	**19010**	B&O Diner, 89 u	36	55
____	**19011**	Lionel Lines Baggage Car, 93	164	290
____	**19015**	Lionel Lines Passenger Coach, 91	108	164
____	**19016**	Lionel Lines Passenger Coach, 91	95	135
____	**19017**	Lionel Lines Passenger Coach, 91	88	118
____	**19018**	Lionel Lines Observation Car, 91	90	117
____	**19019**	SP Baggage Car "9019," 93	120	153
____	**19023**	SP Passenger Coach "9023," 92	125	160
____	**19024**	SP Passenger Coach "9024," 92	85	100
____	**19025**	SP Passenger Coach "9025," 92	100	115
____	**19026**	SP Observation Car "9026," 92	85	100
____	**19038**	Adolphus Busch Observation Car, 92-93 u		85
____	**19039**	Pere Marquette Baggage Car, 93		75
____	**19040**	Pere Marquette Passenger Coach "1115," 93		75
____	**19041**	Pere Marquette Passenger Coach "1116," 93		75
____	**19042**	Pere Marquette Observation Car "36," 93		75
____	**19047**	Baltimore & Ohio Combination Car "9047," 96		55
____	**19048**	Baltimore & Ohio Passenger Coach "9048," 96		50
____	**19049**	Baltimore & Ohio Diner "9049," 96		42
____	**19050**	Baltimore & Ohio Observation Car "9050," 96		42
____	**19056**	NYC Heavyweight Baggage Car, 96		105
____	**19057**	NYC Willow Run Heavyweight Coach, 96		95

		Exc	Like New	
19058	NYC Willow Trail Heavyweight Coach, 96		90	___
19059	NYC Seneca Valley Heavyweight Observation Car, 96		100	___
19060	Pullman Heavyweight Set, 96		479	___
19061	Wabash Passenger Set, 97		235	___
19062	Wabash City of Columbia Coach "2361," 97		90	___
19063	Wabash City of Danville Coach "2362," 97		75	___
19064	Wabash REA Baggage Car "2360," 97		47	___
19065	Wabash Windy City Observation Car "2363," 97		90	___
19066	Commodore Vanderbilt Pullman Heavyweight 2-pack, 97		190	___
19067	Commodore Vanderbilt Willow River Pullman "2543," 97		115	___
19068	Commodore Vanderbilt Willow Valley Pullman "2544," 97		100	___
19069	Pullman Baby Madison Set "9500-02," 97		155	___
19070	Baby Madison Combination Car "9501," 97		40	___
19071	Laurel Gap Baby Madison Coach "9500," 97		34	___
19072	Laurel Summit Baby Madison Coach "9500," 97		40	___
19073	Catskill Valley Baby Madison Observation Car "9502," 97		34	___
19074	Legends of Lionel Madison Set, 97	65	385	___
19075	Mazzone Lionel Legends Coach "2621," 97		105	___
19076	Caruso Lionel Legends Coach "2624," 97		90	___
19077	Raphael Lionel Legends Coach "2652," 97		90	___
19078	Cowen Lionel Legends Observation Car "2600," 97		95	___
19079	NYC Heavyweight Passenger Car Set, 97		275	___
19080	NYC Heavyweight REA Baggage Car "2564," 97		100	___
19081	NYC Park Place Heavyweight Coach "2565," 97		100	___
19082	NYC Star Beam Heavyweight Coach "2566," 97		100	___
19083	NYC Hudson Valley Heavyweight Observation "2567," 97		100	___
19085	N&W Operating Hopper, 97		84	___
19087	C&O Heavyweight Passenger Car 4-pack, "2571-74," 97	80	290	___
19088	C&O Heavyweight Baggage Car "2571," 97		100	___
19089	C&O Heavyweight Sleeper Car "2572," 97		100	___
19090	C&O Heavyweight Diner "2573," 97		110	___
19091	C&O Heavyweight Observation Car "2574," 97		100	___
19093	Commodore Vanderbilt Heavyweight Sleeper Car 2-pack, 98		170	___
19094	Commodore Vanderbilt Niagara Falls Sleeper, 98		75	___
19095	Commodore Vanderbilt Highland Falls Sleeper, 98		75	___
19096	Legends of Lionel Madison Car 2-pack, 98		130	___
19097	Bonnano Lionel Legends Coach "2653," 98		80	___
19098	Pagano Lionel Legends Coach "2654," 98		105	___
19099	PRR Liberty Gap Baggage Car "2623," 99		80	___
19100	Amtrak Baggage Car "9100," 89	125	165	___
19101	Amtrak Combination Car "9101," 89	75	85	___
19102	Amtrak Passenger Coach "9102," 89	75	85	___
19103	Amtrak Vista Dome Car "9103," 89	70	90	___
19104	Amtrak Diner "9104," 89	65	80	___
19105	Amtrak Full Vista Dome Car "9105," 89 u	70	80	___
19106	Amtrak Observation Car "9106", 89	75	90	___
19107	SP Full Vista Dome Car, 90 u	70	88	___
19108	N&W Full Vista Dome Car "576", 91 u	75	85	___
19109	Santa Fe Baggage Car "3400", 91	168	263	___
19110	Santa Fe Combination Car "3500", 91	70	108	___
19111	Santa Fe Diner "601", 91	85	123	___
19112	Santa Fe Passenger Coach, 91	90	135	___
19113	Santa Fe Vista Dome Car, 91	100	135	___

MODERN 1970-2025		Exc	Like New
19116	Great Northern Baggage Car "1200," 92	135	165
19117	Great Northern Combination Car "1240," 92	65	80
19118	Great Northern Passenger Coach "1212," 92	75	95
19119	Great Northern Vista Dome Car "1322," 92	75	95
19120	Great Northern Observation Car "1192," 92	75	95
19121	Union Pacific Vista Dome Car "9121," 92 u	90	100
19122	D&RGW California Zephyr Baggage Car, 93	170	210
19123	D&RGW California Zephyr Silver Bronco Vista Dome Car, 93	95	115
19124	D&RGW California Zephyr Silver Colt Vista Dome Car, 93	95	115
19125	D&RGW California Zephyr Silver Mustang Vista Dome Car, 93	100	125
19126	D&RGW California Zephyr Silver Pony Vista Dome Car, 93	95	115
19127	D&RGW California Zephyr Vista Dome Car, 93	85	100
19128	Santa Fe Full Vista Dome Car "507," 92 u	143	163
19129	IC Full Vista Dome Car "9129," 93	75	85
19130	Lackawanna Passenger Cars, set of 4, 94	280	350
19131	Lackawanna Baggage Car "2000" (see 19130)		150
19132	Lackawanna Diner "469" (see 19130)		100
19133	Lackawanna Passenger Coach "260" (see 19130)		100
19134	Lackawanna Observation Car "789" (see 19130)		85
19135	Lackawanna Combination Car "425," 94	85	100
19136	Lackawanna Passenger Coach "211," 94	65	75
19137	New York Central Roomette Car, 95	71	105
19138	Santa Fe Roomette Car, 95	75	95
19139	N&W Baggage Car "577," 95	150	200
19140	N&W Combination Car "494," 95	60	80
19141	N&W Diner "495," 95	105	135
19142	N&W Passenger Coach "538," 95	75	95
19143	N&W Passenger Coach "537," 95	75	95
19144	N&W Observation Car "582," 95	80	95
19145	C&O Combination Car "1403," 96		65
19146	C&O Passenger Coach "1623," 96		60
19147	C&O Passenger Coach "1803," 96		55
19148	C&O Chessie Club Coach "1903," 96		55
19149	C&O Coach/Diner "1950," 96		50
19150	C&O Observation Car "2504," 96		55
19151	Norfolk & Western Duplex Roomette car, 96		108
19152	Union Pacific Duplex Roomette Car, 96		75
19153	C&O Passenger Cars, set of 4, 96	60	340
19154	Atlantic Coast Line Passenger Car Set, 96	90	340
19155	ACL Combination Car "101," 96		90
19156	ACL Talladega Diner, 96		90
19157	ACL Moultrie Coach, 96		95
19158	ACL Observation Car "256," 96		90
19159	N&W Passenger Cars, set of 4, 95 u	300	385
19160	LL REA Baggage Car, 96		90
19161	LL Silver Mesa Coach, 96		80
19162	LL Silver Sky Vista Dome Car, 96		75
19163	LL Silver Rail Observation Car, 96		75
19164	C&O Passenger Car Add-on, 2-pack, 96		160
19165	ATSF Super Chief Set, 96		305
19166	NP Vista Dome Car Set, 97	113	323
19167	NP Pullman Coach "2571," 97		105
19168	NP Pullman Coach "2571," 97		105

MODERN 1970-2025		Exc	Like New	
19169	NP Pullman Coach "2570," 97		95	___
19170	NP Pullman Coach "2571," 97		100	___
19171	NYC Streamliner Car 4-pack, 97		290	___
19172	NYC Aluminum Passenger/Baggage Car "2570," 97		95	___
19173	NYC Manhattan Island Aluminum Passenger Diner, 97		100	___
19174	NYC Queensboro Bridge Aluminum Passenger Coach, 97		100	___
19175	NYC Windgate Brook Aluminum Observation Car, 97		90	___
19176	ATSF Indian Arrow Diner "2572," 97		90	___
19177	ATSF Grass Valley Coach "2573," 97		90	___
19178	ATSF Citrus Valley Coach "2574," 97		90	___
19179	ATSF Vista Heights Coach "2575," 97		90	___
19180	ATSF Surfliner Passenger Car 4-pack, 97		250	___
19181	GN Empire Builder Prairie View Full Vista Dome Car, 98	33	78	___
19182	GN Empire Builder River View Full Vista Dome Car, 98	38	93	___
19183	GN Empire Builder Vista Dome Car 2-pack, 98	75	163	___
19184	Milwaukee Road Passenger Car 4-pack, 99		390	___
19185	MILW Red River Valley Aluminum Passenger Coach "194," 99		125	___
19186	MILW Aluminum Coach/Diner "170," 99		110	___
19187	MILW Cedar Rapids Aluminum Observation Car "186," 99		120	___
19188	MILW Aluminum REA Passenger/Baggage Car "1336," 99		95	___
19194	KCS Aluminum Passenger Car 4-pack, 00		380	___
19195	KCS Aluminum Baggage Car "19195," 00-01		95	___
19196	KCS Aluminum Coach "Texarkana," 00-01		95	___
19197	KCS Aluminum Coach "Joplin," 00-01		95	___
19198	KCS Aluminum Observation "New Orleans,", 00-01		95	___
19200	Tidewater Southern Boxcar, 87	14	21	___
19201	Lancaster & Chester Boxcar, 87	23	37	___
19202	PRR Boxcar, 87	22	30	___
19203	D&TS Boxcar, 87	11	18	___
19204	Milwaukee Road Boxcar (FF 2), 87	30	43	___
19205	Great Northern DD Boxcar (FF 3), 88	19	24	___
19206	Seaboard System Boxcar, 88	18	23	___
19207	CP Rail DD Boxcar, 88	17	22	___
19208	Southern DD Boxcar, 88	11	13	___
19209	Florida East Coast Boxcar, 88	15	19	___
19210	Soo Line Boxcar, 89	19	23	___
19211	Vermont Railway Boxcar, 89	18	21	___
19212	PRR Boxcar, 89	21	25	___
19213	SP&S DD Boxcar, 89	17	25	___
19214	Western Maryland Boxcar (FF 4), 89	23	27	___
19215	Union Pacific DD Boxcar, 90	17	21	___
19216	Santa Fe Boxcar, 90	17	22	___
19217	Burlington Boxcar, 90	16	21	___
19218	New Haven Boxcar, 90	16	20	___
19219	Lionel Lines 1900-1906 Boxcar, diesel RailSounds, 90	120	145	___
19220	Lionel Lines 1926-1934 Boxcar, 90	27	30	___
19221	Lionel Lines 1935-1937 Boxcar, 90	27	30	___
19222	Lionel Lines 1948-1950 Boxcar, 90	27	30	___
19223	Lionel Lines 1979-1989 Boxcar, 90	18	25	___
19228	Cotton Belt Boxcar, 91	16	22	___
19229	Frisco Boxcar, diesel RailSounds (FF 5), 91	75	90	___
19230	Frisco DD Boxcar (FF 5), 91	21	26	___
19231	TA&G DD Boxcar, 91	13	16	___

	MODERN 1970-2025		Exc	Like New
___	19232	Rock Island DD Boxcar, 91	17	20
___	19233	Southern Pacific Boxcar, 91	15	19
___	19234	NYC Boxcar, 91	60	65
___	19235	MKT Boxcar, 91	55	65
___	19236	NKP DD Boxcar (FF 6), 92	21	30
___	19237	C&IM Boxcar, 92	17	24
___	19238	Kansas City Southern Boxcar, 92	17	24
___	19239	Toronto, Hamilton & Buffalo DD Boxcar, 92	15	20
___	19240	Great Northern DD Boxcar, 92	17	23
___	19241	Mickey Mouse 60th Anniversary Hi-Cube Boxcar, 91 u	135	180
___	19242	Donald Duck 50th Anniversary Hi-Cube Boxcar, 91 u	143	152
___	19243	Clinchfield Boxcar "9790," 91 u	35	41
___	19244	L&N Boxcar "9791," 92	35	38
___	19245	Mickey's World Tour Hi-Cube Boxcar, 92 u	35	40
___	19246	Disney World 20th Anniversary Hi-Cube Boxcar, 92 u	33	40
___	19247	Postwar "6464" Series Boxcar Set I, 3 cars, 93	323	550
___	19248	Western Pacific Boxcar "6464," 93	75	95
___	19249	Great Northern Boxcar "6464," 93	75	95
___	19250	M&StL Boxcar "6464," 93	80	105
___	19251	Montana Rail Link DD Boxcar "10001," 93	21	34
___	19254	Erie Boxcar (FF 7), 93	21	25
___	19255	Erie DD Boxcar (FF 7), 93	22	26
___	19256	Goofy Hi-Cube Boxcar, 93	23	26
___	19257	Postwar "6464" Series Boxcar Set II, 3 cars, 94	73	116
___	19258	Rock Island Boxcar "6464," 94	25	34
___	19259	Western Pacific Boxcar "6464100," 94	33	46
___	19260	Western Pacific Boxcar "6464100," 94	35	49
___	19261	Perils of Mickey Hi-Cube Boxcar #1, 93	20	30
___	19262	Perils of Mickey Hi-Cube Boxcar #2, 93	20	28
___	19263	NYC DD Boxcar (SSS), 94	36	42
___	19264	Perils of Mickey Hi-Cube Boxcar #3, 94	28	31
___	19265	Mickey Mouse 65th Anniversary Hi-Cube Boxcar, 94	22	44
___	19266	Postwar "6464" Series Boxcar Set III, 3 cars, 95	43	98
___	19267	NYC Pacemaker Boxcar "6464125," 95	37	42
___	19268	Missouri Pacific Boxcar "6464150," 95	25	29
___	19269	Rock Island Boxcar "6464," 95	25	26
___	19270	Donald Duck 60th Anniversary Hi-Cube Boxcar, 95	30	34
___	19271	Minnie Mouse Hi-Cube Boxcar, 95	21	43
___	19272	Postwar "6464" Series Boxcar Set IV, 3 cars, 96	73	103
___	19273	BAR State of Maine Boxcar "6464275," 96		35
___	19274	SP Overnight Boxcar "6464225," 96		28
___	19275	Pennsylvania Boxcar "6464," 96		44
___	19276	Postwar "6464" Series Boxcar Set V, 3 cars, 96	56	103
___	19277	Rutland Boxcar "6464-300," 96		26
___	19278	B&O Boxcar "6464-325," 96		40
___	19279	Central of Georgia Boxcar "6464-375," 96		29
___	19280	Mickey's Wheat Hi-Cube Boxcar, 96		32
___	19281	Mickey's Carrots Hi-Cube Boxcar, 96		40
___	19282	Santa Fe "Super Chief" Boxcar "6464-196," 96		24
___	19283	Erie Boxcar "6464-296," 96		22
___	19284	Northern Pacific Boxcar "6464-396," 96	10	35
___	19285	B&A State of Maine Boxcar "6464-275," 96	10	30
___	19286	Tweety and Sylvester Boxcar, 96		46

MODERN 1970-2025		Exc	Like New	
19287	NYC/PC Merger Boxcar "6464-125X" (SSS), 97	50	75	___
19288	PRR/CR Merger Boxcar "6464-200X" (SSS), 97	43	56	___
19289	Monon "Hoosier Line" Boxcar "6464," 97		27	___
19290	Seaboard "Silver Meteor" Boxcar "6464," 97		24	___
19291	GN Boxcar "6464-397," 97	14	33	___
19292	Postwar "6464" Series Boxcar Set VI, 3 cars, 97	25	70	___
19293	MKT Boxcar "6464-350," 97	28	32	___
19294	B&O Boxcar "6464-400," 97	27	37	___
19295	NH Boxcar "6464-425," 97	25	34	___
19300	PRR Ore Car, 87	15	23	___
19301	Milwaukee Road Ore Car, 87	19	26	___
19302	Milwaukee Road Quad Hopper with coal (FF 2), 87	23	35	___
19303	Lionel Lines Quad Hopper with coal, 87 u	20	36	___
19304	GN Covered Quad Hopper (FF 3), 88	17	27	___
19305	Chessie System Ore Car, 88	18	23	___
19307	B&LE Ore Car with load, 89	19	25	___
19308	GN Ore Car with load, 89	18	23	___
19309	Seaboard Covered Quad Hopper, 89	16	19	___
19310	L&C Quad Hopper with coal, 89	16	30	___
19311	SP Covered Quad Hopper, 90	15	18	___
19312	Reading Quad Hopper with coal, 90	21	36	___
19313	B&O Ore Car with load, 90-91	20	25	___
19315	Amtrak Ore Car with load, 91	22	30	___
19316	Wabash Covered Quad Hopper, 91	18	23	___
19317	Lehigh Valley Quad Hopper with coal, 91	47	55	___
19318	NKP Quad Hopper with coal (FF 6), 92	29	32	___
19319	Union Pacific Covered Quad Hopper, 92	19	23	___
19320	PRR Ore Car with load, 92	21	30	___
19321	B&LE Ore Car with load, 92	21	30	___
19322	C&NW Ore Car with load, 93	27	34	___
19323	Detroit & Mackinac Ore Car with load, 93	20	29	___
19324	Erie Quad Hopper with coal (FF 7), 93	25	33	___
19325	N&W 4-bay Hopper "6446-1" with coal, 97		65	___
19326	N&W 4-bay Hopper "6446-2" with coal, 96		60	___
19327	N&W 4-bay Hopper "6446-3" with coal, 96		60	___
19328	N&W 4-bay Hopper "6446-4" with coal, 96		60	___
19329	N&W 4-bay Hopper "6436" with coal, 97		48	___
19330	Cotton Belt 4-bay Hopper "64661" with coal, 98		45	___
19331	Cotton Belt 4-bay Hopper "64662" with coal, 98		45	___
19332	Cotton Belt 4-bay Hopper "64663" with coal, 98		45	___
19333	Cotton Belt 4-bay Hopper "64664" with coal, 98		45	___
19338	Cotton Belt 4-bay Hopper 2-pack, 99		120	___
19339	Cotton Belt 4-bay Hopper "64469," 99		60	___
19340	Cotton Belt 4-bay Hopper "64470," 99		60	___
19341	LV 2-bay Hopper "6456," 99		30	___
19344	D&RGW 3-bay Cylindrical Hopper "15990," 99-00		42	___
19345	CN 3-bay Cylindrical Hopper "370708," 99-00	35	98	___
19346	PRR 4-bay Hopper with coal "744433," 01		40	___
19347	LV 2-bay Hopper "643657," 01		40	___
19348	Duluth, Missabe & Iron Range Ore Car "28000," 03		25	___
19349	U.S. Steel Ore Car "19349," 03		29	___
19350	Postwar "6636" Alaska Quad Hopper, 03		34	___
19357	N&W Hopper "6446-25," Archive Collection, 07		50	___

MODERN 1970-2025			Exc	Like New
___	**19361**	Twizzlers Quad Hopper, 10		55
___	**19362**	Coursers Christmas Hopper with gifts, 10		60
___	**19364**	Milk Duds Covered Hopper, 11		55
___	**19365**	Coca-Cola Quad Hopper, 10		60
___	**19366**	Santa's Little Hopper, 10-11		55
___	**19367**	ATSF Quad Hopper, 11		60
___	**19368**	Southern Offset Hopper "106723," (std O), 11		70
___	**19369**	Alaska Quad Hopper "20756," 12		60
___	**19371**	Burlington Northern I-Beam Car, 04		60
___	**19374**	NS Bathtub Gondola 2-pack (std O), 15		140
___	**19377**	DETX Bathtub Gondola 2-pack (std O), 15		140
___	**19380**	CSX Bathtub Gondola 2-pack (std O), 15		140
___	**19383**	UP PS-4 Flatcar "57125" (std O), 13		70
___	**19384**	ATSF PS-4 Flatcar "90088" (std O), 13		70
___	**19385**	CNJ PS-4 Flatcar "339" (std O), 13		70
___	**19386**	BN PS-4 Flatcar "613200" (std O), 13		70
___	**19388**	BN 89' Auto Carrier (std O), 13-14		110
___	**19389**	SP 89' Auto Carrier (std O), 13-14		110
___	**19390**	CP 89' Auto Carrier (std O), 13-14, 16		110
___	**19391**	Soo Line 89' Auto Carrier (std O), 13-14, 16		110
___	**19393**	BNSF Auto Carrier 2-pack (std O), 12		220
___	**19394**	UP Auto Carrier 2-pack (std O), 12		220
___	**19395**	Grand Trunk Auto Carrier 2-pack (std O), 12		220
___	**19396**	CSX Auto Carrier 2-pack (std O), 12		220
___	**19397**	CN Auto Carrier 2-pack (std O), 12		220
___	**19398**	Conrail Auto Carrier 2-pack (std O), 12		220
___	**19400**	Milwaukee Road Gondola with cable reels (FF 2), 87	21	33
___	**19401**	GN Gondola with coal (FF 3), 88	19	25
___	**19402**	GN Crane Car (FF 3), 88	47	65
___	**19403**	WM Gondola with coal (FF 4), 89	20	25
___	**19404**	Trailer Train Flatcar with WM trailers (FF 4), 89	29	33
___	**19405**	Southern Crane Car, 91	42	65
___	**19406**	West Point Mint Car, 91	38	50
___	**19408**	Frisco Gondola with coil covers (FF 5), 91	26	31
___	**19409**	Southern Flatcar with stakes, 91	18	22
___	**19410**	NYC Gondola with canisters, 91	47	55
___	**19411**	NKP Flatcar with Sears trailer (FF 6), 92	30	59
___	**19412**	Frisco Crane Car, 92	49	65
___	**19413**	Frisco Flatcar with stakes, 92	16	21
___	**19414**	Union Pacific Flatcar with stakes (SSS), 92	19	26
___	**19415**	Erie Flatcar with trailer "7200" (FF 7), 93	28	39
___	**19416**	ICG TTUX Flatcar Set with trailers (SSS), 93	70	75
___	**19419**	Charlotte Mint Car, 93	25	32
___	**19420**	Lionel Lines Vat Car, 94	18	22
___	**19421**	Hirsch Brothers Vat Car, 95	16	21
___	**19423**	Circle L Racing Flatcar "6424" with stock cars, 96		27
___	**19424**	Edison Electric Flatcar "6461" w/transformer, 97		31
___	**19427**	Evans Auto Loader "6414," 99		55
___	**19428**	Evans Boat Loader "6414," 99		70
___	**19429**	Culvert Gondola "6342," 98-99		48
___	**19430**	ATSF Flatcar "6411" with Beechcraft Bonanza, 98		47
___	**19438**	Christmas Gondola (std O), 98		42
___	**19439**	Flatcar with safes, 98		35

MODERN 1970-2025		Exc	Like New	
19440	Flatcar with FedEx trailer, 98		34	___
19441	Lobster Vat Car, 98		35	___
19442	Water Supply Flatcar with tank (SSS), 98		31	___
19444	Flatcar with VW Bug, 98		38	___
19445	Borden Milk Tank Car "520," 99		38	___
19446	Pittsburgh Paint Vat Car, 99		43	___
19447	Mama's Baked Beans Vat Car, 99		35	___
19448	Easter Gondola "6462" with candy, 99		27	___
19449	Liquified Gas Tank Car "6469," 99		31	___
19450	Barrel Ramp Car "6343," 99		31	___
19451	Wheel Car "6262," 99		32	___
19454	PRR Flatcar "6424" with gondola, 99		25	___
19455	Lionel Lines Flatcar "6430" with Cooper-Jarrett trailers, 99		60	___
19457	Lionel Lines Extension Searchlight Car, 99		40	___
19459	Valentine Gondola "6462" with candy, 99		50	___
19471	Mobil Flatcar with 2 trailers, 00 u		96	___
19472	Mobil Bulkhead Flatcar with tank, 00 u		68	___
19474	L&N Flatcar "6424" with trailer frames, 99		26	___
19476	Zoo Gondola "6462" with animals, 99-00		43	___
19477	Monday Night Football Flatcar with trailer, 01		30	___
19478	Culvert Gondola "6342," 99		45	___
19479	Borden Milk Car "521," 00		38	___
19480	Valentine's Vat Car "6475," 99-00		30	___
19481	Easter Vat Car, 99-00		38	___
19482	NYC Flat with trailer "6424," 00		50	___
19483	VW Beetle Flatcar, 00		48	___
19484	Flatcar "6264" with timber, 00		34	___
19485	PRR Culvert Gondola "347004", 01		41	___
19486	NYC Lumber Flatcar, 01		34	___
19487	Flatcar "6800" with airplane, 00		41	___
19489	Evans Auto Loader "500085," 00		50	___
19490	Postwar "6475" Libby's Vat Car, 01-02		36	___
19491	Christmas Vat Car, 01		30	___
19492	WM Skeleton Log Car 3-pack, 01		95	___
19496	Westside Lumber Skeleton Log Car 3-pack, 01		112	___
19500	Milwaukee Road Reefer (FF 2), 87	30	44	___
19502	C&NW Reefer, 87	30	33	___
19503	Bangor & Aroostook Reefer, 87	22	25	___
19504	Northern Pacific Reefer, 87	16	22	___
19505	Great Northern Reefer (FF 3), 88	29	35	___
19506	Thomas Newcomen Reefer, 88	18	23	___
19507	Thomas Edison Reefer, 88	21	27	___
19508	Leonardo da Vinci Reefer, 89	19	27	___
19509	Alexander Graham Bell Reefer, 89	17	20	___
19510	PRR Stock Car (FARR 5), 89 u	18	26	___
19511	WM Reefer (FF 4), 89	22	28	___
19512	Wright Brothers Reefer, 90	17	21	___
19513	Ben Franklin Reefer, 90	17	20	___
19515	Milwaukee Road Stock Car (FF 2), 90 u	31	43	___
19516	George Washington Reefer, 89 u, 91	14	19	___
19517	Civil War Reefer, 89 u, 91	14	19	___
19518	Man on the Moon Reefer, 89 u, 91	13	17	___
19519	Frisco Stock Car (FF 5), 91	26	31	___

MODERN 1970-2025			Exc	Like New
___	**19520**	CSX Reefer, 91	18	23
___	**19522**	Guglielmo Marconi Reefer, 91	19	23
___	**19523**	Dr. Robert Goddard Reefer, 91	19	23
___	**19524**	Delaware & Hudson Reefer (SSS), 91	29	32
___	**19525**	Speedy Alka Seltzer Reefer, 91 u	31	32
___	**19526**	Jolly Green Giant Reefer, 91 u	21	33
___	**19527**	Nickel Plate Road Reefer (FF 6), 92	20	29
___	**19528**	Joshua L. Cowen Reefer, 92	23	28
___	**19529**	A.C. Gilbert Reefer, 92	18	23
___	**19530**	Rock Island Stock Car, 92 u	34	38
___	**19531**	Rice Krispies Reefer, 92 u	23	33
___	**19532**	Hormel Reefer "901," 92 u	18	24
___	**19535**	Erie Reefer (FF 7), 93	23	26
___	**19536**	Soo Line REA Reefer (SSS), 93	25	30
___	**19537**	Kellogg's Corn Flakes Refrigerator Car, 93 u		NRS
___	**19538**	Hormel Reefer "102," 94	22	25
___	**19539**	Heinz Reefer, 94	33	47
___	**19540**	Broken Arrow Ranch Stock Car "3356," 97		28
___	**19552**	Rutland Reefer "395" (std 0), 00		32
___	**19553**	ATSF Stock Car "23003," 00		37
___	**19554**	Postwar Celebration Milk Car "36621," 00		125
___	**19555**	Swift Reefer "5839," red, 01		33
___	**19556**	Swift Reefer "1020," silver, 01		31
___	**19557**	Circus Stock Car "6376," 00		32
___	**19558**	Postwar "6556" MKT Stock Car, 02		126
___	**19559**	MKT Stock Car, girls set add-on, 02	30	95
___	**19560**	NP 2-door Stock Car "6356," Archive Collection, 02		33
___	**19561**	Norman Rockwell Holiday Reefer, 03		25
___	**19562**	Norman Rockwell Holiday Reefer, 03		25
___	**19563**	Norman Rockwell Holiday Reefer, 03		25
___	**19564**	Postwar "6672" Santa Fe Reefer, 03		35
___	**19565**	Burlington Reefer "6672," Archive Collection, 03		35
___	**19567**	Postwar "6572" Railway Express Agency Reefer, 05		45
___	**19568**	GN Reefer, Archive Collection, 05	18	45
___	**19569**	Pillsbury Reefer, traditional, 05		53
___	**19570**	Nestle Nesquik Reefer, traditional, 05		53
___	**19572**	NYC Reefer "6672," Archive Collection, 06		45
___	**19573**	Postwar "6356" NYC Stock Car, 06-07		50
___	**19574**	GN Stock Car, 08		50
___	**19575**	REA Reefer "6721," 08-09		50
___	**19576**	Alaska Reefer, 08		50
___	**19577**	Krey's Reefer, 10-11		60
___	**19578**	Granny Smith Apples Wood-sided Reefer, 10-11		53
___	**19580**	Nicholas Smith Wood-side Refrigerator Car, 09u	17	30
___	**19582**	Nicholas Smith Wood-side Refrigerator Car, 09u	17	30
___	**19583**	Nicholas Smith Wood-side Refrigerator Car, 09u	17	30
___	**19584**	Nicholas Smith Wood-side Refrigerator Car, 09u	17	30
___	**19585**	NS Transparent Instruction Car, 10-11		75
___	**19586**	Alaska Husky Transport Car, 10-11		75
___	**19587**	Hershey's Chocolate Wood-sided Reefer, 10		75
___	**19588**	Santa's Wish Transparent Gift Car, 10		75
___	**19589**	Blood Transfusion Bunk Car, 10-11		60
___	**19590**	Wood-sided Reefer 2-pack, 10		110

MODERN 1970-2025		Exc	Like New	
19593	Hershey's Kisses Wood-sided Reefer, 11-15		60	___
19594	York Peppermint Patty Wood-sided Reefer, 10-11		55	___
19595	AT&SF Warbonnet Refrigerator Car, 10-11	30	55	___
19599	Old Glory Reefers, set of 3, 89 u, 91	37	47	___
19600	Milwaukee Road 1-D Tank Car (FF 2), 87	30	45	___
19601	North American 1-D Tank Car (FF 4), 89	21	32	___
19602	Johnson 1-D Tank Car (FF 5), 91	24	30	___
19603	GATX 1-D Tank Car (FF 6), 92	32	41	___
19604	Goodyear 1-D Tank Car (SSS), 93	33	36	___
19605	Hudson's Bay 1-D Tank Car (SSS), 94	25	29	___
19607	Sunoco 1-D Tank Car "6315," 96	10	31	___
19608	Sunoco Aviation Services 1-D Tank Car "6315" (SSS), 97		38	___
19611	Gulf Oil 1-D Tank Car "6315," 98		33	___
19612	Gulf Oil 3-D Tank Car "6425," 98		30	___
19614	BASF 1-D Tank Car "UTLX 78252," 99-00		25	___
19615	Vulcan Chemicals 1-D Tank Car, 99-00		25	___
19621	Centennial 1-D Tank Car "6015-1," 99		55	___
19622	Centennial 1-D Tank Car "6015-2," 99		62	___
19623	Centennial 1-D Tank Car "6015-3," 99		62	___
19624	Centennial 1-D Tank Car "6015-4," 99		58	___
19625	Ethyl Tank Car "6236," 01		31	___
19626	Diamond Chemical Tank Car "19419," 01		29	___
19627	Shell 1-D Tank Car "1227," 01		37	___
19628	Lion Oil 1-D Tank Car "2256," 01		35	___
19634	General American 1-D Tank Car, 01		30	___
19635	U.S. Army 1-D Tank Car "10936," 01		31	___
19636	Hooker Chemicals 1-D Tank Car "6180," 01		36	___
19637	GATX TankTrain Intermediate Car "44589" (std O), 02		55	___
19638	CN TankTrain Intermediate Car "75571" (std O), 02		65	___
19639	GATX TankTrain Intermediate Car 3-pack (std O), 02		140	___
19644	Union Texas 1-D Tank Car "9922," 02		33	___
19645	Penn Salt 1-D Tank Car "4730," 02		33	___
19646	CN TankTrain Intermediate Car "75571" (std O), 03		45	___
19647	GATX TankTrain Intermediate Car "44589" (std O), 03		45	___
19649	Scrooge McDuck Mint Car, 05	90	207	___
19651	Santa Fe Tool Car, 87	30	35	___
19652	Jersey Central Bunk Car, 88	25	33	___
19653	Jersey Central Tool Car, 88	26	28	___
19654	Amtrak Bunk Car, 89	22	25	___
19655	Amtrak Tool Car, 90-91	23	30	___
19656	Milwaukee Road Bunk Car, smoke, 90	38	44	___
19657	Wabash Bunk Car, smoke, 91-92	36	42	___
19658	Norfolk & Western Tool Car, 91	24	29	___
19660	Mint Car, 98		40	___
19663	Pratt's Hollow Bunk Car "5717," 99		40	___
19664	Ambassador Award Bunk Car, bronze, 99 u	213	463	___
19665	Ambassador Engineer Bunk Car, silver, 99 u	NRS	630	___
19666	Ambassador Cowen Bunk Car, gold, 99 u		443	___
19667	Wellspring Gold Bullion Car, 99		58	___
19669	King Tut Museum Car "9660," 99		70	___
19670	NY Federal Reserve Bullion Car "6445," 00		44	___
19671	Lionel Model Shop Display Car "6445-01," 99-00		50	___
19672	Lionel Mines Mint Car, 00 u		250	___

		MODERN 1970-2025	Exc	Like New
___	**19673**	Wellspring Capital Management Mint Car, 99 u		220
___	**19674**	Lionel Lines Platinum Car, 00		43
___	**19675**	Lionel Model Shop Display "6445-2," 01		42
___	**19676**	Philadelphia Mint Car, 01		40
___	**19677**	Fort Knox Mint Car "6445," 00	15	50
___	**19678**	U.S. Army Bunk Car, 02		45
___	**19679**	St. Louis Federal Reserve Mint Car, 02		38
___	**19681**	Area 51 Alien Suspension Car, 02		47
___	**19682**	Alaska Klondike Mining Mint Car, 02		40
___	**19683**	Pony Express Mint Car, 02	13	50
___	**19686**	Chicago Federal Reserve Mint Car "6445," 03-04		45
___	**19687**	UP Bunk Car "3887," smoke, 03		40
___	**19688**	Postwar "6445" Fort Knox Mint Car, 02-03		39
___	**19689**	CIBRO TankTrain Intermediate Car 3-pack (std 0), 03		100
___	**19694**	Pony Express Mint Car, 03		50
___	**19696**	U.S. Savings Bond Mint Car, 00		150
___	**19697**	U.S. Bureau of Engraving and Printing Mint Car "19697," 04		40
___	**19698**	San Francisco Federal Reserve Mint Car, 04		40
___	**19700**	Chessie System Extended Vision Caboose, 88	43	50
___	**19701**	Milwaukee Road N5c Caboose (FF 2), 88	50	65
___	**19702**	PRR N5c Caboose, 87	44	55
___	**19703**	GN Extended Vision Caboose (FF 3), 88	41	51
___	**19704**	WM Extended Vision Caboose, smoke (FF 4), 89	42	49
___	**19705**	CP Rail Extended Vision Caboose, smoke, 89	44	64
___	**19706**	UP Extended Vision Caboose "9706," smoke, 89	40	56
___	**19707**	SP Work Caboose with searchlight, smoke, 90	55	60
___	**19708**	Lionel Lines Bay Window Caboose, 90	43	46
___	**19709**	PRR Work Caboose, smoke, 89, 91	49	70
___	**19710**	Frisco Extended Vision Caboose, smoke (FF 5), 91	43	47
___	**19711**	NS Extended Vision Caboose, smoke, 92	47	65
___	**19712**	PRR N5c Caboose, 91	44	47
___	**19714**	NYC Work Caboose with searchlight, smoke, 92	70	110
___	**19715**	DM&IR Extended Vision Caboose "C-217," 92 u	50	60
___	**19716**	IC Extended Vision Caboose "9405," smoke, 93	105	135
___	**19717**	Susquehanna Bay Window Caboose "0121," 93	44	55
___	**19718**	C&IM Extended Vision Caboose "74," 92 u	38	45
___	**19719**	Erie Bay Window Caboose "C-300" (FF 7), 93	47	55
___	**19720**	Soo Line Extended Vision Caboose (SSS), 93	32	41
___	**19721**	GM&O Extended Vision Caboose "2956," 93 u	47	50
___	**19723**	Disney Extended Vision Caboose, 94	36	45
___	**19724**	JCPenney MKT Extended Vision Caboose "125," 94 u	38	43
___	**19726**	NYC Bay Window Caboose (SSS), 95	50	60
___	**19727**	Pennsylvania N5c Caboose "477938," 96	18	42
___	**19728**	N&W Bay Window Caboose, 96	21	75
___	**19732**	ATSF Bay Window Caboose "6517," 96		43
___	**19733**	New York Central Caboose "6357," 96		30
___	**19734**	Southern Pacific Caboose "6357", 96		26
___	**19736**	PRR N5c Caboose "6417", 97		27
___	**19737**	Lackawanna Searchlight Caboose "2420", 97		75
___	**19738**	Conrail N5c Caboose "6417" (SSS), 97		55
___	**19739**	NYC Wood-sided Caboose "6907," 97	20	60
___	**19740**	Virginian N5c Caboose "6427," 97 u		65
___	**19741**	Pennsylvania N5c Caboose "6417," 98		50

MODERN 1970-2025		Exc	Like New	
19742	Erie Bay Window Caboose "C301," Caboose Talk, 98		95	___
19748	SP&S Bay Window Caboose "6517," 97 u		50	___
19749	SP Bay Window Caboose "6517," 98		100	___
19750	Holiday Music Bay Window Caboose, 98		160	___
19751	PRR N5c Caboose "492418," 98		30	___
19752	NP Bay Window Caboose "407," 98		50	___
19753	UP Extended Vision Caboose "25641," 98		55	___
19754	NYC Caboose "20112," 98		55	___
19755	Centennial Porthole Caboose, 99		68	___
19756	Lionel Lines Bay Window Caboose, 99		50	___
19758	DL&W Work Caboose "6419," 99		55	___
19759	Corvette N5c Caboose, 99		60	___
19772	Lionel Visitor's Center Vat Car, 99 u		40	___
19773	Lionel Kids Club Barrel Ramp Car "6343," 96 u		48	___
19778	Case Cutlery Wood-sided Caboose "1889" (std O), 99 u		30	___
19779	SP Bay Window Caboose "1908," 99		65	___
19780	LV Porthole Caboose "641751," 99-00		43	___
19781	Vapor Records Holiday Porthole Caboose "6417," 99-00	12	63	___
19782	NYC Bay Window Caboose "21719," 00		65	___
19783	Ford Mustang Extended Vision Caboose, 01		50	___
19785	SP Bay Window Caboose "6517," 00		55	___
19786	PRR Extended Vision Caboose, 00 u		40	___
19787	PRR Porthole Caboose "477927," 01		40	___
19790	Postwar "6417" Lehigh Valley Caboose, 02		41	___
19792	Postwar "C301" Erie Bay Window Caboose, 03		45	___
19796	C&O Bay Window Caboose, 03		50	___
19800	Circle L Ranch Operating Cattle Car, 88	75	95	___
19801	Poultry Dispatch Chicken Car, 87	20	27	___
19802	Carnation Milk Car, 87	87	102	___
19803	Reading Ice Car, 87	38	44	___
19804	Wabash Operating Hopper, 87	25	34	___
19805	Santa Fe Operating Boxcar, 87	28	36	___
19806	PRR Operating Hopper, 88	28	38	___
19807	PRR Extended Vision Caboose, smoke, 88	39	53	___
19808	NYC Ice Car, 88	38	49	___
19809	Erie-Lackawanna Operating Boxcar, 88	27	35	___
19810	Bosco Milk Car, 88	80	89	___
19811	Monon Brakeman Car, 90	43	55	___
19813	Northern Pacific Ice Car, 89 u	41	46	___
19815	Delaware & Hudson Brakeman Car, 92	49	60	___
19816	Madison Hardware Operating Boxcar "190991," 91 u	90	105	___
19817	Virginian Ice Car, 94	31	35	___
19818	Dairymen's League Milk Car "788," 94	65	80	___
19819	Poultry Dispatch Car (SSS), 94	36	43	___
19820	Die-cast Tender, RailSounds II, 95-96		175	___
19821	UP Operating Boxcar, 95	27	36	___
19822	Pork Dispatch Car, 95	29	44	___
19823	Burlington Ice Car, 94 u, 95	39	49	___
19824	U.S. Army Target Launcher, 96		32	___
19825	Generator Car, 96		53	___
19827	NYC Operating Boxcar, 97		37	___
19828	C&NW Animated Stock Car "3356" and Stockyard, 96-97	50	125	___
19830	U.S. Mail Operating Boxcar "3428," 97		39	___

MODERN 1970-2025		Exc	Like New
____ 19831	GM Generator Car "3530," power pole and wire, 97		50
____ 19832	Cola Ice Car "6352," 97		47
____ 19833	Tender "2426RS," RailSounds II, 97	65	240
____ 19834	LL 6-wheel Crane Car "2460," 97		61
____ 19835	FedEx Animated Boxcar "3464X," 97		40
____ 19837	Bucyrus 6-wheel Crane Car "2460," 99		54
____ 19845	Aquarium Car "3435," CC, 98		151
____ 19846	Animated Giraffe Car "3376C," 98		105
____ 19850	Stock Car "33760," RailSounds, 00		130
____ 19853	Firefighting Instruction Generator Car (SSS), 98		60
____ 19854	Lionelville Fire Car (SSS), 98		55
____ 19855	Christmas Aquarium Car, 98	15	60
____ 19856	Mermaid Transport, 98		65
____ 19857	NYC Firefighting Instruction Car "19853," 98-99		175
____ 19858	Lionelville Operating Searchlight Car "19854," 99		65
____ 19859	REA Boxcar "6267," steam RailSounds, 99		170
____ 19860	Conrail Boxcar "169671," diesel RailSounds, 99		140
____ 19864	Animated Ostrich Boxcar, 99		37
____ 19867	Operating Poultry Dispatch Car "3434," 99		48
____ 19868	Shark Aquarium Car "3435," 99		190
____ 19869	Alien Aquarium Car "3435," 99		49
____ 19877	ATSF Operating Barrel Car, 99		55
____ 19878	Operating Helium Tank Flatcar "3362," 99		40
____ 19880	Lionel Lines Extension Searchlight Car, 00		50
____ 19882	Sanderson Farms Poultry Car "3434," 99		41
____ 19883	LL Bucyrus Erie Crane Car "64608," 99		45
____ 19884	Atlantis Travel Aquarium Car, 00 u		95
____ 19885	N&W Operating Hopper Car, 00		31
____ 19886	Seaboard Boxcar "16126," steam RailSounds, 00		140
____ 19887	SP Boxcar "651663," diesel RailSounds, 00		140
____ 19888	Christmas Music Boxcar, 01		65
____ 19889	PRR Bay Window Caboose "477719," Crewtalk, 00		140
____ 19890	Santa Fe Bay Window Caboose "999211," Crewtalk, 00		100
____ 19894	Hood's Operating Milk Car with platform, 03-04		95
____ 19895	3356 Santa Fe Horse Car with corral, 04		120
____ 19896	USMC Missile Launch Sound Car "45," 03-04		165
____ 19897	NYC Crane Car, TMCC, 04	159	263
____ 19898	Nestle Nesquik Operating Milk Car with platform, 04-05		95
____ 19899	Pennsylvania Crane Car "19899" CC, 03-05	63	260
____ 19900	Toy Fair Boxcar, 87 u	65	80
____ 19901	"I Love Virginia" Boxcar, 87	25	35
____ 19902	Toy Fair Boxcar, 88 u	55	80
____ 19903	Christmas Boxcar, 87 u	22	34
____ 19904	Christmas Boxcar, 88 u	32	43
____ 19905	"I Love California" Boxcar, 88	20	24
____ 19906	"I Love Pennsylvania" Boxcar, 89	26	32
____ 19907	Toy Fair Boxcar, 89 u	38	55
____ 19908	Christmas Boxcar, 89 u	30	39
____ 19909	"I Love New Jersey" Boxcar, 90	19	25
____ 19910	Christmas Boxcar, 90 u	35	38
____ 19911	Toy Fair Boxcar, 90 u	75	95
____ 19912	"I Love Ohio" Boxcar, 91	21	28
____ 19913	Christmas Boxcar, 91	34	52

MODERN 1970-2025		Exc	Like New	
19913	Lionel Employee Christmas Boxcar, 91 u	150	200	___
19914	Toy Fair Boxcar, 91 u	38	50	___
19915	"I Love Texas" Boxcar, 92	35	60	___
19916	Lionel Employee Christmas Boxcar, 92 u	190	220	___
19917	Toy Fair Boxcar, 92 u	45	53	___
19918	Christmas Boxcar, 92 u	49	70	___
19919	"I Love Minnesota" Boxcar, 93	40	60	___
19920	Lionel Visitor's Center Boxcar, 92 u	16	28	___
19921	Lionel Employee Christmas Boxcar, 93 u	93	185	___
19922	Christmas Boxcar, 93	33	41	___
19923	Toy Fair Boxcar, 93 u	65	95	___
19925	Lionel Employee Learning Center Boxcar, 93 u	55	63	___
19926	"I Love Nevada" Boxcar, 94	21	26	___
19927	Lionel Visitor's Center Boxcar, 93 u	26	33	___
19928	Lionel Employee Christmas Boxcar, 94 u	205	230	___
19929	Christmas Boxcar, 94	30	40	___
19931	Toy Fair Boxcar, 94 u	49	65	___
19932	Lionel Visitor's Center Boxcar, 94 u	26	33	___
19933	"I Love Illinois" Boxcar, 95	21	27	___
19934	Lionel Visitor's Center Boxcar, 95 u	18	22	___
19937	Toy Fair Boxcar, 95 u	55	75	___
19938	Christmas Boxcar, 95	19	34	___
19939	Lionel Employee Christmas Boxcar, 95 u	100	128	___
19941	"I Love Colorado" Boxcar, 95	23	30	___
19942	"I Love Florida" Boxcar, 96	19	27	___
19943	"I Love Arizona" Boxcar, 96	20	25	___
19944	Lionel Visitor's Center Tank Car, 96 u		35	___
19945	Holiday Boxcar, 96		29	___
19946	Lionel Employee Christmas Boxcar, 96 u		195	___
19947	Lionel Toy Fair Boxcar, 96 u		200	___
19948	Visitor's Center Flatcar with trailer, 96 u		34	___
19949	"I Love NY" Boxcar, 97		50	___
19950	"I Love Montana" Boxcar, 97		30	___
19951	"I Love Massachusetts" Boxcar, 98		26	___
19952	"I Love Indiana" Boxcar, 98		31	___
19955	Lionel Visitor's Center Gondola with coil covers, 98 u		20	___
19956	Toy Fair Boxcar "777," 98 u		65	___
19957	Ambassador Caboose, 97 u		512	___
19958	Ambassador Caboose, silver (std 0), 98 u		558	___
19959	Ambassador Caboose, gold (std 0), 98 u	518	778	___
19964	U.S. JCI Senate Boxcar, 92 u	55	63	___
19968	"I Love Maine" Boxcar, 99		40	___
19969	"I Love Vermont" Boxcar, 99		40	___
19970	"I Love New Hampshire" Boxcar, 99		34	___
19971	"I Love Rhode Island" Boxcar, 99		34	___
19976	Lionel Employee Holiday Boxcar, 99 u	23	150	___
19977	Toy Fair Boxcar, 99 u		50	___
19981	Lionel Centennial Boxcar, 99		36	___
19982	Lionel Centennial Boxcar, 99		36	___
19983	Lionel Centennial Boxcar, 99		36	___
19984	Lionel Centennial Boxcar, 99		36	___
19985	"I Love Georgia" Boxcar, 99-00		45	___
19986	"I Love North Carolina" Boxcar, 99-00		40	___

	MODERN 1970-2025		Exc	Like New
___	**19987**	"I Love South Carolina" Boxcar, 99-00		40
___	**19988**	"I Love Tennessee" Boxcar, 99-00		55
___	**19989**	Toy Fair Boxcar, 00 u		55
___	**19996**	Toy Fair Boxcar, 01 u		50
___	**19997**	Lionel Employee Boxcar, 01 u		125
___	**19998**	Christmas Boxcar, 01		33
___	**19999**	Lionel Visitor's Center 4-bay Hopper, 02 u		153
___	**20000**	PRR Senator Coach 4-pack (std 0), 13, 15		640
___	**20005**	SP Sunset Limited Coach 4-pack (std 0), 13, 15		640
___	**20010**	UP City of Los Angeles Coach 4-pack (std 0), 13, 15		640
___	**20015**	B&O Capitol Limited Coach 4-pack (std 0), 13		640
___	**20020**	FEC City of Miami Coach 4-pack (std 0), 13		640
___	**20025**	KCS Southern Belle Coach 4-pack (std 0), 13		640
___	**20030**	MILW Olympian Coach 4-pack (std 0), 13, 15		640
___	**21029**	World of Little Choo Choo Set, 94u, 95	36	43
___	**21141**	North Dakota State Quarter Gondola Bank, 07		60
___	**21142**	South Dakota State Quarter Hopper Bank, 07		60
___	**21163**	SuperStreets FasTrack Grade Crossing, 08-10		20
___	**21164**	SuperStreets 10" Transition to FasTrack, 08-10		9
___	**21165**	SuperStreets Transition to FasTrack, 2 pieces, 08-10		17
___	**21168**	City Traction Trolley Add-on, 08		75
___	**21169**	City Traction Speeder Add-on, 08		75
___	**21170**	NYC 15" Heavyweight Passenger Car 4-pack, 07		250
___	**21175**	NYC 15" Heavyweight Passenger Car 2-pack, 07		125
___	**21198**	ATSF Alco Diesel AA Set, horn, 08		200
___	**21199**	ATSF Midnight Chief Streamliner Car 4-pack, 08		200
___	**21204**	ATSF Midnight Chief Streamliner Car 2-pack, 08		100
___	**21207**	SP Diesel Work Train, 07		175
___	**21212**	NH Diesel Freight Set, 07		250
___	**21217**	Southern Diesel Executive Inspection Train, 07		175
___	**21229**	Ringling Bros. S2 Diesel Switcher, horn, 07		80
___	**21230**	Ringling Bros. Porter Locomotive, 07		105
___	**21231**	Ringling Bros. Streamliner Car 4-pack, 07		210
___	**21234**	Ringling Bros. Streamliner Car 2-pack, 07		105
___	**21237**	Ringling Bros. Flatcar with 3 wagons, 07		50
___	**21238**	Ringling Bros. Flatcar with 3 wagons, 07		50
___	**21239**	Ringling Bros. Flatcar with crates, 07		45
___	**21240**	Ringling Bros. Flatcar with front end loader and poles, 07		45
___	**21252**	Boy Flying Kite, 08		60
___	**21253**	Operating Bunk Car Yard Office, 07		80
___	**21261**	SuperStreets 2.5" Straight-to-Curve Connector, 4 pieces, 08-10		9
___	**21265**	Operating Voltmeter Car, 07		75
___	**21266**	SuperStreets Intersection, 4 pieces, 08-10		40
___	**21267**	PRR Boxcab Electric Locomotive, horn, 07		77
___	**21271**	WP Operating Coal Dump Car with vehicle, 07		33
___	**21276**	Congressional Diner, smoke, 07		110
___	**21277**	Operating Flagman's Shanty, 08		70
___	**21279**	Roach Wranglers Pest Control Van, 08		30
___	**21281**	SuperStreets D21 Curve, 08-10		3
___	**21282**	SuperStreets 2.5" Curve-to-Curve Connector, 4 pieces, 08-10		9
___	**21283**	SuperStreets Tubular Track Grade Crossing, 08-10		18
___	**21284**	SuperStreets 10" Tubular Transition, 08-10		8

MODERN 1970-2025		Exc	Like New	
21285	SuperStreets 10" Tubular Transition, 2 pieces, 08-10		14	___
21286	SuperStreets Intersection, 08-10		10	___
21287	SuperStreets Y Roadway, 08-10		12	___
21288	SuperStreets O Gauge Conversion Pins, 08-10		2	___
21289	SuperStreets Connector Pins, 08-10		2	___
21290	SuperStreets Hookup Wires, 2 pieces, 08-10		3	___
21291	Dogbone Expander pack, 08-10		25	___
21296	City Traction Classic Truck, 07		30	___
21298	NYC 4-6-4 Hudson Locomotive "5279," CC, 07		500	___
21316	PE RS3 Diesel "2815," CC, 07		350	___
21324	Acrobats and Clowns Figures, 10 pieces, 08-10		12	___
21325	Ringmaster Circus Figures, 5, with accessories, 08-10		12	___
21326	PRR 15" Interurban Car 2-pack, 07		200	___
21354	Fresh Never Frozen Fish Transport Car, 07		80	___
21355	Dump Bin, 08-10		20	___
21358	Special Addition Boxcar, Girl, 08-10		25	___
21359	Special Addition Boxcar, Boy, 08-10		25	___
21368	Passenger Coach Figures, 9 pieces, 08-10		11	___
21369	Walking Figures, 8 pieces, 08-10		11	___
21370	Sitting Figures, 6, with benches, 08-10		11	___
21371	Standing Figures, 8 pieces, 08-10		11	___
21372	Railroad Station Figures, 6, with accessories, 08-10		11	___
21373	School Figures, 7, with accessories, 08-10		11	___
21374	Service Station Figures, 5, with accessories, 08-10		11	___
21375	Police Figures, 10, with dog, 08		20	___
21376	Seated Passenger Figures, 40 pieces, 08		27	___
21377	Mounted Police, 3, with horses, 08-10		11	___
21378	Factory, 08-10		18	___
21379	Police Station, 08-10		16	___
21380	Colonial House, 08-10		16	___
21381	Suburban Station, 08-10		16	___
21382	School, 08-10		17	___
21383	Suburban Ranch House, 08-10		15	___
21384	Service Station with gas pumps, 08-10		17	___
21385	Barn and Chicken Coop, 08-10		20	___
21386	Firehouse, 08-10		17	___
21387	Church, 08-10		15	___
21388	Country L-shaped Ranch House, 08-10		16	___
21389	Supermarket, 08-10		12	___
21390	Diner, 08-10		15	___
21394	Rotating Beacon, 08-09		31	___
21396	Single Tunnel Portals, pair, 08-10		15	___
21397	SuperSnap 31" Remote Switch, left hand, 08-09		55	___
21398	SuperSnap 31" Remote Switch, right hand, 08-09		55	___
21399	SuperSnap 72" Remote Switch, left hand, 08-09		70	___
21400	SuperSnap 72" Remote Switch, right hand, 08-09		70	___
21412	NYC Plymouth Switcher Freight Set, 07		155	___
21430	SuperStreets D16 Curve, 08-10		2	___
21431	SuperStreets 10" Straight Track, 08-10		2	___
21432	SuperStreets D16 Curved Track, 8 pieces, 08-10		18	___
21433	SuperStreets 5" Straight Track, 4 pieces, 08-10		14	___
21434	SuperStreets 10" Straight Track, 8 pieces, 08-10		19	___
21435	World War II Seated Soldiers, 9, with benches, 08-09		20	___

MODERN 1970-2025		Exc	Like New
____ **21436**	Rings and Things Circus Accessories, 08-09		10
____ **21438**	Remote Controller, 07-10		35
____ **21442**	City Figures, 7, with scooter, 08-10		11
____ **21443**	Factory Figures, 6, with accessories, 08-10		11
____ **21444**	Church Figures, 5, with accessories, 08-10		11
____ **21445**	Firefighting Figures, 11, with accessories, 08-10		20
____ **21449**	Operating Loading Platform with flatcar, 07-08		80
____ **21450**	Unloading Station with dump bins, 07		100
____ **21451**	Girder Bridge with stone piers, 07		40
____ **21452**	Graduated Trestle Set, 26 pieces, 07		50
____ **21453**	Elevated Trestle Set, 10 pieces, 07		40
____ **21454**	Double Tunnel Portals, 2 pieces, 08-10		20
____ **21456**	UPS Step Van, 07		30
____ **21466**	Ringling Bros. 15" Aluminum Advertising Car, 07		110
____ **21469**	Ringling Bros. Flatcar, white, with container, 07		45
____ **21470**	Ringling Bros. Flatcar, blue, with container, 07		45
____ **21471**	Ringling Bros. Flatcar with 2 trailers, 08-10		60
____ **21472**	Ringling Bros. Flatcar with 2 trailers, 08-10		60
____ **21476**	Strasburg Plymouth Diesel Switcher, 07		100
____ **21494**	WM RS3 Diesel "189," CC, 07		350
____ **21529**	Montana State Quarter Boxcar Bank, 08		45
____ **21542**	Washington State Quarter Tank Car Bank, 08		45
____ **21543**	Boyd Bros. Ford Classic Truck, 08		33
____ **21549**	Ringling Bros. Crew Bus, 08		33
____ **21552**	S.W.A.T. Team Step Van, 08		30
____ **21560**	Reading Flatcar with rail load, 07		25
____ **21567**	School Bus SuperStreets Set, 08		110
____ **21568**	Dirty Dogz Van SuperStreets Set, 08		100
____ **21569**	Angelo's Pizza Delivery Van, 08		30
____ **21570**	Flying Colors Painting Van, 08		30
____ **21571**	SuperStreets 10" Insulated Roadway, 2 pieces, 08-10		8
____ **21572**	SuperStreets 5" Straight School, 2 pieces, 08-10		8
____ **21573**	SuperStreets 5" Straight Stop Ahead, 2 pieces, 08-10		8
____ **21574**	SuperStreets 5" Straight Crosswalk, 2 pieces, 08-10		8
____ **21575**	SuperStreets 10" Crossing, 2 pieces, 08-10		10
____ **21576**	SuperStreets Skid Mark Roadway Pack, 08-10		13
____ **21577**	Snack-On Step Van, 08		30
____ **21582**	Keystone Coal Porter Locomotive, 08		100
____ **21583**	Keystone Coal Freight Car 4-pack, 08		100
____ **21590**	ATSF "Midnight Chief" 2-bay Hopper "162277," 08		25
____ **21591**	ATSF "Midnight Chief" Flatcar "94468" with trailer, 08		43
____ **21592**	ATSF "Midnight Chief" Caboose, 08		25
____ **21593**	ATSF "Midnight Chief" Boxcar "621593," 08		35
____ **21594**	NYC Empire State Express 15" Aluminum Car 4-pack, 08-09		420
____ **21599**	SP flatcar with wheel load, 07		35
____ **21600**	B&M RS3 Diesel "1538," CC, 08-09	113	350
____ **21607**	Jack Frost Hopper "327" with sugar load, 08		25
____ **21609**	Elephants and Giraffes, 2 pair, 08-10		13
____ **21610**	Lions and Tigers, 2 pair, 08-10		13
____ **21611**	Horses, 4 pieces, 08		13
____ **21621**	ATSF Operating Boxcar "22658," 08-09		90
____ **21623**	Rutland Operating Milk Car with platform, 08-10		150
____ **21626**	Rath Wood-sided Reefer "622," 09		45

MODERN 1970-2025		Exc	Like New	
21627	Greenlee Packing Wood-sided Reefer “3862,” 10		45	___
21628	CNJ Reefer “1438,” 08-09		35	___
21629	C&O Reefer “7783,” 08-09		35	___
21630	UP Stock Car “42005,” 09		45	___
21631	Reading Boxcar “107984,” 08-09		35	___
21632	GN Boxcar “34285,” 08-09		35	___
21633	RI “Route of the Rockets” Boxcar “21110,” 09-10		40	___
21634	Tidewater Flying A 1-D Tank Car “1367,” 09		40	___
21635	Southern Depressed Center Flatcar, 2 transformers, 09		43	___
21636	NS Flatcar with bulkheads and stakes, 08-09		35	___
21637	Ontario Northland Ribbed Hopper with coal, 09		40	___
21639	Pan Am Boxcar “32126,” 08-09		55	___
21640	UP Modern Steel-sided Reefer “499030,” 08-09		55	___
21641	Ringling Bros. Merchandise Flatcar, 08		50	___
21643	PRR Die-cast Gondola with covers, 09		73	___
21644	PRR 16-wheel Flatcar with transformer, 08-09		80	___
21646	DT&I Work Crane and Boom Car, 09		85	___
21649	City Traction Trolley with Ringling Bros. banner, 08-09		80	___
21651	Moo-Town Creamery Step Van, 08-09		38	___
21656	Quikrete Step Van, 08-09		42	___
21658	Ringling Bros. Vintage Truck, 08-09		42	___
21659	DT&I Flatcar “90059” with Ford trailer, 08-09		60	___
21662	Moo-Town Creamery Vending Machine, 08-09		13	___
21663	Moo-Town Creamery Bunk Car Ice Cream Shop, 08-09		115	___
21664	RI Operating Coal Dump Car with vehicle, 08-09		40	___
21665	Alaska Operating Log Dump Car with vehicle, 09		40	___
21667	Red River Lumber Boxcab Diesel with horn, 08-09		100	___
21668	CP Operating Hopper “9628,” 08-09		45	___
21675	Mountain View Creamery Loading Depot, 08-10		130	___
21676	Beaver Creek Logging Die-cast Porter Locomotive, 08-09		120	___
21677	Ford Factory, 09		22	___
21679	Assured Comfort HVAC Van, 08-09		38	___
21680	Division of Prisons Bus SuperStreets Set, 08-09		150	___
21688	Ringling Bros. Heavyweight Coach 2-pack, 08-11		240	___
21691	Ringling Bros. Flatcar with 2 trailers, 08-10		60	___
21692	C&NW MP15 Diesel with Ringling Bros. banner, 08-09		140	___
21693	Southern MP15 Diesel Pair, powered and dummy, 10		200	___
21696	Ford Flatcar with 2 trucks, 08-09		53	___
21698	Lionel Van SuperStreets Set, 08-10		130	___
21701	Star Spangled GG1 Electric Locomotive “4837,” 08-10		260	___
21702	Milwaukee Road Girder Bridge, 08-09	8	20	___
21703	ATSF Black Mesa Aluminum Business Car, 09-10		160	___
21704	C&O Double Searchlight Car with vehicle, 08-09		50	___
21706	Chatham Police Van, 08-09		38	___
21707	NYC Aluminum Business Car, 09		160	___
21708	CN Operating Log Dump Car, 10		120	___
21709	PRR Girder Bridge, 08-09		15	___
21715	Ringling Bros. Stock Car, 08-09		60	___
21717	Pullman-Standard 1-D Tank Car, 08-09		35	___
21719	NYC Bay Window Caboose, 99		70	___
21720	Ringling Bros. Billboard Set #2, 08-09		10	___
21721	Warning Sign Pack, 12 pieces, 08-10		25	___
21730	Regulatory Sign Pack, 12 pieces, 08-10		25	___

MODERN 1970-2025			Exc	Like New
___	**21738**	Railroad Crossing Sign Pack, 6 pieces, 08-10		21
___	**21750**	NKP Rolling Stock 4-pack, 98		160
___	**21751**	PRR Rolling Stock 4-pack, 98		145
___	**21752**	Conrail Unit Trailer Train, 98		285
___	**21753**	Service Station Fire Rescue Train, 98	365	590
___	**21754**	BNSF 3-bay Covered Hopper 2-pack (std 0), 98	30	73
___	**21755**	4-bay Covered Hoppers 2-pack, 98		65
___	**21756**	Conrail Overstamped Boxcars 2-pack, 98		65
___	**21757**	UP Freight Car Set, 98	117	188
___	**21758**	Bethlehem Steel "44" (SSS), 99	169	375
___	**21759**	Canadian Pacific F3 Diesel Passenger Set, 99	394	985
___	**21761**	B&M Boxcar Set, 4-pack, 99		180
___	**21763**	New Haven Freight Set, 99		265
___	**21766**	ACL Passenger Car 2-pack, 99		385
___	**21769**	Centennial 1-D Tank Car Set, 4-pack, 99	NRS	260
___	**21770**	NYC Reefer Set, 4-pack, 99	88	225
___	**21771**	D&RGW Stock Car Set, 4-pack, 99		230
___	**21774**	Custom Series Consist I, 3-pack, 99		150
___	**21775**	Train Wreck Recovery Set, 99	95	220
___	**21778**	ATSF Train Master Diesel Freight Set, 99		950
___	**21779**	Seaboard Freight Car Set, 99	143	280
___	**21780**	NYC Aluminum Passenger Car 2-pack, 99		160
___	**21781**	Case Cutlery Freight Set, 99 u	725	1038
___	**21782**	PRR Congressional Set, 00	282	930
___	**21783**	Monday Night Football 2-pack, 01-02		50
___	**21784**	QVC PRR Coal Freight Steam Set, 00 u		360
___	**21785**	QVC Gold Mine Freight Steam Set, 00 u		300
___	**21786**	Santa Fe F3 Diesel ABBA Passenger Set, 00	659	1693
___	**21787**	Blue Comet Steam Passenger Set, 01-02		1525
___	**21788**	Postwar Missile Launch Freight Set, 02-03	203	350
___	**21789**	Norfolk Southern Piggyback Set, CC (SSS), 01		370
___	**21790**	CN TankTrain Dash 9 Diesel Freight Set, 02	200	630
___	**21791**	Freedom Train Diesel Passenger Set, RailSounds, 03	313	645
___	**21792**	C&O Coal Hopper 6-pack #2 (std 0), 01		145
___	**21793**	Virginian Coal Hopper 6-pack #2 (std 0), 01		160
___	**21794**	Pioneer Seed GP7 Diesel Freight Set, 01 u	630	925
___	**21795**	Case Farmall Freight Set, 01 u	540	750
___	**21796**	NJ Medical Steam Freight Set, 01 u		487
___	**21797**	SP Daylight Passenger Set, 01		670
___	**21852**	MILW PS-2CD Hopper 3-pack (std 0), 06		155
___	**21853**	BNSF PS-2CD Hopper 3-pack (std 0), 06		155
___	**21854**	N&W PS-2CD Hopper 3-pack (std 0), 06		155
___	**21855**	A&P Milk Car 3-pack, 06		150
___	**21856**	Bowman Dairy Milk Car 3-pack (std 0), 06		150
___	**21857**	Western Dairy Milk Car 3-pack (std 0), 06		150
___	**21858**	NP PS-4 Flatcar with trailers, 2-pack (std 0), 06		170
___	**21859**	C&NW PS-4 Flatcar with trailers, 2-pack (std 0), 06		170
___	**21860**	UP PS-4 Flatcar with trailers, 2-pack (std 0), 06		170
___	**21861**	PRR PS-4 Flatcar with trailers (std 0), 06		170
___	**21863**	ADM Unibody Tank Car 3-pack (std 0), 06		135
___	**21864**	Cerestar Unibody Tank Car 3-pack (std 0), 06		135
___	**21865**	Coe Rail Husky Stack Car 2-pack (std 0), 06		170
___	**21866**	Santa Fe Husky Stack Car 2-pack (std 0), 06		170

		Exc	Like New	
21872	C&O Offset Hopper 3-pack (std O), 05		130	___
21873	P&LE Offset Hopper 3-pack (std O), 06		145	___
21874	TTX Trailer Train 2-pack (std O), 06		170	___
21875	CSX Husky Stack Car 2-pack (std O), 06		170	___
21876	Disney Villain Hi-Cube Boxcar 3-pack, 05-06		135	___
21877	Domino Sugar 1-D Tank Car 3-pack (std O), 07		135	___
21878	Procor 1-D Tank Car 3-pack (std O), 07		135	___
21879	C&EI Offset Hopper 3-pack (std O), 07		145	___
21880	Erie Offset Hopper 3-pack (std O), 07		145	___
21881	Frisco Offset Hopper 3-pack (std O), 07-08		200	___
21882	Chessie System Offset Hopper 3-pack (std O), 07		145	___
21883	C&O 3-bay Hopper 2-pack (std O), 07-08		140	___
21884	Pennsylvania Power & Light 3-bay Hopper 2-pack (std O), 07		140	___
21885	Santa Fe 3-bay Hopper 2-pack (std O), 07		140	___
21886	C&NW 3-bay Hopper 2-pack (std O), 07-08		140	___
21888	IMC Canada Cylindrical Hopper 2-pack, 06		130	___
21893	Greenbrier Husky Stack Car 2-pack (std O), 07		170	___
21894	CSX Husky Stack Car 2-pack (std O), 07		170	___
21895	BN Husky Stack Car 2-pack (std O), 07		170	___
21896	Arizona & California Husky Stack Car 2-pack (std O), 07		170	___
21897	REA PS-4 Flatcar with trailers, 2-pack (std O), 07-08		170	___
21898	NYC PS-4 Flatcar with trailers, 2-pack (std O), 07-08		170	___
21899	Lackawanna PS-4 Flatcar with trailers, 2-pack (std O), 07		170	___
21900	Civil War Union Train Set, 99	138	375	___
21901	Civil War Confederate Train Set, 99	158	375	___
21902	MILW PS-4 Flatcar with trailers, 2-pack (std O), 07-08		170	___
21902	Construction Zone Set, 99 u		87	___
21904	UP PS-2 Covered Hopper 2-pack (std O), 07		120	___
21904	Safari Adventure Set, 99 u		90	___
21905	NYC Flyer Set, 99 u		100	___
21909	AGFA Film Steam Freight Set, 98 u		1464	___
21914	Lionel Lines Freight Set, 99		120	___
21916	Lionel Village Trolley, 99		75	___
21917	N&W Freight Set, 99		70	___
21918	PC PS-2 Covered Hopper 2-pack (std O), 07		120	___
21918	Thomas Circus Play Set, 00		100	___
21921	Imco PS-2 Covered Hopper 2-pack (std O), 07-08		120	___
21924	Holiday Trolley Set, 99		65	___
21925	Thomas the Tank Engine Island of Sodor Train Set, 99-00		150	___
21930	NYC PS-2 Covered Hopper 2-pack (std O), 07		120	___
21932	JCPenney NYC Freight Flyer Steam Set, 00 u		170	___
21934	Custom Series Consist II, 3-pack, 99		140	___
21936	Looney Tunes Train Set, 00 u		413	___
21937	NYC Steel-sided Reefer 2-pack (std O), 07		130	___
21939	Dubuque Steel-sided Reefer 2-pack (std O), 07-08		130	___
21940	ADM Steel-sided Reefer 2-pack (std O), 07		130	___
21941	National Car Steel-sided Reefer 2-pack (std O), 07		130	___
21944	Celebrate a Lionel Christmas Steam Set, 00-01		165	___
21945	Christmas Trolley Set, 00		100	___
21948	NYC Freight Flyer Set, air whistle, 00		240	___
21950	Maersk SD70 Diesel Maxi-Stack Set, 00	523	900	___
21951	World War II Troop Train, 00	225	410	___
21952	Lionel Lines Service Station Special Set, 00	138	294	___

		MODERN 1970-2025	Exc	Like New
___	**21953**	Ford Mustang GP7 Diesel Set, CC, 01		348
___	**21955**	D&RGW F3 Diesel AA Passenger Set, CC, 01	163	740
___	**21956**	New York Central Freight Set, 99-00	152	355
___	**21969**	Lionel Village Trolley Set, 00		85
___	**21970**	SP RS3 Diesel Freight Set, horn, 00-01		110
___	**21971**	Pennsylvania Flyer Steam Set, 00	75	195
___	**21972**	Frisco GP7 Diesel Freight Set, horn, 00		150
___	**21973**	ATSF Passenger Set, RailSounds, 00-01		375
___	**21974**	ATSF Passenger Set, SignalSounds, 00-01	75	240
___	**21975**	Burlington Steam Freight Set, SignalSounds, 00		275
___	**21976**	Centennial Steam Freight Starter Set, 00	292	709
___	**21977**	NYC Train Master Steam Freight Set, 99-00		620
___	**21978**	ATSF Train Master Diesel Freight Set, 99-00		500
___	**21981**	JCPenney NYC Flyer Set, 00 u		150
___	**21988**	NYC Freight Set, RailSounds, 00		325
___	**21989**	Burlington Steam Freight Set, RailSounds, 00		338
___	**21990**	NYC Flyer Freight Set, RailSounds, 00		175
___	**21995**	D&RGW F3 Diesel Passenger Set, CC, 00		405
___	**21999**	Whirlpool Steam Freight Set, 00 u	513	745
___	**22103**	PRR A5 Scale Switcher "411," CC, 08-09		330
___	**22104**	PRR Freight Car 3-pack, 08		135
___	**22105**	NYC Empire State Express 4-6-4 Hudson Locomotive "5429," CC, 08-09		420
___	**22113**	NYC Empire State Express 15" Aluminum Car 2-pack, 08-10		210
___	**22116**	Ringling Bros. Diesel Freight Set, 08-10		245
___	**22121**	Ringling Bros. Freight Set, 08-10		390
___	**22126**	Ringling Bros. Expansion Pack, 08-10		135
___	**22131**	NH Streamliner Car 3-pack, 07		150
___	**22135**	CB&Q S2 Diesel Switcher "9305," horn, 07		80
___	**22136**	Erie S2 Diesel Switcher "522," horn, 07		80
___	**22137**	Alaska MP15 Diesel "1552," horn, 07		100
___	**22138**	Astoria Heat & Power Porter Locomotive "4," 07		100
___	**22139**	LIRR Speeder, 08		50
___	**22140**	CNJ Boxcab Diesel "1000," horn, 08		90
___	**22141**	Lackawanna 15" Interurban Car 2-pack, 07		200
___	**22142**	FEC Operating Dump Car, 07		70
___	**22143**	B&A Operating Log Dump Car, 08-09		70
___	**22144**	Alaska Operating Coal Dump Car with vehicle, 08		33
___	**22145**	WM Operating Log Dump Car with vehicle, 08		33
___	**22146**	PFE Operating Boxcar, 08		80
___	**22147**	B&O Operating Hopper with coal, 08		35
___	**22148**	GN Operating Hopper with coal, 08		35
___	**22149**	Dairymen's League Operating Milk Car, green, w/platform, 08		140
___	**22150**	D&RGW Bunk Car, smoke, 08		65
___	**22151**	Alaska Searchlight Car with vehicle, 08		45
___	**22152**	NKP 2-bay Outside-braced Hopper "31299," 08		50
___	**22153**	L&N 2-bay Offset Hopper "78660," 08		50
___	**22154**	D&H 2-bay Rib Side Hopper "5737," 07		50
___	**22155**	Erie-Lack. 2-bay Aluminum Hopper "21353," 08		60
___	**22156**	ACF Demonstrator 2-bay Aluminum Hopper "44586," 07		60
___	**22157**	GN Aluminum Tank Car "74787," 08		60
___	**22158**	MILW Bulkhead Flatcar "967116" with wood, 08-09		43
___	**22159**	BNSF Flatcar "585011" with trailer, 08		43

MODERN 1970-2025		Exc	Like New
22160	UP Flatcar "58059" with container, 08		43
22161	Conrail Flatcar "705910" with NS container, 08		43
22162	Foppiano Wine 3-D Tank Car "1112," 08		45
22163	PRR Weed Control Car "6321226," 07		45
22166	PRR Reefer "19492," 08		25
22167	Seaboard Reefer "16622," 08		25
22168	N&W Boxcar "645772," 08		25
22169	ATSF Reefer "11744," 07		25
22170	P&LE Reefer "22300," 07		25
22171	B&O DD Boxcar "495289," 08		25
22172	CB&Q Stock Car "52731," 08		25
22174	Erie-Lack Transfer Caboose, 07		25
22176	PRR Caboose "478884," 07		25
22177	L&N Caboose "100," 07		25
22179	NYC Depressed Center Flatcar "66256" with 2 girders, 08		25
22180	IC Depressed Center Flatcar with 2 transformers, 07		25
22182	RI Gondola "180043" with coils, 08		25
22184	B&O Covered Hopper "604321," 08		25
22185	UP Covered Hopper "53186," 08		25
22186	P&LE (NYC) Gondola "17243," 08-09		35
22187	PRR 2-D Tank Car "6351815," 07		25
22188	Deep Rock 3-D Tank Car "2152," 08		25
22189	NP Java Diner, smoke, 08		110
22190	C&O Operating Billboard, 08		65
22191	Operating Passenger Station, 08-09		105
22192	Hot Box Operating BBQ Shack, 07		80
22193	Cold Drinks Vending Machine, 08		12
22194	Water Tower with light, 08-09		20
22199	City Traction Trolley Barn, 08-09		65
22202	Loading Ramp, 08-10		20
22203	Dairymen's League Operating Milk Car, white, w/platform, 07		140
22204	Snacks Vending Machine, 08		12
22205	Soup and Sandwich Vending Machine, 08		12
22206	PRR Crew Bus, 08		30
22222	Ringling Bros. Speeder Chase Set, 08-10		92
22225	Ringling Bros. Jomar Heavyweight Private Car, 08-11		120
22226	Ringling Bros. 18" Caledonia Heavyweight Private Car, 08		100
22227	Ringling Bros. 18" Advertising Car, 08		100
22228	Ringling Bros. Flatcar with 3 wagons, 08		50
22231	Ringling Bros. Flatcar with 3 wagons, 08		50
22235	Ringling Bros. Flatcar with pole wagon and truck, 08		75
22238	Ringling Bros. Work Caboose with calliope wagon, 08		40
22240	Ringling Bros. Flatcar/Stock Car with wagon, 08		50
22243	Ringling Bros. Human Cannonball Car, 08		45
22244	Ringling Bros. Operating Searchlight Car with 3 spotlights, 08		60
22247	Ringling Bros. Stock Car "54," 08		50
22248	Ringling Bros. Stock Car "47," 08		50
22249	Ringling Bros. Dining Dept. Billboard Reefer, 08		80
22250	Ringling Bros. Dining Dept. Wood-sided Reefer, 08-09		90
22251	Ringling Bros. Dormitory Bunk Car "22," 08		75
22252	Ringling Bros. Operating Billboard, 08-09		75
22253	Ringling Bros. Vintage Billboard Set #1, 08		9
22255	Ringling Bros. Aluminum Coach "40010," 08-10		165

			Exc	Like New
____	**22257**	Ringling Bros. Aluminum Shop Car "63002," 08-10		165
____	**22258**	Ringling Bros. 18" Aluminum Large Animal Car, 08-10		165
____	**22259**	Ringling Bros. Flatcar with trailer, 08		53
____	**22260**	Ringling Bros. Tractor Trailer, 08		30
____	**22261**	Idaho State Quarter Hopper Bank, 08		65
____	**22262**	Wyoming State Quarter Tank Car Bank, 08		50
____	**22263**	Utah State Quarter Boxcar Bank, 08		45
____	**22264**	SuperStreets Figure-8 Expander Pack, 08-10		35
____	**22267**	Mulligan Spring Water Step Van, 08		30
____	**22270**	Quikrete Classic Truck with 2 pallets, 08		33
____	**22271**	MILW EP-5 Electric Locomotive "E20," CC, 08-09		460
____	**22272**	MILW Olympian Hiawatha 18" Aluminum Car 4-pack, 08		480
____	**22277**	MILW Olympian Hiawatha 18" Aluminum Car 2-pack, 08		250
____	**22280**	Erie-Lack. RS3 Diesel "933," CC, 08-09		350
____	**22281**	Southern Train Master Diesel "6300," CC, 08-09		420
____	**22282**	Southern Bay Window Caboose "X270," 08-09		70
____	**22283**	UP S2 Diesel Switcher "1103" and Caboose "25384," 08		130
____	**22286**	GN Boxcab Electric Locomotive "5008-A," horn, 08		90
____	**22287**	North Shore Line 15" Interurban Car 2-pack, 08		230
____	**22288**	Commuter Train Station, 6 road name stickers, 09		25
____	**22289**	Ringling Bros. 18" Aluminum Passenger Car 2-pack, 08		270
____	**22290**	Erie Boxcar "86448" with graffiti, 08		46
____	**22291**	C&NW Stock Car "14303," 08		46
____	**22292**	Land o' Lakes Butter Billboard Reefer, 08		75
____	**22293**	PRR 4-bay Hopper "253776", 08		65
____	**22294**	Montana Rail Link 3-bay Aluminum Hopper "50049," 08		70
____	**22295**	Canada Wheat 4-bay Aluminum Hopper "606418," 08		73
____	**22296**	Eaglebrook Aluminum Tank Car "19039," 08		70
____	**22297**	Petri Wine 3-D Tank Car "904," 08-09		45
____	**22298**	Cotton Belt Offset Cupola Wood-sided Caboose "2230," 08		80
____	**22299**	MILW Bay Window Caboose "980502," 08-09		70
____	**22300**	Detroit, Toledo & Ironton Coil Car "1352," 08		60
____	**22301**	NYC Flatcar "506090" with freight kit, 08		35
____	**22302**	C&O Flatcar "80951" with freight kit, 08		35
____	**22303**	Extruded Aluminum I-Beam, 3 pieces, 08-09		6
____	**22304**	Rails, 12 pieces, 08-09		6
____	**22305**	Small Transformer Load, pair, 08-09		15
____	**22306**	Large Transformer Load, 08		19
____	**22307**	Forklifts, 3, with pallets, 08-09		27
____	**22308**	Loaders with crates, pair, 08-09		13
____	**22309**	Loaders with logs, pair, 08-09		13
____	**22310**	KBL Logistics Container 2-pack, 08		40
____	**22312**	Commemorative Quarter Extended Vision Caboose, 09		80
____	**22313**	ATSF Boxcar "137460," 08		25
____	**22314**	Coastal King Seafood Wood-sided Reefer, 08		25
____	**22315**	Wisconsin & Southern "God Bless America" Boxcar, 09		43
____	**22316**	NP Depressed Center Flatcar "66130" with water tank, 08		25
____	**22317**	U.S. Air Force Hopper "55175" with ballast load, 08		25
____	**22318**	DM&IR Ore Car "29991", 08		25
____	**22319**	Celanese Chemicals 1-D Tank Car "12730," 08		25
____	**22320**	Baldwin Locomotives Works 1-D Tank Car "6809," 08		25
____	**22321**	B&O Operating Boxcar, 08		45
____	**22322**	PRR Operating Ballast Dump Car, 08		75

MODERN 1970-2025		Exc	Like New	
22323	FEMA Voltmeter Car, 08		75	___
22324	C&NW Cop and Robber Chase Gondola, 08-09		55	___
22325	White Milk Cans, 10 pieces, 08-10		8	___
22326	Twin Searchlight Tower, 08-10		33	___
22327	Tommy's Bunk Car Grill, 08-09		100	___
22328	Santa Fe Operating Freight Transfer Platform, 08-09		130	___
22329	Dual Track Signal Bridge, 08-10		45	___
22330	Stella's Heavyweight Diner, smoke, 08-09		140	___
22331	Coffee Vending Machine, 08		12	___
22332	Spring Water Vending Machine, 08		12	___
22333	Candy Vending Machine, 08		12	___
22334	Ford Plymouth Diesel Switcher and Ore Car 6-pack, 08		200	___
22335	NS Operating Paint Shop with boxcar, 08-09		140	___
22344	KBL Logistics ISO Tank, 08		19	___
22346	Tableau Circus Wagons, 08		13	___
22349	Forklift with 6 pallets, 08-09		23	___
22350	Twin Lamp Posts, 3 pieces, 08-09		22	___
22352	Lamp Posts, 4 pieces, 08-09		20	___
22354	Portable Spotlights, 3 pieces, 08-09		15	___
22356	High Tension Poles, 4 pieces, 08-09		8	___
22358	Rail Yard Signs, 12 pieces, 08-09		10	___
22360	Telephone Poles, 6 pieces, 08-09		7	___
22362	Girder Bridge, 08-09		8	___
22363	Stone Bridge Piers, pair, 08-10		27	___
22365	Heavyweight Passenger Coach 6-wheel Scale Trucks, pair, 08-09		25	___
22366	Aluminum Passenger Coach 4-wheel Scale Trucks, pair, 08-09		25	___
22367	Timkin Scale Sprung Trucks, pair, 08-09		19	___
22368	Bettendorf Scale Sprung Trucks, pair, 08-09		19	___
22369	Scale Couplers, pair, 08-09		6	___
22379	SuperStreets Barricade, 2 pieces, 08-10		11	___
22387	Kiosk with 3 vending machines, 08-09		40	___
22391	Ford MP15 Diesel "10021," horn, 08		115	___
22392	Ford Farming Boxcar "1681," 08		30	___
22393	Ford Stampings DD Boxcar "101," 08		35	___
22394	Ford 2-bay Covered Hopper "1667," 08		30	___
22395	Ford Speeder "14," 08		65	___
22396	Ford Water Tower, 08		25	___
22397	Ford Rotating Sign Tower, 08		55	___
22398	Boyd Bros. and Ford Barn and Chicken Coop, 08		25	___
22399	Ford ISO Tank, 08-09		21	___
22402	PRR Streamlined K4 4-6-2 Pacific Locomotive, tender, 09-10		500	___
22408	Ringling Bros. Tractor Trailer #1, 08-09		35	___
22411	Tableau Wagon Set #2, 08-10		18	___
22412	PRR Operating Flagman's Shanty, 08-09		90	___
22414	Linde Union Carbide Boxcar with aluminum tank, 08-09		70	___
22415	Ringling Bros. Flatcar with circus wagon, 08		50	___
22417	Ringling Bros. Flatcar with container, 09		55	___
22420	PRR Broadway Limited Aluminum Passenger Car 2-pack, 09-10		300	___
22423	GN Aluminum Passenger Car 2-pack, 09-10		360	___
22426	Ford Gondola "13447" with coils, 08-09		43	___
22427	Ford Operating Billboard, 08-09		75	___
22428	Ford Tin Sign Replica 4-pack, 08-09		17	___

MODERN 1970-2025		Exc	Like New
___ **22433**	PRR Broadway Limited Aluminum Passenger Car 4-pack, 09-10		600
___ **22438**	Mail Crane, 08-10		30
___ **22439**	Milwaukee Road Aluminum Passenger Car 2-pack, 09-11		360
___ **22447**	Wabash Die-cast 2-bay Ribbed Hopper "37751," 08-09		60
___ **22449**	UP Crew Bus, 08-09		38
___ **22450**	Seaboard Die-cast Hopper with gravel, 10		80
___ **22454**	Oklahoma State Quarter Die-cast Hopper Bank, 08-09		75
___ **22455**	New Mexico State Quarter Die-cast Gondola Bank, 08-09		74
___ **22456**	Arizona State Quarter Tank Car Bank, 08-09		55
___ **22457**	Alaska State Quarter Boxcar Bank, 09		55
___ **22458**	Hawaii State Quarter Die-cast Hopper Bank, 09		75
___ **22459**	Southern Aluminum Passenger Car 2-pack #1, 09		300
___ **22460**	Southern Aluminum Passenger Car 2-pack #2, 09		300
___ **22461**	Scale Skeleton Log Car 4-pack, 08-09		160
___ **22467**	Railroad Water Tower, 08-09		23
___ **22468**	Fast Eddie's Used Car Lot with 2 die-cast vehicles, 08-09		50
___ **22469**	Cola Illuminated Vending Machine, 08-09		13
___ **22470**	SuperStreets Guard Rails, 08-10		20
___ **22472**	Ringling Bros. Tin Sign Replica 4-pack, 08-09		17
___ **22477**	Lionel Tin Sign Replica 4-pack, 08-09		15
___ **22482**	Vintage Tin Sign Replica 4-pack, 08-09		15
___ **22487**	Scooter Gang with scooters, 09-10		13
___ **22492**	Airport Revolving Searchlight, 10		40
___ **22493**	Ringling Bros. Lighted Clown Wood-sided Reefer, 09		75
___ **22494**	Ford Flatcar with 2 Thunderbird convertibles, 09		53
___ **22496**	Vita O Flavored Water Vending Machine, 09		13
___ **22497**	Top Pop Soda Illuminated Vending Machine, 09		13
___ **22498**	Ringling Bros. Flatcar with 3 circus wagons, 09-10		55
___ **22500**	Defense Dept. Flatcar with 2 jeeps and soldier, 09		50
___ **22501**	C&NW Railroad Van, CC, 09-10		100
___ **22502**	Ringling Bros. Flatcar with 3 circus wagons, 09-10		55
___ **22504**	Ford Water Tower with vintage Ford logo, 09-10		25
___ **22505**	Sparkling Springs Beverage Truck, 09		45
___ **22506**	SuperStreets Fishtail Roadway, 09		25
___ **22507**	Ringling Bros. Flatcar with boxcar and ticket wagon, 09		60
___ **22509**	Pallet Pack with banded loads, 09		20
___ **22510**	Lionel Step Van, CC, 09-10		100
___ **22511**	BNSF Flatcar with helicopter, 09		50
___ **22513**	Ringling Bros. Heavyweight Advertising Car, 09		120
___ **22514**	NYC Girder Bridge, 09-10		15
___ **22515**	Milwaukee Road/REA Scale Boxcar "6436," 09		55
___ **22516**	BNSF MP15 Diesel "3704" with horn, 09		120
___ **22517**	Quick Lane Ford Motorcraft Auto Parts Van, 09-10		42
___ **22518**	Lionel Tank Container Leasing ISO Tank, 09-10		23
___ **22519**	Roma Wine Wood-sided Billboard Reefer, 09-10		70
___ **22520**	WWII Soldiers in Action, 10 pieces, 09-10		20
___ **22521**	1959 Ford Billboard Set, 09		10
___ **22523**	American Flyer Vintage Truck, 09		38
___ **22524**	Ford Coil Car "749772," 09		73
___ **22525**	Vermont Railway Operating Boxcar "177," 09		50
___ **22526**	Crabby Matt's Smoking Heavyweight Diner, 09		150
___ **22527**	Toledo, Peoria & Western Boxcar "5067," 09-10		55
___ **22528**	GN Stock Car "55973," 09-10		55

		Exc	Like New	
22529	U.S. Army 1-D Tank Car "11278," 09		35	___
22530	Milwaukee Road Aluminum Coach "627," 09-11		180	___
22531	Southern Girder Bridge, 09		15	___
22532	Montana Rail Link 1-D Tank Car "100017," 09		35	___
22533	GN Aluminum Coach "1377," 09-10		180	___
22534	SuperStreets D16 Curve Guard Rails, 09-10		20	___
22536	SuperStreets D21 Curve Guard Rails, 09-10		22	___
22538	Ford Modern Aluminum Tank Car "30166," 09		90	___
22539	BNSF Flatcar "922267" with Ford trailer, 09-10		60	___
22542	PRR Flatcar "480227" with freight kit, 09		40	___
22543	Biodiesel 2-D Tank Car "1544," 09		40	___
22544	Ringling Bros. Wood-sided Gondola with equipment, 09		63	___
22548	Kiosk #2 with 3 illuminated vending machines, 09		40	___
22553	Convenience Mart, 09-10		25	___
22554	Auto Parts Store, 09-10		20	___
22555	Ringling Bros. Tractor with Gold Tour container, 09-10		55	___
22558	PRR Flatcar "469301" with milk containers, 09		50	___
22559	UP Gondola "229794" with freight kit, 09-10		80	___
22560	CB&Q Wood-sided Gondola "85150" with spools, 09-10		60	___
22561	Gondola Scrap Load, 09		9	___
22562	Operation Lifesaver Boxcar with flashing LEDs, 09		65	___
22563	Ringling Bros. Handcar and Trailer Set, 10-11		70	___
22566	SuperStreets 2.5" Straight Roadway, 4 pieces, 10		12	___
22568	Generators, 2 pieces, 09		9	___
22570	Large transformer, 09		22	___
22571	Cage Wagon Set, 09-10		18	___
22573	Display Base, 09		20	___
22574	Ringling Bros. Flatcar "39" with trailer, 09		60	___
22577	Biodiesel Storage Tank with 2 figures, 09-10		40	___
22578	Ringling Bros. Heavyweight Coach "70," 09		120	___
22579	Circus Horses, 4 pieces, 09-10		15	___
22580	Bollards and Chains, 09-10		20	___
22582	Pipe Stack Load, 09		30	___
22583	KBL Operating Wind Turbine, 09-10		75	___
22584	KBL Die-cast 16-wheel Flatcar "34807," 09		85	___
22587	Old Reading Flatcar Foot Bridge with stone piers, 09-10		50	___
22590	Roadside Fender Bender, 09-10		75	___
22592	SuperStreets D16 Turn Roadways, left and right, 10		35	___
22595	SuperStreets D21 Turn Roadways, left and right, 10		39	___
22598	SuperStreets Adjustable Straight Kit, 09-10		20	___
22600	Wire Spool Load, 6 pieces, 09		20	___
22610	Napa Valley Wine Train Alco FA Diesel AA Set, 10		230	___
22611	Napa Valley Wine Train Alco FA Diesel "71," powered, 10		150	___
22612	Napa Valley Wine Train Alco FA Diesel "72," unpowered, 10		80	___
22613	Napa Valley Wine Train 15" Passenger Car 4-pack, 10		450	___
22614	Napa Valley Wine Train Heavyweight Observation "1018," 10		110	___
22615	Napa Valley Wine Train Heavyweight Observation "1011," 10		110	___
22616	Napa Valley Wine Train Heavyweight Diner "1090," 10		115	___
22617	Napa Valley Wine Train Heavyweight Diner "1015,", 10		115	___
22618	Signal Oil Co. 1-D Tank Car, 10		40	___
22619	PRR Paoli MU Commuter Train 2-pack, 10		290	___
22622	RR Paoli Motorized Combine, 10		200	___

			Exc	Like New
____	**22623**	PRR Commuter Train Station, 10		35
____	**22624**	NH Die-cast Plymouth Switcher with snowplow, 10		160
____	**22625**	Ringling Bros. 18" Aluminum Generator Car, 10-11		180
____	**22627**	Ringling Bros. Lighted Clown Wood-sided Reefer, 10-11		90
____	**22628**	Ringling Bros. 18" Aluminum Advertising Car, 10-11		180
____	**22629**	Ringling Bros. Stock Car, 10-11		60
____	**22630**	Ringling Bros. Tractor and Trailer, 10-11		35
____	**22633**	Ringling Bros. 18" Aluminum Coach, 10-11		180
____	**22634**	Ringling Bros. 18" Heavyweight Advertising Car, 10-11		146
____	**22635**	Ringling Bros. Operating Dual Searchlight Car, 10-11		60
____	**22637**	Quikrete Step Van, 10		48
____	**22638**	PRR Crew Bus, 10		45
____	**22639**	B&O Boxcab Diesel "195," 10		100
____	**22640**	Central of Georgia Boxcar "5823," 10		45
____	**22641**	New Haven Boxcar "36438," 10		45
____	**22642**	Ringling Bros. Operating Large Animal Feed Car, 10-11		150
____	**22643**	Ford MP15 Diesel "10022," 10-11		135
____	**22644**	Ford Motorcraft 48' Aluminum Tank Car, 10-11		95
____	**22645**	Ringling Bros. Operating Tent Pole Dump Car, 10-11		130
____	**22646**	Ford Speeder, 10-11		75
____	**22647**	Rock Island Gondola "180044," 10		35
____	**22648**	PRR Gondola "353381," 10		35
____	**22651**	Central Vermont Operating Milk Car with platform, 10		175
____	**22653**	Starlite Diner with parking lot, 10		200
____	**22654**	Ringling Bros. Flatcar with 3 circus wagons, 10-11		60
____	**22656**	Ringling Bros. Flatcar with 3 circus wagons, 10-11		60
____	**22658**	Operating Flagman's Shanty, 10		100
____	**22659**	Union 76 1-D Tank Car "6322," 10		40
____	**22660**	Moose Pond Creamery Operating Loading Depot, 10		140
____	**22661**	WM 2-Bay Covered Hopper "5051," 10		35
____	**22662**	PRR Reefer "19494," 10		45
____	**22663**	New Haven Illuminated Caboose, 10		40
____	**22667**	Acme Scrap Platform Crane, 10		60
____	**22670**	ATSF Operating Boxcar, 10		140
____	**22671**	Smoking Southern Bay Window Caboose, 10		90
____	**22672**	Ringling Bros. 18" Sarasota Observation Car, 10-11		146
____	**22673**	Ford Water Tower with light, 10		27
____	**22674**	MILW 21" Aluminum Passenger Car 2-pack, 10-11		400
____	**22679**	Ringling Bros. Operating Billboard, 10-11		100
____	**22902**	Quonset Hut, 98-99	30	45
____	**22907**	Die-cast Girder Bridge, 98-01		10
____	**22910**	Gilbert Tractor Trailer, 98		20
____	**22914**	PowerHouse Lockon, 98-01		24
____	**22915**	Municipal Building, 98-99		28
____	**22916**	190-watt Power Accessory System, 98		425
____	**22918**	Locomotive Backshop, 98	288	460
____	**22919**	ElectroCouplers Kit for GP9 Diesel, 98-00		20
____	**22922**	Intermodal Crane, 98		195
____	**22931**	Die-cast Cantilever Signal Bridge, 98-06		35
____	**22934**	Walkout Cantilever Signal, 98-03		42
____	**22936**	Coaling Tower, 3 pieces, 98		85
____	**22940**	Mast Signal, 98-00		37

MODERN 1970-2025		Exc	Like New	
22942	Accessories Box, 98-01		20	___
22944	Automatic Operating Semaphore, 98-03, 08	17	35	___
22945	Block Target Signal, 98-00		39	___
22946	Automatic Crossing Gate and Signal, 98-99		45	___
22947	Auto Crossing Gate, 98-00		36	___
22948	Gooseneck Street Lamps, set of 2, 98-00		30	___
22949	Highway Lights, set of 4, 98-99		20	___
22950	Classic Street Lamps, set of 3, 98-02		20	___
22951	Dwarf Signal, 98-00		24	___
22952	Classic Billboards, set of 3, 98-00		15	___
22953	Linex Gasoline Tall Oil Tank, 98-99		6	___
22954	Linex Gasoline Wide Oil Tank, 98-99		6	___
22955	ElectroCouplers Kit for J Class and B&A tenders, 98-00		20	___
22956	ElectroCouplers Kit for NW2 Switcher, 98		20	___
22957	ElectroCouplers Kit for F3 Diesel, 98-01		20	___
22958	ElectroCouplers Kit for Dash 9 Diesel, 98-01		20	___
22959	ElectroCoupler Conversion Kit for Atlantic Locomotive, 98-01		13	___
22960	Trainmaster Command Basic Upgrade Kit, 98-01		34	___
22961	Standard GP9 Diesel B Unit Upgrade Kit, 98-01		30	___
22962	Deluxe GP9 Diesel B Unit Upgrade Kit, black trucks, 98-01		44	___
22963	RailSounds Upgrade Kit, steam RailSounds, 98-01		55	___
22964	RailSounds Upgrade Kit, diesel RailSounds, 98-01		55	___
22965	Culvert Loader, CC, 98-01	160	255	___
22966	Figure-8 Add-on Track Pack (027), 98-16	10	17	___
22967	Double Loop Add-on Track Pack (027), 98-16		62	___
22968	Double Loop Track Pack (027), 98-03		65	___
22969	Deluxe Complete Track Pack (0), 98-16		120	___
22972	Bascule Bridge, 98-99	114	337	___
22973	Lionel Corporation Tractor and Trailer, 98		15	___
22975	Culvert Unloader, CC, 99-00		225	___
22979	GP9 Diesel B-Unit Deluxe Upgrade Kit, silver trucks, 98-01		34	___
22980	TMCC SC-2 Switch Controller, 99-16		130	___
22982	Postwar ZW Controller and Transformer Set, 98		265	___
22983	180-watt PowerHouse Power Supply, 99-16. 18		125	___
22990	Flatcar with Route 66 autos, 4-pack, 99		37	___
22991	Christmas Tree and Blue Comet Train, 99-00		60	___
22993	Route 66 Sinclair Dino Cafe, 99-00		215	___
22997	Oil Drum Loader, 99-00		100	___
22998	Triple Action Magnetic Crane, 99		220	___
22999	Sound Dispatching Station, 99-00		90	___
23000	NYC Dreyfuss Hudson Operating Base, 2-rail, 92 u		190	___
23001	NYC Dreyfuss Hudson Operating Base, 3-rail, 93 u		190	___
23002	NYC Hudson Operating Base, 92 u, 93-94		190	___
23003	PRR B-6 Switcher Operating Base, 92 u, 93-94		190	___
23004	NP 4-8-4 Operating Base, 92 u, 93-94		190	___
23005	Reading T-1 Operating Base, 92 u, 93-94		190	___
23006	Chessie System T-1 Operating Base, 92 u, 93-94		190	___
23007	SP Daylight Operating Base, 92 u, 93-94		190	___
23008	NYC L-3 Mohawk Operating Base, 92 u, 93-94		190	___
23009	PRR S2 Turbine Locomotive Operating Base, 92 u, 93-94		190	___
23010	31" Remote Switch, left hand (0), 95-99	30	37	___
23011	31" Remote Switch, right hand (0), 95-99	20	30	___
23012	F3 Diesel ABA Operating Base, 92 u, 93-94		190	___

			Exc	Like New
___	**24018**	PRR Boxcar, 05		25
___	**24101**	Mainline Color Position Signal, 04-08		25
___	**24102**	Industrial Water Tower, 03		55
___	**24103**	Double Floodlight Tower, 03, 05-09		42
___	**24104**	Hobo Tower, 03-05		70
___	**24105**	Track Gang, 03-06		70
___	**24106**	Exploding Ammunition Dump, 02		25
___	**24107**	Missile Firing Range Set, 02		60
___	**24108**	World War II Pylon, 03		80
___	**24109**	Santa Fe Railroad Tugboat, 03	60	125
___	**24110**	Pennsylvania Railroad Tugboat, 03		259
___	**24111**	Swing Bridge, 03		215
___	**24112**	Oil Field with bubble tubes, 03		135
___	**24113**	Lionelville Ford Auto Dealership, 03		225
___	**24114**	AMC/ARC Gantry Crane, CC, 03		195
___	**24115**	AMC/ARC Log Loader, CC, 03, 06-07		140
___	**24117**	Illuminated Covered Bridge, 02-25		100
___	**24119**	Big Bay Lighthouse, 04-05		170
___	**24122**	Lionelville People Pack, 03, 08-09, 15-17		27
___	**24123**	Passenger Station People Pack, 03, 08-09, 15-20		27
___	**24124**	Carnival People Pack, 03, 08-11, 13-16, 18-20	5	27
___	**24130**	TMCC 135/180 PowerMaster, 04-12		79
___	**24131**	Dumbo Pylon, 03		70
___	**24134**	Bethlehem Steel Gantry Crane, 02		200
___	**24135**	Lionel Lighthouse, 02-03		100
___	**24137**	Mr. Spiff and Puddles, 03, 08		34
___	**24138**	Playtime Playground, 03, 08		50
___	**24139**	Duck Shooting Gallery, 03		110
___	**24140**	Charles Bowdish Homestead, 03		60
___	**24147**	Lionel Sawmill, 03		90
___	**24148**	Coal Tipple Coal Pack, 02, 08-10, 13-20		15
___	**24149**	NYC Hobo Hotel, 02		42
___	**24151**	Hobo Campfire, 03		25
___	**24152**	Conveyor Lumber Loader, 03		65
___	**24153**	Railroad Control Tower, 03, 08-10	30	63
___	**24154**	Maiden Rescue, 03		35
___	**24155**	Blinking Light Billboard, 04-10		21
___	**24156**	Lionelville Street Lamps, 4-pack, 04-23		35
___	**24159**	Illuminated Station Platform, 04-08		32
___	**24160**	Rub-a-Dub-Dub, 04		42
___	**24161**	Test O' Strength, 04-06		70
___	**24164**	Summer Vacation, 04-05		80
___	**24168**	Tire Swing, 04-05		70
___	**24170**	Rover's Revenge, 04-05		70
___	**24171**	Campbell's Soup Water Tower, 04		45
___	**24172**	Balancing Man, 04-05		70
___	**24173**	Derrick Platform, 03-05		60
___	**24174**	Icing Station, 04-06		100
___	**24176**	Irene's Diner, 06-07		65
___	**24177**	Hot Air Balloon Ride, 04-06		95
___	**24179**	Scrambler Amusement Ride, 04-07	87	165
___	**24180**	Choo Choo Barn Lionelville Zoo, 04-05	53	236
___	**24182**	Lionelville Firehouse, 04		100

	MODERN 1970-2025	Exc	Like New	
24183	Lionelville Gas Station, 04, 06-09		115	___
24187	Classic Billboard Set: 3 stands and 5 inserts, 04-08		10	___
24190	Station Platform, 05-09		17	___
24191	Park People Pack, 04-18		27	___
24192	Park Benches People Pack, 04-09		23	___
24193	Railroad Yard People Pack, 04-08, 14-18	10	19	___
24194	Civil Servants People Pack, 04-18		27	___
24196	Farm People Pack, 04-09		23	___
24197	City Accessory Pack, 04-17		27	___
24200	Lionel FasTrack Book, 07-10, 13-15		35	___
24201	UPS Centennial Operating Billboard Signmen, 07		100	___
24203	Polar Express Original Figures, 4 pieces, 08-25		30	___
24204	Christmas Tractor Trailer with trees, 08		25	___
24205	Classic Billboard Set, 08-10		20	___
24206	MOW Gantry Crane, 08		280	___
24212	Lionel Art Blinking Billboard, 08-09		23	___
24213	Universal Lockon, 12-16		4	___
24214	Postwar "395" Floodlight Tower, 08		75	___
24215	MTA Metro-North Passenger Station, 07		53	___
24218	Sunoco Elevated Tank, 08-09		75	___
24219	PRR Plastic Girder Bridge, 08		18	___
24220	ATSF Girder Bridge, 08-09		18	___
24221	UP Die-cast Girder Bridge, 08		30	___
24222	UPS Die-cast Girder Bridge, 08		30	___
24223	Santa's Sleigh Pylon, 08		150	___
24224	Postwar "38" Water Tower, 08-09		150	___
24226	Christmas Toy Store, 08		52	___
24227	Halloween Animated Billboard, 08-09		54	___
24228	Christmas Operating Billboard, 08		38	___
24229	Pennsylvania Water Tower, 08-09		23	___
24230	Maiden Rescue, 08		60	___
24232	Burning Switch Tower, 08		80	___
24233	Exploding Ammunition Dump, 08		36	___
24234	Missile Firing Range, 08		43	___
24235	UPS Water Tower, 08		80	___
24236	Wimpy's All-Star Burger Stand, 08		97	___
24238	Sunoco Oil Derrick, 08		90	___
24240	MTA Metro-North Blinking Billboard, 07		21	___
24242	Postwar "352" Icing Station, 08		100	___
24243	Rosie's Roadside Diner, 08		85	___
24244	Commuter People, 08, 13-18		27	___
24245	MTA Metro-North Illuminated Station Platform, 07		32	___
24248	Manual Crossing Gate, 08-23		20	___
24250	Mainline Gooseneck Lamps, pair, 08-09		32	___
24251	Polar Express Caribou Pack, 08-25		30	___
24252	Polar Express Wolves and Rabbits Figures, 08-25		30	___
24264	Halloween People, 08-12		23	___
24265	Trick or Treat People, 08-13		23	___
24270	Operating Forklift Platform, 08-09		280	___
24272	Train Orders Building, 08		80	___
24273	Christmas Water Tower, 08-10		23	___
24274	Christmas Girder Bridge, 08		18	___
24279	PowerMaster Bridge, 08-13		55	___

	MODERN 1970-2025		Exc	Like New
___	**24283**	NYC Girder Bridge, 09-10		21
___	**24284**	Halloween Girder Bridge, 09-11		21
___	**24285**	CP Rail Girder Bridge, 08-09		30
___	**24286**	Polar Express Girder Bridge, 09-14		21
___	**24287**	ATSF Blinking Light Water Tower, 09		30
___	**24288**	NYC Blinking Light Water Tower, 09		30
___	**24293**	Legacy Module Garage, 08-09		50
___	**24294**	AEC Nuclear Reactor, 09-10		338
___	**24295**	Cowen's Corner Hobby Shop, 09		420
___	**24296**	Engine House, 09-12, 14		70
___	**24298**	Franklin Mutual Bank, 08		60
___	**24299**	Main Street Ice Cream Parlor, 08		37
___	**24500**	D&RGW Alco PA Diesel AA Set, 04-05		530
___	**24503**	D&RGW Alco PB Diesel, 04-05		150
___	**24504**	Santa Fe E6 Diesel AA Set, CC, 03		530
___	**24507**	Milwaukee Road E6 Diesel AA Set, CC, 03		530
___	**24511**	Burlington FT Diesel AA Set, RailSounds, 03		225
___	**24516**	Santa Fe F3 Diesel B Unit, 03		235
___	**24517**	NYC F3 Diesel B Unit "2404," powered, CC, 03		250
___	**24518**	WP F3 Diesel B Unit, 03		275
___	**24519**	B&O F3 Diesel B Unit, 03		270
___	**24520**	Alaska F3 Diesel AA Set, 03		650
___	**24521**	Alaska F3 Diesel B Unit, nonpowered, 03		200
___	**24522**	Alaska F3 Diesel B Unit "1519," powered, CC, 03		300
___	**24528**	Postwar "2379T" Rio Grande F3 Diesel A Unit, nonpowered, 04		175
___	**24529**	Santa Fe F3 Diesel AA Set, CC, 04	213	690
___	**24532**	Santa Fe F3 Diesel B Unit "18A," nonpowered, 04		150
___	**24533**	Santa Fe F3 Diesel B Unit "18B," 04		200
___	**24534**	Erie-Lack. F3 Diesel ABA Set, CC, 05		900
___	**24538**	Erie-Lack. F3 Diesel B Unit "8042," powered, CC, 05	60	225
___	**24544**	NYC FA2 Diesel AA Set, CC, 05		600
___	**24547**	NYC FB2 Diesel B Unit "3330" (std O), 05		150
___	**24548**	CN FPA-4 Diesel AA Set, CC, 05		600
___	**24551**	CN FPB-4 Diesel B Unit "6865" (std O), 05		150
___	**24552**	UP F3 Diesel ABA Set, CC, 05	340	895
___	**24556**	UP F3 Diesel B Unit "900C," powered, CC, 05		285
___	**24562**	Santa Fe F3 Diesel B Unit, powered, 04-05	100	300
___	**24563**	PRR F3 Diesel B Unit, powered, 04-05		195
___	**24566**	Napa Valley Wine Train FPA-4 A Unit "71," powered, 05		400
___	**24567**	Napa Valley Wine Train FPA-4 B Unit "72," nonpowered, 05		100
___	**24570**	Santa Fe FT Diesel B Unit, nonpowered, 05		85
___	**24571**	Postwar "2383" ATSF F3 Diesel A Unit, powered, 05		400
___	**24572**	Postwar "2383" ATSF F3 Diesel A Unit, nonpowered, 05		100
___	**24573**	Postwar "2383C" Santa Fe F3 Diesel B Unit, nonpowered, 05	50	180
___	**24574**	UP E7 Diesel AA Set '988/989," CC, 06		700
___	**24577**	UP E7 Diesel B Unit "990," nonpowered (std O), 06		150
___	**24578**	UP E7 Diesel B Unit "988," powered, 06		300
___	**24579**	NYC E7 Diesel AA Set "4008/4009," CC, 06		700
___	**24582**	NYC E7 Diesel B Unit "4105," nonpowered (std O), 06		150
___	**24583**	NYC E7 Diesel B Unit "4104," powered, 06		300
___	**24584**	Pennsylvania F7 Diesel ABA Set "9642/9643," CC, 06		900
___	**24588**	Pennsylvania F7 Diesel B Unit "9643B," powered, 06-07		300

MODERN 1970-2025		Exc	Like New	
24589	Santa Fe F7 Diesel ABA Set "332/333," CC, 06-07		900	___
24593	Santa Fe F7 Diesel B Unit "332B," powered, 06-07		300	___
24594	PRR F7 Diesel Breakdown B Unit, RailSounds, 06-07		160	___
24595	Santa Fe F7 Diesel Breakdown B Unit, RailSounds, 06-07	95	270	___
24596	UP E7 Diesel Breakdown B Unit, RailSounds, 06		270	___
24597	NYC E7 Diesel Breakdown B Unit, RailSounds, 06		270	___
24814	Battle of Bunker Hill 250th Anniversary Boxcar, 25		110	___
25002	P&LE Boxcar "20982," 05	20	25	___
25003	WP Boxcar, orange with silver feather, 05		30	___
25008	Holiday Boxcar, 06		50	___
25009	Santa Fe Hi-Cube Boxcar "14064," 06		30	___
25010	NP Boxcar "48189," 06		30	___
25011	Angela Trotta Thomas "Santa's Break" Boxcar, 06		50	___
25014	PRR Boxcar, silver, 10		30	___
25016	ATSF Boxcar, 10		35	___
25022	NYC Boxcar, 06		35	___
25024	GM&O Boxcar, 07		30	___
25025	Reading Boxcar "106502", 07-08		35	___
25026	RI Hi-Cube Boxcar, 07-08		35	___
25030	Billboard Boxcar with catalog art, 06		20	___
25033	Holiday Boxcar, 07	15	50	___
25034	Angela Trotta Thomas "Santa's Workshop" Boxcar, 07		50	___
25035	Disney Holiday Boxcar, 06		50	___
25041	UPS Centennial Boxcar #1, 06		60	___
25042	UPS Centennial Boxcar #2, 07		60	___
25043	Macy's Parade Boxcar, 06		40	___
25047	"It's a Wonderful Life" Bedford Falls Boxcar, 07 u		75	___
25048	"It's a Wonderful Life" Happy Holidays Boxcar, 07 u		75	___
25050	British Columbia Hi-Cube Boxcar "8008," 08		35	___
25051	Seaboard Boxcar, 08		35	___
25052	Disney Holiday Boxcar, 07		75	___
25053	NYC DD Boxcar "75500," 08		55	___
25054	Angela Trotta Thomas "Christmas Memories" Boxcar, 08		55	___
25057	PRR Boxcar "19751," 08		20	___
25058	Santa Fe Boxcar, 10		30	___
25059	Democrat 2008 Election Boxcar, 08		50	___
25060	Republican 2008 Election Boxcar, 08		50	___
25061	Holiday Boxcar, 08		55	___
25063	Conrail Boxcar "25063," 09		40	___
25064	CP Rail Hi-Cube Boxcar, 09-10	18	40	___
25065	Disney Holiday Boxcar, 08		40	___
25066	Holiday Boxcar, 09		65	___
25067	Angela Trotta Thomas "General Delivery" Boxcar, 09	33	84	___
25068	D&H Boxcar, 08 u		60	___
25077	Milwaukee Road Boxcar "8484," 09-10	13	40	___
25083	Wizard of Oz Boxcar, 1, 09		50	___
25084	Wizard of Oz Boxcar, 2, 09		50	___
25087	Wabash Boxcar "6439," 10-11		40	___
25088	Georgia Power Boxcar, 10		40	___
25093	Seaboard Boxcar, 10		30	___
25095	Texas Special Boxcar, 10		100	___
25096	CN Boxcar, 10		45	___
25103	Chessie "Steam Special" Madison Car 2-pack, 05		100	___

	MODERN 1970-2025		Exc	Like New
___	25106	Pennsylvania Madison Car 4-pack, 05		210
___	25111	Pennsylvania Madison Car 2-pack, 05		120
___	25114	Lionel Lines Passenger Car 3-pack, 05		120
___	25118	Lionel Lines Passenger Car 2-pack, 05		80
___	25121	Southern Streamliner Car 4-pack, 05		210
___	25126	Southern Streamliner Car 2-pack, 05-06		120
___	25134	Polar Express Add-on Diner, 05-17		70
___	25135	Polar Express Add-on Baggage Car, 05-17		70
___	25142	NYC Combination Car, “5018,” 05		40
___	25143	NYC Coach, “3807,” 05		45
___	25144	NYC Observation, “4152,” 05		40
___	25148	B&O Madison Car 4-pack, 06-07		220
___	25153	B&O Madison Car 2-pack, 06-07		125
___	25156	California Zephyr Streamliner Car 4-pack (std 0), 06-07		220
___	25161	California Zephyr Streamliner Car 2-pack, 06-07		125
___	25164	UP Madison Car 4-pack, 06-07		220
___	25169	UP Madison Car 2-pack, 06-07		125
___	25176	B&O Baggage Car, TrainSounds, 06-07		160
___	25177	UP Baggage Car, TrainSounds, 06-07		160
___	25178	California Zephyr Streamliner Baggage Car, TrainSounds, 06-07		160
___	25186	Polar Express Hot Chocolate Car Add-on, 06-14, 16-17		72
___	25187	GN Streamliner Car 4-pack, 07		220
___	25188	GN Streamliner Car 2-pack, 07		125
___	25189	GN Streamliner Baggage Car, TrainSounds, 07		160
___	25196	North Pole Central Vista Dome Car, 07-08		45
___	25197	North Pole Central Baggage Car, 07-10		45
___	25198	PRR Vista Dome Car “4058,” 07-08		45
___	25199	PRR Baggage Car “9359,” 07-09		45
___	25307	B&M Operating Boxcar, 07		55
___	25404	FEC Champion Aluminum Passenger Car 2-pack, 04-05		290
___	25407	FEC Champion Aluminum Diner, StationSounds, 04-05		290
___	25408	Santa Fe El Capitan Aluminum Passenger Car 2-pack, 05		290
___	25411	Santa Fe El Capitan Aluminum Diner, StationSounds, 05		290
___	25412	B&O Columbian Aluminum Passenger Car 2-pack, 05		275
___	25415	B&O Columbian Aluminum Diner, StationSounds, 05		290
___	25416	SP Daylight Aluminum Passenger Car 2-pack, 04-05		290
___	25419	SP Daylight Aluminum Diner, StationSounds, 04-05		290
___	25420	PRR Trail Blazer Aluminum Passenger Car 2-pack, 04-05		290
___	25423	PRR Trail Blazer Aluminum Diner, StationSounds, 04-05		290
___	25433	UP City of Denver Aluminum Passenger Car 4-pack (std 0), 05		1000
___	25438	Union Pacific Aluminum Passenger Car 2-pack, 05		250
___	25441	UP City of Denver 18” Aluminum Diner, StationSounds, 05		290
___	25442	REA Baggage Car, 05		60
___	25443	Santa Fe Super Chief Vista Dome “Regal Pass,” 05		60
___	25444	Santa Fe Super Chief Coach “Indian Falls,” 05		60
___	24445	Santa Fe Super Chief Observation “Vista Valley,” 05		60
___	25446	Santa Fe Super Chief Streamliner Car 2-pack, 05		150
___	25447	Santa Fe Super Chief Vista Dome “Royal Gorge,” 05		70
___	25448	Santa Fe Super Chief Coach “Indian Arrow,” 05		70
___	25450	PRR Congressional Aluminum Passenger Car 4-pack (std 0), 06-07	175	580
___	25455	PRR Congressional Aluminum Passenger Car 2-pack (std 0), 06-07		300
___	25458	PRR Congressional Diner, StationSounds (std 0), 06-07		363

		Exc	Like New	
25473	NYC Commodore Vanderbilt Aluminum Passenger Car 2-pack (std O), 06		300	___
25476	NYC Commodore Vanderbilt Diner, StationSounds (std O), 06		300	___
25496	Texas Special 21" Streamliner Diner, StationSounds (std O), 07		300	___
25503	Santa Fe Heavyweight Passenger Car 4-pack (std O), 07-09		495	___
25504	Santa Fe Heavyweight Passenger Car 2-pack (std O), 07-09		265	___
25505	Santa Fe Heavyweight Diner, StationSounds (std O), 07-09		295	___
25506	SP Heavyweight Passenger Car 4-pack (std O), 07		495	___
25507	SP Heavyweight Passenger Car 2-pack (std O), 07-08		265	___
25508	SP Heavyweight Diner, StationSounds (std O), 07-08	50	295	___
25512	Texas Special Streamliner Car 2-pack (std O), 07		300	___
25514	Best Friend of Charleston Coach, 08		125	___
25515	MILW Heavyweight Passenger Car 4-pack (std O), 07		495	___
25516	MILW Heavyweight Passenger Car 2-pack (std O), 07		265	___
25517	MILW Heavyweight Diner, StationSounds (std O), 07-08		295	___
25518	PRR Heavyweight Passenger Car 4-pack (std O), 07		495	___
25519	PRR Heavyweight Passenger Car 2-pack (std O), 07		265	___
25520	PRR Heavyweight Diner, StationSounds (std O), 07-08		295	___
25521	B&O Heavyweight Passenger Car 4-pack (std O), 07		495	___
25522	B&O Heavyweight Passenger Car 2-pack (std O), 07		265	___
25523	B&O Heavyweight Diner, StationSounds (std O), 07-08		295	___
25559	Phantom IV Passenger Car 4-pack, 08		380	___
25574	UP Streamlined Diner, StationSounds (std O), 08		325	___
25575	Polar Express Heavyweight Car 2-pack, 09		400	___
25576	Polar Express Scale Observation Car, 14, 16		210	___
25578	Polar Express Heavyweight Add-on Coach, 09		200	___
25582	New York City Transit R30 Subway 2-pack, 10		400	___
25586	Polar Express Heavyweight Baggage Car, 10, 12-14		210	___
25587	Polar Express Abandoned Toy Car, 10, 13		200	___
25595	New York City Transit R16 Subway 2-pack, 10		400	___
25598	Polar Express Heavyweight Combination Car, 12-14		210	___
25600	Postwar Scale CP 18" Aluminum Passenger Car 4-pack , 11		640	___
25605	Postwar Scale CP 18" Aluminum Passenger Car 2-pack , 11		320	___
25608	ATSF Super Chief 18" Aluminum Passenger Cars 4-pack, 11		640	___
25613	ATSF Super Chief 18" Aluminum Passenger Cars 2-pack, 11		320	___
25616	UP 18" Passenger Car 2-pack (std O), 11		320	___
25619	PRR "Lindbergh Special" Passenger Car 2-pack, 11		280	___
25622	Milwaukee Road 18" Passenger Car 4-pack, 11		640	___
25623	Milwaukee Road 18" Passenger Car 2-pack, 11		320	___
25630	Polar Express Scale Heavyweight Diner, 12-14, 16		210	___
25631	Lionel Funeral Set Add-on 2-pack (std O), 13		300	___
25635	PRR Red Arrow Heavyweight Coach 3-pack (std O), 13		430	___
25639	PRR Red Arrow Heavyweight Diner (std O), 13		150	___
25646	ATSF Scout Heavyweight Coach 4-pack (std O), 12-14		550	___
25651	ATSF Scout Heavyweight Coach 2-pack (std O), 12-14		280	___
25654	Southern Crescent Limited Heavyweight Passenger Car 2-pack, 12		550	___
25655	Blue Comet Heavyweight Passenger Car 2-pack, 12-13		550	___
25656	Alton Limited Heavyweight Passenger Car 2-pack, 12-14	113	550	___
25665	Amtrak Acela Passenger Car 2-pack, 12		500	___
25713	NYC 20th Century Limited Heavyweight 4-pack (std O), 12-14		550	___
25714	NYC 20th Century Limited Van Twiller Combo Car (std O), 12		140	___

	MODERN 1970-2025		Exc	Like New
___	**25715**	NYC 20th Century Limited Schuyler Mansion Sleeper Car(std O), 12		140
___	**25716**	NYC 20th Century Limited Macomb House Sleeper Car (std O), 12		140
___	**25717**	NYC 20th Century Limited Catskill Valley Observation Car (std O), 12		140
___	**25718**	NYC 20th Century Limited Heavyweight Passenger Car 2-pack, 12-14		280
___	**25719**	NYC 20th Century Limited Baggage Car "4857" (std O), 12		140
___	**25720**	NYC 20th Century Limited Poplar Highlands Sleeper Car (std O), 12		140
___	**25721**	NYC 20th Century Limited Heavyweight Diner "655" (std O), 12		280
___	**25722**	D&RGW California Zephyr 18" Aluminum Passenger Car 4-pack, 12		640
___	**25727**	WP California Zephyr 18" Aluminum Passenger Car 2-pack, 12		320
___	**25731**	CB&Q California Zephyr 18" Aluminum Passenger Car 2-pack, 12		320
___	**25757**	Texas Special Passenger Car 2-pack, 13-14		400
___	**25760**	PRR Passenger Car 2-pack, 13-14		400
___	**25773**	SAL Round-roof Boxcar "19297" (std O), 14		80
___	**25790**	NYC 20th Century Limited Heavyweight Diner (std O), 12		140
___	**25795**	Polar Express 10th Anniversary Scale Coach, 14		215
___	**25795**	Polar Express Gold Coach, 17		200
___	**25796**	Polar Express 10th Anniversary Scale Observation Car, 14, 16		215
___	**25910**	KCS Hi-Cube Boxcar, 12-13		75
___	**25922**	NS Caboose, 13-14	10	25
___	**25923**	Interstate 1-D Tank Car, 13-14	12	30
___	**25930**	John Adams Boxcar, 13, 15-16		70
___	**25931**	Andrew Johnson Boxcar, 13, 15-16		70
___	**25932**	Calvin Coolidge Boxcar, 13, 15-16		70
___	**25933**	Harry S. Truman Boxcar, 13, 15-16		70
___	**25934**	Santa Fe Reefer 3-pack, 14-17		145
___	**25938**	PRR Freight Expansion 3-pack, 13		155
___	**25942**	Western Freight Expansion 3-pack, 13-16		155
___	**25946**	SP Hi-Cube Boxcar "128132," 13, 15		50
___	**25947**	North Pole Express Jack Frost Reefer, 13		43
___	**25958**	Gingerbread Dough Vat Car, 13-14		60
___	**25959**	Gingerbread 3-D Tank Car, 13		55
___	**25960**	Christmas Tree Transparent Boxcar, 13-14		75
___	**25961**	Thanksgiving on Parade Boxcar, 13		60
___	**25962**	Thanksgiving Poultry Car, 13		70
___	**25963**	A Christmas Story 30th Anniversary Boxcar, 13-14		65
___	**25964**	Silver Bell Casting Co. Ore Car, 13		55
___	**25965**	Polar Express 10th Anniversary Boxcar, 13		65
___	**25972**	MILW Scale Round-roof Boxcar "714305" (std O), 15	35	61
___	**25973**	Seaboard Round-roof Boxcar "19297" (std O), 14		80
___	**25977**	A Christmas Story Leg Lamp Mint Car, 13		80
___	**26000**	C&O Flatcar with pipes, 01		20
___	**26001**	BP Flatcar "6424" with trailers, 01 u		150
___	**26002**	Monopoly Pennsylvania Ave. Flatcar w/Airplane, 00 u		60
___	**26003**	Lackawanna Flatcar with NH trailer, 01		60
___	**26004**	Conrail Flatcar "71693" with trailer, 01		50
___	**26005**	Nickel Plate Flatcar with trailer, 01		55
___	**26006**	Southern Flatcar "50126" with trailer, 01		50
___	**26007**	NW Flatcar "203029" with trailer, 01		50
___	**26008**	Farmall Flatcar, 01 u		100
___	**26011**	B&M Bulkhead Flatcar, 01 u	20	30

		Exc	Like New	
26013	CN Flatcar with Zamboni ice resurfacing machine, 01		48	___
26014	JCPenney Flatcar, 01 u		145	___
26016	Soo Line Flatcar with trucks, 01 u		120	___
26017	Soo Line Flatcar with trailer, 01 u		120	___
26018	Soo Line Flatcar with trailer, 01 u		120	___
26019	Alaska Gondola "13801," 02		30	___
26020	Postwar "3830" Flatcar with submarine, 02		46	___
26021	CN Flatcar with trailer, 02		44	___
26022	PFE Flatcar with trailer, 02		32	___
26023	Postwar "6816" Flatcar with bulldozer, 02		65	___
26024	Postwar "6817" Flatcar with scraper, 02		65	___
26025	Postwar "6407" Flatcar with rocket, 02		42	___
26026	Postwar "6413" Flatcar with Mercury capsules, 02		95	___
26027	Flatcar "6425" with U.S. Army boat, 02		30	___
26028	Conrail Well Car "768121," 02		40	___
26030	NYC Flatcar "601172" with stakes and bulkheads, 02		22	___
26033	NYC Gondola "6462," 01		30	___
26035	LL Flatcar with traffic helicopter, 01		50	___
26039	Lions Flatcar with 2 Zamboni ice resurfacing machines, 02		39	___
26042	B&O Gondola "601272" with canisters, 03		19	___
26043	Seaboard Flatcar "48109" with trailer, 03		30	___
26044	NYC Flatcar "506089" with trailers, 03		35	___
26045	Postwar "2411" Flatcar with pipes, 03		40	___
26046	Postwar "6561" Flatcar with cable reels, 03		30	___
26047	Postwar "2461" Flatcar with transformer, 03		25	___
26048	Postwar "6801" Flatcar with boat, 02		29	___
26049	Speedboat Willie Flatcar with boat, 03		29	___
26053	PRR Gondola with canisters, 04–05		20	___
26055	C&O Flatcar "475227" w/Trailer Train Truck, 03		50	___
26056	Southern Bulkhead Flatcar "50125", 02		19	___
26057	SP Flatcar "599365" w/Tractors, 02		37	___
26058	SP Flatcar "599366" w/Trailer Frames, 02		35	___
26060	Postwar "6467" Flatcar w/Bulkheads, 03		42	___
26061	Lionelville Tree Transport Gondola, 03		40	___
26062	NYC Gondola "26062" with cable reels, 03		19	___
26063	Pennsylvania Bulkhead Flatcar "26063", 03		19	___
26064	Rock Island Flatcar "90088" with trailer, 04		34	___
26065	REA Flatcar with trailers "TLCX2," 04		35	___
26066	Great Northern Bulkhead Flatcar "26066," 04		20	___
26067	Southern Gondola "60141" with cable reels, 04		20	___
26070	Nestle Nesquik Flatcar "26070" with trailer, 03		70	___
26077	LL Flatcar "6424" with autos, girls set add-on, 03		44	___
26078	LL Flatcar "6801" with boat, boys set add-on, 03		40	___
26080	NJ Medical School Flatcar with handcar, 03		80	___
26082	Frisco Auto Carrier, 2-tier, 04		20	___
26085	New York Auto Carrier, 2-tier, 05		27	___
26086	Alaska Flatcar with bulkheads, 05		25	___
26087	Rock Island Gondola with canisters, traditional, 05		27	___
26089	LRRC Western Union Telegraph Gondola w/Handcar, 10		70	___
26090	Elvis Presley Flatcar w/Billboards, 05		45	___
26091	Elvis Flatcar with tractor and trailer, traditional, 05		60	___
26092	WC Gondola "54214" w/Canisters, 04		50	___
26093	Hobby Town USA Gondola w/Canisters, 04 u		45	___

	MODERN 1970-2025		Exc	Like New
____	26094	UP Screened Auto Carrier, 04		55
____	26095	CSX Screened Auto Carrier, 04		55
____	26096	BNSF Screened Auto Carrier, 04		55
____	26097	ATSF Screened Auto Carrier "89474" (std 0), 04	26	45
____	26099	PRR Auto Carrier "500423," 3-tier, 07		30
____	26100	PRR 1-D Tank Car, 00		27
____	26101	Lenoil 1-D Tank Car "6015," 00		34
____	26102	AEC Glow-in-Dark 1-D Tank Car, 00		58
____	26103	GATX Tank Train 1-D Tank Car "44588," 00		34
____	26107	BP Petroleum 3-D Tank Car, 00 u		105
____	26108	Lionel Visitor's Center Reefer "206482," 00 u		38
____	26109	NYC (P&LE) 1-D Tank Car, 00		42
____	26110	SP 3-D Tank Car "6415," 00-01		15
____	26111	Frisco Tank Car, 00		29
____	26112	Gulf Oil Tank Car, 00		40
____	26113	U.S. Army 1-D Tank Car, 00		35
____	26114	Service Station 1-D Tank Car (SSS), 00		32
____	26115	Lionel Centennial Tank Car, 00 u		95
____	26116	Pepe LePew 1-D Tank Car, 00 u		85
____	26118	NYC Tank Car "101900," 01		23
____	26119	Protex 3-D Tank Car "1054," 00		29
____	26120	KCS Tank Car "1229," 00		32
____	26122	Pioneer Seed Tank Car, 00 u		60
____	26123	Santa Fe Stock Car "23002," 01		35
____	26124	C&O 1-D Tank Car "X1019," 01		30
____	26125	Winter Wonderland Clear Tank Car with confetti, 00		50
____	26126	Cheerios Boxcar, 98		70
____	26127	Wellspring Capital Management Tank Car with confetti, 00 u	115	239
____	26131	Santa Fe 1-D Tank Car "335268," 02		22
____	26132	UP 1-D Tank Car "69015, 02		40
____	26133	Tootsie Roll 1-D Tank Car "26133," 02		40
____	26135	Whirlpool Tank Car, 01		60
____	26136	Southern 1-D Tank Car "8790011," 03		20
____	26137	Jack Frost 1-D Tank Car "106," 03		32
____	26138	Nestle Nesquik 1-D Tank Car "26138," 03		40
____	26139	Lionel Lines Stock Car "26139" with horses, 03		39
____	26141	Whirlpool 1-D Tank Car, 03 u		97
____	26143	Airco 1-D Tank Car "1137," 03		45
____	26144	Chessie System 1-D Tank Car "2233," 02		22
____	26145	Do It Best 1-D Tank Car, 03 u		82
____	26146	Valspar 1-D Tank Car, 03 u		95
____	26147	Diamond Chemicals 1-D Tank Car "6315," Archive Collection, 02		33
____	26149	Egg Nog 1-D Tank Car, 03		43
____	26150	Alaska 3-D Tank Car "26150," 03		23
____	26151	NP Wood-sided Reefer "26151," 03	13	29
____	26152	Morton Salt 1-D Tank Car "26152," 04		40
____	26153	Pillsbury 1-D Tank Car "26153," 04		40
____	26154	NYC 3-D Tank Car "26154," 04		25
____	26155	Pennsylvania 1-D Tank Car "26155," 04		20
____	26156	North Western Wood-sided Reefer "15356," 04		20
____	26157	Ballyhoo Brothers Circus Stock Car "26157," 04		35
____	26158	Campbell's Soup 1-D Tank Car, 04		35
____	26164	LL 1-D Tank Car "6315," girls set add-on, 03		43

MODERN 1970-2025		Exc	Like New	
26167	New Haven 1-D Tank Car, traditional, 05		27	___
26168	Conrail 3-D Tank Car, traditional, 05		27	___
26169	Santa Fe Wood-sided Reefer, traditional, 05		27	___
26170	Atlanta States Gas 1-D Tank Car, 05	20	25	___
26171	Alaska 1-D Tank Car, 05		30	___
26176	Tidmouth Milk 1-D Tank Car, 05		35	___
26179	GN 3-D Tank Car, 06	15	35	___
26180	DM&IR 1-D Tank Car "S15," 06		30	___
26181	NYC Wood-sided Reefer, 06		30	___
26193	UP 1-D Tank Car, 07		20	___
26194	Hooker Chemical 1-D Tank Car, 06		45	___
26195	PRR 3-D Tank Car "2280," 06		20	___
26196	Candy Cane 1-D Tank Car, 06		60	___
26197	D&H 1-D Tank Car "55", 07-08		35	___
26198	D&RGW 3-D Tank Car, 07		30	___
26199	WP PFE Wood-sided Reefer "55327," 07		30	___
26200	NKP Boxcar "18211," 98		35	___
26201	Operation Lifesaver Boxcar, 98		29	___
26203	D&H Boxcar "1829," 98		25	___
26204	Alaska Boxcar "10806," 98-99		35	___
26205	Rocky & Bullwinkle Boxcar, 99		36	___
26206	Curious George Boxcar, 99		40	___
26208	Vapor Records Boxcar #2, 98		60	___
26214	Celebrate the Century Stamp Boxcar, 98 u		97	___
26215	AEC Glow-in-the-Dark Boxcar, 98		105	___
26216	Cheerios Boxcar, 98 u		83	___
26218	Quaker Oats Boxcar, 98 u		475	___
26219	Ace Hardware Boxcar, 98 u		NRS	___
26220	Smuckers Boxcar, 98 u		99	___
26222	Penn Central Boxcar "125962," 99		31	___
26223	FEC Boxcar "5027," 99		31	___
26224	D&H Boxcar, 99		24	___
26228	Vapor Records Holiday Boxcar, 99 u		135	___
26230	AEC Glow-in-the-Dark Boxcar #2, 99		59	___
26232	Martin Guitar Lumber Boxcar "9823," 99		50	___
26234	NYC Boxcar, 99		29	___
26235	Valentine Boxcar, 99		40	___
26236	Aircraft Boxcar, 99		28	___
26237	Boy Scout Boxcar, 99		85	___
26238	Detroit Historical Museum Boxcar, 99		29	___
26239	M.A.D.D. Boxcar, 99		19	___
26240	RailBox Boxcar, 99-00		24	___
26241	Norfolk & Western Boxcar, 99-00		17	___
26242	D.A.R.E. Boxcar, 99		30	___
26243	Christmas Boxcar, 99		35	___
26244	Woody Woodpecker Boxcar, 99		43	___
26247	Lionel Lines Boxcar, 99		38	___
26253	Acme Explosives Boxcar, 99 u		NRS	___
26254	Keebler Boxcar, 99 u		NRS	___
26255	NYC Boxcar "200495," 99 u		30	___
26256	Salvation Army Charity Boxcar, 99		29	___
26257	Wheaties Boxcar, 99		91	___
26264	Lionel Station Boxcar, 99		44	___

MODERN 1970-2025			Exc	Like New
___	**26265**	NYC Pacemaker Boxcar, 00		30
___	**26271**	AEC Glow-in-the-Dark Boxcar, 99		62
___	**26272**	Christmas Boxcar, 00	6	42
___	**26275**	Boy Scout Boxcar, 00		55
___	**26276**	C&O Boxcar "23296," 99-00		23
___	**26277**	UP Boxcar "491050," 00		20
___	**26278**	Cap'n Crunch Christmas Boxcar, 99		694
___	**26280**	Tinsel Town Express Boxcar, music, 00		50
___	**26284**	Toy Fair Preview Boxcar, 99 u		725
___	**26285**	NYC Pacemaker Boxcar, 00		40
___	**26288**	AEC Glow-in-Dark Boxcar, 99		55
___	**26290**	SP Boxcar, 00		20
___	**26291**	Pennsylvania Boxcar "47158," 00		20
___	**26292**	Frisco Boxcar "22015," 00		20
___	**26293**	Burlington Boxcar, 00		30
___	**26294**	Centennial Express Boxcar, 00		NRS
___	**26295**	Trainmaster Boxcar, 99 u		55
___	**26296**	Service Station Boxcar Set (SSS), 00		105
___	**26298**	Taz Bobbing Boxcar, 00		70
___	**26300**	UPS Flatcar with trailers, 04		50
___	**26301**	UPS Flatcar with airplane, traditional, 05		53
___	**26302**	Troublesome Truck #1, 05		35
___	**26303**	Troublesome Truck #2, 05		35
___	**26305**	SP Auto Carrier, 2-tier, 06		30
___	**26306**	D&RGW Gondola "56135" with canisters, 06		30
___	**26307**	Chessie System Bulkhead Flatcar, 06		30
___	**26308**	Hard Rock Cafe Flatcar with billboards, 06		55
___	**26309**	Alaska Depressed Center Flatcar with cable reels, 06		50
___	**26310**	CGW Flatcar "3707" with trailer, 06		55
___	**26311**	Santa Fe Flatcar with pickups, 06		60
___	**26317**	AEC Gondola with toxic waste containers (red), 06		30
___	**26318**	AEC Gondola with toxic waste containers (white), 06		30
___	**26327**	NYC Gondola w/Canisters, 06	10	15
___	**26330**	Gondola with trees and presents, 06		60
___	**26331**	Lionel Lines Bulkhead Flatcar, 07		30
___	**26332**	CP Rail Gondola "337061" with canisters, 07		30
___	**26335**	Domino Sugar Flatcar with trailer, 07-08		60
___	**26355**	Kasey Kahne Auto Loader w/2 Autos, 07	25	80
___	**26357**	CSX Flatcar "600514" with pipes , 07-08		50
___	**26366**	REA Flatcar with trailers, 07		60
___	**26367**	Santa's Egg Nog Flatcar with container, 07		60
___	**26368**	Gondola with trees and presents, 07		60
___	**26378**	Conrail Auto Carrier "786414," 2-tier, 08		35
___	**26379**	PRR Gondola with cable reels, 08-09		35
___	**26380**	NYC Bulkhead Flatcar, 08		35
___	**26389**	ATSF Flatcar "108477" with 2 pickups, 08		60
___	**26390**	ATSF Flatcar with bulkheads, 09-10		40
___	**26391**	NYC Gondola "263910" with containers, 09		40
___	**26392**	BNSF Auto Carrier, 09		40
___	**26400**	C&NW Hopper, 07-08		35
___	**26401**	NP Ore Car "78540," 08		35
___	**26410**	Chessie System Hopper "47806," 08		35
___	**26411**	Lionel Lines Ore Car "2026," 08-09		35

		Exc	Like New	
26412	Chessie System 4-bay Hopper "60573," 08		35	___
26418	B&M Hopper, 09		40	___
26421	PRR Ore Car, 11		40	___
26422	White Pass Ice Breaker Car, 09		50	___
26423	Soo Line Ore Car, 10		40	___
26424	LV Hopper, 11		30	___
26425	UP Hopper, 11		40	___
26429	PRR Hopper, 11		40	___
26430	CP Hopper w/Coal, 11		60	___
26431	CN ACF 2-Bay Hopper "370088," 10-11		40	___
26435	B&M Ice Breaker Hopper , 11		50	___
26437	CSX Hopper, 11		40	___
26439	Central of Georgia Hopper, 11-12		40	___
26443	M&StL Ore Car "6700," 11		40	___
26445	Polar Hopper with presents, 11-14		60	___
26446	Thomas & Friends Troublesome Trucks Christmas 2-pack, 11-15		70	___
26448	U.S. Army Gondola with reels, 11		40	___
26449	CN Hi-Cube Boxcar "799346," 13		55	___
26451	DM&IR Ore Car "28003," 13		43	___
26452	PRR Hopper "153935," 13		43	___
26457	PRR Ore Car, 12		40	___
26467	Central of Georgia 2-Bay Grain Hopper, 13-14	12	30	___
26473	Lackawanna NS Heritage 2-bay Hopper, 13		55	___
26474	NYC NS Heritage Quad Hopper, 13		55	___
26477	Monopoly Electric Company Hopper, 13		65	___
26481	Boy Scouts of America Christmas Gondola, 13		65	___
26488	Hershey's Ice Breakers Hopper, 13		66	___
26489	Hershey's Chistmas Bells Boxcar, 13		65	___
26491	Pennsylvania Power & Light Gondola with canisters, 13		43	___
26492	Area 51 3-D Tank Car, 13		43	___
26493	Monopoly Water Works 3-D Tank Car, 13		65	___
26494	PRR Truss Rod Gondola with vats, 13		60	___
26495	C&NW Poultry Car, 13		60	___
26496	Lionelville Aquarium Co. Fish Food Vat Car, 13-16		65	___
26497	Bethlehem Steel Depressed Flatcar with reels, 13		43	___
26499	CN Hi-Cube Boxcar "799346," 14		55	___
26502	UP Bay Window Caboose "6517," 97		47	___
26503	ATSF High-Cupola Caboose "7606R," 97		85	___
26504	Mobil Oil Square Window Caboose "6257," 97 u		37	___
26505	Rescue Unit Caboose, 98		50	___
26506	N&W Square Window Caboose "562748", 98		15	___
26507	D&H Square Window Caboose "35707", 98		20	___
26508	Alaska Square Window Caboose "1081", 98		28	___
26509	ATSF Square Window Caboose, 98	15	20	___
26511	Quaker Oats Square Window Caboose, 98 u		52	___
26513	NYC Emergency Caboose "26505," 99		47	___
26515	Lionel Lines Bobber Caboose, 99		10	___
26516	Safari Bobber Caboose, 99 u		10	___
26519	Christmas Work Caboose "6496," 99		41	___
26520	Bethlehem Steel Work Caboose "6130" (SSS), 99		55	___
26523	Keebler Cheezit Square Window Caboose, 99 u		NRS	___
26524	NYC Square Window Caboose "295," 99 u		20	___
26526	Santa Fe Square Window Caboose "999471," 01		30	___

MODERN 1970-2025		Exc	Like New
___ 26527	Christmas Work Caboose with presents, 02		27
___ 26528	PRR Square Window Caboose "6257," 99		21
___ 26530	LL Square Window Caboose "6257," 99		22
___ 26532	NYC Square Window Caboose "296," 00		20
___ 26533	SP Square Window Caboose, 00		20
___ 26534	PRR Square Window Caboose "6257," 00		20
___ 26535	Frisco Square Window Caboose "1700," 00		20
___ 26536	Centennial Express Square Window Caboose, 00		NRS
___ 26537	Lionel Mines Square Window Caboose, 00 u		45
___ 26539	Whirlpool Square Window Caboose, 00 u		NRS
___ 26542	ACL Square Window Caboose "069," 01		31
___ 26543	GN Square Window Caboose "X66", 00-01		28
___ 26544	Alaska Square Window Caboose "1084", 01		25
___ 26545	Snap-On Square Window Caboose, 00 u		NRS
___ 26548	Pioneer Seed Square Window Caboose, 00 u		NRS
___ 26549	PRR Square Window Caboose "4977947," 01		20
___ 26550	NYC Square Window Caboose "19293," 01		20
___ 26551	Chessie System Center Cupola Caboose, 01		25
___ 26552	Santa Fe Square Window Caboose "999472," 01		25
___ 26553	C&O Center Cupola Caboose "A918," 01		30
___ 26554	Monopoly Short Line Square Window Caboose, 00 u		65
___ 26556	NH Center Cupola Caboose, 01		35
___ 26557	Farmall Square Window Caboose, 01 u		NRS
___ 26559	N&W Center Cupola Caboose "518408," 01		20
___ 26560	B&M Square Window Caboose, 01 u		20
___ 26564	Soo Line Center Cupola Caboose, 01 u		20
___ 26565	Lionel Employee Square Window Caboose, 01 u		165
___ 26566	WP Square Window Caboose "731," 02		25
___ 26568	NKP Square Window Caboose "1155," 02		25
___ 26569	Southern Square Window Caboose "252," 02		25
___ 26570	B&O Square Window Caboose "295", 02		25
___ 26572	Lionel 20th Century Square Window Caboose, 00 u		25
___ 26580	Wabash Square Window Caboose "2805," 03		22
___ 26581	C&O Square Window Caboose "C-1831," 03		20
___ 26582	L&N Square Window Caboose "318," 03		20
___ 26583	PRR Square Window Caboose "477814," 03		25
___ 26584	World of Disney Caboose, 03		40
___ 26589	PRR Square Window Caboose "982234," 03-05	15	20
___ 26590	Southern Square Window Caboose "X250," 04		50
___ 26591	Indiana RR Caboose "2001," 01		79
___ 26592	GN Caboose "X-242,", 03-04		30
___ 26593	Erie Square Window Caboose "C-101," 03	25	40
___ 26594	Ontario Northland Work Caboose "26594," 03		25
___ 26595	UP Caboose "26595," 03		18
___ 26596	NYC Caboose "17716," 04		25
___ 26597	Great Northern Caboose "X295," 04		25
___ 26598	UP Caboose "26598," 04		25
___ 26599	DM&IR Work Caboose "26599," 04		25
___ 26600	American Fire and Rescue Water Tank Car, 09-11		55
___ 26603	LV Depressed Flatcar with reels, 09		40
___ 26604	Halloween Spooky Grave Gondola, 09		58
___ 26609	NYC Gondola with Pacemaker canisters		40
___ 26612	Christmas Gifts Gondola, 09		60

		Exc	Like New	
26614	Tupelo Dairy Farms Milk Car, 10-11		60	___
26616	UP Bulkhead Flatcar with pipes, 10		40	___
26617	B&O Depressed Center Flatcar with generator, 10		40	___
26629	PRR Flatcar w/Generators, 10		35	___
26630	Soo Flatcar w/Menards trailer, 10		40	___
26631	CP Flatcar w/Log, 11		65	___
26632	CN Boat Loader, 10-11		65	___
26633	CP Flatcar w/Generators, 10-11		35	___
26634	Texas Special Flatcar w/Navajo trailers, 10		40	___
26635	US Army Flatcar w/Helicopter, 11		23	___
26636	Postwar "6830" Flatcar w/Submarine, 10 u		120	___
26637	Postwar "6640" Missile Launching Car, 10 u		65	___
26638	Pennsylvania Power & Light Flatcar w/Reels, 11		40	___
26639	Cities Service 3-Tier Auto Carrier, 11-12		40	___
26640	CN Maple Syrup Barrel Ramp Car, 11-12		40	___
26641	Coca-Cola Flatcar with trailer, 11		78	___
26642	CN Jet Snowblower, 11-12		65	___
26643	D&RGW Jet Snowblower, 11-13		65	___
26644	BNSF Flatcar with generator, 11		40	___
26645	BNSF Flatcar with trailer, 11		40	___
26646	Pennsylvania Power & Light Flatcar with transformer, 11-12		40	___
26647	IC Bulkhead Flatcar with pipes, 11		40	___
26649	Erie-Lack. Gondola with canisters, 11		40	___
26650	M&StL Flatcar with pipes, 11		40	___
26651	ATSF Scout Heavyweight Passenger Car 2-pack (std O), 12		280	___
26652	NYC Gondola with canisters, 11		40	___
26653	PC Flatcar with generator, 11		35	___
26654	Boy Scouts Flatcar with Pinewood Derby Kit, 11-13	33	75	___
26660	Coca-Cola Vat Car, 11-16		75	___
26661	Reindeer Feed Barrel Ramp Car, 09		60	___
26665	Hershey's Special Dark Flatcar with trailer, 11		60	___
26666	Boy Scouts Flatcar with trailer, 11		70	___
26667	Flatcar with Santa's sleigh, 12		70	___
26668	Strasburg Flatcar with wheels, 11		55	___
26669	U.S. Navy Flatcar with Shark submarine, 12-13		60	___
26673	B&M Flatcar with Milk Tank, 12	33	60	___
26674	AT&SF Barrel Ramp Car, 10-11	10	20	___
26675	Monopoly Auto Loader, 12		80	___
26676	Heinz Baked Beans Vat Car, 12		60	___
26677	LIRR Gondola with canisters, 12		40	___
26679	ATSF Gondola with reels, 12-13		55	___
26683	Christmas Track Maintenance Car, 12-13		67	___
26684	Georgia Power Flatcar w/Generator, 12		45	___
26685	Flatcar with Santa's plane, 12		55	___
26686	Hershey's Cocoa Vat Car, 12-13		63	___
26687	Lone Ranger Gondola with gunpowder vats, 12-14		65	___
26691	UP Flatcar w/Trailers, 12-13	39	66	___
26692	UP Gondola w/Coil Covers, 12-13	28	40	___
26693	Hershey's Krackel Piggyback Flatcar with trailer, 12-13		78	___
26694	Carnegie Science Center Flatcar with submarine, 13	50	73	___
26695	NJ Transit Flatcar "9907" w/Trailer, 12	36	55	___
26696	NJ Transit Gondola "9412" w/Wood ties, 12	40	75	___
26699	PRR Flatcar with wheel load, 12-14		55	___

	MODERN 1970-2025		Exc	Like New
___	**26706**	Lighted Christmas Boxcar, 00		47
___	**26707**	Lionel Steel Operating Welding Flatcar "1108," 00		90
___	**26708**	ABC Monday Night Football TV Car, 01		50
___	**26709**	Postwar "6511" Flatcar w/Psychedelic submarine, 99		32
___	**26710**	Southern Stock Car, Carsounds, 99		95
___	**26712**	Churchill Downs Horse Car "6473," 99-00		38
___	**26713**	Shay Log Car 3-pack, 99		113
___	**26714**	Westside Lumber Flatcar with logs (std O), 99		45
___	**26715**	Westside Lumber Flatcar with logs (std O), 99		45
___	**26716**	Westside Lumber Flatcar with logs (std O), 99		45
___	**26717**	Orion Star Boxcar 9600, 00		30
___	**26718**	Christmas Boxcar, RailSounds, 00		160
___	**26719**	Bobbing Ghost Halloween Boxcar, 00		46
___	**26721**	Lionel Lines Coal Dump Car "3379," 00		31
___	**26722**	Lionel Lines Log Dump Car "3351," 00		31
___	**26723**	Lion Chasing Trainer Gondola "3444," 00		49
___	**26724**	Veterans Day Boxcar, 00		70
___	**26725**	NYC Jumping Hobo Boxcar "88160," 00		38
___	**26726**	T. Rex Bobbing Boxcar, 00		41
___	**26727**	San Francisco City Lights Boxcar, 00		50
___	**26736**	Lionel Birthday Boxcar, 02 u		40
___	**26737**	Operating Santa Gondola "6462," 00 u		65
___	**26738**	Lionel Mines Animated Gondola, 00 u		90
___	**26739**	Santa and Snowman Boxcar, 00		46
___	**26740**	Reindeer Car, 00		43
___	**26741**	Operating Santa Boxcar, 00		50
___	**26743**	Christmas Reindeer Car, 01		55
___	**26745**	Traveling Aquarium Car "506," 01		70
___	**26746**	Bobbing Vampire Boxcar, 01		46
___	**26747**	Halloween Bats Aquarium Car, 01		75
___	**26748**	T&P Operating Hopper Car "9699," 01		38
___	**26749**	Alaska Log Dump Car, 01		29
___	**26751**	Chessie Coal Dump Car, 01		27
___	**26752**	Christmas Aquarium Car, 01	20	55
___	**26753**	Christmas Operating Dump Car, 01		43
___	**26757**	Operating Barrel Car "35621," 00		55
___	**26758**	AEC Nuclear Gondola "719766," 01		95
___	**26759**	Postwar "3459" Coal Dump Car, 02		60
___	**26760**	Postwar "3461" Log Dump Car, 02		60
___	**26761**	AEC Security Caboose 3535, 01		64
___	**26762**	Postwar "3665" Minuteman Car, 01	24	55
___	**26763**	Postwar "6448" Exploding Boxcar, 01		40
___	**26764**	Bethlehem Steel Operating Welding Car, 01		75
___	**26765**	Postwar "3370" Sheriff and Outlaw Car, 01-02	40	49
___	**26766**	Priority Mail Operating Boxcar, 01-02		32
___	**26768**	Postwar "6520" Searchlight Car, 02		49
___	**26769**	Santa Fe Crane Car "199793," CC, 03		255
___	**26770**	Wabash Brakeman Car "3424," 01		70
___	**26773**	Chessie Searchlight Car, 01		20
___	**26774**	Santa Fe Log Dump Car, 01		25
___	**26775**	U.S. Army Searchlight Car, 00		50
___	**26776**	U.S. Army Operating Boxcar "26413," 00		55
___	**26777**	U.S. Flag Boxcar, 01 u		250

MODERN 1970-2025		Exc	Like New	
26779	Burlington Operating Hopper "189312," 02		40	___
26780	Postwar "3376" Bronx Zoo Giraffe Car, 02	25	36	___
26781	Postwar "3540" Operating Radar Car, 02		35	___
26782	Lenny the Lion Bobbing Head Car, 02		38	___
26784	Stingray Express Aquarium Car, 02		35	___
26785	Flatcar with powerboat, 02		31	___
26786	Lionelville Operating Parade Car, 02		40	___
26787	Erie Jumping Hobo Boxcar, 01-02		43	___
26788	Christmas Music Boxcar, 02		46	___
26789	Kiss Kringle Chase Gondola, 02		35	___
26790	Lighted Christmas Boxcar, 02		34	___
26791	UP Animated Gondola, 02	40	50	___
26792	REA Operating Boxcar "6299," 03		39	___
26793	Alaska Extension Searchlight Car, 01		44	___
26794	Postwar "6352" PFE Ice Car, 01-02		85	___
26795	NYC Stock Car "3121," Cattle Sounds, 02		50	___
26796	Lionel Farms Poultry Dispatch Car, 01		55	___
26797	GN Log Dump Car "60011," 02		48	___
26798	Bethlehem Steel Coal Dump Car "26798," 02		70	___
26801	Jumping Bart Simpson Boxcar, 04		44	___
26802	Simpsons Animated Gondola, 04		46	___
26803	Santa Fe Derrick Car "26803," 04		25	___
26804	NYC Coal Dump Car "26804," 04		36	___
26805	Pennsylvania Log Dump Car "26805," 04		24	___
26806	Pillsbury Operating Boxcar "3428," Archive Collection, 04		40	___
26807	Blue Chip Line Motorized Animated Gondola, 04		40	___
26808	Egg Nog Barrel Car, 04		55	___
26809	Santa's Extension Searchlight Car, 04		42	___
26810	NYC Operating Searchlight Car, 05		33	___
26811	Pennsylvania Coal Dump Car, 05		33	___
26812	Santa Fe Log Dump Car, 05		33	___
26813	Lionel Lines Derrick Car, 05	17	39	___
26814	NYC Walking Brakeman Car "174226," 05		40	___
26815	PRR "Workin' on the Railroad" Boxcar "24255," 05		42	___
26816	REA Boxcar, steam TrainSounds, 05		105	___
26817	Alaska Boxcar, diesel TrainSounds, 05		145	___
26818	Christmas Music Boxcar, 05		63	___
26819	Holiday Animated Gondola, 05		55	___
26820	Penguin Transport Aquarium Car, 05		60	___
26821	NP Moe & Joe Lumber Flatcar, 05		75	___
26824	Elvis Presley Searchlight Car, 04		40	___
26825	GN Log Dump Car, 04		35	___
26826	Alaska Searchlight Car, 05		40	___
26827	UPS Operating Boxcar "9237," Archive Collection, 05		62	___
26828	Tornado Chaser Radar Tracking Car, 05		63	___
26829	UPS Holiday Operating Boxcar, 05	30	66	___
26832	Lionel Lines Tender, TrainSounds, 07-08		105	___
26833	Wellspring Radar Car, 04	40	75	___
26834	PFE Ice Car "20042" (std O), 05-06		63	___
26835	MOW Track Cleaning Car, 05		140	___
26836	Halloween Boxcar, SpookySounds, 05		105	___
26841	PRR Log Dump Car, 05		27	___
26842	NYC Coal Dump Car, 05		27	___

	No.	Description	Exc	Like New
___	**26843**	Christmas Flatcar w/Handcar, 06		60
___	**26844**	Christmas Reindeer Transport Car, 06		30
___	**26845**	Southern Derrick Car, 06		35
___	**26846**	GN Coal Dump Car, 06		38
___	**26847**	C&O Coal Dump Car, 06-07		80
___	**26848**	Lionel Lines Moe & Joe Flatcar, 06		80
___	**26849**	SP Log Dump Car, 06-07		80
___	**26850**	D&RGW Searchlight Car, 06		75
___	**26851**	WM Log Dump Car, 06		35
___	**26852**	Postwar "3562-25" Santa Fe Barrel Car, 06		75
___	**26853**	SeaWorld Aquarium Car, 06		75
___	**26854**	UP Walking Brakeman Car, 06-07		75
___	**26855**	Halloween Animated Gondola, 06		65
___	**26856**	Christmas Chase Gondola, 06		65
___	**26857**	Alien Radar Tracking Car, 06		65
___	**26858**	Christmas Music Boxcar, 06		65
___	**26859**	Christmas Parade Boxcar, 06		75
___	**26860**	B&O Boxcar "466035," steam TrainSounds (std O), 06-07		75
___	**26861**	Santa Fe Boxcar, diesel TrainSounds (std O), 06-07		110
___	**26862**	Hard Rock Cafe Boxcar, 06		35
___	**26863**	Railway Express Operating Milk Car with platform, 06		140
___	**26864**	Domino Sugar Operating Boxcar, 06-07		40
___	**26865**	CP Animated Caboose, 06-07	35	80
___	**26866**	BN Searchlight Car, 06		35
___	**26867**	Groom Lake Boxcar, AlienSounds, 06-07		110
___	**26868**	U.S. Steel Operating Welding Car, 06		75
___	**26869**	REA Jumping Hobo Boxcar, 06-07		70
___	**26870**	Christmas Dump Car with presents, 06		80
___	**26871**	PRR Tender, steam TrainSounds (std O), 06		105
___	**26872**	U.S. Army Security Car, 06		75
___	**26876**	Missile Firing Trail Car, 06		75
___	**26877**	U.S. Army Missile Launch Sound Car, 06-07		190
___	**26881**	Neiman Marcus Holiday Musical Boxcar, 05		90
___	**26882**	NYC Animated Caboose "17719," 06		120
___	**26883**	Weyerhaeuser Timber Co. Log Dump Car "117," 06		25
___	**26884**	Hammacher Schlemmer Music Boxcar, 08		45
___	**26885**	WC Log Dump Car, 06		50
___	**26886**	Lionel Lines Log Dump Car, 06	20	53
___	**26887**	Postwar "6470" Exploding Target Car, 06		120
___	**26888**	Weyerhaeuser Timber Co. Log Dump Car "115," 06	11	40
___	**26889**	Weyerhaeuser Timber Co. Log Dump Car "116," 06		40
___	**26891**	PRR Coal Dump Car, 05		30
___	**26897**	Great Western Flatcar with handcar, 07		65
___	**26898**	NYC Log Dump Car, 05		25
___	**26905**	Bethlehem Steel Gondola "6462" with canisters, 98		29
___	**26906**	SP Flatcar "9823" with Corgi '57 Chevy, 98		40
___	**26908**	TTUX Flatcar "6300" with Apple trailers, 98		70
___	**26913**	East St. Louis Gondola "9820," 98		29
___	**26920**	Union Pacific Die-cast Ore Car "64861," 97		70
___	**26921**	Union Pacific Die-cast Ore Car "64862," 97		55
___	**26922**	Union Pacific Die-cast Ore Car "64863", 97		65
___	**26923**	Union Pacific Die-cast Ore Car "64864," 97		55
___	**26924**	Union Pacific Die-cast Ore Car "64865," 97		55

MODERN 1970-2025		Exc	Like New	
26925	Union Pacific Die-cast Ore Car "64866," 97		60	____
26926	Union Pacific Die-cast Ore Car, 98		55	____
26927	Union Pacific Die-cast Ore Car, 98		55	____
26928	Union Pacific Die-cast Ore Car, 98		55	____
26929	Union Pacific Die-cast Ore Car, 98		40	____
26936	Die-cast Tank Car 4-pack, 98		335	____
26937	Die-cast Hopper 4-pack, 98	75	325	____
26938	NYC Reefer, 99		80	____
26940	Rio Grande Stock Car "37710," 99		80	____
26946	D&H Semi-Scale Hopper "9642"		85	____
26947	Gulf Die-cast Tank Car, 98		120	____
26948	P&LE Die-cast Hopper, 98		65	____
26949	NP Flatcar with trailer "6424-2017," 98		47	____
26950	NP Flatcar with trailer "6424-2016," 98		47	____
26951	TTX Flatcar "475185" with PRR trailer, 98		55	____
26952	J.B. Hunt Flatcar with trailer, 98		40	____
26953	J.B. Hunt Flatcar with trailer, 98		40	____
26954	J.B. Hunt Flatcar with trailer, 98		40	____
26955	J.B. Hunt Flatcar with trailer, 98		40	____
26956	C&O Gondola (027), 98-99		15	____
26957	Delaware & Hudson Flatcar with stakes, 98		20	____
26971	Lionel Steel 16-wheel Depressed Center Flatcar, 98		135	____
26972	Pony Express Animated Gondola, 98		36	____
26973	Getty Die-cast Tank Car 3-pack, 98		270	____
26974	Getty Die-cast 1-D Tank Car "4003," 98		80	____
26975	Getty Die-cast 1-D Tank Car "4004," 98	45	125	____
26976	Getty Die-cast 1-D Tank Car "4005," 98		80	____
26977	Sinclair Die-cast Tank Car 3-pack, 98		275	____
26978	Sinclair Tank Car UTLX "64026," 98		105	____
26979	Sinclair Tank Car UTLX "64027," 98		85	____
26980	Sinclair Tank UTLX "64028," 98		90	____
26981	Gulf Die-cast Tank Car 2-pack, 99		165	____
26985	B&O Die-cast Hopper 2-pack, 99		160	____
26987	Chessie System (B&O) Die-cast 4-bay Hopper "235154," 99		90	____
26991	Lionelville Ladder Fire Car, 99		47	____
26992	NYC Reefer, 99		75	____
26993	NYC Reefer, 99		85	____
26994	NYC Reefer, 99		135	____
26995	Rio Grande Stock Car "37714," 99		80	____
26996	Rio Grande Stock Car "37715," 99		80	____
26997	Rio Grande Stock Car "37716," 99		80	____
27000	C&EI Offset Hopper "97393" (std 0), 07		65	____
27001	Erie Offset Hopper "28001" (std 0), 07		65	____
27002	Frisco Offset Hopper "92399" (std 0), 07		65	____
27003	Chessie System Offset Hopper "234355" (std 0), 07		65	____
27016	UP PS-2 Covered Hopper "1312" (std 0), 07-08		60	____
27019	Imco PS-2 Covered Hopper "41001" (std 0), 07-08		60	____
27022	PC PS-2 Covered Hopper "74217" (std 0), 07		60	____
27025	NYC PS-2 Covered Hopper "883180" (std 0), 07		60	____
27026	NYC PS-2 Covered Hopper "883181" (std 0), 07		60	____
27027	NYC PS-2 Covered Hopper "883182" (std 0), 07		60	____
27028	C&O Offset Hopper "27028" (std 0), 07		65	____
27029	ATSF Offset Hopper 3-pack (std 0), 08-09		200	____

			Exc	Like New
____	**27030**	Monon Offset Hopper 3-pack (std O), 08-09		200
____	**27031**	MoPac Offset Hopper 3-pack (std O), 08-09		200
____	**27032**	NYC Offset Hopper 3-pack (std O), 08-09		200
____	**27033**	Chessie System PS-2 Hopper 3-pack (std O), 08-09		180
____	**27034**	Nickel Plate Road PS-2 Hopper 3-pack (std O), 08-09		180
____	**27053**	CB&Q ACF 2-bay Covered Hopper "183925" (std O), 08-09		55
____	**27059**	Bakelite Plastics PS-2 Hopper "61445" (std O), 10-11		70
____	**27061**	Clinchfield Freight Car 2-pack (std O), 10		150
____	**27064**	PRR Flatcar with PRR piggyback trailers (std O), 12		98
____	**27065**	SP Flatcar with SP piggyback trailers (std O), 12		98
____	**27066**	IC Flatcar with IC piggyback trailers (std O), 12		98
____	**27067**	C&O Flatcar with REA piggyback trailers (std O), 12		98
____	**27068**	ATSF Flatcar with Santa Fe piggyback trailers (std O), 12		98
____	**27069**	Conrail PS-2 Hopper "878330" (std O), 12-13		70
____	**27070**	N&W Scale Offset Hopper "279850" (std O), 12		70
____	**27071**	CSX 4-Bay Covered Hopper "256300" (std O), 12		90
____	**27072**	C&NW Scale PS-1 Boxcar "7" (std O), 12-13		70
____	**27073**	PRR Scale Offset Hopper 3-pack (std O), 12		200
____	**27077**	L&N Scale Offset Hopper "88494" (std O), 12-13		70
____	**27078**	Frisco Scale 3-Bay Open Hopper "88299" (std O), 12-14		75
____	**27079**	NYC Boxcar, 09		30
____	**27080**	Lionel Vision Boxcar, 14-15		60
____	**27081**	BN PS-2 Hopper "424796" (std O), 12-13		70
____	**27082**	Grand Trunk 4-Bay Covered Hopper "38111" (std O), 12		90
____	**27083**	RI PS-2 Hopper "500751" (std O), 12-13		70
____	**27084**	Seaboard 8000-gallon 1-D Tank Car "27084" (std O), 12		70
____	**27085**	Wabash PS-2 Hopper "30425" (std O), 12-13		70
____	**27086**	Grand Trunk 60' Boxcar "383575" (std O), 12, 14		85
____	**27087**	CN 60' Boxcar "799424" (std O), 12, 14		85
____	**27088**	MKT PS-5 Gondola "12447" (std O), 12-13		65
____	**27089**	LIRR PS-5 Gondola "6053" (std O), 12		65
____	**27090**	NP 8000-gallon 1-D Tank Car "27090" (std O), 12		70
____	**27091**	WM Scale 3-Bay Open Hopper "85125" (std O), 12		80
____	**27092**	CSX Heritage 60' Boxcar "176740" (std O), 12		85
____	**27093**	Boy Scouts PS-2 Hopper "2013" (std O), 13		70
____	**27094**	BNSF PS-2 Hopper 2-pack (std O), 13-14		130
____	**27095**	KCS PS-2 Hopper 2-pack (std O), 13		130
____	**27096**	C&NW PS-2 Hopper 2-pack (std O), 13		130
____	**27099**	North Pole Central PS-1 Boxcar "125025" (std O), 13		70
____	**27100**	C&NW PS-2CD 4427 Hopper "450669" (std O), 04		40
____	**27101**	Morton Salt PS-2CD 4427 Hopper "504" (std O), 04		43
____	**27102**	Pillsbury PS-2CD 4427 Hopper "3980" (std O), 04		42
____	**27103**	Soo Line PS-2CD 4427 Hopper "70207" (std O), 04		49
____	**27104**	Wabash Cylindrical Hopper "33007" (std O), 03		43
____	**27105**	PC Cylindrical Hopper "884312" (std O), 03		42
____	**27113**	Govt. of Canada Cylindrical Hopper, 04-05		60
____	**27114**	Canadian National Cylindrical Hopper, 04-05		60
____	**27115**	D&H 3-bay ACF Hopper "3454" (std O), 05-06		65
____	**27116**	NYC 3-bay ACF Hopper "886270" (std O), 05-06		65
____	**27117**	DM&IR 3-bay ACF Hopper "5017" (std O), 05		65
____	**27118**	WP 3-bay ACF Hopper "11774" (std O), 05-06		65
____	**27119**	Firestone 3-Bay ACF Hopper (std O), 05	35	45
____	**27129**	N&W 3-bay ACF Hopper "10717" (std O), 06		70

MODERN 1970-2025		Exc	Like New	
27130	PRR 3-bay ACF Hopper "180658" (std 0), 06		70	____
27131	Conrail 3-bay ACF Hopper "473877" (std 0), 06		70	____
27132	UP 3-bay ACF Hopper "18137" (std 0), 06		70	____
27133	MILW PS-2CD Hopper "98606" (std 0), 06		70	____
27134	BNSF PS-2CD Hopper "414367" (std 0), 06		70	____
27135	N&W PS-2CD Hopper "71573" (std 0), 06		70	____
27142	CP Rail 3-bay Hopper, 06		48	____
27146	CP Soo 3-bay Hopper, 06		48	____
27165	C&O 3-bay Hopper "86912" (std 0), 07		70	____
27166	Pennsylvania Power & Light 3-bay Hopper "347" (std 0), 07		70	____
27167	Santa Fe 3-bay Hopper "178558" (std 0), 07-08		70	____
27168	C&NW 3-bay Hopper "135000" (std 0), 07		70	____
27169	CN Cylindrical Hopper "370708" (std 0), 06		65	____
27172	IMC Canada Cylindrical Hopper "45726" (std 0), 06		65	____
27177	Union Starch Cylindrical Hopper 3-pack (std 0), 08		210	____
27186	PRR Cylindrical Hopper 3-pack (std 0), 08		210	____
27187	TH&B Cylindrical Hopper 3-pack (std 0), 08		210	____
27188	KCS 3-bay Covered Hopper 3-pack, 08		225	____
27189	BNSF 3-bay Aluminum Covered Hopper 3-pack, 08		225	____
27190	C&NW PS-2CD Covered Hopper 3-pack (std 0), 08		225	____
27191	RI PS-2CD Covered Hopper 3-pack, 08		225	____
27192	NP PS-2CD Covered Hopper 3-pack (std 0), 08		225	____
27203	NYC DD Boxcar "75509" (std 0), 05		63	____
27204	Grand Trunk Western DD Boxcar "596377" (std 0), 05		63	____
27205	D&RGW DD Boxcar "63798" (std 0), 05		40	____
27206	UP PS 60' Boxcar "960342" (std 0), 08		75	____
27207	IC PS 60' Boxcar "44295" (std 0), 08		75	____
27208	ATSF PS 60' Boxcar "37287" (std 0), 08		75	____
27209	D&RGW PS 60' Boxcar "63835" (std 0), 08		75	____
27210	PRR PS-1 Boxcar "47009" (std 0), 05		60	____
27211	MKT PS-1 Boxcar "948" (std 0), 05		60	____
27212	Rutland PS-1 Boxcar "358" (std 0), 05		60	____
27213	N&W DD Boxcar, 05		35	____
27214	Chessie System PS-1 Boxcar "23770" (std 0), 06		60	____
27215	Rock Island PS-1 Boxcar "57607" (std 0), 06		60	____
27216	Erie-Lack. PS-1 Boxcar "84433" (std 0), 06		60	____
27217	Frisco PS-1 Boxcar "17826" (std 0), 06		59	____
27218	Santa Fe DD Boxcar "9870" (std 0), 06-07		70	____
27219	GN DD Boxcar "35449" (std 0), 06-07		70	____
27220	L&N DD Boxcar "41237" (std 0), 06-07		70	____
27221	CB&Q DD Boxcar "48500" (std 0), 06-07		70	____
27224	CGW PS-1 Boxcar "5180" (std 0), 06		60	____
27225	WP PS-1 Boxcar "19528" (std 0), 06		60	____
27226	NH PS-1 Boxcar "32196" (std 0), 06		60	____
27227	UP PS-1 Boxcar "100306" (std 0), 06		60	____
27228	UP DD Boxcar "454400" (std 0), 07		70	____
27229	Nickel Plate Road DD Boxcar "87100" (std 0), 08		70	____
27230	LV DD Boxcar "8505" (std 0), 08	21	70	____
27231	GN USRA Double-sheathed Boxcar (std 0), 07		65	____
27232	UP USRA Double-sheathed Boxcar (std 0), 07		65	____
27233	Cotton Belt USRA Double-sheathed Boxcar (std 0), 07		65	____
27234	C&NW USRA Double-sheathed Boxcar (std 0), 07		65	____
27235	Railbox Boxcar "10011" (std 0), 07		55	____

			Exc	Like New
____	**27236**	D&RGW DD Boxcar "63799" (std 0), 07		35
____	**27237**	MP USRA Double-sheathed Boxcar (std 0), 07		65
____	**27238**	Nickel Plate DD Boxcar "87101" (std 0), 07		35
____	**27239**	SP DD Boxcar "232852" with auto rack (std 0), 08		75
____	**27240**	Pere Marquette DD Boxcar with auto rack (std 0), 08		75
____	**27241**	C&O PS-1 Boxcar "18719," 08		60
____	**27242**	LV PS-1 Boxcar "62080," 08		60
____	**27243**	SP PS-1 Boxcar "128131," 08		60
____	**27244**	GN PS-1 Boxcar "39404," 08	36	60
____	**27246**	SP Double-sheathed Boxcar "133" (std 0), 08		70
____	**27247**	MP Double-sheathed Boxcar "45111" (std 0), 08		70
____	**27249**	GN Express Boxcar "2500" (std 0), 08		65
____	**27250**	CN Express Boxcar "11061" (std 0), 08-09		65
____	**27251**	WP Express Boxcar "220116," 08-09		65
____	**27254**	Western Pacific UP Heritage Boxcar (std 0), 09-11, 13		85
____	**27259**	PRR ACF Stock Car "128988" (std 0), 10		70
____	**27260**	ATSF Tool Car "190021" (std 0), 09-10		80
____	**27261**	D&RGW Double-sheathed Boxcar "3282," 09		80
____	**27263**	Polar Railroad PS-1 Boxcar, 09		70
____	**27264**	C&O Double-sheathed Boxcar "3502," 10		80
____	**27265**	Virginian PS-1 Boxcar "63300" (std 0), 10		70
____	**27266**	PRR Express Boxcar "504141" (std 0), 10		70
____	**27267**	SP UP Heritage 60' Boxcar "6991" (std 0), 10		85
____	**27268**	NYC DD Boxcar "47100" (std 0), 10		70
____	**27270**	B&O PS-1 Boxcar 2-pack (std 0), 10-11		140
____	**27273**	Ann Arbor PS-1 Boxcar "1314" (std 0), 11		70
____	**27274**	Polar Railroad Double-sheathed Boxcar "1201," 10		70
____	**27275**	SP Overnight PS-1 Boxcar "97938" (std 0), 10		70
____	**27276**	NKP Double-sheathed Boxcar "10580" (std 0), 10-11		70
____	**27277**	WP Scale PS-1 Boxcar "1925" (std 0), 11		70
____	**27278**	Cryo-Trans Trans-Mechanical Reefer (std 0), 10		95
____	**27282**	UP DD Boxcar "163100" (std 0), 10		70
____	**27283**	Postwar Scale Boxcar 2-pack, 10		140
____	**27286**	Postwar Scale 6464 Boxcar 2-pack #2, 11-13		140
____	**27287**	LV Boxcar and Caboose Set (std 0), 10-11		160
____	**27289**	Jersey Central Boxcar and Caboose Set (std 0), 10-11		160
____	**27291**	PRR Double-sheathed Boxcar "539335" (std 0), 10-11		70
____	**27294**	ATSF 57' Mechanical Reefer "3006" (std 0), 10		85
____	**27296**	Cryo-Trans 57' Mechanical Reefer (std 0), 11		85
____	**27299**	WM Steel-sided Reefer (std 0), 11		80
____	**27300**	Western Dairy General American Milk Car (std 0), 06		65
____	**27305**	GN Steel-sided Reefer "70290" (std 0), 06		65
____	**27306**	Santa Fe Steel-sided Reefer "3494" (std 0), 06		42
____	**27307**	Pepper Packing Steel-sided Reefer "2330" (std 0), 06		65
____	**27327**	BNSF Mechanical Reefer "798870" (std 0), 07		70
____	**27328**	SP Fruit Express Reefer "456465" (std 0), 07-09		70
____	**27329**	UP Fruit Express Reefer "55962" (std 0), 07		70
____	**27330**	Great Northern WFE Reefer "8873" (std 0), 07-08		70
____	**27331**	Alderney Dairy General American Milk Car (std 0), 07		65
____	**27332**	Freeport General American Milk Car (std 0), 07		65
____	**27345**	Milwaukee Road 40' Steel-sided Reefer "5317" (std 0), 12	54	80
____	**27349**	ADM Steel-sided Reefer "7019" (std 0), 07		65
____	**27350**	National Car Steel-sided Reefer "2430" (std 0), 07		48

MODERN 1970-2025		Exc	Like New	
27355	NYC Steel-sided Reefer "2570" (std O), 07-08		65	____
27358	Dubuque Steel-sided Reefer "63648" (std O), 07		65	____
27361	PFE Wood-sided Reefer "97680" (std O), 06		65	____
27364	Erie URTX Steel-sided Reefer (std O), 11		80	____
27365	Sheffield Farms Milk Car 2-pack (std O), 08		140	____
27368	CNJ 40' Steel-sided Reefer "1443" (std O), 12		80	____
27369	Borden's Milk Car 2-pack (std O), 08		140	____
27372	PFE Steel-sided Reefer 3-pack (std O), 08		210	____
27373	MILW Reefer 3-pack (std O), 08-09		225	____
27374	Alaska Reefer 3-pack (std O), 08-09		225	____
27375	NP Reefer 3-pack (std O), 08-09		225	____
27394	Detroit, Toledo & Ironton Steel-sided Reefer (std O), 09-10		80	____
27395	Amtrak ExpressTrak Baggage Car, 10		75	____
27396	C&NW UP Heritage Mechanical Reefer (std O), 10		85	____
27409	ATSF Water Tank Car "100844" (std O), 09-10		70	____
27410	30,000-gallon Ethanol Tank Car 3-pack, sound, 09		270	____
27411	30,000-gallon Ethanol Tank Car 3-pack, 09		210	____
27412	GATX TankTrain Car "53782" (std O), 10		70	____
27418	PRR NS Heritage Unibody Tank Car (std O), 10		70	____
27419	Pennsylvania Power & Light 3-bay Open Hopper, 08		80	____
27421	MoPac UP Heritage Cylindrical Hopper (std O), 09-11		80	____
27422	N&W 3-bay Open Hopper "1776" (std O), 09		80	____
27424	Penn Central PS-2 Hopper "440774" (std O), 10-11		80	____
27425	Saskatchewan Cylindrical Hopper "397015" (std O), 09		80	____
27426	Stourbridge Lion Anthracite Coal Car 2-pack, 09-10		130	____
27429	MKT UP Heritage PS2-CD Hopper (std O), 09		80	____
27431	CSX B&O Quad Hopper, 11		50	____
27432	UP 3-bay Open Hopper "78123" (std O), 10		80	____
27433	Conrail NS Heritage Cylindrical Hopper (std O), 10-11		80	____
27434	D&RGW UP Heritage PS2-CD Hopper (std O), 10		80	____
27435	Polar Railroad Tank Car, 09		70	____
27436	Alberta Cylindrical Hopper "396363" (std O), 10		80	____
27438	Virginian NS Heritage 3-bay Open Hopper (std O), 10		80	____
27439	NS Heritage Unibody Tank Car "14098" (std O), 10		70	____
27440	BN Cylindrical Hopper "458456" (std O), 10		80	____
27441	D&M PS-2 Hopper "6133" (std O), 11		70	____
27445	N&W NS Heritage PS-2CD Hopper (std O), 10		80	____
27446	Southern NS Heritage Cylindrical Hopper (std O), 10		80	____
27448	PRR NS Heritage 3-Bay Open Hopper (std O), 11		80	____
27449	UP Boy Scouts 100th Anniversary Cylindrical Hopper (std O), 11		80	____
27450	NW NS Heritage 3-Bay Open Hopper (std O), 11		80	____
27451	Conrail NS Heritage Unibody 1-D Tank Car (std O), 11		70	____
27452	PRR NS Heritage PS-1 Boxcar "45540" (std O), 11		70	____
27453	NS Heritage PS-1 Boxcar "67850" (std O), 11		70	____
27454	CP Cylindrical Hopper (std O), 11	48	77	____
27455	Amtrak 57' Mechanical Reefer (std O), 11		85	____
27456	Soo Line PS2 Covered Hopper "70702" (std O), 11		70	____
27457	NS 3-Bay Open Hopper "148028" (std O), 11		80	____
27458	UP Mechanical Reefer "457244" (std O), 11		85	____
27459	WP DD Boxcar "19404" (std O), 11		70	____
27460	M&StL Double-sheathed Boxcar "26002" (std O), 11		70	____
27461	UP ACF 4-Bay Covered Hopper "91341" (std O), 11		85	____
27462	Chessie ACF 4-Bay Covered Hopper "601878" (std O), 11		85	____

	MODERN 1970-2025		Exc	Like New
____	27463	PRR ACF 3-Bay Covered Hopper "259900" (std O), 11-12		80
____	27464	BNSF ACF 3-Bay Covered Hopper "453403" (std O), 11		80
____	27465	CSX 89' Auto Rack Car "604540" (std O), 12-13		150
____	27466	UP 89' Auto Rack Car (std O), 12-13		150
____	27467	ATSF 89' Auto Rack Car (std O), 12-13		150
____	27468	Grand Truck 89' Auto Rack Car (std O), 12-13		150
____	27469	Frisco Cylindrical Hopper "81021" (std O), 11		80
____	27470	MKT Scale 1-D Tank Car (std O), 11		70
____	27471	DT&I 3-Bay Hopper "2070" (std O), 11		80
____	27472	CP Scale 1-D Tank Car "9943" (std O), 11		70
____	27473	Conrail 89' Auto Rack Car "456249" (std O), 12		150
____	27474	SP Cylindrical Hopper "491020" (std O), 11		80
____	27475	Lionelville & Western Scale 1-D Tank Car "2747" (std O), 11		80
____	27476	U.S. Army Scale 1-D Tank Car (std O), 11		70
____	27477	D&RGW 3-Bay Hopper "14901" (std O), 11		80
____	27478	NYC 3-Bay Hopper "922158" (std O), 11		80
____	27479	BN Scale 3-Bay Open Hopper "516400" (std O), 12		80
____	27480	NKP Scale Offset Hopper "33060" (std O), 12		70
____	27481	W&LE Scale Offset Hopper "62240" (std O), 12		70
____	27482	CP Scale Offset Hopper "354000" (std O), 12	33	69
____	27483	SP Unibody 1-D Tank Car "67200" (std O), 12		70
____	27484	D&H Unibody 1-D Tank Car "59" (std O), 12		70
____	27485	KCS Unibody 1-D Tank Car "996" (std O), 12		70
____	27488	Clinchfield CSX Heritage 3-Bay Open Hopper (std O), 12		80
____	27489	Chessie System CSX Heritage 3-Bay Open Hopper (std O), 12		80
____	27490	ATSF 3-Bay Covered Hopper "314000" (std O), 12-13		85
____	27491	GN 3-Bay Covered Hopper "171400" (std O), 12		85
____	27492	CN 89' Auto Rack Car "710833" (std O), 12		150
____	27493	CN PS-4 Flatcar with piggyback trailers (std O), 12		98
____	27494	CN PS-4 Flatcar with piggyback trailers (std O), 12		98
____	27495	CN PS-4 Flatcar with piggyback trailers (std O), 12		98
____	27496	Polar PS-2 Covered Hopper "1245" (std O), 12, 14		70
____	27497	UP Offset Hopper "74556" (std O), 12		80
____	27498	DM&I 8000-gallon 1-D Tank Car "S19" (std O), 12		70
____	27499	Monon Scale PS-1 Boxcar "916" (std O), 12		70
____	27510	WP PS-4 Flatcar "2001" (std O), 05-06		53
____	27511	P&LE PS-4 Flatcar "1154" (std O), 05-06		35
____	27512	Reading PS-4 Flatcar "9314" (std O), 05		53
____	27513	UP 40' Flatcar "51219" (std O), 06		55
____	27514	CP 40' Flatcar "307401" (std O), 06		55
____	27515	Pennsylvania 40' Flatcar "473567" (std O), 06		55
____	27516	N&W 40' Flatcar "32900" (std O), 06		55
____	27517	NP PS-4 Flatcar "62829" with trailers (std O), 06		85
____	27518	C&NW PS-4 Flatcar "44503" with trailers (std O), 06		85
____	27519	UP PS-4 Flatcar "53007" with trailers (std O), 06		85
____	27520	Coe Rail Husky Stack Car "5540" (std O), 06		85
____	27521	Santa Fe Husky Stack Car "254220" (std O), 06		85
____	27535	UP PS-4 Flatcar "53008" with trailers (std O), 07		65
____	27536	UP PS-4 Flatcar "53009" with trailers (std O), 08		65
____	27537	UP Flatcar with wood load, 06		39
____	27541	NYC 40' Flatcar "496299" with load (std O), 07		63
____	27542	NH 40' Flatcar "17808" with load (std O), 07-08		70
____	27543	ATSF 40' Flatcar "191549" with load (std O), 07-08		70

		Exc	Like New	
27544	GT 40' Flatcar "64301" with load (std 0), 07-08		70	___
27545	REA PS-4 Flatcar "81003" with trailers (std 0), 07-08		85	___
27546	Greenbrier Husky Stack Car "1993" (std 0), 07		85	___
27552	Arizona & California Husky Stack Car (std 0), 07		85	___
27562	NYC PS-4 Flatcar "506075" with trailers (std 0), 07-08		85	___
27563	Lackawanna PS-4 Flatcar "16540" with trailers (std 0), 07		85	___
27564	Milwaukee Road PS-4 Flatcar w/trailers "64074" (std 0), 07-08		85	___
27583	UP 40' Flatcar "59292" with load (std 0), 08		70	___
27584	Reading Flatcar with covered load (std 0), 08-09		70	___
27585	B&M 40' Flatcar "33773" with stakes (std 0), 08-09		65	___
27586	Cass Scenic Skeleton Log Car 3-pack, 07		170	___
27587	Birch Valley Lumber Skeleton Log Car 3-pack, 07		170	___
27594	Wabash PS-4 Flatcar with stakes (std 0), 08-09		65	___
27600	RI Bay Window Caboose "17070" (std 0), 07		90	___
27601	MILW Extended Vision Caboose "992300" (std 0), 07		90	___
27602	C&O Wood-side Caboose "90332" (std 0), 07		90	___
27603	MP UP Heritage Ca-4 Caboose "2891" (std 0), 08		95	___
27604	UP Caboose "3881" (std 0), 08		90	___
27605	Pere Marquette Northeastern Caboose "A986" (std 0), 08		90	___
27606	LL Northeastern Caboose "4679" (std 0), 08		90	___
27607	Monongahela NS Heritage Caboose (std 0), 12		95	___
27608	WM Caboose "1863" (std 0), 08		85	___
27609	B&O Caboose "C-2445" (std 0), 07		90	___
27612	WP Bay Window Caboose "446" (std 0), 08		90	___
27615	NYC Bay Window Caboose "20383" (std 0), 07		90	___
27617	D&H Bay Window Caboose "35725" (std 0), 08		90	___
27618	MKT UP Heritage Ca-4 Caboose "8891" (std 0), 08		95	___
27619	WP UP Heritage Ca-4 Caboose "3891" (std 0), 08		95	___
27623	N&W Northeastern Caboose "500837" (std 0), 09		90	___
27624	D&RGW UP Heritage CA-4 Caboose (std 0), 09		95	___
27625	C&NW UP Heritage CA-4 Caboose (std 0), 09		95	___
27626	SP UP Heritage CA-4 Caboose (std 0), 09		95	___
27628	Wabash Northeastern Caboose "02222" (std 0), 09-10		90	___
27629	C&O Northeastern Caboose (std 0), 10		90	___
27630	Virginian NS Heritage CA-4 Caboose (std 0), 10		95	___
27631	NS Heritage CA-4 Caboose (std 0), 10		95	___
27633	UP CA-3 Caboose (std 0), 10		95	___
27634	ATSF Extended Vision Caboose (std 0), 10		85	___
27635	B&O I-12 Caboose (std 0), 10		85	___
27636	NKP Northeastern Caboose (std 0), 10-11		85	___
27638	Southern NS Heritage CA-4 Caboose (std 0), 10-11		95	___
27639	N&W NS Heritage CA-4 Caboose (std 0), 10		95	___
27640	Clinchfield Northeastern CA-3 Caboose, 10-11		90	___
27642	Virginian Scale Caboose with smoke, 10-13		90	___
27645	UP Boy Scouts 100th Anniversary Ca-3 Caboose (std 0), 11		95	___
27648	PRR NS Heritage Ca-3 Caboose (std 0), 11		105	___
27649	Baldwin Locomotive Works I-12 Caboose "6000" (std 0), 12-13		85	___
27650	CSX Heritage Scale Bay Window Caboose "2510" (std 0), 12		90	___
27651	B&O CSX Heritage I-12 Caboose (std 0), 11		90	___
27652	CSX Heritage Chessie System Scale Caboose (std 0), 12		90	___
27653	Family Lines CSX Heritage Ca-4 Caboose (std 0), 11		90	___
27654	CSX/Clinchfield Scale Bay-Window Caboose (std 0), 12		90	___
27655	WM CSX Heritage Extended Vision Caboose (std 0), 11		90	___

			Exc	Like New
___	**27656**	Polar Express I-12 Caboose, 11		85
___	**27657**	Central of Georgia NE Caboose "X 17" (std O), 10		90
___	**27658**	Pennsylvania Power & Light Work Caboose (std O), 11		80
___	**27659**	Bethlehem Steel Work Caboose (std O), 11		80
___	**27660**	UP George Bush Extended Vision Caboose (std O), 11		90
___	**27661**	KCS Extended Vision Caboose (std O), 11		90
___	**27662**	GTW Northeastern Caboose (std O), 11		90
___	**27663**	IC Extended Vision Caboose (std O), 11		90
___	**27664**	Lionel & Western Northeastern Caboose (std O), 11-12		90
___	**27665**	BN Bicentennial Extended Vision Caboose (std O), 11		90
___	**27666**	NH Scale Northeastern Caboose "C-666" (std O), 12		90
___	**27667**	UP Scale Ca-4 Caboose "3857" (std O), 12-13		95
___	**27668**	UP Scale Ca-3 Caboose "3779" (std O), 12-13		95
___	**27669**	PC Scale Northeastern Caboose "18420" w/smoke (std O), 12-13		90
___	**27670**	CP Scale Northeastern Caboose "400501" (std O), 12-13		90
___	**27671**	West Side Lumber Scale Work Caboose "8" (std O), 12		80
___	**27672**	Weyerhaeuser Timber Scale Work Caboose "12" (std O), 12-13		80
___	**27673**	NYC Scale Northeastern Caboose "20090" (std O), 12		90
___	**27674**	Elk River Lumber Work Caboose "6" (std O), 12, 14, 17		80
___	**27676**	CN Wood-Sided Caboose (std O), 12		90
___	**27677**	UP Work Caboose "907306" (std O), 12		80
___	**27678**	ATSF Wood-Sided Caboose "1790" (std O), 12		85
___	**27679**	NP Wood-Sided Caboose "1282" (std O), 12		85
___	**27680**	GN Wood-Sided Caboose "X499" (std O), 12		85
___	**27681**	Southern NS Heritage Caboose (std O), 12		95
___	**27682**	Conrail NS Heritage Caboose (std O), 12		95
___	**27683**	Erie NS Heritage Caboose (std O), 12, 14-15		95
___	**27684**	Illinois Terminal NS Heritage Caboose (std O), 12, 14-15		95
___	**27685**	Central of Georgia NS Heritage Caboose (std O), 12		95
___	**27686**	LV NS Heritage Caboose (std O), 12		95
___	**27687**	Reading NS Heritage Caboose (std O), 13-15		95
___	**27688**	NYC NS Heritage Caboose (std O), 13		95
___	**27689**	Wabash NS Heritage Caboose (std O), 13-15		95
___	**27690**	Virginian NS Heritage Caboose (std O), 13		95
___	**27691**	PRR NS Heritage Caboose (std O), 12		95
___	**27692**	N&W NS Heritage Caboose (std O), 12		95
___	**27693**	CNJ NS Heritage Caboose (std O), 13-14		95
___	**27694**	NS Heritage Caboose (std O), 12		95
___	**27695**	DL&W NS Heritage Caboose (std O), 13-15		95
___	**27696**	Savannah & Atlanta NS Heritage Caboose (std O), 13-15		95
___	**27697**	Nickel Plate Road NS Heritage Caboose (std O), 12		95
___	**27698**	Interstate NS Heritage Caboose (std O), 12		95
___	**27699**	PC NS Heritage Caboose (std O), 13		95
___	**27702**	Maersk Husky Stack Car 2-pack (std O), 09		225
___	**27705**	ATSF Wedge Plow Flatcar "191369" (std O), 09		90
___	**27706**	ATSF Idler Flatcar "191852" with load (std O), 09		75
___	**27707**	UP Husky Stack Car 2-pack (std O), 09-10		225
___	**27710**	No. 6464 Variation Boxcar 2-pack #2, 09		110
___	**27767**	Santa Fe Passenger 4-pack, 11-12		240
___	**27771**	Postwar "6572" REA Reefer, 11-13		60
___	**27772**	Santa Fe Baggage Car and Diner 2-pack, 11-12		120
___	**27775**	Postwar "2414" Santa Fe Blue-stripe Coach, 11-13		60
___	**27776**	No. 6464 Variation Boxcar 2-pack #3, 11		105

		Exc	Like New	
27779	Postwar Archive UP Caboose "8561," 11-12		48	___
27791	Archive 6464-50 M&StL Boxcar, 12		55	___
27792	Archive Pastel Freight Car 3-pack, 12		170	___
27800	B&M Gondola with coke containers, 09-11		80	___
27816	D&RGW Flatcar "22177" with pipes, 09-10		80	___
27820	Wabash PS-4 Flatcar with piggyback trailers (std 0), 09-10		98	___
27824	MILW 40' Flatcar with metal pipes (std 0), 10		80	___
27825	West Side Lumber Skeleton Log Car, 11		70	___
27826	CP Skeleton Log Car 2-pack (std 0), 10		133	___
27827	UP Bathtub Gondola "28081" (std 0), 10		65	___
27828	CN Bathtub Gondola "193140" (std 0), 10		65	___
27829	WM Skeleton Log Car 2-pack, 10		133	___
27834	Pere Marquette PS-5 Gondola "18400," 11		70	___
27835	P. Bunyan Lumber Skeleton Log Car, 11-12		70	___
27836	Elk River Lumber Skeleton Log Car "11203" (std 0), 11		70	___
27837	B&M PS-4 Flatcar with bulkheads (std 0), 10-11		80	___
27838	PRR PS-4 Flatcar with bulkheads (std 0), 10		80	___
27840	Polar Railroad PS-4 Flatcar with trailers, 10		98	___
27841	CSX Bathtub Gondola 2-pack (std 0), 11		130	___
27842	UP Scale Flatcar with bulkheads "15775" (std 0), 11		70	___
27843	WP Scale PS-5 Gondola "6774" (std 0), 11		70	___
27844	BNSF Bathtub Gondola 3-pack (std 0), 10		200	___
27848	Virginian NS Heritage 60' Boxcar (std 0), 11		85	___
27849	Southern NS Heritage 60' Boxcar (std 0), 11		85	___
27850	CSX 60' Boxcar "196911" (std 0), 11		85	___
27851	BNSF Bathtub Gondola 2-pack, 11		130	___
27854	B&O Double-sheathed Boxcar "196500" (std 0), 11		70	___
27855	NYC 60' DD Boxcar "53423" (std 0), 11		85	___
27856	KCS PS-1 Boxcar "18741" (std 0), 11		70	___
27857	PRR DD Boxcar "81919" (std 0), 11, 14		75	___
27858	MP DD Boxcar "90103" (std 0), 11		70	___
27860	Sugar Creek Lumber Skeleton Log Car "1749" (std 0), 11		70	___
27863	Merrill & Ring Lumber Skeleton Log Car, 11-12		70	___
27868	NS Bathtub Gondola 2-pack (std 0), 11		130	___
27871	NS 60' Boxcar "499646" (std 0), 11		85	___
27872	Polar Hot Cocoa Milk Car, 11, 13		70	___
27873	Polar Reindeer Stock Car, 11, 13		70	___
27874	Grove's Mortuary Double-sheathed Boxcar (std 0), 11		70	___
27875	NYC DD Boxcar "45395" (std 0), 11		70	___
27876	State of Maine PS-1 Boxcar "5141" (std 0), 11		70	___
27877	NH DD Boxcar "40510" (std 0), 11		70	___
27882	Southern ACF 40-ton Stock Car "45655" (std 0), 11		70	___
27883	T&P ACF 40-ton Stock Car "24042" (std 0), 11		70	___
27884	RI ACF 40-ton Stock Car "77601" (std 0), 11		70	___
27885	ATSF ACF 40-ton Stock Car "60390" (std 0), 11		70	___
27886	GN PS-1 Boxcar "11310" (std 0), 11		70	___
27887	D&RGW PS-5 Gondola "56316" with covers (std 0), 11		65	___
27888	LIRR 40' Flatcar with wheels (std 0), 11		70	___
27889	Erie 40' Flatcar "6361" with wheels (std 0), 11		70	___
27890	L&N 40' Flatcar "22269" with wheels (std 0), 11		70	___
27891	NKP Heritage PS-4 Flatcar with trailers (std 0), 11		98	___
27892	Conrail PS-5 Gondola "612690" with covers (std 0), 11		65	___
27893	GTW PS-1 Boxcar "516650" (std 0), 11		70	___

			Exc	Like New
___	**27894**	C&O PS-5 Gondola "362600" with covers (std O), 11		65
___	**27895**	ATSF PS-4 Bulkhead Flatcar "90085" (std O), 11		80
___	**27896**	CP 40' Flatcar with pipe load (std O), 11		80
___	**27899**	UP Scale PS-1 Boxcar "196889" (std O), 12		70
___	**27903**	Sager Place Observation Car, 09	23	74
___	**27912**	Postwar "2445" Elizabeth Coach, 08		60
___	**27917**	Postwar "2550" Baggage-Mail Rail Diesel Car, nonpowered, 13-14		83
___	**27928**	UP Boy Scouts 100th Anniversary PS-1 Boxcar (std O), 11		70
___	**27929**	Postwar Nos. 2484/2485 UP Passenger Car 2-pack, 12-13		120
___	**27935**	Postwar "6820" Aerial Missile Transport Car, 13		60
___	**27941**	Postwar "3854" Merchandise Car, 12	28	78
___	**27946**	Postwar "6050-25" Christmas Savings Boxcar, 13-14		55
___	**27947**	Postwar "6473-25" Reindeer Transport Car, 13		60
___	**27948**	Postwar "6464-25" Great Northern Christmas Boxcar, 13		60
___	**27949**	Postwar "3854-25" PRR Christmas Merchandise Car, 13-14		75
___	**27953**	Reading PS-2 Hopper 2-pack (std O), 13-14		140
___	**27962**	L&N PS-2 Hopper 2-pack (std O), 13-14		140
___	**27965**	P&WV Offset Hopper 3-pack (std O), 13-15		210
___	**27969**	N&W Offset Hopper 3-pack (std O), 13-15		210
___	**27973**	C&O Offset Hopper 3-pack (std O), 13-15		210
___	**27977**	GN Offset Hopper 3-pack (std O), 13-15	90	210
___	**27981**	PRR USRA Double-sheathed Boxcar (std O), 13		70
___	**27982**	SP USRA Double-sheathed Boxcar (std O), 13-14		80
___	**27983**	UP USRA Double-sheathed Boxcar (std O), 13-14		70
___	**27984**	Procor 30,000-gallon 1-D Tank Car 3-pack (std O), 13		240
___	**27988**	UTLX 30,000-gallon 1-D Tank Car 3-pack (std O), 13	255	400
___	**27992**	ADM 30,000-gallon 1-D Tank Car 3-pack (std O), 13		240
___	**27996**	ACFX 30,000-gallon 1-D Tank Car 3-pack (std O), 13		240
___	**28000**	C&NW 4-6-4 Hudson Locomotive "3005," 99		205
___	**28004**	B&O 4-4-2 E6 Atlantic Locomotive, traditional, 99-00		410
___	**28005**	PRR 4-4-2 E6 Atlantic Locomotive, traditional, 99-00		345
___	**28006**	ATSF 4-4-2 E6 Atlantic Locomotive, traditional, 99-00		285
___	**28007**	NYC 4-6-4 Hudson Locomotive "5406," 99		380
___	**28008**	C&O 4-6-4 Hudson Locomotive "306," 99		345
___	**28009**	Santa Fe 4-6-4 Hudson Locomotive "3463," 99		330
___	**28011**	C&O 2-6-6-6 Allegheny Locomotive "1601," 99	800	1800
___	**28012**	4-6-4 Commodore Vanderbilt Locomotive, red, 00 u	717	1700
___	**28013**	NH 4-6-2 Pacific Locomotive "1335," 99		325
___	**28014**	NYC 4-6-2 Pacific Locomotive "4930", 99		305
___	**28015**	Santa Fe Pacific 4-6-2 Pacific Locomotive "3449," 99		340
___	**28016**	Southern 4-6-2 Pacific Locomotive "1407," 99		345
___	**28017**	Case Cutlery 4-6-2 Pacific Locomotive, 99 u		313
___	**28018**	Reading 4-6-0 Camelback Locomotive "571," CC, 01		495
___	**28020**	Lionel Lines 4-6-2 Pacific Locomotive "3344," 99		250
___	**28022**	West Side Lumber Shay Locomotive "800," 99	263	810
___	**28023**	PRR K4 4-6-2 Pacific Locomotive "3755," CC, 99	93	375
___	**28024**	4-6-4 Commodore Vanderbilt Locomotive, blue, 00 u	500	1663
___	**28025**	PRR K4 4-6-2 Pacific Locomotive, traditional, 99		330
___	**28026**	LL 4-6-2 Pacific Locomotive, CC, 99		325
___	**28027**	NYC 4-6-4 Hudson Locomotive "5413," 00		590
___	**28028**	Virginian 2-6-6-6 Allegheny Locomotive "1601," 99	213	1318
___	**28029**	UP 4-8-8-4 Big Boy Locomotive "4006," 99-00	475	1500

MODERN 1970-2025		Exc	Like New	
28030	NYC 4-6-4 Hudson Locomotive "5450," gray, CC, 00		315	___
28032	B&O 4-6-2 Pacific Locomotive, CC, 00		315	___
28033	B&O 4-6-2 Pacific Locomotive, traditional, 00		195	___
28034	UP 4-6-2 Pacific Locomotive, CC, 00		310	___
28035	UP 4-6-2 Pacific Locomotive, traditional, 00		210	___
28036	SP 2-8-0 Consolidation Locomotive "2685," CC, 00-01	113	270	___
28037	SP 2-8-0 Consolidation Locomotive "2686," traditional, 00-01		295	___
28038	UP 2-8-0 Consolidation Locomotive "324," CC, 00-01	113	315	___
28039	UP 2-8-0 Consolidation Locomotive "326," traditional, 00-01		308	___
28044	NYC 4-6-4 Hudson Locomotive, 04		250	___
28051	B&O 2-8-8-4 EM-1 Articulated Locomotive "7617," 00	388	970	___
28052	N&W 2-6-6-4 Class A Locomotive "1218," 00	350	870	___
28055	GN 4-6-4 Hudson Locomotive "1725," traditional, 00-01		170	___
28057	Southern 4-8-2 Mountain Locomotive "1491," CC, 00		690	___
28058	NH 4-8-2 Mountain Locomotive "3310," CC, 00		670	___
28059	WP 4-8-2 Mountain Locomotive "179," CC, 00		630	___
28062	LL Gold-plated 700E J-1E 4-6-4 Hudson Locomotive, display case, 00	534	1067	___
28063	PRR T-1 4-4-4-4 Duplex Locomotive "5511," CC, 00	415	952	___
28064	UP Challenger Coal Tender "3985," CC, 00 u	788	1800	___
28065	NYC Hudson 4-6-4 Locomotive "5412," RailSounds, 00		290	___
28066	B&O President Polk 4-6-2 Locomotive, CC, 01	413	826	___
28067	Erie 4-6-2 Locomotive "2934," CC, 01	138	570	___
28068	D&RGW 4-6-4 Hudson Locomotive, traditional, 01 u	65	300	___
28070	SP Daylight 4-4-2 Atlantic Locomotive "3000," CC, 01		425	___
28071	NP 4-4-2 Atlantic Locomotive "604," CC, 01		415	___
28072	NYC 4-6-4 Hudson J3a Locomotive "5444," CC, 01	302	788	___
28074	NP 2-8-4 Berkshire Locomotive "759," CC, 01	150	640	___
28075	C&O 2-6-6-2 Locomotive "1521," CC, 01		930	___
28076	NKP 2-6-6-2 Locomotive "921," CC, 01	225	960	___
28077	UP 4-6-6-4 Challenger Locomotive "3983," CC, 01		680	___
28078	PRR 2-10-4 J1a Locomotive "6496," CC, 01	369	880	___
28079	C&O 2-10-4 Class T Locomotive "3004," CC, 01	275	882	___
28080	NYC 0-8-0 Locomotive "7745," CC, 01-02	175	540	___
28081	C&O 0-8-0 Locomotive "75," CC, 01-02		520	___
28084	NYC Dreyfuss Hudson 4-6-4 Locomotive "5452," CC, 01-02	338	790	___
28085	N&W 2-8-8-2 Y6b Class Locomotive "2200," CC, 03		1207	___
28086	PRR H9 Consolidation Locomotive "1111," CC, 01		480	___
28087	UP Auxiliary Tender, yellow, CC, 01		210	___
28088	N&W Auxiliary Water Tender, CC, 01-02		200	___
28089	PRR 4-4-4-4 T-1 Duplex Locomotive "5511," 2-rail, 00		1150	___
28090	UP Challenger Oil Tender "3977," 2-rail, 00 u		1800	___
28095	PRR K4 4-6-2 Pacific Locomotive w/RailSounds, 01-02		350	___
28098	NYC 4-6-0 10-wheel Locomotive "1916," CC, 01-02	125	520	___
28099	UP Challenger Oil Tender "3977," CC, 00 u		1700	___
28200	D&H U30C Diesel "702", CC (SSS), 02		375	___
28201	UP SD90MAC Diesel "8049," 03		345	___
28202	Conrail SD80MAC Diesel "7203," 03		325	___
28203	CSX SD80MAC Diesel "803," 03		325	___
28204	NS SD80MAC Diesel "7201," 03		345	___
28205	Chessie System SD9 Diesel "1833," CC, 03		230	___
28207	Erie-Lackawanna U33C Diesel "3304," CC, 02	113	355	___
28208	BN U33C Diesel "5734," CC, 02		355	___

MODERN 1970-2025		Exc	Like New
____ **28211**	CP SD90MAC Diesel "9107," 03		300
____ **28213**	Amtrak GE Dash 8 Diesel "516," CC, 02		300
____ **28214**	BNSF GE Dash 8 Diesel "582," CC, 02		325
____ **28215**	B&O GP30 Diesel "6939," CC, 02		315
____ **28216**	Reading GP30 Diesel "5518," CC, 02		315
____ **28217**	Rio Grande GP30 Diesel "3013," CC, 02		315
____ **28218**	Lehigh Valley Alco C420 Switcher "407," CC, 04		325
____ **28219**	Seaboard Alco C420 Switcher "136," CC, 04		300
____ **28220**	CSX SD60 Diesel "3329," 05		250
____ **28222**	Santa Fe Dash 9 Diesel "605," CC, 05		250
____ **28223**	BNSF SD70MAC Diesel "9433," CC, 05		250
____ **28224**	Jersey Central SD40-2 Diesel "3067," CC, 04		350
____ **28225**	SPSF SD40T-2 Diesel "8521," CC, 04-05		430
____ **28226**	NS SD80MAC Diesel "7204," CC, 04-05		430
____ **28227**	UP SD70MAC Diesel "4979," CC, 04		375
____ **28228**	C&NW Dash 9-44CW Diesel "8669," CC, 03		350
____ **28229**	SP Dash 9-44CW Diesel "8132", CC, 03		350
____ **28230**	Amtrak Dash 8 Diesel "505," CC, 04		295
____ **28235**	Great Northern U33C Diesel "2543," CC, 05		455
____ **28237**	Reading U30C Diesel "6301," CC, 05		455
____ **28239**	Union Pacific SD70 Diesel, TMCC, 04		360
____ **28241**	C&NW U30C Diesel "935," CC, 06		455
____ **28242**	SP U33C Diesel "8773," CC, 06		475
____ **28243**	LIRR Alco C420 Hi-nose Switcher "206," CC, 06		420
____ **28244**	N&W Alco C420 Hi-nose Switcher "417," CC, 06-07		420
____ **28245**	Chessie System SD40T-2 Diesel "7617," RailSounds, 06		265
____ **28246**	Chessie System SD40T-2 Diesel "7618," nonpowered (std 0), 06		168
____ **28247**	Rio Grande SD40T-2 Diesel "5348," RailSounds, 06		265
____ **28248**	Rio Grande SD40T-2 Diesel "5349," nonpowered (std 0), 06		160
____ **28250**	N&W Alco C420 Hi-nose Switcher "416," nonpowered (std 0), 06-07		160
____ **28251**	LIRR Alco C420 Hi-nose Switcher "206," nonpowered (std 0), 06		160
____ **28252**	SP U33C Diesel "8771," nonpowered (std 0), 06		160
____ **28253**	C&NW U30C Diesel "936," nonpowered (std 0), 06		160
____ **28255**	UP SD40T-2 Diesel "4551," traditional, CC, 07-08		265
____ **28256**	UP SD40T-2 Diesel "4596," nonpowered (std 0), 07		170
____ **28257**	NS SD40-2 Diesel "3340," CC, 06		430
____ **28258**	NS SD40-2 Diesel "3341," nonpowered (std 0), 06		450
____ **28259**	CN SD40-2 Diesel "5383," CC, 06		430
____ **28260**	CN SD40-2 Diesel "5384," nonpowered (std 0), 06		170
____ **28261**	UP (MP) SD70ACe Diesel "1982," CC, 07		450
____ **28262**	UP (WP) SD70ACe Diesel "1983," CC, 07	163	450
____ **28263**	UP (MKT) SD70ACe Diesel "1988," CC, 07		450
____ **28264**	UP "Building America" SD70ACe Diesel "8348", CC, 07		450
____ **28265**	MILW U30C Diesel "5657," CC, 07		455
____ **28266**	MILW U30C Diesel "5657," nonpowered (std 0), 07-08		170
____ **28267**	Conrail U30C Diesel "6837," CC, 07		455
____ **28268**	Conrail U30C Diesel "6838," nonpowered (std 0), 07-08		170
____ **28269**	ATSF Dash 8-40BW Diesel "562," CC, 08		500
____ **28270**	ATSF Dash 8-40CW Diesel "563," nonpowered, 08		220
____ **28272**	"I Love USA" SD60 Diesel "1776," traditional, 06	80	250
____ **28279**	UP SD70ACe Diesel "1989," CC, 07		450
____ **28280**	UP (C&NW) SD70ACe Diesel "1995," CC, 07		450

MODERN 1970-2025		Exc	Like New	
28281	UP (SP) SD70ACe Diesel "1996," CC, 07		450	___
28283	UP "Building America" SD70AC3 Diesel, nonpowered (std O), 07		170	___
28284	Ferromex SD70ACe Diesel "4011," CC, 08		495	___
28287	KCS SD70ACe Diesel "4050," CC, 08		495	___
28292	Chessie System U30C Diesel "3312," CC, 02		300	___
28293	Santa Fe U28CG Diesel "354," CC, 02		375	___
28295	Conrail LionMaster SD80MAC Diesel, nonpowered, 08		200	___
28296	UP AC6000 Diesel "7526," CC, 08		660	___
28297	SP GP9 Diesel "446," CC, 10		390	___
28298	CSX AC6000 Diesel "608," CC, 08		660	___
28299	CSX AC6000 Diesel "609," nonpowered, 08		370	___
28300	NS Dash 9 Diesel "9607," nonpowered, 08		220	___
28302	BNSF SD70ACe Diesel "9380," CC, 08		495	___
28305	CSX AC6000 Diesel "610," nonpowered, RailSounds, 08		430	___
28306	GE ES44AC Evolution Hybrid Diesel "2010," CC, 09-10	699	1349	___
28307	Wabash Train Master Diesel "550," CC, 09-10	150	495	___
28311	UP DD35A Diesel "70," CC, 11		600	___
28312	BN SD60 Diesel "8301," CC, 09	163	800	___
28314	UP 3GS21B Genset Switcher "2701," CC, 10		675	___
28316	PRR NS Heritage SD70ACe Diesel "1854," CC, 10	188	500	___
28318	Conrail NS Heritage SD70ACe Diesel "1209," CC, 10		500	___
28320	CP Evolution Hybrid Diesel, 10		1320	___
28323	NS Genset Switcher, CC, 11		800	___
28327	UP AC6000 Diesel "7050," CC, 10	188	700	___
28328	UPAC6000 Diesel "7055," nonpowered, CC, 10		350	___
28330	UP SD70ACe Diesel "8444," CC, 10		500	___
28331	CSX AC6000 Diesel "618," CC, 10	138	700	___
28333	Virginian NS Heritage SD70ACe Diesel, CC, 10		500	___
28334	NS Heritage SD70ACe Diesel "1982," CC, 10		550	___
28338	PRR NS Heritage SD70ACe Diesel, CC, 11		500	___
28339	ATSF AC6000 Diesel "9876," CC, 10		550	___
28340	WP GP7 Diesel "705," CC, 10	138	450	___
28343	Amtrak Dash 9 Diesel "519," CC, 10	138	500	___
28344	Southern NS Heritage SD70ACe Diesel, CC, 10		500	___
28345	N&W NS Heritage SD70ACe Diesel "247," CC, 10		500	___
28347	UP Boy Scouts 100th Anniversary ES44AC Diesel, CC, 11		1538	___
28350	BNSF ES44AC Diesel, CC, 11		850	___
28351	KCS ES44AC Diesel "4655," CC, 11		850	___
28353	Erie GP7 Diesel, CC, 11		450	___
28354	CSX Genset Switcher "1303," CC, 11		800	___
28355	BNSF Genset Switcher "1249," CC, 11		800	___
28356	CSX SD60 Diesel, CC, 11		500	___
28357	CSX SD60 Diesel, CC, 11		500	___
28358	Soo Line SD60 Diesel, CC, 11		500	___
28359	Soo Line SD60 Diesel, CC, 11		500	___
28360	WP GP7 Diesel "707," CC, 11		450	___
28361	WM GP7 Diesel "21," CC, 11		450	___
28362	WM GP7 Diesel "23," CC, 11		450	___
28363	BN SD60 Diesel "8302," CC, 11		500	___
28364	BNSF Dash-9 Diesel "4081," CC, 11		500	___
28365	BNSF Dash-9 Diesel "5121," CC, 11		500	___
28366	CN Dash-9 Diesel "2643," CC, 11		500	___
28367	CN Dash-9 Diesel "2692," CC, 11		500	___

			Exc	Like New
___	**28368**	Amtrak Dash-9 Diesel, CC, 11		500
___	**28369**	NYC DD35A Diesel "9950," CC, 11		600
___	**28370**	UP DD35 Diesel "84," CC, 12		600
___	**28371**	UP DD35A Diesel "72," CC, 11		600
___	**28372**	NYC DD35A Diesel "9955," CC, 11	240	600
___	**28373**	C&NW UP Heritage SD70ACe Diesel, CC, 11		500
___	**28374**	SP UP Heritage SD70ACe Diesel, CC, 11	188	500
___	**28375**	Katy UP Heritage SD70ACe Diesel, CC, 11		500
___	**28376**	MoPac UP Heritage SD70ACe Diesel, CC, 11		500
___	**28377**	Rio Grande UP Heritage SD70ACe Diesel, CC, 11		500
___	**28378**	WP UP Heritage SD70ACe Diesel, CC, 11		500
___	**28380**	NYC DD35A Diesel, nonpowered, 11		440
___	**28381**	ATSF GP30 Diesel, CC, 11		500
___	**28382**	U.S. Army Genset Switcher, CC, 11		800
___	**28383**	Conrail Genset Switcher, CC, 11		800
___	**28384**	CN Genset Switcher "7990," CC, 11-12		800
___	**28385**	ATSF GP30 Diesel "1214," CC, 11		500
___	**28386**	ATSF GP30 Diesel "2710," 11		380
___	**28387**	ATSF GP30 Diesel "2715," nonpowered, 11		240
___	**28388**	ICG GP30 Diesel "2268," CC, 11		500
___	**28389**	ICG GP30 Diesel "2271," CC, 11		500
___	**28390**	UP DD35 Diesel "79," nonpowered, 12		440
___	**28394**	ICG GP30 Diesel "2277," 11		380
___	**28395**	ICG GP30 Diesel "2279," nonpowered, 11		240
___	**28396**	UP ES44AC Diesel "7454," CC, 11		850
___	**28397**	UP ES44AC Diesel "7459," CC, 11		850
___	**28398**	BNSF ES44AC Diesel "6436," CC, 11		850
___	**28399**	KCS ES44AC Diesel "4682," CC, 11	373	850
___	**28400**	Amtrak Rail Bonder, 05		65
___	**28403**	Pennsylvania Ballast Tamper, traditional, 05-06		105
___	**28404**	Maintenance Car, 05		105
___	**28405**	Picatinny Arsenal Switcher, CC, 05		290
___	**28406**	CSX Rail Bonder "92794," traditional, 05		65
___	**28407**	UP Speeder, 05		65
___	**28408**	CNJ Speeder "MW840," traditional, 06		70
___	**28409**	Conrail Rail Bonder "X409," traditional, 06		70
___	**28411**	U.S. Army Missile Launcher Locomotive, 06-07		300
___	**28412**	Santa's Speeder, 06		70
___	**28413**	Milwaukee Road Snowplow "X903," traditional, 06		210
___	**28414**	Lionel Lines Burro Crane, traditional, 06		160
___	**28415**	Third Avenue Trolley "1651," traditional, 06		70
___	**28416**	Hobo Handcar, traditional, 06		70
___	**28417**	Christmas Rotary Snowplow, 06		180
___	**28418**	Christmas Trolley, 06		70
___	**28419**	Lionel Lines Speeder, 07-08		70
___	**28420**	D&RGW Handcar, 07-08		70
___	**28421**	Fort Collins Trolley, 07		73
___	**28422**	PRR Burro Crane, 07-08		160
___	**28423**	Alaska Rotary Snowplow, 06-07		220
___	**28424**	Postwar "51" Navy Switcher, 07		210
___	**28425**	Polar Express Elf Handcar, 06-23		120
___	**28427**	Christmas Snowplow, 08-10	67	210
___	**28428**	Halloween Handcar, 07		70

MODERN 1970-2025		Exc	Like New	
28430	Wellspring Capital Management Trolley, 06	50	85	___
28432	Bethlehem Steel Switcher, traditional, 07		210	___
28434	Christmas Trolley, 07		70	___
28438	Portland Birney Trolley, 08-09		65	___
28440	PRR Inspection Vehicle, 08-09		170	___
28441	Transylvania Trolley, 08	60	72	___
28442	Postwar "50" Gang Car, 08		120	___
28444	NH Handcar, 08-09		75	___
28445	AEC Burro Crane Car		100	___
28446	Silver Bell Trolley, 09		90	___
28447	4850TM Factory Trackmobile, CC, 10		300	___
28448	CSX 4850TM Trackmobile, CC, 10		300	___
28449	UP 4850TM Trackmobile, CC, 10		300	___
28450	CP Rail Trackmobile, CC, 11		300	___
28451	Christmas Track Cleaning Car, 10-13		150	___
28452	MOW Early Era Inspection Vehicle, 10		130	___
28453	PRR Early Era Inspection Vehicle, 10		130	___
28454	CP Early Era Inspection Vehicle, 10		130	___
28455	NYC Trackmobile, CC, 11-13		300	___
28456	Coca-Cola Trolley, 10		90	___
28457	B&M Rotary Snowplow "8457," 11		250	___
28466	U.S. Army Trackmobile, CC, 11		300	___
28467	PRR Trackmobile, CC, 11		300	___
28468	Amtrak Trackmobile, CC, 11		300	___
28469	BNSF Trackmobile, CC, 11		300	___
28470	NYC Early Era Inspection Vehicle , 11		130	___
28471	ATSF Early Era Inspection Vehicle, CC, 11		130	___
28472	Southern Early Era Inspection Vehicle, 11		130	___
28473	GN Early Era Inspection Vehicle, CC, 11		130	___
28474	North Pole Central Elf Handcar, 11		80	___
28475	UP Early Era Insprection Vehicle, 11		130	___
28476	IC Early Era Inspection Vehicle, 11		130	___
28478	Frisco Early Era Inspection Vehicle, CC, 11		130	___
28479	Christmas Early Era Inspection Vehicle, 11		130	___
28480	Grand Trunk Early Era Inspection Vehicle, CC, 11		130	___
28500	Mopac GP20 Diesel "2274," 99-00	100	205	___
28501	ATSF GP9 Diesel "2924," traditional, 99		200	___
28502	ATSF GP9 Diesel "2925," CC, 99-00		255	___
28503	ACL GP7 Diesel, CC, 00		245	___
28504	ACL GP7 Diesel, traditional, 00		170	___
28505	Monon Alco C420 Switcher "505," CC, 00-01		230	___
28506	Monon Alco C420 Switcher "506," traditional, 00-01	70	170	___
28507	NH Alco C420 Switcher "2556," CC, 00-01		275	___
28508	NH Alco C420 Switcher "2557," traditional, 00-01		290	___
28509	FEC GP7 Diesel Set, 99		560	___
28514	B&O GP9 Diesel "6590," 00		85	___
28515	Lionel Service Station Alco C420 Switcher, CC, 00		205	___
28516	Lehigh & Hudson River Alco C420 Diesel, 00		160	___
28517	C&NW GP7 Diesel "1518," CC, 00-01		275	___
28518	PRR EP-5 Electric Locomotive "2352," CC, 00	115	410	___
28519	NP GP9 Diesel "2349," CC, 01	98	270	___
28521	SP Alco RS11 Switcher "5725," CC, 01-02		280	___
28522	MP Alco RS11 Switcher "4611," CC, 01-02		305	___

			Exc	Like New
___	**28523**	Soo SD40-2 Diesel "6622," CC, 01		375
___	**28524**	Chessie SD40-2 Diesel "7616", CC, 01		355
___	**28527**	AEC GP9 Diesel "2001," CC, 01		432
___	**28528**	NH Alco RS11 Diesel "1406," 01-02	150	300
___	**28529**	Norfolk Southern GP9 Diesel, CC, 02		200
___	**28530**	NP Alco S4 Diesel "722," CC, 02		285
___	**28531**	Santa Fe Alco S2 Switcher "2337," CC, 02		285
___	**28532**	LV Alco S2 Switcher "150," CC, 02		280
___	**28533**	Seaboard Air Line Alco S4 Diesel "1489," CC, 02		290
___	**28536**	Rock Island GP7 Diesel "1274," CC, 02-03		230
___	**28538**	WP Alco S2 Switcher "553," CC, 03		340
___	**28539**	B&O Alco S2 Switcher "9045," CC, 03	163	320
___	**28540**	UP SD40T-2 Diesel "4455," CC, 03		390
___	**28541**	SP SD40T-2 Diesel "8239," CC, 03		400
___	**28542**	Rio Grande SD40T-2 Diesel "5350," CC, 03		400
___	**28543**	Ontario Northland RS3 Diesel "1308," 03		80
___	**28544**	Pennsylvania Alco RS11 Switcher "8618," CC, 04		350
___	**28545**	NP Alco RS11 Switcher "900," CC, 03		325
___	**28547**	SP SD40T-2 Diesel "8232," CC, 04		400
___	**28548**	Chessie System Alco S-4 Diesel "9009," CC, 05	125	400
___	**28553**	PRR Alco RS11 Switcher "8620," traditional, 07-08	90	285
___	**28554**	PRR Alco RS11 Diesel "8621," nonpowered, 08		170
___	**28555**	Alaska GP38-2 Diesel "2001," CC, 06		400
___	**28556**	Alaska GP38-2 Diesel "2002," nonpowered (std O), 06		160
___	**28557**	CP GP30 Diesel "5000," CC, 06-07		400
___	**28558**	CP GP30 Diesel "5001," nonpowered (std O), 06-07		150
___	**28559**	Chessie System GP30 Diesel "3044," CC, 06-07		400
___	**28560**	Chessie System GP30 Diesel "3045," nonpowered (std O), 06-07		150
___	**28561**	NYC GP7 Diesel "5628," CC, 07-08		340
___	**28562**	NYC GP7 Diesel "5629," nonpowered (std O), 07		170
___	**28563**	GN GP7 Diesel "626," CC, 07	138	400
___	**28564**	GN GP7 Diesel "627," nonpowered (std O), 07		170
___	**28565**	RI GP7 Diesel "1265," CC, 07		400
___	**28566**	RI GP7 Diesel "1266," nonpowered (std O), 07		170
___	**28567**	UP GP7 Diesel "105," CC, 07		400
___	**28568**	UP GP7 Diesel "106," nonpowered (std O), 07		170
___	**28570**	D&RGW GP7 Diesel "5101," CC, 08		440
___	**28573**	PRR GP7 Diesel "8512," CC, 08		440
___	**28578**	D&H GP38-2 Diesel "7307," CC, 08		440
___	**28587**	PRR GP7 Diesel "8510," CC, 10		450
___	**28592**	N&W GP7 Diesel "2446," CC, 09		500
___	**28594**	White Pass & Yukon NW2 Diesel Switcher, traditional, 09-10	100	300
___	**28595**	ATSF SD40 Diesel "5004," CC, 09		380
___	**28596**	Erie GP7 Diesel "1210," CC, 11		450
___	**28598**	ATSF GP7 Diesel "2791," CC, 10		450
___	**28599**	Erie GP9 Diesel "1261," CC, 10		390
___	**28601**	Winter Wonderland 4-4-2 Atlantic Locomotive "34," 02		85
___	**28602**	PRR 4-4-2 Atlantic Locomotive, 01-02		90
___	**28603**	NYC 4-4-2 Atlantic Locomotive, 01-02		90
___	**28604**	ATSF 4-6-4 Hudson Locomotive "3458," 02		150
___	**28606**	Monopoly 4-4-2 Atlantic Locomotive, 00 u		200
___	**28611**	ATSF 4-6-4 Hudson Locomotive "3459," 02		100

		Exc	Like New	
28612	WP 4-4-2 Atlantic Locomotive, traditional, 02		80	___
28613	Reading 0-6-0 Dockside Switcher "1251," traditional, 04		113	___
28615	B&O 4-6-4 Hudson Locomotive, traditional, 02		225	___
28616	Nickel Plate 2-8-4 Berkshire Locomotive, traditional, 02		190	___
28617	Southern 2-8-4 Berkshire Locomotive, traditional, 02		235	___
28624	Santa Fe 0-6-0 Dockside Switcher "2174," traditional, 04		175	___
28625	Wabash 4-4-2 Atlantic Locomotive "8625," traditional, 03		85	___
28626	PRR 4-6-4 Hudson Locomotive "626," traditional, 03		175	___
28627	C&O 2-8-4 Berkshire Locomotive "2755," traditional, 03		200	___
28628	L&N 2-8-4 Berkshire Locomotive "1970," traditional, 03	150	200	___
28633	JCPenney B&O 2-8-4 Berkshire Locomotive, 07		153	___
28636	D&RGW 4-4-2 Atlantic Locomotive "8636," traditional, 04		95	___
28637	UP 4-6-4 Hudson Locomotive "673," traditional, 04		160	___
28638	GN 2-8-4 Berkshire Locomotive "3414," traditional, 04		200	___
28639	NYC 2-8-4 Berkshire Locomotive "9401," traditional, 04		200	___
28646	North Pole Central 2-8-4 Berkshire "1900," traditional, 04		315	___
28649	Polar Express 2-8-4 Berkshire Locomotive, 03–10		120	___
28650	NYC 0-6-0 Dockside Switcher "X-8688," traditional, 05		80	___
28651	Bethlehem Steel 0-6-0 Dockside Switcher "72," traditional, 05		80	___
28652	LL 4-4-2 Locomotive "8652," traditional, 05		105	___
28655	Erie 2-8-4 Berkshire Locomotive "3338," traditional, 05		240	___
28656	PRR 2-8-4 Berkshire Locomotive "56," traditional, 05	55	240	___
28660	North Pole Central 0-6-0 Dockside Switcher "25," traditional, 05		105	___
28661	Santa Fe 0-4-0 Locomotive "2300" traditional, 05		160	___
28662	C&O 0-4-0 Locomotive "39," traditional, 05		160	___
28663	Nieman Marcus 4-4-2 Atlantic Locomotive, traditional, 06 u		125	___
28665	LRRC Western Union 2-8-4 Berkshire Locomotive "665," 10 u		200	___
28667	Elvis "He Dared to Rock" 2-8-4 Berkshire Locomotive, 04		200	___
28669	Copper Range 0-6-0 Locomotive "194," 05		155	___
28671	ATSF 2-8-4 Berkshire Locomotive "4193," 06-07		225	___
28674	C&O 0-6-0 Dockside Switcher "67," traditional, 06-07		110	___
28675	SP 0-6-0 Dockside Switcher "675," traditional, 06-07		110	___
28676	U.S. Steel 0-6-0 Dockside Switcher "76," traditional, 06-07		110	___
28677	WM 4-4-2 Atlantic Locomotive "103," traditional, 06		110	___
28678	Rio Grande 0-4-0 Locomotive "55," traditional, 06-07		170	___
28679	U.S. Army Transportation Corps 0-4-0 Locomotive "40," traditional, 06		170	___
28680	Reading 0-4-0 Locomotive "1152," traditional, 06		170	___
28681	Virginian 2-8-4 Berkshire Locomotive "509," traditional, 06		260	___
28683	B&O 2-8-2 Mikado Locomotive "1520," TrainSounds, 06-07		260	___
28684	UP 2-8-2 Mikado Locomotive "2498," TrainSounds, 06-07		260	___
28693	B&O 4-4-2 Locomotive "28," traditional, 05		105	___
28694	NYC 4-4-2 Atlantic Locomotive "8637," traditional, 06		100	___
28695	Halloween 0-6-0 Dockside Switcher "X-131," traditional, 06-07		85	___
28699	Holiday 2-8-2 Mikado Locomotive "25," red, RailSounds, 08		260	___
28700	CB&Q 0-8-0 Locomotive "543," RailSounds, 05		650	___
28701	NP 0-8-0 Locomotive "1178," RailSounds, 05	138	650	___
28702	Boston & Albany 0-8-0 Locomotive "53," RailSounds, 05		650	___
28704	PRR 4-4-2 Atlantic Locomotive "68," CC, 05		550	___
28706	PRR Reading Seashore 4-4-2 Atlantic Locomotive "6064," CC, 05		550	___
28742	B&O 4-6-0 Camelback Locomotive "1630," CC, 03		335	___
28743	B&O 4-6-0 Camelback Locomotive "1632," traditional, 03		300	___

			Exc	Like New
___	**28744**	D&H 4-6-0 Camelback Locomotive "548," CC, 03		325
___	**28745**	D&H 4-6-0 Camelback Locomotive "555," traditional, 03		300
___	**28746**	Erie 4-6-0 Camelback Locomotive "860," CC, 03	113	375
___	**28747**	Erie 4-6-0 Camelback Locomotive "878," traditional, 03		300
___	**28748**	Jersey Central 4-6-0 Camelback Locomotive "772," CC, 03		300
___	**28749**	Jersey Central 4-6-0 Camelback Locomotive "773," traditional, 03		300
___	**28750**	Lackawanna 4-6-0 Camelback Locomotive "690," CC, 03	125	375
___	**28751**	Lackawanna 4-6-0 Camelback Locomotive "1031," traditional, 03		300
___	**28752**	LIRR 4-6-0 Camelback Locomotive "126," CC, 03		300
___	**28753**	LIRR 4-6-0 Camelback Locomotive "127," traditional, 03		300
___	**28754**	NYO&W 4-6-0 Camelback Locomotive "249," CC, 03		300
___	**28755**	NYO&W 4-6-0 Camelback "253" Locomotive, traditional, 03		300
___	**28756**	PRR Reading Seashore 4-6-0 Camelback Locomotive "6000," CC, 03	95	325
___	**28757**	PRR Reading Seashore 4-6-0 Camelback "6001," 03		300
___	**28758**	Susquehanna 4-6-0 Camelback Locomotive "30," CC, 03		365
___	**28759**	Susquehanna 4-6-0 Camelback Locomotive "36," traditional, 03		300
___	**28800**	N&W GP7 Diesel "507," 99-00		80
___	**28801**	Lionel Lines 44-ton Switcher, 99		135
___	**28806**	Jersey Central FM H16-44 Diesel "1516," CC, 01		335
___	**28811**	Santa Fe FM H16-44 Diesel "3003," CC, 01		290
___	**28813**	Milwaukee Road FM H16-44 Diesel "406," CC, 01		315
___	**28815**	B&O GP30 Diesel "6935," CC, 02		295
___	**28817**	Reading GP30 Diesel "5513," CC, 02		310
___	**28819**	Rio Grande GP30 Diesel "3013," CC, 02		310
___	**28821**	GT GP7 Diesel "4438," 01		100
___	**28822**	Southern RS3 Diesel "2127," 01		70
___	**28823**	Virginian Electric Locomotive "234," 01		122
___	**28826**	Pioneer Seed GP7 Diesel "2001," traditional, 00 u		NRS
___	**28827**	Chessie GP38 Diesel, traditional, 01		100
___	**28830**	Soo Line GP9 Diesel, traditional, 01 u	95	270
___	**28831**	Conrail U36B Diesel "2971," traditional, 02	40	100
___	**28832**	Santa Fe RS3 Diesel "2099," traditional, 02		70
___	**28836**	NYC FM H-16-44 Diesel "7000," CC, 02		330
___	**28837**	NH FM H-16-44 Diesel "591," CC, 02		325
___	**28838**	UP FM H-16-44 Diesel "1340," CC, 02		325
___	**28839**	Alaska GP 30 Diesel "2000," CC, 04		315
___	**28840**	Burlington GP30 Diesel "945," CC, 03		325
___	**28841**	Seaboard GP30 Diesel "1315," CC, 03		220
___	**28842**	C&O GP9 Diesel, horn, 04		160
___	**28843**	Southern GP38 Diesel, horn, 04		140
___	**28845**	Amtrak RS3 Diesel "106," 03		70
___	**28846**	Western Pacific U36B Diesel "3067," traditional, 04		100
___	**28847**	DM & IR GP38 Diesel "203," traditional, 04		170
___	**28848**	JCPenney Santa Fe GP38 Diesel, 04	50	125
___	**28849**	Western Maryland GP7 Diesel, horn, 04		185
___	**28850**	NYC GP30 Diesel "6115" CC, 04	104	360
___	**28851**	Pennsylvania RS3 Diesel, 04-05		75
___	**28852**	CSX U36B Diesel "1976," traditional, 05		140
___	**28853**	Santa Fe GP38 Diesel "2371," traditional, 05		210
___	**28855**	B&O/Chessie System GP30 Diesel "6945," CC, 05-06	225	425
___	**28857**	Alaska GP9 Diesel, 05		125

		Exc	Like New	
28859	Pennsylvania GP30 Diesel "2206," nonpowered, 06		160	___
28860	UP GP30 Diesel "844," CC, 06		360	___
28861	UP GP30 Diesel "845," nonpowered (std O), 06		150	___
28862	CSX GP30 Diesel "4249," CC, 06		400	___
28863	CSX GP30 Diesel "4250," nonpowered (std O), 06		150	___
28864	UP RS3 Diesel "1195," traditional, 06		85	___
28865	GN GP9 Diesel "688," traditional, 06		160	___
28866	NYC GP20 Diesel "6110," traditional, 06		140	___
28868	ATSF GP38 Diesel		140	___
28873	NYC RS3 Diesel "8226," traditional, 06		85	___
28874	UP GP9 Diesel "178," traditional, 06-07		210	___
28875	Santa Fe GP20 "1107," traditional, 06		140	___
28876	GN FT Diesel "418," traditional, 07-08	75	245	___
28879	UPS Centennial GP38 Diesel, traditional, 06		210	___
28881	Conrail GP20 Diesel "2107," traditional, 07		140	___
28882	Alaska RS3 Diesel "1079," traditional, 07		85	___
28883	Diesel, 07-13		120	___
28884	PRR GP38 Diesel "2389," traditional, 08-09		210	___
28886	RI RS3 Diesel "492," traditional, 08		95	___
28887	Southern RS3 Diesel "2028," traditional, 08		95	___
28890	CN GP9 Diesel "4573," traditional, 08		210	___
28897	Seaboard U36B Diesel "1762," traditional, 08		140	___
28900	Iron 'Arry and Iron Bert 2-pack, 08-09		240	___
28905	ATSF FT Diesel "160," nonpowered, 09-10		120	___
29000	PRR Caleb Strong Madison Coach "2622," 99		80	___
29001	PRR Villa Royal Madison Coach "2621," 99		80	___
29002	PRR Philadelphia Madison Coach "2624," 99	30	80	___
29003	PRR Madison Car 4-pack, 98		220	___
29004	NYC Heavyweight Passenger Car 2-pack, 99		170	___
29007	NYC Pullman Passenger Car 2-pack, 98 u		143	___
29008	NYC Heavyweight Diner "383," 98		95	___
29009	NYC Van Twiller Heavyweight Combination Car, 98		95	___
29010	C&O Heavyweight Passenger Car 2-pack, 99		150	___
29039	Lionel Lines Recovery Combination Car "9501," 99	65	85	___
29041	Alaska Streamliner Car 4-pack, 99-00	59	230	___
29042	Alaska Streamliner Baggage Car "6310," 99-00		50	___
29043	Alaska Streamliner Coach "5408," 99-00		65	___
29044	Alaska Streamliner Vista Dome Car "7014," 99-00		65	___
29046	B&O Streamliner Car 4-pack, 99-00		165	___
29047	B&O Streamliner Baggage Car, 99-00		35	___
29048	B&O Streamliner Coach, 99-00		50	___
29049	B&O Streamliner Vista Dome Car, 99-00		50	___
29050	B&O Streamliner Observation Car, 99-00		40	___
29051	ATSF Streamliner Car 4-pack, 99-00		200	___
29052	ATSF Streamliner Baggage Car, 99-00		40	___
29053	ATSF Streamliner Coach, 99-00		60	___
29054	ATSF Streamliner Vista Dome Car, 99-00		60	___
29055	ATSF Streamliner Observation Car, 99-00		40	___
29056	NYC Streamliner Car 4-pack, 99-00		180	___
29057	NYC Streamliner Baggage Car, 99-00		40	___
29058	NYC Streamliner Coach, 99-00		50	___
29059	NYC Streamliner Vista Dome Car, 99-00		50	___
29060	NYC Streamliner Observation Car, 99-00		45	___

		MODERN 1970-2025	Exc	Like New
____	**29061**	PRR Madison Passenger Car 4-pack, 99-00		190
____	**29062**	PRR Indian Point Madison Baggage Car, 99-00		50
____	**29063**	PRR Christopher Columbus Madison Coach, 99-00		50
____	**29064**	PRR Andrew Jackson Madison Coach, 99-00		50
____	**29065**	PRR Broussard Madison Observation Car, 99-00		50
____	**29066**	CNJ Madison Passenger Car 4-pack, 99-00		210
____	**29067**	CNJ Madison Baggage Car "420," 99-00		50
____	**29068**	CNJ Beachcomber Madison Coach, 99-00		50
____	**29069**	CNJ Echo Lake Madison Coach, 99-00		50
____	**29070**	CNJ Madison Observation Car "1178," 99-00		50
____	**29071**	NYC Baby Madison Car 4-pack, 00	78	203
____	**29072**	NYC Baby Madison Baggage Car "1001," 00		50
____	**29073**	NYC Baby Madison Coach "1005," 00		50
____	**29074**	NYC Baby Madison Coach "1006," 00		50
____	**29075**	NYC Detroit Baby Madison Observation Car "1019," 00		40
____	**29076**	Southern Baby Madison Car 4-pack, 00		155
____	**29077**	Southern Delaware Madison Baggage Car "702," 00		30
____	**29078**	Southern North Carolina Madison Coach "800," 00		50
____	**29079**	Southern Maryland Madison Coach "801," 00		50
____	**29080**	Southern Madison Observation Car "1100," 00		40
____	**29081**	ATSF Baby Madison Car 4-pack, 00		160
____	**29082**	ATSF Baby Madison Baggage Car "1765," 00		30
____	**29083**	ATSF Baby Madison Coach "3040," 00		50
____	**29084**	ATSF Baby Madison Coach "1535," 00		50
____	**29085**	ATSF Baby Madison Observation Car "10," 00		45
____	**29086**	Madison Car 3-pack, 99		280
____	**29090**	Lionel Liontech Madison Car "2656," 99		75
____	**29091**	Lawrence Cowen Lionel Legends Madison Coach "2657," 99-00		75
____	**29105**	PRR Trail Blazer Aluminum Passenger Car 4-pack, 04-05		550
____	**29108**	Searchlight Car, 00		30
____	**29110**	B&O Columbian Aluminum Passenger Car 4-pack, 04		425
____	**29115**	SP Daylight Aluminum Passenger Car 4-pack, 04-05		550
____	**29122**	EL F3 Diesel Passenger Set, 99	200	840
____	**29123**	Erie-Lack. Aluminum Coach/Baggage Car "203", 99		100
____	**29124**	Erie-Lack. Aluminum Coach/Diner "770", 99		100
____	**29125**	Erie-Lack. Eleanor Lord Aluminum Coach, 99		100
____	**29126**	Erie-Lack. Tavern Lounge Aluminum Observation Car "789," 99		125
____	**29127**	ACL Aluminum Baggage Car "152," 99		100
____	**29128**	ACL North Hampton Aluminum Coach, 99		100
____	**29129**	Texas Special Passenger Car 4-pack, 99	650	700
____	**29130**	Texas Special Edward Burleson Aluminum Coach "1200," 99	58	125
____	**29131**	Texas Special David G. Burnett Aluminum Coach "1201," 99	58	125
____	**29132**	Texas Special J. Pinckney Henderson Aluminum Coach "1202," 99	38	122
____	**29133**	Texas Special Stephen F. Austin Aluminum Observation Car "1203," 99	50	118
____	**29135**	California Zephyr Silver Poplar Aluminum Vista Dome Car, 99		150
____	**29136**	California Zephyr Silver Palm Aluminum Vista Dome Car, 99		150
____	**29137**	California Zephyr Silver Tavern Aluminum Vista Dome Car, 99		150
____	**29138**	California Zephyr Silver Planet Aluminum Vista Dome Car, 99		150
____	**29139**	Kughn Lionel Legends Madison Car "2655," 99		113
____	**29140**	NYC Castleton Bridge Aluminum Sleeper Car, 99		120

MODERN 1970-2025		Exc	Like New	
29141	NYC Martin Van Buren Aluminum Combination Car, 99		120	___
29142	CP Skyline Aluminum Vista Dome Car "596," 99		125	___
29143	CP Banff Park Aluminum Observation Car, 99		125	___
29144	Santa Fe El Capitan Aluminum Passenger Car 4-pack, 04		400	___
29149	CB&Q California Zephyr Aluminum Passenger Car 2-pack, 03		300	___
29152	Santa Fe Super Chief Aluminum Passenger Car 2-pack, 03		190	___
29155	D&H Aluminum Passenger Car 2-pack, 03		190	___
29158	Southern Aluminum Passenger Car 2-pack, 03		205	___
29165	Amtrak Superliner Passenger Car 2-pack, Phase IV, 04		195	___
29168	Amtrak Superliner Diner, StationSounds, Phase IV, 04		200	___
29169	Alaska Superliner Passenger Car 2-pack, 04		200	___
29172	Alaska Superliner Diner, StationSounds, 04		200	___
29179	NYC Empire State Express Aluminum Parlor Car, 04			___
29182	N&W Powhatan Arrow Aluminum Passenger Car 4-pack (std O), 05		550	___
29187	N&W Powhatan Arrow Aluminum Passenger Car 2-pack (std O), 05		290	___
29190	N&W Powhatan Arrow Aluminum Diner, StationSounds, 05		290	___
29191	MILW Hiawatha Passenger Car 4-pack, 06		370	___
29192	MILW Hiawatha Combination Car "153," 06		95	___
29193	MILW Hiawatha Coach "437," 06		95	___
29194	MILW Hiawatha Coach "438," 06		95	___
29195	MILW Hiawatha Observation "Miller," 06		95	___
29196	MILW Hiawatha Passenger Car 2-pack, 06		190	___
29197	MILW Hiawatha Baggage Car "1305," 06		95	___
29198	MILW Hiawatha Coach "439," 06		95	___
29199	MILW Hiawatha Diner, StationSounds, 06		190	___
29202	Santa Fe Map Boxcar "6464," 97 u		53	___
29203	Maine Central Boxcar "6464-597," 97 u	10	35	___
29205	Mickey Mouse Hi-Cube Boxcar "9555," 97		70	___
29206	Vapor Records Boxcar #1, 97		90	___
29209	Postwar "6464" Boxcar Series VII, 3 cars, 98	23	97	___
29210	GN Boxcar "6464-450," 98		33	___
29211	B&M Boxcar "6464-475," 98		27	___
29212	Timken Boxcar "6464-500," 98		28	___
29213	ATSF Grand Canyon Route 6464 Boxcar "6464-198," 98		26	___
29214	Southern 6464 Boxcar "6464-298," 98	32	86	___
29215	Canadian Pacific 6464 Boxcar "6464-398," 98	9	28	___
29217	1997 Toy Fair Airex Boxcar, 97		78	___
29218	Vapor Records Boxcar "6464-496," 97 u	20	49	___
29220	Lionel Centennial Series Hi-Cube Boxcar Set, 4 cars, 97		243	___
29221	Centennial Series Hi-Cube Boxcar "9697-1", 97		65	___
29222	Centennial Series Hi-Cube Boxcar "9697-2", 97		72	___
29223	Centennial Series Hi-Cube Boxcar "9697-3", 97		65	___
29224	Centennial Series Hi-Cube Boxcar "9697-4", 97		62	___
29225	H.O.R.D.E. Music Festival Boxcar, 97	48	70	___
29229	Vapor Records Holiday Car, 98		165	___
29231	Halloween Animated Boxcar, 98		42	___
29233	Conrail PC Overstamped Boxcar "6464-598," 98		38	___
29234	Conrail Erie Overstamped Boxcar "6464-698," 98		32	___
29235	NYC Boxcar "6464-510," 99		47	___
29236	MKT Boxcar "6464-515," 99		40	___
29237	M&StL Boxcar "6464-525," 99	13	35	___

MODERN 1970-2025			Exc	Like New
___	**29247**	Classic Green Street Lamps, 3-pack, 08-25		40
___	**29250**	Phoebe Snow Boxcar "6464-199," 99		41
___	**29251**	BN Boxcar "6464-299," 99	13	36
___	**29252**	CP Boxcar "6464-399," 99	13	37
___	**29253**	B&M Boxcar "76032," 99		50
___	**29254**	B&M Boxcar "76033," 99		50
___	**29255**	B&M Boxcar "76034," 99		50
___	**29256**	B&M Boxcar "76035," 99		50
___	**29257**	Southern Boxcar "9464-199," 99		38
___	**29258**	Reading Boxcar "9464-299," 99		36
___	**29259**	NP Bicentennial Boxcar "9464-399," 99		34
___	**29265**	Maine Central Boxcar "8661," 99	10	36
___	**29266**	Frisco Boxcar "8722," 99	15	38
___	**29267**	No. 6464 Boxcar 3-pack, Series VIII, 99	38	86
___	**29268**	Rio Grande Boxcar "63067," 99		40
___	**29271**	Lionel Cola Tractor and Trailer, 98		12
___	**29279**	Conrail Jersey Central Overstamped Boxcar "6464-28X," 99		40
___	**29280**	Conrail LV Overstamped Boxcar "6464-31X," 99		41
___	**29281**	Conrail Overstamped Boxcar 2-pack, 99		70
___	**29282**	Postwar "6464" Boxcar 3-pack, 99	43	125
___	**29283**	NYC Boxcar, 99		55
___	**29284**	GN Boxcar, 99	14	39
___	**29285**	Seaboard Boxcar, 99		36
___	**29286**	Overstamped Boxcar 2-pack, 99		65
___	**29287**	NH PC Overstamped Boxcar "6464-29X," 99	18	34
___	**29288**	Conrail Reading Overstamped Boxcar "6464-32X," 99		38
___	**29289**	Postwar "6464" Series IX, 3 cars, 99-00	35	85
___	**29290**	D&RGW Boxcar "6464-650," 00		41
___	**29291**	ATSF Boxcar "6464-700", 00		38
___	**29292**	NH Boxcar "6464-725", 00		39
___	**29293**	NH Boxcar "6464-425," 99		95
___	**29294**	Hellgate Bridge Boxcar "1900-2000," 99 u		38
___	**29295**	PRR "Don't Stand Me Still" Boxcar "24018," 99-00		65
___	**29296**	PRR "Merchandise" Boxcar "29296," 99-00		65
___	**29297**	PRR "No Damage" Boxcar "47158," 99-00		65
___	**29298**	Lionel Boxcar "6464-2000," 00		46
___	**29300**	50th Anniversary Clear Shell Aquarium Car, 10		85
___	**29301**	Postwar "3662" Transparent Milk Car with platform, 11, 13		155
___	**29302**	Christmas Music Reefer, 10		75
___	**29303**	North Pole Central Crane Car, 10-11		65
___	**29305**	UP Chisholm Trail Stock Car, Cattle Sounds, 11, 13		200
___	**29306**	PRR Hi-Cube Lighted Garland Boxcar, 10-11		70
___	**29309**	GN Pullman-Standard Diesel Freight Set, CC, 13		830
___	**29310**	Marine Science Deep Sea Exhibition Aquarium Car, 11		75
___	**29311**	Strasburg Derrick Car, 11		45
___	**29312**	Santa's Operating Boxcar, 11-12		75
___	**29314**	SP DD Boxcar "214051" (std 0), 13-14		75
___	**29317**	CN DD Boxcar "551334" (std 0), 13-14	40	80
___	**29318**	NJ Transit Gondola "9422" w/Ballast Load, 12-13		35
___	**29319**	NJ Transit BW Caboose "905," 12-13	70	90
___	**29320**	CNJ DD Boxcar "25031" (std 0), 13-14	40	75
___	**29320**	UP Walking Brakeman Car "454400," 12	52	70
___	**29321**	Ice Skating Aquarium Car, 12		80

		Exc	Like New	
29322	Koi Aquarium Car, 13-14		80	___
29323	UP DD Boxcar "500019" (std 0), 13-14		75	___
29324	Walking Zombie Brakeman Car, 12		80	___
29326	NP "Pig Palace" Operating Stock Car "84144," 12		200	___
29327	Bethlehem Steel Operating Hopper "2025," 12		60	___
29328	Beatles "Nothing is Real" Aquarium Car, 12-13		85	___
29329	Peanuts Halloween Aquarium Car, 12-13		85	___
29333	ATSF 89' Auto Carrier 2-pack (std 0), 13-16		220	___
29338	BN 89' Auto Carrier 2-pack (std 0), 13-14		220	___
29344	C&NW DD Boxcar "57766" (std 0), 13		75	___
29345	ATSF 89' Auto Carrier (std 0), 13-14		110	___
29346	Soo Line 89' Auto Carrier 2-pack (std 0), 13-16		220	___
29349	SP 89' Auto Carrier 2-pack (std 0), 13-16		220	___
29364	NYC Water Level Steam Freight Set, CC, 12-13		1600	___
29365	N&W Pocahontas Steam Passenger Set, CC, 12		1950	___
29366	SP TankSet Diesel Set, CC, 12		850	___
29372	BNSF 89' Auto Carrier "300267" (std 0), 13		110	___
29373	CN 89' Auto Carrier "710771" (std 0), 13, 16		110	___
29376	Conrail 89' Auto Carrier "964444" (std 0), 13		110	___
29377	CP 89' Auto Carrier 2-pack (std 0), 13-16		220	___
29380	CSX 89' Auto Carrier "604544" (std 0), 13		110	___
29381	GTW 89' Auto Carrier "50450" (std 0), 14-15		110	___
29382	UP 89' Auto Carrier "604545" (std 0), 13		110	___
29384	DL&W USRA Double-sheathed Boxcar "44153" (std 0), 13		70	___
29385	ATSF USRA Double-sheathed Boxcar "39012" (std 0), 13		70	___
29386	PRR PS-4 Flatcar with stakes "469614" (std 0), 13		70	___
29387	GN PS-4 Flatcar with stakes "629387" (std 0), 13		70	___
29400	Bethlehem Steel Slag Car 3-pack (std 0), 03		185	___
29404	Bethlehem Steel Hot Metal Car 3-pack (std 0), 03	60	210	___
29408	PRR Coil Car, 01		40	___
29411	Sherwin-Williams Vat Car, 02		35	___
29412	Tabasco Brand Vat Car, 02		36	___
29413	Airex Boat Loader Car "29413," 02		42	___
29414	PRR Evans Auto Loader "480123," 01		56	___
29415	WM Skeleton Log Car 3-pack #2 (std 0), 02		90	___
29419	West Side Lumber Skeleton Log Car 3-pack #2 (std 0), 02		90	___
29423	Wellspring Capital Management Happy Holidays Vat Car, 03 u		255	___
29424	Meadow River Lumber Skeleton Log Car 3-pack (std 0), 03		90	___
29429	Campbell's Soup Vat Car "29429," 03		38	___
29430	Meadow River Lumber Skeleton Log Car 3-pack #2 (std 0), 03		90	___
29434	Weyerhauser Skeleton Log Car 3-pack, 05		108	___
29438	Trailer Train Flatcar with 2 UP trailers, 03		60	___
29439	Postwar "6414" Evans Auto Loader, 02		43	___
29441	UP Flatcar "53471" with grader, 02		43	___
29442	CSX Flatcar "600513" with backhoe, 02		43	___
29449	Weyerhaeuser Timber Skeleton Log Car 3-pack #2 (std 0), 03		90	___
29453	Elk River Lumber Skeleton Log Car 3-pack #2 (std 0), 03		90	___
29457	NS Flatcar "157590" with Caterpillar loader, 03		42	___
29458	BNSF Flatcar "922268" with Caterpillar truck, 03		44	___
29459	Water Barrel Car "1878," Archive Collection, 03		40	___
29460	LL Flatcar "3460" with trailers, Archive Collection, 03		39	___
29461	Postwar "6500" Flatcar with red-and-white airplane, 03		32	___
29462	Postwar "6500" Flatcar with white-and-red airplane, 03		31	___

MODERN 1970-2025		Exc	Like New
29463	Postwar "6414" Evans Auto Loader, 03		30
29464	U.S. Army Vat Car "29464," 04		35
29465	U.S. Steel Slag Car 3-pack (std O), 04-05		160
29469	U.S. Steel Hot Metal Car 3-pack (std O), 04-05	70	190
29473	Youngstown Sheet & Tube Slag Car 3-pack (std O), 03		150
29477	Youngstown Sheet & Tube Hot Metal Car 3-pack (std O), 03		170
29481	Cass Scenic Railroad Skeleton Log Car 3-pack (std O), 03		80
29487	Boat-loader with 4 boats, 04		65
29488	Cass Scenic Railroad Skeleton Log Car 3-pack #2 (std O), 04		90
29492	Pickering Lumber Skeleton Log Car 3-pack #1 (std O), 04		100
29496	Pickering Lumber Skeleton Log Car 3-pack #2 (std O), 04		90
29602	Celanese Chemicals 1-D Tank Car, 05		45
29603	Comet 1-D Tank Car, traditional, 05		53
29604	Meadow Brook Molasses 1-D Tank Car, traditional, 05		53
29606	Elvis Presley Gold Record Transport Car, 04		120
29607	Las Vegas Mint Car, traditional, 05		58
29609	Alien Suspension Car, 06		60
29610	Dixie Honey 1-D Tank Car, 06		60
29611	Sunoco 1-D Tank Car, 06	30	63
29612	Las Vegas Poker Chip Car, 06		40
29613	Postwar "6463" Rocket Fuel 2-D Tank Car, 06		75
29614	Postwar "6315" Gulf Chemical Tank Car, 06	15	49
29617	Postwar "6465" Cities Service 2-D Tank Car, 06-07		48
29618	Hooker Chemicals 3-D Tank Car, 07		60
29619	Grave's Formaldehyde 1-D Tank Car, 07		60
29622	Fort Knox Mint Car, lilac, Archive Collection, 07		60
29624	Monopoly Mint Car with money, 08		65
29626	"Case Closed" Mint Car with shredded documents, 08		109
29628	Poinsettia Mint Car, 09		70
29629	AEC Glow-in-the-Dark Tank Car, 09-10		65
29633	Christmas Ornament Lighted Mint Car, 10		70
29634	Federal Reserve Bailout Mint Car, 10		70
29635	Monopoly "Go To Jail" Mint Car, 10		70
29636	Vampire Transport Mint Car, 10-11		70
29637	Candy Cane 2-D Tank Car, 10-11		55
29638	Fort Knox Mint Car, 10-11	40	65
29640	Coca-Cola Tank Car, 10		65
29642	Jolly Rancher 1-D Tank Car, 11		55
29643	Hershey's Syrup 1-D Tank Car, 11		58
29644	ATSF 1-D Tank Car, 11		55
29645	Atlantic City Casino Mint Car, 11		70
29646	Alaska Oil 2-D Tank Car, 11		50
29647	Gingerbread Man Mint Car, 11		70
29648	Kansas City Federal Reserve Mint Car, 11		70
29649	Lionel SP Smoke Pellets Mint Car, 12-13		70
29650	Cleveland Federal Reserve Mint Car, 11		70
29651	Richmond Federal Reserve Mint Car, 12		70
29654	Boston Federal Reserve Mint Car, 13		70
29655	PRR 16-wheel Flatcar with girders "469846," 12		75
29656	ATSF 16-wheel Flatcar with transformer "90096," 12		75
29671	Smoke Pellet Mint Car #2, 13-15		70
29694	Hershey's Mint Car, 14	64	95
29695	Trailer Set Maxi-Stack Pair "48," 13		120

		Exc	Like New	
29697	Santa's Flatcar with submarine, 13		70	___
29698	Tree Topper Star Transport Car, 13-14		80	___
29699	Silver and Gold Christmas Mint Car, 13-14		70	___
29703	Postwar "6427-500" Girl's PRR Porthole Caboose, 01		45	___
29704	Postwar "6427" Boy's Set PRR Porthole Caboose, 02		50	___
29705	PRR Porthole Caboose "477951" (std 0), 04		40	___
29706	Postwar "6437" PRR Porthole Caboose, 04		40	___
29707	NIckel Plate BW Caboose "408" (std 0), 04		80	___
29708	C&O Bay Window Caboose "8315," 04		45	___
29709	PRR Porthole Caboose "477938," 04		40	___
29710	Postwar "6657" D&RGW Caboose, 04-05		33	___
29711	ATSF Bay Window Caboose, 04-05		60	___
29712	Postwar "2420" Searchlight Caboose, 04		50	___
29713	Postwar "6437" PRR Porthole Caboose, 05		20	___
29714	Postwar "6557" Lionel Lines Smoking Caboose, 05-07		120	___
29715	PRR Porthole Caboose "477953," 05		45	___
29716	UP EV Caboose "25462," 04		40	___
29717	NS EV Caboose "555533," 05	40	50	___
29718	Postwar "6419-100" N&W Work Caboose, 05-06		48	___
29719	ATSF Porthole Caboose "6427," Archive Collection, 05-06		48	___
29720	PRR Porthole Caboose "477861," 06		45	___
29721	PRR Work Caboose "491064," 06		50	___
29722	Postwar "6517" LL BW Caboose w/Strobe light, 06		49	___
29723	LL Porthole Caboose "64273" Archive Collection, 06-08	27	50	___
29724	Postwar "6517" LL BW Caboose, 06-07		50	___
29725	CP EV Caboose "43615," 06		50	___
29726	Virginian Porthole Caboose "6427-60," Archive Collection, 06-07		50	___
29727	"I Love U.S.A." Bay Window Caboose "1985," 06		60	___
29728	UP Smoking EV Caboose, 07		60	___
29729	Bethlehem Steel Searchlight Caboose, 06		90	___
29730	Postwar "6427-3" LL Porthole Caboose, 07		45	___
29732	PRR Porthole Caboose "477871," 08		45	___
29733	White Pass & Yukon EV Caboose, 09-10		90	___
29734	PRR NS Heritage CA-4 Caboose (std 0), 09-10		95	___
29735	Conrail NS Heritage CA-4 Caboose (std 0), 10		95	___
29736	NYC Smoking NE Caboose "20883," 09-10		55	___
29737	ATSF Bay Window Caboose, traditional, 10-11		70	___
29738	Postwar "6517" Transparent Smoking BW Caboose, 10-11		80	___
29739	B&M Transfer Caboose, 10-11		50	___
29761	GATX TankTrain A-End "44570," 12		100	___
29762	GATX TankTrain Intermediate Car "44559," 12		80	___
29763	GATX TankTrain Intermediate Car "44580," 12		80	___
29764	GATX TankTrain B-End "44575," 12		100	___
29765	GATX TankSet Add-on 3-pack (std 0), 12		240	___
29766	GATX TankTrain Intermediate Car "44598," 12		80	___
29767	GATX TankTrain Intermediate Car "44581," 12		80	___
29768	GATX TankTrain Intermediate Car "44578," 12		80	___
29769	NYC/MC Double-sheathed Boxcar "51071," 12-13		100	___
29770	B&M Offset Hopper "7168," 12-13		40	___
29771	CN TankSet 2-pack (std 0), 12		160	___
29772	CN TankTrain Intermediate Car "75565," 12	18	66	___
29773	CN TankTrain Intermediate Car "75561," 12		80	___

	MODERN 1970-2025		Exc	Like New
____	29774	GATX TankSet 2-pack (std O), 12		160
____	29775	GATX TankTrain Intermediate Car "57009," 12		80
____	29776	GATX TankTrain Intermediate Car "48671," 12		80
____	29777	CIBRO TankSet 2-pack (std O), 12		160
____	29778	CIBRO TankTrain Intermediate Car "26251," 12		80
____	29779	CIBRO TankTrain Intermediate Car "26255," 12		80
____	29780	NYC 1-D Tank Car, 12-13		90
____	29781	NYC Smoking Wood-sided Caboose, 12-13		200
____	29786	Bethlehem Steel PS-2 3-bay Hopper (std O), 13		80
____	29787	PRR PS-2 3-bay Hopper (std O), 13		80
____	29788	PRR Porthole Caboose "477939," 13-17		35
____	27789	Penn Salt Chemicals 3-D Tank Car "4727,", 13-17		35
____	29790	PRR Boxcar "539339," 13-17		36
____	29791	Wizard of Oz Anniversary Boxcar, 13-15		70
____	29792	Angela Trotta Thomas "Toyland Express" Boxcar, 13		65
____	29793	"Where the Wild Things Are" Boxcar, 13-15		70
____	29800	MOW Crane Car, TMCC, 04		300
____	29801	ATSF Operating Barrel Ramp Car, 04-05		89
____	29802	Postwar "3530" EMD Generator Car, 04-05		89
____	29803	Postwar "3444" Erie Animated Gondola, 04-05		89
____	29804	UP Crane Car "JPX 250," CC, 05		320
____	29805	Conrail Crane Car "50202," CC, 05		320
____	29806	Weyerhaeuser Log Dump Car, 05		75
____	29807	DM&IR Coal Dump Car, 05		75
____	29808	Candy Cane Dump Car, 05		55
____	29809	Santa's Delivery Service Dump Car w/Presents, 05		60
____	29810	Operating Egg Nog Car with platform, 05		140
____	29811	NYC Merchant's Despatch Transit Hot Box Reefer, 05-06	85	110
____	29812	Santa Fe Hot Box Reefer "20699," 05-06		90
____	29813	Santa Fe Boom Car "19144," Crane Sounds, 05		270
____	29814	Pennsylvania Boom Car "491063," Crane Sounds, 05		210
____	29815	NYC Boom Car "X923," Crane Sounds, 05		210
____	29816	MOW Boom Car "X-816," Crane Sounds, 05		210
____	29817	UP Boom Car "909438," Crane Sounds, 05		210
____	29818	Conrail Boom Car, Crane Sounds, 05		210
____	29820	Postwar "3356" Operating Horse Car and Corral, 05		75
____	29821	Postwar "2460" Lionel Lines Crane Car, gray cab, 05		48
____	29822	Postwar "773W" NYC Tender, whistle, 05		48
____	29823	Postwar "3484" Pennsylvania Operating Boxcar, 05		38
____	29824	Postwar "3662" Operating Milk Car and Platform, 05		59
____	29825	Postwar "3434" Poultry Dispatch Car, 05		60
____	29826	Postwar "3530" Generator Car and Light Pole, 05		48
____	29827	Postwar "3419" Helicopter Launching Car, 06		49
____	29828	Postwar "3666" Minuteman Car with cannon, 06		85
____	29829	Postwar "6805" Radioactive Waste Car, 06		85
____	29830	PFE Hot Box Reefer "5890" (std O), 06		105
____	29831	Swift Hot Box Reefer "15342" (std O), 06		150
____	29832	Chessie System Crane Car "940504," CC, 06		320
____	29833	Chessie System Boom Car "940561," CC, 06		210
____	29834	LL Bay Window Caboose "834," TrainSounds (std O), 06-07		110
____	29835	SP Bay Window Caboose "4667," TrainSounds (std O), 06-07		160
____	29838	Postwar "3666" Cannon Firing Boxcar, 05		149
____	29839	Postwar "6512" Cherry Picker Car, 06		63

MODERN 1970-2025		Exc	Like New	
29841	PRR Ballast Dump Car, 06		28	___
29842	REA Express Hot Box Refrigerator Car w/Smoke, 06-07		125	___
29843	Postwar "3356" ATSF Operating Horse Car and Corral, 06-07		110	___
29844	Postwar "3512" Fireman and Ladder Car, 06-08		50	___
29845	Postwar "6812" Track Maintenance Car, 06-08		50	___
29846	Postwar "6650" Operating Missile Launching Car, 06-07		30	___
29847	Postwar "3419" Helicopter Launching Car, 06-07		60	___
29648	Postwar "3540" Operating Radar Car, 06-07		50	___
29849	Lionel Lines Crane Car, silver cab, 05-06		60	___
29850	N&W J Class Tender, air whistle, 06-07		73	___
29851	NYC Operating Crane Car "X-15," CC, 06		180	___
29852	NYC Boom Car w/Sounds, 06		220	___
29853	Postwar "6651" Big John Cannon Car, 08		75	___
29854	Satellite Launching Car, 07		70	___
29855	Lionel Lines Operating Milk Car with platform, 07		140	___
29856	Postwar "3494-550" Monon Operating Boxcar, 06-07		65	___
29857	Postwar "6660" Lionel Lines Boom Car, 06-07		55	___
29858	CP Rail Crane Car "414475," CC, 07		320	___
29859	CP Rail Boom Car "412567," CC, 07		210	___
29865	Southern Operating Barrel Car, 07-08		75	___
29866	Pirates Aquarium Car, 07		75	___
29867	NYC Jet Snow Blower "X27207," 07		120	___
29868	Alaska Jet Snow Blower, 07		120	___
29869	Bethlehem Steel Crane Car, 06		60	___
29870	MOW Jet Snow Blower "MWX-16," 07		120	___
29871	Postwar "3359" Twin Bin Dump Car, 07		40	___
29872	Postwar "3494-275" State of Maine Operating Boxcar, 07		55	___
29873	Postwar "3361" LL Log Dump Car, 07		40	___
29874	Peanuts Halloween Aquarium Car, 12		85	___
29877	Southern Crane Car "D76," CC, 08		350	___
29878	Southern Boom Car "T-193," CC, 08		230	___
29882	Witches Operating Brew Car, 08		150	___
29883	C&NW Operating Crane Car, CC, 10 u		340	___
29884	CNJ Twin Dump Car, 08		85	___
29885	BN Crane Car "S-104," CC, 10		340	___
29886	BN Boom Car "S-1040," CC, 10		220	___
29888	Postwar "3494-625" Soo Line Operating Boxcar, 08		70	___
29891	ATSF Operating Crane Car, CC, 09-10		340	___
29892	ATSF Boom Car, CC, 09-10		220	___
29893	PRR Operating Stock Car "129893," RailSounds, 09		150	___
29894	Christmas Chase Gondola, 09		65	___
29895	Christmas Operating Snow Globe Car, 10		75	___
29897	CSX Chessie System Research Car "3440," 11		65	___
29900	"I Love Wisconsin" Boxcar, 01		35	___
29901	"I Love Kentucky" Boxcar, 01		30	___
29902	"I Love Iowa" Boxcar, 01		31	___
29903	"I Love Missouri" Boxcar, 01		31	___
29904	2002 Toy Fair Boxcar, 02		22	___
29905	2002 Lionel Employee Christmas Boxcar, 02		80	___
29906	"I Love Connecticut" Boxcar, 02		33	___
29907	"I Love West Virginia" Boxcar, 02		33	___
29908	"I Love Delaware" Boxcar, 02		33	___

	MODERN 1970-2025		Exc	Like New
____	**29909**	"I Love Maryland" Boxcar, 02		65
____	**29910**	Toy Fair Centennial Boxcar, 03		40
____	**29911**	2003 Lionel Employee Christmas Boxcar, 03 u		90
____	**29912**	"I Love Alabama" Boxcar, 03		30
____	**29913**	"I Love Mississippi" Boxcar, 03		35
____	**29914**	"I Love Louisiana" Boxcar, 03		35
____	**29915**	"I Love Arkansas" Boxcar, 03		30
____	**29918**	2003 Toy Fair Boxcar, 03 u		48
____	**29919**	2004 Toy Fair Boxcar, 04 u		37
____	**29920**	"I Love North Dakota" Boxcar, 03		35
____	**29921**	"I Love South Dakota" Boxcar, 03		40
____	**29922**	"I Love Nebraska" Boxcar, 03		30
____	**29923**	"I Love Kansas" Boxcar, 03		30
____	**29924**	2004 Lionel Employee Christmas Boxcar, 04 u	23	110
____	**29925**	Toy Fair Polar Express Boxcar, 05 u		250
____	**29926**	2005 Lionel Employee Christmas Boxcar, 05 u		90
____	**29927**	"I Love Washington" Boxcar, 05		45
____	**29928**	"I Love Oregon" Boxcar, 05		40
____	**29929**	"I Love Idaho" Boxcar, 05		45
____	**29930**	"I Love Utah" Boxcar, 05		45
____	**29931**	LRRC Season's Greetings Boxcar, 05 u		40
____	**29932**	"I Love Oklahoma" Boxcar, 06		45
____	**29933**	"I Love New Mexico" Boxcar, 06		45
____	**29934**	"I Love Hawaii" Boxcar, 06		45
____	**29935**	"I Love Alaska" Boxcar, 06		45
____	**29936**	"I Love Wyoming" Boxcar, 06		45
____	**29937**	2006 Toy Fair Boxcar, 06		38
____	**29938**	2006 Lionel Employee Christmas Boxcar, 06 u		25
____	**29939**	LRRC Anniversary Boxcar, 06 u		26
____	**29941**	LRRC 2006 Christmas Boxcar, 06 u		40
____	**29942**	Santa Fe Railroad Art Boxcar, 06		50
____	**29943**	Texas Special Railroad Art Boxcar, 06		50
____	**29944**	1957 Lionel Art Boxcar, 06	10	50
____	**29945**	1947 Lionel Art Boxcar, 06		50
____	**29946**	LRRC 2007 Christmas Boxcar, 07 u		40
____	**29947**	LRRC 2007 Commemorative Boxcar, 07 u		42
____	**29949**	2007 Lionel Employee Christmas Boxcar, 07 u		60
____	**29950**	1948 Lionel Art Boxcar, 08		50
____	**29951**	1954 Lionel Art Boxcar, 08	18	50
____	**29952**	GN Art Boxcar, 08		50
____	**29953**	SP Art Boxcar, 08		50
____	**29954**	2007 Lionel Dealer Christmas Boxcar, 07 u		50
____	**29955**	2008 Lionel Dealer Appreciation Boxcar, 08 u		70
____	**29956**	2008 Lionel Employee Christmas Boxcar, 08 u		60
____	**29957**	LRRC 2008 Christmas Boxcar, 08 u		42
____	**29958**	2009 Lionel Dealer Appreciation Boxcar, 09 u		40
____	**29959**	1952 Lionel Art Boxcar, 09	33	58
____	**29960**	Rock Island Art Boxcar, 09-10		58
____	**29961**	Meet the Beatles Boxcar 2-pack, 10-14		130
____	**29962**	Meet the Beatles Boxcar, 10-14		65
____	**29963**	The Beatles' Second Album Boxcar, 10-14		65
____	**29964**	2009 Lionel Employee Christmas Boxcar, 09 u		25
____	**29965**	Lionel Art Boxcar 2-pack, 10-11		116

MODERN 1970-2025		Exc	Like New	
29966	Lionel Art Boxcar, 12	45	55	___
29967	Lionel Santa Fe Art Boxcar, 10-11		35	___
29968	Beatles "A Hard Day's Night" Boxcar, 11-14		65	___
29969	Beatles "Something New" Boxcar, 11-14		65	___
29970	2010 Lionel Employee Christmas Boxcar, 10 u		25	___
29971	2011 Lionel Employee Christmas Boxcar, 11 u		25	___
29972	2012 Lionel Employee Christmas Boxcar, 12 u		25	___
29973	NYC Pacemaker Boxcar "175005," 10-11		60	___
29974	SP Boxcar "128133," 11		60	___
29975	Holiday Boxcar, 11		60	___
29976	Holiday Boxcar, 12-13		65	___
29977	2011 LRRC Holiday Boxcar, 11 u		60	___
29978	Railroad Museum of Pennsylvania Boxcar, 12		65	___
29979	Angela Trotta Thomas "Christmas Morning" Boxcar, 12-13		60	___
29980	Elvis Presley 35th Anniversary Boxcar, 12		70	___
29982	CV Milk Car "575" (std 0), 15-16		80	___
29985	B&M Milk Car "1903" (std 0), 15-16		80	___
29989	PFE Steel-sided Refrigerator Car 3-pack (std 0), 14-15		240	___
29990	PFE Steel-sided Refrigerator Car "8383" (std 0), 14-15		80	___
29991	PFE Steel-sided Refrigerator Car "8171" (std 0), 14-15		80	___
29992	PFE Steel-sided Refrigerator Car "8080" (std 0), 14-15		80	___
29994	U.S. Army Boxcar, 13-15		70	___
29995	U.S. Navy Boxcar, 13-15		70	___
29996	U.S. Marines Boxcar, 13-15		70	___
29997	U.S. Air Force Boxcar, 13-15		70	___
29998	U.S. National Guard Boxcar, 13-16		70	___
29999	U.S. Coast Guard Boxcar, 13-16		70	___
30000	PRR Keystone Super Freight Steam Train, TMCC, 05		450	___
30001	Santa Fe El Capitan Passenger Set, TrainSounds, 05-10	150	370	___
30002	Neil Young's Greendale Diesel Freight Set, 04		420	___
30003	Pennsylvania Flyer Operating Freight Expansion Pack, 05		99	___
30004	Pennsylvania Flyer Passenger Expansion Pack, 05-08		120	___
30005	Disney Passenger Train, 05		190	___
30007	NYC Flyer Operating Freight Expansion Pack, 05		99	___
30008	NYC Flyer Passenger Expansion Pack, 05-08		120	___
30011	Holiday Expansion Pack, 05		100	___
30012	Thomas the Tank Engine Expansion Pack, 05-13, 16		150	___
30016	NYC Flyer Steam Freight Set, 06-08		290	___
30018	Pennsylvania Flyer Steam Freight Set, 06-07	100	240	___
30020	North Pole Central Christmas Steam Train, 06-07		208	___
30021	Cascade Range Steam Logging Train, 06-08		190	___
30022	Southwest Diesel Freight Set, TrainSounds, 06	80	295	___
30024	UP Fast Freight Steam Set, TrainSounds, 06-07		340	___
30025	Chesapeake Super Freight Steam Set, TMCC, 06-07	238	488	___
30026	CP Diesel Freight Set, TMCC, 06		540	___
30029	Amtrak Coast Limited Set, TMCC, 06			___
30034	Great Western Train Set with Lincoln Logs, 07-09	115	315	___
30035	Sodor Freight Expansion Pack, 06-09		120	___
30036	Great Western Expansion Pack, 07-08		120	___
30037	Pennsylvania Flyer Operating Freight Expansion Pack, 06-08		120	___
30038	NYC Flyer Operating Freight Expansion Pack, 06-08		120	___
30039	North Pole Central Passenger Expansion Pack, 06-11	55	155	___
30040	North Pole Central Freight Expansion Pack, 06-11		110	___

	MODERN 1970-2025		Exc	Like New
___	**30041**	Southwest Diesel Freight Expansion Pack, 06		110
___	**30042**	Cascade Range Expansion Pack, 06		110
___	**30044**	NYC Empire Builder Steam Freight Set, TMCC, 06	1073	2800
___	**30045**	Alaska Steam Work Train, 07-09	80	270
___	**30046**	Alaska Work Train Expansion Pack, 07-08		110
___	**30047**	Northwest Special Diesel Freight Set, TrainSounds, 07-08		295
___	**30048**	Northwest Special Freight Expansion Pack, 07-08		110
___	**30049**	D&RGW Fast Freight Set, TrainSounds, 08-09		320
___	**30050**	Pennsylvania Super Freight Set, CC, 08		450
___	**30051**	UP Diesel Freight Set, TMCC, 07		500
___	**30056**	Halloween Steam Freight Set, 07-10	85	225
___	**30061**	UPS Centennial Stream Freight Set, 07-08	100	230
___	**30063**	"It's a Wonderful Life" Christmas Steam Freight Set, 07 u	375	450
___	**30064**	Pennsylvania Speeder Set, traditional, K-Line, 06		75
___	**30065**	Best Friend of Charleston Locomotive, 07		425
___	**30066/67**	C&O Empire Builder Steam Freight Set, CC, 07-09		2700
___	**30068**	North Pole Central Christmas Freight Set, 08		220
___	**30069**	Thomas & Friends Passenger Train, 08-12		170
___	**30070**	Lionel Lines 4-4-2 Steam Freight Set, 07		300
___	**30076**	Disney Christmas Train, 07		400
___	**30081**	UP Merger Special GP38 Freight Set, 08	83	300
___	**30082**	UP Heritage Freight Car 3-pack, 08		100
___	**30084**	British Great Western Shakespeare Express Passenger Train, 08		300
___	**30085**	MTA Metro-North M-7 Commuter Car Set, 07-08	140	536
___	**30087**	Alien Spaceship Recovery Freight Set, 08-09	85	230
___	**30088**	John Bull Passenger Train, 08		430
___	**30089**	Pennsylvania Flyer Freight Set, 08-10		200
___	**30091**	ATSF Steam Freight Set, 08-09		270
___	**30094**	Chicago & North Western Passenger Set, 08		150
___	**30096**	Pennsylvania Keystone Special Steam Freight Set, 09		260
___	**30103**	NYC 0-8-0 Steam Freight Set, 09-10	167	291
___	**30108**	American Fire and Rescue GP20 Freight Set, 09-10		400
___	**30109**	Nutcracker Route Christmas Train Set, 10-11		270
___	**30111**	Pullman Passenger Expansion Pack, 09-16		155
___	**30112**	Eastern Freight Expansion Pack, 09-17		155
___	**30114**	MTA LIRR M-7 Commuter Set, 09		320
___	**30116**	Lone Ranger Wild West Freight Set, 09-13		400
___	**30118**	A Christmas Story Steam Freight Set, 09-12		340
___	**30120**	Menards C&NW Steam Passenger Set, 09		250
___	**30121**	ATSF Baby Madison Car 3-pack, 10-11		190
___	**30122**	Wizard of Oz Steam Freight Set, 10-12		310
___	**30123**	Boy Scouts of America Steam Freight Set, 10		310
___	**30124**	Thunder Valley Quarry Steam Freight Set, 10-11		300
___	**30125**	Rio Grande Ski Train, TrainSounds, 10-11		340
___	**30126**	Pennsylvania Flyer Steam Freight Set, 10		230
___	**30127**	Scout Steam Freight Set, 10-12		200
___	**30128**	Western Freight Expansion Pack, 10-12		138
___	**30131**	Chessie System Merger Diesel Freight Set, 10		300
___	**30133**	Strasburg Steam Passenger Set, 10-13		330
___	**30135**	Scout Freight Expansion Pack, 11-15		115
___	**30136**	Thunder Valley Quarry Freight Car Add-on 2-pack, 10-11		110
___	**30138**	Chessie System Merger Freight Car Add-on 2-pack, 10-11		120

MODERN 1970-2025		Exc	Like New	
30139	Santa Fe Flyer Steam Freight Set, 10		270	___
30141	Sodor Tank and Wagon Expansion Pack, 10-16		150	___
30142	Texas Special Freight Set, TrainSounds, 10-11		700	___
30144	Operation Eagle Justice Diesel Freight Set, 10-11	138	500	___
30145	Maple Leaf Diesel Freight Set, 10-11		550	___
30146	Menards Soo Line Freight Set, 10	175	275	___
30147	MTA Long Island M-7 Commuter Set, 11		320	___
30149	Bass Pro Shops North Pole Central Christmas Set, 08 u		220	___
30153	CSX Diesel Freight Set, 11		330	___
30154	BNSF Diesel Freight Set, 11		340	___
30155	M&StL Diesel Freight Set, 11-12		230	___
30156	NYC Flyer Freight Set, TrainSounds, 11		300	___
30157	M&StL Flatcar and Erie-Lack. Gondola 2-pack, 11-15		110	___
30158	Norfolk Southern GP38 Diesel Freight Train Set, 11		320	___
30159	Wabash Blue Bird Passenger Set, 11-12		360	___
30161	Boy Scouts Steam Freight Set, 11-13		320	___
30162	Thomas & Friends Christmas Set, 13-15		200	___
30164	Santa's Flyer Steam Freight Set, 11-13		250	___
30165	Candy Cane Transit Commuter 2-pack, 11-13		180	___
30166	Coca-Cola 125th Anniversary Steam Set, 11-12		355	___
30167	SP Merger Steam Freight Train Set , 12		400	___
30168	Rio Grande General Set, TrainSounds, 11-12		325	___
30169	NJ Transit Train Set, 11		350	___
30170	Sodor Freight 3-pack, 11-13		100	___
30171	GG1 Electric Freight Train Set, 11-13		550	___
30173	Santa Fe Flyer Freight Set, 11-12		270	___
30174	Pennsylvania Flyer Freight Set, 11-13	80	290	___
30176	Wegmans Steam Freight Train Set, 11 u		300	___
30177	Menards Milwaukee Road Steam Freight Set, 11 u		175	___
30178	ATSF Super Chief Diesel Passenger Train Set, 12-13		400	___
30179	RI Rocket Diesel Freight Train Set, 12-13	175	400	___
30180	Horseshoe Curve Steam Freight Train Set, 12-13		440	___
30181	CP Diesel Passenger Set, RailSounds, 13, 15		450	___
30183	Scout Remote Steam Freight Set, 13, 15		220	___
30184	Polar Express Steam Freight Set, 13		420	___
30185	NJ Transit Diesel MOW Train Set, 12-13		350	___
30186	KCS Southern Belle Diesel Freight Train Set, 12-13		350	___
30187	Titanic Centennial Diesel Freight Train Set, 12-13		450	___
30188	UP Flyer Steam Freight Train Set, 12-13		330	___
30189	LIRR Diesel Passenger Train Set, 12-13		330	___
30190	Thomas & Friends Set, LionChief, 12-16		200	___
30191	Sodor Work Set 3-pack, 12-15		100	___
30193	Peanuts Christmas Steam Freight Set, 12-15		370	___
30194	North Pole Express Steam Freight Set, 12-13		290	___
30195	Grand Central Express Diesel Passenger Train Set, 12-14		440	___
30196	Hershey's Steam Freight Train Set, 12-13		312	___
30200	NYC Flyer Steam Freight Train Set, 12-13		350	___
30205	Silver Bells Christmas Steam Freight Set, 513-14		240	___
30206	Area 51 RS3 Diesel Freight Set, 13		250	___
30207	Santa Fe RS3 Diesel Freight Set, 13		200	___
30210	CP Rail Grain SetDiesel Freight Set, 13		390	___
30211	BNSF Maxi Stack Diesel Freight Set, 13		440	___
30213	Northeast NS Heritage Diesel Freight Set, 13		410	___

	MODERN 1970-2025		Exc	Like New
___	**30214**	Peanuts Halloween Steam Freight Set, 13, 15-16		320
___	**30217**	SP Black Widow Diesel Freight Set, 13, 15		460
___	**30218**	Polar Express Steam Passenger Set, 13-16		400
___	**30218**	Polar Express Steam Passenger Set w/Personalized Tender, LionChief, 18		440
___	**30219**	Gingerbread Junction Steam Freight Set, 13-14		290
___	**30220**	Polar Express 10th Anniversary Passenger Set, 13-14, 16		500
___	**30221**	Diesel Remote Control Set, 13-16		200
___	**30222**	Percy Remote Control Set, 13-15		200
___	**30223**	James Remote Control Set, 13-15		200
___	**30224**	Pennsylvania Limited Steam Passenger Set, 13		340
___	**30225**	Medal of Honor Train, 13	113	430
___	**30226**	NS Diesel Freight Set, RailSounds, 13		410
___	**30228**	Chattanooga Express Steam Passenger Set, 13		250
___	**30233**	Pennsylvania Flyer Remote Steam Freight Set, 13-17		280
___	**31569**	Western & Atlantic Passenger Car 2-pack, 08		100
___	**31700**	Postwar Girls Freight Set, 01	350	570
___	**31701**	Postwar Boys Freight Set, 02	46	462
___	**31704**	Alton Limited Steam Passenger Set, 02		870
___	**31705**	50th Anniversary Hudson Passenger Set, 02	288	910
___	**31706**	UP Burro Crane Set, 02	60	210
___	**31707**	C&O Diesel Freight Set, 03	80	280
___	**31708**	Postwar "1805" Marines Missile Launch Train, 03	300	419
___	**31710**	BN Diesel Coal Train, RailSounds, 03	345	745
___	**31711**	Postwar "1563W" Wabash Diesel Freight Set, RailSounds, 03	200	570
___	**31712**	UP Alco PA Diesel Passenger Set, RailSounds, 03	475	1495
___	**31713**	Southern Crescent Limited Steam Passenger Set, RailSounds, 03		1195
___	**31714**	Amtrak Acela Diesel Passenger Set, RailSounds, 04-05	800	2000
___	**31715**	Fire Rescue Steam Freight Set, 02		300
___	**31716**	Fire Rescue Steam Freight Set, 03		280
___	**31717**	CP Rail Snow Removal Train, 03	90	255
___	**31718**	SP "Oil Can" Tank Train Freight Set, 03	525	1600
___	**31719**	Western Maryland Fireball Diesel Freight Set, 04	193	363
___	**31720**	FEC Champion Diesel Passenger Set, RailSounds, 04	400	900
___	**31721**	Postwar "13138" Majestic Electric Freight Set, RailSounds, 04	277	580
___	**31724**	Nabisco 3-car Passenger Set, 03		110
___	**31727**	Postwar "2291W" D&RGW Diesel Freight Set, RailSounds, 04	421	640
___	**31728**	Elvis "He Dared to Rock" Steam Freight Set, 04		325
___	**31730**	Norman Rockwell Boxcar 4-pack, 05		95
___	**31733**	Jones & Laughlin Steel Slag Train, 05	NRS	338
___	**31734**	Chessie Steam Special Passenger Set, TMCC, 05		405
___	**31735**	Chessie Diesel Freight Set, TMCC, 05-06		670
___	**31736**	CP Diesel Grain Train, TMCC, 05	457	813
___	**31737**	Napa Valley Diesel Wine Train, CC, 05		1000
___	**31739**	Postwar "13150" Hudson Steam Freight Set, Super O, 05	350	940
___	**31740**	Postwar "2519W" Virginian Diesel Freight Set, TMCC, 05-07	428	710
___	**31742**	Postwar "2544W" ATSF Super Chief Passenger Set, 05	288	700
___	**31746**	GN Mountain Mover Steam Freight Set, 12-13		430
___	**31747**	Pennsylvania Electric Ballast Train, TMCC, 06	205	550
___	**31748**	Santa Fe U28CG Diesel Freight Set (std O), TMCC, 06-07		770

Item	Description	Exc	Like New	
31749	Pennsylvania Diesel Coal Train, TMCC, 06	231	770	___
31750	NYC Hotbox Reefer Steam Freight Set, TMCC, 06-07		530	___
31751	New York City Transit Authority R27 Subway Train, CC, 07		700	___
31752	Postwar 2269W B&O Diesel Freight Set, TMCC, 06-07	233	740	___
31753	Postwar 2551W GN Diesel Freight Set, TMCC, 06-08	219	740	___
31754	Postwar "2545WS" N&W Space Freight Set, TMCC, 06-07	250	957	___
31755	Texas Special Diesel Passenger Set, CC, 07-08	640	1550	___
31757	Postwar "2289WS" Berkshire Freight Set, CC, 07	225	750	___
31758	Postwar "2270W" JC Diesel Passenger Set, CC, 08		750	___
31760	CSX SD40-2 Diesel Husky Stack Car Set, CC, 07-08		770	___
31765	Postwar "11268" C&O Diesel Freight Set, 08		580	___
31767	Bethlehem Steel Rolling Stock Set, K-Line, 06		100	___
31768	B&O Rolling Stock Set, K-Line, 06		100	___
31772	Conrail LionMaster Diesel Freight Set, CC, 08-09		535	___
31773	NS Dash 9 Diesel TankTrain Set, CC, 08	167	798	___
31774	AEC Burro Crane Set, traditional, 09-11		605	___
31775	Postwar "1562" Burlington GP Passenger Set, 08	113	470	___
31776	"2219W" Lackawanna Train Master Freight Set, 08		415	___
31777	"2124W" GG1 Passenger Set, 08	238	452	___
31778	"1484WS" Steam Passenger Set, 08		610	___
31779	Amtrak HHP-8 Amfleet Passenger Set, CC, 09		500	___
31782	ATSF Crane Car and Boom Car, CC (std O), 09-10		560	___
31783	BNSF Ice Cold Express Diesel Freight Set, CC, 10		1000	___
31784	No. 1593 UP Work Train Set, 09	128	470	___
31787	CN SD70M-2 Diesel Coal Train, CC, 09	275	800	___
31790	PRR GG1 Passenger Set, 10		500	___
31791	NYC LionMaster Diesel Freight Set, CC, 10	150	700	___
31793	White Pass & Yukon Freight Car Add-on 3-pack, 10-11, 13		195	___
31794	New York City Transit R30 Subway 4-pack, 10	375	700	___
31795	Pere Marquette Freight Car 3-pack (std O), 10-11		210	___
31796	Feather Route Freight Car 3-pack (std O), 10-11		210	___
31797	New York City Transit R16 Subway Set, CC, 10	1050	1460	___
31799	GN Empire Steam Freight Express Set, 10		430	___
31901	Christmas Steam Freight Set, 02		145	___
31902	PRR K4 Freight Set, 01-02		580	___
31904	C&O Steam Freight Set, RailSounds, 01		400	___
31905	NH Diesel Freight Set, CC, 01		660	___
31907	PRR Atlantic Freight Set, 01 u		400	___
31908	Reading Hobo Express Freight Set, 01 u		365	___
31909	Santa Fe Shell Tank Car Freight Set, 01 u		320	___
31910	Soo Line Diesel Freight Set, 01 u		365	___
31911	Snap-On Anniversary Steam Freight Set, 00 u	113	615	___
31913	PRR Flyer Steam Freight Set, 01		126	___
31914	NYC Flyer Steam Freight Set, RailSounds, 01-02		170	___
31915	Chessie GP38 Diesel Freight Set, 01-02	70	155	___
31916	Santa Fe Steam Freight Set, 01		300	___
31918	C&O Steam Freight Set, SignalSounds, 01		315	___
31919	T&P Steam Passenger Set, RailSounds, 01		210	___
31920	L.L. Bean Freight Set, 01 u		270	___
31922	Snap-On Tool Diesel Freight Set, 01 u	90	356	___
31923	PRR Flyer Freight Set, 01 u		130	___
31924	Union Pacific RS3 Diesel Freight Set, 02		95	___
31926	Area 51 FA Diesel Freight Set, 02		205	___

			Exc	Like New
____	**31928**	Great Train Robbery Set, 02	70	180
____	**31931**	Ballyhoo Brothers Circus Train, 02	90	190
____	**31932**	NYC Limited Passenger Set, RailSounds, 02		285
____	**31933**	Santa Fe Steam Freight Set, RailSounds, 02		320
____	**31934**	Lionel 20th Century Express Steam Freight Set, 00 u		285
____	**31936**	Pennsylvania Flyer Steam Freight Set, 03-05		158
____	**31938**	Southern Diesel Freight Set, 03-04	75	160
____	**31939**	Great Train Robbery Steam Freight Set, 03		185
____	**31940**	NYC Flyer Steam Freight Set, RailSounds, 03		225
____	**31941**	Winter Wonderland Railroad Christmas Train, 03		150
____	**31942**	Norman Rockwell Christmas Train, 03	70	330
____	**31944**	NYC Limited Diesel Passenger Set, RailSounds, 03		250
____	**31945**	Santa Fe Steam Super Freight Set, RailSounds, 03		350
____	**31946**	Disney Christmas Steam Train, 04-05		310
____	**31947**	World of Disney Steam Freight Set, 03		215
____	**31950**	Kraft Holiday UP RS3 Diesel Freight Set, 02 u	35	149
____	**31952**	Great Northern Glacier Route Diesel Freight Set, 03-04		110
____	**31953**	"Riding the Rails" Hobo Train Set, 03-04		225
____	**31956**	Thomas the Tank Engine Set, 04-07	88	195
____	**31958**	Santa Fe Flyer Steam Freight Set, RailSounds, 04		205
____	**31960**	Polar Express Steam Passenger Set, 04-13	190	420
____	**31961**	Bloomingdale's Pennsylvania Flyer Steam Freight Set, 02 u		160
____	**31962**	Nickel Plate Road Super Freight Set, RailSounds, 04		350
____	**31963**	Southern Pacific Overnight Steam Freight Set, 04		340
____	**31966**	Holiday Tradition Steam Freight Set, 04-05		210
____	**31969**	NYC Flyer Steam Freight Set, RailSounds, 04		205
____	**31976**	Yukon Special Diesel Freight Set, 05		225
____	**31977**	New York Central Flyer Steam Freight Set, 05		250
____	**31985**	Santa Fe Steam Fast Freight Set, TrainSounds, 05		320
____	**31987**	Mickey's Holiday Express Train, 04		280
____	**31989**	UP Overland Freight Express Set, 04		880
____	**31990**	Copper Range Steam Freight Mine Set, 05		175
____	**31993**	NS Black Diamond Diesel Freight Set, TMCC, 05		500
____	**32900**	DC Billboard, 99		24
____	**32902**	Construction Zone Signs, set of 6, 99-19		10
____	**32904**	Hellgate Bridge, 99	207	427
____	**32905**	Irvington Factory, 99-00	140	295
____	**32910**	Rotary Coal Tipple with bathtub gondola, 02	261	575
____	**32919**	Animated Maiden Rescue, 99		65
____	**32920**	Animated Pylon with airplane, 99	50	130
____	**32921**	Electric Coaling Station, 99-01		125
____	**32922**	Orange Highway Barrels, set of 6, 99-25		10
____	**32923**	Accessory Transformer, 99-03, 06-16		46
____	**32929**	Icing Station with Santa, 99		90
____	**32930**	Power Supply Set w/ZW controller, 99-02, 06-09	240	425
____	**32933**	Christmas Stocking Hanger Set, 4-piece, 99-00		50
____	**32934**	Stocking Hanger, gondola, 99-00		15
____	**32935**	Stocking Hanger, boxcar, 99-00		15
____	**32960**	Hindenburger Cafe, 99		210
____	**32961**	Route 66 UFO Cafe, 99	80	213
____	**32987**	Hobo Campfire, 99-00	25	48
____	**32988**	Postwar "192" Railroad Control Tower, 99-00		75
____	**32989**	Postwar "464" Sawmill, 99-00		75

MODERN 1970-2025		Exc	Like New	
32990	Linex Oil Derrick, 99-00		55	___
32991	WLLC Radio Station, 99		75	___
32996	Postwar "362" Barrel Loader, 00		125	___
32997	Aluminum Rico Station, 00		300	___
32998	Hobby Shop, 99-00	80	300	___
32999	Hellgate Bridge, 99-00	196	400	___
33000	GP9 Diesel "3000," RailScope video camera system, 88-90	130	175	___
33002	RailScope Television Monitor, 88-90	53	78	___
34102	Amtrak Shelter, 04-08		25	___
34108	Lionelville Suburban House, 03		20	___
34109	Lionelville Large Suburban House, 03		15	___
34110	Lionelville Estate House, 03		30	___
34111	Lionelville Deluxe Fieldstone House, 03		17	___
34112	Lionelville Fieldstone House, 03		17	___
34113	Lionelville Large Suburban House, 03		17	___
34114	Late Illuminated Station and Terrace, red trim, 03		475	___
34117	Early Illuminated Station and Terrace, green trim, 03		475	___
34119	Early Illuminated Terrace, 03		300	___
34120	TMCC Direct Lockon, 04-25		60	___
34121	Lionelville Bungalow, 04		20	___
34122	Lionelville Bungalow with garage, 04		20	___
34123	Lionelville Bungalow with addition, 04		20	___
34124	Lionelville Anastasia's Bakery, 04		20	___
34125	Lionelville Cotton's Candy, 04		20	___
34126	Lionelville Market, 04		20	___
34127	Lionelville O'Grady's Tavern, 04		22	___
34128	Lionelville Pharmacy, 04		15	___
34129	Lionelville Kiddie City Toy Store, 04		20	___
34130	Lionelville Jim's 5&10, 04		25	___
34131	Lionelville Al's Hardware, 04		30	___
34144	Santa Fe Scrap Yard, 05-06		80	___
34145	New Haven Scrap Yard, 06		100	___
34149	Sly Fox and the Hunter, 05-07		80	___
34150	Reading Room, 05-06		70	___
34158	Ring Toss Midway Game, 05-06		20	___
34159	Camel Race Midway Game, 05-06		20	___
34162	Operating Oil Pump, 04-09		53	___
34163	Speeder Shed, 04-06		30	___
34164	Nutcracker Operating Gateman, 05-08		80	___
34190	Carousel, 04-06		165	___
34191	Hobo Depot, 04-05		70	___
34192	Operating Lumberjacks, 04-06		60	___
34193	UPS Animated Billboard, 04		30	___
34194	UPS Package Station, 05		120	___
34195	UPS People Pack, 05-11		27	___
34210	TMCC Direct Lockon, 09		52	___
34359	2011 Lionel Dealer Appreciation Boxcar, 11 u		40	___
34360	2012 Lionel Dealer Appreciation Boxcar, 12 u		40	___
34500	Rio Grande FT Diesel "5484," traditional, 06		245	___
34501	Southern FT Diesel "4102," traditional, 06		400	___
34502	B&O F3 Diesel A Unit, "2368," CC, 06-07		400	___
34503	B&O F3 Diesel B Unit, "2368," unpowered, 06-07		300	___
34504	B&O F3 Diesel A Unit "2368," nonpowered, 06-07	173	300	___

MODERN 1970-2025		Exc	Like New
____ **34505**	B&O E7 Diesel AA Set, CC, 07		700
____ **34508**	PRR E7 Diesel AA Set, CC, 07		700
____ **34509**	PRR E7 Diesel B Unit, nonpowered (std O), 07		170
____ **34510**	PRR E7 Diesel B Unit, powered, CC, 07		300
____ **34511**	NYC F7 Diesel ABA Set, CC, 07-08		900
____ **34512**	NYC F7 Diesel B Unit "2439," powered, CC, 07-08		300
____ **34513**	WP F7 Diesel ABA Set, CC, 07-08		900
____ **34514**	WP F7 Diesel B Unit "918C," powered, CC, 07-08		300
____ **34515**	NYC F7 Diesel Breakdown B Unit "2440," RailSounds, 07		270
____ **34518**	PRR E7 Diesel Breakdown B Unit, RailSounds, 07		270
____ **34519**	NYC Sharknose RF-16 Diesel AA Set, CC, 07-08		630
____ **34520**	NYC Sharknose Diesel B Unit "3818," nonpowered (std O), 07-08		160
____ **34521**	Santa Fe F3 Diesel A Unit "17," traditional, 07		265
____ **34522**	Santa Fe F3 Diesel B Unit "17," nonpowered (std O), 07		150
____ **34544**	ATSF F3 Diesel B Unit, CC, 08		270
____ **34545**	D&RGW F3 Diesel B Unit, CC, 08		270
____ **34546**	Southern F3 Diesel B Unit, CC, 08		270
____ **34547**	Texas Special F3 Diesel B Unit, CC, 08		270
____ **34559**	Archive New Haven F3 Diesel AA Set, 10		500
____ **34564**	SP Alco PA Diesel AA Set, CC, 10-11		750
____ **34567**	SP Alco PB B Unit, CC, 10-11		400
____ **34568**	ATSF Alco PA AA Diesel Set, CC, 11		750
____ **34569**	ATSF Alco PB Diesel, CC, 11		400
____ **34570**	B&O FA Diesel AA Set, CC, 10		650
____ **34573**	Postwar Scale ATSF F3 AA Diesel Set, CC, 11		700
____ **34576**	Postwar Scale NYC F3 AA Diesel Set, CC, 11		700
____ **34579**	Postwar Scale ATSF F3 B Unit, CC, 11		380
____ **34580**	Postwar Scale NYC F3 B Unit, CC, 11		380
____ **34581**	Postwar "2331" Virginian Train Master Diesel, CC, 10		495
____ **34582**	Postwar "2373" CP F3 Diesel AA Set, CC, 10		673
____ **34585**	Postwar "2375" CP F3 B Unit, CC, 10		350
____ **34586**	Postwar "2378" MILW F3 Diesel AB Set, CC, 10		700
____ **34589**	Postwar "2377" MILW F3 A, powered, CC, 10		425
____ **34594**	UP Alco PA AA Diesel Set, CC, 11		750
____ **34597**	UP Alco PB Diesel, CC, 11		400
____ **34600**	SP GP30 Diesel "5010," CC, 11		500
____ **34601**	SP GP30 Diesel "5012," CC, 11		500
____ **34602**	SP GP30 Diesel "5014," 11		380
____ **34603**	SP GP30 Diesel "5017," nonpowered, 11		240
____ **34604**	Conrail GP30 Diesel "2178," CC, 11		500
____ **34605**	Conrail GP30 Diesel "2180," CC, 11		500
____ **34606**	Conrail GP30 Diesel "2182," 11		380
____ **34607**	Conrail GP30 Diesel "2185," nonpowered, 11		240
____ **34608**	Lionelville & Western GP30 Diesel "1100," CC, 11		450
____ **34609**	Lionelville & Western GP30 Diesel "1103," CC, 11		450
____ **34610**	Lionelville & Western GP30 Diesel "1107," 11		330
____ **34611**	Lionelville & Western GP30 Diesel "1112," nonpowered, 11		190
____ **34612**	NS SD70M-2 Diesel "2658," CC, 11		550
____ **34613**	NS SD70M-2 Diesel "2663," CC, 11		550
____ **34614**	CN SD70M-2 Diesel "8020," CC, 11		550
____ **34615**	CN SD70M-2 Diesel "8024," CC, 11		550
____ **34616**	FEC SD70M-2 Diesel "101," CC, 11		550

MODERN 1970-2025		Exc	Like New	
34617	FEC SD70M-2 Diesel "103," CC, 11		550	___
34618	George Bush SD70ACe Diesel "4141," CC, 11	219	611	___
34619	NH SD70ACe Diesel "8696," CC, 11		550	___
34620	NH SD70ACe Diesel "8699," CC, 11		550	___
34623	Texas Special SD70ACe Diesel "6340," CC, 11		550	___
34624	Texas Special SD70ACe Diesel "6344," CC, 11		550	___
34625	NP F3 AA Diesel Set, CC, 11		700	___
34628	NP F3 Diesel B Unit "6005C," CC, 11		380	___
34629	NP F3 Diesel B Unit "6006C," nonpowered, 11		240	___
34630	Frisco F3 AA Diesel Set, CC, 11		700	___
34633	Frisco F3 Diesel B Unit, CC, 11		380	___
34634	Frisco F3 Diesel B Unit, nonpowered, 11		260	___
34635	ATSF F3 AA Diesel Set, CC, 11		700	___
34638	ATSF F3 Diesel B Unit, CC, 11		380	___
34639	ATSF F3 Diesel B Unit, nonpowered, 11		240	___
34640	GTW F3 AA Diesel Set, CC, 11		700	___
34643	GTW F3 Diesel B Unit, CC, 11		380	___
34644	GTW F3 Diesel B Unit, nonpowered, 11		260	___
34645	CN F3 AA Diesel Set, CC, 11		700	___
34648	CN F3 Diesel B Unit, CC, 11		380	___
34649	CN F3 Diesel B Unit, nonpowered, 11		260	___
34650	MILW DD35A Diesel "1535," CC, 11		600	___
34651	MILW DD35A Diesel "1537," nonpowered, 11		440	___
34662	RI GP9 Diesel "1331," CC, 12-13		480	___
34663	RI GP9 Diesel "1327," CC, 12-13		480	___
34664	GN GP9 Diesel "688," CC, 12-13		480	___
34665	GN GP9 Diesel "695," CC, 12-13		480	___
34666	L&N GP9 Diesel "504," CC, 12-13		480	___
34667	L&N GP9 Diesel "525," CC, 12-13		480	___
34668	CN GP90 Diesel "4463," CC, 12		480	___
34669	CN GP90 Diesel "4455," CC, 12		480	___
34670	C&O GP9 Diesel "6240," CC, 12-13		480	___
34671	C&O GP9 Diesel "6243," CC, 12		480	___
34672	PRR Baldwin Centipede Diesel AA, CC, 12-13		2200	___
34673	UP Baldwin Centipede Diesel AA, CC, 12		2200	___
34676	PRR Baldwin Centipede Diesel "5821," CC, 12-14		1100	___
34677	Seaboard Baldwin Centipede Diesel "4503," CC, 12-14		1100	___
34680	NdeM Baldwin Centipede Diesel "6402," CC, 12-14	525	1100	___
34681	UP GP9 Diesel "256," CC, 12		480	___
34682	UP GP9 Diesel "261," CC, 12		480	___
34683	PRR Baldwin Centipede Diesel AA, CC, 12-13		2200	___
34686	Baldwin Demonstrator Centipede AA, CC, 12		2200	___
34689	WM F7 AA Diesel Set, CC, 12-13		730	___
34692	WM F7 B Unit "410," CC, 12-13		400	___
34693	WM F7 B Unit, 12-13		250	___
34694	L&N F7 AA Diesel Set, CC, 12		730	___
34697	L&N F7 B Unit "900," CC, 12-13		400	___
34698	L&N F7 B Unit, 12-13		250	___
34701	PRR Baldwin RF-16 Diesel AA Set, CC, 12-14		730	___
34704	PRR Baldwin RF-16 Diesel B Unit, CC, 12-14		400	___
34705	PRR Baldwin RF-16 Diesel B Unit, nonpowered, 12-14		250	___
34731	NH Alco RS-11 Diesel "1413," nonpowered, 12		240	___
34732	LV Alco RS-11 Diesel "7640," CC, 12		480	___

			Exc	Like New
___	**34733**	LV Alco RS-11 Diesel "7642," CC, 12		480
___	**34734**	LV Alco RS-11 Diesel "7643," nonpowered, 12		240
___	**34735**	ATSF GP9 Diesel "726," CC, 12		480
___	**34736**	ATSF GP9 Diesel "741," CC, 12		480
___	**34737**	NP GP9 Diesel "202," CC, 12		480
___	**34738**	NP GP9 Diesel "317," CC, 12-13		480
___	**34739**	RI GP9 Diesel "1325," nonpowered, 12		240
___	**34740**	GN GP9 Diesel "668," nonpowered, 12		240
___	**34741**	L&N GP9 Diesel "531," nonpowered, 12		240
___	**34742**	CN GP90 Diesel "4527," nonpowered, 12		240
___	**34743**	C&O GP9 Diesel "6249," nonpowered, 12		240
___	**34744**	UP GP9 Diesel "268," nonpowered, 12		240
___	**34745**	Monon Alco C-420 Diesel "509," CC, 12-13		530
___	**34746**	Monon Alco C-420 Diesel "512," CC, 12-13		530
___	**34747**	Monon Alco C-420 Diesel "514," nonpowered, 12-13		260
___	**34748**	LV Alco C-420 Diesel "404," CC, 12		530
___	**34749**	LV Alco C-420 Diesel "412," CC, 12		530
___	**34750**	LV Alco C-420 Diesel "414," nonpowered, 12		260
___	**34754**	Alaska Alco C-420 Diesel "1210," CC, 12		530
___	**34755**	Alaska Alco C-420 Diesel "1214," CC, 12		530
___	**34756**	Alaska Alco C-420 Diesel "1217," nonpowered, 12		260
___	**34757**	Seaboard Alco C-420 Diesel "127," CC, 12-13		530
___	**34758**	Seaboard Alco C-420 Diesel "129," CC, 12-13		530
___	**34759**	Seaboard Alco C-420 Diesel "134," nonpowered, 12-13		260
___	**34760**	NKP Alco C-420 Diesel "578," CC, 12-13		530
___	**34761**	NKP Alco C-420 Diesel "575," CC, 12-13		530
___	**34762**	NKP Alco C-420 Diesel "572," nonpowered, 12-13		260
___	**34763**	CNJ Scale NW2 Diesel Switcher "1060," CC, 12		470
___	**34764**	CNJ Scale NW2 Diesel Switcher "1061," CC, 12		470
___	**34765**	KCS Scale NW2 Diesel Switcher "1221," CC, 12		470
___	**34766**	KCS Scale NW2 Diesel Switcher "1224," CC, 12		470
___	**34767**	L&N Scale NW2 Diesel Switcher "2203," CC, 12		470
___	**34768**	L&N Scale NW2 Diesel Switcher "2206," CC, 12		470
___	**34769**	MKT Scale NW2 Diesel Switcher "8," CC, 12		470
___	**34770**	MKT Scale NW2 Diesel Switcher "12," CC, 12		470
___	**34771**	Reading Scale NW2 Diesel Switcher "102," CC, 12		470
___	**34772**	Reading Scale NW2 Diesel Switcher "104," CC, 12		470
___	**34773**	PRR Scale NW2 Diesel Switcher "9163," CC, 12		470
___	**34774**	PRR Scale NW2 Diesel Switcher "9171," CC, 12		470
___	**34775**	N&W SD40-2 Diesel "6106," nonpowered, 12-13		240
___	**34776**	N&W SD40-2 Diesel "6121," CC, 12-13		530
___	**34777**	N&W SD40-2 Diesel "6109," CC, 12-14		530
___	**34778**	CSX SD40-2 Diesel "8023," nonpowered, 12-13		240
___	**34779**	CSX SD40-2 Diesel "8028," CC, 12-13		530
___	**34780**	CSX SD40-2 Diesel "8033," CC, 12-13		530
___	**34781**	BN SD40-2 Diesel "7140," nonpowered, 12-13		240
___	**34782**	BN SD40-2 Diesel "7153," CC, 12-13		530
___	**34783**	BN SD40-2 Diesel "7162," CC, 12-13		530
___	**34784**	Frisco SD40-2 Diesel "957," CC, 12-13		530
___	**34785**	Frisco SD40-2 Diesel "950," nonpowered, 12-13		240
___	**34786**	Frisco SD40-2 Diesel "952," CC, 12-13		530
___	**34787**	C&NW SD40-2 Diesel "6816," nonpowered, 12-13		240
___	**34788**	C&NW SD40-2 Diesel "6820," CC, 12-13		530

		Exc	Like New	
34789	C&NW SD40-2 Diesel "6832," CC, 12-13		530	___
34790	MKT SD40-2 Diesel "602," nonpowered, 12-13		240	___
34791	MKT SD40-2 Diesel "609," CC, 12-13		530	___
34792	MKT SD40-2 Diesel "620," CC, 12-13		530	___
35100	NYC Vista Dome Car "7012", 07-09		45	___
35101	NYC Baggage Car "5028," 07		40	___
35102	Santa Fe El Capitan Streamliner Diner, 07		65	___
35124	Alton Limited Madison Passenger Car 4-pack, 08-10		240	___
35128	ATSF El Capitan Baggage Car "2103," 08		70	___
35129	ATSF El Capitan Vista Dome Car "3153," 08		70	___
35130	Polar Express Disappearing Hobo Car, 08-14, 16-17	45	77	___
35133	MTA Metro-North M-7 Commuter Add-on 2-pack, 07-08		85	___
35134	North Pole Central Vista Dome Car, 08	23	182	___
35135	North Pole Central Diner, 08-10		45	___
35136	Alaska Heavyweight Passenger Car 4-pack, 08		240	___
35137	Alaska Baggage Car w/TrainSounds, 08		200	___
35138	Alton Limited Baggage Car w/TrainSounds, 08		200	___
35144	Alton Limited Heavyweight Coach "Webster Groves," 08		60	___
35145	Alton Limited Heavyweight Combination Car "Missouri," 08		60	___
35146	Alton Limited Heavyweight Diner "Bloomington," 08		60	___
35147	Alton Limited Heavyweight Observation "Chicago," 08		60	___
35167	PRR Diner "2044," 10		52	___
35168	PRR Coach "4046," 09		52	___
35173	North Pole Central Blitzen Coach, 09	23	133	___
35174	MTA LIRR M-7 Add-on 2-pack, 09		98	___
35184	Western & Atlantic Baggage Car, 09		60	___
35185	Great Western Passenger Car 2-pack, 09		100	___
35193	PRR Streamliner 4-pack, 10-11		250	___
35200	Strasburg Observation Car, 10		60	___
35202	Rio Grande Ski Train Vista Dome "California," 10-11		80	___
35203	Rio Grande Ski Train Baggage Car "1230," 10-11		75	___
35204	Rio Grande Ski Train Observation "Kansas", 10-11		75	___
35205	D&RGW Pikes Peak Add-on Coach, 10-11		70	___
35211	Strasburg Passenger Car Add-on 2-pack, 10		100	___
35214	Rio Grande Winter Park Diner, 11		70	___
35219	Hallow's Eve Express Passenger Car 2-pack, 11		120	___
35229	Hogwarts Express Dementors Coach, 11-15		60	___
35239	NJ Transit 2-pack Passenger Car Add-on, 11-14		100	___
35247	Grand Central Express Passenger Car 2-pack, 12-13		140	___
35250	North Pole Coach 2-pack, 12-13		120	___
35256	Hallow's Eve Express Passenger Car 2-pack #2, 12		120	___
35257	ATSF Vista Dome, 12		70	___
35258	ATSF Baggage Car, 12-13		70	___
35259	LIRR Passenger Car 2-pack, 12-15		110	___
35281	ATSF Super Chief Diner "1495", 13		70	___
35282	LIRR Jamaica Coach, 13-15		60	___
35283	CP Baggage Car and Diner 2-pack, 13		130	___
35286	Peanuts Coach 3-pack, 13		165	___
35290	Polar Express Passenger Car Add-on 2-pack, 13-14, 16		150	___
35293	Angela Trotta Thomas "Toyland Express" Boxcar, 13		45	___
35294	Polar Express Snow Tower, 13-14		28	___
35295	Christmas Billboard Set, 13-14, 16		13	___

			Exc	Like New
___	**35403**	NYC 20th Century Limited 18" Aluminum Passenger Car 4-pack (std O), 08		625
___	**35408**	NYC 20th Century Limited 18" Aluminum Passenger Car 2-pack (std O), 08		325
___	**35411**	NYC 20th Century Limited Diner, StationSounds (std O), 08		325
___	**35412**	Lenny Dean Passenger Coach, 08		100
___	**35413**	LL Streamliner Car 2-pack, 08		270
___	**35415**	UP 18" Streamliner Car 4-pack (std O), 08		625
___	**35423**	UP 18" Streamliner Car 2-pack (std O), 08		325
___	**35430**	Amtrak Coach		45
___	**35431**	Amtrak Coach		45
___	**35432**	Amtrak Coach		45
___	**35433**	Amfleet Phase IVB Coach 2-pack (std O), 10		140
___	**35445**	SP Shasta Daylight 18" Passenger Car 4-pack (std O), 11		640
___	**35446**	SP Shasta Daylight 18" Passenger Car 2-pack (std O), 11		320
___	**35454**	Amfleet Cab Control End Car (std O), 10		250
___	**35473**	Amfleet Capstone Coach 3-pack (std O), 10		180
___	**35481**	NYC Add-on Passenger Car "M-498," 11		120
___	**35490**	Alaska Budd RDC Combination Car "702," nonpowered, 11		130
___	**35497**	RI Budd RDC Combination Car "751," nonpowered, 11		130
___	**35498**	RI Budd RDC Coach "750," nonpowered, 11		130
___	**35499**	Alaska Budd RDC Coach "712," nonpowered, 11		130
___	**36000**	Route 66 Flatcar with 2 red sedans, 98		44
___	**36001**	Route 66 Flatcar with 2 wagons, 98		42
___	**36002**	Pratt's Hollow Passenger Car 4-pack, 98		445
___	**36006**	Uranium Flatcar "6508," 99		60
___	**36016**	Flatcar with propellers, 98		45
___	**36020**	Flatcar "TT-6424" with auto frames, 99		32
___	**36021**	Alaska Flatcar "6424" with airplane, 99		44
___	**36024**	J.B. Hunt Flatcar "64245" with trailer, 99		44
___	**36025**	J.B. Hunt Flatcar "64246" with trailer, 99		50
___	**36026**	Flatcar with J.B. Hunt trailers 2-pack, 99		85
___	**36027**	Tredegar Iron Works Flatcar with cannon, 99		45
___	**36028**	Heavy Artillery Flatcar with cannon, 99		45
___	**36029**	SP Auto Carrier "516712", 99		44
___	**36030**	Troublesome Truck #1, 99		35
___	**36031**	Troublesome Truck #2, 99		35
___	**36032**	Christmas Gondola "6462" with presents, 99		35
___	**36036**	C&O Gondola, 99		20
___	**36038**	Construction Zone Gondola, 99 u	11	20
___	**36040**	Bethlehem Flatcar with block (SSS), 99		75
___	**36041**	Bethlehem Ore Car (SSS), 99		40
___	**36043**	Custom Consist Flatcar with pickup truck, 99		40
___	**36044**	Custom Consist Flatcar with dragster, 99		40
___	**36045**	Flatcar with dragster, 04		30
___	**36046**	Flatcar with custom truck, 04		30
___	**36047**	Construction Zone Gondola, 99 u	11	20
___	**36048**	Construction Zone Gondola, 99 u	11	20
___	**36051**	NYC Flatcar w/Bulkhead, 04	8	20
___	**36054**	Archaeological Expedition Gondola with eggs, 00 u		55
___	**36055**	Flatcar with dragster, 01 u		30
___	**36056**	Flatcar with roadster, 01 u		30
___	**36059**	"Season's Greetings" Gondola, 99 u		50

MODERN 1970-2025		Exc	Like New	
36062	NYC 6462 Gondola, 99-00		22	___
36063	Conrail Gondola "604768," 99-00		20	___
36064	Billboard Flatcar "6424," 00		41	___
36065	Wabash Flatcar "25536" with trailer, 00		35	___
36066	Christmas Gondola with presents, 00		32	___
36067	King Auto Sales Flatcar "6424" with pink Cadillac, 00		40	___
36068	Pine Peak Tree Transport Gondola, 00	38	55	___
36079	Service Station Ltd. Flatcar with trailer, 00		34	___
36082	D&H Flatcar "16533" w/Whirlpool trailer, 00	27	45	___
36083	Santa Fe Gondola "168998," 01		17	___
36084	Grand Trunk Western Coil Car, 00		32	___
36085	FEC Coil Car, 00		29	___
36086	SP Flatcar with trailer, 01	34	35	___
36087	Flatcar "6424" with wooden whistle, 01		25	___
36088	Allis Chalmers Condenser Car "6519," 00		43	___
36089	Frisco Flatcar with airplane, 00		35	___
36090	TT Flatcar "6424" with Pepsi truck, 01		44	___
36091	Maersk Flatcar "250129" with die-cast tractors, 00		55	___
36092	Maersk Flatcar "250130" with die-cast frames, 00		55	___
36093	Soo TT Auto Carrier "906760," 00		49	___
36094	PC F9 Well Car "768122," 01		41	___
36095	Christmas Chase Gondola, 01		37	___
36098	PRR Gondola "385186," 01		20	___
36099	NYC Flatcar with stakes and bulkheads, 01		25	___
36104	Area 51 3-D Tank Car, 07		60	___
36105	Skelly Oil 1-D Tank Car, 08		55	___
36107	WC Wood-sided Refrigerator Car, 08		35	___
36108	Candy Cane 1-D Tank Car, 07		60	___
36109	Alaska 3-D Tank Car, 07		40	___
36110	CP 1-D Tank Car, 07		30	___
36111	D&RGW 1-D Tank Car, 07		24	___
36112	NP 3-D Tank Car, 08		35	___
36113	IC 1-D Tank Car, 08		35	___
36114	ART Wood-sided Reefer, 08		35	___
36117	Lionel Lines 2-D Tank Car, 08		50	___
36118	NYC Pastel Stock Car "63561," 08-09		55	___
36128	Texas & Pacific 3-D Tank Car, 09		40	___
36129	British Columbia 1-D Tank Car, 09		38	___
36130	Jiminy Cricket 1-D Tank Car, 09		70	___
36131	Lackawanna Wood-sided Reefer "7000," 09-10		40	___
36132	Southern 1-D Tank Car, 08		35	___
36145	Philadelphia Quartz 3-D Tank Car "606," 10		40	___
36146	Cities Service 1-D Tank Car "11800," 10		40	___
36149	Strasburg Wood-sided Reefer "105," 10		55	___
36151	Grave's Blood Bank Tank Car, 10		50	___
36156	Pennsylvania Power & Light 1-D Tank Car, 10		40	___
36162	Diamond Chemicals 3-D Tank Car, 11		40	___
36163	Celanese 2-D Tank Car, 11-12		40	___
36166	Polar Express Reefer, 11-12		55	___
36169	Coca-Cola 3-D Tank Car, 11		55	___
36170	Partridge in a Pear Tree Reefer, 11-13		55	___
36172	Bubble Yum 1-D Tank Car, 11		55	___
36173	Santa's Flyer Hot Cocoa 3-D Tank Car, 11		40	___

			Exc	Like New
___	**36176**	C&O 1-D Tank Car, 13		43
___	**36177**	WP 3-D Tank Car, 12		40
___	**36178**	Frisco 2-D Tank Car, 12-13		40
___	**36182**	Eggnog Unibody 1-D Tank Car, 12		70
___	**36191**	GN Waffle-sided Boxcar, 13		43
___	**36195**	PRR Flatcar with patrol helicopter, 13		60
___	**36200**	Quaker Life Cereal Boxcar, 00		513
___	**36203**	Whirlpool Boxcar, 00 u		150
___	**36205**	eBay Boxcar, 00		288
___	**36206**	REA Boxcar, 01		25
___	**36207**	Vapor Records Christmas Boxcar, 01		80
___	**36208**	Father's Day Boxcar, 00		35
___	**36210**	Burlington Hi-Cube Boxcar "19825," 01		40
___	**36211**	NP Hi-Cube Boxcar "659999," 01	18	40
___	**36212**	Lionel Employee Christmas Boxcar, 00 u		410
___	**36213**	Vapor Records Christmas Boxcar, 00		50
___	**36214**	GN Boxcar (Lionel Service Station), 00 u	49	55
___	**36215**	Train Station 25th Anniversary Boxcar, 00 u		48
___	**36218**	Snap-On Boxcar, 00 u		150
___	**36219**	UP Boxcar "183518," 02		78
___	**36220**	Pioneer Seed Boxcar, 00 u		NRS
___	**36221**	PRR Boxcar "569356," 01		20
___	**36222**	NYC Boxcar "162440," 01		20
___	**36223**	Chessie System Boxcar, 01		20
___	**36224**	Santa Fe Boxcar "16263," 01		20
___	**36225**	C&O Boxcar "250549," 01		20
___	**36226**	E-Hobbies Boxcar, 01 u		227
___	**36227**	Monopoly Community Chest Boxcar, 00 u		50
___	**36228**	Lionel Visitor Center Boxcar, 01 u		34
___	**36229**	Island Trains 20th Anniversary Boxcar, 01 u		29
___	**36232**	Farmall McCormick Boxcar, 01 u		285
___	**36236**	TM Books "I Love Lionel" Boxcar "7474-1," 01 u		43
___	**36238**	Snap-On Tool Team ASE Racing Boxcar, 01 u		NRS
___	**36239**	L.L. Bean Boxcar, 01 u		150
___	**36240**	Do It Best Boxcar, 01 u		100
___	**36242**	Erie-Lackawanna Boxcar "73113," 02		24
___	**36243**	Christmas Boxcar "2002," 02		31
___	**36244**	Teddy Bear Centennial Boxcar, 02		36
___	**36245**	Lionel 20th Century Boxcar "1900-1925," 00 u		30
___	**36246**	Lionel 20th Century Boxcar "1926-1950," 00 u		30
___	**36247**	Lionel 20th Century Boxcar "1951-1975," 00 u		30
___	**36248**	Lionel 20th Century Boxcar "1976-2000," 00 u		30
___	**36250**	NYC Early Bird Boxcar, 04		20
___	**36253**	Christmas Boxcar (O), 03		32
___	**36254**	Goofy Hi-Cube Boxcar, 03		37
___	**36255**	Donald Duck Hi-Cube Boxcar, 03		40
___	**36256**	GN Boxcar "6341," 03		23
___	**36261**	PRR Boxcar, 03-05		15
___	**36262**	Southern Central of Georgia Boxcar, 03–04		20
___	**36264**	Santa Fe Boxcar "600196," 02		18
___	**36265**	Angela Trotta Thomas "Window Wishing" Boxcar, 02		38
___	**36267**	Mickey Mouse Hi-Cube Boxcar, 03		50

Item	Description	Exc	Like New	
36270	Angela Trotta Thomas "Home for the Holidays" Boxcar, 02-03		30	___
36272	New Haven Boxcar "6501", 04		20	___
36273	Railbox Hi-Cube Boxcar "15000", 04		21	___
36275	Christmas Boxcar, 04		35	___
36276	Angela Trotta Thomas "Tis the Season" Boxcar, 04		34	___
36277	Pluto Hi-Cube Boxcar, 04-05		50	___
36278	Winnie the Pooh Hi-Cube Boxcar, 04-05		50	___
36281	B&O Boxcar, 04		35	___
36291	Simpsons Boxcar, 04-05		44	___
36294	UP Hi-Cube Boxcar, traditional, 05		27	___
36295	CN Boxcar, traditional, 05		27	___
36296	2005 Holiday Boxcar, 05		48	___
36297	Angela Trotta Thomas "Christmas Eve" Boxcar, 05		48	___
36299	Hammacher Schlemmer Music Boxcar, 04		65	___
36305	eBay Boxcar, 00 u		120	___
36339	Caterpillar Caboose	22	50	___
36500	Western Pacific Caboose "36500", 04		23	___
36501	D&RGW Caboose "36501", 04		22	___
36502	Reading Caboose "36502", 04		25	___
36515	North Pole Central Lines Caboose "36515", 04		36	___
36519	Lionel Lines Caboose, 04		22	___
36520	Santa Fe Caboose "36520", 04		22	___
36525	CSX Work Caboose, lighted, 05		35	___
36526	Pennsylvania Work Caboose, traditional, 05		27	___
36527	Santa Fe Work Caboose, traditional, 05		28	___
36528	Chesapeake & Ohio Work Caboose, traditional, 05		40	___
36529	North Pole Central Work Caboose with presents, traditional, 05		38	___
36530	Pennsylvania Caboose, traditional, 05		33	___
36531	Erie Caboose "C150", traditional, 05		33	___
36532	SP Caboose "1097", traditional, 05		48	___
36533	Reading Caboose "92803", traditional, 05		33	___
36534	NYC Center Cupola Caboose, traditional, 05		40	___
36535	LL Center Cupola Caboose, traditional, 05		28	___
36536	Southern Center Cupola Caboose, traditional, 05		40	___
36539	Elvis Presley Caboose, 04		40	___
36541	Copper Range Caboose, 05		28	___
36542	NYC Caboose, 05		28	___
36543	ATSF Square-Window Caboose, 05		40	___
36544	Alaska Caboose, 05		35	___
36547	Bethlehem Steel Transfer Caboose, traditional, 05		38	___
36548	Transylvania RR Work Caboose, traditional, 05		45	___
36550	Halloween Transfer Caboose, traditional, 06-07		45	___
36551	Christmas Caboose, 06		45	___
36552	U.S. Steel Work Caboose, traditional, 06-07		45	___
36553	NYC Caboose, 08		20	___
36554	SP Work Caboose, traditional, 06		45	___
36555	Pennsylvania Transfer Caboose, 06		45	___
36556	Lionel Lines Work Caboose, 06-07		30	___
36557	D&RGW Work Caboose, traditional, 06		29	___
36558	Virginian Center Cupola Caboose "316", traditional, 06		45	___
36559	WM Center Cupola Caboose "1863", traditional, 06		45	___
36560	C&O Center Cupola Caboose "90876", traditional, 06		45	___

			Exc	Like New
___	**36562**	Army Transportation Work Caboose, traditional, 06		45
___	**36563**	Reading Work Caboose, traditional, 06		45
___	**36565**	UP SP-type Caboose, traditional, 06		48
___	**36566**	NYC SP-type Caboose, traditional, 06		48
___	**36567**	GN SP-type Caboose, traditional, 06		48
___	**36571**	PRR Caboose, 08		20
___	**36580**	B&O Center Cupola Caboose "C2047", traditional, 05		40
___	**36582**	C&O Caboose, 05		22
___	**36583**	Holiday Caboose, 07		50
___	**36587**	SP Caboose "1121", 07-09		40
___	**36589**	PRR Work Caboose, 07		40
___	**36590**	UP Work Caboose, 07		45
___	**36591**	Southern Caboose "X99", 08		45
___	**36592**	Santa Fe Caboose "999471", 06		48
___	**36593**	NYC Caboose, 06		48
___	**36601**	UP Caboose, 06		48
___	**36602**	UPS Centennial Caboose, 06		45
___	**36604**	Pennsylvania Caboose, 06		25
___	**36607**	K-Line Caboose, 06		40
___	**36611**	Conrail Caboose "19674", 07		40
___	**36612**	Alaska Caboose "1080", 07		40
___	**36613**	NYC Caboose, 07		30
___	**36618**	"It's a Wonderful Life" Caboose, 07		75
___	**36621**	Marriott Caboose, 07		75
___	**36622**	C&O Caboose "C-1838", 08-09		40
___	**36623**	ATSF Caboose, 07-09		40
___	**36624**	Lionel Lines Caboose, 08-09		40
___	**36625**	B&M Caboose, 08		50
___	**36626**	Erie Caboose "C101", 08-09		45
___	**36632**	PRR Center Cupola Caboose, 08	8	20
___	**36634**	Holiday Porthole Caboose, green, 08		50
___	**36646**	Monopoly Caboose, 10		48
___	**36647**	Strasburg Caboose, 10		48
___	**36648**	Wizard of Oz Caboose, 09		50
___	**36649**	Pennsylvania Power & Light Work Caboose, 10		45
___	**36657**	Western & Atlantic Caboose, 10-11		48
___	**36659**	PRR Illuminated Porthole Caboose, 11		35
___	**36668**	CSX Illuminated Square Window Caboose, 10		35
___	**36672**	NS Caboose, 11		25
___	**36674**	Polar RR Caboose "C-1225", 11-12		53
___	**36690**	UP Overland Freight Caboose, 12		25
___	**36701**	Baldwin Locomotive Works Operating Welding Car "36701", 02		68
___	**36702**	Bosco Operating Milk Car with platform, 02		115
___	**36703**	Circus Horse Car with corral, 06		132
___	**36704**	Animated Reindeer Stock Car and Corral, 02		145
___	**36718**	AEC Security Caboose, 02		45
___	**36719**	Lionel Lion Bobbing Head Car, 02		20
___	**36720**	Aladdin Aquarium Car, 03		40
___	**36721**	101 Dalmatians Animated Gondola, 03		45
___	**36722**	Peter Pan Bobbing Head Boxcar, 03		45
___	**36726**	Santa Fe Searchlight Car "36726", 03		50
___	**36727**	Weyerhaeuser Moe & Joe Flatcar, 03		65

		Exc	Like New	
36728	SP Walking Brakeman Boxcar 163143," 03		42	___
36729	Lionel Lines Animated Caboose, 04-05	60	68	___
36730	U.S. Army Missile Launch Sound Car "44," 03		175	___
36731	Motorized Aquarium Car "3435," 03		83	___
36732	C&NW Jumping Hobo Car, 03		41	___
36733	Christmas Music Boxcar, 03		45	___
36734	Santa Fe Operating Searchlight Car "20611," 02		25	___
36735	WP Ice Car "7045," 02		55	___
36736	D&RGW Stock Car "39268," RailSounds, 04		45	___
36738	T&P Poultry Dispatch Car "36738," 02		50	___
36739	Postwar "3461" Lionel Lines Log Dump Car, 03		50	___
36740	Postwar "3469" Lionel Lines Coal Dump Car, 03		49	___
36743	Santa Claus Bobbing Head Boxcar, 03		40	___
36744	Little Mermaid Aquarium Car, 03		55	___
36745	Toy Story Animated Gondola, 03		70	___
36753	LFD Firecar with ladder, 02		60	___
36757	Southern Searchlight Car "51422," 03-04		40	___
36758	Patriotic Lighted Boxcar, 02		60	___
36760	B&O Sentinel Brakeman Car "3424," Archive Collection, 02		65	___
36761	Wellspring Capital Management Lighted Boxcar, 02 u		220	___
36764	West Side Lumber Log Dump Car "36764," 03		55	___
36765	Alaska Coal Dump Car "401," 03		50	___
36766	Erie Chase Gondola, 03		50	___
36767	Santa's Radar Tracking Car, 03		40	___
36769	Fourth of July Lighted Boxcar, 03		70	___
36770	American Refrigerator Transit Ice Car "23701," 04		42	___
36771	CN Barrel Car "74208,"04		48	___
36772	Spokane, Portland & Seattle Log Dump Car "36772," 04		46	___
36773	Jersey Central Coal Dump Car "92926," 04		45	___
36774	PRR Moe & Joe Lumber Flatcar, 04		50	___
36775	Santa Fe Animated Caboose "999010", 05		75	___
36776	Santa Fe Walking Brakeman Car "19938", 04		43	___
36778	C&O Searchlight Car "216614," 04		30	___
36780	Sea-Monkeys Motorized Aquarium Car, 04		45	___
36781	Finding Nemo Aquarium Car, 04		50	___
36782	Goofy and Pete Jumping Boxcar, 05		70	___
36783	Disney Operating Boxcar, 04-05		65	___
36784	Monsters Inc. Bobbing Head Boxcar, 04		40	___
36786	Postwar "3494-150" MP Operating Boxcar, 03		40	___
36787	MOW Remote Control Searchlight Car, 04		45	___
36788	Lionel Lines Tender, TrainSounds, 04		75	___
36789	Railbox Boxcar, TrainSounds, 04-05		105	___
36790	Christmas Music Boxcar, 04		70	___
36791	Kinzua Pine Mills Operating Log Dump Car, 96		40	___
36793	Pennsylvania Derrick Car, 03		22	___
36794	NYC Log Dump Car, 03		25	___
36795	Southern Coal Dump Car, 03		25	___
36796	GN Searchlight Car, 03		24	___
36797	"Operation Iraqi Freedom" Minuteman Car, 03		45	___
36803	Santa Animated Caboose, 06		75	___
36804	Candy Cane Dump Car, 06		80	___
36805	Reindeer Jumping Boxcar, 06		70	___
36809	NYC Derrick Car, 07-08		35	___

	MODERN 1970-2025		Exc	Like New
___	36810	PRR Searchlight Car, 07		35
___	36811	UP Dump Coal Dump Car, 07		35
___	36812	British Columbia Log Dump Car, 07-08		35
___	36813	State of Maine Brakeman Car, 08		80
___	36814	D&RGW Animated Caboose "01415," 07-09		80
___	36815	Santa Fe Moe & Joe Flatcar, 07-08		80
___	36816	Virginian Coal Dump Car, 08		80
___	36818	U.S. Steel Searchlight Car, 07-08		75
___	36821	"Naughty or Nice" Dump Car, 07		80
___	36823	Halloween SpookySmoke Boxcar, 07		115
___	36824	Alien Smoking Boxcar, 07		110
___	36825	Lionel Lines Boom w/Crane, 07		35
___	36826	Home Depot/Tony Stewart Searchlight Car, 07		30
___	36829	Alien Radioactive Car, 07		70
___	36830	Trick or Treat Aquarium Car, 07		75
___	36831	MOW Welding Car, 07-08		75
___	36833	Christmas Music Boxcar, 07	27	65
___	36834	Santa Fe Transparent Instruction Car, 07-08		65
___	36838	Lionel Power Co. Voltmeter Car, K-Line, 06		75
___	36839	Operating Milk Car with platform, K-Line, 06		140
___	36841	Visitor Center 15th Anniversary Lighted Boxcar, 06		70
___	36847	Polar Express Tender, TrainSounds, 08-14		130
___	36848	Candy Cane Dump Car, 07		80
___	36849	Tell-Tale Reindeer Car, 07		53
___	36850	Santa and Snowman Boxcar, 07		75
___	36851	Generator Car with Christmas tree, 07		75
___	36853	U.S. Army Exploding Boxcar, 08		60
___	36855	GW Horse Car and Corral, 08		160
___	36856	W&ARR Sheriff and Outlaw Car, 08		75
___	36857	Bobbing Ghost Boxcar, 08		65
___	36859	Lionel Lines Aquarium Car, 08		80
___	36861	PRR Poultry Dispatch Car, 08-09		80
___	36863	Alien Security Car, 08		80
___	36864	Bethlehem Steel Searchlight Car, 08		40
___	36866	WP Coal Dump Car "52369," 08		40
___	36868	NH Barrel Ramp Car, 08		40
___	36869	Bobbing Santa Boxcar, 08		65
___	36870	Postwar "6812" Track Maintenance Car, 08		65
___	36874	PRR Searchlight Car, 09		35
___	36875	Polar Express Coach, sound, 08-14, 16		132
___	36878	NYC Track Cleaning Car, 08		150
___	36879	REA Ice Car "1221," 08		65
___	36880	Koi Fish Aquarium Car, 10		75
___	36881	Christmas Music Boxcar, 08		70
___	36887	Great Western Animated Gondola, 08-09		65
___	36888	Casper Aquarium Car, 09-10		90
___	36889	PRR Barrel Ramp Car, 09-10		46
___	36893	UP Transparent Instruction Car "195220," 09-10		75
___	36896	Christmas Music Boxcar, 09		80
___	36897	Pennsylvania Power & Light Coal Dump Car, 09-10		46
___	36898	Wisconsin Central Log Dump Car, 09		46
___	36900	Depressed Center Flatcar with backshop load, 99	45	115
___	36913	Allied Chemical 1-D Tank Car 2-pack, 00		150

MODERN 1970-2025		Exc	Like New	
36914	Allied Chemical 1-D Tank Car "68075," die-cast, white, 00		90	___
36915	Allied Chemical 1-D Tank Car "68076," die-cast, white, 00		90	___
36916	Allied Chemical 1-D Tank Car 2-pack, 00		175	___
36917	Allied Chemical 1-D Tank Car "65124," die-cast, black, 00		95	___
36918	Allied Chemical 1-D Tank Car "65125," die-cast, black, 00		90	___
36919	Maersk Maxi-Stack Car, 00		33	___
36927	B&O DC Hopper 6-pack, "435040-45," 01		520	___
36935	Maersk Maxi-Stack Car 2-pack, "250131-32," 00		135	___
36937	SP Maxi-Stack Car "513957," 02		65	___
36998	Gingerbread Man Gateman, 12-13		80	___
37001	No. 3444 Erie Animated Gondola, 09		70	___
37002	Operating Plutonium Car 2-pack, 10-11		140	___
37003	PRR Jet Snow Blower "491252," 09-10		138	___
37004	Area 51 Searchlight Car, 09		46	___
37006	Lionel Flatcar with operating LCD billboard, 09		180	___
37009	Smoking Mount St. Helens Boxcar, 10-11		125	___
37010	Pennsylvania Power & Light Searchlight Car, 10		46	___
37011	B&M Operating Milk Car with platform, 10		155	___
37012	GN Jumping Hobo Boxcar, 10		75	___
37015	Jack-o-Lantern Flatcar, 11-13		75	___
37016	Radioactive Plutonium Flatcar, 11		70	___
37017	Plutonium Boom Car, 11		70	___
37022	ATSF Blinking Billboard, 12		25	___
37032	Postwar "3562" Operating Barrel Car, 11		75	___
37033	Casper Animated Gondola , 11		70	___
37035	Santa's Operating Snow Globe Car, 11		75	___
37036	Halloween Operating Globe Car, 11		78	___
37038	Halloween Searchlight Car, 12-13		45	___
37039	Minuteman Searchlight Car, 11		45	___
37040	UP Derrick Car, 11-12		46	___
37041	Pennsylvania Power & Light Coal Dump Car, 11		80	___
37042	IC Coal Dump Car, 11		46	___
37043	Seaboard Log Dump Car, 11		46	___
37044	CP Rail Log Dump Car, 11, 13		80	___
37045	Beatles Yellow Submarine Aquarium Car, 11		85	___
37047	Santa's Flyer Animated Gondola, 11		55	___
37053	EL Derrick Car, 12		45	___
37054	CSX Coal Dump Car, 12		46	___
37055	SP Log Dump Car, 12		46	___
37056	Zombie Aquarium Car, 12		80	___
37057	Bethlehem Steel Culvert Car, 12		65	___
37058	Ghost Globe Halloween Car, 12-15		80	___
37059	Christmas Snow Globe Car, 12		85	___
37060	LIRR Derrick Car, 13-14		50	___
37061	UP Railroad Speeder, CC, 12-14		150	___
37062	NS Railroad Speeder, CC, 12-14		150	___
37063	PRR Railroad Speeder, CC, 12-14, 16		150	___
37064	CSX Railroad Speeder, CC, 12-14		150	___
37065	BNSF Railroad Speeder, CC, 12-14		150	___
37066	MOW Railroad Speeder, CC, 12-14		150	___
37067	NYC Railroad Speeder, CC, 12-14		150	___
37068	CN Railroad Speeder, CC, 12-14		150	___
37069	Strasburg RR Crane Car, 12		65	___

	MODERN 1970-2025		Exc	Like New
____	37070	Gingerbread Man and Santa Animated Gondola, 12		55
____	37071	MOW Searchlight Car, 12		46
____	37073	U.S. Marine Corps Cannon Car, 12		75
____	37075	Boy Scouts of America Crane Car, 13		75
____	37076	Bethlehem Steel Coal Dump Car, 13		50
____	37078	RI Searchlight Car, 13		50
____	37079	Santa Fe Derrick Car, 13		50
____	37081	Peanuts Pumpkin Jack-O-Lantern Car, 13		85
____	37082	Peanuts Animated Trick or Treat Chase Gondola, 14-16		75
____	37083	Strasburg Coal Dump Car, 13		50
____	37084	PRR Cop and Hobo Animated Gondola, 13		65
____	37085	BN Log Dump Car, 13		50
____	37086	Lionelville Aquarium Co. Aquarium Car, 13		80
____	37087	NH Walking Brakeman Car, 13-14		75
____	37089	Santa's List Snow Globe Car, 13		90
____	37090	Polar Express Searchlight Car, 13		60
____	37094	Wizard of Oz Aquarium Car, 13-15		85
____	37095	North Pole Sleigh Repair Welding Car, 13		85
____	37097	Where the Wild Things Are Aquarium Car, 13-15		85
____	37099	North Pole Central EV Caboose "2510" (std 0), 13		95
____	37100	Barrel Loader Building, 12-14		43
____	37101	Smiley Water Tower, 12-14		23
____	37102	Watchman Shanty, 12-14		30
____	37103	FasTrack 031 Curved Track, 13-25		6
____	37110	FasTrack Terminal Section, LionChief, 14-25		10
____	37112	Helicopter 2-pack, 13-20		35
____	37115	Pedestrian Walkover, green, 16-18		55
____	37120	Railroad Crossing Signs, 13-20		10
____	37121	Christmas Station Platform, 13		25
____	37122	Santa Fe Blinking Billboard, 13		25
____	37123	Weyerhaeuser Timber Operating Sawmill, 12-13		140
____	37124	West Side Lumber Operating Sawmill, 12-13		140
____	37125	Legacy Writable Utility Mobile, 12-16, 20		20
____	37127	Angela Trotta Thomas Gallery, 12		75
____	37129	Boy Scouts of America Girder Bridge, 13		23
____	37130	Boy Scouts of America Covered Bridge, 13		60
____	37139	Tis the Season Accessories, 12-13		310
____	37140	All Aboard Accessories, 12-13		65
____	37141	Rail Yard Accessories, 12-13		277
____	37142	Welcome Home Accessories, 12-13		154
____	37146	Legacy PowerMaster, 12-25		130
____	37147	CAB-1L/Base-1L Command Set, 12-16, 18-20		250
____	37149	FasTrack Modular Layout Straight Section Kit, 13		200
____	37150	FasTrack Modular Layout Template, 13-16		30
____	37151	Red Christmas Classic Street Lamps, 3-pack, 14-25		40
____	37152	Operating Coaling Station, 13-14		180
____	37153	FasTrack Modular Layout 45-Degree Reversible Corner Kit, 13		225
____	37154	FasTrack Modular Layout 45-Degree Corner Kit, 13		225
____	37155	CAB-1L Remote Controller, 12-16, 20-25	75	165
____	37156	Base-1L, 12-16		125
____	37158	Hershey's Water Tower, 13		30
____	37159	Peanuts Figure Pack, 13-15		30

MODERN 1970-2025		Exc	Like New	
37160	Strasburg Girder Bridge, 13		21	___
37161	Container 4-pack, 13		40	___
37162	Lionelville Water Tower, 13		25	___
37163	LIRR Girder Bridge, 13		21	___
37164	NS Girder Bridge, 13		21	___
37165	CP Water Tower, 13		25	___
37166	Crossing Shanty, 13-14, 16		25	___
37167	Freight Platform, 13		30	___
37169	Peanuts Psychiatric Booth, 13-16		40	___
37172	Black Gooseneck Lamps, 2-pack, 13-25	13	35	___
37173	Globe Lamp 3-pack, 13-14, 16-19		25	___
37174	Black Classic Street Lamps, 3-pack, 13-25		40	___
37176	Santa Fe Shanty, 13		25	___
37183	Polar Express 10th Anniversary Snowman and Children, 13-17		37	___
37184	Christmas Half Covered Bridge, 13		43	___
37185	Christmas Railroad Signs, 13-14, 16-18		10	___
37187	Kris Kringle's Kloseout Shop, 13		50	___
37191	36-watt Power Supply, LionChief, 14		36	___
37195	Grand Central Terminal 100th Anniversary, 13-15		280	___
37196	Christmas Extension Bridge, 13, 16-18		15	___
37197	North Pole Central Girder Bridge, 13-14, 16-17		30	___
37530	Santa Animated Caboose, 11		80	___
37807	Station Platform, 10-15		23	___
37808	Sunoco Spherical Oil Tank, 10-11		100	___
37810	Curved O Gauge Tunnel, 11-17		65	___
37813	Christmas Tractor and Trailer with trees, 10		27	___
37814	Christmas Crossing Shanty, 10-14		30	___
37816	Rockville Bridge, 11-12		700	___
37820	Lionel Auto Loader Cars 4-pack, 12-13, 16-17		25	___
37821	Smoke Fluid Loader, 11		250	___
37826	Classic Travel Billboard Set, 11-14		13	___
37827	Coca-Cola Covered Bridge, 11		45	___
37828	Vintage Boy Scouts Figure Pack, 11-14		30	___
37829	Polar Express Station Platform, 11-18		40	___
37831	NJ Transit Blinking Light Water Tower, 11-12		30	___
37834	Lionel Boat 4-pack, 11-20		25	___
37836	Monopoly Auto 4-pack, 12		25	___
37837	Polar Express Straight Tunnel, 12-14		80	___
37840	Santa Fe Diorama, 12-17		15	___
37841	Premium Smoke Fluid, 12-16		7	___
37842	CN Tractor with piggyback trailer, 12, 15		90	___
37846	PRR Tractor Trailer, 12		90	___
37847	SP Tractor Trailer, 12		90	___
37848	IC Tractor Trailer, 12		90	___
37849	ATSF Tractor Trailer, 12		90	___
37850	REA Tractor Trailer, 12		90	___
37851	Scale Telephone Poles, 6-pack, 12-25		40	___
37852	Christmas People Pack, 12-14, 16-18		20	___
37853	Alien Billboard, 13, 15		13	___
37854	Classic Christmas Billboard , 12		11	___
37855	Lionel Airplane 2-pack, 12-20		37	___
37900	Silver Truss Bridge, 11		70	___

MODERN 1970-2025		Exc	Like New
____ 37901	Lehigh Valley Tugboat, 10		270
____ 37902	Illuminated Barge, 10		180
____ 37903	Cell Tower, 10-25		85
____ 37904	Boy Scouts Billboard Set, 10		13
____ 37907	Christmas Street Lamps with wreaths, 10-14		30
____ 37909	North Pole Central Jet Snowblower, 11-14		138
____ 37910	Operating Lighthouse, 10		180
____ 37911	D&RGW Blinking Light Water Tower, 10-11		30
____ 37912	Lighted Coaling Tower, 10-15		180
____ 37913	Hopper Shed, 10-15		35
____ 37914	Illuminated Work House, 10-18		40
____ 37916	Beige Brick Suburban House, 10		80
____ 37917	Red Brick Suburban House, 10		80
____ 37919	Operating Sawmill, 10		130
____ 37920	Bascule Bridge, 10		350
____ 37921	ZW-L Transformer, 11-25	659	1000
____ 37922	Coca-Cola Blinking Light Billboard, 10-11		28
____ 37923	Coca-Cola Blinking Light Water Tower, 11		28
____ 37928	Passenger Station, sounds, 11		90
____ 37929	Coca-Cola Diner, 11, 13		75
____ 37930	Rotary Aircraft Beacon, 11-12		81
____ 37933	MG Switch Tower, 11-13		300
____ 37935	Operating Track Gang, 11		100
____ 37939	Assorted Telephone Poles, 6-pack, 11-25		45
____ 37940	PRR Hobo Hotel, 12		150
____ 37941	House Under Construction, 11		90
____ 37942	Christmas Hobo Hotel, 12-13		150
____ 37944	Weathered 50,000-gallon Water Tank, 11-12		170
____ 37946	House Under Construction #2, 12-13		90
____ 37947	GW-180 180-watt Transformer, 12-25		360
____ 37948	Boy Scouts Flagpole with lights, 11		30
____ 37951	Postwar "342" Culvert Loader, 11		165
____ 37952	Postwar "345" Culvert Unloader, 11		190
____ 37953	Jacobs Pharmacy, 11		50
____ 37954	Halloween Station Platform, 11-13		35
____ 37955	Sodor Station Platform, 11-15		35
____ 37957	Deluxe Holiday House, 11		85
____ 37958	SP Scrap Yard, 11-14		110
____ 37959	Midway Basketball Shot Game, 11-13		21
____ 37960	Burning Switch Tower, 11-13		100
____ 37961	NYC Scrap Yard, 11-13		110
____ 37962	NJ Transit Station Platform, 11		37
____ 37964	Archive Operating Freight Terminal, 11-14		150
____ 37965	Christmas Operating Freight Terminal, 11-14, 16-17		150
____ 37966	Lionel Cylindrical Oil Tank, 11-17		100
____ 37967	Boy Scouts Troop Cabin, 12-13		80
____ 37971	Bethlehem Steel Culvert Loader, 11		165
____ 37972	Bethlehem Steel Culvert Unloader, 11		190
____ 37973	Coca-Cola Station Platform, 12		37
____ 37975	PFE Operating Freight Terminal, 11-16		150
____ 37977	Hooker Tank Car Accident, 11-17		130
____ 37978	Deluxe Suburban House, 11-13		80
____ 37979	Rotary Coal Tipple, 12		540

MODERN 1970-2025		Exc	Like New	
37980	Operating Coal Conveyor, 12		90	___
37984	Santa's Repair Work House, 12-14		40	___
37985	Operating Wind Turbine, 12-15		75	___
37986	NJ Transit Blinking Billboard, 12-13		28	___
37989	Sodor Train Shed, 12-16		60	___
37993	Snoopy and the Red Baron Animated Pylon, 12		160	___
37994	Deluxe Holiday House #2, 12-14		120	___
37995	Illuminated Scale Telephone Poles, 6-pack, 12-25		55	___
37996	Postwar 192 Control Tower, 12		70	___
37997	Christmas Lawn Figure Pack, 12-14, 16-18		20	___
37998	Halloween Haunted Passenger Station, 12-13, 15		75	___
38004	Virginian 4-6-0 10-wheel Locomotive "203," CC, 01-02		570	___
38005	Long Island 4-6-0 10-wheel Locomotive "138," CC, 01-02		510	___
38007	UP Auxiliary tender, black, CC, 01		280	___
38008	UP Auxiliary tender, gray, CC, 01	80	205	___
38009	D&RGW 4-6-6-4 Challenger Locomotive "3803," CC, 01	263	1550	___
38010	Clinchfield 4-6-6-4 Challenger Locomotive "673," CC, 01	200	1400	___
38012	Wheeling & Lake Erie 2-6-6-2 Locomotive "8005," CC, 01		610	___
38013	D&H 4-6-6-4 Challenger Locomotive "1527," CC, 01		720	___
38014	D&RGW 4-6-6-4 Challenger Locomotive "3800," CC, 01		710	___
38015	NYC 4-6-4 Hudson Locomotive "773," CC, 01		900	___
38016	Southern 0-8-0 Yard Goat Locomotive "6536," CC, 01-02, 05		530	___
38017	CN 2-6-0 Mogul Locomotive "86," CC, 03, 05		600	___
38018	Wabash 2-6-0 Mogul Locomotive "826," CC, 03		485	___
38019	B&M 2-6-0 Mogul Locomotive "1455," CC, 03, 05	150	600	___
38020	PRR 4-4-4-4 T1 Duplex Locomotive "5514," 02-03		630	___
38021	WP 4-6-6-4 Challenger Locomotive "402," CC, 02	235	650	___
38022	WM 4-6-6-4 Challenger Locomotive "1206," CC, 02		690	___
38023	UP 4-6-6-4 Challenger Locomotive "3976," CC, 02		620	___
38024	PRR 6-4-4-6 S-1 Duplex Locomotive "6100," TMCC, 03	300	1000	___
38025	PRR 4-6-2 K4 Pacific Locomotive "1361," CC, 02	175	950	___
38026	N&W 4-8-4 J Class Northern Locomotive "606," CC, 02	538	1450	___
38027	Meadow River Lumber Heisler Geared Locomotive "6," CC, 03	446	880	___
38028	PRR 6-8-6 S2 Steam Turbine Locomotive, 01	150	650	___
38029	UP 4-12-2 Locomotive "9000," CC, 03		633	___
38030	Santa Fe 2-8-8-2 Locomotive "1795," CC, 03	175	920	___
38031	SP 2-8-8-4 AC-9 Locomotive "3809," CC, 04		1100	___
38032	Virginian 2-8-8-2 Locomotive "741," CC, 03		928	___
38036	Long Island 2-8-0 Consolidation Locomotive, 01		500	___
38037	PRR Reading Seashore 2-8-0 Consolidation "6072," CC, 01		495	___
38038	D&RGW Auxiliary Water Tender, 01	65	230	___
38039	Clinchfield Auxiliary Water Tender, 01	75	220	___
38040	LV 4-6-0 Camelback Locomotive, 01		405	___
38042	C&NW 4-6-0 10-wheel Locomotive "361," CC, 02		450	___
38043	Frisco 4-6-0 10-wheel Locomotive "719," CC, 02		525	___
38044	PRR 4-6-2 K4 Pacific Locomotive "5385," CC, 02	275	920	___
38045	NYC Hudson J-3a 4-6-4 Locomotive "5418," CC, 03		495	___
38046	GN 0-8-0 Locomotive "815," CC, 02	263	530	___
38047	N&W 0-8-0 Locomotive "266," CC, 02		550	___
38048	NPR 0-8-0 Locomotive "303," CC, 02		530	___
38049	N&W 2-6-6-4 Locomotive "1234," CC, 02		690	___
38050	Nickel Plate 2-8-4 Berkshire Locomotive "779," CC, 03	200	925	___
38051	Erie 2-8-4 Berkshire Locomotive "3315," CC, 03	175	810	___

MODERN 1970-2025			Exc	Like New
____	38052	Pere Marquette 2-8-4 Berkshire Locomotive "1225," CC, 03		1000
____	38053	NYC 4-8-2 Mohawk L-2a Locomotive "2793," CC, 03	200	915
____	38055	Santa Fe 4-8-4 Northern Locomotive "3751" CC, 04	175	1100
____	38056	PRR 4-8-2 Mountain M1a Locomotive "6759," CC, 03	163	850
____	38057	Weyerhaeuser Shay Locomotive, CC, 03		1000
____	38058	C&O 2-8-8-2 H7 Locomotive "1580," CC, 04		1200
____	38060	UP 2-8-8-2 H7 Locomotive "3590," CC, 04	350	1200
____	38061	Cass Scenic Heisler Geared Locomotive "6," CC, 03		940
____	38062	Lionel Lines 4-6-2 Pacific Locomotive "8062," CC, 02-03		275
____	38065	UP 2-8-8-2 Mallet Locomotive "3672," CC, 02		1002
____	38066	Elk River Shay Locomotive, CC, 03		1000
____	38067	MILW 4-6-2 Pacific Locomotive "6316," CC, 03		300
____	38068	WM 4-6-2 Pacific Locomotive "204," CC, 03		300
____	38069	Erie Hudson Locomotive, whistle, 05		150
____	38070	C&O 4-6-2 Pacific Locomotive "489," CC, 04	90	300
____	38071	SP Cab Forward AC-12 Locomotive "4294," CC, 05	450	1550
____	38075	UP 4-8-8-4 Big Boy Locomotive "4024," LionMaster, 03		800
____	38076	C&O 2-8-4 Berkshire Locomotive "2699," CC, 04	138	860
____	38077	Virginian 2-8-4 Berkshire Locomotive "508," CC, 04		1000
____	38079	SP 4-8-4 Northern GS-2 Locomotive "4410," CC, 04	225	980
____	38080	WP 4-8-4 Northern GS-64 Locomotive "485," CC, 04	325	1000
____	38081	C&O 2-6-6-6 Allegheny Locomotive "1650," CC, 05-07	313	1700
____	38082	Pennsylvania 2-8-8-2 Y3 Locomotive "374," CC, 04		1000
____	38083	N&W 2-8-8-2 Y3 Locomotive "2009," CC, 04	275	910
____	38085	NYC 4-6-4 Hudson J-3a Locomotive "5422," CC, 03		495
____	38086	B&A 4-6-4 Hudson Locomotive "607," CC, 03		495
____	38087	Nickel Plate 2-8-4 Berkshire Locomotive, RailSounds, 05		190
____	38088	NYC 2-6-0 Mogul Locomotive "1924," CC, 03, 05		600
____	38089	Pennsylvania 4-6-2 Pacific Locomotive "3678," CC, 04		300
____	38090	Clinchfield 4-6-6-4 Challenger Locomotive "672" CC, 04		640
____	38091	NP 4-6-6-4 Challenger Locomotive "5121," CC, 04		660
____	38092	Pickering Lumber Heisler Locomotive "5," CC, 04		1000
____	38093	UP 4-6-6-4 Challenger Locomotive "3980," CC, 04	307	700
____	38094	MILW Hiawatha 4-4-2 Atlantic Locomotive, CC, 06		950
____	38095	N&W 4-8-4 J Class Locomotive "611," CC, 05-06	300	1250
____	38100	Texas Special F3 Diesel AB Set, 99	580	930
____	38103	Texas Special F3 Diesel "2245", 99	435	510
____	38104	CP F3 A Unit "2373," powered, 99		400
____	38105	CP F3 A Unit "2373," nonpowered, 99		100
____	38106	NYC F3 A Unit "2333," powered, 99		400
____	38107	NYC F3 A Unit "2333," nonpowered, 99		250
____	38114	ATSF FT Diesel B Unit, 99-00		170
____	38115	NYC FT Diesel B Unit "2403," nonpowered, 99-00		130
____	38116	B&O FT Diesel B Unit, 99-00		130
____	38144	C&O F3 Diesel AA Set "7019, 7021," 00	138	700
____	38147	GN Alco FA2 AA Diesel Set, CC, 02		405
____	38150	Platinum Ghost "2333," 99	198	495
____	38153	"Spirit of the Century" F3 Diesel AA Set, 99		800
____	38160	Pennsylvania Alco FB2 Diesel, 02		125
____	38161	MKT Alco FB2 Diesel, 02		125
____	38162	Burlington FT Diesel B Unit, 01		0
____	38167	Burlington FT Diesel AA Set, 01		225
____	38176	Pennsylvania Alco FA2 AA Diesel Set, CC, 02		405

MODERN 1970-2025		Exc	Like New	
38182	MKT Alco FA2 AA Diesel Set, CC, 02		360	___
38188	Southern F3 Diesel ABA Set, 00	264	557	___
38194	GN Alco FB2 Diesel, 02		125	___
38195	Santa Fe FT Diesel A Unit "170," 00		125	___
38196	Santa Fe FT Diesel A Unit "171," 00		175	___
38197	SP F3 Diesel ABA Set, 00	209	640	___
38202	Wild West Handcar, 10		75	___
38203	Holly Jolly Trolley 2-car Set, 10		160	___
38204	ATSF FT B Unit, nonpowered, 10		120	___
38210	PRR Alco Diesel AA Set, CC, 10		400	___
38213	Rio Grande Ski Train FT A Unit "541," powered, 10-11		200	___
38214	Rio Grande Ski Train FT B Unit, nonpowered, 11		120	___
38215	ATSF FT Diesel "165," RailSounds, 10-11		280	___
38216	Rio Grande Ski Train FT A Unit, nonpowered, 11		120	___
38219	Texan FT B Unit Diesel, nonpowered, 11, 13-14	25	120	___
38221	CNJ Alco AA Diesel Set, 11		300	___
38224	Alaska Alco AA Diesel Set, 11		300	___
38234	Classic PRR GG1 Electric Locomotive "4866," 12		330	___
38235	Classic PC GG1 Electric Locomotive "4840," 12		330	___
38240	Elf Gang Car, 12		120	___
38241	MOW Gang Car, 12-13		120	___
38248	NS GP38 Diesel "1030," 13-14	180	300	___
38252	CP GE U36B Diesel, "4245," 13	155	200	___
38300	Postwar "2331" Virginian Train Master Diesel, 08	190	230	___
38303	Postwar "2340" GG1 Electric Locomotive, 08		280	___
38305	Postwar "2338" Milwaukee Road GP7 Diesel, 08		220	___
38308	Postwar 2146WS Berkshire Passenger Set, 12	200	460	___
38310	Postwar "2185W" NYC F3 Diesel Freight Set, 09	163	600	___
38311	Postwar "2276W" B&O RDC Commuter Set, 09	110	470	___
38312	Postwar "2343" Santa Fe F3 Diesel AA Set, 09	138	500	___
38313	B&O Budd RDC 2-pack, 09	100	350	___
38323	Postwar "2348" M&StL GP9 Diesel, CC, 10		390	___
38324	Postwar 2507W NH F3 Diesel Freight Set, 10	138	600	___
38328	Postwar 1623W NP GP9 Diesel Freight Set, 10	225	750	___
38329	Postwar 2261W Freight Hauler Set, 10	183	610	___
38334	Postwar 11288 Orbitor Diesel Freight Set, 10	188	500	___
38338	Postwar 2129WS Berkshire Freight Set, 12	188	550	___
38339	Postwar 2505W Virginian Rectifier Freight Set, 10	163	470	___
38340	Postwar 1587S Girl's Steam Freight Set, 10	175	580	___
38342	Postwar 1619W Santa Fe Freight Set, 10-11	125	470	___
38348	Postwar "2339" Transparent Wabash GP7 Diesel, 11		290	___
38349	Postwar 12885-500 C&O GP7 Freight Set, 11-12		600	___
38351	Postwar Archive UP GP7 Diesel, 11		290	___
38353	Postwar X-628 Promotional U.S. Navy Diesel Freight Set, 12-14		600	___
38354	Postwar 1464W UP Anniversary Alco Diesel Passenger Set, 12-14	230	480	___
38357	Postwar 221 U.S. Marine Corps Alco Diesel A Unit, 12-14		300	___
38358	Postwar 2239 IC F3 Freight Set, 12-14		600	___
38365	Archive ATSF Black Bonnet F3 AA Diesel Set, 12-14	333	727	___
38368	Archive NYC Red Lightning F3 AA Diesel Set, 12-14		500	___
38371	Postwar 2031 RI Alco Diesel AA Set, 12-13		400	___
38374	Postwar 221 U.S. Marine Corps Alco Diesel B Unit, 12-14		120	___
38377	Postwar 2363T F3 A Unit, nonpowered, 12-14		170	___

			Exc	Like New
____	**38379**	Archive ATSF Black Bonnet F3 B Unit, 12-14		170
____	**38380**	Archive NYC Red Lightning F3 B Unit, 12-14		248
____	**38386**	Postwar "2367" Wabash F3 Diesel AB Units, 12-14		500
____	**38388**	Postwar "2367" Wabash F3 Diesel A Unit, nonpowered, 12-14		170
____	**38389**	Postwar "2362" UP F3 Diesel AA Set, 14		460
____	**38392**	Postwar "2362" F3 Diesel B Unit, nonpowered, 14		170
____	**38393**	PRR Round-roof Boxcar "76648" (std 0), 14		80
____	**38401**	NYC M-497 Jet-Powered Rail Car, 10		600
____	**38402**	Amtrak HHP-8 Electric Locomotive, RailSounds, 10		400
____	**38403**	B&O CSX Heritage AC6000 Diesel "6607," CC, 11		550
____	**38404**	B&O CSX Heritage AC6000 Diesel "7812," CC, 11		550
____	**38405**	Chessie System CSX Heritage AC6000 Diesel, CC, 11-14	250	550
____	**38406**	Chessie System CSX Heritage AC6000 Diesel, CC, 11-14		550
____	**38407**	WM CSX Heritage AC6000 Diesel "2652," CC, 11		550
____	**38408**	WM CSX Heritage AC6000 Diesel "2659," CC, 11	200	550
____	**38409**	Clinchfield CSX Heritage AC6000 Diesel, CC, 11-13	282	550
____	**38410**	Clinchfield CSX Heritage AC6000 Diesel, CC, 11-14		550
____	**38411**	Family Lines CSX Heritage AC6000 Diesel "4825," CC, 11		550
____	**38412**	Family Lines CSX Heritage AC6000 Diesel "4837," CC, 11		550
____	**38413**	CSX Heritage AC6000 Diesel "607," CC, 11-13		550
____	**38414**	CSX Heritage AC6000 Diesel "654," CC, 11-13		550
____	**38415**	PRR U28C Diesel "6531," CC, 11-12		530
____	**38416**	PRR U28C Diesel "6534," CC, 11-12		530
____	**38417**	BN Bicentennial U30C Diesel "1776," CC, 11		530
____	**38418**	BN Bicentennial U30C Diesel "1777," CC, 11		530
____	**38419**	UP U30C Diesel "2918," CC, 11-12		530
____	**38420**	UP U30C Diesel "2897," CC, 11-12		530
____	**38421**	NP U33C Diesel "3305," CC, 11-12		530
____	**38422**	NP U33C Diesel "3307," CC, 11-12		530
____	**38423**	Southern U30C Diesel "3801," CC, 11-12		530
____	**38424**	Southern U30C Diesel "3804," CC, 11-12		530
____	**38425**	RI Budd RDC Jet Car, 11		330
____	**38426**	Central of Georgia GP7 Diesel "126," CC, 11		450
____	**38427**	Central of Georgia GP7 Diesel "128," CC, 11		450
____	**38428**	Alaska Budd RDC Coach, 11		300
____	**38429**	NYC Budd RDC M-497 Jet Car, 11		330
____	**38432**	MKT H16-44 Diesel "1591," CC, 11		500
____	**38433**	MKT H16-44 Diesel "1731," CC, 11		500
____	**38434**	MKT H16-44 Diesel "1732", 11		380
____	**38435**	MKT H16-44 Diesel "1733," nonpowered, 11		240
____	**38436**	LIRR H-16-44 Diesel "1501," CC, 11		500
____	**38437**	LIRR H-16-44 Diesel "1504," CC, 11		500
____	**38438**	LIRR H-16-44 Diesel "1507", 11		380
____	**38439**	LIRR H-16-44 Diesel "1509," nonpowered, 11		240
____	**38440**	UP H-16-44 Diesel "1341," CC, 11	113	500
____	**38441**	UP H-16-44 Diesel "1342," CC, 11		500
____	**38442**	UP H-16-44 Diesel "1343," 11		380
____	**38443**	UP H-16-44 Diesel "1344," nonpowered, 11		240
____	**38444**	PRR H16-44 Diesel "8807," CC, 11		500
____	**38445**	PRR H16-44 Diesel "8810," CC, 11		500
____	**38446**	PRR H16-44 Diesel "8812," 11		380
____	**38447**	PRR H16-44 Diesel "8815," nonpowered, 11		240

MODERN 1970-2025		Exc	Like New	
38452	PC Alco RS-11 Diesel "7605," CC, 12		480	___
38453	PC Alco RS-11 Diesel "7608," CC, 12		480	___
38454	PRR Alco RS-11 Diesel "9622," CC, 12		480	___
38455	PC Alco RS-11 Diesel "7625," nonpowered, 12		240	___
38456	N&W Alco RS11 Diesel "308," CC, 12-13		480	___
38457	N&W Alco RS-11 Diesel "318," CC, 12		480	___
38458	PRR Alco RS-11 Diesel "8631," CC, 12		480	___
38459	N&W Alco RS-11 Diesel "330," nonpowered, 12		240	___
38460	NKP Alco RS-11 Diesel "855," CC, 12		480	___
38461	NKP Alco RS-11 Diesel "859," CC, 12		480	___
38462	PRR Alco RS-11 Diesel "8639," nonpowered, 12		240	___
38463	NKP Alco RS-11 Diesel "863," nonpowered, 12		240	___
38464	Alaska Alco RS-11 Diesel "3602," CC, 12		480	___
38465	Alaska Alco RS-11 Diesel "3604," CC, 12		480	___
38466	NH Alco RS-11 Diesel "1403," CC, 12		480	___
38467	Alaska Alco RS-11 Diesel "3607," nonpowered, 12		240	___
38468	Seaboard Alco RS-11 Diesel "101," CC, 12-13		480	___
38469	Seaboard Alco RS-11 Diesel "102," CC, 12		480	___
38470	NH Alco RS-11 Diesel "1405," CC, 12		480	___
38471	Seaboard Alco RS-11 Diesel "104," nonpowered, 12		240	___
38472	C&O Alco S2 Diesel Switcher "5001," CC, 11		470	___
38473	C&O Alco S2 Diesel Switcher "5505," CC, 11	113	480	___
38474	C&O Alco S2 Diesel Switcher "5020", 11		360	___
38475	C&O Alco S2 Diesel Switcher "5027," nonpowered, 11		220	___
38476	CN Alco S2 Diesel Switcher "7946," CC, 11		480	___
38477	CN Alco S2 Diesel Switcher "7949," CC, 11		480	___
38478	CN Alco S2 Diesel Switcher "7951," 11		360	___
38479	CN Alco S2 Diesel Switcher "7954," 11		360	___
38480	NYC Alco S2 Diesel Switcher "8504," CC, 11		480	___
38481	NYC Alco S2 Diesel Switcher "8507," CC, 11		480	___
38482	NYC Alco S2 Diesel Switcher "8514," 11		360	___
38483	NYC Alco S2 Diesel Switcher "8521," nonpowered, 11		220	___
38484	Southern Alco S2 Diesel Switcher "2209," CC, 11		480	___
38485	Southern Alco S2 Diesel Switcher "2211," CC, 11		480	___
38486	Southern Alco S2 Diesel Switcher "2215," 11		360	___
38487	Southern Alco S2 Diesel Switcher "2218," nonpowered, 11		220	___
38488	MP Alco S2 Diesel Switcher "9108," CC, 11		480	___
38489	MP Alco S2 Diesel Switcher "9113," CC, 11		480	___
38490	MP Alco S2 Diesel Switcher "9116," 11		360	___
38491	MP Alco S2 Diesel Switcher "9131," nonpowered, 11		220	___
38493	ATSF Early Era Inspection Vehicle, CC, 12		150	___
38494	CP DD35 Diesel "9864," CC, 12		600	___
38495	CP DD35 Diesel "9868," nonpowered, 12		440	___
38496	SP DD35A Diesel "9903," CC, 11		600	___
38497	SP DD35A Diesel "9914," nonpowered , 11		440	___
38498	PRR DD35A Diesel "2380," CC, 11		600	___
38499	PRR DD35A Diesel "2383," nonpowered, 11		440	___
38505	CSX GP-38 Diesel, 11		140	___
38521	PRR GG1 Electric "4839," 11		330	___
38522	Amtrak GG1 Electric "926," 11		330	___
38524	NYC GP35 Diesel "6131," CC, 12		500	___
38525	NYC GP35 Diesel "6138," CC, 12		500	___
38526	NYC GP35 Diesel "6147," nonpowered, 12		260	___

			Exc	Like New
____	**38527**	UP GP35 Diesel "742," CC, 12		500
____	**38528**	UP GP35 Diesel "753," CC, 12		500
____	**38529**	UP GP35 Diesel "760," nonpowered, 12		260
____	**38530**	SP GP35 Diesel "7465," CC, 12		500
____	**38531**	SP GP35 Diesel "7474," CC, 12		500
____	**38532**	SP GP35 Diesel "7481," nonpowered, 12		260
____	**38533**	CP GP35 Diesel "5014," CC, 12		500
____	**38534**	CP GP35 Diesel "5018," CC, 12		500
____	**38535**	CP GP35 Diesel "5023," nonpowered, 12		260
____	**38536**	PRR GP35 Diesel "2297," CC, 12		500
____	**38537**	PRR GP35 Diesel "2302," CC, 12		500
____	**38538**	PRR GP35 Diesel "2305," nonpowered, 12		260
____	**38539**	N&W Alco RS-11 Diesel "308," CC, 12		480
____	**38539**	Conrail GP35 Diesel "2297," CC, 12		500
____	**38540**	Conrail GP35 Diesel "2302," CC, 12		500
____	**38541**	Conrail GP35 Diesel "2305," nonpowered, 12		260
____	**38542**	Milwaukee Road GP35 Diesel "361," CC, 12		500
____	**38543**	Milwaukee Road GP35 Diesel "363," CC, 12		500
____	**38544**	Milwaukee Road GP35 Diesel "366," nonpowered, 12		260
____	**38545**	Pacific Harbor Line Genset Switcher "31," CC, 11		800
____	**38546**	KCS Genset Switcher "1404," CC, 11-12	225	800
____	**38547**	Santa Fe Genset Switcher "9910," CC, 11		800
____	**38548**	EL GP35 Diesel "2555," CC, 12		500
____	**38549**	EL GP35 Diesel "2558," CC, 12		500
____	**38550**	EL GP35 Diesel "2561," nonpowered, 12		260
____	**38558**	D&H Baldwin RF-16 Diesel AA Set, CC, 12	250	730
____	**38561**	D&H Baldwin RF-16 Diesel B Unit, CC, 12		400
____	**38562**	D&H Baldwin RF-16 Diesel B Unit, nonpowered, 12		250
____	**38563**	B&O Baldwin RF-16 Diesel AA Set, CC, 12-14		730
____	**38566**	B&O Baldwin RF-16 Diesel B Unit, CC, 12-14		400
____	**38567**	B&O Baldwin RF-16 Diesel B Unit, nonpowered, 12-14		250
____	**38568**	NYC Baldwin RF-16 Diesel AA Set "3806-3808," CC, 12-14		730
____	**38571**	NYC Baldwin RF-16 Diesel B Unit, CC, 12-14		400
____	**38572**	NYC Baldwin RF-16 Diesel B Unit, nonpowered, 12-14		250
____	**38573**	SP Baldwin RF-16 Diesel AA Set, CC, 12-14		730
____	**38576**	SP Baldwin RF-16 Diesel B Unit, CC, 12-14		400
____	**38577**	SP Baldwin RF-16 Diesel B Unit, nonpowered, 12-14		250
____	**38579**	ATSF GP9 Diesel "744," nonpowered, 12		240
____	**38580**	NP GP9 Diesel "324," nonpowered, 12		240
____	**38581**	CSX SD80MAC Diesel "809," CC, 12-13		530
____	**38582**	CSX SD80MAC Diesel "812," CC, 12		530
____	**38583**	CSX SD80MAC Diesel "804," nonpowered, 12		260
____	**38584**	NS SD80MAC Diesel "7207," CC, 12		530
____	**38585**	NS SD80MAC Diesel "7203," CC, 12		530
____	**38586**	NS SD80MAC Diesel "7209," nonpowered, 12		260
____	**38587**	Conrail SD80MAC Diesel "4126," CC, 12	138	530
____	**38588**	Conrail SD80MAC Diesel "4129," CC, 12		530
____	**38589**	Conrail SD80MAC Diesel "4103," nonpowered, 12		260
____	**38593**	UP NW2 Diesel Switcher Locomotive "1028," CC, 12		470
____	**38594**	UP NW2 Diesel Switcher Locomotive "1043," CC, 12		470
____	**38595**	CB&Q Scale NW2 Diesel Switcher "9227," CC, 12		470
____	**38596**	CB&Q Scale NW2 Diesel Switcher "9245," CC, 12		470
____	**38597**	CB&Q F3 AA Diesel Set "9962A-9962C," CC, 12-13		730

MODERN 1970-2025		Exc	Like New	
38600	UP 0-6-0 Dockside Switcher "87," traditional, 07-09		110	___
38601	Lionel Lines 0-6-0 Dockside Switcher, traditional, 07-09		110	___
38605	PRR 0-4-0 Locomotive "94," traditional, 07		170	___
38606	SP 0-4-0 Locomotive "71," traditional, 07-08		170	___
38607	Southern 2-8-4 Berkshire Locomotive "2718," RailSounds, 07-08		175	___
38608	LL 2-8-2 Mikado Locomotive "57," RailSounds, 07	95	251	___
38609	NYC 2-8-2 Mikado Locomotive "1843," CC, 07		370	___
38610	NKP 2-8-4 Berkshire Locomotive "779," CC, 07-08		370	___
38619	Santa Fe 4-6-2 Pacific Locomotive "2037," traditional, K-Line, 06		260	___
38620	B&O Porter Locomotive "16," traditional, K-Line, 06		100	___
38621	4-6-2 Pacific Locomotive, traditional, K-Line, 06		260	___
38626	Holiday 2-8-2 Mikado Locomotive "25," green, RailSounds, 08		260	___
38627	GN 4-4-2 Atlantic Locomotive "1702," traditional, 08-09		110	___
38630	U.S. Army 0-6-0 Switcher "486," traditional, 08-09		110	___
38634	NYC 4-6-4 Hudson Locomotive "5417," TrainSounds, 07		200	___
38635	C&O 4-6-4 Hudson Locomotive "309," TrainSounds, 08		200	___
38636	ATSF 4-6-4 Hudson Locomotive "3459," TrainSounds, 07		200	___
38637	LL 4-6-4 Hudson Locomotive "5242," TrainSounds, 08		200	___
38638	UP 4-6-2 Pacific Locomotive "2888," RailSounds, 08		300	___
38639	Erie 4-6-2 Pacific Locomotive "2939," RailSounds, 08		300	___
38640	Southern 4-6-2 Pacific Locomotive "1317," RailSounds, 08		300	___
38641	B&M 4-6-2 Pacific Locomotive "3713," RailSounds, 08		300	___
38642	PRR 4-6-2 Pacific Locomotive "5385," RailSounds, 08		300	___
38643	Alaska Mikado 2-8-2 Locomotive "701," CC, 08-09		280	___
38644	T&P Mikado 2-8-2 Locomotive "810," CC, 08-09		400	___
38649	Christmas 4-6-4 Hudson Locomotive, traditional, 08		210	___
38651	Lionel Lines 0-8-0 Locomotive "100," traditional, 08-09		120	___
38654	Bethlehem Steel 0-4-0 Locomotive, traditional, 08-09		170	___
38657	Alton Limited Pacific 4-6-2 Locomotive "659," traditional, 08		300	___
38658	W&ARR 4-4-0 General "1892," TrainSounds, 08-09		165	___
38664	LL 4-4-2 Atlantic Locomotive "1058," traditional, 08-09		110	___
38671	Santa Flyer 4-6-0 Locomotive, 09	100	210	___
38677	Strasburg 0-6-0 Dockside Switcher "1252," 10		130	___
38678	Monopoly Hudson Locomotive, TrainSounds, 10		240	___
38679	ATSF 0-4-0 Switcher "1387," 10-11		190	___
38684	Pennsylvania Power & Light Docksider Switcher, 10		110	___
38687	Western & Atlantic 0-4-0 Locomotive "1897," 10-11		190	___
38689	AT&SF 0-8-0 Steam Locomotive "8689," 10-11	140	255	___
38691	North Pole Central Santa Flyer "2," 10-11		190	___
38692	Angela Trotta Thomas Signature Express, 10-11		190	___
38700	CB&Q F3 B Unit "9962B," CC, 12-13		400	___
38701	CB&Q F3 B Unit, 12-13		250	___
38702	D&RGW F3 AA Diesel Set "5531-5533," CC, 12-14		730	___
38705	D&RGW F3 B Unit "5532," CC, 12-14		400	___
38706	D&RGW F3 B Unit, 12-14		250	___
38707	WP F3 AB Diesel Set "803A-803B," CC, 12-14		730	___
38710	WP F3 A Unit, nonpowered, 12-14		380	___
38711	WP F3 B Unit "803C," CC, 12-14		400	___
38712	Wabash F7 AA Diesel Set "1102A-1102C," CC, 12-13		730	___
38715	Wabash F7 B Unit "1102B," CC, 12-13		400	___
38716	Wabash F7 B Unit, 12-13		250	___
38717	Milwaukee Road F7 AA Diesel Set, CC, 12		730	___

	MODERN 1970-2025		Exc	Like New
___	**38720**	Milwaukee Road F7 B Unit "109B," CC, 12		400
___	**38721**	Milwaukee Road F7 B Unit, 12		250
___	**38722**	Grand Trunk SD80MAC Diesel "9085," CC, 12		530
___	**38723**	Grand Trunk SD80MAC Diesel "9088," CC, 12		530
___	**38724**	Grand Trunk SD80MAC Diesel "9079," nonpowered, 12		260
___	**38725**	CB&Q SD80MAC Diesel "9654," CC, 12		530
___	**38726**	CB&Q SD80MAC Diesel "9651," CC, 12		530
___	**38727**	CB&Q SD80MAC Diesel "9660," nonpowered, 12		260
___	**38728**	PRR SD80MAC Diesel "9942," CC, 12	175	530
___	**38729**	PRR SD80MAC Diesel "9945," CC, 12		530
___	**38730**	PRR SD80MAC Diesel "9947," nonpowered, 12-13	85	260
___	**38731**	Polar SD80MAC Diesel, CC, 12		530
___	**38732**	CB&Q BNSF Heritage SD70ACe Diesel "1848," CC, 12-13		530
___	**38733**	CB&Q BNSF Heritage SD70ACe Diesel "1852," CC, 12-13	188	530
___	**38734**	CB&Q BNSF Heritage SD70ACe Diesel "1856," nonpowered, 12-13		260
___	**38735**	ATSF BNSF Heritage SD70ACe Diesel "1996," CC, 12-13		530
___	**38736**	ATSF BNSF Heritage SD70ACe Diesel "1997," CC, 12-13		530
___	**38737**	ATSF BNSF Heritage SD70ACe Diesel "1999," nonpowered, 12-13		260
___	**38738**	Frisco BNSF Heritage SD70ACe Diesel "1876," CC, 12-13		530
___	**38739**	Frisco BNSF Heritage SD70ACe Diesel "1896," CC, 12-14		530
___	**38740**	Frisco BNSF Heritage SD70ACe Diesel "1916," nonpowered, 12-13		260
___	**38741**	BN BNSF Heritage SD70ACe Diesel "1970," CC, 12-13		530
___	**38742**	BN BNSF Heritage SD70ACe Diesel "1975," CC, 12-13		530
___	**38743**	BN BNSF Heritage SD70ACe Diesel "1980," nonpowered, 12-13		260
___	**38744**	GN BNSF Heritage SD70ACe Diesel "1889," CC, 12-13		530
___	**38745**	GN BNSF Heritage SD70ACe Diesel "1891," CC, 12-13		530
___	**38746**	GN BNSF Heritage SD70ACe Diesel "1893," nonpowered, 12-13		260
___	**38747**	NP BNSF Heritage SD70ACe Diesel "1870," CC, 12-13		530
___	**38748**	NP BNSF Heritage SD70ACe Diesel "1872," CC, 12-13		530
___	**38749**	NP BNSF Heritage SD70ACe Diesel "1875," nonpowered, 12-13		260
___	**38750**	EMD Demonstrator SD70ACe Diesel "2012," CC, 12-13		530
___	**38751**	CNJ F3 AA Diesel Set, CC, 13-14		730
___	**38752**	Vision Centipede AA Pilot Diesels, CC, 13	425	2200
___	**38754**	C&NW F7 AA Diesel Set, CC, 13-14		730
___	**38757**	SP F7 AA Diesel Set, CC, 13-14		730
___	**38760**	CNJ F3 B Unit, CC, 13-14		400
___	**38761**	CNJ F3 B Unit, 13-14		250
___	**38762**	C&NW F7 B Unit "410," CC, 13-14		400
___	**38763**	C&NW F7 B Unit, 13-14		250
___	**38764**	SP F7 B Unit "8219," CC, 13		400
___	**38765**	SP F7 B Unit, 13		250
___	**38768**	N&W GP35 Diesel "1306," CC, 13-14		500
___	**38769**	N&W GP35 Diesel "1308," nonpowered, 13-14		260
___	**38770**	RI GP35 Diesel "307," CC, 13-14		500
___	**38771**	RI GP35 Diesel "309," CC, 13-14		500
___	**38772**	RI GP35 Diesel "323," nonpowered, 13-14		260
___	**38773**	WP GP35 Diesel "3002," CC, 13-14		500
___	**38774**	WP GP35 Diesel "3009," CC, 13-14		500
___	**38775**	WP GP35 Diesel "3014," nonpowered, 13-14		260

MODERN 1970-2025		Exc	Like New	
38778	C&NW RS3 Diesel "1621," LionChief, 14-16		330	___
38779	NYC RS3 Diesel "8244," LionChief, 14-16		330	___
38782	C&BQ GP35 Diesel "990," CC, 13		500	___
38783	C&BQ GP35 Diesel "996," nonpowered, 13		500	___
38784	CN GP35 Diesel "4000," CC, 13		500	___
38785	CN GP35 Diesel "4005," CC, 13		500	___
38786	CN GP35 Diesel "4001," nonpowered, 13		260	___
38787	D&RGW GP35 Diesel "3031," CC, 13		500	___
38788	D&RGW GP35 Diesel "3034," CC, 13		500	___
38789	D&RGW GP35 Diesel "3038," nonpowered, 13		260	___
38790	DT&I GP35 Diesel "351," CC, 13		500	___
38791	DT&I GP35 Diesel "353," CC, 13	470	900	___
38792	DT&I GP35 Diesel "355," nonpowered, 13		260	___
38794	GN GP35 Diesel "3018," CC, 13-14		500	___
38795	GN GP35 Diesel "3036," nonpowered, 13-14		260	___
38796	Chessie System GP35 Diesel "1125," CC, 13		500	___
38797	Chessie System GP35 Diesel "1128," CC, 13		500	___
38798	Chessie System GP35 Diesel "1113," nonpowered, 13		260	___
38799	N&W GP35 Diesel "1302," CC, 13-14		500	___
38800	B&M Early Era Inspection Vehicle, CC, 12		150	___
38801	KCS Trackmobile, CC, 12-13		300	___
38802	North Pole Central Trackmobile, CC, 12		300	___
38803	MOW Trackmobile, CC, 12		300	___
38804	LIRR Trackmobile, CC, 12		300	___
38805	Conrail Trackmobile, CC, 12		300	___
38806	NS Trackmobile, CC, 12		300	___
38807	NP Trackmobile, CC, 12-13		300	___
38808	Chessie System Trackmobile, CC, 12		300	___
38809	CN Trackmobile, CC, 12		300	___
38810	PRR Early Era Inspection Vehicle, CC, 12		150	___
38811	D&RGW Early Era Inspection Vehicle, CC, 12		150	___
38812	SP Early Era Inspection Vehicle, CC, 12-13		150	___
38813	C&O Early Era Inspection Vehicle, CC, 12-13		150	___
38814	Milwaukee Road Early Era Inspection Vehicle, CC, 12		150	___
38815	Transylvania Early Era Inspection Vehicle, CC, 12		150	___
38816	PRR RS3 Diesel "5620," LionChief, 14-16		330	___
38819	D&RGW RS3 Diesel "5202," LionChief, 14-16		330	___
38821	AT&SF GP7 Diesel "2656," LionChief, 14-15		330	___
38824	NP GP7 Diesel "563," LionChief, 14-15		330	___
38825	UP GP7 Diesel "121," LionChief, 14-15		330	___
38827	CB&Q GP7 Diesel "1596," LionChief, 14-15		330	___
38848	Christmas Pioneer Zephyr Set, CC, 13-14	363	1100	___
38853	Santa and Mrs. Claus Handcar, 13		90	___
38855	GN GP35 Diesel "2519," CC, 13-14		500	___
38856	CB&Q Mark Twain Zephyr, CC, 13-14		1100	___
38860	CB&Q Pioneer Zephyr, CC, 13-14		1100	___
38864	Lionel Lines Zephyr, CC, 13-14		1100	___
38865	L&N GP35 Diesel "1105," CC, 13		500	___
38866	L&N GP35 Diesel "1109," CC, 13		500	___
38867	L&N GP35 Diesel "1114," nonpowered, 13		260	___
38868	C&BQ GP35 Diesel "978," CC, 13		500	___

			Exc	Mint
____	**38874**	B&O GP9 Diesel "6448," CC, 13-14		480
____	**38875**	B&O GP9 Diesel "6456," CC, 13-14		480
____	**38876**	B&O GP9 Diesel "6461," nonpowered, 13-14		240
____	**38877**	B&M GP9 Diesel "1705," CC, 13		480
____	**38878**	B&M GP9 Diesel "1714," CC, 13		480
____	**38879**	B&M GP9 Diesel "1722," nonpowered, 13		240
____	**38883**	C&NW GP9 Diesel "701," CC, 13		480
____	**38884**	C&NW GP9 Diesel "704," CC, 13		480
____	**38885**	C&NW GP9 Diesel "712," nonpowered, 13		240
____	**38886**	Erie GP9 Diesel "1260," CC, 13		480
____	**38887**	Erie GP9 Diesel "1263," CC, 13		480
____	**38888**	Erie GP9 Diesel "1265," nonpowered, 13		240
____	**38889**	Nickel Plate Road GP9 Diesel "514," CC, 13		480
____	**38890**	Nickel Plate Road GP9 Diesel "452," CC, 13		480
____	**38891**	Nickel Plate Road GP9 Diesel "457," nonpowered, 13		240
____	**38892**	SP GP9 Diesel "3411," CC, 13		480
____	**38893**	SP GP9 Diesel "3415," CC, 13		480
____	**38894**	SP GP9 Diesel "3419," nonpowered, 13		240
____	**38895**	Wabash GP9 Diesel "484," CC, 13		480
____	**38896**	Wabash GP9 Diesel "488," CC, 13		480
____	**38897**	Wabash GP9 Diesel "491," nonpowered, 13		240
____	**38918**	Chessie System SD40-2 Diesel "7609," CC, 13		530
____	**38919**	Chessie System SD40-2 Diesel "7611," CC, 13		530
____	**38920**	Chessie System SD40-2 Diesel "7614," nonpowered, 13		240
____	**38921**	SP SD40T-2 Diesel Locomotive "8322," CC, 13		530
____	**38922**	SP SD40T-2 Diesel Locomotive "8326," CC, 13		530
____	**38923**	SP SD40T-2 Diesel, nonpowered, 13		260
____	**38924**	B&O SD40-2 Diesel "7602," CC, 13		530
____	**38925**	B&O SD40-2 Diesel "7607," CC, 13		530
____	**38926**	B&O SD40-2 Diesel "7611," nonpowered, 13		240
____	**38933**	Conrail SD40-2 Diesel "6424," CC, 13	163	530
____	**38934**	Conrail SD40-2 Diesel "6437," CC, 13		530
____	**38935**	Conrail SD40-2 Diesel "6468," nonpowered, 13		240
____	**38936**	UP SD40-2 Diesel "2929," CC, 13		530
____	**38937**	UP SD40-2 Diesel "2932," CC, 13		530
____	**38938**	UP SD40-2 Diesel "2947," nonpowered, 13		240
____	**38939**	NS SD40-2 Diesel "3355," CC, 13		530
____	**38940**	NS SD40-2 Diesel "3365," CC, 13		530
____	**38941**	NS SD40-2 Diesel "3379," nonpowered, 13		240
____	**38942**	Central of Georgia NS Heritage ES44AC Diesel, CC, 12		550
____	**38943**	Central of Georgia NS Heritage ES44AC Diesel, CC, 12		550
____	**38944**	Central of Georgia NS Heritage ES44AC Diesel, nonpowered, 12		280
____	**38945**	Conrail NS Heritage ES44AC Diesel, CC, 12		550
____	**38946**	Conrail NS Heritage ES44AC Diesel, CC, 12		550
____	**38947**	Conrail NS Heritage ES44AC Diesel, nonpowered, 12		280
____	**38948**	Interstate NS Heritage ES44AC Diesel Locomotive "8105," CC, 12		550
____	**38949**	Interstate NS Heritage ES44AC Diesel, CC, 12		550
____	**38950**	Interstate NS Heritage ES44AC Diesel, nonpowered, 12		280
____	**38951**	LV NS Heritage ES44AC Diesel, CC, 12		550
____	**38952**	LV NS Heritage ES44AC Diesel, CC, 12		550
____	**38953**	LV NS Heritage ES44AC Diesel, nonpowered, 12		280
____	**38954**	Nickel Plate Road NS Heritage ES44AC Diesel, CC, 12		550

		Exc	Mint
38955	Nickel Plate Road NS Heritage ES44AC Diesel, CC, 12		550 ___
38956	Nickel Plate Road NS Heritage ES44AC Diesel, nonpowered, 12		280 ___
38957	N&W NS Heritage ES44AC Diesel, CC, 12		550 ___
38958	N&W NS Heritage ES44AC Diesel, CC, 12		550 ___
38959	N&W NS Heritage ES44AC Diesel, nonpowered, 12		280 ___
38960	PRR NS Heritage ES44AC Diesel, CC, 12		550 ___
38961	PRR NS Heritage ES44AC Diesel, CC, 12		550 ___
38962	PRR NS Heritage ES44AC Diesel, nonpowered, 12		280 ___
38963	Southern NS Heritage ES44AC Diesel, CC, 12		550 ___
38964	Southern NS Heritage ES44AC Diesel, CC, 12		550 ___
38965	Southern NS Heritage ES44AC Diesel, nonpowered, 12		280 ___
38966	NS Heritage ES44AC Diesel, CC, 12		550 ___
38967	NS Heritage ES44AC Diesel, CC, 12		550 ___
38968	NS Heritage ES44AC Diesel, nonpowered, 12		280 ___
38969	North Pole Central GP35 Diesel "2525," CC, 13		500 ___
38970	North Pole Central GP35 Diesel "2512," CC, 13		500 ___
38971	North Pole Central GP35 Diesel "2513," nonpowered, 13		260 ___
38972	Reading GP35 Diesel "3625," CC, 13		500 ___
38973	Reading GP35 Diesel "3630," CC, 13		500 ___
38974	Reading GP35 Diesel "3633," nonpowered, 13		260 ___
38975	AT&SF GP35 Diesel "3312," CC, 13		500 ___
38976	AT&SF GP35 Diesel "3318," CC, 13		500 ___
38977	AT&SF GP35 Diesel "3329," nonpowered, 13		260 ___
38978	Alaska GP35 Diesel "2501," CC, 13		500 ___
38979	Alaska GP35 Diesel "2503," CC, 13		500 ___
38980	Alaska GP35 Diesel "2502," nonpowered, 13		260 ___
38981	B&O GP35 Diesel "2506," CC, 13-14		500 ___
38982	B&O GP35 Diesel "2511," CC, 13-14		500 ___
38983	B&O GP35 Diesel "2517," nonpowered, 13-14		260 ___
38984	C&O GP35 Diesel "3515," CC, 13-14		500 ___
38985	C&O GP35 Diesel "3521," CC, 13-14		500 ___
38986	C&O GP35 Diesel "3526," nonpowered, 13-14		260 ___
38987	MP GP35 Diesel "603," CC, 13		500 ___
38988	MP GP35 Diesel "607," CC, 13		500 ___
38989	MP GP35 Diesel "611," nonpowered, 13		260 ___
38990	GM&O GP35 Diesel "603," CC, 13-14		500 ___
38991	GM&O GP35 Diesel "607," CC, 13-14		500 ___
38992	GM&O GP35 Diesel "611," nonpowered, 13-14		260 ___
38993	WM GP35 Diesel "3576," CC, 13		500 ___
38994	WM GP35 Diesel "3578," CC, 13		500 ___
38995	WM GP35 Diesel "3580," nonpowered, 13		260 ___
38996	CSX GP35 Diesel "4355," CC, 13		500 ___
38997	CSX GP35 Diesel "4363," CC, 13		500 ___
38998	CSX GP35 Diesel "4390," nonpowered, 13		260 ___
38999	NS GP35 Diesel "2916," CC, 13		500 ___
39008	PRR Heavyweight Passenger Car 4-pack, 00		225 ___
39009	PRR Indian Rock Heavyweight Combination Car, 00		50 ___
39010	PRR Andrew Carnegie Heavyweight Passenger Coach, 00		60 ___
39011	PRR Solomon P. Chase Heavyweight Passenger Coach, 00		60 ___
39012	PRR Skyline View Heavyweight Observation Car, 00		50 ___
39013	B&O Heavyweight Passenger Car 4-pack, 00		400 ___
39014	B&O Harper's Ferry Heavyweight Combination Car, 00		50 ___
39015	B&O Youngstown Heavyweight Passenger Coach, 00		50 ___

	MODERN 1970-2025		Exc	Mint
____	**39016**	B&O New Castle Heavyweight Passenger Coach, 00		50
____	**39017**	B&O Chicago Heavyweight Observation Car, 00		50
____	**39028**	LL Heavyweight Passenger Car 3-pack, 00		195
____	**39029**	LL Irvington Heavyweight Coach "2625", 00		60
____	**39030**	LL Madison Heavyweight Coach "2627", 00		60
____	**39031**	LL Manhattan Heavyweight Coach "2628", 00		60
____	**39032**	UP Madison Passenger Car 4-pack, 00		275
____	**39038**	SP Madison Baggage Car "6015", 01		100
____	**39039**	SP Madison Coach Car "1978", 01		100
____	**39040**	SP Madison Coach "1975", 01		NRS
____	**39041**	SP Madison Observation Car "2951", 01		100
____	**39042**	N&W Heavyweight Passenger Car 4-pack, 00		325
____	**39047**	B&O Heavyweight Passenger Car 2-pack, 01		160
____	**39050**	PRR Heavyweight Passenger Car 2-pack, 01		215
____	**39053**	Alaska Streamliner Car 2-pack, 01		90
____	**39056**	NYC Streamliner Car 2-pack, 01		75
____	**39059**	Santa Fe Streamliner Car 2-pack, 01		100
____	**39062**	B&O Streamliner Car 2-pack, 01		75
____	**39065**	PRR Streamliner Car 4-pack, 01	63	165
____	**39082**	Blue Comet Heavyweight Passenger Car 2-pack, 02		325
____	**39085**	Freedom Train Heavyweight Passenger Car 3-pack, 03		305
____	**39092**	PRR Streamliner Car 2-pack, 01		70
____	**39099**	Alton Limited Heavyweight Passenger Car 2-pack, 03		230
____	**39100**	William Penn Congressional Coach, 00		115
____	**39101**	Molly Pitcher Congressional Coach, 00		100
____	**39102**	Betsy Ross Congressional Vista Dome Car, 00		100
____	**39103**	Alexander Hamilton Congressional Observation Car, 00		100
____	**39104**	Phoebe Snow Car, StationSounds, 99		255
____	**39105**	Milwaukee Road Hiawatha Car, StationSounds, 99		235
____	**39106**	CP Aluminum Passenger Car 2-pack, 00	40	185
____	**39107**	CP Blair Manor Aluminum Passenger Coach "2553", 00		115
____	**39108**	CP Craig Manor Aluminum Passenger Coach "2554", 00		110
____	**39109**	"Spirit of the Century" Aluminum Passenger Car 4-pack, 99		520
____	**39110**	"Spirit of the Century" Full Vista Dome Car, 99-00		100
____	**39111**	"Spirit of the Century" Full Vista Dome Car, 99-00		100
____	**39112**	"Spirit of the Century" Full Vista Dome Car, 99-00		100
____	**39113**	"Spirit of the Century" Skytop Observation Car, 99-00		100
____	**39118**	Texas Special Garland Coach "1203," w/StationSounds, 99-00		220
____	**39119**	Southern Aluminum Passenger Car 4-pack, 00		335
____	**39120**	Southern Grand Junction Aluminum Passenger/Baggage Car, 00		280
____	**39121**	Southern Charlottesville Aluminum Passenger Coach "812", 00		90
____	**39122**	Southern Roanoke Aluminum Passenger Coach "814", 00		250
____	**39123**	Southern Memphis Aluminum Observation Car "1152", 00		90
____	**39124**	Amtrak Superliner Aluminum Passenger Car 4-pack, 02		405
____	**39129**	Santa Fe Superliner Aluminum Passenger Car 4-pack, 02		305
____	**39141**	RI Aluminum Passenger Car 4-pack, 01		400
____	**39146**	UP Aluminum Passenger Car 4-pack, 01	100	285
____	**39151**	CP Aluminum Passenger Car 2-pack, 01		315
____	**39154**	PRR Congressional Aluminum Passenger Car 2-pack, 02		195
____	**39155**	PRR Congressional Baggage Car, 02		105
____	**39156**	PRR Robert Morris Congressional Coach, 02		100

		Exc	Mint	
39157	Southern Aluminum Passenger Car 2-pack, 01		290	___
39160	KCS Aluminum Passenger Car 2-pack, 01	170	260	___
39163	Erie-Lack. Aluminum Passenger Car 2-pack, 01		230	___
39166	Texas Special Aluminum Passenger Car 2-pack, 01	300	430	___
39169	ACL Aluminum Passenger Car 4-pack, 01		360	___
39170	ACL Aluminum Baggage Car "1634", 01		90	___
39171	ACL Aluminum Coach "1090", 01		90	___
39172	ACL Aluminum Coach "1111", 01		90	___
39173	ACL Aluminum Observation "1115", 01		90	___
39179	NP Aluminum Passenger Car 2-pack, 02	118	298	___
39182	WP Aluminum Passenger Car 2-pack, 02		280	___
39185	Rio Grande Aluminum Passenger Car 2-pack, 02		290	___
39194	UP Aluminum Passenger Car 2-pack, 02		220	___
39197	CP Aluminum Passenger Coach, StationSounds, 02		225	___
39198	PRR Aluminum Passenger Coach, StationSounds, 02		210	___
39200	Hellgate Bridge Boxcar #2 "1900-2000", 00 u		55	___
39202	Lionel Centennial Boxcar "1900-2000", 00		46	___
39203	Postwar "6464" Series X, 3 cars, 01	38	105	___
39204	New Haven Boxcar "6464-725", 01		44	___
39205	Alaska Boxcar "6464-825", 01		55	___
39206	NYC Boxcar "6464-900", 01		40	___
39207	UP Boxcar "508500," red, 00	23	55	___
39208	UP Boxcar "903658," silver, 00		42	___
39209	UP Boxcar "500200," yellow, 00		40	___
39210	6530 Fire Fighting Car, 00		37	___
39211	Postwar "6464" Boxcar 3-pack #2, 00	28	88	___
39212	Postwar "6464" SP&S Boxcar, 00		30	___
39213	Postwar "6464" Wabash Boxcar, 00		30	___
39214	Postwar "6464" Kansas, Oklahoma & Gulf Boxcar, 00		30	___
39216	PRR DD Boxcar "47211", 01		46	___
39220	B&LE Heavyweight Boxcar "82101", 01		41	___
39221	L&N Heavyweight Boxcar "109829", 01		41	___
39222	Conrail Heavyweight Boxcar "269198", 01		44	___
39223	Postwar "6464" Archive Boxcar Set, 3-pack, 02		125	___
39224	Postwar "6464" Monon Boxcar, 02		45	___
39225	Postwar "6464" Tidewater Southern Boxcar, 02		40	___
39226	Postwar "6464" SP Boxcar, 02		45	___
39227	Postwar "6468" Automobile Boxcar 3-pack, 01		95	___
39228	Postwar "6468" B&O DD Boxcar, Blue, 01		30	___
39229	Postwar "6468" B&O DD Boxcar, Tuscan, 01		40	___
39230	Postwar "6468" NH DD Boxcar, 01		30	___
39236	WP Boxcar "6464-250", 01		55	___
39238	Elvis Boxcar, 03		36	___
39239	P&LE Boxcar "22300, 02		35	___
39240	Pennsylvania Boxcar "118747", 02		32	___
39241	PC Boxcar "252455", 02		28	___
39242	Postwar "6464" Boxcar 3-pack #1, Archive Collection, 03-04	50	105	___
39243	Soo Line Boxcar, Archive Collection, 03-04		35	___
39244	D&RGW Cookie Box Boxcar, Archive Collection, 03-04		35	___
39245	Duluth, South Shore & Atlantic Boxcar, Archive Collection, 03-04		30	___
39246	Century Club PRR Sharknose Diesel Boxcar, 00		50	___
39247	NYC DD Boxcar "6468", 02-03		32	___

		MODERN 1970-2025	Exc	Mint
___	**39248**	Lackawanna DD Boxcar w/Hobo, 03		45
___	**39249**	LRRC 2003 Christmas Boxcar, 03 u		40
___	**39250**	Campbell's Kids Centennial Boxcar, 03-04		40
___	**39252**	Lenny Dean 60th Anniversary Boxcar, 04		38
___	**39253**	No. 6464 Boxcar 3-pack #2, Archive Collection, 04		100
___	**39254**	Detroit & Mackinac Boxcar, Archive Collection, 04		35
___	**39255**	NS Boxcar, Archive Collection, 04		35
___	**39256**	L&N Boxcar, Archive Collection, 04		35
___	**39257**	WP Boxcar "6464-100," boys set add-on, 03		50
___	**39258**	Elvis Presley "All Shook Up" Boxcar, 03-04		40
___	**39259**	Buick Centennial Boxcar, 03		40
___	**39260**	New Haven Boxcar, 04		40
___	**39262**	Elvis Presley "Elvis Has Left the Building" Boxcar, 04		38
___	**39263**	M&StL Boxcar, Postwar Celebration Series, 05		35
___	**39267**	No. 6464 Boxcar 3-pack #3, Archive Collection, 05		100
___	**39271**	State of Maine Boxcar, 04		35
___	**39273**	No. 6464 Boxcar 3-pack #4, Archive Collection, 06		100
___	**39274**	NP Boxcar, Archive Collection, 06		35
___	**39275**	US Air Force Boxcar, Archive Collection, 06		35
___	**39276**	Lilly Paper Cup Boxcar, Archive Collection, 06		35
___	**39281**	Florida State University Boxcar, 07	32	50
___	**39282**	Purdue University Boxcar, 08		50
___	**39283**	University of Virginia Boxcar, 08		50
___	**39284**	Penn State University Boxcar, 06-07		45
___	**39285**	U.S. Military Academy at West Point Boxcar, 08		50
___	**39286**	University of Illinois Boxcar, 06-07		45
___	**39287**	University of Alabama Boxcar, 06-07		45
___	**39289**	University of Oklahoma Boxcar, 06-08		50
___	**39290**	Postwar "6464" Boxcar 2-pack, rare variations, 08	50	108
___	**39291**	University of Michigan Boxcar, 06-07		45
___	**39292**	Monopoly Boxcar 3-pack, 08		135
___	**39296**	UPS Centennial Boxcar #3, 08-09		55
___	**39297**	Macy's Parade Boxcar, 07		55
___	**39298**	Monopoly Boxcar 3-pack #2, 08		145
___	**39299**	Lenny Dean Commemorative Boxcar, 08		50
___	**39300**	Postwar "6464-1" WP Boxcar, red lettering, 08		70
___	**39301**	Postwar "6464-300" Rutland Boxcar, 08		80
___	**39302**	University of Maryland Boxcar, 08		50
___	**39303**	Villanova University Boxcar, 08		50
___	**39304**	Auburn University Boxcar, 08		50
___	**39305**	Monopoly Virginia Ave. Boxcar, 08		50
___	**39306**	Monopoly Connecticut Ave. Boxcar, 08		50
___	**39307**	Monopoly Marvin Gardens Boxcar, 08		50
___	**39308**	CP Rail "6565" Boxcar "58700", 08-10		55
___	**39309**	Macy's Parade Boxcar, 08		50
___	**39310**	Monopoly Boxcar 3-pack #3, 09-10		170
___	**39316**	New Haven Automobile Boxcar, 09-10		60
___	**39317**	Wizard of Oz Boxcar #1, 09-10		60
___	**39318**	Wizard of Oz Boxcar #2, 09-10		60
___	**39319**	Boy Scouts "Scout Law" Add-on Boxcar, 10		60
___	**39321**	Lionel Art Boxcar 2-pack, 10		116
___	**39325**	Macy's Parade Boxcar, 09		45
___	**39326**	UPS Centennial Boxcar #4, 10-11		60

MODERN 1970-2025		Exc	Mint	
39328	Monopoly Boxcar 3-pack #4, 10-11		220	___
39332	Holiday Boxcar, 10		60	___
39334	Coca-Cola Christmas Boxcar, 10		70	___
39335	Thomas Kinkade Boxcar, 10, 12		60	___
39336	Angela Trotta Thomas "My Turn Yet, Dad?" Boxcar, 10		60	___
39337	George Washington Boxcar, 11-12		60	___
39338	Abraham Lincoln Boxcar, 11-12		60	___
39339	Theodore Roosevelt Boxcar, 11-12		60	___
39340	Thomas Jefferson Boxcar, 11-12		60	___
39341	2010 Lionel Dealer Appreciation Boxcar, 10 u		40	___
39342	Strasburg Boxcar, 11		55	___
39343	New Jersey Central Boxcar, 10		45	___
39344	Monopoly Boxcar 3-pack #5, 11-12		165	___
39345	Monopoly Tennessee Avenue Boxcar, 11		55	___
39346	Monopoly Atlantic Avenue Boxcar, 11		55	___
39347	Monopoly Illinois Avenue Boxcar, 11		55	___
39348	Lionel NASCAR Collectables Boxcar, 11-12		60	___
39350	Thomas Kinkade "All Aboard for Christmas" Boxcar, 12-13		60	___
39351	Peanuts Thanksgiving Boxcar, 12		70	___
39354	Monopoly North Carolina Avenue Boxcar, 12		70	___
39358	Boy Scouts "Prepared For Life" Boxcar, 12		60	___
39359	Thanksgiving Boxcar, 12		60	___
39360	Boy Scouts Cub Scout Boxcar, 12-13		60	___
39361	Coca-Cola Polar Bear Boxcar, 14		70	___
39362	Thomas Kinkade "Emerald City" Boxcar, 12-15		75	___
39363	Peanuts Halloween Boxcar, 12		65	___
39364	2013 Lionel Employee Christmas Boxcar, 13		60	___
39372	Southern Hi-Cube Boxcar, 13-14	12	30	___
39376	Monopoly Boxcar 2-pack, States and Vermont Avenues, 13-15		140	___
39379	Monopoly Boxcar 2-pack, Med. and St. James Ave, 13-15		140	___
39383	Prewar "2719" Boxcar, 13		65	___
39385	U.S. Navy 1-D Tank Car, 13-15		70	___
39386	U.S. Marines 1-D Tank Car, 13-15		70	___
39387	U.S. Air Force 1-D Tank Car, 13-15		70	___
39388	U.S. National Guard 1-D Tank Car, 13-16		70	___
39389	U.S. Coast Guard 1-D Tank Car, 13-16		70	___
39391	U.S. Army Flatcar, 13-16		70	___
39392	U.S. Navy Flatcar, 13-16		70	___
39393	U.S. Marines Flatcar, 13-16		70	___
39394	U.S. Air Force Flatcar, 13-16		70	___
39395	U.S. National Guard Flatcar, 13-16		70	___
39396	U.S. Coast Guard Flatcar, 13-16	33	70	___
39398	Santa's Flyer Reefer, 13		43	___
39399	U.S. Army 1-D Tank Car, 13-15		70	___
39400	Republic Steel Slag Car 3-pack (std 0), 04		100	___
39404	Republic Steel Hot Metal Car 3-pack (std 0), 04		130	___
39411	Jones & Laughlin Hot Metal Car 3-pack (std 0), 05	80	190	___
39423	Postwar "3460" LL Flatcar with trailers, 05		48	___
39424	U.S. Steel 16-wheel Flatcar with girders, 05		70	___
39425	Hood's Flatcar with milk container, traditional, 05		55	___
39426	Nestle Nesquik Flatcar with milk container, traditional, 05		55	___
39428	Bethlehem Steel Slag Car #4 (std 0), 05		60	___
39429	Bethlehem Steel Hot Metal Car #8 (std 0), 05		70	___

	MODERN 1970-2025		Exc	Mint
____	**39430**	Youngstown Sheet & Tube Slag Car #7 (std O), 05		60
____	**39431**	Youngstown Sheet & Tube Hot Metal Car #11 (std O), 05		70
____	**39435**	Postwar "6477" Flatcar with pipes, 06		53
____	**39436**	Postwar "6262" Wheel Car, 06		50
____	**39437**	Supplee Flatcar with milk container, 06		60
____	**39438**	6518 Double Truck Transformer Flatcar, 06-07		
____	**39439**	"6827" Flatcar with P&H power shovel, 04		50
____	**39440**	"6828" Flatcar with P&H truck crane, 04		50
____	**39443**	U.S. Steel Slag Car 3-pack #2 (std O), 06		170
____	**39447**	Postwar "6561" LL Cable Reel Car, Archive Collection, 06-07		55
____	**39450**	Postwar "6414" Evans Auto Loader, Archive Collection, 06		70
____	**39452**	White Bros. Flatcar with milk container, 07		60
____	**39454**	6430 Flatcar w/Vans, 07		60
____	**39457**	Postwar "6175" Flatcar with rocket, 08		55
____	**39458**	Postwar "6844" Flatcar with missiles, 08		55
____	**39463**	Postwar "6430" Flatcar with trailers, 08		55
____	**39468**	Allis-Chalmers Car "52369", 08-09	28	60
____	**39469**	Christmas Egg Nog Barrel Car, 08		50
____	**39470**	UP Well Car "147128", 08		65
____	**39471**	Postwar "6264" Flatcar, 08		60
____	**39472**	ATSF Culvert Gondola, 08		60
____	**39473**	Play-Doh Vat Car, 08		55
____	**39475**	UPS Flatcar with trailer, 08		65
____	**39476**	Bethlehem Steel 16-wheel Flatcar, 08		75
____	**39477**	Christmas Flatcar with reindeer trailers, 08		60
____	**39478**	Postwar "6475" Pickles Vat Car, 08		55
____	**39479**	Postwar "6404" Flatcar with brown automobile, 08		50
____	**39480**	Western & Atlantic Cannon Flatcar, 09		60
____	**39482**	CSX WM Track Maintenance Car "6812", 11		65
____	**39483**	CSX P&LE Gondola "69812", 11		65
____	**39484**	Cocoa Marsh Vat Car, 10-12		60
____	**39486**	Deep Sea Challenger Submarine Car, 11		60
____	**39487**	BN I-Beam Flatcar "870798", 11		60
____	**39488**	Reese's Vat Car, 10		60
____	**39490**	Western & Atlantic Cannonball Flatcar, 10		55
____	**39497**	Christmas Reindeer Stock Car, 10-11		60
____	**39498**	CNJ Gondola with culvert pipes, 11		55
____	**39499**	Alaska Oil Barrel Ramp Car, 11		50
____	**39502**	Monongahela NS Heritage ES44AC Diesel, nonpowered, 13		280
____	**39530**	PRR 1955 Pickup Truck, CC, 13		180
____	**39531**	UP 1955 Pickup Truck, CC, 13		180
____	**39532**	ATSF 1955 Pickup Truck, CC, 13-14		180
____	**39533**	CP 1955 Pickup Truck, CC, 13-14		180
____	**39534**	D&RGW 1955 Pickup Truck, CC, 13		180
____	**39535**	GN 1955 Pickup Truck, CC, 13		180
____	**39536**	MKT 1955 Pickup Truck, CC, 13-14		180
____	**39537**	NYC 1955 Pickup Truck, CC, 13		180
____	**39538**	Nickel Plate Road 1955 Pickup Truck, CC, 13		180
____	**39539**	NP1955 Pickup Truck, CC, 13-14		180
____	**39540**	Southern 1955 Pickup Truck, CC, 13		180
____	**39541**	SP 1955 Pickup Truck, CC, 13-14		180
____	**39542**	Weyerhaeuser 1955 Pickup Truck, CC, 13-14		180
____	**39543**	Texas Special F3 B Unit, 13-14		230

		Exc	Mint
39544	Texas Special F3 B Unit, CC, 13-14		380 ____
39547	PRR F3 B Unit, 13-14		230 ____
39548	PRR F3 B Unit, CC, 13-14		380 ____
39554	NS GP35 Diesel "3918," CC, 13		500 ____
39555	NS GP35 Diesel "2915," nonpowered, 13		260 ____
39556	CP GP35 Diesel "5004," CC, 13-14		500 ____
39557	CP GP35 Diesel "5007," CC, 13-14		500 ____
39558	CP GP35 Diesel "5009," nonpowered, 13-14		260 ____
39562	BN GP35 Diesel "2533," CC, 13-14		500 ____
39563	BN GP35 Diesel "2509," CC, 13-14		500 ____
39564	BN GP35 Diesel "2523," nonpowered, 13-14		260 ____
39565	ATSF Dash-9 Diesel "612," CC, 13		530 ____
39566	ATSF Dash-9 Diesel "623," CC, 13		530 ____
39567	ATSF Dash-9 Diesel "631," nonpowered, 13		260 ____
39568	BC Rail Dash-9 Diesel "4641," CC, 13		530 ____
39569	BC Rail Dash-9 Diesel "4647," CC, 13		530 ____
39570	BC Rail Dash-9 Diesel "4652," nonpowered, 13		260 ____
39571	BNSF Dash-9 Diesel "4023," CC, 13		530 ____
39572	BNSF Dash-9 Diesel "4037," CC, 13		530 ____
39573	BNSF Dash-9 Diesel "4046," nonpowered, 13		260 ____
39574	C&NW Dash-9 Diesel "8605," CC, 13		530 ____
39575	C&NW Dash-9 Diesel "8610," CC, 13		530 ____
39576	C&NW Dash-9 Diesel "8622," nonpowered, 13		260 ____
39577	SP Dash-9 Diesel "8112," CC, 13		530 ____
39578	SP Dash-9 Diesel "8123," CC, 13		530 ____
39579	SP Dash-9 Diesel "8129," nonpowered, 13		260 ____
39580	UP Dash-9 Diesel "9599," CC, 13		530 ____
39581	UP Dash-9 Diesel "9714," CC, 13		530 ____
39582	UP Dash-9 Diesel "9717," nonpowered, 13		260 ____
39583	CSX Dash-9 Diesel "9036," CC, 13		530 ____
39584	CSX Dash-9 Diesel "9048," CC, 13		530 ____
39585	CSX Dash-9 Diesel "9051," nonpowered, 13		260 ____
39586	NS Dash-9 Diesel "9310," CC, 13		530 ____
39587	NS Dash-9 Diesel "9322," CC, 13		530 ____
39588	NS Dash-9 Diesel "9334," nonpowered, 13		260 ____
39589	CN Dash-9 Diesel "2534," CC, 13		530 ____
39590	CN Dash-9 Diesel "2547," CC, 13		530 ____
39591	CN Dash-9 Diesel "2570," nonpowered, 13		260 ____
39592	CNJ NS Heritage SD70ACe Diesel "1071," CC, 13		530 ____
39593	CNJ NS Heritage SD70ACe Diesel "1831," CC, 13		530 ____
39594	CNJ NS Heritage SD70ACe Diesel "1834," nonpowered, 13		260 ____
39595	DL&W NS Heritage SD70ACe Diesel "1074," CC, 13		530 ____
39596	DL&W NS Heritage SD70ACe Diesel "1853," CC, 13		530 ____
39597	DL&W NS Heritage SD70ACe Diesel "1856," nonpowered, 13		260 ____
39598	Monongahela NS Heritage ES44AC Diesel "8025," CC, 12		550 ____
39599	Monongahela NS Heritage ES44AC Diesel "1901," CC, 12		550 ____
39600	PRR E8 AA Diesel Set, CC, 13		930 ____
39603	B&O E9 AA Diesel Set, CC, 13		930 ____
39606	FEC E9 AA Diesel Set, CC, 13		930 ____
39609	SP E9 AA Diesel Set, CC, 13		930 ____
39612	UP E9 AA Diesel Set, CC, 13		930 ____
39615	CB&Q E9 AA Diesel Set, CC, 13		930 ____
39618	MILW E9 AA Diesel Set, CC, 13		930 ____

			Exc	Mint
____	**39621**	KCS E9 AA Diesel Set, CC, 13		930
____	**39624**	Erie NS Heritage SD70ACe Diesel "1068," CC, 13		530
____	**39625**	Erie NS Heritage SD70ACe Diesel "1832," CC, 13		530
____	**39626**	Erie NS Heritage SD70ACe Diesel "1835," nonpowered, 13		260
____	**39627**	Illinois Terminal NS Heritage SD70ACe Diesel "1072," CC, 13		530
____	**39628**	Illinois Terminal NS Heritage SD70ACe Diesel "1896," CC, 13		530
____	**39629**	Illinois Terminal NS Heritage SD70ACe Diesel "1899," nonpowered, 13		260
____	**39630**	NYC NS Heritage SD70ACe Diesel "1066," CC, 13		530
____	**39631**	NYC NS Heritage SD70ACe Diesel "1831," CC, 13		530
____	**39632**	NYC NS Heritage SD70ACe Diesel "1834," nonpowered, 13		260
____	**39633**	Reading NS Heritage SD70ACe Diesel "1067," CC, 13		530
____	**39634**	Reading NS Heritage SD70ACe Diesel "1833," CC, 13		530
____	**39635**	Reading NS Heritage SD70ACe Diesel "1836," nonpowered, 13		260
____	**39636**	Savannah & Atlanta NS Heritage SD70ACe Diesel "1065," CC, 13		530
____	**39637**	Savannah & Atlanta NS Heritage SD70ACe Diesel "1915," CC, 13		530
____	**39638**	Savannah & Atlanta NS Heritage SD70ACe "1918," nonpowered, 13		260
____	**39639**	Virginian NS Heritage SD70ACe Diesel "1069," CC, 13		530
____	**39640**	Virginian NS Heritage SD70ACe Diesel "1907," CC, 13		530
____	**39641**	Virginian NS Heritage SD70ACe Diesel "1910," nonpowered, 13		260
____	**39642**	Wabash NS Heritage SD70ACe Diesel "1070," CC, 13		530
____	**39643**	Wabash NS Heritage SD70ACe Diesel "1877," CC, 13		530
____	**39644**	Wabash NS Heritage SD70ACe Diesel "1880," nonpowered, 13		260
____	**39645**	PC NS Heritage SD70ACe Diesel "1073," CC, 13		530
____	**39646**	PC NS Heritage SD70ACe Diesel "1968," CC, 13		530
____	**39647**	PC NS Heritage SD70ACe Diesel "1971," nonpowered, 13		260
____	**39680**	Wizard of Oz 4-4-2 Atlantic Locomotive, 09		150
____	**51000**	MILW Hiawatha Streamlined Steam Passenger Set, 88		700
____	**51008**	Burlington Pioneer Zephyr Diesel Passenger Set, RailSounds, 04	350	863
____	**51009**	Prewar “269E” Steam Freight Set, TrainSounds, 06		630
____	**51010**	Prewar “246E” Steam Passenger Set, TrainSounds, 07-08	150	630
____	**51012**	Christmas Tinplate Freight Set, 08		675
____	**51014**	Prewar “291W” Red Comet Passenger Car Set, 08	410	675
____	**51220**	NYC Imperial Castle Passenger Coach, 93 u		500
____	**51221**	NYC Niagara County Passenger Coach, 93 u		500
____	**51222**	NYC Cascade Glory Passenger Coach, 93 u		500
____	**51223**	NYC City of Detroit Passenger Coach, 93 u		500
____	**51224**	NYC Imperial Falls Passenger Coach, 93 u		500
____	**51225**	NYC Westchester County Passenger Coach, 93 u		500
____	**51226**	NYC Cascade Grotto Passenger Coach, 93 u		500
____	**51227**	NYC City of Indianapolis Passenger Coach, 93 u		500
____	**51228**	NYC Manhattan Island Observation Car, 93 u		500
____	**51229**	NYC Diner “680”, 93 u		500
____	**51230**	NYC Baggage Car “5017”, 93 u		500
____	**51231**	NYC Century Club Passenger Coach, 93 u		500
____	**51232**	NYC Thousand Islands Observation Car, 93 u		500
____	**51233**	NYC Diner “684”, 93 u		500
____	**51234**	NYC Baggage Car “5020”, 93 u		500
____	**51235**	NYC Century Tavern Passenger Coach, 93 u		500
____	**51236**	NYC City of Toledo Passenger Coach, 93 u		500

		Exc	Mint
51237	NYC Imperial Mansion Passenger Coach, 93 u		500
51238	NYC Imperial Palace Passenger Coach, 93 u		500
51239	NYC Cascade Spirit Passenger Coach, 93 u		500
51240	NYC Diner "681", 93 u		500
51241	NYC City of Chicago Passenger Coach, 93 u		500
51242	NYC Imperial Garden Passenger Coach, 93 u		500
51243	NYC Imperial Fountain Passenger Coach, 93 u		500
51244	NYC Cascade Valley Passenger Coach, 93 u		500
51245	NYC Diner "685", 93 u		500
51300	Shell Semi-Scale 1-D Tank Car "8124", 91	50	135
51301	Lackawanna Semi-Scale Reefer "7000", 92	119	161
51401	PRR Semi-Scale Boxcar "100800", 91	84	128
51402	C&O Semi-Scale Stock Car "95250", 92	94	138
51422	Southern Searchlight Car, 91-92	15	36
51501	B&O Semi-Scale Hopper "532000", 91	78	108
51502	LL Steel Die-cast Ore Car "6486-3" (SSS), 96		80
51503	LL Steel Die-cast Ore Car "6486-1" (SSS), 96		80
51504	LL Steel Die-cast Ore Car "6486-2" (SSS), 96		70
51600	NYC Depressed Center Flatcar with transformer "6418", 96		105
51701	NYC Semi-Scale Caboose "19400", 91	90	132
51702	PRR N-8 Caboose "478039", 91-92	300	385
52038	Southern Hopper "360794" w/Coal (std O), 94 u	36	46
52040	GTW Flatcar w/Tractor and trailer, 94 u	42	51
52044	Mogen David Wine Vat Car, 95 u	21	30
52053	TTOS Carail Convention Boxcar, 94	50	55
52054	Carail Boxcar, 94 u		300
52066	Trainmaster Tractor and Trailer, 94 u	80	125
52068	Toy Train Parade Contadina Boxcar "16245", 94	15	28
52069	Carail Tractor and Trailer, 94 u		75
52070	Knoebel's Boxcar #1, 95 u		94
52075	United Auto Workers Boxcar, 95 u		90
52082	Steamtown Lackawanna Boxcar, 95 u		90
52096	Snow Village Boxcar "9756", 95 u	55	85
52126	MILW Boxcar "21027" with CTT Logo, 97 u		50
52132	Knoebel's Boxcar #2, 99 u		95
52133	Knoebel's Boxcar #3, 98 u		108
52134	Knoebel's Boxcar #4, 00 u		105
52136A	Christmas Special Tractor and Trailer, 97 u		100
52136B	Frisco Special Tractor and Trailer, 98 u		100
52137	Red Wing Shoes Boot Oil Tank Car, 98		65
52141	Zep Manufacturing Boxcar, 96	86	132
52158	Monopoly Mint Car "M-0539", 98		340
52159	Monopoly Depressed Center Flatcar with transformer, 98		95
52160	Monopoly Water Works Tank Car, 98		105
52161	Monopoly SP-type Caboose "M-1006", 98		55
52168	Carail Flatcar with Trailer "17455", 99 u		120
52169	Zep Manufacturing Flatcar with trailer "62734", 99 u		90
52181	Monopoly Set #2, 4-pack, 99		295
52182	Monopoly Railroads Boxcar "M0636", 99 u		78
52183	Monopoly Jail Car "M-1131", 99		75
52184	Monopoly Free Parking Flatcar with 2 autos, 99		60
52185	Monopoly Chance Gondola "M-0893", 99		50
52187	Madison Hardware Flatcar with 2 trailers, 99		98

	MODERN 1970-2025		Exc	Mint
____	52188	Carail Aquarium with 2 autos, 25th Anniversary, 99		95
____	52189	Monopoly 4-6-4 Hudson Locomotive, 99	300	555
____	52200	TTOS SW SP Overnight Merchandise Service Boxcar, 00 u		40
____	52207	Lionel Lines SD40 Diesel, traditional, 00	167	600
____	52208	Lionel Lines Extended Vision Caboose, 00 u		200
____	52218	Monopoly 4-4-2 Steam Freight Set, 00 u	100	391
____	52219	Monopoly 4-6-4 Hudson Locomotive, bronze, 00 u		530
____	52224A	SP Flatcar with Navajo tractor and trailer, 01		25
____	52224B	SP Flatcar with Trailer Flatcar Service tractor and trailer, 01		25
____	52225	Monopoly 4-6-4 Hudson Locomotive, pewter, 01 u		495
____	52231	British Columbia 1-D Tank Car, 00 u		65
____	52249	Knoebel's Amusement Park 75th Anniversary Boxcar, 01 u		117
____	52262	Plasticville Boxcar, 01 u		120
____	52282	WP Feather Boxcar, red, 03		365
____	52315/20	PRR FM Diesel and Caboose, 04 u		440
____	52330	B&O Museum Fundraiser Boxcar, 03 u		100
____	52334	TTOS Smokey Bear 60th Anniversary 1-D Tank Car, 04 u		80
____	52335	TTOS Smokey Bear 60th Anniversary Boxcar, 04 u		70
____	52371	NYC Flatcar with tanker trailer, 05 u		150
____	52422	Christmas Festival of Trees Boxcar, 06u		80
____	52435	Georgia Power Caboose, 08 u		26
____	52447	LCCA NH Alco Diesel and Passenger Cars, 09 u		140
____	52452	Grzybowski's Trains 30th Anniversary Boxcar, 07 u		39
____	52495	LCCA UP Water Tower, 08 u		30
____	52597	U.S. Navy Flatcar w/trailer, "832011", 11		60
____	55452	Norscot Caterpillar Steam Freight Set, 08 u	270	325
____	58032	CTT 30th Anniversary Boxcar “69013”, 17 u		50
____	58213	LCCA B&M GP7 Diesel “2335,” LionChief Plus , 15 u	135	250
____	58226	TCA Cumbres & Toltec Boxcar, 16 u		75
____	58253	LCCA Lionel 115th Anniversary Trailer, 15 u		25
____	58255	LCCA Lionelville Transit Tractor, 15 u	25	40
____	58262	U.S. Coast Guard Flatcar w/trailer "832011", 11 u		60
____	58267	LCCA KCS Inspection Truck, 16 u	56	90
____	58269	LCCA Tacoma Pickup Truck, 17 u		75
____	58270	LCCA NP Pickup Truck, 17 u		75
____	58504	Lionel Flatcar w/Madison Hardware Trailer, 15 u		120
____	58510	Frisco Flatcar w/trailer "100011"		50
____	58513	LCCA Reading Blue Coal 2-bay Hopper w/ETD, 12 u		75
____	58515	LCCA NS Vulcan Switcher, 12 u		50
____	58517	NLOE LIRR Alco Diesels, 13 u		300
____	58522	TCA Los Alamos Mint Car, 16 u		75
____	58527	LCCA Vulcan Switcher, 13 u		80
____	58528	LCCA Reading Vulcan Switcher, 14 u		80
____	58539	LCCA Texas Special B-W Caboose, 13 u		95
____	58545	LCCA Vulcan Switcher, Gold, 12 u		75
____	58550	LCCA Texas Special Unibody Tank Car, 13 u	70	95
____	58578	New York Air Brake PS-1 Boxcar “1890”, 13u		200
____	58585	LCCA Wabash Auto Loader, white, 14 u		110
____	58586	LCCA South Shore Lines Trolley, 14 u		95
____	58598	TCA Philly Pretzel Boxcar, 14 u		80
____	58599	LCCA UP Cylindrical Hopper, 11 u	28	75
____	59002	LCCA TVRM Boxcar, 13 u		150
____	59015	LCCA Conway Scenic RR Boxcar, 15 u		200

No.	Description	Exc	Mint
62162	Postwar "262" Automatic Crossing Gate and Signal, 99-14		60
62180	Railroad Signs, set of 14, 99-04, 08-25		10
62181	Telephone Pole Set, 10-pack, 99-04, 08-24		15
62283	Die-cast Illuminated Bumpers, 99-17		27
62709	Rico Station Kit, 99-00		46
62716	Short Extension Bridge, 99-03, 07-25		15
62900	Lockon, 99-13		3
62901	Ives Track Clips, 12 pieces (027), 99-10, 13-16		5
62905	Lockon with wires, 99-10, 13-14		7
62909	Smoke Fluid, 99-12		7
62927	Lubrication/Maintenance Set, 99-25		25
62985	The Lionel Train Book, 99-03		12
65014	Half Curved Track (027), 99-16		1
65019	Half Straight Track (027), 99-16		1
65020	90-degree Crossover (027), 99-16		11
65021	27" Manual Switch, left hand (027), 99-16		17
65022	27" Manual Switch, right hand (027), 99-16		18
65023	45-degree Crossover (027), 99-16		11
65024	35" Straight Track (027), 99-16		5
65033	27" Diameter Curved Track (027), 99-16		2
65038	9" Straight Track (027), 99-16		2
65041	Insulator Pins, dozen (027), 99-04, 06, 13-14		3
65042	Steel Pins, dozen (027), 99-04, 06-09, 13-14		3
65049	42" Diameter Curved Track (027), 99-16		3
65113	54" Diameter Curved Track (027), 99-16		3
65121	27" Path Remote Switch, left hand (027), 99-14		43
65122	27" Path Remote Switch, right hand (027), 99-14		43
65149	Uncoupling Track (027), 99-14		12
65165	72" Path Remote Switch, right hand (0), 99-14		125
65166	72" Path Remote Switch, left hand (0), 99-14		125
65167	42" Remote Switch, right hand (027), 99-14		25
65168	42" Remote Switch, left hand (027), 99-14		25
65500	10" Straight Track (0), 99-16		2
65501	31" Diameter Curved Track (0), 99-16		2
65504	Half Curved Track (0), 99-16		2
65505	Half Straight Track (0), 99-16		2
65514	Half Curved Track (027), 99-03		3
65523	40" Straight Track (0), 99-16		7
65530	Remote Control Track (0), 99-16		38
65540	90-degree Crossover (0), 99-14		16
65543	Insulator Pins, dozen (0), 99-16		3
65545	45-degree Crossover (0), 99-14		27
65551	Steel Pins, dozen (0), 99-16		3
65554	54" Diameter Curved Track (0), 99-16		4
65572	72" Diameter Curved Track (0), 99-16		5
65824	NLOE LIRR Hopper w/Coal load, 17u		95
68677	Frisco Flatcar w/trailer "832013", 98 u		45
71998	LCCA Amtrak Refrigerator Car (Std 0), 10 u		45
81000	BNSF Waffle-sided Boxcar "496464", 14-15		50
81001	SP&S Flatcar with bulkheads, 14-16		50
81002	UP 3-D Tank Car, 14-15		50
81003	CP Bilevel Auto Carrier, 14-16		50
81004	B&O Depressed-Center Flatcar with transformer, 14-15		50

			Exc	Mint
____	**81005**	Maine Central 2-bay Hopper "1005", 14-16		50
____	**81006**	PRR Hi-Cube Boxcar "31010", 14-16		50
____	**81007**	Seaboard Waffle-sided Boxcar "25335", 14-16		50
____	**81008**	Central of Georgia Boxcar "5818", 14-17		50
____	**81009**	Southern 2-D Tank Car "951005", 14-16		50
____	**81010**	FEC Gondola "6121" with reels, 14-16		50
____	**81011**	PFE Reefer "33280", 14-16		50
____	**81012**	T&P 1-D Tank Car , 14-16		50
____	**81013**	Frisco Boxcar "700117", 14-16		50
____	**81014**	D&RGW Ore Car "31101", 14-15		50
____	**81015**	B&M Reefer "1878", 14-16		50
____	**81016**	Coaling Station, 14, 16-20		110
____	**81017**	Barrel Loading Building, 14-18		43
____	**81018**	Shell Vat Car, 17		80
____	**81019**	Short Tunnel, 14-16-17		45
____	**81021**	B&M Paul Revere GP9 Diesel Freight Set, 14-15		500
____	**81023**	Jersey Central Yard Boss 0-4-0 Steam Freight Set, 14-15		500
____	**81024**	Christmas Train Set, 02-04		150
____	**81025**	Lackawanna Pocono Berkshire Steam Freight Set, 14-15		480
____	**81027**	Thomas the Tank Engine Set, 01-04		120
____	**81028**	Marquette GP38 Diesel Freight Set, 14-15		430
____	**81029**	C&NW Windy City GP38 Diesel Freight Set, 14-15		400
____	**81030**	UP Gold Coast Flyer Steam Freight Set, 14-15		455
____	**81031**	Dinosaur Diesel Freight Set, LionChief, 14-16		175
____	**81038**	MILW Heavy Mikado Locomotive "8693" CC, 15	588	1300
____	**81063**	Plug-Expand-Play Classic Automatic Gateman, 14-25		130
____	**81064**	Construction Zone Signs #2, 14-19		10
____	**81066**	Milwaukee Road Double-sheathed Boxcar "8775" (std O), 14	33	83
____	**81067**	Monopoly Aquarium Car, 14-15		85
____	**81073**	Monopoly Boxcar 2-pack, Ventnor and Indiana Avenues, 14-15		135
____	**81076**	Pennsylvania Salt 8,000-gallon 1-D Tank Car "4724" (std O), 14		73
____	**81077**	Pere Marquette 8,000-gallon 1-D Tank Car "71710" (std O), 14		73
____	**81078**	NYC 8,000-gallon 1-D Tank Car "107898" (std O), 14		73
____	**81079**	NKP 8,000-gallon 1-D Tank Car "50277" (std O), 14		73
____	**81080**	BN 8,000-gallon 1-D Tank Car "977100" (std O), 14		73
____	**81081**	Alaska Steel-sided Reefer "10806" (std O), 14		80
____	**81090**	NS Hi-Cube Boxcar 2-pack (std O), 14-15		190
____	**81093**	2013 Lionel Dealer Appreciation Boxcar, 13 u		40
____	**81094**	Conrail "Big Blue" High-Cube Boxcar Diesel Freight Set, CC, 14-15		970
____	**81095**	Conrail Hi-Cube Boxcar 2-pack (std O), 14-16		190
____	**81101**	Polar Express 10th Anniversary Steam Passenger Set, 14-15		430
____	**81113**	SP 50' DD Boxcar "214051" (std O), 14-15		75
____	**81122**	Christmas 1955 MOW Inspection Truck, CC, 15		180
____	**81126**	WP 1955 MOW Inspection Truck, CC, 15		180
____	**81127**	Alaska 1955 MOW Inspection Truck, CC, 15		180
____	**81129**	MILW 1955 MOW Inspection Truck, CC, 15		180
____	**81130**	CNJ 1955 MOW Inspection Truck, CC, 15		180
____	**81132**	N&W 1955 MOW Inspection Truck, CC, 15		180
____	**81134**	BN SD70MAC Diesel "9424," CC, 14		550
____	**81135**	BN SD70MAC Diesel "9431," CC, 14		550
____	**81137**	BNSF SD70MAC Diesel "9858," CC, 14		550

MODERN 1970-2025		Exc	Mint
81138	BNSF SD70MAC Diesel "9860," CC, 14		550
81141	Conrail SD70MAC Diesel "4138," CC, 14		550
81142	PFE Steel-sided Reefers 3-pack (std 0), 14		300
81144	CSX SD70MAC Diesel "781," CC, 14		550
81147	KCS SD7CMAC Diesel "3950," CC, 14		550
81148	KCS SD7CMAC Diesel "3953," CC, 14		550
81151	Alaska SD7CMAC Diesel "4002," CC, 14		550
81152	Alaska SD7CMAC Diesel "4005," CC, 14		550
81153	CSX SD70MAC Diesel "778," CC, 14		550
81154	UP ES44AC Diesel "7361," CC, 14		550
81155	UP ES44AC Diesel "7388," CC, 14		550
81160	CSX ES44AC Diesel "937," CC, 14		550
81161	CSX ES44AC Diesel "944," CC, 14		550
81169	Iowa Interstate ES44AC Diesel "504," CC, 14		550
81170	Iowa Interstate ES44AC Diesel "507," CC, 14		550
81171	Ferromex ES44AC Diesel "4617," CC, 14		550
81172	Ferromex ES44AC Diesel "4626," CC, 14		550
81176	CN ES44AC Diesel "2812," CC, 14		550
81177	CN ES44AC Diesel "2818," CC, 14		550
81179	2-8-2 Heavy Mikado Pilot Locomotive, CC, 14		1300
81180	2-8-2 Heavy Mikado Locomotive, CC, 15		1300
81181	Southern 2-8-2 Heavy Mikado Locomotive "4866," CC, 15		1300
81182	L&N 2-8-2 Heavy Mikado Locomotive "1757," CC, 14		1300
81183	MP 2-8-2 Heavy Mikado Locomotive "1496," CC, 14		1300
81184	P&WV 2-8-2 Heavy Mikado Locomotive "1152," CC, 14		1300
81185	CNJ 2-8-2 Heavy Mikado Locomotive "845," CC, 14		1300
81186	Frisco 2-8-2 Heavy Mikado Locomotive "4126," CC, 14		1300
81187	C&IM 2-8-2 Heavy Mikado Locomotive "551," CC, 14		1300
81188	NYC 2-8-2 Heavy Mikado Locomotive "9506," CC, 14		1300
81189	CB&Q 2-8-2 Heavy Mikado Locomotive "5509," CC, 15		1300
81190	WP 2-8-2 Heavy Mikado Locomotive "334," CC, 15		1300
81191	Erie 2-8-2 Heavy Mikado Locomotive "3207," CC, 15		1300
81192	GN 2-8-2 Heavy Mikado Locomotive "3148," CC, 14		1300
81193	Wheeling & Lake Erie 2-8-2 Heavy Mikado Locomotive "6012," CC, 15		1300
81194	NKP 2-8-2 Heavy Mikado Locomotive "689," CC, 15	250	1300
81195	PRR Boxcar, 14-15		70
81196	Timken Boxcar, 14-15		70
81197	Santa Fe Boxcar, 14-15		70
81198	GN Boxcar, 14-16		70
81199	PRR 1-D Tank Car, 14-15		70
81200	Timken 1-D Tank Car, 14-16		70
81201	GN 1-D Tank Car, 14-16		70
81202	Santa Fe 1-D Tank Car, 14-15		70
81203	PRR Flatcar, 14-15	24	70
81204	Santa Fe Flatcar, 14-16	37	70
81205	Timken Flatcar, 14-16		70
81206	GN Flatcar, 14-16		70
81207	CP H-24-66 Train Master Diesel "8900," CC, 14		550
81208	CP H-24-66 Train Master Diesel "8903," CC, 14		550
81209	CNJ H-24-66 Train Master Diesel "2401," CC, 14		550
81210	CNJ H-24-66 Train Master Diesel "2406," CC, 14		550
81211	Reading H-24-66 Train Master Diesel "801," CC, 14		550

	MODERN 1970-2025		Exc	Mint
___	**81212**	Reading H-24-66 Train Master Diesel "804," CC, 14		550
___	**81213**	SP H-24-66 Train Master Diesel "4803," CC, 14		550
___	**81214**	SP H-24-66 Train Master Diesel "4809," CC, 14		550
___	**81215**	Southern H-24-66 Train Master Diesel "6300," CC, 14		550
___	**81216**	Southern H-24-66 Train Master Diesel "6303," CC, 14		550
___	**81217**	N&W H-24-66 Train Master Diesel "151," CC, 14		550
___	**81218**	N&W H-24-66 Train Master Diesel "164," CC, 14		550
___	**81219**	Santa Fe E8 Diesel AA Set "84/85," CC, 14		930
___	**81222**	PC E8 Diesel AA Set "4289/4325," CC, 14	238	930
___	**81225**	RI E8 Diesel AA Set "647/648," CC, 14		930
___	**81228**	C&O E8 Diesel AA Set "4027/4028," CC, 14		930
___	**81231**	Erie E8 Diesel AA Set "822/823," CC, 14		930
___	**81234**	MKT E8 Diesel AA Set "131/132," CC, 14		930
___	**81237**	SAL E8 Diesel AA Set "3051/3055," CC, 14		930
___	**81240**	Wabash E8 Diesel AA Set "1007/1011," CC, 14		930
___	**81243**	Pilot M1a 4-8-2 Locomotive, CC, 14		1500
___	**81245**	PRR M1a 4-8-2 Locomotive "6671," CC, 14		1500
___	**81246**	PRR M1a 4-8-2 Locomotive "6764," CC, 14		1500
___	**81247**	PRR M1a Coal Hauler Twin-hopper Steam Freight Set, CC, 14		1800
___	**81248**	10" Girder Bridge Track, 14-25		25
___	**81249**	Christmas Girder Bridge Track, 14, 16-18		25
___	**81250**	FasTrack 0-96 Curve, 14-25		8
___	**81251**	FasTrack 0-31 Manual Switch, right-hand, 14-25		55
___	**81252**	FasTrack 0-31 Manual Switch, left-hand, 14-25	25	55
___	**81253**	FasTrack 0-31 Remote Switch, right-hand, 14-25		130
___	**81254**	FasTrack 0-31 Remote Switch, left-hand, 14-25		130
___	**81256**	Personalized Birthday Message Boxcar, 14-15		85
___	**81257**	Amtrak Water Tower, 14-18		35
___	**81259**	PRR Broadway Limited Steam Passenger Set, 14		370
___	**81261**	NYC Early Bird Special Steam Freight Set, 16-17		380
___	**81262**	UP Steam Freight Set, LionChief, 15		400
___	**81263**	CNJ Diesel Passenger Set, LionChief, 14-16		390
___	**81264**	Western Union Telegraph Steam Freight Set, 14-16		390
___	**81266**	Amtrak FT Diesel Passenger Set, LionChief, 14-15		460
___	**81269**	PRR Allegheny Hauler Steam Freight Set, 16-17		420
___	**81270**	Bethlehem Steel Steam Work Train, LionChief, 15		340
___	**81279**	Albert Hall European Steam Passenger Set, LionChief, 14-15		430
___	**81280**	Victorian Christmas Steam Passenger Set, 14		400
___	**81284**	Frosty the Snowman Steam Freight Set, LionChief, 14-16		320
___	**81286**	Lionel Junction "Little Steam" Freight Set, 14-15		175
___	**81287**	Lionel Junction UP Steam Freight Set, 14-15		175
___	**81288**	Pet Shop Diesel Freight Set, 14-16		175
___	**81290**	Thomas Kinkade Holiday Covered Bridge, 14		70
___	**81292**	Valley Central 1-D Tank Car "45003", 14-17		45
___	**81294**	LCS FasTrack IR Sensor Track, 13-25		100
___	**81295**	AT&SF 2-8-2 Locomotive "3158," LionChief, 14-16	138	430
___	**81296**	GN 2-8-2 Locomotive "3123," LionChief, 14-15		430
___	**81297**	PRR 2-8-2 Locomotive "9633," LionChief, 14-15		430
___	**81299**	Chessie System 2-8-2 Locomotive "2103," LionChief, 14-15		430
___	**81301**	NYC 4-6-4 Hudson Locomotive "5421," LionChief, 14-15		430
___	**81302**	C&O 4-6-4 Hudson Locomotive "308," LionChief Plus, 14-17		430
___	**81303**	UP 4-6-4 Hudson Locomotive "674," LionChief Plus, 14-17		430
___	**81304**	CN 4-6-4 Hudson Locomotive "5702," LionChief Plus, 14-17		430

		Exc	Mint
81307	B&O 4-6-2 Locomotive "5307," LionChief, 14-17		430
81308	CP 4-6-2 Pacific Locomotive "2469," LionChief Plus, 14-17		430
81309	SP 4-6-2 Pacific Locomotive "3106," LionChief Plus, 14-17		430
81311	Alaska 4-6-2 Pacific Locomotive "652," LionChief Plus, 14-17		430
81313	FasTrack Power Lockon, 15-25		25
81314	FasTrack Power Block Lockon, 15-25		44
81315	Coaling Station, 15-17, 19-20		160
81316	Personalized Christmas Message Boxcar, 15		80
81317	FasTrack Plug-Expand-Play Accessory Activator Track Pack, 15-25		27
81325	LCS WiFi Module, 13-16, 18-20		180
81326	LCS Serial Converter #2, 14-25		70
81331	Iron Arry Locomotive with Remote, LionChief, 14-15		140
81332	Iron Bert Locomotive with Remote, LionChief, 14-15		140
81373	Candy Cane Flatcar with bulkheads, 15		60
81395	Thomas Kinkade Christmas Passenger Set, LionChief, 14-15		380
81419	Alien Ooze 1-D Tank Car, 14-15		65
81420	PRR Truss-rod Gondola with tarp, 14-16		65
81422	NS Water Tower, 14		31
81423	Sodor Coal and Scrap Cars 2-pack, 14-16		70
81424	Sodor Crane Car and Work Caboose 2-pack, 14		70
81425	Frosty the Snowman Passenger Station, 14		65
81426	Frosty the Snowman Animated Gondola, 14		75
81427	Frosty the Snowman Aquarium Car, 14		85
81428	Frosty the Snowman Boxcar, 14		65
81430	Lionelville Shanty, 14		22
81432	PRR Girder Bridge, 14-15		21
81433	PRR Crossing Shanty, 14		22
81434	Pennsylvania Station Platform, 14-15		23
81435	N&W NS Heritage Quad Hopper with coal, 14-15		60
81436	Intermodal Container 4-pack, 14		43
81437	York Peppermint Patty Vat Car, 14-15		70
81439	Halloween Pumpkinheads Handcar, 14-16		90
81440	Western Union Handcar, 14-16		100
81441	North Pole Central Snowplow, CC , 15-20		280
81442	PRR Rotary Snowplow "1442," CC, 15-20		280
81443	D&RGW Rotary Snowplow "443," CC, 15-20		280
81444	PRR Tie-Jector, CC, 14-16		200
81445	MOW Tie-Jector, CC, 14-16		200
81446	Santa Fe Tie-Jector, CC, 14-18		200
81447	NS Tie-Jector, CC, 14-18		200
81448	Amtrak Tie-Jector, CC, 14-18	90	200
81449	Zombie Motorized Trolley, 14		100
81450	Polar Express Trolley, 14		110
81451	St. Louis Motorized Trolley, 14		100
81452	Neil Young Texas Special F3 AA Diesels, CC, 13-14		650
81453	Neil Young PRR F3 AA Diesels, CC, 13-14		650
81462	PRR Broadway Limited Add-on Baggage Car, 14-17		70
81463	CNJ Water Tower, 14-17		31
81464	CNJ Montclair Add-on Passenger Car, 14-16		60
81465	SP Flatcar with piggyback trailers, 14-16		75
81466	BN Maxi-Stack Pair, 14-16		140
81469	GN Bilevel Stock Car "65385", 14-17		65

No.	Description	Exc	Mint
81470	DC Comics Batman Phantom Train, 16-17		400
81475	DC Comics Batman M7 Subway Set, LionChief, 14-15		370
81479	Batman Add-on M7 Subway Car 2-pack, 14-15		140
81480	John Deere RS3 Diesel Freight Set, LionChief, 14-16	128	325
81486	NYC Patrol Flatcar with helicopter, 14-15	28	65
81487	Ronald Reagan Presidential Boxcar, 14-15		70
81488	Andrew Jackson Presidential Boxcar, 14-16, 18		70
81489	Warren G. Harding Presidential Boxcar, 14-16, 18, 20		75
81490	Dwight D. Eisenhower Presidential Boxcar, 14-16		70
81491	Jersey Central Coal Dump Car, 14-15		65
81492	Strasburg RR Searchlight Car, 14		50
81493	Postwar "6844" U.S.A.F. Missile Carrying Car, 15-16		65
81494	Santa's Sleigh Rocket Fuel Tank Car, 16		65
81495	40-watt Power Supply, 15-18		65
81496	2014 Lionel Dealer Appreciation Boxcar, 14 u		40
81497	2015 Lionel Dealer Appreciation Boxcar, 15 u		40
81499	LCS Power Supply with DB9 cable, 13-16, 18-20		37
81500	LCS PDI Sensor Track 1' Cable, 13-25		15
81501	LCS PDI Sensor Track 3' Cable, 13-25		16
81502	LCS PDI Sensor Track 10' Cable, 13-25		20
81503	LCS PDI Sensor Track 20' Cable, 13-25		20
81504	Ann Arbor FA-2 Diesel AA Set "53/53A," CC, 14		750
81507	B&O FA-2 Diesel AA Set "817/827," CC, 14-15		750
81510	Erie FA-2 Diesel AA Set "736A/736D," CC, 14-15		750
81513	MKT FA-2 Diesel AA Set "331A/331C," CC, 14		750
81516	NYC FA-2 Diesel AA Set "1075/1078," CC, 14-15		750
81519	PRR FA-2 Diesel AA Set "9608/9609," CC, 14-15		750
81522	Ann Arbor FB2 Diesel "53B", CC, 14	80	450
81523	B&O FB2 Diesel "817B," CC, 14-15		450
81524	Erie FB2 Diesel "736B," CC, 14-15		450
81525	MKT FB2 Diesel "331B," CC, 14		450
81526	NYC FB2 Diesel "3327," CC, 14-15		450
81527	PRR FB2 Diesel "9608B," CC, 14		450
81528	Ann Arbor FB2 Diesel, nonpowered, 14		350
81529	B&O FB2 Diesel, nonpowered, 14-15		350
81530	Erie FB2 Diesel, nonpowered, 14-15		350
81531	MKT FB2 Diesel, nonpowered, 14		350
81532	NYC FB2 Diesel, nonpowered, 14-15		350
81533	PRR FB2 Diesel, nonpowered, 14-15		350
81534	Christmas Toys Stock Car, 14		70
81545	Operation Eagle Missile Launcher Car, CC, 15		350
81546	Operation Eagle Sound Car, CC, 15		240
81568	4th of July Parade Boxcar, 14-16		80
81596	Weathered UP 4-12-2 Locomotive "9000," CC, 13		1400
81597	Weathered B&O RF-16 Sharknose AA Diesels "855-857," CC, 13		830
81600	Weathered PRR RF-16 Sharknose AA Diesels "2020A-2021A," CC, 13		830
81603	72-watt Power Supply, LionChief, 14-24		60
81605	Santa Fe PS-1 Boxcar 5-pack (std O), 14		380
81615	UP 1-D Tank Car, 14		45
81617	Pet Shop 1-D Tank Car, 14-16		45
81619	Reading PS-1 Boxcar "109448" (std O), 14		80

MODERN 1970-2025		Exc	Mint	
81620	Zombie Figure Pack, 14-15		23	___
81621	John Deere Billboard Set, 15		25	___
81622	John Deere Water Tower, 15		40	___
81625	Amtrak Add-on Baggage Car, 14-16		85	___
81626	Barrel Shed, 14-16, 18-20		40	___
81627	Christmas Hopper Shed, 14, 16-17		45	___
81628	Grain Elevator, 15		80	___
81629	Lumber Shed Kit, 14-25		35	___
81635	Water Tower, 14		35	___
81639	LCS Accessory Switch Controller #2, 14-25		130	___
81640	LCS Block Power Controller #2, 14-25		130	___
81641	LCS Accessory Motor Controller, 17-25		130	___
81644	Chessie System Baby Madison Passenger Car 3-pack, 14-16		270	___
81649	SP Baby Madison Passenger Car 3-pack, 14-16		270	___
81654	Philadelphia Energy Solutions 1-D Tank Car "0765", 15-18	25	60	___
81662	FasTrack O-31 Quarter Curved Track, 14-25		5	___
81668	Philadelphia Energy Solutions 1-D Tank Car "0771", 15-16, 18		60	___
81680	Dinosaur 1-D Tank Car, 14-16		45	___
81686	PRR GL-a 2-bay Hopper 3-pack (std O), 14		220	___
81687	LV GL-a 2-bay Hopper 2-pack (std O), 14-15		146	___
81688	CB&Q GL-a 2-bay Hopper 3-pack (std O), 14-16		220	___
81689	C&O GL-a 2-bay Hopper 3-pack (std O), 14-16		220	___
81693	Aerial Target Launcher, 15-16		90	___
81699	Polar Express Scale Twin Hopper, 15		80	___
81703	Santa Fe Hi-Cube Boxcar 2-pack (std O), 14-16		190	___
81704	Grand Trunk Hi-Cube Boxcar 2-pack (std O), 14-16		190	___
81705	Milwaukee Road Hi-Cube Boxcar 2-pack (std O), 14-16		190	___
81706	Frisco Hi-Cube Boxcar 2-pack (std O), 14-16		190	___
81707	NYC Hi-Cube Boxcar 2-pack (std O), 14-16		190	___
81708	Santa Fe Hi-Cube Boxcar "36715" (std O), 14-15		95	___
81710	Milwaukee Road Hi-Cube Boxcar "4980" (std O), 14-15		95	___
81711	Frisco Hi-Cube Boxcar "9125" (std O), 14-15		95	___
81712	NYC Hi-Cube Boxcar "67282" (std O), 14-15		95	___
81723	Postwar “3413” Mercury Capsule Launcher Car, 15		80	___
81725	UP Operating Merchandise Car, 14-15		68	___
81726	REA Operating Merchandise Car, 14-15		80	___
81729	Great Western Passenger Car Add-on 2-pack, 14		130	___
81733	Christmas Boxcar, 14	38	65	___
81734	FasTrack Oval Track and Power Pack, 14-17		200	___
81735	FasTrack Figure-8 Track and Power Pack, 14-17		250	___
81736	Classic Lionel Catalogs Billboard Pack, 14-15		13	___
81737	Passenger Station, 14-15		60	___
81738	Lionel Auto Loader Cars 4-pack, 14-15, 17		25	___
81739	Santa Fe Baby Madison Passenger Car 3-pack, 14-16		270	___
81744	CP Baby Madison Passenger Car 3-pack, 14-16		270	___
81749	Pullman Baby Madison Passenger Car 3-pack, 14-16		270	___
81754	NYC Baby Madison Passenger Car 3-pack, 14-16		270	___
81759	NYC Coach/Diner 2-pack, 14-16		180	___
81760	NYC Coach/Baggage Car 2-pack, 14-16		180	___
81763	Pullman Baby Madison Passenger Car 3-pack, 14-16		180	___
81764	Pullman Coach/Baggage Car 2-pack, 14, 16		180	___
81768	Chessie System Coach/Diner 2-pack, 14-16		180	___
81769	Chessie System Coach/Baggage Car 2-pack, 14-16		180	___

			Exc	Mint
___	**81773**	SP Coach/Diner 2-pack, 14-16		180
___	**81774**	SP Coach/Baggage Car 2-pack, 14-16		180
___	**81778**	Santa Fe Coach/Diner 2-pack, 14-16		180
___	**81779**	Santa Fe Coach/Baggage Car 2-pack, 14-16		180
___	**81783**	CP Coach/Diner 2-pack, 14-16		180
___	**81784**	CP Coach/Baggage Car 2-pack, 14-16		180
___	**81789**	NH GL-a 2-bay Hopper 2-pack (std O), 14-16		146
___	**81793**	Berwind GL-a 2-bay Hopper 3-pack (std O), 14-15		220
___	**81800**	Southern 18" Aluminum Observation/Coach Car, 2-pack (std O), 14		320
___	**81801**	Southern 18" Combination/Vista Dome Car, 2-pack (std O), 14		320
___	**81806**	PRR N5b Caboose "477814" (std O), 14		95
___	**81807**	Conrail N5b Caboose "22882" (std O), 14-15		95
___	**81808**	PC N5b Caboose "22802" (std O), 14-16		95
___	**81809**	LIRR N5b Caboose "2" (std O), 14-15		95
___	**81810**	Lionel Lines N5b Caboose "1402" (std O), 14-16		95
___	**81811**	Polar Express N5b Caboose, 16		95
___	**81812**	RI 18" Aluminum Observation/Coach Car, 2-pack (std O), 14		320
___	**81813**	RI 18" Aluminum Combination/Vista Dome Car, 2-pack (std O), 14		320
___	**81818**	C&O 18" Aluminum Observation/Coach Car, 2-pack (std O), 14		320
___	**81819**	C&O 18" Aluminum Combination/Vista Dome Car, 2-pack (std O), 14		320
___	**81824**	P&WV GL-a 2-bay Hopper 2-pack (std O), 14-16		146
___	**81827**	PC Round-roof Boxcar "100104" (std O), 14		80
___	**81828**	GN Round-roof Boxcar "5885" (std O), 14		80
___	**81829**	WP Round-roof Boxcar "10211" (std O), 14-15		80
___	**81830**	MKT 18" Aluminum Observation/Coach Car, 2-pack (std O), 14		320
___	**81831**	MKT 18" Aluminum Baggage/Diner Car, 2-pack (std O), 14		320
___	**81836**	Erie Double-sheathed Boxcar "71107" (std O), 14-15		80
___	**81837**	Frisco Double-sheathed Boxcar "128528" (std O), 14-15		80
___	**81838**	CNJ Double-sheathed Boxcar "14014" (std O), 14-15		80
___	**81839**	Pacific Fright Express Steel-sided Reefer (std O), 14		80
___	**81840**	UP Ca-4 Caboose with smoke "3880" (std O), 14		90
___	**81841**	UP MOW Caboose "903224" (std O), 14		90
___	**81842**	Wabash 18" Dome-Observation/Coach Car, 2-pack (std O), 14		320
___	**81843**	Wabash 18" Aluminum Combination/Vista Dome Car, 2-pack (std O), 14		320
___	**81858**	PRR GL-a 2-bay Hopper 3-pack (std O), 14		220
___	**81862**	FasTrack 0-31 Curved Track 4-pack, 14-25		25
___	**81866**	RI 18" Aluminum Baggage/Diner Car, 2-pack (std O), 14		320
___	**81869**	C&O 18" Aluminum Baggage/Diner Car, 2-pack (std O), 14		320
___	**81871**	Loggers Figure Pack, 15-23		30
___	**81872**	Wabash 18" Aluminum Baggage/Diner Car, 2-pack (std O), 14		320
___	**81875**	MKT 18" Aluminum Combination/Vista Dome Car, 2-pack (std O), 14		320
___	**81878**	Southern 18" Aluminum Baggage/Diner Car, 2-pack (std O), 14		320
___	**81881**	SP Crane Car, CC, 14-16		500
___	**81882**	DT&I Crane Car, CC, 14-16		500
___	**81883**	CSX Crane Car, CC, 14-16		500
___	**81884**	Bethlehem Steel Crane Car, CC, 14		500
___	**81885**	MOW Crane Car, CC, 14-16		500
___	**81886**	SP Boom Car, RailSounds, CC, 14-16		240
___	**81887**	DT&I Boom Car, RailSounds, CC, 14-16		240
___	**81888**	CSX Boom Car, RailSounds, CC, 14-16		240

MODERN 1970-2025		Exc	Mint
81889	MOW Boom Car, RailSounds, CC, 14-16		240 ___
81890	Bethlehem Steel Boom Car, RailSounds, CC, 14		240 ___
81891	BNSF 52' Gondola "523300" with 3-piece covers (std O), 14		80 ___
81892	Bethlehem Steel 52' Gondola "303022" with 3-piece covers (std O), 14		80 ___
81893	GTW 52' Gondola "145391" with 3-piece covers (std O), 14		80 ___
81894	CSX 52' Gondola "709190" with 3-piece covers (std O), 14		80 ___
81895	North Pole Central 52' Gondola "128925" w/covers (std O), 14		80 ___
81896	NYC PS-5 Flatcar "506266" with piggyback trailers (std O), 14		100 ___
81897	Milwaukee Road PS-5 Flatcar "64660" with piggyback trailers (std O), 14	43	108 ___
81898	Lionel PS-5 Flatcar with piggyback trailers (std O), 14		100 ___
81899	CP PS-5 Flatcar "301000" with piggyback trailers (std O), 14		100 ___
81900	UP PS-5 Flatcar "258255" with piggyback trailers (std O), 14		100 ___
81901	NYC Tractor and Piggyback Trailer, 14, 17		90 ___
81902	Milwaukee Road Tractor and Piggyback Trailer, 14		90 ___
81903	Lionel Tractor and Piggyback Trailer, 14		90 ___
81904	CP Tractor and Piggyback Trailer, 14-15, 17		90 ___
81905	UP Tractor and Piggyback Trailer, 14		90 ___
81908	PFE Steel-sided Reefers 3-pack (std O), 14		240 ___
81912	New York Yankees Boxcar, 14		70 ___
81913	St. Louis Cardinals Boxcar, 14		70 ___
81914	Oakland Athletics Boxcar, 14		70 ___
81915	San Francisco Giants Boxcar, 14		70 ___
81916	Boston Red Sox Boxcar, 14		70 ___
81917	Los Angeles Dodgers Boxcar, 14		70 ___
81918	Cincinnati Reds Boxcar, 14		70 ___
81919	San Diego Padres Boxcar, 14		70 ___
81920	Detroit Tigers Boxcar, 14		70 ___
81921	Atlanta Braves Boxcar, 14		70 ___
81922	Baltimore Orioles Boxcar, 14		70 ___
81923	Minnesota Twins Boxcar, 14		70 ___
81924	Chicago White Sox Boxcar, 14		70 ___
81925	Chicago Cubs Boxcar, 14		70 ___
81926	Philadelphia Phillies Boxcar, 14		70 ___
81927	Cleveland Indians Boxcar, 14		70 ___
81928	New York Mets Boxcar, 14		70 ___
81929	Toronto Blue Jays Boxcar, 14		70 ___
81930	Miami Marlins Boxcar, 14		70 ___
81931	Angels Baseball Boxcar, 14		70 ___
81932	Pittsburgh Pirates Boxcar, 14		70 ___
81933	Texas Rangers Boxcar, 14		70 ___
81934	Milwaukee Brewers Boxcar, 14		70 ___
81935	Houston Astros Boxcar, 14		70 ___
81936	Colorado Rockies Boxcar, 14		70 ___
81937	Tampa Bay Rays Boxcar, 14		70 ___
81938	Seattle Mariners Boxcar, 14		70 ___
81939	Washington Nationals Boxcar, 14		70 ___
81940	Arizona Diamondbacks Boxcar, 14		70 ___
81941	Kansas City Royals Boxcar, 14		70 ___
81944	Rotary Beacon, yellow, 14-19		85 ___
81945	Polar Express Scale Coach, 14		210 ___
81946	FasTrack O-36 Remote Switch, right-hand, 14-25		130 ___
81947	FasTrack O-36 Remote Switch, left-hand, 14-25		130 ___

	MODERN 1970-2025		Exc	Mint
____	**81948**	FasTrack O-48 Remote Switch, right-hand, 14-25	60	140
____	**81949**	FasTrack O-48 Remote Switch, left-hand, 14-25	60	140
____	**81950**	FasTrack O-60 Remote Switch, right-hand, 14-25	60	140
____	**81951**	FasTrack O-60 Remote Switch, left-hand, 14-25	65	140
____	**81952**	FasTrack O-72 Remote Switch, right-hand, 14-25	45	130
____	**81953**	FasTrack O-72 Remote Switch, left-hand, 14-25		140
____	**81954**	FasTrack O-72 Remote Switch, wye, 14-25		140
____	**81968**	Halloween Pacific Fright Express Caboose (std O), 14		90
____	**81969**	PRR 18" Aluminum Parlor/Coach Car, 2-pack (std O), 14-15		320
____	**81972**	B&O 18" Aluminum Baggage/Sleeper Car, 2-pack (std O), 14		320
____	**81975**	SP 18" Aluminum Sleeper/Coach Car, 2-pack (std O), 14-15		320
____	**81978**	UP 18" Aluminum Sleeper/Coach Car, 2-pack (std O), 14-15		320
____	**81981**	KCS 18" Aluminum Sleeper/Coach Car, 2-pack (std O), 14		320
____	**81984**	Postwar "1887" Christmas Flatcar with reindeer, 14		70
____	**81985**	Postwar "6428" Christmas Mail Car, 14		60
____	**81986**	Christmas Wish 1-D Tank Car, 14		60
____	**81987**	Angela Trotta Thomas "Santa's Letter" Boxcar, 14		65
____	**81988**	Angela Trotta Thomas Christmas Billboard Pack, 14		15
____	**81990**	Christmas Gondola with reindeer feed vats, 14		65
____	**81992**	Santa Claus Bobbing Head Boxcar, 14		65
____	**81993**	North Pole Central Santa Finder Searchlight Car, 14		55
____	**81999**	PRR Gondola with Christmas gifts and trees, 14		65
____	**82000**	PRR Christmas Crane Car, 14		75
____	**82001**	Merry & Bright Hot Cocoa Car, 14		70
____	**82002**	Old St. Nick Operating Billboard, 14, 16		60
____	**82003**	Christmas Blinking Water Tower, 14		35
____	**82005**	Christmas Wreath Clock Tower, 14, 16-17		43
____	**82008**	Bungalow House, 15-17		80
____	**82009**	Suburban House, 15-16		80
____	**82010**	Joe's Bait & Tackle Shop, 15-16		65
____	**82011**	Keystone Cafe, 15-16		80
____	**82012**	Single Floodlight Tower, 15-23		80
____	**82013**	Plug-Expand-Play Double Floodlight Tower, 15-25		90
____	**82014**	Postwar "192" Control Tower, 15-16		100
____	**82015**	Wind Turbine, 15-18, 24		80
____	**82016**	Oil Pump, 15-24		120
____	**82017**	Lionel Art Operating Billboard, 15-20		70
____	**82018**	Track Gang, 15-16		100
____	**82020**	Burning Switch Tower, 15-17		130
____	**82021**	Bascule Bridge, 15		450
____	**82022**	Lionel Steel Gantry Crane, CC, 15-19		400
____	**82023**	Operating Sawmill w/Sounds, CC, 15-17		350
____	**82024**	Postwar "164" Log Loader, 15		340
____	**82026**	Postwar "497" Coaling Station, 15-17		300
____	**82028**	Postwar "352" Icing Station, 15-17		150
____	**82029**	Culvert Loader, CC, 15-20		300
____	**82030**	Culvert Unloader, CC, 15-20		300
____	**82033**	MOW Trackside Crane, CC, 16-19		600
____	**82034**	Loading Station, 16		350
____	**82035**	Work House, crane sounds, 15-19		150
____	**82036**	Luxury Diner, 15-17		80
____	**82038**	8" Female Pigtail Power Cable, 15-25		11
____	**82039**	36" Male Pigtail Power Cable, 15-25		12

MODERN 1970-2025		Exc	Mint
82043	Plug-n-Play 6' 3-position Power Cable Extension, 15-25		18 ___
82045	Plug-n-Play 6' 6-position Power Cable Extension, 15-24		22 ___
82046	Plug-Expand-Play 36" Power Tap Cable, 15-25		18 ___
82047	Lionel Lines Log Dump Car, 15-16		65 ___
82048	AT&SF Ice Car, 15-17		75 ___
82049	Santa's Work Shoppe Log Dump Car, 16		65 ___
82050	Santa's Work Shoppe Sawmill, 16-20		240 ___
82051	North Pole Central Icing Station, 16-17		150 ___
82052	PFE Ice Car, 15-17		75 ___
82053	North Pole Central Icing Car, 16-17		75 ___
82054	Weyerhaeuser Log Dump Car, 15-17		65 ___
82055	Bethlehem Steel Trackside Crane, CC, 16-19		600 ___
82056	Operating Freight Station, 18-19		110 ___
82064	Halloween Operating Billboard , 15-19		80 ___
82066	PRR Log Dump Car, 15		65 ___
82067	Lionel Lines Coal Dump Car, 15-17		65 ___
82068	NS Coal Dump Car, 15		65 ___
82069	Conrail Coal Dump Car, 15-17		65 ___
82072	Philadelphia Quartz Hopper "755", 15-18		50 ___
82073	CN Ore Car, 15-17		50 ___
82074	SP 1-D Tank Car, 15-17		50 ___
82075	NYC Waffle-sided Boxcar, 15-17		50 ___
82076	Chessie System Gondola with containers, 16-18		50 ___
82077	D&H Hi-Cube Boxcar, 16		50 ___
82078	NP 1-D Tank Car, 16		50 ___
82079	UP Wood-sided Reefer, 16		50 ___
82080	C&NW 3-D Tank Car , 16-18		50 ___
82081	CSX Auto Carrier, 16-18		50 ___
82082	NS Flatcar with pipes, 16-18		50 ___
82083	Central of Georgia Gondola with cable reels, 16		50 ___
82084	Virginian Boxcar, 16-18		50 ___
82085	AT&SF Waffle-sided Boxcar, 16-17		50 ___
82086	MKT Reefer, 16		50 ___
82087	WP Depressed Flatcar with generator, 16-18		50 ___
82088	Log Pack, 15-20		10 ___
82091	PRR Tie Work Car "82091", 14-16		75 ___
82092	MOW Tie Work Car "77", 14-16		75 ___
82093	AT&SF Tie Work Car "82093", 14-16		75 ___
82094	NS Tie Work Car "51", 14-16		75 ___
82095	Amtrak Tie Work Car "67", 14-16		75 ___
82096	Lionel Steel Culvert Gondola, 15-16		65 ___
82097	Bucyrus-Erie Gantry Crane, CC, 15-19		400 ___
82098	Bucyrus-Erie Culvert Gondola, 15		65 ___
82099	Zombie Apocalypse Survivors GP38 Diesel Freight Set, LionChief, 15		415 ___
82100	Polar Express Hero Boy's Home, 16-17		90 ___
82101	Postwar "6512" Mercury Capsule Astronaut Car, 15-16		80 ___
82102	Lumberjacks, 15-16		65 ___
82103	Playground Swing, 15-16		75 ___
82104	Playground Playtime, 15-16		100 ___
82105	Tire Swing, 15-16		100 ___
82106	Pony Ride, 15-17		75 ___
82107	Tug-of-War, 15-17		65 ___

	MODERN 1970-2025		Exc	Mint
___	82108	Hobo Campfire, 15		100
___	82110	FasTrack 30" Truss Bridge, 15-25		330
___	82111	Lionel Industrial Coal 2-bay Hopper "28111", 15-17		60
___	82112	B&M Alco S2 Diesel Switcher "1260," CC, 15		650
___	82113	B&M Alco S2 Diesel Switcher "1263," CC, 15		650
___	82114	CB&Q Alco S2 Diesel Switcher "9306," CC, 15		650
___	82115	CB&Q Alco S2 Diesel Switcher "9308," CC, 15		650
___	82116	CP Alco S2 Diesel Switcher "7020," CC, 15		650
___	82117	CP Alco S2 Diesel Switcher "7024," CC, 15		650
___	82118	GM&O Alco S2 Diesel Switcher "1001," CC, 15		650
___	82119	GM&O Alco S2 Diesel Switcher "1007," CC, 15		650
___	82120	GN Alco S2 Diesel Switcher "2," CC, 15		650
___	82121	GN Alco S2 Diesel Switcher "5," CC, 15		650
___	82122	PRR Alco S2 Diesel Switcher "5648," CC, 15		650
___	82123	PRR Alco S2 Diesel Switcher "5652," CC, 15		650
___	82124	South Buffalo Alco S2 Diesel Switcher "102," CC, 15		650
___	82125	South Buffalo Alco S2 Diesel Switcher "104," CC, 15		650
___	82126	UP Alco S2 Diesel Switcher "1111," CC, 15		650
___	82127	UP Alco S2 Diesel Switcher "1138," CC, 15		650
___	82128	C&O GP30 Diesel Locomotive "3011," CC, 15		650
___	82129	C&O GP30 Diesel Locomotive "3018," CC, 15		650
___	82130	EMD Demonstrator GP30 Diesel Locomotive "1962," CC, 15		650
___	82131	TP&W GP30 Diesel Locomotive "700," CC, 15		650
___	82132	PC GP30 Diesel Locomotive "2202," CC, 15		650
___	82133	PC GP30 Diesel Locomotive "2246," CC, 15		650
___	82134	GM&O GP30 Diesel Locomotive "501," CC, 15		650
___	82135	GM&O GP30 Diesel Locomotive "521," CC, 15		650
___	82136	N&W GP30 Diesel Locomotive "522," black, CC, 15		650
___	82137	N&W GP30 Diesel Locomotive "542," blue, CC, 15		650
___	82138	MILW GP30 Diesel Locomotive "344," CC, 15		650
___	82139	MILW GP30 Diesel Locomotive "350," CC, 15		650
___	82140	Southern GP30 Diesel Locomotive "2594," CC, 15		650
___	82141	Southern GP30 Diesel Locomotive "2601," CC, 15		650
___	82142	UP GP30 Diesel Locomotive "803" CC, 15		650
___	82143	UP GP30 Diesel Locomotive "830," CC, 15		650
___	82146	Soo Line PS-1 Boxcar "45025" , 15		80
___	82147	N&W PS-1 Boxcar "44292", 15		80
___	82148	GB&W PS-1 Boxcar "777", 15		80
___	82150	Duluth, South Shore & Atlantic PS-1 Boxcar "15091", 15		80
___	82163	B&O NW2 Diesel Locomotive "9555," LionChief, 15-16		300
___	82164	BN NW2 Diesel Locomotive "546," LionChief, 15-16		300
___	82165	CB&Q NW2 Diesel Locomotive "9412A," LionChief, 15-16		300
___	82166	Southern NW2 Diesel Locomotive "2401A," LionChief, 15-16		300
___	82171	BNSF GP20 Diesel Locomotive "2050," LionChief Plus, 15-17		340
___	82172	NYC GP20 Diesel Locomotive "2102," LionChief Plus, 15-17		340
___	82173	NS GP20 Diesel Locomotive "10," LionChief Plus, 15-17		340
___	82174	NYS&W GP20 Diesel Locomotive "1800," LionChief Plus, 15-17		340
___	82175	Virginian Rectifier Locomotive "135," LionChief Plus, 15-17		340
___	82176	N&W Rectifier Locomotive "235," LionChief Plus, 15-17	105	340
___	82177	NH Rectifier Locomotive "306," LionChief Plus, 15-17		340
___	82178	Conrail Rectifier Locomotive "4605," LionChief Plus, 15-17		340
___	82179	PRR Rectifier Locomotive "4466," LionChief Plus, 15-17		340

MODERN 1970-2025		Exc	Mint	
82180	Nickel Plate 2-8-0 Consolidation Locomotive "458," CC, 15		800	____
82181	WM 2-8-0 Consolidation Locomotive "734," CC, 15		800	____
82182	MILW 2-8-0 Consolidation Locomotive "1201," CC, 15		800	____
82183	UP 2-8-0 Consolidation Locomotive "618," CC, 15		800	____
82184	PRR B6sb 0-4-0 Locomotive "1670," CC, 15		700	____
82185	D&RGW Bicentennial Gondola with canisters, 16		50	____
82186	Patriot Chemicals 1-D Tank Car "2015", 15, 18		60	____
82187	Bethlehem Steel Water Tower, 15		35	____
82188	Metro-North M7 Subway Set, LionChief, 15		350	____
82192	MTA LIRR M7 Set, LionChief, 18-19		400	____
82196	Metro-North Add-on 2-pack, 15		130	____
82199	MTA LIRR Add-on Passenger 2-pack, 18		175	____
82202	UP Big Boy Commemorative CA-4 Caboose, 15		95	____
82203	Plug-Expand-Play Remote Control Box, 15-25		30	____
82205	BNSF Golden Swoosh ES44AC Diesel Locomotive "7695," CC, 15	188	650	____
82206	N&W 2-6-6-4 Locomotive "1218," CC, 16		1000	____
82207	Iowa Interstate/Rock Island ES44AC Diesel Locomotive "513," CC, 15		650	____
82208	N&W 2-6-6-4 Locomotive "1212," CC, 16		1000	____
82209	NS ES44AC Diesel Locomotive "8056," CC, 15		650	____
82210	NS ES44AC Diesel Locomotive "8065," CC, 15		650	____
82213	KCS ES44AC Diesel Locomotive "4696," CC, 15		650	____
82214	KCS ES44AC Diesel Locomotive "4685," CC, 15		650	____
82215	AT&SF ES44AC Diesel Locomotive "440," CC, 15		650	____
82216	AT&SF ES44AC Diesel Locomotive "444," CC, 15		650	____
82218	FEC ES44AC Diesel Locomotive "802," CC, 15		650	____
82219	FEC ES44AC Diesel Locomotive "804," CC, 15		650	____
82220	SP Alco PA AA Diesel Locomotive Set "6006, 6015," CC, 15		1000	____
82223	D&RGW Alco PA AA Diesel Locomotive Set "6001, 6003," CC, 15		1000	____
82226	LV Alco PA AA Diesel Locomotive Set "601, 602," CC, 15		1000	____
82229	MP Alco PA AA Diesel Locomotive Set "8018, 8018," CC, 15		1000	____
82232	NKP Alco PA AA Diesel Locomotive Set "190, 189," CC, 15		1000	____
82235	PRR Alco PA AA Diesel Locomotive Set "5070A, 5071A," CC, 15		1000	____
82238	Southern Alco PA AA Diesel Locomotive Set "6900, 6901," CC, 15		1000	____
82241	Wabash Alco PA AA Diesel Locomotive Set "1020, 1020A," CC, 15		1000	____
82244	SP Alco PB Diesel Locomotive, CC, 15		530	____
82245	B&O 2-6-6-4 Locomotive "7620," CC, 16		1000	____
82246	D&RGW Alco PB Diesel Locomotive, CC, 15		530	____
82247	AT&SF 2-6-6-4 Locomotive "1798," CC, 16		1000	____
82248	LV Alco PB Diesel Locomotive, CC, 15		530	____
82249	Bethlehem Steel Boom Car, 15		55	____
82250	MP Alco PB Diesel Locomotive, CC, 15		530	____
82251	Zombie Animated Gondola, 15		75	____
82252	Nickel Plate Road Alco PB Diesel Locomotive, CC, 15		530	____
82253	John Deere 1-D Tank Car, 15		65	____
82254	PRR Alco PB Diesel Locomotive, CC, 15		530	____
82256	Southern Alco PB Diesel Locomotive, CC, 15		530	____
82258	Wabash Alco PB Diesel Locomotive, CC, 15		530	____
82260	PC 50' DD Boxcar "267210" (std 0), 16-17		80	____
82261	Frisco 50' DD Boxcar "7002" (std 0), 16-17		80	____

			Exc	Mint
____	**82263**	PRR Scrapyard, 15-17		130
____	**82265**	MOW Welding Car, 15-16		80
____	**82266**	CN 4-6-0 Steam Locomotive "1158," CC, 15		900
____	**82267**	C&NW 4-6-0 Steam Locomotive "1385," CC, 15		900
____	**82268**	Frisco 4-6-0 Steam Locomotive "633," CC, 15		900
____	**82269**	NP 4-6-0 Steam Locomotive "1382," CC, 15		900
____	**82270**	SP 4-6-0 Steam Locomotive "2353," CC, 15	188	900
____	**82271**	NYC 4-6-0 Steam Locomotive "1258," CC, 15		900
____	**82272**	NH 4-6-0 Steam Locomotive "816," CC, 15		900
____	**82273**	ACL 4-6-0 Steam Locomotive "1031," CC, 15		900
____	**82274**	Chessie SD40 Diesel Locomotive "7500," CC, 15		650
____	**82275**	Chessie SD40 Diesel Locomotive "7593," CC, 15		650
____	**82276**	BN SD40 Diesel Locomotive "6314," CC, 15		650
____	**82277**	BN SD40 Diesel Locomotive "6320," CC, 15		650
____	**82278**	GT SD40 Diesel Locomotive "5922," CC, 15		650
____	**82279**	GT SD40 Diesel Locomotive "5927," CC, 15		650
____	**82280**	MP SD40 Diesel Locomotive "3007," CC, 15		650
____	**82281**	MP SD40 Diesel Locomotive "3014," CC, 15		650
____	**82282**	Conrail SD40 Diesel Locomotive "6308," CC, 15		650
____	**82283**	Conrail SD40 Diesel Locomotive "6350," CC, 15		650
____	**82284**	Conrail SD40 Diesel Locomotive "6300," CC, 15		650
____	**82285**	SP SD40 Diesel Locomotive "8402," CC, 15		650
____	**82286**	SP SD40 Diesel Locomotive "8451," CC, 15		650
____	**82287**	SP Daylight SD40 Diesel Locomotive "7342," CC, 15		650
____	**82288**	Clinchfield SD40 Diesel Locomotive "3000," CC, 15		650
____	**82289**	Clinchfield SD40 Diesel Locomotive "3006," CC, 15		650
____	**82290**	AT&SF FT AA Diesel Locomotive Set, LionChief Plus, 15-17		500
____	**82293**	ACL FT AA Diesel Locomotive Set, LionChief Plus, 15-17		500
____	**82296**	Erie FT AA Diesel Locomotive Set, LionChief Plus, 15-17		500
____	**82299**	D&RGW FT AA Diesel Locomotive Set, LionChief Plus, 15-17		500
____	**82302**	AT&SF FT B Unit, LionChief Plus, 15-17		280
____	**82303**	ACL FT B Unit, LionChief Plus, 15-17		280
____	**82304**	Erie FT B Unit, LionChief Plus, 15-17		280
____	**82305**	D&RGW FT B Unit, LionChief Plus, 15-17		280
____	**82307**	PRR B6sb 0-4-0 Locomotive "5244," CC, 15		700
____	**82308**	PRR B6sb 0-4-0 Locomotive "3233," CC, 15		700
____	**82309**	PRR-Reading Seashore Lines B6sb 0-4-0 Locomotive "6096," CC, 15		700
____	**82310**	LIRR B6sb 0-4-0 Locomotive "2015," CC, 15		700
____	**82311**	Polar RR B6sb 0-4-0 Locomotive "2515," CC, 15		700
____	**82312**	UP ACF 40-ton Stock Car "48133" , 15		80
____	**82313**	GN ACF 40-ton Stock Car "55989" , 15		80
____	**82314**	MILW ACF 40-ton Stock Car "104954" , 15		80
____	**82315**	NP ACF 40-ton Stock Car "84161" , 15		80
____	**82316**	NKP ACF 40-ton Stock Car "42040" , 15		80
____	**82324**	Chessie Diesel Freight Set, LionChief, 15		400
____	**82330**	U.S.A.F. Minuteman Missile Launcher Car, CC, 15		350
____	**82331**	U.S.A.F. Missile Launch Sound Car, CC, 15		240
____	**82333**	Illuminated Hopper Shed, 15-25		45
____	**82334**	Ulysses S. Grant Presidential Boxcar, 15		70
____	**82335**	Franklin D. Roosevelt Presidential Boxcar, 15		70
____	**82340**	N&W Y6b 2-8-8-2 Steam Locomotive "2171," CC, 15		2000
____	**82341**	N&W Y6b 2-8-8-2 Steam Locomotive "2175," CC, 15		2000

MODERN 1970-2025		Exc	Mint
82342	N&W Y6b 2-8-8-2 Steam Locomotive "2195," CC, 15		2000
82343	Lionel Steel Welding Car, 15		80
82344	WM Wood Chip Hopper "2945", 15-16		65
82349	Friday the 13th Jason Voorhees Boxcar, 16		85
82394	UP Auxiliary Water Tender "907853," CC, 15		380
82395	UP Auxiliary Water Tender "907856," CC, 15		380
82396	UP Commemorative Auxiliary Water Tender "809," CC, 15		380
82410	Virginian 2-bay Hopper "13168", 15-17		60
82411	N&W 2-bay Hopper "113733", 15-17		60
82412	Reading Birney Trolley, 15, 18		100
82413	Lionel Transit Birney Trolley, 15		100
82414	CNJ 4-6-0 Camelback Locomotive "777," LionChief, 15-16		440
82415	DL&W 4-6-0 Camelback Locomotive "1035," LionChief Plus, 15-17		440
82416	LV 4-6-0 Camelback Locomotive "1602," LionChief Plus, 15-17		440
82417	Philadelphia & Reading 4-6-0 Camelback Locomotive "675," LionChief Plus, 15-17		440
82418	Erie 4-6-0 Camelback Locomotive "861," LionChief Plus, 15-17		440
82419	UP 8-door Hi-Cube Boxcar "980212", 15-16		100
82420	SP 8-door Hi-Cube Boxcar "615270", 15-16		100
82421	B&O 8-door Hi-Cube Boxcar "192021", 15-16		100
82422	PRR 8-door Hi-Cube Boxcar "110125", 15-16		100
82423	C&NW 8-door Hi-Cube Boxcar "92046", 15-16		100
82424	Chessie 8-door Hi-Cube Boxcar "492025", 15-16		100
82425	PC 8-door Hi-Cube Boxcar "295443", 15-16		100
82426	RI 8-door Hi-Cube Boxcar "532591", 15-16		100
82427	Patriot U36B Diesel Freight Set, LionChief, 15-17		360
82436	Pennsylvania Keystone GP38 Diesel Freight Set, LionChief, 15		450
82442	Five-Star General Old-Time Steam Set, LionChief, 17-18		400
82447	Sheriff & Outlaw Car, 17		80
82453	Amtrak F40PH Diesel Phase II "200," CC, 16		550
82454	Amtrak F40PH Diesel Phase II "207," CC, 16		550
82455	Amtrak F40PH Diesel Phase III "364," CC, 16		550
82456	Amtrak F40PH Diesel Phase III "388," CC, 16		550
82460	CSX F40PH Diesel "9998," CC, 16		550
82461	CSX F40PH Diesel "9999," CC, 16		550
82473	N&W Early Era Inspection Vehicle, CC, 15		200
82474	BN Early Era Inspection Vehicle, CC, 15		200
82475	Bethlehem Steel Early Era Inspection Vehicle, CC, 15		200
82476	NH Early Era Inspection Vehicle, CC, 15		200
82477	Virginian Early Era Inspection Vehicle, CC, 15		200
82478	Reading Early Era Inspection Vehicle, CC, 15		200
82486	Weathered Virginian USRA Y-3 2-8-8-2 Locomotive "737," CC, 14		1450
82487	Weathered AT&SF USRA Y-3 2-8-8-2 Locomotive "1797," CC, 14		1450
82488	Weathered N&W USRA Y-3 2-8-8-2 Locomotive "2029," CC, 14		1450
82489	MILW Olympian 18" Aluminum Passenger Car 2-pack , 14-15		320
82494	Turbo Missile Launch Flatcar, 15		60
82495	D&RGW Scrapyard, 15-19		130
82498	Polar Express Mail Car, 16-17		70
82500	Polar Express Covered Bridge, 15		70

	MODERN 1970-2025		Exc	Mint
___	**82501**	Providence & Worcester 89' Auto Carrier "190091" , 15-16		110
___	**82502**	C&NW 89' Auto Carrier "962255" , 15-16		110
___	**82503**	Chessie 89' Auto Carrier "255798" , 15-16		110
___	**82504**	TFM 89' Auto Carrier "987408", 15-16		110
___	**82505**	BNSF 89' Auto Carrier "212878" , 15-16		110
___	**82506**	UP 89' Auto Carrier "992579" , 15-16		110
___	**82508**	NYC Milk Car "6589" (std 0), 15-16		80
___	**82510**	Polar Express Aquarium Car, 16		85
___	**82512**	Polar Express Work Caboose with presents, 15		85
___	**82514**	Polar Express Reindeer Stock Car, 15		90
___	**82518**	Moon Pie Boxcar, 15		85
___	**82528**	NYC Empire State Express Steam Passenger Set, CC, 15		1950
___	**82534**	NYC J3a 4-6-4 Hudson Locomotive "5429," tender, 15		1500
___	**82535**	NYC J3a 4-6-4 Hudson Locomotive "5426," tender, 15		1500
___	**82536**	NYC J3a 4-6-4 Hudson Locomotive "5429," tender, 15		1500
___	**82537**	NYC J3a 4-6-4 Hudson Locomotive "5426," tender, 15	288	1500
___	**82543**	Postwar "943" Exploding Ammunition Dump, 15-20		50
___	**82544**	Missile Firing Range, 15-16, 19		65
___	**82545**	Santa's Helper Steam Freight Set, 16-17		238
___	**82550**	Wabash 21" Streamlined Passenger Car 4-pack , 15		600
___	**82555**	Wabash 21" Streamlined Passenger Car 2-pack , 15		300
___	**82558**	Southern 21" Streamlined Passenger Car 4-pack , 15		600
___	**82563**	Southern 21" Streamlined Passenger Car 4-pack , 15		300
___	**82566**	RI 21" Streamlined Passenger Car 4-pack , 15		600
___	**82571**	RI 21" Streamlined Passenger Car 4-pack , 15		300
___	**82574**	Texas Special 21" Streamlined Passenger Car 4-pack , 15		600
___	**82579**	Texas Special 21" Streamlined Passenger Car 4-pack , 15		300
___	**82582**	C&O 21" Streamlined Passenger Car 4-pack , 15		600
___	**82587**	C&O 21" Streamlined Passenger Car 4-pack , 15		300
___	**82590**	Amtrak 21" Passenger Car 4-pack, 16		600
___	**82595**	Amtrak 21" Passenger Car 2-pack, 16		300
___	**82598**	NYC Empire State Passenger Car Add-on 2-pack, 15		300
___	**82611**	PRR GL-a 2-bay Hopper 3-pack , 15		220
___	**82615**	B&O GL-a 2-bay Hopper 2-pack , 15		146
___	**82618**	CNJ GL-a 2-bay Hopper 2-pack , 15		146
___	**82621**	Buffalo Creek Flour PS-1 Boxcar "2366" , 15		80
___	**82622**	U.S. Army PS-1 Boxcar "26875 , 15		80
___	**82623**	West India Fruit & Steamship Co. PS-1 Boxcar "321" , 15		80
___	**82624**	Linde Air Products PS-1 Boxcar "3019" , 15		80
___	**82625**	Air Reduction Products PS-1 Boxcar "100" , 15		80
___	**82629**	PRR N5b Caboose "478883" , 15-16		95
___	**82630**	PRR N5b Caboose with trainphone antenna, 15-16		95
___	**82631**	B&M N5b Caboose "C-16" , 15-16		95
___	**82639**	MILW Milk Car "370" (std 0), 15-16, 20, 23		100
___	**82640**	UTLX 1-D Tank Car 3-pack , 15		250
___	**82644**	Philadelphia Energy Solutions 1-D Tank Car 3-pack , 15		250
___	**82648**	Midwest Ethanol Transport 1-D Tank Car 3-pack , 15		250
___	**82652**	Global Ethanol Transport 1-D Tank Car 3-pack , 15		250
___	**82656**	Conrail 60' Boxcar "216010" , 15-17		90
___	**82657**	WM 60' Boxcar "38020" , 15-17		90
___	**82658**	BN 60' Boxcar "355145" , 15-17		90
___	**82659**	RI 60' Boxcar "33825" , 15-17		90
___	**82660**	N&W 60' Boxcar "600949" , 15-17		90

MODERN 1970-2025		Exc	Mint	
82661	P&LE PS-5 Gondola and PS-4 Flatcar , 15-16		175	___
82664	B&LE PS-5 Gondola and PS-4 Flatcar , 15-16		175	___
82667	DT&I PS-5 Gondola and PS-4 Flatcar , 15-16		175	___
82670	Conrail PS-5 Gondola and PS-4 Flatcar , 15-16		175	___
82674	UP Bathtub Gondola 2-pack , 15		140	___
82677	Strasburg 3-D Tank Car , 16		656	___
82678	Angela Trotta Thomas Christmas Boxcar, 16		85	___
82683	Batman and Flash Justice League Boxcar 2-pack, 15-16		170	___
82684	Superman and Green Lantern Boxcar 2-pack, 15-16		170	___
82685	New York Giants Cooperstown Boxcar, 15		85	___
82686	Washington Senators Cooperstown Boxcar, 15		85	___
82687	Detroit Tigers Cooperstown Boxcar, 15		85	___
82688	Pittsburgh Pirates Cooperstown Boxcar, 15		85	___
82689	Operation Eagle Missile Carrying Car, 15-17		65	___
82690	Coca-Cola Anniversary Bottle Boxcar, 15		90	___
82691	Christmas Boxcar, 15		75	___
82693	Santa's Helper Crane, 15		85	___
82694	UP LionMaster 4-6-6-4 Challenger Locomotive "3985," CC , 15		1000	___
82695	UP LionMaster 4-6-6-4 Challenger Locomotive "3977," CC , 15		1000	___
82696	UP LionMaster 4-6-6-4 Challenger Locomotive "3989," CC , 15		1000	___
82697	D&RGW LionMaster 4-6-6-4 Challenger Locomotive "3803," CC , 15		1000	___
82698	WM LionMaster 4-6-6-4 Challenger Locomotive "1201," CC , 15		1000	___
82699	Angela Trotta Thomas Lionelville Christmas Boxcar, 15	38	89	___
82701	Escaping Snowmen Handcar, 15		90	___
82702	Ontario Northland PS-4 Flatcar with covered load , 15		90	___
82703	BN PS-4 Flatcar with covered load , 15		90	___
82704	D&RGW PS-4 Flatcar with covered load , 15		90	___
82705	Reading PS-4 Flatcar with covered load , 15		90	___
82706	Southern PS-4 Flatcar with covered load , 15		90	___
82708	Christmas Gingerbread Shanty, 16-19		40	___
82709	PRR Silver & Gold Ore Car 2-pack, 16-17		130	___
82710	PRR Ice Breaker Tunnel Car, 16-17		65	___
82711	Santa's Favorites Transparent Gift Car, 16		85	___
82713	Christmas Music Boxcar, 15		80	___
82716	Mickey's Holiday to Remember Freight Set, 16		400	___
82717	W. E. Disney Girder Bridge, 16-18		33	___
82718	Disney Villains Hi-Cube Boxcar 2-pack, 16-19		160	___
82721	Dumbo 75th Anniversary Boxcar, 16-17		85	___
82726	Postwar Alco FA Diesel Green Passenger Set, 17-19		550	___
82728	LCS Switch Throw Monitor, 17-25		110	___
82734	New York Yankees Cooperstown Boxcar, 15	41	85	___
82735	Polar Express Conductor Gateman, 18-24	70	133	___
82736	North Pole Central Water Tower, 15		40	___
82737	Coca-Cola Santa Boxcar, 15		85	___
82739	North Pole Central Boxcar, 16-18		80	___
82740	Winter Wonderland Aquarium Car, 15		95	___
82741	Christmas Tinsel Vat Car, 16		70	___
82742	Candy Mountain Christmas Quad Hopper, 16-17		65	___
82743	Santa's Reindeer Station Platform, 15		50	___

	MODERN 1970-2025		Exc	Mint
___	**82744**	Santa Claus Automatic Gateman, 16-17		100
___	**82745**	Christmas Cocoa Barrel Shed, 15		50
___	**82746**	Christmas Floodlight Tower, 16		75
___	**82747**	Christmas Red Arch Under Bridge, 16		30
___	**82748**	Silver Bell Casting Co. Hopper, 15		70
___	**82749**	PRR GG1 Electric "4935," CC, 16		1400
___	**82751**	PRR GG1 Electric "4913," CC, 16		1400
___	**82752**	PRR GG1 Electric "4877," CC, 16		1400
___	**82754**	PC GG1 Electric "4828," CC, 16		1400
___	**82755**	Amtrak GG1 Electric "926," CC, 16		1400
___	**82757**	CP SD90MAC Diesel "9116," CC, 16		650
___	**82758**	CP SD90MAC Diesel "9130," CC, 16		650
___	**82759**	NS SD90MAC Diesel "7230," CC, 16		650
___	**82760**	NS SD90MAC Diesel "7245," CC, 16		650
___	**82761**	UP SD90MAC Diesel "8130," CC, 16		650
___	**82762**	UP SD90MAC Diesel "8133," CC, 16		650
___	**82763**	UP SD90MAC Diesel "8025," CC, 16		650
___	**82764**	UP SD90MAC Diesel "8055," CC, 16		650
___	**82765**	Indiana SD90MAC Diesel "9003," CC, 16		650
___	**82766**	Indiana SD90MAC Diesel "9006," CC, 16		738
___	**82767**	C&O 2-6-6-6 Locomotive "1601," CC, 16		2200
___	**82768**	C&O 2-6-6-6 Locomotive "1604," CC, 16		2200
___	**82769**	C&O 2-6-6-6 Locomotive "1608," CC, 16		2200
___	**82770**	Virginian 2-6-6-6 Locomotive "906," CC, 16		2200
___	**82875**	Southern 2-8-0 Consolidation Locomotive “630,” CC, 15		800
___	**82876**	SP 2-8-0 Consolidation Locomotive “2521,” CC, 15		800
___	**82798**	DM&IR SD38 Diesel “221,” CC, 15		650
___	**82800**	EJ&E SD38 Diesel “650,” CC, 15		650
___	**82784**	BN GP9 Diesel “1706,”CC, 15		550
___	**82785**	BN GP9 Diesel “1804,”CC, 15		550
___	**82786**	Chessie System GP9 Diesel “5903,”CC, 15		550
___	**82787**	Chessie System GP9 Diesel “6240,”CC, 15		550
___	**82788**	D&RGW GP9 Diesel “5911,” CC, 15		550
___	**82789**	D&RGW GP9 Diesel “5914,” CC, 15		550
___	**82790**	NYC GP9 Diesel “5940,” CC, 15		550
___	**82791**	NYC GP9 Diesel “5948,” CC, 15		550
___	**82792**	PRR GP9 Diesel “7006,” CC, 15		550
___	**82793**	PRR GP9 Diesel “7048,” CC, 15		550
___	**82794**	Southern GP9 Diesel “6256,” CC, 15		550
___	**82795**	Southern GP9 Diesel “6257,” CC, 15		550
___	**82796**	Conrail SD38 Diesel “6935,” CC, 15		650
___	**82797**	Conrail SD38 Diesel “6953,” CC, 15		650
___	**82799**	DM&IR SD38 Diesel “223,” CC, 15		650
___	**82801**	EJ&E SD38 Diesel “654,” CC, 15		650
___	**82808**	PCI SD38 Diesel “6940,” CC, 15		650
___	**82803**	PC SD38 Diesel “6945,” CC, 15		650
___	**82804**	Reading & Northern SD38 “2000,” CC, 15		650
___	**82805**	Reading & Northern SD38 “2003,” CC, 15		650
___	**82806**	UP FEF-3 4-8-4 Northern “844,” CC, 15		1700
___	**82807**	UP FEF-3 4-8-4 Northern Greyhound “844,” CC, 15		1700
___	**82808**	UP FEF-3 4-8-4 Northern “8444,” CC, 15		1700
___	**82809**	UP FEF-3 4-8-4 Northern “838,” CC, 15		1700
___	**82810**	UP FEF-3 4-8-4 Northern Greyhound “835,” CC, 15		1700

MODERN 1970-2025		Exc	Mint
82811	Meadow River Lumber Heisler Locomotive "6," CC, 15		1300 ___
82812	Pickering Lumber Heisler Locomotive "10," CC, 15		1300 ___
82813	Cass Scenic Heisler Locomotive "6," CC, 15		1300 ___
82814	Kinzua Pine Mills Heisler Locomotive "102," CC, 15		1300 ___
82815	Mount Rainier Scenic Heisler Locomotive "91," CC, 15		1300 ___
82816	St. Regis Paper Heisler Locomotive "92," CC, 15		1300 ___
82825	CP GP38 Diesel "3019," LionChief Plus, 16-17		340 ___
82826	CSX GP38 Diesel "2145," LionChief Plus, 16-17		340 ___
82827	SP GP38 Diesel "4846," LionChief Plus, 16-18		340 ___
82828	UP GP38 Diesel "905," LionChief Plus, 16-17		340 ___
82829	B&O E7 Diesel AA Set "1422/1428," CC, 15		1000 ___
82830	CB&Q E7 Diesel AA Set "9917A/9917B," CC, 15		1000 ___
82831	GN E7 Diesel AA Set "501A/501B," CC, 15		1000 ___
82832	MILW E7 Diesel AA Set "17A/17B," CC, 15		1000 ___
82833	Pere Marquette E7 Diesel AA Set "101/102," CC, 15		1000 ___
82834	SAL E7 Diesel AA Set "3019/3020," CC, 15		1000 ___
82840	AT&SF PS-4 Flatcar with trailer (std 0), 15-16		110 ___
82841	E-L PS-4 Flatcar with trailer (std 0), 15-16		110 ___
82842	GN PS-4 Flatcar with trailer (std 0), 15-16		110 ___
82843	WM PS-4 Flatcar with trailer (std 0), 15-16		110 ___
82844	PRR PS-4 Flatcar with trailer (std 0), 15-16		110 ___
82845	B&O Truck with 40' trailer, 15-16		90 ___
82846	MILW Truck with 40' trailer, 15-17		90 ___
82847	MKT Truck with 40' trailer, 15-17		90 ___
82848	Logging Disconnect with load, 15-16		65 ___
82849	Logging Disconnect with load 2-pack, 15-16		125 ___
82850	MILW 40' Flatcar with lumber (std 0), 15-17		90 ___
82851	NP 40' Flatcar with lumber (std 0), 15-17		90 ___
82852	Meadow River 40' Flatcar with lumber (std 0), 15-17		90 ___
82853	Pickering 40' Flatcar with lumber (std 0), 15-17		90 ___
82854	PRR 40' Flatcar with lumber (std 0), 15-16		90 ___
82855	ADM Unibody Tank Car "190516" (std 0), 16		75 ___
82856	GATX Unibody Tank Car "4415" (std 0), 16		75 ___
82857	AFPX Unibody Tank Car "413303" (std 0), 16		75 ___
82858	Shell Unibody Tank Car "82858" (std 0), 16		85 ___
82859	Engelhard Unibody Tank Car "24586" (std 0), 16		75 ___
82860	PC PS-5 Gondola "557065" (std 0), 15-16		90 ___
82861	E-L PS-5 Gondola "14552" (std 0), 15-16		90 ___
82862	Frisco PS-5 Gondola "61442" (std 0), 15-16		90 ___
82863	CB&Q PS-5 Gondola "82050" (std 0), 15-16		90 ___
82864	NYC PS-5 Gondola "712603" (std 0), 15-16		90 ___
82865	PRR N5b Caboose "5017" (std 0), 16		90 ___
82866	PRR N5b Caboose "477746" (std 0), 16		90 ___
82867	PRR N5b Caboose "477625" (std 0), 16		90 ___
82868	NH N5 Caboose "C-507" (std 0), 16		90 ___
82869	IR Sensor Track 0 Gauge Tubular Compatible, 17-25		100 ___
82870	Loading Ramp, 15-20		25 ___
82872	Loader/Unloader Workers Figure Pack, 15-20		30 ___
82873	Loggers Cabin, sound, 15-16		140 ___
82874	Early Intermodal Work House, sound, 15-19		130 ___
82877	Thomas Kinkade Polar Express Boxcar, 16		85 ___
82878	Smithsonian Boxcar, 15-16		85 ___
82879	Coca-Cola Christmas Boxcar, 16-17		85 ___

		MODERN 1970-2025	Exc	Mint
___	**82883**	Legacy 360-watt PowerMaster, 15-25		240
___	**82884**	Wabash 21" Streamlined Dining Car, StationSounds, 15		300
___	**82885**	Southern 21" Streamlined Dining Car, StationSounds, 15		300
___	**82886**	RI 21" Streamlined Dining Car, StationSounds, 15		300
___	**82887**	Texas Special 21" Streamlined Dining Car, StationSounds, 15		300
___	**82888**	C&O 21" Streamlined Dining Car, StationSounds, 15		300
___	**82889**	Amtrak 21" Diner, StationSounds, 16		300
___	**82890**	NYC Empire State Express Diner, StationSounds, 15		300
___	**82906**	Pluto Walking Brakeman Car, 16-18		100
___	**82908**	Mickey's Christmas Shanty, 16-18		50
___	**82913**	Winnie the Pooh Boxcar, 16-17		85
___	**82914**	Disney Aquarium Car, 16-18		85
___	**82917**	Disney Station Platform, 17-19		55
___	**82918**	36" Power Cable Extension (3-pin, M/F), 17-25		14
___	**82921**	Evil Queen Hi-Cube Boxcar, 17-19		80
___	**82922**	Scar Hi-Cube Boxcar, 17-19		80
___	**82925**	Scrooge McDuck Mint Car, 17-18		80
___	**82942**	James Monroe Presidential Boxcar, 16, 18		70
___	**82943**	John F. Kennedy Presidential Boxcar, 16		70
___	**82944**	Herbert Hoover Presidential Boxcar, 16		70
___	**82945**	James Madison Presidential Boxcar, 16		70
___	**82947**	Wonder Woman/Green Arrow Boxcar 2-pack, 16		170
___	**82950**	Aquaman/Martian Manhunter Boxcar 2-pack, 16		170
___	**82953**	Joker/Lex Luthor Boxcar 2-pack, 16		170
___	**82954**	Lionel Christmas Boxcar, 16		65
___	**82958**	Christmas Floodlight, 17-18		75
___	**82959**	115th Anniversary 2-8-4 Berkshire Locomotive, 15		2000
___	**82960**	NYC 2-8-2 Mikado Locomotive "1548," LionChief Plus, 15-18		430
___	**82961**	UP 2-8-2 Mikado Locomotive "2537," LionChief Plus, 15-18		430
___	**82962**	Southern 2-8-2 Mikado Locomotive "4501," LionChief Plus, 15-18		430
___	**82963**	Rio Grande 2-8-2 Mikado Locomotive "1208," LionChief Plu, 15-18		430
___	**82964**	MILW 4-6-4 Hudson Locomotive "125," LionChief Plus, 15-18		430
___	**82965**	AT&SF 4-6-4 Hudson Locomotive "3450," LionChief Plus, 15-18		430
___	**82966**	DL&W 4-6-4 Hudson Locomotive "1151," LionChief Plus, 15-18		430
___	**82967**	CB&Q 4-6-4 Hudson Locomotive "3007," LionChief Plus, 15-18		430
___	**82968**	LL 4-6-2 Pacific Locomotive "462," LionChief Plus, 16-17		430
___	**82969**	WM 4-6-2 Pacific Locomotive "202," LionChief Plus, 16-18		430
___	**82970**	Reading & Northern 4-6-2 Pacific Locomotive "425," LionChief Plus, 16-17		450
___	**82971**	C&NW 4-6-2 Pacific Locomotive "600," LionChief Plus, 16-18		300
___	**82972**	Lionel Junction PRR Diesel Freight Set, 16-17		175
___	**82973**	PRR A5 0-4-0 Locomotive "3891", 16-18		450
___	**82974**	SP A5 0-4-0 Locomotive "1040", 16-18		450
___	**82975**	B&O A5 0-4-0 Locomotive "317", 16-18		450
___	**82976**	Bethlehem Steel A5 0-4-0 Locomotive "140," LionChief, 16-18		450
___	**82982**	Christmas Express Steam Freight Set, LionChief, 17-18		320
___	**82984**	NYC RS3 Diesel Freight Set, 16-17		260
___	**82992**	115th Anniversary Boxcar, 16		90
___	**82993**	Weathered UP Y-3 2-8-8-2 Steam Engine, 3595, CC, 15		1450
___	**82994**	Weathered C&O H-7 2-8-8-2 Steam Engine, 1578, CC, 15		1450
___	**82995**	Weathered UP Y-3 2-8-8-2 Steam Engine, 3671, CC, 15		1450

		Exc	Mint
82996	Weathered PRR Y-3 2-8-8-2 Steam Engine, 376, CC, 15		1450
83002	PRR Broadway Limited 21" Diner 2-pack, StationSounds, 16		450
83003	PC 21" StationSounds Diner "4552", 16		300
83006	UP 21" Excursion Diner, StationSounds, 16		300
83007	PRR Broadway Limited 21" Passenger Car 2-pack, 16		300
83010	PC 21" Passenger Car 2-pack, 16		300
83019	UP 21" Excursion Passenger Car 2-pack, 16		300
83022	PRR Broadway Limited 21" Passenger Car 4-pack, 16		600
83027	PC 21" Passenger Car 4-pack, 16		600
83042	UP 21" Excursion Passenger Car 4-pack, 16		675
83063	AT&SF Super Chief Boxcar "143093", 16-19		50
83071	LC Universal Remote, 16-23		55
83072	PRR "Keystone Special" Steam Freight Set, LionChief, 17-20		300
83080	Rio Grande 0-4-0 Switcher Freight Set, 16-17		300
83092	Steel City Switcher Freight Set, CC, 16		1300
83102	SP 21" Passenger Car 4-pack, 16		600
83107	SP 21" Passenger Car 2-pack, 16		300
83110	SP 21" Diner "290," StationSounds, 16		300
83111	American Freedom Train 21" Passenger Car 4-pack, 16-17		675
83116	American Freedom Train 21" Passenger Car 2-pack, 16-17		300
83119	American Freedom Train 21" Exhibit Car, StationSounds, 16-17		300
83120	CSX Office Car Special 21" Passenger Car 4-pack, 16-17		600
83125	CSX Office Car Special 21" Passenger Car 2-pack, 16-17		300
83128	CSX Office Car Special 21" Diner, StationSounds, 16-17		300
83147	Lighted Yard Tower, 16		60
83148	Christmas Express Boxcar, 16-17		53
83157	Smithsonian Air & Space Boxcar 2-pack, 16		170
83162	Nightmare on Elm Street Boxcar, 16		85
83163	Thomas Kinkade Christmas Boxcar, 16-17		85
83164	Frosty the Snowman 1-D Tank Car, 16-17		60
83165	PRR GG1 Electric "4899," CC, 16	375	1400
83166	PRR GG1 Electric "4800," CC, 16		1400
83167	Conrail Bicentennial GG1 Electric "4800," CC, 16		1400
83168	Iron Workers Figure Pack, 16-23		30
83169	NYC Flatcar with piggyback trailers, 16-19		75
83170	Steel Mill Structure, sound, 16-19		130
83171	MOW Workers Figure Pack, 16-22		30
83172	MOW Work Structure, sound, 16-19		130
83173	Single Signal Bridge, 16-25		90
83174	Double Signal Bridge, 16-25		120
83175	Christmas Music Boxcar, 16		80
83176	Lionel Lines Christmas Caboose, 16-17		75
83177	Angela Trotta Thomas Caboose, 16-17		80
83178	Coca-Cola Caboose, 16		75
83179	Conrail Caboose "23878", 16-19		75
83180	PRR Caboose "477100", 16-17		7
83181	AT&SF Caboose "999316", 16-17		75
83182	ACL Caboose "0634", 16-19		75
83183	Erie Caboose "C226", 16-19		75
83184	UP Caboose "25214", 16-18		75
83185	Polar Express Elves Figure Set, 16-25		33
83186	NYC Caboose "21777", 16-18		75
83190	Moon Pie 1-D Tank Car, 16-17		75

			Exc	Mint
___	**83191**	Snow Transport Christmas 1-D Tank Car, 16, 19		85
___	**83192**	Smithsonian Dinosaur Aquarium Car, 16-17		85
___	**83193**	SP GS-4 4-8-4 Locomotive "4449," CC, 16		1700
___	**83194**	SP GS-4 4-8-4 Locomotive "4449," CC, 16		1700
___	**83195**	SP GS-4 4-8-4 Locomotive "4443," CC, 16		1700
___	**83196**	SP GS-4 4-8-4 Locomotive "4444," CC, 16		1700
___	**83197**	American Freedom Train GS-4 4-8-4 Locomotive, CC, 16		1700
___	**83198**	Reading T1 4-8-4 Locomotive "2100," CC, 16		1700
___	**83199**	Reading T1 4-8-4 Locomotive "2119," CC, 16		1700
___	**83200**	Reading T1 4-8-4 Locomotive "2102," CC, 16		1700
___	**83201**	Reading T1 4-8-4 Locomotive "2124," CC, 16		1700
___	**83202**	American Freedom Train T1 4-8-4 Locomotive, CC, 16		1700
___	**83203**	Chessie T1 4-8-4 Locomotive "2101," CC, 16		1700
___	**83204**	B&O 0-8-0 Locomotive "1695," CC, 16		900
___	**83205**	GTW 0-8-0 Locomotive "8380," CC, 16		900
___	**83206**	Indiana Harbor Belt 0-8-0 Locomotive "312," CC, 16		900
___	**83208**	Wabash 0-8-0 Locomotive "1526," CC, 16		900
___	**83209**	Terminal Railroad 0-8-0 Locomotive, CC, 16		900
___	**83214**	North Pole Central 4-6-2 Locomotive "1225", 16-17		430
___	**83215**	Transformer 2-pack, 16-19		15
___	**83223**	Steel I-Beam 12-pack, 16-20		15
___	**83230**	Amtrak Metal Girder Bridge, 16-20		43
___	**83231**	Polar Express Metal Girder Bridge, 16-17		43
___	**83232**	Bethlehem Steel Metal Girder Bridge, 16-19		40
___	**83233**	CSX Metal Girder Bridge, 16-19		37
___	**83234**	John Deere Plastic Girder Bridge, 16-19		33
___	**83238**	John Deere Flatcar with spreaders, 16-17		80
___	**83239**	Polar Express Bells Mint Car, 16-17		80
___	**83240**	Shell Operating Oil Derrick, 16		120
___	**83241**	Shell Oil Storage Tank with Light, 16		85
___	**83242**	Shell 1-D Tank Car, 15-16		75
___	**83243**	Shell 3-D Tank Car, 16-17		75
___	**83244**	Shell Elevated Oil Tank, 17		100
___	**83246**	Shell Boxcar, 16		85
___	**83247**	Shell Billboard Pack, 16-17		25
___	**83248**	"It's a Boy" Boxcar, 16		90
___	**83249**	Polar Express Combination Car, 16-17		70
___	**83250**	"It's a Girl" Boxcar, 16		90
___	**83251**	Poultry Dispatch Sweep Car, 16-18		120
___	**83252**	Gold Medal Milk Car with platform, 17-19		180
___	**83253**	D&RGW Searchlight Car, 16-17		63
___	**83254**	Western Union Animated Gondola, 16-18		70
___	**83256**	GN Horse Transport , 16		80
___	**83257**	Bobbing Werewolf Boxcar, 16-17		75
___	**83258**	CP Boom Car, 16		63
___	**83266**	Lionel Junction Santa Fe Steam Freight Set, 16		175
___	**83275**	Sugar Cookie Scented Smoke Fluid, 17-25		9
___	**83276**	Peppermint Scented Smoke Fluid, 17-25		9
___	**83277**	Pine Scented Smoke Fluid, 17-24		9
___	**83278**	Hot Chocolate Scented Smoke Fluid, 17-25		9
___	**83279**	Wood Stove Scented Smoke Fluid, 17-25		9
___	**83280**	Unscented Smoke Fluid, 17-25		9
___	**83284**	Peekaboo Reindeer Operating Boxcar, 16-17	35	75

		Exc	Mint
83286	John Deere Steam Freight Set, 16-17		400
83291	Christmas Half-covered Bridge, 16-19		70
83292	Christmas Cookies & Candies Store, 16-17		85
83304	North Pole Elves Work Shanty, 16		40
83305	Illuminated Winter Covered Bridge, 16-25		100
83308	North Pole Central Tank Car "122416", 16-17		75
83311	"Santa's Favorites" Egg Nog Reefer, 16-18		65
83312	Santa's Cookies Vat Car, 16-17		70
83313	Reindeer Express Agency Flatcar with trailer, 16-17		70
83315	Christmas Toys Stock Car, 16-18		70
83316	Santa's Sleigh Aquarium Car, 16-18		80
83317	BNSF 65' Mill Gondola "518357" (std 0), 17		80
83318	C&NW 65' Mill Gondola "342036" (std 0), 17		80
83319	CSX 65' Mill Gondola "491600" (std 0), 17		80
83320	NS 65' Mill Gondola "195015" (std 0), 17		80
83321	SP 65' Mill Gondola "365117" (std 0), 17		80
83322	UP 65' Mill Gondola "96257" (std 0), 17		80
83340	Boxcar Children Boxcar, 16		85
83347	ACL USRA Double-sheathed Boxcar, 16		85
83348	B&M USRA Double-sheathed Boxcar, 16		85
83349	RI USRA Double-sheathed Boxcar, 16		85
83350	Northwestern Pacific USRA Double-sheathed Boxcar, 16		85
83351	Wabash USRA Double-sheathed Boxcar, 16		85
83352	Polar Express USRA Double-sheathed Boxcar, 16		95
83353	D&RGW Flatcar with snowplow (std 0), 16		95
83354	NYC Flatcar with snowplow (std 0), 16		95
83355	UP Flatcar with snowplow (std 0), 16		95
83356	MOW Flatcar with Snowplow (std 0), 16		95
83357	Reading NE-style Caboose "92882" (std 0), 16		90
83358	Reading NE-style Caboose "92902" (std 0), 16		90
83359	Reading & Northern NE-style Caboose "92884" (std 0), 16		90
83360	C&O NE-style Caboose "90352" (std 0), 16		90
83361	N&W NE-style Caboose "500830" (std 0), 16		90
83362	WM NE-style Caboose "1887" (std 0), 16		90
83368	EL SD45 Diesel Locomotive "3607," CC, 16		650
83369	EL SD45 Diesel Locomotive "3618," CC, 16		650
83370	EL Bicentennial SD45 Diesel Locomotive "3632," CC, 16		650
83371	GN "Hustle Muscle" SD45 Diesel Locomotive "400," CC, 16		650
83372	GN SD45 Diesel Locomotive "402," CC, 16		650
83373	GN SD45 Diesel Locomotive "407," CC, 16		650
83374	PC SD45 Diesel Locomotive "6235," CC, 16		650
83375	PC SD45 Diesel Locomotive "6237," CC, 16		650
83376	Southern SD45 Diesel Locomotive "3137," CC, 16		650
83377	Southern SD45 Diesel Locomotive "3156," CC, 16		650
83378	SP SD45 Diesel Locomotive "8801," CC, 16		650
83379	SP SD45 Diesel Locomotive "8820," CC, 16		650
83380	UP SD45 Diesel Locomotive "1," CC, 16		650
83381	UP SD45 Diesel Locomotive "21," CC, 16		650
83382	AT&SF NW2 Diesel Locomotive "2405," CC, 16		500
83383	B&M NW2 Diesel Locomotive "1200," CC, 16		500
83384	B&O NW2 Diesel Locomotive "9527," CC, 16		500
83385	CSX NW2 Diesel Locomotive "9565," CC, 16		500
83387	NYO&W NW2 Diesel Locomotive "116," CC, 16	305	500

			Exc	Mint
___	**83388**	PRR NW2 Diesel Locomotive "9171," CC, 16		500
___	**83389**	Philadelphia, Bethlehem & New England NW2 Diesel "27," CC, 16		500
___	**83390**	SP NW2 Diesel Locomotive "1423," CC, 16		500
___	**83391**	SP&S NW2 Diesel Locomotive "41," CC, 16		500
___	**83392**	Union NW2 Diesel Locomotive "555," CC, 16		500
___	**83393**	UP NW2 Diesel Locomotive "1011," CC, 16		500
___	**83395**	AC&Y H16-44 Diesel "201," CC, 16		550
___	**83396**	AC&Y H16-44 Diesel "202," CC, 16		550
___	**83397**	AT&SF H16-44 Diesel "2801," CC, 16		550
___	**83398**	AT&SF H16-44 Diesel "2807," CC, 16		550
___	**83399**	B&O H16-44 Diesel "6705," CC, 16		550
___	**83400**	B&O H16-44 Diesel "6708," CC, 16		550
___	**83401**	MILW H16-44 Diesel "402," CC, 16		550
___	**83402**	MILW H16-44 Diesel "404," CC, 16		550
___	**83403**	DL&W H16-44 Diesel "931," CC, 16		550
___	**83404**	DL&W H16-44 Diesel "934," CC, 16		550
___	**83405**	Southern H16-44 Diesel "6547," CC, 16		550
___	**83406**	Southern H16-44 Diesel "6550," CC, 16		550
___	**83420**	NS Honoring Veterans SD60E Diesel “6920,” CC, 15		650
___	**83421**	NS Go Rail SD60E Diesel “6963,” CC, 15		650
___	**83422**	NS First Responders SD60E Diesel “911,” CC, 15		650
___	**83423**	NS SD60E Diesel “6900,” CC, 15		650
___	**83424**	NS SD60E Diesel “6916,” CC, 15		650
___	**83426**	Johnstown Birney Trolley, 16		100
___	**83434**	Polar Express Passenger Station, 16-17		95
___	**83435**	World War II Pylon, 17		160
___	**83437**	Polar Express Conductor Announcement Car, 16-17, 19		110
___	**83438**	Miller Coors Operating Billboard, 17		80
___	**83440**	Rico Station Kit, 16-25		60
___	**83442**	Large Suburban House, 17-18		95
___	**83443**	Deluxe Bungalow House, 17-18		95
___	**83444**	Illuminated Station Platform, 16-17		43
___	**83445**	Smithsonian Old St. Nick Boxcar, 16-18		85
___	**83455**	Polar Express Operating Billboard, 16-17		85
___	**83462**	Bethlehem Steel Slag Car 3-pack, 16		240
___	**83466**	U.S. Steel Slag Car 3-pack (std 0), 16		240
___	**83470**	Slag Car 3-pack (std 0), 16		240
___	**83474**	Weathered Slag Car 3-pack (std 0), 16		240
___	**83478**	Bethlehem Steel Hot Metal Car 2-pack, 16		200
___	**83481**	U.S. Steel Hot Metal Car 2-pack (std 0), 16		200
___	**83484**	Hot Metal Car 2-pack (std 0), 16		200
___	**83487**	Weathered Hot Metal Car 2-pack (std 0), 16		200
___	**83490**	Lighted Concrete Coaling Tower, 15-18		180
___	**83491**	Boston Red Sox Cooperstown Boxcar, 16		85
___	**83492**	St. Louis Cardinals Cooperstown Boxcar, 16		85
___	**83493**	Philadelphia Phillies Cooperstown Boxcar, 16		85
___	**83494**	Baltimore Orioles Cooperstown Boxcar, 16		85
___	**83496**	Station Platform, 16-18, 21-25		40
___	**83497**	2016 National Train Day Boxcar, 16-17		85
___	**83503**	Thomas with remote, 16-18		120
___	**83504**	Birthday Thomas with remote, 16-18		120
___	**83510**	Thomas & Friends Passenger Set, LionChief, 16-24		250

		Exc	Mint
83511	Thomas, Sodor Locomotive, LionChief, 18-23		160
83512	Thomas & Friends Christmas Freight Set, 16-17		200
83518	PRR Boxcar "83518" (std O), 16		100
83519	REA SensorCar Steel Reefer "7844" (std O), 16, 19		130
83520	North Pole Central Flatcar with snowplow, 16		95
83527	AT&SF PS-1 Boxcar "142501," sound (std O), 16		130
83528	BAR PS-1 Boxcar "5149," sound (std O), 16		130
83529	B&O PS-1 Boxcar "467931," sound (std O), 16		130
83530	BN PS-1 Boxcar "132909," sound (std O), 16		130
83531	C&NW PS-1 Boxcar "5," sound (std O), 16		130
83532	NYC PS-1 Boxcar "175001," sound (std O), 16		130
83533	PRR PS-1 Boxcar "47005," sound (std O), 16		130
83534	UP PS-1 Boxcar "196883," sound (std O), 16		130
83535	PRR GL-a 2-bay Hopper 3-pack #1 (std O), 16		220
83539	PRR GL-a 2-bay Hopper 3-pack #2 (std O), 16		220
83544	PRR N5b Caboose "477797" (std O), 16		95
83545	PFE Reefer 3-pack (std O), 16		170
83549	AT&SF Reefer 3-pack (std O), 16		300
83553	Heisler Log Train Set, CC, 16		1450
83555	Red Logging Disconnect Caboose "1" (std O), 16		40
83556	Brown Logging Disconnect Caboose "6" (std O), 16		40
83557	Logging Disconnect Boxcar (std O), 16		40
83558	Logging Disconnect Flatcar (std O), 16		35
83559	Logging Disconnect Gondola (std O), 16		40
83560	Logging Disconnect Tank Car (std O), 16		40
83561	ATSF Express 50' DD Boxcar "1342" (std O), 16-17		80
83562	CNJ PS-1 Express Boxcar "22487" (std O), 16-17		80
83563	C&EI PS-1 Express Boxcar "2" (std O), 16-17		80
83564	GN PS-1 Express Boxcar "2538" (std O), 16-17		80
83565	KCS PS-1 Express Boxcar "400" (std O), 16-17		80
83566	SP PS-1 Express Boxcar "5712" (std O), 16-17		80
83567	T&P PS-1 Express Boxcar "1721" (std O), 16-17		80
83568	C&S Grain-door PS-1 Boxcar "1650" (std O), 16-17		80
83569	CP Grain-door PS-1 Boxcar "260293" (std O), 16-17		80
83570	GN Grain-door PS-1 Boxcar "18119" (std O), 16-17		80
83571	CGW Grain-door PS-1 Boxcar "5450" (std O), 16-17		80
83572	IC Grain-door PS-1 Boxcar "19000" (std O), 16-17		80
83573	MKT Grain-door PS-1 Boxcar "92463" (std O), 16-17		80
83574	UP CA-4 Caboose "3824" (std O), 16		90
83575	UP CA-4 Caboose "25121" (std O), 16		90
83576	B&O Milk Car "847" (std O), 16-17, 20		90
83577	Supplee Milk Car "7" (std O), 16-17, 20		90
83578	Hood Milk Car "807" (std O), 16-17, 20		90
83579	Rutland Milk Car "351" (std O), 16-17, 20		90
83580	BAR State of Maine 40' Trailer, 2-pack, 16-17		65
83581	C&NW 40' Trailer, 2-pack, 16-17		65
83582	PFE 40' Trailer, 2-pack, 16-17		65
83583	PC 40' Trailer, 2-pack, 16-17		65
83584	SP 40' Trailer, 2-pack, 16-17		65
83585	UP 40' Trailer, 2-pack, 16-17		65
83586	PRR Broadway Limited 21" Passenger Car 2-pack #2 (std O), 16		300
83589	American Freedom Train Add-On 2-pack #2, 16-17		300
83592	American Freedom Train Add-On 2-pack #3, 16-17		300

			Exc	Mint
___	**83595**	Conrail Office Car Special Diesel Passenger Set, CC, 17		1250
___	**83601**	Conrail Office Car Special Add-on 2-pack, 17		310
___	**83604**	Conrail Office Car Special 21" Dome Car "55," StationSounds , 17		320
___	**83605**	Presidents 2-8-2 Mikado Locomotive "1789," LionChief Plus, 16-17		430
___	**83606**	Halloween 2-8-2 Mikado Locomotive "1031," LionChief Plus, 16-17		430
___	**83607**	USRA 2-8-2 Mikado Locomotive "4500," LionChief Plus, 16-18		430
___	**83608**	B&O 2-8-2 Mikado Locomotive "4500," LionChief Plus, 16-17		430
___	**83609**	C&O 2-8-2 Mikado Locomotive "1067," LionChief Plus, 16-17		430
___	**83610**	MKT 2-8-2 Mikado Locomotive "851," LionChief Plus, 16-17		430
___	**83611**	NYC Empire State Express 21" Coach 4-pack #2, 17		620
___	**83616**	NYC Empire State Express 21" Combine/Observation Car 2-pack #2, 17		310
___	**83617**	NYC Empire State Express Martin Van Buren Combine, 19		155
___	**83618**	NYC Empire State Express Franklin Roosevelt Observation, 19		155
___	**83619**	NYC Empire State Express 21" Diner #2, StationSounds, 17		310
___	**83620**	Hogwarts Express Passenger Set, 16-17		400
___	**83624**	UP Sherman Hill Scout RS3 Freight Set, 16-17		500
___	**83633**	Alaska Gold Mint Car, 17		70
___	**83634**	Keystone Smoke Fluid Loader, 16-20		350
___	**83635**	North American Smoke Fluid Loader, 16-19		350
___	**83636**	2015 Contest Winning Boxcar, 15		85
___	**83637**	Mets-Phillies Mascot Aquarium Car, 16		85
___	**83644**	Macy's Dry Goods Boxcar, 15 u		100
___	**83645**	Polar Express Boxcar 2-pack, 16-18		170
___	**83648**	New York Yankees Subway Set, 16		390
___	**83653**	Scale Passenger Car Figures, 24-pack, 16-24		33
___	**83655**	Hamm's Heritage Beer Wood-sided Reefer, 16-17		80
___	**83656**	Coors Heritage Beer Wood-sided Reefer, 16-17		80
___	**83657**	Miller Heritage Beer Wood-sided Reefer, 16-17		80
___	**83658**	Lionelville School Kit, 16-17		60
___	**83659**	PRR Keystone Special Steam Freight Set, 16-17		280
___	**83688**	Trackside Railroad Details Pack, 16-25		33
___	**83689**	Angela Trotta Thomas Christmas Covered Bridge, 17-20		70
___	**83690**	Company Row House, blue, 16-17		60
___	**83691**	Company Row House, yellow, 16-17		60
___	**83692**	Company Row House, white, 16-17		60
___	**83693**	Company Row House, red, 16-17		60
___	**83694**	Toymaker Limited Trolley Set, 18		200
___	**83696**	NYC "Pacemaker" Lionel Junction Diesel Freight Set, 17		175
___	**83701**	Alaska Gold Mine 0-4-0 Steam Freight Set, LionChief, 17		320
___	**83716**	BNSF RS3 Diesel Scout Freight Set, LionChief, 17		280
___	**83733**	Lighted Aquarius Hi-Cube Boxcar, 17		90
___	**83734**	Lighted Pegasus Hi-Cube Boxcar, 17		90
___	**83745**	Lionelville Hospital Kit, 17-18		80
___	**83751**	Illuminated Yard Tower, 18-19, 22-24		65
___	**83752**	W&A Horse Car and Corral, 17-18		180
___	**83762**	Personalized Christmas Boxcar, 16		90
___	**83763**	Personalized Holiday Boxcar, 16		90
___	**83764**	Happy Birthday Boxcar, 16		90
___	**83765**	Anniversary Boxcar, 16-17		90
___	**83766**	Personalized Polar Express Baggage Car, 16-18		95

		Exc	Mint	
83779	Pearl Harbor 75th Anniversary Boxcar, 16-17		85	___
83783	Rosie the Riveter Boxcar, 17		85	___
83784	Heavies and Little Friends Boxcar, 17		85	___
83785	Doolittle Raid Boxcar, 16-17		85	___
83786	D-Day Boxcar, 17		85	___
83788	Uncle Sam "Enlist Now" Boxcar, 16-17		85	___
83790	Mickey Mouse Happy Holidays Boxcar, 17	25	85	___
83791	Donald Duck Happy Holidays Boxcar, 17		85	___
83792	Goofy Happy Holidays Boxcar, 17		85	___
83794	75th Anniversary of Bambi Boxcar, 17		80	___
83795	50th Anniversary of The Jungle Book Boxcar, 17		80	___
83796	100th Anniversary Moon Pie Boxcar, 17		85	___
83800	Happy Thanksgiving Boxcar, 17		80	___
83801	Happy Hanukkah Boxcar, 17		80	___
83802	Disney Happy Halloween Boxcar, 17		85	___
83913	Personalized Halloween Boxcar, 17		95	___
83918	Smithsonian Boxcar, John Bull, 17		85	___
83923	Angela Trotta Thomas Santa's Cookies Boxcar, 17		85	___
83924	Caddyshack Boxcar, 17		80	___
83925	Frosty the Snowman Boxcar, 17		85	___
83926	Personalized Polar Express Boxcar, 17-20		95	___
83927	Lionel Smoke Fluid 1-D Tank Car, 17		75	___
83928	Lionel Paint 1-D Tank Car, 17		75	___
83929	Lionel Hydraulic Oil 1-D Tank Car, 17		75	___
83938	Harry Potter Hogwarts House Gryffindor Boxcar, 17		80	___
83939	Harry Potter Hogwarts House Ravenclaw Boxcar, 17		80	___
83940	Harry Potter Hogwarts House Hufflepuff Boxcar, 17		80	___
83941	Harry Potter Hogwarts House Slytherin Boxcar, 17		80	___
83943	Polar Express Boxcar, 17-18		85	___
83944	John Deere Boxcar, 17		85	___
83945	Richard Nixon Presidential Boxcar, 17		70	___
83946	Jimmy Carter Presidential Boxcar, 17, 19		70	___
83947	Woodrow Wilson Presidential Boxcar, 17, 19-20		75	___
83948	William Howard Taft Presidential Boxcar, 17, 19-20		75	___
83950	Personalized "It's A Boy" Boxcar, 17-23		100	___
83951	Personalized "It's A Girl" Boxcar, 17-23		100	___
83952	Minnie Mouse Happy Holidays Boxcar, 17		85	___
83959	Macy's Parade 90th Anniversary Boxcar, 16 u		30	___
83964	Mickey Mouse Christmas Express Steam Freight Set, LionChief, 17-18		420	___
83972	Harry Potter Hogwarts Steam Passenger Set, LionChief, 17-19		420	___
83974	CSX Diesel Intermodal Set, LionChief, 17-18		460	___
83979	Mickey & Friends B337 Express Steam Freight Set, LionChief, 17, 19-20		370	___
83984	Pennsylvania Flyer 0-8-0 Steam Freight Set, LionChief, 17, 19-20		300	___
83994	C&NW Boxcar, 17		100	___
84000	DETX Rotary Gondola 4-pack (std O), 16-17, 20-23		310	___
84005	CSX Rotary Gondola 4-pack (std O), 16-17, 20-22		310	___
84010	UP Rotary Gondola 4-pack (std O), 16-17, 20-22		310	___
84015	NS Rotary Gondola 4-pack (std O), 16-17, 20-22		310	___
84020	PPLX Rotary Gondola 4-pack (std O), 16-17, 20-23		310	___
84025	PPLX Rotary Gondola 2-pack (std O), 16-17, 20-23		155	___
84028	BNSF Rotary Gondola 4-pack (std O), 16-17, 20-22		310	___

			Exc	Mint
___	**84033**	BNSF Rotary Gondola 2-pack (std O), 16-17, 20-23		155
___	**84045**	BN 21" Passenger Car 4-pack, 17		620
___	**84050**	BN 21" Coach 2-pack, 17		310
___	**84053**	BN 21" Diner, StationSounds , 17		310
___	**84063**	Weathered N&W Y6B 2-8-8-2 Locomotive "2186," CC, 16		2200
___	**84064**	MILW 4-8-4 Northern Locomotive "261," CC, 17		1700
___	**84065**	MILW 4-8-4 Northern Locomotive "265," CC, 17		1700
___	**84066**	MILW 4-8-4 Northern Locomotive "262," CC, 17		1700
___	**84067**	MILW 4-8-4 Northern Locomotive "260 Hiawatha," CC, 17		1700
___	**84068**	DL&W 4-8-4 Northern Locomotive "1661," CC, 17		1700
___	**84069**	B&M 2-6-0 Mogul Locomotive "1397," CC, 16		700
___	**84070**	CV 2-6-0 Mogul Locomotive "397," CC, 16		700
___	**84071**	DL&W 2-6-0 Mogul Locomotive "565," CC, 16	225	700
___	**84072**	Everett 2-6-0 Mogul Locomotive "11," CC, 16		700
___	**84073**	GT 2-6-0 Mogul Locomotive "713," CC, 16		700
___	**84074**	Rutland 2-6-0 Mogul Locomotive "145," CC, 16		700
___	**84075**	ACL E8 Diesel AA Set "544, 545," CC , 17		1000
___	**84078**	BN E8 Diesel AA Set "9935, 9940," CC , 17		1000
___	**84081**	Conrail E8 Diesel AA Set "4020, 4021," CC , 17		1000
___	**84084**	EMD Demonstrator E8 Diesel A Unit "950," CC, 17		650
___	**84085**	L&N E8 Diesel AA Set "796, 797," CC , 17		1000
___	**84088**	NYC E8 Diesel AA Set "4036, 4037," CC , 17		1000
___	**84091**	PRR E8 Diesel AA Set "5763, 5764," CC , 17		1000
___	**84094**	Arkansas & Missouri SD70ACe Diesel Locomotive "70," CC, 16		650
___	**84095**	Arkansas & Missouri SD70ACe Diesel Locomotive "71," CC, 16		650
___	**84096**	BNSF SD70ACe Diesel Locomotive "9372," CC, 16		650
___	**84097**	BNSF SD70ACe Diesel Locomotive "9385," CC, 16		650
___	**84098**	CN SD70ACe Diesel Locomotive "8100," CC, 16		650
___	**84099**	CN SD70ACe Diesel Locomotive "8102," CC, 16		650
___	**84100**	CSX SD70ACe Diesel Locomotive "4837," CC, 16		650
___	**84101**	CSX SD70ACe Diesel Locomotive "4843," CC, 16		650
___	**84102**	EMDX SD70ACe Diesel Locomotive "72," CC, 16		650
___	**84103**	EMDX SD70ACe Diesel Locomotive "73," CC, 16		650
___	**84104**	Montana Rail Link SD70ACe Diesel Locomotive "4309," CC, 16		650
___	**84105**	Montana Rail Link SD70ACe Diesel Locomotive "4312," CC, 16		650
___	**84106**	UP SD70ACe Diesel Locomotive "8360," CC, 16		650
___	**84107**	UP SD70ACe Diesel Locomotive "8415," CC, 16		650
___	**84108**	GN GP7 Diesel "601," LionChief Plus, 16-18		330
___	**84109**	L&N GP7 Diesel "405," LionChief Plus, 16-18		330
___	**84110**	Reading GP7 Diesel "619," LionChief Plus, 16-18		330
___	**84111**	WP GP7 Diesel "707," LionChief Plus, 16-18		330
___	**84112**	Cotton Belt 50' DD Boxcar "47509" (std O), 16-17		80
___	**84113**	D&RGW 50' DD Boxcar "63689" (std O), 16-17		80
___	**84114**	Seaboard 50' DD Boxcar "10090" (std O), 16-17		80
___	**84115**	PRR K4s 4-6-2 Pacific Locomotive "5385," CC, 16	300	1300
___	**84116**	PRR K4s 4-6-2 Pacific Locomotive "5432," CC, 16		1300
___	**84117**	Burlington Refrigerator Express 40' Steel Reefer "76060" (std O), 17		85
___	**84118**	BAR 40' Steel Reefer "7342" (std O), 17		85
___	**84119**	BN 40' Steel Reefer "70609" (std O), 17		85

MODERN 1970-2025		Exc	Mint
84120	Eastern States ERDX 40' Steel Reefer "10060" (std 0), 17		85
84121	National Car Co. 40' Steel Reefer "2430" (std 0), 17		85
84122	FGE 40' Steel Reefer "41475" (std 0), 17		85
84123	B&M PS-2CD Covered Hopper "5717" (std 0), 17		90
84124	L&N PS-2CD Covered Hopper "37399" (std 0), 17		90
84125	MILW PS-2CD Covered Hopper "98333" (std 0), 17		90
84126	NP PS-2CD Covered Hopper "75675" (std 0), 17		90
84127	AT&SF PS-2CD Covered Hopper "304713" (std 0), 17		90
84128	TLDX Demonstrator PS-2CD Covered Hopper "91" (std 0), 17, 19		90
84129	AT&SF Wide Vision Caboose "999705" (std 0), 17		95
84130	BN Freedom Train Wide Vision Caboose "12618" (std 0), 17		95
84131	BNSF Wide Vision Caboose "12584" (std 0), 17		95
84132	CSX Wide Vision Caboose "903180" (std 0), 17		95
84133	D&H Wide-Vision Caboose "35712," 18		100
84134	GN Wide-Vision Caboose "X-109," 18		100
84135	C&O Northeast Caboose "A918" (std 0), 17		90
84137	Conrail Northeast Caboose "18866" (std 0), 17		90
84138	Pere Marquette Northeast Caboose "A909" (std 0), 17		90
84139	WM Northeast Caboose circle herald "1874" (std 0), 17		90
84140	WM Northeast Caboose circus herald "1882" (std 0), 17		90
84141	WM USRA 2-bay Hopper 3-pack #1 (std 0), 17		220
84145	WM USRA 2-bay Hopper 3-pack #2 (std 0), 17		220
84149	Reading USRA 2-bay Hopper 3-pack (std 0), 17		220
84153	B&O 1905 2-bay Hopper 3-pack (std 0), 17		220
84157	Bethlehem Steel 1905 2-bay Hopper 3-pack (std 0), 17		220
84161	Logging Disconnect Stock Car, 17		40
84163	Logging Disconnect Christmas 4-pack (std 0), 17		160
84165	Logging Disconnect Dinner Train 4-pack (std 0), 17, 19		160
84166	Logging Disconnect, 1-pair, brown (std 0), 17, 19		65
84167	Logging Disconnect, 2-pair, brown (std 0), 17		125
84187	B&O 18" Heavyweight Coach 2-pack #1, 18		400
84190	B&O 18" Heavyweight Coach 2-pack #2, 18		400
84193	Reading, Blue Mountain & Northern 18" Heavyweight Coach 2-pack #1, 18		400
84196	Reading, Blue Mountain & Northern 18" Heavyweight Coach 2-pack #2, 18		400
84199	MILW 18" Heavyweight Coach 2-pack #1, 18		400
84202	MILW 18" Heavyweight Coach 2-pack #2, 18		400
84205	Nickel Plate Road 18" Heavyweight Coach 2-pack #1, 18		400
84208	Nickel Plate Road 18" Heavyweight Coach 2-pack #2, 18		400
84211	TH&B 18" Heavyweight Coach 2-pack #1, 18		400
84214	TH&B 18" Heavyweight Coach 2-pack #1, 18		400
84217	Wabash 18" Heavyweight Coach 2-pack #1, 18		400
84220	Wabash 18" Heavyweight Coach 2-pack #2, 18		400
84226	American Freedom Train Add-On 2-pack #4, 17		300
84229	Conrail 21" Theater Inspection Car "9," 17		340
84230	NS 21" Theater Inspection Car Buena Vista, 17		340
84231	CSX 21" Theater Inspection Car Alabama, 17		340
84232	UP 21" Theater Inspection Car Fox River, 17		340
84237	Cass Scenic RR 3-Truck Shay Locomotive "6," CC, 17		1500
84238	Elk River Lumber Co. 3-Truck Shay Locomotive "20," CC, 17		1500
84239	WM 3-Truck Shay Locomotive "6," CC, 17		1500
84240	West Side Lumber Co. 3-Truck Shay Locomotive "3," CC, 17		1500

	MODERN 1970-2025		Exc	Mint
____	**84248**	SP AC-9 2-8-8-4 Locomotive "3800," CC, 17	400	2000
____	**84249**	SP AC-9 2-8-8-4 Locomotive "3805," CC, 17		2000
____	**84250**	SP AC-9 Daylight 2-8-8-4 Locomotive "3811," CC, 17		2000
____	**84251**	ATSF 2-8-4 Berkshire Locomotive "4103," LionChief Plus, 17-18		450
____	**84252**	Nickel Plate Road 2-8-4 Berkshire Locomotive "767," LionChief Plus, 17-18		450
____	**84253**	Pere Marquette 2-8-4 Berkshire Locomotive "1223," LionChief Plus, 17-18		450
____	**84254**	IC 2-8-4 Berkshire Locomotive "8006," LionChief Plus, 17-18		450
____	**84255**	Lionel Lines 2-8-4 Berkshire "726," LionChief Plus, 17-18		450
____	**84256**	AT&SF SD40 Diesel "5006," CC, 17		650
____	**84257**	AT&SF SD40 Diesel "5018," CC, 17		650
____	**84258**	UP SD40 Diesel "4057," CC, 17		650
____	**84259**	UP SD40 Diesel "4062," CC, 17		650
____	**84260**	CSX SD40 Diesel "4614," CC, 17		650
____	**84261**	CSX SD40 Diesel "4621," CC, 17		650
____	**84262**	PRR SD40 Diesel "6041," CC, 17		650
____	**84263**	PRR SD40 Diesel "6089," CC, 17		650
____	**84264**	Southern SD40 Diesel "3170," CC, 17		650
____	**84265**	Southern SD40 Diesel "3200," CC, 17		650
____	**84267**	SP SD40R Diesel "7372," CC, 17		650
____	**84268**	WM SD40 Diesel "7547," CC, 17		650
____	**84269**	WM SD40 Diesel "7549," CC, 17		650
____	**84270**	B&O EMD Torpedo GP9 Diesel "3414," CC, 18		550
____	**84271**	B&O EMD Torpedo GP9 Diesel "3419," CC, 18		550
____	**84272**	C&NW EMD Torpedo GP9 Diesel "1725," CC, 18		550
____	**84273**	C&NW EMD Torpedo GP9 Diesel "1730," CC, 18		550
____	**84274**	MILW EMD Torpedo GP9 Diesel "202," CC, 18		550
____	**84275**	MILW EMD Torpedo GP9 Diesel "208," CC, 18		550
____	**84276**	Nickel Plate Road EMD Torpedo GP9 Diesel "482," CC, 18		550
____	**84277**	Nickel Plate Road EMD Torpedo GP9 Diesel "484," CC, 18		550
____	**84278**	TH&B EMD Torpedo GP9 Diesel "402," CC, 18		550
____	**84279**	TH&B EMD Torpedo GP9 Diesel "403," CC, 18		550
____	**84280**	Wabash EMD Torpedo GP9 Diesel "484," CC, 18		550
____	**84281**	Wabash EMD Torpedo GP9 Diesel "486," CC, 18		550
____	**84282**	BN GE U33C Diesel "5716," CC, 18		580
____	**84283**	BN GE U33C Diesel "5723," CC, 18		580
____	**84284**	D&H GE U33C Diesel "757," CC, 18		580
____	**84285**	D&H GE U33C Diesel "762," CC, 18		580
____	**84286**	Guilford D&H GE U33C Diesel "650," CC, 18		580
____	**84287**	Guilford D&H GE U33C Diesel "654," CC, 18		580
____	**84288**	GN GE U33C Diesel "2530," CC, 18		580
____	**84289**	GN GE U33C Diesel "2541," CC, 18		580
____	**84290**	IC GE U33C Diesel "5052," CC, 18		580
____	**84291**	IC GE U33C Diesel "5054," CC, 18		580
____	**84292**	PC GE U33C Diesel "6547," CC, 18		580
____	**84293**	PC GE U33C Diesel "6561," CC, 18		580
____	**84294**	Sacramento Trolley, 17-18		100
____	**84295**	Connecticut Trolley, 17-18		100
____	**84296**	SP Salad Bowl Express Diesel Freight Set, CC, 17		900
____	**84297**	Logging Disconnect Steel Tank Car (std O), 17		40
____	**84303**	Bucking Feed and Tack, 17		85
____	**84304**	CB&Q Gondola with covers, 17		55

		Exc	Mint
84306	Illuminated John Deere Flagpole, 17-18		60 ___
84307	Lionel Illuminated Flagpole, 17-18, 22-25		45 ___
84308	Gray Half-Covered Bridge, 17		60 ___
84309	PRR Blinking Water Tower, 17-18		45 ___
84310	Modular Train Car Repair Facility, 16-17		110 ___
84312	Alaska RR Gondola with canisters, 17, 19		55 ___
84314	BNSF ACF Covered Hopper "405850," 18		60 ___
84315	Branchline Water Tank Kit, 16-25		40 ___
84317	Passenger Station, 17		80 ___
84318	Illuminated Station Platform, 17-25		55 ___
84327	Santa Fe Operating Billboard, 17		70 ___
84328	Polar Express Steam Passenger Set, LionChief, 17-19		420 ___
84328P	Polar Express Steam Passenger Set w/Personalized Tender, 19-20		420 ___
84330	Witches Brew 1-D Tank Car, 17-18		70 ___
84332	Halloween Boxcar, SpookySounds, 17-18		80 ___
84333	Strasburg RR Gondola with vats, 17, 19		65 ___
84334	Strasburg Half-covered Bridge, 17-18		60 ___
84335	PRR Culvert Gondola "374200," 17, 19		65 ___
84336	UP Log Car, 17		65 ___
84337	MKT Wood-chip Hopper, 17		65 ___
84338	CSX Wood-chip Hopper, 17-18		65 ___
84339	SP Jumping Hobo Boxcar, 17		80 ___
84340	Santa and Snowman Operating Boxcar, 17-18		90 ___
84341	Tell-Tale Reindeer Car, 17		80 ___
84366	PRR Wood-chip Hopper, 17-19		65 ___
84367	Christmas Pylon, 17		160 ___
84369	NYC Welding Car "X939," 17		80 ___
84369	L&N Hummingbird 21" Diner w/StationSounds, 18		330 ___
84370	Polar Express Hopper with silver, 17-18		70 ___
84371	Mickey's Holiday Hopper with presents, 17-18		70 ___
84372	Christmas Station Platform, 17-18		43 ___
84373	Special Trolley Announcement Track, 18-25		60 ___
84374	Christmas Music Boxcar, 17		80 ___
84375	Christmas Boxcar, 17		65 ___
84376	Angela Trotta Thomas Signature Express Aquarium Car, 17-18		85 ___
84377	Christmas Peppermint 1-D Tank Car, 17-18		60 ___
84378	Santa's Choice Milk Car with platform, 17-18		180 ___
84380	Reading & Northern Auxiliary Tender "425-A," CC, 18		300 ___
84383	Elevated Oil Tank, 17-18		95 ___
84388	FasTrack 10" Girder Bridge, gray, 17-25		25 ___
84400	BN "Pulling for Freedom" SD60M Diesel "1991," CC, 17		650 ___
84401	BN SD60M Diesel "9200," CC, 17		650 ___
84402	BN SD60M Diesel "9225," CC, 17		650 ___
84403	Soo Line SD60M Diesel "6058," CC, 17		650 ___
84404	Soo Line SD60M Diesel "6061," CC, 17		650 ___
84405	Conrail SD60M Diesel "5504," CC, 17		650 ___
84406	Conrail SD60M Diesel "5510," CC, 17		650 ___
84407	CSX SD60M Diesel "8783," CC, 17		650 ___
84408	CSX SD60M Diesel "8784," CC, 17		650 ___
84409	NS SD60M Diesel "6808," CC, 17		760 ___
84410	NS SD60M Diesel "6815," CC, 17		650 ___
84411	UP SD60M Diesel "6165," CC, 17		650 ___

			Exc	Mint
____	**84412**	UP SD60M Diesel "6187," CC, 17		650
____	**84413**	B&O FA A-A Diesel Set, "814, 815," LionChief Plus, 17-18		500
____	**84416**	GN FA A-A Diesel Set, "278A, 278B," LionChief Plus, 17-18		500
____	**84419**	NH FA A-A Diesel Set, "417, 418," LionChief Plus, 17-18		500
____	**84422**	UP FA A-A Diesel Set, "1616, 1617," LionChief Plus, 17-18		500
____	**84433**	Polar Express 40' Scale Reefer "122517," 17		90
____	**84434**	NS 30,000-gallon 1-D Tank Car 3-pack (std 0), 16		250
____	**84438**	NS 30,000-gallon 1-D Tank Car "362785" (std 0), 16		80
____	**84439**	UTLX 30,000-gallon 1-D Tank Car 3-pack (std 0), 16		250
____	**84443**	PESX 30,000-gallon 1-D Tank Car 3-pack (std 0), 16, 19		250
____	**84447**	TILX 30,000-gallon 1-D Tank Car 3-pack (std 0), 16, 19		250
____	**84451**	PRR Flatcar 6-pack, 17		120
____	**84452**	AT&SF Flatcar 6-pack, 17-18		120
____	**84453**	UP Flatcar 6-pack, 17-18		120
____	**84454**	Trailer Train Flatcar 6-pack, 17		120
____	**84455**	Assorted Flatcar 6-pack, 17-18		120
____	**84456**	B&O Gondola 6-pack, 17-18		120
____	**84457**	UP Gondola 6-pack, 17-18		120
____	**84458**	East Assorted Gondola 6-pack, 17		120
____	**84459**	Midwest Assorted Gondola 6-pack, 17		120
____	**84460**	West Assorted Gondola 6-pack, 17-18		120
____	**84462**	2-Rail Conversion Kit, 50-ton Scale Trucks, 16-25		20
____	**84463**	2-Rail Conversion Kit, 70-ton Scale Trucks, 16-25		20
____	**84465**	B&O 2-8-2 Light Mikado Locomotive "4500," CC, 17		1300
____	**84466**	GTW 2-8-2 Light Mikado Locomotive "3734," CC, 17		1300
____	**84467**	Maine Central 2-8-2 Light Mikado Locomotive "624," CC, 17		1300
____	**84468**	NYC 2-8-2 Light Mikado Locomotive "5187," CC, 17		1300
____	**84469**	PRR 2-8-2 Light Mikado Locomotive "9630," CC, 17		1300
____	**84470**	Southern 2-8-2 Light Mikado Locomotive "4758," CC, 17		1300
____	**84471**	UP 2-8-2 Light Mikado Locomotive "2537," CC, 17		1300
____	**84472**	AT&SF 2-8-2 Mikado Locomotive, Brass Hybrid "3222," CC, 17		1300
____	**84480**	John Deere Covered Bridge, 17-18		70
____	**84481**	John Deere General Store, 17-18		85
____	**84482**	John Deere Gondola with hay bales, 17-18		75
____	**84483**	John Deere Grain Vat Car, 17		75
____	**84485**	Disney Covered Bridge, 17-18		70
____	**84486**	MILW NW2 Diesel Locomotive "1649," CC, 16		500
____	**84487**	Donald Duck Holiday 1-D Tank Car, 17		70
____	**84489**	Polar Express Covered Bridge, 17-18		70
____	**84490**	NS First Responders Diesel Freight Set, LionChief, 17-18		450
____	**84496**	Shell Service Station, 17		150
____	**84498**	NS Fire Rescue Car, 17-18		75
____	**84499**	Mickey Mouse & Friends Industrial Water Tower, 17-20		100
____	**84500**	NS Unibody 1-D Tank Car "490112," 17-18		75
____	**84507**	New York Central & Hudson River S2 Electric "3207," CC, 17		800
____	**84508**	NYC S2 Electric "113," CC, 17		800
____	**84509**	NYC S2 Electric "115," CC, 17		800
____	**84510**	PC S2 Electric "4710," CC, 17		800
____	**84511**	NYC "Lightning Stripe" S2 Electric "101," CC, 17		800
____	**84512**	S2 Electric Scale Tinplate Freight Set, CC, 17		1000
____	**84514**	Prewar 514 Tinplate Lionel Lines Refrigerator Car, 17		100
____	**84515**	Prewar 515 Tinplate Lionel Lines Hopper Car, 17		100
____	**84516**	Prewar 516 Tinplate Lionel Lines Caboose, 17		100

		Exc	Mint
84525	Uptown Apartment Building, 17		100 ___
84526	Leuzure Marble Co. Warehouse, 17		110 ___
84529	NS Veterans Wide Vision Caboose "6920" (std 0), 17-18		95 ___
84530	NS First Responders Wide Vision Caboose "9-1-1" (std 0), 17-18		95 ___
84532	Nickel Plate Road 2-8-2 Light Mikado Locomotive "587," CC, 17		1300 ___
84538	NS 65' Mill Gondola "195029" (std 0), 17		80 ___
84539	NS 65' Mill Gondola "195065" (std 0), 17		80 ___
84553	Logging Disconnect Reindeer Train 4-pack A, 17		160 ___
84554	Logging Disconnect Reindeer Train 4-pack B, 17		160 ___
84555	Logging Disconnect Santa Claus Observation (std 0), 17		45 ___
84562	BN "Pulling for Freedom" SD60M Diesel "1991," LionChief, 17		500 ___
84563	BN SD60M Diesel "9215," LionChief, 17		500 ___
84564	Soo Line SD60M Diesel "6060," LionChief, 17		500 ___
84565	Conrail SD60M Diesel "5509," LionChief, 17		500 ___
84566	CSX SD60M Diesel "8757," LionChief, 17		500 ___
84567	NS SD60M Diesel "6810," LionChief, 17		500 ___
84568	UP SD60M Diesel "6170," LionChief, 17		500 ___
84570	First Responders EMT Boxcar, 17-22		100 ___
84571	First Responders Personalized Police Boxcar, 17-23		100 ___
84572	First Responders Fire Fighter Boxcar, 17-22		100 ___
84573	Happy Birthday Boxcar, 17		90 ___
84574	Personalized 2017 Merry Christmas Boxcar, 17		90 ___
84575	U.S. Army Boxcar, 17-23		100 ___
84576	U.S. Marine Boxcar, 17-23		100 ___
84577	U.S. Air Force Boxcar, 17-23		100 ___
84578	U.S. Navy Boxcar, 17-23		100 ___
84579	U.S. Coast Guard Boxcar, 17-22		100 ___
84580	"From The Home Front" Boxcar, blue, 17-22		100 ___
84581	"From The Home Front" Boxcar, green, 17-22		100 ___
84582	BNSF 65' Mill Gondola "518375" (std 0), 17		80 ___
84583	BNSF 65' Mill Gondola "518392" (std 0), 17		80 ___
84584	C&NW 65' Mill Gondola "342045" (std 0), 17		80 ___
84585	C&NW 65' Mill Gondola "342049" (std 0), 17		80 ___
84586	CSX 65' Mill Gondola "491616" (std 0), 17		80 ___
84587	CSX 65' Mill Gondola "491638" (std 0), 17		80 ___
84590	SP 65' Mill Gondola "365136" (std 0), 17		80 ___
84591	SP 65' Mill Gondola "365142" (std 0), 17		80 ___
84592	UP 65' Mill Gondola "96267" (std 0), 17		80 ___
84593	UP 65' Mill Gondola "96281" (std 0), 17		80 ___
84599	Bucking Feed & Tack Building, 18-20		85 ___
84600	Polar Express Combination Car, 18-25		85 ___
84601	Polar Express Letters to Santa Mail Car, 18-25		85 ___
84602	Polar Express Disappearing Hobo Car, 18-25		90 ___
84603	Polar Express Hot Chocolate Car, 18-19, 22-25		85 ___
84604	Polar Express Diner, 18-25		85 ___
84605	Polar Express Baggage Car, 18-25		85 ___
84605P	Personalized Polar Express Baggage Car, 19-20		95 ___
84608	Smithsonian Boxcar, Southern "1401", 17		85 ___
84611	Lionel BlueTooth Radio Tower, 17		100 ___
84616	Wonder Woman Boxcar, 17		80 ___
84621	2017 National Lionel Train Day Boxcar, 17		85 ___

			Exc	Mint
___	**84622**	D&RGW EMD SD40T-2 Diesel "5401," CC, 17		600
___	**84623**	D&RGW EMD SD40T-2 Diesel "5405," CC, 17		600
___	**84624**	KCS EMD SD40T-2 Diesel "6102," CC, 17		600
___	**84625**	KCS EMD SD40T-2 Diesel "6110," CC, 17		600
___	**84626**	Lancaster & Chester EMD SD40T-2 Diesel "6002," CC, 17		600
___	**84627**	GECX EMD SD40T-2 Diesel "8661," CC, 17		600
___	**84628**	GECX EMD SD40T-2 Diesel "8678," CC, 17		600
___	**84629**	Ohio Central EMD SD40T-2 Diesel "4026," CC, 17		600
___	**84630**	Ohio Central EMD SD40T-2 Diesel "4027," CC, 17		600
___	**84631**	RJ Corman EMD SD40T-2 Diesel "5361," CC, 17		600
___	**84632**	RJ Corman EMD SD40T-2 Diesel "5409," CC, 17		600
___	**84633**	SP EMD SD40T-2 Diesel "8532," CC, 17		600
___	**84634**	SP EMD SD40T-2 Diesel "8548," CC, 17		600
___	**84635**	UP EMD SD40T-2 Diesel "8593," CC, 17		600
___	**84636**	UP EMD SD40T-2 Diesel "8715," CC, 17		600
___	**84637**	Cotton Belt EMD SD40T-2 Diesel "9389," Bicentennial, CC, 17		600
___	**84638**	ACL EMD E6 A-A Diesel Set "500-501," CC, 17		1000
___	**84641**	AT&SF EMD E6 A-A Diesel Set "12-13," CC, 17		1000
___	**84644**	C&NW EMD E6 A-A Diesel Set "5005A-5005B," CC, 17		1000
___	**84647**	FEC EMD E3 A-A Diesel Set "1001-1002," CC, 17		1000
___	**84650**	IC EMD E6 A-A Diesel Set "4003-4004," CC, 17		1000
___	**84653**	KCS EMD E3 A-A Diesel Set "2-3," CC, 17		1000
___	**84656**	L&N EMD E6 A-A Diesel Set "754-755," CC, 17		1000
___	**84659**	MILW EMD E6 A-A Diesel Set "15A-15B," CC, 17		1000
___	**84662**	UP EMD E6 A-A Diesel Set "996-997," CC, 17		1000
___	**84666**	Battle for Guadalcanal, 17		85
___	**84667**	Battle of the Bulge Boxcar, 17		85
___	**84668**	Silent Service Boxcar, 17		85
___	**84669**	Desert Storm Boxcar, 18, 20		90
___	**84670**	Korean War Boxcar, 18, 20		85
___	**84671**	Vietnam War Boxcar, 18, 20		85
___	**84672**	Memorial Day Boxcar, 18, 20		90
___	**84674**	AT&SF 2-8-2 Mikado , Brass Hybrid, Painted, Unlettered, CC, 17		1300
___	**84675**	AT&SF 2-8-2 Mikado Locomotive, Brass Hybrid, Unpainted, CC, 17		1300
___	**84676**	Peanuts Hilltop Boxcar, 18		90
___	**84677**	Peanuts Meadow Boxcar, 18		90
___	**84678**	Peanuts Winter Boxcar, 18		90
___	**84679**	AT&SF 4-6-2 Pacific Locomotive "1369," LionChief Plus, 17-18		450
___	**84680**	CNJ 4-6-2 Pacific Locomotive "832," LionChief Plus, 17-18		450
___	**84681**	Alton 4-6-2 Pacific Locomotive "5299," LionChief Plus, 17-18		450
___	**84682**	Southern 4-6-2 Pacific Locomotive "1401," LionChief Plus, 17-18		450
___	**84683**	MILW 4-6-2 Pacific Locomotive "810," LionChief Plus, 17-18		450
___	**84685**	Polar Express Scale 2-8-4 Berkshire Locomotive "1225," CC, 17	425	1500
___	**84686**	Nickel Plate Road 2-8-4 Berkshire Locomotive "759," CC, 17		1500
___	**84687**	Nickel Plate Road 2-8-4 Berkshire Locomotive "765," CC, 17		1500
___	**84688**	Nickel Plate Road 2-8-4 Berkshire Locomotive "767," CC, 17		1500
___	**84689**	Southern 2-8-4 Berkshire Locomotive "2716," CC, 17		1500
___	**84690**	W&LE 2-8-4 Berkshire Locomotive "6401," CC, 17		1500

MODERN 1970-2025		Exc	Mint
84691	American Railroads 2-8-4 Berkshire Locomotive "759," CC, 17		1500 ____
84692	RF&P 2-8-4 Berkshire Locomotive "752," CC, 17		1500 ____
84693	Pere Marquette 2-8-4 Berkshire Locomotive "1225," CC, 17		1500 ____
84694	Pere Marquette 2-8-4 Berkshire Locomotive "1223," CC, 17		1500 ____
84695	L&N 2-8-4 Berkshire Locomotive "1992," CC, 17		1500 ____
84696	D&H Alco RS3 Diesel "4121," LionChief Plus, 17-18		350 ____
84697	AT&SF Alco RS3 Diesel "2099," LionChief Plus, 17-18		350 ____
84698	Peabody Coal Short Line RS3 Diesel "101," LionChief Plus, 17-19		350 ____
84699	B&M Alco RS3 Diesel "1536," LionChief Plus, 17-18		350 ____
84700	Hot Wheels Diesel Freight Set, LionChief, 17-19		400 ____
84705	Hot Wheels 50th Anniversary Auto Rack, 17-18		85 ____
84706	Hot Wheels 50th Anniversary Auto Loader, 17-18		90 ____
84707	Hot Wheels 50th Anniversary Flatcar w/Piggyback Trailers, 17-18		85 ____
84708	Hot Wheels Auto Rack, 18		85 ____
84709	NH RS3 Diesel Freight Set, LionChief, 18		300 ____
84719	AT&SF Super Chief Diesel Passenger Set, LionChief, 18-22		500 ____
84724	ATSF Add-on Baggage Car "1386," 18-25		100 ____
84725	ATSF Add-on Vista Dome Car "500," 18-25		100 ____
84726	SP Rising Sun 0-8-0 Steam Freight Set, LionChief, 17-18		320 ____
84732	BNSF Tier 4 Modern Freight Set, LionChief, 18-20		400 ____
84737	Construction Railroad Diesel Freight Set, LionChief, 18-19		350 ____
84747	18 Christmas Boxcar, 18		65 ____
84748	Christmas Music Boxcar #18, 18		80 ____
84754	Anheuser-Busch Clydesdale Old-Time Steam Freight Set, 18-19		420 ____
84760	Daisy Duck 1-D Tank Car, 18-20		75 ____
84761	Chip 'n' Dale Chasing Gondola, 18-20		80 ____
84762	SP Daylight 1-D Tank Car, 17-19		60 ____
84763	Disney Villains Ursula Hi-Cube Boxcar, 18, 20		80 ____
84764	Disney Villains Queen of Hearts Hi-Cube Boxcar, 18, 20		80 ____
84765	Angela Trotta Thomas Christmas Passenger Car 2-pack, 18, 20		300 ____
84766	Gondola w/Construction Signs, 18-19		65 ____
84767	Harry Potter Dementors Coach w/Sound, 18-25		95 ____
84768	Moe & Joe Lumber Flatcar, 18-19		90 ____
84769	Wile E. Coyote & Road Runner Ambush Shack, 18-19		120 ____
84770	Peabody Coal Hopper 6-pack, 18-20		150 ____
84771	PRR Hopper 6-pack, 18-19		150 ____
84772	N&W Hopper 6-pack, 18-20		150 ____
84773	UP Hopper 6-pack, 18-20		150 ____
84774	NS Hopper 6-pack, 18-20		150 ____
84775	DM&IR Ore Car 6-pack, 18-19		150 ____
84776	C&NW Ore Car 6-pack, 18-20		150 ____
84777	GN Ore Car 6-pack, 18-20		150 ____
84778	MILW Ore Car 6-pack, 18-19		150 ____
84779	B&LE Ore Car 6-pack, 18-20		150 ____
84780	U.S. Caboose, 18		75 ____
84781	ELX Halloween Caboose, 18-20		75 ____
84782	Presidential Caboose, 18-20		75 ____
84784	John Deere Harvest Dump Car, 18-19		80 ____
84785	Naughty or Nice Ore Car 2-pack, 18		80 ____

MODERN 1970-2025			Exc	Mint
___	84786	Christmas Essentials Barrel Car, 18-19		70
___	84787	Santa Freight Lines Steam Set, LionChief, 18-19		300
___	84792	House Under Construction, 18-19		100
___	84794	Budweiser Bar & Grille, 18		90
___	84795	Deluxe Christmas House, 18, 20		130
___	84797	Christmas Industrial Water Tower, 18, 20		85
___	84798	Hunting Rabbit Car, 18-19		85
___	84799	Marvin the Martian Earth Stomper Flatcar, 18-19		95
___	84801	Justice League Boxcar, 17		85
___	84802	Gibson Wine 1-D Tank Car "66719," 17		75
___	84803	Tidewater 1-D Tank Car "1367," 17		75
___	84804	A.E. Staley 1-D Tank Car "704," 17		75
___	84805	Mid-Continent Petroleum 1-D Tank Car "1018," 17		75
___	84806	Shell 1-D Tank Car "662," 17		75
___	84807	John Deere 1-D Tank Car "236," 17		75
___	84810	Polar Express 1-D Tank Car "122518," 17		75
___	84811	Polar Express Scale Baggage Car, 17, 24	100	213
___	84812	Polar Express Scale Combine, 17, 24		200
___	84813	Polar Express Scale Coach, 17, 24	100	213
___	84814	Polar Express Scale Diner, 17, 24	100	213
___	84815	Polar Express Scale Observation, 17		200
___	84816	PRR 1930 Broadway Limited Steam Passenger Set, CC, 17		2000
___	84821	PRR Heavyweight Combine Liberty Hill, 17-18		200
___	84822	PRR Heavyweight Sleeper Cent Fawn, 17-18		200
___	84823	PRR Heavyweight Sleeper Central Park, 17-18		200
___	84824	PRR Heavyweight Sleeper Lafayette Square, 17-18		200
___	84825	PRR Heavyweight Diner "4498," 17-18		200
___	84826	PRR Heavyweight Observation Colonel Lindbergh, 17-18		200
___	84827	PRR Heavyweight Observation Washington Circle, 17-18		200
___	84828	BNSF 66' Mill Gondola "518726," w/Graffiti, 17		80
___	84829	BNSF 66' Mill Gondola "518770," 17		80
___	84830	BNSF 66' Mill Gondola "518795," 17		80
___	84831	GNTX Railgon 66' Mill Gondola "290146," w/Graffiti, 17		80
___	84832	GNTX Railgon 66' Mill Gondola "290087," 17		80
___	84833	GNTX Railgon 66' Mill Gondola "290102," 17		80
___	84834	Atlantic & Western 66' Mill Gondola "400704," w/Graffiti, 17		80
___	84835	Atlantic & Western 66' Mill Gondola "400664," 17		80
___	84836	Atlantic & Western 66' Mill Gondola "400675," 17		80
___	84837	Arkansas & Oklahoma 66' Mill Gondola "35018," w/Graffiti, 17		80
___	84838	Arkansas & Oklahoma 66' Mill Gondola "35007," 17		80
___	84839	Arkansas & Oklahoma 66' Mill Gondola "35055," 17		80
___	84840	Steelton & Highspire 66' Mill Gondola "125," w/Graffiti, 17		80
___	84841	Steelton & Highspire 66' Mill Gondola "117," 17		80
___	84842	Steelton & Highspire 66' Mill Gondola "118," 17		80
___	84843	Demonstrator GE AC6000 Diesel "6000," CC, 17		650
___	84844	Demonstrator GE AC6000 Diesel "6001," CC, 17		650
___	84845	Demonstrator GE AC6000 Diesel "6002," CC, 17		650
___	84846	CSX GE AC6000 Diesel "691," CC, 17		650
___	84847	CSX GE AC6000 Diesel "5014," CC, 17		650
___	84848	CSX GE AC6000 Diesel "Diversity 5000," CC, 17		650
___	84849	CSX GE AC6000 Diesel "Diversity 5001," CC, 17		650
___	84850	SP GE AC6000 Diesel "601," CC, 17		650

		Exc	Mint
84851	SP GE AC6000 Diesel "602," CC, 17		650
84852	UP GE AC6000 Diesel "7566," CC, 17		650
84853	UP GE AC6000 Diesel "7579," CC, 17		650
84854	TTX Husky Double-Stack Car "56210," w/Trailers, 17		130
84855	TTX Husky Double-Stack Car "56289," w/Trailers, 17		130
84856	TTX Husky Double-Stack Car "56368," w/Trailers, 17		130
84857	TTX Husky Double-Stack Car "56150," w/Trailers, 17		130
84858	TTX Husky Double-Stack Car "56168," w/Trailers, 17		130
84859	TTX Husky Double-Stack Car "56174," w/Trailers, 17		130
84860	BNSF Husky Double-Stack Car "203003," w/Trailers, 17		130
84861	BNSF Husky Double-Stack Car "203015," w/Trailers, 17		130
84862	BNSF Husky Double-Stack Car "203032," w/Trailers, 17		130
84863	ARZC Husky Double-Stack Car "100000," w/Trailers, 17		130
84864	ARZC Husky Double-Stack Car "100002," w/Trailers, 17		130
84865	ARZC Husky Double-Stack Car "100005," w/Trailers, 17		130
84866	Southwind Husky Double-Stack Car "5003," w/Trailers, 17		130
84867	Southwind Husky Double-Stack Car "5005," w/Trailers, 17		130
84868	Southwind Husky Double-Stack Car "5008," w/Trailers, 17		130
84869	Hot Wheels Boxcar, 18		85
84870	NP 50' Flatcar "65110" w/NPT 40' Trailer, 17		120
84871	NP 50' Flatcar "65126" w/NPT 40' Trailer, 17		120
84872	PRR 50' Flatcar "469615" w/PRRZ 40' Trailer, 17		120
84873	PRR 50' Flatcar "469675" w/PRRZ 40' Trailer, 17		120
84874	Trailer Train 50' Flatcar "475227" w/SOUZ 40' Trailer, 17		120
84875	Trailer Train 50' Flatcar "475274" w/SOUZ 40' Trailer, 17		120
84876	UP 50' Flatcar "53017" w/UPZ 40' Trailer, 17		120
84877	UP 50' Flatcar "53022" w/UPZ 40' Trailer, 17		120
84878	Wabash 50' Flatcar "25535" w/WABZ 40' Trailer, 17		120
84879	Wabash 50' Flatcar "25549" w/WABZ 40' Trailer, 17		120
84880	D&RGW 50' Flatcar "21032" w/RGMW 40' Trailer, 17		120
84881	D&RGW 50' Flatcar "21036" w/RGMW 40' Trailer, 17		120
84882	C&O 40' Trailer 2-pack, 17		65
84883	GM&O 40' Trailer 2-pack, 17		65
84884	L&N 40' Trailer 2-pack, 17		65
84885	SAL 40' Trailer 2-pack, 17		65
84886	Frisco 40' Trailer 2-pack, 17		65
84887	WP 40' Trailer 2-pack, 17		65
84888	PRR X31 Boxcar "78401," w/Circle Keystone, 17		120
84889	PRR X31 Boxcar "78498," w/Circle Keystone, 17		80
84890	PRR X31 Boxcar "68408," w/Shadow Keystone, 17		80
84891	PRR X31 Boxcar "77061," w/Shadow Keystone, 17		80
84892	PRR X31 Boxcar "76803," w/Plain Keystone, 17		80
84893	PRR X31 Boxcar "77734," w/Plain Keystone, 17		80
84894	PRR X31 Boxcar "497310," w/Stores, 17		80
84895	PRR X31 Boxcar "497329," w/Stores, 17		80
84896	N&W X31 Boxcar "46146," 17		80
84897	N&W X31 Boxcar "46340," 17		80
84898	Personalized Man's Best Friend Boxcar, 18-23		100
84899	Personalized World's Best Cat Boxcar, 18-22		100
84904	BNSF Scale Autorack, Orange "965375," 18		120
84905	BNSF Scale Autorack, Orange "965530," 18		120
84906	Ferromex Scale Autorack "705473," 18		120
84907	Ferromex Scale Autorack "953615," 18		120

			Exc	Mint
____	**84908**	Southern Scale Autorack "159162," 18		120
____	**84909**	Southern Scale Autorack "159166," 18		120
____	**84910**	CSX Scale Autorack "156256," 18		120
____	**84911**	CSX Scale Autorack "973924," 18		120
____	**84912**	NS Scale Autorack "983818," 18		120
____	**84913**	NS Scale Autorack "992879," 18		120
____	**84914**	MKT Scale Autorack "254176," 18		120
____	**84915**	MKT Scale Autorack "942194," 18		120
____	**84916**	Union Tank Car Cylindrical Covered Hopper "44072," 18-19		90
____	**84917**	Union Tank Car Cylindrical Covered Hopper "44094," 18-19		90
____	**84918**	Davis Industries Cylindrical Covered Hopper "1002," 18-19		90
____	**84919**	Davis Industries Cylindrical Covered Hopper "1003," 18-19		90
____	**84920**	Conrail Cylindrical Covered Hopper "884244," 18-19		90
____	**84921**	Conrail Cylindrical Covered Hopper "884270," 18-19		90
____	**84922**	CSX Cylindrical Covered Hopper "225370," 18-19		90
____	**84923**	CSX Cylindrical Covered Hopper "225382," 18-19		90
____	**84924**	Wilkes-Barre Mining Cylindrical Covered Hopper "104," 18		90
____	**84925**	Wilkes-Barre Mining Cylindrical Covered Hopper "106," 18		90
____	**84926**	SP Cylindrical Covered Hopper "1002," 18		90
____	**84927**	SP Cylindrical Covered Hopper "1027," 18		90
____	**84928**	John Quincy Adams Presidential Boxcar, 18		70
____	**84929**	James K. Polk Presidential Boxcar, 18		70
____	**84930**	Benjamin Harrison Presidential Boxcar, 18		70
____	**84934**	NYC 4-6-4 Hudson Locomotive "5425," LionChief Plus, 17-18		450
____	**84935**	B&A 4-6-4 Hudson Locomotive "616," LionChief Plus, 17-18		450
____	**84936**	Nickel Plate 4-6-4 Hudson "170," LionChief Plus, 17-18		450
____	**84937**	GN 4-6-4 Hudson Locomotive "171," LionChief Plus, 17-18		450
____	**84938**	AT&SF EMD GP38 Diesel "3441," LionChief Plus, 17-18		350
____	**84939**	NS First Responders GP38 "5642," LionChief Plus, 17-18		350
____	**84940**	Seaboard System EMD GP38 Diesel "543," LionChief Plus, 17-18		350
____	**84941**	FEC EMD GP38 Diesel "506," LionChief Plus, 17-18		350
____	**84942**	PRR 4-4-2 Atlantic Locomotive "460," CC, 17		800
____	**84943**	PRR 4-4-2 Atlantic Locomotive "68," CC, 17		800
____	**84944**	PRR 4-4-2 Atlantic Locomotive "1163," CC, 17		800
____	**84945**	PRSL 4-4-2 Atlantic Locomotive "6009," CC, 17		800
____	**84946**	LIRR 4-4-2 Atlantic Locomotive "1611," CC, 17		800
____	**84947**	GN 4-4-2 Atlantic Locomotive "1707," CC, 17		800
____	**84948**	PRR 2-8-0 Consolidation Locomotive "1288," CC, 18		750
____	**84949**	PRSL 2-8-0 Consolidation Locomotive "8072," CC, 18		750
____	**84950**	LIRR 2-8-0 Consolidation Locomotive "109," CC, 18		750
____	**84951**	Bellefonte Central 2-8-0 Consolidation Locomotive "21," CC, 18		750
____	**84952**	PRR 2-8-0 Consolidation Locomotive "3529," Weathered, CC, 18		750
____	**84953**	Pennsylvania Coal Hauler Steam Freight Set, CC, 18		1100
____	**84964**	Angela Trotta Thomas 4-6-4 Hudson Locomotive, LionChief Plus, 18		450
____	**84965**	Rio Grande A5 0-4-0 Locomotive "62," LionChief Plus, 18		480
____	**84966**	NYC A5 0-4-0 Locomotive "1662," LionChief Plus, 18		480
____	**84967**	PRR A5 0-4-0 Locomotive "577," LionChief Plus, 18		480
____	**84968**	UP A5 0-4-0 Locomotive "218," LionChief Plus, 18		480
____	**84985**	LIRR B60 Baggage Car "7715," 17-18		160
____	**84986**	LIRR B60 Baggage Car "7724," 17-18		160

		Exc	Mint
84987	PRR B60 Baggage Car, Clerestory "7918," 17-18		160 ___
84988	PRR B60 Baggage Car, Clerestory "7941," 17-18		160 ___
84989	PRR B60 Baggage Car, Round Roof "7919," 17-18		160 ___
84990	PRR B60 Baggage Car, Round Roof "7938," 17-18		160 ___
84991	PRR B60 Baggage Car, Round Roof, Messenger "9352," 17-18		160 ___
84992	PRR B60 Baggage Car, Round Roof, Messenger "9379," 17-18		160 ___
84993	PRR B60 Baggage Car, Round Roof, 1960s "9356," 17-18		160 ___
84994	PRR B60 Baggage Car, Round Roof, 1960s "9384," 17-18		160 ___
84995	PRSL Baggage Car "5437," 17-18		160 ___
84996	PRSL B60 Baggage Car "6403," 17-18		160 ___
84997	LIRR 18" Heavyweight Passenger Coach 2-pack, #1, 17-18		400 ___
85000	LIRR 18" Heavyweight Passenger Coach 2-pack, #2, 17-18		400 ___
85003	PRSL 18" Heavyweight Passenger Coach 2-pack, #1, 17-18		400 ___
85006	PRSL 18" Heavyweight Passenger Coach 2-pack, #2, 17-18		400 ___
85009	PRR 18" Heavyweight Passenger Coach 2-pack, #1, 17-18		400 ___
85012	PRR 18" Heavyweight Passenger Coach 2-pack, #2, 17-18		400 ___
85015	ACL/PRR Champion Passenger Car 4-pack, 17-18		620 ___
85016	ACL/PRR Champion Passenger Car 2-pack, 17-18		310 ___
85017	ACL Champion 21" Diner, w/StationSounds, 17-18		310 ___
85018	ACL EMD SW7 Diesel "648," CC, 18		500 ___
85019	BN EMD SW7 Diesel "111," CC, 18		500 ___
85020	Conemaugh & Black Lick EMD SW7 Diesel "106," CC, 18		500 ___
85021	Chessie System EMD SW7 Diesel "5224," CC, 18		500 ___
85022	LV EMD SW7 Diesel "222," CC, 18		500 ___
85023	MEC EMD SW7 Diesel "331," CC, 18		500 ___
85024	NYC EMD SW7 Diesel "8853," CC, 18		500 ___
85025	Frisco EMD SW7 Diesel "303," CC, 18		500 ___
85026	Southern EMD SW7 Diesel "1100," CC, 18		500 ___
85027	UP EMD SW7 Diesel "1808," CC, 18		500 ___
85028	AT&SF EMD SD45 Diesel "5305," CC, 18		600 ___
85029	AT&SF EMD SD45 Diesel "5319," CC, 18		600 ___
85030	B&P EMD SD45 Diesel "453," CC, 18		600 ___
85031	B&P EMD SD45 Diesel "455," CC, 18		600 ___
85032	C&NW EMD SD45 Diesel "6485," CC, 18		600 ___
85033	C&NW EMD SD45 Diesel "6568," CC, 18		600 ___
85034	Montana Rail Link EMD SD45 Diesel "320," CC, 18		600 ___
85035	Montana Rail Link EMD SD45 Diesel "331," CC, 18		600 ___
85036	MPI EMD SD45 Diesel "9009," CC, 18		600 ___
85037	MPI EMD SD45 Diesel "9011," CC, 18		600 ___
85038	N&W EMD SD45 Diesel "1776," CC, 18		600 ___
85039	N&W EMD SD45 Diesel "1790," CC, 18		600 ___
85040	NYS&W EMD SD45 Diesel "3612," CC, 18		600 ___
85041	NYS&W EMD SD45 Diesel "3614," CC, 18		600 ___
85042	WC EMD SD45 Diesel "6525," CC, 18		600 ___
85043	WC EMD SD45 Diesel "6580," CC, 18		600 ___
85046	BNSF EMD SD70ACe Diesel "9214," CC, 18		600 ___
85047	BNSF EMD SD70ACe Diesel "9287," CC, 18		600 ___
85048	CN EMD SD70ACe Diesel "8101," CC, 18		600 ___
85049	CN EMD SD70ACe Diesel "8103," CC, 18		600 ___
85050	CSX EMD SD70ACe Diesel "4849," CC, 18		600 ___
85051	Demonstrator EMD SD70ACe Diesel "1201," CC, 18		600 ___
85052	Demonstrator EMD SD70ACe Diesel "1202," CC, 18		600 ___

			Exc	Mint
____	**85053**	KCS EMD SD70ACe Diesel "4156," CC, 18		600
____	**85054**	KCS EMD SD70ACe Diesel "4164," CC, 18		600
____	**85055**	NS EMD SD70ACe Diesel "1030," CC, 18		600
____	**85056**	NS EMD SD70ACe Diesel "1111," CC, 18		600
____	**85057**	UP EMD SD70ACe Diesel "8650," CC, 18		600
____	**85058**	UP EMD SD70ACe Diesel "8665," CC, 18		600
____	**85059**	MKT EMD NW2 Diesel "7," LionChief Plus, 18		320
____	**85060**	PRR EMD NW2 Diesel "9172," LionChief Plus, 18		320
____	**85061**	Nickel Plate Road EMD NW2 Diesel "13," LionChief Plus, 18		320
____	**85062**	UP EMD NW2 Diesel "1037," LionChief Plus, 18		320
____	**85063**	MILW EMD NW2 Diesel "1649," LionChief Plus, 18		320
____	**85065**	Hot Wheels 50th Anniversary Boxcar, 17-18		85
____	**85066**	TTX Husky Double-Stack Car "56210," w/EOT Device, 17		150
____	**85067**	TTX Husky Double-Stack Car "56180," w/EOT Device, 17		150
____	**85068**	BNSF Husky Double-Stack Car "203054," w/EOT Device, 17		150
____	**85069**	ARZC Husky Double-Stack Car "100008," w/EOT Device, 17		150
____	**85070**	Southwind Husky Double-Stack Car "5009," w/EOT Device, 17		150
____	**85071**	AT&SF Wide-Vision Caboose w/Camera "999718," 18		125
____	**85072**	BN Wide-Vision Caboose w/Camera "12345," 18		125
____	**85073**	Chessie System Wide-Vision Caboose w/Camera "903118," 18		125
____	**85074**	CSX Wide-Vision Caboose w/Camera "903282," 18		125
____	**85075**	Reading Wide-Vision Caboose w/Camera "94116," 18		125
____	**85076**	UP Wide-Vision Caboose w/Camera "13605," 18		125
____	**85077**	NS Wide-Vision Caboose w/Camera "555059," 18		125
____	**85078**	PRR Wide-Vision Caboose w/Camera "477900," 18		125
____	**85079**	DODX Wide-Vision Caboose "902," 18		100
____	**85080**	Montana Rail Link Wide-Vision Caboose "1005," 18		100
____	**85081**	UTLX 30,000-Gallon 1-D Tank Car "212189" w/ FreightSounds, 18		150
____	**85082**	GATX 30,000-Gallon 1-D Tank Car "36323" w/ FreightSounds, 18		150
____	**85083**	Philadelphia Energy Solutions 30,000-Gallon 1-D Tank Car "0756" w/FreightSounds, 18		150
____	**85084**	TILX 30,000-Gallon 1-D Tank Car "254088" w/ FreightSounds, 18		150
____	**85085**	ADM 30,000-Gallon 1-D Tank Car "29248" w/ FreightSounds, 18		150
____	**85086**	Cargill 30,000-Gallon 1-D Tank Car "7964" w/ FreightSounds, 18		150
____	**85087**	UTLX 30,000-Gallon 1-D Tank Car "212187" w/EOT Device, 18		150
____	**85088**	GATX 30,000-Gallon 1-D Tank Car "36328" w/EOT Device, 18		120
____	**85089**	ADM 30,000-Gallon 1-D Tank Car "29252" w/EOT Device, 18		120
____	**85090**	Cargill 30,000-Gallon 1-D Tank Car "7968" w/EOT Device, 18		120
____	**85091**	ACFX 30,000-Gallon 1-D Tank Car "89990" w/EOT Device, 18		120
____	**85092**	Procor 30,000-Gallon 1-D Tank Car "43579" w/EOT Device, 18		120
____	**85093**	American Potash PS-2 Covered Hopper "31259," 17		75
____	**85094**	American Potash PS-2 Covered Hopper "31275," 17		75
____	**85095**	Bucyrus Erie PS-2 Covered Hopper "1114," 17		75
____	**85096**	Bucyrus Erie PS-2 Covered Hopper "1118," 17		75

		Exc	Mint	
85097	Georgia Marble PS-2 Covered Hopper "31340," 17		75	___
85098	Georgia Marble PS-2 Covered Hopper "31341," 17		75	___
85099	Ready Mixed Concrete PS-2 Covered Hopper "331," 17		75	___
85100	Ready Mixed Concrete PS-2 Covered Hopper "340," 17		75	___
85101	Linde PS-2 Covered Hopper "209," 17		75	___
85102	Linde PS-2 Covered Hopper "211," 17		75	___
85103	U.S. Borax PS-2 Covered Hopper "31064," 17		75	___
85104	U.S. Borax PS-2 Covered Hopper "31066," 17	35	75	___
85105	Tank Train 2-Pack with EOT Device, #1, 17		200	___
85108	Tank Train 2-Pack with EOT Device, #2, 17		200	___
85111	Tank Train 2-Pack with EOT Device, #3, 17		200	___
85114	GATX Tank Train 2-Pack with EOT Device, 17		200	___
85117	CN Tank Train 2-Pack with EOT Device, 17		200	___
85120	Cibro Tank Train 2-Pack with EOT Device, 17		200	___
85126	Tank Train Car #1, 17		90	___
85127	Tank Train Car #2, 17		90	___
85128	Tank Train Car #3, 17		90	___
85129	Tank Train Car #4, 17		90	___
85130	Tank Train Car #5, 17		88	___
85131	Tank Train Car #6, 17		90	___
85132	Tank Train Car #1, 17		90	___
85133	Tank Train Car #2, 17		90	___
85134	Tank Train Car #3, 17		90	___
85135	Tank Train Car #4, 17		90	___
85136	Tank Train Car #5, 17		90	___
85137	Tank Train Car #6, 17		90	___
85138	Tank Train Car #1, 17		90	___
85139	Tank Train Car #2, 17		90	___
85140	Tank Train Car #3, 17		90	___
85141	Tank Train Car #4, 17		93	___
85142	Tank Train Car #5, 17		90	___
85143	Tank Train Car #6, 17		90	___
85144	GATX Tank Train Car #1, 17		90	___
85145	GATX Tank Train Car #2, 17	35	90	___
85146	GATX Tank Train Car #3, 17		90	___
85147	GATX Tank Train Car #4, 17		90	___
85148	GATX Tank Train Car #5, 17	35	90	___
85149	GATX Tank Train Car #6, 17		90	___
85150	CN Tank Train Car #1, 17		90	___
85151	CN Tank Train Car #2, 17		90	___
85152	CN Tank Train Car #3, 17		90	___
85153	CN Tank Train Car #4, 17		90	___
85154	CN Tank Train Car #5, 17		90	___
85155	CN Tank Train Car #6, 17		90	___
85156	Cibro Tank Train Car #1, 17		90	___
85157	Cibro Tank Train Car #2, 17		90	___
85158	Cibro Tank Train Car #3, 17		90	___
85159	Cibro Tank Train Car #4, 17	35	90	___
85160	Cibro Tank Train Car #5, 17	35	90	___
85161	Cibro Tank Train Car #6, 17		90	___
85168	Tacoma Rail EMD SD70ACe Diesel "7001," CC, 18		600	___
85169	Tacoma Rail EMD SD70ACe Diesel "7002" CC, 18		600	___

MODERN 1970-2025			Exc	Mint
___	**85170**	Atlanta & West Point USRA 4-6-2 Pacific Locomotive "290," CC, 18		1400
___	**85171**	B&O USRA 4-6-2 Pacific Locomotive "5300," CC, 18		1400
___	**85172**	Reading & Northern USRA 4-6-2 Pacific Locomotive "425," CC, 18		1400
___	**85173**	NP USRA 4-6-2 Pacific Locomotive "2256," CC, 18		1400
___	**85174**	Southern USRA 4-6-2 Pacific Locomotive "1372," CC, 18		1400
___	**85175**	Halloween USRA 4-6-2 Pacific Locomotive "1031," CC, 18		1400
___	**85176**	C&O USRA 2-6-6-2 Locomotive "1522," CC, 18		1600
___	**85177**	W&LE USRA 2-6-6-2 Locomotive "8007," CC, 18		1600
___	**85178**	B&O USRA 2-6-6-2 Locomotive "7555," CC, 18		1600
___	**85179**	Buffalo, Rochester & Pittsburgh USRA 2-6-6-2 "755," CC, 18		1600
___	**85180**	GN USRA 2-6-6-2 Locomotive "1855," CC, 18		1600
___	**85181**	MEC USRA 2-6-6-2 Locomotive "1205," CC, 18		1600
___	**85182**	NYC USRA 2-6-6-2 Locomotive "1400," CC, 18		1600
___	**85183**	SP USRA 2-6-6-2 Locomotive "3932," CC, 18		1600
___	**85184**	WM USRA 2-6-6-2 Locomotive "960," CC, 18		1600
___	**85185**	Renz Hobby Shop, 17		300
___	**85186**	AT&SF EMD F3 A-A Diesel Set, CC, 17	275	850
___	**85189**	AT&SF Powered EMD F3 B Diesel, CC, 17		450
___	**85190**	At&SF SuperBass EMD F3 B Diesel, CC, 17		300
___	**85191**	GN EMD F3 A-A Diesel Set, CC, 17		850
___	**85194**	GN Powered EMD F3 B Diesel, CC, 17		450
___	**85195**	GN SuperBass EMD F3 B Diesel, CC, 17		300
___	**85196**	T&P EMD F7 A-A Diesel Set, CC, 17		850
___	**85199**	T&P Powered EMD F7 B Diesel, CC, 17		450
___	**85200**	T&P SuperBass EMD F3 B Diesel, CC, 17		300
___	**85201**	NYO&W EMD F3 A-A Diesel Set, CC, 17		850
___	**85204**	NYO&W Powered EMD F3 B Diesel, CC, 17		450
___	**85205**	NYO&W SuperBass EMD F3 B Diesel, CC, 17		300
___	**85206**	PRR EMD F7 A-A Diesel Set, CC, 17		850
___	**85209**	PRR Powered EMD F7 B Diesel, CC, 17		450
___	**85210**	PRR SuperBass EMD F7 B Diesel, CC, 17		300
___	**85211**	Reading EMD F3 A-A Diesel Set, CC, 17		850
___	**85214**	Reading Powered EMD F3 B Diesel, CC, 17		450
___	**85215**	ReadingSuperBass EMD F3 B Diesel, CC, 17		300
___	**85216**	Conrail EMD F7 A-A Diesel Set "1792-1730," CC, 17		850
___	**85219**	Conrail Powered EMD F7 B Diesel "3861," CC, 17		450
___	**85220**	Conrail SuperBass EMD F7 B Diesel "3872," CC, 17		300
___	**85222**	CSX Maxi-Stack "85222," 17		75
___	**85223**	BNSF Maxi-Stack "237342," 17-C55718		75
___	**85226**	180-Watt PowerHouse Power Supply, 10-amp, 19-25		230
___	**85227**	GN Oriental Ltd Heavyweight Baggage/Coach, 17-18		400
___	**85230**	GN Oriental Ltd Heavyweight Sleeper/Coach, 17-18		400
___	**85233**	GN Oriental Ltd Heavyweight Sleeper/Diner, 17-18		400
___	**85236**	GN Oriental Ltd Heavyweight Sleeper/Observation, 17-18		400
___	**85241**	Mystery Machine FT Diesel Freight Set, Lionchief, 18-20		430
___	**85246**	Anheuser-Busch Vintage Refrigerator Car, 18-20		80
___	**85247**	Budweiser Clydesdale Vintage Refrigerator Car, 18-19		80
___	**85248**	Budweiser Vintage Refrigerator Car, 18-20		80
___	**85253**	End of the Line Express Diesel Freight Set, LionChief, 18-20		330
___	**85258**	AT&SF FT Ranger Diesel Freight Set, LionChief, 18		430
___	**85263**	Tomb of the Unknown Soldier Walking Brakeman Car, 18		100

MODERN 1970-2025		Exc	Mint	
85264	Harry Potter Hogwarts Add-on Coach "99721," 18-25		90	___
85269	Scooby Doo Sam Witches Café, 18-20		100	___
85270	Hot Wheels Checkered Flagpole, 18		45	___
85271	Polar Express Flagpole, 18-25		45	___
85274	PRR Gla Hopper 3-pack #1, 18		225	___
85278	PRR Gla Hopper 3-pack #2, 18		225	___
85282	PRR Coal Goes To War Gla Hopper 3-pack #3, 18		225	___
85286	Berwind Gla Hopper 3-pack, 18		225	___
85290	PRR MOW PRR Gla Hopper 3-pack #4, 18		225	___
85294	Lionelville Hobby Shop, 18		300	___
85295	LCS CSM2, 18-25		120	___
85296	Layout Control System IRV2, 18-20, 24-25		100	___
85297	PRR N5 Caboose "477819," 18		100	___
85298	PRR N5 Caboose "478884," 18		100	___
85299	Reading & Northern N5 Caboose "477514," 18		100	___
85300	PRSL N5 Caboose "202," 18		100	___
85301	RJ Corman N5 Caboose, 18		100	___
85309	Flight Night Halloween Pylon, 18-19		150	___
85310	Witches Brew Storage Tank, 18-19		85	___
85311	Warehouse Kit, 18-19		60	___
85312	Modular Office Building Kit, 17-19	80	100	___
85314	Hometown Brewery Kit, 19		70	___
85315	UP EMD SD70ACe Diesel "1943," CC, 18		600	___
85316	UP Wide-Vision Caboose, Spirit of Union Pacific "1943," 18		100	___
85317	UP Spirit of the Union Pacific Boxcar, 18		85	___
85318	Personalized Happy Birthday Boxcar, 18		90	___
85319	Personalized 18 Merry Christmas Boxcar, 18		90	___
85320	Personalized Happy Anniversary Boxcar, 18-19		90	___
85321	John Deere Flatcar w/Tractor Load, 18		80	___
85322	Personalized 18 Halloween Boxcar, 18		90	___
85323	Scooby Doo Boxcar, 18		85	___
85324	Thomas & Friends Christmas Freight Set, LionChief, 18-25	100	250	___
85326	NYC Vision Baggage Car "9152," 18		330	___
85327	NYC Baggage Car 2-pack #1, 18		350	___
85330	NYC Baggage Car 2-pack #2, 18		350	___
85333	NYC Baggage/Combine 2-pack, 18		400	___
85336	NYC 18" Heavyweight Baggage Car 2-pack, 18		350	___
85339	SP Scale RPO Passenger Car "5124," 18		160	___
85340	L&N Scale RPO Passenger Car "1099," 18		160	___
85341	LIRR Scale RPO Passenger Car "737," 18		160	___
85342	MILW Scale RPO Passenger Car "2105," 18		160	___
85343	NYC Scale RPO Passenger Car "4819," 18		160	___
85344	PRR Scale RPO Passenger Car "5265," 18		160	___
85345	PRR Scale RPO Passenger Car "5269," 18		160	___
85346	PC Scale RPO Passenger Car "5267," 18		160	___
85347	UP Scale RPO Passenger Car "2060," 18		160	___
85348	MILW 18" Columbian Passenger Car 2-pack #A, 18		400	___
85351	MILW 18" Columbian Passenger Car 2-pack #B, 18		400	___
85354	MILW 18" Columbian Passenger Car 2-pack #C, 18		400	___
85357	MILW 18" Columbian Passenger Car 2-pack #D, 18		400	___
85360	UP Challenger 21" Passenger Car 4-pack, 18		700	___
85361	UP Challenger 21" Passenger Car 2-pack, 18		350	___
85362	UP Challenger 21" Diner w/StationSounds, 18		330	___

		MODERN 1970-2025	Exc	Mint
___	**85367**	L&N Hummingbird 21" Passenger Car 4-pack, 18		700
___	**85368**	L&N Hummingbird 21" Passenger Car 2-pack, 18		350
___	**85370**	R&N 18" Excursion and Business Car 2-pack, A, 18		400
___	**85373**	R&N 18" Excursion and Business Car 2-pack, B, 18		400
___	**85376**	Reading & Northern 21" Dome Car w/StationSounds, 18		350
___	**85377**	MOW Disconnect Work Car 4-pack, 18		160
___	**85378**	PRR Disconnect Work Car 4-pack, 18		160
___	**85379**	AT&SF Disconnect Work Car 4-pack, 18		160
___	**85380**	UP Disconnect Work Car 4-pack, 18		160
___	**85381**	NYC Disconnect Work Car 4-pack, 18		160
___	**85382**	D&RGW Disconnect Work Car 4-pack, 18		160
___	**85383**	Layout Control System IRV2 Sensor Add-on, 18-20, 24-25		30
___	**85384**	Orange 10" Straight FasTrack 4-pack, 18-20		25
___	**85386**	Pennsylvania Lines 2-8-0 Consolidation Locomotive "7109," CC, 18		750
___	**85387**	Western Allegheny 2-8-0 Consolidation Locomotive "85," CC, 18		750
___	**85389**	FasTrack White 10" Straight, 4-pack, 18-25		28
___	**85390**	FasTrack White O-36 Curve, 4-pack, 18-25		28
___	**85391**	White PEP Activation Track, 18-20		25
___	**85392**	White 10" Terminal FasTrack, 18-20		10
___	**85400**	Polar Express Skiing Hobo Observation w/Snowy Roof, 19-20		90
___	**85401**	UP LED Flag Boxcar, Yellow and Gray "1862," 18		120
___	**85402**	UP LED Flag Boxcar, C&NW Heritage "1995," 18		120
___	**85403**	UP LED Flag Boxcar, MKT Heritage "1988," 18		120
___	**85404**	UP LED Flag Boxcar, MP Heritage "1982," 18		120
___	**85405**	UP LED Flag Boxcar, D&RGW Heritage "1989," 18		120
___	**85406**	UP LED Flag Boxcar, SP Heritage "1996," 18		120
___	**85407**	UP LED Flag Boxcar, WP Heritage "1983," 18		120
___	**85408**	UP LED Flag Boxcar, Spirit of Union Pacific "1943," 18		120
___	**85409**	UP LED Flag Boxcar, Steam Program "4-8-8-4," 18		120
___	**85410**	Polar Express Hero Boy's Home, 18-25		130
___	**85411**	Pylon with World War II Planes, 18		145
___	**85412**	Santa's Sleigh Pylon, 18		135
___	**85413**	FasTrack 10" Straight Terminal Track, unpackaged, 23-25		
___	**99000**	Keebler Elf Express Steam Freight Set, 99 u	775	1196
___	**99001**	Mickey's Holiday Express Freight Set, 99 u	163	180
___	**99002**	Looney Tunes Square Window Caboose, 99 u		65
___	**99006**	Keebler Bulkhead Flatcar, 99 u		200
___	**99007**	Smuckers Fudge 1-D Tank Car, 99 u		90
___	**99008**	Mickey's Merry Christmas Boxcar, 99 u		55
___	**99009**	Mickey's Holiday Express Square Window Caboose, 99 u		45
___	**99013**	Case Cutlery Tank Car "1889," 00 u		70
___	**99014**	Case Cutlery Gondola "1889," 00 u		70
___	**99015**	Case Cutlery Boxcar "1889," 00 u		70
___	**99018**	Case Cutlery Rolling Stock 3-pack, 00 u	140	215
___	**1823010**	Thomas' Best Buddies LionChief Set: Percy, 18-19		200
___	**1823011**	Percy, Sodor Locomotive, LionChief, 18-19		120
___	**1823020**	Thomas' Best Buddies LionChief Set: James, 18-19		200
___	**1823021**	James, Sodor Locomotive, LionChief, 18-19		120
___	**1823030**	Sodor Railway Troublemaker Diesel LionChief Set, 18-19		200
___	**1823031**	Thomas & Friends Sodor Diesel Locomotive, LionChief, 18-19, 23		160

		Exc	Mint
1823040	Thomas Kinkade Christmas LionChief Steam Freight Set, 18, 20		400 ___
1823050	Mickey Mouse Celebration LionChief Steam Freight Set, 18		400 ___
1830010	Polar Express Snowman & Children People Pack, 19-24		30 ___
1831010	N&W Brass Hybrid USRA 4-8-2 K2 Locomotive "118," CC, 18		1400 ___
1831020	N&W Brass Hybrid USRA 4-8-2 K2 Locomotive "123," CC, 18		1400 ___
1831030	N&W Brass Hybrid USRA 4-8-2 K2 Locomotive "116," CC, 18		1400 ___
1831040	N&W Brass Hybrid USRA 4-8-2 K2 Locomotive "125," CC, 18		1400 ___
1831050	N&W Brass Hybrid USRA 4-8-2 K2 Locomotive "9999," CC, 18		1400 ___
1831060	PRR 4-6-2 Pacific K4 w/Long-haul Tender "5453," CC, 18		1300 ___
1904010	58" x 86" Lionel Train Table, 19-25		1000 ___
1908010	LCS CSM2 DZ-2500 Breakout Board, 18-25		30 ___
1908080	Improved CW80 Transformer, 19-25		170 ___
1918210	Anheuser-Busch Malt Tonics Woodside Refrigerator Car, 19		80 ___
1922010	UP Sherman Hill 4-8-8-4 Steam Freight Set, LionChief Plus 2.0, 19		1600 ___
1922020	Nickel Plate 2-8-4 Steam Freight Set, LionChief Plus 2.0, 19, 22		880 ___
1922030	Warren G. Harding Funeral Steam Passenger Train, CC, 18		2000 ___
1922040	AT&SF Gold Bonnet Streamlined Passenger Set, CC, 19		1000 ___
1922050	NYC Pacemaker Steam Passenger Set, CC, 19		2000 ___
1922060	BNSF Diesel Freight Oil Train Set, CC, 19		1000 ___
1922070	Pennsylvania Limited 2-8-4 Steam Passenger Set, 19, 22		880 ___
1922080	Lionel GE Bi-Polar Electric State Set, CC, 19		1800 ___
1922090	Erie Mining Diesel Ore Set, CC, 19		900 ___
1923020	NYC Flyer 0-8-0 Steam Freight Set, LionChief, 18-19		350 ___
1923030	Polar Express 15th Anniversary Steam Passenger Set, LionChief, 19		450 ___
1923040	UP Flyer 0-8-0 Steam Freight Set, LionChief, 19-22		370 ___
1923050	NS Tier 4 GE ET44C4 Diesel Freight Set, LionChief, 19-20		400 ___
1923070	Blue Comet Steam Passenger Set, LionChief, 19-20		370 ___
1923080	Promontory Summit 150th Anniversary Steam Locomotive Set, 19		550 ___
1923090	LV GE U36B Diesel Freight Set, LionChief, 19-20		330 ___
1923100	U.S. Steam 0-8-0 Steam Freight Set, LionChief, 19-20		400 ___
1923110	UP America Proud GP38 Diesel Freight Set, LionChief, 19-20		400 ___
1923130	Polar Express Trolley Set, 19		200 ___
1923140	Disney Christmas Express Steam Freight Set, LionChief, 19-25		400 ___
1923150	Winter Wonderland Steam Freight Set, LionChief, 19-22		400 ___
1925001	FasTrack Screws, 100-pack, 19-20		10 ___
1926011	CSX 86-foot 4-Door High Cube Boxcar (Boxcar Logo) "181032," 18		100 ___
1926012	CSX 86-foot 4-Door High Cube Boxcar (Boxcar Logo) "181056," 18		100 ___
1926013	CSX 86-foot 4-Door High Cube Boxcar "181053," 18		100 ___
1926014	CSX 86-foot 4-Door High Cube Boxcar "180455," 18		100 ___
1926021	DT&I 86-foot 4-Door High Cube Boxcar, Green "26341," 18		100 ___
1926022	DT&I 86-foot 4-Door High Cube Boxcar, Purple/Pink "26888," 18		100 ___
1926023	DT&I 86-foot 4-Door High Cube Boxcar, Blue "26443," 18		100 ___
1926024	DT&I 86-foot 4-Door High Cube Boxcar, Blue w/Graffiti "26834," 18		100 ___
1926031	N&W 86-foot 4-Door High Cube Boxcar "355155," 18		100 ___
1926032	N&W 86-foot 4-Door High Cube Boxcar "355197," 18		100 ___

			Exc	Mint
___	**1926041**	Southern 86-foot 4-Door High Cube Boxcar "42954," 18		100
___	**1926042**	Southern 86-foot 4-Door High Cube Boxcar "42995," 18		100
___	**1926051**	UP 86-foot 4-Door High Cube Boxcar "980421," 18		100
___	**1926052**	UP 86-foot 4-Door High Cube Boxcar "980434," 18		100
___	**1926053**	UP 86-foot 4-Door High Cube Boxcar w/Graffiti "980455," 18		100
___	**1926061**	Wabash 86-foot 4-Door High Cube Boxcar "55023," 18		100
___	**1926062**	Wabash 86-foot 4-Door High Cube Boxcar "55055," 18		100
___	**1926070**	ART Refrigerator Car w/FreightSounds "31823," 18		150
___	**1926080**	FGE Refrigerator Car w/FreightSounds "38947," 18		150
___	**1926090**	GN Refrigerator Car w/FreightSounds "68112," 18		150
___	**1926100**	NYC (MDT) Refrigerator Car w/FreightSounds "19091," 18		150
___	**1926110**	PFE Refrigerator Car w/FreightSounds "5860," 18		150
___	**1926120**	AT&SF Refrigerator Car w/FreightSounds "3526,", 18		150
___	**1926131**	PRR Bunk Car "498393," 18		100
___	**1926132**	PRR Bunk Car "498396," 18		100
___	**1926133**	PRR Bunk Car "498398," 18		100
___	**1926141**	AT&SF Bunk Car "196752," 18		100
___	**1926142**	AT&SF Bunk Car "196754," 18		100
___	**1926143**	AT&SF Bunk Car "196459," 18		100
___	**1926151**	NYC Bunk Car "x19075," 18		100
___	**1926152**	NYC Bunk Car "x19076," 18		100
___	**1926153**	NYC Bunk Car "x19078," 18		100
___	**1926161**	D&RGW Bunk Car "x2380," 18		100
___	**1926162**	D&RGW Bunk Car "x2384," 18		100
___	**1926163**	D&RGW Bunk Car "x2387," 18		100
___	**1926171**	UP Bunk Car "906115," 18		100
___	**1926172**	UP Bunk Car "906118," 18		100
___	**1926173**	UP Bunk Car "906121," 18		100
___	**1926181**	MOW Bunk Car "99832," 18		100
___	**1926182**	MOW Bunk Car "99835," 18		100
___	**1926183**	MOW Bunk Car "99837," 18		100
___	**1926190**	PRR Kitchen Car w/Sounds "492774," 18		150
___	**1926200**	AT&SF Kitchen Car w/Sounds "194200," 18		150
___	**1926210**	NYC Kitchen Car w/Sounds "x22483," 18		150
___	**1926220**	D&RGW Kitchen Car w/Sounds "x4013," 18		150
___	**1926230**	UP Kitchen Car w/Sounds "903675," 18		150
___	**1926240**	MOW Kitchen Car w/Sounds "99402," 18		150
___	**1926250**	PRR Tool Car "493551," 18		90
___	**1926260**	AT&SF Tool Car "190455," 18		90
___	**1926270**	NYC Tool Car "x13568," 18		90
___	**1926280**	D&RGW Tool Car "x4510," 18		90
___	**1926290**	UP Tool Car "915129," 18		90
___	**1926300**	MOW Tool Car "99500," 18		90
___	**1926311**	Chessie 52-foot Coil Gondola "305005," 18		90
___	**1926312**	Chessie 52-foot Coil Gondola "305012," 18		90
___	**1926321**	C&SS 52-foot Coil Gondola "3859," 18		90
___	**1926322**	C&SS 52-foot Coil Gondola "3862," 18		90
___	**1926331**	DT&I 52-foot Coil Gondola "9326," 18		90
___	**1926332**	DT&I 52-foot Coil Gondola "9372," 18		90
___	**1926341**	EJ&E 52-foot Coil Gondola "4144," 18		90
___	**1926342**	EJ&E 52-foot Coil Gondola "4156," 18		90
___	**1926351**	P&LE 52-foot Coil Gondola "50062," 18		90

MODERN 1970-2025		Exc	Mint
1926352	P&LE 52-foot Coil Gondola "50086," 18		90 ___
1926361	Union RR 52-foot Coil Gondola "3021," 18		90 ___
1926362	Union RR 52-foot Coil Gondola "3163," 18		90 ___
1926370	Polar Express 52-foot Coil Gondola "122519" w/Presents, 18		95 ___
1926381	ACL 50-foot Bulkhead Flatcar "78310," 19		100 ___
1926382	ACL 50-foot Bulkhead Flatcar "78348," 19		100 ___
1926391	B&O 50-foot Bulkhead Flatcar "8831," 19		100 ___
1926392	B&O 50-foot Bulkhead Flatcar "8844," 19		100 ___
1926401	D&RGW 50-foot Bulkhead Flatcar "22392," 19		100 ___
1926402	D&RGW 50-foot Bulkhead Flatcar "22420," 19		100 ___
1926411	MKT 50-foot Bulkhead Flatcar "13912," 19		100 ___
1926421	SAL 50-foot Bulkhead Flatcar "48102," 19		100 ___
1926422	SAL 50-foot Bulkhead Flatcar "48124," 19		100 ___
1926431	Frisco 50-foot Bulkhead Flatcar "4052," 19		100 ___
1926432	Frisco 50-foot Bulkhead Flatcar "4058," 19		100 ___
1926441	AT&SF Grand Canyon Line 50-foot Double-Door Boxcar "10206," 18		80 ___
1926442	AT&SF Scout 50-foot Double-Door Boxcar "10295," 18		80 ___
1926443	AT&SF El Capitan 50-foot Double-Door Boxcar "10350," 18		80 ___
1926444	AT&SF Super Chief 50-foot Double-Door Boxcar "10410," 18		80 ___
1926445	AT&SF Chief 50-foot Double-Door Boxcar "10456," 18		80 ___
1926451	KCS 50-foot Double-Door Boxcar "20825," 18		80 ___
1926452	KCS 50-foot Double-Door Boxcar "20856," 18		80 ___
1926461	Monon 50-foot Double-Door Boxcar "1423," 18		80 ___
1926462	Monon 50-foot Double-Door Boxcar "1426," 18		80 ___
1926471	T&P 50-foot Double-Door Boxcar "70707," 18		80 ___
1926472	T&P 50-foot Double-Door Boxcar "70735," 18		80 ___
1926480	ELX Halloween 50-foot Double-Door Boxcar "103119," 18		80 ___
1926491	UP CA-4 Caboose "3830," 18		100 ___
1926492	UP CA-4 Caboose "3830," 18		100 ___
1926493	UP CA-4 Caboose "3859,"18		100 ___
1926501	Bartlett Grain PS-2CD 4427-cu-ft Covered Hopper "5509," 19		100 ___
1926502	Bartlett Grain PS-2CD 4427-cu-ft Covered Hopper "5511," 19		100 ___
1926511	BN PS-2CD 4427-cu-ft Covered Hopper "439397,"19		100 ___
1926512	BN PS-2CD 4427-cu-ft Covered Hopper "450621," 19		100 ___
1926521	Cargill PS-2CD 4427-cu-ft Covered Hopper "2819," 19		100 ___
1926522	Cargill PS-2CD 4427-cu-ft Covered Hopper "2853," 19		100 ___
1926531	Conrail PS-2CD 4427-cu-ft Covered Hopper "886283," 19		100 ___
1926532	Conrail PS-2CD 4427-cu-ft Covered Hopper "886304," 19		100 ___
1926540	Ely Thomas Logging Cars 2-pack A, 19		150 ___
1926550	Ely Thomas Logging Cars 2-pack B, 19		150 ___
1926560	Long Bell Logging Cars 2-pack A, 19		150 ___
1926570	Long Bell Logging Cars 2-pack B, 19		150 ___
1926580	NY&P Logging Cars 2-pack A, 19		150 ___
1926590	NY&P Logging Cars 2-pack B, 19		150 ___
1926600	Unlettered Logging Cars 2-pack A, 19		150 ___
1926610	Unlettered Logging Cars 2-pack B, 19		150 ___
1926620	B&O Sentinel PS-1 Boxcar "466024" w/FreightSounds, 19		135 ___
1926630	GN PS-1 Boxcar "39412" w/FreightSounds, 19		135 ___
1926640	PRR PS-1 Boxcar "24267" w/FreightSounds, 19		135 ___
1926650	D&RGW Cookie Box PS-1 Boxcar "60034" w/FreightSounds, 19		135 ___

MODERN 1970-2025			Exc	Mint
___	1926660	Southern PS-1 Boxcar "330434" w/FreightSounds, 19		135
___	1926670	SP Overnight PS-1 Boxcar "97945" w/FreightSounds, 19		135
___	1926680	NYS&W PS-1 Boxcar "501" w/FreightSounds, 19		135
___	1926690	WP PS-1 Boxcar "19531" w/FreightSounds, 19		135
___	1926701	B&M 40-foot Flatcar "33700" w/Sherman Tank Load, 19		130
___	1926702	B&M 40-foot Flatcar "33745" w/Sherman Tank Load, 19		130
___	1926711	NYC 40-foot Flatcar "496250" w/Sherman Tank Load, 19		130
___	1926712	NYC 40-foot Flatcar "496271" w/Sherman Tank Load, 19		130
___	1926721	PRR 40-foot Flatcar "925148" w/Sherman Tank Load, 19		130
___	1926722	PRR 40-foot Flatcar "925164" w/Sherman Tank Load, 19		130
___	1926731	SP 40-foot Flatcar "140014" w/Sherman Tank Load, 19		130
___	1926732	SP 40-foot Flatcar "140125" w/Sherman Tank Load, 19		130
___	1926741	UP 40-foot Flatcar "51125" w/Sherman Tank Load, 19		130
___	1926742	UP 40-foot Flatcar "51196" w/Sherman Tank Load, 19		130
___	1926751	US Army 40-foot Flatcar "35351" w/Sherman Tank Load, 19		130
___	1926752	US Army 40-foot Flatcar "35359" w/Sherman Tank Load, 19		130
___	1926760	CTCX 30,000-gallon 1-D Tank Car 3-pack, 19		250
___	1926770	GATX 30,000-gallon 1-D Tank Car 3-pack, 19		250
___	1926780	SCMX 30,000-gallon 1-D Tank Car 3-pack, 19		250
___	1926790	TILX (Black) 30,000-gallon 1-D Tank Car 3-pack, 19		250
___	1926800	TILX (White) 30,000-gallon 1-D Tank Car 3-pack, 19		250
___	1926810	VMSX 30,000-gallon 1-D Tank Car 3-pack, 19		250
___	1926820	Polar Express 15th Anniversary Boxcar w/FreightSounds, 19		145
___	1926830	C&NW NE Caboose "10808," 19		100
___	1926840	Conrail (RDG patch) NE Caboose "19730," 19		100
___	1926850	D&H NE Caboose "35802," 19		100
___	1926860	L&HR NE Caboose "17," 19		100
___	1926870	LV NE Caboose "95003," 19		100
___	1926880	Halloween (ELX) NE Caboose "1313," 19		100
___	1926890	Alaska RR EV Caboose "1086" w/CupolaCam, 19		130
___	1926900	C&O EV Caboose "3160" w/CupolaCam, 19		130
___	1926910	Conrail EV Caboose "22137" w/CupolaCam, 19		130
___	1926920	D&RGW EV Caboose "01510" w/CupolaCam, 19		130
___	1926930	Milwaukee Road EV Caboose "992303" w/CupolaCam, 19		130
___	1926940	MKT EV Caboose "100" w/CupolaCam, 19		130
___	1926950	N&W EV Caboose "555100" w/CupolaCam, 19		130
___	1926960	Lionel Lines EV Caboose "6960" w/CupolaCam, 19		130
___	1926971	Detroit Salt PS-2CD 4427-cu-ft Covered Hopper "5436," 19		100
___	1926972	Detroit Salt PS-2CD 4427-cu-ft Covered Hopper "5446," 19		100
___	1926981	Producers Grain PS-2CD Covered Hopper "3926," 19		100
___	1926982	Producers Grain PS-2CD Covered Hopper "3940," 19		100
___	1927010	AT&SF 21-inch Passenger Car 4-pack, 19		700
___	1927020	AT&SF 21-inch Passenger Car 2-pack #1, 19		350
___	1927030	AT&SF 21-inch Dome Car "550" w/StationSounds, 19		340
___	1927040	AT&SF 21-inch Passenger Car 2-pack #2, 19		350
___	1927050	UP Excursion 21-inch Passenger Car Expansion Set, 19		350
___	1927060	UP Challenger 21-inch Passenger Car Expansion Set, 19		350
___	1927070	Midnight Special 18-inch Passenger Car 2-pack #1, 18		400
___	1927080	Midnight Special 18-inch Passenger Car 2-pack #2, 18		400
___	1927090	Midnight Special 18-inch Passenger Car 2-pack #3, 18		400
___	1927100	Midnight Special Diner "1305," w/StationSounds, 18		330
___	1927110	SP 18-inch Passenger Car 2-pack #1, 18-19		400
___	1927120	SP 18-inch Passenger Car 2-pack #2, 18-19		400

MODERN 1970-2025		Exc	Mint
1927130	SP 18-inch Passenger Car 2-pack #3, 18-19		400
1927140	SP 18-inch Passenger Car 2-pack #4, 18-19		400
1927150	NYC Pacemaker 2-car Add-on Set, 19		400
1927160	NYC Pacemaker Diner "617" w/StationSounds, 19		330
1927170	N&W Cavalier 18-inch Passenger Car 2-pack A, 19		400
1927180	N&W Cavalier 18-inch Passenger Car 2-pack B, 19		400
1927190	N&W Cavalier 18-inch Diner "1018" w/StationSounds, 19		330
1927200	611 Excursion Train NS Coach 4-pack, 19		700
1927210	611 Excursion Train Private Car 2-pack A, 19		350
1927220	611 Excursion Train Private Car 2-pack B, 19		350
1927230	611 Excursion Train Dome Car w/StationSounds, 19		340
1927241	611 Excursion Train N&W Tool Car "1407," 19		180
1927242	N&W Cavalier Baggage "110," 19		180
1927243	N&W Cavalier Baggage "114," 19		180
1927251	PC 60-foot Baggage "7533," 19		180
1927252	PC 60-foot Baggage "7551," 19		180
1927261	SP 60-foot Baggage "6340," 19		180
1927262	SP 60-foot Baggage "6344," 19		180
1927271	REA 60-foot Baggage "1631," 19		180
1927272	REA 60-foot Baggage "1650," 19		180
1927281	UP 60-foot Baggage "1830" (Greyhound), 19		180
1927282	UP 60-foot Baggage "1841" (Greyhound), 19		180
1927283	UP 60-foot Baggage "1830" (Yellow), 19		180
1927284	UP 60-foot Baggage "1837" (Yellow), 19		180
1927291	ACL 60-foot Baggage "555," 19		180
1927292	ACL 60-foot Baggage "559," 19		180
1927300	ACL 60-foot Railway Post Office "11," 19		180
1927310	N&W Cavalier Railway Post Office "96," 19		180
1927320	Southern 60-foot Railway Post Office "39," 18-19		160
1927330	AT&SF 60-foot Railway Post Office "65," 19		180
1927340	UP 60-foot Railway Post Office "2062", 19		180
1927351	Polar Express Railway Post Office, White Roof, 19, 22-24		200
1927352	Polar Express Railway Post Office, Black Roof, 19, 22-24		200
1927360	LIRR 21-inch Streamlined Coach 4-pack, 19		700
1927370	LIRR 21-inch Streamlined Coach 2-pack, 19		350
1927380	UP 1860s Wood Coach w/RailSounds, 2-pack, 19		350
1927390	Central Pacific 1860s Wood Coach w/RailSounds, 2-pack, 19		350
1927461	Southern 60-foot Baggage "100," 18-19		160
1927462	Southern 60-foot Baggage "109," 18-19		160
1927470	Southern 18-inch Passenger Car 2-pack #1, 18-19		400
1927480	Southern 18-inch Passenger Car 2-pack #2, 18-19		400
1927490	Southern 18-inch Passenger Car 2-pack #3, 18-19		400
1927500	Southern Diner "3168" w/StationSounds, 18-19		330
1927510	MP Sunshine Special 18-inch Passenger Car 2-pack #1, 18-19		400
1927520	MP Sunshine Special 18-inch Passenger Car 2-pack #2, 18-19		400
1927530	MP Sunshine Special 18-inch Passenger Car 2-pack #3, 18-19		400
1927540	MP Sunshine Special Diner "10042" w/StationSounds, 18-19		330
1927550	MP Sunshine Special 60-foot RPO "45", 18-19		160
1927560	Defense Special Heavyweight Passenger Car 2-pack A, 19		400
1927570	Defense Special Heavyweight Passenger Car 2-pack B, 19		400
1927580	Defense Special Heavyweight Passenger Car 2-pack C, 19		400

			Exc	Mint
___	**1927590**	Defense Special Heavyweight Passenger Car 2-pack D, 19		400
___	**1927600**	611 Excursion Train NS Coach 2-pack, 19		350
___	**1927610**	CP 21-inch Passenger Car 4-pack, 19		700
___	**1927620**	CP 21-inch Passenger Car 2-pack, 19		350
___	**1927630**	Polar Express Hot Chocolate Car w/StationSounds, 19		330
___	**1927640**	Polar Express Abandoned Toy Car, 19, 24		200
___	**1927650**	Polar Express 15th Anniversary Coach, 19		200
___	**1927660**	Pennsylvania Limited Suetonius Coach, 19		75
___	**1927670**	Lionel State Set Add-on 2-pack, 19		530
___	**1927680**	Northern Central 1860s Wood Coach w/RailSounds, 2-pack, 19		350
___	**1927690**	Woodruff Sleeping and Parlor 1860s Wood Coach, 2-pack, 19		300
___	**1927700**	Blue Comet Heavyweight Coach, 19-20		75
___	**1927710**	CP 21-inch Diner "550" w/StationSounds, 19		330
___	**1927730**	PRR 1860s Wood Coach w/RailSounds, 2-pack, 19		350
___	**1928011**	BN Auto Rack "159173," 18-19		80
___	**1928012**	BN Auto Rack "159433," 18-19		80
___	**1928021**	Conrail Auto Rack "980139," 18-19		80
___	**1928022**	Conrail Auto Rack "456249," 18-19		80
___	**1928031**	GT Auto Rack "50454," 18-19		80
___	**1928032**	GT Auto Rack "50490," 18-19		80
___	**1928041**	SP Auto Rack "518027," 18-19		80
___	**1928042**	SP Auto Rack "518114," 18-19		80
___	**1928051**	TTX Auto Rack "710866," 18-19		80
___	**1928052**	TTX Auto Rack "710877," 18-19		80
___	**1928060**	Mickey Mouse Celebration Aquarium Car, 18		100
___	**1928070**	NYC Flatcar w/Boat "28070," 18-19		70
___	**1928080**	Hot Wheels Fuel 1-Dome Tank Car, 18-19		75
___	**1928091**	Branch Line Passenger Car 2-pack, 18-19		75
___	**1928092**	James Trucks Wagon Car 2-pack, 18-19		75
___	**1928093**	S.C. Ruffey Wagon Car, 18-19		45
___	**1928110**	BN Hopper 6-pack, 19		150
___	**1928120**	C&NW Hopper 6-pack, 19		150
___	**1928130**	CSX Hopper 6-pack, 19-20		150
___	**1928140**	PP&L Hopper 6-pack, 19-20		150
___	**1928150**	Reading Lines Hopper 6-pack, 19-20		150
___	**1928160**	Bethlehem Steel Ore Car 6-pack, 19-20		150
___	**1928170**	CN Ore Car 6-pack, 19-20		150
___	**1928180**	Erie Mining Ore Car 6-pack, 19		150
___	**1928190**	PRR Ore Car 6-pack, 19-20		150
___	**1928200**	UP Ore Car 6-pack, 19-20		150
___	**1928210**	Malt Tonics Refrigerator Car, 19-22		90
___	**1928220**	Anheuser-Busch 1890s Woodside Refrigerator Car, 19		80
___	**1928240**	Anheuser-Busch Uni-Body 1-D Tank Car "4271," 19		75
___	**1928250**	Anheuser-Busch Barrel Car "28250," 19		80
___	**1928260**	Miller High Life Woodside Refrigerator Car, 19-20		80
___	**1928270**	Coors Golden Beer Woodside Refrigerator Car, 19-20		80
___	**1928280**	Hamm's Beer Woodside Refrigerator Car, 19, 22		90
___	**1928330**	Pez Mint Car, 19		80
___	**1928340**	John Deere Mower Stockcar, 19		80
___	**1928350**	John Deere Flatcar "28350" w/Piggyback Trailers, 19		85
___	**1928360**	Scooby-Doo Aquarium Car, 19-20		100

MODERN 1970-2025		Exc	Mint
1928370	Spy Vs. Spy Challenge Boxcar, 19		85 ___
1928380	Trick or Treat Boxcar w/HalloweenSounds, 19		80 ___
1928390	Undead Gondola, 19		70 ___
1928400	Polar Express Hero Boy Walking Brakeman Car, 19		100 ___
1928410	Polar Express Reindeer Car, 19		80 ___
1928420	Polar Express Searchlight Car, 19		70 ___
1928430	Polar Express Barrel Car, 19		80 ___
1928440	Sweetest Helper Refrigerator Car, 19-20		80 ___
1928450	Snowball Fight Animated Gondola, 19-20		75 ___
1928460	Santa Mobile Rest Stop Flatcar, 19-20		75 ___
1928470	Santa Freight Lines Christmas Transfer Caboose, 19-20		70 ___
1928480	Santa Freight Lines Santa Finder Searchlight Car, 19-20		65 ___
1928490	Christmas Boxcar 2019, 19		65 ___
1928500	Christmas Music Boxcar, 19		80 ___
1928510	UP Barrel Ramp Car "28510," 19-20		75 ___
1928520	BNSF Maxi-Stack, 18-19		80 ___
1928530	CSX Maxi-Stack, 18-19		80 ___
1928540	TTX Maxi-Stack, 18-19		80 ___
1928550	NPR Flatcar "1937" w/Trailer, 19		70 ___
1928560	Batman & Robin Boxcar, 19-20		80 ___
1928570	Batman Bat-Signal Searchlight Car, 19		70 ___
1928580	Batman The Joker Laughing Gas Missile Car, 19-20		90 ___
1928590	Happy Birthday Scooby-Doo Sound Car, 19-20		85 ___
1928600	Batman Classic Gotham City Villains Boxcar, 19-20		80 ___
1928610	Chevy Auto Rack "1911," 19-20		85 ___
1928620	Chevy Flatcar w/Frames, 19		75 ___
1928630	Looney Tunes Scent-imental Over You Chasing Gondola, 19		80 ___
1928640	Thomas the Tank Engine Boxcar, 19		75 ___
1928650	Percy Boxcar, 19		75 ___
1928660	James Boxcar, 19		75 ___
1928670	Mickey's Wish List Boxcar, 19-20		70 ___
1928680	UP Uni-Body 1-D Tank Car "8665," 19-20		70 ___
1928690	Toyota Auto Rack "1937," 19		85 ___
1928700	Toyota Flatcar w/Frames, 19		75 ___
1929040	Anheuser-Busch Barrel Loader, 19		70 ___
1929050	Polar Express Barrel Loader, 19		70 ___
1929060	Polar Express Station Platform, 19-24		55 ___
1929070	Plug-Expand-Play Winter Wonderland Station Platform, 19-25		55 ___
1929080	Hot Wheels Crash City Café, 18-19		100 ___
1929090	Illuminated Christmas Half-Covered Bridge, 19-25		85 ___
1929100	Defect Detector w/Sounds, 18-25		100 ___
1929110	Halloween House, 18		130 ___
1929130	Elf Tug of War Accessory, 19		75 ___
1929160	Sir Topham Hatt Gateman, 19		120 ___
1929170	Haunted House, 19-22		275 ___
1929230	Burning House, 19-20		120 ___
1929804	Peel and Stick Lights, 4-pack, 19-20		10 ___
1929815	Peel and Stick Lights, 15-pack, 19-20		28 ___
1929904	Peel and Stick LED Lights, 4-pack, 19-20		10 ___
1929915	Peel and Stick LED Lights, 15-pack, 19-20		28 ___
1930010	Steel Coil Load Kit, 18-23		20 ___
1930050	Lumber Load Kit, 19		25 ___

			Exc	Mint
____	**1930060**	Millennial People Pack, 18-25		30
____	**1930070**	Trick or Treat Figures, 18-25		30
____	**1930080**	Halloween Lawn Figures, 18-25		30
____	**1930120**	Mickey Mouse Celebration Billboard 3-pack, 18		20
____	**1930130**	Thomas & Friends Covered Bridge, 18-19		70
____	**1930140**	Trolley House, 19		50
____	**1930150**	Budweiser Billboard 3-pack, 19-22		25
____	**1930170**	Green Iron Fence, 19-20		20
____	**1930180**	Benches, 6-pack, 19-20		10
____	**1930190**	Sitting People with Benches, 6-pack, 19-20		23
____	**1930200**	Winter Action Figures, 6-pack, 19-20		23
____	**1930210**	Sled Kids, 3-pack, 19-20		23
____	**1930220**	Sitting People, 6-pack, 19-20		23
____	**1930230**	People on Sleigh Figure Pack, 19-20		23
____	**1930240**	People Waving, 6-pack, 19-20		23
____	**1930160**	Brown Picket Fence, 19-20		20
____	**1930250**	People Eating, 6-pack, 19-20		23
____	**1930260**	Prisoners (striped), 6-pack, 19-20		23
____	**1930270**	Travelers, 6-pack, 19-20		23
____	**1930280**	Horses, 4-pack, 19-20		23
____	**1930290**	Cows and Calves (brown), 6-pack, 19-20		23
____	**1930300**	Unpainted Figures, 36-pack, 19-20		35
____	**1930310**	Unpainted Animals, 36-pack, 19-20		35
____	**1930320**	"Smoking Tony" Lighted Figure, 19-20		20
____	**1930330**	Railroad Worker with Lamp Lighted Figure, 19-20		20
____	**1930340**	Miner with Headlamp Lighted Figure, 19-20		20
____	**1930350**	Man with Flashlight Lighted Figure, 19-20		20
____	**1930360**	Man with Flashing Jackhammer Lighted Figure, 19-20		20
____	**1930370**	Braga House, 19-20		75
____	**1930380**	Fraser House, 19-20		75
____	**1930390**	Harwell House, 19-20		75
____	**1930400**	Olson House Kit, 19-20		22
____	**1930410**	Morris House Kit, 19-20		22
____	**1930420**	Bishop House Kit, 19-20		22
____	**1930430**	Davis House Kit, 19-20		22
____	**1930440**	Church, 19-20		86
____	**1930450**	Unpainted Steel Coils 2-Pack, 19-24		10
____	**1931060**	L&N USRA 4-8-2 Light Mountain Locomotive "404," CC, 18		1300
____	**1931070**	MP USRA 4-8-2 Light Mountain Locomotive "5307," CC, 18		1300
____	**1931080**	NC&StL USRA 4-8-2 Light Mountain Locomotive "551," CC, 18		1300
____	**1931090**	NH USRA 4-8-2 Light Mountain Locomotive "3301," CC, 18		1300
____	**1931100**	Frisco USRA 4-8-2 Light Mountain Locomotive "1501," CC, 18		1300
____	**1931110**	Soo Line USRA 4-8-2 Light Mountain Locomotive "4005," CC, 18		1300
____	**1931120**	Southern USRA 4-8-2 Light Mountain Locomotive "1483," CC, 18		1300
____	**1931130**	Southern USRA 4-8-2 Light Mountain Locomotive "1495," CC, 18		1300
____	**1931140**	North Pole Central 4-8-2 Light Mountain "1224," CC, 18		1300
____	**1931150**	SP 4-4-2 Atlantic A-6 Locomotive "3001," CC, 18		800
____	**1931160**	SP 4-4-2 Atlantic A-6 Locomotive "3000," CC, 18		800
____	**1931170**	SP 4-4-2 Atlantic A-6 Locomotive "3002," CC, 18		800

MODERN 1970-2025		Exc	Mint
1931180	UP 4-4-2 Atlantic Locomotive "3304," CC, 18		800
1931190	C&NW 4-4-2 Atlantic Locomotive "394," CC, 18		800
1931200	IC 4-4-2 Atlantic Locomotive "1003," CC, 18		800
1931210	Clinchfield 4-6-6-4 Locomotive "675," CC, 18		2000
1931220	D&RGW 4-6-6-4 Locomotive "3800," CC, 18		2000
1931230	D&RGW 4-6-6-4 Locomotive "3805," CC, 18		2000
1931240	UP 4-6-6-4 Challenger Locomotive "3975," CC, 18		2000
1931250	UP 4-6-6-4 Challenger Locomotive "3977," CC, 18		2000
1931260	UP 4-6-6-4 Challenger Locomotive "3985," CC, 18		2000
1931270	UP 4-6-6-4 Challenger Locomotive "3981," CC, 18		2000
1931280	UP 4-6-6-4 Challenger Locomotive "3717," CC, 18		2000
1931290	UP 4-6-6-4 Challenger Locomotive "3949," CC, 18		2000
1931300	Undecorated 4-6-6-4 Challenger Locomotive "9999," CC, 18		2000
1931311	UP Vision Auxiliary Water Tender "907853," CC, 18		500
1931312	UP Vision Auxiliary Water Tender "907856," CC, 18		500
1931313	UP Vision Auxiliary Water Tender "907857," CC, 18		500
1931314	UP Vision Auxiliary Water Tender "809," CC, 18		500
1931315	UP Vision Auxiliary Water Tender "814," CC, 18		500
1931316	UP Vision Auxiliary Water Tender "903026," CC, 18		500
1931320	Clinchfield Vision Auxiliary Water Tender "X675," CC, 18		500
1931330	D&RGW Vision Auxiliary Water Tender "3800A," CC, 18		500
1931340	N&W 4-8-4 Northern J-Class "600," CC, 19		1500
1931350	N&W 4-8-4 Northern J-Class "603," CC, 19		1500
1931360	N&W 4-8-4 Northern J-Class "611" (c1982)," CC, 19		1500
1931370	N&W 4-8-4 Northern J-Class "611" (c2016)," CC, 19		1500
1931380	American Freedom Train 4-8-4 "611," CC, 19		1500
1931390	N&W 4-8-4 Northern J-Class "746," CC, 19		1500
1931400	C&O 2-10-4 Texas T1 "3001," CC, 19		1500
1931410	C&O 2-10-4 Texas T1 "3039," CC, 19		1500
1931420	PRR 2-10-4 Texas J1a "6174," CC, 19		1500
1931430	PRR 2-10-4 Texas J1a "6434," CC, 19		1500
1931440	PRR 2-10-4 Texas J1a "6500," CC (artist conception), 19		1500
1931450	NYC 4-6-4 Hudson J3a "5405," CC, 19		1400
1931460	NYC 4-6-4 Hudson J3a "5413," CC, 19		1500
1931470	NYC 4-6-4 Hudson J3a "5418," CC, 19		1400
1931480	NYC 4-6-4 Hudson J3a "5452," CC, 19		1500
1931490	Ely Thomas Two-Truck Shay Locomotive "6," CC, 19		1200
1931500	Lima Stone Two-Truck Shay Locomotive "10," CC, 19		1200
1931510	Lima Locomotive Works Two-Truck Shay Locomotive "2," CC, 19		1200
1931520	Long Bell Two-Truck Shay Locomotive "5," CC, 19		1200
1931530	NY&P Two-Truck Shay Locomotive "3," CC, 19		1200
1931540	Roaring Camp Two-Truck Shay Locomotive "1," CC, 19		1200
1931550	North Pole Woodworks Two-Truck Shay Locomotive "25," CC, 19		1200
1931560	Sleepy Hollow Casket, Two-Truck Shay Locomotive "31," CC, 19		1200
1931650	Central Pacific 4-4-0 Hybrid Jupiter, CC (painted), 19		1100
1931660	UP 4-4-0 Hybrid, "119," CC (painted), 19		1100
1931670	Schenectady Locomotive Works 4-4-0 Hybrid, CC (unpainted), 19		1100
1931680	Rogers Locomotive Works 4-4-0 Hybrid, CC (unpainted), 19		1100
1931690	C&O 2-10-4 Texas T1 "3020," CC (weathered), 19		1700
1931700	PRR 2-10-4 Texas J1a "6481," CC (weathered), 19		1700

			Exc	Mint
___	**1931710**	B&LE 2-10-4 Texas "643," CC, 19		1500
___	**1931720**	CB&Q 2-10-4 Texas "6328," CC, 19		1500
___	**1931730**	DM&IR 2-10-4 Texas "717," CC, 19		1500
___	**1931740**	KCS 2-10-4 Texas "905," CC, 19		1500
___	**1931750**	D&RGW 2-10-4 Texas "1450," CC, 19		1500
___	**1931760**	Southern 2-10-4 Texas "5300," CC, 19		1500
___	**1931770**	Central Pacific 4-4-0 Hybrid Leviathan, CC (painted), 19		1100
___	**1931780**	Northern Central 4-4-0 Hybrid York, CC (painted), 19		1100
___	**1931820**	PRR 4-4-0 Hybrid, "573," CC (painted), 19		1100
___	**1932010**	ATSF 2-8-4 Berkshire "4101," LionChief Plus 2.0, 19-20		500
___	**1932020**	C&O 2-8-4 Berkshire Locomotive "2687," LionChief Plus 2.0, 19		500
___	**1932030**	NPR 2-8-4 Berkshire Locomotive "765," LionChief Plus 2.0, 19-20		500
___	**1932040**	Pere Marquette 2-8-4 Berkshire "1225," LionChief Plus 2.0, 19-20		500
___	**1932050**	Southern 2-8-4 Berkshire, "2716," LionChief Plus 2.0, 19-20		500
___	**1932080**	Disney 2-8-4 Berkshire "2019," LionChief Plus 2.0, 19-20		525
___	**1932090**	Polar Express 2-8-4 Berkshire "1225," LionChief Plus 2.0, 19-20		525
___	**1932100**	North Pole Central 2-8-4 Berkshire "1224," LionChief Plus 2.0, 19-20		500
___	**1932110**	Halloween (ELX) 2-8-4 Berkshire "1031," LionChief Plus 2.0, 19-20		500
___	**1932120**	GN 2-4-2 Columbia Locomotive "374," LionChief, 19		200
___	**1932130**	PRR 2-4-2 Columbia Locomotive "619" LionChief, 19		200
___	**1932140**	AT&SF 2-4-2 Columbia Locomotive "3452," LionChief, 19		200
___	**1932150**	Southern 2-4-2 Columbia Locomotive "1412," LionChief, 19		200
___	**1932161**	UP 4-8-8-4 Big Boy Locomotive "4012," LionChief Plus 2.0, 19		1200
___	**1932162**	UP 4-8-8-4 Big Boy Locomotive "4014," LionChief Plus 2.0, 19		1200
___	**1932163**	UP 4-8-8-4 Big Boy Locomotive "4017," LionChief Plus 2.0, 19		1200
___	**1932164**	UP 4-8-8-4 Big Boy Locomotive "4018," LionChief Plus 2.0, 19		1200
___	**1932170**	UP 4-8-8-4 Big Boy "4000" (Greyhound), LionChief Plus 2.0, 19		1200
___	**1933011**	BN Alco RS11 Diesel "4186," CC, 18		500
___	**1933012**	BN Alco RS11 Diesel "4190," CC, 18		500
___	**1933021**	CV Alco RS11 Diesel "3601," CC, 18		500
___	**1933022**	CV Alco RS11 Diesel "3611," CC, 18		500
___	**1933031**	Conrail Alco RS11 Diesel "7640," CC, 18		500
___	**1933032**	Conrail Alco RS11 Diesel "7651," CC, 18		500
___	**1933041**	Depew, Lancaster & Western Alco RS11 Diesel "1800," CC, 18		500
___	**1933042**	Depew, Lancaster & Western Alco RS11 Diesel "1804," CC, 18		500
___	**1933051**	L&N Alco RS11 Diesel "952," CC, 18		500
___	**1933052**	L&N Alco RS11 Diesel "955," CC, 18		500
___	**1933061**	SCL Alco RS11 Diesel "1202," CC, 18		500
___	**1933062**	SCL Alco RS11 Diesel "1210," CC, 18		500
___	**1933081**	BN EMD SD40-2 Diesel "6702," CC, 18		550
___	**1933082**	BN EMD SD40-2 Diesel "8002," CC, 18		550
___	**1933083**	BN non-powered EMD SD40-2 Diesel "6772," 18		300
___	**1933091**	FEC EMD SD40-2 Diesel "703," CC, 18		550
___	**1933092**	FEC EMD SD40-2 Diesel "713," CC, 18		550
___	**1933093**	FEC non-powered EMD SD40-2 Diesel "714," 18		300

		Exc	Mint
1933101	FURX EMD SD40-2 Diesel "3012," CC, 18		550
1933102	FURX EMD SD40-2 Diesel "3021," CC, 18		550
1933103	FURX non-powered EMD SD40-2 Diesel "3049," 18		300
1933111	Milwaukee Road Bicentennial EMD SD40-2 Diesel "156," CC, 18		550
1933112	Milwaukee Road EMD SD40-2 Diesel "190," CC, 18		550
1933113	Milwaukee Road EMD SD40-2 Diesel "196," CC, 18		550
1933114	Milwaukee Road non-powered EMD SD40-2 Diesel "197," 18		300
1933121	Soo Line "Bandit" EMD SD40-2 Diesel "6301," CC, 18		550
1933122	Soo Line "Bandit" EMD SD40-2 Diesel "6345," CC, 18		550
1933123	Soo Line "Bandit" non-powered EMD SD40-2 Diesel "6362," 18		300
1933131	UP EMD SD40-2 Diesel "3696," CC, 18		550
1933132	UP EMD SD40-2 Diesel "3707," CC, 18		550
1933133	UP non-powered EMD SD40-2 Diesel "B3641," 18		300
1933141	W&LE EMD SD40-2 Diesel "6310," CC, 18		550
1933142	W&LE EMD SD40-2 Diesel "6311," CC, 18		550
1933143	W&LE non-powered EMD SD40-2 Diesel "6347," 18		300
1933151	W&S EMD SD40-2 Diesel "4001," CC, 18		550
1933152	W&S EMD SD40-2 Diesel "4003," CC, 18		550
1933153	W&S non-powered EMD SD40-2 Diesel "4005," 18		300
1933160	AT&SF Alco PA-PA Diesel Set "54-54," CC, 18		1000
1933163	AT&SF Alco PB w/SuperBass Sound "54A," CC, 18		500
1933170	D&RGW Alco PA-PA Diesel Set "6001-6003," CC, 18		1000
1933173	D&RGW Alco PB w/SuperBass Sound "6002," CC, 18		500
1933180	NYC Alco PA-PA Diesel Set "4903-4904," CC, 18		1000
1933183	NYC Alco PB w/SuperBass Sound "4303," CC, 18		500
1933190	PRR Alco PA-PA Diesel Set "5754-5755+B34," CC, 18		1000
1933193	PRR Alco PB w/SuperBass Sound "5754B," CC, 18		500
1933200	SP Alco PA-PA Diesel Set "6034-6039," CC, 18		1000
1933203	SP Alco PB w/SuperBass Sound "5922," CC, 18		500
1933210	UP Alco PA-PA Diesel Set "606-607," CC, 18		1000
1933213	UP Alco PB w/SuperBass Sound "606B," CC, 18		500
1933221	BNSF (ATSF Patch) GE C44-9W Diesel "599," CC, 18		550
1933222	BNSF (ATSF Patch) GE C44-9W Diesel "662," CC, 18		550
1933223	BNSF (ATSF Patch) non-powered GE C44-9W Diesel "604," 18		300
1933231	BNSF GE C44-9W Diesel "703," CC, 18		550
1933232	BNSF GE C44-9W Diesel "4173," CC, 18		550
1933233	BNSF non-powered GE C44-9W Diesel "5282," 18		300
1933241	Pilbara Rail GE C44-9W Diesel "7079," CC, 18		550
1933242	Pilbara Rail GE C44-9W Diesel "7097," CC, 18		550
1933243	Pilbara Rail non-powered GE C44-9W Diesel "7098," 18		300
1933251	Quebec, North Shore & Labrador GE C44-9W Diesel "405," CC, 18		550
1933252	Quebec, North Shore & Labrador GE C44-B141 Diesel "407," CC, 18		550
1933253	Quebec, North Shore & Labrador non-powered GE C44-9W Diesel "413," 18		300
1933261	UP (SP Patch) GE C44-9W Diesel "9615," CC, 18		550
1933262	UP (SP Patch) GE C44-9W Diesel "9617," CC, 18		550
1933263	UP (SP Patch) non-powered GE C44-9W Diesel "9647," 18		300
1933271	UP GE C44-9W Diesel w/Cheyenne Service Unit Plaque "9700," CC, 18		550

			Exc	Mint
____	**1933272**	UP GE C44-9W Diesel "9650," CC, 18		550
____	**1933273**	UP non-powered GE C44-9W Diesel "9654," 18		300
____	**1933281**	BNSF GE ES44AC Diesel "6411," CC, 19		600
____	**1933282**	BNSF GE ES44AC Diesel "6425," CC, 19		600
____	**1933283**	BNSF non-powered GE ES44AC Diesel "6438," 19		350
____	**1933291**	CitiRail GE ES44AC Diesel "1201," CC, 19		600
____	**1933292**	CitiRail GE ES44AC Diesel "1210," CC, 19		600
____	**1933293**	CitiRail non-powered GE ES44AC Diesel "1212," 19		350
____	**1933301**	GE Demonstrator ES44AC Diesel "2005," CC, 19		600
____	**1933302**	GE Demonstrator ES44AC Diesel "2012," CC, 19		600
____	**1933310**	Iowa Interstate GE ES44AC Diesel "516," CC+B387, 19		600
____	**1933321**	UP GE ES44AC Diesel "7964," CC, 19		600
____	**1933322**	UP GE ES44AC Diesel "8109," CC, 19		600
____	**1933323**	UP non-powered GE ES44AC Diesel "8140," 19		350
____	**1933324**	UP GE ES44AC Diesel, Fantasy Greyhound scheme, "8044," CC, 19		600
____	**1933325**	UP GE ES44AC Diesel, Fantasy 49er scheme, "8149," CC, 19		600
____	**1933326**	UP GE ES44AC Diesel Fantasy "119," CC, 19		600
____	**1933327**	UP GE ES44AC Diesel Fantasy Jupiter "60," CC, 19		600
____	**1933331**	Allegheny RR EMD GP35 Diesel "305," CC, 19		500
____	**1933332**	Allegheny RR EMD GP35 Diesel "306," CC, 19		500
____	**1933341**	AT&SF EMD GP35 Diesel "2835," CC, 19		500
____	**1933342**	AT&SF EMD GP35 Diesel "2858," CC, 19		500
____	**1933343**	AT&SF non-powered EMD GP35 Diesel "2932," 19		300
____	**1933351**	C&NW EMD GP35 Diesel "826," CC, 19		500
____	**1933352**	C&NW EMD GP35 Diesel "830," CC, 19		500
____	**1933353**	C&NW non-powered EMD GP35 Diesel "841," 19		300
____	**1933361**	Conrail EMD GP35 Diesel "2398," CC, 19		500
____	**1933362**	Conrail EMD GP35 Diesel "3630," CC, 19		500
____	**1933363**	Conrail non-powered EMD GP35 Diesel "3692," 19		300
____	**1933371**	BNSF EMD GP35 Diesel "2570," CC, 19		500
____	**1933372**	BNSF EMD GP35 Diesel "2615," CC, 19		500
____	**1933373**	BNSF non-powered EMD GP35 Diesel "2931," 19		300
____	**1933381**	Lycoming Valley EMD GP35 Diesel "5510," CC, 19		500
____	**1933382**	Lycoming Valley EMD GP35 Diesel "5514," CC, 19		500
____	**1933391**	PRR EMD GP35 Diesel "2298," CC, 19		500
____	**1933392**	PRR EMD GP35 Diesel "2333," CC, 19		500
____	**1933393**	PRR non-powered EMD GP35 Diesel "2356," 19		300
____	**1933401**	RF&P EMD GP35 Diesel "131," CC, 19		500
____	**1933402**	RF&P EMD GP35 Diesel "134," CC, 19		500
____	**1933403**	RF&P non-powered EMD GP35 Diesel "138," 19		300
____	**1933411**	Apache RR Alco C-420 Diesel "81," CC, 19		500
____	**1933412**	Apache RR Alco C-420 Diesel "82," CC, 19		500
____	**1933413**	Apache RR non-powered Alco C-420 Diesel "84," 19		300
____	**1933421**	D&H Alco C-420 Diesel "404," CC, 19		500
____	**1933422**	D&H Alco C-420 Diesel "414," CC, 19		500
____	**1933423**	D&H non-powered Alco C-420 Diesel "204," 19		300
____	**1933430**	D&M Alco C-420 Diesel "976," CC, 19		500
____	**1933441**	Erie Mining Alco C-420 Diesel "7220," CC, 19		500
____	**1933442**	Erie Mining non-powered Alco C-420 Diesel "7221," 19		300
____	**1933451**	L&HR Alco C-420 Diesel "21," CC, 19		500
____	**1933452**	L&HR Alco C-420 Diesel "23," CC, 19		500
____	**1933453**	L&HR non-powered Alco C-420 Diesel "21," CC, 19		300
____	**1933461**	LIRR Alco C-420 Diesel "202," CC, 19		500

		Exc	Mint
1933462	LIRR Alco C-420 Diesel "218," CC, 19		500
1933471	P&N Alco C-420 Diesel "2000," CC, 19		500
1933472	P&N Alco C-420 Diesel "2001," CC, 19		500
1933480	NYS&W Alco C-420 Diesel "2010," CC, 19		500
1933490	Alco Demonstrator FA A-A Diesel Set, CC, 19		900
1933498	Alco Demonstrator FB-2 Unit, CC, 19		450
1933499	Alco Demonstrator FB-2 Unit w/RailSounds, 19		430
1933500	C&NW Alco FA A-A Diesel Set, CC, 19		900
1933508	C&NW Alco FB-2 Unit, CC, 19		450
1933509	C&NW Alco FB-2 Unit w/RailSounds, 19		430
1933510	CP Alco FA-2 A-A Diesel Set "4082/4083," CC, 19		900
1933518	CP Alco FB-2 "4469," CC, 19		450
1933519	CP Alco FB-2 Unit w/RailSounds, 19		430
1933520	LV Alco FA A-A Diesel Set, CC, 19		900
1933528	LV Alco FB-2 Unit, CC, 19		450
1933529	LV Alco FB-2 Unit w/RailSounds, 19		430
1933530	MP Alco FA A-A Diesel Set, CC, 19		900
1933538	MP Alco FB-2 Unit, CC, 19		450
1933539	MP Alco FB-2 Unit w/RailSounds, 19		430
1933540	NYC Alco FA A-A Diesel Set, CC, 19		900
1933548	NYC Alco FB-2 Unit, CC, 19		450
1933549	NYC Alco FB-2 Unit w/RailSounds, 19		430
1933550	SP&S Alco FA A-A Diesel Set, CC, 19		900
1933558	SP&S Alco FB-2 Unit, CC, 19		450
1933559	SP&S Alco FB-2 Unit w/RailSounds, 19		430
1933561	LIRR Alco FA Cab Car "607," CC, 19		430
1933562	LIRR Alco FA Cab Car "609," CC, 19		430
1933563	LIRR Alco FA Cab Car "608," CC, 19		430
1933564	LIRR Alco FA Cab Car "610," CC, 19		430
1933571	Milwaukee Road GE Bi-Polar Electric "E-1," CC, 19		1300
1933572	Milwaukee Road GE Bi-Polar Electric "E-2," CC, 19		1300
1933573	Milwaukee Road GE Bi-Polar Electric "E-3," CC, 19		1300
1933574	Milwaukee Road GE Bi-Polar Electric "E-4," CC, 19		1300
1933575	Milwaukee Road GE Bi-Polar Electric "E-5," CC, 19		1300
1933580	GN GE Bi-Polar Electric "5020," CC, 19		1300
1933590	NH GE Bi-Polar Electric "380," CC, 19		1300
1933600	NYC GE Bi-Polar Electric "300," CC, 19		1300
1933610	PRR GE Bi-Polar Electric "4501," CC, 19		1300
1933620	Polar Express GE Bi-Polar Electric "E-25," CC, 19		1300
1933630	NS GE C44-9W Diesel "8520," CC, 18		550
1934011	BNSF GE ET44AC Diesel "3738," LionChief Plus 2.0, 19		400
1934012	BNSF GE ET44AC Diesel "3776," LionChief Plus 2.0, 19		400
1934021	CSX GE ET44AC Diesel "3277," LionChief Plus 2.0, 19		400
1934022	CSX GE ET44AC Diesel "3291," LionChief Plus 2.0, 19		400
1934031	NS GE ET44AC Diesel "3600," LionChief Plus 2.0, 19		400
1934032	NS GE ET44AC Diesel "3619," LionChief Plus 2.0, 19		400
1934041	UP GE ET44AC Diesel "2645," LionChief Plus 2.0, 19		400
1934042	UP GE ET44AC Diesel "2727," LionChief Plus 2.0, 19		400
1934050	BN Alco RS3 Diesel "4068," LionChief, 19		200
1934060	CNJ Alco RS3 Diesel "1552," LionChief, 19		200
1934070	Delaware-Lackawanna Alco RS3 Diesel "4103," LionChief, 19		200

MODERN 1970-2025		Exc	Mint
____ **1934080**	UP Alco RS3 Diesel "1219," LionChief, 19		200
____ **1934090**	AT&SF EMD FT Diesel A-A Set "123/124," LionChief Plus 2.0, 19		550
____ **1934098**	AT&SF EMD FT B Unit, LionChief Plus 2.0, 19		300
____ **1934100**	GN EMD FT Diesel A-A Set "400/401," LionChief Plus 2.0, 19		550
____ **1934108**	GN EMD FT B Unit, LionChief Plus 2.0, 19		300
____ **1934110**	NYC EMD FT Diesel A-A Set "1603/1604," LionChief Plus 2.0, 19		550
____ **1934118**	NYC EMD FT B Unit, LionChief Plus 2.0, 19		300
____ **1934120**	Texas Special FT Diesel A-A "219/220," LionChief Plus 2.0, 19		550
____ **1934128**	Texas Special EMD FT B Unit, LionChief Plus 2.0, 19		300
____ **1935010**	Area 51 Motorized Trackmobile "51," CC, 19		350
____ **1935020**	Bethlehem Steel Motorized Trackmobile "12," CC, 19		350
____ **1935030**	BN Motorized Trackmobile, CC, 19		350
____ **1935040**	Granite Run Quarries Motorized Trackmobile, CC, 19		350
____ **1935050**	Milwaukee Road Motorized Trackmobile, CC, 19		350
____ **1935060**	PP&L Motorized Trackmobile "16," CC, 19		350
____ **1935070**	AT&SF Motorized Trackmobile "8," CC, 19		350
____ **1935080**	SP Motorized Trackmobile "5," CC, 19		350
____ **1935090**	WWII U.S. War Bonds Trolley, 19		100
____ **1938010**	Mickey Mouse Celebration True Original Boxcar, 18		85
____ **1938030**	Well-Stocked Angela Trotta Thomas Boxcar, 18		85
____ **1938040**	Jupiter Anniversary Boxcar, 19		85
____ **1938050**	Southern Ry. 125th Anniversary Boxcar, 19		85
____ **1938060**	Westinghouse Air Brake 150th Anniversary Boxcar, 19		85
____ **1938100**	Pez Vintage Boxcar, 19		85
____ **1938110**	Looney Tunes Duck Dodgers Boxcar, 19		90
____ **1938120**	Looney Tunes Rabbit Season Boxcar, 19		90
____ **1938130**	Looney Tunes Road Runner Boxcar, 19		90
____ **1938180**	Martin Van Buren Presidential Boxcar, 19		70
____ **1938190**	James Buchanan Presidential Boxcar, 19		70
____ **1938200**	William McKinley Presidential Boxcar, 19		70
____ **1938210**	WWII Kiss the Way Goodbye Boxcar, 19		85
____ **1938220**	WWII Sherman Tank Boxcar, 19		85
____ **1938240**	WWII Liberty Ships Boxcar, 19		85
____ **1938260**	Wings of Angels--Blonde Boxcar, 19		90
____ **1938270**	Wings of Angels--Redhead Boxcar, 19		90
____ **1938280**	Wings of Angels--Brunette Boxcar, 19		90
____ **1938290**	Happy Birthday 2019 Boxcar, 19		95
____ **1938300**	Merry Christmas 2019 Boxcar, 19		90
____ **1938310**	Angela Trotta Thomas Christmas Boxcar, 19		90
____ **1938320**	Personalized Christmas Caboose, 19-20		90
____ **1938340**	Happy Birthday Caboose, 19-20		90
____ **1938370**	UP Anniversary Boxcar "199," 19		85
____ **1942170**	UP Vision Challenger Boxcar 6-pack #1, 18		390
____ **1942180**	UP Vision Challenger Boxcar 6-pack #2, 18		390
____ **1942190**	UP Vision Challenger Boxcar 6-pack #3, 18		390
____ **1942200**	UP Vision Challenger Boxcar 6-pack #4, 18		390
____ **1942210**	UP Vision Challenger Express Boxcar 6-pack, 18		390
____ **2001090**	LCCA 50th Anniversary Convention Car 2-pack, 20 u		300
____ **2001100**	LCCA 50th Anniversary UP Registration Mint Car, 20 u		75
____ **2001110**	LCCA UP ET44AC Diesel "2020" LionChief Plus 2.0, 20 u		700

MODERN 1970-2025		Exc	Mint
2001160	LCCA 50th Anniversary UP Unibody 1-D Tank Car, 20 u		75 ___
2022010	Granite Run Quarry Steam Freight Set, LionChief Plus 2.0, 19		350 ___
2022020	Christmas Candies Steam Freight Set, LionChief Plus 2.0, 19		350 ___
2022030	Easter Eggspress Steam Freight Set, LionChief Plus 2.0, 19		350 ___
2022040	Manufacturers Railway Alco S-2 Diesel Freight Set, CC, 19		800 ___
2022050	George H.W. Bush Funeral Diesel Passenger Train, CC, 19		1200 ___
2022060	Pennsylvania Fast Freight Electric Freight Set, LionChief Plus 2.0, 19		700 ___
2022070	B&M E8 Diesel Passenger Set, CC, 20		800 ___
2022080	Preamble Express Diesel Passenger Set, CC, 20		800 ___
2022090	Polar Express Elf Steam Work Train Set, LionChief, 20		450 ___
2022100	Pennsylvania Train Master Diesell Freight Set, CC, 20		900 ___
2022110	CNJ Red Baron SD40 Diesel Freight Set, CC, 20		850 ___
2022120	Lionel 120th Deluxe LionChief Plus 2.0 F3 Diesel Freight Set, CC, 20		1000 ___
2022130	SP Vision Stock Express Steam Freight Train Set, CC, 20		2500 ___
2022140	North Pole Central Snowflake Limited Steam Freight Set, CC, 20		1000 ___
2023010	Strasburg RR Steam Freight Set, LionChief, 19-20		370 ___
2023020	Shark Research & Rescue Diesel Freight Set, LionChief, 19		400 ___
2023030	Budweiser Delivery ET44 Diesel Freight Set, LionChief, 20		370 ___
2023040	Disney Frozen 2 Steam Freight Set, LionChief, 20-24		450 ___
2023050	Area 51 ET44 Diesel Freight Set, LionChief, 20, 23		475 ___
2023070	Lionel Junction North Pole Central Steam Freight Set, LionChief, 20		330 ___
2023080	Christmas Light Express Steam Freight Set, LionChief, 20		430 ___
2023090	Witherslack Hall Steam Passenger Set, LionChief, 20		400 ___
2023100	GE Tier 4 ET44 Diesel Freight Set, LionChief, 20		400 ___
2023110	Toy Story Steam Freight Set, LionChief, 20-25		450 ___
2023120	Lionel Lines LionChief Steam Freight Set, 20		300 ___
2023130	Star Trek Diesel Freight Set, LionChief, 20		450 ___
2023140	Polar Express Steam Passenger Set, LionChief, 20		400 ___
2023150	Alaska GP38 Diesel Freight Set, LionChief, 20		400 ___
2023160	Baldwin Locomotive Works Steam Freight Set, LionChief, 20		400 ___
2023170	Hogwarts Express Steam Passenger Set, LionChief, 20		400 ___
2025010	Lighted FasTrack 10" Straight, 4-pack, 20-25		66 ___
2025020	Lighted Fastrack 0-36 Curve, 4-pack, 20-25		66 ___
2025050	Merry Christmas FasTrack Girder Bridge, 20-24		35 ___
2025070	Lighted FasTrack Terminal Track Pack, 20-25		44 ___
2025080	Lighted FasTrack Oval Track Pack , 20-25		165 ___
2026010	Side Dump Car 4-pack, 19		160 ___
2026020	Christmas Side Dump Car 4-pack, 19		160 ___
2026030	Easter Eggspress Side Dump Car 4-pack, 19		160 ___
2026040	Ely Thomas Lumber Logging Caboose, "1," 19		45 ___
2026050	Safety First Logging Caboose, "3," 19		45 ___
2026061	AT&SF 40' Plug-Door Refrigerator Car, "14180," 19		90 ___
2026062	AT&SF 40' Plug-Door Refrigerator Car, "14193," 19		90 ___
2026071	BAR 40' Plug-Door Refrigerator Car, "7728," 19		90 ___
2026072	BAR 40' Plug-Door Refrigerator Car, "7777," 19		90 ___
2026081	GB&W 40' Plug-Door Refrigerator Car, "21002," 19		90 ___
2026082	GB&W 40' Plug-Door Refrigerator Car, "21038," 19		90 ___
2026091	PFE 40' Plug-Door Refrigerator Car, "18015," 19		90 ___
2026092	PFE 40' Plug-Door Refrigerator Car, "18118," 19		90 ___
2026101	Reading 40' Plug-Door Refrigerator Car, "272," 19		90 ___

			Exc	Mint
____	**2026102**	Reading 40' Plug-Door Refrigerator Car, "278," 19		90
____	**2026111**	Therm Ice 40' Plug-Door Refrigerator Car, "8907," 19		90
____	**2026112**	Therm Ice 40' Plug-Door Refrigerator Car, "8910," 19		90
____	**2026120**	AT&SF PS-1 Boxcar, "17819" w/FreightSounds, 19		135
____	**2026130**	DT&I PS-1 Boxcar, "14253" w/FreightSounds, 19		135
____	**2026140**	EL PS-1 Boxcar, B195 "74210" w/FreightSounds, 19		135
____	**2026150**	GN PS-1 Boxcar, "19038" w/FreightSounds, 19		135
____	**2026160**	Illinois Terminal PS-1 Boxcar, "8427" w/FreightSounds, 19		135
____	**2026170**	NYC PS-1 Boxcar, "163194" w/FreightSounds, 19		135
____	**2026180**	PC PS-1 Boxcar, "253321" w/FreightSounds, 19		135
____	**2026190**	UP PS-1 Boxcar, "125404" w/FreightSounds, 19		135
____	**2026200**	B&O I-12 BW Caboose, "C2428," 19		110
____	**2026210**	B&O I-12 BW Caboose, "C2406," 19		110
____	**2026220**	B&O I-12 BW Caboose, "C2822," 19		110
____	**2026230**	B&O I-12 BW Caboose, "C2457," 19		110
____	**2026240**	Chessie System I-12 BW Caboose, "902440," 19		110
____	**2026250**	Polar Express I-12 BW Caboose, "C2425," 19		110
____	**2026260**	Anheuser Busch 8,000-Gallon 1-D Tank Car, "4274," 19		80
____	**2026270**	Deep Rock 8,000-Gallon 1-D Tank Car, "6516," 19		80
____	**2026280**	Everett Distilling 8,000-Gallon 1-D Tank Car, "41," 19		80
____	**2026290**	Hercules Powder 8,000-Gallon 1-D Tank Car, "10673," 19		80
____	**2026300**	Independence Energy 8,000-Gallon 1-D Tank Car, "1776," 19		80
____	**2026310**	Sinclair 8,000-Gallon 1-D Tank Car, "13103," 19		80
____	**2026320**	Amtrak Veterans 60' LED Flag Boxcar, "70042," 19		120
____	**2026330**	I Love USA 60' LED Flag Boxcar, 19		120
____	**2026340**	KCS 60' LED Flag Boxcar, "4006," 19		120
____	**2026350**	NS First Responders 60' LED Flag Boxcar, "9-1-1," 19		120
____	**2026360**	NS Veterans 60' LED Flag Boxcar, "6920," 19		120
____	**2026370**	UP 60" LED Flag Boxcar "4141," 19		120
____	**2026380**	UP Transcontinental 60' LED Flag Boxcar, "150," 19		120
____	**2026391**	AT&SF 60' Boxcar, "37639," 19		100
____	**2026392**	AT&SF 60' Boxcar, "37719," 19		100
____	**2026401**	CP 60' Boxcar, "205502," 19		100
____	**2026402**	CP 60' Boxcar, "205525," 19		100
____	**2026411**	DT&I 60' Boxcar, "25525," 19		100
____	**2026412**	DT&I 60' Boxcar, "25528," 19		100
____	**2026421**	NYC 60' Boxcar, "56451," 19		100
____	**2026422**	NYC 60' Boxcar, "56516," 19		100
____	**2026431**	PRR 60' Boxcar, "11789," 19		100
____	**2026432**	PRR 60' Boxcar, "11813," 19		100
____	**2026441**	PC 60' Boxcar, "274570," 19		100
____	**2026442**	PC 60' Boxcar, "274584," 19		100
____	**2026450**	Chevrolet 60' Boxcar "26450," 19		100
____	**2026460**	Ford 60' Boxcar, "26460," 19		100
____	**2026470**	Area 51 57' Smoking Mechanical Refrigerator Car w/ FreightSounds, 20		200
____	**2026480**	AT&SF 57' Smoking Mechanical Refrigerator Car w/ FreightSounds, 20		200
____	**2026490**	BNSF 57' Smoking Mechanical Refrigerator Car w/ FreightSounds, 20		200
____	**2026500**	Conrail 57' Smoking Mechanical Refrigerator Car w/ FreightSounds, 20		200
____	**2026510**	Halloween Smoking 57' Mechanical Refrigerator Car, 20		200

		Exc	Mint
2026520	PFE 57' Smoking Mechanical Refrigerator Car w/ FreightSounds, 20		200 ____
2026530	UP 57' Smoking Mechanical Refrigerator Car w/ FreightSounds, 20		200 ____
2026541	AT&SF "Beer Car" Insulated Boxcar, "625355," 20		100 ____
2026542	AT&SF "Beer Car" Insulated Boxcar, "625380," 20		100 ____
2026551	BN "Beer Car" Insulated Boxcar, "3069," 20		100 ____
2026552	BN "Beer Car" Insulated Boxcar, "3116," 20		100 ____
2026561	BNSF "Beer Car" Insulated Boxcar, "782403" w/Graffiti, 20		110 ____
2026562	BNSF "Beer Car" Insulated Boxcar, "782425," 20		100 ____
2026563	BNSF "Beer Car" Insulated Boxcar, "782483," 20		100 ____
2026571	Conrail "Beer Car" Insulated Boxcar, "376045," 20		100 ____
2026572	Conrail "Beer Car" Insulated Boxcar, "376142," 20		100 ____
2026581	Coors "Beer Car" Insulated Boxcar, "24," 20		100 ____
2026582	Coors "Beer Car" Insulated Boxcar, "26," 20		100 ____
2026591	Manufacturers Ry. "Beer Car" Insulated Boxcar, "2520," 20		100 ____
2026592	Manufacturers Ry. "Beer Car" Insulated Boxcar, "2540," 20		100 ____
2026601	SP "Beer Car" Insulated Boxcar, "691783" w/Graffiti, 20		110 ____
2026602	SP "Beer Car" Insulated Boxcar, "691729," 20		100 ____
2026603	SP "Beer Car" Insulated Boxcar, "691745," 20		100 ____
2026611	AT&SF 50' Flatcar, "91156" w/20' Trailers, 20		120 ____
2026612	AT&SF 50' Flatcar, "91220" w/20' Trailers, 20		120 ____
2026621	DT&I 50' Flatcar, "911" w/20' Ford Trailers, 20		120 ____
2026622	DT&I 50' Flatcar, "924" w/20' Ford Trailers, 20		120 ____
2026631	PRR 50' Flatcar, "469469" w/Mason Dixon Trailers, 20		120 ____
2026632	PRR 50' Flatcar, "469625" w/Mason Dixon Trailers, 20		120 ____
2026641	Trailer Train 50' Flatcar, 475231" w/Hennis Trailers, 20		120 ____
2026642	Trailer Train 50' Flatcar, 475293" w/Hennis Trailers, 20		120 ____
2026651	UP 50' Flatcar, "53085" w/Merchants Trailers, 20		120 ____
2026652	UP 50' Flatcar, "53091" w/Merchants Trailers, 20		120 ____
2026661	North Pole Central 50' Flatcar, "2024" w/20' Sled-Ex Trailers, 20		120 ____
2026662	North Pole Central 50' Flatcar, "2025" w/20' Sled-Ex Trailers, 20		120 ____
2026671	Polar Express 50' Flatcar, "122420" w/20' Trailers, 20		125 ____
2026672	Polar Express 50' Flatcar, "122520" w/20' Trailers, 20		125 ____
2026680	Polar Express Elf Work Train, 4-pack, 20		200 ____
2026690	Buffalo, Rochester & Pittsburgh 2-bay Hopper, 3-pack, 20		280 ____
2026700	Blue Coal 2-bay Hopper, 3-pack, 20		280 ____
2026710	NYO&W 2-bay Hopper, 3-pack, 20		280 ____
2026720	Rutland 2-bay Hopper, 3-pack, 20		280 ____
2026730	Waddell Coal 2-bay Hopper, 3-pack, 20		280 ____
2026741	CB&Q Friendship Train PS-1 Boxcar, "36262," 0		75 ____
2026742	C&NW Friendship Train PS-1 Boxcar, "143576," 20		75 ____
2026743	L&N Friendship Train PS-1 Boxcar, "16576," 20		75 ____
2026744	NYC Friendship Train PS-1 Boxcar, "161500," 20		75 ____
2026745	SP Friendship Train PS-1 Boxcar, "97994," 20		75 ____
2026746	UP Friendship Train PS-1 Boxcar, "187989," 20		75 ____
2026750	Chateau Martin Wine Car, "132," 20		100 ____
2026760	Cloverland Dairy Milk Car, "101," 20		100 ____
2026770	D&RGW Milk Car, "1612," 20		100 ____
2026780	Frisco Milk Car, "5009," 20		100 ____
2026790	Reid Ice Cream Milk Car, "103," 20		100 ____

	MODERN 1970-2025		Exc	Mint
___	**2026800**	Scenic Citrus Milk Car, "977," 20		100
___	**2026810**	Armour Vision Stockcar 3-pack w/Sound Car, 20		400
___	**2026820**	AT&SF Vision Stockcar 3-pack w/Sound Car, 20		400
___	**2026830**	CP Vision Stockcar 3-pack w/Sound Car, 20		400
___	**2026840**	CB&Q Vision Stockcar 3-pack w/Sound Car, 20		400
___	**2026850**	C&NW Vision Stockcar 3-pack w/Sound Car, 20		400
___	**2026860**	MKT Vision Stockcar 3-pack w/Sound Car, 20		400
___	**2026870**	PRR N5 Caboose, "476998," 20		100
___	**2026880**	PRR N5 Caboose, "477714," 20		100
___	**2026890**	PRR N5 Caboose, "492418," 20		100
___	**2026900**	PC N5 Caboose, "22838," 20		100
___	**2026910**	Lionel Lines NE Caboose, "120," 20		115
___	**2026930**	NYC Wood Caboose, "19020" w/CupolaCam, 20		190
___	**2026940**	NYC Safety Wood Caboose, "18906" w/CupolaCam, 20		190
___	**2026950**	Ford 2-bay Hopper, 3-pack, 20		280
___	**2026960**	AT&SF Vision Refrigerator Car 3-pack, 20		350
___	**2026970**	PFE Vision Refrigerator Car 3-pack, 20		350
___	**2026980**	MDT Vision Refrigerator Car 3-pack, 20		350
___	**2026990**	PRR Vision Refrigerator Car 3-pack, 20		350
___	**2027011**	Christmas Disconnect Passenger Car, Baggage, 19		45
___	**2027012**	Christmas Disconnect Passenger Car, Coach, 19		45
___	**2027013**	Christmas Disconnect Passenger Car, Diner, 19		45
___	**2027014**	Christmas Disconnect Passenger Car, Sleeper, 19		45
___	**2027015**	Christmas Disconnect Passenger Car, Observation, 19		45
___	**2027021**	NYC Disconnect Passenger Car, Baggage, 19		45
___	**2027022**	NYC Disconnect Passenger Car, Coach, 19		45
___	**2027023**	NYC Disconnect Passenger Car, Diner, 19		45
___	**2027024**	NYC Disconnect Passenger Car, Sleeper, 19		45
___	**2027025**	NYC Disconnect Passenger Car, Observation, 19		45
___	**2027031**	PRR Disconnect Passenger Car, Baggage, 19		45
___	**2027032**	PRR Disconnect Passenger Car, Coach, 19		45
___	**2027033**	PRR Disconnect Passenger Car, Diner, 19		45
___	**2027034**	PRR Disconnect Passenger Car, Sleeper, 19		45
___	**2027035**	PRR Disconnect Passenger Car, Observation, 19		45
___	**2027041**	D&RGW Disconnect Passenger Car, Baggage , 19		45
___	**2027042**	D&RGW Disconnect Passenger Car, Coach, 19		45
___	**2027043**	D&RGW Disconnect Passenger Car, Diner, 19		45
___	**2027044**	D&RGW Disconnect Passenger Car, Sleeper, 19		45
___	**2027045**	D&RGW Disconnect Passenger Car, Observation, 19		45
___	**2027051**	AT&SF Disconnect Passenger Car, Baggage , 19		45
___	**2027052**	AT&SF Disconnect Passenger Car, Coach, 19		45
___	**2027053**	AT&SF Disconnect Passenger Car, Diner, 19		45
___	**2027054**	AT&SF Disconnect Passenger Car, Sleeper, 19		45
___	**2027055**	AT&SF Disconnect Passenger Car, Observation, 19		45
___	**2027061**	SP Disconnect Passenger Car, Baggage, 19		45
___	**2027062**	SP Disconnect Passenger Car, Coach, 19		45
___	**2027063**	SP Disconnect Passenger Car, Diner, 19		45
___	**2027064**	SP Disconnect Passenger Car, Sleeper, 19		45
___	**2027065**	SP Disconnect Passenger Car, Observation, 19		45
___	**2027070**	AT&SF California Limited 18" Passenger Car 2-pack, A, 19		400
___	**2027080**	AT&SF California Limited 18" Passenger Car 2-pack, B, 19		400
___	**2027090**	AT&SF California Limited 18" Passenger Car 2-pack, C, 19		400

MODERN 1970-2025		Exc	Mint	
2027100	AT&SF California Limited 18" Diner "1406" w/StationSounds, 19		330	___
2027110	AT&SF Shadow Line 18" Passenger Car 2-pack, 19		400	___
2027120	Alaska RR 21" Passenger Car 4-pack, 19		720	___
2027130	Alaska RR 21" Passenger Car 2-pack, 19		420	___
2027140	Alaska RR 21" Diner, "400" w/StationSounds, 19		330	___
2027160	Alaska RR VistaVision Camera Dome Car, "501," 19		330	___
2027170	UP Challenger 21" Passenger Car Expansion 2-pack, 3, 19		360	___
2027180	NS Executive Train 21" Passenger Car 4-pack, 19		770	___
2027190	NS Executive Train 21" Passenger Car 2-pack, 19		360	___
2027200	NS 21" Diner, "Delaware," w/StationSounds, 19		340	___
2027210	Philadelphia & Reading Observation, 19-20		85	___
2027220	Ferdinand Magellan Observation, 19		85	___
2027230	UP Excursion 21" Passenger Car Expansion 2-pack, 3, 19		360	___
2027240	UP Excursion 21" Passenger Car Expansion 2-pack, 4, 19		360	___
2027250	Amtrak VistaVision Dome Car, "9463," 19		330	___
2027260	UP Excursion VistaVision Dome Car, "Colorado Eagle," 19		330	___
2027270	UP Challenger VistaVision Dome Car, "7005," 19		330	___
2027280	Auto-Train VistaVision Dome Car, "706," 19		330	___
2027290	PRR VistaVision Dome Car, "Catenary View," 19		330	___
2027300	N&W VistaVision Dome Car, "1613," 19		330	___
2027310	Southern VistaVision Dome Car, "1613," 19		330	___
2027330	Friendship Train 18" Sleeper 2-pack, 20		400	___
2027340	American Freedom Train 18" Passenger Car 2-pack, 1, 20		380	___
2027350	American Freedom Train 18" Passenger Car 2-pack, 2, 20		380	___
2027360	Chessie Steam Special Passenger Car 2-pack, 1, 20		450	___
2027370	Chessie Steam Special Passenger Car 2-pack, 2, 20		450	___
2027380	Chessie Steam Special Passenger Car 2-pack, 3, 20		450	___
2027390	Chessie Steam Special Passenger Car 2-pack, 4, 20		450	___
2027400	SP Golden State 21" Passenger Car 4-pack, 20		730	___
2027410	SP Golden State 21" Passenger Car 2-pack, 20		360	___
2027420	SP Golden State 21" Diner w/StationSounds, 20		360	___
2027430	Reading 18" Passsenger Car 2-pack, 1, 20		380	___
2027440	Reading 18" Passsenger Car 2-pack, 2, 20		380	___
2027450	Reading 18" Passsenger Car 2-pack, 3, 20		380	___
2027460	B&M 18" Passenger Car 2-pack, 20		380	___
2027470	Polar Express 18" Hobo Passenger Car w/Black Roof, 20-24		240	___
2027480	Polar Express 18" Hobo Passenger Car w/Snowy Roof, 20-22		240	___
2027490	PRR/AT&SF 21" Passsenger Car 2-pack, 20		400	___
2027500	PRR/UP 21" Passsenger Car 2-pack, 20		400	___
2027510	PRR/MP 21" Passsenger Car 2-pack, 20		400	___
2027520	SP Lark 21" Passenger Car 4-pack, 20		730	___
2027530	SP Lark 21" Passenger Car 2-pack, 20		360	___
2027540	SP Lark 21" Diner, w/StationSounds , 20		460	___
2027550	SP Daylight 18" Heavyweight Passenger Car 2-pack, A, 20		400	___
2027560	SP Daylight 18" Heavyweight Passenger Car 2-pack, B, 20		400	___
2027570	SP Daylight 18" Heavyweight Passenger Car 2-pack, C, 20		400	___
2027580	UP 21" Baggage Car, "Promontory," 19		180	___
2027590	SP Penn-Golden State 21" Passenger Car 2-pack, 20		360	___
2027600	PRR/Frisco 21" Passsenger Car 2-pack, 20		400	___
2027610	SP Daylight 18" Heavyweight Diner w/StationSounds, 20		330	___
2027620	Chessie Steam Special Dome Car w/StationSounds, 20		400	___
2027630	Lionel Lines 21" VistaVision Dome Car, "Chesterfield," 20		340	___

MODERN 1970-2025			Exc	Mint
____	2027640	SP Cities 21" VistaVision Dome Car, "3601," 20		340
____	2027650	SP Daylight VistaVision Dome Car, 20		340
____	2027660	SP Golden State 21" VistaVision Dome Car, 20		340
____	2027670	SP Lark 21" VistaVision Dome Car, 20		340
____	2027680	GN 21" VistaVision Dome Car, "1325," 20		340
____	2027690	Lionel Lines Vision 21" Baggage, "Madison," 20		350
____	2027700	SP Vision Baggage Car, 20		350
____	2027710	SP Vision Baggage Car, Daylight, 20		350
____	2027720	SP Vision Baggage Car, Golden State, 20		350
____	2027730	SP Vision Baggage Car, Lark, 20		350
____	2027740	REA Vision Baggage Car, 20		350
____	2027750	Lionel Lines 21" Passenger Car 4-pack, 20		730
____	2027760	Lionel Lines 21" Diner, "Mount Clemens," w/StationSounds , 20		330
____	2027770	Milwaukee Road 21" VistaVision Dome Car, "60," 20		340
____	2027780	NYC 21" VistaVision Dome Car, "Hudson Vista," 20		340
____	2027790	NS 21" VistaVision Dome Car, "50", 20		340
____	2027800	Polar Express Skiing Hobo Observation w/Black Roof, 20		85
____	2027810	Great Central Pullman Coach, 20		80
____	2028010	George H.W. Bush Funeral Mint Car, 19-22		95
____	2028020	Shark Aquarium Car, "23020," 19		100
____	2028030	PRR Flatcar w/Trailers, "925030," 19		85
____	2028040	PRR Walking Brakeman Car, "24095," 19, 22		110
____	2028060	Ford Auto Rack, "19032020," 20		85
____	2028090	Finding Nemo Aquarium Car, 20		100
____	2028100	Inside Out Memory Ball Transport Car, 20-23		100
____	2028110	Polar Express Elf Bobbing Car, 20-23		90
____	2028120	Polar Express Hot Cocoa Car, 20-22		200
____	2028130	Olaf's Personal Flurry 1-D Tank Car, 20-22		90
____	2028150	Monster Containment Car, 20		80
____	2028160	Jack O' Lantern Flatcar, 20		80
____	2028170	Thomas & Friends Nia Boxcar, 20		75
____	2028180	Thomas & Friends Rebecca Boxcar, 20		75
____	2028190	Thomas & Friends Gordon Boxcar, 20		75
____	2028200	Christmas Boxcar 2020, 20		65
____	2028210	Christmas Music Boxcar 2020, 20		80
____	2028220	Anheuser Busch Brewing Refrigerator Car, 20-23		90
____	2028230	Enjoy Budweiser Refrigerator Car, 20-23		90
____	2028240	Anheuser Busch Cold Storage Car, 20		90
____	2028250	Miller High Life Woodside Refrigerator Car, 20-23		90
____	2028260	Coors Banquet Woodside Refrigerator Car, 20-23		90
____	2028270	Batman vs. The Joker Duel Car, 20-22		90
____	2028280	Batman Shark Repellent Unibody 1-D Tank Car, 20		75
____	2028290	Batman Hi-Cube Boxcar, 20		80
____	2028300	Christmas Light Express Boxcar, "84746," 20-23		100
____	2028310	Best of Lionel Milk Car, 20		180
____	2028320	Alien Radioactive Flatcar, 20		85
____	2028340	Angela Trotta Thomas Gondola w/Presents and Trees, 20		80
____	2028350	Angela Trotta Thomas Christmas Boxcar, 20		75
____	2028360	Mickey & Friends Christmas 1-D Tank Car, 20		70
____	2028380	John Deere Flatcar, "28380" w/3 Tractors, 20		95
____	2028410	National Lampoon's Christmas Vacation 30th Anniversary Lighted Boxcar, 20		90

MODERN 1970-2025		Exc	Mint	
2028430	Thomas & Friends 75th Birthday Music Car, 20		80	___
2028440	A Christmas Story Leg Lamp Boxcar, 20		75	___
2028450	Angela Trotta Thomas Christmas Hopper, 20		65	___
2028460	Winter Wonderland Wintry Mix 1-D Tank Car, 20		80	___
2028470	Polar Express Present Mint Car, 20-23		100	___
2028480	Angela Trotta Thomas 120th Anniversary Boxcar, 20		75	___
2028500	Lionel Ale 1-D Tank Car, 20		75	___
2028510	Thomas Kinkade Santa's Special Delivery Boxcar, "28510," 20		75	___
2028520	Romulan Ale 1-D Tank Car, 20		80	___
2028530	Tribble Transport Car, 20		80	___
2028540	Captain Kirk Boxcar, 20		75	___
2028550	Captain Picard Boxcar, 20		75	___
2028570	Pizza Planet Aquarium Car, 20-23		120	___
2029010	85th Anniversary Gateman, 20		110	___
2029020	Bluetooth Speaker Bandstand, 20		275	___
2029030	Next Stop, Santa Passenger Station, 20		100	___
2029040	End of the Line Passenger Station, 20-23		110	___
2029050	Polar Express Passsenger Station, 20-25		145	___
2029060	Chuga Chuga Brew Thru Bar, 20		90	___
2029160	J Tower Switch Tower, 20		80	___
2029170	Halloween Freight Station, 20		125	___
2029180	Christmas Operating Freight Station, 20		125	___
2029200	Area 51 Search Tower, 20		100	___
2029210	Santa Tracker Command Tower, 20		100	___
2029220	Roasted Chestnuts Retreat, 20		125	___
2029230	Taco Stand, 20		125	___
2029240	Fake News Stand, 20, 22, 25	125	160	___
2029250	Strasburg RR Groffs Grove Pep Platform, 19		45	___
2029260	Strasburg RR East Strasburg Station, 20		100	___
2029270	Lionelville Freight Station, 20		125	___
2029280	Area 1 Souvenir Stand, 20		125	___
2030010	Strasburg RR Cherry Hill Station, 20		20	___
2030050	Stars & Stripes Billboard, 3-pack, 19-22		25	___
2030060	Fun with Puns Billboard, 3-pack, 19		20	___
2030070	Strasburg RR Billboard 3-pack, 20		20	___
2030130	Crossing Shanty, 20-22		20	___
2030140	Polar Express Elf Warming Shack, 3 pack, 20-23		60	___
2030150	Polar Express Barrel Shed, 20, 23		25	___
2030160	Winter Wonderland Barrel Shed, 20-24		25	___
2030170	Anheuser Busch Barrel Shed, 20-22		25	___
2030180	City Park People, 6-pack, 20		23	___
2030190	Street People, 6-pack, 20		23	___
2030200	Walking Figures, 6-pack, 20		23	___
2030210	City People, 6-pack, 20		23	___
2030220	Highway Lamp Single, 3-pack, 20		27	___
2030230	Highway Lamp Double, 2-pack, 20-22		30	___
2030240	Construction Signs, 5-pack, 20-23		9	___
2030250	Halloween Signs, 5-pack, 20		8	___
2030260	Christmas Signs, 5-pack, 20-25		9	___
2030270	Santa's Elves Houses, 3-pack, 20		60	___
2031010	B&A 4-6-6T, "400," CC, 19		1100	___
2031020	NYC 4-6-6T, "1297," CC, 19		1100	___

MODERN 1970-2025			Exc	Mint
___	**2031030**	CN 4-6-6T, "51," CC, 19		1100
___	**2031040**	CNJ 4-6-6T, "231," CC, 19		1100
___	**2031050**	DL&W 4-6-6T, "428," CC, 19		1100
___	**2031060**	IC 4-6-6T, "205," CC, 19		1100
___	**2031070**	NH 4-6-6T, "1850," CC, 19		1100
___	**2031080**	US Army Transportation Corps 4-6-6T, "1945," CC, 19		1100
___	**2031090**	B&O 2-8-8-4 EM-1, "7609," CC, 19		1700
___	**2031100**	B&O 2-8-8-4 EM-1, "7600," CC, 19		1700
___	**2031110**	D&RGW 2-8-8-4 EM-1, "224," CC, 19		1700
___	**2031120**	DM&IR 2-8-8-4 EM-1, "220," CC, 19		1700
___	**2031130**	NP 2-8-8-4 EM-1, "5011," CC, 19		1700
___	**2031140**	UP 2-8-8-4 EM-1, "4050," CC, 19		1700
___	**2031150**	WM 2-8-8-4 EM-1, "1213," CC, 19		1700
___	**2031160**	AT&SF 4-8-4 Northern, "3751," CC, 19		1600
___	**2031170**	AT&SF 4-8-4 Northern, "3759," CC, 19		1600
___	**2031180**	AT&SF 4-8-4 Northern, "3757," CC, 19		1600
___	**2031190**	AT&SF 4-8-4 Northern, "3765," CC, 19		1600
___	**2031200**	ACL 4-8-4S Northern, "1800," CC, 19		1600
___	**2031210**	Rock Island 4-8-4S Northern, "5100," CC, 19		1600
___	**2031220**	D&RGW 4-8-4S Northern, "1802," CC, 19		1600
___	**2031230**	MP 4-8-4S Northern, "2202," CC, 19		1600
___	**2031240**	Frisco 4-8-4S Northern, "4500," CC, 19		1600
___	**2031250**	Frisco 4-8-4S Northern, "4524," CC, 19		1600
___	**2031261**	UP 4-8-8-4 Big Boy, "4014," Excursion Version, CC, 19		2200
___	**2031262**	UP 4-8-8-4 Big Boy, "4005," CC, 19		2200
___	**2031263**	UP 4-8-8-4 Big Boy, "4012," Greyhouse, CC, 19		2200
___	**2031271**	Reading 4-8-4 T1, "2107," CC, 20		1700
___	**2031272**	Reading 4-8-4 T1, "2111," CC, 20		1700
___	**2031281**	Reading 4-8-4 T1, Rambles, "2100," CC, 20		1700
___	**2031282**	Reading 4-8-4 T1, Rambles, "2101," CC, 20		1700
___	**2031290**	Reading, Blue Mountain & Northern 4-8-4 T1, "2102," CC, 20		1700
___	**2031300**	Reading, Blue Mountain & Northern 4-8-4 T1, "2102," CC, 20		1700
___	**2031310**	Conrail 4-8-4 T1, "2101," CC, 20		1700
___	**2031320**	American Freedom Train Vision 4-8-4 T1, "1," CC, 20		1700
___	**2031330**	PRR B6sb 0-4-0, "525," CC, 20		700
___	**2031340**	PRR B6sb 0-4-0, "660," CC, 20		700
___	**2031351**	PRR B6sb 0-4-0, "711," CC, 20		700
___	**2031352**	PRR B6sb 0-4-0, "1644," CC, 20		700
___	**2031360**	AT&SF B6sb 0-4-0, "2101," CC, 20		700
___	**2031370**	Bethlehem Steet B6sb 0-4-0, "1904," CC, 20		700
___	**2031380**	Milwaukee Road B6sb 0-4-0, "1534," CC, 20		700
___	**2031390**	GN B6sb 0-4-0, "90," CC, 20		700
___	**2031400**	Lionel Lines Vision 4-8-4 GS-4, "120," CC, 20		2000
___	**2031411**	SP Vision 4-8-4 GS-1 Brass Hybrid, "4470," CC, 20		2200
___	**2031412**	SP Vision 4-8-4 GS-1 Brass Hybrid, "4471," CC, 20		2200
___	**2031421**	SP Vision 4-8-4 GS-1 Brass Hybrid, "708," CC, 20		2200
___	**2031422**	SP Vision 4-8-4 GS-1 Brass Hybrid, "4403," CC, 20		2200
___	**2031430**	Vision 4-8-4 GS-1 Brass Hybrid Pilot, "9999," CC, 20		2200
___	**2031440**	SP Vision 4-8-4 GS-2 Black, "4410," CC, 20		2000
___	**2031450**	SP Vision 4-8-4 GS-2 Black, "4411," CC, 20		2000
___	**2031460**	SP Vision 4-8-4 GS-2 Daylight, "4412," CC, 20		2000
___	**2031470**	SP Vision 4-8-4 GS-2 Lark, "4414," CC, 20		2000

		Exc	Mint
2031480	SP Vision 4-8-4 GS-3 Daylight, "4416," CC, 20		2000 ____
2031500	SP Vision 4-8-4 GS-3 Daylight, "4423," CC, 20		2000 ____
2031510	SP Vision 4-8-4 GS-3 Golden State, "4428," CC, 20		2000 ____
2031520	SP Lines Vision 4-8-4 GS-4 Daylight, "4449," CC, 20		2000 ____
2031530	SP Vision 4-8-4 GS-4 Daylight, "4449," CC, 20		2000 ____
2031540	American Freedom Train Vision 4-8-4 GS-4, "4449," CC, 20		2000 ____
2031550	BNSF Vision 4-8-4 GS-4, "4449," CC, 20		2000 ____
2031560	SP Vision 4-8-4 GS-4 Daylight, "4439," CC, 20		2000 ____
2031570	SP Lines Vision 4-8-4 GS-5 Daylight, "4458," CC, 20		2000 ____
2031580	SP Vision 4-8-4 GS-5 Daylight, "4459," CC, 20		2000 ____
2031590	SP Lines Vision 4-8-4 GS-6, "4460," CC, 20		2000 ____
2031600	SP Vision 4-8-4 GS-6, "4462," CC, 20		2000 ____
2031610	SP Vision 4-8-4 GS-6, "4467," CC, 20		2000 ____
2031620	WP Vision 4-8-4 GS-6, "481," CC, 20		2000 ____
2031630	WP Vision 4-8-4 GS-6, "486," CC, 20		2000 ____
2031640	Chessie Steam Special Vision GS-4, "4449," CC, 20		2000 ____
2031650	Chessie Steam Special Auxiliary Water Tender w/RailSounds, CC, 20		350 ____
2031660	Conrail Auxiliary Water Tender w/RailSounds, CC, 20		350 ____
2031671	Freedom Train 1975 Auxiliary Water Tender w/RailSounds, CC, 20		350 ____
2031672	Freedom Train 1976 Auxiliary Water Tender w/RailSounds, CC, 20		350 ____
2031673	American Freedom Train Auxiliary Tender, "4449," CC, 20		350 ____
2031680	SP Daylight Auxiliary Water Tender w/RailSounds, CC, 20		350 ____
2031690	Black Auxiliary Water Tender w/RailSounds, CC, 20		350 ____
2031700	UP 4-8-8-4 Big Boy, "4014," First Run Edition, CC, 19		2200 ____
2032010	AT&SF 0-6-0T, "95," LionChief Plus 2.0, 19-20		250 ____
2032020	Brooklyn Eastern District 0-6-0T, "15," LionChief Plus 2.0, 19-20		250 ____
2032030	Bethlehem Steel 0-6-0T, "76," LionChief Plus 2.0, 19-20		250 ____
2032040	D&RGW 0-6-0T, "27," LionChief Plus 2.0, 19-20		250 ____
2032050	PRR 0-6-0T, "2295," LionChief Plus 2.0, 19-20		250 ____
2032100	C&O Lionmaster 2-6-6-6 Allegheny, "1601," CC, 20		1100 ____
2032110	C&O Lionmaster 2-6-6-6 Allegheny, "1607," CC, 20		1100 ____
2032120	C&O Lionmaster 2-6-6-6 Allegheny, "1611," CC, 20		1100 ____
2032130	Virginian Lionmaster 2-6-6-6 Allegheny, "906," CC, 20		1100 ____
2032200	AT&SF 0-8-0, "729," LionChief, 20		220 ____
2032210	GN 0-8-0, "831," LionChief, 20		220 ____
2032220	Reading 0-8-0, "1493," LionChief, 20		220 ____
2032230	SP 0-8-0, "1849," LionChief, 20		220 ____
2033011	B&LE SD38 Diesel, "861," CC, 19		600 ____
2033012	B&LE SD38 Diesel, "863," CC, 19		600 ____
2033021	Conrail SD38 Diesel, "6929," CC, 19		600 ____
2033022	Conrail SD38 Diesel, "6957," CC, 19		600 ____
2033031	CSX SD38 Diesel, "2461," CC, 19		600 ____
2033032	CSX SD38 Diesel, "2463," CC, 19		600 ____
2033041	GTW SD38 Diesel, "6252," CC, 19		600 ____
2033042	GTW SD38 Diesel, "6254," CC, 19		600 ____
2033051	NS SD38 Diesel, "3806," CC, 19		600 ____
2033052	NS SD38 Diesel, "3808," CC, 19		600 ____
2033061	Rail Logix SD38 Diesel, "2001," CC, 19		600 ____
2033062	Rail Logix SD38 Diesel, "2002," CC, 19		600 ____
2033070	AT&SF Alco S-4 Diesel Switcher, "1527," CC, 19		500 ____

			Exc	Mint
___	**2033080**	EL Alco S-4 Diesel Switcher, "513," CC, 19		500
___	**2033090**	Ford Alco S-2 Diesel Switcher, "10013," CC, 19		500
___	**2033100**	Morristown & Erie Alco S-2 Diesel Switcher, "14," CC, 19		500
___	**2033110**	NYS&W Alco S-2 Diesel Switcher, "206," CC, 19		500
___	**2033120**	Nickel Plate Road Alco S-4 Diesel Switcher, "79," CC, 19		500
___	**2033130**	NP Alco S-4 Diesel Switcher, "717," CC, 19		500
___	**2033140**	Northern Pacific Terminal Alco S-2 Diesel Switcher, "40," CC, 19		500
___	**2033150**	Portland Terminal Alco S-2 Diesel Switcher, "1001," CC, 19		500
___	**2033160**	SP Alco S-4 Diesel Switcher, "1820," CC, 19		500
___	**2033170**	Youngstown Sheet & Tube Alco S-2 Diesel Switcher, "1001," CC, 19		500
___	**2033181**	CITX SD70M-2 Diesel, "140," CC, 19		600
___	**2033182**	CITX SD70M-2 Diesel, "141," CC, 19		600
___	**2033183**	CITX SD70M-2 Diesel, "142," unpowered, 19		300
___	**2033191**	EMD SD70M-2 Diesel, "74," CC, 19		600
___	**2033192**	EMD SD70M-2 Diesel, "75," CC, 19		600
___	**2033193**	EMD SD70M-2 Diesel, "76," unpowered, 19		300
___	**2033201**	FEC SD70M-2 Diesel, "104," CC, 19		600
___	**2033202**	FEC SD70M-2 Diesel, "105," CC, 19		600
___	**2033203**	FEC SD70M-2 Diesel, "106," unpowered, 19		300
___	**2033211**	NS SD70M-2 Diesel, "2717," CC, 19		600
___	**2033212**	NS SD70M-2 Diesel, "2731," CC, 19		600
___	**2033213**	NS SD70M-2 Diesel, "2778," unpowered, 19		300
___	**2033221**	P&W SD70M-2 Diesel, "4301," CC, 19		600
___	**2033222**	P&W SD70M-2 Diesel, "4302," CC, 19		600
___	**2033231**	Vermont Ry. SD70M-2 Diesel, "431," CC, 19		600
___	**2033232**	Vermont Ry. SD70M-2 Diesel, "432," CC, 19		600
___	**2033240**	Alaska RR F7 A-A set, CC, 19		900
___	**2033248**	Alaska RR F7B Diesel, "1503," CC, 19		450
___	**2033249**	Alaska RR F7B SuperBass Diesel, "1517," CC, 19		440
___	**2033250**	BN F7 Diesel A-A set, CC, 19		900
___	**2033258**	BN F7B Diesel, "761," CC, 19		450
___	**2033259**	BN F7B SuperBass Diesel, "741," CC, 19		440
___	**2033260**	CGW F7 Diesel A-A set, CC, 19		900
___	**2033268**	CGW F7B Diesel, "114-B," CC, 19		450
___	**2033269**	CGW F7B SuperBass Diesel, "114-0," CC, 19		440
___	**2033270**	D&RGW F7 Diesel A-A set, CC, 19		900
___	**2033278**	D&RGW F7B Diesel, "5652," CC, 19		450
___	**2033279**	D&RGW F7B SuperBass Diesel, "5653," CC, 19		440
___	**2033280**	NS F9 Diesel A-A set, CC, 19		900
___	**2033288**	NS F7B Diesel, "4275," CC, 19		450
___	**2033289**	NS F7B SuperBass Diesel, "4276," CC, 19		440
___	**2033290**	PC F7 Diesel A-A set, CC, 19		900
___	**2033298**	PC F7B Diesel, "3460," CC, 19		450
___	**2033299**	PC F7B SuperBass Diesel, "712," CC, 19		440
___	**2033300**	Cotton Belt F7 Diesel A-A set, CC, 19		900
___	**2033308**	Cotton Belt F7B Diesel, "926," CC, 19		450
___	**2033309**	Cotton Belt F7B SuperBass Diesel, "928," CC, 19		440
___	**2033310**	UP SD70ACe Diesel, "4141," CC, 19		600
___	**2033319**	UP SD70ACe Diesel, "4141," unpowered, 19		300
___	**2033321**	UP SD70AH Diesel, "9096," CC, 19		600
___	**2033322**	UP SD70AH Diesel, "9069," CC, 19		600

		Exc	Mint
2033323	UP SD70AH Diesel, "9088," CC, 19		600 ___
2033330	KCS SD70ACe Diesel, "4006," CC, 19		600 ___
2033340	Amtrak E8 AA Diesel Set, "4316/249," CC, 20		1000 ___
2033350	DL&W E8 AA Diesel Set, "810/811," CC, 20		1000 ___
2033360	NYC E8 AA Diesel Set, "4038/4041," CC, 20		1000 ___
2033370	PRR E8 AA Diesel Set, "5711/5809," CC, 20		1000 ___
2033380	Southern E8 AA Diesel Set, "6901/6914," CC, 20		1000 ___
2033390	Frisco E8 AA Diesel Set, "2003/2006," CC, 20		1000 ___
2033401	DL&W Train Master Diesel, "853," CC, 20		550 ___
2033402	DL&W Train Master Diesel, "854," CC, 20		550 ___
2033411	FM Demonstrator Train Master Diesel, "TM-3," CC, 20		550 ___
2033412	FM Demonstrator Train Master Diesel, "TM-4," CC, 20		550 ___
2033420	PRR Train Master Diesel, "8703," CC, 20		550 ___
2033430	Donald Trump SD70ACe diesel "4545," CC, 20		550 ___
2033431	Southern Train Master Diesel, "6301," CC, 20		550 ___
2033432	Southern Train Master Diesel, "6302," CC, 20		550 ___
2033441	SP Train Master Diesel, "4800," CC, 20		550 ___
2033442	SP Train Master Diesel, "4812," CC, 20		550 ___
2033451	Virginian Train Master Diesel, "55," CC, 20		550 ___
2033452	Virginian Train Master Diesel, "60," CC, 20		550 ___
2033461	CP SD40 Diesel, "740," CC, 20		550 ___
2033462	CP SD40 Diesel, "752," CC, 20		550 ___
2033471	CNJ SD40 Diesel, "3064," CC, 20		550 ___
2033472	CNJ SD40 Diesel, "3069," CC, 20		550 ___
2033481	C&O SD40 Diesel, "7452," CC, 20		550 ___
2033482	C&O SD40 Diesel, "7464," CC, 20		550 ___
2033490	CSX SD40 Diesel, "4617," CC, 20		550 ___
2033501	C&NW SD40 Diesel, "867," CC, 20		550 ___
2033502	C&NW SD40 Diesel, "876," CC, 20		550 ___
2033520	BNSF GE ES44AC Diesel, "5815," CC, 20		550 ___
2033530	CSX GE ES44AC Diesel, "3010," CC, 20		313 ___
2033539	CSX GE ES44AC Diesel, "3010," unpowered, 20		350 ___
2033541	KCS de Mexico GE ES44AC Diesel, "4748," CC, 20		550 ___
2033542	KCS de Mexico GE ES44AC Diesel, "4762," CC, 20		550 ___
2033549	KCS de Mexico GE ES44AC Diesel, "4764," unpowered, 20		350 ___
2033551	SVTX GE ES44AC Diesel, "1912," CC, 20		550 ___
2033552	SVTX GE ES44AC Diesel, "1982," CC, 20		550 ___
2033559	SVTX GE ES44AC Diesel, "1986," unpowered, 20		350 ___
2033560	UP GE ES44AC Diesel, "8003," CC, 20		550 ___
2033571	Christmas ES44AC Diesel, "1224," CC, 20		550 ___
2033572	Christmas ES44AC Diesel, "1225," CC, 20		550 ___
2033590	UP SD70ACe Diesel, "8937," CC, 19		600 ___
2033600	UP SD70AH+B86 Diesel, "1111," CC, 19		600 ___
2033610	CSX First Responders GE ES44AC Diesel, "911," CC, 20		550 ___
2033619	CSX First Responders GE ES44AC Diesel, "911," unpowered, 20		185 ___
2033620	CSX Veterans GE ES44AC Diesel, "1776," CC, 20		550 ___
2033629	CSX Veterans GE ES44AC Diesel, "1776," unpowered, 20		350 ___
2033630	CSX GE ES44AC Diesel, "3194," CC, 20		550 ___
2033639	CSX GE ES44AC Diesel, "3194," unpowered, 20		350 ___
2034010	PRR GG1 Electric, "4935," LionChief Plus 2.0, 19		500 ___
2034020	PRR GG1 Electric, "4877," LionChief Plus 2.0, 19		500 ___
2034030	PRR GG1 Electric, "4872," LionChief Plus 2.0, 19		500 ___

MODERN 1970-2025		Exc	Mint
___ **2034040**	PRR GG1 Electric, "4890," LionChief Plus 2.0, 19		500
___ **2034050**	PRR GG1 Electric, "4916," LionChief Plus 2.0, 19		500
___ **2034061**	Conrail LionMaster SD80MAC Diesel, "4100," LionChief Plus 2.0, 19		450
___ **2034062**	Conrail LionMaster SD80MAC Diesel, "4102," LionChief Plus 2.0, 19		450
___ **2034071**	CSX LionMaster SD80MAC Diesel, "4592," LionChief Plus 2.0, 19		450
___ **2034072**	CSX LionMaster SD80MAC Diesel, "4594," LionChief Plus 2.0, 19		450
___ **2034081**	NS LionMaster SD80MAC Diesel, "7217," LionChief Plus 2.0, 19		450
___ **2034082**	NS LionMaster SD80MAC Diesel, "7219," LionChief Plus 2.0, 19		450
___ **2034091**	UP LionMaster SD90MAC Diesel, "8025," LionChief Plus 2.0, 19		450
___ **2034092**	UP LionMaster SD90MAC Diesel, "8026," LionChief Plus 2.0, 19		450
___ **2034100**	NYC F3 AA Diesel Set, "1620/1621," LionChief Plus 2.0, 20		700
___ **2034110**	PRR F3 AA Diesel Set, "9542/9542A," LionChief Plus 2.0, 20		700
___ **2034120**	UP F3 AA Diesel Set, "1445/1455," LionChief Plus 2.0, 20		700
___ **2034130**	SP F3 AA Diesel Set, "6148/6157," LionChief Plus 2.0, 20		700
___ **2034180**	Conrail GP38 Diesel, "7670," LionChief, 20		220
___ **2034190**	BN GP38 Diesel, "2085," LionChief, 20		220
___ **2034190**	SP Vision 4-8-4 GS-3 LAUPT Special, "4426," CC, 20		2000
___ **2034200**	Chessie System GP38 Diesel, "3847," LionChief, 20		220
___ **2034210**	North Pole Central GP38 Diesel, "1224," LionChief, 20		220
___ **2034220**	Lightning McQueen GP38 Diesel, "95," LionChief, 20		220
___ **2035010**	ELX Trolley, 20		100
___ **2035020**	Fort Collins Trolley, 20		100
___ **2035030**	Toy Story Handcar, 20-23		120
___ **2035050**	Lionelville Trolley, 20		100
___ **2038010**	B&O 190th Anniversary Boxcar, 19		85
___ **2038020**	D&RGW 150th Anniversary Boxcar, 19		85
___ **2038030**	Casey Jones 120th Anniversary MUSA Boxcar, 20		85
___ **2038040**	BN 50th Anniversary MUSA Boxcar, 20		85
___ **2038050**	George H.W. Bush Boxcar, 19-20		80
___ **2038060**	William Henry Harrison Presidential Boxcar, 20, 24		80
___ **2038070**	James Garfield Presidential Boxcar, 20, 24		80
___ **2038080**	Battlefield Honor--Berlin Wall Boxcar, 20-23		95
___ **2038090**	Battlefield Honor--Candy Bombers Boxcar, 20		90
___ **2038110**	Angela Trotta Thomas Stocked Shelves Boxcar, Middle, 19		85
___ **2038120**	2020 Happy Birthday Boxcar, 20		90
___ **2038130**	Happy Anniversary Boxcar, 20		90
___ **2038140**	2020 Merry Christmas Boxcar, 20		90
___ **2038150**	Foghorn Leghorn Crockett-Doodle Do Boxcar, 20-23		95
___ **2038160**	Picnic With Porky Pig Boxcar, 20-23		95
___ **2038170**	Robin Hood Daffy Duck Boxcar, 20-23		95
___ **2038200**	Wings of Angels--Jessamyne Rose Boxcar, 20		90
___ **2038210**	Wings of Angels--Ashten Goodenough Boxcar, 20		90
___ **2038220**	Wings of Angels--Jessie Ray Boxcar, 20		90
___ **2043011**	BN 50' Boxcar, "217552" (std 0), 20-23		50
___ **2043012**	BN 50' Boxcar, "217618" (std 0), 20-23		50
___ **2043013**	BN 50' Boxcar, "217685" (std 0), 20-23		50

MODERN 1970-2025		Exc	Mint
2043014	BN 50' Boxcar, "217741" (std O), 20-23		50 ___
2043021	Golden West 50' Boxcar, "767130" (std O), 20-23		50 ___
2043022	Golden West 50' Boxcar, "767150" (std O), 20-23		50 ___
2043023	Golden West 50' Boxcar, "767167" (std O), 20-23		50 ___
2043024	Golden West 50' Boxcar, "767193" (std O), 20-23		50 ___
2043031	KCS 50' Boxcar, "117731" (std O), 20-23		50 ___
2043032	KCS 50' Boxcar, "117756" (std O), 20-23		50 ___
2043033	KCS 50' Boxcar, "117782" (std O), 20-23		50 ___
2043034	KCS 50' Boxcar, "117790" (std O), 20-23		50 ___
2043041	Railbox 50' Boxcar, "10051" (std O), 20-22		50 ___
2043042	Railbox 50' Boxcar, "10189" (std O), 20-22		50 ___
2043043	Railbox 50' Boxcar, "10524" (std O), 20-22		50 ___
2043044	Railbox 50' Boxcar, "10582" (std O), 20-22		50 ___
2043051	MILW Road Centerbeam Flatcar, "6300" (std O), 20-23		50 ___
2043052	MILW Centerbeam Flatcar, "6318" (std O), 20-23		50 ___
2043053	MILW Centerbeam Flatcar, "6336" (std O), 20-23		50 ___
2043054	MILW Centerbeam Flatcar, "6354" (std O), 20-23		50 ___
2043061	Trailer Train Centerbeam Flatcar, "83729" (std O), 20-23		50 ___
2043062	Trailer Train Centerbeam Flatcar, "83741" (std O), 20-23		50 ___
2043063	Trailer Train Centerbeam Flatcar, "83754" (std O), 20-23		50 ___
2043064	Trailer Train Centerbeam Flatcar, "83773" (std O), 20-23		50 ___
2043071	UP Centerbeam Flatcar, "217015" (std O), 20-23		50 ___
2043072	UP Centerbeam Flatcar, "217031" (std O), 20-23		50 ___
2043073	UP Centerbeam Flatcar, "217047" (std O), 20-23		50 ___
2043074	UP Centerbeam Flatcar, "217063" (std O), 20-23		50 ___
2043081	WP Centerbeam Flatcar, "1404" (std O), 20-23		50 ___
2043082	WP Centerbeam Flatcar, "1412" (std O), 20-23		50 ___
2043083	WP Centerbeam Flatcar, "1420" (std O), 20-23		50 ___
2043084	WP Centerbeam Flatcar, "1428" (std O), 20-23		50 ___
2043091	BNSF Bulkhead Flatcar, "545475" (std O), 20-23		50 ___
2043092	BNSF Bulkhead Flatcar, "545512" (std O), 20-23		50 ___
2043093	BNSF Bulkhead Flatcar, "545587" (std O), 20-23		50 ___
2043094	BNSF Bulkhead Flatcar, "545628" (std O), 20-23		50 ___
2043101	GN Bulkhead Flatcar, "160325" (std O), 20-23		50 ___
2043102	GN Bulkhead Flatcar, "160331" (std O), 20-23		50 ___
2043103	GN Bulkhead Flatcar, "160350" (std O), 20-23		50 ___
2043104	GN Bulkhead Flatcar, "160374" (std O), 20-23		50 ___
2043111	NS Bulkhead Flatcar, "118024" (std O), 20-23		50 ___
2043112	NS Bulkhead Flatcar, "118033" (std O), 20-23		50 ___
2043113	NS Bulkhead Flatcar, "118045" (std O), 20-23		50 ___
2043114	NS Bulkhead Flatcar, "118068" (std O), 20-23		50 ___
2043121	Trailer Train Bulkhead Flatcar, "81023" (std O), 20-23		50 ___
2043122	Trailer Train Bulkhead Flatcar, "81094" (std O), 20-23		50 ___
2043123	Trailer Train Bulkhead Flatcar, "81118" (std O), 20-23		50 ___
2043124	Trailer Train Bulkhead Flatcar, "81145" (std O), 20-23		50 ___
2043131	Bethlehem Steel Gondola, "3131" (std O), 20-22		50 ___
2043132	Bethlehem Steel Gondola, "3145" (std O), 20-22		50 ___
2043133	Bethlehem Steel Gondola, "3168" (std O), 20-22		50 ___
2043134	Bethlehem Steel Gondola "3192" w/Coil Covers (std O), 20-23		50 ___
2043141	Chessie System Gondola, "305001" (std O), 20		45 ___
2043142	Chessie System Gondola "305014" w/Coil Covers (std O), 20-23		50 ___

			Exc	Mint
___	**2043143**	Chessie System Gondola "305036" w/ Coil Covers (std O), 20-23		50
___	**2043144**	Chessie System Gondola "305055" w/ Coil Covers (std O), 20-23		50
___	**2043151**	MKT Gondola "14025" w/Coil Covers (std O), 20-23		50
___	**2043152**	MKT Gondola "14032" w/Coil Covers (std O), 20-23		50
___	**2043153**	MKT Gondola "14041" w/Coil Covers (std O), 20-23		50
___	**2043154**	MKT Gondola "14049" w/Coil Covers (std O), 20-23		50
___	**2043161**	Reading Gondola "29061" w/ Coil Covers (std O), 20-23		50
___	**2043162**	Reading Gondola "29086" w/Coil Covers std O), 20-23		50
___	**2043163**	Reading Gondola "29169" w/Coil Covers (std O), 20-23		50
___	**2043164**	Reading Gondola "29172" w/Coil Covers (std O), 20-23		50
___	**2043170**	BN Rotary Gondola, 4-pack, A, 20		280
___	**2043180**	BN Rotary Gondola, 4-pack, B, 20		280
___	**2043190**	BN Rotary Gondola, 2-pack, 20		140
___	**2043200**	Conrail Rotary Gondola, 4-pack, A, 20		280
___	**2043210**	Conrail Rotary Gondola, 4-pack, B, 20		280
___	**2043220**	Conrail Rotary Gondola, 2-pack, 20		140
___	**2043230**	CSX Rotary Gondola, 4-pack, A, 20		280
___	**2043240**	CSX Rotary Gondola, 4-pack, B, 20		280
___	**2043250**	CSX Rotary Gondola, 2-pack, 20		140
___	**2043260**	NS Rotary Gondola, 4-pack, A, 20		280
___	**2043270**	NS Rotary Gondola, 4-pack, B, 20		280
___	**2043280**	NS Rotary Gondola, 2-pack, 20		140
___	**2043290**	C&NW NE-5 Caboose "606" (std O), 20		60
___	**2043300**	Monon NE-5 Caboose "81526" (std O), 20		60
___	**2043310**	Monongahela NE-5 Caboose "64" (std O), 20		60
___	**2043320**	NH NE-5 Caboose "C-516" (std O), 20		60
___	**2122010**	Aliquippa Turn P&LE GP7 Diesel Freight Set, CC, 20		850
___	**2122020**	NYC Xplorer Baldwin Sharknose Passenger Set, CC, 20		900
___	**2122030**	Southern GP7 Diesel Freight Set, CC, 20		850
___	**2122040**	PRR John Bull Display Set, 21		800
___	**2122050**	Camden & Amboy John Bull Steam Passenger Set, 21		800
___	**2122060**	"Uncle Sam" John Bull Steam Passenger Set, 21		800
___	**2122070**	LV Asa Packer 4-6-2 Pacific Steam Passenger Set, CC, 21		2200
___	**2122080**	NYC 1926 Cardinals 4-6-2 Pacific Steam Passenger Set, CC, 21		2100
___	**2122090**	Amtrak Acela High Speed Train Set, CC, 21		2500
___	**2122100**	Amtrak Acela Concept High Speed Train Set, CC, 21		2500
___	**2122110**	MILW High Speed Train Set, CC, 21		2500
___	**2122120**	NH High Speed Train Set, CC, 21		2500
___	**2122130**	PRR High Speed Train Set, CC, 21		2500
___	**2122140**	ATSF High Speed Train Set, CC, 21		2500
___	**2122150**	UP High Speed Train Set, CC, 21		2500
___	**2122160**	New Hope & Ivyland GP30 Diesel Passenger Excursion Set, CC, 21		1000
___	**2122170**	ATSF Valley Flyer 4-6-2 Pacific Steam Passenger Set, CC, 21		2200
___	**2122180**	Nickel Plate Road Work Train Set, CC, 21		1000
___	**2122190**	Polar Express High Speed Train Set, CC, 21		2500
___	**2123010**	C&O Steam Freight Set LionChief, 20-23		450
___	**2123030**	KCS Tier 4 ET44 Diesel Freight Set LionChief, 21		425
___	**2123040**	John Deere GP38 Diesel Freight Set LionChief, 21-24		450
___	**2123060**	Hallow's Eve Limited Steam Freight Set LionChief, 21-23		400
___	**2123070**	Polar Express Steam Freight Set LionChief, 21-24		400

		Exc	Mint
2123080	Space Launch GP38 Diesel Freight Set LionChief, 21-24		450
2123090	Lionel Junction North Pole Central Steam Freight Set LionChief, Upgraded, 21		325
2123100	Christmas Light Express Steam Freight Set LionChief, Upgraded, 21-25		500
2123110	Toy Story Steam Freight Set LionChief, Upgraded, 21		425
2123120	Star Trek FT Diesel Freight Set LionChief, Upgraded, 21		480
2123130	Polar Express Steam Passenger Set LionChief, Upgraded, 21-24		480
2123140	Harry Potter Hogwarts Express Steam Passenger Set LionChief, Upgraded, 21-25		480
2123150	Frozen II Steam Freight Set LionChief, Upgraded, 21		425
2123160	Area 51 ET44 Diesel Freight Set LionChief, Upgraded, 21		450
2123200	Pennsylvania Keystone Bluetooth 5.0 Steam Freight Set, 21-25		400
2125010	Halloween FasTrack Girider Bridge, 21-24		35
2126011	B&LE PS-5 Covered Gondola "32001," 20		90
2126012	B&LE PS-5 Covered Gondola "32054," 20		90
2126021	Bethlehem Steel PS-5 Covered Hopper "303025," 20		90
2126022	Bethlehem Steel PS-5 Covered Hopper "303041," 20		90
2126031	BN PS-5 Covered Gondola "577225," 20		90
2126032	BN PS-5 Covered Gondola "577239," 20		90
2126041	DT&I PS-5 Covered Hopper "9502," 20		90
2126042	DT&I PS-5 Covered Hopper "9509," 20		90
2126051	Reading & Northern PS-5 Covered Hopper "3806," 20		90
2126052	Reading & Northern PS-5 Covered Hopper "3810," 20		490
2126061	UP PS-5 Covered Hopper "229812," 20		90
2126062	UP PS-5 Covered Hopper "903044," 20		90
2126071	Central of Georgia Roof-Hatch Boxcar "6161," 20		95
2126072	Central of Georgia Roof-Hatch Boxcar "6165," 20		95
2126081	C&NW Roof-Hatch Boxcar "108610," 20		95
2126082	C&NW Roof-Hatch Boxcar "108614," 20		95
2126091	Monon Roof-Hatch Boxcar "10249," 20		95
2126092	Monon Roof-Hatch Boxcar "10421," 20		95
2126101	Southern Roof-Hatch Boxcar "26922," 20		95
2126102	Southern Roof-Hatch Boxcar "26961," 20		95
2126111	UP Roof-Hatch Boxcar "284225," 20		95
2126112	UP Roof-Hatch Boxcar "284227," 20		95
2126120	B&LE 100-ton Hopper 2-pack, A, 20		250
2126128	B&LE 100-ton Hopper 2-pack, B, 20		250
2126129	B&LE 100-ton Hopper 2-pack, C, 20		250
2126130	CSX 100-ton Hopper 2-pack, A, 20		250
2126138	CSX 100-ton Hopper 2-pack, B, 20		250
2126139	CSX 100-ton Hopper 2-pack, C, 20		250
2126140	PP&L 100-ton Hopper 2-pack, A, 20		250
2126148	PP&L 100-ton Hopper 2-pack, B, 20		250
2126149	PP&L 100-ton Hopper 2-pack, C, 20		250
2126160	P&LE 100-ton Hopper 2-pack, A, 20		250
2126168	P&LE 100-ton Hopper 2-pack, B, 20		250
2126169	P&LE 100-ton Hopper 2-pack, C, 20		250
2126170	Reading & Northern 100-ton Hopper 2-pack, A, 20		250
2126178	Reading & Northern 100-ton Hopper 2-pack, B, 20		250
2126179	Reading & Northern 100-ton Hopper 2-pack, C, 20		250
2126180	Ann Arbor PS-2 Covered Hopper "800," 20		90

			Exc	Mint
___	**2126190**	Central Soya PS-2 Covered Hopper "118," 22		90
___	**2126200**	Monon PS-2 Covered Hopper "30648," 20		90
___	**2126210**	PRR PS-2 Covered Hopper "257808," 20		90
___	**2126220**	T&P PS-2 Covered Hopper "8744," 20		90
___	**2126230**	WM PS-2 Covered Hopper "4940," 20		90
___	**2126240**	Chessie BW Caboose "C-3010," 20		110
___	**2126250**	Conrail BW Caboose "21736," 20		110
___	**2126260**	SLSF BW Caboose "1730," 20		110
___	**2126270**	L&N BW Caboose "1134," 20		110
___	**2126280**	NYC BW Caboose "20284," 20		110
___	**2126290**	SP Railroad Police BW Caboose "4762," 20		110
___	**2126300**	NYC Pacemaker Expansion Set, 21		500
___	**2126310**	American Steel 65' Mill Gondola "1776," 21		100
___	**2126320**	Bethlehem Steel 65' Mill Gondola "206320," 21		100
___	**2126330**	CP 65' Mill Gondola "337185," 21		100
___	**2126340**	Conrail SW8 Diesel Switcher "8657," CC, 21		100
___	**2126350**	CSX 65' Mill Gondola "491038," 21		100
___	**2126360**	PRR 65' Mill Gondola "442650," 21		100
___	**2126370**	B&O Boxcar w/FreightSounds "467434," 21		200
___	**2126380**	M&P Boxcar w/FreightSounds "5624," 21		200
___	**2126390**	MP Boxcar w/FreightSounds "41260," 21		200
___	**2126400**	PRR Boxcar w/FreightSounds "26875," 21		200
___	**2126410**	SP Boxcar w/FreightSounds "163285," 21		200
___	**2126420**	WP Boxcar w/FreightSounds "220086," 21		200
___	**2126431**	BNSF Beer Car "782404," 21		100
___	**2126432**	BNSF Beer Car "782480," 21		110
___	**2126441**	D&RGW Beer Car "50816," 21		100
___	**2126442**	D&RGW Beer Car "50871," 21		100
___	**2126451**	Golden West Beer Car "149000," 21		100
___	**2126452**	Golden West Beer Car "149008," 21		110
___	**2126461**	MP Beer Car "793004," 21		100
___	**2126462**	MP Beer Car "793015," 21		100
___	**2126471**	UP Beer Car "465304," 21		100
___	**2126472**	UP Beer Car "465321," 21		100
___	**2126481**	WP Beer Car "67083," 21		100
___	**2126482**	WP Beer Car "67055," 21		100
___	**2126490**	Nickel Plate Road Work Train Expansion Pack, 21		680
___	**2126500**	CP Tool Car "403503," 21		100
___	**2126510**	CNJ Tool Car "92083," 21		100
___	**2126520**	C&O Tool Car "X509," 21		100
___	**2126530**	MKT Tool Car "X-3257," 21		100
___	**2126540**	N&W Tool Car "526544," 21		100
___	**2126550**	WP Tool Car "MW0995," 21		100
___	**2126560**	CP Kitchen Car "410833," 21		150
___	**2126570**	CNJ Kitchen Car "92111," 21		150
___	**2126580**	C&O Kitchen Car "X41," 21		150
___	**2126590**	MKT Kitchen Car "X-3175," 21		150
___	**2126600**	N&W Kitchen Car "526030", 21		150
___	**2126610**	WP Kitchen Car "MW0912," 21		150
___	**2126621**	CP Bunk Car "411213," 21		100
___	**2126622**	CP Bunk Car "411919," 21		100
___	**2126631**	CNJ Bunk Car "92110," 21		100
___	**2126632**	CNJ Bunk Car "92120," 21		100

MODERN 1970-2025		Exc	Mint
2126641	C&O Bunk Car "B575," 21		100 ___
2126642	C&O Bunk Car "B579," 21		100 ___
2126651	MKT Bunk Car "X-2121," 21		100 ___
2126652	MKT Bunk Car "X-2122," 21		100 ___
2126661	N&W Bunk Car "525502," 21		100 ___
2126662	N&W Bunk Car "525534,"21		100 ___
2126671	WP Bunk Car "MW0556," 21		100 ___
2126672	WP Bunk Car "MW0761," 21		100 ___
2126680	Polar Express 40' Flatcar w/Bell, 21		100 ___
2127010	NYC Xplorer Coach 2-pack, 20		370 ___
2127020	ATSF WiFi Theater Car "89," 20		340 ___
2127030	BNSF WiFi Theater Car "William Barstow Strong," 20		340 ___
2127040	C&NW WiFi Theater Car "Fox River," 20		340 ___
2127050	KCS WiFi Theater Car "Arthur E. Stilwell," 20		340 ___
2127060	NS WiFi Theater Car "Buena Vista," 20		340 ___
2127070	SP WiFi Theater Car "Harriman," 20		340 ___
2127080	NYC 1926 Cardinals Passenger Train Expansion Pack, 21		400 ___
2127090	NYC 1926 Cardinals "St. Mary of the Lake" Diner w/ StationSounds, 21		370 ___
2127100	D&RGW Ski Train Power Car, 21-22		370 ___
2127110	D&RGW Ski Train Passenger Car 4-pack, 21-22		825 ___
2127120	D&RGW Ski Train Passenger Car 2-pack, 21-22		410 ___
2127130	D&RGW Ski Train Diner w/StationSounds, 21-22		400 ___
2127140	Polar Express High Speed Train Expansion Pack, 21		1000 ___
2127150	ATSF Valley Flyer Passenger Train Expansion 2-pack, 21		400 ___
2127160	PRR South Wind 21" Passenger Car 4-pack, 20		750 ___
2127170	PRR South Wind 21" Passenger Car 2-pack, 20		370 ___
2127180	PRR South Wind Diner w/StationSounds, 20		350 ___
2127190	PRR "Fleet of Modernism" B60 "7900," 20		190 ___
2127200	PC B60 Passenger Car "7705," 20		190 ___
2127210	PC B60 Passenger Car "7630," 20		190 ___
2127220	Reindeer Express B60 Passenger Car "2124," 20		190 ___
2127230	PRR "Fleet of Modernism" 18" Pullman 2-pack, 20		400 ___
2127240	Pullman Pool Service 18" Sleeper, Green 2-pack, 20		400 ___
2127250	Pullman Pool Service 18" Sleeper, Gray 2-pack, 20		400 ___
2127260	PRR South Wind 1947 Expansion Passenger Car 2-pack, 20		370 ___
2127270	PRR "Fleet of Modernism" RPO "5260," 20		190 ___
2127280	NYC Southwestern Limited 60' Baggage Car "2979," 20		190 ___
2127290	NYC Southwestern Limited 60' Baggage Car "8424," 20		190 ___
2127300	NYC Southwestern Limited RPO "4814," 20		190 ___
2127310	NYC Southwestern Limited 21" Passenger Car 4-pack, 20		750 ___
2127320	NYC Southwestern Limited 21" Passenger Car 2-pack, 20		370 ___
2127330	NYC Southwestern Limited 21" Diner w/StationSounds, 20		370 ___
2127341	Polar Express Sleeping Car "Believe," Black roof, 21		210 ___
2127342	Polar Express Sleeping Car "North Pole," Black roof, 21		210 ___
2127351	Polar Express Sleeping Car "Believe," White roof, 21, 24		210 ___
2127352	Polar Express Sleeping Car "North Pole," White roof, 21, 24		210 ___
2127360	D&H 21" Passenger Car 4-pack, 21		750 ___
2127370	D&H 21" Passenger Car 2-pack, 21		370 ___
2127380	D&H 21" Diner w/StationSounds, 21		370 ___
2127390	Amtrak Acela High Speed Train Expansion Set, 21		1000 ___
2127400	Amtrak Acela Concept High Speed Train Expansion Set, 21		1000 ___
2127410	MILW High Speed Train Expansion Set, 21		1000 ___

		Exc	Mint
___ 2127420	NH High Speed Train Expansion Set, 21		1000
___ 2127430	PRR Concept High Speed Train Expansion Set, 21		1000
___ 2127440	ATSF High Speed Train Expansion Set, 21		1000
___ 2127450	UP High Speed Train Expansion Set, 21		1000
___ 2127460	E-L 21" Passenger Car 4-pack, 21		750
___ 2127470	E-L 21" Passenger Car 2-pack, 21		370
___ 2127480	E-L 21" Diner w/StationSounds, 21		370
___ 2127490	GM&O 18" Passenger Car 2-pack, A, 21		400
___ 2127500	GM&O 18" Passenger Car 2-pack, B, 21		400
___ 2127510	GM&O 18" Passenger Car 2-pack, C, 21		400
___ 2127520	GM&O 18" Diner w/StationSounds, 21		370
___ 2127530	Texas Special 18" Passenger Car 2-pack, A, 21		400
___ 2127540	Texas Special 18" Passenger Car 2-pack, B, 21		400
___ 2127550	Texas Special 18" Passenger Car 2-pack, C, 21		400
___ 2127560	Texas Special 18" Diner w/StationSounds, 21		370
___ 2128010	C&O Walking Brakeman Car "21299," 20-24		110
___ 2128020	Shark Fin Containment Car, 21-24		110
___ 2128030	Monsters Inc. Chasing Gondola, 21-23		90
___ 2128040	Cars Aquarium Car, 21-23		120
___ 2128050	Candy Cane Flatcar, 21		75
___ 2128060	Christmas Tree Flatcar, 21-23		100
___ 2128070	Dump Car w/Presents, 21-23		90
___ 2128080	LL Flatcar w/Handcar, 21-23		135
___ 2128090	Star Trek Dilithium Crystals Hopper w/illumination, 21		90
___ 2128100	Star Trek Chasing Gondola w/Picard, Riker and Q, 21		85
___ 2128110	This Bud's For You Refrigerator Car, 21-23		90
___ 2128120	Those Who Know Bud Refrigerator Car, 21-23		90
___ 2128130	Vintage High Life Refrigerator Car, 21-23		90
___ 2128140	Vintage Coors Refrigerator Car, 21-23		90
___ 2128150	Ford Vintage Boxcar, 21		75
___ 2128160	Chevy Vintage Boxcar, 21		75
___ 2128170	Halloween Sound Car, 21-22		85
___ 2128180	2021 Christmas Music Car, 21		80
___ 2128190	2021 Christmas Boxcar, 21		65
___ 2128200	PRR Flatcar w/Girder Bridge, 21-23		95
___ 2128210	Polar Express Flatcar w/Girder Bridge, 21-25		95
___ 2128220	Batman Aquarium Car, 21-23		120
___ 2128230	Road Runner Aquarium Car, 21-22		120
___ 2128240	Polar Express Operating Present Car, 21-23		100
___ 2128250	SledEx Present Unloading Car, 21-23		100
___ 2128260	North Pole Central Flatcar w/Handcar, 21-22		135
___ 2128270	John Deere Refrigerator Car, 21-22		90
___ 2128280	Polar Express Boxcar, 21-25		85
___ 2128290	Angela Trotta Thomas Christmas Caboose, 21-22		90
___ 2128300	Angela Trotta Thomas Santa Fe Boxcar, 21-23		85
___ 2128310	Angela Trotta Thomas Hudson Boxcar, 21-23		85
___ 2128320	Star Trek Capt. Janeway Boxcar, 21		75
___ 2128330	Star Trek Capt. Sisko Boxcar, 21		75
___ 2128340	Mickey & Friends Christmas Flatcar w/Girders, 21-23		95
___ 2128350	Mickey & Friends Christmas Present Car, 21-23		100
___ 2128360	Space Launch Allis-Chalmers Car w/Capsules, 21-23		85
___ 2129010	Big Tatz Ink, 20-22		100
___ 2129020	Sofa King Mattresses & Furniture, 20-22		110

Item	Description	Exc	Mint
2129030	Sgt. Stumpy's Red, White & Boom Fireworks, 20-24		300 ___
2129050	Track Laying Crew, 20		100 ___
2129060	Road Crew, 20		100 ___
2129070	Polar Express Present Chute Station, 21-23		200 ___
2129080	SledEx Present Chute Station, 21-22		180 ___
2129090	Angela Trotta Thomas Christmastime Hobby Store, 21-22		300 ___
2129100	Batman Rotary Beacon, 21-22		100 ___
2129110	Classic Rotary Beacon, 21-22		90 ___
2129120	Christmas Rotary Beacon, 21-22		90 ___
2129130	Halloween Rotary Beacon, 21-22		90 ___
2129140	Dr. IP Drips & Sons Plumbing, 20-22		100 ___
2129150	Dominant Jeans , 20-22		120 ___
2129160	McCartney's Wings, 20		100 ___
2129180	T Rex Elevated Oil Tank, 21		90 ___
2129190	Polar Express Elevated Hot Chocolate Tank, 21-24		110 ___
2129200	Lionel Ale Elevated Oil Tank, 21-22		110 ___
2129210	Area 51 Elevated Oil Tank, 21-22		110 ___
2129220	Christmas Joy Flagpole, 21-23		45 ___
2129230	Halloween Flagpole, 21-23		45 ___
2129240	Cowens Towing Garage, 21-22		165 ___
2129250	Talking Passenger Station, 21-22		200 ___
2129260	Ford Water Tower, 21		50 ___
2129270	Chevy Water Tower, 21		50 ___
2129280	Halloween Water Tower, 21-22		50 ___
2129290	Christmas Water Tower, 21-25		60 ___
2129300	Area 51 Water Tower, 21-22		60 ___
2129310	John Deere Service Garage, 21-22		180 ___
2129330	Halloween Lighted Half Covered Bridge, 21-22		90 ___
2129340	Chevrolet Flagpole, 21-24		45 ___
2129350	Ford Flagpole, 21-24		45 ___
2129360	Ford Service Station, 21-22		165 ___
2129370	Chevy Service Station, 21-22		165 ___
2129380	Halloween Elevated Oil Tank, 21-23		100 ___
2130010	Frat House, 20		100 ___
2130020	Santa on the Roof House, 21		85 ___
2130030	Cock & Bull Tavern, 21		75 ___
2130040	Russell House, 21		85 ___
2130050	Garage 2-pack, 20		50 ___
2130060	Turner House Kit, 21		50 ___
2130070	Garage Kit, 2-pack, 20		135 ___
2130080	Design-Your-Own-House Kit, 21		60 ___
2130090	Anheuser-Busch Covered Bridge, 21-22		65 ___
2130100	Polar Express Billboard Pack, 21-24		25 ___
2130110	Log Cabin Scented Smoke Fluid, 21-24		9 ___
2130120	Window Shoppers Figures, 21-23		30 ___
2130130	Thru Truss Bridge Kit, 21-25		70 ___
2131010	American Railroads 6-4-4-6 S1 "6100," CC, 20		1600 ___
2131020	PRR 6-4-4-6 S1 "6100," As-Built, CC, 20		1600 ___
2131030	PRR 6-4-4-6 S1 "6100," Calendar, CC, 20		1600 ___
2131040	PRR 6-4-4-6 S1 "6100," Tuscan Red, CC, 20		1600 ___
2131050	B&M 4-6-0 "2074," CC, 20		750 ___
2131060	CP/Railtours 4-6-0 "972," CC, 20		750 ___
2131070	NYC 4-6-0 "1232," CC, 20		750 ___

MODERN 1970-2025		Exc	Mint
____ **2131080**	Reading & Northern 4-6-0 "225," CC, 20		750
____ **2131090**	Rutland 4-6-0 "79," CC, 20		750
____ **2131100**	Soo Line 4-6-0 "2645," CC, 20		750
____ **2131110**	Southern 4-6-0 "947," CC, 20		375
____ **2131120**	T&P 4-6-0 "316," CC, 20		750
____ **2131130**	ATSF USRA 2-8-8-2 "1796," CC, 20		1900
____ **2131140**	B&O USRA 2-8-8-2 "7150," CC, 20		1900
____ **2131150**	Clinchfield USRA 2-8-8-2 "730," CC, 20		1900
____ **2131160**	D&RGW USRA 2-8-8-2 "3504," CC, 20		1900
____ **2131170**	N&W USRA 2-8-8-2 "2020," CC, 20		1900
____ **2131180**	N&W USRA 2-8-8-2 "2050," CC, 20		1900
____ **2131190**	N&W USRA 2-8-8-2 "2021," Weathered, CC, 20		2050
____ **2131200**	NP USRA 2-8-8-2 "4501," CC, 20		1900
____ **2131210**	PRR USRA 2-8-8-2 "377," CC, 2		1900
____ **2131220**	UP USRA 2-8-8-2 "3672," CC, 20		1900
____ **2131230**	Virginian USRA 2-8-8-2 "702," CC, 20		1900
____ **2131240**	ACL USRA 4-6-2 Pacific "1504," CC, 21		1500
____ **2131250**	GM&O USRA 4-6-2 Pacific "5296," CC, 21		1500
____ **2131260**	GN USRA 4-6-2 Pacific "1385," CC, 21		1500
____ **2131270**	MKT USRA 4-6-2 Pacific "411," CC, 21		1500
____ **2131280**	Nickel Plate Road USRA 4-6-2 Pacific "168," CC, 21		1500
____ **2131290**	SP USRA 4-6-2 Pacific "611," CC, 21		1500
____ **2131300**	UP USRA 4-6-2 Pacific "3218," CC, 21		1500
____ **2131310**	ACL USRA Light 2-8-2 "823," CC, 20		1300
____ **2131320**	Georgia USRA Light 2-8-2 "300," CC, 20		1300
____ **2131330**	GTW USRA Light 2-8-2 "4070," CC, 20		1300
____ **2131340**	L&HR USRA Light 2-8-2 "83," CC, 20		1300
____ **2131350**	Monon USRA Light 2-8-2 "554," CC, 20		1300
____ **2131360**	SLSF USRA Light 2-8-2 "4003," CC, 20		1300
____ **2131370**	Southern USRA Light 2-8-2 "4501," CC, 20		1300
____ **2131380**	Wabash USRA Light 2-8-2 "2202," CC, 20		1300
____ **2131390**	CNJ Blue Comet 4-6-0 Camelback "770," CC, 21		650
____ **2131400**	CNJ 4-6-0 Camelback "774," CC, 21		650
____ **2131410**	D&H 4-6-0 Camelback "810," CC, 21		650
____ **2131420**	LIRR 4-6-0 Camelback "18," CC, 21		650
____ **2131430**	NYO&W 4-6-0 Camelback "255," CC, 21		650
____ **2131440**	Reading 4-6-0 Camelback "652," CC, 21		650
____ **2131450**	Strasburg 4-6-0 Camelback "771," CC, 21		650
____ **2131460**	Hallows Eve Limited 4-6-0 Camelback "1313," CC, 21		650
____ **2131470**	ATSF 2-10-10-2 "3001," CC, 21		2500
____ **2131480**	ATSF 2-10-10-2 "3009," CC, 21		2500
____ **2131490**	ATSF Black Bonnet 2-10-10-2 "3005," CC, 21		2500
____ **2131500**	ATSF Valley Flyer 2-10-10-2 "3008," CC, 21		2500
____ **2131510**	NYC 4-8-2 L2a Mohawk "2700," CC, 21		1600
____ **2131520**	NYC 4-8-2 L2a Mohawk "2790," CC, 21		1600
____ **2131530**	NYC 4-8-2 L2a Mohawk "2728," CC, 21		1600
____ **2131540**	NYC 4-8-2 L2a Mohawk "2775," CC, 21		1600
____ **2131550**	NYC 4-8-2 L2a Mohawk "2727," Gray, CC, 21		1600
____ **2131560**	NYC 4-8-2 L2a Mohawk "2750," Pacemaker, CC, 21		1600
____ **2131570**	NH 4-8-2 L2a Mohawk "3507," CC, 21		1600
____ **2132010**	SP LionMaster AC-12 4-8-8-2 Cab-Forward "4294," CC, 20		1300
____ **2132020**	SP LionMaster AC-12 4-8-8-2 Cab-Forward "4291," CC, 20		1300
____ **2132030**	SP LionMaster AC-12 4-8-8-2 Cab-Forward "4280," CC, 20		1300

		Exc	Mint
2132040	SP LionMaster AC-12 4-8-8-2 Cab-Forward "4290," Daylight, CC, 20		1300 ___
2132050	Christmas 4-4-0 General "1225" LionChief, 21-22		275 ___
2132060	Halloween 4-4-0 General "1031" LionChief, 21-22		275 ___
2132070	PRR 4-4-0 General "573" LionChief, 21		250 ___
2132080	W&A 4-4-0 General "3" LionChief, 21		250 ___
2132090	PRR Baby K4 4-6-2 Pacific "1361" LionChief Plus 2.0, 21		550 ___
2132100	PRR Baby K4 4-6-2 Pacific "3750" LionChief Plus 2.0, 21		550 ___
2132110	PRR Baby K4 4-6-2 Pacific "5400" LionChief Plus 2.0, 21		550 ___
2132120	PRR Baby K4 4-6-2 Pacific "5409" LionChief Plus 2.0, 21		550 ___
2133010	CRI&P E7 AA Diesel Set "632/635," CC, 20		1000 ___
2133019	CRI&P E7B SuperBass, 20		450 ___
2133020	SP Golden State E7 AB Diesel Set "6000/6000B," CC, 20		1000 ___
2133029	SP Golden State E7B SuperBass "6000C," 20		450 ___
2133030	NYC E7 AA Diesel Set "4004/4005," CC, 20		1000 ___
2133039	NYC E7B SuperBass "4104," 20		450 ___
2133040	PRR E7 AA Diesel Set "5900/5901," CC, 20		1000 ___
2133043	PRR E7B SuperBass "5848B," 20		450 ___
2133049	PRR E7B SuperBass "5900B," 20		450 ___
2133050	ACL E7 AA Diesel Set "540/541," CC, 20		1000 ___
2133059	ACL E7B SuperBass "755", 20		450 ___
2133060	UP E7 AB Diesel Set "927A/928B," CC, 20		1000 ___
2133069	UP E7B SuperBass "929B", 20		450 ___
2133070	SP Lark E7 AB Diesel Set "6004/6004B," CC, 20		1000 ___
2133079	SP Lark E7B SuperBass "6004C," 20		225 ___
2133080	NYC E7 AA Diesel Set "4002/4003," Black, CC, 20		1000 ___
2133089	NYC E7B SuperBass "4102," Black, 20		450 ___
2133090	Bethlehem Steel Genset Diesel Switcher "420," CC, 20		600 ___
2133100	BNSF Genset Diesel Switcher "1228," CC, 20		600 ___
2133110	CSX Genset Diesel Switcher "1300," CC, 20		600 ___
2133120	NS Genset Diesel Switcher "301," CC, 20		600 ___
2133130	PRR Genset Diesel Switcher "9910," CC, 20		600 ___
2133140	UP Genset Diesel Switcher "2706," CC, 20		600 ___
2133151	ATSF GP7 Diesel "2676," CC, 20		500 ___
2133152	ATSF GP7 Diesel "2804," CC, 20		500 ___
2133161	SSW GP7 Diesel "304," CC, 20		500 ___
2133162	SSW GP7 Diesel "320," CC, 20		500 ___
2133171	MEC GP7 Diesel "562," CC, 20		500 ___
2133172	MEC GP7 Diesel "565," CC, 20		500 ___
2133181	NP GP7 Diesel "564," CC, 20		500 ___
2133182	NP GP7 Diesel "566," CC, 20		500 ___
2133191	SAL GP7 Diesel "1700," CC, 20		500 ___
2133192	SAL GP7 Diesel "1760," CC, 20		500 ___
2133201	T&P GP7 Diesel "1110," CC, 20		500 ___
2133202	T&P GP7 Diesel "1118," CC, 20		500 ___
2133210	ATSF Baldwin Sharknose AA Diesel Set "400A/400D," CC, 20		950 ___
2133218	ATSF Baldwin Sharknose Powered B Diesel "400B," CC, 20		430 ___
2133219	ATSF Baldwin Sharknose B Diesel SuperBass "400C," 20		400 ___
2133220	Baldwin Sharknose AA Diesel Set "6000/6001," CC, 20		950 ___
2133228	Baldwin Sharknose Powered B Diesel "6000B," CC, 20		430 ___
2133229	Baldwin Sharknose B Diesel SuperBass "6001B," 20		400 ___
2133230	EJ&E Baldwin Sharknose AA Diesel Set "700A/701A," CC , 20		950 ___

		Exc	Mint
____ **2133238**	EJ&E Baldwin Sharknose Powered B Diesel "700B," CC, 20		430
____ **2133239**	EJ&E Baldwin Sharknose B Diesel SuperBass "701B," 20		400
____ **2133240**	Monongahela Sharknose AA Diesel Set "1207/1216," CC, 20		950
____ **2133248**	Monongahela Baldwin Sharknose Powered B Diesel "3708," CC, 20		430
____ **2133249**	Monongahela Sharknose B Diesel SuperBass "3709," 20		400
____ **2133250**	NYC Baldwin Sharknose AA Diesel Set "1206/1213," CC, 20		950
____ **2133258**	NYC Baldwin Sharknose Powered B Diesel "3705," CC, 20		430
____ **2133259**	NYC Baldwin Sharknose B Diesel SuperBass "3706," 20		400
____ **2133260**	PRR Baldwin Sharknose AA Diesel Set "5780A/5781A," CC, 20		950
____ **2133268**	PRR Baldwin Sharknose Powered B Diesel "5780B," CC, 20		430
____ **2133269**	PRR Baldwin Sharknose B Diesel Superbass "5732B," 22		400
____ **2133270**	PRR Baldwin Sharknose AA Diesel Set "9730A/9731A," CC, 20		950
____ **2133278**	PRR Baldwin Sharknose Powered B Diesel "9730B," CC, 20		430
____ **2133279**	PRR Baldwin Sharknose B Diesel SuperBass "9732B," 20		400
____ **2133280**	US Army Baldwin Sharknose AA Diesel Set "1775/1776," CC, 20		950
____ **2133288**	US Army Baldwin Sharknose Powered B Diesel "1926," CC, 20		430
____ **2133289**	US Army Baldwin Sharknose B Diesel SuperBass "1941," 20		400
____ **2133290**	UP Genset Diesel Switcher "2709," Graffiti, CC, 20		625
____ **2133311**	ACL SD70ACe Diesel "1840," CC, 21		600
____ **2133312**	ACL SD70ACe Diesel "1967," CC, 21		600
____ **2133321**	ATSF SD70ACe Diesel "1859," CC, 21		600
____ **2133322**	ATSF SD70ACe Diesel "1995," CC, 21		600
____ **2133330**	KCS SD70ACe Diesel "4409 - Heroes," CC, 21		600
____ **2133331**	B&O SD70ACe Diesel "1828," CC, 21		600
____ **2133332**	B&O SD70ACe Diesel "1987," CC, 21		600
____ **2133341**	B&M SD70ACe Diesel "1835," CC, 21		600
____ **2133342**	B&M SD70ACe Diesel "1983," CC, 21		600
____ **2133351**	CP SD70ACe Diesel "1881," CC, 21		600
____ **2133352**	CP SD70ACe Diesel "2021," CC, 21		600
____ **2133361**	GN SD70ACe Diesel "1889," CC, 21		600
____ **2133362**	GN SD70ACe Diesel "1970," CC, 21		600
____ **2133371**	Monon SD70ACe Diesel "1847," CC, 21		600
____ **2133372**	Monon SD70ACe Diesel "1971," CC, 21		600
____ **2133380**	E-L Alco PA AA Diesel Set "862/863," CC, 21		1000
____ **2133390**	GM&O Alco PA AA Diesel Set "290/291," CC, 21		1000
____ **2133400**	MKT Alco PA AA Diesel Set "152A/152C," CC, 21		1000
____ **2133410**	NH Alco PA AA Diesel Set "0760/0761," CC, 21		1000
____ **2133420**	SSW Alco PA AA Diesel Set "300/301," CC, 21		1000
____ **2133430**	D&H Alco PA AA Diesel Set "16/17," CC, 21		1000
____ **2133441**	BNSF GP30 Diesel "2472," CC, 21		530
____ **2133442**	BNSF GP30 Diesel "2826," CC, 21		530
____ **2133451**	C&NW GP30 Diesel "818," CC, 21		530
____ **2133452**	C&NW GP30 Diesel "823," CC, 21		530
____ **2133461**	CSX (Chessie) GP30 Diesel "4126," CC, 21		530
____ **2133462**	CSX (B&O) GP30 Diesel "4131," CC, 21		530
____ **2133471**	KCS GP30 Diesel "4100," CC, 21		530
____ **2133472**	KCS GP30 Diesel "4109," CC, 21		530
____ **2133481**	Reading & Northern GP30 Diesel "2530," CC, 21		530
____ **2133482**	Reading & Northern GP30 Diesel "2531," CC, 21		530
____ **2133491**	Soo GP30 Diesel "700," CC, 21		530

Item	Description	Exc	Mint
2133492	Soo GP30 Diesel "703," CC, 21		530 ___
2133501	UP Veranda Turbine w/SuperBass Tender "61," CC, 21		1650 ___
2133502	UP Veranda Turbine w/SuperBass Tender "69," CC, 21		1650 ___
2133510	Alaska Veranda Turbine w/SuperBass Tender "4501," CC, 21		1650 ___
2133520	GN Veranda Turbine w/SuperBass Tender "5020," CC, 21		1650 ___
2133530	PRR Veranda Turbine w/SuperBass Tender "6201," CC, 21		1650 ___
2133540	D&RGW Veranda Turbine w/SuperBass Tender "4010," CC, 21		1650 ___
2133550	SP Veranda Turbine w/SuperBass Tender "8505," CC, 21		1650 ___
2133560	US Dept of Defense Veranda Turbine w/SuperBass Tender "1941," CC, 21		1650 ___
2133570	B&M SW8 Diesel Switcher "801," CC, 21		500 ___
2133580	Coors Brewing SW8 Diesel Switcher "991," CC, 21		500 ___
2133590	Conrail SW8 Diesel Switcher "8657," CC, 21		500 ___
2133600	NYC SW8 Diesel Switcher "9606," CC, 21		500 ___
2133610	CRI&P SW8 Diesel Switcher "818," CC, 21		500 ___
2133620	SCL SW8 Diesel Switcher "19," CC, 21		500 ___
2133630	SP SW8 Diesel Switcher "1102," CC, 21		500 ___
2133640	Strasburg SW8 Diesel Switcher "8618," CC, 21		500 ___
2133730	UP Veranda Turbine w/SuperBass Tender "65," CC, 21		1650 ___
2133740	UP Veranda Turbine w/SuperBass Tender "67," CC, 21		1650 ___
2134010	ACL GP7 Diesel "105" LionChief Plus 2.0, 20-21		375 ___
2134020	MKT GP7 Diesel "93" LionChief Plus 2.0, 20-21		375 ___
2134030	B&O GP7 Diesel "6698" LionChief Plus 2.0, 20-21		375 ___
2134040	CRI&P GP7 Diesel "1274" LionChief Plus 2.0, 20-21		375 ___
2134050	ATSF GE U36B Diesel "8733" LionChief, 21-22		250 ___
2134060	UP GE U36B Diesel "8573" LionChief, 21-22		250 ___
2134070	Seaboard System GE U36B Diesel "5701" LionChief, 21-25		250 ___
2134080	CSX GE U36B Diesel "5871" LionChief, 21-22		250 ___
2134090	LV Alco RS3 "216" LionChief Plus 2.0, 21		375 ___
2134100	PRR Alco RS3 "4044" LionChief Plus 2.0, 21		375 ___
2134110	ATSF Alco RS3 "2098" LionChief Plus 2.0, 21		375 ___
2134120	Southern Alco RS3 "520" LionChief Plus 2.0, 21		375 ___
2135010	B&O TMCC Speeder, 21		150 ___
2135020	PC TMCC Speeder, 21		150 ___
2135030	ATSF TMCC Speeder, 21		150 ___
2135040	Sperry TMCC Speeder, 21		150 ___
2135050	Polar Express TMCC Speeder, 21-24		165 ___
2135060	Halloween TMCC Speeder, 21-22		165 ___
2135070	Star Trek TMCC Speeder, 21		150 ___
2135080	BNSF TMCC Tamper, 21		200 ___
2135090	BN TMCC Tamper, 21, 24		200 ___
2135100	Conrail TMCC Tamper, 21		200 ___
2135110	CSX TMCC Tamper, 21		200 ___
2135120	NS TMCC Tamper, 21		200 ___
2135130	SP TMCC Tamper, 21		200 ___
2135140	North Pole Central Trolley, 21-23		120 ___
2138010	Kate Shelley Heritage Boxcar, 20		85 ___
2138020	Angela Trotta Thomas Stocked Shelves Boxcar - Bottom, 20		85 ___
2138030	CP 140th Anniversary Boxcar, 20		85 ___
2138040	Amtrak 50th Anniversary Boxcar, 21		85 ___
2138050	Erie Railroad 170th Anniversary Boxcar, 21		85 ___
2138060	Lyndon B. Johnson Presidential Boxcar, 21		80 ___

	MODERN 1970-2025		Exc	Mint
____	**2138070**	Chester A. Arthur Pesidential Boxcar, 21		80
____	**2138080**	Franklin Pierce Presidential Boxcar, 21		80
____	**2138110**	Wings of Angels Kacie Boxcar, 21-22		95
____	**2138120**	Wings of Angels Victoria Boxcar, 21-22		95
____	**2138130**	World War II Africa Campaign Boxcar, 21		85
____	**2138140**	World War II Fletcher Class Destroyer Boxcar, 21		85
____	**2138150**	2021 Happy Birthday Boxcar, 21		90
____	**2138160**	2021 Christmas Boxcar, 21		90
____	**2138170**	2021 Anniversary Boxcar, 21		90
____	**2138190**	Wings of Angels Jessie Boxcar, 21-22		95
____	**2143011**	ATSF Flatcar w/Stakes "90410" (std 0), 20-22		55
____	**2143012**	ATSF Flatcar w/Stakes "90411" (std 0), 20-22		55
____	**2143021**	N&W Flatcar w/Stakes "32900" (std 0), 20-23		55
____	**2143022**	N&W Flatcar w/Stakes "329019" (std 0), 20-22		55
____	**2143031**	NP Flatcar w/Stakes "69001" (std 0), 20-22		55
____	**2143032**	NP Flatcar w/Stakes "69123" (std 0), 20-22		55
____	**2143041**	PRR Flatcar w/Stakes "497918" (std 0), 20-22		55
____	**2143042**	PRR Flatcar w/Stakes "491301" (std 0), 20-22		55
____	**2143051**	ADM RBL Refrigerator Car "7014" (std 0), 20-22		55
____	**2143052**	ADM RBL Refrigerator Car "7019" (std 0), 20-23		55
____	**2143061**	CN RBL Refrigerator Car "290403" (std 0), 20-22		55
____	**2143062**	CN RBL Refrigerator Car "290936" (std 0), 20-22		55
____	**2143071**	FGE RBL Refrigerator Car "363454" (std 0), 20-22		55
____	**2143072**	FGE RBL Refrigerator Car "363700" (std 0), 20-22		55
____	**2143081**	PRR RBL Refrigerator Car "19103" (std 0), 20-22		55
____	**2143082**	PRR RBL Refrigerator Car "19198" (std 0), 20-22		55
____	**2143091**	CP< DD Boxcar "7751" (std 0), 21		50
____	**2143092**	CP< DD Boxcar "7844" (std 0), 21		50
____	**2143101**	D&M DD Boxcar "2115," 21		50
____	**2143102**	D&M DD Boxcar "2127," 21		50
____	**2143111**	Port of Tillamook Bay RR DD Boxcar "164" (std 0), 21		50
____	**2143112**	Port of Tillamook Bay RR DD Boxcar "187" (std 0), 21		50
____	**2143121**	Sierra RR DD Boxcar "5009" (std 0), 21		50
____	**2143122**	Sierra RR DD Boxcar "5036" (std 0), 21		50
____	**2143131**	NYC Gondola w/Ballast Load "632353" (std 0), 21		50
____	**2143132**	NYC Gondola w/Ballast Load "632361" (std 0), 21		50
____	**2143141**	N&W Gondola w/Ballast Load "591000" (std 0), 21		50
____	**2143142**	N&W Gondola w/Ballast Load "591082" (std 0), 21		50
____	**2143151**	PRR Gondola w/Ballast Load "490075" (std 0), 21		50
____	**2143152**	PRR Gondola w/Ballast Load "490079" (std 0), 21		50
____	**2143161**	UP Gondola w/Ballast Load "908467" (std 0), 21		50
____	**2143162**	UP Gondola w/Ballast Load "908469" (std 0), 21		50
____	**2201290**	LCCA N&W 2-6-6-4 Class A Locomotive "1222," CC, 22 u		2100
____	**2208010**	Legacy Base 3, 22-25		500
____	**2213050**	Strasburg RR 2-10-0 Locomotive (1967/2020) "90," CC, 21		1900
____	**2222010**	BNSF SD70MAC Diesel Coal Train Set, CC, 21		900
____	**2222020**	UP Rocket Booster Diesel Set, CC, 22		1700
____	**2222030**	BN SD45 Hustle Muscle Diesel Freight Set, CC, 21		1100
____	**2222040**	Cambria & Indiana SW9 Bicentennial Diesel Coal Train Set, CC, 21		1000
____	**2222050**	Grand Canyon Ry Steam Passenger Set, CC, 21		1300
____	**2222060**	Amtrak Genesis LionChief Plus 2.0 Set, 22		1000
____	**2222070**	B&LE Diesel Ore Train Set, CC, 22		1600

		Exc	Mint
2222080	Black River & Western Excursion Diesel Passenger Set, CC, 22-24	1100	___
2222090	NS 40th Anniversary Diesel Freight Set, CC, 22	1300	___
2222100	PRR S2 Steam LionChief Plus 2.0 Set, 22	750	___
2223010	U.S. Army LionChief Bluetooth 5.0 Diesel Freight Set, 21-24	450	___
2223020	Christmas Celebration LionChief Bluetooth 5.0 Set, 22-25	400	___
2223040	Emergency Response LionChief Bluetooth 5.0 Set, 22-25	500	___
2223050	Anheuser Busch LionChief Bluetooth 5.0 Set, 22-25	400	___
2223060	Lionel Lines LionChief Bluetooth 5.0 Mixed Freight Set, 22-25	360	___
2223070	Great Locomotive Chase Deluxe LionChief Bluetooth 5.0 Set, 22-25	600	___
2223110	Graffiti LionChief Bluetooth 5.0 Set, 22-25	500	___
2226010	Erie Boxcar "82275" w/HoboSounds, 21	190	___
2226020	RI Boxcar "48582" w/HoboSounds, 21	190	___
2226030	AT&SF AAR 2-Bay Hopper 2-Pack, 21	200	___
2226040	Cambria & Indiana Die-cast AAR 2-Bay Hopper 2-Pack, 21	200	___
2226050	NYC AAR 2-Bay Hopper 2-Pack, 21	200	___
2226060	NS AAR 2-Bay Hopper 2-Pack, 21	200	___
2226070	Pittsburg & Shawmut AAR 2-Bay Hopper 2-Pack, 21	200	___
2226080	Reading AAR 2-Bay Hopper 2-Pack, 21,24	200	___
2226090	Alaska Cylindrical Covered Hopper "14500," 21	110	___
2226100	CSX (ex EL) Cylindrical Covered Hopper "884137," 21	110	___
2226110	EL Cylindrical Covered Hopper "20021," 21	110	___
2226120	GM Cylindrical Covered Hopper "61113," 21, 24	110	___
2226130	NYC Cylindrical Covered Hopper "885950," 21	110	___
2226140	UP Cylindrical Covered Hopper "221000," 21	110	___
2226150	CP Caboose "434604" w/CupolaCam, 21	220	___
2226160	SSW Caboose "3" w/CupolaCam, 21	220	___
2226170	NP Caboose "10401" w/CupolaCam, 21	220	___
2226180	SAL Caboose "5754" w/CupolaCam, 21	220	___
2226190	Soo Caboose "1" w/CupolaCam, 21	220	___
2226200	North Pole Central Caboose "2521" w/CupolaCam, 21	220	___
2226210	UP CA-1 Caboose "2664" (brown), 21	150	___
2226220	UP CA-1 Caboose "2535" (brown), 21	150	___
2226230	UP CA-1 Caboose "2550" (yellow), 21	150	___
2226240	UP CA-1 Caboose "2654" (white), 21	150	___
2226250	SP CA-1 Caboose "703," 21	150	___
2226260	Great Western CA-1 Caboose "1006," 21	150	___
2226270	AT&SF 50' Flatcar "91090" w/Fire Truck, 21	160	___
2226280	C&O 50' Flatcar "81001" w/Fire Truck, 21	160	___
2226290	NYC 50' Flatcar "506261" w/Fire Truck, 21	160	___
2226300	PRR 50' Flatcar "469660" w/Fire Truck, 21	160	___
2226310	Southern 50' Flatcar "51819" w/Fire Truck, 21	160	___
2226320	UP 50' Flatcar "53026" w/Fire Truck, 21	160	___
2226330	Ann Arbor 4-Door Hi-Cube Boxcar "10009," 21	130	___
2226340	CN 4-Door Hi-Cube Boxcar "795101," 21	130	___
2226350	Ford 4-Door Hi-Cube Boxcar "101," 21	130	___
2226360	N&W 4-Door Hi-Cube Boxcar "355173," 21	130	___
2226370	PC 4-Door Hi-Cube Boxcar "237544," 21	130	___
2226380	WP 4-Door Hi-Cube Boxcar "86011," 21	130	___
2226390	CN 4-Door Hi-Cube Boxcar w/graffiti, 21	140	___
2226400	Conrail 4-Door Hi-Cube Boxcar w/graffiti, 21	140	___
2226410	HLMX 4-Door Hi-Cube Boxcar w/graffiti, 21	140	___

		Exc	Mint
____ **2226420**	NS 4-Door Hi-Cube Boxcar w/graffiti, 21		140
____ **2226430**	UP Rocket Booster Flatcar w/Rocket 5-Pack, 22-24		860
____ **2226440**	UP Rocket Booster Flatcar 5-Pack, 22		750
____ **2226451**	Bethlehem Steel Coil Car "216451," 22-24		120
____ **2226452**	Bethlehem Steel Coil Car "216489," 22		120
____ **2226461**	BNSF Coil Car "534321," 22-25		120
____ **2226462**	BNSF Coil Car "534354," 22-25		120
____ **2226471**	Conrail Coil Car "623603," 22-25		120
____ **2226472**	Conrail Coil Car "623624," 22-25		120
____ **2226481**	Ferromex Coil Car "918040," 22-24		120
____ **2226482**	Ferromex Coil Car "918046," 22-25		120
____ **2226491**	Reading Coil Car "99502," 22-25		120
____ **2226492**	Reading Coil Car "99561," 22-25		120
____ **2226501**	UP Coil Car "242081," 22-25		120
____ **2226502**	UP Coil Car "242118," 22-25		120
____ **2226510**	Bethlehem Steel Coil Car w/Graffiti "216469," 22-24		130
____ **2226520**	BNSF Coil Car w/Graffiti "534370," 22		130
____ **2226530**	Conrail (NYC) Coil Car w/Graffiti "623684", 22-25		130
____ **2226540**	Ferromex Coil Car w/Graffiti "918032", 22-24		130
____ **2226550**	NS Coil Car w/Graffiti "167024", 22-25		130
____ **2226560**	Polar Express End Door Boxcar, 22		115
____ **2226571**	BN Husky Stack Car "63345", 22-24		170
____ **2226572**	BN Husky Stack Car w/Graffiti "63361", 22-25		190
____ **2226581**	CRLE Husky Stack Car "5462," 22-24		170
____ **2226582**	CRLE Husky Stack Car w/Graffiti "5496," 22-25		190
____ **2226591**	CSX Husky Stack Car "620360," 22		170
____ **2226592**	CSX Husky Stack Car w/Graffiti "620365," 22		190
____ **2226601**	TT Husky Stack Car "56218," 22-24		170
____ **2226602**	TT Husky Stack Car w/Graffiti "56317," 22-25		190
____ **2226611**	TTX Husky Stack Car "56295," 22-25		170
____ **2226612**	TTX Husky Stack Car w/Graffiti "56363," 22-24		190
____ **2226621**	Pacer Husky Stack Car "6301," 22		170
____ **2226622**	Pacer Husky Stack Car w/Graffiti "6325," 22-25		190
____ **2226630**	AT&SF End Door Boxcar "7176," 22		115
____ **2226640**	CB&Q End Door Boxcar "48520," 22-24		115
____ **2226650**	Conoco End Door Boxcar "50014," 22-24		115
____ **2226660**	Southern End Door Boxcar "42000," 22		115
____ **2226670**	UP End Door Boxcar "161202," 22-24		115
____ **2226680**	Wabash End Door Boxcar "18023," 22-24		115
____ **2226690**	B&O Bobber Caboose "1775," 22		120
____ **2226700**	LV Bobber Caboose "2606," 22		120
____ **2226710**	Maryland & Pennsylvania Bobber Caboose "2003," 22		120
____ **2226720**	Northern Central Bobber Caboose "200," 22		120
____ **2226730**	Strasburg Bobber Caboose "1," 22		120
____ **2226740**	U.S. Military Bobber Caboose "65," 22		120
____ **2226750**	BNSF Anniversary BW Caboose, 22		145
____ **2226760**	CSX Fire BW Caboose, 22		145
____ **2226770**	CSX Police BW Caboose, 22		145
____ **2226780**	CSX Veterans BW Caboose, 22		145
____ **2226790**	CN Veterans BW Caboose, 22		145
____ **2226800**	CP Veterans BW Caboose, 22-24		145
____ **2226810**	BNSF Illuminated Flag Boxcar, 22		160
____ **2226820**	CSX Fire Illuminated Flag Boxcar, 22		160

		Exc	Mint
2226830	CSX Police Illuminated Flag Boxcar, 22		160 ___
2226840	CSX Veterans Illuminated Flag Boxcar, 22		160 ___
2226850	Conrail Veterans Illuminated Flag Boxcar, 22		160 ___
2226860	Montana Rail Link Illuminated Flag Boxcar, 22-24		160 ___
2226870	AT&SF Vision Line Stockcar 3-Pack, 22-25		450 ___
2226880	B&O Vision Line Stockcar 3-Pack, 22-25		450 ___
2226890	NYC Vision Line Stockcar 3-Pack, 22-25		450 ___
2226900	NP Vision Line Stockcar 3-Pack, 22-25		450 ___
2226910	Swift Vision Line Stockcar 3-Pack, 22-25		450 ___
2226920	UP Vision Line Stockcar 3-Pack, 22-24		450 ___
2226930	N&W 2-Bay Hopper 2-Pack, 22		200 ___
2226940	PRR 2-Bay Hopper 2-Pack, 22-24		200 ___
2226950	Pennsylvania Coal & Coke 2-Bay Hopper 2-Pack, 22-24		200 ___
2226960	VGN 2-Bay Hopper 2-Pack, 22-25		200 ___
2226970	Westmoreland Coal 2-Bay Hopper 2-Pack, 22-25		200 ___
2226980	West Penn. Power 2-Bay Hopper 2-Pack, 22		200 ___
2226990	North Pole Central End Door Boxcar, 22-24		115 ___
2226991	UP Desert Victory Illuminated Flag Boxcar, 22-25		160 ___
2227010	Strasburg RR Observation "Paradise," 21		210 ___
2227020	Philadelphia & Reading Observation "10," 21		210 ___
2227030	Strasburg RR Wood Coach 2-Pack #1 (1990s), 21		400 ___
2227040	Strasburg RR Wood Coach 2-Pack #2 (1990s), 21		400 ___
2227050	Strasburg RR Wood Coach 2-Pack #1 (2000s), 21		400 ___
2227060	Strasburg RR Wood Coach 2-Pack #2 (2000s), 21		400 ___
2227070	PRR Wood Coach 2-Pack #1, 21		400 ___
2227080	PRR Wood Coach 2-Pack #2, 21		400 ___
2227090	B&M Wood Coach 2-Pack #1, 21		400 ___
2227100	B&M Wood Coach 2-Pack #2, 21		400 ___
2227110	LIRR 72' Passenger Coach 2-Pack #1, 21, 24		390 ___
2227120	LIRR 72' Passenger Coach 2-Pack #2, 21, 24		390 ___
2227130	NH 18" Passenger Car 2-Pack #1, 21		420 ___
2227140	NH 18" Passenger Car 2-Pack #2, 21		420 ___
2227150	NH 18" Passenger Car 2-Pack #3, 21		420 ___
2227160	NH 18" Diner w/StationSounds, 21		380 ___
2227170	Strasburg RR B380#1 (1990s), 21		400 ___
2227180	Strasburg RR Wood Coach/Combine 2-Pack #2 (2000s), 21		400 ___
2227190	PRR Wood Coach/Combine 2-Pack, 21		400 ___
2227200	B&M Wood Coach/Combine 2-Pack, 21		400 ___
2227210	Grand Canyon Ry Coach 2-Pack, 21		390 ___
2227220	UP Rocket Train Rider Car "Hialeah," 22		225 ___
2227230	AT&SF Chief Add-On Coach "3155," 22-25		100 ___
2227240	AT&SF Chief Add-On Vista-Dome "501," 22-25		100 ___
2227250	NS Excursion Coach 4-Pack, 22-24		900 ___
2227260	Amtrak Phase III 21" Passenger Car 4-Pack, 22		900 ___
2227270	Amtrak Phase III 21" Passenger Car 2-Pack, 22-24		450 ___
2227280	Amtrak Phase III Diner w/StationSounds, 22		400 ___
2227290	Amtrak Amfleet Phase III Coach 2-Pack, 22		400 ___
2227300	Amtrak Amfleet Phase V Coach 2-Pack, 22		400 ___
2227310	Amtrak Amfleet Phase VI Coach 2-Pack, 22		400 ___
2227320	Amtrak Amfleet Phase III Coach/Cab Car 2-Pack, 22		400 ___
2227330	Amtrak Amfleet Phase V Coach 2-Pack, 22-25		400 ___
2227340	Amtrak Amfleet Phase VI Coach/Cab Car 2-Pack, 22		400 ___
2227350	CSX Business Train 21" Passenger Car 4-Pack, 22		900 ___

	MODERN 1970-2025		Exc	Mint
___	**2227360**	CSX Business Train 18" Passenger Car 2-Pack, 22		500
___	**2227370**	CSX Business Train 21" Diner w/StationSounds, 22		400
___	**2227380**	Aberdeen, Carolina & Western 21" Passenger Car 2-Pack, 22		450
___	**2227390**	Aberdeen, Carolina & Western 18" Passenger Car 2-Pack, 22		500
___	**2227400**	MOW Wood Baggage/Coach 2-Pack, 22-24		450
___	**2227410**	MOW Wood Combine/Coach 2-Pack, 22-24		450
___	**2227420**	MOW Wood Coach/Observation 2-Pack, 22		450
___	**2227430**	NYC&HR Wood Baggage/Coach 2-Pack, 22		450
___	**2227440**	NYC&HR Wood Combine/Coach 2-Pack, 22		450
___	**2227450**	NYC&HR Wood Coach/Observation 2-Pack, 22		450
___	**2227460**	Southern Wood Baggage/Coach 2-Pack, 22		450
___	**2227470**	Southern Wood Combine/Coach 2-Pack, 22-24		450
___	**2227480**	Southern Wood Coach/Observation 2-Pack, 22-24		450
___	**2227490**	Wabash Wood Baggage/Coach 2-Pack, 22		450
___	**2227500**	Wabash Wood Combine/Coach 2-Pack, 22		450
___	**2227510**	Wabash Wood Coach/Observation 2-Pack, 22		450
___	**2227520**	AT&SF Vision Line Horse Car "1995," 22		370
___	**2227530**	CP Vision Line Horse Car "4560," 22		370
___	**2227540**	L&N Vision Line Horse Car "1507," 22		370
___	**2227550**	PRR Vision Line Horse Car "5024," 22		370
___	**2227560**	REA Vision Line Horse Car "812," 22		370
___	**2227570**	SP Vision Line Horse Car "7200," 22		370
___	**2227580**	North Pole Central Vision Reindeer Car, 22-24		370
___	**2227590**	Polar Express Vision Reindeer Car, 22		370
___	**2227600**	Bureau of Mines 18" Passenger Car 2-Pack, 22-24		500
___	**2227610**	Wood Chapel Car "Evangel," 22-25		225
___	**2228020**	Angela Trotta Thomas GG1 Boxcar, 21-24		85
___	**2228030**	U.S. Army Missile Flatcar, 21-24		90
___	**2228040**	Vintage Anheuser Busch Clydesdale Refrigerator Car, 22-23		90
___	**2228050**	Budweiser Holiday Stein Refrigerator Car, 22-24		90
___	**2228060**	Miller Refrigerator Car, 22		90
___	**2228070**	Coors Refrigerator Car, 22		90
___	**2228080**	Polar Express Aquarium Car, 22-25		120
___	**2228090**	Polar Express Illuminated Boxcar, 22-24		120
___	**2228100**	Hallow's Eve Monster Gondola, 22-23		90
___	**2228110**	Hallow's Eve Illuminated Caboose, 22-24		90
___	**2228120**	Christmas Parade Aquarium Car, 22-25		120
___	**2228130**	Christmas Chasing Gondola, 22-23		90
___	**2228140**	Night Before Christmas Illuminated Boxcar, 22-23		120
___	**2228150**	2022 Christmas Boxcar, 22		70
___	**2228160**	Christmas Music Boxcar "22," 22-24		85
___	**2228170**	Angela Trotta Thomas Christmas Aquarium Car, 22-25		120
___	**2228180**	Angela Trotta Thomas Blue Comet Boxcar, 22-24		85
___	**2228190**	Angela Trotta Thomas NYC Boxcar, 22-24		85
___	**2228220**	Mickey & Friends Christmas Caboose, 22-24		90
___	**2228230**	Mickey & Friends Christmas Searchlight Car, 22-23		85
___	**2228250**	U.S. Navy Flatcar w/Submarine, 22-25		90
___	**2228270**	U.S. Air Force Minuteman Car, 22-25		120
___	**2228280**	U.S. Marine Corps Rocket Launcher Car, 22-24		110
___	**2228290**	U.S. Army Big Cannon Car, 22-24		110
___	**2228300**	Polar Express Caboose, 22-25		90
___	**2228310**	North Pole Central Illuminated Hopper, 22-24		100
___	**2228320**	Budweiser Tank Car, 22-23		85

Item	Description	Exc	Mint
2228350	Monsters Inc. Scare Tank Car w/LEDs, 22-24	120	___
2228360	Disney Pixar Incredibles Operating Car, 22-25	120	___
2228370	Toy Story Woody Walking Brakeman Car, 22-24	120	___
2228380	John Deere Refrigerator Car, 22-24	90	___
2228390	John Deere Work Caboose, 22-25	85	___
2228400	Fourth of July LED Car w/Sounds, 22-24	150	___
2228410	American Flag LED Boxcar, 22-25	120	___
2228440	Chevrolet Vintage Camaro Boxcar, 22-25	85	___
2228450	Chevrolet Flatcar w/Piggyback Trailers, 22-25	95	___
2228460	Ford Boxcar, 22-24	85	___
2228470	Ford Flatcar w/Piggyback Trailers, 22-25	95	___
2228480	Hallow's Eve Mint Car, 22-24	120	___
2228490	Ghoul Searchlight Car, 22-24	85	___
2228500	Graffiti Hi-Cube Boxcar, 22-25	80	___
2228510	W&A Freight Expansion Pack, 22-25	220	___
2228520	2022 National Lionel Train Day Boxcar, 22-24	70	___
2229010	No. 943 Exploding Ammunition Dump, 21-24	65	___
2229020	Missile Range, 21-24	80	___
2229030	Train Orders Building, 21-22	140	___
2229040	Plug-Expand-Play Mission Control Tower, 21-25	130	___
2229050	Burning House, 21-22	200	___
2229060	Tough Guy Gym & Fitness, 21-24	160	___
2229070	Plug-Expand-Play Barn, 21-25	180	___
2229080	Passenger Station, 21-22	150	___
2229100	Townhouse, 21-24	110	___
2229110	Thistle Stop Flower Shop, 21-24	160	___
2229120	Christmas Barn, 21-24	200	___
2229130	Military Surplus Store, 21-24	160	___
2229140	Welcome Home Troops Townhouse, 21-24	110	___
2229150	Fire Station, 22	330	___
2229160	Plug-Expand-Play Private Investigation Building, 22-25	160	___
2229170	Bail Bonds Building, 22	110	___
2229170	Plug-Expand-Play Bail Bonds Building, 22-25	110	___
2229180	Plug-Expand-Play Donuts & Coffee Shop, 22-25	110	___
2229190	Budweiser Brewery, 22-24	220	___
2229200	Plug-Expand-Play Operating Transfer Station, 22-25	300	___
2229210	Plug-Expand-Play Deer Dash Transfer Station, 22-25	300	___
2229220	Plug-Expand-Play Grim's Repo Depot Transfer Station, 22-25	300	___
2229230	Plug-Expand-Play Western Mercantile, 22-25	80	___
2229250	Plug-Expand-Play Sheriff's Headquarters Building, 22-25	80	___
2229260	Firefighter Tank Car Accident Training, 22-24	130	___
2229270	Plug-Expand-Play Industrial Water Tower w/Graffiti Decals, 22-25	80	___
2229280	Polar Express Hot Chocolate Industrial Tower, 22-24	90	___
2229290	Up on the Rooftop Christmas House, 22-24	100	___
2229300	Rocket Launch Pad, 22-23	430	___
2229310	Illuminated Coaling Station, 22-24	130	___
2229320	Christmas Coal Works Lighted Coaling Station, 22-23	130	___
2230010	Vintage Inspired Space Billboards, 21-24	25	___
2230020	Amtrak Through The Years Billboards, 21-24	25	___
2230030	Quonset Hut, 21-25	45	___
2230050	Thomas & Friends Christmas Girder Bridge, 22-25	35	___
2230060	Red Fire Truck, 21-24	80	___

MODERN 1970-2025		Exc	Mint
___ 2230070	Yellow Fire Truck, 21-24		80
___ 2230080	White Fire Truck, 21-24		80
___ 2230090	Black Fire Truck, 21-24		80
___ 2230100	Smoke Fluid Dropper 2-Pack, 21-24		5
___ 2230110	Airplane Accessory 2-Pack, 22-23		14
___ 2230120	Boats 4-Pack, 22-23		14
___ 2230130	Helicopters 2-Pack, 22-23		14
___ 2230140	Railroad Signs 5-Pack, 22-25		9
___ 2230150	Angela Trotta Thomas Christmas Billboards, 22-24		25
___ 2230160	Halloween Billboards, 22-24		25
___ 2230170	Unique Railroad Signs 5-Pack, 22-25		9
___ 2230180	Firefighter Figures and Dog, 22-25		30
___ 2231010	Great Western 2-10-0 Locomotive "90," CC, 21		1900
___ 2231020	Strasburg RR 2-10-0 Locomotive (1990s) "90," CC, 21		1900
___ 2231030	Strasburg RR 2-10-0 Locomotive (2000s) "90," CC, 21		1900
___ 2231040	Great Western 2-10-0 Locomotive (2000s) "90," CC, 21		1900
___ 2231060	SAL 2-10-0 Locomotive "525," CC, 21		1900
___ 2231070	Osage Ry 2-10-0 Locomotive "10," CC, 21		1900
___ 2231080	AT&SF 2-8-0 Locomotive "2535," CC, 21		750
___ 2231090	Buffalo Creek & Gauley 2-8-0 Locomotive "4," CC, 21		750
___ 2231100	C&O 2-8-0 Locomotive "701," CC, 21		750
___ 2231110	MEC 2-8-0 Locomotive "519," CC, 21		750
___ 2231120	NYC 2-8-0 Locomotive "960," CC, 21		750
___ 2231130	WP 2-8-0 Locomotive "26," CC, 21		750
___ 2231141	AT&SF 2-10-4 Locomotive "5011," CC, 22		1750
___ 2231142	AT&SF 2-10-4 Locomotive "5022," CC, 22		1750
___ 2231150	AT&SF 2-10-4 Locomotive "5001," CC, 22		1750
___ 2231160	KCS 2-10-4 Locomotive "902," CC, 22		1750
___ 2231170	KCS 2-10-4 Locomotive "905," CC, 22		1750
___ 2231180	PRR 2-10-4 Locomotive "6510," CC, 22		1750
___ 2231191	SP AC-12 Cab Forward Locomotive "4294," CC, 21		2000
___ 2231192	SP AC-12 Cab Forward Locomotive "4281," CC, 21		2000
___ 2231200	SP AC-12 Cab Forward Locomotive "4278" w/black tender, CC, 21		2000
___ 2231210	SP AC-12 Cab Forward Locomotive, Daylight scheme, "4290," CC, 21		2000
___ 2231220	SP AC-12 Cab Forward Locomotive, Lark scheme, "4285," CC, 21		2000
___ 2231230	SP AC-12 Cab Forward Locomotive "4278" w/gray boiler, CC, 21		2000
___ 2231241	UP 4-12-2 Locomotive "9000," CC, 21		1700
___ 2231242	UP 4-12-2 Locomotive "9023," CC, 21		1700
___ 2231250	UP/OSL 4-12-2 Locomotive "9514," CC, 21		1700
___ 2231260	UP 4-12-2 Locomotive "9002," CC, 21		1700
___ 2231270	UP 4-12-2 Locomotive "9014," CC, 21		1700
___ 2231280	C&O 4-12-2 Locomotive "560," CC, 21		1700
___ 2231290	D&RGW 4-12-2 Locomotive "1420," CC, 21		1700
___ 2231300	MILW 4-12-2 Locomotive "1500," CC, 21		1700
___ 2231310	SP 4-12-2 Locomotive "2124," CC, 21		1700
___ 2231320	SP&S 4-12-2 Locomotive "651," CC, 21		1700
___ 2231340	B&A 2-8-4 Berkshire Locomotive "1401," CC, 22		1600
___ 2231350	B&M 2-8-4 Berkshire Locomotive "4019," CC, 22		1600
___ 2231360	C&NW 2-8-4 Berkshire Locomotive "2803," CC, 22		1600
___ 2231370	AT&SF 2-8-4 Berkshire Locomotive "4198," CC, 22		1600

		Exc	Mint
2231380	SP 2-8-4 Berkshire Locomotive "3506," CC, 22		1600 ___
2231390	TA&G 2-8-4 Berkshire Locomotive "602," CC, 22		1600 ___
2231400	B&M 4-4-2 Atlantic Locomotive "3243," CC, 22		900 ___
2231410	MP 4-4-2 Atlantic Locomotive "5521," CC, 22		900 ___
2231420	NH 4-4-2 Atlantic Locomotive "1111," CC, 22		900 ___
2231430	NYC 4-4-2 Atlantic Locomotive "4751," CC, 22		900 ___
2231440	Southern 4-4-2 Atlantic Locomotive "1905," CC, 22		900 ___
2231450	Wabash 4-4-2 Atlantic Locomotive "606," CC, 22		900 ___
2231460	N&W 2-6-6-4 Class A Locomotive "1218," CC, 22		2100 ___
2231470	N&W 2-6-6-4 Class A Locomotive "1238," CC, 22		2100 ___
2231470	N&W 2-6-6-4 Class A Locomotive "1238," CC, 22		2100 ___
2231480	N&W 2-6-6-4 Class A Locomotive "1200," CC, 22		2100 ___
2231490	N&W 2-6-6-4 Class A Locomotive "1210," CC, 22		2100 ___
2231500	N&W 2-6-6-4 Class A Locomotive "1211," CC, 22		2100 ___
2231510	N&W 2-6-6-4 Class A Locomotive "1201," CC, 22		2100 ___
2231520	N&W 2-6-6-4 Class A Locomotive, Pilot," CC, 22		2100 ___
2231530	Bethlehem Steel 0-6-0 Locomotive "60," CC, 22		800 ___
2231540	SL&SF 0-6-0 Locomotive "3801," CC, 22		800 ___
2231550	NYC 0-6-0 Locomotive "222," CC, 22		800 ___
2231560	PRR 0-6-0 Locomotive "7007," CC, 22		800 ___
2231570	Strasburg 0-6-0 Locomotive "31," CC, 22		800 ___
2231580	Terminal RR of St. Louis 0-6-0 Locomotive "160," CC, 22		800 ___
2231590	Washington Terminal 0-6-0 Locomotive "32," CC, 22		800 ___
2231600	Unpainted brass 2-10-0 Locomotive, CC, 21		1900 ___
2232010	NYC 4-6-4 Hudson Locomotive "5314," LionChief Plus 2.0, 21-22		650 ___
2232020	UP 4-6-4 Hudson Locomotive "675," LionChief Plus 2.0, 21-22		650 ___
2232030	AT&SF 4-6-4 Hudson Locomotive "3463," LionChief Plus 2.0, 21-22		650 ___
2232040	Lionel Lines 4-6-4 Hudson Locomotive "773," LionChief Plus 2.0, 21-22		650 ___
2232050	Bethlehem Steel 0-4-0 Locomotive "76," CC, 22		700 ___
2232060	B&O 0-4-0 Locomotive "37," CC, 22		700 ___
2232070	U.S. Army 0-4-0 Locomotive "491," CC, 22		700 ___
2232080	PRR 0-4-0 Locomotive "477," CC, 22		700 ___
2232090	LIRR 0-4-0 Locomotive "175," CC, 22		700 ___
2232100	B&O 4-6-2 Pacific Locomotive "5215," LionChief Plus 2.0, 22		650 ___
2232110	D&RGW 4-6-2 Pacific Locomotive "801," LionChief Plus 2.0, 22		650 ___
2232120	LV 4-6-2 Pacific Locomotive "2101," LionChief Plus 2.0, 22		650 ___
2232130	Reading & Northern 4-6-2 Pacific Locomotive "425," LionChief Plus 2.0, 22		650 ___
2232140	North Pole Central 4-6-2 Pacific Locomotive "1224," LionChief Plus 2.0, 22-24		650 ___
2233010	BNSF SD70MAC Diesel "9647," CC, 21		650 ___
2233021	BNSF SD70MAC Diesel "9718," CC, 21		650 ___
2233028	BNSF SuperBass SD70MAC Diesel "9829," 21		550 ___
2233031	BNSF SD70MAC Diesel "9721," CC, 21		650 ___
2233032	BNSF SD70MAC Diesel "9789," CC, 21		650 ___
2233038	BNSF SuperBass SD70MAC Diesel "9819," 21		550 ___
2233041	Conrail SD70MAC Diesel "777," CC, 21		650 ___
2233042	Conrail SD70MAC Diesel "780," CC, 21		650 ___
2233048	Conrail SuperBass SD70MAC Diesel "782," 21		550 ___

	MODERN 1970-2025		Exc	Mint
____	**2233051**	CSX SD70MAC Diesel "4551," CC, 21		650
____	**2233052**	CSX SD70MAC Diesel "4553," CC, 21		650
____	**2233058**	CSX SuperBass SD70MAC Diesel "4558," 21		550
____	**2233061**	NS SD70MAC Diesel "1800," CC, 21		650
____	**2233062**	NS SuperBass SD70MAC Diesel "1801," 21		550
____	**2233071**	P&L SD70MAC Diesel "4501," CC, 21		650
____	**2233072**	P&L SD70MAC Diesel "4504," CC, 21		650
____	**2233078**	P&L SuperBass SD70MAC Diesel "4523," 21		550
____	**2233081**	BN SD45 Diesel "6445," CC, 21		600
____	**2233082**	BN SD45 Diesel "6452," CC, 21		600
____	**2233088**	BN SuperBass SD45 Diesel "6455", 21		500
____	**2233091**	EMD SD45 Diesel "4351," CC, 21		600
____	**2233092**	EMD SD45 Diesel "4352," CC, 21, 24-25		600
____	**2233098**	EMD SuperBass SD45 Diesel "4353," 21		500
____	**2233101**	Guilford/Springfield Terminal SD45 Diesel "681," CC, 21		600
____	**2233102**	Guilford/Springfield Terminal SD45 Diesel "684," CC, 21		600
____	**2233108**	Guilford/Springfield Terminal SuperBass SD45 Diesel "685," 21		500
____	**2233111**	MILW SD45 Diesel "6," CC, 21		600
____	**2233112**	MILW SD45 Diesel "8," CC, 21		600
____	**2233118**	MILW SuperBass SD45 Diesel "10," 21		500
____	**2233121**	NS SD45 Diesel "1716," CC, 21		600
____	**2233122**	NS SD45 Diesel "1766," CC, 21		600
____	**2233128**	NS SuperBass SD45 Diesel "1795," 21		500
____	**2233131**	PRR SD45 Diesel "6186," CC, 21		600
____	**2233132**	PRR SD45 Diesel "6197," CC, 21		600
____	**2233138**	PRR SuperBass SD45 Diesel "6202," 21		500
____	**2233141**	Alaska DD35 Diesel "5000," CC, 21		700
____	**2233142**	Alaska DD35 Diesel "5001," CC, 21		700
____	**2233151**	AT&SF DD35 Diesel "1650," CC, 21		700
____	**2233152**	AT&SF DD35 Diesel "1652," CC, 21		700
____	**2233160**	UP DD35 Diesel "71" (Dependable Transportation), CC, 21		700
____	**2233170**	UP DD35 Diesel "76" (We Can Handle It), CC, 21		700
____	**2233180**	UP DD35 Diesel "77" (Shield herald), CC, 21		700
____	**2233190**	UP DD35 Diesel "81" (American flag), CC, 21		700
____	**2233200**	AT&SF SW1200 Diesel "1441," CC, 21		550
____	**2233210**	BNSF SW1200 Diesel "3505," CC, 21		550
____	**2233220**	D&RGW SW1200 Diesel "134," CC, 21		550
____	**2233230**	EJ&E SW1200 Diesel "306," CC, 21		550
____	**2233240**	PC SW1200 Diesel "9020," CC, 21		550
____	**2233250**	US Steel SW1200 Diesel "13," CC, 21		550
____	**2233261**	FM Demonstrator C-Liner Diesel "4801," CC, 21		600
____	**2233262**	FM Demonstrator C-Liner Diesel "4802," CC, 21		600
____	**2233271**	CN C-Liner Diesel "6701," CC, 21		600
____	**2233272**	CN C-Liner Diesel "6705," CC, 21		600
____	**2233281**	LIRR C-Liner Diesel "2001," CC, 21		600
____	**2233282**	LIRR C-Liner Diesel "2003," CC, 21		600
____	**2233291**	NH C-Liner Diesel "792," CC, 21		600
____	**2233292**	NH C-Liner Diesel "798," CC, 21		600
____	**2233301**	NYC C-Liner Diesel "4500," CC, 21		600
____	**2233302**	NYC C-Liner Diesel "4502," CC, 21		600
____	**2233311**	PRR C-Liner Diesel "9570," CC, 21		600
____	**2233312**	PRR C-Liner Diesel "9571," CC, 21		600
____	**2233321**	Alco Demonstrator RS27 Diesel "640-2," CC, 22		600

		Exc	Mint	
2233322	Alco Demonstrator RS27 Diesel "640-4," CC, 22		600	___
2233331	C&NW Alco RS27 Diesel "900," CC, 22		600	___
2233332	C&NW Alco RS27 Diesel "903," CC, 22		600	___
2233341	Conrail Alco RS27 Diesel "2412," CC, 22		600	___
2233342	Conrail Alco RS27 Diesel "2414," CC, 22		600	___
2233351	GB&W Alco RS27 Diesel "316," CC, 22		600	___
2233352	GB&W Alco RS27 Diesel "318," CC, 22		600	___
2233361	PC Alco RS27 Diesel, "2407," CC, 22		600	___
2233362	PC Alco RS27 Diesel, "2409," CC, 22		600	___
2233371	SOO Alco RS27 Diesel "415," CC, 22		600	___
2233372	SOO Alco RS27 Diesel "416," CC, 22		600	___
2233380	B&O EMD SW1 Diesel "8408," CC, 22		550	___
2233390	BN EMD SW1 Diesel "97," CC, 22		550	___
2233400	Conrail EMD SW1 Diesel "8408," CC, 22		550	___
2233410	Flambeau Paper EMD SW1 Diesel "1," CC, 22		550	___
2233420	SP EMD SW1 Diesel "1000," CC, 22		550	___
2233430	Turtle Creek EMD SW1 Diesel "462," CC, 22		550	___
2233441	BNSF Heritage ES44AC Diesel "6075," CC, 22		700	___
2233442	BNSF Heritage ES44AC Diesel "6111," CC, 22		700	___
2233449	BNSF Heritage ES44AC Diesel "6179" (nonpowered), 22		400	___
2233451	BC Rail Heritage ES44AC Diesel "3115," CC, 22		700	___
2233459	BC Rail Heritage ES44AC Diesel "3115," (nonpowered), 22		400	___
2233461	EJ&E Heritage ES44AC Diesel "3023," CC, 22		700	___
2233469	EJ&E Heritage ES44AC Diesel "3023" (unpowered), 22		400	___
2233471	IC Heritage ES44AC Diesel "3008," CC, 22		700	___
2233479	IC Heritage ES44AC Diesel "3008" (unpowered), 22		400	___
2233481	WC Heritage ES44AC Diesel "3069," CC, 22		700	___
2233489	WC Heritage ES44AC Diesel "3069" (unpowered), 22		400	___
2233491	CN Veterans ES44AC Diesel "3015," CC, 22		700	___
2233492	CN Veterans ES44AC Diesel "3233," CC, 22		700	___
2233499	CN Veterans ES44AC Diesel "3015" (unpowered), 22		400	___
2233501	U.S. Armed Forces ES44AC Diesel "1775," CC, 22		700	___
2233502	U.S. Armed Forces ES44AC Diesel "2022," non-powered, 22-25		400	___
2233511	BN EMD SD40-2 Diesel "1876," CC, 22		650	___
2233519	BN EMD SD40-2 Diesel "1876" (unpowered), 22		350	___
2233521	BN EMD SD40-2 Diesel "8002," CC, 22		650	___
2233529	BN EMD SD40-2 Diesel "8002" (unpowered), 22		350	___
2233531	Louisville & Indiana EMD SD40-2 Diesel "3001," CC, 22		650	___
2233539	Louisville & Indiana EMD SD40-2 Diesel "3001" (unpowered), 22		350	___
2233541	Maersk/Sealand EMD SD40-2 Diesel "3329," CC, 22		650	___
2233549	Maersk/Sealand EMD SD40-2 Diesel "3329" (unpowered), 22		350	___
2233551	Savage EMD SD40-2 Diesel "8638," CC, 22		700	___
2233559	Savage EMD SD40-2 Diesel "8638" (unpowered), 22		400	___
2233561	UP Desert Victory EMD SD40-2 Diesel "3593," CC, 22		700	___
2233569	UP Desert Victory EMD SD40-2 Diesel "3593" (unpowered), 22		400	___
2233570	B&LE EMD F7 A-B Set "722A/722B," CC, 22		1150	___
2233580	Aberdeen, Carolina & Western EMD F9 A-B Set "271/276," CC, 22		1150	___
2233590	Reading & Northern EMD F9 A-B Set "270/275," CC, 22		1150	___
2233601	CP Veterans EMD SD90MAC Diesel "7020," CC, 22		650	___

	Item	Description	Exc	Mint
____	**2233609**	CP Veterans EMD SD90MAC Diesel "7020" (unpowered), 22		400
____	**2233611**	CP Veterans EMD SD90MAC Diesel "7021," CC, 22		650
____	**2233619**	CP Veterans EMD SD90MAC Diesel "7021" (unpowered), 22		400
____	**2233621**	CP Veterans EMD SD90MAC Diesel "7022," CC, 22		650
____	**2233629**	CP Veterans EMD SD90MAC Diesel "7022" (unpowered), 22		400
____	**2233631**	CP Veterans EMD SD90MAC Diesel "7023," CC, 22		650
____	**2233639**	CP Veterans EMD SD90MAC Diesel "7023" (unpowered), 22		400
____	**2233641**	CP Veterans EMD SD90MAC Diesel "6644," CC, 22		650
____	**2233649**	CP Veterans EMD SD90MAC Diesel "6644" (unpowered), 22		400
____	**2233651**	CP Heritage EMD SD90MAC Diesel "7010," CC, 22		650
____	**2233652**	CP Heritage EMD SD90MAC Diesel "7016," CC, 22		650
____	**2233660**	EMD Demonstrator SD90MAC Diesel "8204," CC, 22		650
____	**2233671**	NS (UP Patch) EMD SD90MAC Diesel "7240," CC, 22		650
____	**2233672**	NS (UP Patch) EMD SD90MAC Diesel "73140," CC, 22		650
____	**2233681**	San Luis & Rio Grande EMD SD90MAC Diesel "115," CC, 22		650
____	**2233682**	San Luis & Rio Grande EMD SD90MAC Diesel "116," CC, 22		650
____	**2233711**	Amtrak F40PH Diesel Phase III "206," CC, 22		630
____	**2233712**	Amtrak F40PH Diesel Phase III "226," CC, 22		630
____	**2233721**	Amtrak F40PH Diesel Phase IV "401," CC, 22		630
____	**2233722**	Amtrak F40PH Diesel Phase IV "404," CC, 22		630
____	**2233730**	Amtrak F40PH Diesel Phase V "410," CC, 22		630
____	**2233740**	Amtrak F40PH Diesel Veterans "208," CC, 22		630
____	**2233751**	CSX Business Train Diesel "CSX-1," CC, 22		630
____	**2233752**	CSX Business Train Diesel "CSX-2," CC, 22		630
____	**2233753**	CSX Business Train Diesel "CSX-3," CC, 22		630
____	**2233761**	D&RGW Ski Train Diesel "242," CC, 22		630
____	**2233762**	D&RGW Ski Train Diesel "283," CC, 22		630
____	**2233770**	Amtrak NPCU Diesel Phase IV Downeaster "90214" (unpowered), 22		500
____	**2233780**	Amtrak NPCU Diesel Phase IV "90229" (unpowered), 22		500
____	**2233790**	Amtrak NPCU Diesel Phase V "90413" (unpowered), 22		500
____	**2233800**	Amtrak NPCU Diesel Veterans "90208" (unpowered), 22		500
____	**2233810**	AT&SF EMD F7 A-A Set "341/344," CC, 22		1200
____	**2233818**	AT&SF EMD F7 B Unit "345A," CC, 22		600
____	**2233819**	AT&SF EMD F7 B Unit SuperBass "348A" (unpowered), 22		550
____	**2233820**	LV EMD F7 A-A Set "562/566," CC, 22		1200
____	**2233828**	LV EMD F7 B Unit "519," CC, 22		600
____	**2233829**	LV EMD F7 B Unit SuperBass "521" (unpowered), 22		550
____	**2233830**	SOO EMD F7 A-A Set "2201A/2201B," CC, 22		1200
____	**2233838**	SOO EMD F7 B Unit "2201C," CC, 22		600
____	**2233839**	SOO EMD F7 B Unit SuperBass "2202C" (unpowered), 22		550
____	**2233840**	SP EMD F7 A-A Set "6475/6476," CC, 22		1200
____	**2233848**	SP EMD F7 B Unit "8375," CC, 22		600
____	**2233849**	SP EMD F7 B Unit SuperBass "8376" (unpowered), 22		550
____	**2233850**	UP EMD F7 A-A Set "1468/1469," CC, 22		1200
____	**2233858**	UP EMD F7 B Unit "1468B," CC, 22		600
____	**2233859**	UP EMD F7 B Unit SuperBass "1468C" (unpowered), 22		550
____	**2234010**	Amtrak Genesis Locomotive "100," LionChief Plus 2.0, 22		550
____	**2234020**	Amtrak Genesis Locomotive "108," LionChief Plus 2.0, 22		550
____	**2234030**	Amtrak Genesis Locomotive "160," LionChief Plus 2.0, 22		550
____	**2234040**	Amtrak Genesis Locomotive "161," LionChief Plus 2.0, 22		550
____	**2234050**	Amtrak Genesis Locomotive Phase V "150," LionChief Plus 2.0, 21-22		550

		Exc	Mint
2234060	Amtrak Genesis Locomotive Phase 1V "111," LionChief Plus 2.0, 21-22		550 ___
2234060	Amtrak Genesis Locomotive Phase IV NEC "111," LionChief Plus 2.0, 21-22		550 ___
2234070	Amtrak Genesis Locomotive Phase III "40," LionChief Plus 2.0, 21-22		550 ___
2234080	Amtrak Genesis Locomotive Phase V 50th Anniversary "46," LionChief Plus 2.0, 21-22		550 ___
2234090	PRR LionChief 44-Tonner Locomotive "8312," 22-24		250 ___
2234100	ATSF LionChief 44-Tonner Locomotive "463," 22-24		250 ___
2234110	Ford LionChief 44-Tonner Locomotive "1000," 22-24		250 ___
2234120	U.S. Marine Corps LionChief 44-Tonner Locomotive "234120," 22-25		250 ___
2234130	Amtrak LionChief 44-Tonner Locomotive "1100," 22-25		250 ___
2234140	ATSF EMD GP20 Diesel "3009," LionChief Plus 2.0, 22-25		500 ___
2234150	MILW EMD GP20 Diesel "962," LionChief Plus 2.0, 22-25		500 ___
2234160	Conrail EMD GP20 Diesel "2108," LionChief Plus 2.0, 22-25		500 ___
2234170	BN EMD GP20 Diesel "2054," LionChief Plus 2.0, 22-25		500 ___
2234180	BNSF LionChief Dash-8 Diesel, 22-23		280 ___
2234190	NS LionChief Dash-8 Diesel, 22-23		280 ___
2234200	CSX LionChief Dash-8 Diesel, 22-23		280 ___
2234210	UP LionChief Dash-8 Diesel, 22-23		280 ___
2234220	Amtrak Genesis Operation Lifesaver LionChief Plus 2.0 Diesel, 22		550 ___
2235010	Polar Express Trolley, 22-24		120 ___
2235020	First Ave Rapid Transit Trolley, 22-23		120 ___
2235030	Trippy Trolley, 22, 25		140 ___
2235040	AT&SF Doodlebug, LionChief Plus 2.0, 22-24		400 ___
2235050	UP Doodlebug "DC-2," LionChief Plus 2.0, 22-25		400 ___
2235060	PRR Doodlebug "5266," LionChief Plus 2.0, 22-25		400 ___
2235070	Maryland & Pennsylvania Doodlebug "62," LionChief Plus 2.0, 22-25		400 ___
2235080	Hallows Eve Limited Doodlebug "31," LionChief Plus 2.0, 22-25		400 ___
2235090	North Pole Central Doodlebug "25," LionChief Plus 2.0, 22-25		400 ___
2238010	UP 160th Anniversary Boxcar, 21-22		90 ___
2238020	Great Locomotive Chase 160th Anniversary Boxcar, 21-22		90 ___
2238030	Smithsonian 175th Anniversary Boxcar, 21, 24		90 ___
2238040	Rutherford B. Hayes Presidential Boxcar, 22		90 ___
2238050	Grover Cleveland Presidential Boxcar, 22		90 ___
2238060	Gerald Ford Presidential Boxcar, 22		90 ___
2238070	2022 Birthday Personalized Boxcar, 22		100 ___
2238080	2022 Christmas Personalized Boxcar, 22		100 ___
2238090	2022 Anniversary Personalized Boxcar, 22		100 ___
2238100	World War II Generals Boxcar, 22-25		95 ___
2238110	World War II Aircraft Carrier Boxcar, 22		90 ___
2238120	Wings of Angels Sarah Boxcar, 22-25		95 ___
2238130	Wings of Angels Lisa Boxcar, 22-23		95 ___
2238140	Wings of Angels Raquel Boxcar, 22-25		95 ___
2238150	GM Train of Tomorrow Boxcar, 22-24		90 ___
2238160	Rockville Bridge Boxcar, 22		90 ___
2238180	Bazooka Joe 75th Anniversary Boxcar, 22		90 ___
2238210	MILW 175th Anniversary Boxcar, 22-24		90 ___
2238220	Chevrolet Personalized Boxcar, 22-23		100 ___
2238230	Ford Personalized Boxcar, 22-23		100 ___

	MODERN 1970-2025		Exc	Mint
____	2243010	BNSF Rotary Gondola 4-Pack (std 0), 21		360
____	2243020	CSX Rotary Gondola 4-Pack (std 0), 21, 24		360
____	2243030	NS Rotary Gondola 4-Pack (std 0), 21		360
____	2243040	PRR Rotary Gondola 4-Pack (std 0), 21		360
____	2243050	UP Rotary Gondola 4-Pack (std 0), 21		360
____	2243060	CSX Rotary Gondola 2-Pack (std 0), 21		180
____	2243070	NS Rotary Gondola 2-Pack (std 0), 21		180
____	2243080	PRR Rotary Gondola 2-Pack (std 0), 21		180
____	2243090	UP Rotary Gondola 2-Pack (std 0), 21		180
____	2243101	Ashley, Drew & Northern Modern Boxcar "8134" (std 0), 21, 24		60
____	2243102	Ashley, Drew & Northern Modern Boxcar "8145" (std 0), 21-24		60
____	2243111	Conrail Modern Boxcar "166255" (std 0), 21, 24-25		60
____	2243112	Conrail Modern Boxcar "166422" (std 0), 21, 24		60
____	2243121	RI Modern Boxcar "300032" (std 0), 21		60
____	2243122	RI Modern Boxcar "399370" (std 0), 21		60
____	2243131	Railbox Modern Boxcar "30284" (std 0), 21		60
____	2243132	Railbox Modern Boxcar "30306" (std 0), 21		60
____	2243141	UP Modern Boxcar "357416" (std 0), 21		60
____	2243142	UP Modern Boxcar "357429" (std 0), 21		60
____	2243150	UP Rocket Idler Car 6-Pack, 22		375
____	2243160	B&LE Ore Car 6-Pack #1, 22		200
____	2243170	B&LE Ore Car 6-Pack #2, 22		200
____	2243180	BN Ore Car 6-Pack #1 (std 0), 22-24		200
____	2243190	BN Ore Car 6-Pack #2 (std 0), 22-25		200
____	2243200	C&NW Ore Car 6-Pack #1 (std 0), 22-25		200
____	2243210	C&NW Ore Car 6-Pack #2 (std 0), 22-25		200
____	2243220	DM&IR Ore Car 6-Pack #1 (std 0), 22		200
____	2243230	DM&IR Ore Car 6-Pack #2 (std 0), 22		200
____	2243240	SOO Ore Car 6-Pack #1 (std 0), 22-25		200
____	2243250	SOO Ore Car 6-Pack #2 (std 0), 22-25		200
____	2243260	UP Ore Car 6-Pack #1 (std 0), 22		200
____	2243270	UP Ore Car 6-Pack #2 (std 0), 22-24		200
____	2243281	SSW Insulated Boxcar "30043" (std 0), 22-25		70
____	2243282	SSW Insulated Boxcar "30049" (std 0), 22-25		70
____	2243291	NH State of Maine Insulated Boxcar "45022" (std 0), 22		70
____	2243292	NH State of Maine Insulated Boxcar "45064" (std 0), 22		70
____	2243301	NP Insulated Boxcar "98583" (std 0), 22		70
____	2243302	NP Insulated Boxcar "98621" (std 0), 22-24		70
____	2243311	WM Insulated Boxcar "7" (std 0), 22		70
____	2243312	WM Insulated Boxcar "14" (std 0), 22-24		70
____	2301050	LCCA UP Vision 4-8-8-4 Big Boy Locomotive "4023," CC, 23u		2900
____	2322010	LV Legacy Camelback Steam Freight Set, CC, 23		1100
____	2322020	WM Hagerstown Hotshot Diesel Freight Set, CC, 22		1600
____	2322030	PRR Cumberland Valley Wayfreight Set, CC, 22		1500
____	2322040	UP Vision Big Boy Steam Freight Set, CC, 23		4500
____	2322050	PRR Iron Hippo Legacy Steam Freight Set, CC, 23		2300
____	2322060	Union RR Hot Metal Diesel Freight Set, CC, 23		1300
____	2322070	RI Quad Cities Rocket Legacy Diesel Passenger Set, CC, 23		1000
____	2322080	ATSF Fast Fruit Express Legacy Steam Freight Set, CC, 23		2500
____	2323030	ATSF Dash-8 Diesel Auto Rack Set, 22-24		550
____	2323040	Disney 100 Years of Wonder LionChief Bluetooth 5.0 Steam Passenger Set, CC, 23-24		530

Item	Description	Exc	Mint
2323050	Fast Fright Halloween LionChief Bluetooth 5.0 Diesel Freight Set, CC, 23-25		500
2323060	NYC 2-8-0 Consolidation LionChief Bluetooth 5.0 Steam Freight Set, CC, 23-24		450
2323070	Willy Wonka & the Chocolate Factory LionChief Bluetooth 5.0 Steam Freight Set, CC, 23-25		450
2323080	Texas Special Diesel Passenger LionChief Bluetooth 5.0 Set, CC, 23-25		500
2323090	UP Flyer LionChief Bluetooth 5.0 Steam Freight Set, CC, 23-25		400
2323100	Winter Wonderland LionChief Bluetooth 5.0 Steam Freight Set, CC, 23-25		400
2323110	ATSF Super Chief LionChief Bluetooth 5.0 Diesel Passenger Set, CC, 23-25		500
2323130	Gold Mountain LionChief Bluetooth 5.0 Steam Set, CC, 23-24		470
2325010	Polar Express Ice FasTrack 0-36 Curve 4-pack, 23-24		75
2325030	FasTrack 3" Straight, 22-25		5
2326010	UP Heritage C&NW TOFC Flatcar "231995," 22		150
2326020	UP Heritage D&RGW TOFC Flatcar "231989," 22		150
2326030	UP Heritage MKT TOFC Flatcar "231988," 22		150
2326040	UP Heritage MP TOFC Flatcar "231982," 22		150
2326050	UP Heritage SP TOFC Flatcar "231996," 22		150
2326060	UP Heritage WP TOFC Flatcar "231983," 22		150
2326070	BN 100-ton Hopper 2-pack A, 22		300
2326078	BN 100-ton Hopper 2-pack B, 22		300
2326079	BN 100-ton Hopper 2-pack C, 22		300
2326080	Chessie (B&O) 100-ton Hopper 2-pack, 22-24		300
2326088	Chessie (C&O) 100-ton Hopper 2-pack, 22-24		300
2326089	Chessie (WM) 100-ton Hopper 2-pack, 22		300
2326090	D&RGW 100-ton Hopper 2-pack (blue ends), 22-24		300
2326098	D&RGW 100-ton Hopper 2-pack (white ends), 22		300
2326099	D&RGW 100-ton Hopper 2-pack (blue/white ends), 22-24		300
2326100	NS 100-ton Hopper 2-pack A, 22		300
2326108	NS 100-ton Hopper 2-pack B, 22		300
2326109	NS 100-ton Hopper 2-pack C, 22		300
2326110	Reading 100-ton Hopper 2-pack A, 22-25		300
2326150	Ford 60' Boxcar "236150," 22-25		130
2326118	Reading 100-ton Hopper 2-pack B, 22-25		300
2326119	Reading 100-ton Hopper 2-pack C, 22-24		300
5		300	300
2326120	SP 100-ton Hopper 2-pack A, 22		300
2326181	WCOR 60' Boxcar w/Graffiti "6510," 22-25		140
2326128	SP 100-ton Hopper 2-pack B, 22		300
2326182	WCOR 60' Boxcar w/Graffiti "6521," 22-25		140
2326129	SP 100-ton Hopper 2-pack C, 22		300
2326130	John Deere 60' Boxcar "1837," 22-24		130
2326140	Chevrolet 60' Boxcar "236140," 22-25		130
2326160	Reading & Northern 60' Boxcar "1998," 22-24		130
2326170	USMC 60' Boxcar "1591," 22-25		130
2326190	L&NE NE Caboose "583," 22		130
2326200	MC NE Caboose "662," 22-24		130
2326210	RI NE Caboose "17604," 22-24		130
2326220	USMC NE Caboose "601750," 22-25		130
2326272	PRR N6b Cabin Car "981530," 22-25		120

MODERN 1970-2025		Exc	Mint
____ **2326230**	SSW Hobo Boxcar "35209," 22-24		210
____ **2326271**	PRR N6b Cabin Car "980781," 22-25		120
____ **2326273**	PRR N6b Cabin Car "492891," 22-25		120
____ **2326240**	Frisco Hobo Boxcar "17350," 22		210
____ **2326250**	Ann Arbor Hobo Boxcar "1404," 22-24		210
____ **2326260**	Western of Alabama Hobo Boxcar "18252," 22-24		210
____ **2326280**	C&O Wood Caboose "98076," 22		120
____ **2326290**	Strasburg RR Wood Caboose "12," 22		120
____ **2326300**	ATSF Vision Refrigerator Car w/RailSounds 3-pack, 23		500
____ **2326310**	FGE Vision Refrigerator Car w/RailSounds 3-pack, 23		500
____ **2326320**	GN Vision Refrigerator Car w/RailSounds 3-pack, 23		500
____ **2326330**	PFE Vision Refrigerator Car w/RailSounds 3-pack, 23		500
____ **2326340**	D&RGW Vision Stock Car w/RailSounds 3-pack, 23		500
____ **2326350**	PRR Vision Stock Car w/RailSounds 3-pack, 23-24		500
____ **2326360**	T&P Vision Stock Car w/RailSounds 3-pack, 23-25		500
____ **2326370**	UP Vision Stock Car w/RailSounds 3-pack, 23		500
____ **2326380**	CP 50' Flatcar "505571" w/Reimer Trailer, 23		160
____ **2326390**	MILW 50' Flatcar "57500" w/ICX Trailer, 23		160
____ **2326400**	TTX 50' Flatcar "475326" w/Budweiser Trailer, 23-25		170
____ **2326410**	John Deere 50' Flatcar "26410" w/Trailer, 23-24		170
____ **2326420**	Lionel 50' Flatcar "26420" w/Play World Trailer, 23-24		160
____ **2326440**	UP Vision CA-1 Caboose "2551," 23-24		300
____ **2326450**	UP Vision CA-1 Caboose "2527," 23		300
____ **2326460**	Buffalo Creek & Gauley GLA Hopper 2-pack, 23-24		200
____ **2326470**	Interstate GLA Hopper 2-pack, 23-25		200
____ **2326480**	PRR GLA Hopper 2-pack A, 23-25		200
____ **2326490**	PRR GLA Hopper 2-pack B, 23-25		200
____ **2326500**	Westmoreland Coal GLA Hopper 2-pack, 23-25		200
____ **2326510**	PRR N8 Cabin Car "478125," 23-25		150
____ **2326520**	PRR N8 Cabin Car "478172," 23-25		150
____ **2326530**	PRR N8 Cabin Car "478159," 23		150
____ **2326540**	PC N8 Cabin Car "4710," 23-25		150
____ **2326550**	Conrail N8 Cabin Car "23236," 23-25		150
____ **2326560**	Union RR Hot Metal Car "14," 23-25		200
____ **2326570**	Area 51 Scale Hot Metal Car "AF-57X," 23-24		200
____ **2326580**	Christmas Hot Chocolate Thermos Car, 23-24		200
____ **2326590**	Polar Express Hot Chocolate Thermos Car, 23-24		200
____ **2326601**	Ann Arbor PS-5 Gondola "2023," 23-24		120
____ **2326602**	Ann Arbor PS-5 Gondola "2058," 23		120
____ **2326611**	CN PS-5 Gondola "143035," 23-24		120
____ **2326612**	CN PS-5 Gondola "143211," 23		120
____ **2326621**	Conrail PS-5 Gondola "67014," 23-24		120
____ **2326622**	Conrail PS-5 Gondola "67435," 23		120
____ **2326631**	Erie PS-5 Gondola "10325," 23		120
____ **2326632**	Erie PS-5 Gondola "10359," 23		120
____ **2326641**	LV PS-5 Gondola "32953," 23-25		120
____ **2326642**	LV PS-5 Gondola "33059," 23		120
____ **2326651**	RI PS-5 Gondola "3050," 23		120
____ **2326652**	RI PS-5 Gondola "3091," 23		120
____ **2326660**	Christmas Bobber Caboose, 23-24		110
____ **2326670**	C&NW Grain Boxcar "24154," 23-24		110
____ **2326680**	M&StL Grain Boxcar "53150," 23		110
____ **2326690**	Soo Grain Boxcar "44968," 23		110

		Exc	Mint
2326700	T&P Grain Boxcar "40814," 23		110
2326710	UP Grain Boxcar "196861," 23		110
2326720	Wabash Grain Boxcar "90090,"23-24		110
2326770	PRR Vision N8 Cabin Car "478166," 23-25		300
2326780	PRR Vision N8 Cabin Car w/CrewTalk, "478044," 23-25		300
2327010	C&O 18" Passenger Car 2-pack A, 22-25		500
2327020	C&O 18" Passenger Car 2-pack B, 22-25		500
2327030	C&O 18" Passenger Car 2-pack C, 22-25		500
2327040	C&O 18" Diner w/StationSounds, 22-24		430
2327050	The Chessie 21" Passenger Car 4-pack, 22		900
2327060	The Chessie 21" Passenger Car 2-pack, 22		450
2327070	The Chessie 21" Diner w/StationSounds "1971," 22		400
2327080	Strasburg RR Coach (1970s) 2-pack A, 22-25		450
2327090	Strasburg RR Coach (1970s) 2-pack B, 22-25		450
2327100	Strasburg RR 18" Heavyweight "Pequea Valley" (brown), 22-25		250
2327110	Strasburg RR 18" Heavyweight "Pequea Valley" (green), 22-25		250
2327140	US Army 18" Passenger Car 2-pack A, 22		500
2327150	US Army 18" Passenger Car 2-pack B, 22		500
2327160	US Army 18" Passenger Car 2-pack C, 22		500
2327170	US Army 18" Diner w/StationSounds, 22		430
2327180	CN Wood Passenger Car 2-pack A, 22		450
2327190	CN Wood Passenger Car 2-pack B, 22		450
2327200	CN Wood Passenger Car 2-pack C, 22		450
2327210	Strasburg RR 18" Heavyweight "Pequea Valley" (red), 22-24		250
2327220	Strasburg RR 18" Heavyweight "Pequea Valley" (gray), 22-24		250
2327230	Harry Potter "Slytherin House" Coach, 23-25		90
2327240	Harry Potter "Hufflepuff House" Coach, 23-25		90
2327250	Harry Potter "Ravenclaw House" Coach, 23-25		90
2327260	Harry Potter "Gryffindor House" Coach, 23-25		90
2327270	UP Excursion 21" Passenger Car 4-pack, 23		950
2327280	UP Excursion 21" Passenger Car 2-pack, 23		450
2327290	UP Diner w/StationSounds, 23		400
2327300	Aberdeen, Carolina & Western Diner w/StationSounds 2-pack, 23		650
2327310	NYC 20th Century Limited 21" Passenger Car 4-pack, 23-24		950
2327320	NYC 20th Century Limited 21" Passenger Car 2-pack, 23		450
2327330	NYC 20th Century Limited 21" Diner w/StationSounds 2-pack, 23-24		650
2327340	North Pole Central 21" Passenger Car 4-pack, 23		950
2327350	North Pole Central 21" Passenger Car 2-pack, 23		450
2327360	North Pole Central 21" Diner w/StationSounds, 23		400
2327370	Texas Special "Anson B. Jones" Add-on Baggage Car, 23-25		95
2327380	Texas Special "Tulsa" Add-on Coach, 23-25		100
2327390	Aberdeen, Carolina & Western Dome Car, 23		300
2328060	Gold Medal Flour Flatcar w/Milk Container, 22-25		70
2328070	Lionelville Milk Flatcar w/Milk Container, 22-25		70
2328080	Ferromex Auto Rack, 22-24		100
2328090	Southern Auto Rack, 22-23		100
2328100	DC Justice League Lexcorp Kryptonite Hopper, 23-25		110
2328110	DC Justice League The Flash Mint Car, 23-25		120
2328120	DC Justice League Wonder Woman Invisible Jet Flatcar, 23-25		60

			Exc	Mint
____	**2328130**	DC Justice League Wayne Enterprises Transport Car, 23-25		90
____	**2328140**	John Deere Tractor Co. Refrigerator Car, 23-25		90
____	**2328150**	John Deere Flatcar "28230" w/Combine, 23-24		100
____	**2328160**	Disney 100 Illuminated Boxcar, 23-24		150
____	**2328180**	Pennywise Peekaboo Car, 23		100
____	**2328190**	Exorcist Floating Regan Car, 23		120
____	**2328220**	Anheuser-Busch Budweiser Clydesdale Refrigerator Car, 23-25		90
____	**2328230**	Anheuser-Busch Budweiser Military Heritage Reefer, 23-25		90
____	**2328240**	2023 Christmas Boxcar, 23		85
____	**2328250**	Christmas Music Illuminated Boxcar "23," 23-25		150
____	**2328260**	Santa's Choice Milk Flatcar w/Milk Carton, 23-25		70
____	**2328270**	Snow-Covered Christmas Tree Flatcar, 23-24		100
____	**2328280**	Polar Express Sleigh Bells Mint Car, 23-25		90
____	**2328290**	Polar Express Flatcar w/Hot Chocolate Container, 23-25		75
____	**2328300**	Angela Trotta Thomas Texas Special Boxcar, 23-25		85
____	**2328310**	Angela Trotta Thomas General Boxcar, 23-25		85
____	**2328320**	TTX Maxi Stack w/Container, 23-25		100
____	**2328330**	BNSF Maxi Stack w/Container, 23-24		100
____	**2328340**	Halloween Graffiti Maxi Stack w/Container, 23-25		100
____	**2328350**	Christmas Graffiti Maxi Stack w/Container, 23-24		100
____	**2328360**	Dr. Acula Blood Tonic 1-D Tank Car, 23-25		100
____	**2328370**	Halloween Spooky Sounds Illuminated Boxcar, 23-25		150
____	**2328380**	DC Justice League Boxcar, 23-25		85
____	**2328410**	Willy Wonka 1-D Tank Car, 23		100
____	**2328420**	Disney 100 Mickey Mouse Vault Moments Boxcar, 23-24		90
____	**2328430**	Disney100 Minnie Mouse Vault Moments Boxcar, 23-25		90
____	**2328440**	Disney 100 Goofy Vault Moments Boxcar, 23-24		90
____	**2328450**	Disney 100 Donald Duck Vault Moments Boxcar, 23-24		90
____	**2328460**	Christmas Olde Tyme Rolling Stock 3-pack, 23		220
____	**2328470**	Gold Rush Sluice 1-D Tank Car, 23-25		100
____	**2328480**	NYC Pacemaker Merchandise Boxcar, 23-25		120
____	**2328490**	Willie Wonka Bar Golden Ticket Boxcar, 23-25		90
____	**2328530**	2023 National Lionel Train Day Boxcar, 23-25		80
____	**2329010**	Roadside Diner, 22-25		150
____	**2329020**	Christmas Roadside Diner, 23-24		160
____	**2329030**	Polar Express Illuminated Covered Bridge, 23		80
____	**2329050**	Billups Crossing Gate, 22-25		200
____	**2329060**	Amtrak Passenger Station, 22-24		170
____	**2329070**	Carnival Treats Stand, 22-25		160
____	**2329080**	St. Nick's Nog Shoppe Driver-In Diner, 23		400
____	**2329090**	Area 51 Drive-In Diner, 23		400
____	**2329100**	Franks & Stein's Bar & Ghoul, 23-25		130
____	**2329110**	Roscoe Flattz Automotive & Tire Store, 22-25		130
____	**2329130**	Cowen's Family Creamery NE Caboose w/Deck, 22-25		200
____	**2329140**	Grandpa's Workshop w/Sounds, 22-25		130
____	**2329150**	She Shed w/Sounds, 22-25		130
____	**2329160**	Santa's Workshop w/Sounds, 23-24		130
____	**2329170**	Hot Cocoa NE Caboose w/Deck, 23-24		200
____	**2329190**	Disney Christmas Station Platform, 23-25		55
____	**2329200**	Frankenstein's Monster Halloween Gateman, 23-25		130
____	**2329230**	Area 51 Hazardous Materials Barrel Loader, 23-24		80
____	**2329240**	Warner Bros. 100th Anniversary Water Tower, 23-24		90

MODERN 1970-2025		Exc	Mint
2329250	John Deere Nothing Runs Like a Deere Flagpole, 23-25		45 ___
2329270	Prankster Flagpole, 23-25		45 ___
2329280	Willy Wonka Wonka Bar Packaging Facility, 23		270 ___
2329300	Patriots Salute Gateman, 23-25		130 ___
2329340	Lionelville Theatre, 23-25		130 ___
2329350	Warner Bros. 100th Anniversary Theatre, 23		130 ___
2329360	Disney 100 Theatre, 23		130 ___
2330010	Unique Road Signs 5-Pack 2, 22-25		9 ___
2330020	Ford Billboard 3-pack, 22-25		25 ___
2330030	Chevrolet Billboard 3-pack, 22-25		25 ___
2330040	Area 51 Glow in the Dark Haz-Mat Barrels, 23		13 ___
2330050	Midway Games 3-pack and Figures, 22-25		120 ___
2330060	Thomas & Friends Billboard Pack, 23-25		25 ___
2330080	Warner Bros. Classic Movie Billboard Pack, 23		25 ___
2330110	Budweiser Brew Hut, 23-25		45 ___
2330120	Lionel Ale Quonset Hut, 23-25		45 ___
2330140	Dasher's Buy and Fly Quonset Hut, 23-25		45 ___
2330160	Winter Wonderland Scented Smoke Fluid, 23-25		9 ___
2330170	American Summer (Apple Pie) Scented Smoke Fluid, 23-25		9 ___
2330180	Happy Birthday Scented Smoke Fluid, 23-25		9 ___
2330190	Vanilla Bourbon Scented Smoke Fluid, 23-25		9 ___
2330200	Maple Syrup Scented Smoke Fluid, 23-25		9 ___
2330210	Bay Leaf and Tobacco Scented Smoke Fluid, 23-25		9 ___
2331011	PRR 2-8-2 Mikado L1 Locomotive "496," CC, 22		950 ___
2331012	PRR 2-8-2 Mikado L1 Locomotive "4030," CC, 22		950 ___
2331021	PRR 2-8-2 Mikado L1 Locomotive "1343," CC, 22		950 ___
2331022	PRR 2-8-2 Mikado L1 Locomotive "1627," CC, 22		950 ___
2331030	PRR 2-8-2 Mikado L1 Locomotive "1369," CC, 22		950 ___
2331040	ATSF 2-8-2 Mikado L1 Locomotive "882," CC, 22		1000 ___
2331050	DT&I 2-8-2 Mikado L1 Locomotive "496," CC, 22		950 ___
2331060	L&NE 2-8-2 Mikado L1 Locomotive "501," CC, 22		950 ___
2331070	C&O 4-8-4 Greenbrier Locomotive "614," CC, 22		1700 ___
2331080	C&O 4-8-4 Greenbrier Locomotive "611," CC, 22		1700 ___
2331090	C&O 4-8-4 Greenbrier Locomotive "613," CC, 22		1700 ___
2331100	C&O 4-8-4 Greenbrier Locomotive "612," CC, 22		1700 ___
2331110	Chessie System 4-8-4 Greenbrier Locomotive "614," CC, 22		1700 ___
2331120	Family Lines 4-8-4 Greenbrier Locomotive "614," CC, 22		1700 ___
2331130	CN 2-6-0 Mogul Locomotive "89," CC, 22		800 ___
2331140	Middletown & Hummelstown 2-6-0 Mogul Locomotive "91," CC, 22		800 ___
2331150	San Luis & Rio Grande 2-6-0 Mogul Locomotive "89," CC, 22		800 ___
2331160	SP 2-6-0 Mogul Locomotive "1760," CC, 22		800 ___
2331170	Strasburg RR 2-6-0 Mogul Locomotive "89" (1970s) CC, 22		800 ___
2331180	Strasburg RR 2-6-0 Mogul Locomotive "89" (2000s), CC, 22		800 ___
2331191	UP Brass Hybrid 4-6-6-4 Challenger Locomotive "3819," CC, 22		2500 ___
2331192	UP Brass Hybrid 4-6-6-4 Challenger Locomotive "3826," CC, 22		2500 ___
2331193	UP Brass Hybrid 4-6-6-4 Challenger Locomotive, Unnumbered Style 1, CC, 22		2500 ___
2331200	UP Brass Hybrid 4-6-6-4 Challenger Locomotive Pilot, CC, 22		2500 ___
2331211	UP Brass Hybrid 4-6-6-4 Challenger Locomotive "3836," CC, 22		2500 ___

	Item	Description	Exc	Mint
____	**2331212**	UP Brass Hybrid 4-6-6-4 Challenger Locomotive "3839," CC, 22		2500
____	**2331213**	UP Brass Hybrid 4-6-6-4 Challenger Locomotive, Unnumbered, Style 2, CC, 22		2500
____	**2331220**	UP Brass Hybrid 4-6-6-4 Challenger Locomotive "3835" (Challenger scheme), CC, 22		2500
____	**2331231**	UP Brass Hybrid 4-6-6-4 Challenger Locomotive "3815," CC, 22		2500
____	**2331232**	UP Brass Hybrid 4-6-6-4 Challenger Locomotive "3828," CC, 22		2500
____	**2331233**	UP Brass Hybrid 4-6-6-4 Challenger Locomotive, Unnumbered, Style 3, CC, 22		2500
____	**2331250**	UP Vision 4-8-8-4 Big Boy Locomotive Oil-Burning "4014," CC, 23		2800
____	**2331261**	UP Vision 4-8-8-4 Big Boy Locomotive "4000," CC, 23		2900
____	**2331262**	UP Vision 4-8-8-4 Big Boy Locomotive "4002," CC, 23		2900
____	**2331263**	UP Vision 4-8-8-4 Big Boy Locomotive "4012," CC, 23		2900
____	**2331264**	UP Vision 4-8-8-4 Big Boy Locomotive "4014," CC, 23		2900
____	**2331270**	UP Vision 4-8-8-4 Big Boy Locomotive "4019," CC, 23		2900
____	**2331280**	UP Vision 4-8-8-4 Big Boy Locomotive "4021," CC, 23		2900
____	**2331290**	UP Vision 4-8-8-4 Big Boy Locomotive "4024," CC, 23		2900
____	**2331300**	Erie Russian 2-10-0 Decapod Locomotive "2445," CC, 23-24		1300
____	**2331310**	Frisco Russian 2-10-0 Decapod Locomotive "1630," CC, 23		1300
____	**2331320**	Minneapolis, Northfield & Southern Russian 2-10-0 Decapod Locomotive "505," CC, 23		1300
____	**2331330**	Philadelphia & Reading Russian 2-10-0 Decapod Locomotive "1162," CC, 23		1300
____	**2331340**	SAL Russian 2-10-0 Decapod Locomotive "544," CC, 23		1300
____	**2331350**	USA Russian 2-10-0 Decapod Locomotive "1918," CC, 23		1300
____	**2331361**	PRR I1 2-10-0 Decapod Locomotive "531," CC, 23		1500
____	**2331362**	PRR I1 2-10-0 Decapod Locomotive "4250," CC, 23		1500
____	**2331371**	PRR I1 2-10-0 Decapod Locomotive "4241," CC, 23		1500
____	**2331372**	PRR I1 2-10-0 Decapod Locomotive "4652," CC, 23		1500
____	**2331381**	PRR I1 2-10-0 Decapod Locomotive "4262," CC, 23		1500
____	**2331382**	PRR I1 2-10-0 Decapod Locomotive "4521," CC, 23		1500
____	**2331391**	PRR I1 2-10-0 Decapod Locomotive "4258," CC, 23		1500
____	**2331392**	PRR I1 2-10-0 Decapod Locomotive "4325," CC, 23		1500
____	**2331401**	NYC Dreyfuss J3 4-6-4 Hudson Locomotive "5449," CC, 23-25		1700
____	**2331402**	NYC Dreyfuss J3 4-6-4 Hudson Locomotive "5452," CC, 23		1700
____	**2331411**	NYC Dreyfuss J3 4-6-4 Hudson Locomotive "5445," CC, 23		1800
____	**2331412**	NYC Dreyfuss J3 4-6-4 Hudson Locomotive "5447," CC, 23		1800
____	**2331420**	NYC Dreyfuss J3 4-6-4 Hudson Locomotive "5445" w/short tender, CC, 23-25		1700
____	**2331430**	NYC Dreyfuss J3 4-6-4 Hudson Locomotive "5454," CC, 23		1800
____	**2331451**	ATSF 4-8-4 Northern Locomotive "2903," CC, 23		1800
____	**2331452**	ATSF 4-8-4 Northern Locomotive "2912," CC, 23		1800
____	**2331453**	ATSF 4-8-4 Northern Locomotive "2926," CC, 23		1800
____	**2331460**	ATSF 4-8-4 Northern Locomotive Blue Goose "2900," CC, 23		1800
____	**2331470**	ATSF 4-8-4 Northern Locomotive Warbonnet "2901," CC, 23		1800
____	**2331480**	ATSF 4-8-4 Northern Locomotive Restoration "2926," CC, 23		1800
____	**2331540**	Fezziwig RR Legacy 4-6-0 Camelback Locomotive "1225," CC, 23		700
____	**2331550**	DL&W 4-6-0 Camelback Locomotive "1052," CC, 23		700
____	**2331560**	Erie 4-6-0 Camelback Locomotive "918," CC, 23		700

		Exc	Mint	
2331570	L&NE 4-6-0 Camelback Locomotive "151," CC, 23		700	___
2331580	Atlantic City RR 4-6-0 Camelback Locomotive "610," CC, 23		700	___
2331590	PRR 4-6-0 Camelback Locomotive "824," CC, 23		700	___
2332010	Reading 0-6-0T Locomotive "1251" LionChief Plus 2.0, 22-23		350	___
2332020	Alaska 0-6-0T Locomotive "1" LionChief Plus 2.0, 22-23		350	___
2332030	Lehigh Valley Coal 0-6-0T Locomotive "126" LionChief Plus 2.0, 22-23		350	___
2332040	NH 0-6-0T Locomotive "2305" LionChief Plus 2.0, 22-23		350	___
2332050	Halloween 2-8-2 Mikado Locomotive "1031," LionChief Plus 2.0, 23-24		700	___
2332060	CB&Q 2-8-2 Mikado Locomotive "4978," LionChief Plus 2.0, 23-24		700	___
2332070	MILW 2-8-2 Mikado Locomotive "753," LionChief Plus 2.0, 23-25		700	___
2332080	UP 2-8-2 Mikado Locomotive "2549," LionChief Plus 2.0, 23-25		700	___
2332090	PRR 2-8-2 Mikado Locomotive "9631," LionChief Plus 2.0, 23-24		700	___
2332100	NKP 2-8-0 Consolidation Locomotive "455," LionChief, 23		330	___
2332110	WM 2-8-0 Consolidation Locomotive "754," LionChief, 23		330	___
2332120	ATSF 2-10-0 Consolidation Locomotive "2517," LionChief, 23-25		330	___
2332130	C&O 2-8-0 Consolidation Locomotive "752," LionChief, 23-25		330	___
2333040	SP Alco FA-2 AA set "802A/802D," CC, 22		1100	___
2333050	USMC Alco FA-2 AA set "212/213," CC, 22		1100	___
2333080	D&H Alco FA-2 AA set "20/21," CC, 22		1100	___
2333088	D&H Alco FB-2 "20B," CC, 22		550	___
2333089	D&H Alco FB-2 SuperBass "21B," 22		500	___
2333090	EL Alco FA-2 AA set "7371/7374," CC, 22		1100	___
2333098	EL Alco FB-2 "7382," CC, 22		550	___
2333099	EL Alco FB-2 SuperBass "7383," 22		500	___
2333100	Halloween Alco FA-2 AA set "1030A/1031A," CC, 22		1100	___
2333108	Halloween Alco FB-2 "1030B," CC, 22		550	___
2333109	Halloween Alco FB-2 SuperBass "1031B," 22		500	___
2333110	L&N Alco FA-2 AA set "311/314," CC, 22		1100	___
2333118	L&N Alco FB-2 "392" CC, 22		550	___
2333119	L&N Alco FB-2 SuperBass "394", 22		500	___
2333120	NYC Alco FA-2 AA set "1175/1176," CC, 22		1100	___
2333128	NYC Alco FB-2 "3375," CC, 22		550	___
2333129	NYC Alco FB-2 SuperBass "3376", 22		500	___
2333130	PRR Alco FA-2 AA set "5760A/5762A," CC, 22		1100	___
2333138	PRR Alco FB-2 "5760B," CC, 22		550	___
2333139	PRR Alco FB-2 SuperBass "5762B," 22		500	___
2333148	SP Alco FB-2 "802B," CC, 22		550	___
2333149	SP Alco FB-2 SuperBass "802C," 22		500	___
2333158	USMC Alco FB-2 "212B," CC, 22		550	___
2333159	USMC Alco FB-2 SuperBass "213B," 22		500	___
2333160	Montana Rail Link Essential Workers EMD SD70ACe "4404," CC, 22		650	___
2333170	Montana Rail Link Veterans EMD SD70ACe "4407," CC, 22		650	___
2333180	PRLX EMD SD70ACe "4834," CC, 22		650	___
2333190	UP C&NW Heritage EMD SD70ACe "1995," CC, 22		650	___
2333200	UP D&RGW Heritage EMD SD70ACe "1989," CC, 22		650	___
2333210	UP MKT Heritage EMD SD70ACe "1988," CC, 22		650	___

			Exc	Mint
___	**2333220**	UP MP Heritage EMD SD70ACe “1982,” CC, 22		650
___	**2333230**	UP SP Heritage EMD SD70ACe “1996,” CC, 22		650
___	**2333240**	UP WP Heritage EMD SD70ACe “1983,” CC, 22		650
___	**2333251**	Central of Georgia FM H-15-44 Diesel “101,” CC, 22		600
___	**2333252**	Central of Georgia FM H-15-44 Diesel “102,” CC, 22		600
___	**2333261**	CRI&P FM H-15-44 Diesel “400,” CC, 22		600
___	**2333262**	CRI&P FM H-15-44 Diesel “401,” CC, 22		600
___	**2333271**	D&RGW FM H-15-44 Diesel “151,” CC, 22		600
___	**2333272**	D&RGW FM H-15-44 Diesel “152,” CC, 22		600
___	**2333281**	KCS FM H-15-44 Diesel “40,” CC, 22		600
___	**2333282**	KCS FM H-15-44 Diesel “41,” CC, 22		600
___	**2333291**	Monon FM H-15-44 Diesel “36,” CC, 22		600
___	**2333292**	Monon FM H-15-44 Diesel “37,” CC, 22		600
___	**2333301**	UP FM H-15-44 Diesel “1325,” CC, 22		600
___	**2333302**	UP FM H-15-44 Diesel “1329,” CC, 22		600
___	**2333310**	Aberdeen, Carolina & Western EMD E8 AA set, CC, 23		1200
___	**2333320**	North Pole Central EMD E8 AA set, CC, 23		1200
___	**2333330**	Amtrak EMD E8/E9 AA set “410/422,” CC, 23		1200
___	**2333340**	NYC EMD E8/E9 AA set “4053/4083,” CC, 23		1200
___	**2333350**	Southern EMD E8/E9 AA set “2923/2925,” CC, 23		1200
___	**2333360**	SP EMD E8/E9 AA set “6051/6053,” CC, 23		1200
___	**2333371**	ATSF EMD SD40T-2 “5215,” CC, 22		650
___	**2333372**	EMD SD40T-2 “5226,” CC, 22		650
___	**2333379**	ATSF EMD SD40T-2 SuperBass “5238,” 22		600
___	**2333381**	SP EMD SD40T-2 “8524,” CC, 22		650
___	**2333382**	SP EMD SD40T-2 “8533,” CC, 22		650
___	**2333389**	SP EMD SD40T-2 SuperBass “8548,” 22		600
___	**2333391**	SP EMD SD40T-2 Kodachrome “8286,” CC, 22		650
___	**2333392**	SP EMD SD40T-2 Kodachrome “8530,” CC, 22		650
___	**2333399**	SP EMD SD40T-2 SuperBass Kodachrome “8573,” 22		600
___	**2333401**	NYS&W EMD SD40T-2 “3010,” CC, 22		650
___	**2333402**	NYS&W EMD SD40T-2 “3012,” CC, 22		650
___	**2333409**	NYS&W EMD SD40T-2 SuperBass “3016,” 22		600
___	**2333411**	SP EMD SD40T-2 Black Widow “8520,” CC, 22		650
___	**2333412**	SP EMD SD40T-2 Black Widow “8525,” CC, 22		650
___	**2333419**	SP EMD SD40T-2 SuperBass Black Widow “8529,” 22		600
___	**2333421**	WP EMD SD40T-2 “8625,” CC, 22		650
___	**2333422**	WP EMD SD40T-2 “8794,” CC, 22		650
___	**2333429**	WP EMD SD40T-2 SuperBass “8864,” 22		600
___	**2333431**	BN GE ES44AC “9800,” CC, 23		750
___	**2333432**	BN GE ES44AC “9810,” CC, 23		750
___	**2333439**	BN GE ES44AC SuperBass “9819,” 23		550
___	**2333441**	BNSF GE ES44AC “5555,” CC, 23		750
___	**2333442**	BNSF GE ES44AC “5570,” CC, 23		750
___	**2333449**	BNSF GE ES44AC SuperBass “5586,” 23		550
___	**2333451**	C&NW GE ES44AC “8836,” CC, 23		750
___	**2333452**	C&NW GE ES44AC “8842,” CC, 23		750
___	**2333459**	C&NW GE ES44AC SuperBass “8850”, 23		550
___	**2333461**	Conrail GE ES44AC “4145,” CC, 23-24		750
___	**2333462**	Conrail GE ES44AC “4152,” CC, 23		750
___	**2333469**	Conrail GE ES44AC SuperBass “4163,” 23		550
___	**2333471**	KCS GE ES44AC “4859,” CC, 23		750
___	**2333479**	KCS non-powered GE ES44AC “4859,” CC, 23		400

MODERN 1970-2025		Exc	Mint
2333481	KCS GE ES44AC "4674," CC, 23		750 ___
2333489	KCS non-powered GE ES44AC "4674," CC, 23		400 ___
2333490	BN EMD NW2 Switcher "497," CC, 23		600 ___
2333500	C&O EMD NW2 Switcher "5067," CC, 23		600 ___
2333510	Detroit Terminal EMD NW2 Switcher "115," CC, 23		600 ___
2333520	GN EMD NW2 Switcher "161," CC, 23		600 ___
2333530	Indiana Harbor Belt EMD NW2 Switcher "8827," CC, 23		600 ___
2333540	LV EMD NW2 Switcher "186," CC, 23		600 ___
2333551	ATSF EMD GP20 Diesel "1106," CC, 23		650 ___
2333552	ATSF EMD GP20 Diesel "1171," CC, 23		650 ___
2333561	CB&Q EMD GP20 Diesel "907," CC, 23-25		650 ___
2333562	CB&Q EMD GP20 Diesel "915," CC, 23		650 ___
2333571	Kyle RR EMD GP20 Diesel "2035," CC, 23-25		650 ___
2333572	Kyle RR EMD GP20 Diesel "2039," CC, 23		650 ___
2333581	PC EMD GP20 Diesel "2108," CC, 23		650 ___
2333582	PC EMD GP20 Diesel "2109," CC, 23		650 ___
2333591	SSW EMD GP20 Diesel "801," CC, 23		650 ___
2333592	SSW EMD GP20 Diesel "815," CC, 23		650 ___
2333600	KC Terminal EMD GP20 Diesel "WAMX 2005," CC, 23		650 ___
2334010	ATSF EMD NW2 Diesel "2404," CC, 22-23		450 ___
2334020	NYC EMD NW2 Diesel "622," CC, 22-23		450 ___
2334030	GN EMD NW2 Diesel "162," CC, 22-23		450 ___
2334040	SAL EMD NW2 Diesel "1410," CC, 22-23		450 ___
2334050	CN GE ERT44AC Diesel "3810," CC, 23		400 ___
2334060	KCS GE ERT44AC Diesel "5002," CC, 23		400 ___
2334070	BNSF GE ERT44AC Diesel "6337," CC, 23		400 ___
2334080	NS GE ERT44AC Diesel "3657," CC, 23		400 ___
2334090	ATSF EMD FT Diesel "127," CC, 23		300 ___
2334100	NYC EMD FT Diesel "1687," CC, 23-24		300 ___
2334110	PRR EMD FT Diesel "5888," CC, 23-25		300 ___
2334120	North Pole Central EMD FT Diesel "1225," CC, 23-24		300 ___
2335010	MOW TMCC Rail Bonder "M-4," CC, 23		150 ___
2335020	NH TMCC Rail Bonder "18," CC, 23-24		150 ___
2335030	PE TMCC Rail Bonder "1202," CC, 23		150 ___
2335040	LIRR TMCC Rail Bonder "35040," CC, 23		150 ___
2335050	North Pole Central TMCC Rail Bonder "1225," CC, 23-24		150 ___
2335060	Angela Trotta Thomas Trolley, 23		120 ___
2335070	Alaska Budd RDC Unit 2-pack "702/712," CC, 23		600 ___
2335080	B&O Budd RDC Unit 2-pack "9902/9917," CC, 23		600 ___
2335090	NH Budd RDC Unit 2-pack "120/42," CC, 23		600 ___
2335100	SP Budd RDC Unit 2-pack "SP-9/SP-11," CC, 23		600 ___
2335110	Polar Express Budd RDC Unit 2-pack "1225/25," CC, 23-25		600 ___
2335120	Alaska Budd RDC Unit "711," CC, 23		400 ___
2335130	B&O Budd RDC Unit "9918," CC, 23		400 ___
2335140	NH Budd RDC Unit "41," CC, 23		400 ___
2335150	SP Budd RDC Unit "SP-10," CC, 23-25		400 ___
2335160	Polar Express Budd RDC Unit "24," CC, 23-25		400 ___
2335190	Disney's Mickey Mouse and Minnie Mouse Handcar, red, 23-24		200 ___
2338010	Chicago Railroad Fair Boxcar, 22		90 ___
2338030	Millard Fillmore Presidential Boxcar, 23-24		90 ___
2338040	Zachary Taylor Presidential Boxcar, 23-24		90 ___
2338050	John Tyler Presidential Boxcar, 23-24		90 ___

MODERN 1970-2025		Exc	Mint
___ **2338060**	Chessie System 50th Anniversary Boxcar, 23		90
___ **2338070**	Santa Fe Super Chief 75th Anniversary Boxcar, 23-25		95
___ **2338080**	Battle of Midway Boxcar, 23-24		95
___ **2338090**	Boston Tea Party 250th Anniversary Boxcar, 23-25		90
___ **2338100**	Personalized Family Boxcar, 23		100
___ **2338110**	2023 Happy Birthday Boxcar, 23		100
___ **2338120**	2023 Merry Christmas Boxcar, 23		100
___ **2338130**	2023 Happy Anniversary Boxcar, 23		100
___ **2338140**	Wings of America Ariella Boxcar, 23-25		95
___ **2338150**	Wings of America Jen Boxcar, 23-24		95
___ **2338160**	Wings of America Sarah Boxcar, 2, 23		95
___ **2338170**	Happy Birthday Caboose, 23		90
___ **2338180**	Merry Christmas Caboose, 23		90
___ **2338190**	Battle of Mogadishu Boxcar, 23-25		95
___ **2338200**	Disney 100 Celebration Personalized Boxcar, 23		100
___ **2338210**	James Webb Space Telescope Boxcar, 23		90
___ **2338220**	Wright Brothers 120th Anniversary Boxcar, 23-25		90
___ **2338260**	Gettysburg Address 160th Anniversary Boxcar, 23-25		90
___ **2338290**	Thomas Kinkade Studios Christmas Light Express Boxcar, 24		100
___ **2343011**	Reading & Northern Unibody 1-D Tank Car "101275" (std O), 22-25		75
___ **2343012**	Reading & Northern Unibody 1-D Tank Car "2382" (std O), 22-25		75
___ **2343021**	US Army Unibody 1-D Tank Car "18599" (std O), 22-25		75
___ **2343022**	US Army Unibody 1-D Tank Car "18601" (std O), 22-25		75
___ **2343031**	Cargill Unibody 1-D Tank Car "6274" (std O), 22-24		75
___ **2343032**	Cargill Unibody 1-D Tank Car "6281" (std O), 22-24		75
___ **2343041**	GATX Unibody 1-D Tank Car "2658" w/Graffiti (std O), 22-24		75
___ **2343042**	GATX Unibody 1-D Tank Car "2696" w/Graffiti (std O), 22-24		75
___ **2343051**	Procor Unibody 1-D Tank Car "28030" (std O), 22-24		75
___ **2343052**	Procor Unibody 1-D Tank Car "28040" (std O), 22-24		75
___ **2343061**	BN Centerbeam Flatcar "624189" (std O), 23-25		65
___ **2343062**	BN Centerbeam Flatcar "624220" (std O), 23		65
___ **2343071**	CSX Centerbeam Flatcar "600700" (std O), 23-24		65
___ **2343072**	CSX Centerbeam Flatcar "600712" (std O), 23-24		65
___ **2343081**	NS Centerbeam Flatcar "120112" (std O), 23-24		65
___ **2343082**	NS Centerbeam Flatcar "120231" (std O), 23-24		65
___ **2343091**	TTX Centerbeam Flatcar "83519" (std O), 23-25		65
___ **2343092**	TTX Centerbeam Flatcar "83593" (std O), 23		65
___ **2343101**	WCRC Centerbeam Flatcar "7319" (std O), 23-24		65
___ **2343102**	WCRC Centerbeam Flatcar "7540" (std O), 23		65
___ **2401561**	Disney's D23 Mickey Mouse Boxcar, 24-25		100
___ **2401562**	Disney's D23 Tinkerbell Boxcar, 24-25		100
___ **2401563**	Disney's D23 Toy Story Boxcar, 24-25		100
___ **2401564**	Disney's Lilo and Stitch Boxcar, 24-25		100
___ **2401565**	Disney's D23 Mickey and Friends Caboose, 24-25		110
___ **2401566**	Disney's D23 0-8-0 Locomotive "1923" LionChief, 24-25		900
___ **2422030**	WP Feather River Diesel Freight Set, CC, 23		1600
___ **2422040**	PRR M1 Middle Division Steam Freight Set, CC, 23		2000
___ **2426070**	UP PS-1 WWII Boxcar "194407" w/PatriotSounds, 23-25		210
___ **2426080**	UP PS-1 WWII Boxcar "194414" w/PatriotSounds, 23-25		210
___ **2426200**	NP Double-sheathed Boxcar "11237," 23-25		100
___ **2422010**	Erie Triplex Super Set, CC, 24		4000

Item	Description	Exc	Mint
2422020	Lehigh Gorge Scenic Ry. Diesel Passenger Set, CC, 23		1200 ___
2422050	Nickel Plate Road Fast Freight Steam Set, CC, 24		2500 ___
2422060	Polar Express 20th Anniversary Scale Freight Passenger Set, CC, 24		2400 ___
2422070	North Pole Central Cocoa Steam Milk Train, CC, 24		1200 ___
2422080	Atomic Energy Commission Glow-In-Dark Diesel Freight Set, CC, 24		1000 ___
2422089	Atomic Energy Commission GP9B SuperBass "1946B," CC, 24		500 ___
2422090	IC City of Miami Diesel Passenger Set, CC, 24		1500 ___
2423010	Looney Tunes FT Diesel Freight Set, LionChief, 23-25		530 ___
2423020	GN 2-8-0 Steam Freight Set, LionChief, 23		470 ___
2423030	Polar Express 20th Anniversary Steam Passenger Set, LionChief, 24		530 ___
2423040	Disney Frozen Olaf Steam Freight Set, LionChief, 24-25		480 ___
2423050	LL Prairie Steam Freight Set, LionChief, 24-25		430 ___
2423060	Sleigh Bell Limited FT Diesel Passenger Set, LionChief, 24-25		530 ___
2423070	John Deere Steam Freight Set, LionChief, 24-25		430 ___
2426010	Chessie System PS-1 Boxcar "23764" w/FreightSounds, 24-25		210 ___
2426020	CB&Q PS-1 Boxcar "17302" w/FreightSounds, 24-25		210 ___
2426030	DL&W Friendship Train PS-1 Boxcar "51974" w/FreightSounds, 24-25		210 ___
2426040	GN PS-1 Boxcar "18588" w/FreightSounds, 24-25		210 ___
2426050	ICG PS-1 Boxcar "416224" w/FreightSounds, 24		210 ___
2426060	RF&P PS-1 Boxcar "2872" w/FreightSounds, 24-25		210 ___
2426090	UP WWII PS-1 Boxcar "194421" w/FreightSounds, 24-25		210 ___
2426100	U.S. Army PS-1 Boxcar "26884" w/PatriotSounds, 23		210 ___
2426120	U.S.M.C. PS-1 Boxcar "173232" w/PatriotSounds, 23		210 ___
2426130	U.S.A.F. PS-1 Boxcar "26478" w/PatriotSounds, 23		210 ___
2426140	MILW 40' Flatcar "866981," w/John Deere Tractors , 23-25		170 ___
2426150	PRR 40' Flatcar "925142," w/John Deere Tractors , 23-25		170 ___
2426160	NP 40' Flatcar "200204," w/John Deere Tractors , 23-25		170 ___
2426170	John Deere 40' Flatcar "26170," w/Tractors , 23-25		170 ___
2426180	John Deere Double-sheathed Boxcar "1837," 23-25		120 ___
2426190	NYC Double-sheathed Boxcar "161525," 23		100 ___
2426200	U.S. Navy PS-1 Boxcar "61-02450" w/PatriotSounds, 23		210 ___
2426210	PRR Double-sheathed Boxcar "96451," 23-25		100 ___
2426220	SP Friendship Train Double-sheathed Boxcar "300," 23		100 ___
2426230	Strasburg RR Double-sheathed Boxcar "103," 23		100 ___
2426240	Area 51 PS-5 Covered Gondola "X-51-2645N" , 23		125 ___
2426250	Area 51 PS-5 Gondola "X-51-2650N," w/Coke Containers, 23		135 ___
2426260	Bethlehem Steel PS-5 Gondola "18015," w/Coke Containers, 23-25		130 ___
2426270	LNLX PS-5 Covered Gondola "426270," w/Graffiti, 23		135 ___
2426280	John Deere PS-5 Gondola w/Containers, 23		135 ___
2426290	P&LE PS-5 Gondola "10691," w/Coke Containers, 23		130 ___
2426300	Reading PS-5 Gondola "33079," w/Coke Containers, 23-25		130 ___
2426310	U.S. Army Transportation Corps PS-5 Covered Gondola "41310," 23-25		125 ___
2426320	ATSF Refrigerator Car "7599" w/Hot Box, 24		300 ___

			Exc	Mint
___	**2426330**	FGE Refrigerator Car "38945" w/Hot Box, 24		300
___	**2426340**	NYC MDT Refrigerator Car "6110" w/Hot Box, 24		300
___	**2426350**	PFE Refrigerator Car "5845" w/Hot Box, 24		300
___	**2426370**	NP CA-1 Caboose "1370," 24		130
___	**2426380**	UP WWII CA-1 Caboose "1944," 24		130
___	**2426390**	UP CA-1 Caboose "3349," 24		130
___	**2426400**	UP CA-1 Caboose "2659," 24		130
___	**2426410**	UP CA-1 Caboose "3279," 24		130
___	**2426420**	WP CA-1 Caboose "726," 24		130
___	**2426430**	D&H N6b Wood-sided Caboose "35701," 24		125
___	**2426440**	DT&I N6b Wood-sided Caboose "77," 24		125
___	**2426450**	LL N6b Wood-sided Caboose "231901," 24		125
___	**2426460**	North Pole Central N6b Wood-sided Caboose "2325," 24		125
___	**2426470**	Strasburg RR N6b Wood-sided Caboose "12," 24		125
___	**2426480**	Christmas Egg Nog Milk Car "241225," 24-25		120
___	**2426490**	Erie Milk Car "65," 24		120
___	**2426500**	Dr. Acula's Blood Tonic Milk Car "1476," 24-25		120
___	**2426510**	NC&StL Milk Car "3900," 24		120
___	**2426520**	O'Leary Dairies Milk Car "1871," 24-25		120
___	**2426530**	Strasburg RR Milk Car "17579," 24		120
___	**2426540**	Acme 8,000-Gallon 1-D Tank Car "19491," 24-25		110
___	**2426550**	Paluxy Asphalt 8,000-Gallon 1-D Tank Car "4021," 24-25		100
___	**2426560**	Penn Salt 8,000-Gallon 1-D Tank Car "715," 24-25		100
___	**2426570**	St. Lawrence Starch 8,000-Gallon 1-D Tank Car "49104," 24-25		100
___	**2426580**	Stauffer Chemical 8,000-Gallon 1-D Tank Car "86," 24-25		100
___	**2426590**	Union Oil 8,000-Gallon 1-D Tank Car "8085," 24-25		100
___	**2426620**	C&NW PS-2 Covered Hopper "4110," 24-25		90
___	**2426621**	C&NW PS-2 Covered Hopper "3995, weathered, 24-25		100
___	**2426630**	Conrail PS-2 Covered Hopper "877045," 24-25		90
___	**2426631**	Conrail PS-2 Covered Hopper "8776978," weathered", 24-25		100
___	**2426640**	GN PS-2 Covered Hopper "71464," 24		90
___	**2426641**	GN PS-2 Covered Hopper "71436," weathered, 24-25		100
___	**2426650**	IC PS-2 Covered Hopper "55012," 24-25		90
___	**2426651**	IC PS-2 Covered Hopper "55044," weathered, 24-25		100
___	**2426660**	SP PS-2 Covered Hopper "402148," 24-25		90
___	**2426661**	SP PS-2 Covered Hopper "402148," weathered, 24-25		100
___	**2426670**	Winchester & Western PS-2 Covered Hopper "4013," 24-25		90
___	**2426671**	Winchester & Western PS-2 Covered Hopper "4006," weathered, 24-25		100
___	**2426680**	Looney Tunes Acme Mini-Copter PS-1 Boxcar, 24-25		110
___	**2426690**	Looney Tunes Acme Giant Magnet PS-1 Boxcar, 24		110
___	**2426700**	Looney Tunes Acme 50-foot Flatcar w/Trailers, 24		170
___	**2426710**	Deer Dash 50-foot Flatcar w/Trailers, 24		160
___	**2426720**	MKT 50-foot Flatcar w/Trailers "13458," 24		160
___	**2426730**	REA 50-foot Flatcar w/Trailers "1649," 24		160
___	**2426740**	SP 50-foot Flatcar w/Trailers "563225," 24		160
___	**2426750**	T&P 50-foot Flatcar w/Trailers "99402," 24		160
___	**2426760**	PRR Vision N6b Wood-sided Caboose w/RailSounds "980310," 24		300
___	**2426770**	PRR Vision N6b Wood-sided Caboose w/RailSounds "981827," 24		300
___	**2426780**	Eerie Vision Caboose w/RailSounds "103124," 24		310

		Exc	Mint
2426790	Polar Express 20th Anniversary PS-1 Boxcar w/BellSounds, 24-25		220 ___
2426800	Polar Express 20th Anniversary PS-1 Boxcar, 24		110 ___
2427010	C&O George Washington 18" Passenger Car 2-pack, A, 23-25		500 ___
2427020	C&O George Washington 18" Passenger Car 2-pack, B, 23-25		500 ___
2427030	C&O George Washington 18" Passenger Car 2-pack, C, 23		500 ___
2427040	C&O George Washington 18" Diner w/StationSounds, 23		430 ___
2427050	WM Scenic 21" Passenger Car 2-pack, A, 23-25		500 ___
2427060	WM Scenic 21" Passenger Car 2-pack, B, 23		500 ___
2427070	WM Scenic Dome Car w/StationSounds, 23		500 ___
2427080	GN Empire Builder 21" Passenger Car 4-pack, 23		1000 ___
2427090	GN Empire Builder 21" Passenger Car 2-pack, 23		500 ___
2427100	GN Empire Builder 21" Diner w/StationSounds, 23		450 ___
2427110	Lehigh Gorge Scenic Ry. 72' Passenger Car 2-pack, 23-25		430 ___
2427120	GN Empire Builder Full Dome Car "1392," 23		300 ___
2427130	UP 18" Passenger Car 2-pack, A, 23		500 ___
2427140	UP 18" Passenger Car 2-pack, B, 23		500 ___
2427150	UP 18" Passenger Car 2-pack, C, 23		500 ___
2427160	UP 18" Diner w/StationSounds, 23		430 ___
2427170	Amtrak Phase III Modern Dome Car "10031," w/ StationSounds, 23		500 ___
2427180	American Orient Express Full Dome Car, 23		300 ___
2427190	American Orient ExpressPassenger Car 4-pack, 23		1000 ___
2427200	American Orient Express Passenger Car 2-pack, 23		500 ___
2427210	American Orient Express Zurich Diner w/StationSounds, 23		450 ___
2427220	Southern MOW RPO "960408," 23-25		200 ___
2427230	UP MOW RPO "903688," 23		200 ___
2427240	UP 21" Training Car "211," 23		430 ___
2427250	D&RGW 18" Training Car "X201," 23-25		430 ___
2427260	GN 18" Fire Prevention Car "X1828,", 23		430 ___
2427270	MILW 18" Training Car "X711," 23		430 ___
2427280	NYC 18" Training Car "X-23415," 23		430 ___
2427290	PRR 18" Training Car "492443," 23-25		430 ___
2427300	Polar Express 20th Anniversary 18" Coach, 24		250 ___
2427310	Polar Express Observation w/round end and black roof, 24		270 ___
2427320	Polar Express Observation w/round end and white roof, 24		270 ___
2427330	IC City of Miami Passenger Car 2-pack, 24		500 ___
2427340	IC City of Miami Diner w/StationSounds, 24		450 ___
2427350	NYC Semi-Vestibule Wood Coach 2-pack, 24		500 ___
2427360	PRR Semi-Vestibule Wood Coach 2-pack, 24		500 ___
2427370	MILW Hiawatha No. 2 18" Aluminum Passenger Car 4-pack, 24		1400 ___
2427380	MILW Hiawatha No. 2 18" Aluminum Passenger Car 3-pack, 24		900 ___
2427400	MILW Hiawatha No. 4 18" Aluminum Passenger Car 4-pack, 24		1400 ___
2427410	MILW Hiawatha No. 4 18" Aluminum Passenger Car 3-pack, 24		900 ___
2427430	North Pole Central 18" Aluminum Passenger Car 4-pack, 24		1400 ___
2427440	North Pole Central 18" Aluminum Passenger Car 3-pack, 24		900 ___
2427460	C&NW 18" Aluminum Passenger Car 4-pack, 24		1400 ___
2427470	C&NW 18" Aluminum Passenger Car 3-pack, 24		900 ___

			Exc	Mint
___	**2427490**	SAL 18" Aluminum Passenger Car 4-pack, 24		1400
___	**2427500**	SAL 18" Aluminum Passenger Car 3-pack, 24		900
___	**2427520**	UP 18" Aluminum Passenger Car 4-pack, 24		1400
___	**2427530**	UP 18" Aluminum Passenger Car 3-pack, 24		900
___	**2427550**	B&O Royal Blue Wood Passenger Car 2-pack, A, 24		500
___	**2427560**	B&O Royal Blue Wood Passenger Car 2-pack, B, 24		500
___	**2427570**	B&O Royal Blue Wood Passenger Car 2-pack, C, 24		500
___	**2427640**	ATSF Full Vista Dome Car Add-on "60," 24-25		130
___	**2427650**	Halloween Wood Passenger Car 2-pack, A, 24		520
___	**2427660**	Halloween Wood Passenger Car 2-pack, B, 24		520
___	**2427670**	Halloween Wood Passenger Car 2-pack, C, 24		520
___	**2427680**	CB&Q 21" Passenger Car 4-pack, 24		1000
___	**2427690**	CB&Q 21" Passenger Car 2-pack, 24		500
___	**2427700**	CB&Q 21" Diner w/StationSounds, 24		450
___	**2427710**	RI Al Capone Coach 4-pack, 24-25		1000
___	**2427720**	Polar Express 20th Anniversary Coach, white roof, 24-25		100
___	**2427730**	LL Coach "2024," 24-25		110
___	**2427740**	LL Coach "Joshua," 24-25		110
___	**2427750**	LL Observation Coach "Cowen," 24-25		110
___	**2427760**	LL Baggage Car "Tradition," 24-25		100
___	**2427770**	LL Vista Dome Coach "Vision," 24-25		120
___	**2427780**	PRR Coach "4041," 24-25		110
___	**2427790**	PRR Coach "4049," 24-25		110
___	**2427800**	PRR Observation Coach "1126," 24-25		110
___	**2427810**	PRR Baggage Car "5868," 24-25		100
___	**2427820**	PRR Vista Dome Coach "7820," 24-25		120
___	**2427830**	UP Coach "584," 24-25		110
___	**2427840**	UP Coach "590," 24-25		110
___	**2427850**	UP Observation "1576," 24-25		110
___	**2427860**	UP Baggage Car "5715," 24-25		100
___	**2427870**	UP Vista Dome "Stardust," 24-25		120
___	**2427880**	Christmas Coach "12023," 24-25		110
___	**2427890**	Christmas Coach "12024," 24-25		110
___	**2427900**	Christmas Observation "12025," 24-25		110
___	**2427910**	Christmas Baggage Car "Noel," 24-25		100
___	**2427920**	Christmas Vista Dome "Spirit," 24-25		120
___	**2427930**	Halloween Coach "New Moon," 24-25		110
___	**2427940**	Halloween Coach "Crescent Moon," 24-25		110
___	**2427950**	Halloween Observation Coach "Full Moon," 24-25		110
___	**2427960**	Halloween Baggage Car "Harvest," 24-25		100
___	**2427970**	Halloween Vista Dome "Hunter," 24-25		120
___	**2427980**	Sleigh Bell Limited Passenger Car Add-on 2-pack, 24-25		200
___	**2427990**	Polar Express 20th Anniversary Coach, black roof, 24-25		100
___	**2428010**	Tasmanian Devil Lenticular Boxcar, 23-25		130
___	**2428020**	GN Flatcar "65722," w/Bulkheads, 23		70
___	**2428030**	Bethlehem Steel Flatcar "2054," w/Bulkheads, 23		70
___	**2428040**	Harry Potter Dementors Aquarium Car, 24-25		130
___	**2428050**	Wizard of Oz Red Slippers Illuminated Boxcar, 24-25		150
___	**2428060**	Batman 85th Anniversary Bat Signal Caboose, 24-25		160
___	**2428070**	2024 Christmas Boxcar, 24		90
___	**2428080**	2024 Christmas Music Boxcar, 24		120
___	**2428090**	Peppermint RR Transport Bulkhead Flatcar, 24		70
___	**2428100**	Weather Balloon Defense Car 2-pack, 23-25		230

MODERN 1970-2025		Exc	Mint
2428110	Harry Potter and the Sorcerer's Stone Boxcar, 24-25		100 ___
2428120	Harry Potter and the Chamber of Secrets Boxcar, 24-25		100 ___
2428130	Harry Potter and the Prisoner of Azkaban Boxcar, 24-25		100 ___
2428140	Thomas Kinkade Mickey & Minnie Sweetheart Central Park Boxcar, 24-25		100 ___
2428150	Thomas Kinkade Mickey & Minnie Candy Cane Express Boxcar, 24-25		100 ___
2428160	Thomas Kinkade Mickey & Minnie Christmas Lodge Boxcar, 24-25		100 ___
2428170	Polar Express 20th Anniversary Illuminated Boxcar w/ sounds, 24-25		160 ___
2428180	Fright Liner Auto Rack, 24		85 ___
2428190	Chevrolet Crane Car "8190," 24-25		120 ___
2428200	Ford Crane Car "51," 24-25		120 ___
2428210	Ichabod Crane Car, 24		120 ___
2428220	Bob Ross Boxcar w/sounds, 24-25		120 ___
2428230	Polar Express Present Transport Car, 24-25		110 ___
2428240	Lenny Lager 1-D Tank Car, 24		90 ___
2428250	U.S. Army Boxcar "8250," 24-25		90 ___
2428260	U.S. Army Flatcar "8260" w/tank, 24		100 ___
2428270	U.S. Army 3-D Tank Car "8270," 24-25		90 ___
2428280	Aquaman Seven Seas 1-D Tank Car, 24-25		110 ___
2428290	Superman Flatcar w/steel I-beam, 24-25		100 ___
2428300	Green Lantern Power Ring Searchlight Caboose, 24-25		160 ___
2428310	NYSW Boxcar "8310," 24-25		90 ___
2428320	Blue Coal Hopper w/coal load, "8320," 24-25		90 ___
2428330	DL&W Gondola "8330" w/canisters, 24-25		100 ___
2428340	UP Boxcar "960449," 24-25		90 ___
2428350	WP Gondola "6053," 24-25		90 ___
2428360	SP 1-D Tank Car "62904," 24-25		90 ___
2428370	NS Hi-Cube Boxcar "473177" w/graffiti, 24		90 ___
2428380	UTLX Unibody 1-D Tank Car "X-13878" w/graffiti, 24		90 ___
2428390	Ferromex Auto Rack "705176" w/graffiti, 24		100 ___
2428400	Anheuser-Busch Clydesdale Holiday Refrigerator Car, 24-25		100 ___
2428410	Budweiser Illuminated Bar Sign Refrigerator Car, 24-25		150 ___
2428420	Barbie 65th Anniversary Boxcar, 1959, 24-25		100 ___
2428430	Barbie 65th Anniversary Boxcar, 1960s, 24-25		100 ___
2428440	Barbie 65th Anniversary Boxcar, 1970s, 24-25		100 ___
2428450	Mister Rogers Aquarium Car, 24-25		130 ___
2428460	Mister Rogers Neighborhood Boxcar w/sounds, 24-25		120 ___
2428470	Christmas NE5 Caboose, 24		130 ___
2428480	LL NE5 Caboose, 24-25		130 ___
2428490	2024 National Lionel Train Day Boxcar, 24-25		100 ___
2429010	John Deere Showroom, 23		170 ___
2429020	Acme Dynamite Factory, 24-25		400 ___
2429050	Amtrak Mail & Express Station, 24		150 ___
2429060	Sled-Ex Christmas Operating Freight Station, 24-25		150 ___
2429070	Angela Trotta Thomas Halloween Covered Bridge, 24-25		80 ___
2429080	Bob Ross Gallery Building, 24		130 ___
2429090	Polar Express Billy's House, 24-25		130 ___
2429100	Polar Express Freight Terminal, 24		150 ___
2429110	Haunted Barn w/Blinking lights, 24-25		160 ___
2429120	Farm Animals Barn w/Sounds, 24-25		180 ___

MODERN 1970-2025		Exc	Mint
___ **2429130**	John Deere Barn, 24		170
___ **2429140**	Anheuser-Busch Industrial Water Tower, 24-25		90
___ **2429150**	Lenny Lager Industrial Water Tower, 24		90
___ **2429153**	PEP 153 IR, 24		80
___ **2429160**	Thomas Kinkade Christmas Light Express Covered Bridge, 24-25		90
___ **2429180**	Decorative Street Lamp 3-pack, green, 24		40
___ **2429190**	Decorative Street Lamp 3-pack, black, 24		40
___ **2429200**	Station Lights 3-pack, green, 24		40
___ **2429210**	Station Lights 3-pack, black, 24		40
___ **2429220**	Double-Arm Globe Light 3-pack, 24		40
___ **2429230**	Double-Arm Highway Light 3-pack, 24		40
___ **2429240**	Single-Light Extended Pole Light 3-pack, 24		40
___ **2430010**	Acme Dynamite Powder Barrel Pack, 23-25		16
___ **2430020**	Smoke Fluid Bottle w/Needle Dropper 2-pack, 23		10
___ **2430030**	Amtrak Passenger Shelter, 24-25		50
___ **2430040**	Lionelville Passenger Shelter, 24-25		50
___ **2430050**	Bob Ross Water Tower, 24-25		60
___ **2430060**	Polar Express 20th Anniversary Water Tower, 24-25		60
___ **2430070**	Halloween Water Tower, 24-25		60
___ **2431010**	Erie Triplex Steam Locomotive "2603," CC, 24		2500
___ **2431020**	Erie Triplex Steam Locomotive "5014," CC, 24		2500
___ **2431030**	Erie Triplex Steam Locomotive "5015," CC, 24		2500
___ **2431040**	Erie Triplex Steam Locomotive "5016," CC, 24		2500
___ **2431050**	D&RGW Triplex Steam Locomotive "1090," CC, 24		2500
___ **2431060**	NP Triplex Steam Locomotive "4050," CC, 24		2500
___ **2431070**	Virginian Triplex Steam Locomotive "701," CC, 24		2500
___ **2431080**	Pilot Triplex Steam Locomotive "9999," CC, 24		2500
___ **2431090**	Halloween Triplex Steam Locomotive "3131," CC, 24		2500
___ **2431100**	C&O F-19 4-6-2 Pacific Locomotive "490," CC, 23		1300
___ **2431110**	C&O F-19 4-6-2 Pacific, George Washington "491," CC, 23		1300
___ **2431120**	C&O F-19 4-6-2 Pacific Locomotive "492," ca 1929, CC, 23		1300
___ **2431130**	C&O F-19 4-6-2 Pacific Locomotive "493," CC, 23		1300
___ **2431140**	C&O F-19 4-6-2 Pacific Locomotive "494," CC, 23		1300
___ **2431150**	C&O F-19 4-6-2 Pacific Locomotive "491," CC, 23		1300
___ **2431160**	C&O F-19 4-6-2 Pacific George Washington "492," CC, 23		1300
___ **2431170**	Halloween F-19 4-6-2 Pacific Locomotive "310," CC, 23		1300
___ **2431180**	Pere Marquette F-19 4-6-2 Pacific Locomotive "730," CC, 23		1300
___ **2431190**	RF&P F-19 4-6-2 Pacific Locomotive "350," CC, 23		1300
___ **2431200**	D&RGW 2-6-6-2 Locomotive "3302," CC, 23		1800
___ **2431210**	Nickel Plate 2-6-6-2 Locomotive "942," CC, 23		1800
___ **2431220**	NP 2-6-6-2 Locomotive "3110," CC, 23		1800
___ **2431230**	N&W 2-6-6-2 Locomotive "1303," CC, 23		1800
___ **2431240**	WM 2-6-6-2 Locomotive "1309," CC, 23		1800
___ **2431250**	Weyerhaeuser Lumber 2-6-6-2 Locomotive "120," CC, 23		1800
___ **2431260**	UP FEF-3 4-8-4 Locomotive "844," black, CC, 23		1800
___ **2431270**	UP FEF-3 4-8-4 Locomotive "844," gray/yellow, CC, 23		1800
___ **2431280**	UP FEF-3 4-8-4 Locomotive "843," gray/silver, CC, 23		1800
___ **2431290**	UP FEF-3 4-8-4 Locomotive "838," CC, 23		1800
___ **2431300**	UP FEF-3 4-8-4 Locomotive Challenger "836," CC, 23		1800
___ **2431310**	UP FEF-3 4-8-4 Locomotive "841," CC, 23		1800
___ **2431320**	UP Auxiliary Tender "809," CC, 23-25		500
___ **2431329**	UP Auxiliary Tender "809", 23		350

		Exc	Mint
2431330	UP Auxiliary Tender "814," CC, 23-25		500 ___
2431339	UP Auxiliary Tender "814," 23		350 ___
2431340	Black River & Western 2-8-0 Consolidation "60," CC, 23		900 ___
2431350	Colorado & Southern 2-8-0 Consolidation "641," CC, 23		900 ___
2431360	DM&IR 2-8-0 Consolidation "332," CC, 23		900 ___
2431370	GTW 2-8-0 Consolidation "2683," CC, 23		900 ___
2431380	LV 2-8-0 Consolidation "911," CC, 23		900 ___
2431390	SAL 2-8-0 Consolidation "900," CC, 23		900 ___
2431400	PRR M1 4-8-2 Mountain Locomotive "6855," CC, 23		1600 ___
2431410	PRR M1 4-8-2 Mountain Locomotive "6810," CC, 23		1600 ___
2431420	PRR M1 4-8-2 Mountain Locomotive "6845," CC, 23		1600 ___
2431430	PRR M1 4-8-2 Mountain Locomotive "6871," CC, 23		1600 ___
2431440	PRR M1 4-8-2 Mountain Locomotive "6918," CC, 23		1600 ___
2431450	PRR M1 4-8-2 Mountain Locomotive "6888," CC, 23		1600 ___
2431460	Polar Express 2-8-4 Berkshire Locomotive "1225," CC, 24		1700 ___
2431470	Polar Express 20th Anniversary 2-8-4 Berkshire Plasma-Coat "1225," CC, 24		1700 ___
2431480	Polar Express 2-8-4 Berkshire Special Red "1225," CC, 24-25		1700 ___
2431501	NPR 2-8-4 Berkshire Locomotive "755," CC, 24		1700
2431510	NPR 2-8-4 Berkshire Locomotive "777," CC, 24		1700
2431520	C&O 2-8-4 Berkshire Locomotive "2765," CC, 24		1700 ___
2431530	DT&I 2-8-4 Berkshire Locomotive "705," CC, 24		1700 ___
2431540	Pere Marquette 2-8-4 Berkshire Locomotive "1225," CC, 24		1700 ___
2431550	C&O H7 2-8-8-2 Mallet Locomotive "1572" w/1926 tender, CC, 24		2000 ___
2431560	C&O H7 2-8-8-2 Mallet Locomotive "1553" w/Vanderbilt tender, CC, 24		2000 ___
2431570	C&O H7 2-8-8-2 Mallet Locomotive "1564" w/Short Vanderbilt tender, CC, 24		2000 ___
2431580	C&O H7 2-8-8-2 Mallet Locomotive "1584" w/Allegheny tender, CC, 24		2000 ___
2431590	D&RGW H7 2-8-8-2 Mallet Locomotive "3605," CC, 24		2000 ___
2431600	RF&P H7 2-8-8-2 Mallet Locomotive "1," CC, 24		2000 ___
2431611	UP H7 2-8-8-2 Mallet Locomotive "3589," CC, 24		2000 ___
2431612	UP H7 2-8-8-2 Mallet Locomotive "3592," CC, 24		2000 ___
2431620	Christmas F-19 4-6-2 Pacific Locomotive "1224," CC, 23		1300 ___
2431630	B&O 4-6-0 Ten-Wheeler Locomotive "1315," CC, 24		800 ___
2431640	CNJ 4-6-0 Ten-Wheeler Locomotive "185," CC, 24		800 ___
2431650	NYC&HR 4-6-0 Ten-Wheeler Locomotive "2140," CC, 24		800 ___
2431660	NYC 4-6-0 Ten-Wheeler Locomotive "1244," CC, 24		800 ___
2431670	NP 4-6-0 Ten-Wheeler Locomotive "1372," CC, 24		800 ___
2431680	WP 4-6-0 Ten-Wheeler Locomotive "110," CC, 24		800 ___
2431690	MILW Hiawatha 4-4-2 Atlantic Locomotive "1," CC, 24		1200 ___
2431700	MILW Hiawatha 4-4-2 Atlantic Locomotive "2," CC, 24		1200 ___
2431710	MILW Hiawatha 4-4-2 Atlantic Locomotive "4," CC, 24		1200 ___
2431720	North Pole Central 4-4-2 Atlantic Locomotive "12," CC, 24		1200 ___
2431730	C&NW 4-4-2 Atlantic Locomotive "400," CC, 24		1200 ___
2431740	SAL 4-4-2 Atlantic Locomotive "850," CC, 24		1200 ___
2431750	UP 4-4-2 Atlantic Locomotive "2800," CC, 24		1200 ___
2431830	Lionel Lines 4-4-2 Atlantic Locomotive "2024," CC, 24		1200 ___
2432010	LL 2-8-4 Berkshire Locomotive "726," LionChief Plus 2.0, 23		700 ___
2432020	American Railroads 2-8-4 Berkshire "759," LionChief Plus 2.0, 23		700 ___

		Exc	Mint
____ 2432030	DT&I 2-8-4 Berkshire Locomotive "704," LionChief Plus 2.0, 23		700
____ 2432040	ATSF 2-8-4 Berkshire Locomotive "4106," LionChief Plus 2.0, 23		700
____ 2432050	Polar Express 20th Anniversary 2-8-4 Berkshire "1225," LionChief Plus 2.0, 24-25		600
____ 2432060	Polar Express 2-8-4 Berkshire "1225," LionChief Plus 2.0, 24		600
____ 2432070	NKP 2-8-4 Berkshire "759," LionChief Plus 2.0, 24-25		600
____ 2432080	Pere Marquette 2-8-4 Berkshire "1223," LionChief Plus 2.0, 24-25		600
____ 2432090	C&O 2-8-4 Berkshire "2696," LionChief Plus 2.0, 24-25		600
____ 2432100	L&N 2-8-4 Berkshire "1984," LionChief Plus 2.0, 24-25		600
____ 2432110	Peppermint RR 2-8-4 Berkshire "2524," LionChief Plus 2.0, 24-25		600
____ 2433010	Trump GE ES44AC Diesel "2024," CC, 24 u		750
____ 2433031	UP EMD SD70ACe Diesel "8518," CC, 23		700
____ 2443031	WP DD Boxcar "38291" (std 0), 23		70
____ 2443032	WP DD Boxcar "38314" (std 0), 23		70
____ 2433039	UP EMD SD70ACe Diesel "8522" (unpowered), 23		350
____ 2433040	NS Heritage CNJ EMD SD70ACe Diesel "1071," CC, 23		700
____ 2433049	NS Heritage CNJ EMD SD70ACe Diesel "1071" (unpowered), 23		350
____ 2433050	NS Heritage DL&W EMD SD70ACe Diesel "1074," CC, 23		700
____ 2433059	NS Heritage DL&W EMD SD70ACe Diesel "1074" (unpowered), 23		350
____ 2433060	NS Heritage Erie EMD SD70ACe Diesel "1068," CC, 23		700
____ 2433069	NS Heritage Erie EMD SD70ACe Diesel "1068" (unpowered), 23		350
____ 2433070	NS Heritage IT EMD SD70ACe Diesel "1072," CC, 23		700
____ 2433079	NS Heritage IT EMD SD70ACe Diesel "1072" (unpowered), 23		350
____ 2433080	NS Heritage NYC EMD SD70ACe Diesel "1066," CC, 23		700
____ 2433089	NS Heritage NYC EMD SD70ACe Diesel "1066" (unpowered), 23		350
____ 2433111	Alaska RR EMD GP30 Diesel "2000," CC, 23		600
____ 2433112	Alaska RR EMD GP30 Diesel "2504," CC, 23		600
____ 2433121	Conrail EMD GP30 Diesel "2168," CC, 23		600
____ 2433122	Conrail EMD GP30 Diesel "2196," CC, 23		600
____ 2433131	NYC EMD GP30 Diesel "6118," CC, 23		600
____ 2433132	NYC EMD GP30 Diesel "6121," CC, 23		600
____ 2433141	PRR EMD GP30 Diesel "2211," CC, 23		600
____ 2433142	PRR EMD GP30 Diesel "2233," CC, 23		600
____ 2433151	ATSF EMD GP30 Diesel "1203," CC, 23		600
____ 2433152	ATSF EMD GP30 Diesel "1220," CC, 23		600
____ 2433161	WC EMD GP30 Diesel "2252," CC, 23		600
____ 2433162	WC EMD GP30 Diesel "2253," CC, 23		600
____ 2433170	ATSF EMD F7 AA Diesel Set "332/335," CC, 23		1200
____ 2433178	ATSF EMD F7 B Unit "337A," CC, 23		600
____ 2433179	ATSF EMD F7 B Unit SuperBass "338B", 23		550
____ 2433180	B&M EMD F7 AA Diesel Set "4265/4268," CC, 23		1200
____ 2433188	B&M EMD F7 B Unit "4267B," CC, 23		600
____ 2433189	B&M EMD F7 B Unit SuperBass "4268B", 23		550
____ 2433190	CB&Q EMD F7 AA Diesel Set "167A/167C," CC, 23		1200

MODERN 1970-2025		Exc	Mint
2433198	CB&Q EMD F7 B Unit "167B," CC, 23		600
2433199	CB&Q EMD F7 B Unit SuperBass "168B", 23		550
2433200	GN EMD F7 AA Diesel Set "364A/364C," CC, 23		1200
2433208	GN EMD F7 B Unit "364B," CC, 23		600
2433209	GN EMD F7 B Unit SuperBass "364B," CC, 23		550
2433210	RI EMD F7 AA Diesel Set "120/122," CC, 23		1200
2433218	RI EMD F7 B Unit "22," CC, 23		600
2433219	RI EMD F7 B Unit SuperBass "10," 23		550
2433228	Frisco EMD F7 B Unit "5132," CC, 23		600
2433229	Frisco EMD F7 B Unit SuperBass "5139," 23		550
2433220	Frisco EMD F7 AA Diesel Set "5032/5033," CC, 23		1200
2433231	B&O EMD SD50 Diesel "8577," CC, 23		650
2433232	B&O EMD SD50 Diesel "8584," CC, 23		650
2433239	B&O EMD SD50 Diesel SuperBass "8593" (unpowered), 23		600
2433241	Conrail EMD SD50 Diesel "6709" CC, 23		650
2433249	Conrail EMD SD50 Diesel SuperBass "6720" (unpowered), 23		600
2433250	Conrail EMD SD50 Diesel "6707" CC, 23		650
2433261	D&RGW EMD SD50 Diesel "5503," CC, 23		650
2433262	D&RGW EMD SD50 Diesel "5507," CC, 23		650
2433269	D&RGW EMD SD50 Diesel SuperBass "5515" (unpowered), 23		600
2433271	MP EMD SD50 Diesel "5000," CC, 23		650
2433272	MP EMD SD50 Diesel "5041," CC, 23		650
2433279	MP EMD SD50 Diesel SuperBass "5050" (unpowered), 23		600
2433281	NS EMD SD40E Diesel "6313" CC, 23		650
2433282	NS EMD SD40E Diesel "6319" CC, 23		650
2433289	NS EMD SD40E Diesel SuperBass "6329" (unpowered), 23		600
2433291	Reading & Northern EMD SD50 Diesel "5018" CC, 23		650
2433299	Reading & Northern EMD SD50 SuperBass "5019" (unpowered), 23		600
2433300	ADM Alco S2 Diesel Switcher "1," CC, 23		550
2433310	CP Alco S2 Diesel Switcher "7020," CC, 23		550
2433320	Staten Island RR Alco S2 Diesel Switcher "821," CC, 23		550
2433330	L&NE Alco S2 Diesel Switcher "611," CC, 23		550
2433340	NASA Alco S2 Diesel Switcher "2," CC, 23		550
2433350	U.S. Army Alco S2 Diesel Switcher "7100," CC, 23		550
2433361	BAR EMD GP9 Diesel "76," CC, 24		600
2433362	BAR EMD GP9 Diesel "78," CC, 24		600
2433371	Conrail EMD GP9 Diesel "7020," CC, 24		600
2433372	Conrail EMD GP9 Diesel "7043," CC, 24		600
2433379	Conrail EMD GP9 B unit SuperBass "3812," CC, 24		500
2433381	M&StL EMD GP9 Diesel "702," CC, 24		600
2433382	M&StL EMD GP9 Diesel "705," CC, 24		600
2433391	N&W EMD GP9 Diesel "500," CC, 24		600
2433392	N&W EMD GP9 Diesel "512," CC, 24		600
2433401	PRR EMD GP9 Diesel "7013," CC, 24		600
2433402	PRR EMD GP9 Diesel "7025," CC, 24		600
2433409	PRR EMD GP9 B unit SuperBass "7185B," CC, 24		500
2433411	UP EMD GP9 Diesel "310," CC, 24		600
2433412	UP EMD GP9 Diesel "312," CC, 24		600
2433419	UP EMD GP9 B unit SuperBass "310B," CC, 24		500
2433421	BNSF GE ES44 Diesel "5780," CC, 24		750

			Exc	Mint
____	**2433422**	BNSF GE ES44 Diesel "5856," CC, 24		750
____	**2433429**	BNSF GE ES44 SuperBass "5909," 24		600
____	**2433431**	CP GE ES44 Diesel "8951," CC, 24		750
____	**2433432**	CP GE ES44 Diesel "9370," CC, 24		750
____	**2433439**	CP GE ES44 SuperBass "9369," 24		600
____	**2433441**	CSX GE ES44 Diesel "3000," CC, 24		750
____	**2433442**	CSX GE ES44 Diesel "3035," CC, 24		750
____	**2433449**	CSX GE ES44 SuperBass "3059," 24		600
____	**2433451**	NS GE ES44 Diesel "8034," CC, 24		750
____	**2433452**	NS GE ES44 Diesel "8092," CC, 24		750
____	**2433459**	NS GE ES44 SuperBass "8159," 24		600
____	**2433461**	UP GE ES44 Diesel "5282," CC, 24		750
____	**2433462**	UP GE ES44 Diesel "5283," CC, 24		750
____	**2433469**	UP GE ES44 SuperBass "5251," 24		600
____	**2433471**	NS Heritage Central of Georgia GE ES44 Diesel "8101," CC, 24		750
____	**2433479**	NS Heritage Central of Georgia GE ES44 Diesel "8101," non-powered, 24		430
____	**2433481**	NS Heritage LV GE ES44 Diesel "8104," CC, 24		750
____	**2433489**	NS Heritage LV GE ES44 Diesel "8104," non-powered, 24		430
____	**2433491**	NS Heritage Monongahela GE ES44 Diesel "8025," CC, 24		750
____	**2433499**	NS Heritage Monongahela GE ES44 Diesel "8025," non-powered, 24		430
____	**2433501**	NS Heritage N&W GE ES44 Diesel "8103," CC, 24		750
____	**2433509**	NS Heritage N&W GE ES44 Diesel "8103," non-powered, 24		430
____	**2433511**	NS Heritage PRR GE ES44 Diesel "8102," CC, 24		750
____	**2433519**	NS Heritage PRR GE ES44 Diesel "8102," non-powered, 24		430
____	**2433521**	ATSF EMD SD45 Diesel "5534," CC, 24		650
____	**2433522**	ATSF EMD SD45 Diesel "5543," CC, 24		650
____	**2433529**	ATSF EMD SD45 Diesel SuperBass "5555,", 24		600
____	**2433531**	D&H EMD SD45 Diesel "801," CC, 24		650
____	**2433532**	D&H EMD SD45 Diesel "802," CC, 24		650
____	**2433539**	D&H EMD SD45 Diesel SuperBass "803," 24		600
____	**2433541**	D&RGW EMD SD45 Diesel "5315," CC, 24		650
____	**2433542**	D&RGW EMD SD45 Diesel "5326," CC, 24		650
____	**2433549**	D&RGW EMD SD45 Diesel SuperBass "5340", 24		600
____	**2433551**	Reading EMD SD45 Diesel "7601," CC, 24		650
____	**2433552**	Reading EMD SD45 Diesel "7603," CC, 24		650
____	**2433559**	Reading EMD SD45 Diesel SuperBass "7604," 24		600
____	**2433561**	Frisco EMD SD45 Diesel "911," CC, 24		650
____	**2433562**	Frisco EMD SD45 Diesel "916," CC, 24		650
____	**2433569**	Frisco EMD SD45 Diesel SuperBass "929," 24		600
____	**2433571**	SP EMD SD45 Diesel "7400," CC, 24		650
____	**2433572**	SP EMD SD45 Diesel "7437," CC, 24		650
____	**2433579**	SP EMD SD45 Diesel SuperBass "7401," 24		600
____	**2433580**	CSX Heritage B&O GE ES44 Diesel "1827," CC, 24		750
____	**2433589**	CSX Heritage B&O GE ES44 Diesel "1827," non-powered, 24		430
____	**2433590**	B&O EMD E6 Diesel AB Set "57A/57B," CC, 24		1200
____	**2433599**	B&O EMD E6 B Unit SuperBass "588," 24		500
____	**2433600**	CB&Q RI EMD E5 Diesel AB Set, CC, 24		1200
____	**2433609**	CB&Q EMD E5 B Unit SuperBass "9980B," 24		500
____	**2433610**	GM EMD E6 Diesel AB Set "1939/1940," CC, 24		1200
____	**2433619**	GM EMD E6 B Unit SuperBass "1939B," 24		500
____	**2433620**	MILW EMD E6 Diesel AB Set "15A/15B," CC, 24		1200

		Exc	Mint
2433629	MILW EMD E6 B Unit SuperBass "15C," 24		500 ___
2433630	RI EMD E6 Diesel AB Set "630/631," CC, 24		1200 ___
2433639	RI EMD E7 B Unit SuperBass "610," 24		500 ___
2433640	Southern EMD E6 Diesel AB Set "2902/2952," CC, 24		1200 ___
2433649	Southern EMD E6 B Unit SuperBass "2953," 24		500 ___
2433650	UP City of San Francisco EMD E6 Diesel AB Set "SF4/SF5," CC, 24		1200 ___
2433650	C&NW EMD SW8 Diesel "127," CC, 24		550 ___
2433659	UP City of San Francisco EMD E6 B Unit SuperBass "SF6," 24		500 ___
2433670	Detroit Edison EMD SW8 Diesel "214," CC, 24		550 ___
2433680	EL EMD SW8 Diesel "364," CC, 24		550 ___
2433690	Reading & Northern EMD SW8 Diesel "800," CC, 24		550 ___
2433700	T&P EMD SW8 Diesel "812," CC, 24		550 ___
2433710	USAF EMD SW8 Diesel "2021," CC, 24		550 ___
2433720	CSX Heritage Chessie System GE ES44 Diesel "1973," CC, 24		750 ___
2433729	CSX Heritage Chessie System GE ES44 Diesel "1973," non-powered, 24		430 ___
2433731	Conrail GE U28C Diesel "6521," CC, 24		650 ___
2433732	Conrail GE U28C Diesel "6530," CC, 24		650 ___
2433741	L&N GE U28C Diesel "1527," CC, 24		650 ___
2433742	L&N GE U28C Diesel "1530," CC, 24		650 ___
2433751	PRR GE U28C Diesel "6520," CC, 24		650 ___
2433752	PRR GE U28C Diesel "6528," CC, 24		650 ___
2433761	PC GE U28C Diesel "6526," CC, 24		650 ___
2433762	PC GE U28C Diesel "6533," CC, 24		650 ___
2433771	Seaboard System GE U28C Diesel "1531," CC, 24		650 ___
2433772	Seaboard System GE U28C Diesel "1532," CC, 24		650 ___
2433781	SP GE U28C Diesel "7152," CC, 24		650 ___
2433782	SP GE U28C Diesel "7159," CC, 24		650 ___
2433791	UP GE U28C Diesel "2800," CC, 24		650 ___
2433792	UP GE U28C Diesel "2804," CC, 24		650 ___
2433861	CSX Heritage Seaboard System GE ES44 Diesel "1982," CC, 24		750 ___
2433869	CSX Heritage Seaboard System GE ES44 Diesel "1982," non-powered, 24		430 ___
2433891	CSX Heritage Conrail GE ES44 Diesel "1976," CC, 24		750 ___
2433899	CSX Heritage Conrail GE ES44 Diesel "1976," non-powered, 24		430 ___
2433901	CSX Heritage C&O GE ES44 Diesel "1869," CC, 24		750 ___
2433909	CSX Heritage C&O GE ES44 Diesel "1869," non-powered, 24		430 ___
2434010	D&RGW EMD GP7 Diesel "5102," LionChief Plus 2.0, 23		400 ___
2434020	Aberdeen & Rockfish EMD GP7 Diesel "205," LionChief Plus 2.0, 23		400 ___
2434030	CNJ EMD GP7 Diesel "1522," LionChief Plus 2.0, 23-25		400 ___
2434040	RI EMD GP7 Diesel "1208," LionChief Plus 2.0, 23		400 ___
2434050	Amtrak Genesis Locomotive Phase III "145," LionChief Plus 2.0, 24		550 ___
2434060	Amtrak Genesis Locomotive Phase I "156," LionChief Plus 2.0, 24		550 ___
2434070	Amtrak Genesis Locomotive Phase II "130," LionChief Plus 2.0, 24		550 ___
2434090	Amtrak Genesis Locomotive Phase IV "164," LionChief Plus 2.0, 24		550 ___
2434100	Metro-North Genesis Locomotive "208," LionChief Plus 2.0, 24		550 ___
2434110	Metro-North Genesis Locomotive "209," LionChief Plus 2.0, 24		550 ___

	No.	Description	Exc	Mint
___	**2434130**	Metro-North Heritage Conrail Genesis Locomotive "201," LionChief Plus 2.0, 24		550
___	**2434229**	ATSF EMD FT Diesel "157," non-powered, 24		200
___	**2434239**	Texas Special EMD FT Diesel "2001," non-powered, 24-25		200
___	**2434240**	Polar Express Genesis Locomotive, LionChief Plus 2.0, 24		550
___	**2435010**	Looney Tunes Handcar, 23		120
___	**2435020**	Polar Express 20th Anniversary Windup Handcar, 24-25		200
___	**2435030**	Halloween Trolley, LionChief 2.0, 24-25		150
___	**2435040**	B&O Doodlebug "6041," LionChief Plus 2.0, 24-25		400
___	**2435050**	CB&Q Doodlebug "9841," LionChief Plus 2.0, 24-25		400
___	**2435060**	East Broad Top Doodlebug "M-1," LionChief Plus 2.0, 24		400
___	**2435070**	GM&O Doodlebug "2506," LionChief Plus 2.0, 24-25		400
___	**2435080**	NYC Doodlebug "X-8015," LionChief Plus 2.0, 24-25		400
___	**2435090**	NP Doodlebug "B-20," LionChief Plus 2.0, 24-25		400
___	**2435100**	RI Doodlebug "9070," LionChief Plus 2.0, 24-25		400
___	**2435110**	Polar Express Doodlebug "25," LionChief Plus 2.0, 24-25		400
___	**2435120**	Polar Express TMCC Speeder, 24		200
___	**2435130**	North Pole Central TMCC Speeder, 24-25		200
___	**2435140**	Chessie System TMCC Speeder "6240," 24-25		190
___	**2435150**	C&NW TMCC Speeder "400," 24		190
___	**2435160**	RI TMCC Speeder "4351," 24-25		190
___	**2435170**	US Army Transportation Corps TMCC Speeder, 24-25		190
___	**2435190**	Area 51 TMCC Speeder "51," 24-25		190
___	**2435200**	Polar Express 20th Anniversary Windup Handcar, Gold, 24-25		230
___	**2438010**	Hogwarts Express Boxcar "1," 24		100
___	**2438020**	Hogwarts Express Boxcar "2," 24		100
___	**2438030**	Looney Tunes "Hare Trigger" Boxcar, 23		95
___	**2438040**	Looney Tunes "Devil May Hare" Boxcar, 23		95
___	**2438070**	Polar Express Personalized Boxcar, 24		100
___	**2438090**	2024 Personalized Happy Graduation Boxcar, 24		100
___	**2438100**	2024 Personalized Merry Christmas Boxcar, 24		100
___	**2438110**	2024 Personalized Happy Anniversary Boxcar, 24		100
___	**2438130**	2024 Personalized Happy Father's Day Boxcar, 24		100
___	**2438140**	2024 Personalized Happy Mother's Day Boxcar, 24		100
___	**2438150**	East Broad Top 150th Anniversary Boxcar, 24		100
___	**2438160**	Eads Bridge 150th Anniversary Boxcar, 24-25		100
___	**2438170**	Denver, South Park & Pacific RR 150th Anniversary Boxcar, 24-25		100
___	**2438180**	California Zephyr 75th Anniversary Boxcar, 24-25		100
___	**2438190**	First Continental Congress 250th Anniversary Boxcar, 24-25		110
___	**2438210**	Angela Trotta Thomas Prairie Steam Engine Boxcar, 24		100
___	**2438220**	Angela Trotta Thomas Diesel Flag Boxcar, 24		100
___	**2438230**	Bob Ross Boxcar, 24		110
___	**2438270**	Wings of Angels Tala Boxcar, 24-25		110
___	**2438280**	Wings of Angels Nina Boxcar, 24		110
___	**2438290**	Wings of Angels Caitlin Boxcar, 24		110
___	**2438300**	Looney Tunes Acme Boxcar, 1, 24-25		100
___	**2438310**	Looney Tunes Acme Boxcar, 2, 24-25		100
___	**2438340**	Fred Rogers Boxcar, 24		100
___	**2438370**	Roxey the LIRR Dog Boxcar, 24-25		
___	**2442010**	UP World War II PS-1 Boxcar 3-pack, 1, 23		250
___	**2442020**	UP World War II PS-1 Boxcar 3-pack, 2, 23		250
___	**2442030**	UP World War II PS-1 Boxcar 3-pack, 3, 23		250

MODERN 1970-2025		Exc	Mint
2442040	UP World War II PS-1 Boxcar Art 3-pack, 4, 24-25	250	___
2442050	UP World War II PS-1 Boxcar Art 3-pack, 5, 24-25	250	___
2442060	UP World War II PS-1 Boxcar Art 3-pack, 6, 24-25	250	___
2442070	C&O Composite 2-bay Hopper 2-pack, 1, 23	240	___
2442075	C&O Composite 2-bay Hopper 2-pack, 2, 23	240	___
2442079	C&O Composite 2-bay Hopper "55520," 23	80	___
2442080	CB&Q Composite 2-bay Hopper 2-pack, 1, 23	240	___
2442085	CB&Q Composite 2-bay Hopper 2-pack, 2, 23	240	___
2442089	CB&Q Composite 2-bay Hopper "194501," 23	80	___
2442090	LV Composite 2-bay Hopper 2-pack, 1, 23	240	___
2442095	LV Composite 2-bay Hopper 2-pack, 2, 23	240	___
2442099	LV Composite 2-bay Hopper "14007," 23	80	___
2442100	PRR Composite 2-bay Hopper 2-pack, 1, 23	240	___
2442105	PRR Composite 2-bay Hopper 2-pack, 2, 23	240	___
2442109	PRR Composite 2-bay Hopper "221190," 23	80	___
2442110	ADM PS-2CD Covered Hopper 3-pack, 23	250	___
2442119	ADM PS-2CD Covered Hopper "7281," 23	85	___
2442120	Illinois Terminal PS-2CD Covered Hopper 3-pack, 23	250	___
2442129	Illinois Terminal PS-2CD Covered Hopper "2104," 23	85	___
2442130	Co-op PS-2CD Covered Hopper 3-pack, 1, 23	250	___
2442140	Co-op PS-2CD Covered Hopper 3-pack, 2, 23	250	___
2442150	CSX/Family Lines PS-2CD Covered Hopper 3-pack, 23	250	___
2442159	CSX/Family Lines PS-2CD Covered Hopper "252325," 23	85	___
2442161	B&M Single-sheath Boxcar "70820," 23	80	___
2442162	B&M Single-sheath Boxcar "70919," 23	80	___
2442171	D&H Single-sheath Boxcar "17187," 23	80	___
2442172	D&H Single-sheath Boxcar "17246," 23	80	___
2442181	NP Single-sheath Boxcar "28544," 23	80	___
2442182	NP Single-sheath Boxcar "28531," 23	80	___
2442191	Wellsville, Addison & Galeton Single-sheath Boxcar "5031," 23	80	___
2442192	Wellsville, Addison & Galeton Single-sheath Boxcar "5053," 23	80	___
2442201	Budweiser Wood-sided Refrigerator Car "3601," 24-25	100	___
2442202	Budweiser Wood-sided Refrigerator Car "3605," 24-25	100	___
2442211	A&P Wood-sided Refrigerator Car "12000," 24	80	___
2442212	A&P Wood-sided Refrigerator Car "12021," 24	80	___
2442221	Meyer Kornblum Wood-sided Refrigerator Car "241," 24-25	80	___
2442222	Meyer Kornblum Wood-sided Refrigerator Car "244," 24-25	80	___
2442231	PFE/WP Wood-sided Refrigerator Car "55001," 24-25	80	___
2442232	PFE/WP Wood-sided Refrigerator Car "55759," 24	80	___
2442241	Swift's Premium Wood-sided Refrigerator Car "6001," 24-25	80	___
2442242	Swift's Premium Wood-sided Refrigerator Car "6039," 24-25	80	___
2442250	UP WWII PS1 Boxcar Art 3-pack, 7, 24-25	250	___
2442261	BAR Steel-sided Boxcar "65220," 24	80	___
2442262	BAR Steel-sided Boxcar "65500," 24-25	80	___
2442271	Central of Georgia Steel-sided Boxcar "4095," 24-25	80	___
2442272	Central of Georgia Steel-sided Boxcar "4112," 24-25	80	___
2442281	NS Steel-sided Boxcar "25439," 24-25	80	___
2442282	NS Steel-sided Boxcar "28077," 24-25	80	___
2442291	SOO Steel-sided Boxcar "42204," 24-25	80	___
2442292	SOO Steel-sided Boxcar "42430," 24-25	80	___
2442300	C&O 2-Bay AAR Hopper 3-pack, 1, 24	240	___
2442305	C&O 2-Bay AAR Hopper 3-pack, 2, 24	240	___
2442309	C&O 2-Bay AAR Hopper "49623," 24-25	80	___

		Exc	Mint
____ **2442310**	Erie 2-Bay AAR Hopper 3-pack, 1, 24		240
____ **2442315**	Erie 2-Bay AAR Hopper 3-pack, 2, 24		240
____ **2442319**	Erie 2-Bay AAR Hopper "24133," 24-25		80
____ **2433032**	UP EMD SD70ACe Diesel "8620," CC, 23		700
____ **2442320**	NPR 2-Bay AAR Hopper 3-pack, 1, 24		240
____ **2442325**	NPR 2-Bay AAR Hopper 3-pack, 2, 24		240
____ **2442329**	NKP 2-Bay AAR Hopper "33737," 24-25		80
____ **2442330**	MILW 2-Bay AAR Hopper 3-pack, 1, 24		240
____ **2442335**	MILW 2-Bay AAR Hopper 3-pack, 2, 24		240
____ **2442339**	MILW 2-Bay AAR Hopper "96885," 24		80
____ **2442340**	ADM 50-foot 1-D Tank Car 3-pack, 24		260
____ **2442349**	ADM 50-foot 1-D Tank Car "29481," 24		90
____ **2442350**	BNSF 50-foot 1-D Tank Car 3-pack, 24		260
____ **2442359**	BNSF 50-foot 1-D Tank Car "880302," 24		90
____ **2442360**	Cargill Foods 50-foot 1-D Tank Car 3-pack, 24		260
____ **2442369**	Cargill Foods 50-foot 1-D Tank Car "7852," 24		90
____ **2442370**	GATX 50-foot 1-D Tank Car 3-pack, 24		260
____ **2442379**	GATX 50-foot 1-D Tank Car "209792," 24		90
____ **2443001**	BN DD Boxcar "243832" (std 0), 23		70
____ **2443002**	BN DD Boxcar "243859" (std 0), 23		70
____ **2443011**	SP DD Boxcar "248401" (std 0), 23		70
____ **2443012**	SP DD Boxcar "248515" (std 0), 23		70
____ **2443021**	UP DD Boxcar "38508" (std 0), 23		70
____ **2443022**	UP DD Boxcar "38515" (std 0), 23		70
____ **2445010**	LL 2-4-2 Columbia Locomotive "242," LionChief, 24-25		250
____ **2445020**	ELX 2-4-2 Columbia Locomotive "800," LionChief, 24-25		250
____ **2445030**	CB&Q 2-4-2 Columbia Locomotive "3007," LionChief, 24-25		250
____ **2445040**	NYC 2-4-2 Columbia Locomotive "1939," LionChief, 24-25		250
____ **2445050**	Sleigh Bell Limited 2-4-2 Columbia Locomotive "2424," LionChief, 24-25		250
____ **2445060**	ATSF 2-6-2 Prairie Locomotive "1819," LionChief, 24-25		330
____ **2445070**	PRR 2-6-2 Prairie Locomotive "531," LionChief, 24-25		330
____ **2445080**	U.S. Army 2-6-2 Prairie Locomotive "75," LionChief, 24-25		330
____ **2445090**	Winter Wonderland 2-6-2 Prairie Locomotive "2424," LionChief, 24-25		330
____ **2445100**	Justice League The Flash EMD FT Diesel "1940," LionChief, 24-25		300
____ **2445110**	UP EMD FT Diesel "1468," LionChief, 24-25		300
____ **2445120**	PRR EMD FT Diesel "9656," LionChief, 24-25		300
____ **2445130**	LL EMD FT Diesel "1900," LionChief, 24-25		300
____ **2445140**	Halloween EMD FT Diesel "3124," LionChief, 24-25		300
____ **2445150**	Justice League Batman GE ET44 Diesel "Dark Knight," LionChief, 24-25		300
____ **2445160**	CSX GE ET44 Diesel "3398," LionChief, 24-25		300
____ **2445170**	BNSF GE ET44 Diesel "3970," LionChief, 24-25		300
____ **2445180**	U.S. Army GE ET44 Diesel "1775," LionChief, 24-25		300
____ **2445190**	NPC Snowflake Limited GE ET44 Diesel "240," LionChief, 24-25		300
____ **2522010**	Pennsylvania GG1 Freight Set, CC, 24-25		2600
____ **2522020**	Pennsylvania Postwar-Inspired No. 2124W Madison Set, CC, 24-25		2400
____ **2522030**	LL Hudson Prewar Freight Set, CC, 25		2400
____ **2522040**	NH Minuteman Steam Freight Set, CC, 24-25		2000
____ **2522050**	N&W King Coal Steam Freight Set, CC, 24-25		3000

Item	Description	Exc	Mint
2522060	NYC Twentieth Century Limited Steam Passenger Set, CC, 25		3600
2522070	FEC Diesel Auto Rack Freight Set, CC, 25		1400
2522080	DL&W Postwar-Inspired Train Master Diesel Freight Set, CC, 25		1200
2522090	SP Donner Pass SD40T-2 Diesel Freight Set, CC, 25		1100
2522100	North Pole Toy Works Heisler Steam Freight Set, CC, 25		2000
2523010	Area 51 UFO Recovery Diesel Freight Set, LionChief, 24-25		450
2523020	CPKC ET44 Maxi Stack Diesel Freight Set, LionChief, 24-25		380
2523030	Star Wars Empire RS-3 Diesel Freight Set, LionChief, 25		500
2523040	Star Wars Rebel RS-3 Diesel Freight Set, LionChief, 25		500
2523060	Lionel 125 Anniversary No. 2133W NYC F3 Freight Set, LionChief, 25		1200
2523070	Lionel 125 Anniversary No. 1430WS Prairie Steam Passenger Set, LionChief, 25		550
2523110	US Navy RS-3 Diesel Freight Set, LionChief, 25		400
2523120	Peppermint RR 0-8-0 Christmas Steam Freight Set, LionChief, 25		400
2523130	PRR Keystone 0-8-0 Steam Freight Set, LionChief, 25		400
2523140	Harry Potter Hogwarts Express 4-6-0 Steam Passenger Set, LionChief, 25		500
2526010	Conrail N5 Cabin Car "30008," 24-25		125
2526020	LIRR N5 Cabin Car "1," 24-25		125
2526030	PC N5 Cabin Car "19012," 24-25		125
2526040	PRR N5 Cabin Car "5015," 24-25		125
2526050	PRR N5 Cabin Car "477635," 24-25		125
2526060	Pennsylvania Reading Seashore Lines N5 Cabin Car "2356," 24-25		125
2526070	LIRR Vision N5 Cabin Car "3,"24-25		300
2526080	PRR Vision N5 Cabin Car "477764," 24-25		300
2526090	PRR Vision N5 Cabin Car "477727," 24-25		300
2526100	PC Vision N5 Cabin Car "22885," 24-25		300
2526111	PRR X31 Boxcar "81151" (circle keystone), 24-25		100
2526112	PRR X31 Boxcar "81169" (circle keystone), 24-25		100
2526121	PRR X31 Boxcar "60556" (auto/circle keystone), 24-25		100
2526122	PRR X31 Boxcar "60595" (auto/circle keystone), 24-25		100
2526131	PRR X31 Boxcar "69287" (shadow keystone), 24-25		100
2526132	PRR X31 Boxcar "69371" (shadow keystone), 24-25		100
2526141	PRR X31 Boxcar "69287" (shadow keystone)e Boxcar "69070", 24-25		100
2526142	PRR X31 Merchandise Boxcar "69142," 24-25		100
2526151	PC X31B Boxcar "140006," 24-25		100
2526152	PC X31B Boxcar "140008," 24-25		100
2526161	SAL X31 Boxcar "11041," 24-25		100
2526162	SAL X31 Boxcar "11790," 24-25		100
2526170	Area 51 Heavy Duty Flatcar "XP09D," 24-25		170
2526180	AEC Heavy Duty Flatcar "1948," 24-25		170
2526190	Bethlehem Steel Heavy Duty Flatcar "6190," 24-25		170
2526200	DODX Heavy Duty Flatcar "39474," 24-25		170
2526210	TTX Heavy Duty Flatcar "131003," 24-25		170
2526220	Westinghouse Heavy Duty Flatcar "7100," 24-25		170
2526230	Area 51 8,000-gallon 1-D Tank Car "XTCR4B," 24-25		140
2526240	AEC 8,000-gallon 1-D Tank Car "1956," 24-25		130

			Exc	Mint
___	**2526250**	MEC 8,000-gallon 1-D Tank Car "710", 24-25		100
___	**2526260**	US Army 8,000-gallon 1-D Tank Car "10940", 24-25		100
___	**2526270**	Alaska RR 8,000-gallon 1-D Tank Car "9014", 24-25		100
___	**2526280**	Halloween 8,000-gallon 1-D Tank Car "311025", 24-25		130
___	**2526290**	O'Leary Dairies Hotbox Refrigerator Car "101871", 24-25		300
___	**2526300**	REA Hotbox Refrigerator Car "6360", 24-25		300
___	**2526310**	ACL Hotbox Refrigerator Car "3049", 24-25		300
___	**2526320**	GN Hotbox Refrigerator Car "2240", 24-25		300
___	**2526330**	IC Hotbox Refrigerator Car "51000", 24-25		300
___	**2526340**	Area 51 Hotbox Refrigerator Car, 24-25		300
___	**2526350**	US Army Flatcar "39500" w/Trailers, 24-25		160
___	**2526360**	US Army Flatcar "39514" w/Trailers, 24-25		160
___	**2526370**	CNW Flatcar "44017" w/Trailers, 24-25		160
___	**2526380**	PE Flatcar "563200" w/Trailers, 24-25		160
___	**2526390**	Alaska RR Flatcar "12706" w/Trailers, 24-25		160
___	**2526400**	Frightliner US Army Flatcar "103125" w/Trailers, 24-25		160
___	**2526410**	ATSF Vision Auto Rack "978106", 25		350
___	**2526420**	C&NW Vision Auto Rack "983715", 25		350
___	**2526430**	Conrail Vision Auto Rack "158739", 25		350
___	**2526440**	GTW Vision Auto Rack "964524", 25		350
___	**2526450**	SP Vision Auto Rack "977017", 25		350
___	**2526460**	UP Vision Auto Rack "603597", 25		350
___	**2526470**	D&RGW Auto Rack "256004", 25		160
___	**2526480**	KCS Auto Rack "705075", 25		160
___	**2526490**	L&N Auto Rack "911441", 25		160
___	**2526500**	MILW Auto Rack "910652", 25		160
___	**2526510**	NS Auto Rack "255939", 25		160
___	**2526520**	N&W Auto Rack "156382", 25		160
___	**2526530**	CNJ PS-5 Gondola "89220", 25		120
___	**2526540**	GB&W PS-5 Gondola "33", 25		120
___	**2526550**	LV PS-5 Gondola "33185", 25		120
___	**2526560**	Wabash PS-5 Gondola "11615", 25		120
___	**2526570**	AEC PS-5 Gondola "1951" w/Canisters, 25		130
___	**2526580**	Polar Express PS-5 Gondola "122525" w/Canisters, 25		130
___	**2526590**	Acme Disconnect Rocket Cars, 25		100
___	**2526600**	USA Disconnect Rocket Load, 25		100
___	**2526610**	Halloween Disconnect Candy Dump Cars, 25		180
___	**2526620**	Halloween Disconnect, 4-pack, 25		190
___	**2526630**	Christmas Disconnect Candy Dump Cars, 25		180
___	**2526640**	Christmas Disconnect, 4-pack, 25		190
___	**2526650**	C&EI PS-1 Boxcar "16565" w/FreightSounds, 25		220
___	**2526660**	D&RGW PS-1 Boxcar "67864" w/FreightSounds, 25		220
___	**2526670**	MEC PS-1 Boxcar "8417" w/FreightSounds, 25		220
___	**2526690**	2025 Christmas PS-1 Boxcar, 25		110
___	**2526700**	Lionel 125 Anniverary PS-1 Boxcar, 25		110
___	**2526710**	Chessie BW Caboose "903747", 25		150
___	**2526720**	Susquehanna BW Caboose "0121", 25		150
___	**2526730**	SP Police BW Caboose "4726", 25		150
___	**2526750**	Disconnect Green Caboose "50", 25		50
___	**2526760**	USA Disconnect Caboose "76", 25		50
___	**2526790**	Halloween Disconnect Caboose "13", 25		50
___	**2526800**	Christmas Disconnect Caboose "24", 25		50
___	**2526810**	USA Disconnect Car, 4-pack, 25		190

MODERN 1970-2025		Exc	Mint	
2527010	American Railroads B60 Baggage Car, 3-pack, 24-25		900	___
2527020	American Railroads 21" Passenger Car, 4-pack, 24-25		1000	___
2527030	American Railroads 21" Passenger Car, 2-pack, 24-25		500	___
2527040	American Railroads 21" Twin-Unit Diner w/StationSounds, 24-25		700	___
2527050	PRR Spirit of St. Louis 21" Passenger Car, 4-pack, 24-25		1000	___
2527060	PRR Spirit of St. Louis 21" Passenger Car, 2-pack, 24-25		500	___
2527070	PRR Spirit of St. Louis 21" Twin-Unit Diner w/StationSounds, 24-25		700	___
2527080	PRR Congressional 18" Aluminum Passenger Car, 4-pack, 24-25		1300	___
2527090	PRR Senator 18" Aluminum Passenger Car, 4-pack, 24-25		1300	___
2527100	PRR Congressional 18" Aluminum Passenger Car, 2-pack, 24-25		600	___
2527110	PRR Congressional 18" Aluminum Diner w/StationSounds, 24-25		500	___
2527120	PRR 18" Senator Aluminum Diner w/StationSounds, 24-25		600	___
2527130	PC Congressional 18" Aluminum Passenger Car, 4-pack, 24-25		1300	___
2527140	PC Congressional 18" Aluminum Passenger Car, 2-pack, 24-25		600	___
2527150	PC Congressional 18" Aluminum Diner w/StationSounds, 24-25		500	___
2527160	Amtrak Phase I 18" Aluminum Passenger Car, 4-pack, 24-25			___
2527170	Amtrak Phase I 18" Aluminum Passenger Car, 2-pack, 24-25		600	___
2527180	Amtrak Phase I 18" Aluminum Diner w/StationSounds, 24-25			___
2527190	LL 18" Aluminum Passenger Car, 4-pack, 24-25		1300	___
2527200	LL 18" Aluminum Passenger Car, 2-pack, 24-25		600	___
2527210	LL 18" Aluminum Diner w/StationSounds, 24-25		500	___
2527220	PRR B60 Baggage Car "7926", 24-25		300	___
2527230	PRR B60 Baggage Car "7955", 24-25		300	___
2527240	PRR B60 Baggage Car "9021", 24-25		300	___
2527250	PC B60 Baggage Car "7518", 24-25		300	___
2527260	PC B60 Baggage Car "28197", 24-25		300	___
2527270	LL Vision Baggage Car "Santa Clara", 24-25		500	___
2527280	LL Diner "Chesterfield" w/StationSounds, 24-25		500	___
2527290	LL Observation "Concord", 24-25		300	___
2527300	PRR Vision B60 Baggage Car "9369", 24-25		500	___
2527310	PRR Vision B60 Baggage Car "9328", 24-25		500	___
2527320	REA Vision B60 Baggage Car "1651", 24-25		500	___
2527330	PC Vision B60 Baggage Car "7628", 24-25		500	___
2527340	Amtrak Phase II Power Car "695", 24-25		400	___
2527350	Amtrak Phase I Rainbow 21" Passenger Car, 4-pack, 24-25		1000	___
2527360	Amtrak Phase I Rainbow 21" Passenger Car, 2-pack, 24-25		500	___
2527370	Amtrak Phase I Diner "8017" w/StationSounds, 24-25		480	___
2527380	PRR Senator 18" Aluminum Passenger Car, 2-pack, 24-25		500	___
2527390	PRR Senator 18" Shadowline Passenger Car, 2-pack, 24-25		550	___
2527460	Halloween Doom Liner 21" Passenger Car, 4-pack, 24-25		1000	___
2527470	Halloween Doom Liner 21" Passenger Car, 2-pack, 24-25		500	___
2527480	Halloween Doom Liner 21" Doom Car w/StationSounds, 24-25		500	___
2527490	NKP 21" Passenger Car, 4-pack, 24-25		1000	___
2527500	NKP 21" Passenger Car, 2-pack, 24-25		500	___
2527510	NKP 21" Diner w/StationSounds, 24-25		480	___
2527520	NYC 20th Century Limited 18" Passenger Car, 2-pack, 25		600	___

	MODERN 1970-2025		Exc	Mint
___	2527530	"Dover Cliffs" Green Pullman Car w/SleeperSounds, 25		500
___	2527540	"Dover Hill" Gray Pullman Car w/SleeperSounds, 25		500
___	2527550	"Minute Men" Pullman Car w/SleeperSounds, 25		500
___	2527560	NYC Niagara Falls Passenger Car, 2-pack, A, 25		600
___	2527570	NYC Niagara Falls Passenger Car, 2-pack, B, 25		600
___	2527580	NYC Niagara Falls Passenger Car, 2-pack, C, 25		600
___	2527590	Pullman 20th Century Limited 18" Passenger Car Add-on, 1, 25		600
___	2527600	Pullman 20th Century Limited 18" Passenger Car Add-on, 2, 25		600
___	2527610	NYC Diner "452" w/StationSounds, 25		500
___	2527620	NYC Lines Diner "146" w/StationSounds, 25		500
___	2527630	LL Postwar-Inspired 21" Passenger Car, 4-pack, 25		1000
___	2527640	LL Prewar-Inspired Blue Passenger Car, 4-pack, 25		1100
___	2527650	LL Prewar-Inspired Red Passenger Car, 4-pack, 25		1100
___	2527660	LL 15" Aluminum Passenger Car, 4-pack, 25		1100
___	2527670	LL 15" Aluminum Diner w/StationSounds, 25		400
___	2527680	ATSF 15" Aluminum Passenger Car, 4-pack, 25		1100
___	2527690	ATSF 15" Aluminum Diner w/StationSounds, 25		400
___	2527700	FEC 15" Aluminum Passenger Car, 4-pack, 25		1100
___	2527710	FEC 15" Aluminum Diner w/StationSounds, 25		400
___	2527720	Reading 15" Aluminum Passenger Car, 4-pack, 25		1100
___	2527730	Reading 15" Aluminum Diner w/StationSounds, 25		400
___	2527740	SP 15" Aluminum Passenger Car, 4-pack, 25		1100
___	2527750	SP 15" Aluminum Diner w/StationSounds, 25		400
___	2528010	Beetlejuice Illuminated Boxcar, 24-25		150
___	2528020	Beetlejuice Boxcar, 24-25		100
___	2528030	CPKC Maxi Stack Add-on, 24-25		100
___	2528040	Area 51 Flatcar w/Helicopter Add-on, 24-25		90
___	2528050	Thomas and Friends 80th Anniversary Boxcar, 25		100
___	2528060	Area 51 Maxi Stack, 24-25		100
___	2528070	Harry Potter and the Goblet of Fire Movie Boxcar, 25		100
___	2528080	Harry Potter and the Order of the Phoenix Movie Boxcar, 25		100
___	2528100	2025 Christmas Boxcar, 25		90
___	2528110	Nightmare Before Christmas Lock, Shock & Barrel Chasing Gondola, 25		130
___	2528140	DC 90th Anniversary Superman Boxcar, 25		100
___	2528150	DC 90th Anniversary Batman Boxcar, 25		100
___	2528160	DC 90th Anniversary Wonder Woman Boxcar, 25		100
___	2528170	Thomas Kinkade Studios Superman Boxcar, 25		100
___	2528180	Thomas Kinkade Studios DC "The Trinity I" Boxcar, 25		100
___	2528190	Star Wars X-Wing/Tie Fighter Aquarium Car, 25		140
___	2528200	2025 Christmas Boxcar w/Sounds, 25		120
___	2528220	Star Wars Character Boxcar - Luke Skywalker, 25		110
___	2528230	Star Wars Character Boxcar - R2D2 and C3PO, 25		110
___	2528240	Star Wars Character Boxcar - Darth Vader, 25		110
___	2528250	Star Wars Character Boxcar - Storm Troopers, 25		110
___	2528260	Star Wars Light Saber Series Illuminated Boxcar - Darth Vader v. Obi-Wan Kenobi, 25		150
___	2528270	Star Wars Light Saber Series Illuminated Boxcar - Kylo Ren v. Rey, 25		150
___	2528280	Star Wars Light Saber Series Illuminated Boxcar - Darth Maul v. Qui-Gon Jin, 25		150
___	2528290	Star Wars The Mandalorian Grogu Christmas Boxcar, 25		100

MODERN 1970-2025		Exc	Mint
2528300	Star Wars Christmas Boxcar, 25		100 ___
2528310	Star Wars Rebel Chasing Gondola - Droids, 25		130 ___
2528320	Star Wars Empire Chasing Gondola - Storm Troopers, 25		130 ___
2528330	Disney Frozen Boxcar, 25		100 ___
2528340	Batman Classic TV Illuminated Boxcar, 25		150 ___
2528360	Budweiser Bar Sign Illuminated Boxcar, 2, 25		150 ___
2528370	Ford Maxi Stack "28370", 25		100 ___
2528380	Chevrolet Maxi Stack "28380", 25		100 ___
2528390	Butterbeer Refrigerator Car, 25		100 ___
2528400	Butterbeer 1-D Tank Car, 25		110 ___
2528410	Thomas Kinkade Studios -Disney Mickey & Minnie Evening Sleigh Ride Boxcar, 25		100 ___
2528420	Thomas Kinkade Studios -Disney Mickey's Victorian Christmas Boxcar, 25		100 ___
2528430	Thomas Kinkade Studios -Disney Mickey & Minnie in Florida Boxcar, 25		100 ___
2528440	Bob Ross Happy Trees Gondola, 25		90 ___
2528450	Bob Ross Happy Tree Farm Refrigerator Car, 25		100 ___
2528460	Barbie 1980s Boxcar, 25		100 ___
2528470	Barbie 1990s Boxcar, 25		100 ___
2528480	Disney Mickey & Friends Lonesome Ghosts Boxcar, 25		110 ___
2528490	Disney The Nightmare Before Christmas Halloween Boxcar, 25		110 ___
2528500	Disney Stitch Halloween Boxcar, 25		110 ___
2528510	Lionel 125 Anniversary Boxcar, 25		100 ___
2528520	Tom and Jerry Chasing Gondola, 25		130 ___
2528530	Tom and Jerry Illuminated Cartoon Boxcar, 25		150 ___
2528540	Thomas Kinkade Studios - Harry Potter Hogwarts Express Boxcar, 25		100 ___
2528550	Thomas Kinkade Studios - Harry Potter Great Hall Boxcar, 25		100 ___
2528560	Harry Potter Hogsmeade Flatcar w/Trailers, 25		120 ___
2528570	Acme Dynamite 1-D Tank Car, 25		100 ___
2528580	Surfing Stitch Boxcar, 25		140 ___
2528590	Nightmare Before Christmas Zero Aquarium Car, 25		140 ___
2528600	Mister Rogers' Neighborhood of Make-Believe Character Boxcar, 25		100 ___
2528610	Mr. McFeely Mail Car, 25		130 ___
2528620	Anheuser Busch Refrigerator Car, 25		100 ___
2528630	John Deere Waterloo Boy Refrigerator Car, 25		100 ___
2528640	John Deere Quality Equipment Refrigerator Car, 25		100 ___
2528650	Lionel 125 Anniversary Flatcar w/Trailers, 25		120 ___
2528660	Lionel Kiddie City Flatcar "1960" w/Trailers, 25		120 ___
2528670	Liberty Eagle Rail Flatcar "1776" w/Trailers, 25		120 ___
2528680	Winter Wonderland Flatcar w/Trailers, 25		120 ___
2528690	US Navy Flatcar "28690" w/Trailers, 25		120 ___
2528700	Whispering Rails Flatcar "1800" w/Trailers, 25		120 ___
2528710	Area 51 Take Me To Your Leader Alien Flatcar, 25		80 ___
2528720	Surfing Santa Boxcar, 25		140 ___
2528730	Disney Stitch Christmas Boxcar, 25		100 ___
2528740	Sled-Ex Boxcar, 25		90 ___
2528750	Christmas Gondola w/Trees and Presents, 25		110 ___
2528760	Special Christmas Delivery Mint Car, 25		110 ___
2528770	Haunted Hollow Wings of Raven Boxcar "02531", 25		80 ___
2528780	Haunted Hollow Tonic Water Tank Car "103125", 25		80 ___

		Exc	Mint
____ 2528790	Haunted Hollow Hearts Brand Stock Car "253110", 25		80
____ 2528800	Peanuts "It's the Great Pumpkin Charlie Brown" Illuminated TV Boxcar, 25		150
____ 2528810	Peanuts "A Charlie Brown Christmas Aquarium Car, 25		140
____ 2528820	Mattel Uno Boxcar, 25		100
____ 2528840	Rock 'Em Sock 'Em Robots Chasing Gondola, 25		130
____ 2528850	North Pole Central Track Cleaning Car, 25		180
____ 2528860	Area 51 Track Cleaning Car, 25		180
____ 2528870	PRR Track Cleaning Car, 25		180
____ 2528880	Bert's Sweepover Track Cleaning Car, 25		180
____ 2528890	Star Wars Halloween Boxcar, 25		110
____ 2529010	LL No. 282R Gantry Crane, CC, 25		450
____ 2529020	US Navy Gantry Crane, CC, 25		450
____ 2529030	UP No. 18062 Gantry Crane, CC, 25		450
____ 2529050	Area 51 Tank Car Accident, 24-25		230
____ 2529060	Caboose Stand Accessory, 24-25		220
____ 2529070	FasTrack Grade Crossing w/Gates and Flashers, updated, 24-25		200
____ 2529080	Bob Ross Covered Bridge, 25		85
____ 2529090	Lionel 125 Anniversary Illuminated Station Platform, 25		55
____ 2529100	Halloween Illuminated Station Platform, 25		55
____ 2529110	America/World War II Illuminated Station Platform, 25		55
____ 2529130	Ford Elevated Tank, 25		100
____ 2529140	Chevrolet Elevated Tank, 25		100
____ 2529150	DC Comics Lexcorp Kryptonite Elevated Tank, 25		100
____ 2529160	Butterbeer Tank, 25		100
____ 2529170	Acme Tunnel Paint Tank, 25		100
____ 2529180	Plug-Expand-Play Anheuser Busch Concession Stand, 25		160
____ 2529190	Christmas Trailer Home, 25		120
____ 2529200	Halloween Trailer Home, 25		120
____ 2529210	Beach Trailer Home, 25		100
____ 2529220	Patriotic Trailer Home, 25		100
____ 2529230	Plug-Expand-Play AEC Glow-in-the-Dark Elevated Tank, 25		100
____ 2529240	Work House w/Sounds, 25		150
____ 2529260	Fake News Stand, 2, 25		160
____ 2530010	Area 51 Figures, 24-25		30
____ 2530020	Two-bay Hopper Coal Load, 6-pack, 24-25		24
____ 2530030	Three-bay Hopper Coal Load, 6-pack, 24-25		24
____ 2530040	Four-bay Hopper Coal Load, 6-pack, 24-25		24
____ 2530050	Lionel 125 Anniversary Billboard Pack, 25		30
____ 2530060	Butterbeer Scented Smoke Fluid, 25		10
____ 2531011	N&W Y6B 2-8-8-2 Locomotive "2174," CC, 24-25		2000
____ 2531012	N&W Y6B 2-8-8-2 Locomotive "2194," CC, 24-25		2000
____ 2531020	NYC Vision 4-6-4 Hudson Locomotive "5325," CC, 25u		1800
____ 2531021	N&W Y6B 2-8-8-2 Locomotive "2188," CC, 24-25		2000
____ 2531022	N&W Y6B 2-8-8-2 Locomotive "2197," CC, 24-25		2000
____ 2531030	PRR Y6B 2-8-8-2 Locomotive "380," CC, 24-25		2000
____ 2531040	ATSF Y6B 2-8-8-2 Locomotive "1800," CC, 24-25		2000
____ 2531050	GN Y6B 2-8-8-2 Locomotive "2060," CC, 24-25		2000
____ 2531060	UP Y6B 2-8-8-2 Locomotive "3675," CC, 24-25		2000
____ 2531070	CNJ USRA 2-8-2 Heavy Mikado Locomotive "859," CC, 24-25		1400
____ 2531080	EJ&E USRA 2-8-2 Heavy Mikado Locomotive "738," CC, 24-25		1400

		Exc	Mint
2531090	GN USRA 2-8-2 Heavy Mikado Locomotive "3208," CC, 24-25		1400
2531100	L&N USRA 2-8-2 Heavy Mikado Locomotive "1776," CC, 24-25		1400
2531110	P&LE USRA 2-8-2 Heavy Mikado Locomotive "9510," CC, 24-25		1400
2531120	SOO USRA 2-8-2 Heavy Mikado Locomotive "1003," CC, 24-25		1400
2531125	Gold-Plated Lionel 125 Anniversary Vision 4-6-4 Hudson Locomotive, CC, 25		2000
2531130	ACL 0-6-0 Locomotive "1140," CC, 24-25		900
2531140	B&O 0-6-0 Locomotive "353," CC, 24-25		900
2531150	C&NW 0-6-0 Locomotive "2624," CC, 24-25		900
2531160	GTW 0-6-0 Locomotive "7527," CC, 24-25		900
2531170	NKP 0-6-0 Locomotive "384," CC, 24-25		900
2531180	UP 0-6-0 Locomotive "4603," CC, 24-25		900
2531190	Alaska RR 4-8-2 Mountain Locomotive "801," CC, 24-25		1600
2531200	ATSF 4-8-2 Mountain Locomotive "3706," CC, 24-25		1600
2531210	SAL 4-8-2 Mountain Locomotive "200," CC, 24-25		1600
2531220	NC&StL 4-8-2 Mountain Locomotive "561," CC, 24-25		1600
2531230	NH 4-8-2 Mountain Locomotive "3324," CC, 24-25		1600
2531240	Southern 4-8-2 Mountain Locomotive "1490," CC, 24-25		1600
2531250	Tennessee Central 4-8-2 Mountain Locomotive "551," CC, 24-25		1600
2531260	T&P 4-8-2 Mountain Locomotive "907," CC, 24-25		1600
2531270	NYC Vision 4-6-4 Hudson Locomotive "5344," CC, 25		1800
2531280	NYC Vision 4-6-4 Hudson Locomotive "5403," CC, 25		1800
2531290	NYC Vision 4-6-4 Hudson Locomotive "5320," CC, 25		1800
2531300	NYC Vision 4-6-4 Hudson Locomotive "6620," CC, 25		1800
2531310	NYC Vision 4-6-4 Hudson Locomotive "5401," CC, w/Water Scoop Tender, 25		1900
2531320	NYC Vision 4-6-4 Hudson Locomotive "5315," CC, 25		1800
2531330	NYC Vision 4-6-4 Hudson Locomotive "5330," CC, w/Water Scoop Tender, 25		1900
2531340	NYC Vision 4-6-4 Hudson Locomotive "5340," CC, 25		1800
2531350	TH&B Vision 4-6-4 Hudson Locomotive "502," CC, 25		1800
2531360	NYC Vision Commodore Vanderbilt 4-6-4 Hudson Locomotive w/Spoked Drivers, CC, 25		1780
2531370	NYC Vision Commodore Vanderbilt 4-6-4 Hudson Locomotive w/Disc Drivers, CC, 25		1780
2531380	LL Blue Vision Commodore Vanderbilt 4-6-4 Hudson Locomotive "265E," CC, 25		1800
2531390	LL Red Vision Commodore Vanderbilt 4-6-4 Hudson Locomotive "265E," CC, 25		1800
2531400	Loco of the Year Vision Commodore Vanderbilt 4-6-4 Hudson, CC, 25		1800
2531410	Polar Express Vision 4-6-4 Hudson Locomotive, CC, 25		1800
2531420	North Pole Central Vision Saint Nicholas 4-6-4 Hudson Locomotive, CC, 25		1800
2531430	Halloween Vision Flying Dutchman Streamlined 4-6-4 Hudson Locomotive, CC, 25		1800
2531440	PRR Legacy S2 6-8-6 Turbine Locomotive "6200," as built, CC, 25		1400
2531450	PRR Legacy S2 6-8-6 Turbine Locomotive "6200" w/Smoke Lifters, CC, 25		1400
2531460	PRR Legacy S2 6-8-6 Turbine Locomotive "6200," Loewy-inspired Scheme, CC, 25		1400

		Exc	Mint
___ **2531470**	PRR Legacy S2 6-8-6 Turbine Locomotive "6200," Tuscan, CC, 25		1400
___ **2531480**	PRR Legacy S2 6-8-6 Turbine Locomotive "671," CC, 25		1400
___ **2531490**	C&O Legacy S2 6-8-6 Turbine Locomotive "501," CC, 25		1400
___ **2531500**	SP Daylight Legacy S2 6-8-6 Turbine Locomotive "800," CC, 25		1400
___ **2531510**	Baldwin Locomotive Works Legacy S2 6-8-6 Turbine Locomotive "6200," CC, 25		1400
___ **2531520**	Blue Jay Lumber Legacy Heisler Locomotive "10," CC, 25		1700
___ **2531530**	Clearwater Timber Legacy Heisler Locomotive "91," CC, 25		1700
___ **2531540**	Juniata RR Legacy Heisler Locomotive "22," CC, 25		1700
___ **2531550**	Middle Fork RR Legacy Heisler Locomotive "7," CC, 25		1700
___ **2531560**	Weyerhaeuser Legacy Heisler Locomotive "4," CC, 25		1700
___ **2531570**	Ann Arbor Legacy A6 4-4-2 Atlantic Locomotive "1611," CC, 25		1000
___ **2531580**	ATSF Legacy A6 4-4-2 Atlantic Locomotive "1468," CC, 25		1000
___ **2531590**	C&O Legacy A6 4-4-2 Atlantic Locomotive "284," CC, 25		1000
___ **2531600**	Chicago & Alton Legacy A6 4-4-2 Atlantic Locomotive "554," CC, 25		1000
___ **2531610**	CB&Q Legacy A6 4-4-2 Atlantic Locomotive "2565," CC, 25		1000
___ **2531620**	Erie Legacy A6 4-4-2 Atlantic Locomotive "537," CC, 25		1000
___ **2531630**	LL Legacy 2-4-2 Scout Locomotive "1684," CC, 25		1000
___ **2531650**	US Signal Corps Legacy Heisler Locomotive "2," CC, 25		1700
___ **2532010**	NYC Lionmaster J3a 4-6-4 Hudson Locomotive "5249," CC, 24-25		800
___ **2532020**	NYC Lionmaster J3a 4-6-4 Hudson Locomotive "6001," CC, 24-25		800
___ **2532030**	NYC Lionmaster Pacemaker J3a 4-6-4 Hudson Locomotive "1946," CC, 24-25		800
___ **2532040**	Whispering Rails Halloween J3a 4-6-4 Hudson Locomotive "13," LionChief Plus 2.0, 24-25		800
___ **2532050**	LL Lionmaster J3a 4-6-4 Hudson Locomotive "1900," CC, 24-25		800
___ **2532060**	Angela Trotta Thomas 4-6-2 Pacific Locomotive "1900," LionChief Plus 2.0, 25		700
___ **2532070**	B&O 4-6-2 Pacific Locomotive "President Monroe," LionChief Plus 2.0, 25		700
___ **2532080**	Reading 4-6-2 Pacific Locomotive "119," LionChief Plus 2.0, 25		700
___ **2532090**	T&P 4-6-2 Pacific Locomotive "711," LionChief Plus 2.0, 25		700
___ **2532100**	WP 4-6-2 Pacific Locomotive "100," LionChief Plus 2.0, 25		700
___ **2533010**	American Railroads Vision GG1 "4902," CC, 24-25		1700
___ **2533020**	Amtrak Phase I Vision GG1 "921," CC, 24-25		1700
___ **2533030**	Amtrak Phase I Vision GG1 "929," CC, 24-25		1700
___ **2533040**	Conrail Vision GG1 "4800," CC, 24-25		1700
___ **2533050**	PC Vision GG1 "4906," CC, 24-25		1700
___ **2533060**	PC Vision GG1 "4908," CC, 24-25		1700
___ **2533070**	PRR Vision GG1 "4800," CC, 24-25		1700
___ **2533080**	PRR Vision GG1 "4829," CC, 24-25		1700
___ **2533090**	PRR Vision GG1 "4859," CC, 24-25		1700
___ **2533100**	PRR Vision GG1 "4866," CC, 24-25		1700
___ **2533110**	PRR Vision GG1 "4877," CC, 24-25		1700
___ **2533121**	NS Heritage PC EMD SD70ACe Diesel "1073," CC, 24-25		700
___ **2533129**	NS Heritage PC EMD SD70ACe Diesel "1073," non-powered, 24-25		350
___ **2533131**	NS Heritage Reading EMD SD70ACe Diesel "1067," CC, 24-25		700

		Exc	Mint	
2533139	NS Heritage Reading EMD SD70ACe Diesel "1067," non-powered, 24-25		350	___
2533141	NS Heritage Savannah & Atlanta EMD SD70ACe Diesel "1065," CC, 24-25		700	___
2533149	NS Heritage Savannah & Atlanta EMD SD70ACe Diesel "1065," non-powered, 24-25		350	___
2533151	NS Heritage Virginian EMD SD70ACe Diesel "1069," CC, 24-25		700	___
2533159	NS Heritage Virginian EMD SD70ACe Diesel "1069," non-powered, 24-25		350	___
2533161	NS Heritage Wabash EMD SD70ACe Diesel "1070," CC, 24-25		700	___
2533169	NS Heritage Wabash EMD SD70ACe Diesel "1070," non-powered, 24-25		350	___
2533171	GTW EMD SD70M-2 Diesel "8952," CC, 24-25		700	___
2533179	GTW EMD SD70M-2 Diesel "8952," non-powered, 24-25		350	___
2533181	Ferromex EMD SD70ACe Diesel "4042," CC, 24-25		700	___
2533189	Ferromex EMD SD70ACe Diesel "4053," non-powered, 24-25		350	___
2533191	Maine Northern EMD SD70M-2 Diesel "6405," CC, 24-25		700	___
2533192	Maine Northern EMD SD70M-2 Diesel "6406," CC, 24-25		700	___
2533201	Susquehanna EMD SD70M-2 Diesel "4060," CC, 24-25		700	___
2533202	Susquehanna EMD SD70M-2 Diesel "4062," CC, 24-25		700	___
2533211	CN FM C-Liner Diesel "9300," CC, 24-25		600	___
2533212	CN FM C-Liner Diesel "9302," CC, 24-25		600	___
2533219	CN FM C-Liner Diesel SuperBass "9301," CC, 24-25		500	___
2533221	CP FM C-Liner Diesel "4064," CC, 24-25		600	___
2533222	CP FM C-Liner Diesel "4065," CC, 24-25		600	___
2533229	CP FM C-Liner Diesel SuperBass "4449," CC, 24-25		500	___
2533231	MILW FM C-Liner Diesel "26A," CC, 24-25		600	___
2533232	MILW FM C-Liner Diesel "26C," CC, 24-25		600	___
2533239	MILW FM C-Liner Diesel SuperBass "26B" CC, 24-25		500	___
2533241	NYC FM C-Liner Diesel "6606," CC, 24-25		600	___
2533242	NYC FM C-Liner Diesel "6607," CC, 24-25		600	___
2533249	NYC FM C-Liner Diesel SuperBass "6903," CC, 24-25		500	___
2533251	PRR FM C-Liner Diesel "9492A," CC, 24-25		600	___
2533252	PRR FM C-Liner Diesel "9493A," CC, 24-25		600	___
2533259	PRR FM C-Liner Diesel SuperBass "9492B," CC, 24-25		500	___
2533260	ATSF Alco PA AA Diesels "58L/58B," CC, 24-25		1200	___
2533269	ATSF Alco PB Diesel SuperBass "58A", 24-25		500	___
2533270	Erie Alco PA AA Diesels "854/855," CC, 24-25		1200	___
2533279	Erie Alco PB Diesel SuperBass "854B", 24-25		500	___
2533280	NKP Alco PA AA Diesels "184/185," CC, 24-25		1200	___
2533289	NKP Alco PB Diesel SuperBass "184B", 24-25		500	___
2533290	NH Alco PA AA Diesels "764/765," CC, 24-25		1200	___
2533299	NH Alco PB Diesel SuperBass "764B", 24-25		500	___
2533300	Southern Alco PA AA Diesels "6902/6903," CC, 24-25		1200	___
2533309	Southern Alco PB Diesel SuperBass "6902B", 24-25		500	___
2533310	SP Alco PA AA Diesels "6005A/6005C," CC, 24-25		1200	___
2533319	SP Alco PB Diesel SuperBass "6005B", 24-25		500	___
2533320	Amtrak Phase V EMD SW1 Diesel Switcher "737," CC, 24-25		550	___
2533330	Cargill EMD SW1 Diesel Switcher "62," CC, 24-25		550	___
2533340	Dubuque Sand & Gravel EMD SW1 Diesel Switcher "537," CC, 24-25		550	___
2533350	Manufacturers Jct EMD SW1 Diesel Switcher "23," CC, 24-25		550	___

		Exc	Mint
____ **2533360**	NYC EMD SW1 Diesel Switcher "590," CC, 24-25		550
____ **2533370**	LV EMD SW1 Diesel Switcher "112," CC, 24-25		550
____ **2533380**	WP EMD SW1 Diesel Switcher "501," CC, 24-25		550
____ **2533391**	Aberdeen, Carolina & Western EMD SD40-2 Diesel "6910," CC, 24-25		650
____ **2533392**	Aberdeen, Carolina & Western EMD SD40-2 Diesel "6918," CC, 24-25		650
____ **2533401**	C&NW EMD SD40-2 Diesel "6910," CC, 24-25		650
____ **2533402**	C&NW EMD SD40-2 Diesel "6922," CC, 24-25		650
____ **2533411**	CP EMD SD40-2 Diesel "777," CC, 24-25		650
____ **2533412**	CP EMD SD40-2 Diesel "779," CC, 24-25		650
____ **2533420**	Reading & Northern EMD SD40-2 Diesel "1983," CC, 24-25		650
____ **2533431**	SOO EMD SD40-2 Diesel "6615," CC, 24-25		650
____ **2533432**	SOO EMD SD40-2 Diesel "6601," CC, 24-25		650
____ **2533440**	Susquehanna EMD SD40-2 Diesel "3024," CC, 24-25		650
____ **2533510**	Halloween Alco PA AA Diesels "1030/1031," CC, 24-25		1200
____ **2533519**	Halloween Alco PB SuperBass "1030B", 24-25		500
____ **2533520**	VMV EMD SD40-2 Diesel "2001," CC, 24-25		650
____ **2533541**	CSX Heritage ACL GE ES44 Diesel "1871," CC, 25		750
____ **2533549**	CSX Heritage ACL GE ES44 Diesel "1871," non-powered, 25		430
____ **2533551**	CSX Heritage NYC GE ES44 Diesel "1853," CC, 25		750
____ **2533559**	CSX Heritage NYC GE ES44 Diesel "1853," non-powered, 25		430
____ **2533561**	CSX Heritage Family Lines GE ES44 Diesel "1972," CC, 25		750
____ **2533569**	CSX Heritage Family Lines GE ES44 Diesel "1972," non-powered, 25		430
____ **2533571**	CSX Heritage RF&P GE ES44 Diesel "1836," CC, 25		750
____ **2533579**	CSX Heritage RF&P GE ES44 Diesel "1836," non-powered, 25		430
____ **2533581**	CSX Heritage WM GE ES44 Diesel "1852," CC, 25		750
____ **2533589**	CSX Heritage WM GE ES44 Diesel "1852," non-powered, 25		430
____ **2533591**	NS Heritage Conrail GE ES44 Diesel "8098," CC, 25		750
____ **2533599**	NS Heritage Conrail GE ES44 Diesel "8098," non-powered, 25		430
____ **2533601**	NS Heritage Interstate GE ES44 Diesel "8105," CC, 25		750
____ **2533609**	NS Heritage Interstate GE ES44 Diesel "8105," non-powered, 25		430
____ **2533611**	NS Heritage NKP GE ES44 Diesel "8100," CC, 25		750
____ **2533619**	NS Heritage NKP GE ES44 Diesel "8100," non-powered, 25		430
____ **2533621**	NS Heritage Norfolk Southern GE ES44 Diesel "8114," CC, 25		750
____ **2533629**	NS Heritage Norfolk Southern GE ES44 Diesel "8114," non-powered, 25		430
____ **2533631**	NS Heritage Southern GE ES44 Diesel "8099," CC, 25		750
____ **2533639**	NS Heritage Southern GE ES44 Diesel "8099," non-powered, 25		430
____ **2533640**	FEC GE ES44 Diesel "816," CC, 25		750
____ **2533651**	CPKC GE ES44 Diesel "8721," CC, 25		750
____ **2533652**	CPKC GE ES44 Diesel "9375," CC, 25		750
____ **2533661**	CN GE ES44 Diesel "2917," CC, 25		750
____ **2533662**	CN GE ES44 Diesel "2943," CC, 25		750
____ **2533671**	CNJ FM Train Master Diesel "2404," CC, 25		650
____ **2533672**	CNJ FM Train Master Diesel "2411," CC, 25		650
____ **2533681**	C&NW FM Train Master Diesel "1902," CC, 25		650
____ **2533682**	C&NW FM Train Master Diesel "1906," CC, 25		650
____ **2533691**	MILW FM Train Master Diesel "550," CC, 25		650
____ **2533692**	MILW FM Train Master Diesel "552," CC, 25		650

		Exc	Mint
2533701	PRR FM Train Master Diesel "6700," CC, 25		650
2533702	PRR FM Train Master Diesel "6708," CC, 25		650
2533711	Reading FM Train Master Diesel "801," CC, 25		650
2533712	Reading FM Train Master Diesel "867," CC, 25		650
2533721	SP FM Train Master Diesel "3025," CC, 25		650
2533722	SP FM Train Master Diesel "3033," CC, 25		650
2533751	ATSF EMD GP35 Diesel "1301," CC, 25		650
2533752	ATSF EMD GP35 Diesel "1323," CC, 25		650
2533761	GN EMD GP35 Diesel "3036," CC, 25		650
2533762	GN EMD GP35 Diesel "3038," CC, 25		650
2533771	Chessie System EMD GP35 Diesel "3535," CC, 25		650
2533772	Chessie System EMD GP35 Diesel "3563," CC, 25		650
2533781	Housatonic EMD GP35 Diesel "3601," CC, 25		650
2533782	Housatonic EMD GP35 Diesel "3602," CC, 25		650
2533791	ICG EMD GP35 Diesel "2517," CC, 25		650
2533792	ICG EMD GP35 Diesel "2520," CC, 25		650
2533801	Wabash EMD GP35 Diesel "544," CC, 25		650
2533802	Wabash EMD GP35 Diesel "547," CC, 25		650
2533811	B&LE EMD SD40T-2 Diesel "901," CC, 25		700
2533812	B&LE EMD SD40T-2 Diesel "910," CC, 25		700
2533821	CN EMD SD40T-2 Diesel "902," CC, 25		700
2533822	CN EMD SD40T-2 Diesel "903," CC, 25		700
2533831	D&RGW EMD SD40T-2 Diesel "5412," CC, 25		700
2533832	D&RGW EMD SD40T-2 Diesel "5413," CC, 25		700
2533841	SP EMD SD40T-2 Diesel "8232," CC, 25		700
2533842	SP EMD SD40T-2 Diesel "8236," CC, 25		700
2533851	UP EMD SD40T-2 Diesel "8726," CC, 25		700
2533852	UP EMD SD40T-2 Diesel "8803," CC, 25		700
2533861	W&LE EMD SD40T-2 Diesel "5391," CC, 25		700
2533862	W&LE EMD SD40T-2 Diesel "8795," CC, 25		700
2533870	ATSF Alco FA-2 AA Diesels, CC, 25		1200
2533878	ATSF Alco FB-2 Diesel "205," CC, 25		550
2533879	ATSF Alco FB-2 SuperBass "205", 25		550
2533880	B&O Alco FA-2 AA Diesels, CC, 25		1200
2533888	B&O Alco FB-2 Diesel "5008," CC, 25		550
2533889	B&O Alco FB-2 SuperBass "5009", 25		550
2533890	CP Alco FA-2 AA Diesels, CC, 25		1200
2533898	CP Alco FB-2 Diesel "4468," CC, 25		550
2533899	CP Alco FB-2 SuperBass "4470", 25		550
2533900	C&NW Alco FA-2 AA Diesels, CC, 25		1200
2533908	C&NW Alco FB-2 Diesel "4103B," CC, 25		550
2533909	C&NW Alco FB-2 SuperBass "4104B", 25		550
2533910	PRR Alco FA-2 AA Diesels, CC, 25		1200
2533918	PRR Alco FB-2 Diesel, "9614B "CC, 25		550
2533919	PRR Alco FB-2 SuperBass "9615B", 25		550
2533920	Wabash Alco FA-2 AA Diesels, CC, 25		1200
2533928	Wabash Alco FB-2 Diesel "826," CC, 25		550
2533929	Wabash Alco FB-2 SuperBass "827", 25		550
2534010	CSX EMD GP38 Diesel "2100," LionChief Plus 2.0, 24-25		500
2534020	CP EMD GP38 Diesel "3084," LionChief Plus 2.0, 24-25		500
2534030	Ohio Central EMD GP38 Diesel "2161," LionChief Plus 2.0, 24-25		500

			Exc	Mint
____	**2534040**	Paducah & Louisville EMD GP38 Diesel "3803," LionChief Plus 2.0, 24-25		500
____	**2534050**	Seaboard System EMD GP38 Diesel "517," LionChief Plus 2.0, 24-25		500
____	**2534060**	ATSF EMD F3 AA Diesels, LionChief Plus 2.0, 25		900
____	**2534069**	ATSF EMD F3 B Diesel, LionChief Plus 2.0, 25		500
____	**2534070**	FEC EMD F3 AA Diesels, LionChief Plus 2.0, 25		900
____	**2534079**	FEC EMD F3 B Diesel, LionChief Plus 2.0, 25		500
____	**2534080**	Reading EMD F3 AA Diesels, LionChief Plus 2.0, 25		900
____	**2534089**	Reading EMD F3 B Diesel, LionChief Plus 2.0, 25		500
____	**2534090**	SP EMD F3 AA Diesels, LionChief Plus 2.0, 25		900
____	**2534099**	SP EMD F3 B Diesel, LionChief Plus 2.0, 25		500
____	**2535010**	Lenny/Santa Handcar, blue, 25		200
____	**2535060**	Christmas Illuminated Trolley, 25		160
____	**2535070**	Area 51 Trolley, 25		160
____	**2535080**	Anheuser Busch Vintage Truck, CC, 25		200
____	**2535090**	Area 51 Vintage Truck, CC, 25		200
____	**2535100**	Polar Express Vintage Truck, CC, 25		200
____	**2535110**	Kringle Railway Vintage Truck, CC, 25		200
____	**2535120**	Jack's Patch Halloween Vintage Truck, CC, 25		200
____	**2535130**	John Deere Vintage Truck, CC, 25		200
____	**2535140**	Peanuts Halloween Trolley, 25		160
____	**2535150**	Lenny/Santa Handcar, orange, 25		200
____	**2535160**	Lenny/Santa Handcar, bronze, 25		230
____	**2535170**	Peanuts Christmas Trolley, 25		160
____	**2538010**	Angela Trotta Thomas Commodore Vanderbilt Hudson Boxcar, 25		100
____	**2538020**	Angela Trotta Thomas Christmas Anticipation Boxcar, 25		100
____	**2538040**	Railroad Museum of Pennsylvania 50th Anniversary Boxcar, 25		100
____	**2538050**	Stockton & Darlington 200th Anniversary Boxcar, 25		100
____	**2538060**	Orange Blossom Special 100th Anniversary Boxcar, 25		100
____	**2538080**	Bob Ross "A Walk in the Woods" Boxcar, 25		110
____	**2538090**	"Santa's Final Touch - A Lionel Legacy" Boxcar, 25		100
____	**2538100**	Lionel Moment Personalized Boxcar, 25		100
____	**2538110**	Joshua Lionel Cowen Notable American Boxcar, 25		100
____	**2538130**	Battles of Lexington and Concord 250th Anniversary Boxcar, 25		110
____	**2538150**	Paul Revere's "Midnight Ride" 250th Anniversary Boxcar, 25		110
____	**2538160**	U.S. Navy 250th Anniversary Boxcar, 25		110
____	**2538170**	Wings of Angels Katherine Boxcar, 25		110
____	**2538180**	Wings of Angels Rockin' the Red Boxcar, 25		110
____	**2538190**	Wings of Angels High Altitude Hotties Boxcar, 25		110
____	**2538200**	Mister Rogers "Behind The Scenes" Boxcar, 25		110
____	**2538210**	Tom and Jerry 85th Anniversary Boxcar, 25		110
____	**2538220**	Halloween Personalized Boxcar, 24-25		100
____	**2538230**	Ford Personalized Boxcar, 25		100
____	**2538240**	Chevrolet Personalized Boxcar, 25		100
____	**2538250**	Happy Birthday Personalized Boxcar, 25		100
____	**2538260**	Happy Father's Day Personalized Boxcar, 25		100
____	**2538270**	Happy Mother's Day Personalized Boxcar, 25		100
____	**2538280**	Family Personalized Boxcar, 25		100
____	**2538290**	Happy Graduation Personalized Boxcar, 25		100
____	**2538300**	Merry Christmas Personalized Boxcar, 25		100
____	**2538310**	Happy Anniversary Personalized Boxcar, 25		100

		Exc	Mint
2538320	Merry Christmas Personalized Caboose, 25	100	___
2538330	Happy Birthday Personalized Caboose, 25	100	___
2538340	Polar Express Personalized Boxcar, 25	100	___
2538350	Peanuts 75th Anniversary Boxcar, 25	110	___
2538360	Mattel 80th Anniversary Boxcar, 25	110	___
2538430	Angela Trotta Thomas Well Stocked Shelves Boxcar, 2, 25	100	___
2542011	MILW Rib-sided Boxcar (Hiawatha) "22370", 24-25	80	___
2542012	MILW Rib-sided Boxcar (Hiawatha) "23729", 24-25	80	___
2542021	MILW Rib-sided Boxcar (Olympian) "18253", 24-25	80	___
2542022	MILW Rib-sided Boxcar (Olympian) "18361", 24-25	80	___
2542031	MILW Rib-sided Boxcar "22388", 24-25	80	___
2542032	MILW Rib-sided Boxcar "23853", 24-25	80	___
2542041	MILW Rib-sided Boxcar w/ Roof Hatches "8275", 24-25	80	___
2542042	MILW Rib-sided Boxcar w/ Roof Hatches "8293", 24-25	80	___
2542051	MILW Rib-sided Boxcar w/ Yellow Band "8363", 24-25	80	___
2542052	MILW Rib-sided Boxcar w/ Yellow Band "8376", 24-25	80	___
2542061	MILW Rib-sided Boxcar w/ LRD "8515", 24-25	80	___
2542062	MILW Rib-sided Boxcar w/ LRD "8518", 24-25	80	___
2542071	ACL AC-2 Covered Hopper "87251", 24-25	85	___
2542072	ACL AC-2 Covered Hopper "87259", 24-25	85	___
2542081	DL&W AC-2 Covered Hopper "18506", 24-25	85	___
2542082	DL&W AC-2 Covered Hopper "18520", 24-25	85	___
2542091	GN AC-2 Covered Hopper "71318", 24-25	85	___
2542092	GN AC-2 Covered Hopper "71330", 24-25	85	___
2542101	McMillen Feed Mills AC-2 Covered Hopper "102", 24-25	85	___
2542102	McMillen Feed Mills AC-2 Covered Hopper "105", 24-25	85	___
2542111	Shippers Car Line AC-2 Covered Hopper "25321", 24-25	85	___
2542112	Shippers Car Line AC-2 Covered Hopper "25325", 24-25	85	___
2542121	SOO AC-2 Covered Hopper "8904", 24-25	85	___
2542122	SOO AC-2 Covered Hopper "8915", 24-25	85	___
2542131	ACFX ACF 4-Bay Covered Hopper "52569", 24-25	100	___
2542132	ACFX ACF 4-Bay Covered Hopper "52998", 24-25	100	___
2542140	AEX ACF CenterFlow 4-Bay Covered Hopper "5094" w/ Graffiti, 24-25	100	___
2542150	AEX ACF CenterFlow 4-Bay Covered Hopper "5100" w/ Graffiti, 24-25	100	___
2542161	CSX ACF CenterFlow 4-Bay Covered Hopper "201569", 24-25	100	___
2542162	CSX ACF CenterFlow 4-Bay Covered Hopper "201582", 24-25	100	___
2542171	D&RGW ACF CenterFlow 4-Bay Covered Hopper "15500", 24-25	100	___
2542172	D&RGW ACF CenterFlow 4-Bay Covered Hopper "15590", 24-25	100	___
2542181	Cumberland Chemical ACF CenterFlow 4-Bay Covered Hopper "52206", 24-25	100	___
2542182	Cumberland Chemical ACF CenterFlow 4-Bay Covered Hopper "52208", 24-25	100	___
2542190	Alaska RR 3-Bay Hopper w/Peaked Ends 3-pack, A, 24-25	250	___
2542195	Alaska RR 3-Bay Hopper w/Peaked Ends 3-pack, B, 24-25	250	___
2542199	Alaska RR 3-Bay Hopper w/Peaked Ends "14801", 24-25	85	___
2542200	B&O 3-Bay Hopper w/Peaked Ends 3-pack, A, 24-25	250	___
2542205	B&O 3-Bay Hopper w/Peaked Ends 3-pack, B, 24-25	250	___
2542209	B&O 3-Bay Hopper w/Peaked Ends "12347", 24-25	85	___
2542210	C&O 3-Bay Hopper w/Peaked Ends 3-pack, A, 24-25	250	___

			Exc	Mint
____	**2542215**	C&O 3-Bay Hopper w/Peaked Ends 3-pack, B, 24-25		250
____	**2542219**	C&O 3-Bay Hopper w/Peaked Ends "101241", 24-25		85
____	**2542220**	CSX 3-Bay Hopper w/Peaked Ends 3-pack, A, 24-25		250
____	**2542225**	CSX 3-Bay Hopper w/Peaked Ends 3-pack, B, 24-25		250
____	**2542229**	CSX 3-Bay Hopper w/Peaked Ends "108442", 24-25		85
____	**2542230**	N&W 3-Bay Hopper w/Peaked Ends 3-pack, A, 24-25		250
____	**2542235**	N&W 3-Bay Hopper w/Peaked Ends 3-pack, B, 24-25		250
____	**2542239**	N&W 3-Bay Hopper w/Peaked Ends "21348", 24-25		85
____	**2542240**	PRR 3-Bay Hopper w/Peaked Ends 3-pack, A, 24-25		250
____	**2542245**	PRR 3-Bay Hopper w/Peaked Ends 3-pack, B, 24-25		250
____	**2542249**	PRR 3-Bay Hopper w/Peaked Ends "11458", 24-25		85
____	**2542250**	C&NW 4-Bay Hopper 3-Pack, A, 25		260
____	**2542255**	C&NW 4-Bay Hopper 3-Pack, B, 25		260
____	**2542259**	C&NW 4-Bay Hopper "135737", 25		90
____	**2542260**	Conrail 4-Bay Hopper 3-Pack, A, 25		260
____	**2542265**	Conrail 4-Bay Hopper 3-Pack, B, 25		260
____	**2542269**	Conrail 4-Bay Hopper "497530", 25		90
____	**2542270**	D&RGW 4-Bay Hopper 3-Pack, A, 25		260
____	**2542275**	D&RGW 4-Bay Hopper 3-Pack, B, 25		260
____	**2542279**	D&RGW 4-Bay Hopper "19856", 25		90
____	**2542280**	Southern 4-Bay Hopper 3-Pack, A, 25		90
____	**2542285**	Southern 4-Bay Hopper 3-Pack, B, 25		260
____	**2542280**	Southern 4-Bay Hopper "78304", 25		90
____	**2542291**	Railbox ACF 50' Boxcar "10048", 25		90
____	**2542292**	Railbox ACF 50' Boxcar "10127", 25		90
____	**2542301**	Weathered Railbox ACF 50' Boxcar "32508", 25		100
____	**2542302**	Weathered Railbox ACF 50' Boxcar "32534", 25		100
____	**2542310**	Hillsdale County ACF 50' Boxcar "805", 25		90
____	**2542320**	Middletown & New Jersey ACF 50' Boxcar "120782", 25		90
____	**2542330**	New Hope & Ivyland ACF 50' Boxcar "615", 25		90
____	**2542340**	Norfolk Southern ACF 50' Boxcar "2227", 25		90
____	**2542351**	ACFX 40' 1-D Tank Car "73868", 25		100
____	**2542352**	ACFX 40' 1-D Tank Car "73871", 25		100
____	**2542361**	ADM 40' 1-D Tank Car "15387", 25		90
____	**2542362**	ADM 40' 1-D Tank Car "15596", 25		90
____	**2542371**	Engelhard 40' 1-D Tank Car "65355", 25		90
____	**2542372**	Engelhard 40' 1-D Tank Car "65384", 25		90
____	**2542381**	LLTX 40' 1-D Tank Car w/Graffiti "542381", 25		100
____	**2542382**	LLTX 40' 1-D Tank Car w/Graffiti "542396", 25		100
____	**2542391**	HOKX 40' 1-D Tank Car "111638", 25		90
____	**2542392**	HOKX 40' 1-D Tank Car "111736", 25		90
____	**2542401**	JR Simplot 40' 1-D Tank Car "64244", 25		90
____	**2542402**	JR Simplot 40' 1-D Tank Car "64248", 25		90
____	**2542411**	ACL 40' DD Boxcar "55569", 25		85
____	**2542412**	ACL 40' DD Boxcar "55660", 25		85
____	**2542421**	ATSF 40' DD Boxcar "4625", 25		85
____	**2542422**	ATSF 40' DD Boxcar "29999", 25		85
____	**2542431**	GN 40' DD Boxcar "3057", 25		85
____	**2542432**	GN 40' DD Boxcar "3175", 25		85
____	**2542441**	GTW 40' DD Boxcar "587957", 25		85
____	**2542442**	GTW 40' DD Boxcar "587962", 25		85
____	**2542451**	IC 40' DD Boxcar "36876", 25		85
____	**2542452**	IC 40' DD Boxcar "36978", 25		85

MODERN 1970-2025		Exc	Mint	
2542461	UP 40' DD Boxcar "474000", 25		85	___
2542462	UP 40' DD Boxcar "474372", 25		85	___
2542470	B&LE 4-Bay Hopper 3-pack, A, 25		260	___
2542475	B&LE 4-Bay Hopper 3-pack, B, 25		260	___
2542479	B&LE 4-Bay Hopper "65445", 25		90	___
2542480	UP 4-Bay Hopper 3-pack, A, 25		260	___
2542485	UP 4-Bay Hopper 3-pack, B, 25		260	___
2542489	UP 4-Bay Hopper "44698", 25		90	___
2542499	C&NW Bicentennial 4-Bay Hopper "135799", 25		90	___
2542509	B&LE Bicentennial 4-Bay Hopper "65000", 25		90	___
2545010	Southern 0-8-0 Locomotive "6536," LionChief, 25		240	___
2545020	NP 0-8-0 Locomotive "1190," LionChief, 25		240	___
2545030	UP 0-8-0 Locomotive "4500," LionChief, 25		240	___
2545040	B&O 0-8-0 Locomotive "1701," LionChief, 25		240	___
2545050	Conrail Alco RS-3 Diesel "9931," LionChief, 25		230	___
2545060	NH Alco RS-3 Diesel "529," LionChief, 25		230	___
2545070	SP Alco RS-3 Diesel "5295," LionChief, 25		230	___
Unnumbered Items				
	Amtrak Passenger Car Set, 89, 89 u	640	770	___
	Baltimore & Ohio Set, 94, 96		NRS	___
	Black Cave Flyer Playmat, 82		8	___
	Blue Comet Set, 78-80, 87 u	560	620	___
	Boston & Albany Hudson and Standard O Car Set, 86 u	1500	1700	___
	Burlington Texas Zephyr Set, 80, 80 u	980	1150	___
	Cannonball Freight Playmat, 81-82		8	___
	Chesapeake & Ohio Set, 95-96		NRS	___
	Chessie System Special Set, 80, 86 u	560	620	___
	Chicago & Alton Limited Set, 81, 86 u	560	620	___
	Chicago & North Western Passenger Car Set, 93	385	460	___
	Commando Assault Train Playmat, 83-84		8	___
	D&RGW California Zephyr Set, 92, 93		900	___
	Erie Set (FF 7), 93	385	460	___
	Erie-Lackawanna Passenger Car Set, 93, 94	940	980	___
	Favorite Food Freight Set, 81-82	255	355	___
	Frisco Set (FF 5), 91	405	425	___
	General Set, 77-80	240	285	___
	Great Northern Empire Builder Set, 92, 93	620	730	___
	Great Northern Set (FARR 3), 81, 81 u	620	690	___
	Illinois Central City of New Orleans Set, 85, 87, 93	885	1045	___
	Illinois Central Set, 91-92, 95	255	285	___
	Jersey Central Set, 86	345	370	___
	Joshua Lionel Cowen Set, 80, 80 u, 82	540	580	___
	L.A.S.E.R. Playmat, 81-82		8	___
	Lionel Lines Madison Car Set, 91, 93	560	620	___
	Lionel Lines Set, 82, 84 u, 86, 86 u, 87 u, 94-95	530	620	___
	Mickey Mouse Express Set, 77-78, 78 u	1050	1800	___
	Milwaukee Road Set (FF 2), 87, 90 u	380	405	___
	Mint Set, 79 u, 80-83, 84 u, 86 u, 87, 91 u, 93	940	1073	___
	Missouri Pacific Set, 95		390	___
	NASCAR Dale Earnhardt Steam Freight Set (TX328RRGMDE), 12-14		300	___
	NASCAR Dale Earnhardt Jr. Steam Freight Set (T8828TRAIN), 12-14		300	___

MODERN 1970-2025		Exc	Mint
___	NASCAR Jeff Gordon Steam Freight Set (T2428RRDUJG), 12-14		300
___	NASCAR Jimmy Johnson Steam Freight Set (T4828RRLOJJ), 12-14		300
___	NASCAR Kyle Busch Steam Freight Set (T1828RRMMKB), 12-14		300
___	NASCAR Tony Stewart Steam Freight Set (T1428R-RODTS), 12-14		300
___	New Haven Set, 94-95		400
___	New York Central Set, 89, 91	240	270
___	New York Central 20th Century Limited Set, 83, 83 u, 95	1000	1200
___	Nickel Plate Road Set (FF 6), 92	385	460
___	Norfolk & Western Powhatan Arrow Set, 81, 81 u, 82 u, 91 u	1450	1700
___	Norfolk & Western Powhatan Arrow Passenger Car Set, 95	370	445
___	Northern Pacific Set, 90-92	190	250
___	Pennsylvania Set, 79-80, 79 u, 80 u 81 u, 83 u	1200	1350
___	Pennsylvania Set (FARR 5), 84-85, 89 u	600	660
___	Pennsylvania Set, 87-90, 95	240	270
___	Pere Marquette Set, 93	720	770
___	Rock Island & Peoria Set, 80-82	240	315
___	Rocky Mountain Platform, 83-84		8
___	Santa Fe Set (FARR 1), 79, 79 u	460	580
___	Santa Fe Super Chief Set, 91, 91 u, 92 u, 93, 95	1400	1700
___	Southern Pacific Daylight Diesel Set, 82-83, 82-83 u, 90 u	2150	2300
___	Southern Pacific Daylight Steam Set, 90, 92-93	790	940
___	Southern Ry. Crescent Limited Set, 77-78, 87 u	540	650
___	Southern Ry. Set (FARR 4), 83, 83 u	620	690
___	Spirit of '76 Set, 74-76	600	720
___	Station Platform, 83-84		8
___	Toys "R" Us Thunderball Freight Set, 75 u		NRS
___	UCS Remote Control Track Section, 70	4	7
___	Union Pacific Overland Route Set, 84, 92 u	770	840
___	Union Pacific Set (FARR 2), 80, 80 u	540	580
___	Union Pacific Set, 94	430	500
___	Wabash Set (FF 1), 86, 87	755	905
___	Western Maryland Set (FF 4), 89	345	405

Section 4
LIONEL CORPORATION TINPLATE

			Exc	Mint
____	**11-1001**	No. 400E Locomotive, black, brass trim (std)		900
____	**11-1002**	No. 400E Locomotive, gray, nickel trim (std)		900
____	**11-1003**	No. 400E Locomotive, gray, brass trim (std)		900
____	**11-1005**	No. 390 Locomotive, green		600
____	**11-1006**	No. 400E Locomotive, crackele black, brass trim		900
____	**11-1008**	No. 400E Lionel Lines Locomotive		900
____	**11-1009**	No. 400E Locomotive, blue, brass trim		900
____	**11-1010**	No. 385E Locomotive (std)	300	700
____	**11-1012**	No. 1835E Locomotive, black, nickel trim		700
____	**11-1013**	AF No. 4694 Warrior Passenger Set		1400
____	**11-1014**	AF No. 4694 Iron Monarch Passenger Set		1250
____	**11-1015**	No. 392E Locomotive, black, brass trim		800
____	**11-1016**	No. 392E Locomotive, gray, nickel trim	325	800
____	**11-1017**	No. 400E Locomotive, blue, nickel trim (std)		900
____	**11-1018**	No. 7 Lionel Locomotive (std)	400	900
____	**11-1019**	No. 6 Pennsylvania Locomotive (std)		900
____	**11-1020**	American Flyer No. 4696 Locomotive		1000
____	**11-1021**	No. 400E Presidential Locomotive (std)		1000
____	**11-1022**	No. 400E Red Comet Locomotive (std)		1600
____	**11-1023**	No. 400E Locomotive, blue, brass trim (std)		900
____	**11-1024**	No. 400E Locomotive, black, brass trim (std)		900
____	**11-1025**	No. 400E Lionel Lines Locomotive (std)		900
____	**11-1026**	No. 400E Locomotive, pink (std)		1000
____	**11-1027**	No. 400E Locomotive, state green (std)		1000
____	**11-1028**	No. 400E Locomotive, black, brass trim (std)		1000
____	**11-1029**	No. 6 NYC Locomotive (std)		900
____	**11-1030**	No. 6 General Locomotive (std)		900
____	**11-1031**	No. 6 Texas Locomotive (std)		950
____	**11-1038**	No. 6 B&O Locomotive (std)		900
____	**11-1039**	No. 6 Long Island Locomotive (std)		900
____	**11-1040**	No. 6 Strasburg Locomotive (std)		900
____	**11-1041**	No. 6 PRR Locomotive (std)		900
____	**11-1042**	Great Northern Steam Locomotive (std)		1000
____	**11-1043**	Lehigh Valley Steam Locomotive (std)		1000
____	**11-1045**	PRR Steam Locomotive (std)		1000
____	**11-2003**	No. 8E Electric Locomotive, olive green (std)		500
____	**11-2004**	No. 8E Electric Locomotive, dark olive green (std)		500
____	**11-2005**	No. 8E Electric Locomotive, orange (std)		500
____	**11-2006**	No. 8E Electric Locomotive, red/cream (std)		500
____	**11-2007**	American Flyer Presidential Passenger Set (std)		1800
____	**11-2008**	AF No. 4689 Presidential Locomotive, blue (std)		800
____	**11-2009**	Big Brute Electric Engine, zinc chromate		1500
____	**11-2010**	Big Brute Electric Engine, green		1725

Lionel Corporation Tinplate		Exc	Mint
11-2015	Super 381 Electric Engine, state green (std)		1300 ___
11-2016	Super 381 MILW Electric Engine (std)	475	1300 ___
11-2017	No. 408E Electric Locomotive (std)		900 ___
11-2018	No. 408E Electric Locomotive, Mojave		900 ___
11-2019	No. 408E Electric Locomotive, pink		900 ___
11-2020	No. 9 Electric Locomotive, green		600 ___
11-2021	No. 9 Electric Locomotive, orange	200	600 ___
11-2022	No. 9 Electric Locomotive, gray, nickel trim		600 ___
11-2023	No. 9 Electric Locomotive, dark green		600 ___
11-2024	No. 8 Trolley (std)		530 ___
11-2025	No. 9 Trolley (std)		650 ___
11-2026	No. 8 Christmas Trolley (std)		570 ___
11-2027	No. 381E Electric Locomotive, blue (std)		900 ___
11-2028	No. 381E Electric Locomotive, brown (std)		900 ___
11-2029	No. 381E Great Northern Electric Locomotive (std)		900 ___
11-2031	No. 4689 President's Locomotive, red (std)		900 ___
11-2033	Big Brute Electric Locomotive, brown (std)		1950 ___
11-2034	Big Brute Electric Locomotive, orange (std)		1950 ___
11-2038	Super 381 MILW Electric Locomotive (std)		1300 ___
11-2039	Super 381 PRR Electric Locomotive (std)		1300 ___
11-2040	Super 381 Electric Locomotive, two-tone brown (std)		1300 ___
11-2041	Super 381 New Haven Electric Locomotive (std)		1300 ___
11-5001	No. 384 Locomotive Passenger Set, black, brass trim		600 ___
11-5002	No. 384 Locomotive Christmas Freight Set (std)		600 ___
11-5003	No. 384 Locomotive LV Passenger Set (std)		600 ___
11-5004	No. 384 Locomotive NYC Freight Set		600 ___
11-5006	No. 384E Locomotive Girl's Passenger Set		600 ___
11-5007	No. 386 Freight Set (std)		600 ___
11-5008	No. 340E Coal Freight Set (std)		663 ___
11-5009	No. 342E Baby State Passenger Set (std)		600 ___
11-5010	No. 384E Blue Comet Passenger Set (std)		600 ___
11-5011	No. 386 Christmas Freight Set (std)		600 ___
11-5012	No. 342E Passenger Set (std)		1300 ___
11-5013	No. 318E Christmas Freight Set (std)		600 ___
11-5014	No. 384E PRR Steam Passenger Set (std)		600 ___
11-5501	No. 263E Steam Christmas Freight Set		600 ___
11-5502	No. 263E Steam B&O Freight Set		600 ___
11-5505	No. 249E Christmas Steam Passenger Set		500 ___
11-5506	No. 299 Freight Set		450 ___
11-5507	No. 269E Distant Control Freight Set		500 ___
11-5508	Celebration Passenger Set		480 ___
11-5509	No. 269E Christmas Distant Control Freight Set		500 ___
11-5510	No. 269E Distant Control Freight Set		500 ___
11-6001	No. 263E Locomotive, black, brass trim		430 ___
11-6002	No. 263E Locomotive, blue		430 ___
11-6003	No. 277W Remote Control Work Train		680 ___

	Lionel Corporation Tinplate		Exc	Mint
___	11-6004	Blue Comet Distant Control Passenger Set		650
___	11-6005	No. 275W Distant Control Freight Set		600
___	11-6006	UP Streamliner Passenger Set, silver		800
___	11-6007	UP Streamliner Passenger Set, yellow		800
___	11-6008	No. 249E Steam Passenger Set, black, brass trim		600
___	11-6009	No. 249E Steam Passenger Set, blue		600
___	11-6010	No. 249E Steam Passenger Set, gray, nickel trim		600
___	11-6012	No. 260E Locomotive, black, brass trim		430
___	11-6013	No. 255E Locomotive, gray, nickel trim		430
___	11-6014	No. 255E Lionel Lines Locomotive		430
___	11-6015	No. 279E Distant Control Passenger Set		750
___	11-6016	No. 295E Distant Control Passenger Set		750
___	11-6017	Hiawatha Distance Control Streamliner Set		900
___	11-6018	Hiawatha Passenger Train Set		900
___	11-6019	Hiawatha Distance Control Freight Set		900
___	11-6020	UP City of Denver Passenger Set, green		590
___	11-6021	UP City of Denver Passenger Set, yellow/brown		700
___	11-6022	No. 262E Locomotive, black, brass trim		300
___	11-6023	No. 262E Locomotive, black, nickel trim		300
___	11-6024	No. 260E Locomotive, black, brass trim		450
___	11-6025	No. 214 Armored Motor Car Set		400
___	11-6028	No. 256 Electric Locomotive, orange		450
___	11-6029	No. 214 Armored Motor Car Set		400
___	11-6030	No. 295E Distant Control Passenger Set		750
___	11-6031	No. 279E NYC Distance Control Passenger Set		700
___	11-6033	No. 265E Commodore Vanderbilt Locomotive		430
___	11-6036	No. 263E Baby Blue Comet Locomotive		460
___	11-6037	Girls Freight Set		830
___	11-6038	No. 284E Distant Control Freight Set		700
___	11-6039	No. 616 Flying Yankee Passenger Set, black/chrome		590
___	11-6040	No. 616 Flying Yankee Passenger Set, red/chrome	215	590
___	11-6041	No. 616 Flying Yankee Passenger Set, green/chrome		590
___	11-6046	No. 279E Distant Control Passenger Set		700
___	11-6047	No. 264 Red Comet Locomotive		460
___	11-6048	No. 263E Baby Blue Comet Locomotive, brass trim		500
___	11-6050	No. 256 New Haven Electric Locomotive		500
___	11-6051	No. 256 Great Northern Electric Locomotive		500
___	11-6052	No. 263E Locomotive, black, nickel trim		500
___	11-6053	No. 263E Chessie Locomotive		500
___	11-6054	No. 263E Southern Locomotive		500
___	11-6055	Boys Freight Set		900
___	11-6056	No. 261E LL Locomotive and Tender		350
___	11-6057	No. 216E Locomotive and Tender		350
___	11-6061	No. 256 MILW Electric Locomotive		500
___	11-6062	No. 256 PRR Electric Locomotive		500
___	11-30004	No. 213 Cattle Car, cream/maroon (std)		130

Lionel Corporation Tinplate		Exc	Mint
11-30005	No. 213 Cattle Car, terra-cotta/green (std)		130 ___
11-30006	No. 214 Boxcar, cream/orange (std)		130 ___
11-30007	No. 214 Boxcar, yellow/brown (std)		130 ___
11-30008	No. 214R Refrigerator Car, white/blue (std)		130 ___
11-30009	No. 215 Tank Car, silver, nickel trim (std)		130 ___
11-30010	No. 215 Tank Car, green, brass trim (std)		130 ___
11-30011	No. 215 Tank Car, white (std)		130 ___
11-30012	No. 216 Hopper Car, red (std)		130 ___
11-30013	No. 217 Caboose, orange/maroon (std)		140 ___
11-30014	No. 217 Caboose, red (std)		160 ___
11-30015	No. 513 Cattle Car, green/orange, brass trim (std)		100 ___
11-30016	No. 514 Boxcar, cream/orange (std)		100 ___
11-30017	No. 514R Refrigerator Car, ivory/peacock, brass trim (std)		100 ___
11-30018	No. 515 Tank Car, terra-cotta, brass trim (std)		100 ___
11-30019	No. 516 Hopper Car, red, brass trim (std)		120 ___
11-30020	No. 517 Caboose, pea green/red (std)		120 ___
11-30021	No. 212 Gondola, maroon (std)		110 ___
11-30022	No. 212 Gondola, pea green (std)		110 ___
11-30023	No. 513 Cattle Car, cream/maroon, nickel trim (std)		100 ___
11-30024	No. 514R Refrigerator Car, white/blue, nickel trim (std)		100 ___
11-30025	No. 515 Tank Car, silver, nickel trim (std)	25	100 ___
11-30026	No. 516 Hopper Car, red, nickel trim (std)		100 ___
11-30027	No. 517 Caboose, red, nickel trim (std)		120 ___
11-30028	No. 520 Floodlight Car, green, nickel trim (std)		130 ___
11-30029	No. 520 Floodlight Car, terra-cotta, brass trim (std)		130 ___
11-30030	No. 514R Christmas Refrigerator Car, (std)		100 ___
11-30031	No. 514 Christmas Boxcar (std)		100 ___
11-30032	No. 515 MTH/Lionel Tank Car (std)		100 ___
11-30033	No. 211 Flatcar, black, brass trim, with wood (std)		120 ___
11-30034	No. 211 Flatcar, black, nickel trim, with wood (std)		120 ___
11-30035	No. 218 Dump Car, Mojave, nickel trim (std)		140 ___
11-30036	No. 218 Dump Car, Mojave, brass trim (std)		140 ___
11-30037	No. 219 Crane Car, white (std)		200 ___
11-30038	No. 219 Crane Car, yellow, nickel trim (std)	50	200 ___
11-30039	No. 219 Crane Car, yellow (std)		380 ___
11-30042	No. 514 Boxcar, red/black (std)		100 ___
11-30043	No. 512 Gondola, peacock, brass trim (std)		80 ___
11-30044	No. 512 Gondola, green, nickel trim (std)		80 ___
11-30045	No. 514 Boxcar, yellow/brown (std)		100 ___
11-30046	No. 511 Flatcar, black, brass trim, with wood (std)		100 ___
11-30047	No. 511 Flatcar, black, nickel trim, with wood (std)		100 ___
11-30048	No. 216 Hopper Car, dark green (std)		130 ___
11-30050	No. 219 Crane Car, white, brass trim (std)		380 ___
11-30051	No. 514R NYC Refrigerator Car (std)		100 ___
11-30055	No. 212 Gondola, gray (std)		110 ___
11-30056	No. 213 Cattle Car, Mojave/maroon (std)		130 ___

	Lionel Corporation Tinplate		Exc	Mint
____	**11-30057**	No. 213 Cattle Car, terra-cotta/maroon (std)		130
____	**11-30058**	No. 214 Boxcar, terra-cotta/black, brass trim (std)		130
____	**11-30059**	No. 214R Refrigerator Car, white/peacock, brass trim (std)		130
____	**11-30060**	No. 214R Refrigerator Car, ivory/peacock, brass trim (std)		130
____	**11-30061**	No. 215 Tank Car, silver, brass trim (std)		130
____	**11-30062**	No. 215 Tank Car, silver, nickel trim (std)		130
____	**11-30063**	No. 217 Caboose, olive green (std)		140
____	**11-30064**	No. 217 Lionel Lines Caboose (std)		140
____	**11-30065**	No. 217 Caboose, pea green/red (std)		140
____	**11-30066**	No. 217 Caboose, red/peacock (std)	35	160
____	**11-30067**	No. 218 Dump Car, gray (std)		140
____	**11-30068**	No. 218 Dump Car, pea green (std)		140
____	**11-30069**	No. 218 Dump Car, peacock (std)		140
____	**11-30070**	No. 219 Crane Car, peacock/dark green (std)		200
____	**11-30071**	No. 219 Lionel Lines Crane Car (std)	175	380
____	**11-30072**	No. 220 Floodlight Car, green, nickel trim (std)		140
____	**11-30073**	No. 220 Floodlight Car, terra-cotta, brass trim (std)		140
____	**11-30074**	No. 513 Cattle Car, orange/pea green (std)		100
____	**11-30075**	No. 514 Christmas Boxcar (std)		100
____	**11-30076**	No. 514R Refrigerator Car, ivory/blue (std)	45	100
____	**11-30077**	No. 515 Tank Car, cream (std)		100
____	**11-30078**	No. 515 Tank Car, ivory (std)		100
____	**11-30079**	No. 515 Tank Car, orange (std)		100
____	**11-30080**	No. 516 Christmas Hopper Car (std)		120
____	**11-30081**	No. 516 Hopper Car, red (std)		120
____	**11-30082**	No. 517 Caboose, red/black (std)		120
____	**11-30083**	No. 520 Floodlight Car, green, nickel trim (std)		130
____	**11-30087**	No. 516 Hopper Car, red, brass trim (std)		100
____	**11-30088**	AF 4018 Automobile Car, white/blue		150
____	**11-30089**	AF 4020 Stock Car, blue		150
____	**11-30090**	AF 4006 Hopper Car, red		150
____	**11-30091**	AF 4017 Sand Car, green		150
____	**11-30092**	AF 4010 Tank Car, cream/blue		188
____	**11-30093**	AF 4022 Machine Car, orange		110
____	**11-30094**	AF 4021 Caboose, red		160
____	**11-30095**	AF 4018 Automobile Car, orange/maroon		130
____	**11-30096**	AF 4022 Machine Car, blue		110
____	**11-30097**	AF 4022 Machine Car, orange/green		110
____	**11-30098**	AF 4010 Tank Car, blue		190
____	**11-30099**	AF 4017 Sand Car, maroon		130
____	**11-30100**	AF 4006 Hopper Car, green		130
____	**11-30101**	AF 4020 Stock Car, cream/maroon		130
____	**11-30102**	AF 4021 Caboose, red/maroon		140
____	**11-30103**	AF 4021 Caboose, cream/red		140
____	**11-30104**	No. 215 Tank Car (std)		130
____	**11-30105**	No. 214R Refrigerator Car (std)		130

Lionel Corporation Tinplate		Exc	Mint
11-30107	No. 214R Altoona 36 Lager Refrigerator Car (std)		130 ____
11-30108	No. 214R Budweiser Refrigerator Car (std)		140 ____
11-30109	No. 214R Burp-oh Beer Refrigerator Car (std)		365 ____
11-30110	No. 214R Hood's Dairy Refrigerator Car (std)		130 ____
11-30111	No. 214R Old Reading Refrigerator Car (std)		130 ____
11-30112	No. 214R Palisades Park Refrigerator Car (std)		130 ____
11-30113	No. 214 Circus Boxcar (std)		130 ____
11-30114	No. 214 M&M's Christmas Boxcar (std)		140 ____
11-30115	No. 215 Budweiser Tank Car (std)		140 ____
11-30116	No. 215 Freedomland Tank Car (std)		130 ____
11-30117	No. 215 Gulf Tank Car (std)		130 ____
11-30118	No. 215 Tropicana Tank Car (std)		130 ____
11-30119	No. 513 UP Cattle Car (std)		100 ____
11-30120	No. 513 WM Cattle Car (std)		100 ____
11-30121	No. 514 B&O Boxcar (std)		100 ____
11-30122	No. 514 State of Maine Boxcar (std)		120 ____
11-30123	No. 514R PFE Refrigerator Car (std)		100 ____
11-30124	No. 514R Tropicana Refrigerator Car (std)		120 ____
11-30125	No. 515 Anheuser Busch Tank Car (std)		110 ____
11-30126	No. 515 Hooker Chemicals Tank Car (std)		100 ____
11-30127	No. 516 Blue Coal Hopper Car (std)		100 ____
11-30128	No. 516 Waddell Coal Hopper Car (std)		120 ____
11-30129	No. 517 Pennsylvania Caboose (std)		120 ____
11-30130	No. 517 Santa Fe Caboose (std)		140 ____
11-30131	No. 215 Lionel Lines Tank Car (std)		130 ____
11-30134	No. 515 Christmas Tank Car (std)		100 ____
11-30136	No. 214 Christmas Boxcar (std)		150 ____
11-30137	No. 214 UP Boxcar (std)		150 ____
11-30138	No. 214R Horlacher's Brewing Refrigerator Car (std)		150 ____
11-30139	No. 214R Coors Refrigerator Car (std)		140 ____
11-30140	No. 215 Keystone Gasoline Tank Car (std)		150 ____
11-30141	No. 215 Texaco Tank Car (std)		150 ____
11-30142	No. 216 Peabody Hopper Car (std)		130 ____
11-30143	No. 216 Pennsylvania Power & Light Hopper Car (std)		130 ____
11-30144	No. 213 Cattle Car (std)		130 ____
11-30146	No. 217 Jersey Central Caboose (std)		140 ____
11-30147	No. 214 Jersey Central Boxcar (std)		130 ____
11-30148	No. 214 U.S. Army Boxcar (std)		130 ____
11-30149	No. 215 MTH/Lionel Tank Car		130 ____
11-30150	No. 212 Lionel Lines Gondola (std)		130 ____
11-30151	No. 212 Circus Gondola (std)		240 ____
11-30152	No. 212 NYC Gondola (std)		130 ____
11-30153	No. 214 MKT Boxcar (std)		150 ____
11-30154	No. 214 NYC Boxcar (std)		150 ____
11-30155	No. 215 C&O Tank Car (std)		150 ____
11-30156	No. 215 Shell Tank Car (std)		150 ____

	Lionel Corporation Tinplate		Exc	Mint
___	**11-30157**	No. 216 Hopper Car, red, brass trim (std)		150
___	**11-30158**	No. 216 LV Hopper Car (std)		150
___	**11-30159**	No. 217 Pennsylvania Caboose (std)		160
___	**11-30160**	No. 219 B&O Crane Car (std)		220
___	**11-30161**	No. 219 Crane Car, ivory/red (std)		400
___	**11-30162**	No. 219 Lionel Lines Crane Car (std)		220
___	**11-30163**	No. 219 Crane Car, red/silver (std)		400
___	**11-30164**	No. 514R Christmas Refrigerator Car (std)		120
___	**11-30168**	No. 515 PRR Tank Car (std)		120
___	**11-30169**	No. 515 Texaco Tank Car (std)		120
___	**11-30170**	No. 515 Esso Tank Car (std)		120
___	**11-30180**	No. 219 Crane Car, black/cream (std)		220
___	**11-30182**	No. 217 NYC Illuminated Caboose (std)		160
___	**11-30185**	No. 212 Gondola, pea green (std)		150
___	**11-30193**	No. 514R Altoona Brewing Refrigerator Car (std)		120
___	**11-30194**	No. 514R PFE Refrigerator Car (std)		120
___	**11-30195**	No. 514R REA Refrigerator Car (std)		120
___	**11-30196**	No. 514R Robin Hood Beer Refrigerator Car (std)		120
___	**11-30197**	No. 514 UP Boxcar (std)		120
___	**11-30198**	No. 514 Santa Fe Boxcar (std)		120
___	**11-30199**	No. 514 PRR Boxcar (std)		120
___	**11-30200**	No. 514 B&O Boxcar (std)		120
___	**11-30201**	No. 215-3 Shell 3-D Tank Car (std)		150
___	**11-30202**	No. 215-3 Mazda Lamps 3-D Tank Car (std)		150
___	**11-30203**	No. 215-3 Celanese Chemicals 3-D Tank Car (std)		150
___	**11-30204**	No. 215-3 Clark Oil 3-D Tank Car (std)		150
___	**11-30205**	No. 215-2 Sterling Fuels 2-D Tank Car (std)		150
___	**11-30206**	No. 215-2 Philadelphia Quartz 2-D Tank Car (std)		150
___	**11-30207**	No. 215-2 Cook's Paints 2-D Tank Car (std)		150
___	**11-30208**	No. 215-2 Hercules 2-D Tank Car (std)		150
___	**11-30209**	No. 216-1 PRR Covered Hopper (std)		150
___	**11-30210**	No. 216-1 P&LE Covered Hopper (std)		150
___	**11-30211**	No. 216-1 Jack Frost Covered Hopper (std)		150
___	**11-30212**	No. 216-1 GE Lamps Covered Hopper (std)		150
___	**11-30213**	No. 212-1 PRR Covered Gondola Car (std)		150
___	**11-30214**	No. 212-1 Covered Gondola Car (std)		150
___	**11-30215**	No. 212-1 NYC Covered Gondola Car (std)		150
___	**11-30216**	No. 212-1 GN Covered Gondola Car (std)		150
___	**11-30217**	No. 211 Flatcar with wheel load (std)		150
___	**11-30218**	No. 211 Altoona Shops Flatcar with wheel load (std)		150
___	**11-30219**	No. 211 Baldwin Flatcar with wheel load (std)		150
___	**11-30220**	No. 211 Lima Flatcar with wheel load (std)		150
___	**11-30221**	No. 217-1 Chessie Bay Window Caboose (std)		160
___	**11-30222**	No. 217-1 UP Bay Window Caboose (std)		160
___	**11-30223**	No. 217-1 NYC Bay Window Caboose (std)		160
___	**11-30224**	No. 217-1 Long Island Bay Window Caboose (std)		160

Lionel Corporation Tinplate		Exc	Mint
11-30225	PRR Automobile Car (std)		150 ___
11-30227	Shell Tank Car (std)		150 ___
11-30230	Waddell Coal Hopper (std)		150 ___
11-30232	PRR Caboose (std)		160 ___
11-40001	Presidential Passenger Set, blue (std)		1200 ___
11-40002	No. 339 Pullman Car, green (std)		150 ___
11-40003	No. 332 Mail/Baggage Car, green (std)		150 ___
11-40004	No. 332 LV Ithaca Baggage Car		150 ___
11-40005	No. 339 LV Easton Passenger Coach		150 ___
11-40007	300 Series 3-Car Passenger Set, blue/silver (std)		450 ___
11-40009	3-Car State Passenger Set, green (std)		1200 ___
11-40010	Pennsylvania State Baggage Car, green (std)		400 ___
11-40011	Illinois State Coach, green (std)		400 ___
11-40012	Solarium State Car, green (std)		400 ___
11-40013	MILW 3-Car State Passenger Set (std)	525	1200 ___
11-40014	MILW State Baggage Car (std)		538 ___
11-40015	MILW State Passenger Coach (std)		500 ___
11-40016	MILW Solarium State Car (std)		513 ___
11-40017	3-Car Showroom Passenger Set, green (std)	525	1500 ___
11-40018	Showroom Passenger Coach, green (std)		550 ___
11-40019	3-Car Showroom Passenger Set, zinc chromate (std)		1500 ___
11-40020	Showroom Passenger Coach, zinc chromate (std)		500 ___
11-40021	3-Car Blue Comet Passenger Set (std)		1100 ___
11-40022	No. 432 Olbers Blue Comet Baggage Car (std)	190	403 ___
11-40023	No. 419 Tuttle Blue Comet Passenger Coach (std)		380 ___
11-40024	No. 4343 Diner Car		180 ___
11-40025	339 Series Passenger Car, pink		130 ___
11-40026	332 Series Baggage Car, pink		130 ___
11-40027	309 Series 3-Car State Passenger Set, brown (std)		1200 ___
11-40028	Pennsylvania State Baggage Car, brown (std)		400 ___
11-40029	Illinois State Passenger Coach, brown (std)		400 ___
11-40030	Solarium State Car, brown (std)		400 ___
11-40031	State 3-Car Passenger Set, blue (std)		1200 ___
11-40032	Pennsylvania State Baggage Car, blue (std)		400 ___
11-40033	Illinois State Passenger Coach, blue (std)		400 ___
11-40034	Solarium State Car, blue (std)		400 ___
11-40035	309 Series 3-Car Passenger Set, blue (std)		400 ___
11-40036	309 Series 3-Car Passenger Set, green (std)		463 ___
11-40037	309 Series 3-Car Passenger Set, red (std)	175	400 ___
11-40038	No. 309 Passenger Coach (std)		140 ___
11-40039	No. 310 Baggage Car (std)		140 ___
11-40040	3-Car Blue Comet Passenger Set, nickel trim (std)		1100 ___
11-40041	No. 432 Blue Comet Baggage Car, nickel trim (std)		380 ___
11-40042	No. 423 Blue Comet Passenger Coach, nickel trim (std)		380 ___
11-40043	3-Car Stephen Girard Set, brass trim		600 ___
11-40044	No. 4427 Stephen Girard Baggage Car, brass trim		200 ___

	Lionel Corporation Tinplate		Exc	Mint
____	**11-40045**	No. 427 Stephen Girard Passenger Coach, brass trim		200
____	**11-40046**	3-Car Stephen Girard Set, nickel trim		600
____	**11-40047**	No. 4427 Stephen Girard Baggage Car, nickel trim		200
____	**11-40048**	No. 427 Stephen Girard Passenger Coach, nickel trim		200
____	**11-40049**	No. 418 3-Car Passenger Set, green, brass trim (std)		600
____	**11-40050**	No. 418 Diner, green, brass trim (std)		200
____	**11-40051**	No. 418 3-Car Passenger Set, orange, brass trim (std)		600
____	**11-40052**	No. 418 Diner, orange brass trim (std)		325
____	**11-40053**	No. 418 3-Car Passenger Set, Mojave, brass trim (std)		600
____	**11-40054**	No. 418 Diner, Mojave, brass trim (std)		200
____	**11-40055**	No. 418 3-Car Passenger Set, pink, brass trim (std)		600
____	**11-40056**	No. 418 Diner, pink, brass trim (std)		200
____	**11-40057**	Lionel 3-Car Pullman Passenger Set (std)		700
____	**11-40058**	Pennsylvania 3-Car Pullman Passenger Set (std)		700
____	**11-40059**	No. 332 Baggage Car (std)		140
____	**11-40060**	No. 339 Passenger Coach (std)		140
____	**11-40061**	Great Northern State 3-Car Passenger Set (std)		1200
____	**11-40062**	Great Northern State Baggage Car (std)		430
____	**11-40063**	Great Northern State Passenger Coach (std)		430
____	**11-40064**	Great Northern State Solarium Car (std)		430
____	**11-40065**	Presidential 3-Car Passenger Set (std)		1200
____	**11-40066**	Presidential Baggage Car (std)		430
____	**11-40067**	Presidential Passenger Coach (std)		430
____	**11-40068**	Red Comet 3-Car Passenger Set (std)		2070
____	**11-40069**	Red Comet Baggage Car (std)		650
____	**11-40070**	Red Comet Passenger Coach (std)		400
____	**11-40072**	President's Passenger Set, red (std)		1300
____	**11-40073**	No. 310 Baggage Car (std)		140
____	**11-40074**	No. 309 Passenger Coach (std)		140
____	**11-40076**	Green Comet 3-Car Passenger Set (std)		1140
____	**11-40077**	NYC 3-Car Passenger Set, brown (std)		700
____	**11-40078**	General 3-Car Pullman Passenger Set (std)		700
____	**11-40079**	Green Comet Baggage Car (std)		400
____	**11-40080**	Green Comet Passenger Coach (std)		400
____	**11-40081**	Showroom 3-Car Passenger Set, brown (std)	425	1600
____	**11-40082**	Showroom Passenger Coach, brown (std)	175	540
____	**11-40083**	Showroom 3-Car Passenger Set, orange (std)		2050
____	**11-40084**	Showroom Passenger Coach, orange (std)	263	540
____	**11-40095**	3-car B&O Pullman Passenger Set (std)		700
____	**11-40096**	3-car Long Island Pullman Passenger Set (std)	188	700
____	**11-40097**	3-car Strasburg Pullman Passenger Set (std)		700
____	**11-40098**	3-car PRR Pullman Passenger Set (std)		700
____	**11-40099**	3-car MILW State Passenger Set (std)		1550
____	**11-40100**	MILW State Solarium Car (std)		450
____	**11-40101**	MILW State Passenger Coach (std)		475
____	**11-40102**	MILW State Baggage Car (std)		475

Lionel Corporation Tinplate		Exc	Mint
11-40103	3-car PRR State Passenger Set (std)		1200 ___
11-40104	PRR State Solarium Car (std)		400 ___
11-40105	PRR State Passenger Coach (std)		400 ___
11-40106	PRR State Baggage Car (std)		400 ___
11-40107	3-car State Passenger Set, two-tone brown (std)		1200 ___
11-40108	State Solarium Car, two-tone brown (std)		400 ___
11-40109	State Passenger Coach, two-tone brown (std)		400 ___
11-40110	State Baggage Car, two-tone brown (std)		400 ___
11-40111	3-car Great Northern Presidential Set (std)		1200 ___
11-40112	Great Northern Presidential Diner (std)		400 ___
11-40113	3-car Lehigh Valley Presidential Set (std)		1200 ___
11-40114	Lehigh Valley Presidential Diner (std)		400 ___
11-40115	3-car New Haven State Passenger Set (std)		1200 ___
11-40116	New Haven State Solarium Car (std)		400 ___
11-40117	New Haven State Passenger Coach (std)		400 ___
11-40118	New Haven State Baggage Car (std)		400 ___
11-60033	No. 607 Christmas Coach Passenger		90 ___
11-70002	No. 2814 Boxcar, cream/orange		80 ___
11-70003	No. 2814R Refrigerator Car, white/brown		80 ___
11-70004	No. 2814R Christmas Refrigerator Car		80 ___
11-70005	No. 2814R Refrigerator Car, Ivory/peacock		80 ___
11-70006	No. 2815 Tank Car, silver		90 ___
11-70007	No. 2815 Tank Car, orange, nickel trim		80 ___
11-70008	No. 2817 Caboose, red/green		90 ___
11-70009	No. 2815 Christmas Tank Car		80 ___
11-70010	No. 2813 Cattle Car, cream/maroon		80 ___
11-70011	No. 2812 Gondola, apple green		80 ___
11-70012	No. 2811 Flatcar, silver		70 ___
11-70013	No. 2816 Hopper Car, red		90 ___
11-70014	No. 2816 Hopper Car, olive green		80 ___
11-70015	No. 2820 Floodlight Car, terra-cotta		90 ___
11-70016	No. 2815 Sunoco Tank Car		80 ___
11-70017	No. 2810 Crane Car, terra-cotta/maroon		180 ___
11-70018	No. 2811 Flatcar, maroon		70 ___
11-70019	No. 2814R MTH/Lionel Refrigerator Car		90 ___
11-70024	No. 2814 Christmas Boxcar		80 ___
11-70025	No. 2814 Boxcar, cream/orange		80 ___
11-70026	No. 2814 Boxcar, orange/brown		80 ___
11-70027	No. 2814 Boxcar, white brown		80 ___
11-70028	No. 2816 Christmas Hopper Car		80 ___
11-70029	No. 2817 Caboose, red/brown		90 ___
11-70030	No. 2812 Gondola, dark orange		70 ___
11-70031	No. 813 Cattle Car, brown		80 ___
11-70032	No. 2816 Hopper Car, black		80 ___
11-70033	No. 2820 Floodlight Car, light green		90 ___
11-70034	No. 2814R Refrigerator Car, white/brown		80 ___

	Lionel Corporation Tinplate		Exc	Mint
___	11-70035	No. 2651 Flatcar, green		60
___	11-70036	No. 2652 Gondola, red		60
___	11-70037	No. 2653 Hopper Car, black		60
___	11-70038	No. 2654 Shell Tank Car, yellow		60
___	11-70039	No. 2655 Boxcar, yellow/brown		60
___	11-70040	No. 2656 Cattle Car, red/brown		60
___	11-70041	No. 2657 Caboose, red/maroon		60
___	11-70042	No. 659 Dump Car, green		60
___	11-70043	No. 659 Dump Car, orange		60
___	11-70045	No. 2814 Boxcar, yellow/brown		90
___	11-70046	No. 2817 Caboose, red		100
___	11-70047	No. 2814 Christmas Boxcar		80
___	11-70048	No. 2815 Christmas Tank Car		90
___	11-70049	No. 2814R Refrigerator Car, silver frame		90
___	11-70050	No. 2814R Refrigerator Car, black frame		80
___	11-70051	No. 2817 Caboose, red/maroon		90
___	11-70052	No. 2654 Shell Tank Car, gray		60
___	11-70053	No. 2654 Shell Tank Car, black		60
___	11-70054	No. 2653 Hopper Car, green		60
___	11-70055	No. 2653 Hopper Car, red		60
___	11-70056	No. 2655 Boxcar, yellow/maroon		60
___	11-70057	No. 2655 Boxcar, yellow/brown		60
___	11-70058	No. 2656 Cattle Car, gray/red		60
___	11-70059	No. 2656 Cattle Car, burnt orange		60
___	11-70060	No. 659 Dump Car, blue		60
___	11-70061	No. 900 Ammunition Car, gray		60
___	11-70064	No. 2814R Hoods Dairy Refrigerator Car		80
___	11-70065	No. 2814R Isaly's Refrigerator Car		80
___	11-70066	No. 2814R Sheffield Farms Refrigerator Car		90
___	11-70067	No. 2814R Palisades Park Refrigerator Car		80
___	11-70068	No. 2654 UP Tank Car, yellow		60
___	11-70069	No. 2654 M&M's Tank Car		70
___	11-70070	No. 2654 Baker's Chocolate Tank Car		60
___	11-70071	No. 2654 Budweiser Tank Car		70
___	11-70072	No. 2655 Delaware & Hudson Boxcar		60
___	11-70073	No. 2655 Railbox Boxcar		60
___	11-70074	M&M's Christmas Boxcar		70
___	11-70076	No. 2654 LL Tank Car, orange/blue		70
___	11-70078	No. 900 Ammunition Car, green		60
___	11-70079	No. 2820 LL Floodlight Car, black/orange		120
___	11-70080	No. 2820 U.S. Army Air Corps Floodlight Car		120
___	11-70081	No. 2810 Crane Car, yellow/red		180
___	11-70082	No. 2810 Crane Car, white/red		180
___	11-70083	No. 2660 Crane Car, cream/red		100
___	11-70084	No. 2660 Crane Car, terra-cotta/maroon		100
___	11-70085	No. 2660 Crane Car, yellow/red		100

Lionel Corporation Tinplate		Exc	Mint
11-70086	No. 2660 Crane Car, peacock/dark green		100 ___
11-70087	No. 2813 LL Cattle Car, cream/tuscan		90 ___
11-70088	No. 2813 LL Cattle Car, terra cotta/pea green		90 ___
11-70089	No. 2810 B&O Crane Car		180 ___
11-70091	No. 2815 LL Tank Car, cream, orange/blue		80 ___
11-70092	No. 2810 Crane Car, blue		180 ___
11-70095	No. 2820 LL Floodlight Car, black/peacock		120 ___
11-70096	No. 2814 Southern Boxcar		90 ___
11-70097	No. 2814 Chessie Boxcar		90 ___
11-70098	No. 2814 Blue Comet Boxcar, nickel trim		90 ___
11-70098	No. 2814 Blue Comet Boxcar, brass trim		90 ___
11-70102	No. 2654 Mobilgas Tank Car		70 ___
11-70103	No. 2654 Esso Tank Car		70 ___
11-70104	No. 2653 Blue Coal Hopper		70 ___
11-70105	No. 2653 Peabody Hopper		70 ___
11-70106	No. 2655 Altoona Brewing Boxcar		70 ___
11-70107	No. 2655 Hood's Grade A Milk Boxcar		70 ___
11-70108	No. 2655 LL Boxcar		70 ___
11-70109	No. 2657 LL Caboose, green/red		70 ___
11-70110	No. 2657 LL Caboose, orange/red		70 ___
11-70113	No. 2814 PRR Boxcar		90 ___
11-70114	No. 2814 ATSF Grand Canyon Boxcar		90 ___
11-70115	No. 2814 Long Island Boxcar		90 ___
11-70116	No. 2814 Alaska Boxcar		90 ___
11-70117	No. 2814R M. K. Goetz Brewing Refrigerator Car		90 ___
11-70118	No. 2814R Gerber Refrigerator Car		90 ___
11-70119	No. 2814R Roberts & Oake Meats Refrigerator Car		90 ___
11-70120	No. 2814R Sullivan's Packing Refrigerator Car		90 ___
11-70121	No. 2816 Western Maryland Coal Car		90 ___
11-70122	No. 2816 P&LE Coal Car		90 ___
11-70123	No. 2816 Waddell Mining Coal Car		90 ___
11-70124	No. 2816 Blue Coal Car		90 ___
11-70125	No. 2815 Clark Oil Tank Car		90 ___
11-70126	No. 2815 Celanese Chemicals Tank Car		90 ___
11-70127	No. 2815 Shell Tank Car		90 ___
11-70128	No. 2815 Cook's Paints Tank Car		90 ___
11-70129	No. 2817 C&O Caboose		100 ___
11-70130	No. 2817 Long Island Caboose		100 ___
11-70131	No. 2817 Southern Caboose		100 ___
11-70132	No. 2817 Jersey Central Caboose		100 ___
11-70133	No. 2814R Gerber Refrigerator Car		90 ___
11-70144	No. 2815 Shell Tank Car		90 ___
11-70154	No. 2814 ATSF Grand Canyon Boxcar		90 ___
11-80001	2600 Series 4-Car Blue Comet Passenger Set		430 ___
11-80002	UP Articulated Baggage Car, silver		150 ___
11-80003	UP Articulated Baggage Car, yellow		150 ___

	Lionel Corporation Tinplate		Exc	Mint
___	**11-80004**	UP Articulated Coach, silver		150
___	**11-80005**	UP Articulated Coach, yellow		150
___	**11-80006**	No. 2613 Series Pullman Coach, blue		110
___	**11-80007**	2600 Series 3-Car Passenger Set, red		300
___	**11-80008**	2600 Series 3-Car Passenger Set, green		300
___	**11-80009**	Milwaukee Road Articulated Baggage Car		150
___	**11-80010**	Milwaukee Road Articulated Coach		150
___	**11-80011**	Articulated Streamliner Baggage Car		150
___	**11-80012**	Articulated Streamliner Coach		150
___	**11-80013**	No. 2613 Series Pullman Coach, red		100
___	**11-80014**	No. 2613 Series Pullman Coach, green		100
___	**11-80015**	No. 605 Christmas Baggage Car		90
___	**11-80016**	710 Series 3-Car Passenger Set, blue		350
___	**11-80017**	No. 710 Series Baggage Car, blue		120
___	**11-80018**	No. 710 Series Passenger Coach, blue		120
___	**11-80019**	710 Series 3-Car Passenger Set, orange		350
___	**11-80020**	No. 710 Series Baggage Car, orange		120
___	**11-80021**	No. 710 Series Passenger Coach, orange		120
___	**11-80022**	710 Series 3-Car Passenger Set, red		350
___	**11-80023**	No. 710 Series Baggage Car, red		120
___	**11-80024**	No. 710 Series Passenger Coach, red		120
___	**11-80025**	No. 1695 3-Car Passenger Set, blue/silver		350
___	**11-80026**	No. 1685 Passenger Car, blue/silver		120
___	**11-80027**	1695 Series 3-Car Passenger Set, red/maroon		380
___	**11-80028**	No. 1695 Passenger Coach, red/maroon		130
___	**11-80029**	City of Denver Coach, yellow/green		110
___	**11-80030**	City of Denver Coach, green		110
___	**11-80031**	No. 605 Baggage Car		90
___	**11-80032**	No. 607 Passenger Coach		90
___	**11-80034**	No. 2613 NYC Pullman Car, LCCA 2012 Convention		100
___	**11-80036**	No. 605 Red Comet Baggage Car		90
___	**11-80039**	600 Series 3-Car Red Comet Passenger Set		270
___	**11-80040**	2600 Series 4-Car Blue Comet Passenger Set, brass trim		430
___	**11-80041**	No. 2613 Pullman Coach, brass trim		110
___	**11-80042**	Flying Yankee Chrome Coach		110
___	**11-80047**	710 Series 3-Car NH Passenger Set		400
___	**11-80048**	710 Series 3-Car GN Passenger Set		400
___	**11-80049**	2600 Series 4-Car Chessie Passenger Set		430
___	**11-80050**	2600 Series 4-Car Southern Passenger Set		430
___	**11-80051**	No. 2613 Chessie Pullman Coach		110
___	**11-80052**	No. 2613 Southern Pullman Coach		110
___	**11-80053**	No. 710 NH Baggage Car		140
___	**11-80054**	No. 710 NH Passenger Coach		140
___	**11-80055**	No. 710 GN Baggage Car		140
___	**11-80056**	No. 710 GN Passenger Coach		140
___	**11-80059**	710 Series 3-car MILW Passenger Set		400

Lionel Corporation Tinplate		Exc	Mint
11-80060	No. 713 MILW Baggage Car		140 ___
11-80061	No. 710 MILW Passenger Coach		140 ___
11-80062	710 Series 3-car PRR Passenger Set		400 ___
11-80063	No. 713 PRR Baggage Car		140 ___
11-80064	No. 710 PRR Passenger Coach		140 ___
11-90001	No. 300 Hellgate Bridge, green/cream		500 ___
11-90002	No. 300 Hellgate Bridge, silver/white		500 ___
11-90003	No. 092 Signal Tower, cream/red		70 ___
11-90006	No. 437 Switch Tower		280 ___
11-90007	No. 155 Freight Shed		330 ___
11-90008	No. 116 Passenger Station		400 ___
11-90009	No. 438 Signal Tower		450 ___
11-90010	No. 192 Villa Set		200 ___
11-90011	No. 191 Villa		70 ___
11-90012	No. 54 Street Lamp Set, green		45 ___
11-90013	No. 54 Street Lamp Set, red		45 ___
11-90014	No. 56 Gas Lamp Set, green		35 ___
11-90015	No. 56 Gas Lamp Set, maroon		35 ___
11-90016	No. 57 Corner Lamp Set, black		40 ___
11-90017	No. 57 Corner Lamp Set, red		35 ___
11-90018	No. 58 Lamp Set, single arc, cream		35 ___
11-90019	No. 58 Lamp Set, single arc, dark green		35 ___
11-90020	No. 59 Gooseneck Lamp Set, black		40 ___
11-90021	No. 59 Gooseneck Lamp Set, maroon		40 ___
11-90022	No. 1184 Bungalow (std)		200 ___
11-90023	No. 1184 Bungalow (std)		200 ___
11-90024	No. 1189 Villa (std)		300 ___
11-90025	No. 1191 Villa (std)		300 ___
11-90026	No. 165 Magnetic Crane		300 ___
11-90027	No. 441 Weighing Station (std)		380 ___
11-90028	No. 69 Operating Warning Bell		50 ___
11-90029	No. 78 Automatic Control Signal (std)		70 ___
11-90030	No. 79 Flashing Railroad Signal		70 ___
11-90031	No. 80 Operating Semaphore		70 ___
11-90032	No. 63 Lamp Post Set, aluminum		50 ___
11-90033	No. 87 Railroad Crossing Signal		50 ___
11-90034	No. 92 Floodlight Tower Set		160 ___
11-90035	No. 94 High Tension Tower Set		150 ___
11-90036	No. Automatic Block Signal (std)		70 ___
11-90037	No. 163 Freight Accessory Set, green cart		100 ___
11-90038	No. 163 Freight Accessory Set, orange cart		100 ___
11-90039	No. 208 Tools and Chest, dark gray		80 ___
11-90040	No. 208 Tools and Chest, silver		80 ___
11-90041	No. 550 Miniature Figures		100 ___
11-90042	No. 64 Lamp Post Set, light green		30 ___
11-90043	No. 85 Race Car Set	300	700 ___

	Lionel Corporation Tinplate		Exc	Mint
___	**11-90044**	Straight Race Car Track Section		20
___	**11-90045**	Inside Curve Race Car Track Section		20
___	**11-90046**	Outside Curve Race Car Track Section		20
___	**11-90047**	No. 55 Airplane & No. 49 Airport Set with mat		800
___	**11-90048**	No. 49 Airport Mat		60
___	**11-90049**	No. 90 Flagpole		50
___	**11-90050**	No. 205 Merchandise Containers, 3 pieces (std)		135
___	**11-90052**	No. 442 Diner		160
___	**11-90053**	No. 43 Runabout Boat, red/white		450
___	**11-90054**	No. 44 Speed Boat		450
___	**11-90055**	No. 71 Telegraph Post Set, gray/red		80
___	**11-90056**	Teardrop Lamp Set, pea green		20
___	**11-90057**	No. 46 Crossing Gate		40
___	**11-90058**	Small Oil Drum Set		20
___	**11-90060**	No. 115 Passenger Station, beige/pea green		300
___	**11-90061**	No. 115 Passenger Station, cream, orange/blue		300
___	**11-90062**	No. 134 Lionel City Station with stop		330
___	**11-90063**	No. 444 Roundhouse Section		500
___	**11-90064**	No. 200 Turntable, red/black		200
___	**11-90065**	No. 89 Flagpole, blue base (std)		50
___	**11-90066**	No. 89 Flagpole, white base (std)		50
___	**11-90067**	No. 89 American Flag Pole, white base (std)		50
___	**11-90068**	Operating Industrial Crane		350
___	**11-90069**	Operating Industrial Crane, TCA 2010 Convention		350
___	**11-90070**	No. 552 Diner, orange/blue		200
___	**11-90071**	No. 552 Diner, white/blue		200
___	**11-90072**	No. 911 Country Estate, cream/red		140
___	**11-90073**	No. 911 Country Estate, red/green		140
___	**11-90074**	No. 912 Suburban Home, ivory/peacock		140
___	**11-90075**	No. 912 Suburban Home, mustard/green		140
___	**11-90076**	No. 913 Landscaped Bungalow, white/maroon		110
___	**11-90077**	No. 913 Landscaped Bungalow, light green/peacock		110
___	**11-90078**	AF No. 2050 Old Glory Flag Pole		100
___	**11-90079**	No. 43 Runabout Boat, orange/blue		400
___	**11-90084**	No. 57 Lamp Post Set, Lionel & American Flyer Aves.		40
___	**11-90085**	No. 57 Lamp Post Set, orange, 21st St. & Fifth Ave.		40
___	**11-90086**	AF No. 2013 Corner Lamp Set, yellow		40
___	**11-90089**	No. 436 Power Station, cream		150
___	**11-90090**	No. 436 Power Station, terra-cotta		150
___	**11-90094**	No. 438 Signal Tower		160
___	**11-90095**	No. 116 Passenger Station		400
___	**11-90096**	No. 1184 Bungalow, gray/green		200
___	**11-90097**	No. 1184 Bungalow, white/maroon		200
___	**11-90098**	No. 1189 Villa (std)		300
___	**11-90099**	No. 1191 Villa (std)		300

Lionel Corporation Tinplate		Exc	Mint
11-90100	No. 442 Diner		160 ___
11-90101	No. 54 Lamp Post Set, pea green		45 ___
11-90102	No. 54 Lamp Post Set, state brown		45 ___
11-90103	No. 58 Lamp Post Set, peacock		35 ___
11-90104	No. 58 Lamp Post Set, orange		35 ___
11-90105	No. 59 Lamp Post Set, dark green		40 ___
11-90106	No. 59 Lamp Post Set, light green		40 ___
11-90107	No. 92 Floodlight Tower Set		170 ___
11-90108	No. 79 Flashing Signal		70 ___
11-90109	No. 69 Warning Signal		50 ___
11-90110	No. 94 High Tension Tower Set		170 ___
11-90111	No. 57 Corner Lamp Set, orange, Lionel		40 ___
11-90112	No. 57 Corner Lamp Set, blue, Lionel		40 ___
11-90113	No. 57 Corner Lamp Set, blue/yellow		40 ___
11-90114	No. 152 Operating Crossing Gate		40 ___
11-90115	No. 153 Operating Block Signal		40 ___
11-90116	No. 154 Highway Flashing Signal	15	75 ___
11-90117	No. 437 Switch Signal Tower, cream/orange	80	300 ___
11-90118	No. 437 Switch Signal Tower, terra-cotta/green		300 ___
11-90119	AF No. 4230 Roadside Flashing Signal		100 ___
11-90120	No. 200 Turntable, gray/green		200 ___
11-90121	No. 200 Turntable, orange/blue		200 ___
11-90122	No. 437 Switch Tower		280 ___
11-90123	No. 98 Coal Bunker		180 ___
11-99030	No. 25 Illuminated Track Bumpers (std)		60 ___

Section 5
MODERN TINPLATE

		Exc	Mint
	O Gauge Classics		
___ **1-263E**	Lionel Lines Blue Comet 2-4-2 Locomotive		NRS
___ **350E**	Lionel Lines Hiawatha 4-4-2 Locomotive	113	200
___ **882**	Lionel Lines Combination Car		NRS
___ **883**	Lionel Lines Passenger Car		NRS
___ **884**	Lionel Lines Observation Car		NRS
___ **1612**	Lionel Lines Passenger Car		NRS
___ **1613**	Lionel Lines Passenger Car		NRS
___ **1614**	Lionel Lines Baggage Car		NRS
___ **1615**	Lionel Lines Observation Car		NRS
___ **51000**	Milwaukee Road Hiawatha Set, 88 u	314	882
___ **51001**	Lionel #44 Freight Special Set, 89	230	600
___ **51004**	Blue Comet Set, 91		1600
___ **51100**	Lionel Lines Electric Locomotive "44E", 89		NRS
___ **51201**	Rail Chief Passenger Cars, set of 4, 90	150	458
___ **51202**	Lionel Lines Combination Car "892"		NRS
___ **51203**	Lionel Lines Passenger Car "893"		NRS
___ **51204**	Lionel Lines Passenger Car "894"		NRS
___ **51205**	Lionel Lines Observation Car "895"		NRS
___ **51400**	Lionel Lines Boxcar "8814," 89		NRS
___ **51500**	Lionel Lines Hopper "8816," 89		NRS
___ **51700**	Lionel Lines Caboose "8817," 89		NRS
___ **51800**	Lionel Lines Searchlight Car "8820," 89		NRS
	Standard Gauge Classics		
___ **1-318E**	Lionel Lines Electric Locomotive	180	600
___ **1-4390**	American Flyer West Point Baggage Car		NRS
___ **1-4391**	American Flyer Academy Passenger Car		NRS
___ **1-4392**	American Flyer Army/Navy Observation Car		NRS
___ **5130**	Lionel Lines Flatcar with lumber		NRS
___ **5140**	Lionel Lines Reefer		NRS
___ **5150**	Lionel Lines Shell Tank Car		NRS
___ **5160**	Lionel Lines Caboose		NRS
___ **13001**	1-318E Freight Express Train Set, 90-91		960
___ **13002**	Fireball Express Set, 90 u	350	1600
___ **13003**	American Flyer Mayflower Passenger Car Set, 92		2000
___ **13004**	Milwaukee Road Hiawatha Passenger Set, 01-02		2000
___ **13008**	NYC Commodore Vanderbilt Passenger Set, 02	700	1600
___ **13100**	Lionel Lines 2-4-2 Locomotive "1-390E," 88 u		610
___ **13101**	Lionel Lines 2-4-0 Locomotive "1-384E," 89 u	313	750
___ **13102**	Lionel Lines Electric Locomotive "1-381E," 89 u	383	1490
___ **13103**	Lionel Lines Blue Comet 4-4-4 Locomotive, 90	625	1350
___ **13104**	Lionel Lines "Old #7" 4-4-0 Locomotive, 90		900

MODERN TINPLATE		Exc	Mint
13106	Lionel Lines Fireball Express 2-4-2 Locomotive		NRS ____
13107	Lionel Lines Electric Locomotive "1-408E," 91		990 ____
13108	Lionel Lines 4-4-4 Locomotive "2-400E," Gray, 91	450	1100 ____
13109	American Flyer Mayflower Electric Locomotive, 92		2500 ____
13200	Lionel Lines Searchlight Car "1520," 89 u	55	155 ____
13300	Lionel Lines Gondola "1512," 89 u		75 ____
13303	Lionel Lines Sunoco Tank Car "1-215," 92		135 ____
13400	Lionel Lines Baggage Car "323," 88 u		173 ____
13401	Lionel Lines Passenger Car "324," 88 u		180 ____
13402	Lionel Lines Observation Car "325," 88 u	35	135 ____
13403	Lionel Lines State Passenger Car Set, 89 u		1100 ____
13404	Lionel Lines California Passenger Car "1412," 90	200	360 ____
13405	Lionel Lines Colorado Passenger Car "1413," 90	200	360 ____
13406	Lionel Lines New York Observation Car "1416," 90	200	360 ____
13407	Lionel Lines Illinois Passenger Car "1414," 90	175	450 ____
13408	Lionel Lines Blue Comet Passenger Car Set, 90	413	1500 ____
13409	Lionel Lines Faye Passenger Car "1420"		NRS ____
13410	Lionel Lines Westphal Passenger Car "1421"		NRS ____
52404	PE Birney Trolley, 06		75 ____
13411	Lionel Lines Tempel Observation Car "1422"		NRS ____
13412	Lionel Lines "Old #7" Passenger Car Set, 90	175	800 ____
13413	Lionel Lines Combination Car "183"		NRS ____
13414	Lionel Lines Passenger Car "184"		NRS ____
13415	Lionel Lines Observation Car "185"		NRS ____
13416	Lionel Lines New Jersey Baggage Car "326"		NRS ____
13417	Lionel Lines Connecticut Passenger Car "327"		NRS ____
13418	Lionel Lines New York Observation Car "328"		NRS ____
13420	Lionel Lines State Passenger Car Set, 91		1300 ____
13421	Lionel Lines California Passenger Car "2412,", 90	200	360 ____
13422	Lionel Lines Colorado Passenger Car "2413," 90	200	360 ____
13423	Lionel Lines Illinois Passenger Car "2414," 92 u	200	817 ____
13424	Lionel Lines New York Observation Car "2416," 92	200	360 ____
13425	Lionel Lines Barnard Passenger Car "1423," 91 u	175	1350 ____
13600	Lionel Lines Cattle Car "1513," 89 u		90 ____
13601	"Season's Greetings" Boxcar, 89 u		105 ____
13602	"Season's Greetings" Boxcar, 90 u		100 ____
13604	"Season's Greetings" Boxcar, 91 u		110 ____
13605	Lionel Lines Boxcar "1-214," 92	45	155 ____
13700	Lionel Lines Caboose "1517," 89 u		105 ____
13702	Lionel Lines Caboose "1217," 91		115 ____
13800	Lionelville Passenger Station, 88 u	40	390 ____
13801	Lionelville Station "126," 89 u	55	290 ____
13804	Lionelville Switch Tower "437," 91		400 ____
13900	Electric Rapid Transit Trolley "200," 89 u		290 ____
13901	Electric Rapid Transit Trolley Trailer "201," 89 u		150 ____
51900	Signal Bridge and Control Panel, 89 u		399 ____

Section 6
CLUB CARS AND SPECIAL PRODUCTION

			Exc	Mint
ARTRAIN				
___	**9486**	GTW "I Love Michigan" Boxcar, 87		305
___	**17885**	1-D Tank Car, 90	55	65
___	**17891**	GTW 20th Anniversary Boxcar, 91	70	75
___	**19425**	CSX Flatcar with "Art in Celebration" trailer, 96		80
___	**52013**	Norfolk Southern Flatcar with trailer, 92	160	228
___	**52024**	Conrail Auto Carrier, 93	80	90
___	**52049**	BN Gondola with coil covers, 94	50	56
___	**52097**	Chessie System Reefer, 95		34
___	**52140**	Union Pacific Bunk Car, 97		37
___	**52165**	SP Caboose "6256", 98		60
___	**52197**	Santa Fe GP38 Diesel, 99		243
___	**52227**	"Artistry in Space" Boxcar, 00		75
___	**52255**	30th Anniversary Flatcar with billboard, 01		100
___	**52283**	Paint Vat Car, 02		59
___	**52331**	Flatcar with "America's Railways" trailer, 03		150
___	**52349**	Hometown Art Museum Hopper, purple, 04		35
___	**52350**	"Native Views" 3-bay Hopper, 04		65
___	**52411**	"35 Years" 1-D Tank Car, 06		35
CARNEGIE SCIENCE CENTER				
___	**25085**	Miniature Railroad & Village Boxcar, 09		50
___	**26750**	Great Miniature Railroad & Village Boxcar, 99		78
___	**36202**	Great Miniature Railroad 80th Anniversary Boxcar, 00		110
___	**36234**	Great Miniature Railroad & Village Boxcar, 01		50
___	**52277**	Carnegie Science Center 10th Anniversary Boxcar, 02		60
___	**52332**	Miniature Railroad & Village Boxcar, 03		58
___	**52362**	Miniature Railroad & Village 50th Anniversary Boxcar, 04		50
___	**52399**	MRR&V Express Boxcar, 05		50
___	**52432**	Miniature Railroad & Village Boxcar, 06		50
___	**52510**	Miniature Railroad & Village Caboose, 08		50
___	**26694**	Carnegie Science Center Flatcar w/Submarine, 12	25	50
___	**37098**	Carnegie Science Center Flatcar w/Capsule, 13	25	50
___	**58603**	Carnegie Science Center Boxcar, 11	25	50
CHICAGOLAND RAILROAD CLUB				
___	**52081**	C&NW Boxcar "6464-555", 96	40	68
___	**52101**	BN Maxi-Stack Flatcar "64287" with containers, 97		82
___	**52102**	SF Extended Vision Caboose, red roof, 96		75
___	**52103**	SF Extended Vision Caboose, black roof, 96		75
___	**52120**	Shedd Aquarium Car "3435-557," 98	34	79
___	**52148**	REA/Santa Fe Operating Boxcar, 99	15	70
___	**52170**	SP Operating Boxcar "52170-561," 99		65
___	**52171**	UP Operating Boxcar "52171-561," 99		65

CLUB CARS AND SPECIAL PRODUCTION		Exc	Mint
52178	Burlington Operating Boxcar "52178-559," 00		70
52179	ACL Operating Boxcar "52179-560," 00		73
52215	C&NW 3-bay Cylindrical Hopper, 01		60
52216	C&NW Cylindrical Hopper, 02		60
52223	REA/Santa Fe Centennial Operating Boxcar, 00		65
52251	PRR Express Car, green, 01		67
52259	MP GP20 Diesel, traditional, 01		250
52292	PRR Express Car, tuscan red, 02		50
52327	City of Los Angeles Express Car, 04		65
52328	City of New Haven Express Car, 04		55
52363	City of New Orleans Express Car, 04		55
52364	City of New York Express Car, 04		65
52388	Great Northern Tool Car, 06		48
52389	Great Northern Crew Car, 06		48
52390	Great Northern Welding Caboose, 06		78
52391	Great Northern Racing Crew Car, 06		48
52426	City of San Francisco Express Car, 07		55
52427	Rock Island Rocket Express Car, 07		55
52475	Western Pacific UP Heritage Boxcar, 07		60
18510	C&NW 25th Anniversary Refrigerator Car, 19		65
2001310	ATSF PS-1 Boxcar, 20		70
2201202	Lumber Jack Lager Refrigerator Car, 22		85
Classic Toy Trains			
52126	10th Anniversary MILW Boxcar "21027," 97		50
69013	30th Anniversary CTT Boxcar, 17		75
Dept. 56			
16270	Heritage Village Boxcar "9796," 96		56
52096	Snow Village Boxcar "9756", 95		85
52139	Square Window Caboose "6256," 97		72
52157	Holly Brothers 3-D Tank Car, 98	6	85
52175	4-6-4 Hudson Locomotive, CC, 99	75	350
52199	4-bay Hopper "6756," 00	20	53
52254	"Happy Holidays" Gondola, 01		35
Eastwood Automobilia			
16275	Radio Flyer Boxcar "16275," 96		50
16757	Johnny Lightning Auto Carrier "3435," 96		90
16985	Flatcar with 2 Ford vans, 97		49
52044	Mogen David Wine Vat Car, 95	21	30
52083	PRR Flatcar "21697" with tanker, 95		41
52130	Flatcar with Hot Wheels tanker, 97		60
Houston Tinplate Operators Society (HTOS)			
8900	Sam Houston Mint Car, 00		120
8901	Miracle Petroleum 1-D Tank Car, 01		100
8902	USS Houston Submarine Car, 02		100

	CLUB CARS AND SPECIAL PRODUCTION		Exc	Mint
___	**8903**	Railway Express Boxcar, 03		100
___	**8904**	Lone Star Bay Window Caboose, 04		100
___	**8999**	Lone Star Aquarium Car, mermaid or trout, 99	43	105

INLAND EMPIRE TRAIN COLLECTORS ASSOCIATION (IETCA)

			Exc	Mint
___	**1979**	Boxcar, 79		15
___	**1980**	SP-type Caboose, 80		14
___	**1981**	Quad Hopper, 81		14
___	**1982**	3-D Tank Car, 82		14
___	**1983**	Refrigerator Car, 83		14
___	**1986**	Bunk Car, 86		14
___	**7518**	Carson City Mint Car, 84	36	43

LIONEL CENTRAL OPERATING LINES (LCOL)

			Exc	Mint
___	**1981**	Boxcar, 81		23
___	**1986**	Work Caboose, shell only, 86		14
___	**5724**	Pennsylvania Bunk Car, 84	30	39
___	**6508**	Canadian Pacific Crane Car, 83		40
___	**6907**	NYC Wood-sided Caboose, 97		50
___	**9184**	Erie Bay Window Caboose, 82	17	21
___	**9475**	D&H "I Love NY" Boxcar, 85		34
___	**16342**	CSX Gondola with coil covers, 92		20
___	**17221**	NYC Boxcar, 95		30

LIONEL COLLECTORS ASSOCIATION OF CANADA (LCAC)

			Exc	Mint
___	**5710**	Canadian Pacific Reefer, 83		215
___	**5714**	Michigan Central Reefer, 85	120	150
___	**6100**	Ontario Northland Covered Quad Hopper, 82		250
___	**8103**	Toronto, Hamilton & Buffalo Boxcar, 81		150
___	**8204**	Algoma Central Boxcar, 82		150
___	**8507/08**	Canadian National F3 Diesel AA, shells only, 85		400
___	**8912**	Canada Southern Operating Hopper, 89		95
___	**9413**	Napierville Junction Boxcar, 80		10
___	**9718**	Canadian National Boxcar, 79		20
___	**17893**	BAOC 1-D Tank Car "914," 91		120
___	**52004**	Algoma Central Gondola "9215" with coil covers, 92	70	90
___	**52005**	Canadian National F3 Diesel B Unit "9517," 93		30
___	**52006**	Canadian Pacific Boxcar "930016" (std 0), 93	63	149
___	**52115**	Wabash Lake Railway 2-tier Auto Carrier "9519," 98		100
___	**52125**	TH&B Gondola 2-pack, 99		90
___	**52245**	Northern Alberta Railways Boxcar, 99		160
___	**86009**	Canadian National Bunk Car, 86		115
___	**87010**	Canadian National Express Reefer, 87		115
___	**88011**	Canadian National Caboose (std 0), 88		500
___	**830005**	Canadian National Boxcar, 83		300
___	**840006**	Canadian Wheat Board Covered Quad Hopper, 84		165
___	**900013**	Canadian National Flatcar with trailers, 90		225

LIONEL COLLECTORS CLUB OF AMERICA (LCCA)

■ LCCA National Convention Cars

		Exc	Mint	
6112	Commonwealth Edison Quad Hopper with coal, 83	49	78	___
6323	Virginia Chemicals 1-D Tank Car, 86	47	63	___
6567	Illinois Central Gulf Crane Car "100408," 85	55	63	___
7403	LNAC Boxcar, 84	21	24	___
9118	Corning Covered Quad Hopper, 74	65	92	___
9155	Monsanto 1-D Tank Car, 75	38	47	___
9159	UP Refrigerator Car, 10	50	100	___
9212	Seaboard Coast Line Flatcar with trailers, 76	22	31	___
9259	Southern Bay Window Caboose, 77	11	41	___
9358	Sands of Iowa Covered Quad Hopper, 80	24	33	___
9435	Central of Georgia Boxcar, 81	25	29	___
9460	D&TS Automobile Boxcar, 82	25	34	___
9701	Baltimore & Ohio Automobile Boxcar, 72		170	___
9727	TA&G Boxcar, 73	105	134	___
9728	Union Pacific Stockcar, 78	23	26	___
9733	Airco Boxcar with tank car body, 79	37	50	___
17500	Convention Boxcar 2-pack, 17		120	___
17501	NP PS-1 Boxcar "201706", 17		60	___
17502	GN Mechanical Refrigerator Car "724295," 17		60	___
17510	NP Wood-chip 2-Bay Hopper "724293," 17		85	___
17870	East Camden & Highland Boxcar (std 0), 87	29	33	___
17873	Ashland Oil 3-D Tank Car, 88	55	70	___
17876	Columbia, Newberry & Laurens Boxcar (std 0), 89	32	40	___
17880	D&RGW Wood-sided Caboose (std 0), 90	43	55	___
17887	Conrail Flatcar with Armstrong Tile trailer (std 0), 91	30	49	___
17888	Conrail Flatcar with Ford trailer (std 0), 91	42	80	___
17892	Conrail Flatcar with Armstrong and Ford Trailers (std 0), 91		140	___
17899	NASA Unibody 1-D Tank Car "190" (std 0), 92	47	53	___
27019	Imco PS-2 Covered Hopper, 09		50	___
52023	D&TS 2-bay ACF Hopper "2601" (std 0), 93	27	40	___
52038	Southern Hopper "360794" w/Coal (std 0), 94	36	46	___
52074	Iowa Beef Packers Reefer "197095" (std 0), 95		32	___
52090	Pere Marquette DD Boxcar "71996" (std 0), 96		52	___
52110	CStPM&O Boxcar "71997" (std 0), 97	18	52	___
52151	Amtrak Express Baggage Boxcar "71998" (std 0), 98		64	___
52152	Ben Franklin and Liberty Bell Wood-side Refrigerator Car, 98	65	120	___
52176	Fort Worth & Denver Boxcar "8277" (std 0), 99		55	___
52195	Double-stack Car w/2 containers, 00		100	___
52244	Louisville & Nashville Horse Car "2001," 01		50	___
52266	PRR "Coal Goes To War" Hopper "707025," 02		86	___
52267	PRR "Coal Goes To War" Hopper "707026," 02		92	___
52273	U.S. Navy Flatcar w/Submarine, 02		219	___

	CLUB CARS AND SPECIAL PRODUCTION		Exc	Mint
____	**52299**	Las Vegas Mint Car, 03	23	80
____	**52343**	MILW Milk Car, orange, 04	43	130
____	**52344**	MILW Milk Car, blue, 04	50	172
____	**52393**	MKT Speeder, yellow, nonpowered, 05		20
____	**52394**	Frisco Speeder, red, powered, 05		25
____	**52395**	Frisco Flatcar, silver, 05		25
____	**52396**	Frisco Flatcar w/2 speeders, 05		125
____	**52412**	UP Auxiliary Power Car, 06		55
____	**52455**	C&NW UP Heritage Unibody 1-D Tank Car, 07	65	110
____	**52491**	PS-2 Covered Hopper 2-pack, 08		140
____	**52507**	NYC Water Tower, 08		83
____	**52514**	ATSF Mint Car with Gold, 09		275
____	**52543**	BNSF Mechanical Refrigerator Car, 09		140
____	**52559**	UP Cylindrical Hopper, 10		100
____	**52562**	D&RGW Uranium Transport Mint Car, 10		230
____	**58045**	Chicago Registration Trolley, 18	58	80
____	**58046**	Chicago Banquet Trolley, 18	60	80
____	**58047**	Reno Registration Trolley, 19	60	80
____	**58060**	C&NW UP Heritage Boxcar (std O), 18	75	120
____	**58061**	C&IM Unibody 1-D Tank Car, 18		100
____	**58213**	B&M GP7 Diesel "2335," LionChief Plus, 15	135	250
____	**58214**	B&M GP7 Diesel "2361," non-powered, 15	75	105
____	**58217**	B&M Smoking Caboose, 15	56	77
____	**58251**	MEC PS-4 Flatcar w/Trailers, 15	60	85
____	**58252**	LCCA 45th Anniversary Trailer, 15		35
____	**58253**	Lionel 115th Anniversary Trailer, 15		35
____	**58254**	Providence & Worcester PS-4 Flatcar w/Tractor Cabs, 15	75	100
____	**58267**	KCS Inspection Truck Motorized Unit, 16	56	90
____	**58268**	KCS Inspection Truck Motorized Unit, 16	55	80
____	**58271**	MP Katy and Kansas Maxi Stack, set of 2, 16	47	85
____	**58272**	MKT Maxi-Stack Car and Container, 16	74	110
____	**58273**	Look-A-Like Container, 16	40	70
____	**58509**	NP PS-1 Boxcar w/Illumination, 12		150
____	**58515**	NS Vulcan Switcher, 12		50
____	**58532**	Reading Anthracite Blue Coal Mining Set, 17		190
____	**58560**	Southern "Tennessean" Boxcar, 13	59	90
____	**58561**	Southern "Pelican" DD Boxcar, 13	39	82
____	**58576**	Postwar 3494-550 Monon Operating Boxcar, 14		85
____	**58586**	South Shore Lines Registration Trolley, 14		95
____	**58587**	South Shore Line Banquet Trolley, 14		110
____	**58589**	Boston Electric Banquet Trolley, 15	80	125
____	**59003**	Lionel Trains ACF 2-Bay Hopper, 13		50
____	**59013**	Monon Boxcar, 14		29
____	**59014**	Conway Scenic RR Boxcar, 15	75	100
____	**59017**	BNSF Boxcar, 16		95
____	**72511**	Alamo Mint Car, 11	75	150

CLUB CARS AND SPECIAL PRODUCTION		Exc	Mint	
72512	Richard Kughn Car, 10		120	___
75511	Federal Reserve Mint Car, 11		200	___
83860	Kansas City Custom Container, 16		20	___
83861	BNSF Custom Container, 16		20	___
1901430	SP Daylight Mint Car, 19		120	___
1901440	Virginia & Truckee Boxcar, 19		90	___
2001090	50th Anniversary Convention Car 2-pack, 20		300	___
2001091	50th Anniversary UP Operating Welding Caboose, 20		150	___
2001092	50th Anniversary UP Gondola w/Coil covers, 20		100	___
2001100	50th Anniversary UP Registration Mint Car, 20		75	___
2001110	UP ET44AC Diesel "2020" LionChief Plus 2.0, 20		700	___
2001160	50th Anniversary UP Unibody 1-D Tank Car, 20		75	___
2001270	50th Anniversary Convention Banquet Boxcar, 20		150	___
2001281	50th Anniversary Convention Volunteer Boxcar, 20		80	___
2001282	50th Anniversary Convention Director Boxcar, 20		170	___
2001330	U.S.A.F. Strategic Air Command Boxcar, 20		130	___
2101270	Scranton Electric City Registration Trolley, 21		125	___
2101280	Scranton Electric City Banquet Trolley, 21		190	___
2101520	EL Walking Brakeman Car, 21		115	___
2101540	Texas Special Walking Brakeman Car, 21		90	___
2201210	Tennessee Central Mint Car, 22		90	___
2201220	RJ Corman Flatcar w/Excavator, 22		100	___
2201230	RJ Corman Gondola w/Coil Covers, 22		80	___
2201240	National Corvette Museum Boxcar, 22	105	200	___
2201250	Goo Goo Candy Banquet Boxcar, 22		200	___
2201261	Goo Goo Candy Convention Volunteer Boxcar, 22		175	___
2201262	Goo Goo Candy Boxcar, 22		225	___
2301120	Concord Convention Tank Car 2-pack, 23		180	___
2301121	Southern Heritage Unibody 1-D Tank Car, 23		90	___
2301122	NS Heritage Unibody 1-D Tank Car, 23		90	___
2301130	NASCAR Racing Mint Car, 23		125	___
2301140	Aberdeen, Carolina & Western Boxcar, 23		95	___
2301141	Aberdeen, Carolina & Western Boxcar, 23		95	___
2301142	Aberdeen, Carolina & Western Boxcar, 23		95	___
2301150	Concord Convention Registration Boxcar, 23		90	___
2301200	Lionel Headquarters Tour Boxcar, 23		80	___
2301250	Aberdeen, Carolina & Western Unibody 1-D Tank Car, 23		150	___
2301460	Texas Pete Boxcar, 23		110	___
2301510	Texas Pete Unibody 1-D Tank Car, 23		150	___
2401190	Krispy Kreme Doughnuts Boxcar, 24		95	___
2401200	SP Passenger Train, 24		430	___
2401230	UP Boat Loader, 24		95	___
2401300	SP Gondola w/Coil covers, 24		90	___
2401400	Omaha Steaks Boxcar, 24		99	___
2401450	UP National Convention Banquet Boxcar, 24		150	___

	CLUB CARS AND SPECIAL PRODUCTION		Exc	Mint
___	**2401451**	UP National Convention Volunteer Boxcar, 24		175
___	**2401452**	UP National Convention Director/Officer Boxcar, 24		200
___	**2401490**	Strategic Air Command Museum Boxcar, 24		99

■ LCCA Meet Specials

			Exc	Mint
___	**1130**	Tender, 76		15
___	**6014-900**	Frisco Boxcar (027), 75	17	30
___	**6483**	Jersey Central SP-type Caboose, 82	24	28
___	**9016**	Chessie System Hopper (027), 79	16	20
___	**9036**	Mobilgas 1-D Tank Car (027), 78	20	22
___	**9142**	Republic Steel Gondola, green or blue, with canisters, 77	15	23

■ Other LCCA Production

			Exc	Mint
___	**4001**	RJ Corman Boxcar, 99		80
___	**4002**	RJ Corman Boxcar, 99		40
___	**6464-2002**	Maddox Retirement Boxcar, 02		100
___	**8068**	Rock Island GP20 Diesel, 80	85	143
___	**9739**	D&RGW Boxcar, 78	17	25
___	**9771**	Norfolk & Western Boxcar, 77		32
___	**14154**	Water Tower with LCCA plaque, 04		90
___	**17174**	Great Northern 3-bay Hopper, 03		25
___	**17234**	Port Huron & Detroit Boxcar, 00		45
___	**17377**	American Railway Express Reefer "302," 06	25	48
___	**17412**	Gondola, blue, 02		28
___	**17895**	LCCA Tractor, 91	13	21
___	**17896**	Lancaster Lines Tractor, 91	22	30
___	**18090**	D&RGW 4-6-2 Locomotive and Tender, 90	230	303
___	**18483**	C&O Ballast Tamper, 07		73
___	**18490**	UP Ballast Tamper, yellow, 06		125
___	**19998**	"Seasons Greetings" Boxcar, 03		40
___	**22680**	NH Yankee Clipper Boxcar, 10	80	110
___	**26023**	Flatcar with bulldozer, 04		53
___	**26024**	Flatcar with scraper, 04		63
___	**26049**	Speedboat Willie Flatcar with boat, 05		45
___	**26132**	UP 1-D Tank Car, 06		27
___	**26780**	Operating Giraffe Car, green or pink, 05		70
___	**26791**	UP Chase Gondola, red, 03		32
___	**26791**	Rio Grande Chase Gondola, black, 06		32
___	**26795**	Mrs. O'Leary's Dairy Farm Stock Car, 07		100
___	**26834**	"La Cosa Nostra Railway" Operating Ice Car, 07	25	75
___	**29232**	Lenny the Lion Hi-Cube, signed by Lenny Dean, 98		63
___	**52107**	On-track Pickup, orange, 96		50
___	**52108**	On-track Van, blue, 96		35
___	**52025**	Madison Hardware Tractor and Trailer, 93	13	18

CLUB CARS AND SPECIAL PRODUCTION		Exc	Mint	
52039	"Track 29" Bumper, 94	10	20	___
52055	SOVEX Tractor and Trailer, 94	15	22	___
52056	Southern Tractor and Trailer, 94	17	23	___
52091	Lenox Tractor and Trailer, 95		14	___
52092	Iowa Interstate Tractor and Trailer, 95		20	___
52100	Grand Rapids Station Platform, 98		23	___
52131	Beechcraft Airplane, blue, 97		25	___
52138	Beechcraft Airplane, orange, 97		25	___
52153	6414 Auto Set, 4-pack, 98	43	72	___
52206	LCCA SD40 Diesel and Extended-Vision Caboose, 00		650	___
52257	"Season's Greetings" Gondola, 01		36	___
52300	Halloween General Train, 04		360	___
52348	Halloween General Sheriff and Outlaw Car, 04		115	___
52405	Halloween General Add-on Cars, 06	55	160	___
52406	Halloween General Cannon, 08		135	___
52423	Postwar "1608W" NH Alco Diesel Passenger Set, 09	316	510	___
52468	Postwar "2434" Newark Pullman Coach, 09		75	___
52469	Postwar "2432" Clifton Vista-Dome Car, 09		75	___
52581	Texas Special Milk Car, 10		110	___
52582	Gondola with dinosaurs, 12		45	___
58065	2018 Christmas Boxcar, 18	60	90	___
58224	Walking Brakeman Car, 15	55	80	___
58249	2015 Christmas Boxcar, 15	60	90	___
58255	Lionelville Tractor/Trailer, blue, 15	25	40	___
58256	Lionelville Tractor/Trailer, orange, 15	25	40	___
58264	2016 Christmas Boxcar, 16	50	75	___
58269	NP Inspection Truck Motorized Unit, 17	63	100	___
58526	Texas Special NW2 Cow and Calf Switchers, 14		375	___
58527	Lionel Vulcan Switcher, 13		80	___
58536	Texas Special PS-4 Flatcar w/Helicopter, 12	77	100	___
58539	Texas Special B-W Caboose, 13		95	___
58549	Texas Special Diamonds Mint Car, 14		75	___
58550	Texas Special Unibody Tank Car, 13	70	95	___
58584	Wabash Auto Loader, black, 14		110	___
58585	Wabash Auto Loader, white, 14		110	___
58599	UP Cylindrical Hopper, 11	28	75	___
58613	2014 Christmas Boxcar, 14	62	80	___
59000	Tennessee Valley RR Boxcar, 13		80	___
84609	2017 Christmas Boxcar, 17		40	___
1901420	2019 Christmas Boxcar, 19		125	___
2001300	2020 Christmas Boxcar, 20		60	___
2101320	2021 Christmas Boxcar, 21		85	___
2101530	Salute to First Responders Boxcar, 21	60	85	___
2201290	N&W 2-6-6-4 Class A Locomotive "1222," CC, 22		2100	___
2201470	2022 Christmas Boxcar, 22		80	___

CLUB CARS AND SPECIAL PRODUCTION

	No.	Description	Exc	Mint
____	**2301050**	UP Vision 4-8-8-4 Big Boy Locomotive "4023," CC, 23		2900
____	**2301550**	2023 Christmas Boxcar, 23		90
____	**2401330**	LL Triplex Steam Locomotive "2024," CC, 24		2500
____	**2401570**	2024 Christmas Boxcar, 24		100
____	**2401760**	Alaska RR Doodlebug, 24		360
____	**2401770**	Texas Special Doodlebug, 24		360
____	**2501010**	PRR GG1 "2340," CC, 25		1700
____	**2531020**	NYC Vision 4-6-4 Hudson Locomotive "5325," CC, 25		1800

LIONEL OPERATING TRAIN SOCIETY (LOTS)

■ LOTS National Convention Cars

	No.	Description	Exc	Mint
____	**303**	Stauffer Chemical 1-D Tank Car, 85	85	210
____	**3764**	Kahn's Brine Tank Refrigerator Car, 81	70	85
____	**6111**	L&N Covered Quad Hopper, 83	37	42
____	**6211**	C&O Gondola w/Canisters, 86	60	90
____	**9414**	Cotton Belt Boxcar, 80	39	55
____	**16812**	Grand Trunk ACF 2-Bay Hopper (std O), 96	30	60
____	**16813**	Pennsylvania Power & Light Hopper w/Coal (std O), 97	40	78
____	**17874**	MilLW Log Dump Car "59629," 88	90	148
____	**17875**	Port Huron & Detroit Boxcar "1289," 89	40	48
____	**17882**	B&O DD Boxcar "298011" w/ETD, 90	55	65
____	**17890**	CSX Auto Carrier "151161," 91	75	80
____	**19960**	WP Boxcar "1952" (std O), 92	47	66
____	**38356**	Dow Chemical 3-D Tank Car, 87	85	125
____	**52014**	BN TTUX Flatcar Set "637500" w/N&W trailers, 93	165	205
____	**52041**	BN TTUX Flatcar Set "637500" w/Conrail trailers, 94	60	85
____	**52048**	CN Intermodel Laser Service Tractor-Trailer, 94	28	35
____	**52067**	CB&Q Operating Ice Car "50240," 95	30	60
____	**52135**	ATSF Refrigerator Car "22739,", 98	30	55
____	**52162**	GM&O DD Boxcar "24580," 99	35	65
____	**52196**	CP Maxi-Stack Flatcar "524115" w/Containers, 00	50	95
____	**52217**	LOTS/LCCA 2000 Convention Billboard, 00	5	10
____	**52234**	WM Well Car /Transformer, 01	30	60
____	**52260**	National Aquarium in Baltimore Car, 01	55	110
____	**52261**	Schlitz Beer Refrigerator Car "92132," 02	30	60
____	**52281**	PRR Operating Boxcar "30129," 03	30	55
____	**52342**	Southern Stockcar "70425" w/Sounds, 04		57
____	**52346**	D&H PS-2 Covered Hopper "12041," 06	35	65
____	**52380**	Virginian Coal Hopper "2605" w/ETD, 05	25	50
____	**52381**	Virginian Coal Hopper "2606," 05	25	50
____	**52425**	SP&S Boxcar (std O), 07	54	90
____	**52474**	NYC Evans Auto Loader w/Studebakers, 08	40	82
____	**52550**	NC&StL Dixieland Boxcar, 09	40	73
____	**52553**	Tennessee Aquarium Car, 09	25	52
____	**52566**	NH State of Maine Double-sheathed Boxcar, 10	30	62

CLUB CARS AND SPECIAL PRODUCTION		Exc	Mint	
52580	Robin Hood Beer Double-sheathed Boxcar, 11	40	80	___
58044	B&M Operating Welding Flatcar, 18	90	160	___
58223	CGW Flatcar w/Edelweiss Beer Trailers, 15	50	90	___
58228	CB&Q Zephyr Double-sheathed Boxcar, 15	40	55	___
58236	Tucker Automobile Parts DD Boxcar, 15	60	120	___
58260	Yuengling Beer Double-sheathed Boxcar, 16	100	150	___
58508	Genesee Beer & Ale Double-sheathed Boxcar, 12	35	65	___
58538	NYC Flatcar w/Kodak Trailer, 12	95	115	___
58553	UP Maxi-Stack Car w/WP Containers, 13	40	75	___
58575	H. J. Heinz Double-sheathed Boxcar, 14	35	70	___
80948	Michigan Central Boxcar, 82	145	230	___
83862	Philadelphia Cradle of Liberty Double-sheathed Boxcar, 16	65	85	___
83872	D&RGW Matchless Mine Ore Car "38171,", 17		55	___
83873	D&RGW Matchless Mine Ore Car "38173," 17		55	___
121315	PRR Hi-Cube Boxcar, 84	125	343	___
1901320	L&N Auto Loader w/Corvettes, 19		120	___
2001340	Gorilla Glue Boxcar, 20	120	180	___
2101350	MKT Auto Loader w/Ford Trucks and Thunderbirds, 21		150	___
2401220	ATSF Iron Rail Brewing PS-1 Boxcar, 24		85	___

■ LOTS Meet Specials

22680	NH Yankee Clipper Boxcar by K-Line, 10		60	___
52413	Saratoga Brewery Refrigerator Car, 06	30	60	___
52456	Alpenrose Dairy Milk Car, 07	50	95	___
52506	Studebaker Automobile Parts Boxcar, 08	40	75	___
52552	Radioactive Waste Removal Car, 09	45	86	___
58558	Virginia & Truckee Ore Car "34132," 13	30	50	___
58559	Virginia & Truckee Ore Car "34133," 13	30	50	___
58593	Porter Locomotive Works Double-sheathed Boxcar, 15	80	95	___
83869	D&RGW Flatcar w/Celestial Seasoning Maxi-Stack, 17	90	130	___
1801050	Woodstock Brewing Boxcar, 18	90	140	___
1901670	L&N Kentucky Bourbon Trail 3-Bay Covered Hopper, 19	80	125	___
2001450	U.S.A.F. Wright-Patterson Unibody 1-D Tank Car, 20	80	120	___
2301330	Joshua Dairy Farm Flatcar "44232" w/Milk Container, 23	45	65	___
2401240	CPKC Sunflower Oil Unibody 1-D Tank Car, 24		77	___

■ Other LOTS Production

1223	Seattle & North Coast Hi-Cube Boxcar, 86	300	400	___
18890	UP Alco RS-3 Diesel "8805," 89	120	145	___
52042	BN TTUX Flatcar "637500" w/CN trailer, 94	50	60	___
52129	Lighted Billboard with Angela Trotta Thomas art, 97	15	28	___
52280	"More Precious than Gold" Mint Car, 02	45	90	___
52309	Patriotic 1-D Tank Car, 03	35	68	___
52347	ATSF EMD SD80MAC Diesel "2504," CC, 04	170	350	___
52359	Silver Anniversary Ore Car "1979," 04	20	40	___

CLUB CARS AND SPECIAL PRODUCTION			Exc	Mint
___	**52360**	Silver Anniversary Ore Car "2004," 04	20	40
___	**52382**	ATSF Warbonnet EV Caboose "2505," 05	165	325
___	**52419**	Touring Layout Aquarium Car, 056	45	90
___	**52477**	ATSF Warbonnet Boxcar "2807," 07	125	170
___	**52523**	ATSF Warbonnet Flatcar w/Trailer, 08	45	88
___	**52567**	ATSF Warbonnet ACF 2-Bay Hopper "2809," 10	30	58
___	**52590**	ATSF Warbonnet Mint Car, 11	40	75
___	**58535**	ATSF Warbonnet Transparent Boxcar, 12	40	75
___	**58566**	Virginia & Truckee Carson City Mint Car, 13	35	70
___	**58594**	ATSF Warbonnet Crane Car "35143," 14	150	270
___	**58595**	ATSF Warbonnet Work Caboose "35144," 14	140	230
___	**83863**	ATSF Warbonnet Unibody 1-D Tank Car," 16	140	170
___	**83874**	ATSF Warbonnet Gondola "38172" w/Coil Covers, 17	80	120
___	**1801030**	Samuel Adams Lager Beer Boxcar, 18		55
___	**1901330**	BNSF Warbonnet 3-Bay Hopper "40192," 19		160
___	**2001350**	CSX Flatcar w/Kroger Trailer, 20		55
___	**2101371**	ATSF Warbonnet Ore Car "42213," 21		60

LIONEL CENTURY CLUB (LCC)				
___	**14532**	PRR Sharknose Diesel AA Set, LCC II, 00		690
___	**18053**	2-8-4 Berkshire Locomotive "726," 97	192	705
___	**18057**	6-8-6 PRR S2 Steam Turbine Locomotive "671," 98	250	568
___	**18058**	4-6-4 Hudson Locomotive "773," 97	331	840
___	**18068**	Tender for PRR Steam Turbine Locomotive "773," 99	43	232
___	**18135**	NYC F3 Diesel AA Set, 99	329	650
___	**18178**	NYC F3 Diesel B Unit, 99		230
___	**18314**	PRR GG1 Electric "2332," 97	347	560
___	**18340**	FM Train Master Set, LCC II, 00	275	900
___	**24510**	PRR Sharknose Diesel B Unit, LCC II, 00		200
___	**28069**	NYC 4-8-6 Niagara Locomotive "6024," CC, LCC II, 00	325	920
___	**29173**	Empire State Express Passenger Car 4-pack, LCC II, 02		372
___	**29178**	Empire State Express Passenger Car 2-pack, LCC II, 02	88	178
___	**29181**	Empire State Express Diner, LCC II, 02	70	195
___	**29204**	Boxcar "1900-2000," 96		331
___	**29226**	Berkshire Boxcar, 97	115	145
___	**29227**	GG1 Boxcar, 98		55
___	**29228**	PRR Turbine Boxcar "671," 99		60
___	**29248**	F3 Boxcar "2333," 99		67
___	**31716**	Niagara Milk Train Set, LCC II, 00	113	300
___	**31726**	PRR Sharknose Coal Train Set, LCC II, 00		180
___	**31731**	Train Master Freight Train Set, LCC II, 00	103	180
___	**38000**	NYC 4-6-4 Hudson Empire State Locomotive, LCC II, 02	338	990
___	**38106**	NYC F3 Diesel "2333," powered, 99	230	430
___	**38107**	NYC F3 Diesel "2333," non-powered, 99	110	210
___	**39201**	Hudson Boxcar "773," 00		58
___	**39215**	Niagara Boxcar, LCC II, 01		48

CLUB CARS AND SPECIAL PRODUCTION		Exc	Mint	
39217	Boxcar, LCC II, 00		60	___
39218	Gold Boxcar, LCC II, 00		85	___
39237	M-10000 Boxcar, LCC II, 00		70	___
39246	PRR Sharknose Boxcar, LCC II, 00		55	___
39265	Fairbanks-Morse Train Master Boxcar, LCC II, 00		60	___
39266	Empire State Boxcar, LCC II, 00		40	___
51007	UP M-10000 4-car Passenger Set, LCC II, 00	600	970	___
51249	UP Overland Route Sleeper Car, LCC II, 02	60	15	___

LIONEL RAILROADER CLUB (LRRC)				
780	Boxcar, 82	55	67	___
781	Flatcar with trailers, 83	40	50	___
782	1-D Tank Car, 85	40	43	___
784	Covered Quad Hopper, 84	50	60	___
11183	Lincoln Funeral Train, 13		800	___
11319	PRR Tuscan K4 4-6-2 Pacific Locomotive "5409," CC, 13		900	___
11320	PRR Tuscan K4 4-6-2 Pacific Locomotive "5436," 13		750	___
12875	Tractor and Trailer, 94	13	18	___
12921	Illuminated Station Platform, 95	19	22	___
14274	Water Tower, 07		20	___
15034	50th Anniversary Mail Car, 10		50	___
15035	Holiday Boxcar, 10		50	___
16800	Ore Car, yellow, 86	60	69	___
16801	Bunk Car, blue, 88	20	33	___
16802	Tool Car, 89	24	35	___
16803	Searchlight Car, 90	23	27	___
16804	Bay Window Caboose, 91	25	30	___
16838	Illuminated Station Platform, 09	30	50	___
16839	Covered Bridge, 11		50	___
16840	Flagpole, 09	20	40	___
18680	4-6-4 Hudson Locomotive, 00		300	___
18684	4-6-2 Pacific Locomotive, 99		220	___
18818	GP38-2 Diesel, 92	100	117	___
19399	Christmas Boxcar, 13		60	___
19437	Flatcar with trailer, 97	11	55	___
19473	Operating Log Dump Car "3351," 99		38	___
19685	Western Union Dining Car, 02		47	___
19695	Western Union 1-D Tank Car, 03		22	___
19774	Porthole Caboose, 99		49	___
19775	Stock Car, 99		51	___
19924	Boxcar, 93	10	22	___
19930	Quad Hopper with coal, 94	14	20	___
19935	1-D Tank Car, 95	19	24	___
19940	Vat Car, 96		32	___
19953	6464 Boxcar, 97		35	___
19965	Aquarium Car "3435,", 99		56	___

	CLUB CARS AND SPECIAL PRODUCTION		Exc	Mint
____	**19966**	Gondola "9820" (std 0), 98	18	32
____	**19967**	Kids Club Animated Gondola, 98	25	32
____	**19978**	Gold Membership Boxcar, 99		46
____	**19991**	Gold Membership Boxcar, 00		65
____	**19992**	Western Union Tool Car "3550," 00		50
____	**19993**	Gold Membership Boxcar, 01		65
____	**19994**	Western Union Passenger Car "1307," 01		60
____	**19995**	25th Anniversary Boxcar (std 0), 01		49
____	**22013**	Christmas Ornament Keepsake, 13	10	18
____	**24217**	Animated Billboard, 08		30
____	**25073**	2009 Holiday Boxcar, 09	15	30
____	**25631**	Lincoln Train Passenger Car 2-pack, 13		300
____	**25635**	Red Passenger Car 3-pack, 12		420
____	**25639**	Red Arrow Diner, 12		140
____	**26089**	Western Union Gondola with handcar, 05		65
____	**26165**	Western Union Refrigerator Car, 04		30
____	**26382**	Flatcar with tractor and tanker, 08		60
____	**26413**	Commemorative 4-bay Hopper, 08		68
____	**26601**	Flatcar w/Pipes, 10		50
____	**26636**	50th Anniversary 6830 Flatcar with submarine, 11		55
____	**26637**	50th Anniversary 6640 USMC Missile Launching Car, 11		65
____	**27058**	ACF 2-Bay Covered Hopper "27058," 09	30	60
____	**27940**	Postwar 6469 Liquified Gas Tank Car, 13		50
____	**27943**	Postwar 6416 Boat Loader, 13		50
____	**27944**	Postwar 3413 Mercury Capsule Launch Car, 13		60
____	**27945**	50th Anniversary 6446-60 LV Covered Quad Hopper, 13		55
____	**28062**	4-6-4 Hudson Locomotive, 00		1150
____	**28571**	GP9 Diesel, CC, 07		250
____	**28665**	Western Union 2-8-4 Berkshire Locomotive "665," 05	63	175
____	**29200**	Lionel Boxcar "9700," 96		38
____	**29313**	50th Anniversary 3409 Helicopter Car, 11		70
____	**29657**	50th Anniversary 6413 Mercury Capsule Car, 12		55
____	**29658**	50th Anniversary 6465 Cities Service 2-D Tank Car, 12		50
____	**29876**	Crane and Boom Car 2-Car Set, CC, 10	450	750
____	**29879**	Crane Car, CC, 10		450
____	**29883**	Boom Car w/RailSounds, 10		300
____	**29931**	Holiday Boxcar, 05		25
____	**29939**	30th Anniversary Boxcar, 06		50
____	**29941**	Holiday Boxcar, 06		25
____	**29946**	Holiday Boxcar, 07		37
____	**29947**	Commemorative Boxcar, 07		30
____	**29957**	Holiday Boxcar, 08		50
____	**29977**	Holiday Boxcar, 11		60
____	**36521**	Western Union Searchlight Caboose, 05		32
____	**36769**	4th of July Lighted Boxcar, 03		70
____	**36841**	Visitor Center 15th Anniversary Lighted Boxcar, 06		70

CLUB CARS AND SPECIAL PRODUCTION		Exc	Mint	
37968	Clock Tower with wreath, 11		43	___
39249	Holiday Boxcar, 03		30	___
39264	Holiday Boxcar, 04		50	___
39352	50th Anniversary 6445 Fort Knox Mint Car, 12		70	___
39353	50th Anniversary Santa Fe Boxcar, 11		55	___
39357	2012 Christmas Boxcar, 12	35	50	___
39496	"6475" 50th Anniversary Vat Car, 10		60	___
58632	1955 Maintenance of Way Truck, 13		165	___
81116	Polar Express Operating Billboard, 14		60	___
81117	Polar Express Flatcar with silver bell, 14		45	___

LIONEL RAILROAD CLUB OF MILWAUKEE

52116	MILW Flatcar "194797," black, with tractor and trailer, 97		71	___
52163	CMStP&P "Hiawatha" DD Automobile Boxcar, 98	25	63	___
52180	MILW Flatcar "194799," tuscan, with trailer, 99	25	70	___
52228	CMStP&P 1-D Water Tank Car "908309," 00		50	___
52229	MILW 1-D Diesel Fuel Tank Car "907797," 00		50	___
52230	1-D Tank Car 2-pack, 00		142	___
52246	CMStP&P "Olympian" Boxcar "194701," 01	19	61	___
52265	MILW/Zoological Society Aquarium Car "4701," orange, 02		55	___
52278	MILW/Zoological Society Aquarium Car "4702," blue, 03		95	___
52297	MILW Reefer "194703," yellow, 03		67	___
52298	MILW Flatcar "194704" with orange trailer, 04		115	___
52337	MILW/Zoological Society Motorized Aquarium Car, 04		90	___
52368	MILW Flatcar "472004," black, 05		65	___
52369	MILW Trailer Train Auto Carrier "194705," 05		85	___
52370	CMStP&P Milk Car "364," tan, 05	57	86	___
52387	CMStP&P Flatcar "194706," gray, 06	30	59	___
52400	MILW PS-2 2-bay Hopper "99607," orange, 06		85	___
52401	MILW PS-2 2-bay Hopper "98809," yellow, 06	33	73	___
52402	CMStP&P URTX Operating Ice Car "4706," 06	54	85	___
52428	CMStP&P 0-4-0 Switcher and Caboose Set, 60th Anniversary, 06		275	___
52429	CMStP&P 0-4-0 Switcher, 06		200	___
52430	CMStP&P Offset Cupola Caboose, 06	20	65	___
52458	MILW Stock Car "102721" (std O), 07	24	69	___
52466	CMStP&P Stock Car "105254" (std O), 07	35	76	___
52551	MILW "Big M" DD Boxcar "200947," yellow, 09		60	___
52572	MILW Reiman Aquarium Car, 11		75	___
52599	MILW 2-bay ACF Hopper, 12		60	___
58263	Breast Cancer Awareness Boxcar, 16		60	___
58563	CMStP&P Round-Roof Boxcar, 13	30	73	___
58591	MILW Flatcar with auto frames, 14,	14	60	___
2201070	Delafield Brewhaus Beer Wood-side Refrigerator Car, 22		75	___

LONG ISLAND TOY TRAIN LOCOMOTIVE ENGINEERS

58520	Entenmann's Vat Car, 12		65	___

CLUB CARS AND SPECIAL PRODUCTION			Exc	Mint
___	**58556**	Flatcar with U.S. Navy airplane, 13		70
___	**58562**	Entenmann's Quad Hopper, 14		74

NASSAU LIONEL OPERATING ENGINEERS (NLOE)

			Exc	Mint
___	**8389**	Long Island Boxcar, 89	70	100
___	**8390**	Long Island Covered Quad Hopper, 90	70	100
___	**8391A**	Long Island Bunk Car, 91	70	90
___	**8391B**	Long Island Tool Car, 91	70	90
___	**17893**	Long Island 1-D Tank Car "8392," 92	80	105
___	**52007**	Long Island Alco RS-3 Diesel "1552," 93	120	250
___	**52019**	Long Island Boxcar "8393," 93	39	65
___	**52020**	Long Island Bay Window Caboose "8393," 93	65	95
___	**52026**	Long Island Flatcar "8394" w/Grumman trailer, 94	275	465
___	**52061**	Long Island Stern's Pickle Products Vat Car "8395," 95		200
___	**52072**	Grumman Tractor, 94	40	75
___	**52076**	Long Island Observation"9683," 96	175	350
___	**52112**	Long Island Ronkonkoma Vista Dome "9783," 97	150	300
___	**52122**	Meenan Oil 1-D Tank Car "8397" (std O), 97	30	60
___	**52123**	Long Island Hicksville Diner "9883," 98	150	300
___	**52144**	Long Island Flatcar "8398" w/Grumman van, 99	50	94
___	**52145**	Long Island Jamaica Coach "99831," 99	150	300
___	**52145**	Long Island Penn Station Coach "99832," 99	150	300
___	**52166**	Long Island Flatcar "8399" w/Grumman trailer, 98	40	77
___	**52173**	Long Island EMD F3 Diesel A-A Set "2000/2001," 00		260
___	**52174**	U.S. Mail RPO Aluminum Baggage Car, 00		220
___	**52186**	Grucci Fireworks Boxcar "2000," 00	35	72
___	**52209**	Long Island World's Fair Sleeper/Roomette, 01		80
___	**52232**	Central RR of Long Island Boxcar "8301," 01	30	60
___	**52235**	Long Island World's Fair Vista Dome, 02		80
___	**52256**	New York & Atlantic Boxcar "8302," 02	30	58
___	**52263**	Long Island World's Fair Combination Car, 02		80
___	**52296**	Long Island Flatcar w/Republic tank truck, 03	40	78
___	**52329**	New York & Atlantic Caboose, 04	40	80
___	**52341**	Long Island Flatcar w/Pan Am trailer, 05	45	85
___	**52365**	Long Island Flatcar w/Lilco transformer, 05	70	135
___	**52420**	Long Island 80th Anniversary Boxcar, 06	25	45
___	**52480**	Long Island Flatcar w/Pipes, 08	25	50
___	**52489**	Long Island Flatcar w/P.C. Richard & Son trailer, 07	35	67
___	**52555**	Martha Clara Vineyards Vat Car, 09	30	58
___	**52568**	Long Island Flatcar w/NY Islanders Trailer, 10	30	62
___	**52586**	Flatcar w/Cradle of Aviation Museum Trailer, 11	25	52
___	**52592**	Petland Discounts Aquarium Car, 11	35	70
___	**58212**	Cross Harbor Round-roof Boxcar "8315," 15	45	90
___	**58239**	Long Island GLa Hopper 2-pack, 16	90	160
___	**58240**	Long Island GLa Hopper, Tuscan, 16	40	80

CLUB CARS AND SPECIAL PRODUCTION		Exc	Mint	
58241	Long Island GLa Hopper, Black, 16	40	80	___
58266	Nathan's Famous 100th Anniversary Refrigerator Car, 16	95	120	___
58500	Nassau County Firefighters Museum Tank Car, 12	30	55	___
58517	Long Island Alco C-420 Diesel, CC, 12	275	485	___
58567	Nathan's Famous Steel-side Refrigerator Car "83131," 13	40	74	___
58568	Nathan's Famous Steel-side Refrigerator Car "83132," 13	40	74	___
58573	Long island PS-1 Boxcar "8312," 14		125	___
58574	Long Island Flatcar "8313" w/Tractor and Trailer, 13	50	150	___
58581	Long Island Double-sheathed Boxcar "8314," 14	100	170	___
83870	Long Island PS-2CD Covered Hopper, 17	60	120	___
1901070	Long Island 50' DD Boxcar "8318," 18		80	___
2001320	Long Island Milk Car "8319,", 19		130	___
2001570	Long Island 50' Flatcar "8320" w/Trailers, 20	60	85	___
2101231	Long Island MOW Bunk Car, 21		95	___
2101232	Long Island MOW Tool Car, 21		95	___
2101510	Long Island MOW Kitchen Car w/RailSounds, 21		140	___
2136150	Long Island 4-6-0 Camelback Locomotive "19," CC, 21		200	___
2301270	Long Island Center-Beam Flatcar "8323," 23		65	___
2401280	Long Island Bobber Caboose "22," 24		130	___

NICHOLAS SMITH TRAINS				
19580	Wood-side Refrigerator Car, 09	17	30	___
19582	Wood-side Refrigerator Car, 09	17	30	___
19583	Wood-side Refrigerator Car, 09	17	30	___
19584	Wood-side Refrigerator Car, 09	17	30	___
1831070	PRR K4 4-6-2 Pacific Locomotive "295," CC, 18		1295	___
1933740	Reading FA/FA Diesels, CC, 19		849	___
1933748	Reading FA-2 Diesel, CC, 19		350	___
1933749	Reading FB-2 SuperBass, 19		350	___
1933750	ATSF FA/FA Diesels, CC, 19		849	___
1933758	ATSF FA-2 Diesel, CC, 19		350	___
1933759	ATSF FB-2 SuperBass, 19		350	___
2133860	LV EMD SW8 Diesel "253," CC, 21		470	___
2133870	PC EMD SW8 Diesel "8623," CC, 21		470	___
2233861	Alaska EMD SD70MAC Diesel "4001," CC, 22		700	___
2233868	Alaska EMD SD70MAC SuperBass "4006," 22		600	___
2333730	L&NE EMD FA/FB/FA Diesels, CC, 23		1450	___
2333731	L&NE EMD FA-2 Diesel "701," CC, 23		600	___
2333732	L&NE EMD FA-2 Diesel "704," CC, 23		600	___
2333739	L&NE EMD FB-2 SuperBass "751," 23		350	___

RAILROAD MUSEUM OF LONG ISLAND				
52416	RMLI 15th Anniversary LIRR Boxcar, 05	120	170	___
52433	Atlantis Marine World Aquarium Car, 06	95	145	___
52453	North Fork Bank Mint Car, 07	50	90	___
52497	LIRR Flatcar w/Entenmann's trailer and tractor, 08	65	110	___

	CLUB CARS AND SPECIAL PRODUCTION		Exc	Mint
___	**52498**	Boeing Fairchild Container Car, 10	40	75
___	**52548**	Celebrating 175 Years of Railroading Boxcar, 09	50	90
___	**52557**	Entenmann's Operating Boxcar, 10	50	90
___	**52570**	Riverhead Building Supply Boxcar, 11	30	60
___	**52571**	Riverhead Visitor's Center Boxcar, 11	30	60
___	**52577**	King Kullen Boxcar, 11	30	60
___	**52595**	J. P. Holland Submarine Car, 12	30	60
___	**58054**	Mason Candies Dots and Crows Boxcar, 18	35	65
___	**58069**	Steam Up! LIRR 39 Blue Boy Boxcar, 18	35	65
___	**58521**	Wonder Bread PS-2 Covered Hopper, 12	30	60
___	**58227**	World's Fair Crew Car, 15	30	60
___	**58259**	Steam Union Pacific LIRR 39 Boxcar, 16	35	65
___	**58551**	Flatcar with White Castle refrigerated trailer, 13	30	60
___	**58554**	RCA Operating Radar Car, 13	30	60
___	**58555**	Grown on Long Island Flatcar w/Trailers, 16	40	65
___	**58579**	World's Fair Exhibit Car, 14	40	70
___	**58580**	World's Fair Tool Car, 15	40	70
___	**84598**	North Fork Potato Chips Boxcar, 17	35	65
___	**2001260**	Long Island Duckling Stockcar, 20	40	70
___	**2101100**	White Rock Products Boxcar, 21	40	70
___	**2201150**	Tribute B60 Baggage Car, 22	40	70

ST. LOUIS LIONEL RAILROAD CLUB

			Exc	Mint
___	**52099**	MP Flatcar with St. Louis trailer, 96		65
___	**52104**	St. Louis tractor and trailer, 96		20
___	**52117**	Wabash Flatcar with REA tractor and trailer, 97		65
___	**52136A**	Christmas Tractor and Trailer, 97		100
___	**52136B**	Frisco Tractor and Trailer, 98		100
___	**52147**	Frisco Campbell TOFC Flatcar, 98		75
___	**52150**	Frisco Campbell TOFC Flatcar, 98		130
___	**52167**	ATSF Flatcar "831999" with Navajo trailer, 99		75
___	**52190**	IC Flatcar with trailers, 00		80
___	**52222**	Cotton Belt Flatcar with SP tractor and trailer, 01		50
___	**52224A**	SP Flatcar with Navajo tractor and trailer, 01		25
___	**52224B**	SP Flatcar with service tractor and trailer, 01		25
___	**52258**	UP Flatcar with UP tractor and trailer, 02		55
___	**52290**	UP Flatcar with tractor trailer, 03		75
___	**52336**	U.S. Army Flatcar with tanker truck, 04		125
___	**52371**	NYC Flatcar with Fire Company tanker truck, 05		145
___	**52392**	PRR Flatcar with Hood's Milk tanker truck, 06		100
___	**52440**	U.S.M.C. Flatcar with tractor and trailer, 07		135
___	**52490**	Silver Special Flatcar with USA tractor and trailer, 08		100
___	**52513**	Frisco Flatcar with U.S.A.F. trailer, 09		120
___	**52597**	U.S. Navy Flatcar w/Trailer, 12		120
___	**58052**	Frisco Boxcar, 18		70

CLUB CARS AND SPECIAL PRODUCTION		Exc	Mint
58261	Monsanto Boxcar, 15		70 ___
68677	Frisco/Route 66 Flatcar w/Trailer, 13		120 ___
1901310	Anheuser Busch Beer Car, 19		80 ___

TRAIN COLLECTORS ASSOCIATION (TCA)

■ TCA National Convention Cars

		Exc	Mint
511	St. Louis Baggage Car, 81	36	41 ___
2671-1968	TCA Tender, shell only, 68	10	54 ___
5734	REA Refrigerator Car, 85	42	51 ___
6315	Pittsburgh 1-D Tank Car, 72	55	60
6436-1969	Open Quad Hopper, red, 69	45	70 ___
6464-1965	Pittsburgh Boxcar, blue, 65	128	191 ___
6464-1970	Chicago Boxcar, 70	60	93 ___
6464-1971	Disneyland Boxcar, 71	210	240 ___
6517-1966	Bay Window Caboose, 66	163	268 ___
6926	New Orleans Extended Vision Caboose, 86	27	39 ___
7205	Denver Combination Car, 82	37	50 ___
7206	Louisville Passenger Car, 83	40	55 ___
7212	Pittsburgh Passenger Car, 84	41	50 ___
7812	Houston Stock Car, 77	12	25 ___
8476	4-6-4 Locomotive "5484," 85	255	310 ___
9123	Dearborn 3-tier Auto Carrier, 73	25	36 ___
9319	"Silver Jubilee" Mint Car, 79	54	130 ___
9544	Chicago Observation Car, 80		50 ___
9611	Boston Hi-Cube Boxcar, 78	21	26 ___
9774	Orlando "Southern Belle" Boxcar, 75	13	35 ___
9779	Philadelphia Boxcar "9700-1976," 76	26	34 ___
9864	Seattle Refrigerator Car, 74	37	52 ___
11737	TCA 40th Anniversary F3 Diesel ABA Set, 93	254	528 ___
17879	Valley Forge Dining Car, 89		60 ___
17883	New Georgia Passenger Car, 90	52	64 ___
17898	Wabash Reefer "21596," 92	41	44 ___
19211	Vermont Railway Flatcars (2) with 4 trailers, 08		160 ___
21608	"Fang" Snake Exhibition Car, 09	35	50 ___
21612	Oil Creek & Titusville Operating Boxcar, 08		90 ___
21714	Copper Basin Hopper w/Load, 09		225 ___
22609	Old Bay Seasoning Boxcar, 10		75 ___
32660	Valley Forge Dining Car, 89		100 ___
52008	Bucyrus Erie Crane Car, 93	44	49 ___

	CLUB CARS AND SPECIAL PRODUCTION		Exc	Mint
___	**52035**	Yorkrail GP9 Diesel "1750," shell only, 94	44	55
___	**52036**	TCA 40th Anniversary Bay Window Caboose, 94	35	40
___	**52037**	Yorkrail GP9 Diesel "1754," 94	125	150
___	**52059**	Clinchfield Quad Hopper "16413" with coal, 94	85	110
___	**52062**	Skytop Observation Car, 95	210	360
___	**52085**	Full Vista Dome Car, 96		115
___	**52106**	City of Phoenix Diner, 97	16	100
___	**52142**	Massachusetts Central Maxi-Stack Flatcar "5100-01," 98		120
___	**52143**	City of Providence Passenger Car, 98	16	140
___	**52146**	Ocean Spray Refrigerator Car, 98		235
___	**52155**	City of San Francisco Baggage Car, 99		140
___	**52191**	City of Grand Rapids Aluminum Passenger Car, 00		135
___	**52210**	Rico Station, 00		29
___	**52220**	City of Chattanooga Vista Dome Car, 01		140
___	**52221**	Norfolk Southern Boxcar, 01		50
___	**52237**	Lionel Gondola, yellow, 01		110
___	**52238**	Lionel Gondola, red, 01		110
___	**52239**	Lionel Gondola, silver, 01		110
___	**52240**	Lionel Gondola 3-pack, 01	155	330
___	**52241**	Lionel Gondola, black, 02		15
___	**52242**	Lionel Gondola, blue, 02		35
___	**52250**	City of Chicago Combination Car, 02		130
___	**52272**	Lionel Gondola, gold, 02		80
___	**52274**	UP City of Los Angeles RPO Car, 03		95
___	**52276**	California Gold Mint Car, 03		65
___	**52333**	Harmony Dairy Milk Car, 04		90
___	**52338**	Lionel 50th Anniversary Mint Car, 04		75
___	**52339**	50th Anniversary Convention Banquet Car with coin, 04	88	360
___	**52340**	Train Order Building, 04		90
___	**52373**	Montana Rail Link 2-car Set, 05		90
___	**52374**	Montana Rail Link 2-bay Hopper, 05		50
___	**52375**	Montana Rail Link Flatcar with pulpwood logs, 05		50
___	**52376**	GN Refrigerator Car, 05		60
___	**52403**	T&P Stockcar (std O), 06		75
___	**52414**	Flatcar w/3 snowmobiles, 07		80
___	**52415**	Denver Operating Sheriff and Outlaw Car, 07	35	75
___	**52417**	Denver Mint Banquet Car, 07		200
___	**52481**	Ben & Jerry's Refrigerator Car, 08		95
___	**52482**	Vermont Ry. Maxi-Stack Car w/4 Containers, 08		165
___	**52483**	Rutland PS-1 Boxcar "358," 08		50
___	**52500**	ATSF Grand Canyon Reefer, 09		60
___	**52508**	Celebrate America Mint Car, 09		95
___	**52554**	Bethlehem Steel Hot Metal Car, 10		70
___	**52573**	Sierra RR Stockcar, 11		50
___	**52576**	Crystal Creamery General American Milk Car, 11		75

CLUB CARS AND SPECIAL PRODUCTION		Exc	Mint	
52584	Phillips Seafood Aquarium Car, 10		100	___
52593	LN PS-1 Boxcar, 12		45	___
52594	Quikrete Cement & Concrete ACF 4-Bay Covered Hopper, 12		85	___
58042	Heinz Pickle Refrigeration Line Boxcar, 18		190	___
58062	Mermaid Oysters Boxcar, 18		300	___
58067	Manhattan Project Trinity Site Mint Car, 19		275	___
58068	Manhattan Project Mint Car, 19		300	___
58216	NYC Merchants Despatch Transit Steel-sided Refrigerator Car, 15		60	___
58237	Coney Island & Brooklyn RR Trolley, 15		100	___
58238	Bergen County Traction Co. Trolley, 15		100	___
58258	Texas Mexican Ry. Boxcar, 16		70	___
58511	Chick-Fil-A Poultry Dispatch Operating Boxcar, 12		125	___
58516	C&NW PS-1 Boxcar, 13		75	___
58544	St. Louis Refrigeration Co. Refrigerator Car, 13	85	125	___
58547	Cotton Belt Blue Streak Merchandise Boxcar, 13		75	___
58571	Bethlehem Steel PS-1 Boxcar, 14	80	100	___
58572	Reading Philadelphia Mint Car, 14	45	80	___
84595	Carnegie Steel Boxcar, gray, 17		40	___
84596	Carnegie Steel Boxcar, brown, 17		40	___
1901051	Sierra Blanca Brewing Wood-side Refrigerator Car, 19		75	___
2001060	Jacksonville Naval Air Station Boxcar , 20		50	___
2001070	Department 56 Convention Boxcar, 20		100	___
2001581	SAL Flatcar w/Trailer "32211," 20		100	___
2101130	WP Boxcar "6464-100," reverse colors, 21		70	___
2201040	Quikrete Cement & Concrete PS-1 Boxcar w/Roof hatch "30328," 22		200	___
2201090	Mountain Man Moonshine Boxcar, 22		200	___
2201310	Quikrete Cement & Concrete PS-1 Boxcar "1940,", 22		200	___

■ TCA Museum-Related and Other Cars

		Exc	Mint	
1018-1979	Mortgage Burning Hi-Cube Boxcar, 79	32	35	___
5731	L&N Reefer, 90		95	___
7780	TCA Museum Boxcar, 80		26	___
7781	Hafner Boxcar, 81		26	___
7782	Carlisle & Finch Boxcar, 82		26	___
7783	Ives Boxcar, 83		26	___
7784	Voltamp Boxcar, 84		23	___
7785	Hoge Boxcar, 85		23	___
9771	Norfolk & Western Boxcar, 77	24	31	___
16811	Rutland Boxcar "5477096," 96	18	47	___
19906	"I Love Pennsylvania" Boxcar: President's Car, 94		40	___
52045	Pennsylvania Dutch Milk Car "61052," 94		90	___
52051	Baltimore & Ohio Sentinel Boxcar "6464095," 95	36	42	___
52052	TCA 40th Anniversary Boxcar, 94		90	___

	CLUB CARS AND SPECIAL PRODUCTION		Exc	Mint
___	**52063**	NYC Pacemaker Boxcar "6464125," 95		345
___	**52064**	Missouri Pacific Boxcar "6464150," 95		370
___	**52065**	Pennsylvania Dutch Grain Operating Boxcar "9208," 96		100
___	**52118**	Rio Grande Boxcar "5477097," 97		53
___	**52119**	TCA Museum 20th Anniversary Boxcar, 97		70
___	**52128**	Pennsylvania Dutch Pretzels Boxcar, 99		80
___	**52172**	L&N "Share the Freedom Boxcar" "5477099," 99		56
___	**52198**	Frisco Boxcar "5477000," 00		43
___	**52215**	Museum Work Train Gondola with pipes, 03		53
___	**52226**	Angela Trotta Thomas Boxcar "2000," 01		100
___	**52243**	Museum Work Train 1-D Tank Car, 01		50
___	**52271**	Museum Work Train Flatcar with wheel load, 02		20
___	**52289**	National Toy Train Museum 25th Anniversary Bullion Car, 02		75
___	**52295**	National Toy Train Museum Gondola with pipes, 03		16
___	**52310**	Museum Work Train Boxcar, 04		53
___	**52311**	TCA 50th Anniversary Train Master 5-Car Freight Set, 04	327	450
___	**52315**	TCA 50th Anniversary PRR Train Master and Caboose, 04		400
___	**52320**	TCA 50th Anniversary PRR Porthole Caboose, 04		100
___	**52321**	SP Train Master Diesel, 04		375
___	**52322**	MKT 8,000-Gallon 1-D Tank Car Shell, 04		25
___	**52323**	C&NW PS-5 Gondola Shell, 04		25
___	**52324**	B&M PS-2 3-Bay Covered Hopper Shell, 04		25
___	**52325**	SAL PS-1 Boxcar, 04		65
___	**52326**	SP Smoking Caboose, 04		200
___	**52361**	National Toy Train Museum 50th Anniversary Boxcar, 04		70
___	**52372**	Museum Work Train Baggage Car, 05		70
___	**52408**	N&W Caboose, 06		55
___	**52409**	Museum Work Train Idler Caboose, 06		68
___	**52437**	Museum Work Train Crane Car, 07		78
___	**58040**	U.S. Navy Seabees Boxcar, 18		170
___	**58313**	TCA 50th Anniversary SP Train Master 5-Car Freight Set, 04		430
___	**58314**	TCA 50th Anniversary SP Train Master and Caboose, 04		350
___	**61052**	Penn Dutch Dairy Operating Milk Car, 15		100
___	**1901460**	Pennsylvania RR Christmas Boxcar "6464-200," 19		150
___	**1901700**	York Train Meet October 2019 Boxcar, 19		300
___	**2101400**	WP Boxcar "6464-100," black lettering, 21		120
___	**2101480**	B&O Sentinel Boxcar "6464-325," 21		165
___	**2101570**	SP Boxcar "6464-225," 21		165
___	**2101600**	York TCA Meet Boxcar October 2021, 21		125
___	**2201031**	ATSF Bicentennial EMD SD45 Diesel "5700," CC, 22		600

■ TCA Bicentennial Special Set

			Exc	Mint
___	**1973**	Bicentennial Observation Car, 76	34	50

CLUB CARS AND SPECIAL PRODUCTION		Exc	Mint	
1974	Bicentennial Passenger Car, 76	34	50	___
1975	Bicentennial Passenger Car, 76	34	50	___
1976	Bicentennial U36B Diesel, 76	115	165	___

■ Atlantic Division

1980	Atlantic Division Flatcar with trailers, 80	28	34	___
6101	Burlington Northern Covered Quad Hopper, 82	21	34	___
9186	Conrail N5c Caboose, 79	22	30	___
9193	Budweiser Vat Car, 84	80	110	___
9466	Wanamaker Boxcar, 83	105	135	___
9788	Lehigh Valley Boxcar, 78	19	24	___
58564	Tastykake Cupcake Boxcar 1, 18		90	___
58565	Tastykake Cupcake Boxcar 2, 18		90	___
58582	Philly Pretzel Billboard Refrigerator Car, 14		65	___
58592	Tastykake Butterscotch Krimpets Hi-Cube Boxcar, 11	80	125	___
84594	Wawa Hoagiefest Boxcar, 17		90	___
1901410	Yuengling Beer Boxcar, 19		95	___

■ Desert Division

52088	Desert Division 25th Anniversary On-track Step Van, 96		120	___
52105	Superstition Mountain Operating Gondola "61997," 97		80	___
52442	Verde Canyon Boxcar, 07		55	___
52443	Grand Canyon Boxcar, 07		55	___
58222	AEC Los Alamos Mint Car, 16		165	___
58226	Cumbres & Toltec Double-sheathed Boxcar, 17		150	___
84597	Fred Harvey House Boxcar, 17		50	___
2001150	El Tova Musa Boxcar, 20		110	___

■ Dixie Division

52127	Dixie Division 10th Anniversary Southern 3-bay Hopper, 98		70	___
52438	Southern PS-1 Boxcar "27007," 06	40	80	___
52444	Southern PS-1 Boxcar "27087," 06	40	80	___

■ Eastern Division

9412	Richmond, Fredericksburg & Potomac Boxcar, 79		26	___
9740	Chessie System Boxcar w/Trolley Overstamp, 76		23	___
9771	Norfolk & Western Boxcar, 78		30	___
9783	B&O Time-Saver Boxcar, 77		30	___

■ Fort Pitt Division

1984-30X	Heinz Ketchup Boxcar, 84		500	___

Great Lakes Division

	No.	Description	Exc	Mint
___	**1983**	Churchill Downs Boxcar, 83		200
___	**1983**	Churchill Downs Reefer, 83		250
___	**8957**	Season's Greetings BN GP20 Diesel, powered, 80		230
___	**8958**	Season's Greetings BN GP20 Diesel, non-powered, 80		150
___	**9119**	Detroit & Mackinac Covered Quad Hopper, 77	19	22
___	**9272**	New Haven Bay Window Caboose, 79	19	22
___	**9401**	Great Northern Boxcar, 78		23
___	**9730**	Season's Greetings CP Rail Boxcar, 76		27
___	**9740**	10th Anniversary Chessie System Boxcar, 76		23
___	**52000**	Detroit-Toledo Division Flatcar with trailer, 92	70	85

Great Lakes Division: Three Rivers Chapter

	No.	Description	Exc	Mint
___	**9113**	Norfolk & Western Quad Hopper, 76	27	30

Great Lakes Division: Western Michigan Chapter

	No.	Description	Exc	Mint
___	**9730**	5th Anniversary CP Rail Boxcar, 74		25

Lake & Pines Division

	No.	Description	Exc	Mint
___	**52018**	3-M Boxcar, 93		45

Lone Star Division

	No.	Description	Exc	Mint
___	**7522**	New Orleans Mint Car with coin, 86		420
___	**52093**	Lone Star Division Boxcar "6464-696," 96		32
___	**52585**	Texas Special Dallas Federal Reserve Mint Car, 11	35	62
___	**58512**	SP Daylight San Francisco Mint Car, 12		65
___	**58552**	Texas Special Mint Car with silver bars, 12	65	95

Lone Star Division: North Texas Chapter

	No.	Description	Exc	Mint
___	**9739**	D&RGW Boxcar, 76		20

Metropolitan Division (METCA)

	No.	Description	Exc	Mint
___	**10**	CNJ EMD F3 Diesel A Unit Shell, 71	15	25
___	**9272**	NH BW Caboose, 79	21	25
___	**9754**	NYC Pacemaker Boxcar, 76	15	31
___	**52485**	NYC Mint Car w/Copper load, 08	60	120
___	**52486**	PRR Mint Car, green, 09	60	125
___	**52487**	PRR Mint Car, Tuscan, 09	60	125
___	**52488**	NYC Mint Car Lightning Stripe , 10	30	60
___	**52574**	Fort Knox 50th Anniversary Mint Car, 11	50	100
___	**52583**	B&O Mint Car Capitol Dome, 11	50	100
___	**52596**	LIRR Mint Car, 12	50	100
___	**58033**	CNJ Boxcar, 16	100	120
___	**58038**	Charles Chips Boxcar, 17	110	170
___	**58057**	Halloween Boxcar, 18	50	80

CLUB CARS AND SPECIAL PRODUCTION		Exc	Mint	
58112	Spirit of Union Pacific EMD SD70ACe Diesel "9026," CC, 18	425	600	___
58229	NYC Madison Hardware Boxcar, 15	150	200	___
58230	CNJ Madison Hardware Boxcar, 15	180	220	___
58231	NY Connecting RR Madison Hardware Boxcar, 15	175	215	___
58232	Lionel Lines Madison Hardware Boxcar, 15	210	250	___
58237	Coney Island Trolley, 19		100	___
58238	Palisades Park Trolley, 15	80	125	___
58243	Entenmann's Gondola w/Load, 16	100	130	___
58244	PRR Madison Hardware Boxcar, 15	185	225	___
58245	LL Madison Hardware Boxcar, gold, 15		100	___
58246	CNJ Blue Comet Banquet Mint Car, 15	150	230	___
58247	CNJ Mint Car, 15	200	275	___
58248	E-L Banquet Mint Car, 15	235	335	___
58274	LV Boxcar, 16	55	80	___
58280	REA Christmas Boxcar, 16	50	85	___
58285	Brookside Milk Refrigerator Car, 17	120	180	___
58286	Riverside Milk Refrigerator Car, 17	90	125	___
58501	REA Flatcar w/Trailer, 15	95	125	___
58502	NYC Flatcar w/Trailer, 15	95	125	___
58503	Lionel Showroom Layout Delivery Flatcar w/Trailer, 15	100	150	___
58504	Lionel Flatcar w/Madison Hardware Trailer, 15	200	225	___
58523	CNJ Blue Comet Mint Car, 13	35	70	___
58534	CNJ Mint Car, 13	35	70	___
58569	E-L Mint Car, 14	35	70	___
58598	Entenmann's 1-D Tank Car, 15	165	290	___
83866	Susquehanna Boxcar, 16	50	85	___
1801011	Edison Cement 2-Bay Covered Hopper "1899,", 18	25	45	___
1801012	Edison Cement 2-Bay Covered Hopper "1932," 18	25	45	___
1801020	New Hope & Ivyland Boxcar, 18	60	90	___
1801041	Spirit of Union Pacific Boxcar "1943," 18	80	120	___
1801042	Spirit of Union Pacific Boxcar "9026," 18	80	120	___
1901150	PRR EMD SD40-2 Diesel "6100," CC, 19	425	600	___
1901160	Susquehanna EMD SD40-2 Diesel "3018," CC, 19	425	600	___
1901191	PC Boxcar "45612," 19	90	120	___
1901200	LIRR Boxcar "2587," 19	90	135	___
1901210	U.S. Army MASH Boxcar, 19	60	100	___
1901230	United States Lines Boxcar, 19	90	125	___
1901240	Manufacturers Ry. Boxcar "257," 19	60	85	___
1901250	Public Service Boxcar, 19	80	110	___
1901260	Brooklyn Navy Yard Boxcar, 19	200	250	___
1901301	CP Boxcar, 19	55	80	___
1901302	CN Boxcar "1918," 19	55	80	___
1901303	BC Rail Boxcar, 19	65	100	___
1901351	Coors Beer Wood-side Refrigerator Car "1873," 19	65	100	___
1901352	Coors Beer Wood-side Refrigerator Car "1847," 19	65	100	___

	CLUB CARS AND SPECIAL PRODUCTION		Exc	Mint
___	**1901353**	Coors Beer Wood-side Refrigerator Car "1868," 19	65	100
___	**1901354**	Coors Beer Wood-side Refrigerator Car "1880," 19	110	150
___	**1901370**	Conrail FGE Boxcar "3600602," 19	65	100
___	**1901380**	ATSF Ore Car 6-pack, 19	180	230
___	**1901381**	ATSF Ore Car, red, 19	30	55
___	**1901382**	ATSF Ore Car, black, 19	30	55
___	**1901383**	ATSF Ore Car, brown, 19	30	55
___	**1901384**	ATSF Ore Car, blue, 19	30	55
___	**1901385**	ATSF Ore Car, green, 19	30	55
___	**1901386**	ATSF Ore Car, orange, 19	30	55
___	**1901400**	Linde Union Carbide Boxcar "2061," 19	80	110
___	**1901500**	National Bohemian Wood-sided Refrigerator Car, 19	140	200
___	**1901540**	Susquehanna Alco C-420 Diesel "2000," CC, 19	350	500
___	**1904190**	George Bush 4141 PS-1 Boxcar, 19	80	125
___	**2001021**	Budweiser Beer Wood-sided Refrigerator Car "1876," 20		80
___	**2001022**	Budweiser Beer Wood-sided Refrigerator Car "1951," 20		80
___	**2001130**	Conrail GG1 "4800," CC, 20		460
___	**2001140**	PRR GG1 "1776," LionChief Plus 2.0, 20		460
___	**2001180**	GATX EMD SD38 Locomotive "3310," CC, 20		600
___	**2001201**	Morristown & Erie Boxcar, 20	60	90
___	**2001202**	Morristown & Erie Christmas Boxcar, 20		100
___	**2001210**	BAR State of Maine Potatoes Boxcar, 20		120
___	**2001211**	BAR State of Maine Potatoes Boxcar, reverse colors, 20	360	500
___	**2001220**	Norfolk Naval Shipyard Boxcar, 20		100
___	**2001240**	Reedy Creek Fire Department Boxcar, 20	60	90
___	**2001250**	Harley & Davidson Bros. Boxcar, 20		120
___	**2001370**	LIRR Milk Refrigerator Car "3012," 20		100
___	**2001380**	PRR Milk Refrigerator Car, 20		100
___	**2001400**	E-L Train Master Diesel "1856," CC, 20		550
___	**2001441**	Archive No. 2240 Wabash EMD F3 Diesel, LionChief 2.0, 20		350
___	**2001442**	Archive No. 2367 Wabash EMD F3 Diesel, LionChief 2.0, 20		350
___	**2001560**	No. 60 Lionelville Trolley, red lettering, 20		130
___	**2101190**	BAR EMD GP7 Diesel "1776," CC, 21		550
___	**2101220**	Boxcar Brewing Co. Boxcar, 21		100
___	**2101230**	Entenmann's EMD GP7 Diesel "1898," LionChief 2.0, 21		550
___	**2101240**	Entenmann's NE-5 Caboose, 21		90
___	**2101250**	PRR G5 4-6-0 Locomotive "5741," CC, 21	550	800
___	**2101260**	ATSF EMD GP7 Diesel "2210," CC, 21	350	500
___	**2101380**	Alaska RR 6464-825 Boxcar, reverse colors, 21		300
___	**2101381**	Alaska RR 6464-825 Boxcar, yellow roof/ends, 21		300
___	**2101390**	ATSF EMD SD70ACe Diesel "1863," CC, 21		675
___	**2101420**	Air Force One EMD SD70ACe "1776," CC, 21		650
___	**2101440**	Renken's Milk & Cream Milk Refrigerator Car, 21		100
___	**2101460**	METCA 60th Anniversary Boxcar, 21	400	500
___	**2101461**	METCA 60th Anniversary Boxcar, blue, 21	400	500

CLUB CARS AND SPECIAL PRODUCTION		Exc	Mint
2101610	Middleton & New Jersey Boxcar, 21		100 ___
2103890	EMD Demonstrator SW8 Diesel "801," CC, 21	340	500 ___
2133830	We The People 4th of July EMD SD70ACe Diesel "1776," CC, 21		650 ___
2133880	EMD Demonstrator SW8 Diesel "105," CC, 21	340	500 ___
2201320	D&H Blue Coal Boxcar, 22		100 ___
2201330	DL&W Blue Coal Boxcar, 22		100 ___
2201350	Freedom Isn't Free Boxcar, 22		100 ___
2201351	Freedom Isn't Free Boxcar, gold, 22	250	400 ___
2201360	Texas Special EMD SD40-2 Diesel "1915," CC, 22	400	600 ___
2201370	Panama Canal Ry EMD F40PH Diesel "1863," CC, 22	400	575 ___
2201380	Halloween A5 0-4-0 Locomotive "13," CC, 22	500	700 ___
2201390	Christmas A5 0-4-0 Locomotive "25," CC, 22	500	700 ___
2201410	NS EMD SD33ECO Diesel "6224," CC, 22	400	600 ___
2201490	Christmas Silver Hooves Boxcar, 22		65 ___
2201500	Halloween Transylvania Rail Lines Boxcar, 22	65	95 ___
2301040	Military Aviation P-51 Mustang EMD SD70ACe Diesel "1945," CC, 23		800 ___
2301071	Air Force One Unibody 1-D Tank Car "28000," 23	90	120 ___
2301072	Air Force One Unibody 1-D Tank Car "29000," 23	90	121 ___
2301080	George Bush 4141 Unibody 1-D Tank Car, 23	90	122 ___
2301090	Spirit of Union Pacific Unibody 1-D Tank Car, 23	90	123 ___
2301110	CNJ Train Master Diesel "1506," CC, 23		550 ___
2301160	D&RG 2-6-0 Locomotive "260," CC, 23		720 ___
2301210	Postwar No. 6464-510 NYC Pacemaker Boxcar, pink, 23		100 ___
2301211	Postwar No. 6464-510 NYC Pacemaker Boxcar, gold, 23		500 ___
2301240	LV Boxcar "6464-520," purple, 23		95 ___
2301260	Postwar No. 6464-515 MKT Boxcar, pink, 23		100 ___
2301261	Postwar No. 6464-515 MKT Boxcar, gold, 23		500 ___
2301270	PRR Boxcar "6464," dark blue, 23		65 ___
2301360	NYC Pacemaker 0-8-0 Camelback Locomotive "2750," CC, 23		650 ___
2301370	LIRR GE ES44 Diesel "295," CC, 23		700 ___
2301400	Texas Special Trolley, 23		120 ___
2301411	Texas Special Maxi-Stack Car "184597," red/white, 23		100 ___
2301412	Texas Special Maxi-Stack Car "184598," red/gray, 23		100 ___
2301420	Entenmann's 2-8-2 Mikado Locomotive "1905," LionChief Plus 2.0, 23		700 ___
2301430	Entenmann's Trolley, 23		130 ___
2301441	Entenmann's Maxi-Stack "1961," white, 23		110 ___
2301442	Entenmann's Maxi-Stack "2014," blue, 23		110 ___
2301450	PE Trolley, orange/red, 23120120700		110 ___
2401010	Reading & Northern EMD SD50 Diesel "5018," CC, 24		650 ___
2401060	LV Heritage GE ES44AC Diesel "8104," CC, 24700		575 ___
2401070	New York & Greenwood Lake EMD GP9 Diesel "1267," CC, 24		575 ___
2401080	Mustang P-51 Red Tail EMD SD70ACe Diesel "72," CC, 24		800 ___
2401170	LL EMD SD70ACe Diesel "1900/2024," CC, 24		800 ___

	CLUB CARS AND SPECIAL PRODUCTION		Exc	Mint
___	**2401180**	New Hope & Ivyland 2-8-0 Locomotive "40," CC, 24		900
___	**2401220**	Postwar 6464-515 MKT Boxcar, black, 24		85
___	**2401280**	LV Alco S2 Diesel "164," CC, 24		520
___	**2401340**	Navy Corsair EMD GP9 Diesel "427," CC, 24		600
___	**2401380**	Texas Special EMD GP9 Diesel "245," CC, 24		600
___	**2401430**	Aberdeen, Carolina & Western EMD GP9 Diesel "902," CC, 24		600
___	**2401480**	C&O 2-8-4 Berkshire Locomotive "2769," CC, 24		1600
___	**2401590**	ATSF EMD E6 A and B Units "91," CC, clear shells, 24		700
___	**2401591**	ATSF EMD E6 SuperBass B Unit "91A," clear shell, 24		400
___	**2401640**	Aberdeen, Carolina & Western Milk Refrigerator Car "6455," 24		120
___	**2401650**	Entenmann's Milk Refrigerator Car, 24		120
___	**2401660**	LV Milk Refrigerator Car "1132-A," 24		120
___	**2401670**	King Syrup 8,000-gallon 1-D Tank Car "801," 24		95
___	**2401680**	Conoco 8,000-gallon 1-D Tank Car "44," 24		95
___	**2401690**	Aberdeen, Carolina & Western PS-2 Covered Hopper "770," 24		100
___	**2401730**	Air Force One BW Caboose "1776," 24	140	650
___	**2401740**	Entenmann's BW Caboose "1973," 24		140
___	**2501060**	Hellcat EMD SD70ACe Diesel "45," CC, 25650		60
___	**2501071**	USS California Battleship EMD SD70 Diesel "BB-44," CC, 25		680
___	**2501079**	USS Tennessee Battleship EMD SD70 Diesel "BB-43," unpowered, 25		350
___	**2501080**	Checkpoint Charlie Boxcar, 25		100
___	**2501090**	MILW Hiawatha EMD SD70ACe Diesel "1935," CC, 25		650
___	**2501100**	PRR GG1 "4939," Loewy scheme, CC, 25		650
___	**2501110**	Panama Canal Ry. EMD SD40-2 "1867," CC, 25		600
___	**2501111**	Panama Canal Ry. EMD SD40-2 "1867," unpowered, 25		350
___	**2501130**	Aberdeen, Carolina & Western PS-1 Boxcar "1987," 25		100
___	**2501140**	Aberdeen, Carolina & Western PS-1 Boxcar "6940," 25		100
___	**2501150**	C&O PS-1 Boxcar "1942," 25		100
___	**2501170**	Aberdeen, Carolina & Western REA Steel-sided Refrigerator Car "1918," 25		100
___	**2501220**	Texas Special Steel-sided Refrigerator Car "250," 25		100
___	**2501280**	George S. Patton 4-6-4 Hudson "1945" w/Water-scoop Tender, CC, 25		750
___	**2533209**	Susquehanna EMD SD70M-2 "4064," unpowered, 25		340

■ Midwest Division

___	**4**	C&NW F3 Diesel A Unit, shell only, 77		80
___	**5**	Midwest Division Covered Quad Hopper, 78		43
___	**1287**	C&NW Refrigerator Car, 84		0
___	**1988**	IC Boxcar, 88		40
___	**7600**	Frisco "Spirit of '76" N5c Caboose "00003," 76		38
___	**9872**	PFE Reefer "00006," 79		410
___	**52516**	UP Boxcar "6464-5909," 09		90

■ Midwest Division: Museum Express

		Exc	Mint
9264	ICG Covered Quad Hopper, 78	22	26 ___
9289	C&NW N5c Caboose, 80	37	44 ___
9785	Conrail Boxcar, 77		35 ___
9786	C&NW Boxcar, 79		20 ___

■ New England Division (NETCA)

		Exc	Mint
1203	Boston & Maine NW2 Diesel, shell only, 72		65 ___
5710	Canadian Pacific Reefer, 82	38	45 ___
5716	Vermont Central Reefer, 83	25	30 ___
6124	Delaware & Hudson Covered Quad Hopper, 84	25	30 ___
8051	Hood's Milk Boxcar, 86	44	75 ___
9181	Boston & Maine N5c Caboose, 77	23	35 ___
9400	Conrail Boxcar, Tuscan or blue, 78	23	27 ___
9415	Providence & Worcester Boxcar, 79	28	34 ___
9423	NYNH&H Boxcar, 80	25	30 ___
9445	Vermont Northern Boxcar, 81	29	39 ___
9753	Maine Central Boxcar, 75	24	34 ___
9768	Boston & Maine Boxcar, 76	32	39 ___
9785	Conrail Boxcar, 78	22	26 ___
16911	B&M Flatcar with trailer, 95		150 ___
22677	B&M Baked Beans Boxcar, 10		45 ___
52001	B&M Quad Hopper with coal, 92	50	75 ___
52016	B&M Gondola with coil covers, 93	55	65 ___
52043	L.L. Bean Boxcar, 94	115	215 ___
52080	B&M Flatcar "91095" with trailer, 95		215 ___
52111	Ben & Jerry's Flatcar with trailer, 96		313 ___
52212	Berkshire Brewing Reefer, 00		155 ___
52236	Moxie Boxcar, 01		160 ___
52270	Jenney Manufacturing Tank Car, 02		150 ___
52306	NH Flatcar with New England Transportation trailer, 03		150 ___
52352	Poland Spring Boxcar, 04		131 ___
52379	CP Rail Flatcar w/W.B. Mason trailer, 05		75 ___
52383	Fisk Tire Boxcar, 05		108 ___
52397	D&H Flatcar w/Vermont Railway trailer, 06		90 ___
52418	Indian Motocycle Boxcar, 06		190 ___
52434	New England Central Flatcar w/Cabot's trailer, 07		95 ___
52448	Oilzum Tank Car Set of 2, 08		105 ___
52457	Cape Cod Potato Chip Boxcar, 07		93 ___
52484A	Cabot's Reefer, 08	100	250 ___
52484B	Bay State Beer Reefer, 09		90 ___
52589	B&M Flatcar w/Howard Johnson trailer, 11		100 ___
58221	G. Fox & Co. Boxcar, 15	45	90 ___
58522	Grafton & Upton Flatcar with Spag's trailer, 12		90 ___

Ozark Division: Gateway Chapter

	No.	Description	Exc	Mint
___	**5700**	Oppenheimer Refrigerator Car, 81	55	110
___	**9068**	Reading Bobber Caboose, 76		20
___	**9601**	Illinois Central Gulf Hi-Cube Boxcar, 77		21
___	**9767**	Railbox Boxcar, 78		20
___	**52003**	"Meet Me In St. Louis" Flatcar with trailer, 92		520
___	**58510**	Frisco Flatcar w/Trailers, 11		100

Pacific Northwest Division

	No.	Description	Exc	Mint
___	**52077**	Great Northern Hi-Cube Boxcar "9695," 95		460

Rocky Mountain Division

	No.	Description	Exc	Mint
___	**1971-1976**	Fifth Anniversary Division Refrigerator Car, 76		75
___	**52511**	Colorado Yule Marble Co. Depressed-Center Flatcar "3," 08		90
___	**52512**	Colorado Yule Marble Co. Depressed-Center Flatcar "6," 08		90

Sacramento Sierra Chapter

	No.	Description	Exc	Mint
___	**6401**	Virginian Bay Window Caboose, 84		35
___	**9301**	U.S. Mail Operating Boxcar, 76	26	38
___	**9414**	Cotton Belt Boxcar, 80		35
___	**9427**	Bay Line Boxcar, 81		30
___	**9444**	Louisiana Midland Boxcar, 82		35
___	**9452**	Western Pacific Boxcar, 83		35
___	**9705**	D&RGW Boxcar, 75		38
___	**9723**	Western Pacific Boxcar, 73		29
___	**9726**	Erie-Lackawanna Boxcar, 79		23
___	**9730**	CP Rail Boxcar w/Chapter logo decal, 77		30
___	**9785**	Conrail Boxcar, 78		22

Southern Division

	No.	Description	Exc	Mint
___	**1976**	FEC F3 Diesel ABA, shells only, 76		275
___	**1986**	Southern Division Bunk Car, 86		30
___	**6111**	L&N Covered Quad Hopper, 83	20	22
___	**9287**	Southern N5c Caboose, 77	15	22
___	**9352**	Trailer Train Flatcar with circus trailers, 80	29	55
___	**9403**	Seaboard Coast Line Boxcar, 78		18
___	**9405**	Chattahoochie Boxcar, 79		21
___	**9443**	Florida East Coast Boxcar, 81		23
___	**9471**	ACL Boxcar, 84		23
___	**9482**	Norfolk & Southern Boxcar, 85		23
___	**16606**	Southern Searchlight Car, 88	17	24
___	**19942**	Southern Division 30th Anniversary Boxcar, 96		20

Western Division

		Exc	Mint	
6464-1967	WP Convention Boxcar	217	280	___
52275	Western Pacific Boxcar, 03		105	___

TOY TRAIN OPERATING MUSEUM (GADSDEN-PACIFIC DIVISION)

		Exc	Mint	
17872	Anaconda Ore Car, 88	60	72	___
17878	Magma Ore Car, 89	45	55	___
17881	Phelps Dodge Ore Car, 90	36	40	___
17886	Cyprus Ore Car, 91	26	31	___
19961	Inspiration Consolidated Copper Ore Car, 92	23	30	___
52011	Tucson, Cornelia & Gila Bend Ore Car, 93	20	29	___
52027	Pinto Valley Mine Ore Car, 94	20	29	___
52071	Copper Basin Railway Ore Car, 95		30	___
52089	SMARRCO Ore Car, 96		26	___
52124	El Paso & Southwestern Ore Car, 97		40	___
52164	SP Ore Car, 98		35	___
52177	Arizona Southern Ore Car, 99		35	___
52213	BHP Copper Ore Car, 00		29	___
52248	Tombstone & Western Ore Car, 01		40	___
52279	Dragoon & Northern Ore Car, 02		50	___
52307	Twin Buttes Ore Car, 03		35	___
52358	AJO & Southwestern Ore Car, 04		45	___
52386	Ray & Gila Bend Ore Car, 05		45	___
52421	Calabasas, Tuscon & Northwestern Ore Car, 06		45	___
52473	Mascot & Western Ore Car, 07		90	___
52524	Tucson, Globe & Northern Ore Car, 08		42	___
52558	Port of Tucson Ore Car, 09		45	___
52579	Rosemont Copper Ore Car, 10		40	___
52588	ASARCO Ore Car, 11		40	___
58234	ASARCO Hayden Smelter Ore Car, 15	20	45	___
58262	UP Ore Car, 16	20	45	___
58513	Freeport-McMoRan Ore Car, 12		40	___
58557	San Pedro & Southwestern Ore Car, 13		40	___
58583	Arizona Eastern Ore Car, 14		42	___

TOY TRAIN OPERATING SOCIETY (TTOS)

TTOS National Convention Cars

		Exc	Mint	
1984	Sacramento Northern Boxcar, 84	65	85	___
1985	Snowbird Covered Quad Hopper, 85	42	55	___
6017	SP-type Caboose, blue, 68	125	210	___
6017	SP-type Caboose, brown, 69	200	300	___
6057	SP-type Caboose, orange, 69	125	210	___
6076	Santa Fe Hopper (027), 70		103	___

CLUB CARS AND SPECIAL PRODUCTION			Exc	Mint
___	**6167-1967**	Hopper, olive drab with gold lettering, 67	25	85
___	**6257**	SP-type Caboose, red, 69	125	210
___	**6476-1**	LV Hopper, gray, 69	45	73
___	**6582**	Portland Flatcar with wood, 86	44	55
___	**9326**	Burlington Northern Bay Window Caboose, 82		25
___	**9347**	Niagara Falls 3-D Tank Car, 79	38	46
___	**9355**	Delaware & Hudson Bay Window Caboose, 82		50
___	**9361**	C&NW Bay Window Caboose, 82	47	55
___	**9382**	Florida East Coast Bay Window Caboose, 82		70
___	**9512**	Summerdale Junction Passenger Car, 74	38	53
___	**9520**	Phoenix Combination Car, 75	29	33
___	**9526**	Snowbird Observation Car, 76	36	51
___	**9535**	Columbus Baggage Car, 77	33	51
___	**9678**	Hollywood Hi-Cube Boxcar, 78	25	32
___	**9684**	Museum Exhibit Hi-Cube Boxcar, 84		50
___	**9868**	Oklahoma City Reefer, 80	36	44
___	**9883**	Phoenix Reefer, 83		50
___	**17871**	NYC Flatcar "81487" with Kodak and Xerox trailers, 87	185	217
___	**17877**	MKT 1-D Tank Car "3739469," 89	55	70
___	**17884**	Columbus & Dayton Terminal Boxcar (std O), 90	32	41
___	**17889**	SP Flatcar "15791" (std O) with trailer, 91	43	63
___	**19963**	Union Equity 3-bay ACF Hopper "86892" (std O), 92	30	38
___	**52010**	Weyerhaeuser DD Boxcar "838593" (std O), 93	25	42
___	**52028**	Ford Freight Car 3-pack, 94		100
___	**52029**	Ford 1-D Tank Car "12" (027), 94	33	40
___	**52030**	Ford Gondola "4023," 94	23	29
___	**52031**	Ford Hopper "1458" (027), 94	28	33
___	**52057**	Western Pacific Boxcar "64641995," 95	45	48
___	**52087**	New Mexico Central Boxcar "64641996," 96		55
___	**52114**	NYC Flatcar with Gleason and SASIB trailers, 97		58
___	**52149**	Conrail Flatcar with Blum coal shovel, 98		60
___	**52192**	SP Crane and Gondola Set, 00		75
___	**52193**	SP Gondola "6060," 00		50
___	**52194**	SP Crane Car "7111," 00		35
___	**52231**	British Columbia 1-D Tank Car, 01		25
___	**52253**	San Pedro, Los Angeles & Salt Lake Ry. Boxcar, 02	27	35
___	**52288**	D&RGW Cookie Boxcar, 03		20
___	**52293**	D&RGW 1-D Tank Car, 03		40
___	**52334**	Forest Service/Smokey Bear 60th Anniversary Boxcar, 04		80
___	**52335**	Forest Service/Smokey Bear 60th Anniversary i-D Tank Car, 04		80
___	**52351**	BNSF Icicle Refrigerator Car w/EOT Device, 04	75	150
___	**52378**	Las Vegas & Tonopah Boxcar, 05		70

CLUB CARS AND SPECIAL PRODUCTION		Exc	Mint	
52410	SP Flatcar with 2 trailers, 06		70	___
52441	Pennsylvania Operating Hopper, 07		60	___
52445	Pennsylvania RR Boxcar, 07		68	___
52545	Erie "6464" Boxcar, 09		50	___
58053	Nevada Southern Generator Car, 17		110	___
58235	Forest Service/Smokey Bear Gondola, 15		70	___
58257	50th Anniversary Mint Car, 16		50	___
58333	Sierra Railroad Sierra Beer Boxcar, 13		70	___
1901480	Arkansas Valley Terminal Ry. Boxcar, 19		75	___

■ TTOS Division Cars

		Exc	Mint	
52009	Sacramento Valley Division WP Boxcar, 93	34	44	___
52040	Wolverine Division GTW Flatcar w/Tractor and trailer, 94	42	51	___
52058	Central California Division Santa Fe Boxcar, 95	32	42	___
52086	Canadian Division Pacific Great Eastern Boxcar, 96	15	48	___
52113	Northeastern Division Genesee & Wyoming 3-bay Hopper, 97		34	___
52264	New Mexico Division Durango & Silverton Operating Hopper, 02		55	___

■ TTOS Southwestern Division

		Exc	Mint	
19962	Southern Pacific 3-bay ACF Hopper "496035" (std 0), 92	50	65	___
52047	Cotton Belt Wood-sided Caboose (std 0), smoke, 93-94	60	68	___
52073	Pacific Fruit Express Reefer "459402" (std 0), 95		65	___
52098	National Bureau of Standards Boxcar (std 0), 96		47	___
52121	Mobilgas Tank Car "238" (std 0), 97	40	75	___
52154	Pacific Fruit Express Reefer "459403" (std 0), 98		53	___
52287	Operating MX Missile Car, 02		55	___
52385	Ward Kimball Boxcar, 05		55	___
52431	Operating MX Missile Car, 06		60	___
52476	Life Savers Tank Car, 07		85	___
52515	Life Savers Wild Cherry Tank Car, 08		77	___
52565	Life Savers Pep O Mint Tank Car, 09		60	___
52569	Life Savers Butter Rum Tank Car, 10		62	___
52591	Life Savers Wint O Green Tank Car, 11		84	___
58208	Life Savers Peppermint Tank Car, 14		110	___
58548	Life Savers Bay-Window Caboose, 13		82	___

■ Other TTOS Production

		Exc	Mint	
1983	Phoenix 3-D Tank Car, 83		100	___
17894	Southern Pacific Tractor, 91	17	21	___
27148	BNSF "4427" PS2 Hopper, 06		50	___
52021	Weyerhaeuser Tractor and Trailer, 93	24	31	___
52022	Union Pacific Boxcar, 93		400	___
52032	Ford 1-D Tank Car (027) with Kughn inscription, 94	70	95	___
52046	ACL Boxcar "16247," 94		110	___
52053	Carail Boxcar, Contadina Boxcar "16245," 94		55	___
52078	Southern Pacific SD9 Diesel "5366," 96	105	235	___

	CLUB CARS AND SPECIAL PRODUCTION		Exc	Mint
___	**52079**	Southern Pacific Bay Window Caboose, 96	45	55
___	**52084**	Union Pacific I-Beam Flatcar "16380" with load, 95		155
___	**52201**	SP Overnight Merchandise Service Boxcar "6400-201," 00		50
___	**52202**	SP Overnight Merchandise Service Boxcar "6400-202," 00		50
___	**52203**	SP Overnight Merchandise Service Boxcar "6400-203," 00		45
___	**52204**	SP Overnight Merchandise Service Boxcar "6400-204," 00		35
___	**52205**	SP Overnight Merchandise Service Boxcar 5-pack, 00		185
___	**52384**	Transparent Damage Control Boxcar, 03		71
___	**52451**	Pennsylvania "X2454" Boxcar, 07	107	175
___	**52505**	Forest Service/Smokey Bear Flatcar with airplane, 08		45
___	**52525**	SP "X6454" Boxcar, 08		50
___	**52526**	SP "X6454" Boxcar, 08	8	165
___	**52547**	C&NW Reefer, 09		84

VIRGINIA TRAIN COLLECTORS (VTC)

___	**7679**	Boxcar	79	17
___	**7681**	N5c Caboose	81	23
___	**7682**	Covered Quad Hopper	82	26
___	**7683**	Virginia Fruit Express Reefer	83	26
___	**7684**	Vitraco 3-D Tank Car	84	26
___	**7685**	Boxcar	85	27
___	**7686**	GP7 Diesel	86	100
___	**7692-1**	Baggage Car (027)	92	35
___	**7692-2**	Combination Car (027)	92	35
___	**7692-3**	Dining Car (027)	92	35
___	**7692-4**	Passenger Car (027)	92	35
___	**7692-5**	Vista Dome Car (027)	92	35
___	**7692-6**	Passenger Car (027)	92	35
___	**7692-7**	Observation Car (027)	92	35
___	**7696**	20th Anniversary Station	96	65
___	**52002**	Shenandoah Dining Car	92	65
___	**52060**	Tender "7694" with whistle	94	70

Section 7
BOXES 1945-1969

		Good P-5	Exc P-7
___ **020**	90-Degree Crossover, 45-61	3	8
___ **020X**	45-Degree Crossover	3	8
___ **022**	Switch Controller	2	4
___ **020**	0 90 Degree Crossover	3	6
___ **020X**	0 45 Degree Crossover	3	7
___ **022**	Remote Control Switches, pair (with both inserts)	3	9
___ **022**	Remote Control Switches, pair (yellow, with both inserts)	4	10
___ **022A**	Remote Control Switches, pair (with both inserts)	6	15
___ **25**	Bumper	2	4
___ **26**	Bumper	2	4
___ **30**	Water Tower	8	24
___ **35**	Boulevard Lamp	3	11
___ **36**	Operating Car Remote Control Set	5	13
___ **37**	Uncoupling Track Set	2	4
___ **38**	Operating Water Tower	19	68
___ **40**	Hookup Wire, 8 reels (dealer box)	30	259
___ **41**	U.S. Army Switcher	12	45
___ **42**	Manual Switches	2	11
___ **42**	Picatinny Arsenal Switcher	22	71
___ **44**	U.S. Army Mobile Launcher	17	76
___ **44**	U.S. Army Mobile Launcher (with orange sleeve)	30	115
___ **45**	U.S. Marines Mobile Launcher	33	99
___ **45/45N**	Automatic Gateman	5	19
___ **48**	Super O Insulated Straight Track, 6 pieces (dealer box)	9	28
___ **49**	Super O Insulated Curved Track, 6 pieces (dealer box)	8	26
___ **50**	Section Gang Car (early classic)	9	28
___ **50**	Section Gang Car (brown corrugated)	5	15
___ **50**	Section Gang Car (orange picture)	11	33
___ **51**	Navy Yard Switcher	16	51
___ **52**	Fire Car	19	58
___ **53**	Rio Grande Snowplow	24	72
___ **54**	Ballast Tamper	11	34
___ **55**	PRR Tie-Jector Car	12	33
___ **56**	Lamp Post	3	12
___ **56**	M&StL Mine Transport	36	110
___ **57**	AEC Switcher	45	177
___ **58**	Lamp Post	6	21
___ **58**	Great Northern Rotary Snow Blower	48	186
___ **59**	Minuteman Switcher	60	196
___ **60**	Lionelville Rapid Transit Trolley (classic)	10	34
___ **60**	Lionelville Rapid Transit Trolley (brown corrugated)	8	27
___ **64**	Highway Lamp Post	6	19
___ **65**	Handcar	26	107

BOXES		Good P-5	Exc P-7	
68	Executive Inspection Car	23	60	___
69	Maintenance Car	24	65	___
70	Yard Light	2	7	___
71	Lamp Post	2	5	___
75	Goose Neck Lamps	3	11	___
76	Boulevard Street Lamps	4	12	___
76	Boulevard Street Lamps (Hillside Checkerboard)	13	44	___
89	Flagpole	5	21	___
91	Circuit Breaker	3	11	___
92	Circuit Breaker		10	___
93	Water Tower	8	28	___
97	Coal Elevator	13	45	___
108	Trestle Set (overstamped)	6	17	___
110	Graduated Trestle Set	1	4	___
111	Elevated Trestle Set	2	7	___
112	Remote Control Switches, pair (Super O)	6	16	___
112LH	Remote Control Super O Switch, left-hand	5	13	___
112RH	Remote Control Super O Switch, right-hand	5	14	___
114	Newsstand with horn	6	22	___
115	Passenger Station (113-1, Star Corp. stamped on box)	20	94	___
118	Newsstand with whistle	6	21	___
122	Lamp Assortment	18	87	___
123	Lamp Assortment	18	87	___
123-60	Replacement Lamp Assortment	5	55	___
125	Whistle Shack	5	14	___
128	Animated Newsstand	9	26	___
130	60-degree Crossing (Super O)	2	5	___
132	Passenger Station	7	22	___
133	Passenger Station	7	21	___
138	Water Tower	8	31	___
140	Automatic Banjo Signal (classic)	3	8	___
142	Manual Switches, pair (Super O)	4	14	___
145	Automatic Gateman (brown corrugated)	6	15	___
145	Automatic Gateman (cellophane), 66	13	39	___
148	Dwarf Trackside Signal	5	18	___
150	Telegraph Pole Set	4	12	___
151	Automatic Semaphore	3	8	___
151	Automatic Semaphore (narrower box, earlier postwar)	5	14	___
151	Automatic Semaphore (blister pack enclosure)	14	57	___
152	Automatic Crossing Gate	3	13	___
153	Automatic Block Control Signal	4	11	___
154	Automatic Highway Signal (cellophane)	5	18	___
154	Automatic Highway Signal (all other boxes)	3	8	___
155	Blinking Light Signal	6	25	___
156	Station Platform	9	45	___
157	Station Platform	6	17	___

	BOXES		Good P-5	Exc P-7
___	160	Unloading Bin	20	68
___	161	Mail Pickup Set (with liner)	8	30
___	163	Single Target Block Signal (white box)	15	45
___	164	Log Loader	15	50
___	167	Whistle Controller	2	4
___	175	Rocket Launcher	18	54
___	175-50	Rocket, separate sale	41	134
___	175-50	Dealer Display Box, 6 rockets	75	402
___	182	Magnetic Crane	16	51
___	192	Operating Control Tower	34	129
___	193	Industrial Water Tower	11	39
___	195	Floodlight Tower	6	20
___	195	Floodlight Tower (cellophane)	7	27
___	195-75	Floodlight Extension, 8-bulb (classic)	6	26
___	195-75	Floodlight Extension, 8-bulb (white box)	9	39
___	197	Rotating Radar Antenna	9	32
___	197-15	Separate Sale Radar Head	23	77
___	199	Microwave Relay Tower	6	28
___	202	UP Alco Diesel A Unit	10	39
___	204	Santa Fe Alco AA Set (master carton)	53	176
___	204	Santa Fe Alco AA Set (P and T boxes)	22	85
___	204P	Santa Fe A Unit	13	39
___	204T	Santa Fe Diesel Dummy A Unit	14	48
___	208	Santa Fe Alco AA Set (master carton)	56	229
___	208	Santa Fe Alco AA Set (P and T boxes)	23	91
___	208P	Santa Fe Alco A Unit	17	53
___	208T	Santa Fe Alco Dummy A Unit	32	76
___	209	New Haven Alco AA Set (master carton)	77	303
___	209	New Haven Alco AA Set (P and T boxes)	64	236
___	209P	New Haven Alco A Unit	24	80
___	209T	New Haven Diesel Dummy A Unit	36	127
___	210	Texas Special Alco AA Set (P and T boxes)	19	68
___	210P	Texas Special Alco A Unit	10	37
___	210T	Texas Special Alco Dummy A Unit	21	67
___	211	Texas Special Alco AA Set (P and T boxes)	29	100
___	211P	Texas Special Alco A Unit (brown corrugated)	14	45
___	212	Santa Fe AA Master Carton	32	170
___	212P	USMC Alco Diesel A Unit	31	104
___	212T	USMC Diesel Dummy A Unit	215	665
___	214	Plate Girder Bridge (classic)	3	8
___	214	Plate Girder Bridge (Hillside orange picture)	6	19
___	216	Burlington Alco Diesel A Unit	26	94
___	217	B&M Alco AB Set (C and P boxes)	34	125
___	217C	B&M Alco B Unit	18	57
___	217P	B&M Alco A Unit	24	69
___	217-16	Sleeve for 217 and 218 outer boxes	26	81

BOXES		Good P-5	Exc P-7	
218	Santa Fe Alco AA Set (master carton)	19	80	___
218C	Santa Fe Alco Diesel B Unit	20	76	___
218P	Santa Fe Alco Diesel A Unit	16	60	___
218T	Santa Fe Diesel Dummy A Unit	23	64	___
220	Santa Fe Alco AA Set (P and T boxes)	21	79	___
220T	Santa Fe Alco Dummy A Unit	20	69	___
221	2-6-4 Locomotive	19	64	___
221T	Tender	13	40	___
221W	Whistling Tender	18	49	___
223P	Santa Fe Alco A Unit	15	51	___
224	2-6-2 Locomotive	21	77	___
224	U.S. Navy Alco AB Set (C and P boxes)	36	153	___
224C	U.S. Navy B Unit	33	101	___
224P	U.S. Navy Alco A unit	33	123	___
225	C & O Alco Diesel A Unit	10	37	___
226	B&M Alco Diesel AB Set (C and P boxes)	25	79	___
226C	B&M Alco Diesel B Unit	13	30	___
226P	B&M Alco Diesel A Unit	13	44	___
228P	CN Alco Diesel A Unit	20	70	___
229C	M&StL Alco B Unit	13	45	___
229P	M&StL Alco A Unit (brown corrugated)	12	41	___
230P	C&O Alco A Unit	12	42	___
231P	Rock Island Alco A Unit	12	53	___
233	2-4-2 Scout Locomotive	12	35	___
234W	Whistle Tender	10	32	___
235	2-4-2 Scout Locomotive	18	75	___
236	2-4-2 Scout Locomotive	9	26	___
237	2-4-2 Scout Locomotive	9	28	___
239	2-4-2 Scout Locomotive	18	39	___
238	Engine and Tender Master Carton	15	34	___
243	2-4-2 Scout Locomotive	8	23	___
243W	Tender	9	23	___
244T	Tender (overstamped 1625T box)	17	52	___
245	2-4-2 Scout Locomotive	15	45	___
246	2-4-2 Scout Locomotive	11	33	___
247	2-4-2 Scout Locomotive	11	30	___
247T	Tender	8	25	___
248	2-4-2 Scout Locomotive	10	34	___
249	2-4-2 Scout Locomotive	15	40	___
250	2-4-2 Scout Locomotive	10	27	___
250T	Tender	8	22	___
252	Crossing Gate	2	6	___
253	Block Control Signal	3	8	___
256	Illuminated Freight Station	11	32	___
257	Freight Station with diesel horn	10	29	___
260	Bumper (Hagerstown checkerboard)	3	8	___

BOXES		Good P-5	Exc P-7
___ 260	Bumper (all other boxes)	2	4
___ 262	Highway Crossing Gate	4	16
___ 264	Operating Forklift Platform	18	56
___ 282	Portal Gantry Crane	26	66
___ 299	Code Transmitter Beacon Set	11	34
___ 308	Railroad Sign Set	3	9
___ 309	Yard Sign Set	3	9
___ 310	Billboard Set	2	5
___ 313	Bascule Bridge	32	128
___ 314	Scale Model Girder Bridge	4	12
___ 315	Illuminated Trestle Bridge	21	68
___ 316	Trestle Bridge	6	21
___ 317	Trestle Bridge	6	19
___ 321	Trestle Bridge	5	15
___ 321-100	Trestle Bridge	8	20
___ 332	Arch-Under Trestle Bridge	5	15
___ 334	Operating Dispatching Board	11	44
___ 342	Culvert Loader	22	69
___ 345	Culvert Unloader	22	69
___ 348	Manual Culvert Unloader	21	60
___ 350	Engine Transfer Table	14	66
___ 350-50	Transfer Table Extension	15	48
___ 352	Ice Depot	17	53
___ 353	Trackside Control Signal	5	15
___ 356	Operating Freight Station	9	33
___ 356-35	Baggage Trucks Set	11	35
___ 362	Barrel Loader	7	28
___ 362-78	Wooden Barrels	2	5
___ 364	Conveyor Lumber Loader	7	23
___ 365	Dispatching Station	10	33
___ 375	Turntable	17	61
___ 394	Rotary Beacon	6	21
___ 394-37	Rotating Beacon Cap	2	6
___ 395	Floodlight Tower	6	21
___ 397	Operating Coal Loader	7	26
___ 397	Operating Coal Loader (separate label on box)	12	42
___ 400	B&O Passenger Rail Diesel Car	15	138
___ 404	B&O Baggage-Mail Rail Diesel Car	27	119
___ 410	Billboard Blinker	4	15
___ 413	Countdown Control Panel	6	17
___ 415	Diesel Fueling Station	11	42
___ 419	Heliport Control Tower	32	120
___ 443	Missile Launching Platform	9	30
___ 445	Switch Tower	8	32
___ 448	Missile Firing Range Set	12	46
___ 450	Operating Signal Bridge	4	15

BOXES		Good P-5	Exc P-7	
452	Overhead Gantry Signal	10	36	___
455	Operating Oil Derrick	15	54	___
456	Coal Ramp	14	47	___
460	Piggyback Transportation Set	12	42	___
460-150	Two Trailers	56	196	___
461	Platform with truck and trailer	13	51	___
462	Derrick Platform Set	41	152	___
464	Lumber Mill	10	37	___
465	Sound Dispatching Station	11	35	___
470	Missile Launching Platform	7	26	___
494	Rotary Beacon (classic)	6	22	___
497	Coaling Station	16	48	___
600	MKT NW2 Switcher	22	64	___
601	Seaboard NW2 Switcher	23	79	___
602	Seaboard NW2 Switcher	25	87	___
610	Erie NW2 Switcher	15	57	___
611	Jersey Central NW2 Switcher (overstamped 621 box)	37	111	___
613	UP NW2 Switcher	24	81	___
614	Alaska NW2 Switcher	44	148	___
616	Santa Fe NW2 Switcher	24	98	___
617	Santa Fe NW2 Switcher	32	100	___
621	Jersey Central NW2 Switcher	21	65	___
622	Santa Fe NW2 Switcher	29	95	___
623	Santa Fe NW2 Switcher	19	77	___
624	C&O NW2 Switcher	22	75	___
625	LV GE 44-ton Switcher	57	210	___
626	B&O GE 44-ton Switcher	44	159	___
628	Northern Pacific GE 44-ton Switcher	20	73	___
629	Burlington GE 44-ton Switcher	43	162	___
634	Santa Fe NW2 Switcher	28	135	___
637	2-6-4 Locomotive	15	48	___
637LTS	2-6-4 Locomotive and Tender (master carton)	47	185	___
646	4-6-4 Locomotive	16	48	___
665	4-6-4 Locomotive	16	46	___
665LTS	4-6-4 Locomotive and Tender (master carton)	60	226	___
671	6-8-6 Steam Turbine Locomotive	20	66	___
671R	6-8-6 Steam Turbine Locomotive	44	178	___
671W	Whistle Tender	17	76	___
671-75	Smoke Lamp, 12 volt	3	7	___
675	2-6-2 Locomotive (classic)47-49	17	64	___
675	2-6-2 Locomotive (brown corrugated)52	30	85	___
681	6-8-6 Steam Turbine Locomotive	35	115	___
681LTS	6-8-6 Steam Turbine Locomotive and Tender (master carton)	119	419	___
682	6-8-6 Steam Turbine Locomotive	42	145	___
682LTS	6-8-6 Steam Turbine Locomotive and Tender (master carton)	338	875	___

BOXES			Good P-5	Exc P-7
___	685	4-6-4 Hudson Locomotive	22	127
___	685LTS	4-6-4 Hudson Locomotive and Tender (master carton)	155	457
___	726	2-8-4 Berkshire Locomotive46	47	158
___	726	2-8-4 Berkshire Locomotive (after 1946)	36	120
___	726RR	2-8-4 Berkshire Locomotive	22	71
___	736	2-8-4 Berkshire Locomotive, 50	27	89
___	736	2-8-4 Berkshire Locomotive	22	73
___	736X	2-8-4 Berkshire Locomotive	26	87
___	736LTS	2-8-4 Berkshire Locomotive and Tender (master carton)	81	260
___	736W	Pennsylvania Tender	17	68
___	746	N&W 4-8-4 Locomotive	59	190
___	746LTS	N&W 4-8-4 Locomotive and Tender (master carton)	246	668
___	746W	N&W Whistle Tender	32	126
___	746WX	N&W Whistle Tender, long stripe	47	165
___	760	Curved Track	7	22
___	773	4-6-4 Hudson Locomotive50	88	264
___	773	4-6-4 Hudson Locomotive, 64-66	66	175
___	773LTS	4-6-4 Hudson Locomotive and Tender (master carton), 50	166	631
___	773LTS	4-6-4 Hudson and Whistle Tender (master carton), 64-66	96	307
___	773W	NYC Tender	34	98
___	810	Milwaukee Road Freight Set	70	320
___	920-2	Tunnel Portals	5	15
___	920	Scenic Display Set	13	39
___	927	Lubricating Kit	2	6
___	928	Maintenance and Lubricating Kit	5	18
___	943	Ammo Dump	5	14
___	951	Farm Set	12	40
___	952	Figure Set	11	35
___	953	Figure Set	13	53
___	957	Farm Building and Animal Set	15	46
___	959	Barn Set	15	45
___	960	Barnyard Set	10	44
___	961	School Set	28	120
___	963	Frontier Set	15	158
___	965	Farm Set	12	47
___	966	Firehouse Set	12	47
___	969	Construction Set	11	40
___	970	Ticket Booth	11	50
___	972	Landscape Tree Assortment	8	33
___	981	Freight Yard Set	10	33
___	983	Farm Set	11	38
___	984	Railroad Set	12	48
___	986	Farm Set	18	68
___	987	Town Set		185
___	1000W	Steam Freight Set	21	75

BOXES		Good P-5	Exc P-7	
1001	Diesel Freight Set	18	65	___
1001	2-4-2 Scout Locomotive	6	27	___
1001T	Tender	4	12	___
1002	Gondola	3	8	___
X1004	PRR Baby Ruth Boxcar	3	8	___
1005	Sunoco 1-D Tank Car	3	8	___
1007	LL SP-type Caboose	3	8	___
1009	Manumatic Track Section	3	8	___
1019	Remote Control Track Set (027)	2	5	___
1024	Manual Switches for 027 Track Set	5	13	___
1024	Manual Switches	3	6	___
1025	Illuminated Bumper (027)	2	5	___
1032	Transformer, 75 watts	2	5	___
1033	Transformer, 90 watts	2	8	___
1034	Transformer, 75 watts	2	14	___
1041	Transformer, 50 watts	2	7	___
1041	Transformer, 60 watts	2	8	___
1043	Transformer, 50 watts	3	9	___
1043-500	Transformer, 50 watts, ivory	33	85	___
1044	Transformer, 90 watts	3	11	___
1045	Operating Watchman	5	18	___
1047	Operating Switchman	19	68	___
1060	2-4-2 Locomotive (brown corrugated)	13	49	___
1107	Steam Freight Set	13	45	___
1109	Steam Freight Set	12	40	___
1110	2-4-2 Locomotive	5	18	___
1112	Scout Set	6	22	___
1113	Scout Set	8	26	___
1117	Scout Steam Freight Set	14	35	___
1119	Scout Set	9	30	___
1120	2-4-2 Scout Locomotive	5	16	___
1121	027 Remote Control Switches, pair	2	6	___
1121LH	027 Remote Control Switch, left-hand	2	6	___
1121RH	027 Remote Control Switch, right-hand	2	6	___
1122	027 Remote Control Switches, pair	2	12	___
1130	2-4-2 Locomotive	5	19	___
1130T	Tender (classic)	4	13	___
1130T	Tender (orange perforated)	8	25	___
1130T-500	Tender, pink, from Girls Set	46	171	___
1232	Transformer, 75 watts, made for export	4	11	___
1407B	Steam Switcher Work Set	57	249	___
1417WS	Steam Work Train Set	24	101	___
1423W	Steam Freight Set	18	79	___
1425B	Steam Switcher Freight Set	50	203	___
1429WS	Steam Freight Set	24	95	___
1431	Steam Freight Set	21	64	___

	BOXES		Good P-5	Exc P-7
___	**1432W**	027 Steam Passenger Set	50	208
___	**1433W**	Steam Freight Set	14	37
___	**1435WS**	Steam Freight Set	10	35
___	**1447WS**	Turbine Locomotive Set	35	134
___	**1451WS**	027 Steam Freight Set	19	78
___	**1453WS**	027 Steam Freight Set	18	77
___	**1455WS**	Steam Freight Set	23	82
___	**1457B**	Santa Fe Freight Set (marked "1457"), 49	35	136
___	**1457B**	Santa Fe Freight Set50	43	153
___	**1459WS**	Steam Freight Set	27	83
___	**1463WS**	Steam Freight Set	46	85
___	**1464W**	Union Pacific Diesel Passenger Set	110	436
___	**1465**	Steam Freight Set	16	58
___	**1467W**	Union Pacific Freight Set	33	119
___	**1469WS**	Steam Freight Set	19	68
___	**1471**	Steam Freight Set	18	64
___	**1471WS**	Steam Freight Set	21	66
___	**1473WS**	Steam Freight Set	23	81
___	**1475WS**	Steam Freight Set	19	80
___	**1479WS**	Steam Freight Set	28	109
___	**1481WS**	Steam Freight Set	22	75
___	**1483WS**	Steam Freight Set	28	94
___	**1485WS**	Steam Freight Set	21	65
___	**1500**	Steam Freight Set	12	45
___	**1502WS**	Steam Freight Set	115	424
___	**11480**	Diesel Freight Set	44	163
___	**1503WS**	Steam Freight Set	25	68
___	**1505WS**	Steam Freight Set	28	89
___	**1507WS**	Steam Freight Set	23	79
___	**1511S**	Steam Freight Set	18	59
___	**1513S**	Steam Freight Set	20	66
___	**1515WS**	Steam Freight Set	28	95
___	**1517W**	Texas Special Freight Set	40	148
___	**1519WS**	Steam Freight Set	44	154
___	**1520W**	Texas Special Passenger Set	170	651
___	**1521WS**	Steam Work Train Set	57	213
___	**1523**	Diesel Freight Set	35	131
___	**1525**	Diesel Freight Set	19	52
___	**1527**	027 Steam Work Train Set	39	144
___	**1529**	Pennsylvania Diesel Freight Set	54	201
___	**1531W**	Diesel Freight Set	29	100
___	**1533WS**	Steam Freight Set	19	64
___	**1534W**	Burlington Diesel Passenger Set	98	351
___	**1535W**	Diesel Freight Set	56	215
___	**1536W**	Diesel Passenger Set	80	346
___	**1537WS**	Steam Freight Set	34	128

BOXES		Good P-5	Exc P-7	
1538WS	Hudson Passenger Set	172	659	___
1539W	Santa Fe Diesel Freight Set	63	223	___
1541WS	Steam Freight Set	44	165	___
1542	Electric Freight Set	12	49	___
1543	Lehigh Valley Freight Set	13	50	___
1547S	Steam Freight Set	15	53	___
1549	Steam Work Train Set	23	83	___
1551W	Diesel Freight Set	10	43	___
1552W	Diesel Passenger Set	133	251	___
1553W	Diesel Freight Set	23	76	___
1555WS	027 Steam Freight Set	19	61	___
1557	Diesel Freight Set	24	80	___
1559W	MILW Diesel Freight Set	25	88	___
1561WS	Steam Freight Set	21	55	___
1562W	Burlington GP7 Diesel Passenger Set	35	132	___
1569	UP Diesel Freight Set	16	59	___
1571	LV Diesel Freight Set	18	62	___
1573	Steam Freight Set	18	64	___
1575	Diesel Freight Set	21	61	___
1577S	Steam Freight Set	26	75	___
1578S	Steam Passenger Set	132	495	___
1579S	Steam Freight Set	20	65	___
1581	Jersey Central Mixed Set	22	77	___
1583WS	Steam Freight Set	17	61	___
1585W	Diesel Freight Set	21	72	___
1586	Diesel Passenger Set	29	145	___
1587S	Girls Train Set	630	1418	___
1589WS	027 Steam Freight Set	33	122	___
1590	Steam Freight Set	16	62	___
1591	USMC Military Set	111	500	___
1593	UP Diesel Work Train Set	28	95	___
1599W	Texas Special Freight Set	27	96	___
1600	Diesel Passenger Set	137	532	___
1601W	Wabash GP7 Diesel Set	46	202	___
1603WS	Steam Freight Set	27	89	___
1605W	Santa Fe Diesel Freight Set	43	160	___
1607WS	Steam Work Train Set	13	44	___
1608W	New Haven Passenger Set	130	715	___
1609W	Steam Freight Set	22	81	___
1611	027 Alaska Diesel Freight Set	55	196	___
1612	027 General Set	30	112	___
1613S	Steam Freight Set	24	84	___
1615	B&M Diesel Freight Set	22	77	___
1615	0-4-0 Locomotive	19	64	___
1615LTS	0-4-0 Locomotive and Tender (master carton)	42	137	___
1615T	Tender	10	42	___

	BOXES		Good P-5	Exc P-7
____	**1617S**	Steam Work Train	63	140
____	**1619W**	Santa Fe Diesel Freight Set	29	104
____	**1621WS**	027 Steam Freight Set (brown corrugated)	56	199
____	**1621WS**	027 Steam Freight Set (suitcase)	28	103
____	**1623W**	NP Diesel Freight Set	48	180
____	**1625**	0-4-0 Locomotive	29	108
____	**1625T**	Tender	23	76
____	**1625WS**	Steam Freight Set	28	101
____	**1626W**	Santa Fe Diesel Passenger Set	66	215
____	**1627S**	Stream Freight Set	20	41
____	**1629WS**	C&O Diesel Freight Set	18	72
____	**1631WS**	027 Steam Freight Set	18	62
____	**1633**	U.S. Navy Diesel Freight Set	94	339
____	**1635WS**	Steam Freight Set	32	119
____	**1637**	Santa Fe Diesel Freight Set	19	73
____	**1639WS**	Steam Freight Set	16	38
____	**1640-100**	Presidential Kit	13	50
____	**1643**	C&O Diesel Freight Set	14	54
____	**1645**	Diesel Freight Set	28	88
____	**1647**	U.S. Marines Military Set	33	111
____	**1648**	Steam Freight Set	10	43
____	**1649**	Santa Fe Diesel Freight Set	21	72
____	**1650**	Steam Military Set	28	95
____	**1651**	Passenger Train Set	36	136
____	**1654**	2-4-2 Locomotive	8	29
____	**1654W**	Whistle Tender	14	23
____	**1655**	2-4-2 Locomotive	13	40
____	**1656**	0-4-0 Locomotive	26	115
____	**1656LTS**	4-4-0 Locomotive and Tender (master carton)	53	200
____	**1665**	0-4-0 Locomotive	37	146
____	**1666**	2-6-2 Locomotive	14	53
____	**1682T**	Tender	6	27
____	**1800**	General Gift Pack	24	101
____	**1805**	Marine Land Sea and Air Gift Pack	532	1199
____	**1809**	Western Gift Pack	14	60
____	**1862**	4-4-0 Civil War General Locomotive	22	80
____	**1862T**	Tender	13	47
____	**1865**	Western & Atlantic Coach	10	41
____	**1866**	Western & Atlantic Mail-Baggage Car	10	41
____	**1872**	4-4-0 Civil War General Locomotive	29	100
____	**1872LTS**	4-4-0 Locomotive and Tender (master carton)	100	400
____	**1872T**	Tender	16	49
____	**1875**	Western & Atlantic Coach	38	148
____	**1875W**	Western & Atlantic Coach, whistle	20	94
____	**1876**	Western & Atlantic Baggage Car	16	65
____	**1877**	Flatcar with fence and horses	14	51

BOXES		Good P-5	Exc P-7	
2001	Track Make-up Kit (027)	650	2000	___
2002	Track Make-up Kit (027)	475	1400	___
2016	2-6-4 Locomotive	9	34	___
2018	2-6-4 Locomotive	10	34	___
2018-14	Sleeve for Outer Box	6	20	___
2020	6-8-6 Steam Turbine Locomotive	18	72	___
2020W	Tender	12	55	___
2023	Union Pacific Alco AA Set (master carton), 50	31	115	___
2023	Union Pacific Alco AA Set (master carton), 51	28	94	___
2025	2-6-2 or 2-6-4 Locomotive	15	67	___
2026	2-6-2 or 2-6-4 Locomotive	12	48	___
2028	Pennsylvania GP7 Diesel	29	118	___
2029	2-6-4 Locomotive	12	93	___
2031	Rock Island Alco AA Set (master carton)52	47	163	___
2032	Erie Alco AA Set (master carton)	35	111	___
2033	Uinion Pacific Alco AA Set (master carton)	26	92	___
2034	2-4-2 Scout Locomotive	10	39	___
2035	2-6-4 Locomotive	18	66	___
2036	2-6-4 Locomotive	12	45	___
2036LTS	2-6-4 Locomotive and Tender (master carton)	100	256	___
2037	2-6-4 Locomotive (brown corrugated)	9	32	___
2037-500	2-6-4 Locomotive, pink, from Girls Set	80	334	___
2046	4-6-4 Locomotive	22	82	___
2046LTS	4-6-4 Locomotive and Tender (master carton)	77	289	___
2046T	Lionel Lines Tender, for export	21	72	___
2046W	Lionel Lines Tender (early classic, with liner)	16	63	___
2046W	Lionel Lines Tender (marked "2046")	21	78	___
2046W	Pennsylvania Tender	23	80	___
2046W-50	Pennsylvania Tender	12	55	___
2055	4-6-4 Locomotive	18	51	___
2055LTS	4-6-4 Locomotive and Tender (master carton)	60	221	___
2056	4-6-4 Locomotive	19	59	___
2065	4-6-4 Locomotive	17	56	___
2103W	Steam Freight Set	25	90	___
2105WS	Steam Freight Set	32	114	___
2113WS	Steam Freight Set	44	182	___
2120WS	Steam Passenger Set	100	565	___
2121WS	Steam Freight Set	34	154	___
2124W	GG1 Passenger Set	180	952	___
2125WS	Steam Freight Set	35	110	___
2126WS	Steam Turbine Passenger Set	79	402	___
2129WS	Steam Freight Set	113	600	___
2136WS	Steam Passenger Set	42	164	___
2139W	GG1 Freight Set	146	669	___
2140WS	Steam Turbine Passenger Set	56	388	___
2141WS	Steam Turbine Freight Set	35	153	___

	BOXES		Good P-5	Exc P-7
____	**2145WS**	Steam Freight Set	81	291
____	**2146W**	Berkshire Passenger Set	197	504
____	**2147WS**	Steam Freight Set	53	140
____	**2148WS**	Hudson Passenger Set	450	1666
____	**2149**	Santa Fe Diesel Freight Set	71	311
____	**2151W**	F3 Freight Set	59	300
____	**2153WS**	Steam Freight Set	54	173
____	**2155WS**	Berkshire Freight Set	76	231
____	**2159W**	GG1 Freight Set	107	452
____	**2161W**	Santa Fe Twin Diesel Freight Set	40	161
____	**2163WS**	Steam Freight Set	40	160
____	**2165WS**	Steam Freight Set	40	150
____	**2167WS**	Steam Freight Set	36	147
____	**2171W**	NYC Diesel Freight Set	43	185
____	**2173WS**	Steam Freight Set	47	174
____	**2175W**	Santa Fe Diesel Freight Set	80	173
____	**2177WS**	Steam Freight Set	18	68
____	**2179WS**	Steam Freight Set	26	88
____	**2183WS**	Steam Freight Set	34	113
____	**2185W**	NYC Diesel Freight Set	34	116
____	**2187WS**	Steam Freight Set	20	75
____	**2190W**	Santa Fe Diesel Passenger Set	38	157
____	**2191W**	Santa Fe Diesel Freight Set	37	160
____	**2193W**	NYC Diesel Freight Set	36	124
____	**2201WS**	Steam Freight Set	55	126
____	**2203WS**	Steam Freight Set	43	231
____	**2205WS**	Steam Freight Set	27	98
____	**2207W**	Santa Fe Diesel Freight Set	36	137
____	**2209W**	NYC Diesel Freight Set	41	142
____	**2211WS**	Steam Freight Set	33	134
____	**2213WS**	Steam Freight Set	30	108
____	**2217WS**	Steam Turbine Freight Set	54	201
____	**2219W**	Diesel Freight Set	75	308
____	**2221WS**	Steam Freight Set	32	127
____	**2222WS**	Hudson Passenger Set	123	528
____	**2223W**	Lackawanna FM Freight Set	121	443
____	**2225T**	Tender	18	77
____	**2225WS**	Steam Freight Set	43	170
____	**2226W**	Tender	29	101
____	**2226WX**	Lionel Lines Tender	35	122
____	**2227W**	Santa Fe Diesel Freight Set	62	264
____	**2229W**	NYC Diesel Freight Set	34	125
____	**2231W**	Southern Diesel Freight Set	75	313
____	**2234W**	Santa Fe Passenger Set	149	321
____	**2235W**	Milwaukee Road Diesel Freight Set	41	164
____	**2237WS**	Steam Freight Set	36	142

BOXES		Good P-5	Exc P-7	
2239W	Illinois Central Freight Set	92	405	___
2240	Wabash F3 AB Set (C and P boxes)	59	217	___
2240	Wabash F3 AB Set (master carton)	137	610	___
2240C	Wabash F3 B Unit	40	143	___
2240P	Wabash F3 A Unit	28	93	___
2241WS	Steam Freight Set	21	84	___
2242	New Haven F3 AB Set (C and P boxes)	102	542	___
2242	New Haven F3 AB Set (master carton)	354	939	___
2242C	New Haven F3 B Unit	78	319	___
2242P	New Haven F3 A Unit	79	301	___
2243	Santa Fe F3 AB Set (C and P boxes)	35	91	___
2243	Santa Fe F3 AB Set (master carton)	43	177	___
2243C	Santa Fe F3 B Unit	22	76	___
2243P	Santa Fe F3 A Unit	22	74	___
2243W	Diesel Freight Set	32	128	___
2244W	Wabash Passenger Set	197	815	___
2245	Texas Special F3 AB Set (C and P boxes)	50	181	___
2245	Texas Special F3 AB Set (master carton)	213	714	___
2245C	Texas Special F3 B Unit	34	119	___
2245P	Texas Special F3 A Unit	22	83	___
2247W	Wabash F3 Diesel Freight Set	67	322	___
2251W	Diesel Freight Set	43	170	___
2254W	Pennsylvania GG1 Passenger Set55	242	1185	___
2255W	Diesel Work Train Set	43	140	___
2257	SP-type Caboose	5	18	___
2257WS	Steam Freight Set	29	106	___
2259W	New Haven Electric Freight Set	40	144	___
2261WS	Steam Freight Set	28	90	___
2263W	New Haven Freight Set	44	192	___
2265WS	Steam Freight Set	28	102	___
2267W	Diesel Freight Set	51	205	___
2269W	B&O Diesel Freight Set	160	569	___
2270W	Jersey Central Passenger Set	290	1104	___
2271W	Pennsylvania GG1 Freight Set	81	323	___
2273W	Milwaukee Road Diesel Freight Set	128	486	___
2274W	Pennsylvania Passenger Set	176	671	___
2275W	Wabash GP7 Freight Set	42	131	___
2276W	Budd Passenger Set	67	320	___
2277WS	Work Train Set	41	153	___
2285W	Diesel Freight Set	74	242	___
2279W	NH Electric Freight Set	68	215	___
2283W	Steam Freight Set	35	123	___
2289WS	Berkshire Super O Freight Set	53	201	___
2291W	Rio Grande Diesel Freight Set	116	585	___
2292WS	Steam Passenger Set	110	604	___
2293W	Pennsylvania GG1 Freight Set	177	812	___

	BOXES		Good P-5	Exc P-7
___	**2295WS**	N&W Steam Freight Set	168	699
___	**2296W**	Canadian Pacific Passenger Set	308	1143
___	**2297WS**	N&W Steam Freight Set	129	689
___	**2321**	Lackawanna FM Train Master Diesel	33	122
___	**2322**	Virginian FM Train Master Diesel	35	158
___	**2328**	Burlington GP7 Diesel	38	123
___	**2329**	Virginian Electric Locomotive	52	223
___	**2330**	Pennsylvania GG1 Electric Locomotive	67	231
___	**2331**	Virginian FM Train Master Diesel	34	148
___	**2332**	Pennsylvania GG1 Electric Locomotive	40	179
___	**2333**	NYC F3 AA Set (master carton)	41	151
___	**2333**	NYC F3 AA Set (P and T boxes)	40	157
___	**2333P**	NYC F3 A Unit (brown corrugated)	21	78
___	**2333**	Santa Fe F3 AA Set (master carton)	81	191
___	**2333**	Santa Fe F3 AA Set (P and T boxes)	30	109
___	**2333T**	Santa Fe F3 Dummy A Unit	29	133
___	**2333P**	Santa Fe F3 A Unit	21	82
___	**2337**	Wabash GP7 Diesel, 58	28	121
___	**2338**	MILW GP7 Diesel (classic)	25	100
___	**2338**	MILW GP7 Diesel (brown corrugated)	16	58
___	**2338X**	MILW GP7 Diesel (brown corrugated marked "2338X")	25	125
___	**2339**	Wabash GP7 Diesel, 57	30	114
___	**2340-1**	Pennsylvania GG1 Electric, tuscan	96	226
___	**2340-25**	Pennsylvania GG1 Electric, green, gold stripes	34	263
___	**2341**	Jersey Central FM Train Master Diesel	218	868
___	**2343**	Santa Fe F3 AA Set (master carton)	42	155
___	**2343**	Santa Fe F3 AA Set (P and T boxes)	34	121
___	**2343C**	Santa Fe F3 B Unit	23	92
___	**2343P**	Santa Fe F3 A Unit	20	68
___	**2343T**	Santa Fe F3 Dummy Unit	27	88
___	**2344**	NYC F3 AA Set (master carton)	65	255
___	**2344**	NYC F3 AA Set (P and T boxes)	51	191
___	**2344C**	NYC F3 B Unit	26	93
___	**2344P**	NYC F3 A Unit	38	112
___	**2344T**	NYC F3 Dummy Unit	34	155
___	**2345**	Western Pacific F3 AA Set (master carton)	163	634
___	**2345**	Western Pacific F3 AA Set (P and T boxes, brown corrugated)	55	276
___	**2345P**	Western Pacific F3 A Unit	38	140
___	**2345T**	Western Pacific F3 Dummy A Unit	57	199
___	**2346**	B&M GP9 Diesel	33	120
___	**2347**	C&O GP9 Diesel	463	1425
___	**2348**	M&StL GP9 Diesel	33	128
___	**2349**	Northern Pacific GP9 Diesel	57	206
___	**2349-12**	Sleeve for 2349 and 2359 outer boxes	20	83
___	**2350**	New Haven EP-5 Electric Locomotive	25	86

BOXES		Good P-5	Exc P-7	
2351	Milwaukee Road EP-5 Electric Locomotive	38	141	___
2352	Pennsylvania EP-5 Electric Locomotive	48	184	___
2353	Santa Fe F3 AA Set (master carton)	55	197	___
2353	Santa Fe F3 AA Set (P and T boxes)	42	165	___
2353P	Santa Fe F3 A Unit (brown corrugated)	19	62	___
2353T	Santa Fe F3 Dummy Unit	23	86	___
2354	NYC F3 AA Set (master carton)	51	228	___
2354P	NYC F3 A Unit (brown corrugated)	37	111	___
2354T	NYC F3 Dummy Unit	39	123	___
2355	Western Pacific F3 AA Set (master carton)	113	546	___
2355	Western Pacific F3 AA Set (P and T boxes)	60	240	___
2355P	Western Pacific F3 A Unit	44	171	___
2355T	Western Pacific F3 Dummy A Unit	44	153	___
2356	Southern F3 AA Set (master carton)	87	440	___
2356C	Southern F3 B Unit	56	201	___
2356P	Southern F3 A Unit	33	121	___
2356T	Southern F3 Dummy Unit	59	193	___
2357	SP-type Caboose	4	14	___
2358	Great Northern EP5 Electric Locomotive	55	218	___
2358-12	Outer Box Sleeve	44	160	___
2359	Boston & Maine GP9 Diesel	23	86	___
2360-10	Pennsylvania GG1 Electric Locomotive, tuscan	99	288	___
2360-25	Pennsylvania GG1 Electric Locomotive, green	43	178	___
2363	Illinois Central F3 AB Set (master carton)	143	552	___
2363	Illinois Central F3 AB Set (C and P boxes)	76	309	___
2363C	Illinois Central F3 B Unit	42	132	___
2363P	Illinois Central F3 A Unit	34	150	___
2365	C&O GP7 Diesel	21	74	___
2367	Wabash F3 AB Diesel Set Master Carton	45	89	___
2367C	Wabash F3 B Unit	48	234	___
2367P	Wabash F3 A Unit	44	160	___
2368	B&O F3 AB Set (master carton)	216	1293	___
2368C	B&O F3 B Unit	167	362	___
2368P	B&O F3 A Unit	46	269	___
2373	CP F3 AA Set (P and T boxes)	147	499	___
2373P	CP F3 A Unit	50	657	___
2373T	CP F3 Dummy A Unit	69	225	___
2378	Milwaukee Road F3 AB Set (master carton)	159	684	___
2378C	Milwaukee Road F3 B Unit	71	264	___
2378P	Milwaukee Road F3 A Unit	67	315	___
2379	Denver and Rio Grande F3 AB Set (master carton)	155	1057	___
2379C	Rio Grande F3 B Unit	59	199	___
2379P	Rio Grande F3 A Unit	45	161	___
2383	Santa Fe F3 AA Units (master carton)	60	280	___
2383P	Santa Fe F3 A Unit	22	79	___
2383T	Santa Fe F3 Dummy Unit	27	96	___

	BOXES		Good P-5	Exc P-7
___	**2400**	Maplewood Pullman Car	14	48
___	**2401**	Hillside Observation Car	13	47
___	**2402**	Chatham Pullman Car	14	49
___	**2403B**	Tender with bell	23	81
___	**2404**	Santa Fe Vista Dome Car	11	38
___	**2405**	Santa Fe Pullman Car	11	38
___	**2406**	Santa Fe Observation Car	11	38
___	**2408**	Santa Fe Vista Dome Car	12	38
___	**2409**	Santa Fe Pullman Car	13	43
___	**2410**	Santa Fe Observation Car	10	40
___	**2411**	Lionel Lines Flatcar	9	32
___	**2412**	Santa Fe Vista Dome Car	13	47
___	**2414**	Santa Fe Pullman Car	13	47
___	**2416**	Santa Fe Observation Car (orange perforated)	14	58
___	**2416**	Santa Fe Observation Car (orange picture)	13	46
___	**2419**	DL&W Work Caboose	10	33
___	**2420**	DL&W Work Caboose with searchlight	18	57
___	**2421**	Maplewood Pullman Car	13	44
___	**2422**	Chatham Pullman Car	13	44
___	**2423**	Hillside Observation Car	13	45
___	**2426W**	Hudson Tender (early classic)	73	269
___	**2426W**	Hudson Tender (middle classic)	66	243
___	**2429**	Livingston Pullman Car	21	69
___	**2430**	Pullman Car, blue	13	44
___	**2431**	Observation Car, blue	13	45
___	**2432**	Clifton Vista Dome Car	12	43
___	**2434**	Newark Pullman Car	12	41
___	**2435**	Elizabeth Pullman Car	18	59
___	**2436**	Mooseheart Observation Car	13	42
___	**2436**	Mooseheart Observation Car (classic)	12	40
___	**2440**	Pullman Car, green	12	43
___	**2441**	Observation Car, green	12	43
___	**2442**	Pullman Car, brown	12	45
___	**2442**	Clifton Vista Dome Car	14	46
___	**2443**	Observation Car, brown	10	43
___	**2444**	Newark Pullman Car	15	47
___	**2445**	Elizabeth Pullman Car	25	89
___	**2446**	Summit Observation Car	13	43
___	**2452**	Pennsylvania Gondola	5	17
___	**2452X**	Pennsylvania Gondola	4	13
___	**X2454**	Pennsylvania Boxcar (marked "Box Car")	13	47
___	**X2454**	Pennsylvania Boxcar (marked "Merchandise Car")	19	69
___	**2456**	Lehigh Valley Hopper	4	15
___	**2457**	Pennsylvania N5-type Caboose	6	28
___	**2458**	Pennsylvania Automobile Boxcar	10	41
___	**2460**	Bucyrus Erie Crane Car (box with toy logo)	20	50

BOXES		Good P-5	Exc P-7	
2460	Bucyrus Erie Crane Car (box without toy logo)	29	116	___
2461	Transformer Car	14	47	___
2465	Sunoco 2-D Tank Car	3	9	___
2466T	Tender	8	26	___
2466W	Tender	11	36	___
2466WX	Tender	11	41	___
2472	PRR N5-type Caboose	4	18	___
2481	Plainfield Pullman Car	39	154	___
2482	Westfield Pullman Car	39	154	___
2483	Livingston Observation Car	39	154	___
2501W	M&StL Diesel Freight Set	52	225	___
2502W	Budd RDC Set	112	205	___
2503WS	Super O Steam Freight Set	24	93	___
2505W	Super O Electric Freight Set	51	219	___
2507W	New Haven Diesel Freight Set	76	351	___
2509WS	Super O Steam Freight Set	42	190	___
2511W	Pennsylvania Electric Work Set	56	241	___
2513W	Virginian Rectifier Set	79	349	___
2515WS	Super O Steam Freight Set	73	305	___
2517W	Rio Grande Diesel Freight Set	77	372	___
2518W	Pennsylvania Electric Passenger Set	235	491	___
2519W	Virginian Train Master Super O Freight Set	69	390	___
2521	President McKinley Observation Car	21	79	___
2521WS	Super O Steam Freight Set	89	570	___
2522	President Harrison Vista Dome Car	22	81	___
2523	President Garfield Pullman Car	23	82	___
2523W	Santa Fe Super O Freight Set	66	297	___
2525WS	Super O Steam Work Train Set	131	511	___
2526W	Santa Fe Passenger Set	126	371	___
2527	Missile Launcher Set, yellow	18	73	___
2528WS	Super O General Set	39	169	___
2530	REA Baggage Car	26	119	___
2530	REA Baggage Car (orange perforated)	73	290	___
2531	Silver Dawn Observation Car	17	69	___
2531WS	Super O Steam Freight Set	37	137	___
2532	Silver Range Vista Dome Car	20	90	___
2533	Silver Cloud Pullman Car	17	67	___
2533W	Super O GN Electric Freight Set	95	439	___
2534	Silver Bluff Pullman Car	16	55	___
2535WS	Steam Freight Set	45	170	___
2537W	New Haven Freight Set	65	311	___
2541	Alexander Hamilton Observation Car	25	101	___
2541W	Santa Fe Super O Freight Set	129	446	___
2542	Betsy Ross Vista Dome Car	22	79	___
2543	William Penn Pullman Car	21	79	___
2543WS	Berkshire Freight Set	110	528	___

	BOXES		Good P-5	Exc P-7
___	**2544**	Molly Pitcher Pullman Car	21	79
___	**2544W**	Santa Fe Passenger Set	109	572
___	**2545WS**	Super O Military Set	179	772
___	**2547WS**	Super O Steam Freight Set	38	161
___	**2549W**	Super O Military Set	75	210
___	**2550**	B&O Baggage-Mail Rail Diesel Car	39	151
___	**2551**	Banff Park Observation Car	32	113
___	**2551W**	GN Electric Set	124	515
___	**2552**	Skyline 500 Vista Dome Car	32	111
___	**2553**	Blair Manor Pullman Car	52	204
___	**2553WS**	Berkshire Freight Set	57	277
___	**2554**	Craig Manor Pullman Car	56	201
___	**2555**	Sunoco 1-D Tank Car	10	38
___	**2555**	Sunoco 1-D Tank Car (overstamped 2755 box)	22	73
___	**2559**	B&O Passenger Rail Diesel Car	40	143
___	**2560**	Lionel Lines Crane Car	14	48
___	**2561**	Vista Valley Observation Car	34	119
___	**2561**	Vista Valley Observation Car (orange perforated)	46	154
___	**2562**	Regal Pass Observation Car	36	130
___	**2562**	Regal Pass Observation Car (orange perforated)	50	166
___	**2563**	Indian Falls Pullman Car	39	142
___	**2570**	Super O Santa Fe Work Train Set	55	212
___	**2572**	Boston & Maine Military Set	39	159
___	**2574**	Santa Fe Military Set	63	273
___	**2625**	Irvington Pullman Car	42	175
___	**2627**	Madison Pullman Car	29	113
___	**2628**	Manhattan Pullman Car	30	112
___	**2671T**	Pennsylvania Tender, for export	18	59
___	**2671W**	Pennsylvania Tender	20	69
___	**2671WX**	Lionel Lines Tender	27	76
___	**2755**	Sunoco 1-D Tank Car	17	54
___	**X2758**	PRR Automobile Boxcar	10	34
___	**2855**	Sunoco 1-D Tank Car	32	118
___	**3330**	Flatcar with submarine kit	22	72
___	**3330-100**	Operating Submarine Kit, separate sale	47	159
___	**3349**	Turbo Missile Launch Car	7	33
___	**3356**	Operating Horse Car and Corral Set (classic)	17	66
___	**3356**	Operating Horse Car and Corral Set (orange picture)	20	74
___	**3356-2**	Horse Car	75	342
___	**3356-100**	Black Horses (classic)	4	13
___	**3356-100**	Black Horses (white box)	8	21
___	**3356-150**	Horse Car Corral	97	473
___	**3357**	Hydraulic Maintenance Car	11	43
___	**3357-27**	Trestle Components for Cop and Hobo Car	8	27
___	**3359**	Lionel Lines Twin-bin Coal Dump Car	11	41
___	**3360**	Operating Burro Crane	19	72

BOXES		Good P-5	Exc P-7	
3361	Operating Log Dump Car	5	20	___
3361X	Operating Log Dump Car	6	26	___
3362	Helium Tank Unloading Car	13	41	___
3362/3364	Operating Unloading Car (Hagerstown checkerboard)	17	50	___
3364	Log Unloading Car	8	28	___
3366	Circus Car Corral Set	36	140	___
3366-100	White Horses	10	34	___
3370	W&A Outlaw Car	9	34	___
3376	Bronx Zoo Car	11	41	___
3376-160	Bronx Zoo Car, green	14	48	___
3410	Helicopter Car	15	57	___
3413	Mercury Capsule Car	17	65	___
3419	Helicopter Car	17	73	___
3424	Wabash Operating Boxcar	22	59	___
3424-75	Low Bridge Signal (marked "3424-75" or overstamped on 3424-100 box)	56	203	___
3424-100	Low Bridge Signal	5	19	___
3428	U.S. Mail Operating Boxcar	11	42	___
3434	Poultry Dispatch Car	19	63	___
3435	Traveling Aquarium Car	30	112	___
3444	Erie Operating Gondola	10	34	___
3451	Operating Log Dump Car	8	28	___
3454	PRR Operating Merchandise Car	23	82	___
3456	N&W Operating Hopper	13	40	___
3459	LL Operating Coal Dump Car (no toymaker's logo)	18	60	___
3459	LL Operating Coal Dump Car (toymaker's logo)	12	43	___
3461	LL Operating Log Car	8	26	___
3461X	Automatic Lumber Car	9	35	___
3461-25	Lionel Lines Operating Log Car, green	12	45	___
3462	Automatic Milk Car	16	123	___
3462-70	Milk Cans	2	10	___
3464	NYC Operating Boxcar	5	25	___
3464	Santa Fe Operating Boxcar	5	12	___
3469	LL Operating Coal Dump Car	11	39	___
3469X	LL Operating Coal Dump Car	8	30	___
3470	Target Launching Car	13	41	___
3472	Automatic Milk Car	10	37	___
3474	Western Pacific Operating Boxcar	11	43	___
3482	Automatic Milk Car	14	52	___
3484	Pennsylvania Operating Boxcar	10	31	___
3484-25	ATSF Operating Boxcar	9	33	___
3494	NYC Operating Boxcar	12	43	___
3494-150	Missouri Pacific Operating Boxcar	15	51	___
3494-275	State of Maine Operating Boxcar	13	98	___
3494-550	Monon Operating Boxcar	45	180	___
3494-625	Soo Operating Boxcar	48	185	___

	BOXES		Good P-5	Exc P-7
____	**3509**	Satellite Launching Car	12	50
____	**3512**	Fireman and Ladder Car	17	73
____	**3519**	Satellite Launching Car	11	39
____	**3520**	Searchlight Car	9	31
____	**3530**	GM Generator Car	16	51
____	**3530-50**	Searchlight with pole and base, separate sale	34	104
____	**3535**	Security Car with searchlight	13	67
____	**3540**	Operating Radar Car	21	75
____	**3545**	Operating TV Monitor Car	23	92
____	**3559**	Operating Coal Dump Car	11	35
____	**3562-1**	ATSF Operating Barrel Car	27	131
____	**3562-25**	ATSF Operating Barrel Car, gray	13	50
____	**3562-50**	ATSF Operating Barrel Car, yellow	15	53
____	**3562-75**	ATSF Operating Barrel Car, orange	18	54
____	**3619**	Helicopter Reconnaissance Car	12	52
____	**3620**	Searchlight Car with insert	11	38
____	**3650**	Extension Searchlight Car	10	37
____	**3656**	Operating Cattle Car	10	36
____	**3656**	Stockyard with cattle (set box with car box)	14	68
____	**3656-9**	Cattle (marked "3656" on 4 sides, unnumbered tuck flaps)	5	16
____	**3656-9**	Cattle (marked "3656" on 4 sides, "3656-44" on 1 tuck flap)	3	10
____	**3656-9**	Cattle (marked "3656-34" on 4 sides, "3656-44" on 1 tuck flap)	3	10
____	**3656-9**	Cattle (marked "3656" on 4 sides, "3656-44" on 1 tuck flap, OPS markings)	5	18
____	**3656-9**	Cattle (unnumbered sides, marked "3656-44" on 1 tuck flap)	6	20
____	**3656-9**	Cattle (unnumbered sides, marked "3656-34" on 1 tuck flap)	9	29
____	**3656-150**	Corral Platform, separate sale	135	628
____	**3662**	Automatic Milk Car (classic), 55	18	88
____	**3662**	Automatic Milk Car (orange picture), 64	18	65
____	**3662**	Automatic Milk Car (white box), 66	23	79
____	**3665**	Minuteman Operating Car	17	47
____	**3672**	Bosco Operating Milk Car	68	178
____	**3820**	USMC Operating Submarine Car	21	74
____	**3830**	Operating Submarine Car	14	46
____	**3854**	Automatic Merchandise Car	86	432
____	**3927**	Lionel Lines Track Cleaning Car	8	28
____	**4109WS**	Electronic Control Set	103	485
____	**4357**	SP-type Caboose, electronic	29	103
____	**4452**	PRR Gondola, electronic	23	85
____	**4454**	Baby Ruth PRR Boxcar, electronic	26	105
____	**4457**	PRR N5-type Caboose, tintype, electronic	25	93
____	**4671W**	Tender	46	151
____	**5160**	Viewing Stand	12	52

BOXES		Good P-5	Exc P-7	
5459	LL Coal Dump Car, electronic	25	113	___
6001T	Tender	3	8	___
6002	NYC Gondola	2	7	___
6004	Baby Ruth PRR Boxcar	3	8	___
6007	Lionel Lines SP-type Caboose	1	6	___
6009	Remote Control Uncoupling Track	2	4	___
6012	Gondola	3	9	___
6014	Boxcar	3	10	___
6014-60	Frisco Boxcar, white (middle classic)	5	18	___
6014-60	Frisco Boxcar, white	5	16	___
6014-85	Bosco or Frisco Boxcar, orange (classic)	6	22	___
6014-85	Boxcar (Hagerstown production)		19	___
6014-100	Airex Boxcar, red	7	20	___
6014-100	Airex Boxcar, red (orange perforated)	9	30	___
6014-150	Wix Boxcar	40	173	___
6014-335	Frisco Boxcar	6	19	___
6014-410	Frisco Boxcar	13	50	___
6015	Sunoco 1-D Tank Car	3	10	___
6017	Lionel Lines SP-type Caboose	2	9	___
6017-1	Caboose	5	16	___
6017-50	U.S. Marine Corps SP-type Caboose (box marked "6017-60")	16	54	___
6017-60	USMC Caboose	5	18	___
6017-85	Lionel Lines SP-type Caboose, gray	11	36	___
6017-100	B&M SP-type Caboose	12	40	___
6017-185	ATSF SP-type Caboose	5	17	___
6017-200	U.S. Navy SP-type Caboose	64	375	___
6017-235	ATSF SP-type Caboose	10	33	___
6019	Remote Control Track	2	5	___
6020W	Tender	9	36	___
6024	Nabisco Shredded Wheat Boxcar	5	22	___
6024-60	RCA Whirlpool Boxcar	15	54	___
6025	Gulf 1-D Tank Car (classic)	4	14	___
6025-60	Gulf 1-D Tank Car	5	18	___
6025-60	Gulf 1-D Tank Car (classic, overstamped 6024 box)	10	35	___
6025-85	Gulf 1-D Tank Car (classic)	9	32	___
6026T	Lionel Lines Tender	8	23	___
6026W	Lionel Lines Tender (classic or picture)	9	35	___
6027	Alaska SP-type Caboose	50	200	___
6029	Remote Control Uncoupling Track (classic)	2	5	___
6029	Remote Control Uncoupling Track (orange picture)	4	11	___
6032	Short Gondola	3	10	___
6034	Boxcar (Hagerstown production)	2	9	___
X6034	Baby Ruth PRR Boxcar	3	10	___
6035	Sunoco 1-D Tank Car	4	10	___
6037	Lionel Lines SP-type Caboose	2	6	___

	BOXES		Good P-5	Exc P-7
___	**6050**	Lionel Savings Bank Boxcar	6	23
___	**6050-110**	Swift Boxcar	7	23
___	**6057**	Lionel Lines SP-type Caboose	6	24
___	**6059**	M&StL SP-type Caboose	6	20
___	**6059-50**	M&StL SP-type Caboose (Hagerstown checkerboard)	10	32
___	**6062**	NYC Gondola	5	18
___	**6066T**	Tender	8	23
___	**6110**	2-4-2 Locomotive	7	25
___	**6111-75**	Flatcar with logs	14	46
___	**6111-110**	Flatcar	15	48
___	**6112-1**	Canister Car	10	28
___	**6112-25**	Canister Set	12	38
___	**6112-85**	Short Gondola (marked "Canister Car")	6	22
___	**6112-110**	Gondola Car with Canisters	6	25
___	**6112-135**	Short Gondola (marked "Canister Car")	6	23
___	**6119**	DL&W Work Caboose, red	6	21
___	**6119-25**	DL&W Work Caboose, orange	9	29
___	**6119-50**	DL&W Work Caboose, brown	10	28
___	**6119-75**	DL&W Work Caboose	10	34
___	**6119-100**	DL&W Work Caboose (classic)	8	27
___	**6119-100**	DL&W Work Caboose (picture, perforated, or window)	14	55
___	**6121**	Flatcar with pipes	14	45
___	**6121-60**	Flatcar with pipes	15	56
___	**6121-85**	Flatcar with pipes (classic)	15	55
___	**6130**	ATSF Work Caboose (cellophane)	13	40
___	**6130**	ATSF Work Caboose (Hagerstown checkerboard)	13	44
___	**6130**	ATSF Work Caboose (all other boxes)	6	23
___	**6149**	Remote Control Uncoupling Track, 64-69	2	5
___	**6151**	Flatcar with patrol truck	11	42
___	**6162-60**	Alaska Gondola	34	124
___	**6162-110**	NYC Gondola, blue (orange picture)	9	32
___	**6162-110**	NYC Gondola, red, separate sale (orange picture with label)	18	66
___	**6167-85**	Union Pacific SP-type Caboose	16	53
___	**6175**	Flatcar with rocket	10	36
___	**6220**	Santa Fe NW2 Switcher	22	90
___	**6250**	Seaboard NW2 Switcher	31	123
___	**6257**	SP-type Caboose	3	9
___	**6257X**	SP-type Caboose	12	41
___	**6257-25**	SP-type Caboose	4	11
___	**6257-50**	SP-type Caboose	5	12
___	**6262**	Flatcar with wheel load	8	29
___	**6264**	Flatcar with lumber, separate sale	53	146
___	**6311**	Flatcar with pipes	11	40
___	**6315**	Gulf 1-D Chemical Tank Car (classic)	13	43
___	**6315**	Gulf 1-D Chemical Tank Car (Hagerstown checkerboard)	18	50

BOXES		Good P-5	Exc P-7	
6315-60	Gulf 1-D Chemical Tank Car (orange picture)	10	37	___
6342	NYC Gondola	73	577	___
6343	Barrel Ramp Car	10	36	___
6346	Alcoa Quad Hopper	11	37	___
6356	NYC Stock Car	10	31	___
6357	SP-type Caboose (classic)	4	14	___
6357	Caboose (orange perforated)	8	20	___
6357	SP-type Caboose (orange perforated, overstamped)	19	71	___
6357-50	ATSF SP-type Caboose	155	543	___
6361	Timber Transport Car	12	40	___
6361	Timber Transport Car (Hagerstown checkerboard)	18	61	___
6362	Truck Car	10	39	___
6376	LL Circus Stock Car	12	43	___
6401	Flatcar, gray	23	85	___
6403B	Tender with bell	20	68	___
6405	Flatcar with piggyback van	8	28	___
6407	Flatcar with rocket	82	399	___
6411	Flatcar with logs	5	20	___
6413	Mercury Capsule Carrying Car	17	57	___
6414	Evans Auto Loader (classic)	23	67	___
6414	Evans Auto Loader (orange picture)	25	88	___
6414	Evans Auto Loader (orange picture, overstamped 6416 box)	31	97	___
6414	Evans Auto Loader (orange perforated), 59	20	80	___
6414	Evans Auto Loader (cellophane), 66	29	126	___
6414-25	Four Automobiles, separate sale	149	559	___
6414-85	Evans Auto Loader (orange picture)	125	414	___
6415	Sunoco 3-D Tank Car (classic)	9	26	___
6415	Sunoco 3-D Tank Car (orange picture)	13	35	___
6415	Sunoco 3-D Tank Car (cellophane)	21	68	___
6415	Sunoco 3-D Tank Car (Hillside checkerboard)	17	49	___
6415	Sunoco 3-D Tank Car (orange picture with label)	25	84	___
6416	Boat Transport Car	32	115	___
6417	PRR N5c Porthole Caboose	4	21	___
6417-25	Lionel Lines N5c Porthole Caboose	7	26	___
6417-50	Lehigh Valley N5c Porthole Caboose	27	75	___
6418	Machinery Car	16	59	___
6419	DL&W Work Caboose	9	32	___
6419-25	DL&W Work Caboose	6	22	___
6419-50	DL&W Work Caboose	9	33	___
6419-100	N&W Work Caboose	23	74	___
6420	DL&W Work Caboose with searchlight	13	41	___
6424	Twin Auto Flatcar	11	38	___
6424-60	Twin Auto Flatcar	15	62	___
6424-85	Twin Auto Flatcar	13	51	___
6424-110	Twin Auto Flatcar	22	82	___

BOXES			Good P-5	Exc P-7
___	**6425**	Gulf 3-D Tank Car	9	32
___	**6427**	Lionel Lines N5c Porthole Caboose	8	21
___	**6427-1**	Caboose	8	28
___	**6427-60**	Virginian N5c Porthole Caboose	66	238
___	**6427-500**	PRR N5c Porthole Caboose, sky blue, from Girls Set	46	168
___	**6428**	U.S. Mail Boxcar	11	40
___	**6429**	DL&W Work Caboose	33	132
___	**6430**	Flatcar with trailers	11	61
___	**6431**	Flatcar with vans and tractor (cellophane), 66	44	159
___	**6434**	Poultry Dispatch Stock Car	13	44
___	**6436**	Lehigh Valley Open Quad Hopper, black	11	39
___	**6436-25**	Lehigh Valley Open Quad Hopper, maroon	9	633
___	**6436-110**	Lehigh Valley Open Quad Hopper, red	10	33
___	**6436-500**	Lehigh Valley Open Quad Hopper, lilac, from Girls Set	53	230
___	**6436-1969**	TCA Hopper (Hagerstown checkered)	13	42
___	**6437**	PRR N5c Porthole Caboose	6	21
___	**6440**	Flatcar with vans	12	41
___	**6440**	Green Pullman Car	11	43
___	**6441**	Green Observation Car	11	42
___	**6442**	Brown Pullman Car	11	43
___	**6443**	Brown Observation Car	11	43
___	**6445**	Fort Knox Gold Reserve Car	13	44
___	**6446**	N&W Covered Quad Hopper	9	33
___	**6446**	N&W Covered Quad Hopper (orange picture)	17	63
___	**6446-25**	N&W Covered Quad Hopper	11	39
___	**6446-60**	Lehigh Valley Covered Quad Hopper	62	264
___	**6447**	PRR N5c Porthole Caboose	55	226
___	**6448**	Exploding Target Range Boxcar	9	31
___	**6452**	Pennsylvania Gondola	4	13
___	**X6454**	Santa Fe, NYC, or Baby Ruth Boxcar	7	24
___	**X6454**	PRR Boxcar	3	10
___	**X6454**	PRR Boxcar (classic, overstamped 3464 box)	7	26
___	**X6454**	SP Boxcar	7	25
___	**X6454**	Erie Boxcar	6	24
___	**6456**	Lehigh Valley Short Hopper	5	14
___	**6456-25**	LV Short Hopper ("25" rubber-stamped on end flaps)	8	50
___	**6456-75**	Lehigh Valley Short Hopper	33	122
___	**6457**	SP-type Caboose	5	14
___	**6460**	Bucyrus Erie Crane Car	11	40
___	**6460-25**	Bucyrus Erie Crane Car, red cab	16	56
___	**6461**	Transformer Car	9	33
___	**6462**	NYC Gondola, black	3	9
___	**6462-25**	NYC Gondola, green	5	16
___	**6462-75**	NYC Gondola, red	4	13
___	**6462-100**	NYC Gondola, red	11	34

BOXES		Good P-5	Exc P-7	
6462-125	NYC Gondola, red plastic	4	14	___
6462-500	NYC Gondola, pink, from Girls Set	49	180	___
6463	Rocket Fuel 2-D Tank Car	12	46	___
6464-1	Western Pacific Boxcar	13	44	___
6464-25	Great Northern Boxcar	15	50	___
6464-50	M&StL Boxcar	14	47	___
6464-50	M&StL Boxcar (overstamped with "S" and "Silver")	20	66	___
6464-75	Rock Island Boxcar	12	42	___
6464-100	Western Pacific Boxcar	29	121	___
6464-125	NYC Pacemaker Boxcar	15	54	___
6464-150	Missouri Pacific Boxcar	14	77	___
6464-175	Rock Island Boxcar	15	60	___
6464-175	Rock Island Boxcar (overstamped with "S" and "Silver")	31	117	___
6464-200	Pennsylvania Boxcar	17	64	___
6464-200	Pennsylvania Boxcar (Hagerstown checkerboard)	21	69	___
6464-225	SP Boxcar	13	46	___
6464-250	Western Pacific Boxcar (orange picture with label)	49	141	___
6464-250	Western Pacific Blue Feather Boxcar (classic for 6464-100), 54	115	512	___
6464-250	Western Pacific Boxcar (cellophane)	22	79	___
6464-275	State of Maine Boxcar	19	65	___
6464-300	Rutland Boxcar55	23	86	___
6464-325	B&O Sentinel Boxcar	60	209	___
6464-350	MKT Boxcar	43	180	___
6464-375	Central of Georgia Boxcar	18	57	___
6464-400	B&O Time-Saver Boxcar	12	41	___
6464-425	New Haven Boxcar (classic)	10	41	___
6464-425	New Haven Boxcar (Hagerstown)	12	41	___
6464-450	Great Northern Boxcar	12	51	___
6464-450	Great Northern Boxcar (cellophane)	17	60	___
6464-475	B&M Boxcar (classic)	12	46	___
6464-475	B&M Boxcar (orange picture)	22	79	___
6464-500	Timken Boxcar	22	80	___
6464-510	NYC Pacemaker Boxcar	75	271	___
6464-515	MKT Boxcar	75	271	___
6464-525	M&StL Boxcar	22	43	___
6464-650	D&RGW Boxcar (cellophane)	20	71	___
6464-700	Santa Fe Boxcar	14	50	___
6464-725	New Haven Boxcar (orange picture, "735" on box)	11	39	___
6464-725	New Haven Boxcar (Hagerstown checkerboard)	18	64	___
6464-825	Alaska Boxcar	58	221	___
6464-900	NYC Boxcar	12	42	___
6464-960	TCA Boxcar, 1965	25	69	___
6465	Gulf 2-D Tank Car, black (classic)	4	13	___
6465	Sunoco 2-D Tank Car (classic, overstamped 2465 box)	5	19	___
6465	Sunoco 2-D Tank Car (classic, overstamped 6555 box)	6	20	___

BOXES			Good P-5	Exc P-7
___	6465-60	Gulf 2-D Tank Car (classic)	5	17
___	6465-60	Sunoco 2-D Tank Car (classic)	3	12
___	6465-85	Lionel Lines 2-D Tank Car (orange perforated)	25	112
___	6465-110	Cities Service 2-D Tank Car (orange perforated)	13	46
___	6465-160	Lionel Lines Tank Car (orange picture)	34	122
___	6466T	Lionel Lines Tender	5	19
___	6466W	Lionel Lines Tender (with liner)	15	46
___	6466WX	Lionel Lines Tender (with liner)	15	47
___	6467	Miscellaneous Car	13	42
___	6468	B&O Auto Boxcar, tuscan (marked "X")	54	157
___	6468	B&O Auto Boxcar, blue	10	32
___	6468-25	NH Auto Boxcar	12	43
___	6469	Liquified Gas Tank Car	20	102
___	6470	Explosives Boxcar	10	37
___	6472	Refrigerator Car	5	18
___	6473	Horse Transport Car	10	35
___	6473	Horse Transport Car (end flaps half white, half orange)	22	84
___	6475	Pickles Vat Car (orange picture)	18	63
___	6476	Lehigh Valley Short Hopper	5	18
___	6476	Lehigh Valley Short Hopper (orange perforated)	11	40
___	6476-85	Lehigh Valley Short Hopper	12	46
___	6476-135	Lehigh Valley Short Hopper	7	27
___	6476-160	Lehigh Valley Short Hopper (Hagerstown checkerboard)	8	31
___	6477	Miscellaneous Car with pipes	11	39
___	6482	Refrigerator Car	8	30
___	6500	Flatcar with Bonanza airplane	79	290
___	6501	Flatcar with jet boat	23	75
___	6511	Flatcar with pipes	10	34
___	6512	Cherry Picker Car	12	40
___	6517	Lionel Lines Bay Window Caboose	14	41
___	6517-60	Bay Window Caboose (TCA)	28	105
___	6517-75	Erie Bay Window Caboose	63	236
___	6518	Transformer Car	15	48
___	6519	Allis-Chalmers Flatcar (classic)	33	69
___	6519	Allis-Chalmers Flatcar (orange perforated)	30	101
___	6520	Searchlight Car 2 City	13	41
___	6520	Searchlight Car 3 City	32	105
___	6530	Firefighting Instruction Car	16	56
___	6536	M&StL Open Quad Hopper	18	65
___	6544	Missile Firing Car	21	79
___	6555	Sunoco 1-D Tank Car	10	32
___	6556	MKT Stock Car	45	172
___	6557	SP-type Smoking Caboose	30	119
___	6560	Bucyrus Erie Crane Car (Hagerstown checkerboard)	17	59
___	6560	Bucyrus Erie Crane Car (all other boxes)	11	41
___	6560-25	Bucyrus Erie Crane Car, 8-wheel (with liner)	17	48

BOXES		Good P-5	Exc P-7	
6561	Cable Car, 2 reels	10	39	___
6562-1	NYC Gondola, gray	7	24	___
6562-25	NYC Gondola, red	5	22	___
6562-50	NYC Gondola, black	5	19	___
6572	REA Reefer (classic)	13	53	___
6572	REA Reefer (orange picture)	12	41	___
6636	Alaska Open Quad Hopper	15	63	___
6646	Lionel Lines Stock Car	6	21	___
6650	IRBM Rocket Launcher	8	30	___
6654W	Whistle Tender	10	31	___
6656	Stock Car	7	27	___
6657	Rio Grande SP-type Caboose	23	102	___
6660	Boom Car	11	43	___
6670	Derrick Car	13	49	___
6672	Santa Fe Refrigerator Car	9	32	___
6736	Detroit & Mackinac Open Quad Hopper	14	49	___
6800	Flatcar with airplane (classic)	15	51	___
6800	Flatcar with airplane (orange perforated)	17	63	___
6800-60	Airplane, separate sale	68	195	___
6801	Flatcar with brown and white boat	9	33	___
6801-50	Flatcar with yellow and white boat	12	41	___
6801-60	Boat, separate sale	33	104	___
6801-75	Flatcar with blue and white boat	12	42	___
6802	Flatcar with girders (late classic)	7	25	___
6802	Flatcar with girders (orange perforated)	14	50	___
6803	Flatcar with USMC tank and sound truck	27	100	___
6804	Flatcar with USMC trucks	27	98	___
6805	Atomic Energy Disposal Flatcar	21	80	___
6806	Flatcar with USMC trucks	29	98	___
6807	Flatcar with boat	22	84	___
6808	Flatcar with military units	26	99	___
6809	Flatcar with USMC trucks	27	99	___
6810	Flatcar with trailer	8	29	___
6812	Track Maintenance Car	17	58	___
6814	Rescue Caboose	18	63	___
6816	Flatcar with Allis-Chalmers bulldozer	48	183	___
6816-100	Allis-Chalmers bulldozer	185	419	___
6817	Flatcar with Allis-Chalmers motor scraper	56	184	___
6818	Flatcar with transformer	8	26	___
6819	Flatcar with helicopter	10	45	___
6820	Aerial Missile Transport Car with helicopter	64	235	___
6821	Flatcar with crates	7	26	___
6822	Searchlight Car	7	26	___
6823	Flatcar with IRBM missiles	16	62	___
6825	Flatcar with arch trestle bridge	6	22	___

	BOXES		Good P-5	Exc P-7
___	**6826**	Flatcar with Christmas trees	19	63
___	**6827**	Flatcar with Harnischfeger power shovel	26	95
___	**6827-100**	Harnischfeger Power Shovel	26	83
___	**6828**	Flatcar with Harnischfeger crane (cellophane, no crane kit box)	28	83
___	**6828**	Flatcar with Harnischfeger crane (orange picture, no crane kit box)	18	69
___	**6828**	Harnischfeger Crane Kit, used with flatcar	14	62
___	**6828-100**	Harnischfeger Crane, separate sale	39	139
___	**6830**	Flatcar with submarine	16	56
___	**6844**	Missile Carrying Car	18	75
___	**11001**	Steam Freight Set (advance catalog 1962)	7	28
___	**11011**	Diesel Freight Set	20	75
___	**11201**	Steam Freight Set	15	55
___	**11212**	Diesel Freight Set	23	85
___	**11222**	027 Steam Freight Set	17	56
___	**11232**	NH Diesel Freight Set	18	67
___	**11242**	Steam Freight Set	16	59
___	**11252**	Diesel Space Set	22	74
___	**11268**	Military Set	28	109
___	**11278**	Steam Freight Set	16	58
___	**11288**	Steam Freight Set	28	102
___	**11321**	Diesel Freight Set	17	34
___	**11331**	Steam Freight Set	11	40
___	**11341**	Diesel Freight Set	10	26
___	**11375**	027 Steam Freight Set	12	48
___	**11415**	Steam Freight Set (advance catalog 1963)	21	95
___	**11420**	Steam Freight Set	8	30
___	**11430**	Steam Freight Set	20	65
___	**11440**	Diesel Freight Set	16	58
___	**11450**	Steam Freight Set	18	62
___	**11460**	Steam Freight Set	10	36
___	**11490**	Santa Fe Passenger Set	30	113
___	**11500**	Steam Freight Set	26	96
___	**11520**	Steam Freight Set	22	78
___	**11530**	Diesel Freight Set	27	82
___	**11540**	Steam Freight Set	13	33
___	**11550**	Steam Freight Set	17	57
___	**11560**	Texas Special Set	10	37
___	**11590**	Santa Fe Passenger Set	25	94
___	**11710**	Steam Freight Set	21	75
___	**11750**	Steam Freight Set	21	79
___	**12710**	Steam Freight Set	31	126
___	**12730**	Santa Fe Diesel Freight Set	44	155
___	**12760**	Berkshire Freight Set	77	288
___	**12780**	Santa Fe Passenger Set	106	409

BOXES		Good P-5	Exc P-7	
12800	B&M Diesel Freight Set	22	80	___
12800X	B&M Diesel Freight Set	42	167	___
12820	Virginian Train Master Freight Set	62	243	___
12840	Steam Freight Set	43	245	___
12850	Diesel Freight Set	38	156	___
13008	Super O Introductory Set	20	74	___
13018	Santa Fe Space-age Military Set	158	622	___
13028	Super O Space Set	56	225	___
13048	Super O Steam Freight Set	47	230	___
13058	Santa Fe Space-age Military Set	72	295	___
13088	Santa Fe Passenger Set	196	736	___
13098	Steam Freight Set	67	251	___
13108	Santa Fe Space Set	60	168	___
13118	Berkshire Freight Set	69	287	___
13128	Santa Fe Space-age Military Set	158	587	___
13150	Hudson Freight Set	229	884	___
A	Transformer, 90 watts	3	10	___
CTC	Master Carton		167	___
CO-1	Track Clips, 100	3	8	___
ECU-1	Electronic Control Unit	33	119	___
KW	Transformer, 190 watts	5	19	___
KW	Transformer, 190 watts (yellow)	5	17	___
LTC	Lockon	1	5	___
LW	Transformer, 125 watts	5	15	___
R	Transformer, 110 watts	4	11	___
RCS	Remote Control Track	2	4	___
RW	Transformer, 110 watts	4	12	___
S	Transformer, 80 watts	4	15	___
SW	Transformer, 130 watts	4	13	___
TW	Transformer, 175 watts	4	16	___
UCS	Remote Control Track (0)	2	4	___
UTC	Lockon	3	6	___
VW	Transformer, 150 watts	5	25	___
Z	Transformer, 250 watts	25	83	___
ZW	Transformer, 250 Watts	10	23	___
ZW	Transformer, 275 watts (classic)	9	33	___
ZW	Transformer, 275 watts (orange, with inserts)	10	35	___
ZW	Transformer, 275 watts (yellow, with inserts)	11	37	___
ZW	Transformer, 275 watts (classic)	11	35	___
ZW	Transformer, 275 watts (orange, with inserts)	11	35	___
ZW	Transformer, 275 watts (yellow, with inserts)	13	35	___

Section 8
CATALOGED SETS 1945-1969

			Good	Exc
___	**463W**	Steam Freight Set, 45	516	1019
___	**1000W**	027 Steam Freight Set, 55	147	365
___	**1001**	027 Diesel Freight Set, 55	67	202
___	**1105**	027 Diesel Freight Set (1055, 6042, 6044, 6045, 6047), 59		145
___	**1107**	027 Diesel Freight Set (1055, 6042, 6044, 6047), 60	56	120
___	**1111**	027 Scout Freight Set, 48	30	190
___	**1112**	027 Scout Freight Set, 48	61	219
___	**1113**	027 Scout Freight Set, 50	51	116
___	**1115**	027 Scout Freight Set, 49	59	137
___	**1117**	027 Scout Freight Set, 49	50	172
___	**1119**	027 Freight Scout Set, 51-52	55	160
___	**1123**	027 Steam Freight Set (1060, 1060T, 6042, 6406, 6067), 60-62	50	98
___	**1400**	027 Steam Passenger Set, 46	110	614
___	**1400W**	027 Steam Passenger Set, 46	63	720
___	**1401**	027 Steam Freight Set, 46	50	248
___	**1401W**	027 Steam Freight Set, 46	60	220
___	**1402**	027 Steam Passenger Set, 46	88	550
___	**1402W**	027 Steam Passenger Set, 46	125	550
___	**1403**	027 Steam Freight Set, 46	100	515
___	**1403W**	027 Steam Freight Set, 46	208	618
___	**1405**	027 Steam Freight Set, 46	95	250
___	**1405W**	027 Steam Freight Set, 46	88	363
___	**1407B**	027 Steam Switcher Set, 46	175	1804
___	**1409**	027 Steam Freight Set, 46	88	425
___	**1409W**	027 Steam Freight Set, 46	93	435
___	**1411W**	027 Steam Freight Set, 46	188	702
___	**1413WS**	027 Steam Freight Set, 46	68	350
___	**1415WS**	027 Steam Freight Set, 46	93	530
___	**1417WS**	027 Steam Work Train Set, 46	113	720
___	**1419WS**	027 Steam Freight Set, 46	123	880
___	**1421WS**	027 Steam Freight Set, 46	208	1100
___	**1423W**	027 Steam Freight Set, 48-49	65	239
___	**1425B**	027 Steam Switcher Freight Set, 48	239	713
___	**1425B**	027 Steam Switcher Freight Set, 49	172	825
___	**1426WS**	027 Steam Passenger Set, 48-49	236	779
___	**1427WS**	027 Steam Freight Set, 48	169	294
___	**1429WS**	027 Steam Freight Set, 48	200	530
___	**1430WS**	027 Steam Passenger Set, 48-49		894
___	**1431**	027 Steam Freight Set, 47	20	235
___	**1431W**	027 Steam Freight Set, 47	50	168
___	**1432**	027 Steam Passenger Set, 47	148	850
___	**1432W**	027 Steam Passenger Set, 47		795
___	**1433**	027 Steam Freight Set, 47	83	521
___	**1433W**	027 Steam Freight Set, 47	161	374
___	**1434WS**	027 Steam Passenger Set, 47	53	555
___	**1435WS**	027 Steam Freight Set, 47	33	240
___	**1437WS**	027 Steam Freight Set, 47	110	611
___	**1439WS**	027 Steam Freight Set, 47	45	470
___	**1441WS**	027 Steam Work Train Set, 47	155	1225
___	**1443WS**	027 Steam Freight Set, 47	55	400

SETS		Good	Exc	
1445WS	027 Steam Freight Set, 48	129	362	___
1447WS	027 Steam Work Train Set, 48	60	460	___
1447WS	027 Steam Work Train Set, 49	353	1442	___
1449WS	027 Steam Freight Set, 48		430	___
1451WS	027 Steam Freight Set, 49	75	290	___
1453WS	027 Steam Freight Set, 49		386	___
1455WS	027 Steam Freight Set, 49		318	___
1457B	027 Diesel Freight Set, 49-50	145	710	___
1459WS	027 Steam Freight Set, 49		1090	___
1461S	027 Steam Freight Set, 50		175	___
1463W	027 Steam Freight Set, 50		268	___
1463WS	027 Freight Set, 51	88	244	___
1464W	027 UP Diesel Passenger Set, 50	447	1570	___
1464W	027 UP Passenger Set, 51	238	880	___
1464W	027 UP Passenger Set, 52-53	282	804	___
1465	027 Steam Freight Set, 52	75	188	___
1467W	027 UP Diesel Freight Set, 50-51	126	795	___
1467W	027 Erie Diesel Freight Set, 52-53	79	641	___
1469WS	027 Steam Freight Set, 50-51	187	329	___
1471WS	027 Steam Freight Set, 50-51	161	450	___
1473WS	027 Steam Freight Set, 50	110	560	___
1475WS	027 Steam Freight Set, 50	63	735	___
1477S	027 Steam Freight Set, 51-52	158	275	___
1479WS	027 Steam Freight Set, 52	234	396	___
1481WS	027 Steam Freight Set, 51	230	469	___
1483WS	027 Steam Freight Set, 52	527	1023	___
1484WS	027 Steam Passenger Set, 52		705	___
1485WS	027 Steam Freight Set, 52		270	___
1500	027 Steam Freight Set, 53	43	193	___
1500	027 Steam Freight Set, 54		172	___
1501S	027 Steam Freight Set, 53	95	234	___
1502WS	027 Steam Passenger Set, 53	375	1523	___
1503WS	027 Steam Freight Set, 53-54	216	442	___
1505WS	027 Steam Freight Set, 53	316	592	___
1507WS	027 Steam Freight Set, 53	173	558	___
1509WS	027 Steam Freight Set, 53	188	500	___
1511S	027 Steam Freight Set, 53	91	250	___
1513S	027 Steam Freight Set, 54-55	99	248	___
1515WS	027 Steam Freight Set, 54	208	517	___
1516WS	027 Passenger Set, 54	208	650	___
1517W	027 Diesel Freight Set, 54	688	2075	___
1519WS	027 Steam Freight Set, 54		615	___
1520W	027 Texas Special Passenger Set, 54	809	1925	___
1521WS	027 Steam Work Train Set, 54		758	___
1523	027 Diesel Work Train Set, 54	138	671	___
1525	027 Diesel Freight Set, 55		245	___
1527	027 Steam Work Train Set, 55	332	727	___
1529	027 PRR Diesel Freight Set, 55	320	652	___
1531W	027 Diesel Freight Set, 55	288	1094	___
1533WS	027 Steam Freight Set, 55	113	577	___
1534W	027 Diesel Passenger Set, 55	332	1000	___
1535W	027 Diesel Freight Set, 55	175	1650	___
1536W	027 Texas Special Passenger Set, 55	1045	2195	___

	SETS		Good	Exc
___	**1537WS**	027 Steam Freight Set, 55		508
___	**1538WS**	027 Steam Passenger Set, 55		900
___	**1539W**	027 Santa Fe Diesel Freight Set, 55		850
___	**1541WS**	027 Steam Freight Set, 55		600
___	**1542**	027 Electric Freight Set, 56	108	322
___	**1543**	027 Diesel Freight Set, 56	133	255
___	**1545**	027 Diesel Freight Set, 56		265
___	**1547S**	027 Steam Freight Set, 56		125
___	**1549**	027 Steam Work Train Set, 56		980
___	**1551W**	027 Diesel Freight Set, 56		566
___	**1552**	027 Diesel Passenger Set, 56	183	842
___	**1553W**	027 MILW Diesel Freight Set, 56	0	505
___	**1555WS**	027 Steam Freight Set, 56	266	404
___	**1557W**	027 Diesel Work Train Set, 56	334	466
___	**1559W**	027 MILW Diesel Freight Set, 56		800
___	**1561WS**	027 Steam Freight Set, 56		733
___	**1562W**	027 Diesel Passenger Set, 56	822	2134
___	**1563W**	027 Wabash Diesel Freight Set, 56		1570
___	**1565WS**	027 Steam Freight Set, 56	311	535
___	**1567W**	027 Santa Fe Diesel Freight Set, 56		1200
___	**1569**	027 UP Diesel Freight Set, 57	63	220
___	**1571**	027 LV Diesel Freight Set, 57	195	845
___	**1573**	027 Steam Freight Set, 57	93	212
___	**1575**	027 MP Diesel Freight Set, 57	118	320
___	**1577S**	027 Steam Freight Set, 57	126	235
___	**1578S**	027 Steam Passenger Set, 57	408	775
___	**1579S**	027 Steam Freight Set, 57		260
___	**1581**	027 Jersey Central Diesel Freight Set, 57		495
___	**1583WS**	027 Steam Freight Set, 57	78	268
___	**1585W**	027 Seaboard Diesel Freight Set, 57		493
___	**1586**	027 Santa Fe Diesel Passenger Set, 57	213	670
___	**1587S**	027 Steam Freight Set (Girls Set), 57-58	1363	3787
___	**1589WS**	027 Steam Freight Set, 57	123	500
___	**1590**	027 Steam Freight Set, 58	87	457
___	**1591**	027 Military Set, 58	663	1719
___	**1593**	027 UP Diesel Work Set, 58	75	590
___	**1595**	027 Military Set, 58		2050
___	**1597S**	027 Steam Freight Set, 58		355
___	**1599**	027 Texas Special Freight Set, 58		529
___	**1600**	027 Burlington Diesel Passenger Set, 58		750
___	**1601W**	027 Wabash Diesel Freight Set, 58		766
___	**1603WS**	027 Steam Freight Set, 58		433
___	**1605W**	027 Santa Fe Diesel Freight Set, 58		945
___	**1607WS**	027 Steam Work Train Set, 58		483
___	**1608W**	027 NH Diesel Passenger Set, 58	825	1865
___	**1609**	027 Steam Freight Set, 59-60	73	177
___	**1611**	027 Alaska Diesel Freight Set, 59	158	494
___	**1612**	027 General Set, 59-60	181	399
___	**1613S**	027 B&O Steam Freight Set, 59		254
___	**1615**	027 B&M Diesel Freight Set, 59	320	644
___	**1617S**	027 Steam Work Train Set, 59		800
___	**1619W**	027 Santa Fe Diesel Freight Set, 59	225	975
___	**1621WS**	027 Steam Freight Set, 59	255	587

SETS		Good	Exc	
1623W	027 NP Diesel Freight Set, 59	800	1958	___
1625WS	027 Steam Freight Set, 59		563	___
1626W	027 Santa Fe Diesel Passenger Set, 59	288	875	___
1627S	027 Steam Freight Set, 60	23	175	___
1629	027 C&O Diesel Freight Set, 60	120	361	___
1631WS	027 Steam Freight Set, 60	192	275	___
1633	027 U.S. Navy Diesel Freight Set, 60	477	1199	___
1635WS	027 Steam Freight Set, 60		400	___
1637W	027 Santa Fe Diesel Freight Set, 60	459	676	___
1639WS	027 Steam Freight Set, 60		1250	___
1640W	027 Santa Fe Diesel Passenger Set, 60	150	750	___
1641	027 Steam Freight Set, 61		175	___
1642	027 Steam Freight Set, 61		225	___
1643	027 C&O Diesel Freight Set, 61		328	___
1644	027 General Set, 61	53	375	___
1645	027 Diesel Freight Set, 61		250	___
1646	027 Steam Freight Set, 61		325	___
1647	027 U.S. Marines Military Set, 61	685	1203	___
1648	027 Steam Freight Set, 61	168	1120	___
1649	027 Santa Fe Diesel Freight Set, 61		538	___
1650	027 Steam Military Set, 61	105	506	___
1651	027 Santa Fe Diesel Passenger Set, 61		671	___
1800	General Gift Pack, 59-60	231	395	___
1805	027 Military Set (Land-Sea and Air Gift Pack), 60	585	3048	___
1809	Western Gift Pack, 61		300	___
1810	Space Age Gift Pack, 61	736	1165	___
2100	Steam Passenger Set, 46		550	___
2100W	Steam Passenger Set, 46	330	640	___
2101	Steam Freight Set, 46		350	___
2101W	Steam Freight Set, 46	99	395	___
2103W	Steam Freight Set, 46		467	___
2105WS	Steam Freight Set, 46		464	___
2110WS	Steam Passenger Set, 46		1875	___
2111WS	Steam Freight Set, 46		895	___
2113WS	Steam Freight Set, 46		4247	___
2114WS	Steam Passenger Set, 46	782	2500	___
2115WS	Steam Work Train Set, 46	422	1288	___
2120S	Steam Passenger Set, 47		500	___
2120WS	Steam Passenger Set, 47		500	___
2121S	Steam Freight Set, 47		400	___
2121WS	Steam Freight Set, 47		405	___
2123WS	Steam Freight Set, 47		645	___
2124W	PRR Electric Passenger Set, 47	936	3200	___
2125WS	Steam Freight Set, 47	238	568	___
2126WS	Steam Passenger Set, 47	463	1950	___
2127WS	Steam Work Train Set, 47		670	___
2129WS	Steam Freight Set, 47		2250	___
2131WS	Steam Work Train Set, 47		1200	___
2133W	Diesel Freight Set, 48		1350	___
2135WS	Steam Freight Set, 48	148	399	___
2135WS	Steam Freight Set, 49	230	670	___
2136WS	Steam Passenger Set, 48		674	___
2136WS	Steam Passenger Set, 49	86	802	___

SETS		Good	Exc
2137WS	Steam Freight Set, 48	263	720
2139W	PRR Electric Freight Set, 48		1425
2139W	PRR Electric Freight Set, 49	475	1360
2140WS	Steam Passenger Set, 48-49	225	1600
2141WS	Steam Freight Set, 48	188	519
2143WS	Steam Work Train Set, 48		795
2144W	PRR Electric Passenger Set, 48-49	1163	1903
2145WS	Steam Freight Set, 48		815
2146WS	Steam Passenger Set, 48-49	1050	2000
2147WS	Steam Freight Set, 49	125	454
2148WS	Hudson Passenger Set, 50	1850	5700
2149B	Diesel Work Train Set, 49		690
2150WS	Steam Passenger Set, 50		1000
2151W	Diesel Freight Set, 49		888
2153WS	Steam Work Train Set, 49		1010
2155WS	Steam Freight Set, 49		1053
2159W	Electric Freight Set, 50	875	2514
2161W	Santa Fe Diesel Freight Set, 50		1550
2163WS	Steam Freight Set, 50		550
2163WS	Steam Freight Set, 51	363	1164
2165WS	Steam Freight Set, 50		678
2167WS	Steam Freight Set, 50-51	110	618
2169WS	Hudson Freight Set, 50	1100	3205
2171W	NYC Diesel Freight Set, 50		1335
2173WS	Steam Freight Set, 50	177	947
2173WS	Steam Freight Set, 51		523
2175W	Santa Fe Diesel Freight Set, 50	305	836
2175W	Santa Fe Diesel Freight Set, 51	285	893
2177WS	Steam Freight Set, 52	163	363
2179WS	Steam Freight Set, 52	204	589
2183WS	Steam Freight Set, 52	313	945
2185W	NYC Diesel Freight Set, 50		960
2185W	NYC Diesel Freight Set, 51		1018
2187WS	Steam Freight Set, 52	280	650
2189WS	Steam Freight Set, 52	227	837
2190W	Santa Fe Diesel Passenger Set, 52	925	2000
2190W	Santa Fe Diesel Passenger Set, 53	1018	2125
2191W	Santa Fe Diesel Freight Set, 52		1355
2193W	NYC Diesel Freight Set, 52	388	1487
2201WS	Steam Freight Set, 53	234	1036
2203WS	Steam Freight Set, 53	338	1135
2205WS	Steam Freight Set, 53	371	1123
2207W	Santa Fe Diesel Freight Set, 53	614	1832
2209W	NYC Diesel Freight Set, 53	714	1433
2211WS	Steam Freight Set, 53	225	740
2213WS	Steam Freight Set, 53	325	1274
2217WS	Steam Freight Set, 54	629	1075
2219W	Diesel Freight Set, 54	870	1543
2221WS	Steam Freight Set, 54		500
2222WS	Steam Passenger Set, 54	1423	2613
2223W	Diesel Freight Set, 54	1178	3098
2225WS	Steam Work Train Set, 54	223	960
2227W	Santa Fe Diesel Freight Set, 54	777	1614
2229W	NYC Freight Set, 54	650	1525

SETS		Good	Exc	
2231W	Southern Diesel Freight Set, 54	797	2829	___
2234W	Santa Fe Diesel Passenger Set, 54	248	1990	___
2235W	MILW Diesel Freight Set, 55	188	654	___
2237WS	Steam Freight Set, 55		393	___
2239W	Illinois Central Diesel Freight Set, 55	288	1366	___
2241WS	Steam Freight Set, 55		615	___
2243W	Diesel Freight Set, 55	488	1375	___
2244W	Wabash Diesel Passenger Set, 55	1654	3650	___
2245WS	Steam Freight Set, 55		1150	___
2247W	Wabash Diesel Freight Set, 55	1596	2583	___
2249WS	Steam Freight Set, 55	341	872	___
2251W	Diesel Freight Set, 55	1250	2842	___
2253W	PRR Electric Freight Set, 55	950	2788	___
2254W	PRR Electric Passenger Set, 55	950	5500	___
2255W	Diesel Work Train Set, 56	224	843	___
2257WS	Steam Freight Set, 56	95	925	___
2259W	NH Electric Freight Set, 56	346	692	___
2261WS	Steam Freight Set, 56	285	636	___
2263W	NH Electric Freight Set, 56	162	978	___
2265WS	Steam Freight Set, 56		1003	___
2267W	Diesel Freight Set, 56		2210	___
2269W	B&O Diesel Freight Set, 56		2967	___
2270W	Jersey Central Diesel Passenger Set, 56	877	5730	___
2271W	PRR Electric Freight Set, 56	1272	2332	___
2273W	MILW Diesel Freight Set, 56	2036	4480	___
2274W	PRR Electric Passenger Set, 56	1493	3834	___
2275W	Wabash Diesel Freight Set, 57	115	820	___
2276W	Budd RDC Set, 57	1035	2035	___
2277WS	Steam Work Train Set, 57		585	___
2279W	NH Electric Freight Set, 57	370	837	___
2281W	Santa Fe Diesel Freight Set, 57	213	1040	___
2283WS	Steam Freight Set, 57		750	___
2285W	Diesel Freight Set, 57	525	2132	___
2287W	MILW Electric Freight Set, 57	600	2650	___
2289WS	Super O Steam Freight Set, 57	277	1850	___
2291W	Super O Rio Grande Diesel Freight Set, 57	1532	2617	___
2292WS	Super O Steam Passenger Set, 57	1000	1982	___
2293W	Super O PRR Electric Freight Set, 57	950	2400	___
2295WS	Super O Steam Freight Set, 57	1050	2157	___
2296W	Super O CP Diesel Passenger Set, 57	1590	4227	___
2297WS	Super O Steam Freight Set, 57	750	2375	___
2501W	Super O Diesel Work Train Set, 58	188	914	___
2502W	Super O Budd RDC Set, 58		2375	___
2503WS	Super O Steam Freight Set, 58	150	715	___
2505W	Super O Electric Freight Set, 58	375	1400	___
2507W	Super O Diesel Freight Set, 58	763	3000	___
2509WS	Super O Steam Freight Set, 58		927	___
2511W	Super O Electric Work Set, 58		1100	___
2513W	Super O Electric Freight Set, 58	1633	3000	___
2515WS	Super O Steam Freight Set, 58		892	___
2517W	Super O Rio Grande Diesel Freight Set, 58	1275	2625	___
2518W	Super O PRR Electric Passenger Set, 58		1850	___
2519W	Super O Diesel Freight Set, 58	1267	3400	___

SETS		Good	Exc
2521WS	Super O Steam Freight Set, 58	1000	2409
2523W	Super O Santa Fe Diesel Freight Set, 58		1300
2525WS	Super O Steam Work Train Set, 58	1358	3448
2526W	Super O Santa Fe Diesel Passenger Set, 58	894	4034
2527	Super O Missile Launcher Set, 59-60	482	861
2528WS	Super O General Set, 59-61	492	752
2529W	Super Electric Work Train Set, 59	950	1634
2531WS	Super O Steam Freight Set, 59	650	1294
2533W	Super O GN Electric Freight Set, 59		1910
2535WS	Super O Steam Freight Set, 59		840
2537W	Super O NH Diesel Freight Set, 59	332	2500
2539WS	Super O Steam Freight Set, 59		1483
2541W	Super O Santa Fe Diesel Freight Set, 59	398	2400
2543WS	Super O Steam Freight Set, 59		1590
2544W	Super O Santa Fe Diesel Passenger Set, 59-60	1370	2490
2545WS	Super O Military Set, 59		3000
2547WS	Super O Steam Freight Set, 60		484
2549W	Super O Military Set, 60	580	1237
2551W	Super O GN Electric Freight Set, 60	1150	3392
2553WS	Super O Steam Freight Set, 60	1077	2672
2555W	Super O Santa Fe Freight Set with matching HO Set, 60		10000
2570	Super O Santa Fe Work Train Set, 61	543	875
2571	Super O Steam Freight Set, 61		520
2572	Super O B&M Diesel Freight Set, 61		813
2573	Super O Steam Freight Set, 61	650	1433
2574	Super O Santa Fe Diesel Freight Set, 61	750	1875
2575	Super O PRR Electric Freight Set, 61	1250	3300
2576	Super O Santa Fe Diesel Passenger Set, 61		3065
4109WS	Electronic Control Set, 46-47		1493
4110WS	Electronic Control Set, 48-49	265	2500
11011	027Diesel Freight Set, 62		286
11201	027 Steam Freight Set, 62		129
11212	027 Santa Fe Diesel Freight Set, 62		375
11222	027 Steam Freight Set, 62		243
11232	027 NH Diesel Freight Set, 62		535
11242	027 Steam Freight Set, 62		167
11252	027 Texas Special Space Set, 62	190	477
11268	027 C&O Diesel Freight Set, 62	817	1425
11278	027 Steam Freight Set, 62		239
11288	027 Space Set, 62	500	1215
11298	027 Steam Freight Set, 62	238	565
11308	027 Santa Fe Diesel Passenger Set, 62		730
11311	027 Steam Freight Set, 63		232
11321	027 Rio Grande Diesel Freight Set, 63		400
11331	027 Steam Freight Set, 63	35	105
11341	027 Santa Fe Diesel Freight Set, 63		831
11351	027 Steam Freight Set, 63		190
11361	027 Texas Special Space Set, 63		750
11375	027 Steam Freight Set, 63		700
11385	027 Santa Fe Space Set, 63		2000
11395	027 Steam Freight Set, 63		600
11405	027 Santa Fe Diesel Passenger Set, 63		750
11420	027 Steam Freight Set, 64		200

SETS		Good	Exc	
11430	027 Steam Freight, 64	97	170	___
11440	027 Rio Grande Diesel Freight Set, 64	143	346	___
11450	027 Steam Freight Set, 64	98	298	___
11460	027 Steam Freight Set, 64	50	150	___
11470	027 Steam Freight Set, 64	81	305	___
11480	027 Diesel Freight Set, 64		619	___
11490	027 Diesel Passenger Set, 64-65		397	___
11500	027 Steam Freight Set, 64		438	___
11500	027 Steam Freight Set, 65		275	___
11500	027 Steam Freight Set, 66	105	275	___
11510	027 Steam Freight Set, 64		300	___
11520	027 Steam Freight Set, 65-66	70	143	___
11530	027 Santa Fe Diesel Freight, 65-66	113	439	___
11540	027 Steam Freight Set, 65-66		260	___
11550	027 Steam Freight Set, 65-66	60	219	___
11560	027 Texas Special Freight Set, 65-66	191	360	___
11590	027 Santa Fe Diesel Passenger Set, 66		646	___
11600	027 Steam Freight Set, 68	640	1540	___
11710	027 Steam Freight Set, 69	137	176	___
11720	Diesel Freight Set, 69	100	746	___
11730	027 UP Diesel Freight Set, 69		800	___
11740	027 RI Diesel Freight Set, 69	60	310	___
11750	027 Steam Freight Set, 69		360	___
11760	027 Steam Freight Set, 69		355	___
12502	Prairie-Rider Gift Pack, 62		600	___
12512	Enforcer Gift Pack, 62		1100	___
12700	Steam Freight Set, 64		1000	___
12710	Steam Freight Set, 64-66	350	1182	___
12720	Santa Fe Diesel Freight Set, 64		1500	___
12730	Santa Fe Diesel Freight Set, 64-66	448	1136	___
12740	Santa Fe Diesel Freight Set, 64		1500	___
12760	Steam Freight Set, 64		1100	___
12780	Santa Fe Diesel Passenger, 64-66	1108	4678	___
12800	B&M Diesel Freight Set, 65-66	390	834	___
12820	Diesel Freight Set, 65	509	2304	___
12840	Steam Freight Set, 66	771	1791	___
12850	Diesel Freight Set, 66	425	2400	___
13008	Super 0 Steam Freight Set, 62		500	___
13018	Super 0 Santa Fe Diesel Freight Set, 62	646	1200	___
13028	Super 0 Space Set, 62		1000	___
13036	Super 0 General Set, 62	490	1160	___
13048	Super 0 Steam Freight Set, 62	360	941	___
13058	Super 0 Space Set, 62	800	2048	___
13068	Super 0 PRR Electric Freight Set, 62		3200	___
13078	Super 0 PRR Electric Passenger Set, 62		3500	___
13088	Super 0 Santa Fe Diesel Passenger Set, 62	1250	3300	___
13098	Super 0 Steam Freight Set, 63		2133	___
13108	Super 0 Santa Fe Space Set, 63		1000	___
13118	Super 0 Steam Freight Set, 63		1500	___
13128	Super 0 Santa Fe Space Set, 63		1750	___
13138	Super 0 PRR Electric Freight Set, 63		3800	___
13148	Super 0 Santa Fe Diesel Passenger Set, 63		2500	___
13150	Super 0 Hudson Steam Freight Set, 64	1538	4450	___

ABBREVIATIONS

Descriptions

AAR	Association of American Railroads (truck type)
AEC	Atomic Energy Commission
AF	American Flyer
CC	Command Control
DD	Double-door
EMD	Electro-Motive Division
ETD	End-of-train device
FARR	Famous American Railroad Series
FF	Fallen Flag Series
FM	Fairbanks-Morse
GE	General Electric
LL	Lionel Lines
MOW	Maintenance-of-way
MU	Multiple unit (commuter cars)
O	Lionel gauge (1¼" between outside rails)
OO	Lionel gauge (¾" between outside rails)
PFE	Pacific Fruit Express
REA	Railway Express Agency
SSS	Service Station Special
std	Standard gauge (2⅛" between outside rails)
std O	Standard O (scale length and dimension)
TMCC	TrainMaster Command Control
USMC	United States Marine Corps
1-D	One dome
2-D	Two dome
3-D	Three dome

Railroad names

ACL	Atlantic Coast Line
ATSF	Atchison, Topeka & Santa Fe
B&A	Boston & Albany
BAR	Bangor & Aroostook
B&LE	Bessemer & Lake Erie
B&M	Boston & Maine
BN	Burlington Northern
BNSF	Burlington Northern Santa Fe
B&O	Baltimore & Ohio
CB&Q	Chicago, Burlington & Quincy
CMStP&P	Chicago, Milwaukee, St. Paul & Pacific (Milwaukee Road)
CN	Canadian National
CGW	Chicago Great Western
CNJ	Central of New Jersey
C&NW	Chicago & North Western
C&O	Chesapeake & Ohio
CP	Canadian Pacific
CRI&P	Chicago, Rock Island & Pacific (Rock Island)
C&S	Colorado & Southern
CUVA	Cuyahoga Valley Railway
D&H	Delaware & Hudson
D&RGW	Denver & Rio Grande Western
DT&I	Detroit, Toledo & Ironton
DM&IR	Duluth, Missabe & Iron Range
E-L	Erie-Lackawanna (Erie-Lack.)
FEC	Florida East Coast
FWD	Fort Worth & Denver
FY&P	Franklin & Pittsylvania
GM&O	Gulf, Mobile & Ohio
GN	Great Northern
GN&W	Genesee & Wyoming
GTW	Grand Trunk Western
IC	Illinois Central
ICG	Illinois Central Gulf
IGN	International-Great Northern
KCS	Kansas City Southern
L&N	Louisville & Nashville
LNE	Lehigh & New England
LV	Lehigh Valley
MEC	Maine Central
MILW	Milwaukee Road
MKT	Missouri-Kansas-Texas (Katy)
MNS	Minnesota, Northfield & Southern
MP	Missouri Pacific
M&StL	Minneapolis & St. Louis
NdeM	Nacionales de Mexico Railway
NH	New Haven
NKP	Nickel Plate Road
NOT&M	New Orleans, Texas & Mexico
NP	Northern Pacific
NS	Norfolk Southern
N&W	Norfolk & Western
NWP	Northwestern Pacific
NYC	New York Central
NYO&W	New York, Ontario & Western
NYNH&H	New York, New Haven & Hartford (New Haven)
OSL	Oregon Short Line
P&LE	Pittsburgh & Lake Erie
PC	Penn Central
PRR	Pennsylvania Railroad
PMKY	Pittsburgh, McKeesport & Youghiogheny
PTM	ST Rail System
RFP	Richmond, Fredericksburg & Potomac
SF	Santa Fe
SLSF	St. Louis-San Francisco (Frisco)
SP	Southern Pacific
SSW	St. Louis Southwestern (Cotton Belt)
T&P	Texas & Pacific
TP&W	Toledo, Peoria & Western
UP	Union Pacific
WM	Western Maryland
WP	Western Pacific

NOTES

NOTES

BUILD YOUR TOY TRAIN LIBRARY

Display Layouts and Showrooms

In this 100-page special issue from *Classic Toy Trains*, you will discover 60 of the greatest postwar Lionel and American Flyer layouts. Display Layou and Showrooms contains information and pictures you've never seen before

CT18241001-C - $13.99

Track Plans for Lionel FasTrack

Featuring 25 mostly small and mid-sized plans designed specifically for FasTrack, this collection includes detailed plans, a brief overview of FasTrack, and track-planning tips.

10-8804 - $16.99

25-195

Shop.Trains.com